The Official SAT Study Guide™

THE COLLEGE BOARD, NEW YORK

ABOUT THE COLLEGE BOARD

The College Board is a mission-driven not-for-profit organization that connects students to college success and opportunity. Founded in 1900, the College Board was created to expand access to higher education. Today, the membership association is made up of over 6,000 of the world's leading educational institutions and is dedicated to promoting excellence and equity in education. Each year, the College Board helps more than seven million students prepare for a successful transition to college through programs and services in college readiness and college success — including the SAT® and the Advanced Placement Program®. The organization also serves the education community through research and advocacy on behalf of students, educators, and schools. For further information, visit collegeboard.org.

Copies of this book are available from your bookseller or may be ordered from College Board Publications at store.collegeboard.org or by calling 800-323-7155.

Editorial inquiries concerning this book should be submitted at sat.collegeboard.org/contact.

This publication was written and edited by the College Board, with primary authorship by Carolyn Lieberg, Jim Patterson, Andrew Schwartz, Jessica Marks, and Sergio Frisoli. Cover and layout design: Iris Jan. Project manager: Jim Gwyn. Product owner: Aaron Lemon-Strauss. Invaluable contributions and review from the College Board's Assessment Design & Development team led by Sherral Miller, Laurie Moore, and Nancy Burkholder.

ISBN-13: 978-1-4573-0928-1

Printed in the United States of America

1 2 3 4 5 6 7 8 9 23 22 21 20 19 18 17

Distributed by Macmillan

Dear Student:

Congratulations on taking an important step toward preparing for the redesigned SAT®. *The Official SAT Study Guide*™ is a tool to help you practice for the newest version of the exam. By investing in SAT practice, you are making a commitment to your college, career, and life success.

As you start to familiarize yourself with the new exam, we are excited to share with you some of the many benefits it has to offer. It is important to remember that the questions that make up the exam are modeled on the work you are already doing in school. You will recognize topics and ideas from your math, English language arts, science, history, and social studies classes. These questions are also aligned with the skills that research says matter most for college and career readiness. This means that, by practicing for the redesigned SAT, you are reinforcing the knowledge and skills that will help you excel both in your course work and in your future pursuits.

The new SAT is clearer than ever. The questions will not be tricky, nor will there be any obscure vocabulary or penalties for guessing. By being transparent about what is on the test and making materials easily available, we are providing you the foundation for successful practice. The best source of information about the SAT is found right here in the pages of this book, and you have taken an important step by equipping yourself with these key facts.

The redesigned SAT is just one component of the College Board's commitment to increasing students' access to and success in college and career. We have also partnered with colleges and universities to offer college application fee waivers to every income-eligible senior who takes the SAT using a fee waiver (to learn more visit http://sat.org/fee-waivers). The College Board wants you to succeed in your pursuits, and defraying the cost of admission for eligible students is just one way that we can make it easier for you to reach your goals.

Now that you have this great study guide as a tool, we encourage you to begin practicing today.

Keep up the good work.

Cynthia B. Schmeiser

Cynthia B. Schmeiser
Chief of Assessment
The College Board

Dear Student:

I took the SAT more than 20 years ago. But even back in the prehistoric times of the early '90s, an earlier version of this book played a big role in helping me prepare not just for the SAT, but for life. For several weeks, I would wake up early on Saturday mornings, do push-ups while blasting "Eye of the Tiger," take a practice test, and review the items I found difficult. Eventually, I worked through every test in the book. By the time test day came around, I found I was just as prepared as anyone to put my best foot forward for the SAT. I also showed myself that I could develop a plan and stick to it to reach a goal, and that skill has proven essential ever since.

But you have much more than even I had at your disposal.

Khan Academy® is a nonprofit with the mission of providing a free, world-class education for anyone, anywhere, and we've partnered with the College Board to create the world's best online SAT practice program, which also happens to be free. Yes, FREE! On Khan Academy (khanacademy.org/sat), we've designed a program that gives you unlimited practice and help with the skills you find challenging so you can show up on test day ready to rock the SAT. More than three million students have already used these free, official tools. If you take the PSAT, you can share your score with us (through the click of a button!), and we'll automatically create a personalized SAT practice plan for you based on your PSAT results.

So take a breath. Force a smile. Strike a power pose (look that up on YouTube if you don't know what a "power pose" is). Realize that your brain is like a muscle: The more you practice and get feedback, the stronger it gets. Realize that when you get a question wrong in practice, that is when your brain actually grows and strengthens. Realize that the SAT is just a measure of college readiness, and the best way to get college ready is to really hone your language and math abilities through deliberate practice. No matter how long you have until the exam, realize that you have the power to create a study plan for yourself and stick to it. This isn't about SAT prep, but life prep. And of course, the more practice, the better; so if you can, start regularly practicing with this book and the resources on Khan Academy weeks or months before the exam.

I envy you. You're at the most exciting stage of your life. Embrace the challenge. Enjoy the process. As you prepare, remember that you can arm yourself now with tools and habits that will help you be the best version of yourself, not just on the SAT but throughout your life.

And don't forget to smile!

Onward,

Sal Khan
Founder, Khan Academy

Contents

PART 4 Eight Official Practice Tests with Answer Explanations

PART 1

Getting Ready for the SAT

CHAPTER 1

Introducing the SAT

Welcome to the *Official SAT Study Guide*! This guide is designed for you. Return to it again and again in the coming weeks and months. Reading it is an excellent way to become familiar with the SAT — its content, structure, timing, question types, and more. The information, advice, and sample questions will help you prepare to take the test with confidence.

Tackling new things makes most of us nervous, but when we can learn a great deal about a new situation in advance, we feel much more able to take a deep breath and meet the challenge. Learning about the SAT through this guide and taking practice tests will help you be well prepared when your test date arrives.

How Does the SAT® Measure Academic Achievement?

Questions on the SAT will not ask you to recall details of *Hamlet* or to name the capital of Nevada or the location of the Rappahannock River. If you recall those facts, good for you, but the SAT will ask for something different. Instead of asking you to show what you've memorized, the questions invite you to exercise your thinking skills.

REMEMBER

The SAT isn't designed to assess how well you've memorized a large set of facts; rather, the SAT assesses your ability to apply the knowledge and skills you'll need in college and career.

All of the learning you've done — from childhood to now — contributes to how you think, how your mind manages information. Even if you don't recall the details of a history or science lesson, the process of learning information and blending it with previously learned information is key to becoming a skilled thinker.

The world needs more people who can use their thinking skills to solve problems, communicate clearly, and understand complex relationships. The best high school courses promote thinking skills, and colleges are looking for students who are skilled thinkers. The SAT is designed to measure the thinking skills you'll need to succeed in college and career.

REMEMBER

The SAT has been carefully crafted by many people, experts in their fields, to ensure that it's a fair test that assesses the knowledge and skills you'll need to succeed in college and career.

How Is the SAT Developed?

The process of developing a test given to millions of students around the world is complex and involves many people. The SAT is developed by the College Board, a not-for-profit organization that was founded more than a century ago to expand access to higher education. The College Board is a large organization, with more than 6,000 schools, colleges, and universities as members.

College Board test developers are content experts in physics, biology, statistics, math, English, history, computer science, sociology, education, psychology, and other disciplines. They use their expertise to create questions for the SAT that will allow students to demonstrate their best thinking.

Committees of high school and college instructors review every potential SAT question to make sure that each one measures important knowledge and skills, that the questions are fair to all students, and that they're written in a way that models what students are learning in the best high school classrooms.

REMEMBER

Colleges care about your SAT score because it's a strong predictor of how you'll perform in college. By doing well on the SAT, you can show colleges that you're ready to succeed.

Colleges want to admit students who will have successful college experiences and go on to have successful careers. Colleges use the SAT in admissions because it's developed according to rigorous specifications, with input from numerous experts, to assess what matters most for college and career readiness and success. Independent research demonstrates that the single most important factor for demonstrating college readiness is high school GPA. Even more predictive than GPA, though, is GPA combined with an SAT score.

How Is the SAT Organized?

The SAT has four tests, with the Essay being optional. The three tests that everyone will take are (1) the Reading Test, (2) the Writing and Language Test, and (3) the Math Test. The timing and number of questions are as follows:

Component	Time Allotted (minutes)	Number of Questions/Tasks
Reading	65	52
Writing and Language	35	44
Math	80	58
Essay (optional)	50	1
Total	180 (230 with Essay)	154 (155 with Essay)

REMEMBER

More scores = more information. The scores reported on the SAT provide detailed information about your achievement and readiness for college and career.

The Essay is optional, but some high schools and colleges require it. Depending on your high school and your college choices, you may already know whether or not you'll take the Essay. If you have any uncertainty — for instance, if you can imagine that you might transfer from a school that doesn't require it to one that does — consider taking the SAT with Essay.

How Is the SAT Scored?

When you take the SAT, you don't get just one score. The SAT reports a total score, but there are also section scores, test scores, cross-test scores, and subscores. This wide array of scores provides insight into your achievement and your readiness for college and career.

You earn points on the SAT by answering questions correctly. No points are deducted for wrong answers, so go ahead and give your best answer to every question — there's no advantage to leaving any blank.

Total Score and Section Scores

The total score is the number most commonly associated with the SAT. The total score ranges from 400 to 1600. This score is the sum of the scores on the Evidence-Based Reading and Writing section (which includes the Reading and Writing and Language Tests) and the Math section. Of the 154 questions in the entire SAT (not counting the Essay), 96 questions are on the Reading and the Writing and Language Tests and 58 questions are on the Math Test.

Section scores for Evidence-Based Reading and Writing and for Math are reported on a scale from 200 to 800. The Evidence-Based Reading and Writing section score is derived in equal measure from the scores on the Reading and the Writing and Language Tests. The Math section score is derived from the score on the Math Test.

Test Scores

Test scores are reported on a scale of 10 to 40 for each of the three required tests: Reading, Writing and Language, and Math.

Cross-Test Scores

Cross-test scores — one for **Analysis in History/Social Studies** and one for **Analysis in Science** — are reported on a scale of 10 to 40 and are based on selected questions in the Reading, Writing and Language, and Math Tests that reflect the application of reading, writing, language, and math skills in history/social studies and science contexts.

Subscores

Subscores are reported on a scale of 1 to 15. They provide more detailed information about how you're doing in specific areas of literacy and math.

Two subscores are reported for Writing and Language: Expression of Ideas and Standard English Conventions.

The **Expression of Ideas** subscore is based on questions focusing on topic development, organization, and rhetorically effective use of language.

The **Standard English Conventions** subscore is based on questions focusing on sentence structure, usage, and punctuation.

REMEMBER

Subscores provide additional insight into your performance on specific topics and skills.

The Math Test reports three subscores: Heart of Algebra, Problem Solving and Data Analysis, and Passport to Advanced Math.

Heart of Algebra focuses on linear equations, systems of linear equations, and functions.

Problem Solving and Data Analysis focuses on quantitative reasoning, the interpretation and synthesis of data, and problem solving in rich and varied contexts.

Passport to Advanced Math focuses on topics important for progressing to more advanced mathematics, such as understanding the structure of expressions, reasoning with more complex equations, and interpreting and building functions.

The final two subscores — Words in Context and Command of Evidence — are based on questions in both the Reading and the Writing and Language Tests.

Words in Context questions address word and phrase meanings in context as well as rhetorical word choice.

Command of Evidence questions ask you to interpret and use evidence found in a wide range of passages and informational graphics, such as graphs, tables, and charts.

REMEMBER

Test scores will reflect your performance on each of the three required tests on the SAT. The three different Essay scores serve a similar role.

Essay Scores

The scores for the optional SAT Essay are reported separately and aren't factored into any other scores. The Essay yields three scores, one each on three dimensions:

Reading: How well you demonstrate your understanding of the included passage

Analysis: How well you analyze the passage and carry out the task of explaining how the author of the passage builds an argument to persuade an audience

Writing: How skillfully you craft your response

Two raters read each response and assign a score of 1 to 4 to each of the three dimensions. The two raters' scores are combined to yield Reading, Analysis, and Writing scores, each on a scale of 2 to 8.

The SAT Score Report

You'll be able to access all of your scores online through your free College Board account. This account will be the same one you use to register for the SAT. Learn more at sat.org.

Score Range

The SAT Score Report includes a score range for each of the scores described above. This range indicates where your scores would likely fall if you took the test several times within a short period of time (for instance, on three consecutive days). If you were to do that, you would see numbers that differ, but not by much.

Percentiles

Your SAT Score Report includes the percentile rank for each score and subscore. Percentile ranks are a way of comparing scores in a particular group. For the SAT, separate percentile ranks are reported based on your state and on the total group of test takers. Each percentile rank can range from 1 to 99 and indicates the percentage of test takers who attained a score equal to or lower than yours. For instance, a perfect total score of 1600 would have a percentile rank of 99, meaning that 99% of people taking the test achieved a 1600 or lower score. A percentile rank of 50 means that half of students taking the test scored at or below your score.

REMEMBER

Your percentile rank indicates the percentage of test takers who scored at or below your score.

Online Score Report

The SAT Online Score Report gives you the meaning behind your numbers by providing a summary of how you did on each section, including how many questions you got right, got wrong, or didn't answer. The tool offers insight into your strengths and weaknesses by showing your results grouped by subject and question difficulty. The online report provides other information as well:

- Percentiles to help you see how your results compare with those of other students
- A search tool for career and college majors, with suggestions based on information you provide in your profile
- If you took the Essay, a scanned copy of your response and the prompt

Being able to review your response to the Essay gives you an opportunity to reconsider how well you understood the passage, the effectiveness of your analysis, and the quality of your writing. You can reflect on whether your points were clear, how well you provided support for your points, and how effectively you structured your response.

REMEMBER

You'll be able to access your online score report through your free College Board account. This report will give you a detailed breakdown of your performance.

Additional SAT Services

When you register for the SAT, you'll be able to choose reports and services that can be helpful in a number of ways. Depending on which date you test on, there are different options for receiving detailed feedback. Browse through the types of information that each of the following reports and services offers you.

Additional Score Reports

Registering for the SAT allows you to send your results to up to four institutions; you can identify these institutions within nine days of taking the test. Take advantage of all four score reports, whether you send them to colleges or to scholarship sites. Sending your scores to colleges early in the college application process is a great way to show your interest. Use your online account to order additional score reports.

REMEMBER

Within nine days of taking the test, you can decide to have your SAT results sent, free of charge, to four institutions.

REMEMBER

The Score Choice service allows you to select which scores (by test date) to send to your chosen colleges. Keep in mind, however, that you can't choose to submit specific section scores from different test dates.

Score Choice™

If you take the SAT more than once, you can use the Score Choice service. Score Choice allows you to select which scores, by test date, to send to your chosen colleges or scholarship programs, in accordance with each institution's individual score use practices. Note that this service is optional. If you don't select Score Choice when registering, all of your scores will be sent to institutions receiving your results. Most colleges consider only your best scores when they review your application, though this varies by institution. If you want only your best scores to be seen, you should use Score Choice.

Each school or program has its own deadlines and policies for how scores are used. Check with the individual school or scholarship program to make sure you're following its guidelines.

Note that you can't select one section score from one test date and another section score from another date. (For example, you won't be able to send your Evidence-Based Reading and Writing score from one date and your Math score from a different date.) Also, if you took the SAT with Essay, you won't be able to send scores without the Essay scores as well.

Student Answer Verification Services

The SAT Program offers two answer verification services for the SAT. These services are intended to help you feel confident that your test was scored accurately by providing information about the questions and how you answered them. Depending on when and where you take the SAT, you can order either the Student Answer Service (SAS) or the Question-and-Answer Service (QAS). You can order the services when you register for the SAT or up to five months after your test date.

Both SAS and QAS tell you which questions you answered correctly, which ones you didn't answer correctly, and which ones you didn't answer. You'll also see information about the type and difficulty of questions. QAS provides additional information, including the test questions themselves. The Essay prompt is only released as part of the Question-and-Answer Service.

REMEMBER

Enrolling in the optional Student Search Service allows colleges and scholarship programs to contact you to invite you to apply.

Student Search Service

All students who take the SAT are eligible to opt in to the Student Search Service, which helps colleges and scholarship recognition organizations find you. If you sign up during registration, your name and contact information, GPA, date of birth, grade level, high school, email address, extracurricular activities, and intended college major will be put into a database that colleges and scholarship programs use when they want to locate and recruit students with particular characteristics or interests.

Please note:

- Joining Student Search Service is voluntary.
- Colleges that participate in the program don't receive your scores as part of their membership. They may request information about students whose scores are in a particular range, but your scores will not be provided through this service.
- Any colleges that contact you are doing so to invite you to apply. Going through the application process is the only way to be admitted to a college. Colleges use the service to locate potential students who they think should apply.
- Student Search Service is restricted to colleges and scholarship programs. Your information will never be sold to a commercial marketing firm or retailer of merchandise or services (such as a test-preparation company).

SAT Fee Waivers

Students who face financial barriers to taking the SAT can receive SAT fee waivers to cover the cost of testing. Seniors who use a fee waiver to take the SAT will also receive four college application fee waivers to use in applying to colleges that accept the waivers. You can learn about eligibility and the other benefits offered to help you in the college application process at sat.org/fee-waivers.

REMEMBER

Visit sat.org/fee-waivers to learn more about SAT fee waivers and college application fee waivers.

CHAPTER 2

Doing Your Best on the SAT

The SAT is an important test, one that can have a big impact on your future. And getting ready for the SAT involves a lot of time and hard work. In order to do your best on the SAT, it's important not to think of the test as an obstacle that's in your way or an ordeal that you have to endure. Instead, think of the SAT as an opportunity to show colleges and scholarship programs that you're ready to succeed at the next level. You can make best use of your opportunity by learning the essential skills and knowledge covered on the test, getting familiar with the test itself, practicing in smart ways, and having a good test day strategy.

Building Important Knowledge and Skills Measured on the SAT

The Key: Working Hard in School

The best preparation for the SAT occurs every day as you study hard in school and acquire important reading, writing, language, and math knowledge and skills. You don't have to discover secret tricks or go into training for test day. The SAT is focused on the skills and knowledge at the heart of education. It will measure:

- What you learn in high school
- What you need to succeed in college and career

The same habits and choices that lead to success in school will help you get ready for the SAT. The best way to prepare for the test is to:

- Take challenging courses
- Do your homework
- Prepare for tests and quizzes
- Ask and answer lots of questions

In short, take charge of your education and learn as much as you can.

REMEMBER

The best way to prepare for the SAT is to work hard in school. The SAT has been designed to reflect what you're being taught in school, as well as the skills and knowledge you need to succeed in college and workforce training programs.

Reading Knowledge and Skills

To succeed in college and career, you'll need a range of reading skills — and the ability to use those skills when you engage with challenging texts in a wide array of subjects. Not coincidentally, you'll also need those skills to do well on the SAT.

Some SAT questions ask you to locate a piece of information or an idea stated directly. But there's much more to reading than understanding the things that an author writes explicitly. You'll also need to understand what the author's words imply.

Authors are often subtle, and readers have to make reasonable inferences or draw logical conclusions on their own. In other words, they have to read between the lines to reach a deeper meaning — or just to follow the author's train of thought.

REMEMBER

SAT Reading Test and Essay passages are drawn from high-quality, previously published sources. Reading Test passages are drawn from the subject areas of U.S. and world literature, history/social studies, and science, while Essay passages are arguments written for a broad audience. Practice reading and analyzing essays or articles from each of these areas to prepare yourself for the SAT.

Some SAT questions ask you to use clearly stated information and ideas in a passage or pair of related passages to figure out meanings that are only suggested. You'll also need to apply this skill when you read the complex texts assigned in college. Because you'll encounter such texts in your earliest classes, you'll see them on the SAT, too.

Complex texts often:

- Include uncommon words
- Use sophisticated sentence structures
- Present large amounts of information and ideas quickly
- Discuss abstract ideas (such as justice or freedom)
- Describe subtle or complicated relationships among concepts

Not all passages on the SAT are this challenging, but you should be ready to use your reading skills to draw out meaning from those that are.

Vocabulary Knowledge and Skills

The SAT doesn't have a vocabulary section, but it does test how well you know, interpret, and use words and phrases.

On the Reading Test, you'll be asked to read a passage and figure out the precise meaning of a word or phrase as it is used in a given context. The word or phrase will probably have more than one dictionary meaning, so you'll have to use context clues to figure out which meaning is intended in the passage. You may also be asked to analyze how words and phrases are used to convey meaning, style, tone, or the like.

Both the Writing and Language Test and the Essay test your ability to use words and phrases appropriately and precisely. On the Writing and Language Test, for example, you may be asked to choose the word or phrase that best expresses an idea or creates a particular mood.

Writing and Language Knowledge and Skills

Writing is another central component of your post–high school future. The SAT divides the skills assessed on the Writing and Language Test into two broad categories: Expression of Ideas and Standard English Conventions.

Expression of Ideas questions focus on revision of text for topic development; organization, logic, and cohesion; and rhetorically effective use of language. You may be asked to:

- Replace a sentence with one that states the main claim more clearly.
- Add evidence that supports an argument.
- Remove an example that's not relevant to the passage's central idea.
- Correct the writer's interpretation of the data presented in a graph.
- Ensure that information and ideas are presented in the clearest and most logical order.
- Decide which word or phrase expresses an idea most clearly.
- Choose between similar words with different connotations.
- Revise language to get rid of wordiness or repetition.
- Change a sentence so that it is more consistent with the passage's style or tone.
- Revise sentence structure to shift emphasis.
- Combine two sentences effectively.

Standard English Conventions questions focus on editing text following the conventions of standard written English sentence structure, usage, and punctuation. These questions may ask you to recognize and correct:

- Grammatically incomplete sentences, run-ons, and comma splices
- Problems with coordination or subordination of clauses in sentences
- Lack of parallelism in sentence construction
- Dangling and other misplaced modifiers
- Inappropriate shifts in verb tense, voice, and mood and in pronoun person and number
- Vague or ambiguous pronouns
- Confusion between the words *its/it's*, *your/you're*, and *their/they're/there* as well as other commonly confused words (for example, *affect* and *effect*)

- Lack of agreement between pronouns and antecedents, between subjects and verbs, and between nouns
- Illogical comparisons of unlike terms
- Cases of nonstandard expression (when words and phrases are used in a way not typical to standard written English)
- Problems with using end-of-sentence punctuation or punctuation within sentences (particularly colons, semicolons, and dashes) to signal sharp breaks in thought
- Confusion between plurals and possessives and between singular and plural possessives
- Problems with punctuating a series of items
- Confusion between restrictive/essential and nonrestrictive/nonessential sentence elements
- Unnecessary punctuation (for example, between a subject and a verb)

REMEMBER

The SAT Essay is optional for students. Some school districts and colleges, however, will require it. The Essay has been designed to mirror some of the kinds of work often required in college and career.

Your writing skills will also be evaluated if you choose to take the optional SAT Essay. The Essay, in part, will be scored according to how well you've expressed your ideas and to what extent, if any, mistakes in applying standard written English conventions impair the quality of your expression.

Math Knowledge and Skills

The SAT Math Test covers a range of math practices, with an emphasis on problem solving, modeling, using tools strategically, and using algebraic structure. The Math Test is your chance to show that you have mathematical fluency, an understanding of mathematical concepts, and skill in applying your math knowledge to real-world problems.

Demonstrating fluency on the Math Test means being able to carry out procedures flexibly, accurately, efficiently, and strategically. You'll need to show that you can solve problems quickly by identifying and using the most efficient solution approaches. This may involve solving a problem by inspection, finding a shortcut, or reorganizing the information you've been given.

The Math Test will also give you the opportunity to demonstrate your grasp of math concepts, operations, and relations. For instance, you may be asked to make connections between properties of linear equations, their graphs, and the contexts they represent.

Application problems on the SAT Math Test are your chance to show that you can apply the math skills you've been learning in class. These real-world problems ask you to analyze a situation, determine the essential elements required to solve the problem, represent the problem mathematically, and carry out a solution.

Getting Familiar with the SAT

Know the Test Directions

Knowing the directions for the SAT before test day will give you an advantage. By learning in advance what the directions say, you can minimize the amount of time you spend reading them on test day and be more focused on the actual questions. The directions for each portion of the SAT are reprinted on the following pages. Study them now and you'll be better prepared to do your best on test day.

REMEMBER

By knowing in advance how long the test is, when the breaks are scheduled, what formats the questions come in, what the test directions are, and how the test is scored, you won't have any surprises on test day and will be able to focus on performing your best.

Know the Test Question Formats

In addition to knowing the test directions, you should also know how questions on the various parts of the SAT are asked. Doing so will help prevent surprises on test day and free you up to focus on the content rather than the format. For example, you'll want to become familiar with the two-column presentation and the use of underlined portions of text in the Writing and Language Test. For the Math Test, you'll definitely want to become familiar with the format of the student-produced response questions (SPRs), sometimes referred to as "grid-ins." For each of these questions, you won't have answer choices to select from. Rather, you must solve the problem and "grid" the answer you came up with on the answer sheet.

The more you practice with official SAT practice tests and sample questions, the more comfortable you'll become with the question formats. And be sure to read through this book's information about the format of each test and work through the sample questions in Chapter 9 (the Reading Test), Chapter 13 (the Writing and Language Test), and Chapters 20 and 21 (the Math Test).

Reading Test

65 MINUTES, 52 QUESTIONS

Turn to Section 1 of your answer sheet to answer the questions in this section.

DIRECTIONS

Each passage or pair of passages below is followed by a number of questions. After reading each passage or pair, choose the best answer to each question based on what is stated or implied in the passage or passages and in any accompanying graphics (such as a table or graph).

Writing and Language Test

35 MINUTES, 44 QUESTIONS

Turn to Section 2 of your answer sheet to answer the questions in this section.

DIRECTIONS

Each passage below is accompanied by a number of questions. For some questions, you will consider how the passage might be revised to improve the expression of ideas. For other questions, you will consider how the passage might be edited to correct errors in sentence structure, usage, or punctuation. A passage or a question may be accompanied by one or more graphics (such as a table or graph) that you will consider as you make revising and editing decisions.

Some questions will direct you to an underlined portion of a passage. Other questions will direct you to a location in a passage or ask you to think about the passage as a whole.

After reading each passage, choose the answer to each question that most effectively improves the quality of writing in the passage or that makes the passage conform to the conventions of standard written English. Many questions include a "NO CHANGE" option. Choose that option if you think the best choice is to leave the relevant portion of the passage as it is.

Math Test – No Calculator

25 MINUTES, 20 QUESTIONS

Turn to Section 3 of your answer sheet to answer the questions in this section.

DIRECTIONS

For questions 1-15, solve each problem, choose the best answer from the choices provided, and fill in the corresponding circle on your answer sheet. **For questions 16-20**, solve the problem and enter your answer in the grid on the answer sheet. Please refer to the directions before question 16 on how to enter your answers in the grid. You may use any available space in your test booklet for scratch work.

NOTES

1. The use of a calculator **is not permitted**.
2. All variables and expressions used represent real numbers unless otherwise indicated.
3. Figures provided in this test are drawn to scale unless otherwise indicated.
4. All figures lie in a plane unless otherwise indicated.
5. Unless otherwise indicated, the domain of a given function f is the set of all real numbers x for which $f(x)$ is a real number.

REFERENCE

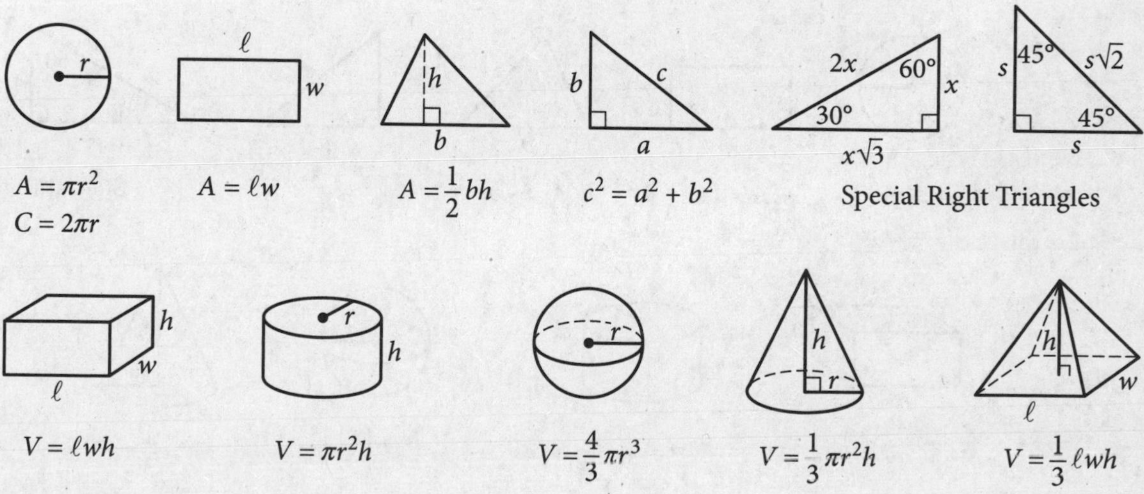

The number of degrees of arc in a circle is 360.

The number of radians of arc in a circle is 2π.

The sum of the measures in degrees of the angles of a triangle is 180.

Math Test – Calculator

55 MINUTES, 38 QUESTIONS

Turn to Section 4 of your answer sheet to answer the questions in this section.

DIRECTIONS

For questions 1-30, solve each problem, choose the best answer from the choices provided, and fill in the corresponding circle on your answer sheet. **For questions 31-38**, solve the problem and enter your answer in the grid on the answer sheet. Please refer to the directions before question 31 on how to enter your answers in the grid. You may use any available space in your test booklet for scratch work.

NOTES

1. The use of a calculator **is permitted**.
2. All variables and expressions used represent real numbers unless otherwise indicated.
3. Figures provided in this test are drawn to scale unless otherwise indicated.
4. All figures lie in a plane unless otherwise indicated.
5. Unless otherwise indicated, the domain of a given function f is the set of all real numbers x for which $f(x)$ is a real number.

REFERENCE

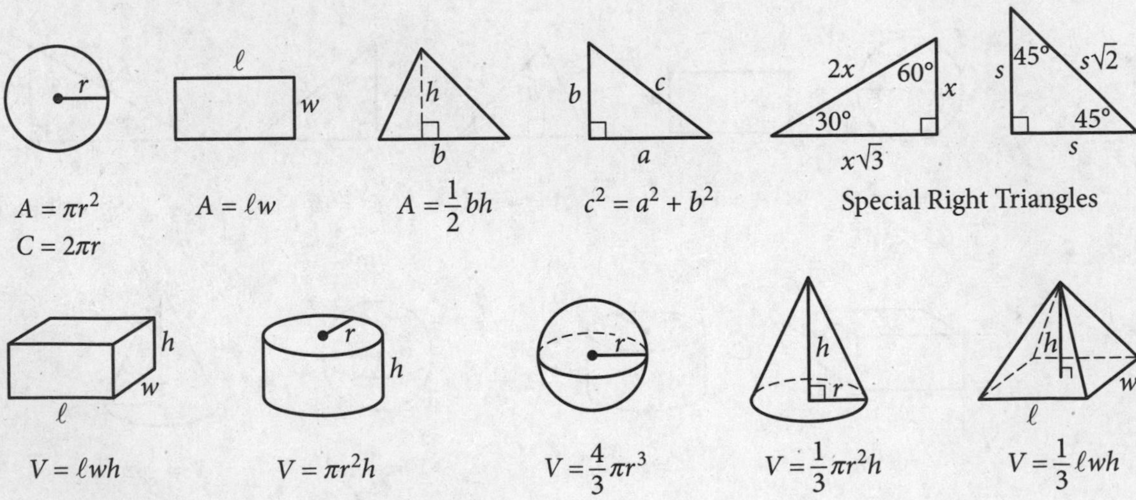

The number of degrees of arc in a circle is 360.
The number of radians of arc in a circle is 2π.
The sum of the measures in degrees of the angles of a triangle is 180.

DIRECTIONS

For questions 16-20, solve the problem and enter your answer in the grid, as described below, on the answer sheet.

1. Although not required, it is suggested that you write your answer in the boxes at the top of the columns to help you fill in the circles accurately. You will receive credit only if the circles are filled in correctly.
2. Mark no more than one circle in any column.
3. No question has a negative answer.
4. Some problems may have more than one correct answer. In such cases, grid only one answer.
5. **Mixed numbers** such as $3\frac{1}{2}$ must be gridded as 3.5 or 7/2. (If 3 1 / 2 is entered into the grid, it will be interpreted as $\frac{31}{2}$, not $3\frac{1}{2}$.)
6. **Decimal answers:** If you obtain a decimal answer with more digits than the grid can accommodate, it may be either rounded or truncated, but it must fill the entire grid.

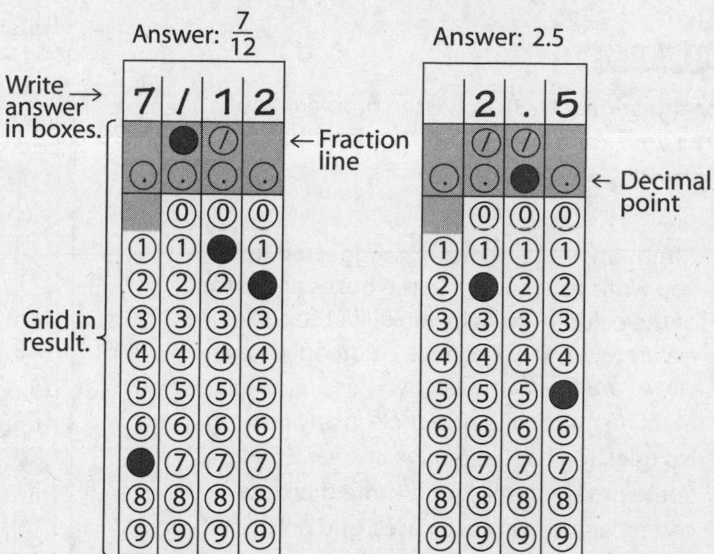

Acceptable ways to grid $\frac{2}{3}$ are:

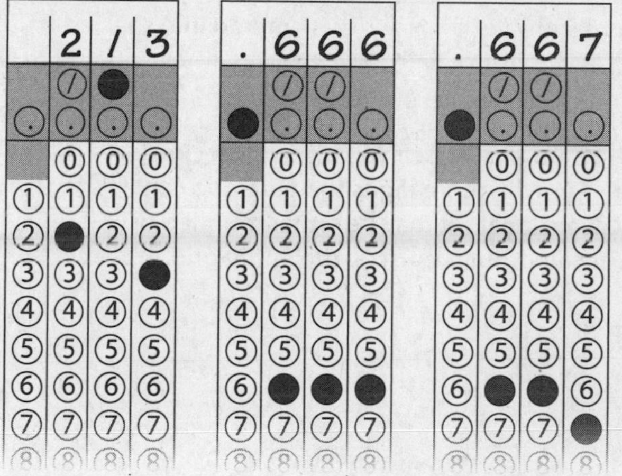

Answer: 201 – either position is correct

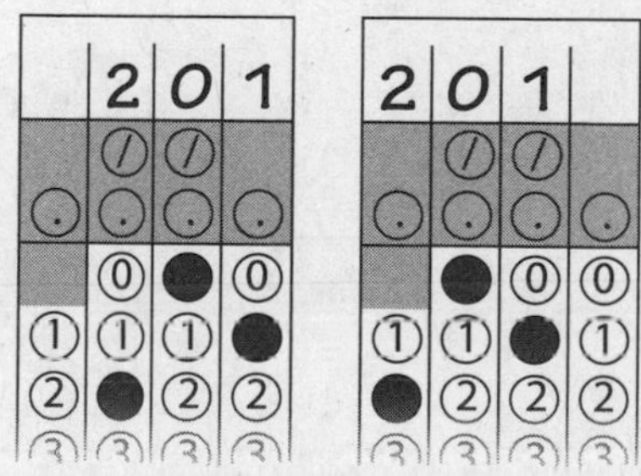

NOTE: You may start your answers in any column, space permitting. Columns you don't need to use should be left blank.

DIRECTIONS

For questions 31-38, solve the problem and enter your answer in the grid, as described below, on the answer sheet.

1. Although not required, it is suggested that you write your answer in the boxes at the top of the columns to help you fill in the circles accurately. You will receive credit only if the circles are filled in correctly.
2. Mark no more than one circle in any column.
3. No question has a negative answer.
4. Some problems may have more than one correct answer. In such cases, grid only one answer.
5. **Mixed numbers** such as $3\frac{1}{2}$ must be gridded as 3.5 or 7/2. (If 3 1 / 2 is entered into the grid, it will be interpreted as $\frac{31}{2}$, not $3\frac{1}{2}$.)
6. **Decimal answers:** If you obtain a decimal answer with more digits than the grid can accommodate, it may be either rounded or truncated, but it must fill the entire grid.

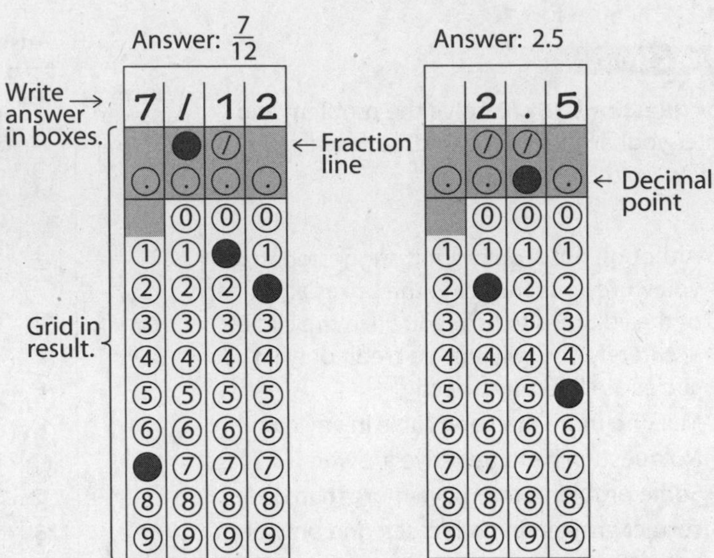

Acceptable ways to grid $\frac{2}{3}$ are:

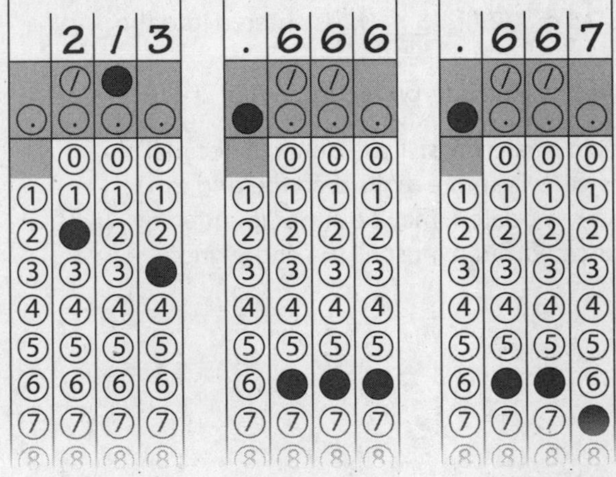

Answer: 201 – either position is correct

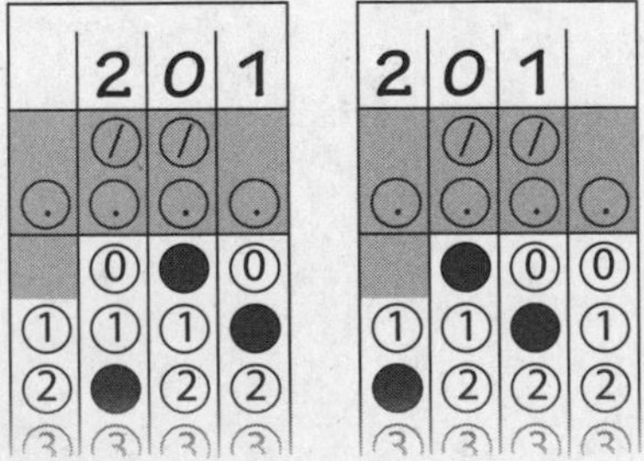

NOTE: You may start your answers in any column, space permitting. Columns you don't need to use should be left blank.

Essay

DIRECTIONS

The essay gives you an opportunity to show how effectively you can read and comprehend a passage and write an essay analyzing the passage. In your essay, you should demonstrate that you have read the passage carefully, present a clear and logical analysis, and use language precisely.

Your essay must be written on the lines provided in your answer booklet; except for the Planning Page of the answer booklet, you will receive no other paper on which to write. You will have enough space if you write on every line, avoid wide margins, and keep your handwriting to a reasonable size. Remember that people who are not familiar with your handwriting will read what you write. Try to write or print so that what you are writing is legible to those readers.

You have <u>50 minutes</u> to read the passage and write an essay in response to the prompt provided inside this booklet.

REMINDERS:

— Do not write your essay in this booklet. Only what you write on the lined pages of your answer booklet will be evaluated.

— An off-topic essay will not be evaluated.

As you read the passage below, consider how [the author] uses

- evidence, such as facts or examples, to support claims.
- reasoning to develop ideas and to connect claims and evidence.
- stylistic or persuasive elements, such as word choice or appeals to emotion, to add power to the ideas expressed.

The passage follows the box above.

Write an essay in which you explain how [the author] builds an argument to persuade [his/her] audience that [author's claim]. In your essay, analyze how [the author] uses one or more of the features listed above (or features of your own choice) to strengthen the logic and persuasiveness of [his/her] argument. Be sure that your analysis focuses on the most relevant aspects of the passage.

Your essay should not explain whether you agree with [the author's] claims, but rather explain how the author builds an argument to persuade [his/her] audience.

The Best Practice

The Sat Suite of Assessments

The SAT is part of an integrated system called the SAT Suite of Assessments. The other tests in the suite are the PSAT/NMSQT®, PSAT™ 10, and PSAT™ 8/9. The tests are connected by the same underlying continuum of knowledge and skills that research shows are the most essential for college and career readiness and success. The PSAT 8/9 is administered to eighth- and ninth-graders, and the PSAT/NMSQT and PSAT 10 are administered to high school sophomores and juniors. The tests in the SAT Suite of Assessments measure the same skills and knowledge in ways that make sense for different grade levels. As you progress through the suite, the tests keep pace, matching the scope and difficulty of the work you're doing in the classroom.

Because the content is aligned across all tests in the suite, taking the earlier tests is a great way to get ready for the SAT. Plus, if you take any test in the SAT Suite of Assessments, you'll get access to video lessons and personalized SAT study resources from Khan Academy®. Talk to your school counselor or visit collegereadiness.collegeboard.org to learn more about the SAT Suite of Assessments.

PRACTICE AT
satpractice.org

Throughout this book, you'll see notes like this one that give you specific ideas on how to improve your SAT score. To learn more about the College Board's partnership with Khan Academy and how it can help you succeed on the SAT, go to **satpractice.org**.

Official Sat Practice from Khan Academy

The College Board's test developers and the online learning experts at Khan Academy worked together to create Official SAT Practice. And it's free — just go to satpractice.org and create a Khan Academy account to get started. Don't miss out on these practice tools:

- Personalized recommendations for practice on the knowledge and skills you need the most help with
- Thousands of questions written by authors trained by College Board test developers
- Video lessons that explain problems step-by-step
- Full-length practice tests

If you've already taken the PSAT 8/9, PSAT 10, PSAT/NMSQT, or the SAT, you can connect your College Board account to your Khan Academy account and automatically get personalized practice recommendations based on your test results. If you haven't yet taken a test in the SAT Suite of Assessments, you'll be able to get personalized practice recommendations after taking diagnostic quizzes.

Daily Practice App

It's easy to make practice a part of your daily routine with the Daily Practice for the New SAT app. You'll get a new question to answer each day, and you'll get immediate feedback. The free app makes it easy to:

- Answer an official Reading, Writing and Language, or Math Test question
- Get a hint if you're stuck
- Read answer explanations and learn from your mistakes
- Keep at it — daily practice can only enhance your knowledge and skills

Daily Practice for the New SAT also has a Scan and Score feature to use when you're practicing on paper. Here's how Scan and Score works:

1. Take a complete SAT practice test, using the official answer sheet to bubble in your answers.
2. Open the Daily Practice app and activate your phone's camera.
3. Keeping the app open, scan your answer sheet with your phone's camera.

You'll have your scores instantly, along with a summary of how you did on each question. Your scores will be saved so you can review your answers and discover what you did right — and wrong.

Daily Practice for the New SAT is available for iPhone, iPad, and iPod Touch in the App Store and for Android devices on Google Play.

Sat Study Group

Creating a study plan and sticking to it are important parts of getting ready for the SAT. Having an SAT study group can help. Working with a group united around a common goal — to do your best on the SAT — can help you stay on track with your study plan and obtain support when you get stuck. And research shows that students who study together learn 2.5 times as much as students who study alone.

To start a successful study group, you'll need to figure a few things out: who, where, and when. You'll want to find other students who plan to take the SAT the same day as you so the same study timeline can work for everyone. An ideal study group will be big enough to be a strong resource, with students who are strong in different areas, and small enough so that everyone stays involved asking and answering questions. Look for five to eight members. Once you have your study group, you'll need to figure out the where and the when. You'll want a place where you can talk and solve problems together and a quiet room where you can take full-length SAT practice tests together. And agreeing on a meeting schedule that works for everyone is important. Try for one or two 45- to 60-minute meetings each week.

Your SAT study group needs someone to keep things running smoothly, doing things such as making sure everyone knows about schedule changes and tracking progress toward goals. A group sponsor — such as a teacher, coach, or parent — could take on these responsibilities, but so can you or another group member. It's good experience, and leading an extracurricular activity is a plus on college applications. Talk to your school counselor or visit collegereadiness.collegeboard.org to find out more about starting an SAT study group.

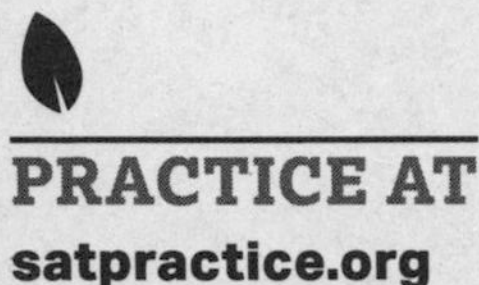

PRACTICE AT
satpractice.org

Resist the temptation to cram hours and hours of test preparation into those last few days before the SAT. Cramming has been shown to be an ineffective study technique and may lead to fatigue and increased anxiety.

Test Day

Counting Down to the Test

In the months and weeks leading up to test day, you'll probably spend a good amount of time preparing for the test: brushing up on old skills, developing new ones, going over sample questions and tests, and so on. In the days immediately preceding the test, you might want to consider taking a different approach by focusing on maintaining your physical health and readiness.

If exercise is part of your daily routine, keep it up. If you like to walk or do other physical activity during times of stress, plan to include these activities in your preparation time. And eat well in the days preceding the test. Your brain operates optimally when you feed your body a balanced diet. On test day, it's good to include proteins and whole grains in your breakfast to help you with lasting energy and focus.

PRACTICE AT
satpractice.org

It's important to get plenty of sleep during the nights leading up to your SAT. But don't drastically alter your sleep schedule by, for instance, going to sleep much earlier than usual. Stick with a sleep schedule that works for you and allows you to do your best.

Get a good night's sleep. In a TED talk, neuroscientist Jeff Iliff explains that our brains use one-quarter of our energy and that a remarkable "cleaning" goes on while we slumber. Many adults and teens know how hard it is to turn off electronics at night. For many, phones, tablets, and computers have become companions, keeping us up-to-date on the latest, well, everything. Using them at night, though, can interfere with sleep. If that sounds like you, you'll find it an interesting experiment to set a time to turn them off.

Readying Yourself the Day Before the Test

- **Plan how you will get to the test site.** If it's in a large school or office building, be sure to find out which door will be open. If you haven't been in the building before, find out how to get to the room.
- **Set two alarms.** Even though alarms rarely fail, it can happen. You'll sleep better knowing you have a backup.
- **Review the list of things you need to take with you, and pack them all in a bag.**
- **Review the test directions once more.**

Understanding What to Pack

- **Photo admission ticket** (remember that the photo must resemble how you'll look on the day of the test and must comply with the rules posted on collegeboard.org/sat)
- **Valid photo ID** (driver's license or other state-issued photo ID, school identification card, valid passport, or student ID form prepared by your school with a photo and the school seal overlapping the photo)
- **Several number 2 pencils** with soft erasers (mechanical pencils are not permitted)
- **Approved calculator** (see collegereadiness.collegeboard.org/sat/taking-the-test for calculator guidance)
- **Watch** (one that only tells time; nothing that can be used to record, transmit, receive, or play back audio, photographic, text, or video content)
- **A drink or snacks** (for your break)

Understanding What Not to Pack

- Cell phones or smartphones
- Audio players or recorders
- Tablets, laptops, notebooks, or any other personal computing devices, including wearable technology
- Separate timers of any type
- Cameras or any other photographic equipment
- Smartwatches or any other devices that can be used to record, transmit, receive, or play back audio, photographic, text, or video content
- Pens, highlighters, or mechanical or colored pencils
- Books, dictionaries, or references of any kind
- Compasses, rulers, protractors, or cutting devices
- Notes, pamphlets, or papers of any kind, including scratch paper
- Earplugs
- Unacceptable calculators that have typewriter-like keypads, use paper tape, make noise, or use a power cord

If you're seen using any of the items above, they'll be held by a test administrator, you'll be asked to leave, or you may be denied admission. Obviously, the better choice is to leave them at home.

REMEMBER

You won't be permitted to take the test if you arrive late. Make sure you know exactly how to get to the test site, and plan to arrive early to account for unexpected transportation delays.

Avoiding Problems on Test Day

You will not be allowed to take the test if:

- The photo on the admission ticket doesn't look like you or otherwise doesn't comply with the rules posted on collegeboard .org/sat (for example, it's too light or too dark, it includes another person, or your face is covered)
- You're missing either the admission ticket or a valid photo ID
- You're late

Please note:

- Changes to where you take the test are not permitted on test day. You can take the test only at the center or school where you're registered to take it.
- Test-type changes are not guaranteed on test day. You can only switch from SAT to SAT with Essay if space and materials allow.
- Walk-in (or standby) testing is not permitted.

Using Good Test-Taking Strategies

Try these strategies out as you practice, and be ready to use them on test day:

- Pace yourself by keeping track of the time using either a clock or a watch that's on your desk. Each section of the test has its own time limit. Check yourself one-quarter, one-half, and three-quarters of the way through the allotted time to make sure you're still on pace.
- While you need to keep your answer sheet free of stray marks, you're welcome to mark up the test booklet as much as you want. Annotating your test booklet can, if done judiciously, help you recall important facts or work through challenging problems.
- Consider skimming the questions in the Reading and the Writing and Language Tests prior to reading each of the passages in order to get a sense of what issues will be important.
- Before reading the answer choices for each multiple-choice question, try to come up with the right answer on your own. Then read the possible answers to find the one closest to your own.
- Always read all the answer choices. You don't want a hasty decision to cause you to select the wrong answer to a question.
- Don't dwell on questions that stump you. Circle ones you decide to skip so that you can return to them quickly later. Remember that a question you answer easily and quickly is worth as much as a question that you struggle with or take a lot of time on.

PRACTICE AT

satpractice.org

Formulating an answer, or at least an approximation of an answer, to a multiple-choice question before reading the answer choices will help you to select the correct answer more accurately and efficiently.

- Remember that there's no penalty for guessing, so you should answer all questions before time is up. When you're not sure of an answer, make an educated guess. For multiple-choice questions, draw lines through each of the answer choices you eliminate. Eliminating even one answer choice substantially increases your odds of choosing correctly.
- **Important:** Be sure to check often to make sure that the number of the question you're about to answer matches the number in the test booklet. Erase and adjust if needed.
- You may finish some sections before time runs out. Review, but do so carefully. You don't want to second-guess yourself and change answers just to change them.

REMEMBER

Answer every question. Points aren't deducted for wrong answers. For multiple-choice questions, eliminate as many answer choices as you can and make an educated guess from among those remaining.

Dealing with Nerves and Distractions

It's not uncommon to feel nervous about the test. Try to consider that adrenaline rush as an aid. It's chemical energy, after all; your body is trying to help. If the energy feels like too much help, take a few slow, deep breaths and remember that you're prepared for this test. Combine that thought with the fact that while this test is important, it's only one of several factors that colleges consider when they review your application.

PRACTICE AT
satpractice.org

It's perfectly normal to feel nervous or anxious on test day. Research has shown that when facing an important event, students who view nervousness as a normal and even a positive response by the body perform better than students who view nervousness as detrimental.

You'll want to put distractions out of your mind as much as possible. If you're momentarily struggling, a nearby student turning a page, for example, can break your concentration and make you feel like you're falling behind (even if you're not). Remember: You have no idea how well other people are doing on the test, and being the fastest doesn't mean being the most successful. Stay focused on your own effort, and push unhelpful thoughts away as quickly as they enter your mind.

One more way to quiet your nerves is to remember that you can take the SAT again. More than half of the students who take the SAT take it twice — once in the spring of their junior year and once in the fall of their senior year. Most students who do so have higher scores on the later test. If you choose this path, make sure you spend time between tests to brush up on areas that you struggled with the first time.

PART 2

Evidence-Based Reading and Writing

CHAPTER 3

Command of Evidence

Despite important differences in purpose, topic, format, content, and style, well-executed pieces of writing still have a lot in common. Authors of all kinds, writing for all sorts of reasons, must make use of support — details, examples, reasons, facts, figures, and so on — to help make their ideas compelling, their points clear, and their claims convincing.

The SAT asks you to pay attention to how authors use support in texts that cover a range of subjects and styles. One important way that the SAT does this is by including questions that ask you to identify the part of the text that provides the best evidence (textual support) for the answer to another question. You'll also be asked to make sense of information presented in graphics, such as tables, graphs, and charts, and to draw connections between that information and the information presented in the passage. You might be asked other sorts of related questions as well, such as how the focus of a piece of writing could be improved (perhaps by deleting irrelevant information) or what role a piece of evidence plays in an author's argument.

REMEMBER

You'll frequently be asked to use evidence to create or defend an argument, or to critically assess someone else's argument, in college and in the workforce.

Your command of evidence will be tested throughout much of the SAT, including the Reading Test, the Writing and Language Test, and the optional Essay. Command of Evidence questions accompany each Reading and Writing and Language passage and contribute to a Command of Evidence subscore. While your response to the Essay prompt doesn't contribute to this subscore, it will still make use of your skill in understanding how an author uses support to make an argument effective.

What We Mean by Command of Evidence

The Command of Evidence category includes questions that focus on many of the ways in which authors use support. These include:

- Determining the best evidence in a passage (or pair of passages) for the answer to a previous question or the best evidence for a specified conclusion (Reading Test)

- Interpreting data presented in informational graphics (such as tables, graphs, and charts) and drawing connections between words and data (Reading Test, Writing and Language Test)
- Understanding how the author of an argument uses (or fails to use) evidence to support the claims he or she makes (Reading Test)
- Revising a passage to clarify main ideas, strengthen support, or sharpen focus (Writing and Language Test)

REMEMBER

While separate from the Command of Evidence score, the Analysis score on the Essay is largely based on knowledge and skills related to those required for Command of Evidence questions.

Having a strong command of evidence is also central to the Essay. Your Analysis score on the Essay is based in large part on how well you can explain how the author of a passage uses evidence, reasoning, stylistic or persuasive techniques, and/or other means to persuade an audience.

Ten Reading Test questions — generally two per passage or pair of passages — contribute to the Command of Evidence subscore. Eight Writing and Language Test questions — again, generally two per passage — also contribute to the subscore. Although not part of the Command of Evidence subscore, the Essay's Analysis score is based heavily on skills related to Command of Evidence questions.

REMEMBER

A total of 18 questions — 10 from the Reading Test and 8 from the Writing and Language Test — contribute to the Command of Evidence subscore.

Let's consider the types of questions in a little more detail.

Determining the Best Evidence (Reading Test)

Sometimes the Reading Test will ask you a question and then present you with another question that asks for the "best evidence" to support the answer to the first question. This is actually simpler than it might seem at first.

You should begin by reading and answering the first question to the best of your ability. This question will often ask you to draw a reasonable conclusion or inference from the passage. As you're reaching that conclusion or inference, you're using textual evidence. Textual evidence can be as simple as a small piece of information, such as a fact or a date, but it can also be more complex or subtle, such as the words an author uses to signal his or her point of view on an issue. Textual evidence helps you defend the answer you might give to a teacher asking how you reached a particular interpretation of a text. Consider the following examples:

- "I think the author supports clearer labeling on food because . . ."
- "The narrator seems to feel sympathy for the main character because . . ."

What would follow "because" in each of these examples is likely to be textual evidence — the "how I know it" part of the statement.

All that the second question in a pair of SAT Reading Test questions is asking you to do, then, is to make explicit what you're already doing when you answer the first question in a pair. Typically, the second question will present you with four excerpts from the passage and ask you which one provides the best evidence for the answer to the previous question. All you need to do is figure out which one does the best job of answering the question of "how I know it" — in other words, which one provides the best textual evidence.

It could be that looking at the choices in the second question makes you reconsider your answer to the first one. That can be OK. Maybe rereading particular parts of the passage made something clearer than it'd been before or drew your attention to a crucial detail you hadn't considered. While you don't want to second-guess yourself endlessly, sometimes it can be a good idea to rethink an answer based on new information.

You may also see questions that present you with a conclusion already drawn and ask you to determine which of the four answer options provides the best evidence from the passage for that conclusion. You can treat these questions just like the textual evidence questions described earlier, except this time you don't have to draw the conclusion yourself in a separate question.

Interpreting Data in Informational Graphics (Reading Test, Writing and Language Test)

Some passages in both the Reading Test and the Writing and Language Test are accompanied by one or more informational graphics. These graphics, which are typically tables, graphs, or charts, usually represent numerical data in visual form, such as results from a scientific experiment. On the Reading Test, you may be asked to locate or interpret information in the graphic, but you may also or instead be asked to draw connections between the graphic and the accompanying passage. For instance, you may be asked how data in the graphic support a particular conclusion reached by the author of the passage. On the Writing and Language Test, you may be asked to revise a passage to correct an error in the writer's interpretation of a table, replace a general description with precise figures, or add accurate and relevant information in support of a claim.

PRACTICE AT
satpractice.org

When a question refers to a table, graph, or chart, carefully examine the graphic to get a clear understanding of the data being displayed. This may include reading the title, identifying what the *x*- and *y*-axes represent, noting the increment values on the axes, and reading any captions.

It's important to note that these Reading and Writing and Language questions aren't math questions in disguise. You won't need to add, subtract, multiply, or divide (and you won't have access to a calculator). The questions instead ask you to "read" graphics and draw conclusions, much as you do when you read and interpret written texts.

Understanding How an Argument Uses (or Doesn't Use) Evidence (Reading Test)

Being able to figure out how an author constructs an argument is an important skill needed for success in college and workforce training programs — and on the SAT. Arguments seek to convince readers

PRACTICE AT
satpractice.org

Questions on the Reading Test that ask about the use of evidence may require you to take a step back from what the author is saying and to focus instead on how the author's argument is put together.

(or listeners or viewers) of the rightness of one or more claims, or assertions. To do this, authors of arguments make use of evidence, reasoning, and stylistic and persuasive elements such as vivid imagery or appeals to emotion to flesh out their claims. A reader convinced by an author's argument may end up changing his or her view on a topic or be persuaded to take a particular action.

Arguments are a consistent part of the Reading Test (as well as the Writing and Language Test and the Essay). Reading Test questions that focus on evidence use may ask you to identify what type of evidence a particular author relies on most heavily (personal anecdotes or survey results, for example), to determine what evidence in the passage supports a particular claim, or to decide whether a new piece of information (such as a research finding) would strengthen or weaken an author's case.

Analyzing an argument, including its use of evidence, is the main focus of the optional Essay, which we'll turn to momentarily.

Improving a Passage's Structure, Support, and Focus (Writing and Language Test)

PRACTICE AT
satpractice.org

Developing a clear understanding of the writer's overall purpose in a Writing and Language Test passage is critical to answering many Command of Evidence questions. Be sure you're always thinking about the writer's purpose as you read passages on the SAT.

As noted earlier, the Writing and Language Test may ask you to revise a passage to better incorporate information from one or more graphics into the text. The test will ask you to show your command of evidence in other ways as well. You may end up adding or revising a topic sentence to improve the clarity and structure of a passage. You may also add or revise supporting material, such as a description or an example, to make the writer's claim or point more robust. Other questions may ask you to think about whether adding, revising, or removing a particular sentence would sharpen or blur the focus of a certain paragraph or the passage as a whole. The element that these Writing and Language questions (along with questions about informational graphics) have in common is that they require you to think about how a writer develops a topic through making and building up claims or points.

A Note About the Essay

PRACTICE AT
satpractice.org

Another reason preparing for and taking the SAT Essay is a good idea is that in doing so, you'll be practicing many of the skills you need to do well on multiple-choice Command of Evidence questions.

The optional Essay's three scores aren't combined with scores on the multiple-choice portion of the SAT and thus don't contribute to the Command of Evidence subscore. However, as we mentioned before, the heart of the Essay task is analyzing an argument and explaining how the author builds the argument to persuade an audience through evidence, reasoning, and/or stylistic or persuasive elements (or other elements you identify). The main focus of the Essay — and the foundation for its Analysis score — is, therefore, connected to your command of evidence in the broad sense. Receiving a good Analysis score requires making use of many of the same skills called on by the Command of Evidence questions on the multiple-choice Reading Test and Writing and Language Test.

Chapter 3 Recap

The Command of Evidence subscore on the SAT is based on questions from both the Reading Test and the Writing and Language Test. These questions are designed to see whether you understand how authors make use of information and ideas to develop and support their claims and points.

You'll find three types of questions on the **Reading Test** that address command of evidence.

1. **Determining the best evidence:** You'll be asked to figure out which part of a passage offers the strongest support for the answer to another question or for a conclusion that the question itself provides. These sorts of questions accompany every passage on the test.
2. **Interpreting data presented in informational graphics:** You'll be asked to locate particular information in tables, graphs, charts, and the like; draw conclusions from such data; and make connections between the data and the information and ideas in a passage. These sorts of questions accompany select passages, as only some passages on the test include graphics.
3. **Understanding how an argument uses (or doesn't use) evidence:** You'll be asked to think about how an author makes (or fails to make) use of supporting information, such as facts, figures, and quotations, to develop claims. These sorts of questions accompany select passages on the test — those that stake out one or more claims and seek to make those claims convincing through the use of evidence, reasoning, and stylistic and persuasive elements.

You'll find two types of questions on the **Writing and Language Test** that address command of evidence.

1. **Interpreting data presented in informational graphics:** You'll be asked to use data in tables, graphs, charts, and the like when you're revising passages to make the passage more accurate, clear, precise, or convincing. These sorts of questions accompany select passages, as only some passages on the test include graphics.
2. **Improving a passage's structure, support, and focus:** You'll be asked to revise passages to make the writer's central ideas sharper; add or revise supporting information, such as facts, figures, and quotations; and eliminate information that's irrelevant or that just doesn't belong at a particular point in a passage. These sorts of questions accompany nearly every passage on the test.

Although not contributing to the subscore, the optional **Essay** is very much about command of evidence, as its task centers on analyzing how an author builds an argument to persuade an audience. To do well on the Essay — especially in terms of getting a good Analysis score — you'll have to consider how the author uses evidence, reasoning, stylistic or persuasive elements, or other techniques to influence readers.

As you approach all of these questions and tasks, you'll want to think like an author. Answering for yourself such questions as "What evidence in the passage is being used to support the author's interpretation?" and "How relevant is this information to the passage as a whole?" is critical to getting a good Command of Evidence subscore on the SAT.

CHAPTER 4

Words in Context

You'll see questions on the SAT about the meaning and use of words and phrases. These questions will always refer to multiparagraph passages, and the words and phrases focused on will be ones that are important to readings in many subject areas. Having questions about words and phrases embedded in extended passages means that there'll be context clues to draw on as you determine meaning, analyze rhetorical impact, and make choices about which word or phrase to use in a particular writing situation. It also means that the meaning and use of these words and phrases will be shaped, often in complex or subtle ways, by context. Moreover, the test's emphasis on words and phrases used fairly frequently means that you'll be able to devote your attention to acquiring vocabulary knowledge that's likely to be of use to you throughout your academic career instead of focusing on words and phrases that you're unlikely to encounter again after taking the test.

Let's consider the kinds of words and phrases that are tested on the SAT and then briefly examine the sorts of Words in Context questions you'll find on the test.

REMEMBER

The SAT won't test you on the meaning of obscure, seldom-used words and phrases presented with little context. Rather, you'll be tested on words and phrases that often appear in college courses and beyond and that are grounded in rich contexts.

High-Utility Academic Words and Phrases

The SAT focuses on "high-utility academic words and phrases," the type of vocabulary that you can find in challenging readings across a wide range of subjects. You may, for example, come across the word "restrain" — one of these high-utility academic words — in a number of different types of texts. You could find it in a novel in which the main character is trying to restrain, or hold in check, his emotions; you could also find it in a social studies text discussing how embargoes can be used to restrain, or limit, trade among nations. Note, too, how the precise meaning of "restrain" varies to some extent based on the context in which the word appears.

PRACTICE AT
satpractice.org

Since the SAT focuses on academic words and phrases commonly encountered in challenging texts, a good way to prepare is to read texts across a range of subjects and types. As you encounter unfamiliar words or phrases, practice using context clues to determine their meaning.

PRACTICE AT
satpractice.org

We do *not* recommend practicing by poring over long lists of obscure, esoteric vocabulary.

As the above example suggests, high-utility academic words and phrases are different from other kinds of vocabulary you know and will encounter in school and life. High-utility academic words and phrases aren't generally part of conversational language, so if you know the common meanings of a word such as "restrain," it's probably because you either learned it by reading a lot or from vocabulary lessons in school. High-utility academic words and phrases aren't technical terms, either. "Atomic mass," "ductile," and "isotope" may sound like they'd fit into the category of high-utility academic words and phrases, but what makes them different is that they're generally only used in particular types of texts and conversations — in this case, readings about and discussions of science. This doesn't mean that these terms aren't worth knowing — far from it — but it does mean that, in some sense, their value is more limited than that of words and phrases that you might encounter in many different sorts of texts and discussions. Since the SAT can't (and shouldn't) try to test everything, the College Board has chosen to focus on high-utility academic words and phrases because of their great power in unlocking the meaning of the complex texts that you're likely to encounter in high school and postsecondary courses.

Words in Context Questions

Questions in the Words in Context category ask you to consider both the meaning and role of words and phrases as they are used in particular passages. You'll also be asked to think about how to make language use more effective. These questions focus on the following skills:

- Interpreting words and phrases in context (Reading Test)
- Analyzing word choice rhetorically (Reading Test)
- Making effective use of language (Writing and Language Test)

Ten Reading Test questions — generally two per passage; a mix of questions about word/phrase meanings and rhetorical word choice — contribute to the Words in Context subscore. Eight Writing and Language Test questions — again, generally two per passage — also contribute to the subscore; these eight questions will cover a range of skills, from making text more precise or concise to maintaining style and tone to combining two or more sentences into a smoother, more effective single sentence.

Let's consider each of these three main types more fully.

Interpreting Words and Phrases in Context (Reading Test)

A number of questions on the Reading Test will require you to figure out the precise meaning of a given word or phrase based on how it's used in a particular passage. "Precise" is an important qualifier here, as you'll generally be asked to pick the most appropriate meaning of a word or phrase with more than one dictionary definition. The extended context — up to and including an entire passage — gives you more clues to meaning, but you'll have to make good use of those clues to decide on which of the offered meanings makes the most sense in a given passage.

PRACTICE AT
satpractice.org

Often, Reading Test answer choices will each contain one of several possible real-world meanings of the tested word or phrase. Make use of the context clues in the passage to hone in on the precise meaning of the word or phrase as it's used in the passage.

Here's an example: Think about the word "intense," which is a pretty good representative of high-utility academic words and phrases. Maybe you associate this word with emotion or attitude, as in "He's an intense person," or perhaps with determination, as in "She put forth intense effort in order to do well on the quiz." However, neither of these quite matches how "intense" is used in the following excerpt from a longer passage.

PRACTICE AT
satpractice.org

A good strategy here is to use context clues in the paragraph to come up with a word that could replace "intense" while maintaining the intended meaning of the sentence.

> [. . .] The coming decades will likely see more intense clustering of jobs, innovation, and productivity in a smaller number of bigger cities and city-regions. Some regions could end up bloated beyond the capacity of their infrastructure, while others struggle, their promise stymied by inadequate human or other resources.
>
> Adapted from Richard Florida, *The Great Reset*. ©2010 by Richard Florida.

In this case, "intense" is more about degree: the clustering of jobs, innovation, and productivity is, according to the author, likely to be denser, or more concentrated in fewer large cities and city-regions, in the coming decades. While prior knowledge of what "intense" often means could be useful here, you'd also have to read and interpret the context in order to determine exactly how the word is being used in this case.

Analyzing Word Choice Rhetorically (Reading Test)

Other Words in Context questions on the Reading Test may ask you to figure out how the author's particular choice of a word, phrase, or pattern of words or phrases influences the meaning, tone, or style of a passage. Sometimes these questions deal with the connotations, or associations, that certain words and phrases evoke. Consider how you (or an author) might describe someone who wasn't accompanied by other people. Saying that person was "alone" is more or less just pointing out a fact. To say instead that that person was "solitary" offers a stronger sense of isolation. To instead call that person "forlorn" or even "abandoned" goes yet a step further in casting the person's separateness in a particular, negative way. Deciding which word or

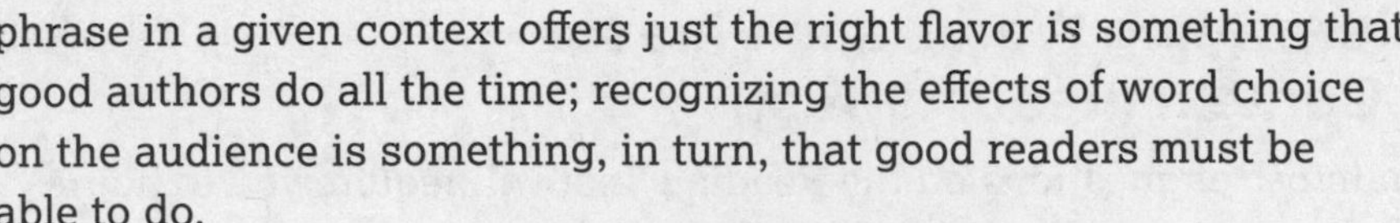

phrase in a given context offers just the right flavor is something that good authors do all the time; recognizing the effects of word choice on the audience is something, in turn, that good readers must be able to do.

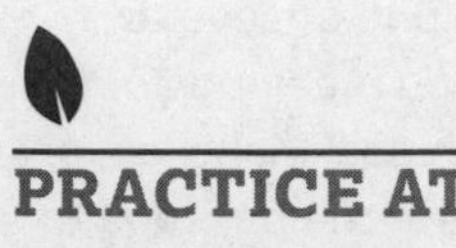

PRACTICE AT
satpractice.org

Taking context into consideration is critical when answering questions about the effective use of language. You may, for instance, need to consider the overall tone or style of the passage or the writer's purpose when choosing your answer.

Making Effective Use of Language (Writing and Language Test)

While the Reading Test asks you to interpret how authors use words and phrases, the Writing and Language Test calls on you to make those kinds of decisions yourself as you revise passages. Questions about effective language use are varied. Some questions may present you with language that's wordy or redundant, and you'll have to choose a more concise way of conveying the same idea without changing the meaning. Other questions may ask you to choose the most precise way to say something or the most appropriate way to express an idea in a given context. Other questions may have you pick out the word or phrase that does the best job of maintaining the style or tone of the passage, or of continuing a particular linguistic pattern, such as repetition for emphasis or cohesion. In these cases, you may have to replace informal language with a more formal expression (or vice versa, depending on the style and tone of the overall passage) or decide which option most effectively maintains a pattern. Still other questions may require you to combine whole sentences or parts of two or more sentences to make choppy or repetitive sentences flow more smoothly or to accomplish some other goal (such as placing emphasis on an action rather than on the person performing the action).

It's worth noting here that these language use questions aren't directly about grammar, usage, or mechanics. Instead, these questions try to get you to think about how language should be used to accomplish particular writerly aims, such as being clearer, more precise, or more economical.

Chapter 4 Recap

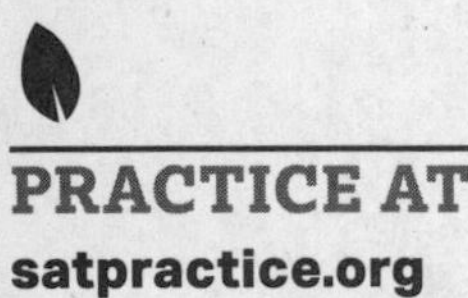

PRACTICE AT
satpractice.org

Since the words and phrases you'll be tested on are set within extended contexts, you'll have clues to help you determine the correct meaning. Don't be discouraged if you're unfamiliar with some of the tested words or phrases.

The Words in Context subscore on the SAT is based on questions from both the Reading Test and the Writing and Language Test. These questions are intended to determine whether you can figure out word and phrase meanings in context and how authors use words and phrases to achieve specific purposes.

There are two types of questions on the **Reading Test** that address words in context.

1. **Interpreting words and phrases in context:** You'll be asked to decide on the precise meaning of particular words and phrases as they're used in context. This will typically involve considering various real-world meanings of words and phrases and picking the

one that most closely matches how the word or phrase is used in the passage. These sorts of questions accompany most passages on the test.

2. **Analyzing word choice rhetorically:** You'll be asked to think about how an author's choice of words and phrases helps shape meaning, tone, and style. These sorts of questions accompany select passages on the test.

REMEMBER

Analyzing word choice is also an integral part of your task on the Essay.

You'll find a single main type of question (and several subtypes) on the **Writing and Language Test** that addresses words in context. In questions about effective language use, you'll be asked to revise passages to improve the precision and concision of expression; ensure that the style and tone of the passage are appropriate and consistent; and combine sentences or parts of sentences to enhance flow or to achieve some other purpose (such as emphasis). These sorts of questions accompany every passage on the test.

While the specific format of Words in Context questions varies within and between the Reading Test and the Writing and Language Test, all of the questions ask you to consider the same kinds of choices about language that skilled authors routinely make. As you approach each question, you'll want to examine the nuances of word and phrase meanings and connotations as well as the impact that particular words, phrases, and language patterns are likely to have on the reader.

CHAPTER 5

About the SAT Reading Test

Whatever your postsecondary plans, reading will be important. Even as other forms of media, such as audiovisual formats, have gained a valuable place in education, the written word remains a vital tool in conveying information and ideas. Whether you're taking a course in literature, history, physics, or accounting, your ability to read and understand text — often largely or wholly on your own — will be critical to doing well in the class. The SAT Reading Test is designed to assess how ready you are to read and interpret the kinds of texts you're likely to encounter in college and career.

REMEMBER

The basic aim of the SAT Reading Test is to determine whether you're able to comprehend the many types of challenging literary and informational texts you're likely to encounter in college and career.

The passages (reading selections) on the Reading Test vary in genre, purpose, subject, and complexity in order to assess your skill in comprehending a diverse range of texts similar to those you'll come across in many different postsecondary courses. The Reading Test will also include a pair of related passages, with some questions asking you to draw connections between the two selections. Some passages will include one or more informational graphics, such as tables, graphs, and charts, and you'll be expected both to understand those graphics and to link the information contained in them with information found in the passage.

You'll be answering questions that deal with both what's stated and what's implied in these texts — that is, what authors say directly and what they suggest but don't come right out and say explicitly. Some questions deal with the information and ideas in passages, while others focus on structure, purpose, and other aspects of the craft of writing; still others ask you to draw connections between pairs of related passages or analyze informational graphics. As a group, these questions require you to use the same close reading skills you're already using in your high school classes and that are important to have in order to be successful in college courses and workforce training programs.

The rest of this chapter is an overview of the Reading Test. Additional information about the question types can be found in the next three chapters.

Reading Test Passages

The passages on the Reading Test are as varied as those you're reading now for your high school classes. Some are literary in nature, while others are primarily informational. They differ in purpose as well: Some tell a story, while others share information, explain a process or concept, or try to convince you to accept or do something. They also cover a wide range of subjects. Some passages are particularly challenging, while others are more straightforward. In addition, some passages are paired, and others are accompanied by one or more informational graphics.

Here are some of the key features of Reading Test passages.

- **Genre:** The Reading Test includes both literary and informational passages. Literary passages are primarily concerned with telling a story, recounting an event or experience, or reflecting on an idea or concept. The Reading Test includes both a fiction selection and a selection from a historically or culturally important document, such as a speech, essay, or letter. Informational passages, as the name implies, are mostly concerned with conveying information and ideas.
- **Purpose:** As noted above, some Reading Test passages are mainly focused on telling a story, recounting an event or experience, or reflecting on an idea or concept. Other passages present information and ideas or explain a process or concept. Still other passages are best described as arguments. Their goal is to convince readers through the use of evidence, reasoning, and/or stylistic and persuasive techniques to believe something or to take some sort of action.
- **Subject:** The Reading Test includes passages in three major subject areas: U.S. and world literature, history/social studies, and science. Literature passages are selections from classic and more recent works of fiction by authors from the United States and around the world. History/social studies passages include selections from fields such as economics, sociology, and political science. This category also includes selections from U.S. founding documents and similar texts in the Great Global Conversation about civic and political life written by authors from the United States and other nations. Science passages deal with information, concepts, and experiments in the fields of Earth science, biology, chemistry, and physics.
- **Complexity:** The reading challenge posed by the passages on the test varies. Some passages are relatively straightforward. They may, for example, have a very clear purpose, present a fairly small amount of information, and use familiar language. Other passages, by contrast, are more complex. They may have multiple levels of

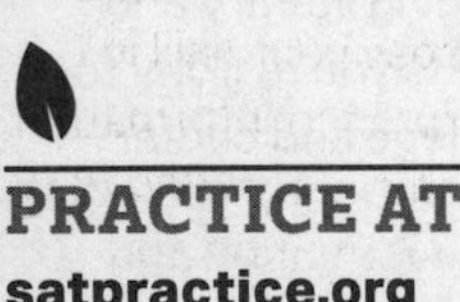

PRACTICE AT
satpractice.org

You may find that you're better at reading and interpreting passages from one subject area — history/social studies, for instance — than from others. It's important, therefore, to practice reading and answering questions about passages from all three subject areas on the SAT Reading Test (U.S. and world literature, history/social studies, and science). In fact, consider devoting more practice time to the type(s) of passages you're less comfortable reading.

meaning (such as a literal and a metaphorical level), require the reader to follow a complicated series of events, and make use of long and involved sentences. (It's important to note here that each administration of the Reading Test has a similar range of passage complexity, so you shouldn't worry about getting a test that has nothing but highly complex passages.) Chapter 9 includes examples of low- and high-complexity passages to give you a sense of the spread of difficulty you'll see on the test.

Two other features of passages are important as well.

- **Paired passages:** Each administration of the Reading Test includes a pair of related passages. These passages are on the same topic and interact with one another in some way. They may, for instance, present different perspectives or opinions on a topic, with the first passage taking one position and the second passage another. In other cases, the two passages may simply contain different information on the same topic. One may be a general overview, for example, while the other zeroes in on one particular element. The set of associated questions will ask about each passage separately as well as about both passages together. History/social studies and science passages may be paired.
- **Informational graphics:** Some passages include one or more tables, graphs, charts, and the like that correspond to the topic of the passage. A graphic may, for instance, display the results of an experiment described in the passage. Questions may ask you to locate information in the graphic, draw reasonable conclusions about the graphic's data, or make connections between the graphic and the passage. Graphics appear with one of the history/social studies and one of the science passages.

REMEMBER

Two passages on the SAT Reading Test will include one or more informational graphics — tables, graphs, charts, or the like. Related questions will assess your skill in locating and interpreting information in the graphic(s) and integrating that information with information and ideas in the passage.

All of the passages on the Reading Test come from previously published, high-quality sources. The Reading Test always includes:

- One passage from a classic or contemporary work of U.S. or world literature
- One passage or a pair of passages from either a U.S. founding document (such as an essay by James Madison) or a text in the Great Global Conversation (such as a speech by Nelson Mandela)
- One passage on a social science topic from a field such as economics, psychology, or sociology
- Two science passages (or one passage and one passage pair) that examine foundational concepts or recent developments in Earth science, biology, chemistry, or physics

Reading Test Questions

All Reading Test questions are multiple-choice and have four answer options. To decide which of the four answer choices makes the most sense, you'll want to consider what's stated and implied in the passage (or passage pair), along with any supplementary material (such as a table or graph). The questions follow something of a natural order. You'll find questions about the passage as a whole — questions about the main idea or point of view, for example — early on in each set, while questions about specific parts of the passage come later. Questions about graphics and questions linking paired passages typically come near the end of the sequence.

REMEMBER

Wrong answer choices are often tempting. You must, therefore, base your answer on a close reading and interpretation of the passage and any associated graphics.

The questions are meant to be like those that you'd ask or answer in a lively, serious discussion about a text. Think of the kinds of questions you'd be asked to consider in your favorite, most engaging class, and you'll have the general idea of what's on the Reading Test. The questions aren't intended to be tricky or trivial, although some will be quite challenging and will require careful reading and thinking. They're designed to determine whether you're reading closely and making reasonable interpretations, so expect to see some answer choices that may seem right or fit your preconceptions but that don't match up with what an author is saying.

REMEMBER

All of the information you need to answer the questions can be found in the passages themselves or in supplementary material such as graphics. You won't be tested directly on your background knowledge of the specific topics covered. In fact, be careful if applying outside knowledge to a passage or its questions, as this may skew your interpretation.

The questions also often reflect the specific sort of passage you're reading. A literature question may ask you to think about plot or character, but a science question won't; instead, it may ask about things such as hypotheses and experimental data. Although passages are taken from texts on various subjects, the questions don't directly test your background knowledge of the specific topics covered. All of the information you'll need to answer the questions can be found in the passages themselves (or in any supplementary material, such as a graphic).

Reading Test questions fall into three general categories: (1) Information and Ideas, (2) Rhetoric, and (3) Synthesis. The questions won't be labeled this way on the test, and it's not crucial that you understand all of the differences. A brief explanation of each category, though, should help you get a sense of what you'll encounter, what knowledge and skills are covered, and how better to prepare for the test.

- **Information and Ideas:** These questions focus on the author's message. In these sorts of questions, you'll be asked to locate stated information, make reasonable inferences, and apply what you've read to another, similar situation. You'll also be asked to figure out the best evidence in the passage for the answer to another question or the best support for a conclusion offered in the question itself. You'll also have to determine central ideas and themes, summarize important information, and understand relationships (including cause-and-effect, comparison-contrast, and sequence). Other questions will ask you to interpret the meaning of words and phrases as they are used in particular contexts.

- **Rhetoric:** These questions focus your attention on how an author puts together a text and how the various pieces contribute to the whole text. You'll be asked to think about how an author's word choice shapes meaning, tone, and style. You'll also be asked to consider how a passage is structured and what purpose its various parts (such as a particular detail) play. Questions about the author's point of view and purpose are also part of this category, as are questions about the claims, reasons, evidence, and stylistic and persuasive devices (such as appeals to fear or emotion) found in arguments. The common thread tying these questions together is their emphasis on the author's craft. Instead of thinking about the author's message per se, you'll be thinking about how the author constructs his or her text to make its message clear, engaging, informative, or convincing.
- **Synthesis:** Unlike questions in the other two categories, Synthesis questions only accompany certain passages. They come in two basic forms. Some Synthesis questions ask you to draw connections between a pair of passages. For example, a question may ask how the author of the first passage in a pair would most likely react to a claim made by the author of the second passage. A question may instead ask you something more general, such as how the two passages are similar or different in content, form, style, or perspective. Other Synthesis questions ask about informational graphics. In these, you may have to find a particular piece of data, figure out which conclusion is the most reasonable given a certain set of results from a study, or integrate information from a table with the information and ideas found in the passage itself.

The Reading Test in Overview

Having a general sense of how the Reading Test is put together will help you to prepare for the test and pace yourself during the test itself.

- Total Questions: 52
- Total Time: 65 minutes (on average, a minute and 15 seconds per question, inclusive of passage reading time)
- Number of Passages: Four single passages plus one pair of passages
- Passage Length: 500 to 750 words; total of 3,250 words
- Passage Subjects: One U.S. and world literature passage, two history/social studies passages (one in social science and one from a U.S. founding document or text in the Great Global Conversation), and two science passages

REMEMBER

You'll have 65 minutes to answer 52 questions on the Reading Test, or 1 minute and 15 seconds per question on average. However, it's important to keep in mind that you'll spend a good portion of this time reading the four single passages along with one pair of passages.

- Passage Complexities: A defined range from grades 9–10 to early postsecondary
- Questions per Passage: 10 or 11
- Scores: In addition to an overall test score, the questions on the Reading Test contribute to various scores in the following ways:
  - Command of Evidence: 10 questions, generally two per passage
  - Words in Context: 10 questions, generally two per passage
  - Analysis in History/Social Studies: 21 questions (all of the questions on the two history/social studies passages)
  - Analysis in Science: 21 questions (all of the questions on the two science passages)

NOTE: *Some Reading Test questions don't contribute to any of these scores (just to the overall test score), and some history/social studies and science questions (such as vocabulary questions) may contribute to two of these scores.*

Chapter 5 Recap

The SAT Reading Test measures your skill in reading and comprehending texts across a wide range of genres, purposes, subjects, and complexities. The questions on the test are all multiple-choice, mirror those that you'd encounter in a good class discussion, and cover three basic areas: Information and Ideas, Rhetoric, and Synthesis. All of the questions can be answered based on what's stated or implied in the passages (and in any supplementary material provided), and no question tests background knowledge of the topic. Each administration of the test includes one passage pair, and two passages (one in history/social studies, one in science) include an informational graphic or graphics.

PRACTICE AT
satpractice.org

Devote ample practice time to reading passages efficiently and strategically, considering the types of things you'll likely be asked in SAT questions. With practice, you'll find that you can read passages more quickly and gain a stronger grasp of the content, structure, and author's purpose.

There's quite a bit to read on the test and also a fair number of questions; the length of the test, however, is balanced by three factors. First, the passages, while often challenging, are like those that you're probably already reading for your high school classes, and they cover many of the same subjects as well. Second, the questions deal with important aspects of the passages rather than trivia, so if you grasp the central ideas and key details of each passage, you're more likely to do well. Finally, enough time is provided (65 minutes) so that you should be able to answer the questions without a lot of rushing as long as you maintain a good, consistent pace and watch the clock.

CHAPTER 6

Reading: Information and Ideas

Questions on the Reading Test can be sorted into three categories: (1) Information and Ideas, (2) Rhetoric, and (3) Synthesis. This chapter focuses on the first category, Information and Ideas.

Information and Ideas: The Author's Message

Information and Ideas questions ask you to think carefully about the author's message. To interpret that message, you'll need to consider both what's stated and what's implied in the passage. By "stated," we mean the things that the author mentions directly and explicitly, such as facts, figures, and other kinds of main points and key details. "Implied," by contrast, refers to what isn't directly stated but is otherwise strongly suggested and can reasonably be inferred.

Let's examine the specific sorts of questions that make up the Information and Ideas category and what kinds of skills and knowledge these questions expect of you.

Questions in this category are of six main types:

- **Reading Closely:** Determining what's stated or implied in a passage and applying what you've learned from it to a new, similar situation
- **Citing Textual Evidence:** Deciding which part of a passage best supports either the answer to another question or a given conclusion
- **Determining Central Ideas and Themes:** Understanding the main point(s) or theme(s) of a passage
- **Summarizing:** Recognizing an effective summary of a passage or of a part of a passage
- **Understanding Relationships**: Establishing connections (such as cause-and-effect, comparison-contrast, and sequence) between people, events, ideas, and the like in a passage

- **Interpreting Words and Phrases in Context:** Figuring out the precise meaning of a particular word or phrase as it's used in a passage

Let's explore each of these types in turn.

Reading Closely

Reading Closely is the most general of the question types on the Reading Test. It includes a broad range of questions that deal with interpreting what an author has said explicitly or implicitly and applying that information to new contexts. You may be asked to locate a point or detail in a passage or to reach a supportable conclusion or inference based on what's been stated directly, or you may be asked to think about how the information and ideas in the passage could be applied to another analogous case or situation.

REMEMBER

Keywords in the question will often clue you in on whether you're being asked about information that was explicitly stated in the passage or about an implicit message that was suggested by the passage. Being aware of this will help you approach questions more effectively.

The questions themselves don't follow an easily recognized pattern, but in each case, you'll have to read attentively and consider what the author is trying to say directly or indirectly. There are also often one or more clues within the question that hint at the kind of work you'll have to do. If the question uses "according to the passage," "states," "indicates," or something similar, it's likely that you should look for something said explicitly in the text. On the other hand, if the question uses "based on the passage," "it can reasonably be inferred," "implies," or the like, you'll probably need to interpret the passage to figure out an implicit message.

Citing Textual Evidence

Questions of this type ask you to determine which portion of the passage provides the best textual evidence for the answer to another question or for a conclusion offered in the question itself.

Consider this brief excerpt from a speech by Congresswoman Barbara Jordan, who was discussing the nature and seriousness of the impeachment of a president in the U.S. political process. The sentences that are the focus of the first of two paired questions have been highlighted here for convenience, but they wouldn't be if this were a real test. (The full passage, along with more thorough answer explanations, can be found in Chapter 9.)

. . . The North Carolina ratification convention: "No one need be afraid that officers who commit oppression will pass with immunity." **"Prosecutions of impeachments will seldom fail to agitate the passions of the whole community," said Hamilton in the *Federalist Papers*, number 65. "We divide into parties more or less friendly or inimical to the accused." I do not mean political parties in that sense.**

The drawing of political lines goes to the motivation behind impeachment; but impeachment must proceed within the confines of the constitutional term "high crime[s] and misdemeanors." Of the impeachment process, it was Woodrow Wilson who said that "Nothing short of the grossest offenses against the plain law of the land will suffice to give them speed and effectiveness. Indignation so great as to overgrow party interest may secure a conviction; but nothing else can." [. . .]

Adapted from a speech delivered by Congresswoman Barbara Jordan of Texas on July 25, 1974, as a member of the Judiciary Committee of the United States House of Representatives.

In lines 46-50 ("Prosecutions . . . sense"), what is the most likely reason Jordan draws a distinction between two types of "parties"?

A) To counter the suggestion that impeachment is or should be about partisan politics

B) To disagree with Hamilton's claim that impeachment proceedings excite passions

C) To contend that Hamilton was too timid in his support for the concept of impeachment

D) To argue that impeachment cases are decided more on the basis of politics than on justice

The above question isn't our main interest here, but we need to consider it briefly in order to make sense of the second of the two questions. The best answer here is choice A. In the paragraph containing the highlighted sentences, Jordan quotes Alexander Hamilton, who talks about how people "divide into parties" of those who oppose or support impeachment (those who are "more or less friendly or inimical to the accused"). She then goes on to say, "I do not mean political parties in that sense." Here, she draws a distinction between informal groups of people — those simply for and against impeachment, as Hamilton meant — and organized political parties, such as the modern-day Republican and Democratic parties. The most likely reason Jordan goes to this trouble is because she's worried about being misinterpreted. (This becomes clear elsewhere in the passage, where she indicates that, in her view, impeachment shouldn't be about pure politics but rather about serious violations of the law by a president.)

PRACTICE AT
satpractice.org

When you're asked to explain why the author of the passage includes a specific statement, carefully consider the context of the statement as well as the author's broader point of view in the passage overall.

REMEMBER

Many Citing Textual Evidence questions will require you to select the statement from a passage that best supports the answer to a previous question.

But how do we know choice A is the best answer? That's where textual evidence comes in, and it's the basis for the second question in the pair. Before we look at the actual question format, though, consider the following brief quotations from the larger passage. Ask yourself: Which one best supports the answer to the previous question?

> It is wrong, I suggest, it is a misreading of the Constitution for any member here to assert that for a member to vote for an article of impeachment means that that member must be convinced that the President should be removed from office.
>
> The division between the two branches of the legislature, the House and the Senate, assigning to the one the right to accuse and to the other the right to judge—the framers of this Constitution were very astute.
>
> The drawing of political lines goes to the motivation behind impeachment; but impeachment must proceed within the confines of the constitutional term "high crime[s] and misdemeanors."
>
> Congress has a lot to do: appropriations, tax reform, health insurance, campaign finance reform, housing, environmental protection, energy sufficiency, and mass transportation.

The first of the four quotations talks about impeachment, but other than that, it doesn't really have anything clearly to do with the answer to the previous question. The second quotation is about a kind of division, but, again, it has little to do with the matter at hand. The fourth quotation merely offers a list of the many things Jordan feels Congress should be concerning itself with.

That leaves the third quotation. In it, Jordan claims that while a desire to achieve political goals can lead some to want to start impeachment proceedings against a president ("the drawing of political lines goes to the motivation behind impeachment"), the process is too serious for that to be a good basis for such proceedings. Instead, impeachment should only be sought if the president is believed to have committed a serious offense ("must proceed within the confines of the constitutional term 'high crime[s] and misdemeanors'"). This third quotation, then, serves as the best of the four options in terms of textual evidence.

In test format, this Citing Textual Evidence question looks like the following:

> Which choice provides the best evidence for the answer to the previous question?
>
> A) Lines 13-16 ("It . . . office")
>
> B) Lines 20-23 ("The division . . . astute")
>
> C) Lines 51-54 ("The drawing . . . misdemeanors")
>
> D) Lines 61-64 ("Congress . . . transportation")

Each of these answer choices refers to one of the quotations presented earlier, only this time, passage line numbers stand in for the full quotation. The words marking the beginning and the end of the quotation are included to make it easier to find the lines in the passage.

You'll see questions like this throughout the Reading Test, and you should approach each in a similar way: finding the best answer to the first question and then deciding which part of the passage offers the best support for that answer. It's OK to work on both of these questions at once and to reconsider your answer to the first question after you read the second. Sometimes looking at the choices in the second question will help you rethink your original answer to the first question. Just don't overthink it or second-guess yourself too much.

It's possible you'll see variations on the above format as well. One sort is when the question itself provides a conclusion (instead of the test asking you to come up with it on your own in another question) and asks you which choice provides the best support for it. This is fundamentally the same sort of question as the previous Citing Textual Evidence example, only it's a one-part instead of a two-part question.

PRACTICE AT
satpractice.org

Citing Textual Evidence questions often come as part of a pair, with the answer to the evidence question being related to the answer to an earlier question. You may sometimes find it helpful to revisit your answer to the previous question after reading the answer choices in the evidence question.

Determining Central Ideas and Themes

Some questions on the Reading Test may ask you to figure out what the main points or themes of a passage are. These two concepts are very similar, although many people (and the Reading Test) tend to refer to "theme" instead of "main idea" when talking about the central message of a literary text. In either case, you're typically looking for an overarching statement that succinctly encapsulates a key point the author is trying to make. Main ideas and themes may be stated explicitly or, especially in more challenging passages, only implied. While "theme" questions tend to be only about a passage as a whole, "main idea" questions can be about one or more paragraphs or an entire passage. Generally, words such as "main idea," "main point," "central idea," or "theme" help signal the intent of the question. Because you're looking for the main idea (or theme), you'll want to avoid picking an answer that only refers to a detail or that fails to capture the entire point the author makes.

PRACTICE AT
satpractice.org

Keywords such as "main idea" and "theme" clue you in to the fact that you're looking for the answer choice that captures the overarching point the author makes in one or more paragraphs or in the passage as a whole. Be wary of answer choices that focus in on specific details.

Summarizing

When you successfully summarize a text, you've conveyed the most important ideas (generally in the order presented) without adding your own interpretation or including minor details. Although the Reading Test doesn't ask you to create your own summary of a passage or a part of a passage, you may be asked to choose which one of four options offers the best summary, or perhaps to recognize where a proposed summary falls short (maybe because it's inaccurate in some way or includes extraneous details). These sorts of questions generally use some form of the word "summary" as a clue to their purpose.

Understanding Relationships

Some questions on the Reading Test may ask you to determine the relationship between people, ideas, events, and the like in passages. These questions tend to fall into one of three subtypes:

- **Cause-and-effect:** Understanding how one thing caused another to happen; often signaled by words such as "because" and "since"
- **Comparison-contrast:** Understanding how two things are similar and/or different; often signaled by words such as "more" and "less"
- **Sequence:** Understanding the order in which things happened; often signaled by words such as "first," "last," "before," and "after"

These sorts of questions can be found with all types of passages. You may, for example, have to determine sequence when figuring out what happened and when in a passage from a novel or which step came first in a science experiment. As noted previously, Understanding Relationships questions will often use words that suggest the kind of relationship you're looking for. This relationship may be directly stated, or you may have to infer it from information in the passage.

PRACTICE AT

satpractice.org

As you read the passage, take special note of keywords that signal causes and effects (e.g., "because"), comparisons ("more," "less"), and sequences ("first," "after"). You may be asked one or more questions that test your understanding of these relationships.

Interpreting Words and Phrases in Context

Interpreting Words and Phrases questions ask you to determine the precise meaning of a particular word or phrase as it's used in a passage. You'll again be offered four answer options, one of which most closely matches how the author is using the word or phrase. Remember from our previous discussion of "intense" in Chapter 4 that these tested words will often have multiple dictionary definitions, meaning that you can't rely solely on your vocabulary knowledge. Having a broad vocabulary can be helpful, but you'll also have to think about how the word or phrase is being used in a particular case.

REMEMBER

On Interpreting Words and Phrases questions, don't rely solely on your vocabulary knowledge. Tested words will often have multiple definitions, so be sure to consider the context in which the word or phrase is being used.

Although there are some variations, Interpreting Words and Phrases questions typically come in the format of "As used in line *x*, '[word or phrase]' most nearly means," where *x* is a line in the passage and *word or phrase* is the tested vocabulary. Often, you can try substituting each answer choice into the relevant sentence of the passage to get a better idea of which choice makes the most sense. Note, however, that simply reading the sentence containing the word or phrase isn't always enough; you may need to consider a larger portion of the text — multiple sentences or the surrounding paragraph — or even the passage as a whole to confirm the intended meaning.

Chapter 6 Recap

Information and Ideas questions are, at heart, questions about the message the author is trying to convey. Questions in this category will ask you to read closely, to cite textual evidence, to determine central ideas and themes, to summarize, to understand relationships, and to interpret words and phrases in context. In some cases, the answer can be found word for word (or nearly so) in the passage, but because the Reading Test is also a test of your reasoning skills, you'll often have to do much of the work yourself by making supportable inferences and drawing logical conclusions.

CHAPTER 7

Reading: Rhetoric

Rhetoric: The Author's Craft

The word "rhetoric" carries several meanings, as you may know — especially if you're involved in speech or debate. One common definition, perhaps the best known today, is "lofty and dishonest language." That meaning is often associated with pronouncements by politicians who are seen as using words to dodge controversy, hide their true position, or prop up a weak argument. The fact that words such as "empty" or "mere" often precede "rhetoric" suggests that the term has a negative connotation for many people.

REMEMBER

Rhetoric questions assess your understanding of how and why the author develops the structure and meaning of the passage. Understanding the author's purpose or point of view is often of central importance to correctly answering Rhetoric questions.

"Rhetoric," however, has another, broader, more positive meaning, and that is "the study of writing or speaking." Rhetoric in this sense stretches back at least to Aristotle and the ancient Greeks, who helped make rhetoric a formal practice with defined rules and conventions. It's in this second sense that the SAT uses the term. Rhetoric questions on the Reading Test assess how well you understand the choices that authors make in structuring and developing their texts. Paralleling what we did with Information and Ideas in Chapter 6, we'll turn now to the kinds of Rhetoric questions you'll find on the Reading Test.

Questions in this category are of five main types:

- **Analyzing word choice:** Understanding how an author selects words, phrases, and language patterns to influence meaning, tone, and style
- **Analyzing text structure:** Describing how an author shapes and organizes a passage and how the parts of the passage contribute to the whole
- **Analyzing point of view:** Understanding the point of view or perspective from which a passage is told and how that point of view or perspective affects the content and style of the passage
- **Analyzing purpose:** Determining the main rhetorical aim of a passage or a significant part of the passage, such as a paragraph

- **Analyzing arguments:** Examining the claims, counterclaims, reasoning, evidence, and stylistic and persuasive techniques an author uses in an argument

We'll consider each of these subcategories in the sections that follow.

PRACTICE AT
satpractice.org

Questions that ask you to analyze word choice aren't assessing your vocabulary knowledge per se. Rather, these questions assess your skill in determining the impact that particular words and phrases have on the meaning, style, and tone of a passage.

Analyzing Word Choice

Questions about analyzing word choice are — with Information and Ideas questions about interpreting the meaning of words and phrases in context — key elements of the Words in Context subscore. In contrast to word/phrase meaning questions, Analyzing Word Choice questions focus less on definitions and more on the rhetorical impact that particular words, phrases, and language patterns (such as repetition) have on the meaning, style, and tone of a passage. While there's no standard phrasing to these types of questions, they'll generally call out certain words, phrases, or sentences and ask you to consider the purpose or effect of this language.

PRACTICE AT
satpractice.org

As you read a passage on the SAT, you'll want to shift back and forth between a focus on the specific content of the passage (the "what") and the structure of the passage (the "how"). Text structure questions require a broader, more abstract rhetorical understanding of the passage.

Analyzing Text Structure

Text structure questions on the Reading Test come in two basic forms. One kind will ask you to characterize in some way the overall structure of the passage. In a few cases, this may be as simple as just recognizing the basic organizing principle of the passage, such as cause-and-effect, sequence, or problem-solution. In most cases, though, such questions will be more complicated and shaped by the content of the individual passage. You may, for example, have to track how the structure shifts over the course of the passage, meaning that the answer will be in two or more parts (as in "the passage begins by doing *x* and then does *y*").

Let's examine the wording of one such question. The literature passage this question is based on and the explanation for the answer can be found in Chapter 9. Our real interest now is only the format and wording of the question and the approach you'd need to take to respond to it.

Over the course of the passage, the main focus of the narrative shifts from the

A) reservations a character has about a person he has just met to a growing appreciation that character has of the person's worth.

B) ambivalence a character feels about his sensitive nature to the character's recognition of the advantages of having profound emotions.

C) intensity of feeling a character has for another person to the character's concern that that intensity is not reciprocated.

D) value a character attaches to the wonders of the natural world to a rejection of that sort of beauty in favor of human artistry.

To answer this question (or one like it), you'll have to both think abstractly (moving beyond just understanding the plot to being able to characterize the structure of the passage as an author might) and identify the major change in focus that occurs in the passage.

The other kind of text structure question asks about the relationship between an identified part of a passage (such as a phrase or sentence or a particular detail) and the passage as a whole. You may be asked, for example, to recognize that a given detail serves mainly as an example of a particular point the author is trying to make — or that it adds emphasis, foreshadows a later development, calls an assumption into question, or the like. You'll again have to think abstractly, considering not only what the author is saying but also the main contribution that a particular element of the passage makes to furthering the author's overall rhetorical purpose.

Analyzing Point of View

When the Reading Test asks you to consider point of view, it's not usually simply a matter of understanding what's often called "narrative point of view" — whether a passage is told from, say, a first person or a third person omniscient perspective. This can be part of it, but on the Reading Test, "point of view" is a broader term that also includes the stance, attitude, or bias of the author, narrator, or speaker. Point of view questions are found not just with fiction passages but with passages of all sorts.

Point of view questions generally identify themselves by words and phrases such as "perspective" and "point of view." The answer choices frequently offer characterizations of the author, narrator, or speaker. Consider, for instance, the following question from the Barbara Jordan speech we discussed in Chapter 6. (Remember: The passage, additional sample questions, and answer explanations can be found in Chapter 9.)

The stance Jordan takes in the passage is best described as that of

A) an idealist setting forth principles.

B) an advocate seeking a compromise position.

C) an observer striving for neutrality.

D) a scholar researching a historical controversy.

In this case, you have to figure out the stance, or perspective, that Jordan brings to the speech she delivers. To decide on the best answer — which in this instance is choice A — you'll want to both form an overall impression of Jordan and confirm (or modify) that impression based on specific elements of the passage — what Jordan says and how she says it. You might note that Jordan describes her faith in the U.S. Constitution as "whole," "complete," and "total" and that she claims that "the powers relating to impeachment are an essential check in the hands of the body of the legislature against and upon the encroachments of the executive." Her description of her faith in the Constitution strongly suggests idealism, and her claim about impeachment powers can be seen as setting forth a principle. As with questions about analyzing text structure, questions about point of view may ask you to note how the perspective from which a passage is told shifts over the course of the text.

PRACTICE AT
satpractice.org

For every SAT passage you read, get in the habit of asking yourself, "Why did the author write this passage?" Or, put differently, "What point or message was the author trying to get across in the passage?" Answering such questions as you read the passage will help you with many of the questions you'll be asked.

PRACTICE AT
satpractice.org

Keep a sharp eye out for evidence, contrast, and conclusion keywords when reading passages that are argumentative in nature. These keywords will help you analyze the content and structure of the passage. Evidence use can be signaled by keywords such as "for example" and "because" as well as references to statistics, surveys, and case studies. Contrast keywords include "however," "despite," and "on the contrary." Conclusion keywords include "therefore," "as a result," and "thus."

Analyzing Purpose

Questions about analyzing purpose are like questions about text structure in that you'll have to think abstractly about the text — not just understanding what the text says but also what the author is trying to achieve. In Analyzing Purpose questions, you'll consider the main purpose or function of the whole passage or of a significant part of the passage, generally one or more paragraphs. The word "purpose" or "function" is often used in such questions, while the answer choices often begin with or include rhetorically focused verbs such as "criticize," "support," "present," or "introduce."

Analyzing Arguments

The Reading Test includes passages that are primarily argumentative in nature. Such passages typically include one or more claims, or assertions, that the author attempts to convince the reader to accept through the use of reasoning (analysis), evidence (facts, statistics, expert testimony, case studies, and the like), and stylistic and persuasive elements (vivid imagery, appeals to emotion, and so on). Arguments also sometimes include counterclaims, or assertions made by those whose opinions are different from or opposed to those of the author, which the author may discuss and attempt to pick apart in order to show that his or her own position is stronger. (Confident, fair-minded authors will often take it upon themselves to point out the weaknesses of their own position and the strengths of the positions of others. On the Reading Test, though, you're usually seeing only part of an argument, so counterarguments won't always be present.)

Practically speaking, you probably won't approach Analyzing Arguments questions much differently than you would similar questions about other kinds of passages. A question that asks about the central claim of an argument, for example, is a lot like a question about the main idea or theme of another sort of passage. You'll have to decide on the primary assertion (main point) that the author is making in the argument and distinguish that from secondary assertions (minor points) and details. Analyzing Arguments questions differ from other kinds of Reading Test questions mainly in that they use words and concepts such as "claim," "counterclaim," "reason," and "evidence" to direct your attention to some of the features that distinguish arguments from texts designed to narrate events or experiences, to inform, or to explain.

Chapter 7 Recap

In contrast to Information and Ideas questions, Rhetoric questions on the SAT Reading Test focus on the author's craft rather than on the informational content of passages. When answering Rhetoric questions, you'll think less about the message the author is trying to convey and more about how that message is conveyed and what the author hopes to accomplish. Questions of this sort will ask you to analyze word choice, text structure, point of view, purpose, and arguments. Whatever their specific type, Rhetoric questions will generally be abstract in nature and ask you to step back from the information and ideas in a passage. You'll have a chance to show that you can think as an author would as you trace how particular words, phrases, sentences, and paragraphs interact with an overarching purpose and structure to shape and express the message that the author is trying to share with the audience.

CHAPTER 8

Reading: Synthesis

Up until now in our discussion of the SAT Reading Test, most of the question types we've examined have focused on taking things (sentences, paragraphs, ideas) apart and examining them closely for their meaning or for their rhetorical purpose or effect. Synthesis questions on the Reading Test, by contrast, focus mainly on putting information and ideas together into a bigger whole to acquire a deeper, broader understanding of a topic. Also in contrast to questions in the Information and Ideas and Rhetoric categories, Synthesis questions appear only with selected passages — either paired passages or passages with one or more informational graphics.

REMEMBER

Synthesis questions appear only with paired passages or passages that are accompanied by one or more informational graphics. Synthesis questions ask you to draw connections between related passages and to locate data in and draw reasonable conclusions from tables, graphs, and charts, as well as integrate information conveyed in graphics and in words.

Questions in this category are of two main types:

- **Analyzing multiple texts:** Making connections between topically related history/social studies or science passages
- **Analyzing quantitative information:** Locating data in informational graphics such as tables, graphs, and charts; drawing reasonable conclusions from such graphics; and integrating information displayed graphically with information and ideas in a passage

Each of these types is discussed in more detail in the following sections.

Analyzing Multiple Texts

Each administration of the Reading Test includes one set of two topically related passages on a subject in either history/social studies or science. These pairings are chosen carefully to ensure that the passages are similar enough that meaningful connections can be drawn between the two.

REMEMBER

The SAT Reading Test includes one set of topically related passages, or "paired passages," drawn from history/social studies or science. You'll be assessed on your understanding of each passage individually as well as your skill in drawing meaningful connections between the two.

The two passages may present opposing positions on the same issue, but it's more likely that the second passage will "respond" to the first in some more general way. The second passage may, for instance, provide a more detailed explanation of an idea that's only touched on in the first passage, or it may offer a practical application of a theoretical concept discussed in the first passage. The two passages will be different enough in content that you should be able to remember who said what if you've read them both carefully, but, as always, you can refer to the test booklet as often as you like and use notations such as underlines, numbers, and arrows if this will help you keep the two passages straight in your mind.

Here's an example that gives you an idea of how paired passages work.

Passage 1 is adapted from Susan Milius, "A Different Kind of Smart." ©2013 by Science News. Passage 2 is adapted from Bernd Heinrich, *Mind of the Raven: Investigations and Adventures with Wolf-Birds*. ©2007 by Bernd Heinrich.

Passage 1

In 1894, British psychologist C. Lloyd Morgan published what's called Morgan's çanon, the principle that suggestions of humanlike mental processes behind an animal's behavior should be rejected if a simpler explanation will do.

Still, people seem to maintain certain expectations, especially when it comes to birds and mammals. "We somehow want to prove they are as 'smart' as people," zoologist Sara Shettleworth says. We want a bird that masters a vexing problem to be employing human-style insight.

New Caledonian crows face the high end of these expectations, as possibly the second-best toolmakers on the planet.

Their tools are hooked sticks or strips made from spike-edged leaves, and they use them in the wild to winkle grubs out of crevices. Researcher Russell Gray first saw the process on a cold morning in a mountain forest in New Caledonia, an island chain east of Australia. Over the course of days, he and crow researcher Gavin Hunt had gotten wild crows used to finding meat tidbits in holes in a log. Once the birds were checking the log reliably, the researchers placed a spiky tropical pandanus plant beside the log and hid behind a blind.

A crow arrived. It hopped onto the pandanus plant, grabbed the spiked edge of one of the long straplike leaves and began a series of ripping motions. Instead of just tearing away one long strip, the bird ripped and nipped in a sequence to create a slanting stair-step edge on a leaf segment with a narrow point and a wide base. The process took only seconds. Then the bird dipped the narrow end of its leaf strip into a hole in the log, fished up the meat with the leaf-edge spikes, swallowed its prize and flew off.

"That was my 'oh wow' moment," Gray says. After the crow had vanished, he picked up the tool the bird had left behind. "I had a go, and I couldn't do it," he recalls. Fishing the meat out was tricky. It turned out that Gray was moving the leaf shard too forcefully instead of gently stroking the spines against the treat.

The crow's deft physical manipulation was what inspired Gray and Auckland colleague Alex Taylor to test other wild crows to see if they employed the seemingly insightful string-pulling solutions that some ravens, kea parrots and other brainiac birds are known to employ. Three of four crows passed that test on the first try.

Passage 2

For one month after they left the nest, I led my four young ravens at least once and sometimes several times a day on thirty-minute walks. During these walks, I wrote down everything in their environment they pecked at. In the first sessions, I tried to be teacher. I touched specific objects—sticks, moss, rocks—and nothing that I touched remained untouched by them. They came to investigate what I had investigated, leading me to assume that young birds are aided in learning to identify food from the parents' example. They also, however, contacted almost everything else that lay directly in their own paths. They soon became more independent by taking their own routes near mine. Even while walking along on their own, they pulled at leaves, grass stems, flowers, bark, pine needles, seeds, cones, clods of earth, and other objects they encountered. I wrote all this down, converting it to numbers. After they were thoroughly familiar with the background objects in these woods and started to ignore them, I seeded the path we would later walk together with objects they had never before encountered. Some of these were conspicuous food items: raspberries, dead meal worm beetles, and cooked corn kernels. Others were conspicuous and inedible: pebbles, glass chips, red winterberries. Still others were such highly cryptic foods as encased caddisfly larvae and moth cocoons. The results were dramatic.

The four young birds on our daily walks contacted all new objects preferentially. They picked them out at a rate of up to tens of thousands of times greater than background or previously contacted objects. The main initial criterion for pecking or picking anything up was its novelty. In subsequent trials, when the previously novel items were edible, they became preferred and the inedible objects became "background" items, just like the leaves, grass, and pebbles, even if they were highly conspicuous. These experiments showed that ravens' curiosity ensures exposure to all or almost all items in the environment.

PRACTICE AT
satpractice.org

Paired passages will be topically related, as are these two passages that broadly deal with bird intelligence. The exact relationship between the two passages, however, may be nuanced.

You can probably easily imagine, even before reading any of the associated questions, why these two passages might have been chosen for pairing. The two texts share a broad topical similarity — animal intelligence — but if that were all, it probably wouldn't be a very meaningful activity to draw connections between them. Examining more closely, we note that both passages deal with the issue of bird intelligence, although Passage 1 mainly discusses New Caledonian crows while Passage 2 mainly discusses ravens. Delving more deeply still, we grasp that both passages deal to some extent with the issue of humans' response to and interpretation of animals' signs of intelligence. Passage 1 is explicit about this, noting in the first three paragraphs that people have a tendency to see animals as thinking in humanlike ways even when simpler and perhaps more defensible explanations are possible. Passage 2 isn't as direct in this respect, but the author (the "I" in the passage) definitely shows some of that tendency with regard to his ravens (e.g., "These experiments showed that ravens' curiosity ensures exposure to all or almost all items in the environment"). However, the two passages are different enough — at the most basic level, one is about crows and the other is about ravens — that it's fairly easy to keep the information and ideas in each passage separate after you've read both.

REMEMBER

Sets of questions associated with paired passages will begin with questions that focus on each passage separately and that will be similar in nature to the questions you'll see on nonpaired passages. Next, you'll see Synthesis questions that require you to draw on an understanding of both passages.

The questions you'll find with paired passages are of two general kinds. The first kind consists of questions about either Passage 1 or Passage 2 separately. These come in order — questions about Passage 1, then questions about Passage 2 — and are of the same types that we discussed in Chapters 6 and 7. The second kind consists of the actual Synthesis questions. These questions require you to draw meaningful connections between the two passages. They may ask about the information and ideas in the passages or about the rhetorical strategies used in them, just like questions about single (non-paired) passages — except in these cases, you'll have to draw on an understanding of both texts to answer the questions correctly.

Let's inspect two of the Synthesis questions associated with the paired passages presented earlier. (The questions and a full answer explanation for each can be found in Chapter 9.)

The first question asks you to recognize a relatively straightforward similarity between the animals discussed in the two passages.

The crows in Passage 1 and the ravens in Passage 2 shared which trait?

A) They modified their behavior in response to changes in their environment.

B) They formed a strong bond with the humans who were observing them.

C) They manufactured useful tools for finding and accessing food.

D) They mimicked the actions they saw performed around them.

To recognize choice A as the best answer, you'll need to recognize that both the crows described in Passage 1 and the ravens described in Passage 2 changed their behavior due to changes in their environment. As Passage 1 notes, the wild crows began "checking [a] log reliably" after the researchers "had gotten [them] used to finding meat tidbits" in holes in the log. Passage 2, meanwhile, mentions that the ravens "picked . . . out" objects newly introduced by the researcher into their environment "at a rate of up to tens of thousands of times greater than background or previously contacted objects." To answer the question correctly, you'll have to connect specific information found in each passage.

The second question we'll consider here concerns a point that we touched on when discussing the passages themselves.

Is the main conclusion presented by the author of Passage 2 consistent with Morgan's canon, as described in Passage 1?

A) Yes, because the conclusion proposes that the ravens' behavior is a product of environmental factors.

B) Yes, because the conclusion offers a satisfyingly simple explanation of the ravens' behavior.

C) No, because the conclusion suggests that the ravens exhibit complex behavior patterns.

D) No, because the conclusion implies that a humanlike quality motivates the ravens' behavior.

Compared to the first question, this one is broader and more abstract and complex. You have to understand (at least) both Morgan's canon, as described in Passage 1, and the main conclusion of Passage 2. We've already hinted at the best answer to this question, which is choice D. Passage 1 defines Morgan's canon as "the principle that suggestions of humanlike mental processes behind an animal's behavior should be rejected if a simpler explanation will do." The author of Passage 2, however, indicates his belief that ravens display curiosity — a humanlike trait — and doesn't show any signs of having seriously considered other, simpler possibilities. The main point to remember here is that Synthesis questions aren't always about drawing simple point-A-to-point-B comparisons; some questions will require you to have a solid working knowledge of the subtleties of the passages.

PRACTICE AT
satpractice.org

Higher difficulty questions associated with paired passages will require you to have a strong understanding of each passage individually and then to draw complex or subtle connections between the two. As you read the second passage in a pair, carefully consider how that passage relates to the first in terms of content, focus, and perspective.

Analyzing Quantitative Information

You'll find one or more informational graphics — tables, graphs, charts, and the like — accompanying one of the history/social studies passages and also one of the science passages on the test. There will be questions about those graphics as well. These questions are of three general kinds (although the first two are fairly similar):

- Questions that ask you to locate information in one or more informational graphics
- Questions that ask you to draw reasonable conclusions from data presented in one or more graphics
- Questions that ask you to connect the information displayed in one or more graphics with the information and ideas in the accompanying passage

The main difference between the first two kinds is simply in how explicit the information is. Sometimes you'll be asked just to locate a particular piece of information; in other cases, you'll need to interpret the data to make a reasonable inference. (This difference is analogous to the stated-implied distinction we talked about previously.) The third sort of question, on the other hand, will require you to understand both the passage and the graphic(s) and to integrate the information found in each.

Let's briefly examine two different questions involving graphics. The first question is a relatively simple one requiring a straightforward reading of a graphic that accompanies a social science passage on traffic. (As always, the passage, graphic, question, and answer explanation can be found in Chapter 9.)

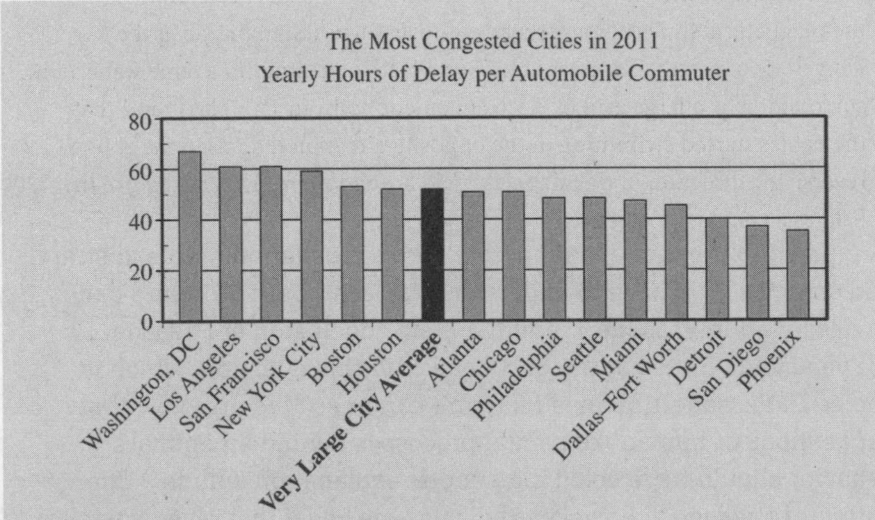

Which claim about traffic congestion is supported by the graph?

A) New York City commuters spend less time annually delayed by traffic congestion than the average for very large cities.

B) Los Angeles commuters are delayed more hours annually by traffic congestion than are commuters in Washington, D.C.

C) Commuters in Washington, D.C., face greater delays annually due to traffic congestion than do commuters in New York City.

D) Commuters in Detroit spend more time delayed annually by traffic congestion than do commuters in Houston, Atlanta, and Chicago.

PRACTICE AT
satpractice.org

Some Analyzing Quantitative Information questions, such as this one, will require you to locate information from a chart, table, or graph or to draw a reasonable conclusion from the data. Carefully analyze the data in the graphic — for instance, by reading the title, determining what the axes represent, and understanding the scale or scales used — before selecting your answer.

You can determine the best answer to this question, choice C, by understanding how the graph displays information. As its title indicates, the graph conveys data about the most congested U.S. cities in 2011 in terms of "yearly hours of delay per automobile commuter." A series of U.S. cities is listed on the horizontal (*x*) axis of the graph, while hours in increments of 20 are marked along the vertical (*y*) axis. Each light gray bar represents the yearly hours of delay per driver for a given city, while the dark gray bar near the middle represents the average delay for very large cities. Higher bars represent greater yearly delays than lower bars, so automobile commuters in the cities listed toward the left-hand side of the graph experienced longer annual delays than did the automobile commuters in the cities listed toward the right-hand side. Given that, it's a fairly simple matter to answer the question, as Washington, D.C., is to the left of New York City (and all other cities) on the graph.

The second question requires more genuine synthesis, as you'll have to understand both the passage and the graphic to get the question right. Because of this, we'll quote the most relevant bit from the passage and then follow that with the graphic. (In a real testing situation, you'd have to find this portion of the passage on your own. Chapter 9 contains the full passage as well as the question, graphic, and answer explanation.)

[. . .] Putman works in the lab of Ken Lohmann, who has been studying the magnetic abilities of loggerheads for over 20 years. In his lab at the University of North Carolina, Lohmann places hatchlings in a large water tank surrounded by a large grid of electromagnetic coils. In 1991, he found that the babies started swimming in the opposite direction if he used the coils to reverse the direction of the magnetic field around them. They could use the field as a compass to get their bearing. [. . .]

Adapted from Ed Yong, "Turtles Use the Earth's Magnetic Field as Global GPS." ©2011 by Kalmbach Publishing Co.

Orientation of Hatchling Loggerheads Tested in Magnetic Fields

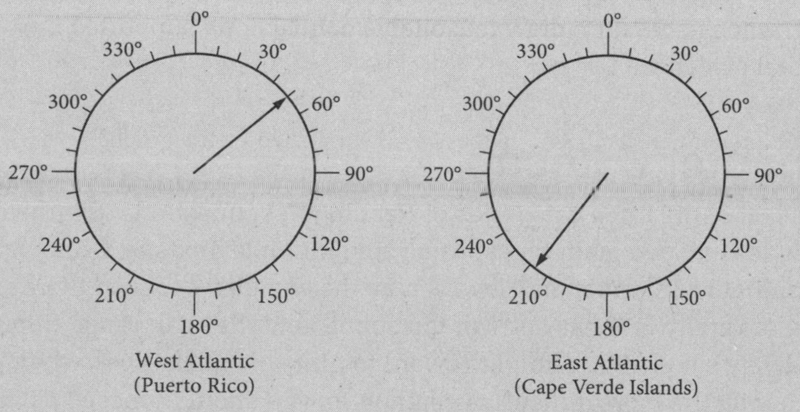

Adapted from Nathan Putman, Courtney Endres, Catherine Lohmann, and Kenneth Lohmann, "Longitude Perception and Bicoordinate Magnetic Maps in Sea Turtles." ©2011 by Elsevier Inc.

Orientation of hatchling loggerheads tested in a magnetic field that simulates a position at the west side of the Atlantic near Puerto Rico (left) and a position at the east side of the Atlantic near the Cape Verde Islands (right). The arrow in each circle indicates the mean direction that the group of hatchlings swam. Data are plotted relative to geographic north (N = 0°).

It can reasonably be inferred from the passage and the graphic that if scientists adjusted the coils to reverse the magnetic field simulating that in the East Atlantic (Cape Verde Islands), the hatchlings would most likely swim in which direction?

A) Northwest

B) Northeast

C) Southeast

D) Southwest

PRACTICE AT
satpractice.org

For passages that are accompanied by one or more informational graphics, be sure to carefully read all of the information given, including the title, labels, and captions of all graphics.

PRACTICE AT
satpractice.org

A more challenging Synthesis question such as this one will require that you integrate a solid understanding of the passage with a reasonable interpretation of data presented in a chart, table, graph, or similar figure.

While the first question we examined was just about finding some information in a graphic, this question requires multiple steps involving both a passage and a graphic. We know from the passage that loggerhead turtle hatchlings in a specially constructed tank in Ken Lohmann's lab will start "swimming in the opposite direction" if the direction of the magnetic field around them is reversed. From the graphic and its accompanying caption, we learn, among other things, that geographic north on the diagram is represented by 0 degrees and that loggerhead hatchlings swimming in a magnetic field simulating that of a position in the East Atlantic Ocean near the Cape Verde Islands will normally move in a southwesterly direction (around 218 degrees). Putting these bits of information together, we can reasonably infer that if the magnetic field affecting these "East Atlantic" turtles were reversed, the hatchlings would also reverse direction, swimming in a northeasterly direction. The best answer here, then, is choice B.

As you can tell, questions involving graphics can sometimes get complicated, but the basic set of knowledge and skills you'll apply is the same as you'd use with any other question on the Reading Test. Read carefully, figure out what the author says directly and indirectly, and, when necessary, draw reasonable conclusions supported by textual evidence.

Chapter 8 Recap

The last of the three categories of Reading Test questions, Synthesis, includes just two main types: Analyzing Multiple Texts and Analyzing Quantitative Information. However, as the samples suggest, there's a lot of variety in these sorts of questions, and they can range from relatively simple and straightforward to quite complex. Even when you encounter the more difficult ones, though, you should proceed calmly and thoughtfully. The knowledge and skills these questions call on are fundamentally the same as those needed for any other question on the test. In the end, it's all about reading closely, making use of textual evidence, and drawing supportable conclusions when needed.

Chapters 5 through 8 have covered the content of the SAT Reading Test in quite a bit of detail. The next chapter will present sample passages and questions, along with detailed explanations of how the answer for each question was reached and why the alternatives were not as good as the indicated answer. Some of the material in the preceding four chapters will be presented again, but additional passages and questions are included as well.

CHAPTER 9

Sample Reading Test Questions

In Chapters 5 to 8, you learned about the basic elements of the SAT Reading Test, including the types of passages you'll encounter and the types of questions the test will include. In this chapter, you'll find five sample passages and associated test questions. Following each question is an explanation for the best answer and some comments about the incorrect answer choices.

These instructions will precede the SAT Reading Test.

REMEMBER

There will be four single passages and one set of paired passages on the Reading Test. Passages are drawn from U.S. and world literature, history/social studies, and science.

Reading Test

65 MINUTES, 52 QUESTIONS

Turn to Section 1 of your answer sheet to answer the questions in this section.

DIRECTIONS

Each passage or pair of passages below is followed by a number of questions. After reading each passage or pair, choose the best answer to each question based on what is stated or implied in the passage or passages and in any accompanying graphics (such as a table or graph).

Sample 1:

History/Social Studies Passage, Lower Text Complexity

The following passage on commuting is of lower complexity, although some aspects of the passage are more challenging than others (as is generally true of the published materials you read). This passage is accompanied by a graphic.

REMEMBER

The text complexity of the passages will range from lower (grades 9–10) to higher (postsecondary entry).

Questions 1-3 are based on the following passage and supplementary material.

This passage is adapted from Richard Florida, *The Great Reset*. ©2010 by Richard Florida.

In today's idea-driven economy, the cost of time is what really matters. With the constant pressure to innovate, it makes little sense to waste countless collective hours commuting. So, the most efficient and productive regions are those in which people are thinking and working — not sitting in traffic.

The auto-dependent transportation system has reached its limit in most major cities and megaregions. Commuting by car is among the least efficient of all our activities — not to mention among the least enjoyable, according to detailed research by the Nobel Prize–winning economist Daniel Kahneman and his colleagues. Though one might think that the economic crisis beginning in 2007 would have reduced traffic (high unemployment means fewer workers traveling to and from work), the opposite has been true. Average commutes have lengthened, and congestion has gotten worse, if anything. The average commute rose in 2008 to 25.5 minutes, "erasing years of decreases to stand at the level of 2000, as people had to leave home earlier in the morning to pick up friends for their ride to work or to catch a bus or subway train," according to the U.S. Census Bureau, which collects the figures. And those are average figures. Commutes are far longer in the big West Coast cities of Los Angeles and San Francisco and the East Coast cities of New York, Philadelphia, Baltimore, and Washington, D.C. In many of these cities, gridlock has become the norm, not just at rush hour but all day, every day.

The costs are astounding. In Los Angeles, congestion eats up more than 485 million working hours a year; that's seventy hours, or nearly two weeks, of full-time work per commuter. In D.C., the time cost of congestion is sixty-two hours per worker per year. In New York it's forty-four hours. Average it out, and the time cost across America's thirteen biggest city regions is fifty-one hours per worker per year. Across the country, commuting wastes 4.2 billion hours of work time annually — nearly a full workweek for every commuter. The overall cost to the U.S. economy is nearly $90 billion when lost productivity and wasted fuel are taken into account. At the Martin Prosperity Institute, we calculate that every minute shaved off America's commuting time is worth $19.5 billion in value added to the economy. The numbers add up fast: five minutes is worth $97.7 billion; ten minutes, $195 billion; fifteen minutes, $292 billion.

It's ironic that so many people still believe the main remedy for traffic congestion is to build more roads and highways, which of course only makes the problem worse. New roads generate higher levels of "induced traffic," that is, new roads just invite drivers to drive more and lure people who take mass transit back to their cars. Eventually, we end up with more clogged roads rather than a long-term improvement in traffic flow.

The coming decades will likely see more intense clustering of jobs, innovation, and productivity in a smaller number of bigger cities and city-regions. Some regions could end up bloated beyond the capacity of their infrastructure, while others struggle, their promise stymied by inadequate human or other resources.

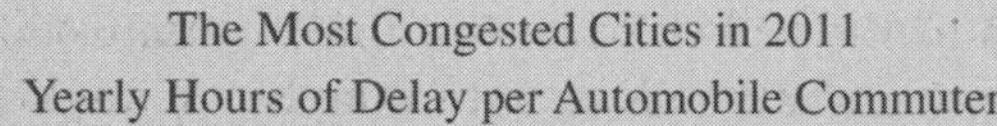

The Most Congested Cities in 2011
Yearly Hours of Delay per Automobile Commuter

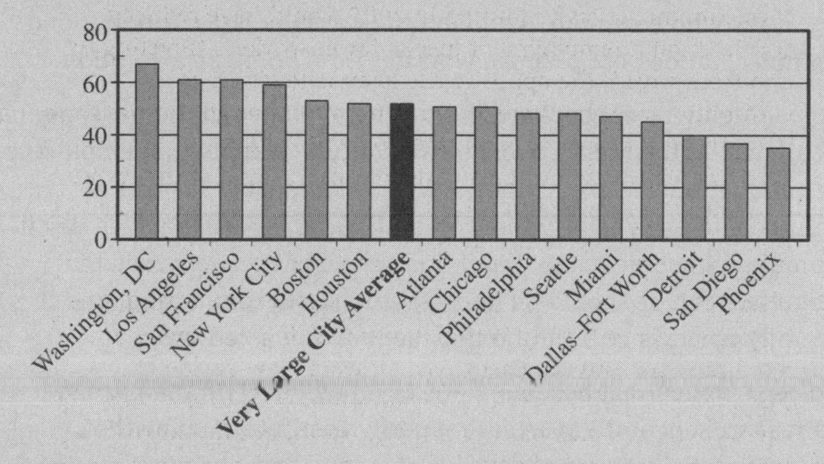

Adapted from Adam Werbach, "The American Commuter Spends 38 Hours a Year Stuck in Traffic." ©2013 by The Atlantic.

REMEMBER

One history/social studies passage and one science passage will be accompanied by an informational graphic such as a chart, table, or graph.

1

The passage most strongly suggests that researchers at the Martin Prosperity Institute share which assumption?

A) Employees who work from home are more valuable to their employers than employees who commute.

B) Employees whose commutes are shortened will use the time saved to do additional productive work for their employers.

C) Employees can conduct business activities, such as composing memos or joining conference calls, while commuting.

D) Employees who have longer commutes tend to make more money than employees who have shorter commutes.

Content: Rhetoric

Key: B

Objective: You must reasonably infer an assumption that is implied in the passage.

Explanation: Choice B is the best answer because details in the third paragraph (lines 28-43) strongly suggest that researchers ("we") at the Martin Prosperity Institute assume that shorter commutes will lead to more productive time for workers. The author notes that "across the country, commuting wastes 4.2 billion hours of work time annually" and that "the overall cost to the U.S. economy is nearly $90 billion when lost productivity and wasted fuel are taken into account" (lines 34-38). Given also that those at the institute "calculate that every minute shaved off America's commuting time is worth $19.5 billion in value added to the economy" (lines 39-41), it can reasonably be concluded that some of that added value is from heightened worker productivity.

PRACTICE AT
satpractice.org

Choice A is tempting, as you might want to draw the inference that people who work from home don't waste time commuting and thus are more valuable to employers. This inference, however, is not supported by the passage, which makes no mention of working from home.

Choice A is incorrect because there is no evidence in the passage that researchers at the Martin Prosperity Institute assume that employees who work from home are more valuable to their employers than employees who commute. Although the passage does criticize long commutes, it does not propose working from home as a solution.

Choice C is incorrect because there is no evidence in the passage that researchers at the Martin Prosperity Institute assume that employees can conduct business activities, such as composing memos or joining conference calls, while commuting. The passage does discuss commuting in some detail, but it does not mention activities that commuters can or should be undertaking while commuting, and it generally portrays commuting time as lost or wasted time.

Choice D is incorrect because there is no evidence in the passage that researchers at the Martin Prosperity Institute assume that employees who have lengthy commutes tend to make more money than employees who have shorter commutes. The passage does not draw any clear links between the amount of money employees make and the commutes they have.

PRACTICE AT
satpractice.org

On questions that ask for the meaning of a word in context, consider the role the word plays in the context in which it appears. Wrong answer choices will often consist of alternate meanings of the word that do not fit the context.

2

As used in line 52, "intense" most nearly means

A) emotional.

B) concentrated.

C) brilliant.

D) determined.

Content: Information and Ideas

Key: B

Objective: You must determine the meaning of a word in the context in which it appears.

Explanation: Choice B is the best answer because the context makes clear that the clustering of jobs, innovation, and productivity will be more concentrated in, or more densely packed into, "a smaller number of bigger cities and city-regions" (lines 53-54).

Choice A is incorrect because although "intense" sometimes means "emotional," it would make no sense in this context to say that the clustering of jobs, innovation, and productivity will be more emotional in "a smaller number of bigger cities and city-regions" (lines 53-54).

Choice C is incorrect because although "intense" sometimes means "brilliant," it would make no sense in this context to say that the clustering of jobs, innovation, and productivity will be more brilliant in "a smaller number of bigger cities and city-regions" (lines 53-54).

Choice D is incorrect because although "intense" sometimes means "determined," it would make no sense in this context to say that the clustering of jobs, innovation, and productivity will be more determined in "a smaller number of bigger cities and city-regions" (lines 53-54).

3

Which claim about traffic congestion is supported by the graph?

A) New York City commuters spend less time annually delayed by traffic congestion than the average for very large cities.

B) Los Angeles commuters are delayed more hours annually by traffic congestion than are commuters in Washington, D.C.

C) Commuters in Washington, D.C., face greater delays annually due to traffic congestion than do commuters in New York City.

D) Commuters in Detroit spend more time delayed annually by traffic congestion than do commuters in Houston, Atlanta, and Chicago.

PRACTICE AT
satpractice.org

This question requires you to locate information from a graph and draw a reasonable conclusion from the data. Carefully analyze the data in the graph, including the title, axes labels, and unit increments, before selecting your answer.

Content: Synthesis

Key: C

Objective: You must interpret data presented graphically.

Explanation: Choice C is the best answer. Higher bars on the graph represent longer annual commuter delays than lower bars; moreover, the number of hours of annual commuter delay generally decreases as one moves from left to right on the graph. The bar for Washington, D.C., is higher than and to the left of that for New York City, meaning that D.C. automobile commuters experience greater amounts of delay each year.

Choice A is incorrect because the graph's bar for New York City is higher than and to the left of that for the average for very large cities, meaning that New York City automobile commuters experience greater, not lesser, amounts of delay each year.

Choice B is incorrect because the graph's bar for Los Angeles is lower than and to the right of that for Washington, D.C., meaning that Los Angeles automobile commuters experience lesser, not greater, amounts of delay each year.

Choice D is incorrect because the graph's bar for Detroit is lower than and to the right of those for Houston, Atlanta, and Chicago, meaning that Detroit automobile commuters experience lesser, not greater, amounts of delay each year.

Sample 2:

History/Social Studies Passage, Higher Text Complexity

The following passage from a text in the Great Global Conversation inspired by U.S. founding documents and is of higher complexity, although some aspects of the passage are less challenging than others.

PRACTICE AT

satpractice.org

Some passages, like this one, are preceded by a brief introduction. Be sure to read the introduction as it may provide context that will help you understand the passage.

Questions 4-8 are based on the following passage.

The passage is adapted from a speech delivered by Congresswoman Barbara Jordan of Texas on July 25, 1974. She was a member of the Judiciary Committee of the United States House of Representatives. In the passage, Jordan discusses how and when a United States president may be impeached, or charged with serious offenses while in office. Jordan's speech was delivered in the context of impeachment hearings against then President Richard M. Nixon.

Today, I am an inquisitor. An hyperbole would not be fictional and would not overstate the solemnness that I feel right now. My faith in the Constitution is whole; it is complete; it is total. And I am not going to sit here and be an idle spectator to the diminution, the subversion, the destruction, of the Constitution.

"Who can so properly be the inquisitors for the nation as the representatives of the nation themselves?" "The subjects of its jurisdiction are those offenses which proceed from the misconduct of public men."* And that's what we're talking about. In other words, [the jurisdiction comes] from the abuse or violation of some public trust.

It is wrong, I suggest, it is a misreading of the Constitution for any member here to assert that for a member to vote for an article of impeachment means that that member must be convinced that the President should be removed from office. The Constitution doesn't say that. The powers relating to impeachment are an essential check in the hands of the body of the legislature against and upon the encroachments of the executive. The division between the two branches of the legislature, the House and the Senate, assigning to the one the right to accuse and to the other the right to judge — the framers of this Constitution were very astute. They did not make the accusers and the judges . . . the same person.

We know the nature of impeachment. We've been talking about it a while now. It is chiefly designed for the President and his high ministers to somehow be called into account. It is designed to "bridle" the executive if he engages in excesses. "It is designed as a method of national inquest into the conduct of public men."* The framers confided in the Congress the power, if need be, to remove the President in order to strike a delicate balance between a President swollen with power and grown tyrannical, and preservation of the independence of the executive.

The nature of impeachment: a narrowly channeled exception to the separation of powers maxim. The Federal Convention of 1787 said that. It limited impeachment to high crimes and misdemeanors, and discounted and opposed the term "maladministration." "It is to be used only for great misdemeanors," so it was said in the North Carolina ratification convention. And in the Virginia ratification convention: "We do not trust our liberty to a particular branch. We need one branch to check the other."

. . . The North Carolina ratification convention: "No one need be afraid that officers who commit oppression will pass with immunity." "Prosecutions of impeachments will seldom fail to agitate the passions of the whole community," said Hamilton in the *Federalist* Papers, Number 65. "We divide into parties more or less friendly or inimical to the accused."* I do not mean political parties in that sense.

The drawing of political lines goes to the motivation behind impeachment; but impeachment must proceed within the confines of the constitutional term "high crime[s] and misdemeanors." Of the impeachment process, it was Woodrow Wilson who said that "Nothing short of the grossest offenses against the plain law of the land will suffice to give them speed and effectiveness. Indignation so great as to overgrow party interest may secure a conviction; but nothing else can."

Common sense would be revolted if we engaged upon this process for petty reasons. Congress has a lot to do: appropriations, tax reform, health insurance, campaign finance reform, housing, environmental protection, energy sufficiency, mass transportation. Pettiness cannot be allowed to stand in the face of such overwhelming problems. So today we're not being petty. We're trying to be big, because the task we have before us is a big one.

*Jordan quotes from *Federalist* No. 65, an essay by Alexander Hamilton, published in 1788, on the powers of the United States Senate, including the power to decide cases of impeachment against a president of the United States.

PRACTICE AT
satpractice.org

As you read a passage on the SAT, be sure to always ask yourself, "Why is the author writing this? What is his or her purpose?" Identifying the author's purpose will help you answer many of the questions you'll face.

4

The stance Jordan takes in the passage is best described as that of

A) an idealist setting forth principles.
B) an advocate seeking a compromise position.
C) an observer striving for neutrality.
D) a scholar researching a historical controversy.

Content: Rhetoric

Key: A

Objective: You must use information and ideas in the passage to determine the speaker's perspective.

Explanation: Choice A is the best answer. Jordan helps establish her idealism by declaring that she is an "inquisitor" (line 1) and that her "faith in the Constitution is whole; it is complete; it is total" (lines 3-4). At numerous points in the passage, Jordan sets forth principles (e.g., "The powers relating to impeachment are an essential check in the hands of the body of the legislature against and upon the encroachments of the executive," lines 17-20) and refers to important documents that do the same, including the U.S. Constitution and *Federalist* No. 65.

Choice B is incorrect because although Jordan is advocating a position, there is no evidence in the passage that she is seeking a compromise position. Indeed, she notes that she is "not going to sit here and be an idle spectator to the diminution, the subversion, the destruction, of the Constitution" (lines 4-6), indicating that she is not seeking compromise.

Choice C is incorrect because Jordan is a participant ("an inquisitor," line 1) in the proceedings, not a mere observer. Indeed, she notes that she is "not going to sit here and be an idle spectator to the diminution, the subversion, the destruction, of the Constitution" (lines 4-6).

Choice D is incorrect because Jordan is identified as a congresswoman and an "inquisitor" (line 1), not a scholar, and because she is primarily discussing events happening at the moment, not researching an unidentified historical controversy. Although she refers to historical documents and individuals, her main emphasis is on the (then) present impeachment hearings.

5

The main rhetorical effect of the series of three phrases in lines 5-6 (the diminution, the subversion, the destruction) is to

A) convey with increasing intensity the seriousness of the threat Jordan sees to the Constitution.

B) clarify that Jordan believes the Constitution was first weakened, then sabotaged, then broken.

C) indicate that Jordan thinks the Constitution is prone to failure in three distinct ways.

D) propose a three-part agenda for rescuing the Constitution from the current crisis.

Content: Rhetoric

Key: A

Objective: You must determine the main rhetorical effect of the speaker's choice of words.

Explanation: Choice A is the best answer because the quoted phrases — building from "diminution" to "subversion" to "destruction" — suggest the increasing seriousness of the threat Jordan sees to the Constitution.

Choice B is incorrect because the passage offers no evidence that the quoted phrases refer to three different events that happened in a strict sequence. It is more reasonable to infer from the passage that Jordan sees "diminution," "subversion," and "destruction" as differing degrees to which the Constitution could be undermined. Moreover, the passage suggests that Jordan sees these three things as products of the same action or series of actions, not as three distinct stages in a process.

Choice C is incorrect because the passage offers no evidence that the quoted phrases refer to three distinct ways in which the Constitution is prone to failure. It is more reasonable to infer from the passage that Jordan sees "diminution," "subversion," and "destruction" as differing degrees in which the Constitution could be undermined. Moreover, the passage suggests that Jordan sees these three things as products of the same action or series of actions, not as three distinct "ways."

Choice D is incorrect because the passage offers no evidence that the quoted phrases refer to three unique elements of a proposal to resolve a crisis. It is more reasonable to infer from the passage that Jordan sees "diminution," "subversion," and "destruction" as differing degrees in which the Constitution could be undermined. Moreover, the passage suggests that Jordan sees these three things as products of the same action or series of actions, not as three distinct "parts."

PRACTICE AT
satpractice.org

What is meant by "rhetorical effect" is the influence or impact that a particular arrangement of words has on the intended meaning of a text.

PRACTICE AT
satpractice.org

To answer this question, first identify what point the author is trying to get across in the paragraph in which the three phrases appear. Next, consider the effect that the series of three phrases has on the author's intended point.

6

As used in line 35, "channeled" most nearly means

A) worn.

B) sent.

C) constrained.

D) siphoned.

Content: Information and Ideas

Key: C

Objective: You must determine the meaning of a word in the context in which it appears.

Explanation: Choice C is the best answer because the context makes clear that the kind of "exception" (line 36) Jordan describes should be narrowly constrained, or limited. As lines 37-39 indicate, the Federal Convention of 1787 "limited impeachment to high crimes and misdemeanors, and discounted and opposed the term 'maladministration,'" presumably because the term implied too broad a scope for the exception.

Choice A is incorrect because while "channeled" sometimes means "worn," it would make no sense in this context to say that the kind of "exception" (line 36) Jordan describes should be narrowly worn.

Choice B is incorrect because while "channeled" sometimes means "sent," it would make no sense in this context to say that the kind of "exception" (line 36) Jordan describes should be narrowly sent.

Choice D is incorrect because while "channeled" sometimes means "siphoned," it would make no sense in this context to say that the kind of "exception" (line 36) Jordan describes should be narrowly siphoned.

PRACTICE AT
satpractice.org

The context clues that indicate the intended meaning of a word may not always be found in the actual sentence in which the word appears. In this question, the strongest clues appear later in the paragraph, when the author states, "It limited impeachment to . . ." and "It is to be used only for great misdemeanors . . ."

7

In lines 46-50 ("Prosecutions . . . sense"), what is the most likely reason Jordan draws a distinction between two types of "parties"?

A) To counter the suggestion that impeachment is or should be about partisan politics

B) To disagree with Hamilton's claim that impeachment proceedings excite passions

C) To contend that Hamilton was too timid in his support for the concept of impeachment

D) To argue that impeachment cases are decided more on the basis of politics than on justice

Content: Rhetoric

Key: A

Objective: You must interpret the speaker's line of reasoning.

PRACTICE AT
satpractice.org

As with Question 5, this question depends on an understanding of the reasoning immediately preceding and following the sentence in which Jordan draws a distinction between types of parties. Be sure, therefore, to consider Jordan's statement in the context in which it appears.

Explanation: Choice A is the best answer. Jordan is making a distinction between two types of "parties": the informal associations to which Alexander Hamilton refers and formal, organized political parties such as the modern-day Republican and Democratic parties. Jordan anticipates that listeners to her speech might misinterpret her use of Hamilton's quotation as suggesting that she thinks impeachment is essentially a tool of organized political parties to achieve partisan ends, with one party attacking and another defending the president. Throughout the passage, and notably in the seventh paragraph, Jordan makes clear that she thinks impeachment should be reserved only for the most serious of offenses — ones that should rankle people of any political affiliation.

Choice B is incorrect because Jordan offers no objection to Hamilton's notion that impeachment proceedings excite passions. Indeed, she quotes Hamilton extensively in a way that indicates that she fundamentally agrees with his view on impeachment. Moreover, she acknowledges that her own speech is impassioned — that she feels a "solemnness" (line 2) and a willingness to indulge in "hyperbole" (line 1).

Choice C is incorrect because Jordan offers no objection to Hamilton's level of support for the concept of impeachment. Indeed, she quotes Hamilton extensively in a way that indicates that she fundamentally agrees with his view on impeachment.

Choice D is incorrect because Jordan suggests that she and her fellow members of Congress are "trying to be big" (line 66), or high-minded, rather than decide the present case on the basis of politics. Indeed, throughout the last four paragraphs of the passage (lines 35-67), she elaborates on the principled and just basis on which impeachment should proceed. Moreover, throughout the passage, Jordan is focused on the present impeachment hearings, not on the justice or injustice of impeachments generally.

8

Which choice provides the best evidence for the answer to the previous question?

A) Lines 13-16 ("It . . . office")

B) Lines 20-23 ("The division . . . astute")

C) Lines 51-54 ("The drawing . . . misdemeanors")

D) Lines 61-64 ("Congress . . . transportation")

Content: Information and Ideas

Key: C

Objective: You must determine which portion of the passage provides the best evidence for the answer to question 7.

PRACTICE AT
satpractice.org

Questions 7 and 8 can be viewed as two-part questions since the answer to Question 8 is dependent on the answer to Question 7. It may be helpful to revisit your answer to the first question after reading the answer choices in the second question.

Explanation: Choice C is the best answer because in lines 51-54, Jordan draws a contrast between political motivations and "high crime[s] and misdemeanors" as the basis for impeachment and argues that impeachment "must proceed within the confines" of the latter concept. These lines thus serve as the best evidence for the answer to the previous question.

Choice A is incorrect because lines 13-16 only address a misconception that Jordan contends some people have about what a vote for impeachment means. Therefore, these lines do not serve as the best evidence for the answer to the previous question.

Choice B is incorrect because lines 20-23 only speak to a division of responsibility between the two houses of the U.S. Congress. Therefore, these lines do not serve as the best evidence for the answer to the previous question.

Choice D is incorrect because lines 61-64 serve mainly to indicate that the U.S. Congress has an extensive and important agenda. Therefore, these lines do not serve as the best evidence for the answer to the previous question.

REMEMBER

One science passage on the Reading Test will be accompanied by an informational graphic.

Sample 3:

Science Passage with Graphic, Lower Text Complexity

The following natural science passage on loggerhead turtles is of lower complexity, although some aspects of the passage are more challenging than others. This passage is accompanied by a graphic.

Questions 9-13 are based on the following passage and supplementary material.

This passage is adapted from Ed Yong, "Turtles Use the Earth's Magnetic Field as Global GPS." ©2011 by Kalmbach Publishing Co.

In 1996, a loggerhead turtle called Adelita swam across 9,000 miles from Mexico to Japan, crossing the entire Pacific on her way. Wallace J. Nichols tracked this epic journey with a satellite tag. But Adelita herself had no such technology at her disposal. How did she steer a route across two oceans to find her destination?

Nathan Putman has the answer. By testing hatchling turtles in a special tank, he has found that they can use the Earth's magnetic field as their own Global Positioning System (GPS). By sensing the field, they can work out both their latitude and longitude and head in the right direction.

Putman works in the lab of Ken Lohmann, who has been studying the magnetic abilities of loggerheads for over 20 years. In his lab at the University of North Carolina, Lohmann places hatchlings in a large water tank surrounded by a large grid of electromagnetic coils. In 1991, he found that the babies started swimming in the opposite direction if he used the coils to reverse the direction of the magnetic field around them. They could use the field as a compass to get their bearing.

Later, Lohmann showed that they can also use the magnetic field to work out their position. For them, this is literally a matter of life or death. Hatchlings born off the sea coast of Florida spend their early lives in the North Atlantic gyre, a warm current that circles between North America and Africa. If they're swept towards the cold waters outside the gyre, they die. Their magnetic sense keeps them safe.

Using his coil-surrounded tank, Lohmann could mimic the magnetic field at different parts of the Earth's surface. If he simulated the field at the northern edge of the gyre, the hatchlings swam southwards. If he simulated the field at the gyre's southern edge, the turtles swam west-northwest. These experiments showed that the turtles can use their magnetic sense to work out their latitude — their position on a north-south axis. Now, Putman has shown that they can also determine their longitude — their position on an east-west axis.

He tweaked his magnetic tanks to simulate the fields in two positions with the same latitude at opposite ends of the Atlantic. If the field simulated the west Atlantic near Puerto Rico, the turtles swam northeast. If the field matched that on the east Atlantic near the Cape Verde Islands, the turtles swam southwest. In the wild, both headings would keep them within the safe, warm embrace of the North Atlantic gyre.

Before now, we knew that several animal migrants, from loggerheads to reed warblers to sparrows, had some way of working out longitude, but no one knew how. By keeping the turtles in the same conditions, with only the magnetic fields around them changing, Putman clearly showed that they can use these fields to find their way. In the wild, they might well also use other landmarks like the position of the sea, sun and stars.

Putman thinks that the turtles work out their position using two features of the Earth's magnetic field that change over its surface. They can sense the field's inclination, or the angle at which it dips towards the surface. At the poles, this angle is roughly 90 degrees and at the equator, it's roughly zero degrees. They can also sense its intensity, which is strongest near the poles and weakest near the Equator. Different parts of the world have unique combinations of these two variables. Neither corresponds directly to either latitude or longitude, but together, they provide a "magnetic signature" that tells the turtle where it is.

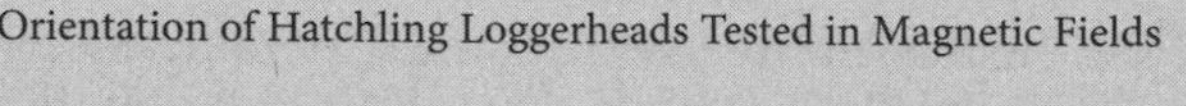

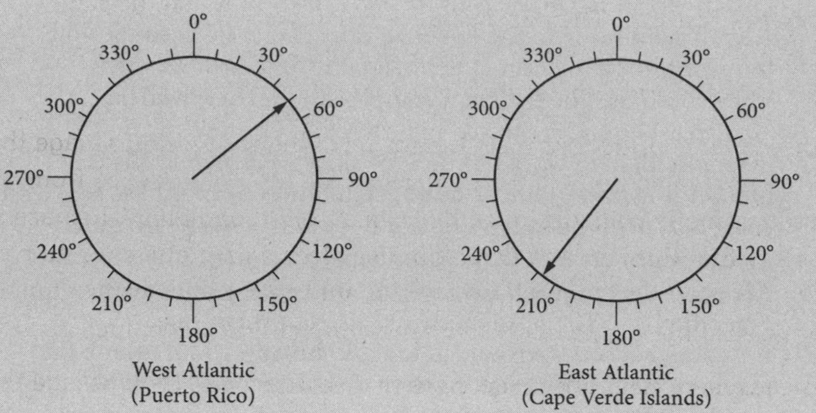

Adapted from Nathan Putman, Courtney Endres, Catherine Lohmann, and Kenneth Lohmann, "Longitude Perception and Bicoordinate Magnetic Maps in Sea Turtles." ©2011 by Elsevier Inc.

Orientation of hatchling loggerheads tested in a magnetic field that simulates a position at the west side of the Atlantic near Puerto Rico (left) and a position at the east side of the Atlantic near the Cape Verde Islands (right). The arrow in each circle indicates the mean direction that the group of hatchlings swam. Data are plotted relative to geographic north (N = 0°).

9

The passage most strongly suggests that Adelita used which of the following to navigate her 9,000-mile journey?

A) The current of the North Atlantic gyre

B) Cues from electromagnetic coils designed by Putman and Lohmann

C) The inclination and intensity of Earth's magnetic field

D) A simulated "magnetic signature" configured by Lohmann

Content: Information and Ideas

Key: C

Objective: You must draw a reasonable inference from the text.

Explanation: Choice C is the best answer. The first paragraph describes the 9,000-mile journey that Adelita made and raises the question, which the rest of the passage tries to answer, of how this loggerhead turtle was able to "steer a route across two oceans to find her destination" (lines 5-6). The answer comes most directly in the last paragraph, which presents Putman's belief that loggerhead turtles "work out their position using two features of the Earth's magnetic field that change over its surface" (lines 50-52): its inclination and its intensity. It is reasonable, therefore, to infer from the passage that this was the method that Adelita used.

Choice A is incorrect because there is no evidence in the passage that Adelita used the current of the North Atlantic gyre to navigate her 9,000-mile journey. The passage does discuss the North Atlantic gyre but only as the place where loggerhead turtle hatchlings "born off the sea coast of Florida spend their early lives" (lines 22-23).

Choice B is incorrect because there is no evidence in the passage that Adelita navigated her 9,000-mile journey with the aid of cues from electromagnetic coils designed by Putman and Lohmann. The passage does say that Putman and Lohmann use electromagnetic coils as part of their research on loggerhead turtles, but the coils are part of tanks used in a laboratory to study loggerhead hatchlings (see lines 12-16).

Choice D is incorrect because there is no evidence in the passage that Adelita navigated her 9,000-mile journey with the aid of a simulated "magnetic signature" configured by Lohmann. The passage does describe how Lohmann and Putman manipulate magnetic fields as part of their research on loggerhead turtle hatchlings (see, for example, lines 14-19), but there is no indication that the two scientists used (or even could use) the kind of equipment necessary for this project outside of laboratory tanks or with Adelita in the wild.

PRACTICE AT
satpractice.org

Many wrong answer choices may be tempting as they often contain information that appears in the passage. The passage does refer to the North Atlantic gyre, as well as electromagnetic coils, for instance. Only choice C, however, is relevant to the question of how Adelita was able to navigate her journey.

10

Which choice provides the best evidence for the answer to the previous question?

A) Lines 1-3 ("In 1996 . . . way")
B) Lines 27-28 ("Using . . . surface")
C) Lines 48-49 ("In the wild . . . stars")
D) Lines 58-60 ("Neither . . . it is")

PRACTICE AT
satpractice.org

Approach this question by going back to Question 9 and rereading the question and your answer. Then assess which choice best supports the answer to Question 9.

Content: Information and Ideas

Key: D

Objective: You must determine which portion of the passage provides the best support for the answer to question 9.

Explanation: Choice D is the best answer because in lines 58-60, the author indicates that "together, [inclination and intensity] provide a 'magnetic signature' that tells the turtle where it is." Therefore, these lines serve as the best evidence for the answer to the previous question.

Choice A is incorrect because in lines 1-3, the author establishes that Adelita made a 9,000-mile journey but does not explain how she navigated it. Therefore, these lines do not serve as the best evidence for the answer to the previous question.

Choice B is incorrect because in lines 27-28, the author indicates that Lohmann is able to "mimic the magnetic field at different parts of the Earth's surface" in his laboratory but does not explain how Adelita navigated her 9,000-mile journey or suggest that Lohmann had any influence over Adelita's trip. Therefore, these lines do not serve as the best evidence for the answer to the previous question.

Choice C is incorrect because, in lines 48-49, the author notes that loggerhead turtles "in the wild" may make use of "landmarks like the position of the sea, sun and stars" but does not indicate that Adelita used such landmarks to navigate her 9,000-mile journey. Therefore, these lines do not serve as the best evidence for the answer to the previous question.

11

As used in line 3, "tracked" most nearly means

A) searched for.

B) traveled over.

C) followed.

D) hunted.

PRACTICE AT
satpractice.org

Here's a strategy you may find helpful if you're struggling on a "word in context" question such as Question 11 — substitute each of the answer choices for the given word in the sentence and determine which fits best in the context.

Content: Information and Ideas

Key: C

Objective: You must determine the meaning of a word in the context in which it appears.

Explanation: Choice C is the best answer because the context makes clear that Nichols followed Adelita's "epic journey with a satellite tag" (lines 3-4).

Choice A is incorrect because while "tracked" sometimes means "searched for," it would make little sense in this context to say that Nichols searched for Adelita's "epic journey with a satellite tag" (lines 3-4). It is more reasonable to conclude from the passage that Nichols knew about Adelita and her journey and used a satellite tag to help follow it.

Choice B is incorrect because while "tracked" sometimes means "traveled over," it would make no sense in this context to say that Nichols traveled over Adelita's "epic journey with a satellite tag" (lines 3-4).

Choice D is incorrect because while "tracked" sometimes means "hunted," it would make no sense in this context to say that Nichols hunted Adelita's "epic journey with a satellite tag" (lines 3-4).

12

Based on the passage, which choice best describes the relationship between Putman's and Lohmann's research?

A) Putman's research contradicts Lohmann's.

B) Putman's research builds on Lohmann's.

C) Lohmann's research confirms Putman's.

D) Lohmann's research corrects Putman's.

Content: Information and Ideas

Key: B

Objective: You must characterize the relationship between two individuals described in the passage.

Explanation: Choice B is the best answer. Putman "works in the lab of Ken Lohmann, who has been studying the magnetic abilities of loggerheads for over 20 years" (lines 12-14). Lohmann had earlier demonstrated that loggerhead turtles "could use the [magnetic] field as a compass to get their bearing" (line 19) and "use their magnetic sense to work out their latitude — their position on a north-south axis" (lines 32-34). Putman has since ("Now," line 34) built on Lohmann's work by demonstrating that the turtles "can also determine their longitude — their position on an east-west axis" (lines 34-35).

Choice A is incorrect because the passage does not indicate that Putman's research contradicts Lohmann's. In fact, Putman's work complements Lohmann's. Lohmann had demonstrated that loggerhead turtles "could use the [magnetic] field as a compass to get their bearing" (line 19) and "use their magnetic sense to work out their latitude — their position on a north-south axis" (lines 32-34). Putman has, in turn, demonstrated that the turtles "can also determine their longitude — their position on an east-west axis" (lines 34-35).

Choice C is incorrect because the research of Lohmann that the passage describes came before that of Putman. Putman "works in the lab of Ken Lohmann, who has been studying the magnetic abilities of loggerheads for over 20 years" (lines 12-14). Lohmann had earlier demonstrated that loggerhead turtles "could use the [magnetic] field as a compass to get their bearing" (line 19) and "use their magnetic sense to work out their latitude — their position on a north-south axis" (lines 32-34). Putman has since ("Now," line 34) built on Lohmann's work by demonstrating that the turtles "can also determine their longitude — their position on an east-west axis" (lines 34-35).

Choice D is incorrect because the passage does not indicate that Lohmann's research corrects Putman's. First, Lohmann's research that the passage describes came before that of Putman (see explanation for choice C) and thus could not "correct" Putman's later research. Second, the passage does not indicate that Putman's research contradicts Lohmann's (see explanation for choice A), meaning that there is nothing for Lohmann to "correct" with his own research.

PRACTICE AT

satpractice.org

On Question 12, begin by determining if Putman's and Lohmann's research is complementary or contradictory; doing so will allow you to eliminate two of the four answer choices. Then, research the passage for additional clues that refine the relationship between their research.

PRACTICE AT
satpractice.org

Another way to phrase this question is, "Why did the author refer to reed warblers and sparrows?" It's often helpful to paraphrase the question in your own words to ensure you understand what it's asking.

13

The author refers to reed warblers and sparrows (line 44) primarily to

A) contrast the loggerhead turtle's migration patterns with those of other species.

B) provide examples of species that share one of the loggerhead turtle's abilities.

C) suggest that most animal species possess some ability to navigate long distances.

D) illustrate some ways in which the ability to navigate long distances can help a species.

Content: Rhetoric

Key: B

Objective: You must determine the main rhetorical effect a part of the passage has on the passage as a whole.

Explanation: Choice B is the best answer because the author indicates that reed warblers and sparrows, like loggerhead turtles, had previously been known to have "some way of working out longitude" (lines 44-45).

Choice A is incorrect because although the author notes that loggerhead turtles, reed warblers, and sparrows are all "animal migrants" (line 43), he offers no specifics about the migration patterns of reed warblers and sparrows, and the only connection he draws among the three animals is their recognized ability of somehow "working out longitude" (line 45).

Choice C is incorrect because the author only mentions three "animal migrants" by name (loggerhead turtles, reed warblers, and sparrows) and indicates that "several" such migrants had previously been known to have "some way of working out longitude" (lines 43-45). He makes no claim in the passage that most animal species have some long-distance navigation ability.

Choice D is incorrect because although the author indicates that reed warblers and sparrows, like loggerhead turtles, are "animal migrants" (line 43), he offers no specifics about how the ability to navigate long distances might help reed warblers and sparrows (nor, for that matter, much information about how this ability might help loggerhead turtles).

Sample 4:

U.S. and World Literature Passage, Higher Text Complexity

The following passage from a literary text is of higher complexity, although some aspects of the passage are less challenging than others.

Questions 14-18 are based on the following passage.

This passage is adapted from Edith Wharton, *Ethan Frome*, originally published in 1911. Mattie Silver is Ethan's household employee.

Mattie Silver had lived under Ethan's roof for a year, and from early morning till they met at supper he had frequent chances of seeing her; but no moments in her company were comparable to those when, her arm in his, and her light step flying to keep time with his long stride, they walked back through the night to the farm. He had taken to the girl from the first day, when he had driven over to the Flats to meet her, and she had smiled and waved to him from the train, crying out, "You must be Ethan!" as she jumped down with her bundles, while he reflected, looking over her slight person: "She don't look much on housework, but she ain't a fretter, anyhow." But it was not only that the coming to his house of a bit of hopeful young life was like the lighting of a fire on a cold hearth. The girl was more than the bright serviceable creature he had thought her. She had an eye to see and an ear to hear: he could show her things and tell her things, and taste the bliss of feeling that all he imparted left long reverberations and echoes he could wake at will.

It was during their night walks back to the farm that he felt most intensely the sweetness of this communion. He had always been more sensitive than the people about him to the appeal of natural beauty. His unfinished studies had given form to this sensibility and even in his unhappiest moments field and sky spoke to him with a deep and powerful persuasion. But hitherto the emotion had remained in him as a silent ache, veiling with sadness the beauty that evoked it. He did not even know whether any one else in the world felt as he did, or whether he was the sole victim of this mournful privilege. Then he learned that one other spirit had trembled with the same touch of wonder: that at his side, living under his roof and eating his bread, was a creature to whom he could say: "That's Orion down yonder; the big fellow to the right is Aldebaran, and the bunch of little ones — like bees swarming — they're the Pleiades . . ." or whom he could hold entranced before a ledge of granite thrusting up through the fern while he unrolled the huge panorama of the ice age, and the long dim stretches of succeeding time. The fact that admiration for his learning mingled with Mattie's wonder at what he taught was not the least part of his pleasure. And there were other sensations, less definable but more exquisite, which drew them together with a shock of silent joy: the cold red of sunset behind winter hills, the flight of cloud-flocks over slopes of golden stubble, or the intensely blue shadows of hemlocks on sunlit snow. When she said to him once: "It looks just as if it was painted!" it seemed to Ethan that the art of definition could go no farther, and that words had at last been found to utter his secret soul. . . .

PRACTICE AT
satpractice.org

Keywords and phrases throughout the final paragraph signal a shift in the focus of the narrative. For instance, " . . . these memories came back with the poignancy of vanished things," signals a temporal shift, and words such as "dull," "indifference," and "fatuity" point to a change in the main character's feelings.

PRACTICE AT
satpractice.org

This question, like many questions from the rhetoric category, asks you to think about the passage on a broader level. Thus, when reading passages on the SAT, pay as much attention to the structure and purpose of the passage (the "how" and "why") as you do to the content of the passage (the "what").

As he stood in the darkness outside the church these memories came back with the poignancy of vanished things. Watching Mattie whirl down the floor from hand to hand he wondered how he could ever have thought that his dull talk interested her. To him, who was never gay but in her presence, her gaiety seemed plain proof of indifference. The face she lifted to her dancers was the same which, when she saw him, always looked like a window that has caught the sunset. He even noticed two or three gestures which, in his fatuity, he had thought she kept for him: a way of throwing her head back when she was amused, as if to taste her laugh before she let it out, and a trick of sinking her lids slowly when anything charmed or moved her.

14

Over the course of the passage, the main focus of the narrative shifts from the

A) reservations a character has about a person he has just met to a growing appreciation that character has of the person's worth.

B) ambivalence a character feels about his sensitive nature to the character's recognition of the advantages of having profound emotions.

C) intensity of feeling a character has for another person to the character's concern that that intensity is not reciprocated.

D) value a character attaches to the wonders of the natural world to a rejection of that sort of beauty in favor of human artistry.

Content: Rhetoric

Key: C

Objective: You must describe the overall structure of a text.

Explanation: Choice C is the best answer. The first paragraph traces the inception of Ethan's feelings for Mattie: Ethan "had taken to the girl from the first day" (lines 6-7) and saw her arrival as "like the lighting of a fire on a cold hearth" (line 14). The second paragraph (lines 20-48) focuses on "their night walks back to the farm" (line 20) and Ethan's elation in perceiving that "one other spirit . . . trembled with the same touch of wonder" that characterized his own (lines 30-31). In other words, the main focus of the first two paragraphs is the intensity of feeling one character, Ethan, has for another, Mattie. The last paragraph shifts the focus of the passage to Ethan's change in perception; he sees Mattie in a social setting interacting with other men, wonders "how he could ever have thought that his dull talk interested her" (lines 52-53), interprets her seeming happiness as "plain proof of indifference" toward him (lines 54-55), and sees betrayal in the "two or three gestures which, in his fatuity, he had thought she kept for him" (lines 57-59).

Choice A is incorrect because while Ethan acknowledges that Mattie "don't look much on housework" (line 11), the first paragraph also notes that Ethan "had taken to the girl from the first day" (lines 6-7);

therefore, there is no support for the notion that Ethan's "reservations" about Mattie lasted for any length of time or ever constituted the main focus of the narrative.

Choice B is incorrect because while Ethan does exhibit ambivalence about his sensitive nature, seeing it as a "mournful privilege" (lines 29-30), the main focus of the narrative does not shift to his recognition of the advantages of having profound emotions. Indeed, in the last paragraph, Ethan's profound emotions give him only grief, as he sees Mattie seemingly rejecting him.

Choice D is incorrect because while the second paragraph (lines 20-48) does discuss in depth the value Ethan attaches to natural beauty, nothing in the passage signifies that he has rejected natural beauty in favor of human artistry. The closest the passage comes to this is in lines 45-46, in which Mattie is said to have likened a natural scene to a painting, an assertion with which Ethan agrees.

15

In the context of the passage, the author's use of the phrase "her light step flying to keep time with his long stride" (lines 4-5) is primarily meant to convey the idea that

A) Ethan and Mattie share a powerful enthusiasm.

B) Mattie strives to match the speed at which Ethan works.

C) Mattie and Ethan playfully compete with each other.

D) Ethan walks at a pace that frustrates Mattie.

Content: Rhetoric

Key: A

Objective: You must determine the main rhetorical effect of the author's choice of words.

Explanation: Choice A is the best answer. The author uses the phrase mainly to introduce a topic discussed at length in the second paragraph (lines 20-48) — namely, the growing connection Ethan sees himself forming with Mattie over the course of many evening walks during which they share similar feelings for the wonders of the natural world. In the context of the passage, the phrase evokes an image of two people walking eagerly and in harmony.

Choice B is incorrect because while the phrase literally conveys Mattie's attempts to keep up with Ethan's pace, the phrase relates to times of leisure during which Ethan and Mattie walked arm-in-arm (see lines 1-4) rather than times of work. Moreover, the phrase is used primarily in a figurative way to suggest shared enthusiasm (see explanation for choice A).

PRACTICE AT
satpractice.org

Choice C may seem tempting, as the relationship between Ethan and Mattie is described in the passage as containing an aspect of playfulness. The idea that Mattie and Ethan playfully compete with one another is not, however, the intended purpose of the phrase referred to in the question.

Choice C is incorrect because while the phrase literally describes Mattie's attempts to keep up with Ethan's pace, the context makes clear that Mattie and Ethan are not in competition with each other; instead, they are enjoying times of leisure during which the two walk arm-in-arm (see lines 1-4). Moreover, the phrase is used primarily in a figurative way to suggest shared enthusiasm (see explanation for choice A).

Choice D is incorrect because while the phrase could in isolation be read as conveying some frustration on the part of Mattie, who had to expend extra effort to keep up with Ethan's pace, the context makes clear that Mattie is not annoyed with Ethan but is instead enjoying times of leisure during which the two walk arm-in-arm (see lines 1-4). The phrase is used primarily to suggest shared enthusiasm (see explanation for choice A).

16

The description in the first paragraph indicates that what Ethan values most about Mattie is her

A) fitness for farm labor.
B) vivacious youth.
C) receptive nature.
D) freedom from worry.

Content: Information and Ideas

Key: C

Objective: You must characterize the relationship between two individuals in the passage.

Explanation: Choice C is the best answer. Lines 8-14 mention many of Mattie's traits: she is friendly ("smiled and waved"), eager ("jumped down with her bundles"), easygoing ("she ain't a fretter"), and energetic ("like the lighting of a fire on a cold hearth"). However, the trait that appeals the most to Ethan, as suggested by it being mentioned last in the paragraph, is her openness to the world around her: "She had an eye to see and an ear to hear: he could show her things and tell her things, and taste the bliss of feeling that all he imparted left long reverberations and echoes he could wake at will" (lines 15-19).

Choice A is incorrect because the passage suggests that Ethan does not actually view Mattie as particularly well suited to farm labor. When first seeing Mattie, Ethan thinks to himself, after "looking over her slight person," that "she don't look much on housework" (lines 10-11).

Choice B is incorrect because the passage suggests that Mattie's youth is not what Ethan values most about Mattie. Although the passage does note that "the coming to his house of a bit of hopeful young life was like the lighting of a fire on a cold hearth" (lines 12-14), the narrator goes on to note that "the girl was more than the bright serviceable creature [Ethan] had thought her" (lines 14-15), indicating that Ethan values something more in Mattie than simply her vivacity.

Choice D is incorrect because although Ethan acknowledges that Mattie "ain't a fretter" (line 12), there is no evidence that Mattie's freedom from worry is what Ethan values the most about Mattie. The first paragraph lists several positive traits that Mattie has, with the most emphasis being placed on her openness to the world around her (see explanation for choice C).

PRACTICE AT
satpractice.org

What makes this question particularly challenging is that there's quite a bit of support for choice B in the first paragraph of the passage. Choice C, however, is the best answer because the first paragraph ends with a strong emphasis on Mattie's receptive nature, underscored by the keyword "But" in line 12.

17

Which choice provides the best evidence for the answer to the previous question?

A) Lines 1-6 ("Mattie . . . farm")
B) Lines 6-12 ("He had . . . anyhow")
C) Lines 12-14 ("But it . . . hearth")
D) Lines 15-19 ("She had . . . will")

PRACTICE AT
satpractice.org

Questions 16 and 17 form an interrelated question pair. The thought process that led you to the answer for Question 16 will help you select the answer for Question 17.

Content: Information and Ideas

Key: D

Objective: You must determine which portion of the passage provides the best evidence for the answer to the previous question.

Explanation: Choice D is the best answer. Lines 15-19 explain that Mattie "had an eye to see and an ear to hear: [Ethan] could show her things and tell her things, and taste the bliss of feeling that all he imparted left long reverberations and echoes he could wake at will." In other words, Mattie is open, or receptive, to ideas and experiences, and the placement of this point at the end of the list of traits Ethan admires ("But it was not only . . .") suggests that her openness is most important to him. Therefore, these lines serve as the best evidence for the answer to the previous question.

Choice A is incorrect because lines 1-6 only describe Ethan and Mattie's living situation and indicate that Ethan enjoys walking with her in the evenings. They do not indicate which quality of Mattie's Ethan values the most. Therefore, these lines do not serve as the best evidence for the answer to the previous question.

Choice B is incorrect because lines 6-12 only indicate Ethan's first impression of Mattie. Mattie comes across as generally friendly and enthusiastic in their first encounter, but it is not these qualities that Ethan values the most. Therefore, these lines do not serve as the best evidence for the answer to the previous question.

Choice C is incorrect because lines 12-14 only convey that there was something special about Mattie beyond her friendliness and enthusiasm. They do not indicate what Ethan values the most about Mattie. Therefore, these lines do not serve as the best evidence for the answer to the previous question.

PRACTICE AT
satpractice.org

The clues that can help you answer this question can be found in the lines immediately preceding the lines referenced in the question. When asked why the author includes a particular detail, always consider the context in which the detail appears.

18

The author includes the descriptions of the sunset, the clouds, and the hemlock shadows (lines 42-45) primarily to

A) suggest the peacefulness of the natural world.
B) emphasize the acuteness of two characters' sensations.
C) foreshadow the declining fortunes of two characters.
D) offer a sense of how fleeting time can be.

Content: Rhetoric

Key: B

Objective: You must analyze the relationship between a particular part of a text and the whole text.

Explanation: Choice B is the best answer. Lines 40-45 indicate that "there were other sensations, less definable but more exquisite, which drew [Ethan and Mattie] together with a shock of silent joy: the cold red of sunset behind winter hills, the flight of cloud-flocks over slopes of golden stubble, or the intensely blue shadows of hemlocks on sunlit snow." In the context of the second paragraph (lines 20-48), which focuses on the connection Ethan and Mattie establish through their shared interest in and sensitivity to nature, the descriptions primarily serve to emphasize the acuteness, or intensity, of the characters' sensations. According to the passage, Ethan and Mattie do not merely appreciate nature or see it as pretty or calm; rather, they experience a powerful "shock of silent joy" when in the presence of natural beauty.

Choice A is incorrect because there is no indication that the descriptions are included primarily to emphasize the peacefulness of the natural world. Some readers may see "the cold red of sunset behind winter hills, the flight of cloud-flocks over slopes of golden stubble, or the intensely blue shadows of hemlocks on sunlit snow" (lines 42-45) as evoking a peaceful, harmonious scene. However, Ethan and Mattie do not merely appreciate nature or see it as pretty or calm; rather, they experience a powerful "shock of silent joy" (line 42) when in the presence of natural beauty.

Choice C is incorrect because there is no evidence in the passage that the descriptions are included primarily to foreshadow Ethan's and Mattie's declining fortunes. In fact, there is no evidence in the passage of decline for either character apart from the agitation that Ethan experiences over his relationship with Mattie.

Choice D is incorrect because there is no evidence in the passage that the descriptions are included primarily to offer a sense of time as fleeting. In fact, the speed at which time passes plays no particular role in the passage.

Sample 5:

Science Passage Pair, Medium Text Complexity

The following pair of passages from a life science text is of medium complexity: it represents the middle range of language difficulty and cognitive demand of passages that you'll find on the Reading Test.

REMEMBER

You'll see one set of paired passages on the SAT Reading Test.

Questions 19-23 are based on the following passages.

Passage 1 is adapted from Susan Milius, "A Different Kind of Smart." ©2013 by Science News. Passage 2 is adapted from Bernd Heinrich, *Mind of the Raven: Investigations and Adventures with Wolf-Birds*. ©2007 by Bernd Heinrich.

Passage 1

In 1894, British psychologist C. Lloyd Morgan published what's called Morgan's canon, the principle that suggestions of humanlike mental processes behind an animal's behavior should be rejected if a simpler explanation will do.

Still, people seem to maintain certain expectations, especially when it comes to birds and mammals. "We somehow want to prove they are as 'smart' as people," zoologist Sara Shettleworth says. We want a bird that masters a vexing problem to be employing human-style insight.

New Caledonian crows face the high end of these expectations, as possibly the second-best toolmakers on the planet.

Their tools are hooked sticks or strips made from spike-edged leaves, and they use them in the wild to winkle grubs out of crevices. Researcher Russell Gray first saw the process on a cold morning in a mountain forest in New Caledonia, an island chain east of Australia. Over the course of days, he and crow researcher Gavin Hunt had gotten wild crows used to finding meat tidbits in holes in a log. Once the birds were checking the log reliably, the researchers placed a spiky tropical pandanus plant beside the log and hid behind a blind.

A crow arrived. It hopped onto the pandanus plant, grabbed the spiked edge of one of the long straplike leaves and began a series of ripping motions. Instead of just tearing away one long strip, the bird ripped and nipped in a sequence to create a slanting stair-step edge on a leaf segment with a narrow point and a wide base. The process took only seconds. Then the bird dipped the narrow end of its leaf strip into a hole in the log, fished up the meat with the leaf-edge spikes, swallowed its prize and flew off.

"That was my 'oh wow' moment," Gray says. After the crow had vanished, he picked up the tool the bird had left behind. "I had a go, and I couldn't do it," he recalls. Fishing the meat out was tricky. It turned out that Gray was moving the leaf shard too forcefully instead of gently stroking the spines against the treat.

The crow's deft physical manipulation was what inspired Gray and Auckland colleague Alex Taylor to test other wild crows to see if they employed the seemingly insightful string-pulling solutions that some ravens, kea parrots and other brainiac birds are known to employ. Three of four crows passed that test on the first try.

Passage 2

For one month after they left the nest, I led my four young ravens at least once and sometimes several times a day on thirty-minute walks. During these walks, I wrote down everything in their environment they pecked at. In the first sessions, I tried to be teacher. I touched specific objects — sticks, moss, rocks — and nothing that I touched remained untouched by them. They came to investigate what I had investigated, leading me to assume that young birds are aided in learning to identify food from the parents' example. They also, however, contacted almost everything else that lay directly in their own paths. They soon became more independent by taking their own routes near mine. Even while walking along on their own, they pulled at leaves, grass stems, flowers, bark, pine needles, seeds, cones, clods of earth, and other objects they encountered. I wrote all this down, converting it to numbers. After they were thoroughly familiar with the background objects in these woods and started to ignore them, I seeded the path we would later walk together with objects they had never before encountered. Some of these were conspicuous food items: raspberries, dead meal worm beetles, and cooked corn kernels. Others were conspicuous and inedible: pebbles, glass chips, red winterberries. Still others were such highly cryptic foods as encased caddisfly larvae and moth cocoons. The results were dramatic.

The four young birds on our daily walks contacted all new objects preferentially. They picked them out at a rate of up to tens of thousands of times greater than background or previously contacted objects. The main initial criterion for pecking or picking anything up was its novelty. In subsequent trials, when the previously novel items were edible, they became preferred and the inedible objects became "background" items, just like the leaves, grass, and pebbles, even if they were highly conspicuous. These experiments showed that ravens' curiosity ensures exposure to all or almost all items in the environment.

19

Within Passage 1, the main purpose of the first two paragraphs (lines 1-10) is to

A) offer historical background in order to question the uniqueness of two researchers' findings.
B) offer interpretive context in order to frame the discussion of an experiment and its results.
C) introduce a scientific principle in order to show how an experiment's outcomes validated that principle.
D) present seemingly contradictory stances in order to show how they can be reconciled empirically.

Content: Rhetoric

Key: B

Objective: You must determine the main purpose of two paragraphs in relation to the passage as a whole.

Explanation: Choice B is the best answer. Passage 1 opens with an explanation of Morgan's canon and continues with a discussion of people's expectations regarding animal intelligence. Taken together, the first two paragraphs indicate that despite cautions to the contrary, people still tend to look for humanlike levels of intelligence in many animals, including birds. These two paragraphs provide a framework in which to assess the work of Gray and Hunt, presented in the rest of the passage. The passage's characterization of the experiment Gray and Hunt conduct, in which they observe a crow's tool-making ability and to which Gray responds by trying and failing to mimic the bird's behavior ("I had a go, and I couldn't do it," line 34), suggests that Shettleworth, quoted in the second paragraph, is at least partially correct in her assessment that "we somehow want to prove [birds] are as 'smart' as people" (lines 6-7).

Choice A is incorrect because while the reference to Morgan's canon in the first paragraph offers a sort of historical background (given that the canon was published in 1894), the second paragraph describes people's continuing expectations regarding animal intelligence. Furthermore, the fact that Gray and Hunt may share with other people the tendency to look for humanlike intelligence in many animals does not by itself establish that the main purpose of the first two paragraphs is to question the uniqueness of Gray and Hunt's findings.

Choice C is incorrect because while the reference to Morgan's canon in the first paragraph does introduce a scientific principle, the discussion in the second paragraph of people's expectations regarding animal intelligence, as well as the passage's characterization of Gray and Hunt's experiment and how the researchers interpret the results, primarily suggest that people tend to violate the canon by attributing humanlike levels of intelligence to many animals.

Choice D is incorrect because although the first two paragraphs do present different perspectives, they are not seemingly or genuinely contradictory. The second paragraph, particularly the quotation from Shettleworth, serves mainly to qualify (not contradict) the position staked out in the first paragraph by suggesting that while Morgan's canon is probably a sound principle, people still tend to project humanlike levels of intelligence onto many animals. Moreover, the experiment depicted in the rest of the passage primarily bears out Shettleworth's claim that "We somehow want to prove [birds] are as 'smart' as people" (lines 6-7) and thus does not reconcile the perspectives found in the opening paragraphs.

PRACTICE AT
satpractice.org

In contrast to Question 19, which requires a broader understanding of the passage, Question 20 asks about a specific detail. On this type of question, it may help to locate and reread the relevant detail in the passage before selecting your answer.

20

According to the experiment described in Passage 2, whether the author's ravens continued to show interest in a formerly new object was dictated primarily by whether that object was

A) edible.
B) plentiful.
C) conspicuous.
D) natural.

Content: Information and Ideas/Understanding relationships

Key: A

Objective: You must identify an explicitly stated relationship between events.

Explanation: Choice A is the best answer. The last paragraph of Passage 2 presents the results of an experiment in which the author scattered unfamiliar objects in the path of some ravens. According to the passage, the birds initially "contacted all new objects preferentially" but in "subsequent trials" only preferred those "previously novel items" that "were edible" (lines 69-74).

Choice B is incorrect because the ravens studied by the author only preferred those "previously novel items" that "were edible," whereas "the inedible objects became 'background' items, just like the leaves, grass, and pebbles" (lines 74-76). In other words, plentiful items did not continue to interest the ravens unless the items were edible.

Choice C is incorrect because the ravens studied by the author only preferred those "previously novel items" that "were edible," whereas "the inedible objects became 'background' items, just like the leaves, grass, and pebbles, even if they were highly conspicuous" (lines 74-77). In other words, conspicuous items did not continue to interest the ravens unless the items were edible.

Choice D is incorrect because the ravens studied by the author only preferred those "previously novel items" that "were edible," whereas "the inedible objects became 'background' items, just like the leaves, grass, and pebbles" (lines 74-76). In other words, natural items did not continue to interest the ravens unless the items were edible.

21

The crows in Passage 1 and the ravens in Passage 2 shared which trait?

A) They modified their behavior in response to changes in their environment.

B) They formed a strong bond with the humans who were observing them.

C) They manufactured useful tools for finding and accessing food.

D) They mimicked the actions they saw performed around them.

Content: Synthesis/Analyzing multiple texts

Key: A

Objective: You must synthesize information and ideas from paired texts.

Explanation: Choice A is the best answer. Both bird species studied modified their behavior in response to changes in their environment. The researchers described in Passage 1 "had gotten wild crows used to finding meat tidbits in holes in a log" (lines 19-20). In other words, the researchers had repeatedly placed meat in the log — that is, changed the crows' environment — and the birds had responded by modifying their behavior, a point reinforced in line 21, which notes that the birds began "checking the log reliably." The ravens in Passage 2 act in analogous fashion, responding to the introduction of new objects in their environment by "pick[ing] them out at a rate of up to tens of thousands of times greater than background or previously contacted objects" (lines 70-72).

Choice B is incorrect because while there is some evidence that the ravens described in Passage 2 formed a bond with the author, going on walks with him and possibly viewing him as their "teacher," there is no evidence that a similar bond formed between the researchers described in Passage 1 and the crows they studied. Indeed, these researchers "hid behind a blind" (line 22) in an effort to avoid contact with their subjects.

Choice C is incorrect because while crows' tool-making ability is the central focus of the experiment described in Passage 1, there is no evidence that the ravens in Passage 2 did anything similar. Passage 1 does mention that "some ravens" use "seemingly insightful string-pulling solutions" (lines 40-41), but nothing in Passage 2 suggests that the ravens in that particular study had or displayed tool-making abilities.

PRACTICE AT
satpractice.org

The incorrect answers to Question 21 are traits that may have been possessed by either the crows in Passage 1 or the ravens in Passage 2. Only choice A describes a trait that the birds from both passages exhibited.

Choice D is incorrect because while there is some evidence that the ravens described in Passage 2 mimicked human behavior, going on walks with the author and possibly viewing him as their "teacher," there is no evidence that the crows in Passage 1 did any mimicking. Passage 1, in fact, suggests that the ability of the crow to produce the meat-fishing tool was innate rather than a skill it had acquired from either humans or other birds.

PRACTICE AT
satpractice.org

This question asks you to identify something the author of Passage 2 did that the researchers discussed in Passage 1 didn't do. Thus, the correct answer must fulfill both of these criteria. If an answer choice fulfills only one of two criteria, eliminate it!

22

One difference between the experiments described in the two passages is that unlike the researchers discussed in Passage 1, the author of Passage 2

A) presented the birds with a problem to solve.
B) intentionally made the birds aware of his presence.
C) consciously manipulated the birds' surroundings.
D) tested the birds' tool-using abilities.

Content: Synthesis/Analyzing multiple texts

Key: B

Objective: You must synthesize information and ideas from paired texts.

Explanation: Choice B is the best answer. The researchers described in Passage 1 "hid behind a blind" (line 22) to avoid being seen by the crow. The author of Passage 2, on the other hand, made no attempt to conceal his presence; in fact, as he describes it, he "led" the ravens in his study on "walks" (lines 44-46), during which he "touched specific objects" (line 48) and then watched to see whether the birds touched the same objects. The author of Passage 2 notes that the ravens "soon became more independent" (lines 54-55), going their own way rather than continuing to follow the author. From this, it is clear that the author of Passage 2, unlike the researchers described in Passage 1, intentionally made the birds aware of his presence.

Choice A is incorrect because while a case could be made that the author of Passage 2 gave the ravens a problem to solve (Which new objects are best to touch?), the researchers described in Passage 1 presented the crows with a problem as well: how to extract meat from a log. Thus, presenting birds with a problem to solve was not a difference between the experiments.

Choice C is incorrect because both the researchers described in Passage 1 and the author of Passage 2 consciously manipulated the birds' surroundings. The crow researchers placed meat pieces in a log and a pandanus plant behind the log (see lines 18-22). The author of Passage 2 put unfamiliar objects on a path for the ravens to find (see lines 61-62). Thus, conscious manipulation of the birds' surroundings was not a difference between the experiments.

Choice D is incorrect because there is no evidence that the author of Passage 2 tested the ravens' tool-using abilities. The passage instead indicates that the author recorded observations about the birds' interactions with objects naturally occurring in and artificially introduced into the environment.

23

Is the main conclusion presented by the author of Passage 2 consistent with Morgan's canon, as described in Passage 1?

A) Yes, because the conclusion proposes that the ravens' behavior is a product of environmental factors.

B) Yes, because the conclusion offers a satisfyingly simple explanation of the ravens' behavior.

C) No, because the conclusion suggests that the ravens exhibit complex behavior patterns.

D) No, because the conclusion implies that a humanlike quality motivates the ravens' behavior.

Content: Synthesis/Analyzing Multiple Texts

Key: D

Objective: You must synthesize information and ideas from paired texts.

Explanation: Choice D is the best answer. According to Passage 1, Morgan's canon is "the principle that suggestions of humanlike mental processes behind an animal's behavior should be rejected if a simpler explanation will do" (lines 2-4). The main conclusion drawn by the author of Passage 2 is that "ravens' curiosity ensures exposure to all or almost all items in the environment" (lines 78-79). In referring to the ravens' behavior as reflecting "curiosity," a human trait, the author of Passage 2 would seem to be ascribing a humanlike mental process to an animal's behavior without explicitly considering alternate explanations.

Choice A is incorrect because the main conclusion drawn by the author of Passage 2 is that "ravens' curiosity ensures exposure to all or almost all items in the environment" (lines 78-79). In referring to the ravens' behavior as reflecting "curiosity," a human trait, the author of Passage 2 would seem to be ascribing a humanlike mental process to an animal's behavior without explicitly considering alternate explanations. Morgan's canon holds that such suggestions should be rejected unless a "simpler explanation" cannot be found (line 4); therefore, the conclusion the author of Passage 2 reaches is not consistent with Morgan's canon. Moreover, by ascribing the ravens' behavior to "curiosity," the author of Passage 2 seems to reject environmental factors as the cause.

PRACTICE AT
satpractice.org

Break this challenging question down into a series of logical steps. First, identify the main conclusion of Passage 2 and refresh your memory of Morgan's canon. Next, determine if the conclusion in Passage 2 is consistent with Morgan's canon, and eliminate two answer choices accordingly. Lastly, examine the differences between the remaining two choices and select the one that is supported by the passages.

Choice B is incorrect because the main conclusion drawn by the author of Passage 2 is that "ravens' curiosity ensures exposure to all or almost all items in the environment" (lines 78-79). In referring to the ravens' behavior as reflecting "curiosity," a human trait, the author of Passage 2 would seem to be ascribing a humanlike mental process to an animal's behavior without explicitly considering alternate explanations. Morgan's canon holds that such suggestions should be rejected unless a "simpler explanation" cannot be found (line 4); therefore, the conclusion the author of Passage 2 reaches cannot be the type of "simpler explanation" Morgan was alluding to.

Choice C is incorrect because while the main conclusion drawn by the author of Passage 2 is not consistent with Morgan's canon (see explanation for choice D), nothing about how the canon is described in Passage 1 precludes the possibility that animals can exhibit complex behavior patterns. The canon merely rejects the idea that humanlike mental processes should quickly or easily be attributed to animals.

CHAPTER 10

About the SAT Writing and Language Test

Writing will be central to your postsecondary education, whether your plans involve college or some form of workforce training. Along with speaking and creating media, writing is a critical communication tool — one that you'll use continually in a variety of ways both informal and formal. You may use notes, journaling, or the like to record information, to aid memory, and to clarify thoughts and feelings for yourself; you may also create essays, poems, reports, and so on to share information and ideas with others in a more structured, fully developed way.

In the latter cases, you'll probably take each piece of writing through a variety of steps, from planning to polishing. Your writing process may differ from that of others, and your own process may change depending on the nature of the writing task, purpose, and audience (not to mention how much time you have), but revising your writing to improve the content and editing your writing to ensure that you've followed the conventions of standard written English are likely to be key parts of most projects. The SAT Writing and Language Test is designed to emulate these two tasks, assessing how well you can revise and edit a range of texts to improve the expression of ideas and to correct errors in sentence structure, usage, and punctuation.

REMEMBER

On the SAT Writing and Language Test, you'll be placed in the role of someone revising and editing the work of another writer.

The passages on the Writing and Language Test vary in purpose, subject, and complexity. Some passages (and possibly questions) will also include one or more informational graphics, such as tables, graphs, and charts, and you'll be expected to use the information in these graphics to inform decisions about revising the associated passage.

Unlike passages on the Reading Test, passages on the Writing and Language Test are written specifically for the test; that way, we can more easily introduce "errors" — our general term for the various rhetorical and mechanical problems we assess on the test. You'll encounter the passages and questions in side-by-side columns, with each passage (spread over multiple pages) in the left-hand column and associated questions in the right-hand column. Question numbers embedded in the passages, along with other forms of annotation (especially underlining), let you know what part of the passage is being tested at any given point; in some cases, questions may ask about a passage as a whole.

PRACTICE AT
satpractice.org

Getting a good score on the Writing and Language Test isn't about rote recall of language "rules." You'll instead need to consider context — often at the paragraph or passage level — when choosing your answer.

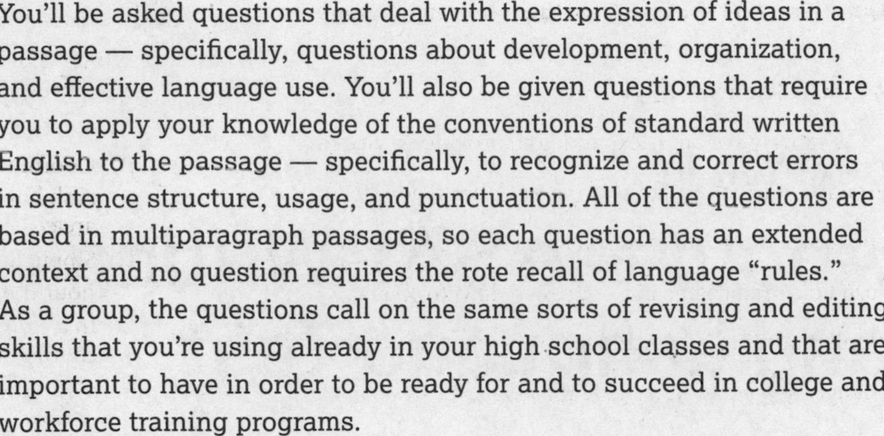

You'll be asked questions that deal with the expression of ideas in a passage — specifically, questions about development, organization, and effective language use. You'll also be given questions that require you to apply your knowledge of the conventions of standard written English to the passage — specifically, to recognize and correct errors in sentence structure, usage, and punctuation. All of the questions are based in multiparagraph passages, so each question has an extended context and no question requires the rote recall of language "rules." As a group, the questions call on the same sorts of revising and editing skills that you're using already in your high school classes and that are important to have in order to be ready for and to succeed in college and workforce training programs.

The rest of this chapter offers a general description of the Writing and Language Test. The following two chapters go into more detail about the question types that are included on the test.

Writing and Language Test Format

Before we delve into the passages and questions, let's take a look at the test format. Understanding how things work will help you get a quick start on test day and allow you to focus your full attention on answering the questions.

A sample of the Writing and Language Test format appears on the next page. Each passage will be headed by a title in boldface type. The passage itself will be spread across multiple pages (so, unless you're on the last question set on the test, don't assume that you've reached the end of a given passage until you see the title of the next one). The passage is positioned in the left-hand column of each page, and the questions related to the portion of the passage on that page appear in order in the right-hand column.

REMEMBER

In many cases, a boxed question number as well as underlining specify the part of the passage that a particular question refers to.

Most questions are "anchored" to a particular location in the passage via a boxed question number in the passage. Sometimes this boxed number will stand alone; in these cases, the associated question will tell you what to do, such as consider adding a sentence at that point. At other times, this boxed number will be followed by underlined text; for these questions, you'll have to consider which of four answer options results either in the most rhetorically effective expression in the context of the passage or in an expression that is correct in terms of standard written English sentence structure, usage, or punctuation. While some questions with an underlined portion include a question-specific direction (as in question 1), others don't (as in question 2). When there are no additional directions, assume that you're to choose the option that's the most rhetorically effective in context or that results in a conventionally correct expression. If a question includes a "NO CHANGE" option — it'll always be the first answer choice — pick it if you think the original version presented in the passage is the best option; otherwise, pick one of the three alternatives.

REMEMBER

Some questions with an underlined portion may not include directions. For these questions, assume that your task is to select the answer that's the most effective or correct.

REMEMBER

Some questions include a "NO CHANGE" option; choose this answer if you think the original text presented in the passage is the best choice.

Questions 1-11 are based on the following passage.

A Life in Traffic

A subway system is expanded to provide service to a growing suburb. A bike-sharing program is adopted to encourage nonmotorized transportation. **1** To alleviate rush hour traffic jams in a congested downtown area, stoplight timing is coordinated. When any one of these changes **2** occur, it is likely the result of careful analysis conducted by transportation planners.

The work of transportation planners generally includes evaluating current transportation needs,

1

Which choice best maintains the sentence pattern already established in the paragraph?

A) NO CHANGE
B) Coordinating stoplight timing can help alleviate rush hour traffic jams in a congested downtown area.
C) Stoplight timing is coordinated to alleviate rush hour traffic jams in a congested downtown area.
D) In a congested downtown area, stoplight timing is coordinated to alleviate rush hour traffic jams.

2

A) NO CHANGE
B) occur, they are
C) occurs, they are
D) occurs, it is

You may come across some other forms of passage annotation as well. If the paragraphs in a passage or the sentences in a paragraph are numbered, one or more questions will refer to those numbers. You may be asked, for example, to consider where a particular sentence should be placed in a paragraph (e.g., "after sentence 3"). You may also, on occasion, be advised that a particular question asks about the passage as a whole. In that case, you'll have to apply your understanding of the entire passage when answering the question.

Writing and Language Test Passages

The passages on the Writing and Language Test are varied in order to better assess whether you can apply your revising and editing knowledge and skills in a wide range of contexts important for college and career. Passages differ in purpose: Some primarily serve to relate events or experiences narratively, while others serve mainly to convey information, explain a process or idea, or argue for a particular way of thinking or acting. Passages also represent numerous different subject areas. In addition, passages vary in complexity, with some being relatively straightforward and others being highly challenging.

Let's consider some of the key features of Writing and Language Test passages.

- **Purpose:** As previously mentioned, some Writing and Language Test passages are focused on narrating experiences in a storylike way. Though there is no fiction passage on the Writing and Language Test (as there is on the Reading Test), a nonfiction narrative, such as one recounting a historical event or relating the steps in a scientific investigation, is found on each test. Other passages on the test serve mainly to inform, to explain, or to argue in support of a claim.

REMEMBER

Passage purpose, subject matter, and complexity will vary in order to provide a broad assessment of your revising and editing knowledge and skills.

- **Subject:** Writing and Language Test passages cover a variety of subject areas, including career-related topics, the humanities, history/social studies, and science. Passages on career-related topics aren't workplace documents, such as memos or reports; instead, they're general-interest pieces on trends, issues, and debates in common career pathways, such as health care and information technology. Humanities passages focus on the arts and letters and include texts on fine art, film, music, literature, and the like. History/social studies passages include texts on topics in history as well as in the social sciences, such as anthropology, archaeology, economics, and psychology. Science passages cover both foundational scientific concepts as well as recent advances in fields such as Earth science, biology, chemistry, and physics.
- **Complexity:** The reading challenge posed by the passages on the test varies. Some passages are relatively straightforward. They may, for example, have a very clear purpose, present a fairly small amount of information, and use familiar language. Other passages, by contrast, are more complex. They may have a more subtle purpose, require the reader to follow a complicated series of events, and make use of long and involved sentences. (It's important to note that each Writing and Language Test has a similar range of passage complexity, so you shouldn't worry about taking a test that has nothing but highly challenging passages.)

PRACTICE AT
satpractice.org

When you answer questions on the Writing and Language Test that relate to informational graphics, you'll be using skills similar to those you'll use on Problem Solving and Data Analysis questions on the SAT Math Test and some Synthesis questions on the SAT Reading Test.

One additional feature of passages is also important to note here.

- **Informational graphics:** Passages (and occasionally questions) on the Writing and Language Test may include one or more tables, graphs, charts, or the like that relate to the topic of the passage. A graphic may, for example, provide additional statistical support for a point made in the passage. Questions may ask you, for example, to use information from the graphic(s) to correct an error in the writer's reporting of data or to replace the passage's vague description of findings with a more precise one using specific quantities.

All of the passages on the Writing and Language Test are high-quality, well-edited pieces of writing developed specifically for the test. They convey interesting information, explore intriguing ideas, and offer new insights. Although the primary purpose of the passages is to help assess your revising and editing knowledge and skills, it's our hope that you find the passages engaging and worth reading.

Writing and Language Test Questions

Now that we've talked about the passages on the Writing and Language Test, it's time to turn to the questions. All of the questions are multiple-choice, which means that you'll pick the best of four answer options for each question. The questions are also all centered in multiparagraph passages, so you won't be tested on isolated rhetorical or grammar, usage, and mechanics skills. Because all questions are passage based, you'll want to consider the passage context carefully before answering each question. Sometimes focusing only on the sentence that a particular question refers to is enough to get that question right, but in other cases you'll have to think about the entire paragraph or the passage as a whole to get a good feel for the best response. Questions are sequenced in order of appearance, meaning that questions addressing the first paragraph come before those addressing the second paragraph, and so on. Any questions about the passage as a whole come last in a set. You'll encounter questions about informational graphics in the most logical spots in the order.

REMEMBER

All questions on the Writing and Language Test are multiple-choice with four answer options.

REMEMBER

All questions are passage based, so consider each question in the context of the passage before selecting your answer.

The questions on the test are designed to reflect as closely as possible the kinds of revising and editing decisions that writers and editors make. Think about a piece of writing that you've written and then gone back to improve. When you reread what you'd written, what came to mind? Maybe you realized that a particular point you were making didn't have enough support, so you added some. Maybe you recognized that you'd forgotten to put in a transition between two ideas, so you clarified the connection. Or maybe you saw that a subject and verb didn't agree, so you corrected the problem. Although you're not working with your own writing on the Writing and Language Test, the thinking process you'll use as you revise and edit the passages on the test is similar.

The questions also often reflect the demands of the specific sort of passage you're working with. In some passages (particularly those with informational graphics), data are important, so you're likely to be working to improve the accuracy, clarity, and precision of the writer's descriptions of those data. In other passages (particularly in narratives), sequence will be central, so a question about the logical order and flow of information and ideas is likely to show up. Although the passages are grounded in particular subject areas, the questions don't test your background knowledge of the specific topics covered. The passages and any supplementary material, such as tables or graphs, will provide all of the information about a given topic that you'll need to make revision and editing decisions.

REMEMBER

You won't need any background knowledge of the topic covered in a passage; all the information you need to answer the questions will be in the passage and in any supplementary material, such as a table or graph.

Writing and Language questions can be sorted into two general categories: (1) Expression of Ideas and (2) Standard English Conventions. The questions won't have those labels on them, but usually it'll be pretty easy to tell the difference. A brief discussion of each category should help you get a sense of what's on the test, what knowledge and skills you're likely to make use of, and how to focus your preparation for the test.

REMEMBER

Expression of Ideas questions ask you to assess and improve the substance and quality of passage text, while Standard English Conventions questions require you to recognize and correct errors in grammar, usage, and punctuation.

1. **Expression of Ideas:** These questions focus on the rhetorical elements of passages. To put it another way, Expression of Ideas questions deal with improving the substance and quality of the writer's message. You'll be asked to revise passages to improve the development of the topic, the organization of information and ideas, and the effectiveness of the language use. Development questions are about main ideas (such as topic sentences and thesis statements), supporting details, focus, and quantitative information in tables, graphs, charts, and so on. Organization questions focus on logical sequence and placement of information and ideas as well as effective introductions, conclusions, and transitions. Effective Language Use questions ask you to improve precision and concision (e.g., eliminating wordiness), consider style and tone (e.g., making sure that the tone is consistent throughout the passage), and combine sentences to improve flow and to achieve particular rhetorical effects (such as emphasis on one point over another).
2. **Standard English Conventions:** These questions focus on recognizing and correcting grammar, usage, and mechanics problems in passages. More specifically, these questions ask you to recognize and correct errors in sentence structure (such as run-on or incomplete sentences), usage (such as lack of subject-verb or pronoun-antecedent agreement), and punctuation (such as missing or unnecessary commas).

The Writing and Language Test in Overview

Some of the basic elements of the Writing and Language Test are listed below. Familiarizing yourself with this overview may help you prepare for the test and pace yourself on test day.

- Total Questions: 44
- Total Time: 35 minutes (on average, slightly under a minute per question, inclusive of passage reading time)
- Number of Passages: Four
- Passage Length: 400 to 450 words; total of 1,700 words
- Passage Subjects: One passage on a career-related topic and one passage each in the humanities, history/social studies, and science
- Passage Writing Modes: One nonfiction narrative, one to two informative/explanatory texts, and one to two arguments

- Passage Complexities: A defined range from grades 9–10 to early postsecondary
- Questions per Passage: 11
- In addition to an overall test score, the questions on the Writing and Language Test contribute to various scores in the following ways:
    - Expression of Ideas: 24 questions, generally six per passage
    - Standard English Conventions: 20 questions, generally five per passage
    - Command of Evidence: Eight questions, generally two per passage
    - Words in Context: Eight questions, generally two per passage
    - Analysis in History/Social Studies: Six questions (all of the Expression of Ideas questions on the history/social studies passage)
    - Analysis in Science: Six questions (all of the Expression of Ideas questions on the science passage)

NOTE: *Some Writing and Language questions contribute to multiple scores.*

Chapter 10 Recap

The SAT Writing and Language Test measures your knowledge and skills in revising and editing texts widely varied in purpose, subject, and complexity. The questions on the test are multiple-choice and passage based; represent the kinds of choices writers and editors routinely have to make; reflect differences in the content and nature of the passages; and cover two basic areas: Expression of Ideas and Standard English Conventions. Questions don't test topic-specific background knowledge; all of the information about each topic needed to answer the questions is provided to you. Some passages and/or questions on the test include one or more informational graphics.

The Writing and Language Test offers a significant but fair challenge to college- and career-ready students. Since the questions are fairly "natural" in the sense that they mimic common revision and editing issues and are based in extended pieces of high-quality writing, you won't have to worry about applying obscure conventions or dealing with highly artificial or brief passages that provide little context for an answer. On the other hand, you *will* have to pay attention to the context as you answer the questions. Sometimes you'll have to "read around" a given place in the passage — looking both before it and after it — or you'll have to think about the whole passage to see how the larger text influences the answer to a particular question. Sometimes, too, what would seem like the best answer in many situations — such as adopting a formal tone — is a weaker choice in a given case, such as in a highly informal passage. The questions themselves will also often state the goal to be accomplished, such as adding support or shifting emphasis. Paying careful attention to the goals indicated in the questions and to the contextual clues provided in the passages will go a long way toward ensuring that you do your best on the Writing and Language Test.

CHAPTER 11

Writing and Language: Expression of Ideas

Questions on the SAT Writing and Language Test fall into two broad categories: (1) Expression of Ideas and (2) Standard English Conventions. This chapter focuses on the first category, Expression of Ideas.

Expression of Ideas: The Art of Writing

Expression of Ideas questions on the Writing and Language Test focus on refining the substance and quality of a writer's message. Specifically, Expression of Ideas questions focus on development, organization, and effective language use in relation to the writer's purpose. Collectively, these questions address rhetorical aspects of the passages on the test. When you answer the rhetorically oriented Expression of Ideas questions, you're using your knowledge of and skill in writing to make each passage clearer, sharper, richer, and more engaging.

Broken down, the Expression of Ideas category consists of these elements:

- **Development:** Refining the content of a passage to achieve the writer's purpose, including:
  - *Proposition:* Adding, revising, or retaining (leaving unchanged) thesis statements, topic sentences, claims, and the like — the "main ideas" of a passage or paragraph
  - *Support:* Adding, revising, or retaining material that supports a passage's points or claims
  - *Focus:* Adding, revising, retaining, or deleting material on the basis of relevance to the purpose (e.g., deleting an irrelevant sentence)
  - *Quantitative information:* Using data from informational graphics (tables, graphs, charts, and the like) to enhance the accuracy, precision, and overall effectiveness of a passage

PRACTICE AT
satpractice.org

On the Writing and Language Test, you'll be asked to step into the role of editor, identifying ways that a writer could improve the development, organization, and use of language in a passage.

REMEMBER

As you can see from the descriptions of these three subcategories, Expression of Ideas questions require you to have a strong understanding of the passage as a whole.

REMEMBER

Proposition questions focus on the "big ideas" in the passage and ask you, for instance, to add or revise thesis statements or topic sentences in order to clarify the writer's points.

- **Organization:** Improving the structure of a passage to enhance logic and cohesion, including:
  - *Logical sequence:* Ensuring that material is presented in a passage in the most logical place and order
  - *Introductions, conclusions, and transitions:* Improving the openings and closings of paragraphs and passages and the connections between and among information and ideas in a passage
- **Effective Language Use:** Revising text to improve written expression and to achieve the writer's purpose, including:
  - *Precision:* Making word choice more exact or more appropriate for the context
  - *Concision:* Making word choice more economical by eliminating wordiness and redundancy
  - *Style and tone:* Making word choice consistent with the overall style and tone of a passage or accomplishing some particular rhetorical goal
  - *Syntax:* Combining sentences to improve the flow of language or to accomplish some particular rhetorical goal

In the following sections, we'll examine each of these subcategories in turn.

Development

Development questions on the Writing and Language Test get to the heart of the substance of the passage. They're the questions that focus most directly on the content of the writer's message. (Note, though, that you won't need background knowledge of the passage's topic to answer the questions; all the information you'll need will be in the passage itself and in any supplementary material, such as a table or graph.) When you answer a Development question, you'll be looking for ways to enhance the writer's message by clarifying the main points, working with supporting details, sharpening the focus, and — in some passages — using data from informational graphics such as tables, graphs, and charts to make the passage more accurate, more precise, and generally more effective. Let's go into a little more detail on each of these points.

Proposition

Proposition questions require you to think about the "big ideas" in the passage and how they can be refined to better clarify and structure the writer's message. The forms these big ideas take vary from passage to passage, but there are several common types: *Thesis statements* express the main idea of the overall passage. *Topic sentences* are used to help structure and clarify the focus of paragraphs. These often (but not always) come at the beginning of a paragraph and serve to preview (and limit) what's to come. *Claims* and *counterclaims* are features specific to arguments. A claim is an assertion that the writer is trying to convey, such as the writer's position on a debate or issue, while a counterclaim is someone else's assertion that differs from, and sometimes opposes, the assertion the writer is making. (You might think of claims and counterclaims this way: In the formula "While many people believe *x*, *y* is actually the case," *y* is the writer's claim and *x* is the counterclaim the writer is arguing against.)

Proposition questions won't always use words and phrases such as "claim" or "topic sentence," but it's helpful to use them here to give you a sense of the nature of these questions. Proposition questions will typically ask you to add or revise topic sentences, thesis statements, and so on in order to clarify and sharpen the writer's points or to leave them as is if the original version presented in the passage is better than any of the alternatives offered.

REMEMBER

Whereas Proposition questions focus on the big ideas, Support questions get into the details of how the writer backs up the big ideas with evidence, examples, and the like.

Support

Support questions are basically the flip side of Proposition questions. When you answer a Support question, you'll be thinking about how best to flesh out and make more effective or convincing the writer's big ideas. Support comes in many forms, but among the most common are descriptive details, facts, figures, and examples. The questions will typically use a word such as "support" and indicate what idea in the passage the writer wants to develop. You'll be asked to add or revise supporting material in order to strengthen a writer's point or to leave supporting material unchanged if the original version in the passage is the best way to accomplish the writer's goal.

REMEMBER

Some Focus questions may ask you to determine what information is irrelevant or insufficiently connected to the writer's purpose. Other Focus questions may ask you to determine what information should be added or retained.

Focus

Focus questions are mainly about relevance in relation to the writer's purpose. Purpose is a key consideration here because while some questions will ask you to remove information or an idea that's clearly irrelevant to the topic, the harder questions of this type will offer a detail that's loosely but not sufficiently tied to the point that the writer is making or that goes off on an interesting but ultimately unhelpful tangent. Focus questions are often about recognizing and deleting material that's irrelevant or only vaguely connected to the writer's aim, and these types of questions will often identify a sentence and ask you whether it should be kept or deleted. Focus questions, however, can also be about adding or retaining relevant information and ideas, so you shouldn't assume that every time you see a Focus question the answer will be to remove something. For these sorts of questions, it's especially important to consider the larger context of a particular paragraph or of the passage as a whole; without an understanding of the goal the writer is trying to achieve, it's very difficult to make informed decisions about relevance.

REMEMBER

Questions on the Writing and Language Test that refer to informational graphics will require you to closely integrate data from one or more graphics with text from the passage.

PRACTICE AT
satpractice.org

To answer this question correctly, you'll need to combine a solid understanding of the text with an accurate interpretation of the data displayed in the graph.

Quantitative Information

We talked at length in the discussion of the Reading Test about comprehension questions related to informational graphics. Although the Writing and Language Test also includes a number of such graphics, the focus of questions about them is significantly different. On both tests, you'll have to read and interpret informational graphics, but on the Writing and Language Test, you'll have to integrate text and graphics in a more direct way than on the Reading Test. Let's look at an example from a passage on traffic congestion. (As with the other samples in this chapter, the full passage text, question, and answer explanation can be found in Chapter 13.)

[. . .] Transportation planners perform critical work within the broader field of urban and regional planning. As of 2010, there were approximately 40,300 urban and regional planners employed in the United States. The United States Bureau of Labor Statistics forecasts steady job growth in this field, **11** projecting that 16 percent of new jobs in all occupations will be related to urban and regional planning. Population growth and concerns about environmental sustainability are expected to spur the need for transportation planning professionals.

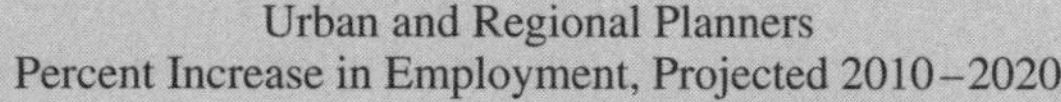

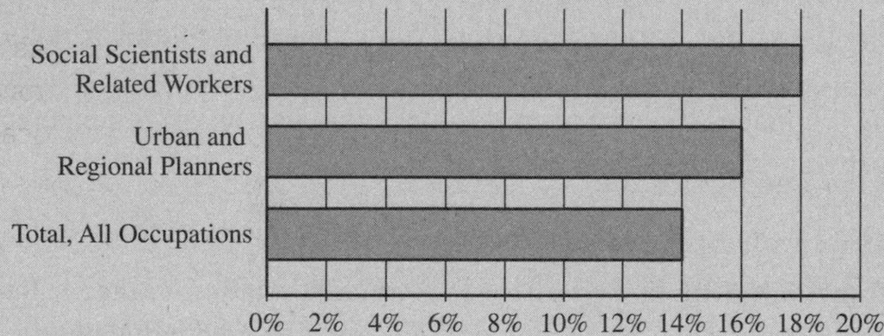

11. Which choice completes the sentence with accurate data based on the graph?
    - A) NO CHANGE
    - B) warning, however, that job growth in urban and regional planning will slow to 14 percent by 2020.
    - C) predicting that employment of urban and regional planners will increase 16 percent between 2010 and 2020.
    - D) indicating that 14 to 18 percent of urban and regional planning positions will remain unfilled.

To answer this question, you need to understand both the passage and the accompanying graph. The question directs you to the underlined portion of the passage excerpt and asks you to complete the sentence with accurate data from the graphic. (Unless told otherwise by a question, you should assume that the graphic itself is accurate, so you don't need to worry about whether you're working with "true" information.)

The basic logic of the question is similar to that of other questions on the test that include a "NO CHANGE" option: If you think the original version in the passage is the best, select choice A; if you think that one of the other choices better meets the goal set out in the question, pick that one instead.

REMEMBER

Pick choice A, "NO CHANGE," if you think the original version presented in the passage provides accurate data from the graph.

In this case, the original version doesn't accurately capture what's in the graph. The graph's title lets us know that the bars represent projected increases in employment between 2010 and 2020. (These increases are "projected" because at the time the graph was put together, actual data on those years weren't available.) The original version (choice A) is inaccurate because the graph indicates that employment in "all occupations" is expected to increase 14 percent between 2010 and 2020, not that 16 percent of new jobs in all occupations during that period will be related to urban and regional planning. So we have to look to the other choices for a better option. Choice C proves to be the best answer because the middle bar in the graph indicates that the employment of urban and regional planners is expected to increase 16 percent over the indicated time period. As is true on the Reading Test, you won't have to use math skills to answer a question such as this; you'll just be "reading" the graphic and locating and interpreting the data.

REMEMBER

Quantitative Information questions may come in a few different forms, but all of them require you to establish a meaningful connection between graphic(s) and passage.

While many Quantitative Information questions will be like this one, you may come across other styles. For instance, you may be asked to replace a general description with a more precise one based on numerical data. (To take a simple example, the preceding passage may simply have said that there's expected to be "a great deal of growth in the employment of urban and regional planners," and you'd replace that vague assertion with the fact that that growth is expected to be 16 percent.) You may also be told that the writer is considering adding a particular graphic to the passage and asked to decide whether doing so would help make a particular point. In any case, you'll need to have a good understanding of the graphic and be able to draw a meaningful connection between the graphic(s) and the passage.

Organization

Questions about organization ask you to consider whether the placement or sequence of material in a passage could be made more logical or whether the openings and closings of a passage and its paragraphs and the transitions tying information and ideas together could be improved. We'll now examine each of these types.

Logical Sequence

REMEMBER

Logical Sequence questions generally ask you to determine the best placement for a given sentence within a paragraph or passage.

If you're recounting an event, you'll typically want to present things in the order in which they happened, and if you're presenting new information or ideas, you'll want to follow a sequence that makes things easy for the reader to understand. Logical Sequence questions address these sorts of issues. One common question of this type directs you to consider the numbered sentences in a paragraph and to decide whether one of those sentences is out of place. In this situation, you'll identify the best placement for the given sentence within the paragraph in terms of logic and cohesion. If you think the sentence is fine in its present location, you'll choose an option such as "where it is now" (similar to the "NO CHANGE" choice found in many other questions); otherwise, you'll pick one of the alternative placements, which are generally phrased in terms of "before" or "after" another numbered sentence (e.g., "before sentence 1," "after sentence 3"). Other questions may ask you to find the most logical place for a sentence within the passage as a whole or to add at the most logical point a new sentence that's not already in the passage; other variations are possible as well. The basic approach is the same in every case: After reading and considering the passage, figure out which order or placement makes the passage most logical and cohesive.

Introductions, Conclusions, and Transitions

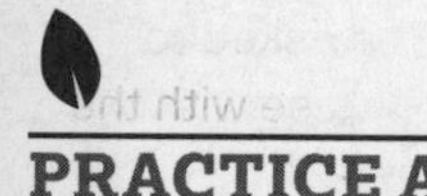

PRACTICE AT
satpractice.org

Context is critical for Development and Organization questions. Always consider the tested element in context as well as how the element relates to the writer's purpose.

Introductions, conclusions, and transitions are, in a sense, the connective tissue that holds a text together. They help orient the reader, generate interest, serve as reminders of the purpose and point of a text, and build conceptual bridges between and among ideas. Questions about introductions, conclusions, and transitions on the Writing and Language Test ask you to think about how to make the reader's movement through a passage smoother and more meaningful. You may, for instance, be asked to add an introduction or conclusion to a passage or paragraph, to revise an existing opening or closing to make it more effective, or to determine which word, phrase, or sentence most successfully creates or clarifies a logical link between sentences or paragraphs. Again, you often have a "NO CHANGE" option, which you should select if you think the original version found in the passage is better than any of the offered alternatives. Once more, context is critical: You'll need to read more than just the tested sentence to know what relationship the writer is trying to establish between and among ideas.

PRACTICE AT
satpractice.org

Be on the lookout for specific words or phrases such as "for instance," "however," and "thus." These keywords signal the logical relationship between information and ideas in the passage and play an important role in some Organization questions.

Many questions about transitions focus on words and phrases commonly used to signal logical relationships. If you see "for instance" in a text, you know that you're getting what the writer hopes is a clarifying example of a general point; if you see "however," you know that the writer is trying to tell you that something is actually the case despite what might seem to be the case. Becoming comfortable with the function of common transition words and phrases such as "by contrast," "additionally," "in spite of that," "thus," and the like will be of great value in answering questions about transitions on the Writing and Language Test. But not all transitions can be reduced to a single word or phrase, so some questions on the Writing and Language Test may ask you to add or revise (or retain) a full-sentence transition between sentences or paragraphs.

Effective Language Use

Effective Language Use questions focus on using language to accomplish particular rhetorical goals. Questions in this subcategory involve improving the precision and economy of expression, making sure that the style and tone of a passage are appropriate and consistent, putting sentences together to make ideas flow more smoothly, and other specified aims. In the following discussion, we'll examine the ways in which Effective Language Use is tested on the SAT.

Precision

Vague language often leaves the reader uncertain or confused. Precision questions on the Writing and Language Test generally require you to replace vague language with something more specific or to recognize that a particular word or phrase doesn't make sense in a given context.

Here's an example, taken from a humanities passage about painter Dong Kingman (available in full in Chapter 13).

> [. . .] As Kingman developed as a painter, his works were often compared to paintings by Chinese landscape artists dating back to CE 960, a time when a strong tradition of landscape painting emerged in Chinese art. Kingman, however, **16** vacated from that tradition in a number of ways, most notably in that he chose to focus not on natural landscapes, such as mountains and rivers, but on cities. [. . .]
>
> 16. A) NO CHANGE
> B) evacuated
> C) departed
> D) retired

All four of the tested words have something to do with "leaving," but only one of them makes good contextual sense. It's not "vacated" — the version already in the passage — because the word implies a literal leaving. You might vacate a building, leaving it empty, but you wouldn't "vacate" from a tradition. Similar problems occur if you try to use "evacuated" or "retired" in that context. "Evacuated" indicates removal or withdrawal, as when a person leaves a dangerous place to get to a safe place. "Retired" also indicates withdrawal, as when a person leaves a job after reaching a certain age. Only "departed" (choice C) has the correct general sense of leaving and makes sense in the context of leaving a tradition.

REMEMBER

If a word or phrase in the passage is vague or not appropriate for the given context, you'll be asked to replace the word or phrase with the best alternative.

PRACTICE AT

satpractice.org

While all four of the answer choices have to do with the concept of "leaving," only one of them is appropriate in the context of this sentence.

While many Precision questions take this approach, other forms are possible. For example, you may simply be presented with language that's imprecise or unclear and asked to sharpen it by using more specific phrasing.

REMEMBER

Concision — stating an idea briefly but also clearly and accurately — is a valued characteristic of writing in both college and the workforce.

Concision

Sometimes language can be repetitive. Concision questions will ask you to recognize such cases and to eliminate wordy or redundant language. Sometimes this repetitiveness will be in the underlined portion of the passage itself, but other times you'll have to recognize that the writer made the same point elsewhere in the passage and that the underlined portion should be deleted for the sake of economy. You'll want to avoid automatically picking the shortest answer in every case, though, because there's such a thing as being too concise, and sometimes a particular phrasing is just too "telegraphic" to be clear or to include all the necessary information.

PRACTICE AT

satpractice.org

The tone of the passages on the Writing and Language Test may range from very casual to very formal. You may be asked to correct instances in which a writer deviates from the established tone.

Style and Tone

Sometimes a writer will lose track of the "voice" he or she is trying to establish in a piece of writing and use language that's "super casual" or that "embodies a stultifying degree of ponderousness" that's not in keeping with the level of formality (or informality) established in the rest of the passage. One common Style and Tone question on the Writing and Language Test asks you to recognize such cases and to revise the passage to improve consistency of tone. To answer such questions, you'll need to have a clear sense of the writer's voice and be able to identify language that fits in with that voice. Across the test, passages exhibit a range of tones, meaning that sometimes a very casual or a highly formal choice may, in fact, be the right one in context.

REMEMBER

On Style and Tone questions, you'll want to factor in what the writer is trying to accomplish in the passage when choosing your answer.

This question type addresses more than just tone, however. A question may specify a particular stylistic effect that the writer wants to create and ask you to determine which choice best achieves that goal. One such approach involves stylistic patterns. Maybe the writer has used a series of sentence fragments (incomplete sentences) for emphasis, and you'll be expected to recognize that only one of the four answer choices maintains that pattern. You might instinctively want a complete sentence since we're often told that fragments are "wrong," but in this case, the goal specified in the question should override that instinct. Fragments aren't the only kind of pattern that a writer might establish to create a particular effect. Perhaps the writer wants to set up a series of short, descriptive sentences ("The wind blew. The trees waved. The leaves spun."), and only one of the four options ("The onlookers shivered.") extends that pattern. We've said it before, but it's true here again: The context provided by the passage (and often a goal named in the question itself) should guide you as you select your answer to such questions.

Syntax

"Syntax" is a fancy term for the arrangement of words into phrases, clauses, and sentences. While there are grammatical "rules" (really, standard practices or conventions, as we'll see in the next chapter) for syntax that most well-edited writing usually follows, what we're talking about here is the arrangement of words to achieve specific rhetorical purposes or effects. Syntax questions will ask you to consider how sentences can be combined — blended together — to improve flow and cohesion or to achieve some other specified end, such as placing emphasis on a particular element. In some cases, you'll be combining two (or sometimes more) full sentences; in others, you'll identify the choice that creates the best link between two sentences. You won't be changing the meaning of the original text, just connecting ideas more effectively.

REMEMBER

On Syntax questions, you'll be asked how two or more sentences can be combined to improve flow or cohesion or to achieve another rhetorical goal.

The following example will give you a good sense of the format. (The full passage, along with this and other questions and their answer explanations, can, again, be found in Chapter 13.)

[. . .] During his career, Kingman exhibited his work **21** internationally. He garnered much acclaim. [. . .]

21. Which choice most effectively combines the sentences at the underlined portion?
    A) internationally, and Kingman also garnered
    B) internationally; from exhibiting, he garnered
    C) internationally but garnered
    D) internationally, garnering

REMEMBER

The best answer to a Syntax question will improve flow or cohesion (or achieve some other rhetorical goal) without altering the meaning of the original sentences.

There's nothing grammatically wrong with having two separate sentences here, but the writing is rather choppy, and a good writer or editor might reasonably want to combine the two sentences to create a clearer, more fluid single thought. The best answer here is choice D, which — importantly, without changing the original meaning — creates a logical, smooth connection between the two ideas (Kingman exhibited his work and Kingman earned recognition). Note how choice C is also grammatical but creates an illogical proposition: Despite exhibiting his work internationally, Kingman garnered acclaim. Note also how choices A and B really don't do anything to improve the sentence flow. Choice A creates two partially redundant independent clauses (". . . Kingman exhibited . . . and Kingman also garnered . . .") and doesn't make clear that the exhibitions were what won Kingman the acclaim. Choice B does draw that connection but, in a clunky way, repeats the idea of exhibiting (". . . Kingman exhibited . . .; from exhibiting . . ."). When you answer Syntax questions, you'll have to think less about what works from a technical, grammatical standpoint and more about what creates the most effective connections between and among phrases, clauses, and sentences.

Chapter 11 Recap

The Expression of Ideas category of Writing and Language Test questions focuses on the rhetorical aspects of writing. In answering these questions, you'll have to revise passages as a writer or editor would, considering the issues of how best to develop the topic and the points the writer is attempting to convey; how to organize information and ideas to create the most logical, smoothest progression; and how to use language purposefully to achieve the most effective results. These questions will often specify a goal that the writer is seeking to accomplish, and you should use this information, along with a full understanding of the passage and its intended purpose, to make the best choice in each case.

CHAPTER 12

Writing and Language: Standard English Conventions

The focus of this chapter is on Standard English Conventions, one of the two broad categories of questions on the SAT Writing and Language Test. Standard English Conventions questions relate to some of the basic elements of writing: sentence structure, usage, and punctuation.

Standard English Conventions: The Craft of Language

"Conventions" is just another way of referring to standard practices and expectations that we follow in all sorts of areas of our lives. We have conventions for how to greet people, make polite requests, and express gratitude. Conventions aren't just about etiquette, though; they're the customs we use and rely on in order to make our dealings with other people function more smoothly.

Like conventions in other parts of our lives, language conventions offer a standard (typical, broadly agreed upon) way to construct written expression in a manner that meets people's expectations and thereby helps ensure that our spoken and, especially, our written utterances are understood. To take a simple but important example, we commonly agree that in most cases a "sentence" in writing consists of a more or less complete thought, that a sentence will have certain parts (at least a subject and a verb), that the start of a new sentence should be signaled by a capital letter, and that the end of a sentence should be indicated with punctuation (a period, question mark, or exclamation point).

Of course, people violate conventions all the time. When the violation is against the law, there are generally clear and obvious penalties. But what's the "penalty" if you break a language convention?

REMEMBER

Observing standard English conventions is about more than ticking off items on a long list of grammar, usage, and mechanics rules; rather, it's closely tied to the meaning a writer wishes to convey.

Sometimes there's none at all. It could be that your reader or listener fully understands what you mean and can essentially skip over the irregularity. Sometimes you may even intentionally deviate from a convention to achieve a particular purpose. A sentence fragment, for instance, breaks convention by lacking key elements of a typical sentence but, in certain cases, can be very effective in creating emphasis, reflecting surprise or shock, or the like.

In most cases, though, following language conventions proves highly useful. When a writer observes conventions, the reader's attention can be focused on the message being sent. When a writer fails to observe them, the reader is likely to be distracted, annoyed, or confused. Conventions aren't truly separate from the meaning that you as a writer are trying to convey; they're part and parcel of it, a critical means by which you ensure that the message you intend to convey is the same as what the reader understands.

As is the case for Expression of Ideas, Standard English Conventions on the Writing and Language Test is an overarching category that includes three subcategories, each of which contains several testing points. Standard English Conventions questions require you to edit passages for sentence structure, usage, and punctuation. (Spelling and capitalization aren't directly tested.) In list form, the conventions category looks like this:

- **Sentence Structure:** Recognizing and correcting sentence formation problems and inappropriate shifts in sentence construction, including
  - *Sentence boundaries:* Recognizing and correcting grammatically incomplete sentences that aren't rhetorically effective (like the "good" — clearly deliberate — sentence fragments we spoke of earlier)
  - *Subordination and coordination:* Recognizing and correcting problems in how major parts of sentences are related
  - *Parallel structure:* Recognizing and correcting problems with parallelism
  - *Modifier placement:* Recognizing and correcting problems with modifier placement, including dangling and misplaced modifiers
  - *Inappropriate shifts in verb tense, mood, and voice* (e.g., changing inappropriately from past to present tense)
  - *Inappropriate shifts in pronoun person and number* (e.g., changing inappropriately from second person "you" to third person "one")

- **Conventions of Usage:** Observing standard usage practices, including
  - *Pronoun clarity:* Recognizing and correcting ambiguous or vague pronouns (pronouns with more than one possible antecedent or no clear antecedent at all)
  - *Possessive determiners:* Distinguishing between and among possessive determiners ("its," "your," "their"), contractions ("it's," "you're," "they're"), and adverbs ("there")
  - *Agreement:* Ensuring agreement between subject and verb, between pronoun and antecedent, and between nouns
  - *Frequently confused words:* Distinguishing between and among words that are commonly mistaken for one another (e.g., "affect" and "effect")
  - *Logical comparison:* Recognizing and correcting cases in which unlike terms are compared
  - *Conventional expression:* Recognizing and correcting cases in which, for no good rhetorical reason, language fails to follow conventional practice
- **Conventions of Punctuation:** Observing standard punctuation practices, including
  - *End-of-sentence punctuation:* Using the correct form of ending punctuation (period, question mark, or exclamation point) when the context makes the writer's intent clear
  - *Within-sentence punctuation:* Correctly using and recognizing and correcting misuses of colons, semicolons, and dashes
  - *Possessive nouns and pronouns:* Recognizing and correcting inappropriate uses of possessive nouns and pronouns and deciding between plural and possessive forms
  - *Items in a series:* Using commas and sometimes semicolons to separate elements in lists
  - *Nonrestrictive and parenthetical elements:* Using punctuation to set off nonessential sentence elements and recognizing and correcting cases in which punctuation is wrongly used to set off essential sentence elements
  - *Unnecessary punctuation:* Recognizing and eliminating unneeded punctuation

PRACTICE AT

satpractice.org

As you can see, there are a lot of English language conventions that may be tested on the SAT. Get comfortable with them, especially those that you know you tend to struggle with. Check out satpractice .org for help.

Three general observations are in order before we discuss the three subcategories in some detail. First, while many Expression of Ideas questions specify what to consider as you answer them, many Standard English Conventions questions don't. You'll most often be presented with an underlined portion of the passage and four choices, generally consisting of a "NO CHANGE" option and three alternatives. Choose "NO CHANGE" if you find no conventions problem; otherwise, choose the alternative that follows the conventions of standard written English. Each question tests one concept or at most two closely related concepts.

PRACTICE AT
satpractice.org

For more practice with the standard English conventions tested on the SAT, visit Khan Academy at satpractice.org.

Second, the main purpose of this chapter is to familiarize you with what's tested in the Standard English Conventions questions on the Writing and Language Test. While you may learn a thing or two about those conventions from reading this chapter, it's beyond the chapter's scope to teach the knowledge and skills you'll need to do well on the test. If a particular concept touched on in this chapter is unclear, take a look at the sample questions in Chapter 13 — each question identifies what's being tested — or consult other sources, such as your teachers, textbooks, or high-quality print and digital reference materials. As always, Khan Academy provides an outstanding resource for SAT readiness at satpractice.org.

Finally, while you may be used to thinking of language conventions as absolute rules, in reality, linguists, educators, writers, and authors of style manuals debate quite a few of these issues. For example, while many books and experts advise using a comma before a coordinating conjunction in a list of three or more items (*x*, *y*, and *z*), others suggest that it's often not necessary (*x*, *y* and *z*). Although the Writing and Language Test includes questions about items in a series, we don't directly test this particular comma usage. In general terms, the test stays away from assessing what's sometimes called "contested usage" — those issues that experts disagree about. There's no definitive list of what we don't test — indeed, that list changes over time as some issues get settled and new ones crop up — but if good reference books disagree on a particular point, it's likely that we don't test the matter directly.

In the following sections, we'll describe the general features of each of the three conventions subcategories and touch on the specific knowledge and skills addressed in each. To keep things manageable, we won't go into detail on each possible testable issue.

Sentence Structure

In Chapter 11, we introduced the concept of syntax, defining it as the arrangement of words into phrases, clauses, and sentences. Sentence Structure questions in the Standard English Conventions category address syntax from a conventions perspective. You'll have to recognize and correct problems in how sentences are formed as well as identify and fix cases in which constructions shift inappropriately within or between sentences. For discussion purposes, let's divide this subcategory into two basic groupings: sentence formation and inappropriate shifts in construction.

Sentence Formation

Questions about sentence formation try to determine whether you can recognize and correct fundamental (but not always simple) problems with how sentences are constructed. Some of these questions may ask you to identify and fix rhetorically ineffective sentence fragments (incomplete sentences), run-ons (independent clauses fused together without punctuation or conjunction), and comma splices (independent clauses joined by only a comma).

PRACTICE AT
satpractice.org

Items in a series should be in similar form. For instance, the sentence "She likes running, swimming, and hiking" exhibits basic but sound parallelism.

Other questions will ask you to identify and fix problems in how the various phrases and clauses within a sentence are related. Sometimes the problem will be with the coordination or subordination of clauses, as when a coordinating conjunction such as "and" or "but" is used when the logic of the sentence calls for a subordinating conjunction such as "although" or "because." In other cases, the problem will be a lack of parallel structure — a failure to treat grammatically similar structures in a series in the same way. The sentence "She likes running, swimming, and to go on hikes," for example, exhibits flawed parallelism because the pattern of gerunds ("running," "swimming") is broken by an infinitive phrase ("to go on hikes"). In yet other instances, a sentence will include a dangling or misplaced modifier — a word, phrase, or clause that doesn't modify what it's supposed to. For example, the sentence "Even after paying for costly repairs, the car still broke down" has a dangling modifier because presumably a person, not the car, paid for the repairs.

Inappropriate Shifts in Construction

Sometimes sentence structure problems emerge because of a failure to be consistent either within or between sentences. If a writer has been using past tense and for no clear reason suddenly switches to using present tense, an inappropriate shift in construction has occurred. On the Writing and Language Test, such problematic shifts can happen with either verbs or pronouns. A question about verb shifts may ask you to edit an inappropriate shift from, say, past to present tense, indicative to conditional mood, or active to passive voice. A question about pronoun shifts may ask you to recognize and correct an inappropriate shift from, for example, a second person to a third person pronoun (such as from "you" to "one") or from a singular to a plural pronoun. Of course, not all shifts are inappropriate; some are, in fact, quite necessary. If a writer has been describing his or her current feelings and then flashes back to the events that led to those feelings,

PRACTICE AT
satpractice.org

The Writing and Language Test may include questions on consistency in verb tense, mood, and voice as well as in pronoun person and number.

a shift from present to past tense is perfectly warranted. It's when these shifts happen inappropriately or for no clear reason that they become fodder for questions on the Writing and Language Test.

Conventions of Usage

"Usage" is a technical term used to describe a range of language practices that are widely accepted and understood by people speaking and writing the same language within a particular culture or community. Particular "rules" for speaking and writing solidify over time (often over many generations) and become the standard by which formal speech and writing are judged. Often these "rules" develop without conscious thought. You'd be hard-pressed to find a rational reason for why native speakers of English would recognize the phrase "A big red balloon" as standard but "A red big balloon" as nonstandard, but nearly all would immediately notice the difference (and probably consider the second an error). It's a little circular, but usage conventions are, ultimately, conventions regarding how particular groups of people customarily use language.

On the Writing and Language Test, the subcategory Conventions of Usage calls on knowledge and skills associated with common practices in formal, well-edited English writing. We'll treat each testing point briefly now.

Pronoun Clarity

In well-written and well-edited writing, all pronouns have a clear and appropriate antecedent, or noun to which they refer. Because writers generally know their subjects better than their audiences do, however, sometimes vague or ambiguous pronouns creep in. These are pronouns that have no clear and appropriate antecedent or that have potentially more than one antecedent. To cite one example: In the sentence "Michael gave Steven his book," the pronoun "his" is ambiguous. Does the writer mean that Michael gave Steven one of Michael's own books or that Michael returned Steven's own book to him? It's not possible to know from the sentence alone. Even if the surrounding text made the intended antecedent clear, it's still not good practice to leave vague or ambiguous pronouns in a text. The Writing and Language Test will sometimes present you with such problematic pronouns and ask you to correct the situation (in many cases by replacing a vague or ambiguous pronoun with a noun).

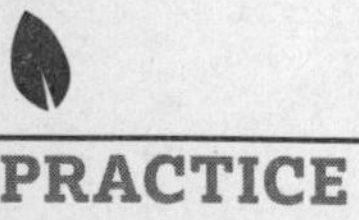

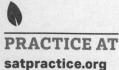

PRACTICE AT
satpractice.org

If you have trouble using homophones such as "its" and "it's" or "their" and "they're" correctly, pay close attention to these words in your everyday writing in school. Becoming more familiar with the proper use of these words will be good practice for the Writing and Language Test (and will serve you well throughout your life).

Possessive Determiners

The bane of many writers' and editors' existence is observing the differences between "its" and "it's"; "your" and "you're"; and "their," "they're," and "there." That so many people have trouble keeping these words straight is probably due to a number of factors. "Its" and "it's," for instance, sound the same and have similar spellings; that "its" lacks the apostrophe generally used to signal possession is no help either. Still, these words do have different functions, many people will recognize when they're confused with one another, and questions about them are likely to appear on the Writing and Language Test. It's worth the time and effort, therefore, to learn how to use these words in a conventional way if you struggle with them.

Agreement

The Writing and Language Test includes questions that cover a range of agreement issues. A question may ask you to recognize and correct problems in agreement between subject and verb, between pronoun and antecedent, and between nouns. You most likely already understand the conventions for subject-verb and pronoun-antecedent agreement, but the concept of noun agreement may be less familiar. In essence, for related nouns to agree they must have the same number — singular noun with singular noun, and plural noun with plural noun. The sentence "Alfredo and Julia became a doctor after many years of study" contains a problem with noun agreement because the compound subject "Alfredo and Julia" is plural but "doctor" is singular. A better version of the sentence would be "Alfredo and Julia became doctors after many years of study."

PRACTICE AT

satpractice.org

There are many words that sound and are spelled similarly but that have different meanings and uses. Practice identifying the correct uses of these words. Examples include:

affect / effect
accept / except
than / then

Frequently Confused Words

The Writing and Language Test may include questions asking you to distinguish between and among frequently confused words — words that have similar or identical sounds and/or similar spellings but that have different meanings and are used in different ways. The "its"/"it's" distinction we discussed earlier is really just a special (and particularly troublesome) case of the more general problem of frequently confused words. "Affect" and "effect" is a commonly cited pair of such words because the two words are relatively common and have similar sounds and spellings. In most cases, "affect" should be used as a verb and "effect" as a noun. (We said "most cases" because psychologists sometimes use "affect" as a noun to refer to emotion and because "effect" is — infrequently — used as a verb, as in "to effect a change.") If you feel that you often get words such as these mixed up, consider consulting one of the many lists of frequently confused words available in language handbooks and on the Internet.

PRACTICE AT

satpractice.org

When a sentence compares two or more things, check to make sure that the items being compared are parallel in nature.

Logical Comparison

Problems with illogical comparisons arise when unlike or dissimilar things are treated as equivalent. For example, the sentence "The cost of living in the city differs from the suburb" contains an illogical comparison because instead of comparing the cost of living in the city and in the suburb — two similar concepts — the sentence actually compares a concept (cost of living) with a location (suburb). One easy way to correct the error is to add the phrase "that in," as in "The cost of living in the city differs from that in the suburb." Another approach is to make "suburb" possessive: "The cost of living in the city differs from the suburb's [cost of living]." Questions on the Writing and Language Test may require you to identify and fix such comparison problems.

Conventional Expression

Conventional Expression questions don't fit neatly into one of the usage types listed earlier, but like them they focus on recognizing and correcting instances in which word choice doesn't conform to the practices of standard written English.

PRACTICE AT
satpractice.org

Conventions of Punctuation questions ask you to correct problematic punctuation or to add punctuation to clarify meaning.

Conventions of Punctuation

A number of questions on the Writing and Language Test concern the use and misuse of various forms of punctuation, including end punctuation (periods, question marks, and exclamation points), commas, semicolons, colons, and dashes, to signal various relationships within and between sentences. In many cases, you'll be expected to recognize and correct problematic punctuation; in some cases, you'll be asked to add punctuation to clarify meaning. There are a number of particular types of Conventions of Punctuation questions, which we'll touch on briefly in the sections that follow.

End-of-Sentence Punctuation

End punctuation — periods, question marks, and exclamation points — is, of course, used to mark the conclusion of sentences and to offer some clue as to their nature (a question mark signaling a question, and the like). By now, you've doubtless mastered the use of such punctuation in most situations, so questions on the Writing and Language Test are limited to challenging cases. One such case is the indirect question — a question that's embedded in a declarative sentence and that takes a period instead of a question mark. "He asked whether I could come along" is an example of an indirect question. While it could easily be rewritten as a typical question, in its present form the question is phrased as a statement and should be concluded with a period.

Within-Sentence Punctuation

On the Writing and Language Test, questions about the appropriate use of colons, semicolons, and dashes to signal sharp breaks in thought come under the heading of Within-Sentence Punctuation. You may be asked to recognize when one of these forms of punctuation is misused and to correct the situation, or you may be expected to use one of these forms properly to establish a particular relationship among words and ideas. The best answer to a particular question of this latter sort may involve using a semicolon to connect two closely related independent clauses or a colon to introduce a list or an idea that builds on one previously introduced in the sentence.

Possessive Nouns and Pronouns

In Writing and Language Test questions about possessive nouns and pronouns, you may be asked to recognize and correct cases in which the incorrect form of a possessive noun or pronoun is used, such as when a singular possessive is used when the context calls for a plural possessive. You may also have to edit instances in which a possessive form is incorrectly used in place of a plural form and vice versa.

Items in a Series

Series that contain more than two elements typically require some form of punctuation to separate the elements. In most cases, commas are used as separators, but in more complex situations (particularly when one or more of the elements has its own commas), semicolons may be used instead. On the Writing and Language Test, you may find questions asking you to add or remove commas (or semicolons) to eliminate ambiguity and to reflect conventional practice. In all cases, the passage context will make clear how many items there are in the series. (As noted earlier, the Writing and Language Test doesn't directly test whether a comma should be placed immediately before the coordinating conjunction in a series of three or more elements.)

Nonrestrictive and Parenthetical Elements

Some questions on the Writing and Language Test may ask you to recognize whether a given part of a sentence is essential or nonessential to the meaning of the sentence and to make punctuation decisions accordingly. Essential (restrictive) sentence elements are critical to the sentence's meaning and aren't set off with punctuation, whereas nonessential (nonrestrictive, parenthetical) sentence elements are set off from the rest of the sentence with commas, dashes, or parentheses. On the Writing and Language Test, you may have to remove punctuation from essential elements, add punctuation to nonessential elements, or correct instances in which nonessential elements are set off with mismatched punctuation (a comma and a dash, for example).

Unnecessary Punctuation

While just the right amount of punctuation can improve the clarity and effectiveness of writing, too much punctuation can slow the reader down and introduce confusion. Some questions on the Writing and Language Test will assess whether you can recognize and remove such extraneous punctuation. Sometimes this stray punctuation will clearly disrupt the meaning and flow of a sentence, as when a comma appears between an adjective and the noun it modifies, but other instances will be trickier to identify because they occur where there seem to be natural "pauses" in sentences, such as between a subject and a predicate. It's true that writers have some freedom in how much punctuation to use and where, so the Writing and Language Test will only test unnecessary punctuation when it clearly falls beyond what is considered typical in well-edited writing.

Chapter 12 Recap

The Standard English Conventions questions on the SAT Writing and Language Test deal with a wide range of sentence structure, usage, and punctuation issues. To answer them correctly, you'll have to apply your knowledge of language conventions and your editing skills to a variety of multiparagraph passages. While the questions on the test deal with matters of standard practice, they focus on more than just correcting surface errors and following "rules" for rules' sake. Instead, Standard English Conventions questions address issues of substance that affect the meaning and communicative power and persuasiveness of text, and answering them correctly goes a long way toward demonstrating that you're ready for the kinds of writing tasks that you'll be expected to undertake in your postsecondary courses of study.

CHAPTER 13

Sample Writing and Language Test Questions

This chapter presents two Writing and Language Test sample passages and associated test questions. Following each question is an explanation of the best answer and some comments about the incorrect answer choices.

These instructions will precede the SAT Writing and Language Test.

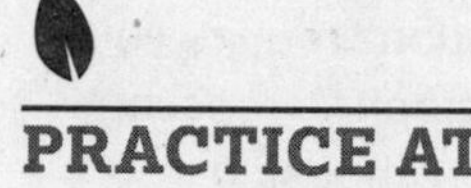

PRACTICE AT
satpractice.org

Carefully read the test directions now so that you won't have to spend much time on them on test day.

Writing and Language Test

35 MINUTES, 44 QUESTIONS

Turn to Section 2 of your answer sheet to answer the questions in this section.

DIRECTIONS

Each passage below is accompanied by a number of questions. For some questions, you will consider how the passage might be revised to improve the expression of ideas. For other questions, you will consider how the passage might be edited to correct errors in sentence structure, usage, or punctuation. A passage or a question may be accompanied by one or more graphics (such as a table or graph) that you will consider as you make revising and editing decisions.

Some questions will direct you to an underlined portion of a passage. Other questions will direct you to a location in a passage or ask you to think about the passage as a whole.

After reading each passage, choose the answer to each question that most effectively improves the quality of writing in the passage or that makes the passage conform to the conventions of standard written English. Many questions include a "NO CHANGE" option. Choose that option if you think the best choice is to leave the relevant portion of the passage as it is.

Sample 1:

Careers Passage with Graphic

REMEMBER

Note how the words, phrases, and sentences tested on the Writing and Language Test are embedded within a fairly lengthy passage (400–450 words). This is because many of the questions require you to consider paragraph- or passage-level context when choosing your answer.

PRACTICE AT
satpractice.org

Read the passage as a whole carefully, identifying things such as the writer's purpose, the organization of the passage, and the writer's style and tone, much as you would on the Reading Test.

Questions 1-11 are based on the following passage and supplementary material.

A Life in Traffic

A subway system is expanded to provide service to a growing suburb. A bike-sharing program is adopted to encourage nonmotorized transportation. [1] To alleviate rush hour traffic jams in a congested downtown area, stoplight timing is coordinated. When any one of these changes [2] occur, it is likely the result of careful analysis conducted by transportation planners.

The work of transportation planners generally includes evaluating current transportation needs, assessing the effectiveness of existing facilities, and improving those facilities or [3] they design new ones. Most transportation planners work in or near cities, [4] but some are employed in rural areas. Say, for example, a large factory is built on the outskirts of a small town. Traffic to and from that location would increase at the beginning and end of work shifts. The transportation [5] planner's job, might involve conducting a traffic count to determine the daily number of vehicles traveling on the road to the new factory. If analysis of the traffic count indicates that there is more traffic than the [6] current road as it is designed at this time can efficiently accommodate, the transportation planner might recommend widening the road to add another lane.

Transportation planners work closely with a number of community stakeholders, such as government officials and other interested organizations and individuals. [7] Next, representatives from the local public health department might provide input in designing a network of trails and sidewalks to encourage people to walk more. [8] According to the American Heart Association, walking provides numerous benefits related to health and well-being. Members of the Chamber of Commerce might share suggestions about designing transportation and parking facilities to support local businesses.

9 People who pursue careers in transportation planning have a wide variety of educational backgrounds. A two-year degree in transportation technology may be sufficient for some entry-level jobs in the field. Most jobs, however, require at least a bachelor's degree; majors of transportation planners are **10** varied, including fields such as urban studies, civil engineering, geography, or transportation and logistics. For many positions in the field, a master's degree is required.

Transportation planners perform critical work within the broader field of urban and regional planning. As of 2010, there were approximately 40,300 urban and regional planners employed in the United States. The United States Bureau of Labor Statistics forecasts steady job growth in this field, **11** projecting that 16 percent of new jobs in all occupations will be related to urban and regional planning. Population growth and concerns about environmental sustainability are expected to spur the need for transportation planning professionals.

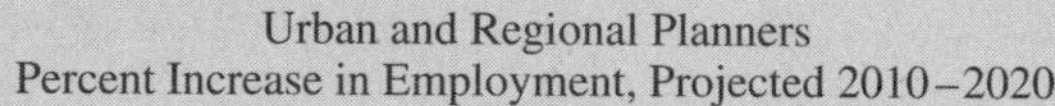
Urban and Regional Planners
Percent Increase in Employment, Projected 2010–2020

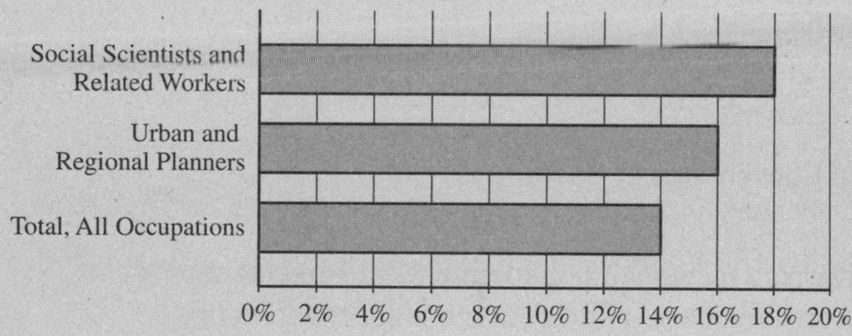

Adapted from United States Bureau of Labor Statistics, Employment Projections program. "All occupations" includes all occupations in the United States economy.

1

Which choice best maintains the sentence pattern already established in the paragraph?

A) NO CHANGE

B) Coordinating stoplight timing can help alleviate rush hour traffic jams in a congested downtown area.

C) Stoplight timing is coordinated to alleviate rush hour traffic jams in a congested downtown area.

D) In a congested downtown area, stoplight timing is coordinated to alleviate rush hour traffic jams.

PRACTICE AT
satpractice.org

To answer this question correctly, you'll want to read the two preceding sentences, determine the pattern that's been established, and choose the answer that's most consistent with that pattern.

Content: Language Use

Key: C

Objective: You must revise text to ensure consistency of style within a series of sentences.

Explanation: Choice C is the best answer because it most closely maintains the sentence pattern established by the two preceding sentences, which begin with noun and passive verb phrases ("A subway system is expanded," "A bike-sharing program is adopted").

Choice A is not the best answer because it does not maintain the sentence pattern established by the two preceding sentences. Rather, it begins the sentence with an infinitive phrase.

Choice B is not the best answer because it does not maintain the sentence pattern established by the two preceding sentences. Rather, it begins the sentence with a gerund phrase.

Choice D is not the best answer because it does not maintain the sentence pattern established by the two preceding sentences. Rather, it places a prepositional phrase, "in a congested downtown area," at the beginning of the sentence.

REMEMBER

When a question has no additional directions, such as Question 2, assume that you're to choose the option that's the most effective or correct.

PRACTICE AT

satpractice.org

This question tests your understanding of both subject-verb agreement and pronoun-antecedent agreement. The key to this question is correctly identifying the subject of the sentence; is it "any one" or "changes"?

2

A) NO CHANGE
B) occur, they are
C) occurs, they are
D) occurs, it is

Content: Conventions of Usage

Key: D

Objective: You must maintain grammatical agreement between pronoun and antecedent and between subject and verb.

Explanation: Choice D is the best answer because it maintains agreement between the pronoun ("it") and the antecedent ("any one") and between the subject ("any one") and the verb ("occurs").

Choice A is not the best answer because the plural verb "occur" does not agree with the singular subject "any one."

Choice B is not the best answer because the plural verb "occur" does not agree with the singular subject "any one" and because the plural pronoun "they" does not agree with the singular antecedent "any one."

Choice C is not the best answer because the plural pronoun "they" does not agree with the singular antecedent "any one."

3

A) NO CHANGE
B) to design
C) designing
D) design

Content: Sentence Structure

Key: C

Objective: You must maintain parallel structure.

Explanation: Choice C is the best answer because "designing" maintains parallelism with "evaluating," "assessing," and "improving."

Choice A is not the best answer because "they design" does not maintain parallelism with "evaluating," "assessing," and "improving."

Choice B is not the best answer because "to design" does not maintain parallelism with "evaluating," "assessing," and "improving."

Choice D is not the best answer because "design" does not maintain parallelism with "evaluating," "assessing," and "improving."

4

Which choice results in the most effective transition to the information that follows in the paragraph?

A) NO CHANGE
B) where job opportunities are more plentiful.
C) and the majority are employed by government agencies.
D) DELETE the underlined portion and end the sentence with a period.

Content: Organization

Key: A

Objective: You must determine the most effective transition between ideas.

Explanation: Choice A is the best answer because it effectively signals the shift in the paragraph to the example of the work a transportation planner might perform if he or she were employed in a rural area and asked to consider the effects of a new factory built "on the outskirts of a small town."

Choice B is not the best answer because noting that job opportunities are more plentiful in cities does not effectively signal the shift in the paragraph to the example of the work a transportation planner might perform if he or she were employed in a rural area.

Choice C is not the best answer because noting that most transportation planners work for government agencies does not effectively signal the shift in the paragraph to the example of the work a transportation planner might perform if he or she were employed in a rural area.

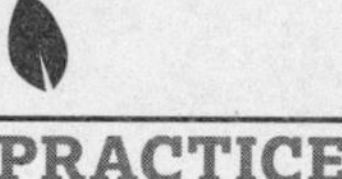

PRACTICE AT

satpractice.org

Don't assume that the best answer will always involve a change to the text in the passage. Sometimes the passage text as originally presented is the best option, in which case you'll choose choice A, "NO CHANGE."

Choice D is not the best answer because the proposed deletion would create a jarring shift from the statement "Most transportation planners work in or near cities" to the example of the work a transportation planner might perform if he or she were employed in a rural area.

PRACTICE AT

satpractice.org

As on Question 2, this question tests two topics — here, possessive nouns and unnecessary punctuation. Be sure the answer you choose is the best option overall. Some answer choices may correct one problem but not the other or may correct one problem but introduce an alternate error.

5

A) NO CHANGE
B) planner's job
C) planners job,
D) planners job

Content: Conventions of Punctuation

Key: B

Objective: You must recognize and correct inappropriate uses of possessive nouns and pronouns as well as differentiate between possessive and plural forms. You must also recognize and correct cases in which unnecessary punctuation appears in a sentence.

Explanation: Choice B is the best answer because it correctly uses an apostrophe to indicate possession and does not introduce any unnecessary punctuation.

Choice A is not the best answer because while it correctly indicates the possessive relationship between "transportation planner" and "job," it introduces an unnecessary comma after the word "job."

Choice C is not the best answer because it does not indicate the possessive relationship between "transportation planner" and "job," and because it introduces an unnecessary comma after the word "job."

Choice D is not the best answer because it does not indicate the possessive relationship between "transportation planner" and "job."

REMEMBER

Economy of expression, or conveying meaning as concisely as possible, may be tested on some questions.

6

A) NO CHANGE
B) current design of the road right now
C) road as it is now currently designed
D) current design of the road

Content: Effective Language Use

Key: D

Objective: You must improve the economy of expression.

Explanation: Choice D is the best answer because it offers a clear and concise wording without redundancy or wordiness.

Choice A is not the best answer because "current" is redundant with "at this time" and because "as it is designed" is unnecessarily wordy.

Choice B is not the best answer because “current” is redundant with “right now.”

Choice C is not the best answer because “now” is redundant with “currently.”

PRACTICE AT
satpractice.org

If a question asks you to choose the most appropriate transitional word or phrase at the beginning of a sentence, carefully consider how that sentence relates to the previous sentence. Does it function as a contradiction, an example, a comparison?

7

A) NO CHANGE
B) For instance,
C) Furthermore,
D) Similarly,

Content: Organization

Key: B

Objective: You must determine the most logical transitional word or phrase.

Explanation: Choice B is the best answer because the transitional phrase “For instance” logically indicates that what follows provides an example related to the previous sentence. “Representatives from the local public health department” is an example of the kinds of people with whom transportation planners work.

Choice A is not the best answer because the transitional word “Next” indicates sequence, which is not logical given that what follows provides an example related to the previous sentence.

Choice C is not the best answer because the transitional word “Furthermore” indicates addition, which is not logical given that what follows provides an example related to the previous sentence.

Choice D is not the best answer because the transitional word “Similarly” indicates comparison or likeness, which is not logical given that what follows provides an example related to the previous sentence.

8

The writer is considering deleting the underlined sentence. Should the sentence be kept or deleted?

A) Kept, because it provides supporting evidence about the benefits of walking.
B) Kept, because it provides an additional example of a community stakeholder with whom transportation planners work.
C) Deleted, because it blurs the paragraph’s focus on the community stakeholders with whom transportation planners work.
D) Deleted, because it doesn’t provide specific examples of what the numerous benefits of walking are.

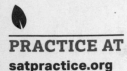

Content: Development

Key: C

Objective: You must delete information that blurs the focus of the paragraph and weakens cohesion.

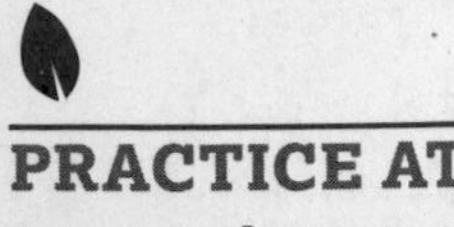

PRACTICE AT
satpractice.org

Information should be kept only if it's clearly relevant and effectively connected to the writer's purpose.

Explanation: Choice C is the best answer because it identifies the best reason the underlined sentence should not be kept. At this point in the passage and paragraph, a general statement about the benefits of walking only serves to interrupt the discussion of the community stakeholders with whom transportation planners work.

Choice A is not the best answer because the underlined sentence should not be kept. Although the sentence theoretically provides supporting evidence about the benefits of walking, the passage has not made a claim that needs to be supported in this way, and including such a statement only serves to interrupt the discussion of the community stakeholders with whom transportation planners work.

Choice B is not the best answer because the underlined sentence should not be kept. Although the American Heart Association could theoretically be an example of "other interested organizations" with which transportation planners work, the sentence does not suggest that this is the case. Instead, the association is merely the source for the general statement about the benefits of walking, a statement that only serves to interrupt the discussion of the actual community stakeholders with whom transportation planners work.

Choice D is not the best answer because although the underlined sentence should be deleted, it is not because the sentence lacks specific examples of the numerous benefits of walking. Adding such examples would only serve to blur the focus of the paragraph further with general factual information, as the paragraph's main purpose is to discuss the community stakeholders with whom transportation planners work.

9

A) NO CHANGE
B) People, who pursue careers in transportation planning,
C) People who pursue careers, in transportation planning,
D) People who pursue careers in transportation planning,

Content: Conventions of Punctuation

Key: A

Objective: You must distinguish between restrictive/essential and nonrestrictive/nonessential sentence elements and avoid unneeded punctuation.

Explanation: Choice A is the best answer because "who pursue careers in transportation planning" is, in context, a restrictive clause that should not be set off with punctuation. "Who pursue careers in transportation planning" is essential information defining who the "people" are.

Choice B is not the best answer because it incorrectly sets off the restrictive clause "who pursue careers in transportation planning" with commas as though the clause were nonrestrictive or not essential to defining who the "people" are.

Choice C is not the best answer because it incorrectly sets off the essential sentence element "in transportation planning" with commas as though the phrase were not essential to the meaning of the sentence. "In transportation planning" is essential information defining what the "careers" are.

Choice D is not the best answer because it introduces an unnecessary comma after the word "planning," incorrectly setting off the subject of the sentence ("people who pursue careers in transportation planning") from the predicate ("have a wide variety of educational backgrounds").

PRACTICE AT
satpractice.org

When examining the underlined portion of the passage being tested, it may be helpful to think about how (if at all) the underlined portion can be improved *before* you look at the answer choices. Doing so may help you more quickly and accurately choose your answer.

10

A) NO CHANGE
B) varied, and including
C) varied and which include
D) varied, which include

Content: Sentence Structure

Key: A

Objective: You must recognize and correct problems in coordination and subordination in sentences.

Explanation: Choice A is the best answer because it effectively uses a comma and "including" to set off the list of varied fields in which transportation planners major.

Choice B is not the best answer because "and including" results in an ungrammatical sentence.

Choice C is not the best answer because "and which include" results in an ungrammatical sentence.

Choice D is not the best answer because it is unclear from this construction to what exactly the relative pronoun "which" refers.

PRACTICE AT
satpractice.org

In Question 11, you must integrate information from the text with data presented in the graph. Make sure that the data cited is both accurate and aligns with the content of the sentence.

11

Which choice completes the sentence with accurate data based on the graph?

A) NO CHANGE
B) warning, however, that job growth in urban and regional planning will slow to 14 percent by 2020.
C) predicting that employment of urban and regional planners will increase 16 percent between 2010 and 2020.
D) indicating that 14 to 18 percent of urban and regional planning positions will remain unfilled.

Content: Development

Key: C

Objective: You must evaluate text based on data presented graphically.

Explanation: Choice C is the best answer because it completes the sentence with an accurate interpretation of data in the graph. The graph displays projections of how much growth in employment there is expected to be between 2010 and 2020 for "social scientists and related workers," for "urban and regional planners," and in "all occupations" in the U.S. economy. According to the graph, the employment of urban and regional planners is expected to increase 16 percent between 2010 and 2020.

Choice A is not the best answer because the data in the graph do not support the claim that 16 percent of new jobs in all occupations will be related to urban and regional planning.

Choice B is not the best answer because the data in the graph do not support the claim that job growth in urban and regional planning will slow to 14 percent by 2020.

Choice D is not the best answer because the data in the graph do not support the claim that 14 to 18 percent of urban and regional planning positions will remain unfilled.

Sample 2:

Humanities Passage

Questions 12-22 are based on the following passage.

Dong Kingman: Painter of Cities

A 1954 documentary about renowned watercolor painter Dong Kingman shows the artist sitting on a stool on Mott Street in New York City's Chinatown. A crowd of admiring spectators **12** watched as Kingman squeezes dollops of paint from several tubes into a tin watercolor **13** box, from just a few primary colors, Kingman creates dozens of beautiful hues as he layers the translucent paint onto the paper on his easel. Each stroke of the brush and dab of the sponge transforms thinly sketched outlines into buildings, shop signs, and streetlamps. The street scene Kingman begins composing in this short film is very much in keeping with the urban landscapes for which he is best known.

[1] Kingman was keenly interested in landscape painting from an early age. [2] In Hong Kong, where Kingman completed his schooling,

teachers at that time customarily assigned students a formal "school name." [3] His interest was so keen, in fact, that he was named after it. [4] The young boy who had been Dong Moy Shu became Dong Kingman. [5] The name Kingman was selected for its two **14** parts, "king" and "man"; Cantonese for "scenery" and "composition." [6] As Kingman developed as a painter, his works were often compared to **15** paintings by Chinese landscape artists dating back to CE 960, a time when a strong tradition of landscape painting emerged in Chinese art. [7] Kingman, however, **16** vacated from that tradition in a number of ways, most notably in that he chose to focus not on natural landscapes, such as mountains and rivers, but on cities. **17**

18 His fine brushwork conveys detailed street-level activity: a peanut vendor pushing his cart on the sidewalk, a pigeon pecking for crumbs around a fire **19** hydrant, an old man tending to a baby outside a doorway. His broader brush strokes and sponge-painted shapes create majestic city skylines, with skyscrapers towering in the background, bridges connecting neighborhoods on either side of a river, and **20** delicately painted creatures, such as a tiny, barely visible cat prowling in the bushes of a park. To art critics and fans alike, these city scenes represent the innovative spirit of twentieth-century urban Modernism.

During his career, Kingman exhibited his work **21** internationally. He garnered much acclaim. In 1936, a critic described one of Kingman's solo exhibits as "twenty of the freshest, most satisfying watercolors that have been seen hereabouts in many a day." **22**

12

A) NO CHANGE
B) had watched
C) would watch
D) watches

Content: Sentence Structure

Key: D

Objective: You must recognize and correct inappropriate shifts in verb tense and mood.

PRACTICE AT
satpractice.org

When a question asks you to choose the tense and mood of a verb, look for consistency with the surrounding text to help determine your answer. Note that while no shift is warranted here, sometimes shifts are necessary.

Explanation: Choice D is the best answer because the simple present tense verb "watches" is consistent with the tense of the verbs in the rest of the sentence and paragraph.

Choice A is not the best answer because "watched" creates an inappropriate shift to the past tense.

Choice B is not the best answer because "had watched" creates an inappropriate shift to the past perfect tense.

Choice C is not the best answer because "would watch" creates an inappropriate shift that suggests a habitual or hypothetical aspect when other verbs in the sentence and paragraph indicate that a specific, actual instance is being narrated.

13

A) NO CHANGE
B) box. From just a few primary colors,
C) box from just a few primary colors,
D) box, from just a few primary colors

Content: Sentence Structure

Key: B

Objective: You must create two grammatically complete and standard sentences.

Explanation: Choice B is the best answer because it provides punctuation that creates two grammatically complete and standard sentences.

Choice A is not the best answer because it results in a comma splice as well as some confusion about what the prepositional phrase "from just a few primary colors" modifies.

Choice C is not the best answer because it results in a run-on sentence as well as some confusion about what the prepositional phrase "from just a few primary colors" modifies.

Choice D is not the best answer because it results in a comma splice.

PRACTICE AT
satpractice.org

A colon is used to signal a break in a sentence; what follows the colon further defines the concept that precedes the colon. A semicolon connects two closely related independent clauses.

14

A) NO CHANGE
B) parts: "king" and "man,"
C) parts "king" and "man";
D) parts; "king" and "man"

Content: Conventions of Punctuation

Key: B

Objective: You must both signal a strong within-sentence break and set off nonessential elements of the sentence.

Explanation: Choice B is the best answer because the colon after "parts" effectively signals that what follows in the sentence further defines what the "two parts" of Kingman's name are and because the comma after "man" properly indicates that "'king' and 'man'" and "Cantonese for 'scenery' and 'composition'" are nonrestrictive appositives.

Choice A is not the best answer because the semicolon after "man" incorrectly joins an independent clause and a phrase. Moreover, the comma after "parts" is arguably a weak form of punctuation to be signaling the strong break in the sentence indicated here.

Choice C is not the best answer because the semicolon after "man" incorrectly joins an independent clause and a phrase and because the absence of appropriate punctuation after "parts" fails to indicate that "two parts" and "'king' and 'man'" are nonrestrictive appositives.

Choice D is not the best answer because the semicolon after "parts" incorrectly joins an independent clause and two phrases and because the absence of appropriate punctuation after "man" fails to indicate that "'king' and 'man'" and "Cantonese for 'scenery' and 'composition'" are nonrestrictive appositives.

15

A) NO CHANGE
B) Chinese landscape artists
C) painters of Chinese landscapes
D) artists

Content: Conventions of Usage

Key: A

Objective: You must ensure that like terms are being compared.

Explanation: Choice A is the best answer because it creates a comparison between like terms: "works" by Kingman and "paintings by Chinese landscape artists."

Choice B is not the best answer because it creates a comparison between unlike terms: "works" by Kingman and "Chinese landscape artists."

Choice C is not the best answer because it creates a comparison between unlike terms: "works" by Kingman and "painters of Chinese landscapes."

Choice D is not the best answer because it creates a comparison between unlike terms: "works" by Kingman and "artists."

PRACTICE AT
satpractice.org

Comparisons must be logical; that is, the items compared must be of a parallel nature. What are Kingman's "works" most logically compared to in sentence 6 of the passage?

16

A) NO CHANGE
B) evacuated
C) departed
D) retired

REMEMBER

Question 16 is very similar to a Words in Context question from the SAT Reading Test. You're asked to determine the most appropriate word given the context of the sentence.

Content: Effective Language Use

Key: C

Objective: You must determine the most contextually appropriate word.

Explanation: Choice C is the best answer because "departed" is the most contextually appropriate way to indicate that Kingman had deviated from the tradition of Chinese landscape painting in a number of ways.

Choice A is not the best answer because while "vacated" does offer some sense of "leaving," it would be awkward and unconventional to say that a person was vacating from a tradition in a number of ways.

Choice B is not the best answer because while "evacuated" does offer some sense of "leaving," it would be awkward and unconventional to say that a person was evacuating from a tradition in a number of ways.

Choice D is not the best answer because while "retired" does offer some sense of "leaving," it would be awkward and unconventional to say that a person was retiring from a tradition in a number of ways.

PRACTICE AT
satpractice.org

Consider the overall meaning of the paragraph when deciding the most logical placement of sentence 3. Also, look for words or concepts found in sentence 3 in other sentences in the paragraph, as these may signal a continuation of ideas.

17

To make this paragraph most logical, sentence 3 should be placed

A) where it is now.
B) before sentence 1.
C) after sentence 1.
D) after sentence 4.

Content: Organization

Key: C

Objective: You must improve the cohesion of a paragraph.

Explanation: Choice C is the best answer because placing sentence 3 after sentence 1 makes the paragraph most cohesive. Sentence 3 refers to Kingman's "interest" being "so keen," a continuation of the idea in sentence 1, which says that "Kingman was keenly interested in landscape painting from an early age."

Choice A is not the best answer because leaving sentence 3 where it is now creates a sequence of sentences that lacks sufficient cohesion. Keeping sentence 3 in its current location disrupts the link between sentence 2 (which describes the concept of "school names" in Hong Kong) and sentence 4 (which reveals that Dong Kingman was the school name of Dong Moy Shu).

Choice B is not the best answer because placing sentence 3 before sentence 1 creates a sequence of sentences that lacks sufficient cohesion. Putting sentence 3 at the beginning of the paragraph would offer a poor introduction to the paragraph, in large part because sentence 3 builds directly on a point made in sentence 1.

Choice D is not the best answer because placing sentence 3 after sentence 4 creates a sequence of sentences that lacks sufficient cohesion. Putting sentence 3 after sentence 4 would disrupt the link between sentence 4 (which mentions that Dong Moy Shu was given the school name Dong Kingman) and sentence 5 (which explains what the two parts composing the name Kingman mean in Cantonese).

18

Which choice most effectively establishes the main topic of the paragraph?

A) Kingman is considered a pioneer of the California Style school of painting.

B) Although cities were his main subject, Kingman did occasionally paint natural landscapes.

C) In his urban landscapes, Kingman captures the vibrancy of crowded cities.

D) In 1929 Kingman moved to Oakland, California, where he attended the Fox Art School.

Content: Development

Key: C

Objective: You must determine which sentence best signals the main topic of a paragraph.

Explanation: Choice C is the best answer because it clearly establishes the main topic of the paragraph: Kingman's urban landscapes.

Choice A is not the best answer because it would begin the paragraph with a loosely related detail about Kingman's painting style and would not clearly establish the main topic of the paragraph.

Choice B is not the best answer because it would suggest that the main topic of the paragraph is the natural landscapes Kingman occasionally painted, which is incorrect given the focus of the rest of the sentences in the paragraph.

Choice D is not the best answer because it would begin the paragraph with a loosely related detail about Kingman's life and would not clearly establish the main topic of the paragraph.

19

A) NO CHANGE

B) hydrant—

C) hydrant:

D) hydrant

Content: Conventions of Punctuation

Key: A

Objective: You must effectively separate items in a series.

Explanation: Choice A is the best answer because a comma after the word "hydrant" separates the phrase "a pigeon pecking for crumbs around a fire hydrant" from the phrase "an old man tending to a baby outside a doorway." A comma is also consistent with the punctuation choice made to separate the first two phrases in the asyndetic series following the colon in the sentence.

Choice B is not the best answer because a dash is not a conventional choice for punctuating items in a series.

Choice C is not the best answer because although a colon can be used to introduce a series, it is not a conventional choice for separating items within a series.

Choice D is not the best answer because it fuses together two items in the series. Separating the phrases "a pigeon pecking for crumbs around a fire hydrant" and "an old man tending to a baby outside a doorway" requires punctuation (and could also involve a coordinating conjunction).

PRACTICE AT
satpractice.org

Consider which answer choice best continues the theme of "majestic city skylines" established by the first two examples in the sentence.

20

The writer wants to complete the sentence with a third example of a detail Kingman uses to create his majestic city skylines. Which choice best accomplishes this goal?

A) NO CHANGE
B) exquisitely lettered street and storefront signs.
C) other details that help define Kingman's urban landscapes.
D) enormous ships docking at busy urban ports.

Content: Development

Key: D

Objective: You must revise supporting information to accomplish a writing goal.

Explanation: Choice D is the best answer because the phrase "enormous ships docking at busy urban ports" effectively continues the sentence's series of details ("skyscrapers towering in the background" and "bridges connecting neighborhoods") conveying the majesty of city skylines as depicted by Kingman.

Choice A is not the best answer because the phrase "delicately painted creatures, such as a tiny, barely visible cat prowling in the bushes of a park" does not convey a sense of the majesty of city skylines as depicted by Kingman and thus does not effectively continue the sentence's series of details ("skyscrapers towering in the background" and "bridges connecting neighborhoods").

Choice B is not the best answer because the phrase "exquisitely lettered street and storefront signs" does not convey a sense of the majesty of city skylines as depicted by Kingman and thus does not effectively continue the sentence's series of details ("skyscrapers towering in the background" and "bridges connecting neighborhoods").

Choice C is not the best answer because the phrase “other details that help define Kingman’s urban landscapes” is too vague and general to constitute a third example that conveys a sense of the majesty of city skylines as depicted by Kingman and thus does not effectively continue the sentence’s series of details (“skyscrapers towering in the background” and “bridges connecting neighborhoods”).

PRACTICE AT
satpractice.org

You’ll want to choose the answer that combines the sentences in the most efficient manner possible without altering the original meaning.

21

Which choice most effectively combines the sentences at the underlined portion?

A) internationally, and Kingman also garnered

B) internationally; from exhibiting, he garnered

C) internationally but garnered

D) internationally, garnering

Content: Effective Language Use

Key: D

Objective: You must combine sentences effectively.

Explanation: Choice D is the best answer because it combines the sentences logically and efficiently, with the original second sentence becoming a participial phrase describing Kingman.

Choice A is not the best answer because it creates a wordy and awkward construction and because it fails to link the acclaim Kingman received with the exhibition of his work.

Choice B is not the best answer because it creates a repetitive and awkward construction.

Choice C is not the best answer because “but” suggests contrast or exception, neither of which makes sense in the context of the sentence.

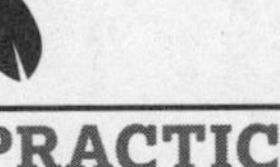

PRACTICE AT
satpractice.org

Always read the question carefully, as it may contain keywords to help you in choosing your answer. The keywords in this question are "an enduring legacy of Kingman’s work."

22

The writer wants to conclude the passage with a sentence that emphasizes an enduring legacy of Kingman’s work. Which choice would best accomplish this goal?

A) Although Kingman’s work might not be as famous as that of some other watercolor painters, such as Georgia O’Keeffe and Edward Hopper, it is well regarded by many people.

B) Since Kingman’s death in 2000, museums across the United States and in China have continued to ensure that his now-iconic landscapes remain available for the public to enjoy.

C) The urban landscapes depicted in Kingman’s body of work are a testament to aptness of the name chosen for Kingman when he was just a boy.

D) Kingman’s work was but one example of a long-lasting tradition refreshed by an innovative artist with a new perspective.

Content: Organization

Key: B

Objective: You must determine the most effective ending of a text given a particular writing goal.

Explanation: Choice B is the best answer because it concludes the passage with a sentence that emphasizes the enduring legacy of Kingman's work by indicating that museums continue to make Kingman's iconic paintings accessible to the public.

Choice A is not the best answer because it concludes the passage with a sentence that acknowledges that the works of other painters are more famous than Kingman's (which downplays, rather than emphasizes, the enduring legacy of Kingman's work) and offers only a general assertion that Kingman's work is "well regarded by many people."

Choice C is not the best answer because instead of referring to the enduring legacy of Kingman's work, it concludes the passage with a sentence that recalls a detail the passage provides about Kingman's early life.

Choice D is not the best answer because it concludes the passage with a sentence that is too vague and general to emphasize effectively an enduring legacy of Kingman's work. It is not clear what the idea of refreshing a long-lasting tradition is intended to mean or how (or even whether) this represents an enduring legacy. Moreover, referring to Kingman's work as "but one example" downplays the significance of any potential legacy that might be suggested.

CHAPTER 14

About the SAT Essay

The SAT Essay is a lot like a typical college writing assignment in which you're asked to analyze a text. To do well on the SAT Essay, you'll want to have a good sense of what the test asks of you as well as the reading, analysis, and writing skills required to compose a response to the Essay prompt. This chapter is intended primarily to get you more familiar with the Essay. After we discuss the test in general, we'll turn to some sample prompts as well as examples of student papers and what scores they would receive.

Important Features of the SAT Essay

The Essay on the SAT is optional, which means that — unless you're required to take the test by your school or some other institution — you need to make an informed, personal choice about whether to take the Essay. You should figure out whether any of the postsecondary institutions that you're applying to require Essay scores; if so, your decision is pretty simple. If that's not the case and you're not otherwise required to take the Essay, you'll have to make up your own mind about it.

REMEMBER

The Essay is optional for students. If your school or the postsecondary institutions you're applying to don't require Essay scores, you'll have to make an informed, personal decision as to whether to take the Essay.

We recommend that you seriously consider taking the Essay. The task the Essay asks you to complete — analyzing how an argument works — is an interesting and engaging one. The Essay also gives you an excellent opportunity to demonstrate your reading, analysis, and writing skills — skills critical to readiness for and success in college and career — and the scores you'll get back will give you insight into your strengths in these areas as well as indications of any skills that may still need work.

Position within the SAT Test

The Essay is administered after the multiple-choice sections of the SAT. This makes it easier to give the test to some students and not to others, since the Essay is not required.

Test Length

The SAT Essay is 50 minutes in length. The passage you'll read and analyze is about the same length as the longest passage you'll see on the SAT Reading Test, and you'll need to spend a fair amount of time reading, selectively rereading, analyzing, and drawing evidence from it in order to do well.

REMEMBER

You'll have 50 minutes to complete the Essay task. While you'll want to pace yourself, this should be enough time for you to produce your best work, especially if you've practiced with some sample passages.

You may find it reassuring to know that the College Board decided to allot 50 minutes for the test only after careful study and review. This process included examining papers from thousands of students who took the Essay as part of our research. From this process, we learned that 50 minutes provided enough time for most students to complete the Essay task without rushing. Although you'll still have to pace yourself and pay attention to the time available, you should have enough time to do your best work on the Essay.

Number of Prompts and Responses

The Essay includes only one prompt, or question. You'll produce a single essay in response to that prompt.

REMEMBER

The Essay *won't* ask you to take a stance on an issue. Rather, your task will be to analyze an argument presented in a passage in order to explain how the author builds the argument to persuade his or her audience.

The Essay Task

The SAT Essay asks you to analyze a provided argument in order to explain how the author builds his or her argument to persuade an audience. The support you provide for your analysis won't come primarily from your own prior knowledge, opinions, or experiences. Instead, you'll be drawing on information and ideas found in the accompanying reading passage and using those to develop your analysis. In other words, you'll be making extensive use of textual evidence to flesh out your response to the question of how the author builds his or her argument in the passage to persuade an audience.

REMEMBER

The Essay task will be the same in every test. What will change is the reading selection you'll be asked to analyze. Familiarizing yourself with the Essay prompt ahead of time, and understanding exactly what your task is, will save you time on test day and will likely result in your writing a stronger essay.

The SAT Essay uses virtually the same prompt in every single test given to students. The reading selection and a sentence describing that selection change each time the test is given, but you'll always know what you're going to be asked to write about. This has huge advantages for you over how most essay tests are administered. You'll be able to focus your preparation on developing important reading, analysis, and writing knowledge and skills instead of on trying to guess what question we'll ask, and on test day you can get right to work instead of spending a lot of valuable time trying to form an opinion on a topic you may not have even thought much about.

We'll come back to that prompt after a brief discussion of how the Essay is evaluated.

Scores

When you take the Essay, you'll receive three scores:

- **Reading:** How well you demonstrated your understanding of the passage

- **Analysis:** How well you analyzed the passage and carried out the task of explaining how the author builds his or her argument to persuade an audience
- **Writing:** How skillfully you crafted your response

Each score will be on a 2–8 scale, the combined result of two raters scoring each dimension independently on a 1–4 scale. These three scores aren't combined with each other or with scores on any other part of the test.

REMEMBER

The three scores you'll receive reflect the three main criteria your Essay will be evaluated on. As you practice for the Essay, focus on each of these three areas and try to assess your performance in each.

By evaluating your performance in three main areas, we're able to better pinpoint your strengths and weaknesses. Perhaps your response shows that you understood the passage very well and were able to produce a clear and cohesive essay but that you struggled some with the analysis task. If we combined that into one score, it might be indistinguishable from the score of a student who did very well in analysis and in demonstrating reading comprehension but less well in putting his or her thoughts into words. By giving you three separate scores, we make it easier for you to know where you did well and where you might have struggled. This, in turn, will help you find ways to improve specific shortcomings.

More details about how the Essay is scored, along with the complete scoring rubric, appear later in this chapter.

The Essay Prompt in Detail

Now let's examine the prompt for the SAT Essay. And we do mean *the* prompt because, as we noted earlier, the prompt is nearly identical on every single administration of the SAT.

REMEMBER

The prompt provided here will be nearly identical to the prompt you'll see on test day. Read it carefully now and make sure you understand what it's asking you to do.

> As you read the passage below, consider how [the author] uses
>
> - evidence, such as facts or examples, to support claims.
> - reasoning to develop ideas and to connect claims and evidence.
> - stylistic or persuasive elements, such as word choice or appeals to emotion, to add power to the ideas expressed.

> Write an essay in which you explain how [the author] builds an argument to persuade [his/her] audience that [author's claim]. In your essay, analyze how [the author] uses one or more of the features listed above (or features of your own choice) to strengthen the logic and persuasiveness of [his/her] argument. Be sure that your analysis focuses on the most relevant features of the passage.
>
> Your essay should not explain whether you agree with [the author's] claims, but rather explain how the author builds an argument to persuade [his/her] audience.

The Passage

Your response to the Essay prompt will be firmly rooted in a reading selection of between 650 and 750 words — about the length of one of the longer passages on the Reading Test. All of your work on the Essay will center on your ability to understand, analyze, and explain your analysis of this passage. While the passage will come from any one of a wide range of high-quality sources and will differ on each administration of the test, all Essay passages take the form of an argument written for a broad audience. By this we mean that the form of the writing will always be argumentative (i.e., the author will always be making a claim, or assertion, and trying to convince an audience to agree with that claim) and that the subject will be generally accessible to a wide readership. You won't see a highly technical argument on a specialized subject that requires background knowledge. All of the relevant information needed to understand the topic will be included in the passage itself.

REMEMBER

The Essay's reading selection will change with each test administration, but it will always take the form of an argument of about 650–750 words in length written for a broad audience. You won't need to bring in any specialized background knowledge; everything you need to write a strong essay will be in the passage.

Building an Argument to Persuade an Audience

By asking you to focus on how the author of the passage "builds an argument to persuade an audience," the Essay prompt is encouraging what may be called rhetorical analysis. In this rhetorical analysis, you're paying attention to how the author uses particular techniques and elements to make his or her writing more convincing, persuasive, and powerful; your discussion should focus on what the author does, why he or she does it, and what effect this is likely to have on readers. You'll definitely want to capture some of the main ideas and key details of the passage in your analysis, but your main task is *not* to summarize that information but rather to assess its contribution to the argument.

REMEMBER

The primary focus of your essay should *not* be on what the author says. Rather, your essay should focus on how the author develops an argument that is persuasive and powerful.

Evidence, Reasoning, and Stylistic and Persuasive Elements

The Essay directions advise you to think about how the author uses evidence, reasoning, and stylistic and persuasive elements to develop his or her argument. These are cornerstones to much argumentative writing, so we should examine briefly what we mean by each of these.

Evidence is information and ideas that the author uses to support a claim. Evidence takes many forms, and the forms vary depending on the kind of argument the author is writing and the nature of the point the author is trying to make. Evidence can come in the form of facts, statistics, quotations from (other) experts, the results of experiments or other research, examples, and the like. The author of any given passage may use some of these or rely on other kinds of sources entirely. It'll be up to you to figure out what constitutes evidence in a particular passage and how the author uses it to support his or her claims.

REMEMBER

Evidence, reasoning, and stylistic and persuasive elements are three main ways authors can develop their arguments. A strong SAT Essay will analyze the author's use of one or more of these components.

Your analysis of an author's use of evidence can take many forms, depending on the particular passage in question. You may end up pointing out that the author relies (perhaps too much) on one kind of evidence or another — or on little or no evidence at all, likely weakening the argument's effectiveness. You may instead or in addition point to specific cases in which the author's choice of evidence was particularly effective in supporting a claim or point. Other approaches are possible as well.

Reasoning is the connective tissue that holds an argument together. It's the "thinking" — the logic, the analysis — that develops the argument and ties the claim and evidence together. Reasoning plays a stronger role in some texts than in others. Some authors are very careful about making their thought processes clear so that readers can follow and critique them. In other cases, texts rely less heavily on logic.

Your analysis of an author's use of reasoning can take a number of different approaches. You may decide to discuss how the author uses (or fails to use) clear, logical reasoning to draw a connection between a claim and the evidence supporting that claim. You may also or instead choose to evaluate the impact that particular aspects of the author's reasoning (e.g., unstated assumptions) have on how convincing the argument is. Other approaches are possible as well.

Stylistic and persuasive elements are rhetorical techniques that an author might bring to bear in order to enhance the power of his or her argument. An author could make use of appeals, such as to the audience's fears or sense of honor, or employ particularly vivid descriptive language to create a mood of anticipation or anxiety, or use one or more of any number of other such devices. There's no definitive list of these techniques, and you don't have to know them all by heart or by name to be able to get good scores on the Essay. The key thing here is to be on the lookout for ways in which the author attempts to influence the audience, sometimes by using something other than a strictly logical, rational approach.

Your analysis of the author's use of stylistic and persuasive elements can follow a number of paths. You may point out instances in which the author uses such devices and evaluate their role or their effectiveness in convincing an audience to action. You may also analyze and evaluate the varying extent to which logic and emotion contribute to the persuasiveness of the text. Other approaches are possible as well.

We've listed some examples of how evidence, reasoning, and stylistic and persuasive elements might be analyzed in a passage, but these are by no means the only ways. For some passages, evidence may be less important than reasoning and/or stylistic and persuasive elements, so it makes sense to devote less attention to evidence in such a case. Indeed, successful responses do *not* need to cover each of these three categories. In fact, it's generally better to focus your essay on a few points that are well made than attempt to check off a long list of rhetorical elements. You can also choose to discuss some aspect of the passage that doesn't fit neatly into one of the three categories but that plays an important part in how the author builds the argument.

PRACTICE AT

satpractice.org

Your analysis does *not* have to focus exclusively on how the author's use of evidence, reasoning, and stylistic and persuasive elements makes the argument stronger or more persuasive. Instead, you may choose to point out ways in which the author's use (or lack of use) of one or more of these elements weakens the effectiveness of the argument.

REMEMBER

Your Essay does *not* have to address the author's use of all three components discussed here (evidence, reasoning, and stylistic and persuasive elements) in order to earn high scores. An essay that provides strong analysis of fewer but well-chosen points will likely score better than an essay that provides little analysis of a long list of points.

The Most Relevant Aspects of the Passage

As the preceding discussion suggests, your analysis should be selective. That is, you should focus your attention on those features of the passage that you feel make the biggest contribution to the persuasive power of the passage. While 50 minutes is a fair amount of time, it's not enough to write about everything that's going on in the passage. Pick and choose what you analyze.

Not Explaining Whether You Agree with the Author's Claims

Remember that when we talked about the concept of "building an argument to persuade an audience," we noted that your main purpose in the Essay is rhetorical. That is, you should focus your analysis on how the author attempts to persuade an audience through such techniques as citing evidence, using reasoning, and employing various stylistic and persuasive techniques. Your main goal is *not* to show why or whether you agree or disagree with the points the author makes.

REMEMBER

While it's tempting to state your opinion on the topic discussed in the Essay passage, remember that this is not your task. Your task is to analyze how the author attempts to persuade an audience through the use of evidence, reasoning, and stylistic and persuasive elements and/or other features you identify.

This can be hard. We all have opinions and the urge to share them. You've also probably done a lot of writing in which you've argued for one position or another. What's more, it can be tough to stay emotionally detached if you read something that you either strongly agree or strongly disagree with. Nevertheless, such detachment is something we all have to demonstrate at times, and it's a skill that postsecondary instructors will expect you to be able to make use of routinely. It's also an important general reading skill. If you make your own judgments too early while reading, you're likely to miss something that the author says and maybe even distort the text's message to fit your own preconceptions. Being able to differentiate your own views from those of others is a critical academic and life skill, and it's something that the SAT Essay will — indirectly — call on you to do.

It's a slightly different case, though, when you feel that the passage on the Essay isn't particularly effective or persuasive. Here, you're on somewhat safer ground, as you're still thinking and analyzing rhetorically — still focusing on the art and craft of writing — only this time on one or more ways that you feel the author is failing to make a strong point. It's okay to fault the author in this sense, but be sure to make clear what you think the author's intent probably was. You could point out, for instance, that the author's description seems too idealized to be truly believable or that the author gives too much attention to anecdotes instead of solid evidence, but you should still devote your main effort to what the author *does* do and what the author *intends* to accomplish (even if he or she sometimes misses the mark).

REMEMBER

Your essay will be scored by two raters, each of whom will assign a score of 1–4 in the categories of Reading, Analysis, and Writing. The two raters' scores for each dimension will be added together. Thus, you'll receive three scores on your essay, each ranging from 2 to 8.

SAT Essay Scoring Rubric

Reproduced in this section is the rubric that two raters will use to assess your essay. Each rater will assign a score of 1–4 in each of three categories: Reading, Analysis, and Writing. These scores will be added together to give you a 2–8 score on each of the three dimensions. Recall that these scores aren't combined with each other or with other scores on the SAT.

Score	Reading	Analysis	Writing
4 Advanced	The response demonstrates thorough comprehension of the source text. The response shows an understanding of the text's central idea(s) and of most important details and how they interrelate, demonstrating a comprehensive understanding of the text. The response is free of errors of fact or interpretation with regard to the text. The response makes skillful use of textual evidence (quotations, paraphrases, or both), demonstrating a complete understanding of the source text.	The response offers an insightful analysis of the source text and demonstrates a sophisticated understanding of the analytical task. The response offers a thorough, well-considered evaluation of the author's use of evidence, reasoning, and/or stylistic and persuasive elements, and/or feature(s) of the student's own choosing. The response contains relevant, sufficient, and strategically chosen support for claim(s) or point(s) made. The response focuses consistently on those features of the text that are most relevant to addressing the task.	The response is cohesive and demonstrates a highly effective use and command of language. The response includes a precise central claim. The response includes a skillful introduction and conclusion. The response demonstrates a deliberate and highly effective progression of ideas both within paragraphs and throughout the essay. The response has wide variety in sentence structures. The response demonstrates a consistent use of precise word choice. The response maintains a formal style and objective tone. The response shows a strong command of the conventions of standard written English and is free or virtually free of errors.
3 Proficient	The response demonstrates effective comprehension of the source text. The response shows an understanding of the text's central idea(s) and important details. The response is free of substantive errors of fact and interpretation with regard to the text. The response makes appropriate use of textual evidence (quotations, paraphrases, or both), demonstrating an understanding of the source text.	The response offers an effective analysis of the source text and demonstrates an understanding of the analytical task. The response competently evaluates the author's use of evidence, reasoning, and/or stylistic and persuasive elements, and/or feature(s) of the student's own choosing. The response contains relevant and sufficient support for claim(s) or point(s) made. The response focuses primarily on those features of the text that are most relevant to addressing the task.	The response is mostly cohesive and demonstrates effective use and control of language. The response includes a central claim or implicit controlling idea. The response includes an effective introduction and conclusion. The response demonstrates a clear progression of ideas both within paragraphs and throughout the essay. The response has variety in sentence structures. The response demonstrates some precise word choice. The response maintains a formal style and objective tone. The response shows a good control of the conventions of standard written English and is free of significant errors that detract from the quality of writing.
2 Partial	The response demonstrates some comprehension of the source text. The response shows an understanding of the text's central idea(s) but not of important details. The response may contain errors of fact and/or interpretation with regard to the text. The response makes limited and/or haphazard use of textual evidence (quotations, paraphrases, or both), demonstrating some understanding of the source text.	The response offers limited analysis of the source text and demonstrates only partial understanding of the analytical task. The response identifies and attempts to describe the author's use of evidence, reasoning, and/or stylistic and persuasive elements, and/or feature(s) of the student's own choosing, but merely asserts rather than explains their importance. Or one or more aspects of the response's analysis are unwarranted based on the text. The response contains little or no support for claim(s) or point(s) made. The response may lack a clear focus on those features of the text that are most relevant to addressing the task.	The response demonstrates little or no cohesion and limited skill in the use and control of language. The response may lack a clear central claim or controlling idea or may deviate from the claim or idea over the course of the response. The response may include an ineffective introduction and/or conclusion. The response may demonstrate some progression of ideas within paragraphs but not throughout the response. The response has limited variety in sentence structures; sentence structures may be repetitive. The response demonstrates general or vague word choice; word choice may be repetitive. The response may deviate noticeably from a formal style and objective tone. The response shows a limited control of the conventions of standard written English and contains errors that detract from the quality of writing and may impede understanding.

(continued)

Score	Reading	Analysis	Writing
1 Inadequate	The response demonstrates little or no comprehension of the source text. The response fails to show an understanding of the text's central idea(s) and may include only details without reference to central idea(s). The response may contain numerous errors of fact and/or interpretation with regard to the text. The response makes little or no use of textual evidence (quotations, paraphrases, or both), demonstrating little or no understanding of the source text.	The response offers little or no analysis or ineffective analysis of the source text and demonstrates little or no understanding of the analytic task. The response identifies without explanation some aspects of the author's use of evidence, reasoning, and/or stylistic and persuasive elements, and/or feature(s) of the student's choosing. Or numerous aspects of the response's analysis are unwarranted based on the text. The response contains little or no support for claim(s) or point(s) made, or support is largely irrelevant. The response may not focus on features of the text that are relevant to addressing the task. Or the response offers no discernible analysis (e.g., is largely or exclusively summary).	The response demonstrates little or no cohesion and inadequate skill in the use and control of language. The response may lack a clear central claim or controlling idea. The response lacks a recognizable introduction and conclusion. The response does not have a discernible progression of ideas. The response lacks variety in sentence structures; sentence structures may be repetitive. The response demonstrates general and vague word choice; word choice may be poor or inaccurate. The response may lack a formal style and objective tone. The response shows a weak control of the conventions of standard written English and may contain numerous errors that undermine the quality of writing.

PRACTICE AT
satpractice.org

Take some time to read the sample passages and student essays below. As you read each student essay, consider how well the student does in each of the three scoring dimensions (Reading, Analysis, and Writing), using the scoring rubric as a guide. Compare your assessment of each essay to the assessment provided.

We've provided two samples that illustrate the sorts of reading passages you can expect to find on the Essay. After you read each passage, you can review samples of the essays that actual students wrote in response to that reading passage.

Each student response has received a separate score for each of the three dimensions assessed: Reading, Analysis, and Writing. The scores are presented directly preceding each sample essay and in order, meaning that a "1/2/1" would refer to a score of 1 in Reading, 2 in Analysis, and 1 in Writing. Scores for the samples were assigned on a 1–4 scale according to the scoring rubric. It's important to note that although these samples are representative of student achievement, neither set comprehensively illustrates the many ways in which students can earn a particular score on a particular dimension.

Although all of the sample essays were handwritten by students, they're shown typed here for ease of reading. Each essay has been transcribed exactly as the student wrote it, without alterations to spelling, punctuation, or paragraph breaks.

Sample Passage 1

As you read the passage below, consider how Peter S. Goodman uses

- evidence, such as facts or examples, to support claims.
- reasoning to develop ideas and to connect claims and evidence.
- stylistic or persuasive elements, such as word choice or appeals to emotion, to add power to the ideas expressed.

PRACTICE AT
satpractice.org

As you read the passage, be on the lookout for the author's use of these three elements (evidence, reasoning, and stylistic and persuasive elements). You may find it helpful to take brief notes in the margins.

Adapted from Peter S. Goodman, "Foreign News at a Crisis Point." ©2013 by TheHuffingtonPost.com, Inc. Originally published September 25, 2013. Peter Goodman is the executive business and global news editor at TheHuffingtonPost.com.

1 Back in 2003, American Journalism Review produced a census of foreign correspondents then employed by newspapers based in the United States, and found 307 full-time people. When AJR repeated the exercise in the summer of 2011, the count had dropped to 234. And even that number was significantly inflated by the inclusion of contract writers who had replaced full-time staffers.

2 In the intervening eight years, 20 American news organizations had entirely eliminated their foreign bureaus.

3 The same AJR survey zeroed in on a representative sampling of American papers from across the country and found that the space devoted to foreign news had shrunk by 53 percent over the previous quarter-century.

4 All of this decline was playing out at a time when the U.S. was embroiled in two overseas wars, with hundreds of thousands of Americans deployed in Iraq and Afghanistan. It was happening as domestic politics grappled with the merits and consequences of a global war on terror, as a Great Recession was blamed in part on global imbalances in savings, and as world leaders debated a global trade treaty and pacts aimed at addressing climate change. It unfolded as American workers heard increasingly that their wages and job security were under assault by competition from counterparts on the other side of oceans.

5 In short, news of the world is becoming palpably more relevant to the day-to-day experiences of American readers, and it is rapidly disappearing.

6 Yet the same forces that have assailed print media, eroding foreign news along the way, may be fashioning a useful response. Several nonprofit outlets have popped up to finance foreign reporting, and a for-profit outfit, GlobalPost, has dispatched a team of 18 senior correspondents into the field, supplemented by dozens of stringers and freelancers. . . .

REMEMBER

The Essay passage is lengthy. Spend sufficient time reading, and selectively rereading, the passage to ensure you understand it well. You'll need a strong understanding of the passage in order to analyze how the author builds his or her argument to persuade an audience.

7 We are intent on forging fresh platforms for user-generated content: testimonials, snapshots and video clips from readers documenting issues in need of attention. Too often these sorts of efforts wind up feeling marginal or even patronizing: "Dear peasant, here's your chance

to speak to the pros about what's happening in your tiny little corner of the world." We see user-generated content as a genuine reporting tool, one that operates on the premise that we can only be in so many places at once. Crowd-sourcing is a fundamental advantage of the web, so why not embrace it as a means of piecing together a broader and more textured understanding of events?

8 We all know the power of Twitter, Facebook and other forms of social media to connect readers in one place with images and impressions from situations unfolding far away. We know the force of social media during the Arab Spring, as activists convened and reacted to changing circumstances. . . . Facts and insights reside on social media, waiting to be harvested by the digitally literate contemporary correspondent.

9 And yet those of us who have been engaged in foreign reporting for many years will confess to unease over many of the developments unfolding online, even as we recognize the trends are as unstoppable as globalization or the weather. Too often it seems as if professional foreign correspondents, the people paid to use their expertise while serving as informational filters, are being replaced by citizen journalists who function largely as funnels, pouring insight along with speculation, propaganda and other white noise into the mix.

10 We can celebrate the democratization of media, the breakdown of monopolies, the rise of innovative means of telling stories, and the inclusion of a diversity of voices, and still ask whether the results are making us better informed. Indeed, we have a professional responsibility to continually ask that question while seeking to engineer new models that can channel the web in the interest of better informing readers. . . .

11 We need to embrace the present and gear for the future. These are days in which newsrooms simply must be entrepreneurial and creative in pursuit of new means of reporting and paying for it. That makes this a particularly interesting time to be doing the work, but it also requires forthright attention to a central demand: We need to put back what the Internet has taken away. We need to turn the void into something fresh and compelling. We need to re-examine and update how we gather information and how we engage readers, while retaining the core values of serious-minded journalism.

12 This will not be easy. . . . But the alternative—accepting ignorance and parochialism—is simply not an option.

Write an essay in which you explain how Peter S. Goodman builds an argument to persuade his audience that news organizations should increase the amount of professional foreign news coverage provided to people in the United States. In your essay, analyze how Goodman uses one or more of the features listed in the box above (or features of your own choice) to strengthen the logic and persuasiveness of his argument. Be sure that your analysis focuses on the most relevant features of the passage.

PRACTICE AT
satpractice.org

If you decide to practice for the SAT Essay, select a passage to use for your analysis. Take several minutes to brainstorm some of the points you may choose to focus on. Next, create an outline in which you decide on the structure and progression of your essay. An outline will help ensure your essay is well organized and cohesive. This strategy may also be useful on test day.

Sample Student Essays

Student Sample 1— Scores: 1/1/1

In the Article, "Foreign News at a Crisis Point" by Peter S. Goodman ©2013 by TheHuffingtonPost.com, the author builds up an argument to persuade his audience. He provided information about American Journalism Review to let people in the community know how it started.

"we need to embrace the present and gear for the future." This means that the author wants to find new ways of communicating with the community now, that will help later on in the future. This is important because the author wants better media to transmit to the public.

"We all know the Power of Twitter, Facebook, and other forms of Social media to connect leaders in one Place with images and

[unfinished]

Sample 1 Scoring Explanation: This response scored a 1/1/1.

Reading—1: This response demonstrates little comprehension of Goodman's text. Although the inclusion of two quotations from the text (*"we need to embrace the present . . ."*; *"We all know the power of Twitter, Facebook . . ."*) suggests that the writer has read the passage, the writer does not provide any actual indication of an understanding of the text. The writer fails to show a clear understanding of Goodman's central claim, saying vaguely that *the author wants better media to transmit to the public.* The response is further limited by vague references to details from the passage that are largely unconnected to the passage's central idea, such as when the writer states that Goodman *provided information about American Journalism Review to let people in the community know how it started.* Overall, this response demonstrates inadequate reading comprehension.

Analysis—1: This response demonstrates little understanding of the analytical task. The writer makes few attempts to analyze the source text. What attempts are offered either repeat the prompt without elaboration (*the author builds up an argument to persuade his audience*) or merely paraphrase the text in a general way (*This means that the author wants to find new ways of communicating*). The brief response consists mostly of quotations taken from the passage, with very few of the writer's own ideas included. Overall, this response demonstrates inadequate analysis.

Writing—1: This response demonstrates little cohesion and inadequate skill in the use and control of language. While the writer does include a very basic central claim (*the author builds up an argument to persuade his audience*), the response does not have a discernible progression of ideas. Much of the brief response is comprised of quotations from Goodman's text, and the language that is the writer's own is repetitive and vague. For example, the writer states that Goodman shares information with his readers to *let people in the community know how it started*, with no clear indication of what "it" refers to. Overall, this response demonstrates inadequate writing.

Student Sample 2 — Scores: 2/1/2

In the article "Foreign News At a Crisis Point", Peter S. Goodman argues that the news orginizations should increase the amount of Foreign news coverage offered to the Americans.

Peter S. Goodman offers many explanations of why the American public needs more profetional Foreign news covarage. He appeals to our emotions when he states that it's seen very often that when news orginization ask for a review by a reader/viewer they might end up to feel marginal. Goodman gives an idea to fix that problem and says, "Crowd-Sourcing is a fundimental advantage of the web, so why not emdrace it as means of piecing together a broader and more textual understanding of events?" He talks about this because he believes that the news should add what the people want to hear and not what the reportors want to talk about.

He also states a fact from the American Journalism Review, the AJR sampled many news papers from across the country and they observed that the space of which belonged to foreign news had shrunk by 53% over the previous quarter-century. Goodman took this into consideration and noticed that the decline was talking place around the time in which America was in the middle of two wars overseas. It was also around the time the government viewed the consequences and merits of global war on terrorism.

Peter S. Goodman offered many reason for which Foreign news should be in creased so the American public could view it and they all have great support and add relavence to the viewer.

Sample 2 Scoring Explanation: This response scored a 2/1/2.

Reading—2: This response demonstrates some comprehension of Goodman's text. The writer shows an understanding of Goodman's central idea, stating that *news orginizations should increase the amount of Foreign news coverage offered to the Americans.* While the writer includes some details from the source text (*it's seen very often that when news orginization ask for a review by a reader/viewer they might end up to feel marginal*); *Goodman . . . noticed that the decline was talking place around the time in which America was in the middle of two wars overseas*), these details are, for the most part, unconnected to the central idea. The use of textual evidence is limited, and therefore it is unclear whether the writer understands how important details relate to the central idea. Further, the writer demonstrates some evidence of having misinterpreted the argument, stating that Goodman *talks about this because he believes that the news should add what the people want to hear and not what the reportors want to talk about.* Overall, the response demonstrates partially successful reading comprehension.

Analysis—1: This response demonstrates very little understanding of the analytical task. The writer does identify an argumentative strategy in Goodman's text when the writer says Goodman *appeals to our emotions*; however, the writer does not analyze this moment further or provide elaboration about how the example appeals to the audience's emotions. Instead, the writer reverts to summary and writes that *Goodman gives an idea to fix that problem.* Throughout the rest of the response, the writer only describes Goodman's use of evidence by summarizing parts of the text rather than providing analysis. Overall, this response demonstrates inadequate analysis.

Writing—2: This response demonstrates limited cohesion and writing skill. The writer includes a central claim, but the introductory paragraph is not effective. Individual paragraphs display some progression of ideas, but there is little to connect ideas between paragraphs or in the response as a whole. The writer's word choice is general, and sentence structures follow a simple, repetitive subject-verb structure (*Peter S. Goodman offers*; *He appeals*; *Goodman gives*; *He talks*). Some language errors (*emdrace*; *talking place*) detract from the quality of writing throughout the essay but do not seriously impede understanding. Overall, this response demonstrates partially successful writing.

PRACTICE AT
satpractice.org

Unlike the previous two responses, this response utilizes a clearer organizational structure. The introductory paragraph summarizes Goodman's primary claim and previews the persuasive elements that will be discussed later in the response.

Student Sample 3 — Scores: 3/2/3

Peter Goodman's purpose in writing "Foreign News at a Crisis Point" was to persuade his audience that the news should include more information about the world as a whole. Goodmans argument becomes powerful through the use of pathos, using evidence, and also embracing reasoning.

Goodman is extremely persuasive in his argument when he brings pathos into effect. He uses pathos to appeal to the emotions of the readers. He plays out the hard times of the U.S. by saying "American workers heard increasingly that their ways and job security were under assault" and "hundreds of thousands of Americans deployed in Iraq and Afghanistan." This information is used to show the reader why the news coverage in foreign countries is diminishing. Goodman wants the reader to know that he understands why coverage is focusing more on the United States but not that its a good thing.

Goodman uses evidence to support his claims that coverage of foreign news is dwindling. Goodman says "20 American news organizations had entirely eliminated their foreign bureaus." He also explains "in the summer of 2011, the count (of full time foreign correspondents) had dropped to 234." This factual information is used so that Goodman can prove that he knows what he's talking about. These facts prove that Goodman had researched the information and persuades readers to believe Goodman's argument.

Goodman also uses reasoning to show readers that there can always be improvement. He says, "these are days in which newsrooms simply must be entreprenuial and creative in pursuit of new means of reporting and paying for it." Goodman uses the argument that we have to take matters into our own hands to prepare and change the future. Goodmans advice to change now internet focused journalism is comes from a strong skill of reasoning.

Goodman uses pathos evidence and reasoning to persuade readers that foreign news coverage needs to be increased. He plays on the reader's emotions by talking about issues that matter to them. He provides facts to show that his argument is valid. He also uses reasoning to come up with a solution to the issue. Goodman uses these features to successfully make a persuasive argument about the amount of professional foreign news coverage provided to Americans.

Sample 3 Scoring Explanation: This response scored a 3/2/3.

Reading—3: This response demonstrates effective comprehension of the source text in terms of both the central idea and important details. The writer accurately paraphrases the central claim of Goodman's text (*Peter Goodman's purpose in writing "Foreign News at a Crisis Point" was to persuade his audience that the news should include more information about the world as a whole*). The writer also makes use of appropriate textual evidence to demonstrate an understanding of key details (*He plays out the hard times of the U.S. by saying "American workers heard increasingly that their ways and job security were under assault" and "hundreds of thousands of Americans deployed in Iraq and Afghanistan"*; *Goodman uses evidence to support his claims that coverage of foreign news is dwindling. Goodman says "20 American* *news organizations had entirely eliminated their foreign bureaus*"). The response is free of errors of fact or interpretation. Overall, this response demonstrates proficient reading comprehension.

Analysis—2: This response demonstrates a limited understanding of the analytical task and offers an incomplete analysis of how Goodman builds his argument. The writer identifies some important pieces of evidence in Goodman's text and attempts to describe their use (*This factual information is used so that Goodman can prove that he knows what he's talking about. These facts prove that Goodman had researched the information and persuades readers to believe Goodman's argument*), but the writer's reliance on assertions leads only to limited analysis. For example, in the third body paragraph, which discusses Goodman's use of reasoning, the writer merely paraphrases a selected quotation from the text (*He says, "these are days in which newsrooms simply must be entreprenuial and creative in pursuit of new means of reporting and paying for it." Goodman uses the argument that we have to take matters into our own hands to prepare and change the future*) and then asserts circularly that Goodman's advice *comes from a strong skill of reasoning.* Overall, this response demonstrates partially successful analysis.

Writing—3: The writer demonstrates effective use and command of language in this response, and the response as a whole is cohesive. The response includes a precise central claim (*Goodmans argument becomes powerful through the use of pathos, using evidence, and also embracing reasoning*). The brief but focused introduction establishes the framework for the writer's organizational structure, which the writer follows faithfully in the body of the response, progressing from idea to idea and ending with a competent conclusion that summarizes the response. The response displays variety in sentence structure (*He uses pathos to appeal to the emotion of the readers*; *coverage of foreign news is dwindling*; *Goodman uses these features to successfully make a persuasive argument about the amount of professional foreign news coverage provided to Americans*) and generally good control of the conventions of standard written English. Overall, this response demonstrates proficient writing.

Student Sample 4 — Scores: 3/3/3

Logic, reason, and rhetoric create a strong persuasive argument. Peter S. Goodman utilizes these tools in his article "Foreign News At a Crisis Point". Goodman presents a cause and effect argument as well, by presenting the facts and revealing their consequences. What truly persuades his audience is his use of logic, reasen, and rhetoric. These occur in forms of examples, explanations and conclusions, and persuasive and rhetorical statements.

Goodman's use of logic occurs throughout his article, but is most prevelant in the beginning. Examples and statistical presentations initially draw interest from readers. Goodman begins with a census from year 2003 and year 2011 that reveals the major decline of foreign correspondents employed by newspapers based in the United States. The numbers themselves raise a concern in the audiences mind, but may not capture their attention. Goodman then presents more apalling examples, including the sharp decrease of space devoted to foreign news over a quarter century, in order to further capture the reader's attention and raise concern. The connection between the decline in foreign news and increased American involvement overseas heightens curiosity for the reader. Goodman employs logic, basic reasoning and evidence presentation in order to raise concern, curiosity, and questions from the reader.

Goodman's use of reason is present throughout the entire article. After Goodman's presentation of his statistics and facts, he raises more concern about how to increase these statistics and factual numbers. Goodman uses reason to recognize that it would be more "genuine" and better informing for readers to hear of first hand experiences. The reader of his article begins to wonder how Goodman plans to increase the amount of professional foreign news coverage for Americans, and Goodman utilizes reason to draw a simple solution. Social media sites provide an outlet for individuals to have a voice "electronically" speaking. Goodman uses reason to reveal to the reader that first-hand knowledge is best and social media sites provide easy access, so why not create an outlet for people who know more to say more? Goodman also utilizes reason to present the problem of inaccurate information on social media sites. He further builds and enhances his argument when he states that there must be a way to "engage readers, while retaining the core values of journalism." Goodman also uses reason to evoke agreement within the reader's mind when he draws simple conclusions and presents simple solutions. Reason allows Goodman to construct upon his solid foundation of evidence that creates his argument.

Rhetoric seals the deal in Goodman's argument. After presenting the facts using logic, and making connections using reason, Goodman utilizes rhetoric to place the cherry on the top of his argument. Rhetoric is crucial in an argument because it determines how the reader feels after reading an article. Goodman utilizes rhetoric after he presents the fundamental advantage of crowd-sourcing on the web, when he asks a rhetorical question. Goodman presents obvious and exciting information that seems more than reasonable, and asks whether this great idea should be practiced or not. A rhetorical question is meant to evoke either disagreement or agreement of the author's purpose. In this case, Goodman's use of rhetoric evokes agreement from the reader. In his final stanza, after presenting all methods of reform, Goodman utilizes rhetoric to once again state the obvious. Goodman presents his solutions, then asks if it is better to stay ignorant and parochial; the answer to his statement is obvious, and causes the reader to agree with him.

Great persuasive essays utilize the tools of persuasion. Goodman began his argument with logic, combined in reason, and finalized with rhetoric. A flow of examples to connections, to solutions, and consequences propels the reader into agreement with the author. Goodman solidifies his argument and builds his argument with logic, reason, and rhetoric, allowing for a reader to be in more agreement and satisfaction of his argument.

Sample 4 Scoring Explanation: This response scored a 3/3/3.

Reading—3: This response demonstrates effective comprehension of the source text. Although the central idea is never explicitly stated in the introduction, the writer accurately captures the main focus of Goodman's argument: his *concern* for *the major decline of foreign correspondents employed by newspapers based in the United States.* The writer also accurately paraphrases (*Goodman begins with a census from year 2003 and year 2011*) and directly quotes important details from the source text, demonstrating effective comprehension. In the second body paragraph, for example, the writer demonstrates understanding of Goodman's discussion of the benefits and drawbacks of social media, effectively tracing Goodman's argument from the value of *first-hand knowledge* to *the problem of inaccurate information on social media sites.* Overall, this response demonstrates proficient reading comprehension.

Analysis—3: This response demonstrates an understanding of the analytical task and offers an effective analysis of the source text. The writer discusses how various elements of the text are used to build Goodman's argument and how they contribute to the text's persuasiveness. For example, the writer discusses Goodman's use of statistical evidence as well as Goodman's use of reasoning in the analysis of the social media argument (*He further builds and enhances his argument when he states that there must be a way to "engage readers, while retaining the core values of journalism"*). The writer then discusses how Goodman makes effective use of rhetoric toward the end of paragraph 7 of the passage by posing a rhetorical question (*Goodman utilizes rhetoric after he presents the fundamental advantage of crowd-sourcing on the web, when he asks a rhetorical question*). Although the response occasionally relies upon assertions about the elements of persuasive arguments (*Goodman's use of logic occurs throughout his article*; *Goodman employs logic, basic reasoning and evidence presentation in order to raise concern, curiosity, and questions from the reader*; *Reason allows Goodman to construct upon his solid foundation of evidence*; *Rhetoric seals the deal*), the writer provides effective support in other places (for example in the discussion of Goodman's use of rhetoric in the third body paragraph). Overall, this response demonstrates proficient analysis.

Writing—3: This response is generally cohesive and demonstrates effective use of language. The writer provides an effective introduction that lays out in broad strokes the ways in which Goodman builds his argument (*What truly persuades his audience is his use of logic, reasen, and rhetoric. These occur in forms of examples, explanations and conclusions, and persuasive and rhetorical statements*). The response also includes a summarizing conclusion. The three body paragraphs are structured around the three features the writer has chosen to focus on: *logic*, *reason*, and *rhetoric.* Within each paragraph, there is a clear progression of ideas, though there are few transitions between paragraphs. Although the response sometimes demonstrates awkwardness and repetitive phrasing (*Goodman's use of reason*;

Goodman uses reason; *Goodman also uses reason*), the writer's word choice is generally effective. The response demonstrates some variety in sentence structure and also maintains a formal style and objective tone. Overall, this response demonstrates proficient writing.

Student Sample 5 — Scores: 3/3/4

Peter S. Goodman builds a solid argument for the growing need for foreign news coverage and utilizes concrete evidence, logical reasoning and persuasive appeals to not only expose the paucity of international news feeds, but also convince his audience that it is crucial that news organizations increase the amount of foreign news coverage provided to Americans.

Goodman begins by clearly laying out the raw statistics from a census produced by the American Journalism Review to show the dramatic decline of foreign correspondents and bureaus that had been "entirely eliminated" by American news organizations over the past decayed. In an attempt to point out the incredulous absurdity of these facts, Goodman goes on to discuss the context of the decrease in foreign coverage by providing examples of real world events that affected all Americans. Goodman uses this irony—that in the wake of pivotal global changes like war, global trade treaties and the war on terror, the foreign coverage in the U.S. was diminishing rather than growing—to try to show the American audience that this argument is very much relevant to their everyday lives. He hones in on examples that resonate with many Americans, like the threat to their wages and job security posed by international counterparts, in order to grab the reader's attention and connect his claims to their "day-to-day experiences". This also serves as a way to persuade leaders of the increasing importance of the need for a stronger stream of foreign news coverage by appealing to the audience's emotions and insinuating that they are missing out on critical information that pertains directly to their lives.

Goodman employs stylistic elements through his careful choice of words that strengthen the argument and make a more powerful impression on the reader. He alludes to the "forces" that have destructively "eroded foreign news", but also remains intent on solving this issue by boldly "forging fresh platforms" that will relay a wider range of news to the American people. He appeals to the individual, always referencing the practical need for "user-generated" content available to all people.

Goldman closes his argument by condemning ignorance and calling for action in an exigency.

[unfinished]

PRACTICE AT
satpractice.org

Keep track of pacing during the Essay to ensure you can complete your response in the allotted time. An unfinished essay won't allow you to demonstrate your full reading, analysis, and writing abilities and may lower your score.

Scoring Explanation Sample 5: This response scored a 3/3/4.

Reading—3: This response demonstrates effective comprehension of the source text, citing both the central idea and important details in Goodman's piece. The writer accurately paraphrases the central claim of Goodman's text (*Goodman builds a solid argument for the growing need for foreign news coverage . . . [to] convince his audience that it is crucial that news organizations increase the amount of foreign news coverage provided to Americans*). The writer also demonstrates an understanding of the details of Goodman's text: Goodman's use of *raw statistics*; *the context* for *the decrease in foreign coverage*; that Goodman *condemn[s] ignorance and call[s] for action.* The response is also free of errors of fact or interpretation. Overall, this response demonstrates proficient reading comprehension.

Analysis—3: The response demonstrates an understanding of the analytical task and offers an effective analysis of the source text. The writer discusses how various elements of the text are used to build Goodman's argument and how they contribute to the text's persuasiveness: *Goodman begins by clearly laying out the raw statistics . . . to show the dramatic decline of foreign correspondents and bureaus*; *Goodman uses this irony—that in the wake of pivotal global changes like war, global trade treaties and the war on terror, the foreign coverage . . . was diminishing rather than growing—to try to show . . . that this argument is very much relevant to their everyday lives.* The writer then discusses how Goodman *employs stylistic elements* to further the argument, competently selecting textual evidence of the author's strong, deliberate language, namely *the "forces" that have destructively "eroded foreign news."* Had the writer elaborated more on this discussion, perhaps by explaining how these words *make a powerful impression on the reader*, this response might have moved from a competent evaluation into a more advanced analysis. Overall, this response demonstrates proficient analysis.

Writing—4: This response is cohesive and demonstrates highly effective use and control of language. The writer presents a generally skillful, concise introduction, which is also the response's central claim: *Peter S. Goodman builds a solid argument for the growing need for foreign news coverage and utilizes concrete evidence, logical reasoning and persuasive appeals to not only expose the paucity of international news feeds, but also convince his audience that it is crucial that news organizations increase the amount of foreign news coverage provided to Americans.* The writer employs precise word choice throughout the response (*dramatic decline, discuss the context of the decrease, uses this irony, hones in on examples, make a more powerful impression on the reader, appeals to the individual, always referencing the practical need*). Although the writer was not able to finish the response, the two existing body paragraphs are tightly focused and deliberately structured to advance the writer's analysis of Goodman's use of *concrete evidence* and *stylistic elements* (mainly *choice of words* and *persuasive appeals*). The response maintains a formal style and objective tone and contains clear transitions (*Goodman begins by clearly laying out*; *Goldman* [sic] *closes his argument*) to guide the reader. Overall, this response demonstrates advanced writing skill.

Student Sample 6 — Scores: 4/3/3

Over the years what is going on in the outside world has started to affect us more. Whether it is a war that is going to effect us physically or even an oil disaster that will effect us economically. However, this news is not always covered. The U.S. news focuses more on what is going on in our own country then outside of it we are not well informed to the world around us. Peter S. Goodman uses many different types of evidence to support his claims and persuade his audience that news organizations should increase the amount of professional foreign news coverage provided to Americans.

Within the first three paragraphs of this article the author offers many statistical evidence. He throws out numbers. As a reader this appeals to a logical thinking audience. Also, many people will start to believe that this author is a credible source. He appears to know what he is talking about. Peter S. Goodman appears to have done some research on this topic and proves this within his first three paragraphs. The author uses the numbers "307" and "234" in the first paragraph. He wanted to illustrate to this audience the decreasing amount of foreign correspondents that are employed by news companies within the U.S. Right away goodman shows the audience the subject of the article. He establishes his purpose. He wants to call for a change. The author never comes out and says this in the first paragraph, but he subtely hints at it. Next he shows how many news organizations no longer have "foreign bureaus." Again he throws out a number, "53 percent" to show how much foreign news has decreased within the United States. All these facts are to support his claim that foreign news has shrunk within the United States over the years. He feels as if this should change so people are better informed. Peter S. Goodman then shifts from using statistical evidence to historical evidence.

Peter S. Goodman talks about things that are going on in the world around us today. He brings up many issues that have just recently occured. As a reader I now start to question whether I know what these issues are all about. Did I ever hear about them or even read about them? These are all questions the author has put into the readers' mind. First, he starts off with the war in Iraq and Afghanistan which almost every reader would know about. There are issues that many of them had to deal with personality. Some of their family members may be serving overseas. The author makes a personal connection with the audience. They know the feeling of not knowing exactly what is going on overseas. They constantly question what is happening and whether their loved ones are safe. The author then claims that world news has started to have an affect on our day to day lives in the US. He illustrates how our wages and economy depend on what is going on outside of the United States. Peter S. Goodman transitions from histerical evidence to things that we use for news such as social media to make a connection to his audience.

The author starts to talk about how we now rely on social media for our world news. He again backs up his claim that we need more "professional" foreign coverage in the United States. He explains how common people are providing the news. This may make for "speculation, propaganda, and other white noise into the mix." These people are not professional writers. Also, most of them are not neutral on an issue. He shows that common people are bias. They all have an opinion and share it. Instead of saying what is actually going on; they may say what they think is going on. The author uses the example of bias saying there was not new organization reporting on this. All of our news came from social media. People talk these accounts as truth. They do not realize that they are not filtered. He compares "professional foreign correspondents" to "informational filters" while he compares "citizen journalists" to "funnels". Professional reporters that would investigate foreign issues would only report back what they know is true. Only facts would be included. However, every day people that are writing on the web would say anything and everything they could think of. He uses this comparison to show his audience the different ways they are given information. He wants to show them that right now they are depending on opinions when in fact they should be depending on facts. The author goes from how people are obtaining their information to how he thinks people should obtain their information.

Peter S. Goodman uses his last few paragraphs to state his claims once again. He renforces the idea that we need to take back "what the Internet has taken away." He supports this earlier in his article when he [shows] how we do not also receive the full story when we rely on day to day people to report the world news. The author wants to journalists to change the way they write. He believes that they will be much more successful in providing information to the public. They need to "engage" their readers. The author's last few paragraphs are used to restate his claims that he supported with evidence through out his article.

The author uses many different types of evidence to back up his claims. He shows that he has researched his topic by providing statistical evidence that agrees with his opinions. He shows the decrease in the amount of foreign correspondents with this evidence. Then he shifts to historical evidence. This evidence is used to show how much the world around us has an impact on our society. Then he transitions to how we obtain information today. He shows we do not always receive the full story. He uses this to claim how we should gain our information. The author believes in more foreign correspondents. Throughout "Foreign News At a Crisis Point" Peter S. Goodman uses evidence to portray why we need to increase the amount of foreign news we receive instead the United States. In using the evidence he shows how and why the world around us constantly has an impact on us; this is why it is so important that the United States citizens have an accurate description of issues and situations that are developing in foreign nations.

Scoring Explanation Sample 6: This response scored a 4/3/3.

Reading—4: This response demonstrates thorough comprehension of the source text and illustrates an understanding of the interrelation between the central idea and the important details of Goodman's article. The writer paraphrases Goodman's central claim (*news organizations should increase the amount of professional foreign news coverage provided to Americans*) and then accurately describes the statistical evidence that undergirds that claim (the decrease of foreign correspondents as well as the decrease of foreign bureaus). The writer goes on to discuss how Goodman ties the central claim to important details such as *the war in Iraq and Afghanistan* and the reliance on *social media for our world news*, thereby showing an understanding of these details. The response is free of errors of fact or interpretation. Overall, this response demonstrates advanced reading comprehension.

Analysis—3: This response demonstrates good understanding of the analytical task and offers an effective analysis of the source text. The writer effectively analyzes how Goodman uses various elements of his text to build a persuasive argument. For example, the writer discusses two statistical pieces of evidence at the beginning of Goodman's argument (*The author uses the numbers "307" and "234" . . . to illustrate . . . the decreasing amount of foreign correspondents; he throws out a number, "53 percent" to show how much foreign news has decreased*). The writer then discusses how Goodman shifts from *statistical evidence to historical evidence* to further his argument. Although the example then given is not historical but current, the writer competently evaluates the effect of this element of Goodman's text (*he starts off with the war in Iraq and Afghanistan which almost every reader would know about. . . . The author makes a personal connection with the audience*). Finally, the writer makes good analytical use of textual evidence, saying that Goodman *compares "professional foreign correspondents" to "informational filters" while he compares "citizen journalists" to "funnels."* The writer then explains what using this comparison illustrates ("filters" present *facts*, while "funnels" convey *anything and everything they could think of*) for Goodman's audience. Overall, this response demonstrates proficient analysis.

Writing—3: The response demonstrates effective use and command of language and as a whole is cohesive. The response includes a precise central claim (*Goodman uses many different types of evidence to support his claims and persuade his audience that news organizations should increase the amount of professional foreign news coverage*). The effective introduction provides context for the analysis that follows and the conclusion effectively encapsulates that analysis. In addition, the writer progresses smoothly from idea to idea within and between paragraphs. Although the response displays a consistently formal and objective tone and good control of the conventions of standard written English, the writer sometimes relies on choppy sentence structure and awkward or repetitive phrasing (. . . *the author offers many statistical evidence. He throws out numbers; He shows that common people are bias. They all have an opinion and share it*). Overall, this response demonstrates proficient writing.

Student Sample 7 — Scores: 4/3/3

Media presentation from across the globe is vital to the upkeep and maintenance of our society. How this information is obtained and presented, if presented at all, is a different story, however. Goodman builds an argument to persuade his audience that news organizations should increase the amount of professional foreign news coverage to the Americas through the presentation of statistics, connections to social media as well as using specific diction to establish his argument.

Goodman uses statistics and facts, as presented by the AJR, in order to show the loss of foreign correspondents reporting to the U.S. in order to persuade his audience that there is a need for more professional coverage. He begins his essay with the statistic saying that the level of professional foreign correspondents dropped from 307 full-time people to 234. This conveys that the number of people providing legitimate and credible information to news services in the U.S. is going down, thus alluding to the overall decrease in foreign Media. Goodman uses this to build his argument by envoking his audience to think that they may not be getting all the true media and facts presented. He uses the statistic of the shrinking correspondents to establish the fact that if this number is continually decreasing, there may be in the future a lack of unbiased media presentation, asking his audience to consider the importance of foreign news coverage.

Goodman connects to the vast implications of bias presented via social media to further build his argument. Reporters "know the power of Twitter, Facebook and other forms of social media" and, as they continue to rise in popularity in the distribution of media, are enabling the genesis of "citizen journalists who function largely as funnels . . . pouring white noise into the mix". Goodman further builds his argument here in order to persuade his audience by showing how with the rise of social media, more biased and superfluous information can be projected and wrongly viewed.

Goodman says this to evoke a concern within his audience about the truth in media. Blatantly put, Goodman accounts for that if you want unbiased foreign media people must turn from social media such as Twitter and Facebook and turn toward professional foreign media presentation. Presenting this idea of a possible falacy within social media greatly establishes his purpose as well as affirms his audience on weather they agree with him or not.

Also, Goodman uses specific diction to further establish his argument to persuade his audience. Goodman uses personal prounouns such as "we" to show that he personally is a part of the media presentation community, not only establishing his credibility on the subject, but also aiding in his persuasion of his audience by allowing them to think he is an expert in the field. Through his word choice, Goodman further establishes his argument by ascribing the need for more foreign reporter not as a burden but as a challenge. This adds in the persuasion of his audience by showing them that this is a real problem and that there are people rising up to it, and so should they.

Goodman's use of up-to-date references as well as connections to social media, use of statistics, and diction establish his argument of the need for more foreign reporters as well as persuading his audience of the need to do so.

Scoring Explanation Sample 7: This response scored a 4/3/3.

Reading—4: This response demonstrates thorough comprehension of the source text and shows an understanding of the relationship between the central idea and the important details in Goodman's piece. The writer includes the central claim of Goodman's text (*news organizations should increase the amount of professional foreign news coverage to the Americas*) and even paraphrases the claim in broader terms (*Media presentation from across the globe is vital to the upkeep and maintenance of our society*). The writer also exhibits an understanding of the details in Goodman's text (*He begins his essay with the statistic saying that the level of professional foreign correspondents dropped from 307 full-time people to 234*; *if you want unbiased foreign media people must turn from social media such as Twitter and Facebook and turn toward professional foreign media presentation*). The response is also free of errors of fact or interpretation. Overall, this response demonstrates advanced reading comprehension.

Analysis—3: This response demonstrates good understanding of the analytical task by offering an effective analysis of the source text. Focusing on the most relevant features of Goodman's argument, the writer thoroughly discusses, for example, the use of Goodman's opening statistic (the drop from 307 full-time foreign correspondents to 234), how it *conveys that the number of people providing legitimate and credible information to news services . . . is going down*, and how, therefore, *Goodman [is] . . . envoking his audience to think that they may not be getting all the true . . . facts*. The writer then follows up the point by saying that Goodman is *asking his audience to consider the importance of foreign news coverage*. The writer also competently selects relevant textual evidence from Goodman's argument about the dangers of social media, citing the evocative quotation *"citizen journalists who function largely as funnels . . . pouring white noise into the mix."* Additionally, the writer analyzes the diction in Goodman's text by discussing the author's deliberate choice of *personal pronouns such as "we"* to establish *credibility on the subject*. Overall, this response demonstrates proficient analysis.

Writing—3: This response demonstrates cohesion as well as effective use and command of language. The response includes a precise central claim (*Goodman builds an argument to persuade his audience that news organizations should increase the amount of professional foreign news coverage to the Americas through the presentation of statistics, connections to social media as well as using specific diction to establish his argument*). The focused introduction establishes context for the writer's analysis and provides the framework for the response's organizational structure. The writer then follows that framework faithfully in the body of the response, progressing clearly from idea to idea. The response displays variety in sentence structure and some precise word choice (*vital to the upkeep and maintenance of our society*, *vast implications of bias*, *superfluous information*), although the writer sometimes uses infelicitous phrasing and vocabulary (*envoking* *his audience to think; a possible falacy within social media greatly establishes his purpose*). Overall, this response demonstrates proficient writing.

Sample Passage 2

As you read the passage below, consider how Adam B. Summers uses

- evidence, such as facts or examples, to support claims.
- reasoning to develop ideas and to connect claims and evidence.
- stylistic or persuasive elements, such as word choice or appeals to emotion, to add power to the ideas expressed.

Adapted from Adam B. Summers, "Bag Ban Bad for Freedom and Environment." ©2013 by The San Diego Union-Tribune, LLC. Originally published June 13, 2013.

1 Californians dodged yet another nanny-state regulation recently when the state Senate narrowly voted down a bill to ban plastic bags statewide, but the reprieve might only be temporary. Not content to tell us how much our toilets can flush or what type of light bulb to use to brighten our homes, some politicians and environmentalists are now focused on deciding for us what kind of container we can use to carry our groceries.

2 The bill . . . would have prohibited grocery stores and convenience stores with at least $2 million in gross annual sales and 10,000 square feet of retail space from providing single-use plastic or paper bags, although stores would have been allowed to sell recycled paper bags for an unspecified amount. The bill fell just three votes short of passage in the Senate . . . and Sen. Alex Padilla, D-Los Angeles, who sponsored the measure, has indicated that he would like to bring it up again, so expect this fight to be recycled rather than trashed.

3 While public debate over plastic bag bans often devolves into emotional pleas to save the planet or preserve marine life (and, believe me, I love sea turtles as much as the next guy), a little reason and perspective is in order.

4 According to the U.S. Environmental Protection Agency, plastic bags, sacks, and wraps of all kinds (not just grocery bags) make up only about 1.6 percent of all municipal solid waste materials. High-density polyethylene (HDPE) bags, which are the most common kind of plastic grocery bags, make up just 0.3 percent of this total.

5 The claims that plastic bags are worse for the environment than paper bags or cotton reusable bags are dubious at best. In fact, compared to paper bags, plastic grocery bags produce fewer greenhouse gas emissions, require 70 percent less energy to make, generate 80 percent less waste, and utilize less than 4 percent of the amount of water needed to manufacture them. This makes sense because plastic bags are lighter and take up less space than paper bags.

6 Reusable bags come with their own set of problems. They, too, have a larger carbon footprint than plastic bags. Even more disconcerting are

the findings of several studies that plastic bag bans lead to increased health problems due to food contamination from bacteria that remain in the reusable bags. A November 2012 statistical analysis by University of Pennsylvania law professor Jonathan Klick and George Mason University law professor and economist Joshua D. Wright found that San Francisco's plastic bag ban in 2007 resulted in a subsequent spike in hospital emergency room visits due to E. coli, salmonella, and campylobacter-related intestinal infectious diseases. The authors conclude that the ban even accounts for several additional deaths in the city each year from such infections.

7 The description of plastic grocery bags as "single-use" bags is another misnomer. The vast majority of people use them more than once, whether for lining trash bins or picking up after their dogs. (And still other bags are recycled.) Since banning plastic bags also means preventing their additional uses as trash bags and pooper scoopers, one unintended consequence of the plastic bag ban would likely be an increase in plastic bag purchases for these other purposes. This is just what happened in Ireland in 2002 when a 15 Euro cent ($0.20) tax imposed on plastic shopping bags led to a 77 percent increase in the sale of plastic trash can liner bags.

8 And then there are the economic costs. The plastic bag ban would threaten the roughly 2,000 California jobs in the plastic bag manufacturing and recycling industry, although, as noted in the Irish example above, they might be able to weather the storm if they can successfully switch to producing other types of plastic bags. In addition, taxpayers will have to pony up for the added bureaucracy, and the higher regulatory costs foisted upon bag manufacturers and retailers will ultimately be borne by consumers in the form of price increases.

9 Notwithstanding the aforementioned reasons why plastic bags are not, in fact, evil incarnate, environmentalists have every right to try to convince people to adopt certain beliefs or lifestyles, but they do not have the right to use government force to compel people to live the way they think best. In a free society, we are able to live our lives as we please, so long as we do not infringe upon the rights of others. That includes the right to make such fundamental decisions as "Paper or plastic?"

Write an essay in which you explain how Adam B. Summers builds an argument to persuade his audience that plastic shopping bags should not be banned. In your essay, analyze how Summers uses one or more of the features listed in the box above (or features of your own choice) to strengthen the logic and persuasiveness of his argument. Be sure that your analysis focuses on the most relevant features of the passage.

Your essay should not explain whether you agree with Summers's claims, but rather explain how Summers builds an argument to persuade his audience.

Sample Student Essays

Student Sample 1 — Scores: 2/1/1

Adams B. Summers argues what the damages of a proposed plastic bag ban would do if the legislation gets passed. Summers presents his argument well, and his use of fact/examples, reasoning to devolope ideas, and persuasive word choice build his argument. He uses examples/facts, such as plastic bags only make up 1.6 percent of all solid waste. His excellent word choice that appeals to your mind such as him saying the politician hopes to bring up the bill again to essentially "recycle rather than trash it". He uses reasoning that makes sense to a reader stating how many jobs may be potentially lost due to the bill and how much waste is really caused by plastic bags v. paper.

Scoring Explanation Sample 1: This response scored a 2/1/1.

Reading—2: This response demonstrates some comprehension of Summers's text. The writer indicates an understanding of the main idea of Summers's argument (*Summers argues what the damages of a proposed plastic bag ban would do if the legislation gets passed*). The writer also selects some important details from the text (*plastic bags only make up 1.6 percent of all solid waste*; *many jobs may be potentially lost due to the bill*). However, the writer does not expand on the significance of these details in relation to the main ideas of Summers's text. The response makes limited and haphazard use of textual evidence with little or no interpretation. Overall, this response demonstrates partially successful reading comprehension.

Analysis—1: This response demonstrates little understanding of the analytical task. Although the writer identifies some argumentative elements in Summers's text (*his use of fact/examples, reasoning to devolope ideas, and persuasive word choice*), the writer does not explain how these elements build Summers's argument. Instead, the writer only identifies these aspects of the text and names an example of each, with no further analysis (*He uses examples/facts, such as plastic bags only make up 1.6 percent of all solid waste*). There are two moments in which the writer attempts to analyze Summers's use of word choice and reasoning (*His excellent word choice that appeals to your mind* and *He uses reasoning that makes sense to a reader*). There is not enough textual evidence given to support these claims, however. For example, the writer does not analyze Summers's use of specific words and instead falls back into summary of the passage. Overall, this response demonstrates inadequate analysis.

Writing—1: This response demonstrates little cohesion and limited skill in the use of language. The response is only one brief paragraph and lacks a recognizable introduction and conclusion. Although there is a central claim, taken directly from the prompt (*Summers presents his argument well, and his use of fact/examples, reasoning to devolope ideas,* *and persuasive word choice build his argument*), there is no discernible progression of ideas in the response. Furthermore, sentence structures are repetitive. Due to the brief nature of the response, there is not enough evidence of writing ability to merit a score higher than 1. Overall, this response demonstrates inadequate writing.

Student Sample 2 — Scores: 3/1/2

> Adam B. Summers brings up several good points as to why plastic shoping bags should not be banned. He explains how the EPA says all plastic bags only make up 1.6 percent of all waste, and plastic shoping bags only contribute 0.3 percent to all the waste. The bags hardly make up any waste and require less energy to make compared to paper or cotton bags. Plastic bags produce fewer greenhouse gasses, 80 percent less waste and less water to make them over paper or cotton reusable bags. Reusable bags also have a higher risk of giving a consumer food poising because of bacteria left in them and then the bags are used again.
>
> Plastic bags are also called "single use" bags, but that is not true because people re-use them for garabge bags. By cutting of plastic shoping bags people would by more garabge bags wich are plastic so it would defeat the purpose. eliminating plastic bags would also cause the people who make them and dispose them lose their jobs too. Enviornmentalist can try to convince people paper is better than plastic but people should also look at it from the other prespective, and choose, "Paper or Plastic?".

Scoring Explanation Sample 2: This response scored a 3/1/2.

Reading—3: This response demonstrates effective comprehension of Summers's text. The writer provides appropriate textual evidence (in this case, paraphrases) to articulate both the central idea (*plastic shoping bags should not be banned*) and important details from the passage (*all plastic bags only make up 1.6 percent of all waste, and plastic shoping bags only contribute 0.3 percent to all the waste*; *Plastic bags produce fewer greenhouse gasses, 80 percent less waste and less water to make them over paper or cotton reusable bags*). The writer also demonstrates a proficient understanding of the entirety of Summers's text by incorporating details from various points throughout Summers's argument (*Plastic bags are also called "single use" bags, but that is not true because people re-use them for garabge bags*; *eliminating plastic bags would also cause the people who make them and dispose them lose their jobs too*). The response, which is essentially summary, is free of substantive errors of fact and interpretation. Overall, this response demonstrates proficient reading comprehension.

Analysis—1: This response demonstrates no understanding of the analytic task, as it is exclusively summary and offers no discernible analysis of Summers's text. The writer fails to identify aspects of evidence, reasoning, or stylistic and persuasive elements that Summers uses to build his argument and instead only provides a

REMEMBER

Your response on the Essay should not simply be a summary of the argument presented in the passage. A critical part of your task is to analyze how the author builds an argument using evidence, reasoning, and stylistic or persuasive elements.

general statement on the quality of the passage (*Adam B. Summers brings up several good points as to why plastic shoping bags should not be banned*). Overall, this response demonstrates inadequate analysis.

Writing—2: This response demonstrates limited cohesion and writing skill. The response includes an ineffective introduction and conclusion based on the brief, general central claim that opens the response (*Adam B. Summers brings up several good points as to why plastic shoping bags should not be banned*) and the concluding sentence of the response (*Enviornmentalist can try to convince people paper is better than plastic but people should also look at it from the other prespective, and choose, "Paper or Plastic?"*). There is no real organization of ideas within paragraphs, and there are no transitions between the two paragraphs that indicate how the ideas in one relate to the other. Although there is some limited progression of ideas over the course of the response, there is little progression of ideas within paragraphs. There are numerous errors that detract from the quality of writing, and the response at times exhibits limited control of language and vague word choice (*By cutting of plastic shoping bags people would by more garabge bags wich are plastic so it would defeat the purpose*). Overall, this response demonstrates partially successful writing.

Student Sample 3 — Scores: 3/2/2

In Adam B Summers' essay he gives valid reasons why plastic bags should not be banned. His essay is persuasive in many ways such as focusing on the effect on the earth and also job cutting. He also gives alternative ways to use a plastic bag. Summers gives examples on how banning plastic bags can lead to worse human damage.

Summers states that a plastic bag is easy to make without using much of anything. Knowing that making a plastic bag takes up to 70% less energy and can also help our earth because it produces less green house gases. Saying this part persuades the earth lovers and it persuades them to side with the no bag ban because it's not as harmful as the reusible bags.

Reusible bags are more harmful than anyone could think and when Summers put in the facts that people die from food born illnesses it catches the doctors and people who care about the well being of others his essay persuades them to not only use the plastic bags but to use cation when using reusible bags because of the illnesses and deaths.

There are many ways to use a plastic bag not just for groceries and when Adam Summers states this it focuses on the renew and reusers where can use plastic bags in the home and daily life. Also being a cheaper alternative. Summers states that if the banning of plastic bags will cost the jobs of 2000 people which to the companies and workers this is a valid argument if they want to keep their jobs.

Summers provides multiple ways to persuade some one and any one with different beliefs. This build many persusive arguments and cause and effects fact based conclusions.

Scoring Explanation Sample 3: This response scored a 3/2/2.

Reading—3: This response demonstrates effective comprehension of Summers's text. The writer accurately paraphrases the central idea (*plastic bags should not be banned*) and important details from the passage — for instance, the environmental impacts of plastic vs. reusable bags (*Knowing that making a plastic bag takes up to 70% less energy and can also help our earth because it produces less green house gases*) and the impact of the bag ban on jobs (*Summers states that if the banning of plastic bags will cost the jobs of 2000 people*). The writer summarizes all of the major points in Summers's argument with no substantive errors of fact or interpretation. Overall, this response demonstrates proficient reading comprehension.

Analysis—2: This response offers a limited analysis of Summers's text, indicating only partial understanding of the analytical task. Although the writer attempts to explain how Summers's use of evidence builds his argument, the writer only asserts the importance of this evidence and its effect on the audience. For example, the fact that plastic bags take 70 percent less energy to make *persuades the earth lovers . . . to side with the no bag ban because it's not as harmful as the reusible bags.* The writer then asserts that this evidence helps build Summers's argument but does not explain how or why. This pattern of assertion without explanation continues in the subsequent paragraph about the health consequences of reusable bags (*when Summers put in the facts that people die from food born illnesses it catches the doctors and people who care about the well being of others . . .* [and] *persuades them to not only use the plastic bags but to use cation when using reusible bags*) and in the paragraph about job cuts (*to the companies and workers this is a valid argument if they want to keep their jobs*). Overall, the response demonstrates partially successful analysis.

Writing—2: This response demonstrates limited cohesion and writing skill. The response does contain a central claim (Summers *gives valid reasons why plastic bags should not be banned*). It also contains an introduction and conclusion; however, they are mostly ineffective due to imprecise word choice (*Summers provides multiple ways to persuade some one and any one with different beliefs. This build many persusive arguments and cause and effects fact based conclusions*). Although each body paragraph is loosely centered on one of three aspects of Summers's argument (ecological, health, and unemployment consequences of the plastic bag ban), there is limited variety in sentence structures and vague word choice throughout the response (*Summers gives examples on how banning plastic bags can lead to worse human damage*; *when Adam Summers states this it focuses on the renew and reusers where can use plastic bags in the home and daily life. Also being a cheaper alternative*). Language and writing errors, such as syntactically awkward sentences, run-on sentences, and sentence fragments, detract from the quality of writing and impede understanding. Overall, this response demonstrates partially successful writing.

Student Sample 4 — Scores: 3/3/3

The style and features an author use can help persuade the audience if clearly used. Adam B. Summers in the essay "Bag ban bad for freedom and environment" uses factual evidence, word choice, and emotion to build his argument. In doing this, Summers successfully persuades his audience into believing "Paper or Plastic" is a personal right.

When using factual evidence, Summers further persuades his reader. Readers are often attracted to facts because they are hard evidence to proving a point. Summers touches upon how plastic bag waste makes up only 0.3 percent out of the 1.6 percent of all munciple solid waste products. By providing this fact Summers shows the low numbered statistics which persuade the reader. The reader sees the small numbers and is immediately taking the authors side. Another use of factual evidence is when Summers discusses Ireland's problem since they've banned the use of plastic bags. By adding in the effects this had on another country, the audience realizes the same situation could happen in California, causing the reader to further his mind to Summer's ideas.

The word choice Summers uses helps lure his readers into his argument. In the first paragraph, Summers uses words such as "dodged", "narrowly", and "down". The usage of words makes the reader feel as if he is in the actual voting process of the bill, taking the rocky road in state government only to get voted down. From the start, Summers makes the audience feel involved which intrigues the reader further. In the second to last paragraph, Summers plays with the phrases "weather the storm" and "pony up" to represent the possibilities to come if a bill banning plastic bags is passed. By telling the reader to "get ready", he puts a negative feeling to the future of the bill and persuades the reader into thinking that the future may not be something they like.

Summers also adds in personal emotion to make the reader feel connected to the author. He writes "I love sea turtles as much as the next guy" to show that he is human too and cares about nature. The claim would touch many readers who are in the same position as Summers; they love nature but think the banning of plastic bags is unreasonable. Summers connects to all readers in his audience when he further helps

[unfinished]

Student Sample 4: This response scored a 3/3/3.

Reading—3: This response demonstrates effective comprehension of the source text by exhibiting proficient understanding of both the central idea and important details in Summers's text. The writer accurately paraphrases the central idea of the passage (*Summers successfully persuades his audience into believing "Paper or Plastic" is a personal right*). The writer also both paraphrases and directly quotes important details from the text (*Summers plays with the phrases "weather the storm" and "pony up" to represent the possibilities to come if a bill banning plastic bags is passed; Summers touches upon how plastic bag waste makes up only 0.3 percent out of the 1.6 percent of all munciple solid waste products*). Although the response is incomplete, as it ends midsentence, there are enough details provided from the text to indicate that the writer adequately understands the entirety of Summers's argument. The response is also free of substantive errors of fact and interpretation. Overall, this response demonstrates proficient reading comprehension.

Analysis—3: This response offers an effective analysis of Summers's argument and demonstrates proficient understanding of the analytical task. The writer identifies three persuasive elements—*factual evidence, word choice, and emotion*—and competently evaluates how these aspects of Summers's text contribute to building his argument. Moreover, the writer explains, with sufficient support, what effects these persuasive elements have on Summers's audience. One example of this type of analysis occurs in the paragraph that analyzes Summers's use of factual evidence, particularly *Ireland's problem since they've banned the use of plastic bags. By adding in the effects this had on another country, the audience realizes the same situation could happen in California, causing the reader to further his mind to Summer's ideas.* Effective analysis continues in the paragraph that analyzes Summers's word choice (*By telling the reader to "get ready", he puts a negative feeling to the future of the bill and persuades the reader into thinking that the future may not be something they like*). Although these moments of analysis are effective, the response lacks the thoroughness and insight seen in responses scoring higher. Overall, this response demonstrates proficient analysis.

Writing—3: The response is mostly cohesive and demonstrates effective use and control of language. The introduction is brief but effectively provides a clear central claim (*Adam B. Summers in the essay "Bag ban bad for freedom and environment" uses factual evidence, word choice, and emotion to build his argument*). The rest of the response is organized according to this three-pronged structure, with each body paragraph remaining on topic. A clear progression of ideas is demonstrated both within paragraphs and throughout the response. The writer integrates quotations and examples from the source text to connect ideas and paragraphs logically. There is a variety of sentence structures (*He writes "I love sea turtles as much as the next guy" to show that he is human too and cares about nature. The claim would touch many readers who are in the same position as Summers; they love nature but think the banning of plastic bags is unreasonable*). There also are some examples of precise word choice (*helps lure his readers into his argument*; *taking the rocky road in state government only to get voted down*; *makes the audience feel involved which intrigues the reader further*). Although the response has no conclusion, this does not preclude the response from demonstrating proficient writing overall.

Student Sample 5 — Scores: 3/3/4

In the wake of environmental concerns in the United States, a bill in California which would ban plastic bags for groceries failed to make it through the state Senate by a small margin. In his article "Bag ban bad for freedom and environment" (2013), Adam Summers asserts that the plastic bag ban would be harmful for consumers and the environment. He conveys this through citing statistics, appealing to the audience's emotions and sense of self-interests, and utilizing sarcastic diction. The intended audience for this article is primarily readers who support the proposed bag ban and intend to help it pass.

The author's statistics cited throughout the article reinforce his argument and provide a solid base. In the fourth paragraph he mentions the most common plastic grocery bags, which "make up just 0.3 percent of solid municipal waste materials. The author also cites the "77 percent increase in the sale of plastic trash can liner bags" as a result of a similar ban in Ireland. These statistics appeal to the reader's logic and ensure that they can follow a logical path to support the author and oppose the ban. The statistics provide solid evidence that are enhanced by the numbers and cannot be easily argued against.

The author's patriotic asides in the first and final paragraphs appeal to the audience's emotions and self-interests. In the first paragraph, the author talks of the rights the government has impeded and talks of a regulation of "what kind of container we can use to carry our groceries." In the final paragraph, the author talks of the fundamental rights to decide "paper or plastic." This causes the readers to feel violated by the government and want to look out for his rights. When the regulations start to harm the individuals themselves, then they are more likely to take measures to oppose the bill.

The author's sarcastic tone throughout the article conveys the conception that those people supporting this bill are misinformed and incorrect. In the sixth paragraph, the author says "The claims that plastic bags are worse for the environment than paper bags or cotton reusable bags are dubious at best." He also leads the reader to infer that supporters of the bill believe plastic bags are "evil incarnate" and "use government force to compel people to live the way they think best." In the first paragraph, the author talks of how "Californians dodged yet another nanny-state regulation." This sarcastic tone causes the audience to lost faith in these Environmentalists. It also causes the reader to question the motives of the bill and its supporters.

Through citing statistics, appealing to self interest and emotions, and utilizing sarcastic diction, Adam Summers conveys his beliefs that California should not pass a law banning plastic grocery bags.

Scoring Explanation Sample 5: This response scored a 3/3/4.

Reading—3: This response demonstrates effective comprehension of the source text, with the writer showing an understanding of both the central idea (*the plastic bag ban would be harmful for consumers and the environment*) and important details of the passage (*the most common plastic grocery bags, which "make up just 0.3 percent" of solid municipal waste; government . . . regulation of "what kind of container we can use to carry our groceries"*). Throughout the response, the writer conveys an understanding of the text with appropriate use of both quotations and paraphrases. There are also no errors of fact or interpretation. Overall, this response demonstrates proficient reading comprehension.

Analysis—3: This response demonstrates an understanding of the analytical task by offering an effective analysis of the source text. The writer centers the analysis on how Summers conveys his argument through *citing statistics, appealing to the audience's emotions and sense of self-interest, and utilizing sarcastic diction.* In each of these areas, the writer competently discusses the effect of Summers's argumentative strategies. For example, in the first body paragraph, the writer cites some of the statistical evidence in the source text and points out that *these statistics appeal to the reader's logic and ensure that they can follow a logical path to support the author and oppose the ban.* Further, the writer states that the statistics *cannot be easily argued against.* The analysis continues in the second body paragraph, in which the writer evaluates Summers's *patriotic asides* and the fact that they cause the reader to *feel violated by the government and want to look out for his rights.* The response is consistently focused on analyzing the effect of various argumentative strategies on the audience, and the writer chooses relevant support for the analysis. Overall, this response demonstrates proficient analysis.

Writing—4: This response demonstrates a highly effective use of language in this cohesive essay. The body paragraphs closely follow the central claim (*Adam Summers asserts that the plastic bag ban would be harmful . . . through citing statistics, appealing to the audience's emotions and sense of self-interests, and utilizing sarcastic diction*) presented in the introduction. There are some slight organizational mistakes that lead to a somewhat clumsy progression of ideas. For example, the last sentence of the introductory paragraph, although informative, does not enhance the introduction in any way or provide a smooth segue into the following paragraphs. However, these organizational mistakes are balanced by a consistent variety of sentence structures and precise word choice (*wake of environmental concerns, take measures to oppose the bill*) and language errors do not impede understanding. Overall, this response demonstrates advanced writing.

Student Sample 6 — Scores: 4/4/4

In Adam B. Summers' "Bag ban bad for freedom and environment" editorial for the San Diego Union-Tribune, he argues against the possible laws hindering Californians from using plastic bags at grocery stores. He believes they would do more harm than good, and that "a little reason and perspective is in order." By the end of this piece the reader will likely find themselves nodding in agreement with what Summers has to say, and this isn't just because he's right. Summers, like any good writer, employs tactical reasoning and persuasive devices to plead with the audience to take his side. In this article, he demonstrates many such devices.

"Plastic bags . . . make up only about 1.6 percent of all municipal solid waste materials," Summers ventures, his first utilization of a cold, hard fact. The truth in the numbers is undeniable, and he cites his sources promptly, making the statement that much more authentic. Knowledge is often viewed as power, and with information as direct as a statistic, Summers is handing that power to the reader – the power to agree with him. Not only does Summers spread the facts with numbers, he also does so with trends. He talks about the price increase in Ireland, and the documented health hazards of reusable bags. He uses the truth, backed by reliable sources, to infiltrate the readers' independent mind. His thoroughness in this regard carefully builds his argument against this piece of legislation, and this is just one of the many ways he spreads his opposition.

Additionally, Summers appeals to the ethnical and emotional side of individuals. With key phrases like "taxpayers will have to pony up" and "borne by consumers," Summers activates the nature of a human to act in their own self-interest. While one might view this as selfish, Summers reassures the reader that they are not alone in feeling this way, further contributing to his argument. With his statement that he "love[s] sea turtles as much as the next guy," Summers adds acceptance to those who don't care to act with regard for the environment. By putting himself beside the reader as a typical consumer, he equals them, and makes himself more likeable in the process. Appealing to environmentalists, too, Summers qualifies that they "have every right to try to convince people to adopt certain beliefs or lifestyles, but they do not have the right to use government force . . ." A statement such as this is an attempt to get readers of either persuasion on his side, and his ingenius qualification only adds to the strength of his argument.

An article focusing on the choice between "paper or plastic," and how that choice might be taken away certainly seems fairly standard, but by adjusting his diction (i.e. using well known phrases, selecting words with strong connotations), Summers creates something out of the ordinary. It is with word choice such as "recycled rather than trashed" that the author reveals the legislations intent to stir up a repeat bill. Because the issue at hand is one of waste and environmental protection, his humorous diction provides a link between he and the audience, revealing not only an opportunity to laugh, but also reinforcement of the concept that Summers is trustworthy and just like everyone else. Negative words with specifically poor connotations also aid

Summers in his persuasive struggle. "Reprieve," "dubious," "bureaucracy," and "evil incarnate" all depict a disparaging tone of annoyance and anger, surely helping Summers to spread his message.

It is through many rhetorical devices that Summers sells his argument. Powerful diction, qualification, ethos, pathos, logos, and informative facts all contribute to an exceptionally well-written argument. It is his utilization of these practices and more that make this article worthy of recognition. Once one reads the piece, they'll be nodding along in accordance with Summers, and it isn't for no reason.

Scoring Explanation Sample 6: This response scored a 4/4/4.

Reading—4: This response demonstrates thorough comprehension of the source text. The writer provides a brief summary of Summers's main point in the introductory paragraph (*he argues against the possible laws hindering Californians from using plastic bags at grocery stores*) and throughout the response uses a mixture of direct quotations and paraphrases to show an understanding of the central idea and important details from the source text interrelate (*He talks about the price increase in Ireland, and the documented health hazards of reusable bags; the legislations intent to stir up a repeat bill*). Further, the writer demonstrates an understanding of how the central idea and important details interrelate by consistently relating details to the main argument of the source text. The response is free from errors of fact or interpretation. Overall, this response demonstrates advanced reading comprehension.

Analysis—4: This response demonstrates a sophisticated understanding of the analytical task by offering an insightful analysis of Summers's employment of *tactical reasoning and persuasive devices to plead with the audience to take his side*. The writer puts forth a thorough evaluation of Summers's use of evidence, reasoning, and stylistic and persuasive elements by continually analyzing even the smallest features of Summers's piece. For example, when citing a fact that Summers provides (*"Plastic bags . . . make up only about 1.6 percent of all municipal solid waste materials"*), the writer focuses on *the truth in the numbers* as well as Summers's deliberate choice to share the fact's source and the effect doing so has on Summers's argument. The writer continues the analysis by broadening the focus to a brief but sophisticated discussion of knowledge as power and the persuasive approach of *handing that power to the reader*. This type of well-considered evaluation continues throughout the response, during which the writer touches on Summers's appeals *to the ethical and emotional side of individuals* and Summers's use of diction to create *something out of the ordinary*. The response is focused on relevant and strategically chosen features of the source text in support of the writer's analysis. Overall, this essay demonstrates advanced analysis.

Writing—4: This response demonstrates highly effective command of language and cohesion. The response is organized around the writer's claim that readers *will likely find themselves nodding in agreement with what Summers has to say, and this isn't just because he's right* but also because of his use of *tactical reasoning and persuasive devices.* The response is highly organized and demonstrates a deliberate progression of ideas, with the writer seamlessly transitioning from point to point. Sentence structures are varied and often sophisticated (*While one might view this as selfish, Summers reassures the reader that they are not alone in feeling this way, further contributing to his argument*). Word choice is precise without tonal missteps (*tactical reasoning; his ingenius qualification only adds to the strength of his argument; disparaging tone of annoyance and anger*). The response shows a strong command of the conventions of standard written English and is virtually free of errors. Minor conventions errors (*Summers adds acceptance to those who don't care to act*; *and it isn't for no reason*) do not detract from the quality of the writing. Overall, this response demonstrates advanced writing ability.

Student Sample 7 — Scores: 4/4/4

"Paper or plastic?" This is often a question we are asked at our weekly and/or bi-weekly trip to the supermarket to purchase groceries to keep our family fed. Adam B. Summers has created a highly plausible argument that may change your answer next time you go grocery shopping. He has developed valid claims that are backed up with crucial evidence and has been able to properly persuade the reader by appealing to logos and other rhetorical strategies.

Summers uses his words and research to reason with the reader and explain to them why plastic bags really are the correct choice. A vast majority of people are misled about all of the waste that plastic bags cause when Summers writes, "... plastic bags, sacks, and wraps of all kinds (not just grocery bags) make up only about 1.6 percent of all municipal solid waste materials." This number is definitely lower that we all assume, going into this passage, and we are left surprised. Using reusable bags is a solution that others have come up with to attempt to create less waste, however Summers delivers an appealing argument. "... plastic bag bans lead to increased health problems due to food contamination from bacteria that remain in the reusable bags." This excerpt creates another claim that leaves the reader wondering if reusable bags are really worth it. These past two claims are connected well because they both draw the reader back to the idea of using plastic bags. Another claim by Summers, "... one unintended consequence of the plastic bag would likely be an increase in plastic bag purchases for these other purposes." These "other purposes" can be for lining trash bins, picking up after your dog on a walk, collecting kitty litter, and many more things we use plastic bags for. When the author brings in all of these additional uses of the plastic bag, we see the significance of the plastic bag and how much money we save by reusing them. A final claim by Summers, "The plastic bag ban would threaten the roughly 2,000 California jobs in the plastic bag manufacturing and recycling industry ..."

PRACTICE AT
satpractice.org

Your response doesn't have to be an exhaustive analysis of the passage. Focusing your essay on a few key points, with ample textual evidence and analysis, can yield a strong score.

Now the reader almost feels guilty because they do not want to take away jobs of others and the fact that some people even depend on shoppers using plastic bags. These two final claims are well connected because the author stressed the economic benefits of using plastic bags. Not only are these bags saving you money, but they also are keeping some people in work. These four ideas are successfully connected and convince the reader to use plastic bags over paper bags and other types of reusable bags.

Evidence is a key component of this passage and Summers is sure to include this when presenting us with key facts. He references important agencies such as the U.S. Environmental Protection Agency and includes a professor from the University of Pennsylvania, Jonathan Klick and a professor from George Mason University, Joshua D. Wright. The inclusion of this agency and these professors make the work of Summers credible and believable because us readers are confident of what we are being told is correct and true. Evidence he also uses are facts such as, ". . . plastic grocery bags produce fewer greenhouse gas emissions, require 70 percent less energy to make, generate 80 percent less waste." These facts back up Summers' claims that plastic bags are the better choice. Without evidence, his passage would not mean a thing to us readers and we would never be able to believe what he has said.

Persuasive elements are what make this passage successful. Summers has excellent ideas and credible evince, but his use of persuasion are what capture the reader. He appeals to logos when stating all of his claims about how using plastic bags can save you money and keep you from getting sick, but he also appeals to pathos because this passage described how plastic bags amount to less waste than most of us think and he wants to help us make the Earth a better place to live. Throwing examples at us, ". . . San Francisco's plastic bag ban in 2007 resulted in a subsequent spike in hospital emercgency room visits due to E. Coli, salmonella, . . ." persuade the reader as well. With rhetorical strategies and direct examples, Summers is clearly able to persuade the reader to choose plastic next time.

So what will you choose next time you're shopping for groceries with your family? Summers has made the choice obvious with his persuasive and effective passage. He has been able to develop several ideas and backed them up with evidence that us readers can trust. After reading this passage, there seems to be no other choice than plastic.

Scoring Explanation Sample 7: This response scored a 4/4/4.

Reading—4: This response demonstrates thorough comprehension of the source text. The writer shows an understanding of Summers's *highly plausible argument* and the important specifics that add detail to one of Summers's central claims: that *plastic bags really are the correct choice.* The writer accurately paraphrases ideas from Summers's text throughout the essay (*These "other purposes" can be for lining trash bins, picking up after your dog on a walk, collecting kitty litter, and many more things we use plastic bags for*), and the writer skillfully incorporates direct quotations within the response (*people are misled about all of the waste that plastic bags cause when Summers writes,*

". . . plastic bags, sacks and wraps of all kinds"). The writer also understands how the details in Summers's text interrelate to convey the main point of the piece (*valid claims that are backed up with crucial evidence; Summers uses his words and research to reason with the reader; These past two claims are connected well because they both draw the reader back to the idea; Summers has . . . credible evince, but his use of persuasion are what capture the reader*). The response is free from errors of fact or interpretation. Overall, this response demonstrates advanced reading comprehension.

Analysis—4: This response demonstrates a sophisticated understanding of the analytical task by offering an insightful analysis of the source text. Rather than relying on assertions as analysis, the writer thoroughly evaluates how Summers uses *words and research to reason with the reader*, how *evidence is a key component*, and how *persuasive elements . . . make this passage successful*. The writer is able to fully discuss each of these aspects of Summers's piece, using relevant examples from the source text as support for the writer's analysis. For example, the writer uses Summers's claim that *"The plastic bag ban would threaten the roughly 2,000 California jobs in the plastic bag manufacturing and recycling industry"* to discuss the guilt the writer perceives the reader feels in reaction to this claim. The writer also explains how Summers uses this claim in conjunction with discussion of alternate uses for plastic bags to stress *the economic benefits of using plastic bags*. The writer consistently focuses on the features of Summers's text that are most relevant and offers well-considered evaluations throughout the response. Overall, this response demonstrates advanced analysis.

Writing—4: This response demonstrates highly effective command of language and cohesion. Beginning with the skillful introduction, the writer constructs a response that demonstrates a deliberate and highly effective progression of ideas, starting with an examination of Summers's claims and evidence and ending with emphasis on the use of persuasive elements. This skillful control over organization occurs at the body paragraph level as well, as the writer connects pieces of evidence from different parts of the source text within each paragraph. The writer's word choice is precise (*a highly plausible argument, a key component, the inclusion of this agency*), and sentence structures are varied and sophisticated. This response demonstrates a strong command of written English and is virtually free of errors. Overall, this response demonstrates advanced writing.

[illegible]

Analysis—1. The [illegible]

[illegible]

[illegible]

PART 3

Math

CHAPTER 15

About the SAT Math Test

Focus on Math That Matters Most

Instead of testing you on every math topic there is, the SAT Math Test focuses on the topics you're most likely to encounter in college and career. The three areas of focus for math in the SAT are

- Heart of Algebra
- Problem Solving and Data Analysis
- Passport to Advanced Math

Heart of Algebra focuses on linear equations, systems of linear equations, and functions that are found in many fields of study. These questions ask you to create equations that represent a situation and solve equations and systems of equations as well as to make connections between different representations of linear relationships.

Problem Solving and Data Analysis includes using ratios, percentages, and proportional reasoning to solve problems in real-world situations, including science, social science, and other contexts. It also includes describing relationships shown graphically and analyzing statistical data. This group of skills is really about being quantitatively literate and demonstrating a command of the math that resonates throughout college courses, career training programs, and everyday life.

These two areas of math provide a powerful foundation for the math you will do in the future.

Passport to Advanced Math is the third area of focus in the SAT Math Test. The problems in this area focus on the math you will need to pursue further study in a discipline such as science or economics and for career opportunities in the STEM fields of science, technology, engineering, and math. The Passport to Advanced Math area requires familiarity with more-complex equations or functions, which will prepare you for calculus and advanced courses in statistics.

REMEMBER

Questions on the SAT Math Test are distributed among these three topics with 19 Heart of Algebra questions, 17 Problem Solving and Data Analysis questions, and 16 Passport to Advanced Math questions. The remaining six questions test your understanding of additional topics in math such as area, volume, circles, triangles, and trigonometry.

REMEMBER

The SAT Math Test requires a stronger and deeper understanding of a relatively small number of math topics that are especially relevant in college and in many careers.

The SAT Math Test also contains questions in **Additional Topics in Math**. Some of these problems focus on key concepts from geometry, including applications of volume, area, surface area, and coordinate geometry; similarity, which is another instance of proportional reasoning; and properties of lines, angles, triangles and other polygons, and circles. There are also problems that focus on the fundamental ideas of trigonometry and radian measure, which are essential for study in STEM fields. Finally, there are problems involving the arithmetic of complex numbers, another concept needed for more-advanced study in math and the STEM fields.

What the Math Test Assesses

The SAT Math Test assesses your understanding of mathematical concepts, your procedural skill and fluency in math, and your ability to apply those concepts and skills to real-world problems.

Conceptual understanding and procedural skill and fluency are complementary. Together, they lead to a thorough understanding of mathematical ideas and methods for solving problems. Questions on the SAT Math Test assess these skills in various ways because the ability to use mathematical ideas and methods flexibly shows an understanding of math that can be applied to a wide variety of settings.

A key to the relationship between fluency and conceptual understanding is recognizing and making use of structure. Recognizing structure allows you to understand mathematical relationships in a coherent manner and making use of it allows you both to apply these relationships more widely and to extend these relationships in useful ways. Many of the examples and sample questions in the following chapters are more simply and deeply understood (and more quickly solved!) if you observe structure in the mathematics of the problem.

PRACTICE AT
satpractice.org

As is mentioned throughout this guide, the best preparation for the SAT is to work hard in your high school classes. Applying your math skills in your science and social studies classes will prepare you for many of the questions you'll come across on the SAT Math Test.

Problems Grounded in Real-World Contexts

The SAT Math Test features multistep problems with applications in science, social science, career scenarios, and other real-life contexts. In some cases, you will be presented with a scenario and then asked several questions related to the same context. You learn specific math skills in your math classes, and these skills are applied in your science and social studies classes. When you use your mathematical skills outside of the math classroom, you are preparing for the SAT.

The Makeup of the SAT Math Test

Calculator and No-Calculator Portions

There are calculator and no-calculator portions on the SAT Math Test. A calculator is a tool, and the ability to determine when to use it is a skill that you're expected to have. In the calculator portion, many questions don't require a calculator and many questions can be completed faster without using a calculator. In general, the questions in the calculator portion are more complex than those in the no-calculator portion. Questions in the no-calculator portion emphasize your ability to do problems efficiently and accurately.

You should bring a calculator to use on the calculator portion of the SAT Math Test. A scientific or graphing calculator is recommended, and familiarity with your calculator may provide an advantage on some questions. Every question on the SAT can be solved without a calculator; however, strategically deciding when to use a calculator will reduce the time required to complete the test. Using a calculator can also help you avoid missing a question because of computation errors.

REMEMBER

You're permitted to use a calculator on one portion of the SAT Math Test, so be sure to bring a calculator with you to the test. However, many questions don't require a calculator and can actually be solved more quickly without one, so use careful judgment in deciding when to use it.

PRACTICE AT
satpractice.org

Make sure that you're very familiar with and comfortable using the calculator you bring with you on test day. Practice using the calculator you'll use on the test throughout your test preparation.

Multiple-Choice and Gridded-Response Questions

About 80% of the questions on the Math Test are multiple-choice. Each multiple-choice question consists of a question followed by four options. There is only one correct answer and there is no penalty for selecting an incorrect answer. Therefore, you should provide an answer to every question on the test.

The other questions on the Math Test are gridded-response questions (also called student-produced response questions), and these questions make up about 20% of the test. The answer to each gridded-response question is a number (fraction, decimal, or positive integer) that you'll enter on the answer sheet into a grid like the one shown on the next page. Like all questions on the SAT, there is no penalty for answering a gridded-response question incorrectly.

Examples of filled-in answer grids are shown on the next page. Note that in addition to whole numbers, you may also enter a fraction line or a decimal point. Further details on how to grid your answers are provided in Chapter 21.

PRACTICE AT
satpractice.org

There is no penalty for selecting an incorrect answer on the SAT, so never leave a question blank! On questions that you're not sure how to solve, eliminate as many answer choices as you can, and then guess from among the remaining choices.

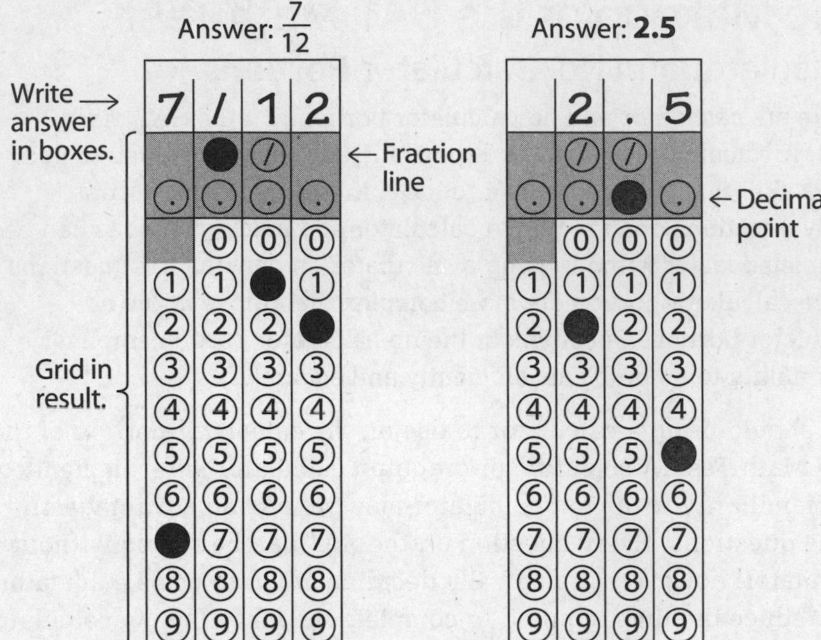

REMEMBER

On gridded-response questions, you must fill in the circles that correspond to your answer. You won't receive credit if you write your answer only in the boxes at the top of the grid.

PRACTICE AT

satpractice.org

Make sure to get lots of practice using the facts and formulas provided in the Reference section in the Math Test directions. Practicing with these facts and formulas will ensure you can use them accurately and efficiently.

Mathematics Reference Information

The Math Test includes the reference information shown below. You may find these facts and formulas helpful as you answer some of the test questions, but make sure you have plenty of practice with this information beforehand. To do well, you'll need to be comfortable working with these facts and formulas.

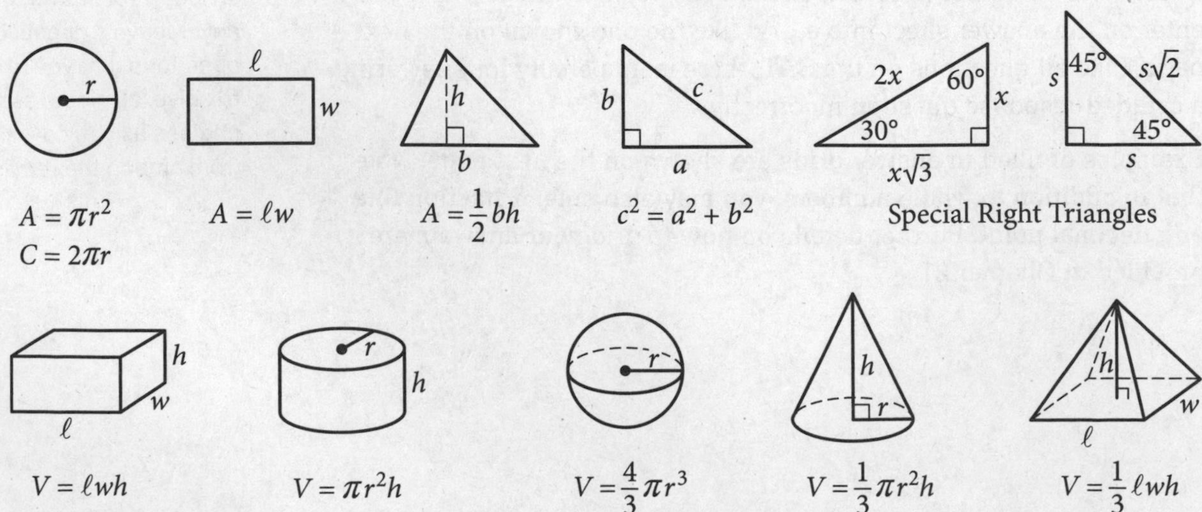

The number of degrees of arc in a circle is 360.

The number of radians of arc in a circle is 2π.

The sum of the measures in degrees of the angles of a triangle is 180.

Test Summary

The following table summarizes the key content dimensions of the SAT Math Test.

SAT Math Test Content Specifications

Time Allotted	**80 minutes**	
Calculator Portion (38 questions)	55 minutes	
No-Calculator Portion (20 questions)	25 minutes	
	Number	**Percentage of Test**
Total Questions	**58 questions**	**100%**
Multiple-Choice (MC, 4 options)	45 questions	78%
Student-Produced Response (SPR—grid-in)	13 questions	22%
Contribution of Questions to Subscores		
Heart of Algebra	**19 questions**	**33%**
Analyzing and fluently solving linear equations and systems of linear equations		
Creating linear equations and inequalities to represent relationships between quantities and to solve problems		
Understanding and using the relationship between linear equations and inequalities and their graphs to solve problems		
Problem Solving and Data Analysis	**17 questions**	**29%**
Creating and analyzing relationships using ratios, proportional relationships, percentages, and units		
Representing and analyzing quantitative data		
Finding and applying probabilities in context		
Passport to Advanced Math	**16 questions**	**28%**
Identifying and creating equivalent algebraic expressions		
Creating, analyzing, and fluently solving quadratic and other nonlinear equations		
Creating, using, and graphing exponential, quadratic, and other nonlinear functions		

PRACTICE AT
satpractice.org

Take plenty of time to familiarize yourself with this table. Knowing exactly what the Math Test consists of, including the number of questions and time allotted as well as the distribution of question categories, will help you to feel confident and prepared on test day.

PRACTICE AT
satpractice.org

As you progress through your test practice, assess which math skills you're strongest in and which you have the greatest room for improvement in. Allocate your study time appropriately, and make use of the many resources available to you on the Khan Academy website (satpractice.org).

Additional Topics in Math*	**6 questions**	**10%**
Solving problems related to area and volume		
Applying definitions and theorems related to lines, angles, triangles, and circles		
Working with right triangles, the unit circle, and trigonometric functions		
Contribution of Questions to Cross-Test Scores		
Analysis in Science	8 questions	14%
Analysis in History/Social Studies	8 questions	14%

*Questions under Additional Topics in Math contribute to the total Math Test score but do not contribute to a subscore within the Math Test.

As indicated in the content specifications previously, the Math Test has two portions. One is a 55-minute portion — 38 questions for which you are permitted to use a calculator. The other is a 25-minute portion — 20 questions for which you are not permitted to use a calculator. The blueprint for each portion is shown below.

Calculator Portion

	Number of Questions	% of Test
Total Questions	**38**	**100%**
Multiple-Choice (MC)	30	79%
Student-Produced Response (SPR—grid-in)	8	21%
Content Categories	**38**	**100%**
Heart of Algebra	11	29%
Problem Solving and Data Analysis	17	45%
Passport to Advanced Math	7	18%
Additional Topics in Math	3	8%
Time Allocated	**55 minutes**	

No-Calculator Portion

	Number of Questions	% of Test
Total Questions	**20**	**100%**
Multiple-Choice (MC)	15	75%
Student-Produced Response (SPR—grid-in)	5	25%
Content Categories	**20**	**100%**
Heart of Algebra	8	40%
Passport to Advanced Math	9	45%
Additional Topics in Math	3	15%
Time Allocated	**25 minutes**	

REMEMBER

Don't be intimidated by the fact that you can't use a calculator on one of the SAT Math portions. Questions in the no-calculator portion are more conceptual in nature and don't require a calculator to be solved.

CHAPTER 16

Heart of Algebra

Heart of Algebra questions on the SAT Math Test focus on the mastery of linear equations, systems of linear equations, and linear functions. The ability to analyze and create linear equations, inequalities, and functions is essential for success in college and career, as is the ability to solve linear equations and systems fluently.

Heart of Algebra questions vary significantly in form and appearance. They may be straightforward fluency exercises or pose challenges of strategy or understanding, such as interpreting the relationship between graphical and algebraic representations or solving as a process of reasoning. You'll be required to demonstrate both procedural skill and a deep understanding of concepts.

The questions in Heart of Algebra include both multiple-choice questions and student-produced response questions. The use of a calculator is permitted for some questions in this domain and not permitted for others.

Heart of Algebra is one of the three SAT Math Test subscores, reported on a scale of 1 to 15.

Let's explore the content and skills assessed by Heart of Algebra questions.

REMEMBER

The SAT Math Test requires you to demonstrate a deep understanding of several core algebra topics, namely linear equations, systems of linear equations, and linear functions. These topics are fundamental to the learning and work often required in college and career.

Linear Equations, Linear Inequalities, and Linear Functions in Context

When you use algebra to analyze and solve a problem in real life, a key step is to represent the context of the problem algebraically. To do this, you may need to define one or more variables that represent quantities in the context. Then you need to write one or more expressions, equations, inequalities, or functions that represent the relationships described in the context. For example, once you write an equation that represents the context, you solve the equation. Then you interpret the solution to the equation in terms of the context. Questions on the SAT Math Test may assess your ability to accomplish any or all of these steps.

Example 1

In 2014, County X had 783 miles of paved roads. Starting in 2015, the county has been building 8 miles of new paved roads each year. At this rate, how many miles of paved road will County X have in 2030? (Assume that no paved roads go out of service.)

PRACTICE AT
satpractice.org

Many Heart of Algebra questions such as this one will require you to accomplish the following steps:

1. Define one or more variables that represent quantities in the question.
2. Write one or more equations, expressions, inequalities, or functions that represent the relationships described in the question.
3. Solve the equation, and interpret the solution in terms of what the question is asking.

Ample practice with each of these steps will help you develop your math skills and knowledge.

The first step in answering this question is to decide what variable or variables you need to define. The question is asking how the number of miles of paved road in County X depends on the year. This can be represented using n, the number of years after 2014. Then, since the question says that County X had 783 miles of paved road in 2014 and is building 8 miles of new paved roads each year, the expression $783 + 8n$ gives the number of miles of paved roads in County X in the year that is n years after 2014. The year 2030 is $2030 - 2014 = 16$ years after 2014; thus, the year 2030 corresponds to $n = 16$. Hence, to find the number of miles of paved roads in County X in 2030, substitute 16 for n in the expression $783 + 8n$, giving $783 + 8(16) = 783 + 128 = 911$. Therefore, at the given rate of building, County X will have 911 miles of paved roads in 2030.

(Note that this example has no choices. It is a student-produced response question. On the SAT, you would grid your answer in the spaces provided on the answer sheet.)

There are different questions that can be asked about the same context.

Example 2

In 2014, County X had 783 miles of paved roads. Starting in 2015, the county has been building 8 miles of new paved roads each year. At this rate, if n is the number of years after 2014, which of the following functions f gives the number of miles of paved road there will be in County X? (Assume that no paved roads go out of service.)

A) $f(n) = 8 + 783n$

B) $f(n) = 2{,}014 + 783n$

C) $f(n) = 783 + 8n$

D) $f(n) = 2{,}014 + 8n$

REMEMBER

There are several different ways you may be tested on the same underlying algebra concepts. Practicing a variety of questions, with different contexts, is a good way to ensure you'll be ready for the questions you'll come across on the SAT.

This question already defines the variable and asks you to create or identify a function that describes the context. The discussion in Example 1 shows that the correct answer is choice C.

Example 3

In 2014, County X had 783 miles of paved roads. Starting in 2015, the county has been building 8 miles of new paved roads each year. At this rate, in which year will County X first have at least 1,000 miles of paved roads? (Assume that no paved roads go out of service.)

In this question, you must create and solve an inequality. As in Example 1, let n be the number of years after 2014. Then the expression $783 + 8n$ gives the number of miles of paved roads in County X. The question is asking when there will first be at least 1,000 miles of paved roads in County X. This condition can be represented by the inequality $783 + 8n \geq 1{,}000$. To find the year in which there will first be at least 1,000 miles of paved roads, you solve this inequality for n. Subtracting 783 from each side of $783 + 8n \geq 1{,}000$ gives $8n \geq 217$. Then dividing each side of $8n \geq 217$ by 8 gives $n \geq 27.125$. Note that an important part of relating the inequality $783 + 8n \geq 1{,}000$ back to the context is to notice that n is counting calendar years, and so the value of n must be an integer. The least value of n that satisfies $783 + 8n \geq 1{,}000$ is 27.125, but the year $2014 + 27.125 = 2041.125$ does not make sense as an answer, and in 2041, there would be only $783 + 8(27) = 999$ miles of paved roads in the county. Therefore, the variable n needs to be rounded up to the next integer, and so the least possible value of n is 28. Therefore, the year that County X will first have at least 1,000 miles of paved roads is 28 years after 2014, which is 2042.

PRACTICE AT
satpractice.org

Solving an equation or inequality is often only part of the problem-solving process. You'll also need to interpret the solution in the context of the question, so be sure to remind yourself of the question's context and the meaning of the variables you solved for before selecting your answer.

In Example 1, once the variable n was defined, you needed to find an expression that represents the number of miles of paved road in terms of n. In other questions, creating the correct expression, equation, or function may require a more insightful understanding of the context.

Example 4

To edit a manuscript, Miguel charges \$50 for the first 2 hours and \$20 per hour after the first 2 hours. Which of the following expresses the amount, C, in dollars, Miguel charges if it takes him x hours to edit a manuscript, where $x > 2$?

A) $C = 20x$

B) $C = 20x + 10$

C) $C = 20x + 50$

D) $C = 20x + 90$

The question defines the variables C and x and asks you to express C in terms of x. To create the correct equation, you must note that since the \$50 that Miguel charges pays for his first 2 hours of editing, he charges \$20 per hour only *after* the first 2 hours. Thus, if it takes x hours for Miguel to edit a manuscript, he charges \$50 for the first 2 hours and \$20 per hour for the remaining time, which is $x - 2$ hours. Thus, his total charge, C, in dollars, can be written as $C = 50 + 20(x - 2)$, where $x > 2$. This does not match any of the choices. But when the right-hand side of $C = 50 + 20(x - 2)$ is expanded, you get $C = 50 + 20x - 40$, or $C = 20x + 10$, which is choice B.

PRACTICE AT
satpractice.org

When the solution you arrive at doesn't match any of the answer choices, consider if expanding, simplifying, or rearranging your solution will cause it to match an answer choice. Sometimes, this extra step is needed to arrive at the correct answer.

As with Examples 1 to 3, there are different questions that could be asked about this context. For example, you could be asked to find how long it took Miguel to edit a manuscript if he charged \$370.

In some questions on the SAT Math Test, you'll be given a function that represents a context and be asked to find the value of the output of the function given an input or the value of the input that corresponds to a given output.

Example 5

A builder uses the function g defined by $g(x) = 80x + 10{,}000$ to estimate the cost $g(x)$, in dollars, to build a one-story home of planned floor area of x square feet. If the builder estimates that the cost to build a certain one-story home is \$106,000, what is the planned floor area, in square feet, of the home?

This question asks you to find the value of the input of a function when you are given the value of the output and the equation of the function. The estimated cost of the home, in dollars, is the output of the function g for a one-story home of planned floor area of x square feet. That is, the output of the function, $g(x)$, is 106,000, and you need to find the value of the input x that gives an output of 106,000. To do this, substitute 106,000 for $g(x)$ in the equation that defines g: $106{,}000 = 80x + 10{,}000$. Now solve for x: First, subtract 10,000 from each side of the equation $106{,}000 = 80x + 10{,}000$, which gives $96{,}000 = 80x$. Then, divide each side of $96{,}000 = 80x$ by 80, which gives $1{,}200 = x$. Therefore, a one-story home with an estimated cost of \$106,000 to build has a planned floor area of 1,200 square feet.

Systems of Linear Equations and Inequalities in Context

You may need to define more than one variable and create more than one equation or inequality to represent a context and answer a question. There are questions on the SAT Math Test that require you to create and solve a system of equations or create a system of inequalities.

PRACTICE AT
satpractice.org

You can use either of two approaches — combination or substitution — when solving a system of linear equations. One may get you to the answer more quickly than the other, depending on the equations you're working with and what you're solving for. Practice using both to give you greater flexibility on test day.

Example 6

Maizah bought a pair of pants and a briefcase at a department store. The sum of the prices of the pants and the briefcase before sales tax was \$130.00. There was no sales tax on the pants and a 9% sales tax on the briefcase. The total Maizah paid, including the sales tax, was \$136.75. What was the price, in dollars, of the pants?

To answer the question, you first need to define the variables. The question discusses the prices of a pair of pants and a briefcase and asks you to find the price of the pants. So it's appropriate to let P be the price, in dollars, of the pants and to let B be the price, in dollars, of the briefcase. Since the sum of the prices before sales tax was

\$130.00, the equation $P + B = 130$ is true. A sales tax of 9% was added to the price of the briefcase. Since 9% is equal to 0.09, the price of the briefcase with tax was $B + 0.09B = 1.09B$. There was no sales tax on the pants, and the total Maizah paid, including tax, was \$136.75, so the equation $P + 1.09B = 136.75$ holds.

Now, you need to solve the system

$$P + B = 130$$
$$P + 1.09B = 136.75$$

Subtracting the sides of the first equation from the corresponding sides of the second equation gives you $(P + 1.09B) - (P + B) = 136.75 - 130$, which simplifies to $0.09B = 6.75$. Now you can divide each side of $0.09B = 6.75$ by 0.09. This gives you $B = \frac{6.75}{0.09} = 75$. This is the value of B, the price, in dollars, of the briefcase. The question asks for the price, in dollars, of the pants, which is P. You can substitute 75 for B in the equation $P + B = 130$, which gives you $P + 75 = 130$, or $P = 130 - 75 = 55$, so the pants cost \$55.

REMEMBER

While this question may seem complex, as it involves numerous steps, solving it requires a strong understanding of the same underlying principles outlined earlier: defining variables, creating equations to represent relationships, solving equations, and interpreting the solution.

Example 7

Each morning, John jogs at 6 miles per hour and rides a bike at 12 miles per hour. His goal is to jog and ride his bike a total of at least 9 miles in no more than 1 hour. If John jogs j miles and rides his bike b miles, which of the following systems of inequalities represents John's goal?

A) $\frac{j}{6} + \frac{b}{12} \le 1$
$j + b \ge 9$

B) $\frac{j}{6} + \frac{b}{12} \ge 1$
$j + b \le 9$

C) $6j + 12b \ge 9$
$j + b \le 1$

D) $6j + 12b \le 1$
$j + b \ge 9$

John jogs j miles and rides his bike b miles; his goal to jog and ride his bike a total of at least 9 miles is represented by the inequality $j + b \ge 9$. This eliminates choices B and C.

Since rate × time = distance, it follows that time is equal to distance divided by rate. John jogs j miles at 6 miles per hour, so the time he jogs is equal to $\frac{j \text{ miles}}{6 \text{ miles/hour}} = \frac{j}{6}$ hours. Similarly, since John rides his bike b miles at 12 miles per hour, the time he rides his bike is $\frac{b}{12}$ hours. Thus, John's goal to complete his jog and his bike ride in no more than 1 hour can be represented by the inequality $\frac{j}{6} + \frac{b}{12} \le 1$. The system $j + b \ge 9$ and $\frac{j}{6} + \frac{b}{12} \le 1$ is choice A.

PRACTICE AT
satpractice.org

In Example 7, the answer choices each contain two parts. Use this to your advantage by tackling one part at a time and eliminating answers that don't work.

PRACTICE AT
satpractice.org

You should be able to quickly rearrange equations such as the distance formula (distance = rate × time) by solving for any of the variables. Example 7 requires you to solve the equation for time.

Fluency in Solving Linear Equations, Linear Inequalities, and Systems of Linear Equations

Creating linear equations, linear inequalities, and systems of linear equations that represent a context is a key skill for success in college and career. It's also essential to be able to fluently solve linear equations, linear inequalities, and systems of linear equations. Some of the Heart of Algebra questions present equations, inequalities, or systems without a context and directly assess your fluency in solving them.

Some fluency questions permit the use of a calculator; other questions do not permit the use of a calculator and test your ability to solve equations, inequalities, and systems of equations by hand. Even for questions where a calculator is permitted, you may be able to answer the question more quickly without using a calculator, such as in Example 9. Part of what the SAT Math Test assesses is your ability to decide when using a calculator to answer a question is appropriate. Example 8 is an example of a question that could appear on the no-calculator portion of the Math Test.

Example 8

$$3\left(\frac{1}{2}-y\right)=\frac{3}{5}+15y$$

What is the solution to the equation above?

Using the distributive property to expand the left-hand side of the equation gives $\frac{3}{2} - 3y = \frac{3}{5} + 15y$. Adding $3y$ to both sides of the equation and then subtracting $\frac{3}{5}$ from both sides of the equation gives $\frac{3}{2} - \frac{3}{5} = 18y$. The equation may be easier to solve if it's transformed into an equation without fractions; to do this, multiply each side of $\frac{3}{2} - \frac{3}{5} = 18y$ by 10, which is the least common multiple of the denominators 2 and 5. This gives $\frac{30}{2} - \frac{30}{5} = 180y$, which can be simplified further to $15 - 6 = 180y$, or $9 = 180y$. Therefore, $y = \frac{1}{20}$.

REMEMBER

While a calculator is permitted on one portion of the SAT Math Test, it's important to not over-rely on a calculator. Some questions, such as Example 9, can be solved more efficiently without using a calculator. Your ability to choose when to use and when not to use a calculator is one of the things the SAT Math Test assesses, so be sure to practice this in your studies.

Example 9

$$-2(3x - 2.4) = -3(3x - 2.4)$$

What is the solution to the equation above?

You could solve this in the same way as Example 8, by multiplying everything out and simplifying. But the structure of the equation reveals that −2 times a quantity, $3x - 2.4$, is equal to −3 times the same quantity. This is only possible if the quantity $3x - 2.4$ is equal to zero. Thus, $3x - 2.4 = 0$, or $3x = 2.4$. Therefore, the solution is $x = 0.8$.

Example 10

$$-2x = 4y + 6$$
$$2(2y + 3) = 3x - 5$$

What is the solution (x, y) to the system of equations above?

This is an example of a system you can solve quickly by substitution. Since $-2x = 4y + 6$, it follows that $-x = 2y + 3$. Now you can substitute $-x$ for $2y + 3$ in the second equation. This gives you $2(-x) = 3x - 5$, which simplifies to $5x = 5$, or $x = 1$. Substituting 1 for x in the first equation gives you $-2 = 4y + 6$, which simplifies to $4y = -8$, or $y = -2$. Therefore, the solution to the system is $(1, -2)$.

In the preceding examples, you have found a unique solution to linear equations and to systems of two linear equations in two variables. But not all such equations and systems have solutions, and some have infinitely many solutions. Some questions on the SAT Math Test assess your ability to determine whether an equation or a system has one solution, no solutions, or infinitely many solutions.

PRACTICE AT
satpractice.org

In Example 6, the elimination method yields an efficient solution to the question. In Example 10, substitution turns out to be an efficient approach. These examples illustrate the benefits of knowing both approaches and thinking critically about which approach may be more efficient on a given question.

The Relationships among Linear Equations, Lines in the Coordinate Plane, and the Contexts They Describe

A system of two linear equations in two variables can be solved by graphing the lines in the coordinate plane. For example, you can graph the equations of the system in the xy-plane in Example 10:

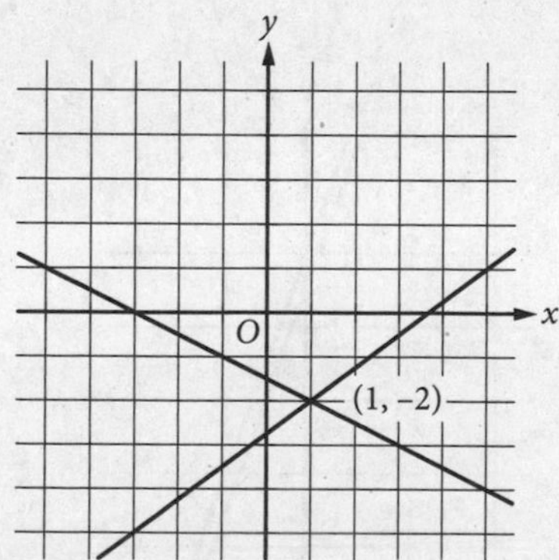

The point of intersection gives the solution to the system.

If the equations in a system of two linear equations in two variables are graphed, each graph will be a line. There are three possibilities:

1. The lines intersect in one point. In this case, the system has a unique solution.

PRACTICE AT

satpractice.org

Graphing systems of two linear equations is another effective approach to solving them. Practice arranging linear equations into $y = mx + b$ form and graphing them in the coordinate plane.

REMEMBER

When the graphs of a system of two linear equations are parallel lines, as in Example 11, the system has zero solutions. If the question states that a system of two linear equations has an infinite number of solutions, as in Example 12, the equations must be equivalent.

PRACTICE AT

satpractice.org

The equations in the system in Example 11 are in a form that allows you to quickly find both the x-intercept and the y-intercept of the graph of the equation. For example, the graph of $y + 3x = 2$ has an x-intercept of $\left(\frac{2}{3}, 0\right)$ because if $y = 0$, then $3x = 2$ and $x = \frac{2}{3}$. Similarly, the graph has a y-intercept of (0, 2) because if $x = 0$, then $y = 2$.

2. The lines are parallel. In this case, the system has no solution.
3. The lines are identical. In this case, every point on the line is a solution, and so the system has infinitely many solutions.

One way that the second and third cases can be identified is to put the equations of the system in slope-intercept form. If the lines have the same slope and different y-intercepts, they are parallel; if both the slope and the y-intercept are the same, the lines are identical.

How are the second and third cases represented algebraically? Examples 11 and 12 answer this question.

Example 11

$$2y + 6x = 3$$

$$y + 3x = 2$$

How many solutions (x, y) are there to the system of equations above?

A) Zero

B) One

C) Two

D) More than two

If you multiply each side of $y + 3x = 2$ by 2, you get $2y + 6x = 4$. Then subtracting each side of $2y + 6x = 3$ from the corresponding side of $2y + 6x = 4$ gives $0 = 1$. This is a false statement. Therefore, the system has zero solutions (x, y).

Alternatively, you could graph the two equations. The graphs are parallel lines, so there are no points of intersection.

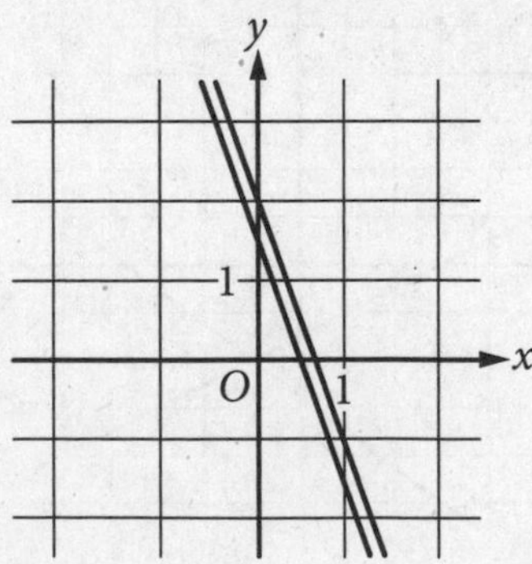

Example 12

$$3s - 2t = a$$

$$-15s + bt = -7$$

In the system of equations above, a and b are constants. If the system has infinitely many solutions, what is the value of a?

If a system of two linear equations in two variables has infinitely many solutions, the two equations in the system must be equivalent. Since the two equations are presented in the same form, the second equation must be equal to the first equation multiplied by a constant. Since the coefficient of s in the second equation is −5 times the coefficient of s in the first equation, multiply each side of the first equation by −5. This gives you the system

$$-15s + 10t = -5a$$
$$-15s + bt = -7$$

Since these two equations are equivalent and have the same coefficient of s, the coefficients of t and the constants on the right-hand side must also be the same. Thus, $b = 10$ and $-5a = -7$. Therefore, the value of a is $\frac{7}{5}$.

There will also be questions on the SAT Math Test that assess your knowledge of the relationship between the algebraic and the geometric representations of a line, that is, between an equation of a line and its graph. The key concepts are

- If the slopes of line ℓ and line k are each defined (that is, if neither line is a vertical line), then
  - Line ℓ and line k are parallel if and only if they have the same slope.
  - Line ℓ and line k are perpendicular if and only if the product of their slopes is −1.

Example 13

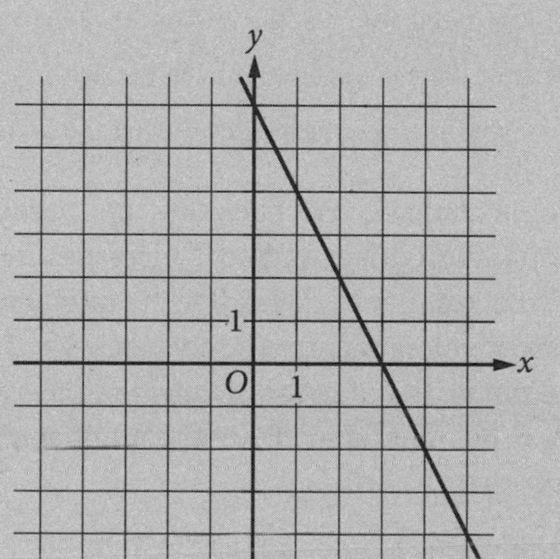

The graph of line k is shown in the xy-plane above. Which of the following is an equation of a line that is perpendicular to line k?

A) $y = -2x + 1$

B) $y = -\frac{1}{2}x + 2$

C) $y = \frac{1}{2}x + 3$

D) $y = 2x + 4$

REMEMBER

The SAT Math Test will further assess your understanding of linear equations by, for instance, asking you to select a linear equation that describes a given graph, select a graph that describes a given linear equation, or determine how a graph may be affected by a change in its equation.

Note that the graph of line k passes through the points (0, 6) and (3, 0). Thus, the slope of line k is $\frac{0-6}{3-0} = -2$. Since the product of the slopes of perpendicular lines is -1, a line that is perpendicular to line k will have slope $\frac{1}{2}$. All the choices are in slope-intercept form, and so the coefficient of x is the slope of the line represented by the equation. Therefore, choice C, $y = \frac{1}{2}x + 3$, is an equation of a line with slope $\frac{1}{2}$, and thus this line is perpendicular to line k.

PRACTICE AT
satpractice.org

Example 13 requires a strong understanding of slope as well as the ability to calculate slope: slope is equal to rise over run, or the change in the y-value divided by the change in the x-value. Parallel lines have slopes that are equal. Perpendicular lines have slopes whose product is -1.

As we've noted, some contexts can be described with a linear equation. The graph of a linear equation is a line. A nonvertical line has geometric properties such as its slope and its y-intercept. These geometric properties can often be interpreted in terms of the context. The SAT Math Test has questions that assess your ability to make these interpretations. For example, look back at the contexts in Examples 1 to 3. You created a linear function, $f(n) = 783 + 8n$, that describes the number of miles of paved road County X will have n years after 2014. This equation can be graphed in the coordinate plane, with n on the horizontal axis and $f(n)$ on the vertical axis. The points of this graph lie on a line with slope 8 and vertical intercept 783. The slope, 8, gives the number of miles of new paved roads added each year, and the vertical intercept gives the number of miles of paved roads in 2014, the year that corresponds to $n = 0$.

Example 14

A voter registration drive was held in Town Y. The number of voters, V, registered T days after the drive began can be estimated by the equation $V = 3{,}450 + 65T$. What is the best interpretation of the number 65 in this equation?

A) The number of registered voters at the beginning of the registration drive

B) The number of registered voters at the end of the registration drive

C) The total number of voters registered during the drive

D) The number of voters registered each day during the drive

The correct answer is choice D. For each day that passes, it is the next day of the registration drive, and so T increases by 1. In the given equation, when T, the number of days after the drive began, increases by 1, V, the number of voters registered, becomes $V = 3{,}450 + 65(T + 1) = 3{,}450 + 65T + 65$. That is, the number of voters registered increased by 65 for each day of the drive. Therefore, 65 is the number of voters registered each day during the drive.

You should note that choice A describes the number 3,450, and the numbers described by choices B and C can be found only if you know how many days the registration drive lasted; this information is not given in the question.

Mastery of linear equations, systems of linear equations, and linear functions is built upon key skills such as analyzing rates and ratios. Several key skills are discussed in the next domain, Problem Solving and Data Analysis.

CHAPTER 17

Problem Solving and Data Analysis

The Problem Solving and Data Analysis questions on the SAT Math Test assess your ability to use your math understanding and skills to solve problems set in the real world. The questions ask you to create a representation of a problem, consider the units involved, pay attention to the meaning of quantities, know and use different properties of mathematical operations and representations, and apply key principles of statistics. Special focus in this domain is given to mathematical models. You may be asked to create and use a model and to understand the distinction between the predictions of a model and the data that has been collected. Models are representations of real-life contexts. They help us to explain or interpret the behavior of certain components of a system and to predict results that are as yet unobserved or unmeasured.

The questions involve quantitative reasoning about ratios, rates, and proportional relationships and may require understanding and applying unit rates. Many of the problems are set in academic and career settings and draw from science, including the social sciences.

Some questions present information about the relationship between two variables in a graph, scatterplot, table, or another form and ask you to analyze and draw conclusions about the given information. The questions assess your understanding of the key properties of, and the differences between, linear, quadratic, and exponential relationships and how these properties apply to the corresponding real-life contexts.

Problem Solving and Data Analysis also includes questions that assess your understanding of essential concepts in statistics. You may be asked to analyze univariate data presented in dot plots, histograms, box plots, and frequency tables, or bivariate data presented in scatterplots, line graphs, and two-way tables. This includes computing, comparing, and interpreting measures of center, interpreting measures of spread, describing overall patterns, and recognizing the effects of outliers on measures of center. These questions may test your understanding of the conceptual meaning of standard deviation (although you will not be asked to calculate a standard deviation).

Other questions may ask you to estimate the probability of a simple event, employing different approaches, rules, or probability models. Special attention is given to the notion of conditional probability, which is tested using two-way tables and in other ways.

Some questions will present you with a description of a study and ask you to decide what conclusion is most appropriate based on the design of the study. Some questions ask about using data from a sample to draw conclusions about an entire population. These questions might also assess conceptual understanding of the margin of error (although you won't be asked to calculate a margin of error) when a population mean or proportion is estimated from sample data. Other questions ask about making conclusions about cause-and-effect relationships between two variables.

REMEMBER

Problem Solving and Data Analysis questions comprise 17 of the 58 questions (29%) on the Math Test.

Problem Solving and Data Analysis questions include both multiple-choice questions and student-produced response questions. The use of a calculator is allowed for all questions in this domain.

Problem Solving and Data Analysis is one of the three SAT Math Test subscores, reported on a scale of 1 to 15.

Let's explore the content and skills assessed by Problem Solving and Data Analysis questions.

Ratio, Proportion, Units, and Percentage

Ratio and proportion is one of the major ideas in mathematics. Introduced well before high school, ratio and proportion is a theme throughout mathematics, in applications, in careers, in college mathematics courses, and beyond.

Example 1

On Thursday, 240 adults and children attended a show. The ratio of adults to children was 5 to 1. How many children attended the show?

A) 40

B) 48

C) 192

D) 200

PRACTICE AT
satpractice.org

A ratio represents a relationship between quantities, not the actual quantities themselves. Fractions are an especially effective way to represent and work with ratios.

Because the ratio of adults to children was 5 to 1, there were 5 adults for every 1 child. Thus, of every 6 people who attended the show, 5 were adults and 1 was a child. In fractions, $\frac{5}{6}$ of the 240 who attended were adults and $\frac{1}{6}$ were children. Therefore, $\frac{1}{6} \times 240 = 40$ children attended the show, which is choice A.

Ratios on the SAT may be expressed in the form 3 to 1, 3:1, $\frac{3}{1}$, or simply 3.

Example 2

On an architect's drawing of the floor plan for a house, 1 inch represents 3 feet. If a room is represented on the floor plan by a rectangle that has sides of lengths 3.5 inches and 5 inches, what is the actual floor area of the room, in square feet?

A) 17.5

B) 51.0

C) 52.5

D) 157.5

Because 1 inch represents 3 feet, the actual dimensions of the room are $3 \times 3.5 = 10.5$ feet and $3 \times 5 = 15$ feet. Therefore, the floor area of the room is $10.5 \times 15 = 157.5$ square feet, which is choice D.

Another classic example of ratio is the length of a shadow. At a given location and time of day, it might be true that a fence post that is 4 feet high casts a shadow that is 6 feet long. This ratio of the length of the shadow to the height of the object, 6 to 4 or 3 to 2, remains the same for any object at the same location and time. This could be considered a unit rate: the ratio of the length of the shadow to the height of the object would be equivalent to $\frac{3}{2}:1$ or the unit rate $\frac{3}{2}$ feet change in height for every 1 foot change in length. So, for example, a tree that is 12 feet tall would cast a shadow that is $\frac{3}{2} \times 12 = 18$ feet long. In this situation, in which one variable quantity is always a fixed constant times another variable quantity, the two quantities are said to be directly proportional.

Variables x and y are said to be directly proportional if $y = kx$, where k is a nonzero constant. The constant k is called the constant of proportionality.

In the preceding example, you would say the length of an object's shadow is directly proportional to the height of the object, with constant of proportionality $\frac{3}{2}$. So if you let L be the length of the shadow and H be the height of the object, then $L = \frac{3}{2}H$.

Notice that both L and H are lengths, so the constant of proportionality, $\frac{L}{H} = \frac{3}{2}$, has no units. In contrast, let's consider Example 2 again. On the scale drawing, 1 inch represents 3 feet. The length of an actual measurement is directly proportional to its length on the scale drawing. But to find the constant of proportionality, you need to keep track of units: $\frac{3\text{ feet}}{1\text{ inch}} = \frac{36\text{ inches}}{1\text{ inch}} = 36$. Hence, if S is a length on the scale drawing that corresponds to an actual length of R, then $R = 36S$, where R and S have the same units.

Many of the questions on the SAT Math Test require you to pay attention to units. Some questions in Problem Solving and Data Analysis require you to convert units either between the English system and the metric system or within those systems.

Example 3

Scientists estimate that the Pacific Plate, one of Earth's tectonic plates, has moved about 1,060 kilometers in the past 10.3 million years. What was the average speed of the Pacific Plate during that time period, in centimeters per year?

A) 1.03

B) 10.3

C) 103

D) 1,030

PRACTICE AT

satpractice.org

Pay close attention to units, and convert units if required by the question. Writing out the unit conversion as a series of multiplication steps, as seen here, will help ensure accuracy. Intermediate units should cancel (as do the kilometers and meters in Example 3), leaving you with the desired unit (centimeters per year).

Since 1 kilometer = 1,000 meters and 1 meter = 100 centimeters, you get $\frac{1{,}060 \text{ kilometers}}{10{,}300{,}000 \text{ years}} \times \frac{1{,}000 \text{ meters}}{1 \text{ kilometer}} \times \frac{100 \text{ centimeters}}{1 \text{ meter}} = 10.3\frac{\text{centimeters}}{\text{year}}$.

Therefore, the correct answer is choice B.

Questions may require you to move between unit rates and total amounts.

Example 4

County Y consists of two districts. One district has an area of 30 square miles and a population density of 370 people per square mile, and the other district has an area of 50 square miles and a population density of 290 people per square mile. What is the population density, in people per square mile, for all of County Y?

REMEMBER

13 of the 58 questions on the Math Test, or 22%, are student-produced response questions for which you'll grid your answers in the spaces provided on the answer sheet.

(Note that this example is a student-produced response question and has no choices. On the SAT, you will grid your answer in the spaces provided on the answer sheet.)

The first district has an area of 30 square miles and a population density of 370 people per square mile, so its total population is $30 \text{ square miles} \times 370 \frac{\text{people}}{\text{square mile}} = 11{,}100$ people. The other district has an area of 50 square miles and a population density of 290 people per square mile, so its total population is $50 \text{ square miles} \times 290 \frac{\text{people}}{\text{square mile}} = 14{,}500$ people. Thus, County Y has total population $11{,}100 + 14{,}500 = 25{,}600$ people and total area $30 + 50 = 80$ square miles. Therefore, the population density of County Y is $\frac{25{,}600}{80} = 320$ people per square mile.

Problem Solving and Data Analysis also includes questions involving percentages, which are a type of proportion. These questions may involve the concepts of percentage increase and percentage decrease.

PRACTICE AT
satpractice.org

Percent is a type of proportion that means "per 100"; 20%, for instance, means 20 out of (or per) 100. Percent increase or decrease is calculated by finding the difference between two quantities, then dividing the difference by the original quantity and multiplying by 100.

Example 5

A furniture store buys its furniture from a wholesaler. For a particular table, the store usually charges its cost from the wholesaler plus 75%. During a sale, the store charged the cost from the wholesaler plus 15%. If the sale price of the table was $299, what is the usual price for the table?

A) $359

B) $455

C) $479

D) $524

The sale price of the table was $299. This is equal to the cost from the wholesaler plus 15%. Thus, $299 = 1.15(cost from the wholesaler), and the cost from the wholesaler is $\frac{\$299}{1.15} = \$260$. The usual price is the cost from the wholesaler, $260, plus 75%. Therefore, the usual price the store charges for the table is $1.75 \times \$260 = \$455$, which is choice B.

Interpreting Relationships Presented in Scatterplots, Graphs, Tables, and Equations

The behavior of a variable and the relationship between two variables in a real-world context may be explored by considering data presented in tables and graphs.

REMEMBER

The ability to interpret and synthesize data from charts, graphs, and tables is a widely applicable skill in college and in many careers and thus is tested on the SAT Math Test.

The relationship between two quantitative variables may be modeled by a function or an equation. The function or equation may be found by examining ordered pairs of data values and by analyzing how the variables are related to one another in the real world. The model may allow very accurate predictions, as for example models used in physical sciences, or may only describe a general trend, with considerable variability between the actual and predicted values, as for example models used in behavioral and social sciences.

Questions on the SAT Math Test assess your ability to understand and analyze the relationships between two variables, the properties of the functions used to model these relationships, and the conditions under which a model is considered to be an appropriate representation of the data. Problem Solving and Data Analysis questions focus on linear, quadratic, and exponential relationships.

Example 6

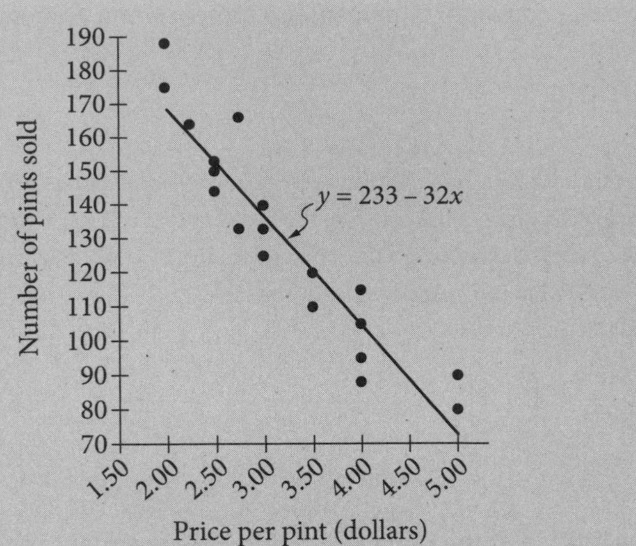

A grocery store sells pints of raspberries and sets the price per pint each week. The scatterplot above shows the price and the number of pints of raspberries sold for 19 weeks, along with a line of best fit for the data and an equation for the line of best fit.

PRACTICE AT

satpractice.org

A line of best fit is a straight line that best represents the association shown on a scatterplot. It's often written in $y = a + bx$ form.

There are several different questions that could be asked about this context.

A. According to the line of best fit, how many pints of raspberries would the grocery store be predicted to sell in a week when the price of raspberries is $4.50 per pint?

Because the line of best fit has equation $y = 233 - 32x$, where x is the price, in dollars, for a pint of raspberries and y is the expected number of pints of raspberries sold, the number of pints the store would be predicted to sell in a week where the price of raspberries is $4.50 per pint is $233 - 32(4.50) = 89$ pints.

B. For how many of the 19 weeks shown was the number of pints of raspberries sold greater than the number predicted by the line of best fit?

For a given week, the number of pints of raspberries sold is greater than the number predicted by the line of best fit if and only if the point representing that week lies above the line of best fit. For example, at the price of $5 per pint, the number sold in two different weeks was approximately 80 and 90, which is more than the 73 predicted by the line of best fit. Of the 19 points, 8 lie above the line of best fit, so there were 8 weeks in which the number of pints sold was greater than what was predicted by the line of best fit.

C. What is the best interpretation of the slope of the line of best fit in this context?

On the SAT, this question would be followed by multiple-choice answer options. The slope of the line of best fit is −32. This means that the correct answer would state that for each dollar that the price of a pint of raspberries increases, the store is predicted to sell 32 fewer pints of raspberries.

D. What is the best interpretation of the *y*-intercept of the line of best fit in this context?

On the SAT, this question would be followed by multiple-choice answer options.

In this context, the *y*-intercept does not represent a likely scenario, so it cannot be accurately interpreted in this context. According to the model, the *y*-intercept means that if the store sold raspberries for $0 per pint — that is, if the store gave raspberries away — 233 people would be expected to accept the free raspberries. However, it is not realistic that the store would give away raspberries, and if they did, it is likely that far more people would accept the free raspberries. Also notice that in this case, the left-most line on the graph is not the *y*-axis. The lower-left corner shows the *x*- and *y*-coordinates of (1.5, 70), not (0, 0).

The fact that the *y*-intercept indicates that 233 people would accept free raspberries is one limitation of the model. Another limitation is that for a price of $7.50 per pint or above, the model predicts that a negative number of people would buy raspberries, which is impossible. In general, you should be cautious about applying a model for values outside of the given data. In this example, you should only be confident in the prediction of sales for prices between $2 and $5.

Giving a line of best fit, as in this example, assumes that the relationship between the variables is best modeled by a linear function, but that is not always true. On the SAT, you may see data that are best modeled by a linear, quadratic, or exponential model.

Example 7

Time (hours)	Number of bacteria
0	1.0×10^3
1	4.0×10^3
2	1.6×10^4
3	6.4×10^4

The table above gives the initial number (at time $t = 0$) of bacteria placed in a growth medium and the number of bacteria in the growth medium over 3 hours. Which of the following functions best models the number of bacteria, $N(t)$, after t hours?

A) $N(t) = 4{,}000t$

B) $N(t) = 1{,}000 + 3{,}000t$

C) $N(t) = 1{,}000(4^{-t})$

D) $N(t) = 1{,}000(4^{t})$

PRACTICE AT

satpractice.org

To determine if a model is linear or exponential, examine the change in the quantity between successive time periods. If the difference in the quantity is constant, the model is linear. If the ratio in the quantity is constant (for instance, 4 times greater than the preceding time period), the model is exponential.

The given choices are linear and exponential models. If a quantity is increasing linearly with time, then the *difference* in the quantity between successive time periods is constant. If a quantity is increasing exponentially with time, then the *ratio* in the quantity between successive time periods is constant. According to the table, after each hour, the number of bacteria in the culture is 4 times as great as it was the preceding hour: $\frac{4.0 \times 10^3}{1.0 \times 10^3} = \frac{1.6 \times 10^4}{4.0 \times 10^3} = \frac{6.4 \times 10^4}{1.6 \times 10^4} = 4$. That is, for each increase of 1 in t, the value of $N(t)$ is multiplied by 4. At $t = 0$, which corresponds to the time when the culture was placed in the medium, there were 10^3 bacteria. This is modeled by the exponential function $N(t) = 1{,}000(4^t)$, which has the value 1,000 at $t = 0$ and increases by a factor of 4 for each increase of 1 in the value of t. Choice D is the correct answer.

The SAT Math Test may have questions on simple and compound interest, which are important examples of linear and exponential growth, respectively.

Example 8

A bank has opened a new branch and, as part of a promotion, the bank branch is offering $1,000 certificates of deposit at simple interest of 4% per year. The bank is selling certificates with terms of 1, 2, 3, or 4 years. Which of the following functions gives the total amount, A, in dollars, a customer will receive when a certificate with a term of k years is finally paid?

A) $A = 1{,}000(1.04k)$

B) $A = 1{,}000(1 + 0.04k)$

C) $A = 1{,}000(1.04)^k$

D) $A = 1{,}000(1 + 0.04^k)$

For 4% simple interest, 4% of the original deposit is added to the original deposit for each year the deposit was held. That is, if the certificate has a term of k years, $4k\%$ is added to the original deposit to get the final amount. Because $4k\%$ is $0.04k$, the final amount paid to the customer is $A = 1{,}000 + 1{,}000(0.04k) = 1{,}000(1 + 0.04k)$. Choice B is the correct answer.

The general formula for simple interest is $A = P(1 + rt)$, where P is the amount, in dollars, of the original deposit, called the principal; r is the annual interest rate expressed as a decimal; and t is the time, in years, the deposit is held. In Example 8, $P = 1{,}000$, $r = 0.04$, and $t = k$; so A, in dollars, is given by $A = 1{,}000[1 + (0.04)k]$.

In contrast, compound interest is an example of exponential growth.

Example 9

A bank has opened a new branch and, as part of a promotion, the bank branch is offering \$1,000 certificates of deposit at an interest rate of 4% per year, compounded semiannually. The bank is selling certificates with terms of 1, 2, 3, or 4 years. Which of the following functions gives the total amount, A, in dollars, a customer will receive when a certificate with a term of k years is finally paid?

A) $A = 1{,}000(1 + 0.04k)$

B) $A = 1{,}000(1 + 0.08k)$

C) $A = 1{,}000(1.04)^k$

D) $A = 1{,}000(1.02)^{2k}$

The interest is compounded semiannually, that is, twice per year. At the end of the first half year, 2% of the original deposit is added to the value of the certificate (4% annual interest multiplied by the time period, which is $\frac{1}{2}$ year, gives 2% interest). When the interest is added, the value, in dollars, of the certificate is now $1{,}000 + 1{,}000(0.02) = 1{,}000(1.02)$. Since the interest is reinvested (compounded), the new principal at the beginning of the second half year is 1,000(1.02). At the end of the second half year, 2% of 1,000(1.02) is added to the value of the certificate; the value, in dollars, of the certificate is now $1{,}000(1.02) + 1{,}000(1.02)(0.02)$, which is equal to $1{,}000(1.02)(1.02) = 1{,}000(1.02)^2$. In general, after n compounding periods, the amount, A, in dollars, is $A = 1{,}000(1.02)^n$.

When the certificate is paid after k years, the value of the certificate will have been multiplied by the factor (1.02) a total of $2k$ times. Therefore, the total amount, A, in dollars, a customer will receive when a certificate with a term of k years is finally paid is $A = 1{,}000(1.02^{2k})$. Choice D is the correct answer.

The general formula for compound interest is $A = P\left(1 + \frac{r}{n}\right)^{nt}$, where P is the amount, in dollars, of the principal, r is the annual interest rate expressed as a decimal, t is the number of years the deposit is held, and n is the number of times the interest is compounded per year. In Example 9, $P = 1{,}000$, $r = 0.04$, $t = k$, and $n = 2$; so A, in dollars, is given by $A = 1{,}000\left(1 + \frac{0.04}{2}\right)^{2k} = 1{,}000(1.02)^{2k}$.

NOTE: Although the stated interest rate is 4% per year in Example 9, the value of the account increases by more than 4% in a year, namely 4.04% per year. (You may have seen banks offer an account in this way, for example, 5.00% annual interest rate, 5.13% effective annual yield.) If you take calculus, you will often see a situation in which a stated rate of change differs from the actual change over an interval. But on the SAT, other than compound interest, the stated rate of change is always equal to the actual rate of change. For example, if a question says that the height of a plant increases by 10% each month, it means that $\frac{\text{height of the plant now}}{\text{height of the plant a month ago}} = 1.1$

PRACTICE AT

satpractice.org

Know the formulas for simple and compound interest.

Simple interest: $A = P(1 + rt)$

Compound interest: $A = P\left(1 + \frac{r}{n}\right)^{nt}$

A is the total amount, P is the principal, r is the annual interest rate expressed as a decimal, t is the time period, and n is the number of times the interest is compounded per year.

(or if a question says that the population of a city is decreasing by 3% per year, it means that $\frac{\text{population of the city}}{\text{population of the city a year ago}} = 0.97$). Then, if the question asks by what percentage the height of the plant will increase in 2 months, you can write

$$\frac{\text{height of the plant in 2 months}}{\text{height of the plant now}} = \frac{\text{height of the plant in 2 months}}{\text{height of the plant in 1 month}} \times \frac{\text{height of the plant in 1 month}}{\text{height of the plant now}}$$

$$= 1.1 \times 1.1 = 1.21$$

Therefore, the answer is that the height of the plant increases by 21% in 2 months.

An SAT Math Test question may ask you to interpret a graph that shows the relationship between two variables.

Example 10

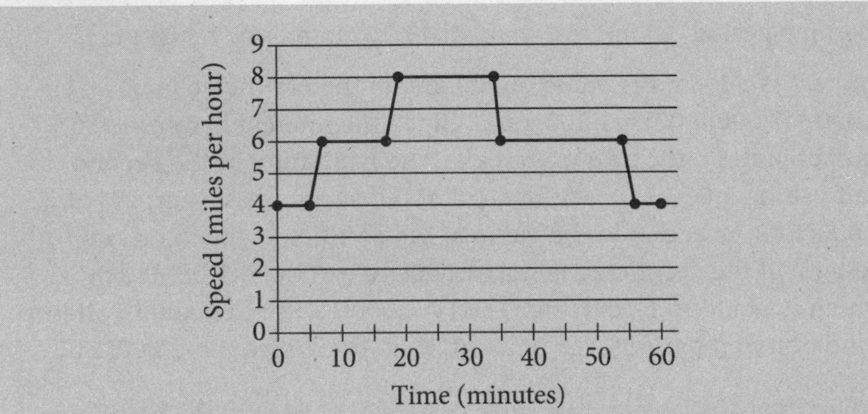

Each evening, Maria walks, jogs, and runs for a total of 60 minutes. The graph above shows Maria's speed during the 60 minutes. Which segment of the graph represents the times when Maria's speed is the greatest?

A) The segment from (17, 6) to (19, 8)

B) The segment from (19, 8) to (34, 8)

C) The segment from (34, 8) to (35, 6)

D) The segment from (35, 6) to (54, 6)

The correct answer is choice B. Because the vertical coordinate represents Maria's speed, the part of the graph with the greatest vertical coordinate represents the times when Maria's speed is the greatest. This is the highest part of the graph, the segment from (19, 8) to (34, 8), when Maria runs at 8 miles per hour (mph). Choice A represents the time during which Maria's speed is increasing from 6 to 8 mph; choice C represents the time during which Maria's speed is decreasing from 8 to 6 mph; and choice D represents the longest period of Maria moving at the same speed, not the times when Maria's speed is the greatest.

More Data and Statistics

Some questions on the SAT Math Test will assess your ability to understand and analyze data presented in a table, bar graph, histogram, line graph, or other display.

Example 11

A store is deciding whether to install a new security system to prevent shoplifting. Based on store records, the security manager of the store estimates that 10,000 customers enter the store each week, 24 of whom will attempt to shoplift. Based on data provided from other users of the security system, the manager estimates the results of the new security system in detecting shoplifters would be as shown in the table below.

	Alarm sounds	Alarm does not sound	Total
Customer attempts to shoplift	21	3	24
Customer does not attempt to shoplift	35	9,941	9,976
Total	56	9,944	10,000

According to the manager's estimates, if the alarm sounds for a customer, what is the probability that the customer did *not* attempt to shoplift?

A) 0.03%

B) 0.35%

C) 0.56%

D) 62.5%

According to the manager's estimates, the alarm will sound for 56 customers. Of these 56 customers, 35 did *not* attempt to shoplift. Therefore, if the alarm sounds, the probability that the customer did *not* attempt to shoplift is $\frac{35}{56} = \frac{5}{8} = 62.5\%$. The correct answer is choice D.

Example 11 is an example of a conditional probability, the probability of an event given that another event occurred. The question asks for the probability that a customer did not attempt to shoplift given that the alarm sounded.

REMEMBER

Mean and median are measures of center for a data set, while range and standard deviation are measures of spread.

You may be asked to answer questions that involve a measure of center for a data set: the mean or the median. A question may ask you to draw conclusions about one or more of these measures of center even if the exact values cannot be calculated. To recall briefly:

The mean of a set of numerical values is the sum of all the values divided by the number of values in the set.

The median of a set of numerical values is the middle value when the values are listed in increasing (or decreasing) order. If the set has an even number of values, then the median is the average of the two middle values.

Example 12

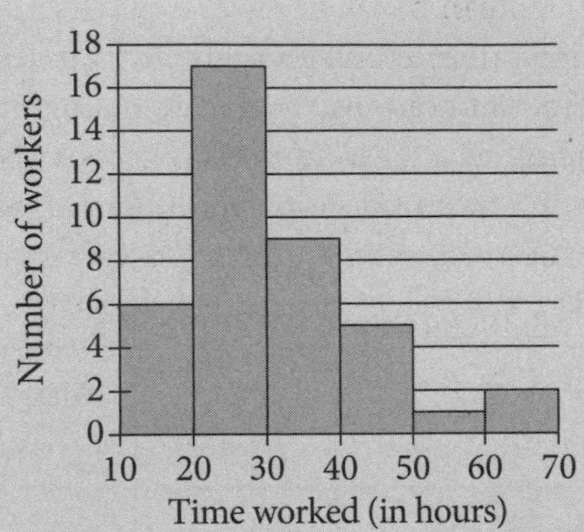

REMEMBER

The distribution of a variable provides the possible values of the variable and how often they occur.

The histogram above summarizes the distribution of time worked last week, in hours, by the 40 employees of a landscaping company. In the histogram, the first bar represents all workers who worked at least 10 hours but less than 20 hours; the second represents all workers who worked at least 20 hours but less than 30 hours; and so on. Which of the following could be the median and mean amount of time worked, in hours, for the 40 employees?

A) Median = 22, Mean = 23

B) Median = 24, Mean = 22

C) Median = 26, Mean = 32

D) Median = 32, Mean = 30

(**Note:** On the SAT, all histograms have the same type of boundary condition. That is, the values represented by a bar include the left endpoint but do not include the right endpoint.)

If the number of hours the 40 employees worked is listed in increasing order, the median will be the average of the 20th and the 21st numbers on the list. The first 6 numbers on the list will be workers represented by the first bar; hence, each of the first 6 numbers will be at least 10 but less than 20. The next 17 numbers, that is, the 7th through the 23rd numbers on the list, will be workers represented by the second bar; hence, each of the next 17 numbers will be at least 20 but less than 30. Thus, the 20th and the 21st numbers on the list will be at least 20 but less than 30. Therefore, any of the median values in choices A, B, or C are possible, but the median value in choice D is not.

Now let's find the possible values of the mean. Each of the 6 employees represented by the first bar worked at least 10 hours but less than 20 hours. Thus, the total number of hours worked by these 6 employees is at least 60. Similarly, the total number of hours worked by the 17 employees represented by the second bar is at least 340; the total number of hours worked by the 9 employees represented by the third bar is at least 270; the total number of hours worked by the 5 employees represented by the fourth bar is at least 200; the total number of hours worked by the 1 employee represented by the fifth bar is at least 50; and the total number of hours worked by the 2 employees represented by the sixth bar is at least 120. Adding all these hours shows that the total number of hours worked by all 40 employees is at least $60 + 340 + 270 + 200 + 50 + 120 = 1{,}040$. Therefore, the mean number of hours worked by all 40 employees is at least $\frac{1{,}040}{40} = 26$. Therefore, only the values of the mean given in choices C and D are possible. Because only choice C has possible values for both the median and the mean, it is the correct answer.

A data set may have a few values that are much larger or smaller than the rest of the values in the set. These values are called *outliers*. An outlier may represent an important piece of data. For example, if a data set consists of rates of a certain illness in various cities, a data point with a very high value could indicate a serious health issue to be investigated.

In general, outliers affect the mean more than the median. Therefore, outliers that are larger than the rest of the points in the data set tend to make the mean greater than the median, and outliers that are smaller than the rest of the points in the data set tend to make the mean less than the median. In Example 12, the mean was larger than the median due to the unusually large amount of time worked by a few employees. One graphical display used to identify outliers is the box plot.

The mean and the median are different ways to describe the center of a data set. Another key characteristic of a data set is the amount of variation, or spread, in the data. One measure of spread is the *range*, which is equal to the maximum value minus the minimum value. Another measure of spread is the *standard deviation*, which is a measure of how far away the points in the data set are from the mean value. On the SAT Math Test, you will *not* be asked to compute the standard deviation of a data set, but you do need to understand that a larger standard deviation corresponds to a data set whose values are more spread out from the mean value.

REMEMBER

You won't be asked to calculate the standard deviation of a set of data on the SAT Math Test, but you will be expected to demonstrate an understanding of what standard deviation measures.

Example 13

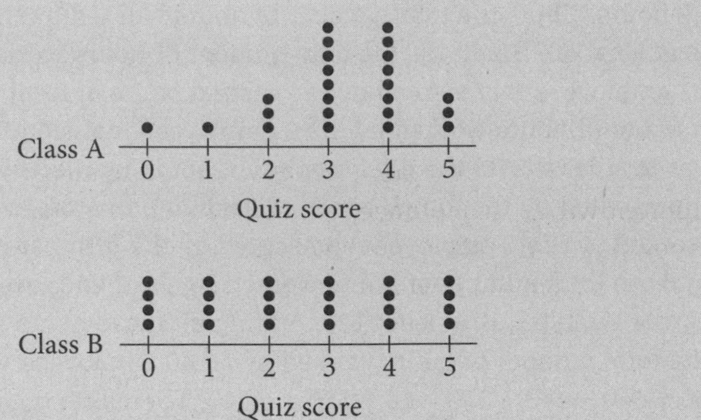

The dot plots above show the distributions of scores on a current events quiz for two classes of 24 students. Which of the following correctly compares the standard deviation of the scores in each of the classes?

A) The standard deviation of quiz scores in Class A is smaller.

B) The standard deviation of quiz scores in Class B is smaller.

C) The standard deviations of quiz scores in Class A and Class B are the same.

D) The relationship cannot be determined from the information given.

PRACTICE AT
satpractice.org

When asked to compare the standard deviations of two data sets, first locate the mean approximately. Then, ask yourself which data set has values that are more closely clustered around the mean. That data set will have the smaller standard deviation.

In Class A, the mean score is between 3 and 4. The large majority of scores are 3 and 4, with only a few scores of 0, 1, 2, and 5. In Class B, the mean score is 2.5, and scores are evenly spread across all possible scores, with many scores not close to the mean score. Because the scores in Class A are more closely clustered around the mean, the standard deviation of the scores in Class A is smaller. The correct answer is choice A.

A *population parameter* is a numerical value that describes a characteristic of a population. For example, the percentage of registered voters who would vote for a certain candidate is a parameter describing the population of registered voters in an election. In another example, the average income of a household in a city is a parameter describing the population of households in that city. An essential purpose of statistics is to estimate a population parameter based on a sample from the population. A common example is election polling, where researchers will interview a random sample of registered voters to estimate the proportion of all registered voters who plan to vote for a certain candidate. The precision of the estimate depends on the variability of the sample data and the sample size. For instance, if household incomes in a city vary widely or the sample is small, the estimate that comes from a sample may differ considerably from the actual value for the population parameter.

For example, a researcher wants to estimate the mean number of hours each week that the 1,200 students at a high school spend on the Internet. Interviewing all 1,200 students would be time consuming, and it would be more efficient to survey a random sample of the students. Suppose the researcher has time to interview 80 students. Which 80 students? In order to have a sample that is representative of the population, students who will participate in the study should be selected *at random*. That is, each student must have the same chance to be selected. Random selection is essential in protecting against bias and increases the reliability of any values calculated. The researcher can select students at random in several different ways; for instance, write each student's name on a slip of paper, put all the slips in a bowl, mix up the slips, and then draw 80 names from the bowl. In practice, a computer is often used to select participants at random.

If you do not select a random sample, the sampling method used may introduce bias. For example, if you found 80 students from those attending a game of the school's football team, those people would be more likely to be interested in sports, and in turn, an interest in sports might be related to the average amount of time the students spend on the Internet. The result would be that the average time those 80 students spend on the Internet might not be an accurate estimate of the average amount of time *all* students at the school spend on the Internet.

Suppose you select 80 students at random from the 1,200 students at the high school. You ask them how much time they spend on the Internet each week, and you calculate that the mean time is 14 hours. You also find that 6 of the 80 students spend less than 2 hours each week on the Internet. Based on these results, what conclusions should be made about the entire population of 1,200 students?

Because the sample was selected at random, the mean of 14 hours is a plausible estimate for the mean time spent on the Internet for all 1,200 students. Also, we can use the sample data to estimate how many students spend less than 2 hours on the Internet each week. In the sample, the percentage is $\frac{6}{80}$, or 7.5%. Applying this percentage to the entire population of 1,200 students, it is plausible that 90 students at the school spend less than 2 hours per week on the Internet.

However, estimated population parameters need to be interpreted carefully. An essential part of statistics is accounting for the variability of the estimate. The estimates above are reasonable, but they are unlikely to be exactly correct. Statistical analysis can also describe how far from the estimates the actual values are expected to be, at most. To describe the precision of an estimate, statisticians use *margins of error*. On the SAT, you will not be expected to compute a margin of error, but you should understand how sample size affects the margin of error and how to interpret a given margin of error in the context.

REMEMBER

You won't need to calculate margins of error on the SAT Math Test, but you should understand what the concept means and be able to interpret in context.

If the example above were an SAT question, you might be given survey results indicating that, for a random sample of 80 students, the estimated mean was 14 hours with an associated margin of error of 1.2 hours. An appropriate interpretation of these data is that a plausible population parameter, or the mean number of hours for all 1,200 students in the population, is greater than 12.8 hours but less than 15.2 hours.

There are some key points to note.

1. The value of the margin of error is affected by two factors: the variability in the data and the sample size. The larger the standard deviation, the larger the margin of error; the smaller the standard deviation, the smaller the margin of error. Furthermore, increasing the size of the random sample provides more information and reduces the margin of error.
2. The margin of error applies to the estimated value of the population parameter only; it does not inform the estimated value for an individual. In the example, plausible values for the population parameter are in the interval from 12.8 hours to 15.2 hours. The time, in hours, that an individual spends on the Internet may or may not fall in this interval.

Example 14

A quality control researcher at an electronics company is testing the life of the company's batteries in a certain camera. The researcher selects 100 batteries at random from the daily output of the batteries and finds that the life of the batteries has a mean of 342 pictures with an associated margin of error of 18 pictures. Which of the following is the most appropriate conclusion based on these data?

A) All the batteries produced by the company that day have a life between 324 and 360 pictures.

B) All the batteries ever produced by the company have a life between 324 and 360 pictures.

C) It is plausible that the mean life of batteries produced by the company that day is between 324 and 360 pictures.

D) It is plausible that the mean life of all the batteries ever produced by the company is between 324 and 360 pictures.

PRACTICE AT
satpractice.org

When a margin of error is provided, determine the value to which the margin of error applies. The margin of error concerns the mean value of a population and does not apply to values of individual objects in the population.

The correct answer is choice C. Choices A and B are incorrect because the margin of error gives information about the mean life of all batteries produced by the company that day, not about the life of any individual battery. Choice D is incorrect because the sample of batteries was taken from the population of all the batteries produced by the company on that day. The population of all batteries the company ever produced may have a different mean life because of changes in the formulation of the batteries, wear on machinery, improvements in production processes, and many other factors.

The statistics examples discussed so far are largely based on investigations intended to estimate some characteristic of a group: the mean amount of time students spend on the Internet, the mean life of a battery, and the percentage of registered voters who plan to vote for a candidate. Another primary focus of statistics is to investigate relationships between variables and to draw conclusions about cause and effect. For example, does a new type of physical therapy help people recover from knee surgery faster? For such a study, some people who have had knee surgery will be randomly assigned to the new therapy, while other people who have had knee surgery will be randomly assigned to the usual therapy. The medical results of these patients can be compared. The key questions from a statistical viewpoint are

- Is it appropriate to generalize from the sample of patients in the study to the entire population of people who are recovering from knee surgery?
- Is it appropriate to conclude that the new therapy *caused* any difference in the results for the two groups of patients?

The answers depend on the use of random selection and random assignment.

- If the subjects in the sample of a study were selected at random from the entire population in question, the results can be generalized to the entire population because random sampling ensures that each individual has the same chance to be selected for the sample.
- If the subjects in the sample were randomly assigned to treatments, it may be appropriate to make conclusions about cause and effect because the treatment groups will be roughly equivalent at the beginning of the experiment other than the treatment they receive.

PRACTICE AT
satpractice.org

In order for results of a study to be generalized to the entire population, and for a cause-and-effect relationship to be established, both random sampling and random assignment of individuals to treatments are needed.

This can be summarized in the following table.

	Subjects Selected at Random	Subjects Not Selected at Random
Subjects randomly assigned to treatments	• Results can be generalized to the entire population. • Conclusions about cause and effect can appropriately be drawn.	• Results *cannot* be generalized to the entire population. • Conclusions about cause and effect can appropriately be drawn.
Subjects not randomly assigned to treatments	• Results can be generalized to the entire population. • Conclusions about cause and effect *should not* be drawn.	• Results *cannot* be generalized to the entire population. • Conclusions about cause and effect *should not* be drawn.

The previous example discussed treatments in a medical experiment. The word *treatment* refers to any factor that is deliberately varied in an experiment.

Example 15

A community center offers a Spanish course. This year, all students in the course were offered additional audio lessons they could take at home. The students who took these additional audio lessons did better in the course than students who didn't take the additional audio lessons. Based on these results, which of the following is the most appropriate conclusion?

A) Taking additional audio lessons will cause an improvement for any student who takes any foreign language course.

B) Taking additional audio lessons will cause an improvement for any student who takes a Spanish course.

C) Taking additional audio lessons was the cause of the improvement for the students at the community center who took the Spanish course.

D) No conclusion about cause and effect can be made regarding students at the community center who took the additional audio lessons at home and their performance in the Spanish course.

PRACTICE AT
satpractice.org

Be wary of conclusions that claim a cause-and-effect relationship or that generalize a conclusion to a broader population. Before accepting a conclusion, assess whether or not the subjects were selected at random from the broader population and whether or not subjects were randomly assigned to treatments.

The correct answer is choice D. The better results of these students may have been a result of being more motivated, as shown in their willingness to do extra work, and not the additional audio lessons. Choice A is incorrect because no conclusion about cause and effect is possible without random assignment to treatments and because the sample was only students taking a Spanish course, so no conclusion can be appropriately made about students taking all foreign language courses. Choice B is incorrect because no conclusion about cause and effect is possible without random assignment to treatments and because the students taking a Spanish course at the community center is not a random sample of all students who take a Spanish course. Choice C is incorrect because the students taking the Spanish course at the community center were not randomly assigned to use the additional audio lessons or to not use the additional audio lessons.

CHAPTER 18

Passport to Advanced Math

Passport to Advanced Math questions include topics that are especially important for students to master *before* studying advanced math. Chief among these topics is the understanding of the structure of expressions and the ability to analyze, manipulate, and rewrite these expressions. These questions also include reasoning with more complex equations and interpreting and building functions.

REMEMBER

16 of the 58 questions (28%) on the SAT Math Test are Passport to Advanced Math questions.

Heart of Algebra questions focus on the mastery of linear equations, systems of linear equations, and linear functions. In contrast, Passport to Advanced Math questions focus on the ability to work with and analyze more complex equations. The questions may require you to demonstrate procedural skill in adding, subtracting, and multiplying polynomials and in factoring polynomials. You may be required to work with expressions involving exponentials, integer and rational exponents, radicals, or fractions with a variable in the denominator. The questions may ask you to solve a quadratic equation, a radical equation, a rational equation, or a system consisting of a linear equation and a nonlinear equation. You may be required to manipulate an equation in several variables to isolate a quantity of interest.

Some questions in Passport to Advanced Math will ask you to build a quadratic or exponential function or an equation that describes a context or to interpret the function, the graph of the function, or the solution to the equation in terms of the context.

Passport to Advanced Math questions may assess your ability to recognize structure. Expressions and equations that appear complex may use repeated terms or repeated expressions. By noticing these patterns, the complexity of a problem can be quickly simplified. Structure may be used to factor or otherwise rewrite an expression, to solve a quadratic or other equation, or to draw conclusions about the context represented by an expression, equation, or function. You may be asked to identify or derive the form of an expression, equation, or function that reveals information about the expression, equation, or function or the context it represents.

Passport to Advanced Math questions also assess your understanding of functions and their graphs. A question may require you to demonstrate your understanding of function notation, including interpreting an expression where the argument of a function is an expression rather than a variable. The questions may assess your understanding of how the algebraic properties of a function relate to the geometric characteristics of its graph.

Passport to Advanced Math questions include both multiple-choice questions and student-produced response questions. Some of these questions are in the no-calculator portion, where the use of a calculator is not permitted, and others are in the calculator portion, where the use of a calculator is permitted. When you can use a calculator, you must decide whether using your calculator is an effective strategy for that particular question.

Passport to Advanced Math is one of the three SAT Math Test subscores, reported on a scale of 1 to 15.

Let's consider the content and skills assessed by Passport to Advanced Math questions.

Operations with Polynomials and Rewriting Expressions

Questions on the SAT Math Test may assess your ability to add, subtract, and multiply polynomials.

Example 1

$$(x^2 + bx - 2)(x + 3) = x^3 + 6x^2 + 7x - 6$$

In the equation above, b is a constant. If the equation is true for all values of x, what is the value of b?

A) 2

B) 3

C) 7

D) 9

REMEMBER

Passport to Advanced Math questions build on the knowledge and skills tested on Heart of Algebra questions. Develop proficiency with Heart of Algebra questions before tackling Passport to Advanced Math questions.

To find the value of b, expand the left-hand side of the equation and then collect like terms so that the left-hand side is in the same form as the right-hand side.

$$(x^2 + bx - 2)(x + 3) = (x^3 + bx^2 - 2x) + (3x^2 + 3bx - 6)$$
$$= x^3 + (3 + b)x^2 + (3b - 2)x - 6$$

Since the two polynomials are equal for all values of x, the coefficient of matching powers of x should be the same. Therefore, comparing the coefficients of $x^3 + (3 + b)x^2 + (3b - 2)x - 6$ and $x^3 + 6x^2 + 7x - 6$ reveals that $3 + b = 6$ and $3b - 2 = 7$. Solving either of these equations gives $b = 3$, which is choice B.

Questions may also ask you to use structure to rewrite expressions. The expression may be of a particular type, such as a difference of squares, or it may require insightful analysis.

Example 2

Which of the following is equivalent to $16s^4 - 4t^2$?

A) $4(s^2 - t)(4s^2 + t)$

B) $4(4s^2 - t)(s^2 + t)$

C) $4(2s^2 - t)(2s^2 + t)$

D) $(8s^2 - 2t)(8s^2 + 2t)$

This example appears complex at first, but it is very similar to the equation $x^2 - y^2$, which factors as $(x - y)(x + y)$. The expression $16s^4 - 4t^2$ is also the difference of two squares: $16s^4 - 4t^2 = (4s^2)^2 - (2t)^2$. Therefore, it can be factored as $(4s^2)^2 - (2t)^2 = (4s^2 - 2t)(4s^2 + 2t)$. This expression can be rewritten as $(4s^2 - 2t)(4s^2 + 2t) = 2(2s^2 - t)(2)(2s^2 + t) = 4(2s^2 - t)(2s^2 + t)$, which is choice C.

Alternatively, a 4 could be factored out of the given equation: $4(4s^4 - t^2)$. The expression inside the parentheses is a difference of two squares. Therefore, it can be further factored as $4(2s^2 + t)(2s^2 - t)$.

PRACTICE AT
satpractice.org

Passport to Advanced Math questions require a high comfort level working with quadratic equations and expressions, including multiplying polynomials and factoring. Recognizing classic quadratic patterns such as $x^2 - y^2 = (x - y)(x + y)$ can also improve your speed and accuracy.

Example 3

$$y^5 - 2y^4 - cxy + 6x$$

In the polynomial above, c is a constant. If the polynomial is divisible by $y - 2$, what is the value of c?

If the expression is divisible by $y - 2$, then the expression $y - 2$ can be factored from the larger expression. Since $y^5 - 2y^4 = (y - 2)y^4$, you have $y^5 - 2y^4 - cxy + 6x = (y - 2)(y^4) - cxy + 6x$. If this entire expression is divisible by $y - 2$, then $-cxy + 6x$ must be divisible by $y - 2$. Thus, $-cxy + 6x = (y - 2)(-cx) = -cxy + 2cx$. Therefore, $2c = 6$, and the value of c is 3.

Quadratic Functions and Equations

Questions in Passport to Advanced Math may require you to build a quadratic function or an equation to represent a context.

Example 4

A car is traveling at x feet per second. The driver sees a red light ahead, and after 1.5 seconds reaction time, the driver applies the brake. After the brake is applied, the car takes $\frac{x}{24}$ seconds to stop, during which time the average speed of the car is $\frac{x}{2}$ feet per second. If the car travels 165 feet from the time the driver saw the red light to the time it comes to a complete stop, which of the following equations can be used to find the value of x?

A) $x^2 + 48x - 3{,}960 = 0$

B) $x^2 + 48x - 7{,}920 = 0$

C) $x^2 + 72x - 3{,}960 = 0$

D) $x^2 + 72x - 7{,}920 = 0$

PRACTICE AT
satpractice.org

Example 4 requires careful translation of a word problem into an algebraic equation. It pays to be deliberate and methodical when translating word problems into equations on the SAT.

During the 1.5-second reaction time, the car is still traveling at x feet per second, so it travels a total of $1.5x$ feet. The average speed of the car during the $\frac{x}{24}$-second braking interval is $\frac{x}{2}$ feet per second, so over this interval, the car travels $\left(\frac{x}{2}\right)\left(\frac{x}{24}\right) = \frac{x^2}{48}$ feet. Since the total distance the car travels from the time the driver saw the red light to the time it comes to a complete stop is 165 feet, you have the equation $\frac{x^2}{48} + 1.5x = 165$. This quadratic equation can be rewritten in standard form by subtracting 165 from each side and then multiplying each side by 48, giving $x^2 + 72x - 7{,}920 = 0$, which is choice D.

Some questions on the SAT Math Test will ask you to solve a quadratic equation. You must determine the appropriate procedure: factoring, completing the square, the quadratic formula, use of a calculator (if permitted), or use of structure. You should also know the following facts in addition to the formulas in the directions:

- The sum of the solutions of $x^2 + bx + c = 0$ is $-b$.
- The product of the solutions of $x^2 + bx + c = 0$ is c.

Each of the facts can be seen from the factored form of a quadratic. If r and s are the solutions of $x^2 + bx + c = 0$, then $x^2 + bx + c = (x - r)(x - s)$. Thus, $b = -(r + s)$ and $c = (-r)(-s) = rs$.
Note: To use either of these facts, the coefficient of x^2 must be equal to 1.

REMEMBER

The SAT Math Test may ask you to solve a quadratic equation. Be prepared to use the appropriate method. Practice using the various methods (below) until you are comfortable with all of them.

1. Factoring
2. Completing the square
3. Quadratic formula
4. Using a calculator

Example 5

What are the solutions x of $x^2 - 3 = x$?

A) $\frac{-1 \pm \sqrt{11}}{2}$

B) $\frac{-1 \pm \sqrt{13}}{2}$

C) $\frac{1 \pm \sqrt{11}}{2}$

D) $\frac{1 \pm \sqrt{13}}{2}$

The equation can be solved by using the quadratic formula or by completing the square. Let's use the quadratic formula. First, subtract x from each side of $x^2 - 3 = x$ to put the equation in standard form: $x^2 - x - 3 = 0$. The quadratic formula states the solutions x of the equation $ax^2 + bx + c = 0$ are $\frac{-b \pm \sqrt{b^2 - 4ac}}{2a}$. For the equation $x^2 - x - 3 = 0$, you have $a = 1$, $b = -1$, and $c = -3$. Substituting these values into the quadratic formula gives $x = \frac{-(-1) \pm \sqrt{(-1)^2 - 4(1)(-3)}}{2(1)} = \frac{1 \pm \sqrt{1 - (-12)}}{2} = \frac{1 \pm \sqrt{13}}{2}$, which is choice D.

PRACTICE AT

satpractice.org

The quadratic formula states that the solutions x of the equation $ax^2 + bx + c = 0$ are $x = \frac{-b \pm \sqrt{b^2 - 4ac}}{2a}$.

Example 6

If $x > 0$ and $2x^2 + 3x - 2 = 0$, what is the value of x?

The left-hand side of the equation can be factored: $2x^2 + 3x - 2 = (2x - 1)(x + 2) = 0$. Therefore, either $2x - 1 = 0$, which gives $x = \frac{1}{2}$, or $x + 2 = 0$, which gives $x = -2$. Since $x > 0$, the value of x is $\frac{1}{2}$.

REMEMBER

Pay close attention to all of the details in the question. In Example 6, x can equal $\frac{1}{2}$ or -2, but since the question states that $x > 0$, the value of x must be $\frac{1}{2}$.

Example 7

What is the sum of the solutions of $(2x - 1)^2 = (x + 2)^2$?

If a and b are real numbers and $a^2 = b^2$, then either $a = b$ or $a = -b$. Since $(2x - 1)^2 = (x + 2)^2$, either $2x - 1 = x + 2$ or $2x - 1 = -(x + 2)$. In the first case, $x = 3$, and in the second case, $3x = -1$, or $x = -\frac{1}{3}$. Therefore, the sum of the solutions x of $(2x - 1)^2 = (x + 2)^2$ is $3 + \left(-\frac{1}{3}\right) = \frac{8}{3}$.

Exponential Functions, Equations, and Expressions and Radicals

We examined exponential functions in Examples 7 and 9 of Chapter 17. Some Passport to Advanced Math questions ask you to build a function that models a given context. As discussed in Chapter 17, exponential functions model situations in which a quantity is multiplied by a constant factor for each time period. An exponential function can be increasing with time, in which case it models exponential growth, or it can be decreasing with time, in which case it models exponential decay.

Example 8

A researcher estimates that the population of a city is increasing at an annual rate of 0.6%. If the current population of the city is 80,000, which of the following expressions appropriately models the population of the city t years from now according to the researcher's estimate?

A) $80{,}000(1 + 0.006)^t$

B) $80{,}000(1 + 0.006^t)$

C) $80{,}000 + 1.006^t$

D) $80{,}000(0.006^t)$

According to the researcher's estimate, the population is increasing by 0.6% each year. Since 0.6% is equal to 0.006, after the first year, the population is $80{,}000 + 0.006(80{,}000) = 80{,}000(1 + 0.006)$. After the second year, the population is $80{,}000(1 + 0.006) + 0.006(80{,}000)(1 + 0.006) = 80{,}000(1 + 0.006)^2$. Similarly, after t years, the population will be $80{,}000(1 + 0.006)^t$ according to the researcher's estimate. This is choice A.

PRACTICE AT
satpractice.org

A quantity that grows or decays by a fixed percent at regular intervals is said to possess exponential growth or decay, respectively.

Exponential growth is represented by the function $y = a(1 + r)^t$, while exponential decay is represented by the function $y = a(1 - r)^t$, where y is the new population, a is the initial population, r is the rate of growth or decay, and t is the number of time intervals that have elapsed.

A well-known example of exponential decay is the decay of a radioactive isotope. One example is iodine-131, a radioactive isotope used in some medical treatments. The decay of iodine-131 emits beta and gamma radiation, and it decays to xenon-131. The half-life of iodine-131 is 8.02 days; that is, after 8.02 days, half of the iodine-131 in a sample will have decayed to xenon-131. Suppose a sample of A milligrams of iodine-131 decays for d days. Every 8.02 days, the quantity of iodine-131 is multiplied by $\frac{1}{2}$, or 2^{-1}. In d days, a total of $\frac{d}{8.02}$ different 8.02-day periods will have passed, and so the original quantity will have been multiplied by 2^{-1} a total of $\frac{d}{8.02}$ times. Therefore, the amount, in milligrams, of iodine-131 remaining in the sample will be $A(2^{-1})^{\frac{d}{8.02}} = A\left(2^{-\frac{d}{8.02}}\right)$.

In the preceding discussion, we used the identity $\frac{1}{2} = 2^{-1}$. Questions on the SAT Math Test may require you to apply this and other laws of exponents and the relationship between powers and radicals.

Some Passport to Advanced Math questions ask you to use properties of exponents to rewrite expressions.

Example 9

Which of the following is equivalent to $\left(\frac{1}{\sqrt{x}}\right)^n$?

A) $x^{\frac{n}{2}}$

B) $x^{-\frac{n}{2}}$

C) $x^{n+\frac{1}{2}}$

D) $x^{n-\frac{1}{2}}$

The square root $\sqrt{x}$ is equal to $x^{\frac{1}{2}}$. Thus, $\frac{1}{\sqrt{x}} = x^{-\frac{1}{2}}$, and $\left(\frac{1}{\sqrt{x}}\right)^n = \left(x^{-\frac{1}{2}}\right)^n = x^{-\frac{n}{2}}$. Choice B is the correct answer.

PRACTICE AT

satpractice.org

Practice your exponent rules. Know, for instance, that $\sqrt{x} = x^{\frac{1}{2}}$ and that $\frac{1}{\sqrt{x}} = x^{-\frac{1}{2}}$.

An SAT Math Test question may also ask you to solve a radical equation. In solving radical equations, you may square both sides of an equation. Since squaring is *not* a reversible operation, you may end up with an extraneous root; that is, a root to the simplified equation that is *not* a root to the original equation. Thus, when solving a radical equation, you should check any solution you get in the original equation.

Example 10

$$x - 12 = \sqrt{x + 44}$$

What are the solutions x of the given equation?

A) 5

B) 20

C) −5 and 20

D) 5 and 20

Squaring each side of $x - 12 = \sqrt{x + 44}$ gives

$$(x - 12)^2 = \left(\sqrt{x + 44}\right)^2 = x + 44$$

$$x^2 - 24x + 144 = x + 44$$

$$x^2 - 25x + 100 = 0$$

$$(x - 5)(x - 20) = 0$$

The solutions to the quadratic are $x = 5$ and $x = 20$. However, since the first step was to square each side of the given equation, which is not a reversible operation, you need to check $x = 5$ and $x = 20$ in the original equation. Substituting 5 for x gives

$$5 - 12 = \sqrt{5 + 44}$$

$$-7 = \sqrt{49}$$

PRACTICE AT
satpractice.org

A good strategy to use when solving radical equations is to square both sides of the equation. When doing so, however, be sure to check the solutions in the original equation, as you may end up with a root that is not a solution to the original equation.

This is not a true statement (since $\sqrt{49}$ represents only the positive square root, 7), so $x = 5$ is *not* a solution to $x - 12 = \sqrt{x + 44}$. Substituting 20 for x gives

$$20 - 12 = \sqrt{20 + 44}$$

$$8 = \sqrt{64}$$

This is a true statement, so $x = 20$ is a solution to $x - 12 = \sqrt{x + 44}$. Therefore, the only solution to the given equation is 20, which is choice B.

Solving Rational Equations

Questions on the SAT Math Test may assess your ability to work with rational expressions, including fractions with a variable in the denominator. This may include finding the solution to a rational equation.

Example 11

$$\frac{3}{t+1} = \frac{2}{t+3} + \frac{1}{4}$$

If t is a solution to the equation above and $t > 0$, what is the value of t?

PRACTICE AT
satpractice.org

When solving for a variable in an equation involving fractions, a good first step is to clear the variable out of the denominators of the fractions Remember that you can only multiply both sides of an equation by an expression when you know the expression cannot be equal to 0.

If both sides of the equation are multiplied by $4(t + 1)(t + 3)$, the resulting equation will not have any fractions, and the variable will no longer be in the denominator. This gives $12(t + 3) = 8(t + 1) + (t + 1)(t + 3)$. Multiplying out the products gives $12t + 36 = (8t + 8) + (t^2 + 4t + 3)$, or $12t + 36 = t^2 + 12t + 11$, which simplifies to $0 = t^2 - 25$. Therefore, the solutions to the equation are $t = 5$ and $t = -5$. Since $t > 0$, the value of t is 5.

Systems of Equations

Questions on the SAT Math Test may ask you to solve a system of equations in two variables in which one equation is linear and the other equation is quadratic or another nonlinear equation.

Example 12

$$3x + y = -3$$

$$(x + 1)^2 - 4(x + 1) - 6 = y$$

If (x, y) is a solution of the system of equations above and $y > 0$, what is the value of y?

PRACTICE AT
satpractice.org

The first step used to solve this example is substitution, an approach you may use on Heart of Algebra questions. The other key was noticing that $(x + 1)$ can be treated as a variable.

One method for solving systems of equations is substitution. If the first equation is solved for y, it can be substituted in the second equation. Subtracting $3x$ from each side of the first equation gives you $y = -3 - 3x$, which can be rewritten as $y = -3(x + 1)$. Substituting $-3(x + 1)$ for y in the second equation gives you

$(x + 1)^2 - 4(x + 1) - 6 = -3(x + 1)$. Since the factor $(x + 1)$ appears as a squared term and a linear term, the equation can be thought of as a quadratic equation in the variable $(x + 1)$, so collecting the terms and setting the expression equal to 0 gives you $(x + 1)^2 - (x + 1) - 6 = 0$. Factoring gives you $((x + 1) - 3)((x + 1) + 2) = 0$, or $(x - 2)(x + 3) = 0$. Thus, either $x = 2$, which gives $y = -3 - 3(2) = -9$; or $x = -3$, which gives $y = -3 - 3(-3) = 6$. Therefore, the solutions to the system are $(2, -9)$ and $(-3, 6)$. Since the question states that $y > 0$, the value of y is 6.

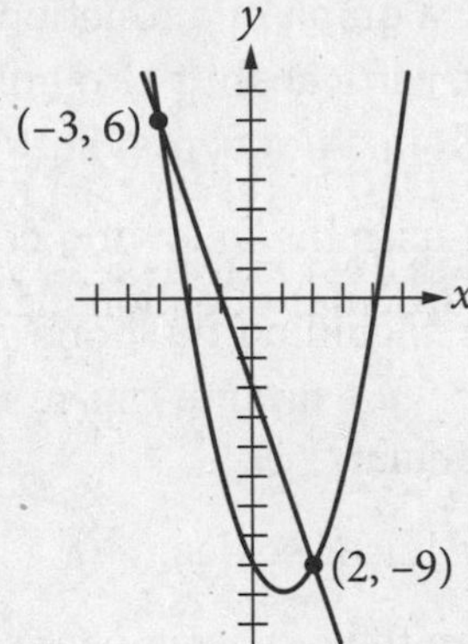

The solutions of the system are given by the intersection points of the two graphs. Questions on the SAT Math Test may assess this or other relationships between algebraic and graphical representations of functions.

Relationships Between Algebraic and Graphical Representations of Functions

A function f has a graph in the xy-plane, which is the graph of the equation $y = f(x)$ (or, equivalently, consists of all ordered pairs $(x, f(x))$). Some Passport to Advanced Math questions assess your ability to relate properties of the function f to properties of its graph, and vice versa. You may be required to apply some of the following relationships:

- **Intercepts.** The x-intercepts of the graph of f correspond to values of x such that $f(x) = 0$, which corresponds to where the graph intersects with the x-axis; if the function f has no zeros, its graph has no x-intercepts, and vice versa. The y-intercept of the graph of f corresponds to the value of $f(0)$, or where the graph intersects with the y-axis. If $x = 0$ is not in the domain of f, the graph of f has no y-intercept, and vice versa.
- **Domain and range.** The domain of f is the set of all x for which $f(x)$ is defined. The range of f is the set of all y such that $y = f(x)$ for some value of x in the domain. The domain and range can be found from the graph of f as the set of all x-coordinates and y-coordinates, respectively, of points on the graph.
- **Maximum and minimum values.** The maximum and minimum values of f can be found by locating the highest and the lowest points on the graph, respectively. For example, suppose P is the

PRACTICE AT
satpractice.org

The domain of a function is the set of all values for which the function is defined. The range of a function is the set of all values that correspond to the values in the domain, given the relationship defined by the function, or the set of all outputs that are associated with all of the possible inputs.

highest point on the graph of f. Then the y-coordinate of P is the maximum value of f, and the x-coordinate of P is where f takes on its maximum value.

- **Increasing and decreasing.** The graph of f shows the intervals over which the function f is increasing and decreasing.
- **End behavior.** The graph of f can indicate if $f(x)$ increases or decreases without limit as x increases or decreases without limit.
- **Transformations.** For a graph of a function f, a change of the form $f(x) + a$ will result in a vertical shift of a units and a change of the form $f(x + a)$ will result in a horizontal shift of a units.

Note: The SAT Math Test uses the following conventions about graphs in the xy-plane *unless* a particular question clearly states or shows a different convention:

- The axes are perpendicular.
- Scales on the axes are linear scales.
- The size of the units on the two axes *cannot* be assumed to be equal unless the question states they are equal or you are given enough information to conclude they are equal.
- The values on the horizontal axis increase as you move to the right.
- The values on the vertical axis increase as you move up.

REMEMBER

Don't assume the size of the units on the two axes are equal unless the question states they are equal or you can conclude they are equal from the information given.

Example 13

The graph of which of the following functions in the xy-plane has x-intercepts at -4 and 5?

A) $f(x) = (x + 4)(x - 5)$

B) $g(x) = (x - 4)(x + 5)$

C) $h(x) = (x - 4)^2 + 5$

D) $k(x) = (x + 5)^2 - 4$

The x-intercepts of the graph of a function correspond to the zeros of the function. All the functions in the choices are defined by quadratic equations, so the answer must be a quadratic function. If a quadratic function has x-intercepts at -4 and 5, then the values of the function at -4 and 5 are each 0; that is, the zeros of the function occur at $x = -4$ and at $x = 5$. Since the function is defined by a quadratic equation and has zeros at $x = -4$ and $x = 5$, it must have $(x + 4)$ and $(x - 5)$ as factors. Therefore, choice A, $f(x) = (x + 4)(x - 5)$, is correct.

The graph in the xy-plane of each of the functions in the previous example is a parabola. Using the defining equations, you can tell that the graph of g has x-intercepts at 4 and -5; the graph of h has its vertex at (4, 5); and the graph of k has its vertex at $(-5, -4)$.

PRACTICE AT

satpractice.org

Another way to think of Example 13 is to ask yourself, "Which answer choice represents a function that has values of zero when $x = -4$ and $x = +5$?"

Example 14

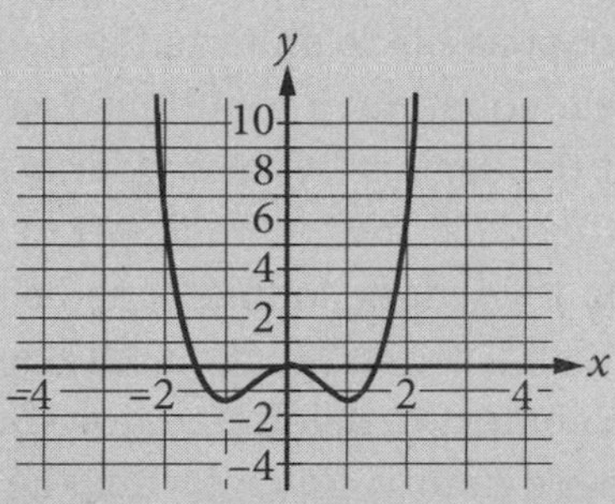

The function $f(x) = x^4 - 2.4x^2$ is graphed in the xy-plane as shown above. If k is a constant such that the equation $f(x) = k$ has 4 solutions, which of the following could be the value of k?

A) 1

B) 0

C) -1

D) -2

Choice C is correct. Since $f(x) = x^4 - 2.4x^2$, the equation $f(x) = k$, or $x^4 - 2.4x^2 = k$, will have 4 solutions if and only if the graph of the horizontal line with equation $y = k$ intersects the graph of f at 4 points. The graph shows that of the given choices, only for choice C, -1, does the graph of $y = -1$ intersect the graph of f at 4 points.

Function Notation

The SAT Math Test assesses your understanding of function notation. You must be able to evaluate a function given the rule that defines it, and if the function describes a context, you may need to interpret the value of the function in the context. A question may ask you to interpret a function when an expression, such as $2x$ or $x + 1$, is used as the argument instead of the variable x.

Example 15

If $g(x) = 2x + 1$ and $f(x) = g(x) + 4$, what is $f(2)$?

You are given $f(x) = g(x) + 4$ and therefore $f(2) = g(2) + 4$. To determine the value of $g(2)$, use the function $g(x) = 2x + 1$. Thus, $g(2) = 2(2) + 1$, and therefore $g(2) = 5$. Substituting $g(2)$ gives $f(2) = 5 + 4$, or $f(2) = 9$.

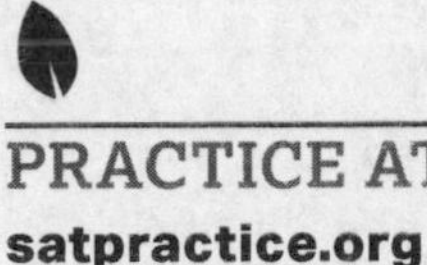

PRACTICE AT

satpractice.org

What may seem at first to be a complex question boils down to straightforward substitution.

Alternatively, since $f(x) = g(x) + 4$ and $g(x) = 2x + 1$, it follows that $f(x)$ must equal $2x + 1 + 4$, or $2x + 5$. Therefore, $f(2) = 2(2) + 5 = 9$.

Interpreting and Analyzing More Complex Equations in Context

Equations and functions that describe a real-life context can be complex. Often, it's not possible to analyze them as completely as you can analyze a linear equation or function. You still can acquire key information about the context by interpreting and analyzing the equation or function that describes it. Passport to Advanced Math questions may ask you to identify connections between the function, its graph, and the context it describes. You may be asked to use an equation describing a context to determine how a change in one quantity affects another quantity. You may also be asked to manipulate an equation to isolate a quantity of interest on one side of the equation. You may be asked to produce or identify a form of an equation that reveals new information about the context it represents or about the graphical representation of the equation.

Example 16

For a certain reservoir, the function f gives the water level $f(n)$, to the nearest whole percent of capacity, on the nth day of 2016. Which of the following is the best interpretation of $f(37) = 70$?

A) The water level of the dam was at 37% capacity for 70 days in 2016.

B) The water level of the dam was at 70% capacity for 37 days in 2016.

C) On the 37th day of 2016, the water level of the dam was at 70% capacity.

D) On the 70th day of 2016, the water level of the dam was at 37% capacity.

PRACTICE AT
satpractice.org

Another way to check your answer in Example 17 is to pick simple numbers for mass and speed and examine the impact on kinetic energy when those values are altered as indicated by the question. If mass and speed both equal 1, kinetic energy is $\frac{1}{2}$.

When mass is halved, to $\frac{1}{2}$, and speed is doubled, to 2, the new kinetic energy is 1. Since 1 is twice the value of $\frac{1}{2}$, you know that kinetic energy is doubled.

The function f gives the water level, to the whole nearest percent of capacity on the nth day of 2016. It follows that $f(37) = 70$ means that on the 37th day of 2016, the water level of the dam was at 70% capacity. This statement is choice C.

Example 17

If an object of mass m is moving at speed v, the object's kinetic energy KE is given by the equation $\text{KE} = \frac{1}{2}mv^2$. If the mass of the object is halved and its speed is doubled, how does the kinetic energy change?

A) The kinetic energy is halved.

B) The kinetic energy is unchanged.

C) The kinetic energy is doubled.

D) The kinetic energy is quadrupled (multiplied by a factor of 4).

Choice C is correct. If the mass of the object is halved, the new mass is $\frac{m}{2}$. If the speed of the object is doubled, its new speed is $2v$. Therefore, the new kinetic energy is $\frac{1}{2}\left(\frac{m}{2}\right)(2v)^2 = \frac{1}{2}\left(\frac{m}{2}\right)(4v^2) = mv^2$. This is double the kinetic energy of the original object, which was $\frac{1}{2}mv^2$.

Example 18

A gas in a container will escape through holes of microscopic size, as long as the holes are larger than the gas molecules. This process is called effusion. If a gas of molar mass M_1 effuses at a rate of r_1 and a gas of molar mass M_2 effuses at a rate of r_2, then the following relationship holds.

$$\frac{r_1}{r_2} = \sqrt{\frac{M_2}{M_1}}$$

This is known as Graham's law. Which of the following correctly expresses M_2 in terms of M_1, r_1, and r_2?

A) $M_2 = M_1\left(\frac{r_1^2}{r_2^2}\right)$

B) $M_2 = M_1\left(\frac{r_2^2}{r_1^2}\right)$

C) $M_2 = \sqrt{M_1}\left(\frac{r_1}{r_2}\right)$

D) $M_2 = \sqrt{M_1}\left(\frac{r_2}{r_1}\right)$

Squaring each side of $\frac{r_1}{r_2} = \sqrt{\frac{M_2}{M_1}}$ gives $\left(\frac{r_1}{r_2}\right)^2 = \left(\sqrt{\frac{M_2}{M_1}}\right)^2$, which can be rewritten as $\frac{M_2}{M_1} = \frac{r_1^2}{r_2^2}$. Multiplying each side of $\frac{M_2}{M_1} = \frac{r_1^2}{r_2^2}$ by M_1 gives $M_2 = M_1\left(\frac{r_1^2}{r_2^2}\right)$, which is choice A.

PRACTICE AT
satpractice.org

Always start by identifying exactly what the question asks. In Example 18, you are being asked to isolate the variable M_2. Squaring both sides of the equation is a great first step as it allows you to eliminate the radical sign.

Example 19

A store manager estimates that if a video game is sold at a price of p dollars, the store will have weekly revenue, in dollars, of $r(p) = -4p^2 + 200p$ from the sale of the video game. Which of the following equivalent forms of $r(p)$ shows, as constants or coefficients, the maximum possible weekly revenue and the price that results in the maximum revenue?

A) $r(p) = 200p - 4p^2$

B) $r(p) = -2(2p^2 - 100p)$

C) $r(p) = -4(p^2 - 50p)$

D) $r(p) = -4(p - 25)^2 + 2{,}500$

PRACTICE AT
satpractice.org

The fact that the coefficient of the squared term is negative for this function indicates that the graph of r in the coordinate plane is a parabola that opens downward. Thus, the maximum value of revenue corresponds to the vertex of the parabola.

Choice D is correct. The graph of r in the coordinate plane is a parabola that opens downward. The maximum value of revenue corresponds to the vertex of the parabola. Since the square of any real number is always nonnegative, the form $r(p) = -4(p - 25)^2 + 2{,}500$ shows that the vertex of the parabola is (25, 2,500); that is, the maximum must occur where $-4(p - 25)^2$ is 0, which is $p = 25$, and this maximum is $r(25) = 2{,}500$. Thus, the maximum possible weekly revenue and the price that results in the maximum revenue occur as constants in the form $r(p) = -4(p - 25)^2 + 2{,}500$.

CHAPTER 19

Additional Topics in Math

In addition to the questions in Heart of Algebra, Problem Solving and Data Analysis, and Passport to Advanced Math, the SAT Math Test includes several questions that are drawn from areas of geometry, trigonometry, and the arithmetic of complex numbers. They include both multiple-choice and student-produced response questions. Some of these questions appear in the no-calculator portion, where the use of a calculator is not permitted, and others are in the calculator portion, where the use of a calculator is permitted.

Let's explore the content and skills assessed by these questions.

REMEMBER

Six of the 58 questions (approximately 10%) on the SAT Math Test will be drawn from Additional Topics in Math, which includes geometry, trigonometry, and the arithmetic of complex numbers.

Geometry

The SAT Math Test includes questions that assess your understanding of the key concepts in the geometry of lines, angles, triangles, circles, and other geometric objects. Other questions may also ask you to find the area, surface area, or volume of an abstract figure or a real-life object. You don't need to memorize a large collection of formulas. Many of the geometry formulas are provided in the reference information at the beginning of each section of the SAT Math Test, and less commonly used formulas required to answer a question are given with the question.

REMEMBER

You do not need to memorize a large collection of geometry formulas. Many geometry formulas are provided on the SAT Math Test in the Reference section of the directions.

To answer geometry questions on the SAT Math Test, you should recall the geometry definitions learned prior to high school and know the essential concepts extended while learning geometry in high school. You should also be familiar with basic geometric notation.

Here are some of the areas that may be the focus of some questions on the SAT Math Test.

- Lines and angles
  - Lengths and midpoints
  - Measures of angles
  - Vertical angles
  - Angle addition
  - Straight angles and the sum of the angles about a point

- Properties of parallel lines and the angles formed when parallel lines are cut by a transversal
- Properties of perpendicular lines

- Triangles and other polygons
  - Right triangles and the Pythagorean theorem
  - Properties of equilateral and isosceles triangles
  - Properties of 30°-60°-90° triangles and 45°-45°-90° triangles
  - Congruent triangles and other congruent figures
  - Similar triangles and other similar figures
  - The triangle inequality
  - Squares, rectangles, parallelograms, trapezoids, and other quadrilaterals
  - Regular polygons
- Circles
  - Radius, diameter, and circumference
  - Measure of central angles and inscribed angles
  - Arc length, arc measure, and area of sectors
  - Tangents and chords
- Area and volume
  - Area of plane figures
  - Volume of solids
  - Surface area of solids

PRACTICE AT

satpractice.org

The triangle inequality theorem states that for any triangle, the length of any side of the triangle must be less than the sum of the lengths of the other two sides of the triangle and greater than the difference of the lengths of the other two sides.

You should be familiar with the geometric notation for points and lines, line segments, angles and their measures, and lengths.

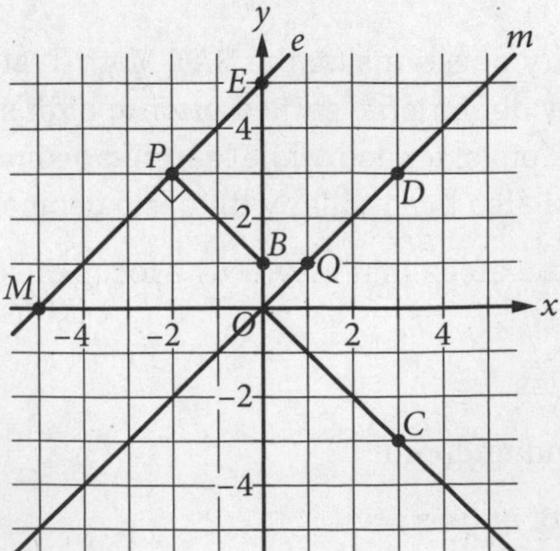

In the figure above, the *xy*-plane has origin *O*. The values of *x* on the horizontal *x*-axis increase as you move to the right, and the values of *y* on the vertical *y*-axis increase as you move up. Line *e* contains point *P*, which has coordinates (−2, 3); point E, which has coordinates (0, 5); and point M, which has coordinates (−5, 0). Line m passes through the origin O (0, 0), the point Q (1, 1), and the point D (3, 3).

Lines e and m are parallel — they never meet. This is written $e \parallel m$.

You will also need to know the following notation:

- $\overleftrightarrow{PE}$: the line containing the points P and E (this is the same as line e)
- $\overline{PE}$ or line segment PE: the line segment with endpoints P and E
- PE: the length of segment PE (you can write $PE = 2\sqrt{2}$)
- $\overrightarrow{PE}$: the ray starting at point P and extending indefinitely in the direction of point E
- $\overrightarrow{EP}$: the ray starting at point E and extending indefinitely in the direction of point P
- $\angle DOC$: the angle formed by $\overrightarrow{OD}$ and $\overrightarrow{OC}$
- $\triangle PEB$: the triangle with vertices P, E, and B
- Quadrilateral $BPMO$: the quadrilateral with vertices B, P, M, and O
- $\overline{BP} \perp \overline{PM}$: segment BP is perpendicular to segment PM (you should also recognize that the right angle box within $\angle BPM$ means this angle is a right angle)

PRACTICE AT
satpractice.org

Familiarize yourself with these notations in order to avoid confusion on test day.

Example 1

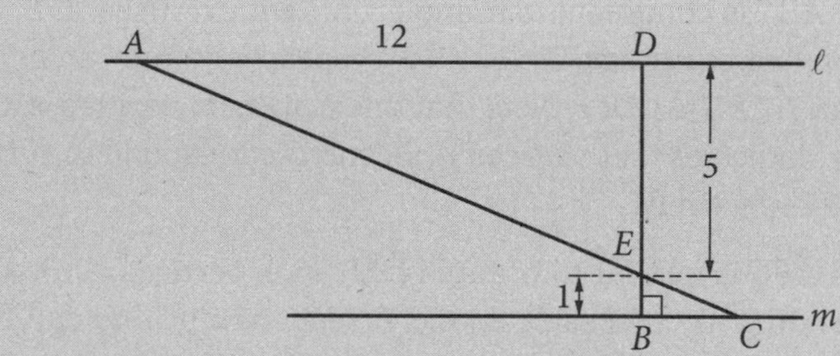

In the figure above, line ℓ is parallel to line m, segment BD is perpendicular to line m, and segment AC and segment BD intersect at E. What is the length of segment AC?

Since segment AC and segment BD intersect at E, $\angle AED$ and $\angle CEB$ are vertical angles, and so the measure of $\angle AED$ is equal to the measure of $\angle CEB$. Since line ℓ is parallel to line m, $\angle BCE$ and $\angle DAE$ are alternate interior angles of parallel lines cut by a transversal, and so the measure of $\angle BCE$ is equal to the measure of $\angle DAE$. By the angle-angle theorem, $\triangle AED$ is similar to $\triangle CEB$, with vertices A, E, and D corresponding to vertices C, E, and B, respectively.

Also, $\triangle AED$ is a right triangle, so by the Pythagorean theorem, $AE = \sqrt{AD^2 + DE^2} = \sqrt{12^2 + 5^2} = \sqrt{169} = 13$. Since $\triangle AED$ is similar to

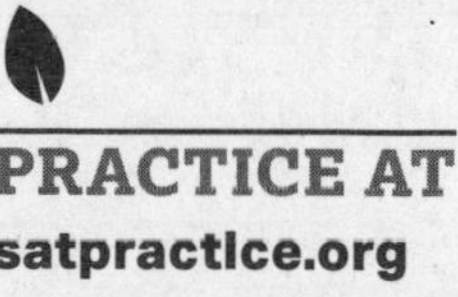

PRACTICE AT
satpractice.org

A shortcut here is remembering that 5, 12, 13 is a Pythagorean triple (5 and 12 are the lengths of the sides of the right triangle, and 13 is the length of the hypotenuse). Another common Pythagorean triple is 3, 4, 5.

$\triangle CEB$, the ratios of the lengths of corresponding sides of the two triangles are in the same proportion, which is $\frac{ED}{EB} = \frac{5}{1} = 5$. Thus, $\frac{AE}{EC} = \frac{13}{EC} = 5$, and so $EC = \frac{13}{5}$. Therefore, $AC = AE + EC = 13 + \frac{13}{5} = \frac{78}{5}$.

Note some of the key concepts that were used in Example 1:

- Vertical angles have the same measure.
- When parallel lines are cut by a transversal, the alternate interior angles have the same measure.
- If two angles of a triangle are congruent to (have the same measure as) two angles of another triangle, the two triangles are similar.
- The Pythagorean theorem.
- If two triangles are similar, then all ratios of lengths of corresponding sides are equal.
- If point *E* lies on line segment *AC*, then $AC = AE + EC$.

PRACTICE AT
satpractice.org

Note how Example 1 requires the knowledge and application of numerous fundamental geometry concepts. Develop mastery of the fundamental concepts and practice applying them on test-like questions.

Note that if two triangles or other polygons are similar or congruent, the order in which the vertices are named does *not* necessarily indicate how the vertices correspond in the similarity or congruence. Thus, it was stated explicitly in Example 1 that "$\triangle AED$ is similar to $\triangle CEB$, with vertices *A*, *E*, and *D* corresponding to vertices *C*, *E*, and *B*, respectively."

You should also be familiar with the symbols for congruence and similarity.

- Triangle *ABC* is congruent to triangle *DEF*, with vertices *A*, *B*, and *C* corresponding to vertices *D*, *E*, and *F*, respectively, and can be written as $\triangle ABC \cong \triangle DEF$. Note that this statement, written with the symbol $\cong$, indicates that vertices *A*, *B*, and *C* correspond to vertices *D*, *E*, and *F*, respectively.
- Triangle *ABC* is similar to triangle *DEF*, with vertices *A*, *B*, and *C* corresponding to vertices *D*, *E*, and *F*, respectively, and can be written as $\triangle ABC \sim \triangle DEF$. Note that this statement, written with the symbol $\sim$, indicates that vertices *A*, *B*, and *C* correspond to vertices *D*, *E*, and *F*, respectively.

Example 2

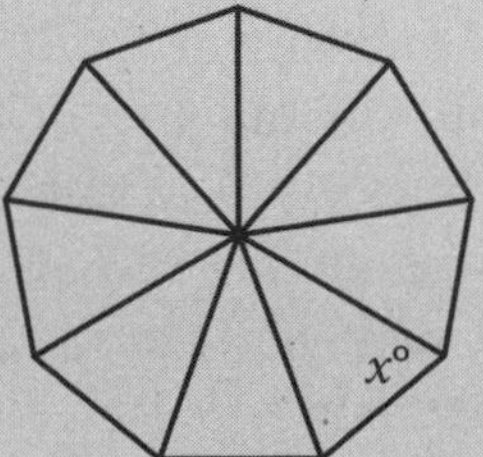

In the figure above, a regular polygon with 9 sides has been divided into 9 congruent isosceles triangles by line segments drawn from the center of the polygon to its vertices. What is the value of *x*?

The sum of the measures of the angles around a point is 360°. Since the 9 triangles are congruent, the measures of each of the 9 angles are equal. Thus, the measure of each of the 9 angles around the center point is $\frac{360°}{9} = 40°$. In any triangle, the sum of the measures of the interior angles is 180°. So in each triangle, the sum of the measures of the remaining two angles is $180° - 40° = 140°$. Since each triangle is isosceles, the measure of each of these two angles is the same. Therefore, the measure of each of these angles is $\frac{140°}{2} = 70°$. Hence, the value of x is 70.

Note some of the key concepts that were used in Example 2:

- The sum of the measures of the angles about a point is 360°.
- Corresponding angles of congruent triangles have the same measure.
- The sum of the measure of the interior angles of any triangle is 180°.
- In an isosceles triangle, the angles opposite the sides of equal length are of equal measure.

Example 3

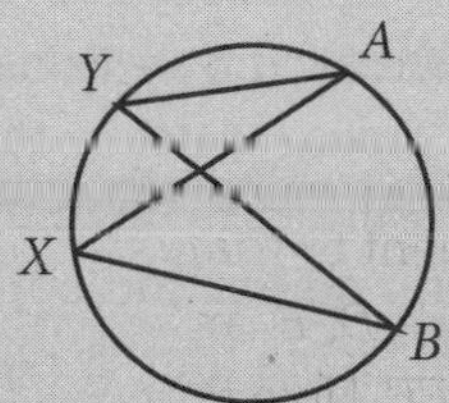

In the figure above, $\angle AXB$ and $\angle AYB$ are inscribed in the circle. Which of the following statements is true?

A) The measure of $\angle AXB$ is greater than the measure of $\angle AYB$.

B) The measure of $\angle AXB$ is less than the measure of $\angle AYB$.

C) The measure of $\angle AXB$ is equal to the measure of $\angle AYB$.

D) There is not enough information to determine the relationship between the measure of $\angle AXB$ and the measure of $\angle AYB$.

Choice C is correct. Let the measure of arc $\overset{\frown}{AB}$ be $d°$. Since $\angle AXB$ is inscribed in the circle and intercepts arc $\overset{\frown}{AB}$, the measure of $\angle AXB$ is equal to half the measure of arc $\overset{\frown}{AB}$. Thus, the measure of $\angle AXB$ is $\frac{d°}{2}$. Similarly, since $\angle AYB$ is also inscribed in the circle and intercepts arc $\overset{\frown}{AB}$, the measure of $\angle AYB$ is also $\frac{d°}{2}$. Therefore, the measure of $\angle AXB$ is equal to the measure of $\angle AYB$.

Note the key concept that was used in Example 3:

- The measure of an angle inscribed in a circle is equal to half the measure of its intercepted arc.

PRACTICE AT

satpractice.org

At first glance, it may appear as though there's not enough information to determine the relationship between the two angle measures. One key to this question is identifying what is the same about the two angle measures. In this case, both angles intercept arc $\overset{\frown}{AB}$.

You also should know these related concepts:

- The measure of a central angle in a circle is equal to the measure of its intercepted arc.
- An arc is measured in degrees, while arc length is measured in linear units.

You should also be familiar with notation for arcs and circles on the SAT:

- A circle may be identified by the point at its center; for instance, "the circle centered at point *M*" or "the circle with center at point *M*."
- An arc named with only its two endpoints, such as arc $\overparen{AB}$, will always refer to a minor arc. A minor arc has a measure that is less than 180°.
- An arc may also be named with three points: the two endpoints and a third point that the arc passes through. So, arc $\overparen{ACB}$ has endpoints at *A* and *B* and passes through point *C*. Three points may be used to name a minor arc or an arc that has a measure of 180° or more.

REMEMBER

Figures are drawn to scale on the SAT Math Test unless explicitly stated otherwise. If a question states that a figure is not drawn to scale, be careful not to make unwarranted assumptions about the figure.

In general, figures that accompany questions on the SAT Math Test are intended to provide information that is useful in answering the question. They are drawn as accurately as possible EXCEPT in a particular question when it is stated that the figure is not drawn to scale. In general, even in figures not drawn to scale, the relative positions of points and angles may be assumed to be in the order shown. Also, line segments that extend through points and appear to lie on the same line may be assumed to be on the same line. A point that appears to lie on a line or curve may be assumed to lie on the line or curve.

The text "Note: Figure not drawn to scale." is included with the figure when degree measures may not be accurately shown and specific lengths may not be drawn proportionally. The following example illustrates what information can and cannot be assumed from a figure not drawn to scale.

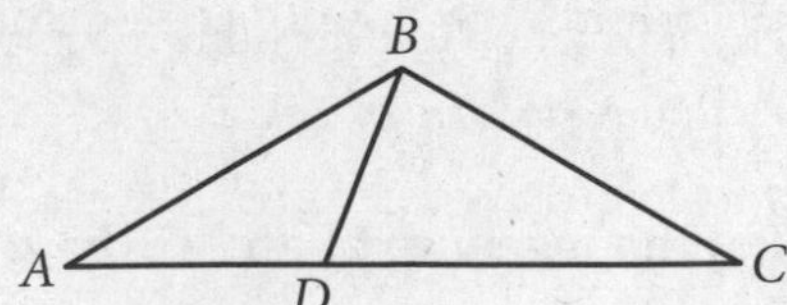

Note: Figure not drawn to scale.

A question may refer to a triangle such as *ABC* above. Although the note indicates that the figure is not drawn to scale, you may assume the following from the figure:

- *ABD* and *DBC* are triangles.
- *D* is between *A* and *C*.
- *A*, *D*, and *C* are points on a line.

- The length of $\overline{AD}$ is less than the length of $\overline{AC}$.
- The measure of angle ABD is less than the measure of angle ABC.

You may *not* assume the following from the figure:

- The length of $\overline{AD}$ is less than the length of $\overline{DC}$.
- The measures of angles BAD and DBA are equal.
- The measure of angle DBC is greater than the measure of angle ABD.
- Angle DBC is a right angle.

Example 4

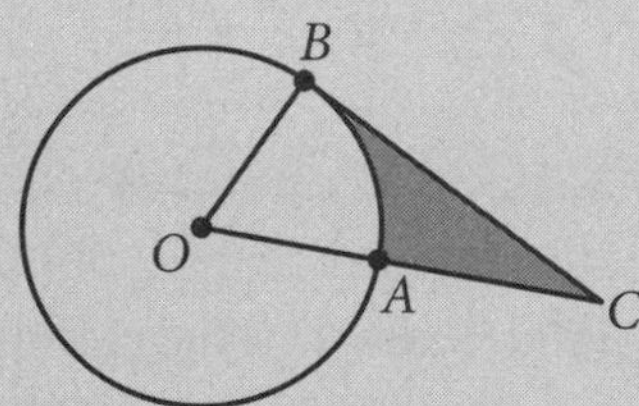

In the figure above, O is the center of the circle, segment BC is tangent to the circle at B, and A lies on segment OC. If $OB = AC = 6$, what is the area of the shaded region?

A) $18\sqrt{3} - 3\pi$

B) $18\sqrt{3} - 6\pi$

C) $36\sqrt{3} - 3\pi$

D) $36\sqrt{3} - 6\pi$

Since segment BC is tangent to the circle at B, it follows that $\overline{BC} \perp \overline{OB}$, and so triangle OBC is a right triangle with its right angle at B. Since $OB = 6$ and OB and OA are both radii of the circle, $OA = OB = 6$, and $OC = OA + AC = 12$. Thus, triangle OBC is a right triangle with the length of the hypotenuse ($OC = 12$) twice the length of one of its legs ($OB = 6$). It follows that triangle OBC is a 30°-60°-90° triangle with its 30° angle at C and its 60° angle at O. The area of the shaded region is the area of triangle OBC minus the area of the sector bounded by radii OA and OB.

In the 30°-60°-90° triangle OBC, the length of side OB, which is opposite the 30° angle, is 6. Thus, the length of side BC, which is opposite the 60° angle, is $6\sqrt{3}$. Hence, the area of triangle OBC is $\frac{1}{2}(6)(6\sqrt{3}) = 18\sqrt{3}$. Since the sector bounded by radii OA and OB has central angle 60°, the area of this sector is $\frac{60}{360} = \frac{1}{6}$ of the area of the circle. Since the circle has radius 6, its area is $\pi(6)^2 = 36\pi$, and so the area of the sector is $\frac{1}{6}(36\pi) = 6\pi$. Therefore, the area of the shaded region is $18\sqrt{3} - 6\pi$, which is choice B.

PRACTICE AT

satpractice.org

On complex multistep questions such as Example 4, start by identifying the task (finding the area of the shaded region) and considering the intermediate steps that you'll need to solve for (the area of triangle OBC and the area of sector OBA) in order to get to the final answer. Breaking up this question into a series of smaller questions will make it more manageable.

PRACTICE AT

satpractice.org

Arc length, area of a sector, and central angle are all proportional to each other in a circle. This proportionality is written as

$$\frac{\text{arc length}}{\text{circumference}} = \frac{\text{central angle}}{\text{360 degrees}} = \frac{\text{area of a sector}}{\text{area of a circle}}$$

Note some of the key concepts that were used in Example 4:

- A tangent to a circle is perpendicular to the radius of the circle drawn to the point of tangency.
- Properties of 30°-60°-90° triangles.
- Area of a circle.
- The area of a sector with central angle $x°$ is equal to $\frac{x}{360}$ of the area of the entire circle.

Example 5

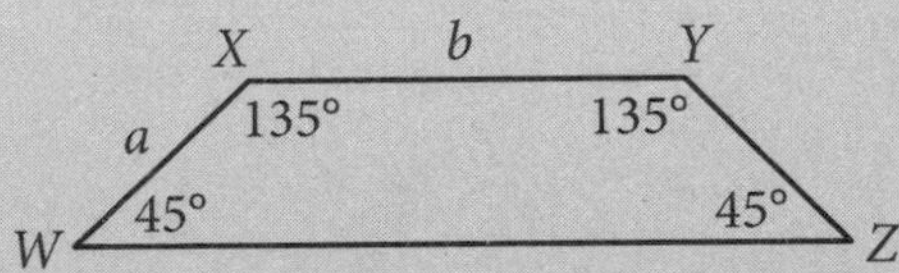

Trapezoid *WXYZ* is shown above. How much greater is the area of this trapezoid than the area of a parallelogram with side lengths *a* and *b* and base angles of measure 45° and 135°?

A) $\frac{1}{2}a^2$

B) $\sqrt{2}a^2$

C) $\frac{1}{2}ab$

D) $\sqrt{2}ab$

PRACTICE AT

satpractice.org

Note how drawing the parallelogram within trapezoid *WXYZ* makes it much easier to compare the areas of the two shapes, minimizing the amount of calculation needed to arrive at the solution. Be on the lookout for time-saving shortcuts such as this one.

In the figure, draw a line segment from *Y* to the point *P* on side *WZ* of the trapezoid such that $\angle YPW$ has measure 135°, as shown in the figure below.

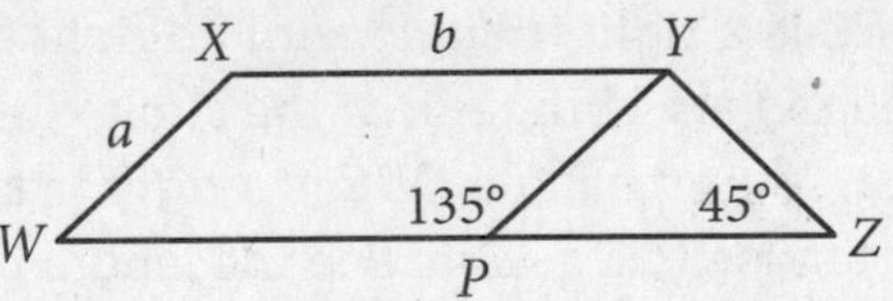

Since in trapezoid *WXYZ* side *XY* is parallel to side *WZ*, it follows that *WXYP* is a parallelogram with side lengths *a* and *b* and base angles of measure 45° and 135°. Thus, the area of the trapezoid is greater than a parallelogram with side lengths *a* and *b* and base angles of measure 45° and 135° by the area of triangle *PYZ*. Since $\angle YPW$ has measure 135°, it follows that $\angle YPZ$ has measure 45°. Hence, triangle *PYZ* is a 45°-45°-90° triangle with legs of length *a*. Therefore, its area is $\frac{1}{2}a^2$, which is choice A.

Note some of the key concepts that were used in Example 5:

- Properties of trapezoids and parallelograms
- Area of a 45°-45°-90° triangle

Some questions on the SAT Math Test may ask you to find the area, surface area, or volume of an object, possibly in a real-life context.

Example 6

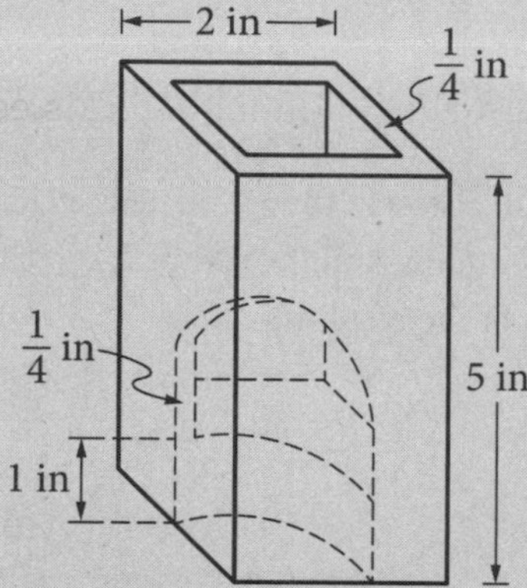

Note: Figure not drawn to scale.

A glass vase is in the shape of a rectangular prism with a square base. The figure above shows the vase with a portion cut out to show the interior dimensions. The external dimensions of the vase are height 5 inches (in), with a square base of side length 2 inches. The vase has a solid base of height 1 inch, and the sides are each $\frac{1}{4}$ inch thick. Which of the following is the volume, in cubic inches, of the glass used in the vase?

A) 6

B) 8

C) 9

D) 11

The volume of the glass used in the vase can be calculated by subtracting the inside volume of the vase from the outside volume of the vase. The inside and outside volumes are different-sized rectangular prisms. The outside dimensions of the prism are 5 inches by 2 inches by 2 inches, so its volume, including the glass, is $5 \times 2 \times 2 = 20$ cubic inches. For the inside volume of the vase, since it has a solid base of height 1 inch, the height of the prism removed is $5 - 1 = 4$ inches. In addition, each side of the vase is $\frac{1}{4}$ inch thick, so each side length of the inside volume is $2 - \frac{1}{4} - \frac{1}{4} = \frac{3}{2}$ inches. Thus, the inside volume of the vase removed is $4 \times \frac{3}{2} \times \frac{3}{2} = 9$ cubic inches. Therefore, the volume of the glass used in the vase is $20 - 9 = 11$ cubic inches, which is choice D.

PRACTICE AT
satpractice.org

Pay close attention to detail on a question such as Example 6. You must take into account the fact that the vase has a solid base of height 1 inch when subtracting the inside volume of the vase from the outside volume of the vase.

Coordinate Geometry

Questions on the SAT Math Test may ask you to use the coordinate plane and equations of lines and circles to describe figures. You may be asked to create the equation of a circle given the figure or

PRACTICE AT
satpractice.org

You should know that the graph of $(x - a)^2 + (y - b)^2 = r^2$ in the xy-plane is a circle with center (a, b) and radius r.

use the structure of a given equation to determine a property of a figure in the coordinate plane. You should know that the graph of $(x - a)^2 + (y - b)^2 = r^2$ in the xy-plane is a circle with center (a, b) and radius r.

Example 7

$$x^2 + (y + 1)^2 = 4$$

The graph of the equation above in the xy-plane is a circle. If the center of this circle is translated 1 unit up and the radius is increased by 1, which of the following is an equation of the resulting circle?

A) $x^2 + y^2 = 5$

B) $x^2 + y^2 = 9$

C) $x^2 + (y + 2)^2 = 5$

D) $x^2 + (y + 2)^2 = 9$

The graph of the equation $x^2 + (y + 1)^2 = 4$ in the xy-plane is a circle with center $(0, -1)$ and radius $\sqrt{4} = 2$. If the center is translated 1 unit up, the center of the new circle will be $(0, 0)$. If the radius is increased by 1, the radius of the new circle will be 3. Therefore, an equation of the new circle in the xy-plane is $x^2 + y^2 = 3^2 = 9$, so choice B is correct.

Example 8

$$x^2 + 8x + y^2 - 6y = 24$$

The graph of the equation above in the xy-plane is a circle. What is the radius of the circle?

The given equation is not in the standard form $(x - a)^2 + (y - b)^2 = r^2$. You can put it in standard form by completing the square. Since the coefficient of x is 8 and the coefficient of y is -6, you can write the equation in terms of $(x + 4)^2$ and $(y - 3)^2$ as follows:

$$x^2 + 8x + y^2 - 6y = 24$$

$$(x^2 + 8x + 16) - 16 + (y^2 - 6y + 9) - 9 = 24$$

$$(x + 4)^2 - 16 + (y - 3)^2 - 9 = 24$$

$$(x + 4)^2 + (y - 3)^2 = 24 + 16 + 9 = 49 = 7^2$$

Therefore, the radius of the circle is 7. (Also, the center of the circle is $(-4, 3)$.)

Trigonometry and Radians

Questions on the SAT Math Test may ask you to apply the definitions of right triangle trigonometry. You should also know the definition of radian measure; you may also need to convert between angle measure in degrees and radians. You may need to evaluate trigonometric functions at benchmark angle measures such as $0, \frac{\pi}{6}, \frac{\pi}{4}, \frac{\pi}{3},$

and $\frac{\pi}{2}$ radians (which are equal to the angle measures 0°, 30°, 45°, 60°, and 90°, respectively). You will *not* be asked for values of trigonometric functions that require a calculator.

For an acute angle, the trigonometric functions sine, cosine, and tangent can be defined using right triangles. (Note that the functions are often abbreviated as sin, cos, and tan, respectively.)

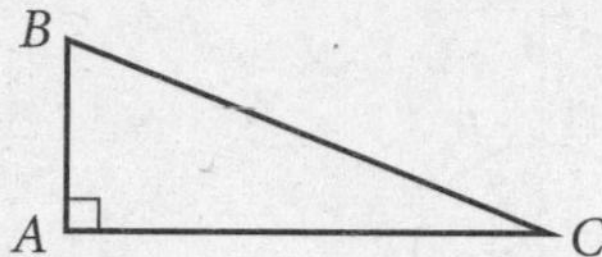

For $\angle C$ in the right triangle above:

- $\sin(\angle C) = \frac{AB}{BC} = \frac{\text{length of leg opposite } \angle C}{\text{length of hypotenuse}}$
- $\cos(\angle C) = \frac{AC}{BC} = \frac{\text{length of leg adjacent to } \angle C}{\text{length of hypotenuse}}$
- $\tan(\angle C) = \frac{AB}{AC} = \frac{\text{length of leg opposite } \angle C}{\text{length of leg adjacent to } \angle C} = \frac{\sin(\angle C)}{\cos(\angle C)}$

The functions will often be written as sin *C*, cos *C*, and tan *C*, respectively.

Note that the trigonometric functions are actually functions of the *measures* of an angle, not the angle itself. Thus, if the measure of $\angle C$ is, say, 30°, you can write sin(30°), cos(30°), and tan(30°), respectively.

Also note that sine and cosine are cofunctions and that $\sin B = \frac{\text{length of leg opposite } \angle B}{\text{length of hypotenuse}} = \frac{AC}{BC} = \cos C$. This is the complementary angle relationship: $\sin(x°) = \cos(90° - x°)$.

PRACTICE AT
satpractice.org

The acronym "SOHCAHTOA" may help you remember how to compute sine, cosine, and tangent. SOH stands for Sine equals Opposite over Hypotenuse, CAH stands for Cosine equals Adjacent over Hypotenuse, and TOA stands for Tangent equals Opposite over Adjacent.

Example 9

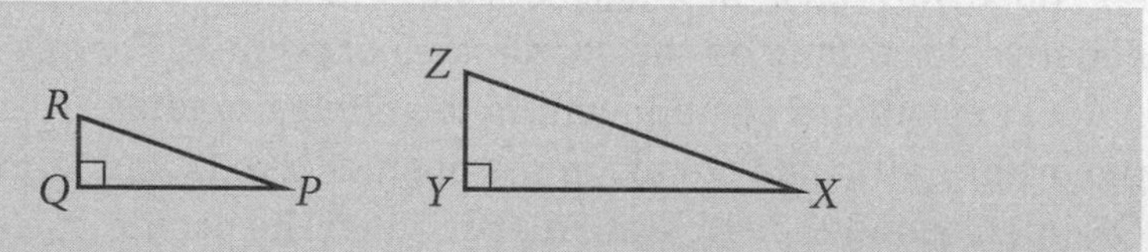

In the figure above, right triangle *PQR* is similar to right triangle *XYZ*, with vertices *P*, *Q*, and *R* corresponding to vertices *X*, *Y*, and *Z*, respectively. If cos *R* = 0.263, what is the value of cos *Z*?

By the definition of cosine, $\cos R = \frac{RQ}{RP}$ and $\cos Z = \frac{ZY}{ZX}$. Since triangle *PQR* is similar to triangle *XYZ*, with vertices *P*, *Q*, and *R* corresponding to vertices *X*, *Y*, and *Z*, respectively, the ratios $\frac{RQ}{RP}$ and $\frac{ZY}{ZX}$ are equal.

Therefore, since $\cos R = \frac{RQ}{RP} = 0.263$, it follows that $\cos Z = \frac{ZY}{ZX} = 0.263$.

Note that this is why, to find the values of the trigonometric functions of, say, *d*°, you can use *any* right triangle with an acute angle of measure *d*° and then take the appropriate ratio of lengths of sides.

Note that since an acute angle of a right triangle has measure between 0° and 90°, exclusive, right triangles can be used only to find values of trigonometric functions for angles with measures between 0° and 90°, exclusive. The definitions of sine, cosine, and tangent can be extended to all values. This is done using radian measure and the unit circle.

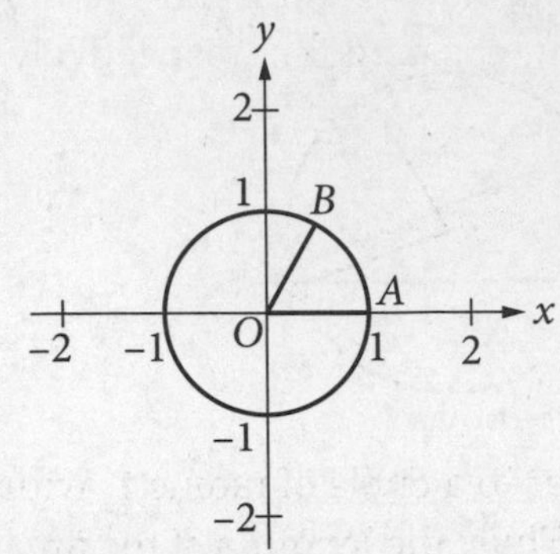

The circle above has radius 1 and is centered at the origin, O. An angle in the coordinate plane is said to be in standard position if it meets these two conditions: (1) its vertex lies at the origin and (2) one of its sides lies along the positive x-axis. Since $\angle AOB$ above, formed by segments OA and OB, meets both these conditions, it is said to be in *standard position*. As segment OB, also called the *terminal side* of $\angle AOB$, rotates counterclockwise about the circle, while OA is anchored along the x-axis, the *radian* measure of $\angle AOB$ is defined to be the length s of the arc that $\angle AOB$ intercepts on the unit circle. In other words, the measure of $\angle AOB$ is s radians.

When an acute $\angle AOB$ is in standard position within the unit circle, the x-coordinate of point B is $\cos(\angle AOB)$, and the y-coordinate of point B is $\sin(\angle AOB)$. When $\angle AOB$ is greater than 90 degrees (or $\frac{\pi}{2}$ radians), and point B extends beyond the boundaries of the positive x-axis and positive y-axis, the values of $\cos(\angle AOB)$ and $\sin(\angle AOB)$ may be negative depending on the coordinates of point B. For any $\angle AOB$, place $\angle AOB$ in standard position within the circle of radius 1 centered at the origin, with side OA along the positive x-axis and terminal side OB intersecting the circle at point B. Then the cosine of $\angle AOB$ is the x-coordinate of B, and the sine of $\angle AOB$ is the y-coordinate of B. The tangent of $\angle AOB$ is the sine of $\angle AOB$ divided by the cosine of $\angle AOB$.

PRACTICE AT
satpractice.org

To convert from degrees to radians, multiply the number of degrees by 2π / 360 degrees. To convert from radians to degrees, multiply the number of radians by 360 degrees / 2π.

An angle with a full rotation about point O has measure 360°. This angle intercepts the full circumference of the circle, which has length 2π. Thus, $\frac{\text{measure of an angle in radians}}{\text{measure of an angle in degrees}} = \frac{2\pi}{360°}$. It follows that measure of an angle in radians $= \frac{2\pi}{360°} \times$ measure of an angle in degrees and measure of an angle in degrees $= \frac{360°}{2\pi} \times$ measure of an angle in radians.

Also note that since a rotation of 2π about point O brings you back to the same point on the unit circle, $\sin(s + 2\pi) = \sin(s)$, $\cos(s + 2\pi) = \cos(s)$, and $\tan(s + 2\pi) = \tan(s)$, for any radian measure s.

Let angle DEF be a central angle in a circle of radius r, as shown in the following figure.

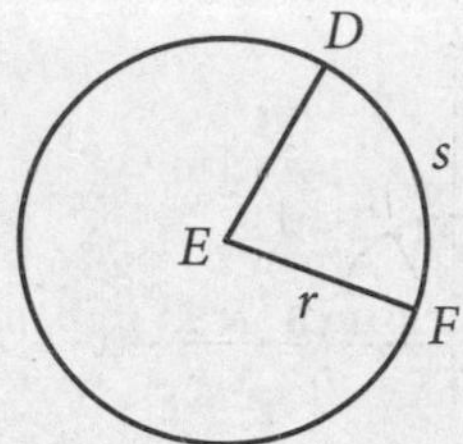

A circle of radius r is similar to a circle of radius 1, with constant of proportionality equal to r. Thus, the length s of the arc intercepted by angle DEF is r times the length of the arc that would be intercepted by an angle of the same measure in a circle of radius 1. Therefore, in the figure above, $s = r \times$ (radian measure of angle DEF), or radian measure of angle $DEF = \frac{s}{r}$.

Example 10

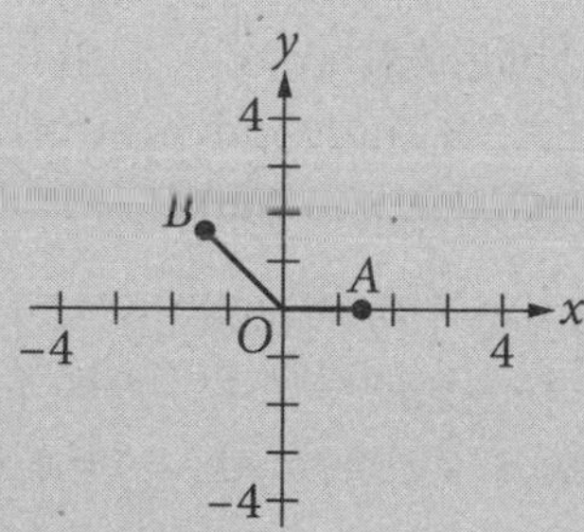

In the figure above, the coordinates of point B are $(-\sqrt{2}, \sqrt{2})$. What is the measure, in radians, of angle AOB?

A) $\frac{\pi}{4}$

B) $\frac{\pi}{2}$

C) $\frac{3\pi}{4}$

D) $\frac{5\pi}{4}$

Let C be the point $(-\sqrt{2}, 0)$. Then triangle BOC, shown in the figure below, is a right triangle with both legs of length $\sqrt{2}$.

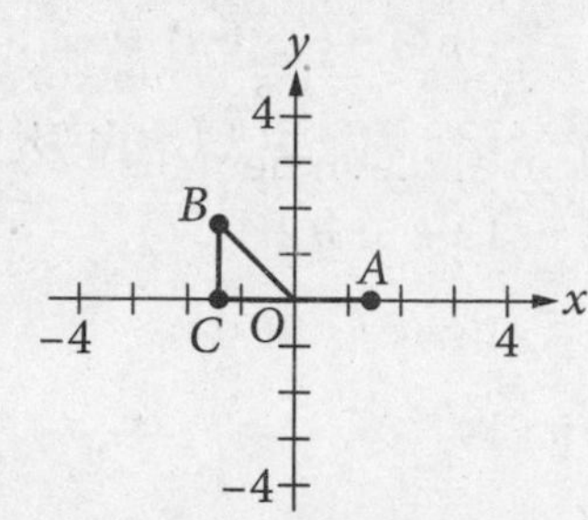

PRACTICE AT

satpractice.org

Always be on the lookout for special right triangles. Here, noticing that segment OB is the hypotenuse of a 45-45-90 triangle makes this question easier to solve.

Hence, triangle *BOC* is a 45°-45°-90° triangle. Thus, angle *COB* has measure 45°, and angle *AOB* has measure 180° − 45° = 135°. Therefore, the measure of angle *AOB* in radians is $135° \times \frac{2\pi}{360°} = \frac{3\pi}{4}$, which is choice C.

Example 11

$$\sin(x) = \cos(K - x)$$

In the equation above, the angle measures are in radians and K is a constant. Which of the following could be the value of K?

A) 0

B) $\frac{\pi}{4}$

C) $\frac{\pi}{2}$

D) π

The complementary angle relationship for sine and cosine implies that the equation $\sin(x) = \cos(K - x)$ holds if $K = 90°$. Since $90° = \frac{2\pi}{360°} \times 90° = \frac{\pi}{2}$ radians, the value of K could be $\frac{\pi}{2}$, which is choice C.

REMEMBER

The number i is defined to be the solution to equation $x^2 = -1$. Thus, $i^2 = -1$, and $i = \sqrt{-1}$.

REMEMBER

If you have little experience working with complex numbers, practice adding, subtracting, multiplying, and dividing complex numbers until you are comfortable doing so. You may see complex numbers on the SAT Math Test.

Complex Numbers

The SAT Math Test includes questions on the arithmetic of complex numbers.

The square of any real number is nonnegative. The number i is defined to be the solution to the equation $x^2 = -1$. That is, $i^2 = -1$, or $i = \sqrt{-1}$. Note that $i^3 = i^2(i) = -i$ and $i^4 = i^2(i^2) = -1(-1) = 1$.

A complex number is a number of the form $a + bi$, where a and b are real number constants and $i = \sqrt{-1}$. This is called the standard form of a complex number. The number a is called the real part of $a + bi$, and the number bi is called the imaginary part of $a + bi$.

Addition and subtraction of complex numbers are performed by adding their real and complex parts. For example,

- $(-3 -2i) + (4 - i) = (-3 + 4) + (-2i + (-i)) = 1 - 3i$
- $(-3 -2i) - (4 - i) = (-3 - 4) + (-2i - (-i)) = -7 - i$

Multiplication of complex numbers is performed similarly to multiplication of binomials, using the fact that $i^2 = -1$. For example,

$$\begin{aligned}(-3 - 2i)(4 - i) &= (-3)(4) + (-3)(-i) + (-2i)(4) + (-2i)(-i)\\ &= -12 + 3i - 8i + (-2)(-1)i^2\\ &= -12 - 5i + 2i^2\\ &= -12 - 5i + 2(-1)\\ &= -14 - 5i\end{aligned}$$

The complex number $a - bi$ is called the conjugate of $a + bi$. The product of $a + bi$ and $a - bi$ is $a^2 - abi + abi - b^2i^2$; this reduces to $a^2 + b^2$, a real number. The fact that the product of a complex number and its conjugate is a real number can be used to perform division of complex numbers.

$$\frac{-3-2i}{4-i} = \frac{-3-2i}{4-i} \times \frac{4+i}{4+i}$$

$$= \frac{(-3-2i)(4+i)}{(4-i)(4+i)}$$

$$= \frac{-12-3i-8i-2i^2}{4^2-i^2}$$

$$= \frac{-10-11i}{17}$$

$$= -\frac{10}{17} - \frac{11}{17}i$$

Example 12

In the complex number system, which of the following is equal to $\frac{1+i}{1-i}$? (Note: $i = \sqrt{-1}$)

A) i

B) $2i$

C) $-1 + i$

D) $1 + i$

Multiply both the numerator and denominator of $\frac{1+i}{1-i}$ by $1 + i$ to remove i from the denominator.

$$\frac{1+i}{1-i} = \frac{1+i}{1-i} \times \frac{1+i}{1+i}$$

$$= \frac{(1+i)(1+i)}{(1-i)(1+i)}$$

$$= \frac{1+2i+i^2}{1^2-i^2}$$

$$= \frac{1+2i-1}{1-(-1)}$$

$$= \frac{2i}{2}$$

$$= i$$

Choice A is the correct answer.

CHAPTER 20

Sample Math Questions: Multiple-Choice

In the previous chapters, you learned about the four areas covered by the SAT Math Test. On the test, questions from the areas are mixed together, requiring you to solve different types of problems as you progress. In each portion, no-calculator and calculator, you'll first see multiple-choice questions and then student-produced response questions. This chapter will illustrate sample multiple-choice questions. These sample questions are divided into no-calculator and calculator portions just as they would be on the actual test.

REMEMBER

It's important not to spend too much time on any question. You'll have on average a minute and fifteen seconds per question on the no-calculator portion and a little less than a minute and a half per question on the calculator portion. If you can't solve a question in a reasonable amount of time, skip it (remembering to mark it in your booklet) and return to it later.

Test-Taking Strategies

While taking the SAT Math Test, you may find that some questions are more difficult than others. Don't spend too much time on any one question. If you can't answer a question in a reasonable amount of time, skip it and return to it after completing the rest of the section. It's important to practice this strategy because you don't want to waste time skipping around to find "easy" questions. Mark each question that you don't answer in your booklet so you can easily go back to it later. In general, questions are ordered by difficulty, with the easier questions first and the harder questions last within each group of multiple-choice questions and again within each group of student-produced response questions. Don't let the question position or question type deter you from answering questions. Read and attempt to answer every question you can.

REMEMBER

In general, questions are ordered by difficulty with the easier questions first and the harder questions last within each group of multiple-choice questions and again within each group of student-produced response questions, so the later questions may take more time to solve than those at the beginning.

Read each question carefully, making sure to pay attention to units and other keywords and to understand exactly what information the question is asking for. You may find it helpful to underline key

REMEMBER

Knowing when to use a calculator is one of the skills that is assessed by the SAT Math Test. Keep in mind that some questions are actually solved more efficiently without the use of a calculator.

information in the problem, to draw figures to visualize the information given, or to mark key information on graphs and diagrams provided in the booklet.

When working through the test, remember to check your answer sheet to make sure you're filling in your answer on the correct row for the question you're answering. If your strategy involves skipping questions, it can be easy to get off track, so pay careful attention to your answer sheet.

On the calculator portion, keep in mind that using a calculator may not always be an advantage. Some questions are designed to be solved more efficiently with mental math strategies, so using a calculator may take more time. When answering a question, always consider the reasonableness of the answer — this is the best way to catch mistakes that may have occurred in your calculations.

REMEMBER

Never leave questions blank on the SAT, as there is no penalty for wrong answers. Even if you're not sure of the correct answer, eliminate as many answer choices as you can and then guess from among the remaining ones.

Remember, there is no penalty for guessing on the SAT. If you don't know the answer to a question, make your best guess for that question. Don't leave any questions blank on your answer sheet. When you're unsure of the correct answer, eliminating the answer choices you know are wrong will give you a better chance of guessing the correct answer from the remaining choices.

On the no-calculator portion of the test, you have 25 minutes to answer 20 questions. This allows you an average of about 1 minute 15 seconds per question. On the calculator portion of the test, you have 55 minutes to answer 38 questions. This allows you an average of about 1 minute 26 seconds per question. Keep in mind that you should spend less time on easier questions so you have more time available to spend on the more difficult ones.

Directions

The directions below precede the no-calculator portion of the SAT Math Test. The same references provided in the no-calculator portion of the SAT Math Test are also provided in the calculator portion of the test.

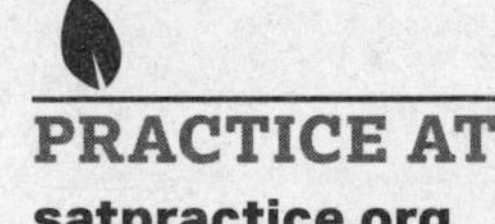

PRACTICE AT

satpractice.org

Familiarize yourself with all test directions now so that you don't have to waste precious time on test day reading the directions.

Math Test – No Calculator

25 MINUTES, 20 QUESTIONS

Turn to Section 3 of your answer sheet to answer the questions in this section.

DIRECTIONS

For questions 1-15, solve each problem, choose the best answer from the choices provided, and fill in the corresponding circle on your answer sheet. **For questions 16-20**, solve the problem and enter your answer in the grid on the answer sheet. Please refer to the directions before question 16 on how to enter your answers in the grid. You may use any available space in your test booklet for scratch work.

NOTES

1. The use of a calculator **is not permitted**.
2. All variables and expressions used represent real numbers unless otherwise indicated.
3. Figures provided in this test are drawn to scale unless otherwise indicated.
4. All figures lie in a plane unless otherwise indicated.
5. Unless otherwise indicated, the domain of a given function *f* is the set of all real numbers *x* for which *f*(*x*) is a real number.

REFERENCE

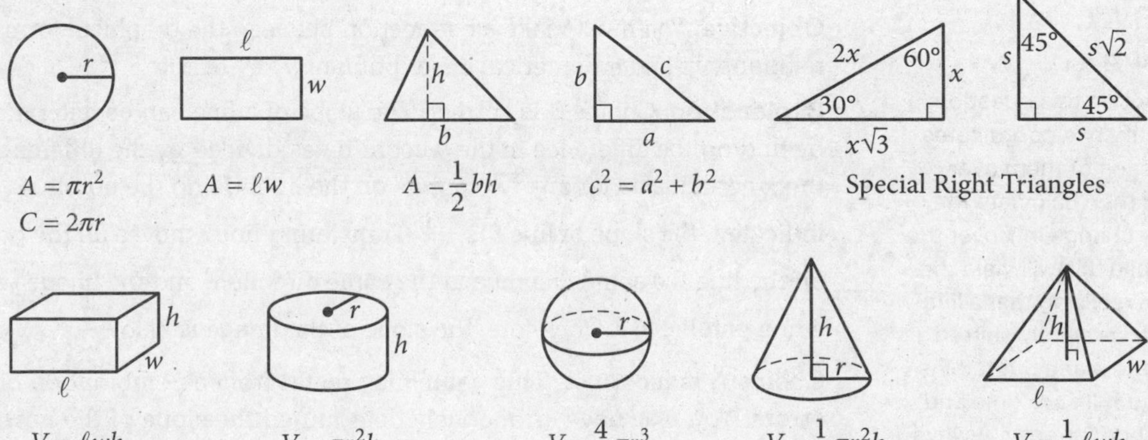

The number of degrees of arc in a circle is 360.
The number of radians of arc in a circle is 2π.
The sum of the measures in degrees of the angles of a triangle is 180.

Sample Questions: Multiple-Choice – No Calculator

1

Line ℓ is graphed in the xy-plane below.

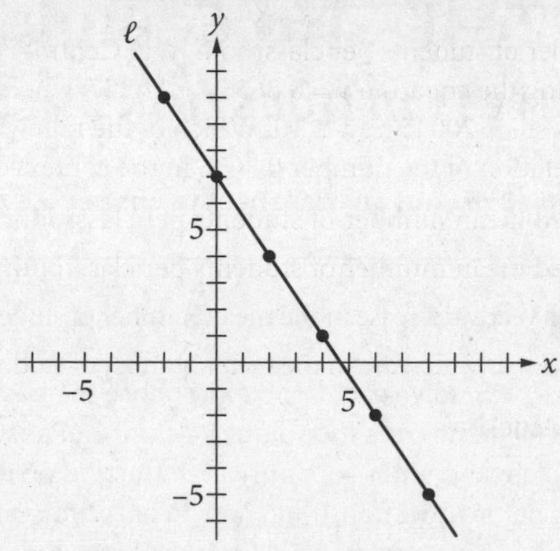

If line ℓ is translated up 5 units and right 7 units, then what is the slope of the new line?

A) $\frac{2}{5}$

B) $-\frac{3}{2}$

C) $-\frac{8}{9}$

D) $-\frac{11}{14}$

Content: Heart of Algebra

Key: B

Objective: You must make a connection between the graphical form of a relationship and a numerical description of a key feature.

Explanation: Choice B is correct. The slope of a line can be determined by finding the difference in the y-coordinates divided by the difference in the x-coordinates for any two points on the line. Using the points indicated, the slope of line ℓ is $-\frac{3}{2}$. Translating line ℓ moves all the points on the line the same distance in the same direction, and the image will be a line parallel to ℓ. Therefore, the slope of the image is also $-\frac{3}{2}$.

Choice A is incorrect. This value may result from a combination of errors. You may have erroneously determined the slope of the new line by adding 5 to the numerator and adding 7 to the denominator in the slope of line ℓ and gotten the result $\frac{(-3+5)}{(-2+7)}$.

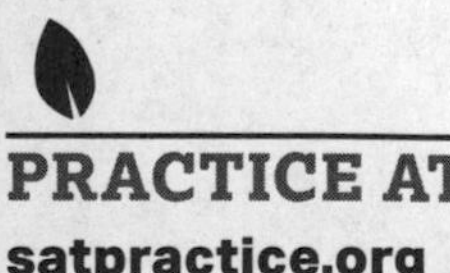

PRACTICE AT
satpractice.org

Your first instinct on this question may be to identify two coordinates on line ℓ, shift each of them over 5 and up 7, and then calculate the slope using the change in y over the change in x. While this will yield the correct answer, realizing that a line that is translated is simply shifted on the coordinate plane but retains its original slope will save time and reduce the chance for error. Always think critically about a question before diving into your calculations.

Choice C is incorrect. This value may result from a combination of errors. You may have erroneously determined the slope of the new line by subtracting 5 from the numerator and subtracting 7 from the denominator in the slope of line ℓ.

Choice D is incorrect and may result from adding $\frac{5}{7}$ to the slope of line ℓ.

2

The mean number of students per classroom, y, at Central High School can be estimated using the equation $y = 0.8636x + 27.227$, where x represents the number of years since 2004 and $x \leq 10$. Which of the following statements is the best interpretation of the number 0.8636 in the context of this problem?

A) The estimated mean number of students per classroom in 2004

B) The estimated mean number of students per classroom in 2014

C) The estimated yearly decrease in the mean number of students per classroom

D) The estimated yearly increase in the mean number of students per classroom

Content: Heart of Algebra

Key: D

Objective: You must interpret the slope of an equation in relation to the real-world situation it models. Also, when the models are created from data, you must recognize that these models only estimate the independent variable, y, for a given value of x.

Explanation: Choice D is correct. When an equation is written in the form $y = mx + b$, the coefficient of the x-term (in this case 0.8636) is the slope. The slope of this linear equation gives the amount that the mean number of students per classroom (represented by y) changes per year (represented by x). The slope is positive, indicating an increase in the mean number of students per classroom each year.

Choice A is incorrect and may result from a misunderstanding of slope and y-intercept. The y-intercept of the equation represents the estimated mean number of students per classroom in 2004.

Choice B is incorrect and may result from a misunderstanding of the limitations of the model. You may have seen that $x \leq 10$ and erroneously used this statement to determine that the model finds the mean number of students in 2014.

Choice C is incorrect and may result from a misunderstanding of slope. You may have recognized that slope models the rate of change but thought that a slope of less than 1 indicates a decreasing function.

3

If $\frac{2}{a-1} = \frac{4}{y}$, and $y \neq 0$ where $a \neq 1$, what is y in terms of a?

A) $y = 2a - 2$

B) $y = 2a - 4$

C) $y = 2a - \frac{1}{2}$

D) $y = \frac{1}{2}a + 1$

PRACTICE AT
satpractice.org

When working with rational equations, you can multiply both sides of the equation by the lowest common denominator to clear denominators. In Example 3, the rational equation consists of two fractions set equal to each other. In this case, cross multiplication produces the same result as multiplying both sides of the equation by the lowest common denominator.

Content: Passport to Advanced Math

Key: A

Objective: You must complete operations with multiple terms and manipulate an equation to isolate the variable of interest.

Explanation: Choice A is correct. Multiplying both sides of the equation by the denominators of the rational expressions in the equation gives $2y = 4a - 4$. You should then divide both sides by 2 to isolate the y variable, yielding the equation $y = 2a - 2$.

Choice B is incorrect. This equation may be the result of not dividing both terms by 2 when isolating y in the equation $2y = 4a - 4$.

Choice C is incorrect. This equation may result from not distributing the 4 when multiplying 4 and $(a - 1)$.

Choice D is incorrect. This equation may result from solving $2y = 4a - 4$ for a, yielding $a = \frac{1}{2}y + 1$. A misunderstanding of the meaning of variables may have resulted in switching the variables to match the answer choice.

4

In the complex number system, which of the following is equal to $(14 - 2i)(7 + 12i)$? (Note: $i = \sqrt{-1}$)

A) 74

B) 122

C) $74 + 154i$

D) $122 + 154i$

Content: Additional Topics in Math

Key: D

Objective: You must apply the distributive property on two complex binomials and then simplify the result.

Explanation: Choice D is correct. Applying the distributive property to multiply the binomials yields the expression $98 + 168i - 14i - 24i^2$. The note in the question reminds you that $i = \sqrt{-1}$, therefore, $i^2 = -1$. Substituting this value into the expression gives you $98 + 168i - 14i - (-24)$, and combining like terms results in $122 + 154i$.

PRACTICE AT
satpractice.org

Multiply complex numbers in the same way you would multiply binomials (by the "FOIL" method or by using the distributive property). Remember that $i = \sqrt{-1}$ and that $i^2 = -1$.

Choice A is incorrect and may result from a combination of errors. You may not have correctly distributed when multiplying the binomials, multiplying only the first terms together and the second terms together. You may also have used the incorrect equality $i^2 = 1$.

Choice B is incorrect and may result from a combination of errors. You may not have correctly distributed when multiplying the binomials, multiplying only the first terms together and the second terms together.

Choice C is incorrect and results from misapplying the statement $i = \sqrt{-1}$.

5

The graph of $y = (2x - 4)(x - 4)$ is a parabola in the xy-plane. In which of the following equivalent equations do the x- and y-coordinates of the vertex of the parabola appear as constants or coefficients?

A) $y = 2x^2 - 12x + 16$

B) $y = 2x(x - 6) + 16$

C) $y = 2(x - 3)^2 + (-2)$

D) $y = (x - 2)(2x - 8)$

Content: Passport to Advanced Math

Key: C

Objective: You must be able to see structure in expressions and equations and create a new form of an expression that reveals a specific property.

Explanation: Choice C is correct. The equation $y = (2x - 4)(x - 4)$ can be written in vertex form, $y = a(x - h)^2 + k$, to display the vertex, (h, k), of the parabola. To put the equation in vertex form, first multiply: $(2x - 4)(x - 4) = 2x^2 - 8x - 4x + 16$. Then, add like terms, $2x^2 - 8x - 4x + 16 = 2x^2 - 12x + 16$. The next step is completing the square.

$y = 2x^2 - 12x + 16$	
$y = 2(x^2 - 6x) + 16$	Isolate the x^2 term by factoring.
$y = 2(x^2 - 6x + 9 - 9) + 16$	Make a perfect square in the parentheses.
$y = 2(x^2 - 6x + 9) - 18 + 16$	Move the extra term out of the parentheses.
$y = 2(x - 3)^2 - 18 + 16$	Factor inside the parentheses.
$y = 2(x - 3)^2 - 2$	Simplify the remaining terms.

Therefore, the coordinates of the vertex, $(3, -2)$, are both revealed only in choice C. Since you are told that all of the equations are equivalent, simply knowing the form that displays the coordinates of the vertex will save all of these steps — this is known as "seeing structure in the expression or equation."

PRACTICE AT

satpractice.org

While you may be asked to write the equation of a parabola in vertex form, sometimes simply knowing the form that displays the coordinates of the vertex will suffice, saving you precious time.

Choice A is incorrect; it is in polynomial form, displaying the y-value of the y-intercept of the graph $(0, 16)$ as a constant.

Choice B is incorrect; it displays the y-value of the y-intercept of the graph $(0, 16)$ as a constant.

Choice D is incorrect; it displays the x-value of one of the x-intercepts of the graph $(2, 0)$ as a constant.

6

If $a^{-\frac{1}{2}} = x$, where $a > 0$ and $x > 0$, which of the following equations gives a in terms of x?

A) $a = \frac{1}{\sqrt{x}}$

B) $a = \frac{1}{x^2}$

C) $a = \sqrt{x}$

D) $a = -x^2$

Content: Passport to Advanced Math

Key: B

Objective: You must demonstrate fluency with the properties of exponents. You must be able to relate fractional exponents to radicals as well as demonstrate an understanding of negative exponents.

Explanation: Choice B is correct. There are multiple ways to approach this problem, but all require an understanding of the properties of exponents. You may rewrite the equation as $\frac{1}{\sqrt{a}} = x$ and then proceed to solve for a, first by squaring both sides, which gives $\frac{1}{a} = x^2$, and then by multiplying both sides by a to find $1 = ax^2$. Finally, dividing both sides by x^2 isolates the desired variable.

Choice A is incorrect and may result from a misunderstanding of the properties of exponents. You may understand that a negative exponent can be translated to a fraction but misapply the fractional exponent.

Choice C is incorrect and may result from a misunderstanding of the properties of exponents. You may recognize that an exponent of $\frac{1}{2}$ is the same as the square root but misapply this information.

Choice D is incorrect and may result from a misunderstanding of the properties of exponents. You may recognize that raising a to the power of $\frac{1}{2}$ is the same as taking the square root of a and, therefore, that a can be isolated by squaring both sides. However, you may not have understood how the negative exponent affects the base of the exponent.

PRACTICE AT
satpractice.org

Know the exponent rules and practice applying them. This question tests several of them:

1) a^{-b} can be written as $\frac{1}{a^b}$

2) $a^{\frac{1}{2}}$ is the same as $\sqrt{a}$

3) $\sqrt{a^2} = a$

4) To eliminate a radical from an equation, as in $\frac{1}{\sqrt{a}} = x$, square both sides of the equation.

7

If $y = x^3 + 2x + 5$ and $z = x^2 + 7x + 1$, what is $2y + z$ in terms of x?

A) $3x^3 + 11x + 11$

B) $2x^3 + x^2 + 9x + 6$

C) $2x^3 + x^2 + 11x + 11$

D) $2x^3 + 2x^2 + 18x + 12$

Content: Passport to Advanced Math

Key: C

Objective: You must substitute polynomials into an expression and then simplify the resulting expression by combining like terms.

Explanation: Choice C is correct. Substituting the expressions equivalent to y and z into $2y + z$ results in the expression $2(x^3 + 2x + 5) + x^2 + 7x + 1$. You must apply the distributive property to multiply $x^3 + 2x + 5$ by 2 and then combine the like terms in the expression.

Choice A is incorrect and may result if you correctly found $2y$ in terms of x but did not pay careful attention to exponents when adding the expression for $2y$ to the expression for z. As a result, you may have combined the x^3 and x^2 terms.

Choice B is incorrect and may result if you failed to distribute the 2 when multiplying $2(x^3 + 2x + 5)$.

Choice D is incorrect and may result from finding $2(y + z)$ instead of $2y + z$.

PRACTICE AT
satpractice.org

Don't worry if you missed this question; there are several ways to make a mistake. Always be methodical when doing calculations or simplifying expressions, and use the space in your test booklet to perform the steps in finding your answer.

8

Which of the following is equal to $\sin\left(\frac{\pi}{5}\right)$?

A) $-\cos\left(\frac{\pi}{5}\right)$

B) $-\sin\left(\frac{\pi}{5}\right)$

C) $\cos\left(\frac{3\pi}{10}\right)$

D) $\sin\left(\frac{7\pi}{10}\right)$

Content: Additional Topics in Math

Key: C

Objective: You must understand radian measure and have a conceptual understanding of trigonometric relationships.

Explanation: Choice C is correct. Sine and cosine are cofunctions, or are related by the equation $\sin(x) = \cos\left(\frac{\pi}{2} - x\right)$. Therefore, $\sin\left(\frac{\pi}{5}\right) = \cos\left(\frac{\pi}{2} - \frac{\pi}{5}\right)$, which reduces to $\cos\left(\frac{3\pi}{10}\right)$.

Choice A is incorrect and may result from a misunderstanding about trigonometric relationships. You may have thought that cosine is the inverse function of sine and therefore reasoned that the negative of the cosine of an angle is equivalent to the sine of that angle.

Choice B is incorrect and may result from a misunderstanding of the unit circle and how it relates to trigonometric expressions. You may have thought that, on a coordinate grid, the negative sign only changes the orientation of the triangle formed, not the value of the trigonometric expression.

Choice D is incorrect. You may have confused the relationship between sine and cosine and erroneously added $\frac{\pi}{2}$ to the given angle measure instead of subtracting the angle measure from $\frac{\pi}{2}$.

9

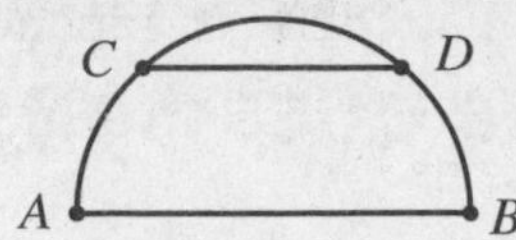

The semicircle above has a radius of r inches, and chord $\overline{CD}$ is parallel to the diameter $\overline{AB}$. If the length of $\overline{CD}$ is $\frac{2}{3}$ of the length of $\overline{AB}$, what is the distance between the chord and the diameter in terms of r?

A) $\frac{1}{3}\pi r$

B) $\frac{2}{3}\pi r$

C) $\frac{\sqrt{2}}{2}r$

D) $\frac{\sqrt{5}}{3}r$

Content: Additional Topics in Math

Key: D

Objective: This problem requires you to make use of properties of circles and parallel lines in an abstract setting. You will have to draw an additional line in order to find the relationship between the distance of the chord from the diameter and the radius of the semicircle. This question provides an opportunity for using different approaches to find the distance required: one can use either the Pythagorean theorem or the trigonometric ratios.

Explanation: Choice D is correct. Let the semicircle have center O. The diameter $\overline{AB}$ has length $2r$. Because chord $\overline{CD}$ is $\frac{2}{3}$ of the length of the diameter, $CD = \frac{2}{3}(2r) = \frac{4}{3}r$. It follows that $\frac{1}{2}CD = \frac{1}{2}\left(\frac{4}{3}\right)r$ or $\frac{2}{3}r$. To find the distance, x, between $\overline{AB}$ and $\overline{CD}$, draw a right triangle connecting center O, the midpoint of chord $\overline{CD}$, and point C. The Pythagorean theorem can then be set up as follows: $r^2 = x^2 + \left(\frac{2}{3}r\right)^2$. Simplifying the right-hand side of the equation yields $r^2 = x^2 + \frac{4}{9}r^2$. Subtracting $\frac{4}{9}r^2$ from both sides of the equation yields $\frac{5}{9}r^2 = x^2$. Finally, taking the square root of both sides of the equation will reveal $\frac{\sqrt{5}}{3}r = x$.

Choice A is incorrect. If you selected this answer, you may have tried to use the circumference formula to determine the distance rather than making use of the radius of the circle to create a triangle.

Choice B is incorrect. If you selected this answer, you may have tried to use the circumference formula to determine the distance rather than making use of the radius of the circle to create a triangle.

Choice C is incorrect. If you selected this answer, you may have made a triangle within the circle, using a radius to connect the chord and the diameter, but then may have mistaken the triangle for a 45-45-90 triangle and tried to use this relationship to determine the distance.

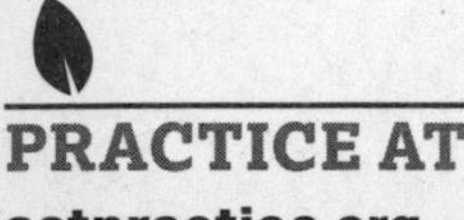

PRACTICE AT
satpractice.org

Question 9 is a particularly challenging question, one that may require additional time to solve. Be careful, however, not to spend too much time on a question. If you're unable to solve a question in a reasonable amount of time at first, flag it in your test booklet and return to it after you've attempted the rest of the questions in the section.

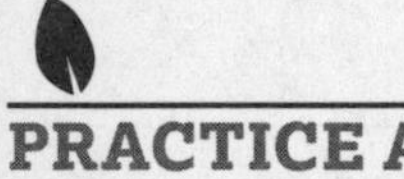

PRACTICE AT
satpractice.org

Advanced geometry questions may require you to draw shapes, such as triangles, within a given shape in order to arrive at the solution.

Math Test – Calculator

55 MINUTES, 38 QUESTIONS

Turn to Section 4 of your answer sheet to answer the questions in this section.

DIRECTIONS

For questions 1-30, solve each problem, choose the best answer from the choices provided, and fill in the corresponding circle on your answer sheet. **For questions 31-38**, solve the problem and enter your answer in the grid on the answer sheet. Please refer to the directions before question 31 on how to enter your answers in the grid. You may use any available space in your test booklet for scratch work.

NOTES

1. The use of a calculator **is permitted**.
2. All variables and expressions used represent real numbers unless otherwise indicated.
3. Figures provided in this test are drawn to scale unless otherwise indicated.
4. All figures lie in a plane unless otherwise indicated.
5. Unless otherwise indicated, the domain of a given function f is the set of all real numbers x for which $f(x)$ is a real number.

REFERENCE

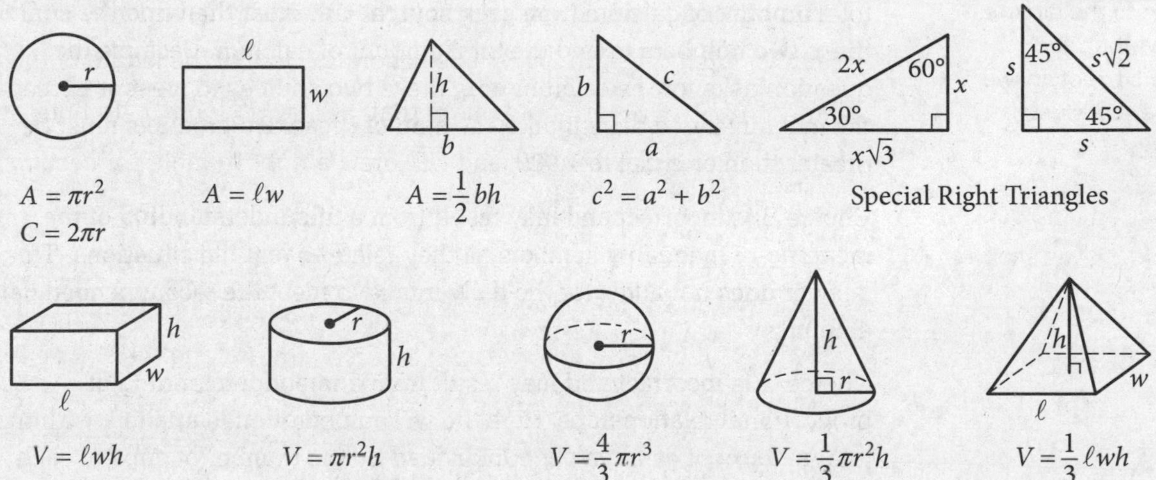

The number of degrees of arc in a circle is 360.
The number of radians of arc in a circle is 2π.
The sum of the measures in degrees of the angles of a triangle is 180.

Sample Questions: Multiple-Choice – Calculator

10

The recommended daily calcium intake for a 20-year-old is 1,000 milligrams (mg). One cup of milk contains 299 mg of calcium and one cup of juice contains 261 mg of calcium. Which of the following inequalities represents the possible number of cups of milk, m, and cups of juice, j, a 20-year-old could drink in a day to meet or exceed the recommended daily calcium intake from these drinks alone?

A) $299m + 261j \geq 1{,}000$

B) $299m + 261j > 1{,}000$

C) $\frac{299}{m} + \frac{261}{j} \geq 1{,}000$

D) $\frac{299}{m} + \frac{261}{j} > 1{,}000$

Content: Heart of Algebra

Key: A

Objective: You must identify the correct mathematical notation for an inequality to represent a real-world situation.

Explanation: Choice A is correct. Multiplying the number of cups of milk by the amount of calcium each cup contains and multiplying the number of cups of juice by the amount of calcium each cup contains gives the total amount of calcium from each source. You must then find the sum of these two numbers to find the total amount of calcium. Because the question asks for the calcium from these two sources to meet or exceed the recommended daily intake, the sum of these two products must be greater than or equal to 1,000.

Choice B is incorrect and may result from a misunderstanding of the meaning of inequality symbols as they relate to real-life situations. This answer does not allow for the daily intake to meet the recommended daily amount.

Choice C is incorrect and may result from a misunderstanding of proportional relationships. Here the wrong operation is applied, with the total amount of calcium per cup divided by the number of cups of each type of drink. These values should be multiplied.

Choice D is incorrect and may result from a combination of mistakes. The inequality symbol used allows the option to exceed, but not to meet, the recommended daily value, and the wrong operation may have been applied when calculating the total amount of calcium intake from each drink.

PRACTICE AT
satpractice.org

On questions involving inequalities, pay close attention to the direction of the inequality symbol, and whether or not the correct answer should include an equal sign.

11

A research assistant randomly selected 75 undergraduate students from the list of all students enrolled in the psychology-degree program at a large university. She asked each of the 75 students, "How many minutes per day do you typically spend reading?" The mean reading time in the sample was 89 minutes, and the margin of error for this estimate was 4.28 minutes. Another research assistant intends to replicate the survey and will attempt to get a smaller margin of error. Which of the following samples will most likely result in a smaller margin of error for the estimated mean time students in the psychology-degree program read per day?

A) 40 randomly selected undergraduate psychology-degree program students

B) 40 randomly selected undergraduate students from all degree programs at the university

C) 300 randomly selected undergraduate psychology-degree program students

D) 300 randomly selected undergraduate students from all degree programs at the university

Content: Problem Solving and Data Analysis

Key: C

Objective: You must first read and understand the statistics calculated from the survey. Then, you must apply your knowledge about the relationship between sample size and subject selection on margin of error.

Explanation: Choice C is correct. Increasing the sample size while randomly selecting participants from the original population of interest will most likely result in a decrease in the margin of error.

Choice A is incorrect and may result from a misunderstanding of the importance of sample size to a margin of error. The margin of error is likely to increase with a smaller sample size.

Choice B is incorrect and may result from a misunderstanding of the importance of sample size and participant selection to a margin of error. The margin of error is likely to increase due to the smaller sample size. Also, a sample of undergraduate students from all degree programs at the university is a different population than the original survey; therefore, the impact to the mean and margin of error cannot be predicted.

Choice D is incorrect. A sample of undergraduate students from all degree programs at the university is a different population than the original survey and therefore the impact to the mean and margin of error cannot be predicted.

PRACTICE AT

satpractice.org

As discussed in Chapter 17, margin of error is affected by two factors: the variability in the data and the sample size. Increasing the size of the random sample provides more information and reduces the margin of error.

12

A company's manager estimated that the cost C, in dollars, of producing n items is $C = 7n + 350$. The company sells each item for \$12. The company makes a profit when the total income from selling a quantity of items is greater than the total cost of producing that quantity of items. Which of the following inequalities gives all possible values of n for which the manager estimates that the company will make a profit?

A) $n < 70$

B) $n < 84$

C) $n > 70$

D) $n > 84$

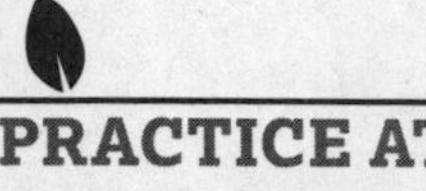

PRACTICE AT
satpractice.org

Remember to solve an inequality just as you would an equation, with one important exception. When multiplying or dividing both sides of an inequality by a negative number, you must reverse the direction of the inequality:

If $-2x > 6$, then $x < -3$.

Content: Heart of Algebra

Key: C

Objective: You must interpret an expression or equation that models a real-world situation and be able to interpret the whole expression (or specific parts) in terms of its context.

Explanation: Choice C is correct. One way to find the correct answer is to create an inequality. The income from sales of n items is $12n$. For the company to profit, $12n$ must be greater than the cost of producing n items; therefore, the inequality $12n > 7n + 350$ can be used to model the context. Solving this inequality yields $n > 70$.

Choice A is incorrect and may result from a misunderstanding of the properties of inequalities. You may have found the number of items of the break-even point as 70 and used the incorrect notation to express the answer, or you may have incorrectly modeled the scenario when setting up an inequality to solve.

Choice B is incorrect and may result from a misunderstanding of how the cost equation models the scenario. If you use the cost of \$12 as the number of items n and evaluate the expression $7n$, you will find the value of 84. Misunderstanding how the inequality relates to the scenario might lead you to think n should be less than this value.

Choice D is incorrect and may result from a misunderstanding of how the cost equation models the scenario. If you use the cost of \$12 as the number of items n and evaluate the expression $7n$, you will find the value of 84. Misunderstanding how the inequality relates to the scenario might lead you to think n should be greater than this value.

13

At a primate reserve, the mean age of all the male primates is 15 years, and the mean age of all female primates is 19 years. Which of the following must be true about the mean age m of the combined group of male and female primates at the primate reserve?

A) $m = 17$

B) $m > 17$

C) $m < 17$

D) $15 < m < 19$

Content: Problem Solving and Data Analysis

Key: D

Objective: You must evaluate the means for two separate populations in order to determine the constraints on the mean for the combined population.

Explanation: Choice D is correct. You must reason that because the mean of the males is lower than that of the females, the combined mean cannot be greater than or equal to that of the females, while also reasoning that because the mean of the females is greater than that of the males, the combined mean cannot be less than or equal to the mean of the males. Therefore, the combined mean must be between the two separate means.

Choice A is incorrect and results from finding the mean of the two means. This answer makes an unjustified assumption that there are an equal number of male and female primates.

Choice B is incorrect and results from finding the mean of the two means and misapplying an inequality to the scenario. This answer makes an unjustified assumption that there are more females than males.

Choice C is incorrect and results from finding the mean of the two means and misapplying an inequality to the scenario. This answer makes an unjustified assumption that there are more males than females.

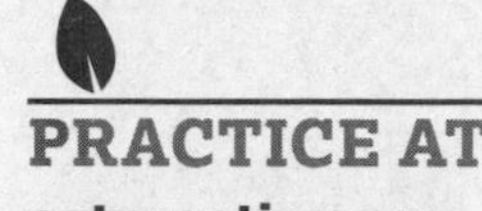

PRACTICE AT
satpractice.org

Question 13 doesn't require extensive calculation, or really any calculation at all. Rather, it relies upon a solid understanding of mean along with careful reasoning. On the SAT, it pays to reason critically about the question before diving into calculations.

14

A researcher wanted to know if there is an association between exercise and sleep for the population of 16-year-olds in the United States. She obtained survey responses from a random sample of 2,000 United States 16-year-olds and found convincing evidence of a positive association between exercise and sleep. Which of the following conclusions is well supported by the data?

A) There is a positive association between exercise and sleep for 16-year-olds in the United States.

B) There is a positive association between exercise and sleep for 16-year-olds in the world.

C) Using exercise and sleep as defined by the study, an increase in sleep is caused by an increase of exercise for 16-year-olds in the United States.

D) Using exercise and sleep as defined by the study, an increase in sleep is caused by an increase of exercise for 16-year-olds in the world.

PRACTICE AT
satpractice.org

When deciding what conclusions are supported by the data from a study or survey, ask yourself:

1. Was the sample of subjects in the study selected at random from the entire population in question? If so, the results can be generalized to the entire population in question. However, check to make sure that the conclusion is referring to the same population as that in the study.

2. Were the subjects randomly assigned to treatments? If so, conclusions about cause and effect can be drawn.

Content: Problem Solving and Data Analysis

Key: A

Objective: You must use information from a research study to evaluate whether the results can be generalized to the study population and whether a cause-and-effect relationship exists. To conclude a cause-and-effect relationship like the ones described in choices C and D, there must be a random assignment of participants to groups receiving different treatments. To conclude that the relationship applies to a population, participants must be randomly selected from that population.

Explanation: Choice A is correct. A relationship in the data can only be generalized to the population that the sample was drawn from.

Choice B is incorrect. A relationship in the data can only be generalized to the population that the sample was drawn from. The sample was from high school students in the United States, not from high school students in the entire world.

Choice C is incorrect. Evidence for a cause-and-effect relationship can only be established when participants are randomly assigned to groups who receive different treatments.

Choice D is incorrect. Evidence for a cause-and-effect relationship can only be established when participants are randomly assigned to groups who receive different treatments. Also, a relationship in the data can only be generalized to the population that the sample was drawn from. The sample was from high school students in the United States, not from high school students in the entire world.

15

A biology class at Central High School predicted that a local population of animals will double in size every 12 years. The population at the beginning of 2014 was estimated to be 50 animals. If P represents the population n years after 2014, then which of the following equations represents the class's model of the population over time?

A) $P = 12 + 50n$
B) $P = 50 + 12n$
C) $P = 50(2)^{12n}$
D) $P = 50(2)^{\frac{n}{12}}$

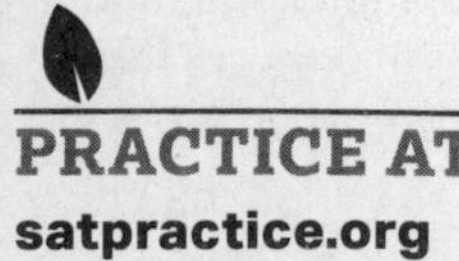

PRACTICE AT
satpractice.org

A good strategy for checking your answer on Question 15 is to pick a number for n and test the answer choices. If $n = 12$, for instance, P should equal 100 (since after 12 years, the initial population of 50 should double to 100). Only choice D yields a value of 100 when you plug in 12 for n.

Content: Passport to Advanced Math

Key: D

Objective: You must identify the correct mathematical notation for an exponential relationship that represents a real-world situation.

Explanation: Choice D is correct. A population that doubles in size over equal time periods is increasing at an exponential rate. In a doubling scenario, an exponential growth model can be written in the form $y = a(2)^{\frac{n}{b}}$, where a is the initial population (that is, the population when $n = 0$) and b is the number of years it takes for the population to double in size. In this case, the initial population is 50, the number of animals at the beginning of 2014. Therefore, $a = 50$. The text explains that the population will double in size every 12 years. Therefore, $b = 12$.

Choice A is incorrect and may result from a misunderstanding of exponential equations or of the context. This linear model indicates that the initial population is 12 animals and the population is increasing by 50 animals each year. However, this is not the case.

Choice B is incorrect and may result from a misunderstanding of exponential equations or of the context. This linear model indicates that the initial population is 50 animals and the population is increasing by 12 animals each year. However, this is not the case.

Choice C is incorrect. This exponential model indicates that the initial population is 50 animals and is doubling. The exponent $12n$ indicates that the population is doubling 12 times per year, not every 12 years. However, this is not the case.

16

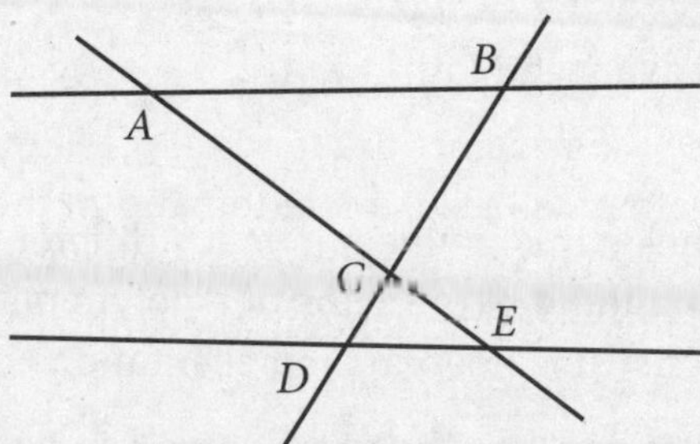

Note: Figure not drawn to scale.

In the figure above, $\triangle ABC$ is similar to $\triangle EDC$. Which of the following must be true?

A) $\overline{AE} \parallel \overline{BD}$
B) $\overline{AE} \perp \overline{BD}$
C) $\overline{AB} \parallel \overline{DE}$
D) $\overline{AB} \perp \overline{DE}$

Content: Additional Topics in Math

Key: C

Objective: You must use spatial reasoning and geometric logic to deduce which relationship is true based on the given information. You must also use mathematical notation to express the relationship between the line segments.

Explanation: Choice C is correct. Given that $\triangle ABC$ is similar to $\triangle EDC$, you can determine that the corresponding $\angle BAC$ is congruent to $\angle CED$. The converse of the alternate interior angle theorem tells us that $\overline{AB} \parallel \overline{DE}$. (You can also use the fact that $\angle ABC$ and $\angle CDE$ are congruent to make a similar argument.)

REMEMBER

When a question explicitly states that a figure is *not* drawn to scale, avoid making unwarranted assumptions. Rely instead on your knowledge of mathematical properties and theorems.

Choice A is incorrect and may result from multiple misconceptions. You may have misidentified the segments as perpendicular and used the wrong notation to express this statement.

Choice B is incorrect and may result from using only the diagram and not considering the given information. The line segments appear to be perpendicular, but need not be, given the information provided.

Choice D is incorrect and may result from misunderstanding either the notation or the vocabulary of parallel and perpendicular lines. You may have incorrectly identified or notated parallel lines as perpendicular.

17

The function f is defined by $f(x) = 2x^3 + 3x^2 + cx + 8$ where c is a constant. In the xy-plane, the graph of f intersects the x-axis at the three points $(-4, 0)$, $\left(\frac{1}{2}, 0\right)$, and $(p, 0)$. What is the value of c?

A) -18

B) -2

C) 2

D) 10

PRACTICE AT

satpractice.org

When a question states that the graph of a function intersects the x-axis at specific points, this means that the dependent variable, ($f(x)$), equals zero for the specified values of the independent variable, (x). Applying this concept leads to the solution on Question 17.

Content: Passport to Advanced Math

Key: A

Objective: You could tackle this problem in many different ways, but the focus is on your understanding of the zeros of a polynomial function and how they are used to construct algebraic representations of polynomials.

Explanation: Choice A is correct. The given zeros can be used to set up an equation to solve for c. Substituting -4 for x and 0 for y yields $-4c = 72$, or $c = -18$. Alternatively, since -4, $\frac{1}{2}$, and p are zeros of the polynomial function, it follows that $f(x) = (2x - 1)(x + 4)(x - p)$. Were this polynomial multiplied out, the constant term would be $(-1)(4)(-p) = 4p$. (We can grasp this without performing the full expansion.) Since it is given that this value is 8, it goes that $4p = 8$ or, rather, $p = 2$. Substituting 2 for p in the polynomial function yields $f(x) = (2x - 1)(x + 4)(x - 2)$, and after multiplying the factors, one finds that the coefficient of the x term, or the value of c, is -18.

Choice B is incorrect. This value may be the result of solving for $p(p = 2)$ and then misunderstanding the relationship between the constants p and c in the equation.

Choice C is incorrect. This is the value of p, not c. Finding the value of p is an intermediate step to finding the value of c, but the value of p is not the final answer.

Choice D is incorrect. This value could be the result of an arithmetic error. Using the value of $p(p = 2)$ and the other zeros, $f(x)$ can be factored as $f(x) = (2x - 1)(x + 4)(x - 2)$. If the x terms in the product were erroneously found to be $14x$ and $-4x$, then combining like terms could result in this incorrect answer.

Sample Question Set

Questions 18 to 20 refer to the following information:

The first metacarpal bone is located in the hand. The scatterplot below shows the relationship between the length of the first metacarpal bone and the height of 9 people. A line of best fit is also shown.

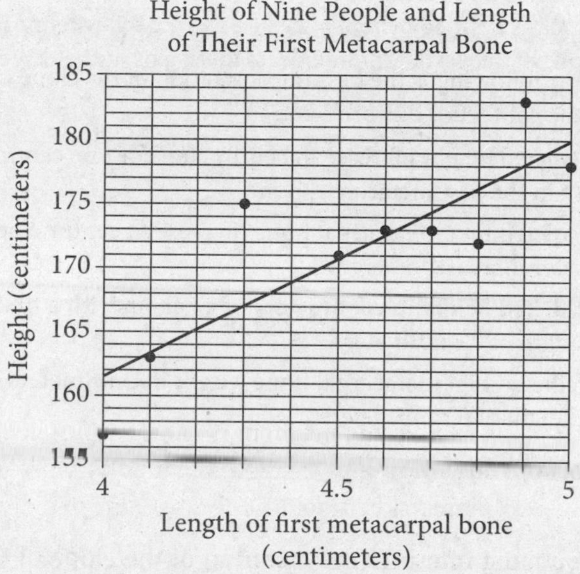

18

How many of the 9 people have an actual height that differs by more than 3 centimeters from the height predicted by the line of best fit?

A) 2

B) 4

C) 6

D) 9

Content: Problem Solving and Data Analysis

Key: B

Objective: You must read and interpret information from a data display.

Explanation: Choice B is correct. The people who have first metacarpal bones of length 4.0, 4.3, 4.8, and 4.9 centimeters have heights that differ by more than 3 centimeters from the height predicted by the line of best fit.

PRACTICE AT

satpractice.org

Pay close attention to axis labels as well as to the size of the units on the two axes.

Choice A is incorrect. There are 2 people whose actual heights are more than 3 centimeters above the height predicted by the line of best fit. However, there are also 2 people whose actual heights are farther than 3 centimeters below the line of best fit.

Choice C is incorrect. There are 6 data points in which the absolute value between the actual height and the height predicted by the line of best fit is greater than 1 centimeter.

Choice D is incorrect. The data on the graph represent 9 different people; however, the absolute value of the difference between actual height and predicted height is not greater than 3 for all of the people.

19

Which of the following is the best interpretation of the slope of the line of best fit in the context of this problem?

A) The predicted height increase in centimeters for one centimeter increase in the first metacarpal bone

B) The predicted first metacarpal bone increase in centimeters for every centimeter increase in height

C) The predicted height in centimeters of a person with a first metacarpal bone length of 0 centimeters

D) The predicted first metacarpal bone length in centimeters for a person with a height of 0 centimeters

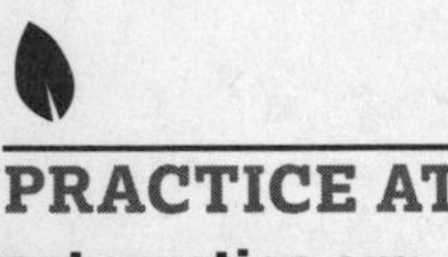

PRACTICE AT
satpractice.org

Throughout the SAT Math Test, you'll be asked to apply your knowledge of math principles and properties, such as slope, to specific contexts, such as the line of best fit in the scatterplot above. To do so requires that you possess a strong understanding of these math concepts.

Content: Heart of Algebra

Key: A

Objective: You must interpret the meaning of the slope of the line of best fit in the context provided.

Explanation: Choice A is correct. The slope is the change in the vertical distance divided by the change in the horizontal distance between any two points on a line. In this context, the change in the vertical distance is the change in the predicted height of a person, and the change in the horizontal distance is the change in the length of his or her first metacarpal bone. The unit rate, or slope, is the increase in predicted height for each increase of one centimeter of the first metacarpal bone.

Choice B is incorrect. If you selected this answer, you may have interpreted slope incorrectly as run over rise.

Choice C is incorrect. If you selected this answer, you may have mistaken slope for the y-intercept.

Choice D is incorrect. If you selected this answer, you may have mistaken slope for the x-intercept.

20

Based on the line of best fit, what is the predicted height for someone with a first metacarpal bone that has a length of 4.45 centimeters?

A) 168 centimeters

B) 169 centimeters

C) 170 centimeters

D) 171 centimeters

Content: Problem Solving and Data Analysis

Key: C

Objective: You must use the line of best fit to make a prediction. You must also demonstrate fluency in reading graphs and decimal numbers.

Explanation: Choice C is correct. First, notice that the scale of the x-axis is 0.1, and therefore the x-value of 4.45 is halfway between the unmarked value of 4.4 and the marked value of 4.5. Then, find the y-value on the line of best fit that corresponds with an x-value of 4.45, which is 170.

Choice A is incorrect. If you mistakenly find the point on the line between the x-values of 4.3 and 4.4, you'll likely find a predicted metacarpal bone length of 168 centimeters.

Choice B is incorrect. If you mistakenly find the point on the line that corresponds to an x-value of 4.4 centimeters, you'll likely find a predicted height of approximately 169 centimeters.

Choice D is incorrect. If you mistakenly find the point on the line that corresponds with an x-value of 4.5 centimeters, you'll likely find a predicted height of approximately 171 centimeters. You might also choose this option if you mistakenly use the data point that has an x-value closest to 4.45 centimeters.

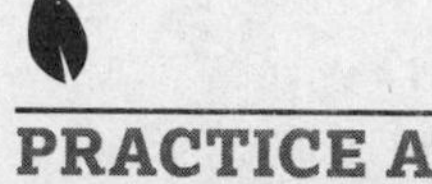

PRACTICE AT

satpractice.org

The answer choices on Question 20 are very close together. Thus, be very precise when examining the scatterplot to find the y-value that corresponds to an x-value of 4.45 on the line of best fit.

CHAPTER 21

Sample Math Questions: Student-Produced Response

In this chapter, you will see examples of student-produced response math questions. This type of question appears in both the calculator and the no-calculator portions of the test. Student-produced response questions can come from any of the four areas covered by the SAT Math Test.

Student-Produced Response Strategies

Student-produced response questions don't have answer choices to select from. You must solve the problem and grid your answer on the answer sheet. There is a space to write your answer, and there are circles below to fill in for your answer. Use your written answer to make sure you fill in the correct circles. The filled-in circles are what determine how your answer is scored. You will not receive credit if you only write in your answer without filling in the circles.

REMEMBER

You must fill in the circles on the answer sheet in order to receive credit. You will not receive credit if you only write in your answer but don't fill in the circles.

Each grid has four columns. If your answer does not fill all four columns, leave the unneeded spaces blank. You may start your answer in any column as long as there is space to fill in the complete answer.

Many of the same test-taking strategies you used on the multiple-choice questions should be used for the student-produced response questions, but here are a few additional tips to consider: First, remember that your answer must be able to fit in the grid on the answer sheet. The grid is four characters long, and there is no grid for negative numbers. If you solve a question and find an answer that is negative or is greater than 9999, you should try to solve the problem a different way to find the correct answer. On some questions, your answer may include a dollar sign, a percent sign, or a degree symbol. These symbols can't be included in the answer grid, and as a reminder, the question will instruct you to disregard them.

When entering a fraction or decimal answer, keep a few things in mind. The scanner can't interpret mixed numbers; therefore, you need to give your answer as an improper fraction or as the decimal equivalent. If your answer is a decimal with more digits than will fit in the grid, you must fill the entire grid with the most accurate value possible, either rounding the number or truncating it. Do not include a leading zero when gridding in decimals. For example, if your answer is $\frac{2}{3}$, you can grid 2/3, .666, or .667; however, 0.6, .66, and 0.67 would all be considered incorrect. Do not round up when truncating a number unless the decimal should be rounded up. For example, if the answer is $\frac{1}{3}$, .333 is an acceptable answer, but .334 is not. It is also not necessary to reduce fractions to their lowest terms as long as the fraction fits in the grid. If your answer is $\frac{6}{18}$, you do not need to reduce it to $\frac{1}{3}$. Giving your answer as an unreduced fraction (if it fits in the grid) can save you time and prevent simple calculation mistakes.

REMEMBER

Answers can't be mixed numbers. Give your answer as an improper fraction or as the decimal equivalent. For instance, do *not* submit $3\frac{1}{2}$ as your answer. Instead, submit either $\frac{7}{2}$ or 3.5.

Make sure to read the question carefully and answer what is being asked. If the question asks for the number of thousands and the correct answer is 2 thousands, grid in 2 as the answer, not 2000. If the question asks for your answer to be rounded to the nearest tenth or hundredth, only a correctly rounded answer will be accepted.

REMEMBER

You don't need to reduce fractions to their lowest terms as long as the fraction fits in the grid. You can save time and prevent calculation errors by giving your answer as an unreduced fraction.

Some student-produced response questions may have more than one correct answer. You should only provide one answer. Do not attempt to grid in more than one answer. You should not spend your time looking for additional answers. Just like multiple-choice questions, there is no penalty for guessing on student-produced response questions. If you are not sure of the correct answer, make an educated guess. Try not to leave questions unanswered.

REMEMBER

Carefully read the directions for the student-produced response questions now so you won't have to spend precious time doing so on test day.

The actual test directions for the student-produced response questions appear on the next page.

DIRECTIONS

For questions 31–38, solve the problem and enter your answer in the grid, as described below, on the answer sheet.

1. Although not required, it is suggested that you write your answer in the boxes at the top of the columns to help you fill in the circles accurately. You will receive credit only if the circles are filled in correctly.
2. Mark no more than one circle in any column.
3. No question has a negative answer.
4. Some problems may have more than one correct answer. In such cases, grid only one answer.
5. **Mixed numbers** such as $3\frac{1}{2}$ must be gridded as 3.5 or 7/2. (If 3 1 / 2 is entered into the grid, it will be interpreted as $\frac{31}{2}$, not $3\frac{1}{2}$.)
6. **Decimal answers:** If you obtain a decimal answer with more digits than the grid can accommodate, it may be either rounded or truncated, but it must fill the entire grid.

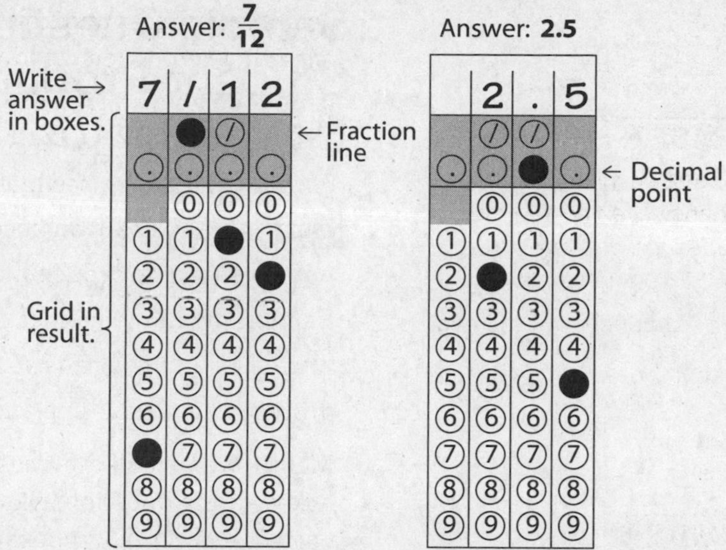

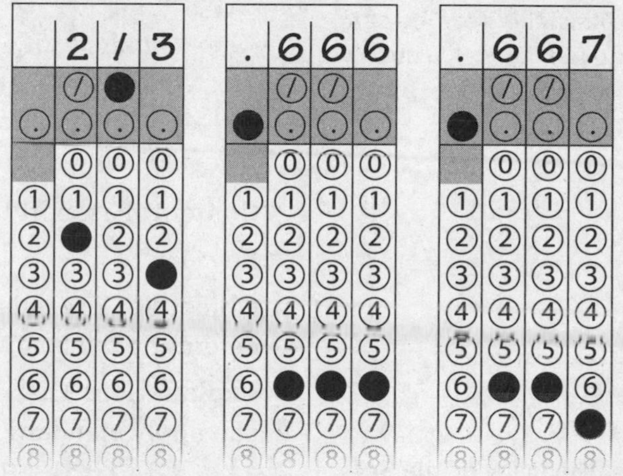

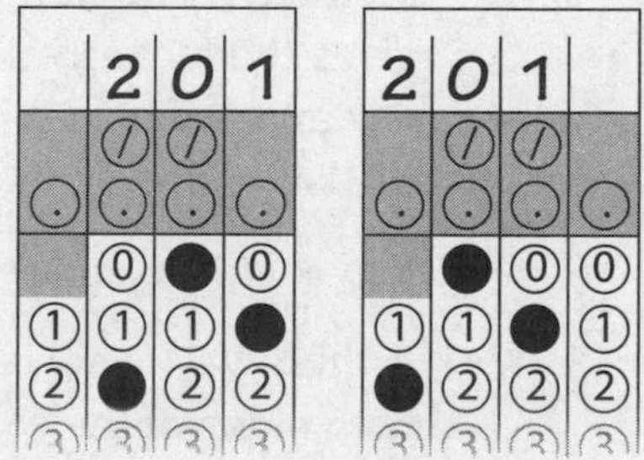

NOTE: You may start your answers in any column, space permitting. Columns you don't need to use should be left blank.

Sample Questions: Student-Produced Response – No Calculator

1

If $a^2 + 14a = 51$ and $a > 0$, what is the value of $a + 7$?

Content: Passport to Advanced Math

Key: 10

Objective: You must use your knowledge of quadratic equations to determine the best way to efficiently solve this problem.

Explanation: There is more than one way to solve this problem. You can apply standard techniques by rewriting the equation $a^2 + 14a = 51$ as $a^2 + 14a - 51 = 0$ and then factoring. Since the coefficient of a is 14 and the constant term is −51, factoring requires writing 51 as the product of two numbers that differ by 14. This is $51 = (3)(17)$, which gives the factorization $(a + 17)(a - 3) = 0$. The possible values of a are −17 and 3. Since it is given that $a > 0$, it must be true that $a = 3$. Thus, the value of $a + 7$ is $3 + 7 = 10$.

You could also use the quadratic formula to find the possible values of a.

A third way to solve this problem is to recognize that adding 49 to both sides of the equation yields $a^2 + 14a + 49 = 51 + 49$, or rather $(a + 7)^2 = 100$, which has a perfect square on each side. Since $a > 0$, the solution to $a + 7 = 10$ is evident.

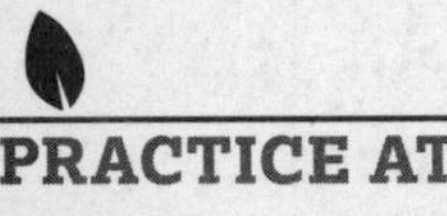

PRACTICE AT

satpractice.org

This question, like many on the SAT Math Test, can be solved in a variety of ways. Use the method that will get you to the correct answer in the least amount of time. Knowing multiple approaches can also help in case you get stumped using one particular method.

2

If $\frac{1}{2}x + \frac{1}{3}y = 4$, what is the value of $3x + 2y$?

Content: Heart of Algebra

Key: 24

Objective: You must use the structure of the equation to efficiently solve the problem.

Explanation: Using the structure of the equation allows you to quickly solve the problem if you see that multiplying both sides of the equation by 6 clears the fractions and yields $3x + 2y = 24$.

PRACTICE AT
satpractice.org

Always be on the lookout for shortcuts. On Question 2, for instance, examining the structure of the equation yields a very efficient solution.

3

What is one possible solution to the equation $\frac{24}{x+1} - \frac{12}{x-1} = 1$?

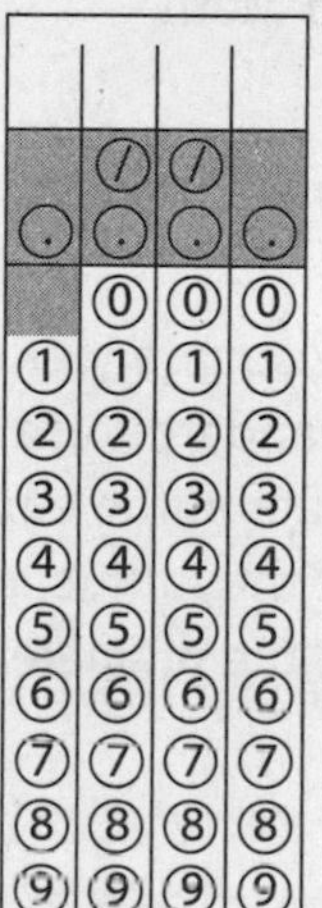

Content: Passport to Advanced Math

Key: 5, 7

Objective: You should seek the best solution method for solving rational equations before beginning. Searching for structure and common denominators at the outset will prove very useful and will help prevent complex computations that do not lead to a solution.

PRACTICE AT

satpractice.org

Eliminating fractions is often a good first step when asked to solve a rational equation. To eliminate the fractions in this equation, multiply both sides of the equation by the common denominator, which is $(x + 1)(x - 1)$.

Explanation: In this problem, multiplying both sides of the equation by the common denominator $(x + 1)(x - 1)$ yields $24(x - 1) - 12(x + 1) = (x + 1)(x - 1)$. Multiplication and simplification then yields $12x - 36 = x^2 - 1$, or $x^2 - 12x + 35 = 0$. Factoring the quadratic gives $(x - 5)(x - 7) = 0$, so the solutions occur at $x = 5$ and $x = 7$, both of which should be checked in the original equation to ensure they are not extraneous. In this case, both values are solutions, and either is a correct answer.

4

$$x^2 + y^2 - 6x + 8y = 144$$

The equation of a circle in the xy-plane is shown above. What is the *diameter* of the circle?

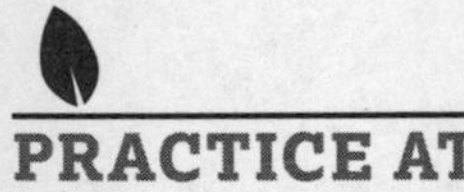

PRACTICE AT

satpractice.org

To solve Question 4, you must know that the standard form of the equation of a circle is $(x - a)^2 + (y - b)^2 = r^2$, where (a, b) is the center of the circle and r is the radius. You also must know how to complete a square.

Content: Additional Topics in Math

Key: 26

Objective: You must determine a circle property given the equation of the circle.

Explanation: Completing the square yields the equation $(x - 3)^2 + (y + 4)^2 = 169$, the standard form of an equation of the circle. Understanding this form results in the equation $r^2 = 169$, which when solved for r gives the value of the radius as 13. Diameter is twice the value of the radius; therefore, the diameter is 26.

Sample Questions: Student-Produced Response – Calculator

5

The table below classifies 103 elements as metal, metalloid, or nonmetal and as solid, liquid, or gas at standard temperature and pressure.

	Solids	Liquids	Gases	Total
Metals	77	1	0	78
Metalloids	7	0	0	7
Nonmetals	6	1	11	18
Total	90	2	11	103

What fraction of all solids and liquids in the table are metalloids?

Content: Problem Solving and Data Analysis

Key: .076, $\frac{7}{92}$

Objective: You must read information from a two-way table and determine the specific relationship between two categorical variables.

Explanation: There are 7 metalloids that are solid or liquid, and there are 92 total solids and liquids. Therefore, the fraction of solids and liquids that are metalloids is $\frac{7}{92}$, or .076.

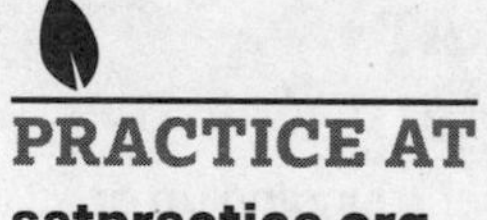

PRACTICE AT
satpractice.org

The denominator of the fraction will be the total number of solids and liquids, while the numerator will be the number of liquids and solids that are metalloids. Carefully retrieve that information from the table, and remember to fill in the circles that correspond to the answer.

6

A typical image taken of the surface of Mars by a camera is 11.2 gigabits in size. A tracking station on Earth can receive data from the spacecraft at a data rate of 3 megabits per second for a maximum of 11 hours each day. If 1 gigabit equals 1,024 megabits, what is the maximum number of typical images that the tracking station could receive from the camera each day?

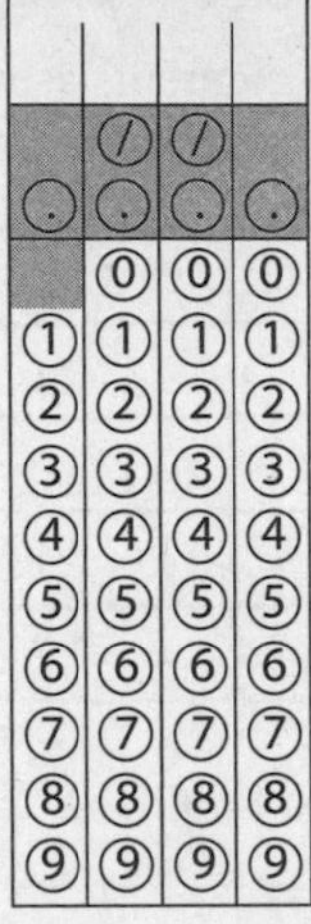

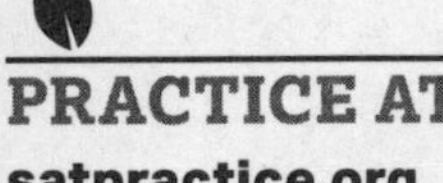

PRACTICE AT
satpractice.org

Unit analysis and conversion is an important skill on the SAT Math Test and features prominently on this question. It may help to write out the conversion, including the units, as illustrated here.

PRACTICE AT
satpractice.org

Consider whether rounding up or down is appropriate based on the question. Here, rounding 10.4 down to 10 is required to receive credit on this question since the question specifically asks for the maximum number of images that the tracking station can receive each day.

Content: Problem Solving and Data Analysis

Key: 10

Objective: In this problem, you must use the unit rate (data-transmission rate) and the conversion between gigabits and megabits as well as conversions in units of time. Unit analysis is critical to solving the problem correctly, and the problem represents a typical calculation that would be done when working with electronic files and data-transmission rates.

Explanation: The tracking station can receive 118,800 megabits each day $\left(\frac{3 \text{ megabits}}{1 \text{ second}} \times \frac{60 \text{ seconds}}{1 \text{ minute}} \times \frac{60 \text{ minutes}}{1 \text{ hour}} \times 11 \text{ hours}\right)$, which is about 116 gigabits each day $\left(\frac{118{,}800}{1{,}024}\right)$. If each image is 11.2 gigabits, then the number of images that can be received each day is $\frac{116}{11.2} \approx 10.4$. Since the question asks for the maximum number of typical images, rounding the answer down to 10 is appropriate because the tracking station will not receive a completed 11th image in one day.

7

If $-\frac{9}{5} < -3t + 1 < -\frac{7}{4}$, what is one possible value of $9t - 3$?

Content: Heart of Algebra

Key: Any decimal with a value greater than 5.25 and less than 5.4. Equivalent fractions in this range that can be entered in the grid are also acceptable.

Objective: You should recognize the structure of the inequality to form a strategy to solve the inequality.

Explanation: Using the structure of the inequality to solve, you could note that the relationship between $-3t + 1$ and $9t - 3$ is that the latter is -3 multiplied by the former. Multiplying all parts of the inequality by -3 reverses the inequality signs, resulting in $\frac{27}{5} > 9t - 3 > \frac{21}{4}$, or rather $\frac{21}{4} < 9t - 3 < \frac{27}{5}$ when written with increasing values from left to right. Any value that is greater than $\frac{21}{4}$ and less than $\frac{27}{5}$ is correct. Therefore, any fraction greater than $\frac{21}{4}$ (equivalent to 5.25) and less than $\frac{27}{5}$ (equivalent to 5.4) that can be entered in the grid is also acceptable.

PRACTICE AT

satpractice.org

When you multiply an inequality by a negative number, remember to reverse the inequality signs.

REMEMBER

When entering your answer to this question, do not enter your answer as a mixed fraction. Rather, enter your answer as a decimal or an improper fraction.

8

An architect drew the sketch below while designing a house roof. The dimensions shown are for the interior of the triangle.

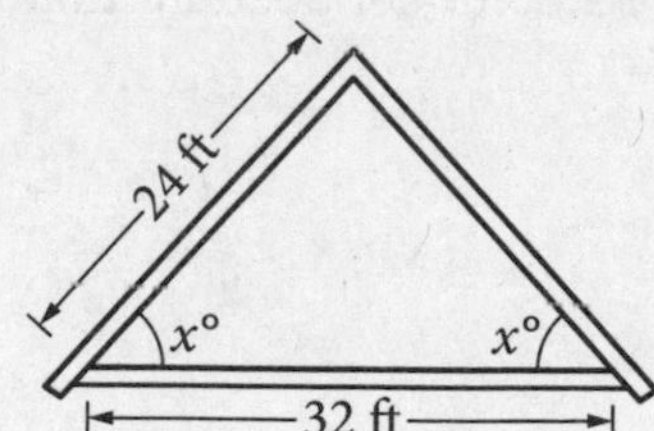

Note: Figure not drawn to scale.

What is the value of cos x?

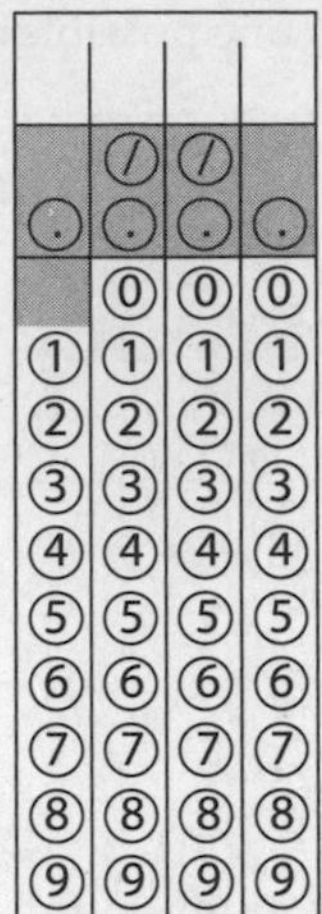

Content: Additional Topics in Math

Key: $\frac{2}{3}$, $\frac{4}{6}$, $\frac{6}{9}$, $\frac{8}{12}$, .666, .667

Objective: You must make use of properties of triangles to solve a problem.

Explanation: Because the triangle is isosceles, constructing a perpendicular from the top vertex to the opposite side will bisect the base and create two smaller right triangles. In a right triangle, the cosine of an acute angle is equal to the length of the side adjacent to the angle divided by the length of the hypotenuse. This gives $\cos x = \frac{16}{24}$, which can be simplified to $\cos x = \frac{2}{3}$. Note that $\frac{16}{24}$ cannot be entered into the answer grid, so this fraction must be reduced. Acceptable answers to grid are 2/3, 4/6, 6/9, 8/12, .666, and .667.

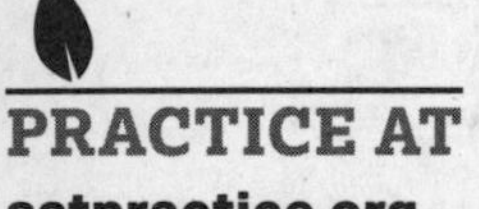

PRACTICE AT

satpractice.org

The cosine of an acute angle is equal to the length of the side adjacent to the angle divided by the length of the hypotenuse. Learn to solve for sine, cosine, and tangent of an acute angle; this may be tested on the SAT.

Sample Question Set

Questions 9 and 10 refer to the following information:

An international bank issues its Traveler credit cards worldwide. When a customer makes a purchase using a Traveler card in a currency different from the customer's home currency, the bank converts the purchase price at the daily foreign exchange rate and then charges a 4% fee on the converted cost.

Sara lives in the United States and is on vacation in India. She used her Traveler card for a purchase that cost 602 rupees (Indian currency). The bank posted a charge of $9.88 to her account that included a 4% fee.

9

What foreign exchange rate, in Indian rupees per one U.S. dollar, did the bank use for Sara's charge? Round your answer to the nearest whole number.

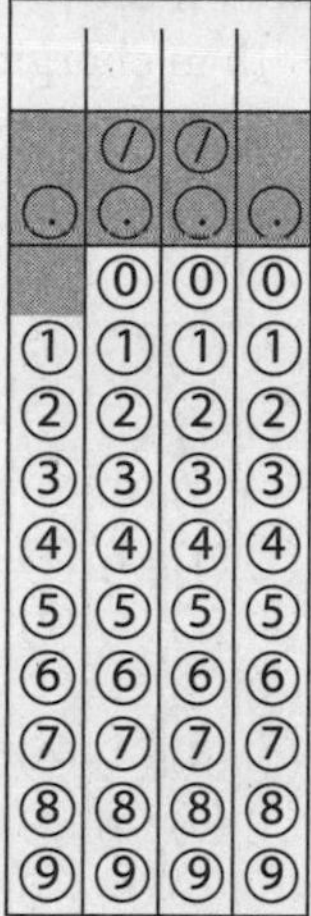

Content: Problem Solving and Data Analysis

Key: 63

Objective: You must use the information in the problem to set up a ratio that will allow you to find the exchange rate.

Explanation: $9.88 represents the conversion of 602 rupees plus a 4% fee on the converted cost. To calculate the original cost of the item in dollars, x, find $1.04x = 9.88$, $x = 9.5$. Since the original cost is $9.50, to calculate the exchange rate r, in Indian rupees per one U.S. dollar:

$9.50 \text{ dollars} \times \frac{r \text{ rupees}}{1 \text{ dollar}} = 602 \text{ rupees}$; solving for r yields approximately 63 rupees.

PRACTICE AT
satpractice.org

It is helpful to divide this question into two steps. First, calculate the original cost of Sara's purchase in dollars. Then, set up a ratio to find the exchange rate, keeping track of your units.

10

A bank in India sells a prepaid credit card worth 7500 rupees. Sara can buy the prepaid card using U.S. dollars at the daily exchange rate with no fee, but she will lose any money left unspent on the prepaid card. What is the least number of the 7500 rupees on the prepaid card Sara must spend for the prepaid card to be cheaper than charging all her purchases on the Traveler card? Round your answer to the nearest whole number of rupees.

Content: Problem Solving and Data Analysis

Key: 7212

Objective: You must set up an inequality to solve a multistep problem.

Explanation: Let d represent the cost, in U.S. dollars, of the 7500-rupee prepaid card. This implies that the exchange rate on this particular day is $\frac{d}{7500}$ dollars per rupee. Suppose Sara's total purchases on the prepaid card were r rupees. The value of r rupees in dollars is $\left(\frac{d}{7500}\right)r$ dollars. If Sara spent the r rupees on the Traveler card instead, she would be charged $1.04\left(\frac{d}{7500}\right)r$ dollars. To answer the question about how many rupees Sara must spend in order to make the Traveler card a cheaper option (in dollars) for spending the r rupees, you must set up the inequality $1.04\left(\frac{d}{7500}\right)r \geq d$. Rewriting both sides reveals $1.04\left(\frac{r}{7500}\right)d \geq (1)d$, from which you can infer $1.04\left(\frac{r}{7500}\right) \geq 1$. Dividing both sides by 1.04 and multiplying both sides by 7500 finally yields $r \geq 7212$. Hence the least number of rupees Sara must spend for the prepaid card to be cheaper than the Traveler card is 7212.

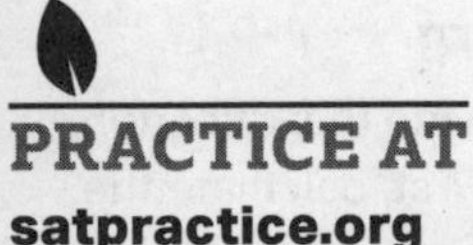

PRACTICE AT
satpractice.org

Another helpful way to think about this question is to keep in mind the fact that Sara will pay 7500 rupees for the prepaid card, regardless of how much money she leaves unspent. For the prepaid card to be cheaper than using the Traveler card, the Traveler card must end up costing Sara more than 7500 rupees. You can set up an inequality to calculate the least amount of purchases Sara needs to make using the Traveler card to exceed 7500 rupees. This value, when rounded to the nearest whole number, yields the correct answer.

PART 4

Eight Official Practice Tests with Answer Explanations

Introduction

Time to Practice

The remainder of this book is composed of eight full SAT practice tests. Each practice test is followed by an answer sheet and answer explanations. These practice tests and explanations were written by the College Board's Assessment Design and Development team using the same processes and review standards used when writing the actual SAT. Everything from the layout of the page to the construction of the questions accurately reflects what you'll see on test day.

The practice tests will provide the most valuable insight into your performance on the actual SAT when completed in a single sitting. As such, we urge you not to leaf through these tests for question practice, but instead to take them under conditions similar to those of a real test. If you are looking for additional questions, you can find them in the Practice section of sat.org

Tips for Taking the Practice Tests

You'll get the most out of the practice tests if you take them under conditions that are as close as possible to those of the real test:

- Leave yourself 3 hours to complete each sample test and an additional 50 minutes to complete the SAT Essay.
- Sit at a desk or table cleared of any other papers or books. Items such as dictionaries, books, or notes won't be allowed when you take the actual SAT.
- For the math questions that allow calculators, use the calculator that you plan to use on test day.
- Set a timer or use a watch or clock to time yourself on each section.
- Tear out or make a copy of the practice test answer sheet located immediately after each practice test and fill it in just as you will on the day of the actual test.

How to Score Your Practice Tests

For more information on how to score your practice tests, go to sat.org/scoring. As you learned earlier, your SAT results will include a number of scores that provide additional information about your achievement and readiness for college and career. The College Board has also produced a free app that will allow you to immediately score your answer sheet by taking a picture of it. This app will take much of the manual labor out of scoring a paper-and-pencil test, and we hope it will encourage you to engage in productive practice. You can find more information on the app as well as how to score your tests without the app at sat.org/scoring.

Connection to Khan Academy

Through the College Board practice app, you'll be able to automatically score your practice tests and send those results to Khan Academy to power your personalized practice. Then, when you log on to its website (khanacademy.org/sat), Khan Academy will recommend specific lessons and resources to target the skills that will most improve your score on the SAT. Since the SAT is a measure of college and career readiness, this practice will also better prepare you for success beyond the SAT.

The SAT®

Practice Test #1

Make time to take the practice test. It's one of the best ways to get ready for the SAT.

After you've taken the practice test, score it right away at **sat.org/scoring**.

CollegeBoard

Test begins on the next page.

Reading Test

65 MINUTES, 52 QUESTIONS

Turn to Section 1 of your answer sheet to answer the questions in this section.

DIRECTIONS

Each passage or pair of passages below is followed by a number of questions. After reading each passage or pair, choose the best answer to each question based on what is stated or implied in the passage or passages and in any accompanying graphics (such as a table or graph).

Questions 1-10 are based on the following passage.

This passage is from Lydia Minatoya, *The Strangeness of Beauty*. ©1999 by Lydia Minatoya. The setting is Japan in 1920. Chie and her daughter Naomi are members of the House of Fuji, a noble family.

Akira came directly, breaking all tradition. Was that it? Had he followed form—had he asked his mother to speak to his father to approach a go-between—would Chie have been more receptive?

He came on a winter's eve. He pounded on the door while a cold rain beat on the shuttered veranda, so at first Chie thought him only the wind. The maid knew better. Chie heard her soft scuttling footsteps, the creak of the door. Then the maid brought a calling card to the drawing room, for Chie.

Chie was reluctant to go to her guest; perhaps she was feeling too cozy. She and Naomi were reading at a low table set atop a charcoal brazier. A thick quilt spread over the sides of the table so their legs were tucked inside with the heat.

"Who is it at this hour, in this weather?" Chie questioned as she picked the name card off the maid's lacquer tray.

"Shinoda, Akira. Kobe Dental College," she read.

Naomi recognized the name. Chie heard a soft intake of air.

"I think you should go," said Naomi.

Akira was waiting in the entry. He was in his early twenties, slim and serious, wearing the black military-style uniform of a student. As he bowed—his hands hanging straight down, a black cap in one, a yellow oil-paper umbrella in the other—Chie glanced beyond him. In the glistening surface of the courtyard's rain-drenched paving stones, she saw his reflection like a dark double.

"Madame," said Akira, "forgive my disruption, but I come with a matter of urgency."

His voice was soft, refined. He straightened and stole a deferential peek at her face.

In the dim light his eyes shone with sincerity. Chie felt herself starting to like him.

"Come inside, get out of this nasty night. Surely your business can wait for a moment or two."

"I don't want to trouble you. Normally I would approach you more properly but I've received word of a position. I've an opportunity to go to America, as dentist for Seattle's Japanese community."

"Congratulations," Chie said with amusement. "That is an opportunity, I'm sure. But how am I involved?"

Even noting Naomi's breathless reaction to the name card, Chie had no idea. Akira's message, delivered like a formal speech, filled her with maternal amusement. You know how children speak so earnestly, so hurriedly, so endearingly about things that have no importance in an adult's mind? That's how she viewed him, as a child.

CONTINUE

It was how she viewed Naomi. Even though Naomi was eighteen and training endlessly in the arts needed to make a good marriage, Chie had made no effort to find her a husband.

Akira blushed.

"Depending on your response, I may stay in Japan. I've come to ask for Naomi's hand."

Suddenly Chie felt the dampness of the night.

"Does Naomi know anything of your . . . ambitions?"

"We have an understanding. Please don't judge my candidacy by the unseemliness of this proposal. I ask directly because the use of a go-between takes much time. Either method comes down to the same thing: a matter of parental approval. If you give your consent, I become Naomi's yoshi.* We'll live in the House of Fuji. Without your consent, I must go to America, to secure a new home for my bride."

Eager to make his point, he'd been looking her full in the face. Abruptly, his voice turned gentle. "I see I've startled you. My humble apologies. I'll take no more of your evening. My address is on my card. If you don't wish to contact me, I'll reapproach you in two weeks' time. Until then, good night."

He bowed and left. Taking her ease, with effortless grace, like a cat making off with a fish.

"Mother?" Chie heard Naomi's low voice and turned from the door. "He has asked you?"

The sight of Naomi's clear eyes, her dark brows gave Chie strength. Maybe his hopes were preposterous.

"Where did you meet such a fellow? Imagine! He thinks he can marry the Fuji heir and take her to America all in the snap of his fingers!"

Chie waited for Naomi's ripe laughter.

Naomi was silent. She stood a full half minute looking straight into Chie's eyes. Finally, she spoke. "I met him at my literary meeting."

Naomi turned to go back into the house, then stopped.

"Mother."

"Yes?"

"I mean to have him."

* a man who marries a woman of higher status and takes her family's name

1

Which choice best describes what happens in the passage?

A) One character argues with another character who intrudes on her home.

B) One character receives a surprising request from another character.

C) One character reminisces about choices she has made over the years.

D) One character criticizes another character for pursuing an unexpected course of action.

2

Which choice best describes the developmental pattern of the passage?

A) A careful analysis of a traditional practice

B) A detailed depiction of a meaningful encounter

C) A definitive response to a series of questions

D) A cheerful recounting of an amusing anecdote

3

As used in line 1 and line 65, "directly" most nearly means

A) frankly.

B) confidently.

C) without mediation.

D) with precision.

4

Which reaction does Akira most fear from Chie?

A) She will consider his proposal inappropriate.

B) She will mistake his earnestness for immaturity.

C) She will consider his unscheduled visit an imposition.

D) She will underestimate the sincerity of his emotions.

5

Which choice provides the best evidence for the answer to the previous question?

A) Line 33 ("His voice . . . refined")
B) Lines 49-51 ("You . . . mind")
C) Lines 63-64 ("Please . . . proposal")
D) Lines 71-72 ("Eager . . . face")

6

In the passage, Akira addresses Chie with

A) affection but not genuine love.
B) objectivity but not complete impartiality.
C) amusement but not mocking disparagement.
D) respect but not utter deference.

7

The main purpose of the first paragraph is to

A) describe a culture.
B) criticize a tradition.
C) question a suggestion.
D) analyze a reaction.

8

As used in line 2, "form" most nearly means

A) appearance.
B) custom.
C) structure.
D) nature.

9

Why does Akira say his meeting with Chie is "a matter of urgency" (line 32)?

A) He fears that his own parents will disapprove of Naomi.
B) He worries that Naomi will reject him and marry someone else.
C) He has been offered an attractive job in another country.
D) He knows that Chie is unaware of his feelings for Naomi.

10

Which choice provides the best evidence for the answer to the previous question?

A) Line 39 ("I don't . . . you")
B) Lines 39-42 ("Normally . . . community")
C) Lines 58-59 ("Depending . . . Japan")
D) Lines 72-73 ("I see . . . you")

CONTINUE

Questions 11-21 are based on the following passage and supplementary material.

This passage is adapted from Francis J. Flynn and Gabrielle S. Adams, "Money Can't Buy Love: Asymmetric Beliefs about Gift Price and Feelings of Appreciation." ©2008 by Elsevier Inc.

Every day, millions of shoppers hit the stores in full force—both online and on foot—searching frantically for the perfect gift. Last year, Americans spent over $30 billion at retail stores in the month of December alone. Aside from purchasing holiday gifts, most people regularly buy presents for other occasions throughout the year, including weddings, birthdays, anniversaries, graduations, and baby showers. This frequent experience of gift-giving can engender ambivalent feelings in gift-givers. Many relish the opportunity to buy presents because gift-giving offers a powerful means to build stronger bonds with one's closest peers. At the same time, many dread the thought of buying gifts; they worry that their purchases will disappoint rather than delight the intended recipients.

Anthropologists describe gift-giving as a positive social process, serving various political, religious, and psychological functions. Economists, however, offer a less favorable view. According to Waldfogel (1993), gift-giving represents an objective waste of resources. People buy gifts that recipients would not choose to buy on their own, or at least not spend as much money to purchase (a phenomenon referred to as "the deadweight loss of Christmas"). To wit, givers are likely to spend $100 to purchase a gift that receivers would spend only $80 to buy themselves. This "deadweight loss" suggests that gift-givers are not very good at predicting what gifts others will appreciate. That in itself is not surprising to social psychologists. Research has found that people often struggle to take account of others' perspectives—their insights are subject to egocentrism, social projection, and multiple attribution errors.

What is surprising is that gift-givers have considerable experience acting as both gift-givers and gift-recipients, but nevertheless tend to overspend each time they set out to purchase a meaningful gift. In the present research, we propose a unique psychological explanation for this overspending problem—i.e., that gift-givers equate how much they spend with how much recipients will appreciate the gift (the more expensive the gift, the stronger a gift-recipient's feelings of appreciation). Although a link between gift price and feelings of appreciation might seem intuitive to gift-givers, such an assumption may be unfounded. Indeed, we propose that gift-recipients will be less inclined to base their feelings of appreciation on the magnitude of a gift than givers assume.

Why do gift-givers assume that gift price is closely linked to gift-recipients' feelings of appreciation? Perhaps givers believe that bigger (i.e., more expensive) gifts convey stronger signals of thoughtfulness and consideration. According to Camerer (1988) and others, gift-giving represents a symbolic ritual, whereby gift-givers attempt to signal their positive attitudes toward the intended recipient and their willingness to invest resources in a future relationship. In this sense, gift-givers may be motivated to spend more money on a gift in order to send a "stronger signal" to their intended recipient. As for gift-recipients, they may not construe smaller and larger gifts as representing smaller and larger signals of thoughtfulness and consideration.

The notion of gift-givers and gift-recipients being unable to account for the other party's perspective seems puzzling because people slip in and out of these roles every day, and, in some cases, multiple times in the course of the same day. Yet, despite the extensive experience that people have as both givers and receivers, they often struggle to transfer information gained from one role (e.g., as a giver) and apply it in another, complementary role (e.g., as a receiver). In theoretical terms, people fail to utilize information about their own preferences and experiences in order to produce more efficient outcomes in their exchange relations. In practical terms, people spend hundreds of dollars each year on gifts, but somehow never learn to calibrate their gift expenditures according to personal insight.

CONTINUE

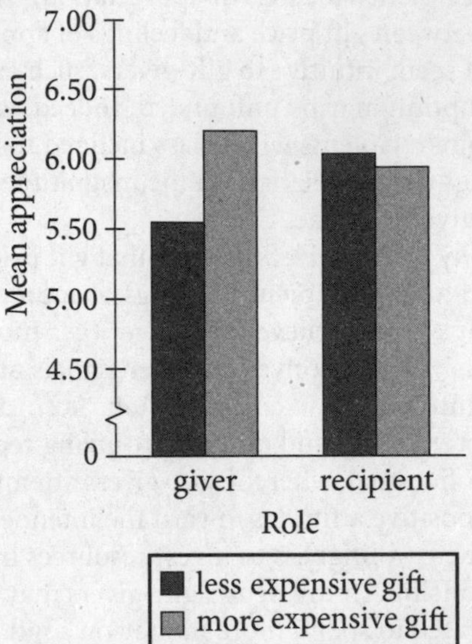

11

The authors most likely use the examples in lines 1-9 of the passage ("Every . . . showers") to highlight the

A) regularity with which people shop for gifts.
B) recent increase in the amount of money spent on gifts.
C) anxiety gift shopping causes for consumers.
D) number of special occasions involving gift-giving.

12

In line 10, the word "ambivalent" most nearly means

A) unrealistic.
B) conflicted.
C) apprehensive.
D) supportive.

13

The authors indicate that people value gift-giving because they feel it

A) functions as a form of self-expression.
B) is an inexpensive way to show appreciation.
C) requires the gift-recipient to reciprocate.
D) can serve to strengthen a relationship.

14

Which choice provides the best evidence for the answer to the previous question?

A) Lines 10-13 ("Many . . . peers")
B) Lines 22-23 ("People . . . own")
C) Lines 31-32 ("Research . . . perspectives")
D) Lines 44-47 ("Although . . . unfounded")

15

The "social psychologists" mentioned in paragraph 2 (lines 17-34) would likely describe the "deadweight loss" phenomenon as

A) predictable.
B) questionable.
C) disturbing.
D) unprecedented.

16

The passage indicates that the assumption made by gift-givers in lines 41-44 may be

A) insincere.
B) unreasonable.
C) incorrect.
D) substantiated.

CONTINUE

17

Which choice provides the best evidence for the answer to the previous question?

A) Lines 53-55 ("Perhaps . . . consideration")
B) Lines 55-60 ("According . . . relationship")
C) Lines 63-65 ("As . . . consideration")
D) Lines 75-78 ("In . . . relations")

18

As it is used in line 54, "convey" most nearly means

A) transport.
B) counteract.
C) exchange.
D) communicate.

19

The authors refer to work by Camerer and others (line 56) in order to

A) offer an explanation.
B) introduce an argument.
C) question a motive.
D) support a conclusion.

20

The graph following the passage offers evidence that gift-givers base their predictions of how much a gift will be appreciated on

A) the appreciation level of the gift-recipients.
B) the monetary value of the gift.
C) their own desires for the gifts they purchase.
D) their relationship with the gift-recipients.

21

The authors would likely attribute the differences in gift-giver and recipient mean appreciation as represented in the graph to

A) an inability to shift perspective.
B) an increasingly materialistic culture.
C) a growing opposition to gift-giving.
D) a misunderstanding of intentions.

CONTINUE

38

Woolf characterizes the questions in lines 53-57 ("For we . . . men") as both

A) controversial and threatening.

B) weighty and unanswerable.

C) momentous and pressing.

D) provocative and mysterious.

39

Which choice provides the best evidence for the answer to the previous question?

A) Lines 46-47 ("We . . . questions")

B) Lines 48-49 ("And . . . them")

C) Line 57 ("The moment . . . short")

D) Line 62 ("That . . . Madam")

40

Which choice most closely captures the meaning of the figurative "sixpence" referred to in lines 70 and 71?

A) Tolerance

B) Knowledge

C) Opportunity

D) Perspective

41

The range of places and occasions listed in lines 72-76 ("Let us . . . funerals") mainly serves to emphasize how

A) novel the challenge faced by women is.

B) pervasive the need for critical reflection is.

C) complex the political and social issues of the day are.

D) enjoyable the career possibilities for women are.

CONTINUE

Questions 42-52 are based on the following passages.

Passage 1 is adapted from Michael Slezak, "Space Mining: the Next Gold Rush?" ©2013 by New Scientist. Passage 2 is from the editors of *New Scientist*, "Taming the Final Frontier." ©2013 by New Scientist.

Passage 1

Follow the money and you will end up in space. That's the message from a first-of-its-kind forum on mining beyond Earth.

Convened in Sydney by the Australian Centre for Space Engineering Research, the event brought together mining companies, robotics experts, lunar scientists, and government agencies that are all working to make space mining a reality.

The forum comes hot on the heels of the 2012 unveiling of two private asteroid-mining firms. Planetary Resources of Washington says it will launch its first prospecting telescopes in two years, while Deep Space Industries of Virginia hopes to be harvesting metals from asteroids by 2020. Another commercial venture that sprung up in 2012, Golden Spike of Colorado, will be offering trips to the moon, including to potential lunar miners.

Within a few decades, these firms may be meeting earthly demands for precious metals, such as platinum and gold, and the rare earth elements vital for personal electronics, such as yttrium and lanthanum. But like the gold rush pioneers who transformed the western United States, the first space miners won't just enrich themselves. They also hope to build an off-planet economy free of any bonds with Earth, in which the materials extracted and processed from the moon and asteroids are delivered for space-based projects.

In this scenario, water mined from other worlds could become the most desired commodity. "In the desert, what's worth more: a kilogram of gold or a kilogram of water?" asks Kris Zacny of HoneyBee Robotics in New York. "Gold is useless. Water will let you live."

Water ice from the moon's poles could be sent to astronauts on the International Space Station for drinking or as a radiation shield. Splitting water into oxygen and hydrogen makes spacecraft fuel, so ice-rich asteroids could become interplanetary refuelling stations.

Companies are eyeing the iron, silicon, and aluminium in lunar soil and asteroids, which could be used in 3D printers to make spare parts or machinery. Others want to turn space dirt into concrete for landing pads, shelters, and roads.

Passage 2

The motivation for deep-space travel is shifting from discovery to economics. The past year has seen a flurry of proposals aimed at bringing celestial riches down to Earth. No doubt this will make a few billionaires even wealthier, but we all stand to gain: the mineral bounty and spin-off technologies could enrich us all.

But before the miners start firing up their rockets, we should pause for thought. At first glance, space mining seems to sidestep most environmental concerns: there is (probably!) no life on asteroids, and thus no habitats to trash. But its consequences —both here on Earth and in space—merit careful consideration.

Part of this is about principles. Some will argue that space's "magnificent desolation" is not ours to despoil, just as they argue that our own planet's poles should remain pristine. Others will suggest that glutting ourselves on space's riches is not an acceptable alternative to developing more sustainable ways of earthly life.

History suggests that those will be hard lines to hold, and it may be difficult to persuade the public that such barren environments are worth preserving. After all, they exist in vast abundance, and even fewer people will experience them than have walked through Antarctica's icy landscapes.

There's also the emerging off-world economy to consider. The resources that are valuable in orbit and beyond may be very different to those we prize on Earth. Questions of their stewardship have barely been broached—and the relevant legal and regulatory framework is fragmentary, to put it mildly.

Space miners, like their earthly counterparts, are often reluctant to engage with such questions. One speaker at last week's space-mining forum in Sydney, Australia, concluded with a plea that regulation should be avoided. But miners have much to gain from a broad agreement on the for-profit exploitation of space. Without consensus, claims will be disputed, investments risky, and the gains made insecure. It is in all of our long-term interests to seek one out.

CONTINUE

42

In lines 9-17, the author of Passage 1 mentions several companies primarily to

A) note the technological advances that make space mining possible.

B) provide evidence of the growing interest in space mining.

C) emphasize the large profits to be made from space mining.

D) highlight the diverse ways to carry out space mining operations.

43

The author of Passage 1 indicates that space mining could have which positive effect?

A) It could yield materials important to Earth's economy.

B) It could raise the value of some precious metals on Earth.

C) It could create unanticipated technological innovations.

D) It could change scientists' understanding of space resources.

44

Which choice provides the best evidence for the answer to the previous question?

A) Lines 18-22 ("Within . . . lanthanum")

B) Lines 24-28 ("They . . . projects")

C) Lines 29-30 ("In this . . . commodity")

D) Lines 41-44 ("Companies . . . machinery")

45

As used in line 19, "demands" most nearly means

A) offers.

B) claims.

C) inquiries.

D) desires.

46

What function does the discussion of water in lines 35-40 serve in Passage 1?

A) It continues an extended comparison that begins in the previous paragraph.

B) It provides an unexpected answer to a question raised in the previous paragraph.

C) It offers hypothetical examples supporting a claim made in the previous paragraph.

D) It examines possible outcomes of a proposal put forth in the previous paragraph.

47

The central claim of Passage 2 is that space mining has positive potential but

A) it will end up encouraging humanity's reckless treatment of the environment.

B) its effects should be thoughtfully considered before it becomes a reality.

C) such potential may not include replenishing key resources that are disappearing on Earth.

D) experts disagree about the commercial viability of the discoveries it could yield.

48

As used in line 68, "hold" most nearly means

A) maintain.

B) grip.

C) restrain.

D) withstand.

CONTINUE

49

Which statement best describes the relationship between the passages?

A) Passage 2 refutes the central claim advanced in Passage 1.

B) Passage 2 illustrates the phenomenon described in more general terms in Passage 1.

C) Passage 2 argues against the practicality of the proposals put forth in Passage 1.

D) Passage 2 expresses reservations about developments discussed in Passage 1.

50

The author of Passage 2 would most likely respond to the discussion of the future of space mining in lines 18-28, Passage 1, by claiming that such a future

A) is inconsistent with the sustainable use of space resources.

B) will be difficult to bring about in the absence of regulations.

C) cannot be attained without technologies that do not yet exist.

D) seems certain to affect Earth's economy in a negative way.

51

Which choice provides the best evidence for the answer to the previous question?

A) Lines 60-63 ("Some . . . pristine")

B) Lines 74-76 ("The resources . . . Earth")

C) Lines 81-83 ("One . . . avoided")

D) Lines 85-87 ("Without . . . insecure")

52

Which point about the resources that will be highly valued in space is implicit in Passage 1 and explicit in Passage 2?

A) They may be different resources from those that are valuable on Earth.

B) They will be valuable only if they can be harvested cheaply.

C) They are likely to be primarily precious metals and rare earth elements.

D) They may increase in value as those same resources become rare on Earth.

STOP

If you finish before time is called, you may check your work on this section only. Do not turn to any other section.

No Test Material On This Page

Writing and Language Test

35 MINUTES, 44 QUESTIONS

Turn to Section 2 of your answer sheet to answer the questions in this section.

DIRECTIONS

Each passage below is accompanied by a number of questions. For some questions, you will consider how the passage might be revised to improve the expression of ideas. For other questions, you will consider how the passage might be edited to correct errors in sentence structure, usage, or punctuation. A passage or a question may be accompanied by one or more graphics (such as a table or graph) that you will consider as you make revising and editing decisions.

Some questions will direct you to an underlined portion of a passage. Other questions will direct you to a location in a passage or ask you to think about the passage as a whole.

After reading each passage, choose the answer to each question that most effectively improves the quality of writing in the passage or that makes the passage conform to the conventions of standard written English. Many questions include a "NO CHANGE" option. Choose that option if you think the best choice is to leave the relevant portion of the passage as it is.

Questions 1-11 are based on the following passage.

Whey to Go

Greek yogurt—a strained form of cultured yogurt—has grown enormously in popularity in the United States since it was first introduced in the country in the late 1980s.

From 2011 to 2012 alone, sales of Greek yogurt in the US increased by 50 percent. The resulting increase in Greek yogurt production has forced those involved in the business to address the detrimental effects that the yogurt-making process may be having on the environment. Fortunately, farmers and others in the

CONTINUE

Greek yogurt business have found many methods of controlling and eliminating most environmental threats. Given these solutions as well as the many health benefits of the food, the advantages of Greek yogurt [1] outdo the potential drawbacks of its production.

[1] The main environmental problem caused by the production of Greek yogurt is the creation of acid whey as a by-product. [2] Because it requires up to four times more milk to make than conventional yogurt does, Greek yogurt produces larger amounts of acid whey, which is difficult to dispose of. [3] To address the problem of disposal, farmers have found a number of uses for acid whey. [4] They can add it to livestock feed as a protein [2] supplement, and people can make their own Greek-style yogurt at home by straining regular yogurt. [5] If it is improperly introduced into the environment, acid-whey runoff [3] can pollute waterways, depleting the oxygen content of streams and rivers as it decomposes. [6] Yogurt manufacturers, food [4] scientists; and government officials are also working together to develop additional solutions for reusing whey. [5]

1

A) NO CHANGE
B) defeat
C) outperform
D) outweigh

2

Which choice provides the most relevant detail?

A) NO CHANGE
B) supplement and convert it into gas to use as fuel in electricity production.
C) supplement, while sweet whey is more desirable as a food additive for humans.
D) supplement, which provides an important element of their diet.

3

A) NO CHANGE
B) can pollute waterway's,
C) could have polluted waterways,
D) has polluted waterway's,

4

A) NO CHANGE
B) scientists: and
C) scientists, and
D) scientists, and,

5

To make this paragraph most logical, sentence 5 should be placed

A) where it is now.
B) after sentence 1.
C) after sentence 2.
D) after sentence 3.

CONTINUE

6 Though these conservation methods can be costly and time-consuming, they are well worth the effort. Nutritionists consider Greek yogurt to be a healthy food: it is an excellent source of calcium and protein, serves 7 to be a digestive aid, and 8 it contains few calories in its unsweetened low- and non-fat forms. Greek yogurt is slightly lower in sugar and carbohydrates than conventional yogurt is. 9 Also, because it is more concentrated, Greek yogurt contains slightly more protein per serving, thereby helping people stay

6

The writer is considering deleting the underlined sentence. Should the writer do this?

A) Yes, because it does not provide a transition from the previous paragraph.

B) Yes, because it fails to support the main argument of the passage as introduced in the first paragraph.

C) No, because it continues the explanation of how acid whey can be disposed of safely.

D) No, because it sets up the argument in the paragraph for the benefits of Greek yogurt.

7

A) NO CHANGE

B) as

C) like

D) for

8

A) NO CHANGE

B) containing

C) contains

D) will contain

9

A) NO CHANGE

B) In other words,

C) Therefore,

D) For instance,

CONTINUE

10 satiated for longer periods of time. These health benefits have prompted Greek yogurt's recent surge in popularity. In fact, Greek yogurt can be found in an increasing number of products such as snack food and frozen desserts. Because consumers reap the nutritional benefits of Greek yogurt and support those who make and sell 11 it, therefore farmers and businesses should continue finding safe and effective methods of producing the food.

10

A) NO CHANGE
B) fulfilled
C) complacent
D) sufficient

11

A) NO CHANGE
B) it, farmers
C) it, so farmers
D) it: farmers

CONTINUE

Questions 12-22 are based on the following passage and supplementary material.

Dark Snow

Most of Greenland's interior is covered by a thick layer of ice and compressed snow known as the Greenland Ice Sheet. The size of the ice sheet fluctuates seasonally: in summer, average daily high temperatures in Greenland can rise to slightly above 50 degrees Fahrenheit, partially melting the ice; in the winter, the sheet thickens as additional snow falls, and average daily low temperatures can drop **12** to as low as 20 degrees.

12

Which choice most accurately and effectively represents the information in the graph?

A) NO CHANGE

B) to 12 degrees Fahrenheit.

C) to their lowest point on December 13.

D) to 10 degrees Fahrenheit and stay there for months.

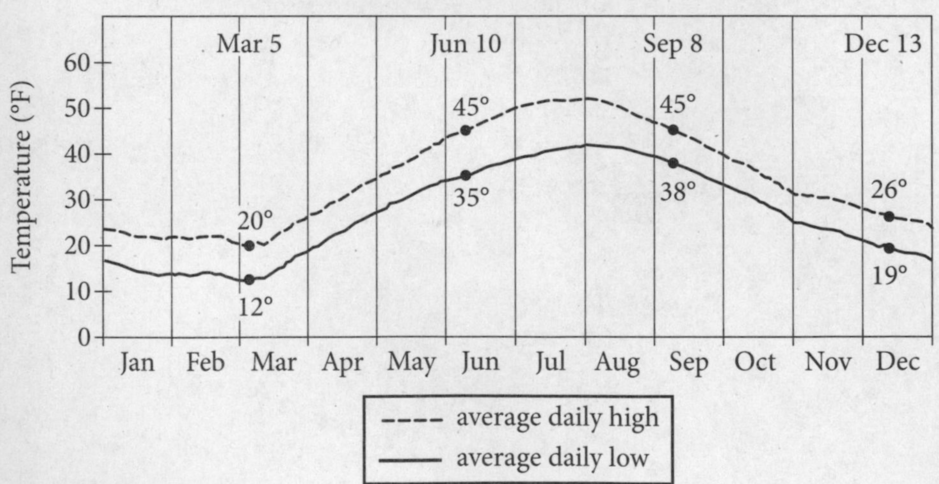

Adapted from WMO. ©2014 by World Meteorological Organization.

CONTINUE

Typically, the ice sheet begins to show evidence of thawing in late **13** summer. This follows several weeks of higher temperatures. **14** For example, in the summer of 2012, virtually the entire Greenland Ice Sheet underwent thawing at or near its surface by mid-July, the earliest date on record. Most scientists looking for the causes of the Great Melt of 2012 have focused exclusively on rising temperatures. The summer of 2012 was the warmest in 170 years, records show. But Jason **15** Box, an associate professor of geology at Ohio State believes that another factor added to the early **16** thaw; the "dark snow" problem.

13

Which choice most effectively combines the two sentences at the underlined portion?

A) summer, following
B) summer, and this thawing follows
C) summer, and such thawing follows
D) summer and this evidence follows

14

A) NO CHANGE
B) However,
C) As such,
D) Moreover,

15

A) NO CHANGE
B) Box an associate professor of geology at Ohio State,
C) Box, an associate professor of geology at Ohio State,
D) Box, an associate professor of geology, at Ohio State

16

A) NO CHANGE
B) thaw; and it was
C) thaw:
D) thaw: being

According to Box, a leading Greenland expert, tundra fires in 2012 from as far away as North America produced great amounts of soot, some **17** of it drifted over Greenland in giant plumes of smoke and then **18** fell as particles onto the ice sheet. Scientists have long known that soot particles facilitate melting by darkening snow and ice, limiting **19** it's ability to reflect the Sun's rays. As Box explains, "Soot is an extremely powerful light absorber. It settles over the ice and captures the Sun's heat." The result is a self-reinforcing cycle. As the ice melts, the land and water under the ice become exposed, and since land and water are darker than snow, the surface absorbs even more heat, which **20** is related to the rising temperatures.

17

A) NO CHANGE
B) soot
C) of which
D) DELETE the underlined portion.

18

A) NO CHANGE
B) falls
C) will fall
D) had fallen

19

A) NO CHANGE
B) its
C) there
D) their

20

Which choice best completes the description of a self-reinforcing cycle?

A) NO CHANGE
B) raises the surface temperature.
C) begins to cool at a certain point.
D) leads to additional melting.

CONTINUE

[1] Box's research is important because the fires of 2012 may not be a one-time phenomenon. [2] According to scientists, rising Arctic temperatures are making northern latitudes greener and thus more fire prone. [3] The pattern Box observed in 2012 may repeat **21** itself again, with harmful effects on the Arctic ecosystem. [4] Box is currently organizing an expedition to gather this crucial information. [5] The next step for Box and his team is to travel to Greenland to perform direct sampling of the ice in order to determine just how much the soot is contributing to the melting of the ice sheet. [6] Members of the public will be able to track his team's progress—and even help fund the expedition—through a website Box has created. **22**

21

A) NO CHANGE
B) itself,
C) itself, with damage and
D) itself possibly,

22

To make this paragraph most logical, sentence 4 should be placed

A) where it is now.
B) after sentence 1.
C) after sentence 2.
D) after sentence 5.

Questions 23-33 are based on the following passage.

Coworking: A Creative Solution

When I left my office job as a website developer at a small company for a position that allowed me to work full-time from home, I thought I had it made: I gleefully traded in my suits and dress shoes for sweatpants and slippers, my frantic early-morning bagged lunch packing for a leisurely midday trip to my refrigerator. The novelty of this comfortable work-from-home life, however, **23** soon got worn off quickly. Within a month, I found myself feeling isolated despite having frequent email and instant messaging contact with my colleagues. Having become frustrated trying to solve difficult problems, **24** no colleagues were nearby to share ideas. It was during this time that I read an article **25** into coworking spaces.

23

A) NO CHANGE
B) was promptly worn
C) promptly wore
D) wore

24

A) NO CHANGE
B) colleagues were important for sharing ideas.
C) ideas couldn't be shared with colleagues.
D) I missed having colleagues nearby to consult.

25

A) NO CHANGE
B) about
C) upon
D) for

CONTINUE

The article, published by *Forbes* magazine, explained that coworking spaces are designated locations that, for a fee, individuals can use to conduct their work. The spaces are usually stocked with standard office **26** equipment, such as photocopiers, printers, and fax machines. **27** In these locations, however, the spaces often include small meeting areas and larger rooms for hosting presentations. **28** The cost of launching a new coworking business in the United States is estimated to be approximately $58,000.

26

A) NO CHANGE
B) equipment, such as:
C) equipment such as:
D) equipment, such as,

27

A) NO CHANGE
B) In addition to equipment,
C) For these reasons,
D) Likewise,

28

The writer is considering deleting the underlined sentence. Should the sentence be kept or deleted?

A) Kept, because it provides a detail that supports the main topic of the paragraph.
B) Kept, because it sets up the main topic of the paragraph that follows.
C) Deleted, because it blurs the paragraph's main focus with a loosely related detail.
D) Deleted, because it repeats information that has been provided in an earlier paragraph.

CONTINUE

What most caught my interest, though, was a quotation from someone who described coworking spaces as "melting pots of creativity." The article refers to a 2012 survey in which **29** <u>64 percent of respondents noted that coworking spaces prevented them from completing tasks in a given time.</u> The article goes on to suggest that the most valuable resources provided by coworking spaces are actually the people **30** <u>whom use</u> them.

29

At this point, the writer wants to add specific information that supports the main topic of the paragraph.

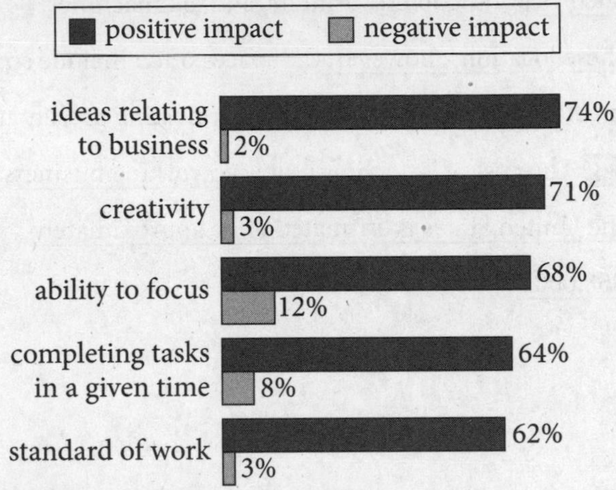

Adapted from "The 3rd Global Coworking Survey." ©2013 by Deskmag.

Which choice most effectively completes the sentence with relevant and accurate information based on the graph above?

A) NO CHANGE
B) 71 percent of respondents indicated that using a coworking space increased their creativity.
C) respondents credited coworking spaces with giving them 74 percent of their ideas relating to business.
D) respondents revealed that their ability to focus on their work improved by 12 percent in a coworking space.

30

A) NO CHANGE
B) whom uses
C) who uses
D) who use

CONTINUE

[1] Thus, even though I already had all the equipment I needed in my home office, I decided to try using a coworking space in my city. [2] Because I was specifically interested in coworking's reported benefits related to creativity, I chose a facility that offered a bright, open work area where I wouldn't be isolated. [3] Throughout the morning, more people appeared. [4] Periods of quiet, during which everyone worked independently, were broken up occasionally with lively conversation. **31**

I liked the experience so much that I now go to the coworking space a few times a week. Over time, I've gotten to know several of my coworking **32** colleagues: another website developer, a graphic designer, a freelance writer, and several mobile app coders. Even those of us who work in disparate fields are able to **33** share advice and help each other brainstorm. In fact, it's the diversity of their talents and experiences that makes my coworking colleagues so valuable.

31

The writer wants to add the following sentence to the paragraph.

> After filling out a simple registration form and taking a quick tour of the facility, I took a seat at a table and got right to work on my laptop.

The best placement for the sentence is immediately

A) before sentence 1.
B) after sentence 1.
C) after sentence 2.
D) after sentence 3.

32

A) NO CHANGE
B) colleagues;
C) colleagues,
D) colleagues

33

A) NO CHANGE
B) give some wisdom
C) proclaim our opinions
D) opine

CONTINUE

Questions 34-44 are based on the following passage.

The Consolations of Philosophy

Long viewed by many as the stereotypical useless major, philosophy is now being seen by many students and prospective employers as in fact a very useful and practical major, offering students a host of transferable skills with relevance to the modern workplace. **34** In broad terms, philosophy is the study of meaning and the values underlying thought and behavior. But **35** more pragmatically, the discipline encourages students to analyze complex material, question conventional beliefs, and express thoughts in a concise manner.

Because philosophy **36** teaching students not what to think but how to think, the age-old discipline offers consistently useful tools for academic and professional achievement. **37** A 1994 survey concluded that only 18 percent of American colleges required at least one philosophy course. **38** Therefore, between 1992 and 1996, more than 400 independent philosophy departments were eliminated from institutions.

34

A) NO CHANGE
B) For example,
C) In contrast,
D) Nevertheless,

35

A) NO CHANGE
B) speaking in a more pragmatic way,
C) speaking in a way more pragmatically,
D) in a more pragmatic-speaking way,

36

A) NO CHANGE
B) teaches
C) to teach
D) and teaching

37

Which choice most effectively sets up the information that follows?

A) Consequently, philosophy students have been receiving an increasing number of job offers.
B) Therefore, because of the evidence, colleges increased their offerings in philosophy.
C) Notwithstanding the attractiveness of this course of study, students have resisted majoring in philosophy.
D) However, despite its many utilitarian benefits, colleges have not always supported the study of philosophy.

38

A) NO CHANGE
B) Thus,
C) Moreover,
D) However,

CONTINUE

More recently, colleges have recognized the practicality and increasing popularity of studying philosophy and have markedly increased the number of philosophy programs offered. By 2008 there were 817 programs, up from 765 a decade before. In addition, the number of four-year graduates in philosophy has grown 46 percent in a decade. Also, studies have found that those students who major in philosophy often do better than students from other majors in both verbal reasoning and analytical **39** writing. These results can be measured by standardized test scores. On the Graduate Record Examination (GRE), for example, students intending to study philosophy in graduate school **40** has scored higher than students in all but four other majors.

These days, many **41** student's majoring in philosophy have no intention of becoming philosophers, instead they plan to apply those skills to other disciplines. Law and business specifically benefit from the complicated theoretical issues raised in the study of philosophy, but philosophy can be just as useful in engineering or any field requiring complex analytic skills. **42** That these skills are transferable across professions

39

Which choice most effectively combines the sentences at the underlined portion?

A) writing as
B) writing, and these results can be
C) writing, which can also be
D) writing when the results are

40

A) NO CHANGE
B) have scored
C) scores
D) scoring

41

A) NO CHANGE
B) students majoring
C) students major
D) student's majors

42

At this point, the writer is considering adding the following sentence.

> The ancient Greek philosopher Plato, for example, wrote many of his works in the form of dialogues.

Should the writer make this addition here?

A) Yes, because it reinforces the passage's main point about the employability of philosophy majors.
B) Yes, because it acknowledges a common counterargument to the passage's central claim.
C) No, because it blurs the paragraph's focus by introducing a new idea that goes unexplained.
D) No, because it undermines the passage's claim about the employability of philosophy majors.

43 which makes them especially beneficial to twenty-first-century students. Because today's students can expect to hold multiple jobs—some of which may not even exist yet—during 44 our lifetime, studying philosophy allows them to be flexible and adaptable. High demand, advanced exam scores, and varied professional skills all argue for maintaining and enhancing philosophy courses and majors within academic institutions.

43

A) NO CHANGE
B) that
C) and
D) DELETE the underlined portion.

44

A) NO CHANGE
B) one's
C) his or her
D) their

STOP

If you finish before time is called, you may check your work on this section only.
Do not turn to any other section.

No Test Material On This Page

Math Test – No Calculator

25 MINUTES, 20 QUESTIONS

Turn to Section 3 of your answer sheet to answer the questions in this section.

DIRECTIONS

For questions 1-15, solve each problem, choose the best answer from the choices provided, and fill in the corresponding circle on your answer sheet. **For questions 16-20**, solve the problem and enter your answer in the grid on the answer sheet. Please refer to the directions before question 16 on how to enter your answers in the grid. You may use any available space in your test booklet for scratch work.

NOTES

1. The use of a calculator **is not permitted**.
2. All variables and expressions used represent real numbers unless otherwise indicated.
3. Figures provided in this test are drawn to scale unless otherwise indicated.
4. All figures lie in a plane unless otherwise indicated.
5. Unless otherwise indicated, the domain of a given function f is the set of all real numbers x for which $f(x)$ is a real number.

REFERENCE

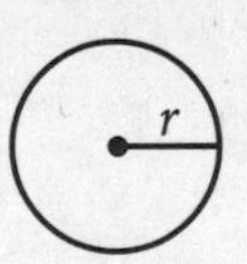

$A = \pi r^2$
$C = 2\pi r$

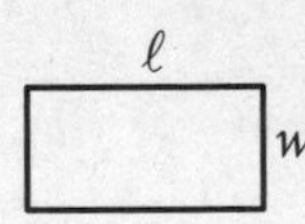

$A = \ell w$

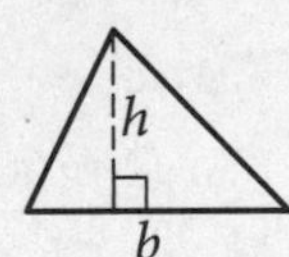

$A = \frac{1}{2}bh$

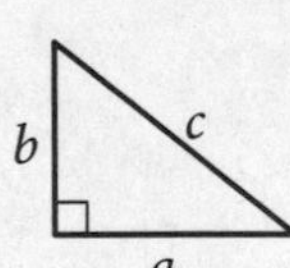

$c^2 = a^2 + b^2$

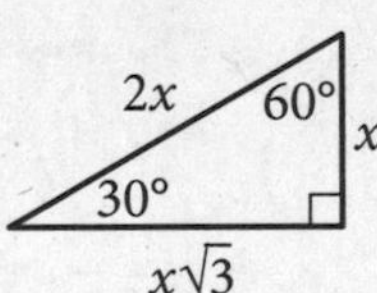

Special Right Triangles

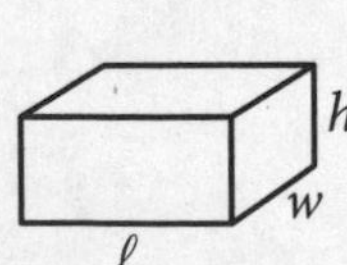

$V = \ell wh$

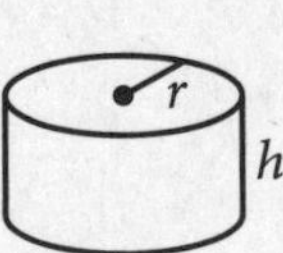

$V = \pi r^2 h$

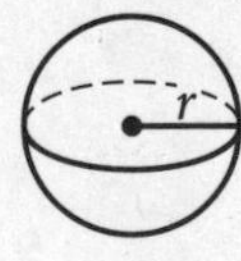

$V = \frac{4}{3}\pi r^3$

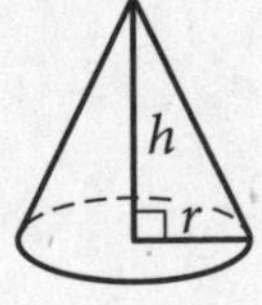

$V = \frac{1}{3}\pi r^2 h$

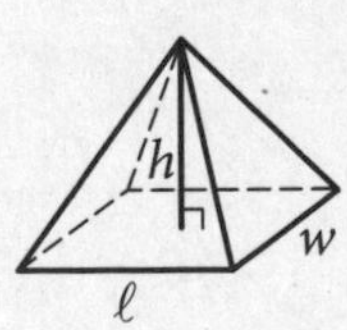

$V = \frac{1}{3}\ell wh$

The number of degrees of arc in a circle is 360.
The number of radians of arc in a circle is 2π.
The sum of the measures in degrees of the angles of a triangle is 180.

CONTINUE

1

If $\frac{x-1}{3} = k$ and $k = 3$, what is the value of x ?

A) 2

B) 4

C) 9

D) 10

2

For $i = \sqrt{-1}$, what is the sum $(7 + 3i) + (-8 + 9i)$?

A) $-1 + 12i$

B) $-1 - 6i$

C) $15 + 12i$

D) $15 - 6i$

3

On Saturday afternoon, Armand sent m text messages each hour for 5 hours, and Tyrone sent p text messages each hour for 4 hours. Which of the following represents the total number of messages sent by Armand and Tyrone on Saturday afternoon?

A) $9mp$

B) $20mp$

C) $5m + 4p$

D) $4m + 5p$

4

Kathy is a repair technician for a phone company. Each week, she receives a batch of phones that need repairs. The number of phones that she has left to fix at the end of each day can be estimated with the equation $P = 108 - 23d$, where P is the number of phones left and d is the number of days she has worked that week. What is the meaning of the value 108 in this equation?

A) Kathy will complete the repairs within 108 days.

B) Kathy starts each week with 108 phones to fix.

C) Kathy repairs phones at a rate of 108 per hour.

D) Kathy repairs phones at a rate of 108 per day.

5

$$(x^2y - 3y^2 + 5xy^2) - (-x^2y + 3xy^2 - 3y^2)$$

Which of the following is equivalent to the expression above?

A) $4x^2y^2$

B) $8xy^2 - 6y^2$

C) $2x^2y + 2xy^2$

D) $2x^2y + 8xy^2 - 6y^2$

6

$$h = 3a + 28.6$$

A pediatrician uses the model above to estimate the height h of a boy, in inches, in terms of the boy's age a, in years, between the ages of 2 and 5. Based on the model, what is the estimated increase, in inches, of a boy's height each year?

A) 3

B) 5.7

C) 9.5

D) 14.3

7

$$m = \frac{\left(\frac{r}{1{,}200}\right)\left(1 + \frac{r}{1{,}200}\right)^N}{\left(1 + \frac{r}{1{,}200}\right)^N - 1} P$$

The formula above gives the monthly payment m needed to pay off a loan of P dollars at r percent annual interest over N months. Which of the following gives P in terms of m, r, and N ?

A) $P = \frac{\left(\frac{r}{1{,}200}\right)\left(1 + \frac{r}{1{,}200}\right)^N}{\left(1 + \frac{r}{1{,}200}\right)^N - 1} m$

B) $P = \frac{\left(1 + \frac{r}{1{,}200}\right)^N - 1}{\left(\frac{r}{1{,}200}\right)\left(1 + \frac{r}{1{,}200}\right)^N} m$

C) $P = \left(\frac{r}{1{,}200}\right) m$

D) $P = \left(\frac{1{,}200}{r}\right) m$

CONTINUE

8

If $\frac{a}{b} = 2$, what is the value of $\frac{4b}{a}$?

A) 0

B) 1

C) 2

D) 4

9

$$3x + 4y = -23$$
$$2y - x = -19$$

What is the solution (x, y) to the system of equations above?

A) $(-5, -2)$

B) $(3, -8)$

C) $(4, -6)$

D) $(9, -6)$

10

$$g(x) = ax^2 + 24$$

For the function g defined above, a is a constant and $g(4) = 8$. What is the value of $g(-4)$?

A) 8

B) 0

C) −1

D) −8

11

$$b = 2.35 + 0.25x$$
$$c = 1.75 + 0.40x$$

In the equations above, b and c represent the price per pound, in dollars, of beef and chicken, respectively, x weeks after July 1 during last summer. What was the price per pound of beef when it was equal to the price per pound of chicken?

A) \$2.60

B) \$2.85

C) \$2.95

D) \$3.35

12

A line in the xy-plane passes through the origin and has a slope of $\frac{1}{7}$. Which of the following points lies on the line?

A) $(0, 7)$

B) $(1, 7)$

C) $(7, 7)$

D) $(14, 2)$

CONTINUE

13

If $x > 3$, which of the following is equivalent to $\dfrac{1}{\dfrac{1}{x+2}+\dfrac{1}{x+3}}$?

A) $\dfrac{2x+5}{x^2+5x+6}$

B) $\dfrac{x^2+5x+6}{2x+5}$

C) $2x+5$

D) x^2+5x+6

14

If $3x - y = 12$, what is the value of $\dfrac{8^x}{2^y}$?

A) 2^{12}

B) 4^4

C) 8^2

D) The value cannot be determined from the information given.

15

If $(ax+2)(bx+7) = 15x^2 + cx + 14$ for all values of x, and $a + b = 8$, what are the two possible values for c ?

A) 3 and 5

B) 6 and 35

C) 10 and 21

D) 31 and 41

CONTINUE

DIRECTIONS

For questions 16–20, solve the problem and enter your answer in the grid, as described below, on the answer sheet.

1. Although not required, it is suggested that you write your answer in the boxes at the top of the columns to help you fill in the circles accurately. You will receive credit only if the circles are filled in correctly.
2. Mark no more than one circle in any column.
3. No question has a negative answer.
4. Some problems may have more than one correct answer. In such cases, grid only one answer.
5. **Mixed numbers** such as $3\frac{1}{2}$ must be gridded as 3.5 or 7/2. (If 3 1 / 2 is entered into the grid, it will be interpreted as $\frac{31}{2}$, not $3\frac{1}{2}$.)
6. **Decimal answers:** If you obtain a decimal answer with more digits than the grid can accommodate, it may be either rounded or truncated, but it must fill the entire grid.

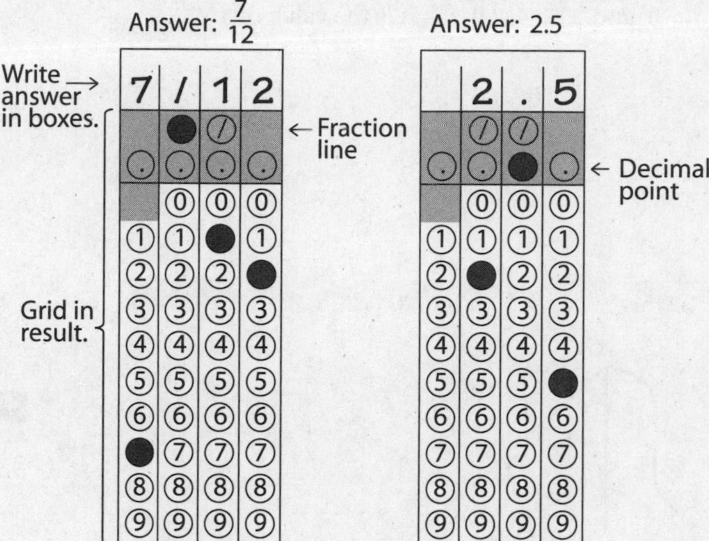

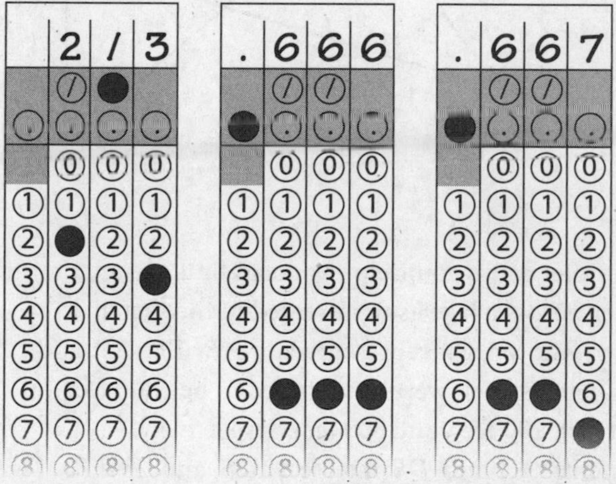

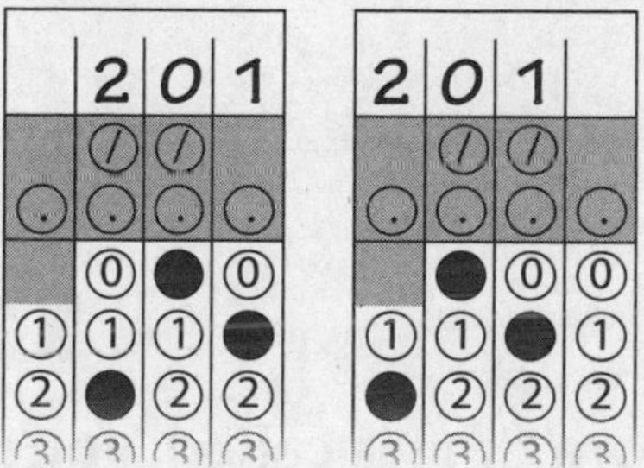

NOTE: You may start your answers in any column, space permitting. Columns you don't need to use should be left blank.

CONTINUE

16

If $t > 0$ and $t^2 - 4 = 0$, what is the value of t ?

17

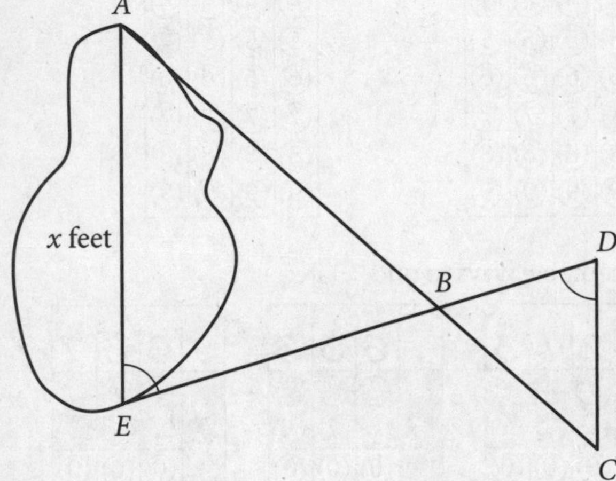

A summer camp counselor wants to find a length, x, in feet, across a lake as represented in the sketch above. The lengths represented by AB, EB, BD, and CD on the sketch were determined to be 1800 feet, 1400 feet, 700 feet, and 800 feet, respectively. Segments AC and DE intersect at B, and $\angle AEB$ and $\angle CDB$ have the same measure. What is the value of x ?

18

$$x + y = -9$$
$$x + 2y = -25$$

According to the system of equations above, what is the value of x ?

19

In a right triangle, one angle measures $x°$, where $\sin x° = \frac{4}{5}$. What is $\cos(90° - x°)$?

20

If $a = 5\sqrt{2}$ and $2a = \sqrt{2x}$, what is the value of x ?

STOP

If you finish before time is called, you may check your work on this section only.

Do not turn to any other section.

No Test Material On This Page

Math Test – Calculator

55 MINUTES, 38 QUESTIONS

Turn to Section 4 of your answer sheet to answer the questions in this section.

DIRECTIONS

For questions 1-30, solve each problem, choose the best answer from the choices provided, and fill in the corresponding circle on your answer sheet. **For questions 31-38**, solve the problem and enter your answer in the grid on the answer sheet. Please refer to the directions before question 31 on how to enter your answers in the grid. You may use any available space in your test booklet for scratch work.

NOTES

1. The use of a calculator **is permitted**.
2. All variables and expressions used represent real numbers unless otherwise indicated.
3. Figures provided in this test are drawn to scale unless otherwise indicated.
4. All figures lie in a plane unless otherwise indicated.
5. Unless otherwise indicated, the domain of a given function *f* is the set of all real numbers *x* for which *f*(*x*) is a real number.

REFERENCE

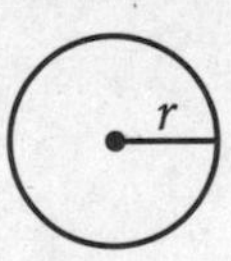

$A = \pi r^2$
$C = 2\pi r$

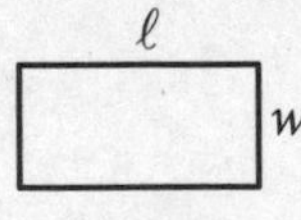

$A = \ell w$

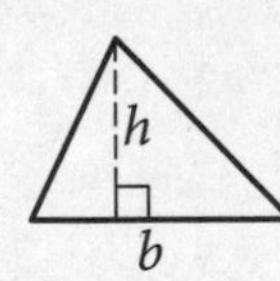

$A = \frac{1}{2}bh$

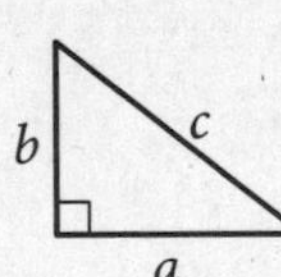

$c^2 = a^2 + b^2$

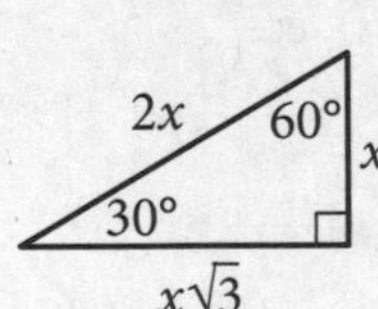

Special Right Triangles

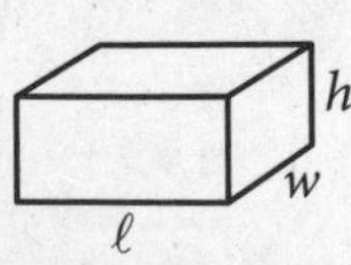

$V = \ell wh$

$V = \pi r^2 h$

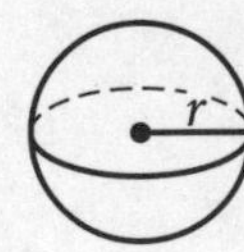

$V = \frac{4}{3}\pi r^3$

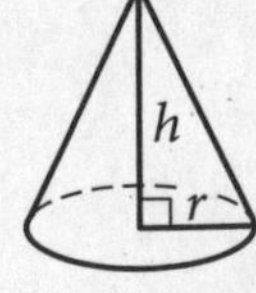

$V = \frac{1}{3}\pi r^2 h$

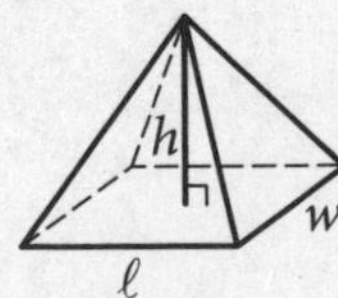

$V = \frac{1}{3}\ell wh$

The number of degrees of arc in a circle is 360.
The number of radians of arc in a circle is 2π.
The sum of the measures in degrees of the angles of a triangle is 180.

CONTINUE

1

John runs at different speeds as part of his training program. The graph shows his target heart rate at different times during his workout. On which interval is the target heart rate strictly increasing then strictly decreasing?

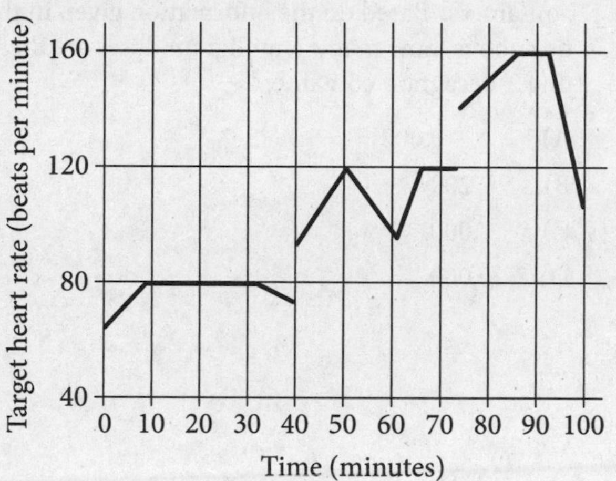

A) Between 0 and 30 minutes

B) Between 40 and 60 minutes

C) Between 50 and 65 minutes

D) Between 70 and 90 minutes

2

If $y = kx$, where k is a constant, and $y = 24$ when $x = 6$, what is the value of y when $x = 5$?

A) 6

B) 15

C) 20

D) 23

3

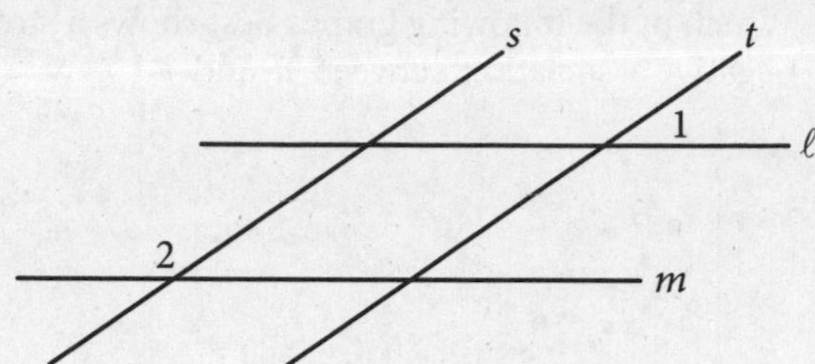

In the figure above, lines ℓ and m are parallel and lines s and t are parallel. If the measure of $\angle 1$ is $35°$, what is the measure of $\angle 2$?

A) 35°

B) 55°

C) 70°

D) 145°

4

If $16 + 4x$ is 10 more than 14, what is the value of $8x$?

A) 2

B) 6

C) 16

D) 80

CONTINUE

5

Which of the following graphs best shows a strong negative association between d and t ?

A) 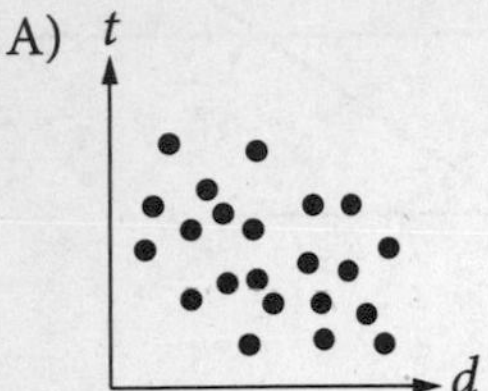

B) 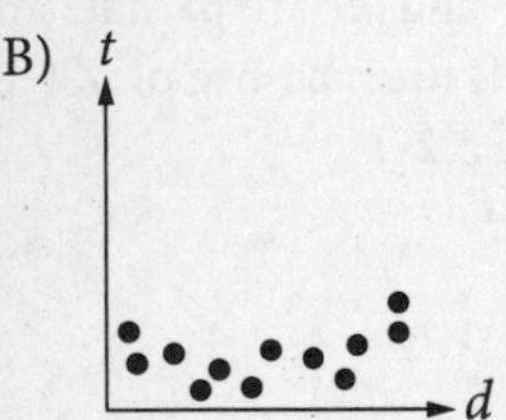

C) 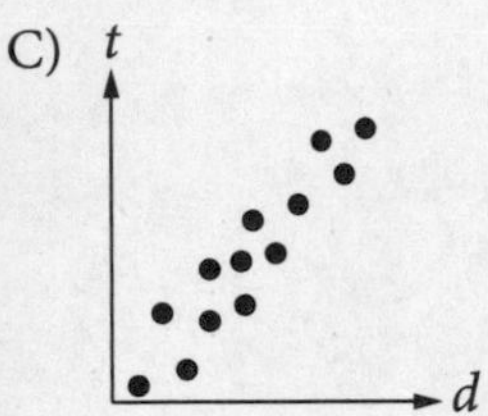

D) 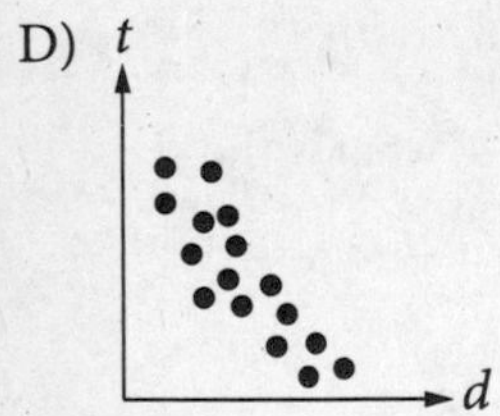

6

1 decagram = 10 grams
1,000 milligrams = 1 gram

A hospital stores one type of medicine in 2-decagram containers. Based on the information given in the box above, how many 1-milligram doses are there in one 2-decagram container?

A) 0.002

B) 200

C) 2,000

D) 20,000

CONTINUE

7

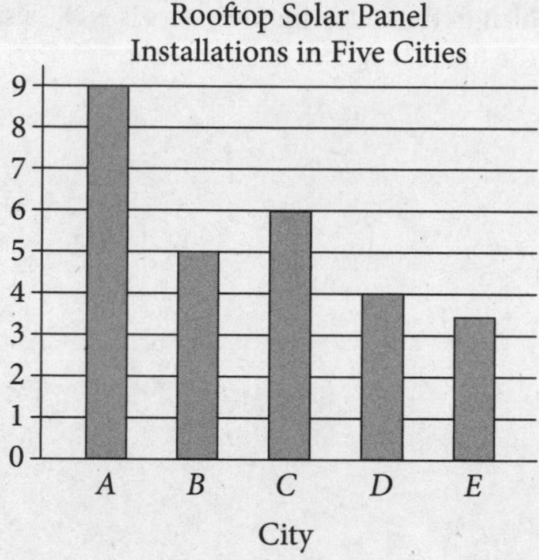

The number of rooftops with solar panel installations in 5 cities is shown in the graph above. If the total number of installations is 27,500, what is an appropriate label for the vertical axis of the graph?

A) Number of installations (in tens)

B) Number of installations (in hundreds)

C) Number of installations (in thousands)

D) Number of installations (in tens of thousands)

8

For what value of n is $|n-1|+1$ equal to 0 ?

A) 0

B) 1

C) 2

D) There is no such value of n.

CONTINUE

Questions 9 and 10 refer to the following information.

$$a = 1{,}052 + 1.08t$$

The speed of a sound wave in air depends on the air temperature. The formula above shows the relationship between a, the speed of a sound wave, in feet per second, and t, the air temperature, in degrees Fahrenheit (°F).

9

Which of the following expresses the air temparature in terms of the speed of a sound wave?

A) $t = \dfrac{a - 1{,}052}{1.08}$

B) $t = \dfrac{a + 1{,}052}{1.08}$

C) $t = \dfrac{1{,}052 - a}{1.08}$

D) $t = \dfrac{1.08}{a + 1{,}052}$

10

At which of the following air temperatures will the speed of a sound wave be closest to 1,000 feet per second?

A) −46°F

B) −48°F

C) −49°F

D) −50°F

11

Which of the following numbers is NOT a solution of the inequality $3x - 5 \geq 4x - 3$?

A) −1

B) −2

C) −3

D) −5

12

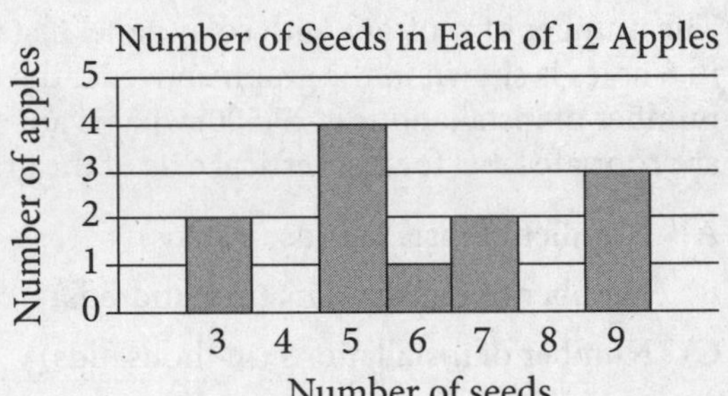

Based on the histogram above, of the following, which is closest to the average (arithmetic mean) number of seeds per apple?

A) 4

B) 5

C) 6

D) 7

13

		Course			
		Algebra I	Geometry	Algebra II	Total
Gender	Female	35	53	62	150
	Male	44	59	57	160
	Total	79	112	119	310

A group of tenth-grade students responded to a survey that asked which math course they were currently enrolled in. The survey data were broken down as shown in the table above. Which of the following categories accounts for approximately 19 percent of all the survey respondents?

A) Females taking Geometry

B) Females taking Algebra II

C) Males taking Geometry

D) Males taking Algebra I

14

Lengths of Fish (in inches)						
8	9	9	9	10	10	11
11	12	12	12	12	13	13
13	14	14	15	15	16	24

The table above lists the lengths, to the nearest inch, of a random sample of 21 brown bullhead fish. The outlier measurement of 24 inches is an error. Of the mean, median, and range of the values listed, which will change the most if the 24-inch measurement is removed from the data?

A) Mean

B) Median

C) Range

D) They will all change by the same amount.

CONTINUE

Questions 15 and 16 refer to the following information.

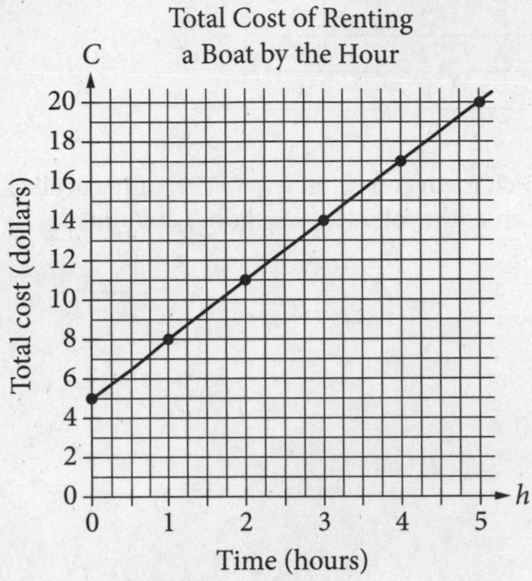

The graph above displays the total cost C, in dollars, of renting a boat for h hours.

15

What does the C-intercept represent in the graph?

A) The initial cost of renting the boat

B) The total number of boats rented

C) The total number of hours the boat is rented

D) The increase in cost to rent the boat for each additional hour

16

Which of the following represents the relationship between h and C ?

A) $C = 5h$

B) $C = \frac{3}{4}h + 5$

C) $C = 3h + 5$

D) $h = 3C$

17

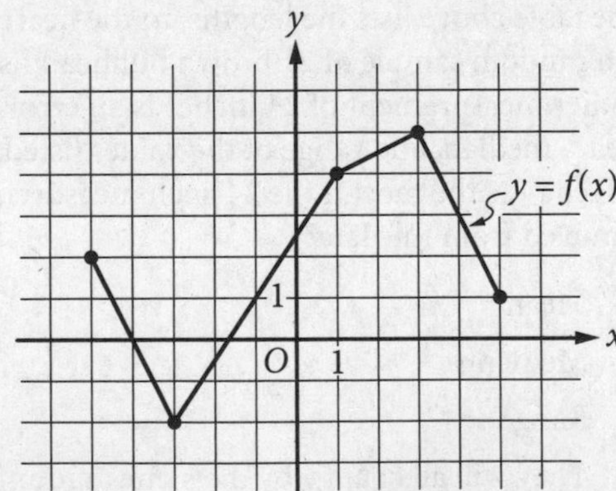

The complete graph of the function f is shown in the xy-plane above. For what value of x is the value of $f(x)$ at its minimum?

A) -5

B) -3

C) -2

D) 3

CONTINUE

18

$$y < -x + a$$
$$y > x + b$$

In the xy-plane, if $(0, 0)$ is a solution to the system of inequalities above, which of the following relationships between a and b must be true?

A) $a > b$

B) $b > a$

C) $|a| > |b|$

D) $a = -b$

19

A food truck sells salads for \$6.50 each and drinks for \$2.00 each. The food truck's revenue from selling a total of 209 salads and drinks in one day was \$836.50. How many salads were sold that day?

A) 77

B) 93

C) 99

D) 105

20

Alma bought a laptop computer at a store that gave a 20 percent discount off its original price. The total amount she paid to the cashier was p dollars, including an 8 percent sales tax on the discounted price. Which of the following represents the original price of the computer in terms of p ?

A) $0.88p$

B) $\frac{p}{0.88}$

C) $(0.8)(1.08)p$

D) $\frac{p}{(0.8)(1.08)}$

21

Dreams Recalled during One Week

	None	1 to 4	5 or more	Total
Group X	15	28	57	100
Group Y	21	11	68	100
Total	36	39	125	200

The data in the table above were produced by a sleep researcher studying the number of dreams people recall when asked to record their dreams for one week. Group X consisted of 100 people who observed early bedtimes, and Group Y consisted of 100 people who observed later bedtimes. If a person is chosen at random from those who recalled at least 1 dream, what is the probability that the person belonged to Group Y ?

A) $\frac{68}{100}$

B) $\frac{79}{100}$

C) $\frac{79}{164}$

D) $\frac{164}{200}$

CONTINUE

Questions 22 and 23 refer to the following information.

Annual Budgets for Different Programs in Kansas, 2007 to 2010

Program	Year			
	2007	2008	2009	2010
Agriculture/natural resources	373,904	358,708	485,807	488,106
Education	2,164,607	2,413,984	2,274,514	3,008,036
General government	14,347,325	12,554,845	10,392,107	14,716,155
Highways and transportation	1,468,482	1,665,636	1,539,480	1,773,893
Human resources	4,051,050	4,099,067	4,618,444	5,921,379
Public safety	263,463	398,326	355,935	464,233

The table above lists the annual budget, in thousands of dollars, for each of six different state programs in Kansas from 2007 to 2010.

22

Which of the following best approximates the average rate of change in the annual budget for agriculture/natural resources in Kansas from 2008 to 2010 ?

A) $50,000,000 per year
B) $65,000,000 per year
C) $75,000,000 per year
D) $130,000,000 per year

23

Of the following, which program's ratio of its 2007 budget to its 2010 budget is closest to the human resources program's ratio of its 2007 budget to its 2010 budget?

A) Agriculture/natural resources
B) Education
C) Highways and transportation
D) Public safety

CONTINUE

24

Which of the following is an equation of a circle in the xy-plane with center $(0, 4)$ and a radius with endpoint $\left(\frac{4}{3}, 5\right)$?

A) $x^2 + (y-4)^2 = \frac{25}{9}$

B) $x^2 + (y+4)^2 = \frac{25}{9}$

C) $x^2 + (y-4)^2 = \frac{5}{3}$

D) $x^2 + (y+4)^2 = \frac{3}{5}$

25

$$h = -4.9t^2 + 25t$$

The equation above expresses the approximate height h, in meters, of a ball t seconds after it is launched vertically upward from the ground with an initial velocity of 25 meters per second. After approximately how many seconds will the ball hit the ground?

A) 3.5

B) 4.0

C) 4.5

D) 5.0

26

Katarina is a botanist studying the production of pears by two types of pear trees. She noticed that Type A trees produced 20 percent more pears than Type B trees did. Based on Katarina's observation, if the Type A trees produced 144 pears, how many pears did the Type B trees produce?

A) 115

B) 120

C) 124

D) 173

27

A square field measures 10 meters by 10 meters. Ten students each mark off a randomly selected region of the field; each region is square and has side lengths of 1 meter, and no two regions overlap. The students count the earthworms contained in the soil to a depth of 5 centimeters beneath the ground's surface in each region. The results are shown in the table below.

Region	Number of earthworms	Region	Number of earthworms
A	107	F	141
B	147	G	150
C	146	H	154
D	135	I	176
E	149	J	166

Which of the following is a reasonable approximation of the number of earthworms to a depth of 5 centimeters beneath the ground's surface in the entire field?

A) 150

B) 1,500

C) 15,000

D) 150,000

CONTINUE

28

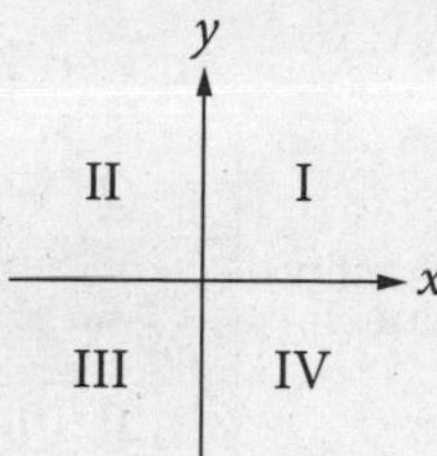

If the system of inequalities $y \geq 2x + 1$ and $y > \frac{1}{2}x - 1$ is graphed in the xy-plane above, which quadrant contains no solutions to the system?

A) Quadrant II
B) Quadrant III
C) Quadrant IV
D) There are solutions in all four quadrants.

29

For a polynomial $p(x)$, the value of $p(3)$ is -2. Which of the following must be true about $p(x)$?

A) $x - 5$ is a factor of $p(x)$.
B) $x - 2$ is a factor of $p(x)$.
C) $x + 2$ is a factor of $p(x)$.
D) The remainder when $p(x)$ is divided by $x - 3$ is -2.

30

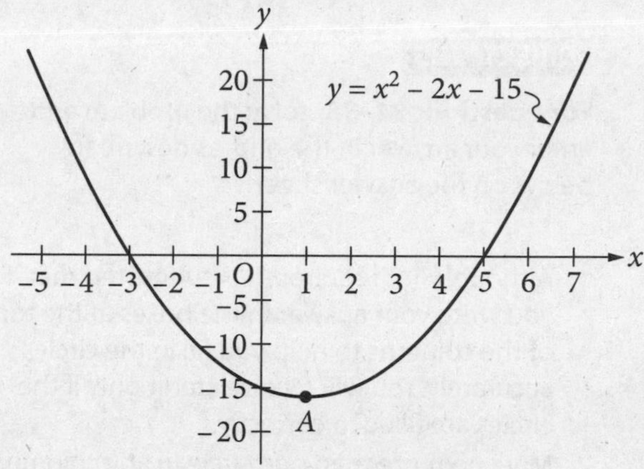

Which of the following is an equivalent form of the equation of the graph shown in the xy-plane above, from which the coordinates of vertex A can be identified as constants in the equation?

A) $y = (x + 3)(x - 5)$
B) $y = (x - 3)(x + 5)$
C) $y = x(x - 2) - 15$
D) $y = (x - 1)^2 - 16$

CONTINUE

DIRECTIONS

For questions 31–38, solve the problem and enter your answer in the grid, as described below, on the answer sheet.

1. Although not required, it is suggested that you write your answer in the boxes at the top of the columns to help you fill in the circles accurately. You will receive credit only if the circles are filled in correctly.
2. Mark no more than one circle in any column.
3. No question has a negative answer.
4. Some problems may have more than one correct answer. In such cases, grid only one answer.
5. **Mixed numbers** such as $3\frac{1}{2}$ must be gridded as 3.5 or 7/2. (If 3 1 / 2 is entered into the grid, it will be interpreted as $\frac{31}{2}$, not $3\frac{1}{2}$.)
6. **Decimal answers:** If you obtain a decimal answer with more digits than the grid can accommodate, it may be either rounded or truncated, but it must fill the entire grid.

Answer: $\frac{7}{12}$

Write answer in boxes. → 7 / 1 2

← Fraction line

Grid in result.

Answer: 2.5

2 . 5

← Decimal point

Acceptable ways to grid $\frac{2}{3}$ are:

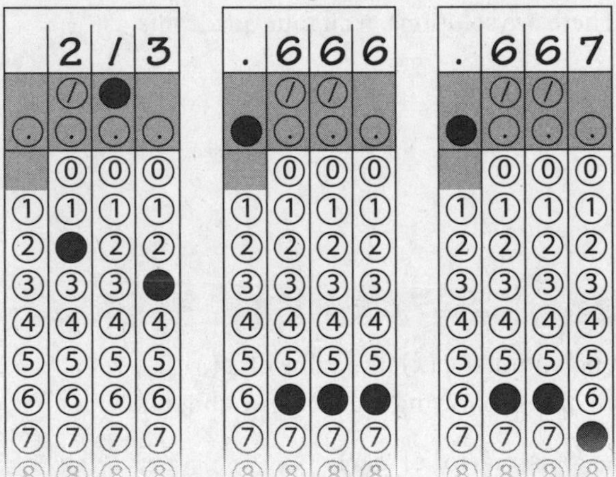

Answer: 201 – either position is correct

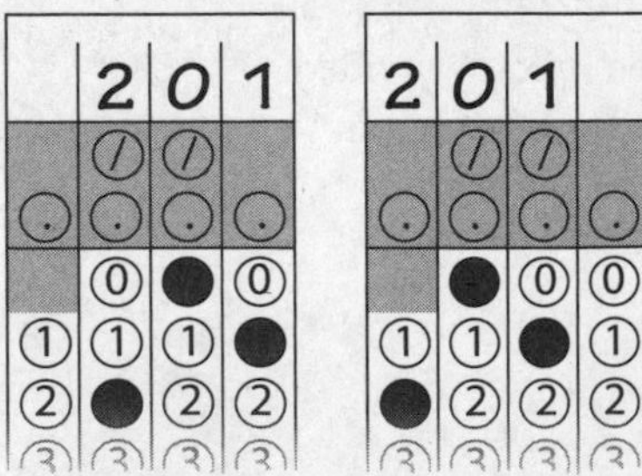

NOTE: You may start your answers in any column, space permitting. Columns you don't need to use should be left blank.

CONTINUE

31

Wyatt can husk at least 12 dozen ears of corn per hour and at most 18 dozen ears of corn per hour. Based on this information, what is a possible amount of time, in hours, that it could take Wyatt to husk 72 dozen ears of corn?

32

The posted weight limit for a covered wooden bridge in Pennsylvania is 6000 pounds. A delivery truck that is carrying x identical boxes each weighing 14 pounds will pass over the bridge. If the combined weight of the empty delivery truck and its driver is 4500 pounds, what is the maximum possible value for x that will keep the combined weight of the truck, driver, and boxes below the bridge's posted weight limit?

33

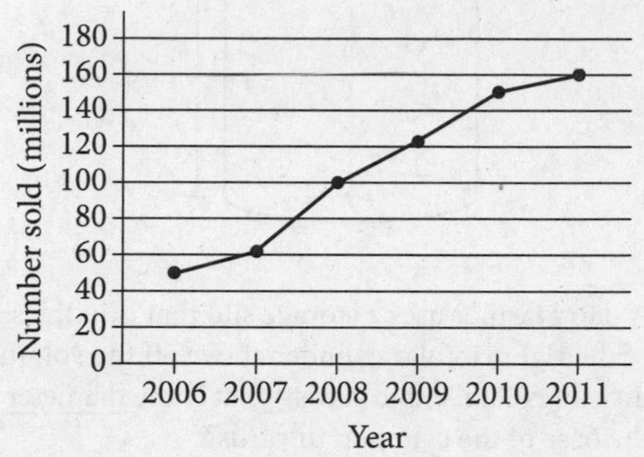

According to the line graph above, the number of portable media players sold in 2008 is what fraction of the number sold in 2011 ?

34

A local television station sells time slots for programs in 30-minute intervals. If the station operates 24 hours per day, every day of the week, what is the total number of 30-minute time slots the station can sell for Tuesday and Wednesday?

CONTINUE

35

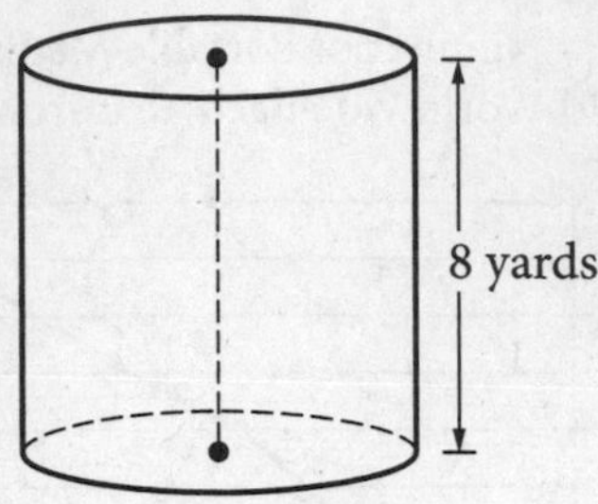

A dairy farmer uses a storage silo that is in the shape of the right circular cylinder above. If the volume of the silo is 72π cubic yards, what is the diameter of the base of the cylinder, in yards?

36

$$h(x) = \frac{1}{(x-5)^2 + 4(x-5) + 4}$$

For what value of x is the function h above undefined?

Questions 37 and 38 refer to the following information.

Jessica opened a bank account that earns 2 percent interest compounded annually. Her initial deposit was \$100, and she uses the expression $\$100(x)^t$ to find the value of the account after t years.

37

What is the value of x in the expression?

38

Jessica's friend Tyshaun found an account that earns 2.5 percent interest compounded annually. Tyshaun made an initial deposit of \$100 into this account at the same time Jessica made a deposit of \$100 into her account. After 10 years, how much more money will Tyshaun's initial deposit have earned than Jessica's initial deposit? (Round your answer to the nearest cent and ignore the dollar sign when gridding your response.)

STOP

If you finish before time is called, you may check your work on this section only.

Do not turn to any other section.

No Test Material On This Page

This page represents the back cover of the Practice Test.

The SAT® Practice Essay #1

The essay gives you an opportunity to show how effectively you can read and comprehend a passage and write an essay analyzing the passage. In your essay, you should demonstrate that you have read the passage carefully, present a clear and logical analysis, and use language precisely.

You have 50 minutes to read the passage and write an essay in response to the prompt provided inside this booklet.

For information on scoring your essay, view the SAT Essay scoring rubric at **sat.org/essay**.

As you read the passage below, consider how Jimmy Carter uses

- evidence, such as facts or examples, to support claims.
- reasoning to develop ideas and to connect claims and evidence.
- stylistic or persuasive elements, such as word choice or appeals to emotion, to add power to the ideas expressed.

Adapted from former US President Jimmy Carter, Foreword to *Arctic National Wildlife Refuge: Seasons of Life and Land, A Photographic Journey* by Subhankar Banerjee. ©2003 by Subhankar Banerjee.

1 The Arctic National Wildlife Refuge stands alone as America's last truly great wilderness. This magnificent area is as vast as it is wild, from the windswept coastal plain where polar bears and caribou give birth, to the towering Brooks Range where Dall sheep cling to cliffs and wolves howl in the midnight sun.

2 More than a decade ago, [my wife] Rosalynn and I had the fortunate opportunity to camp and hike in these regions of the Arctic Refuge. During bright July days, we walked along ancient caribou trails and studied the brilliant mosaic of wildflowers, mosses, and lichens that hugged the tundra. There was a timeless quality about this great land. As the never-setting sun circled above the horizon, we watched muskox, those shaggy survivors of the Ice Age, lumber along braided rivers that meander toward the Beaufort Sea.

3 One of the most unforgettable and humbling experiences of our lives occurred on the coastal plain. We had hoped to see caribou during our trip, but to our amazement, we witnessed the migration of tens of thousands of caribou with their newborn calves. In a matter of a few minutes, the sweep of tundra before us became flooded with life, with the sounds of grunting animals and clicking hooves filling the air. The dramatic procession of the Porcupine caribou herd was a once-in-a-lifetime wildlife spectacle. We understand firsthand why some have described this special birthplace as "America's Serengeti."

4 Standing on the coastal plain, I was saddened to think of the tragedy that might occur if this great wilderness was consumed by a web of roads and pipelines, drilling rigs and industrial facilities. Such proposed developments would forever destroy the wilderness character of America's only Arctic Refuge and disturb countless numbers of animals that depend on this northernmost terrestrial ecosystem.

5 The extraordinary wilderness and wildlife values of the Arctic Refuge have long been recognized by both Republican and Democratic presidents. In 1960, President Dwight D. Eisenhower established the original 8.9 million-acre Arctic National Wildlife Range to preserve its unique wildlife, wilderness, and recreational values. Twenty years later, I signed the Alaska National Interest Lands Conservation Act, monumental legislation that safeguarded more than 100 million acres of national parks, refuges, and forests in Alaska. This law specifically created the Arctic National Wildlife Refuge, doubled the size of the former range, and restricted development in areas that are clearly incompatible with oil exploration.

6 Since I left office, there have been repeated proposals to open the Arctic Refuge coastal plain to oil drilling. Those attempts have failed because of tremendous opposition by the American people, including the Gwich'in Athabascan Indians of Alaska and Canada, indigenous people whose culture has depended on the Porcupine caribou herd for thousands of years. Having visited many aboriginal peoples around the world, I can empathize with the Gwich'ins' struggle to safeguard one of their precious human rights.

7 We must look beyond the alleged benefits of a short-term economic gain and focus on what is really at stake. At best, the Arctic Refuge might provide 1 to 2 percent of the oil our country consumes each day. We can easily conserve more than that amount by driving more fuel-efficient vehicles. Instead of tearing open the heart of our greatest refuge, we should use our resources more wisely.

8 There are few places on earth as wild and free as the Arctic Refuge. It is a symbol of our national heritage, a remnant of frontier America that our first settlers once called wilderness. Little of that precious wilderness remains.

9 It will be a grand triumph for America if we can preserve the Arctic Refuge in its pure, untrammeled state. To leave this extraordinary land alone would be the greatest gift we could pass on to future generations.

> Write an essay in which you explain how Jimmy Carter builds an argument to persuade his audience that the Arctic National Wildlife Refuge should not be developed for industry. In your essay, analyze how Carter uses one or more of the features listed in the box above (or features of your own choice) to strengthen the logic and persuasiveness of his argument. Be sure that your analysis focuses on the most relevant features of the passage.
>
> Your essay should not explain whether you agree with Carter's claims, but rather explain how Carter builds an argument to persuade his audience.

This page represents the back cover of the Practice Essay.

SAT PRACTICE ANSWER SHEET

COMPLETE MARK ● EXAMPLES OF INCOMPLETE MARKS

It is recommended that you use a No. 2 pencil. It is very important that you fill in the entire circle darkly and completely. If you change your response, erase as completely as possible. Incomplete marks or erasures may affect your score.

TEST NUMBER

ENTER TEST NUMBER

For instance, for Practice Test #1, fill in the circle for 0 in the first column and for 1 in the second column.

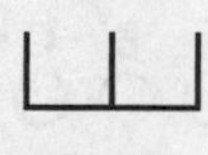

0 ○ ○
1 ○ ○
2 ○ ○
3 ○ ○
4 ○ ○
5 ○ ○
6 ○ ○
7 ○ ○
8 ○ ○
9 ○ ○

SECTION 1

	A B C D		A B C D		A B C D		A B C D
1	○ ○ ○ ○	14	○ ○ ○ ○	27	○ ○ ○ ○	40	○ ○ ○ ○
2	○ ○ ○ ○	15	○ ○ ○ ○	28	○ ○ ○ ○	41	○ ○ ○ ○
3	○ ○ ○ ○	16	○ ○ ○ ○	29	○ ○ ○ ○	42	○ ○ ○ ○
4	○ ○ ○ ○	17	○ ○ ○ ○	30	○ ○ ○ ○	43	○ ○ ○ ○
5	○ ○ ○ ○	18	○ ○ ○ ○	31	○ ○ ○ ○	44	○ ○ ○ ○
6	○ ○ ○ ○	19	○ ○ ○ ○	32	○ ○ ○ ○	45	○ ○ ○ ○
7	○ ○ ○ ○	20	○ ○ ○ ○	33	○ ○ ○ ○	46	○ ○ ○ ○
8	○ ○ ○ ○	21	○ ○ ○ ○	34	○ ○ ○ ○	47	○ ○ ○ ○
9	○ ○ ○ ○	22	○ ○ ○ ○	35	○ ○ ○ ○	48	○ ○ ○ ○
10	○ ○ ○ ○	23	○ ○ ○ ○	36	○ ○ ○ ○	49	○ ○ ○ ○
11	○ ○ ○ ○	24	○ ○ ○ ○	37	○ ○ ○ ○	50	○ ○ ○ ○
12	○ ○ ○ ○	25	○ ○ ○ ○	38	○ ○ ○ ○	51	○ ○ ○ ○
13	○ ○ ○ ○	26	○ ○ ○ ○	39	○ ○ ○ ○	52	○ ○ ○ ○

Download the College Board SAT Practice app to instantly score this test.
Learn more at sat.org/scoring.

SAT PRACTICE ANSWER SHEET

COMPLETE MARK ● EXAMPLES OF INCOMPLETE MARKS 

It is recommended that you use a No. 2 pencil. It is very important that you fill in the entire circle darkly and completely. If you change your response, erase as completely as possible. Incomplete marks or erasures may affect your score.

SECTION 2

1 A B C D	10 A B C D	19 A B C D	28 A B C D	37 A B C D
2 A B C D	11 A B C D	20 A B C D	29 A B C D	38 A B C D
3 A B C D	12 A B C D	21 A B C D	30 A B C D	39 A B C D
4 A B C D	13 A B C D	22 A B C D	31 A B C D	40 A B C D
5 A B C D	14 A B C D	23 A B C D	32 A B C D	41 A B C D
6 A B C D	15 A B C D	24 A B C D	33 A B C D	42 A B C D
7 A B C D	16 A B C D	25 A B C D	34 A B C D	43 A B C D
8 A B C D	17 A B C D	26 A B C D	35 A B C D	44 A B C D
9 A B C D	18 A B C D	27 A B C D	36 A B C D	

If you're scoring with our mobile app we recommend that you cut these pages out of the back of this book. The scoring does best with a flat page.

CollegeBoard

SAT PRACTICE ANSWER SHEET

COMPLETE MARK ● EXAMPLES OF INCOMPLETE MARKS

It is recommended that you use a No. 2 pencil. It is very important that you fill in the entire circle darkly and completely. If you change your response, erase as completely as possible. Incomplete marks or erasures may affect your score.

SECTION 3

1 A B C D
2 A B C D
3 A B C D
4 A B C D
5 A B C D
6 A B C D
7 A B C D
8 A B C D
9 A B C D
10 A B C D
11 A B C D
12 A B C D
13 A B C D
14 A B C D
15 A B C D

Only answers that are gridded will be scored. You will not receive credit for anything written in the boxes.

16 17 18 19 20

/ . 0 1 2 3 4 5 6 7 8 9

NO CALCULATOR ALLOWED

Did you know that you can print out these test sheets from the web? Learn more at sat.org/scoring.

SAT PRACTICE ANSWER SHEET

COMPLETE MARK ● EXAMPLES OF INCOMPLETE MARKS 

It is recommended that you use a No. 2 pencil. It is very important that you fill in the entire circle darkly and completely. If you change your response, erase as completely as possible. Incomplete marks or erasures may affect your score.

SECTION 4

1 Ⓐ Ⓑ Ⓒ Ⓓ	7 Ⓐ Ⓑ Ⓒ Ⓓ	13 Ⓐ Ⓑ Ⓒ Ⓓ	19 Ⓐ Ⓑ Ⓒ Ⓓ	25 Ⓐ Ⓑ Ⓒ Ⓓ
2 Ⓐ Ⓑ Ⓒ Ⓓ	8 Ⓐ Ⓑ Ⓒ Ⓓ	14 Ⓐ Ⓑ Ⓒ Ⓓ	20 Ⓐ Ⓑ Ⓒ Ⓓ	26 Ⓐ Ⓑ Ⓒ Ⓓ
3 Ⓐ Ⓑ Ⓒ Ⓓ	9 Ⓐ Ⓑ Ⓒ Ⓓ	15 Ⓐ Ⓑ Ⓒ Ⓓ	21 Ⓐ Ⓑ Ⓒ Ⓓ	27 Ⓐ Ⓑ Ⓒ Ⓓ
4 Ⓐ Ⓑ Ⓒ Ⓓ	10 Ⓐ Ⓑ Ⓒ Ⓓ	16 Ⓐ Ⓑ Ⓒ Ⓓ	22 Ⓐ Ⓑ Ⓒ Ⓓ	28 Ⓐ Ⓑ Ⓒ Ⓓ
5 Ⓐ Ⓑ Ⓒ Ⓓ	11 Ⓐ Ⓑ Ⓒ Ⓓ	17 Ⓐ Ⓑ Ⓒ Ⓓ	23 Ⓐ Ⓑ Ⓒ Ⓓ	29 Ⓐ Ⓑ Ⓒ Ⓓ
6 Ⓐ Ⓑ Ⓒ Ⓓ	12 Ⓐ Ⓑ Ⓒ Ⓓ	18 Ⓐ Ⓑ Ⓒ Ⓓ	24 Ⓐ Ⓑ Ⓒ Ⓓ	30 Ⓐ Ⓑ Ⓒ Ⓓ

CALCULATOR ALLOWED

If you're using our mobile app keep in mind that bad lighting and even shadows cast over the answer sheet can affect your score. Be sure to scan this in a well-lit area for best results.

CollegeBoard

SAT PRACTICE ANSWER SHEET

COMPLETE MARK | EXAMPLES OF INCOMPLETE MARKS

It is recommended that you use a No. 2 pencil. It is very important that you fill in the entire circle darkly and completely. If you change your response, erase as completely as possible. Incomplete marks or erasures may affect your score.

SECTION 4 (Continued)

Only answers that are gridded will be scored. You will not receive credit for anything written in the boxes.

31

/
.
0
1
2
3
4
5
6
7
8
9

32

/
.
0
1
2
3
4
5
6
7
8
9

33

/
.
0
1
2
3
4
5
6
7
8
9

34

/
.
0
1
2
3
4
5
6
7
8
9

35

/
.
0
1
2
3
4
5
6
7
8
9

Only answers that are gridded will be scored. You will not receive credit for anything written in the boxes.

36

/
.
0
1
2
3
4
5
6
7
8
9

37

/
.
0
1
2
3
4
5
6
7
8
9

38

/
.
0
1
2
3
4
5
6
7
8
9

CALCULATOR ALLOWED

○ I understand that my essay (without my name) may be reproduced in other College Board materials. If I mark this circle, I withhold my permission to reproduce my essay for any purposes beyond score reporting and the assessment of my writing skills. Marking this circle will have no effect on my score, nor will it prevent my essay from being made available to any college to which I send my SAT scores.

IMPORTANT: **USE A NO. 2 PENCIL. DO NOT WRITE OUTSIDE THE BORDER!** Words written outside the essay box or written in ink **WILL NOT APPEAR** in the copy sent to be scored, and your score will be affected.

PLANNING PAGE You may plan your essay in the unlined planning space below, but use only the lined pages following this one to write your essay. Any work on this planning page will not be scored.

Use pages 7 through 10 for your ESSAY →

FOR PLANNING ONLY

Use pages 7 through 10 for your ESSAY →

Page 6

PLEASE DO NOT WRITE IN THIS AREA

SERIAL #

BEGIN YOUR ESSAY HERE.

You may continue on the next page.

PLEASE DO NOT WRITE IN THIS AREA

SERIAL #

DO NOT WRITE OUTSIDE OF THE BOX.

You may continue on the next page.

DO NOT WRITE OUTSIDE OF THE BOX.

You may continue on the next page.

PLEASE DO NOT WRITE IN THIS AREA

SERIAL #

DO NOT WRITE OUTSIDE OF THE BOX.

STOP.

Answer Explanations

SAT Practice Test #1

Section 1: Reading Test

QUESTION 1

Choice B is the best answer. In the passage, a young man (Akira) asks a mother (Chie) for permission to marry her daughter (Naomi). The request was certainly surprising to the mother, as can be seen from line 47, which states that prior to Akira's question Chie "had no idea" the request was coming.

Choice A is incorrect because the passage depicts two characters engaged in a civil conversation, with Chie being impressed with Akira's "sincerity" and finding herself "starting to like him." Choice C is incorrect because the passage is focused on the idea of Akira's and Naomi's present lives and possible futures. Choice D is incorrect because the interactions between Chie and Akira are polite, not critical; for example, Chie views Akira with "amusement," not animosity.

QUESTION 2

Choice B is the best answer. The passage centers on a night when a young man tries to get approval to marry a woman's daughter. The passage includes detailed descriptions of setting (a "winter's eve" and a "cold rain," lines 5-6); character (Akira's "soft, refined" voice, line 33; Akira's eyes "sh[ining] with sincerity," line 35); and plot ("Naomi was silent. She stood a full half minute looking straight into Chie's eyes. Finally, she spoke," lines 88-89).

Choice A is incorrect because the passage focuses on a nontraditional marriage proposal. Choice C is incorrect because the passage concludes without resolution to the question of whether Akira and Naomi will receive permission to marry. Choice D is incorrect because the passage repeatedly makes clear that for Chie, her encounter with Akira is momentous and unsettling, as when Akira acknowledges in line 73 that he has "startled" her.

QUESTION 3

Choice C is the best answer. Akira "came directly, breaking all tradition," (line 1) when he approached Chie and asked to marry her daughter, and he "ask[ed] directly," without "a go-between" (line 65) or "mediation," because doing otherwise would have taken too much time.

Choices A, B, and D are incorrect because in these contexts, "directly" does not mean in a frank, confident, or precise manner.

QUESTION 4

Choice A is the best answer. Akira is very concerned Chie will find his marriage proposal inappropriate because he did not follow traditional protocol and use a "go-between" (line 65). This is clear in lines 63-64, when Akira says to Chie "Please don't judge my candidacy by the unseemliness of this proposal."

Choice B is incorrect because there is no evidence in the passage that Akira worries that Chie will mistake his earnestness for immaturity. Choice C is incorrect because while Akira recognizes that his unscheduled visit is a nuisance, his larger concern is that Chie will reject him due to the inappropriateness of his proposal. Choice D is incorrect because there is no evidence in the passage that Akira worries Chie will underestimate the sincerity of his emotions.

QUESTION 5

Choice C is the best answer. In lines 63-64, Akira says to Chie, "Please don't judge my candidacy by the unseemliness of this proposal." This reveals Akira's concern that Chie may say no to the proposal simply because Akira did not follow traditional practices.

Choices A, B, and D do not provide the best evidence for the answer to the previous question. Choice A is incorrect because line 33 merely describes Akira's voice as "soft, refined." Choice B is incorrect because lines 49-51 reflect Chie's perspective, not Akira's. Choice D is incorrect because lines 71-72 indicate only that Akira was speaking in an eager and forthright matter.

QUESTION 6

Choice D is the best answer because Akira clearly treats Chie with respect, including "bow[ing]" (line 26) to her, calling her "Madame" (line 31), and looking at her with "a deferential peek" (line 34). Akira does not offer Chie utter deference, though, as he asks to marry Naomi after he concedes that he is not following protocol and admits to being a "disruption" (line 31).

Choice A is incorrect because while Akira conveys respect to Chie, there is no evidence in the passage that he feels affection for her. Choice B is incorrect because neither objectivity nor impartiality accurately describes how Akira addresses Chie. Choice C is incorrect because Akira conveys respect to Chie and takes the conversation seriously.

QUESTION 7

Choice D is the best answer. The first paragraph (lines 1-4) reflects on how Akira approached Chie to ask for her daughter's hand in marriage. In these lines, the narrator is wondering whether Chie would have been more likely to say yes to Akira's proposal if Akira had followed tradition: "Akira came directly, breaking all tradition. Was that it? Had he followed form — had he asked his mother to speak to his father to approach a go-between — would Chie have been more receptive?" Thus, the main purpose of the first paragraph is to examine why Chie reacted a certain way to Akira's proposal.

Choice A is incorrect because the first paragraph describes only one aspect of Japanese culture (marriage proposals) but not the culture as a whole. Choice B is incorrect because the first paragraph implies a criticism of Akira's individual marriage proposal but not the entire tradition of Japanese marriage proposals. Choice C is incorrect because the narrator does not question a suggestion.

QUESTION 8

Choice B is the best answer. In line 1, the narrator suggests that Akira's direct approach broke "all tradition." The narrator then wonders if Akira had "followed form," or the tradition expected of him, would Chie have been more receptive to his proposal. In this context, following "form" thus means following a certain tradition or custom.

Choices A, C, and D are incorrect because in this context "form" does not mean the way something looks (appearance), the way it is built (structure), or its essence (nature).

QUESTION 9

Choice C is the best answer. Akira states that his unexpected meeting with Chie occurred only because of a "matter of urgency," which he explains as "an opportunity to go to America, as dentist for Seattle's Japanese community" (lines 41-42). Akira decides to directly speak to Chie because Chie's response to his marriage proposal affects whether Akira accepts the job offer.

Choice A is incorrect because there is no evidence in the passage that Akira is worried his parents will not approve of Naomi. Choice B is incorrect because Akira has "an understanding" with Naomi (line 63). Choice D is incorrect; while Akira may know that Chie is unaware of his feelings for Naomi, this is not what he is referring to when he mentions "a matter of urgency."

QUESTION 10

Choice B is the best answer. In lines 39-42, Akira clarifies that the "matter of urgency" is that he has "an opportunity to go to America, as dentist for Seattle's Japanese community." Akira needs Chie's answer to his marriage proposal so he can decide whether to accept the job in Seattle.

Choices A, C, and D do not provide the best evidence for the answer to the previous question. Choice A is incorrect because in line 39 Akira apologizes for interrupting Chie's quiet evening. Choice C is incorrect because lines 58-59 address the seriousness of Akira's request, not its urgency. Choice D is incorrect because line 73 shows only that Akira's proposal has "startled" Chie and does not explain why his request is time-sensitive.

QUESTION 11

Choice A is the best answer. Lines 1-9 include examples of how many people shop ("millions of shoppers"), how much money they spend ("over $30 billion at retail stores in the month of December alone"), and the many occasions that lead to shopping for gifts ("including weddings, birthdays, anniversaries, graduations, and baby showers."). Combined, these examples show how frequently people in the US shop for gifts.

Choice B is incorrect because even though the authors mention that "$30 billion" had been spent in retail stores in one month, that figure is never discussed as an increase (or a decrease). Choice C is incorrect because lines 1-9 provide a context for the amount of shopping that occurs in the US, but the anxiety (or "dread") it might cause is not introduced until later in the passage. Choice D is incorrect because lines 1-9 do more than highlight the number of different occasions that lead to gift-giving.

QUESTION 12

Choice B is the best answer. Lines 9-10 state "This frequent experience of gift-giving can engender ambivalent feelings in gift-givers." In the subsequent sentences, those "ambivalent" feelings are further exemplified as conflicted feelings, as shopping is said to be something that "[m]any relish" (lines 10-11) and "many dread" (line 14).

Choices A, C, and D are incorrect because in this context, "ambivalent" does not mean feelings that are unrealistic, apprehensive, or supportive.

QUESTION 13

Choice D is the best answer. In lines 10-13, the authors clearly state that some people believe gift-giving can help a relationship because it "offers a powerful means to build stronger bonds with one's closest peers."

Choice A is incorrect because even though the authors state that some shoppers make their choices based on "egocentrism," (line 33) there is no evidence in the passage that people view shopping as a form of self-expression. Choice B is incorrect because the passage implies that shopping is an expensive habit. Choice C is incorrect because the passage states that most people have purchased and received gifts, but it never implies that people are *required* to reciprocate the gift-giving process.

QUESTION 14

Choice A is the best answer. In lines 10-13, the authors suggest that people value gift-giving because it may strengthen their relationships with others: "Many relish the opportunity to buy presents because gift-giving offers a powerful means to build stronger bonds with one's closest peers."

Choices B, C, and D do not provide the best evidence for the answer to the previous question. Choice B is incorrect because lines 22-23 discuss how people often buy gifts that the recipients would not purchase. Choice C is incorrect because lines 31-32 explain how gift-givers often fail to consider the recipients' preferences. Choice D is incorrect because lines 44-47 suggest that the cost of a gift may not correlate to a recipient's appreciation of it.

QUESTION 15

Choice A is the best answer. The "deadweight loss" mentioned in the second paragraph is the significant monetary difference between what a gift-giver would pay for something and what a gift-recipient would pay for the same item. That difference would be predictable to social psychologists, whose research "has found that people often struggle to take account of others' perspectives — their insights are subject to egocentrism, social projection, and multiple attribution errors" (lines 31-34).

Choices B, C, and D are all incorrect because lines 31-34 make clear that social psychologists would expect a disconnect between gift-givers and gift-recipients, not that they would question it, be disturbed by it, or find it surprising or unprecedented.

QUESTION 16

Choice C is the best answer. Lines 41-44 suggest that gift-givers assume a correlation between the cost of a gift and how well-received it will be: ". . . gift-givers equate how much they spend with how much recipients will appreciate the gift (the more expensive the gift, the stronger a gift-recipient's feelings of appreciation)." However, the authors suggest this assumption may be incorrect or "unfounded" (line 47), as gift-recipients "may not construe smaller and larger gifts as representing smaller and larger signals of thoughtfulness and consideration" (lines 63-65).

Choices A, B, and D are all incorrect because the passage neither states nor implies that the gift-givers' assumption is insincere, unreasonable, or substantiated.

QUESTION 17

Choice C is the best answer. Lines 63-65 suggest that the assumption made by gift-givers in lines 41-44 may be incorrect. The gift-givers assume that recipients will have a greater appreciation for costly gifts than for less costly gifts, but the authors suggest this relationship may be incorrect, as gift-recipients "may not construe smaller and larger gifts as representing smaller and larger signals of thoughtfulness and consideration" (lines 63-65).

Choices A and D are incorrect because lines 53-55 and 75-78 address the question of "why" gift-givers make specific assumptions rather than addressing the validity of these assumptions. Choice B is incorrect because lines 55-60 focus on the reasons people give gifts to others.

QUESTION 18

Choice D is the best answer. Lines 53-55 state that "Perhaps givers believe that bigger (i.e., more expensive) gifts convey stronger signals of thoughtfulness and consideration." In this context, saying that more expensive gifts "convey" stronger signals means the gifts send, or communicate, stronger signals to the recipients.

Choices A, B, and C are incorrect because in this context, to "convey" something does not mean to transport it (physically move something), counteract it (act in opposition to something), or exchange it (trade one thing for another).

QUESTION 19

Choice A is the best answer. The paragraph examines how gift-givers believe expensive gifts are more thoughtful than less expensive gifts and will be more valued by recipients. The work of Camerer and others offers an explanation for the gift-givers' reasoning: "gift-givers attempt to signal their positive attitudes toward the intended recipient and their willingness to invest resources in a future relationship" (lines 57-60).

Choices B, C, and D are incorrect because the theory articulated by Camerer and others is used to explain an idea put forward by the authors ("givers believe that bigger . . . gifts convey stronger signals"), not to introduce an argument, question a motive, or support a conclusion.

QUESTION 20

Choice B is the best answer. The graph clearly shows that gift-givers believe that a "more valuable" gift will be more appreciated than a "less valuable gift." According to the graph, gift-givers believe the monetary value of a gift will determine whether that gift is well received or not.

Choice A is incorrect because the graph does not suggest that gift-givers are aware of gift-recipients' appreciation levels. Choices C and D are incorrect because neither the gift-givers' desire for the gifts they purchase nor the gift-givers' relationship with the gift-recipients is addressed in the graph.

QUESTION 21

Choice A is the best answer. Lines 69-75 explain that while people are often both gift-givers and gift-receivers, they struggle to apply information they learned as a gift-giver to a time when they were a gift-receiver: "Yet, despite the extensive experience that people have as both givers and receivers, they often struggle to transfer information gained from one role (e.g., as a giver) and apply it in another, complementary role (e.g., as a receiver)." The authors suggest that the disconnect between how much appreciation a gift-giver thinks a gift merits and how much appreciation a gift-recipient displays for the gift may be caused by both individuals' inability to comprehend the other's perspective.

Choices B and C are incorrect because neither the passage nor the graph addresses the idea that society has become more materialistic or that there is a growing opposition to gift-giving. Choice D is incorrect because the passage emphasizes that gift-givers and gift-recipients fail to understand each other's perspective, but it offers no evidence that the disconnect results only from a failure to understand the other's intentions.

QUESTION 22

Choice B is the best answer. Lines 2-4 of the passage describe DNA as "a very long chain, the backbone of which consists of a regular alternation of sugar and phosphate groups." The backbone of DNA, in other words, is the main structure of a chain made up of repeating units of sugar and phosphate.

Choice A is incorrect because the passage describes DNA on the molecular level only and never mentions the spinal column of organisms. Choice C is incorrect because the passage describes the backbone of the molecule as having "a regular alternation" of sugar and phosphate, not one or the other. Choice D is incorrect because the nitrogenous bases are not the main structural unit of DNA; rather, they are attached only to the repeating units of sugar.

QUESTION 23

Choice D is the best answer. The authors explain that hydrogen bonds join together pairs of nitrogenous bases, and that these bases have a specific structure that leads to the pairing: "One member of a pair must be a purine and the other a pyrimidine in order to bridge between the two chains" (lines 27-29). Given the specific chemical properties of a nitrogenous base, it would be inaccurate to call the process random.

Choice A is incorrect because lines 5-6 describe how nitrogenous bases attach to sugar but not how those bases pair with one another. Choice B is incorrect because lines 9-10 do not contradict the student's claim. Choice C is incorrect because lines 23-25 describe how the two molecules' chains are linked, not what the specific pairing between nitrogenous bases is.

QUESTION 24

Choice D is the best answer. In lines 12-14 the authors state: "the first feature of our structure which is of biological interest is that it consists not of one chain, but of two."

Choices A and B are incorrect because lines 12-14 explicitly state that it is the two chains of DNA that are of "biological interest," not the chemical formula of DNA, nor the common fiber axis those two chains are wrapped around. Choice C is incorrect because, while the X-ray evidence did help Watson and Crick to discover that DNA consists of two chains, it was not claimed to be the feature of biological interest.

QUESTION 25

Choice C is the best answer. In lines 12-14 the authors claim that DNA molecules appear to be comprised of two chains, even though "it has often been assumed . . . there would be only one" (lines 15-17). The authors support this claim with evidence compiled from an X-ray: "the density, taken with the X-ray evidence, suggests very strongly that there are two [chains]" (lines 18-19).

Choices A, B, and D are incorrect because the authors mention density and X-ray evidence to support a claim, not to establish that DNA carries genetic information, present a hypothesis about the composition of a nucleotide, or confirm a relationship between the density and chemical formula of DNA.

QUESTION 26

Choice B is the best answer. The authors explain that "only certain pairs of bases will fit into the structure" (lines 25-26) of the DNA molecule. These pairs must contain "a purine and the other a pyrimidine in order to bridge between the two chains" (lines 27-29), which implies that any other pairing would not "fit into the structure" of the DNA molecule. Therefore, a pair of purines would be larger than the required purine/pyrimidine pair and would not fit into the structure of the DNA molecule.

Choice A is incorrect because this section is not discussing the distance between a sugar and phosphate group. Choice C is incorrect because the passage never makes clear the size of the pyrimidines or purines in relation to each other, only in relation to the space needed to bond the chains of the DNA molecule. Choice D is incorrect because the lines do not make an implication about the size of a pair of pyrimidines in relation to the size of a pair consisting of a purine and a pyrimidine.

QUESTION 27

Choice D is the best answer. The authors explain how the DNA molecule contains a "precise sequence of bases" (lines 43-44), and that the authors can use the order of bases on one chain to determine the order of bases on the other chain: "If the actual order of the bases on one of the pair of chains were given, one could write down the exact order of the bases on the other one, because of the specific pairing. Thus one chain is, as it were, the complement of the other, and it is this feature which suggests how the deoxyribonucleic acid molecule might duplicate itself" (lines 45-51). The authors use the words "exact," "specific," and "complement" in these lines to suggest that the base pairings along a DNA chain is understood and predictable, and may explain how DNA "duplicate[s] itself" (line 51).

Choice A is incorrect because the passage does not suggest that most nucleotide sequences are known. Choice B is incorrect because these lines are not discussing the random nature of the base sequence along one chain of DNA. Choice C is incorrect because the authors are describing the bases attached only to the sugar, not to the sugar-phosphate backbone.

QUESTION 28

Choice C is the best answer. Lines 6-7 state that "Two of the possible bases — adenine and guanine — are purines," and on the table the percentages of adenine and guanine in yeast DNA are listed as 31.3% and 18.7% respectively.

Choices A, B, and D are incorrect because they do not state the percentages of both purines, adenine and guanine, in yeast DNA.

QUESTION 29

Choice A is the best answer. The authors state: "We believe that the bases will be present almost entirely in their most probable forms. If this is true, the conditions for forming hydrogen bonds are more restrictive, and the only pairs of bases possible are: adenine with thymine, and guanine with cytosine" (lines 31-35). The table shows that the pairs adenine/thymine and guanine/cytosine have notably similar percentages in DNA for all organisms listed.

Choice B is incorrect. Although the choice of "Yes" is correct, the explanation for that choice misrepresents the data in the table. Choices C and D are incorrect because the table does support the authors' proposed pairing of nitrogenous bases in DNA molecules.

QUESTION 30

Choice A is the best answer because it gives the percentage of cytosine (17.3%) in sea urchin DNA and the percentage of guanine (17.7%) in sea urchin DNA. Their near similar pairing supports the authors' proposal that possible pairings of nitrogenous bases are "adenine with thymine, and guanine with cytosine" (line 35).

Choices B, C, and D do not provide the best evidence for the answer to the previous question. Choice B (cytosine and thymine), Choice C (cytosine and adenine), and Choice D (guanine and adenine) are incorrect because they show pairings of nitrogenous bases that do not compose a similar percentage of the bases in sea urchin DNA.

QUESTION 31

Choice D is the best answer. The table clearly shows that the percentage of adenine in each organism's DNA is different, ranging from 24.7% in *E.coli* to 33.2% in the octopus. That such a variability would exist is predicted in lines 41-43, which states that "in a long molecule many different permutations are possible."

Choices A and B are incorrect because the table shows that the percentage of adenine varies between 24.7% and 33.2% in different organisms. Choice C is incorrect because lines 36-38 state that adenine pairs with thymine but does not mention the variability of the base composition of DNA.

QUESTION 32

Choice B is the best answer. In this passage, Woolf asks women a series of questions. Woolf wants women to consider joining "the procession of educated men" (lines 56-57) by becoming members of the workforce. Woolf stresses that this issue is urgent, as women "have very little time in which to answer [these questions]" (lines 48-49).

Choice A is incorrect because Woolf argues against the tradition of only "the sons of educated men" (lines 82-83) joining the workforce. Choice C is incorrect because Woolf is not highlighting the severity of social divisions as much as she is explaining how those divisions might be reduced (with women joining the workforce). Choice D is incorrect because Woolf does not question the feasibility of changing the workforce dynamic.

QUESTION 33

Choice A is the best answer. Throughout the passage, Woolf advocates for more women to engage with existing institutions by joining the workforce: "We too can leave the house, can mount those steps [to an office], pass in and out of those doors, . . . make money, administer justice . . ." (lines 30-32). Woolf tells educated women that they are at a "moment of transition" (line 51) where they must consider their future role in the workforce.

Choice B is incorrect because even though Woolf mentions women's traditional roles (lines 68-69: "while they stirred the pot, while they rocked the cradle"), she does not suggest that women will have to give up these traditional roles to gain positions of influence. Choice C is incorrect because though Woolf wonders how "the procession of the sons of educated men" impacts women's roles, she does not argue that this male-dominated society has had grave and continuing effects. Choice D is incorrect because while Woolf suggests educated women can hold positions currently held by men, she does not suggest that women's entry into positions of power will change those positions.

QUESTION 34

Choice C is the best answer. Woolf uses the word "we" to refer to herself and educated women in English society, the "daughters of educated men" (line 64). Woolf wants these women to consider participating in a changing workforce: "For there, trapesing along at the tail end of the procession [to and from work], we go ourselves" (lines 23-24). In using the word "we" throughout the passage, Woolf establishes a sense of solidarity among educated women.

Choice A is incorrect because Woolf does not use "we" to reflect on whether people in a group are friendly to one another; she is concerned with generating solidarity among women. Choice B is incorrect because though Woolf admits women have predominantly "done their thinking" within traditional female roles (lines 64-69), she does not use "we" to advocate for more candor among women. Choice D is incorrect because Woolf does not use "we" to emphasize a need for people in a group to respect one other; rather, she wants to establish a sense of solidarity among women.

QUESTION 35

Choice B is the best answer. Woolf argues that the "bridge over the River Thames, [has] an admirable vantage ground for us to make a survey" (lines 1-3). The phrase "make a survey" means to carefully examine an event or activity. Woolf wants educated women to "fix [their] eyes upon the procession — the procession of the sons of educated men" (lines 9-11) walking to work.

Choice A is incorrect because while Woolf states the bridge "is a place to stand on by the hour dreaming," she states that she is using the bridge "to consider the facts" (lines 6-9). Woolf is not using the bridge for fanciful reflection; she is analyzing "the procession of the sons of educated men" (lines 10-11). Choice C is incorrect because Woolf does not compare the bridge to historic episodes. Choice D is incorrect because Woolf does not suggest that the bridge is a symbol of a male-dominated past, but rather that it serves as a good place to watch men proceed to work.

QUESTION 36

Choice D is the best answer. Woolf writes that the men who conduct the affairs of the nation (lines 15-17: "ascending those pulpits, preaching, teaching, administering justice, practising medicine, transacting business, making money") are the same men who go to and from work in a "procession" (line 10). Woolf notes that women are joining this procession, an act that suggests the workforce has become less exclusionary: "For there, trapesing along at the tail end of the procession, we go ourselves" (lines 23-24).

Choice A is incorrect because the procession is described as "a solemn sight always" (lines 17-18), which indicates that it has always been influential. Choice B is incorrect because the passage does not indicate that this procession has become a celebrated feature of English life. Choice C is incorrect because the passage states only that the procession is made up of "the sons of educated men" (lines 10-11).

QUESTION 37

Choice C is the best answer, as lines 23-24 suggest that the workforce has become less exclusionary. In these lines Woolf describes how women are joining the male-dominated procession that travels to and from the work place: "For there, trapesing along at the tail end of the procession, we go ourselves."

Choices A, B, and D are incorrect because they do not provide the best evidence for the answer to the previous question. Choice A is incorrect because lines 12-17 describe the positions predominantly held by men. Choice B is incorrect because lines 17-19 use a metaphor to describe how the procession physically looks. Choice D is incorrect because lines 30-34 hypothesize about future jobs for women.

QUESTION 38

Choice C is the best answer. Woolf characterizes the questions she asks in lines 53-57 as significant ("so important that they may well change the lives of all men and women for ever," lines 52-53) and urgent ("we have very little time in which to answer them," lines 48-49). Therefore, Woolf considers the questions posed in lines 53-57 as both momentous (significant) and pressing (urgent).

Choice A is incorrect because Woolf characterizes the questions as urgent and important, not as something that would cause controversy or fear. Choice B is incorrect because though Woolf considers the questions to be weighty (or "important"), she implies that they can be answered. Choice D is incorrect because Woolf does not imply that the questions are mysterious.

QUESTION 39

Choice B is the best answer. The answer to the previous question shows how Woolf characterizes the questions posed in lines 53-57 as momentous and pressing. In lines 48-49, Woolf describes these questions as "important," or momentous, and states that women "have very little time in which to answer them," which shows their urgency.

Choices A, C, and D do not provide the best evidence for the answer to the previous question. Choices A and D are incorrect because lines 46-47 and line 62 suggest that women need to think about these questions and not offer trivial objections to them. Choice C is incorrect because line 57 characterizes only the need for urgency and does not mention the significance of the questions.

QUESTION 40

Choice C is the best answer. Woolf writes that women "have thought" while performing traditional roles such as cooking and caring for children (lines 67-69). Woolf argues that this "thought" has shifted women's roles in society and earned them a "brand-new sixpence" that they need to learn how to "spend" (lines 70-71). The "sixpence" mentioned in these lines is not a literal coin. Woolf is using the "sixpence" as a metaphor, as she is suggesting women take advantage of the opportunity to join the male-dominated workforce.

Choices A, B, and D are incorrect because in this context, "sixpence" does not refer to tolerance, knowledge, or perspective.

QUESTION 41

Choice B is the best answer. In lines 72-76, Woolf repeats the phrase "let us think" to emphasize how important it is for women to critically reflect on their role in society. Woolf states this reflection can occur at any time: "Let us think in offices; in omnibuses; while we are standing in the crowd watching Coronations and Lord Mayor's Shows; let us think . . . in the gallery of the House of Commons; in the Law Courts; let us think at baptisms and marriages and funerals."

Choices A, C, and D are incorrect because in lines 72-76 Woolf is not emphasizing the novelty of the challenge faced by women, the complexity of social and political issues, or the enjoyable aspect of women's career possibilities.

QUESTION 42

Choice B is the best answer. The author of Passage 1 identifies specific companies such as the "Planetary Resources of Washington," "Deep Space Industries of Virginia," and "Golden Spike of Colorado" to support his earlier assertion that there are many interested groups "working to make space mining a reality" (line 8).

Choices A, C, and D are incorrect because the author of Passage 1 does not mention these companies to profile the technological advances in space mining, the profit margins from space mining, or the diverse approaches to space mining.

QUESTION 43

Choice A is the best answer. The author of Passage 1 explicitly states that one benefit to space mining is access to precious metals and earth elements: "within a few decades, [space mining] may be meeting earthly demands for precious metals, such as platinum and gold, and the rare earth elements vital for personal electronics, such as yttrium and lanthanum" (lines 18-22).

Choice B is incorrect because Passage 1 does not suggest that precious metals extracted from space may make metals more valuable on Earth. Choice C and Choice D are incorrect because Passage 1 never mentions how space mining could create unanticipated technological innovations or change scientists' understanding of space resources.

QUESTION 44

Choice A is the best answer. Lines 18-22 suggest that space mining may help meet "earthly demands for precious metals . . . and the rare earth elements vital for personal electronics." In this statement, the author is stating materials ("metals," "earth elements") that may be gathered as a result of space mining, and that these materials may be important to Earth's economy.

Choices B, C, and D do not provide the best evidence for the answer to the previous question. Choice B is incorrect because lines 24-28 focus on an "off-planet economy" but never address positive effects of space mining. Choice C is incorrect because lines 29-30 suggest the relative value of water found in space. Choice D is incorrect because lines 41-44 state that space mining companies hope to find specific resources in lunar soil and asteroids but do not address how these resources are important to Earth's economy.

QUESTION 45

Choice D is the best answer. The author suggests in lines 19-22 that space mining may meet "earthly demands for precious metals, such as platinum and gold, and the rare earth elements vital for personal electronics." In this sentence, "earthly demands" suggests that people want, or desire, these precious metals and rare earth elements.

Choices A, B, and C are incorrect because in this context "demands" does not mean offers, claims, or inquiries.

QUESTION 46

Choice C is the best answer. Lines 29-30 introduce the idea that water mined in space may be very valuable: "water mined from other worlds could become the most desired commodity." Lines 35-40 support this assertion by suggesting how mined space water could be used "for drinking or as a radiation shield" (lines 36-37) or to make "spacecraft fuel" (line 38).

Choice A is incorrect because the comparison in the previous paragraph (the relative value of gold and water to someone in the desert) is not expanded upon in lines 35-40. Choice B is incorrect because the question asked in the previous paragraph is also answered in that paragraph. Choice D is incorrect because no specific proposals are made in the previous paragraph; rather, an assertion is made and a question is posed.

QUESTION 47

Choice B is the best answer. The author of Passage 2 recognizes that space mining may prove beneficial to humanity, stating that "we all stand to gain: the mineral bounty and spin-off technologies could enrich us all" (lines 50-52). The author also repeatedly mentions that space mining should be carefully considered before it is implemented: "But before the miners start firing up their rockets, we should pause for thought" (lines 53-54); "But [space mining's] consequences — both here on Earth and in space — merit careful consideration" (lines 57-59).

Choice A is incorrect because the author of Passage 2 concedes that "space mining seems to sidestep most environmental concerns" (lines 55-56) but does not imply that space mining will recklessly harm the environment, either on Earth or in space. Choice C is incorrect because the author of Passage 2 does not address any key resources that may be disappearing on Earth. Choice D is incorrect because the author of Passage 2 admits that "resources that are valuable in orbit and beyond may be very different to those we prize on Earth" (lines 74-76) but does not mention any disagreement about the commercial viabilities of space mining discoveries.

QUESTION 48

Choice A is the best answer. In lines 60-66, the author presents some environmental arguments against space mining: "[space] is not ours to despoil" and we should not "[glut] ourselves on space's riches." The author then suggests that these environmental arguments will be hard to "hold," or maintain, when faced with the possible monetary rewards of space mining: "History suggests that those will be hard lines to hold . . ." (line 68).

Choices B, C, and D are incorrect because in this context, "hold" does not mean grip, restrain, or withstand.

QUESTION 49

Choice D is the best answer. The author of Passage 1 is excited about the possibilities of space mining and how it can yield valuable materials, such as metals and elements (lines 19-20 and lines 41-42), water ice (line 35), and space dirt (line 44). The author of Passage 2, on the other hand, recognizes the possible benefits of space mining but also states that space mining should be thoughtfully considered before being implemented. Therefore, the author of Passage 2 expresses some concerns about a concept discussed in Passage 1.

Choice A is incorrect because the author of Passage 2 does not refute the central claim of Passage 1; both authors agree there are possible benefits to space mining. Choice B is incorrect because the author of Passage 1 does not describe space mining in more general terms than does the author of Passage 2. Choice C is incorrect because the author of Passage 2 is not suggesting that the space mining proposals stated in Passage 1 are impractical.

QUESTION 50

Choice B is the best answer. In lines 18-28, the author of Passage 1 describes many of the possible economic benefits of space mining, including the building of "an off-planet economy" (line 25). The author of Passage 2 warns that there may be ramifications to implementing space mining and building an "emerging off-world economy" (line 73) without regulation: "But miners have much to gain from a broad agreement on the for-profit exploitation of space. Without consensus, claims will be disputed, investments risky, and the gains made insecure" (lines 83-87).

Choices A, C, and D are incorrect because the author of Passage 2 does not suggest that the benefits to space mining mentioned in lines 18-28 of Passage 1 are unsustainable, unachievable, or will negatively affect Earth's economy. Rather, the author recognizes the benefits of space mining but advocates for the development of regulation procedures.

QUESTION 51

Choice D is the best answer. In lines 85-87, the author of Passage 2 states that the future of space mining will prove difficult without regulations because "claims will be disputed, investments risky, and the gains made insecure."

Choices A, B, and C are incorrect because they do not provide the best evidence for the answer to the previous question. Choice A is incorrect because lines 60-63 present some environmental concerns toward space mining. Choice B is incorrect because lines 74-76 focus on how space mining may discover valuable resources that are different from the ones found on Earth. Choice C is incorrect because lines 81-83 simply describe one person's objections to the regulation of the space mining industry.

QUESTION 52

Choice A is the best answer because both Passage 1 and Passage 2 indicate a belief that the resources most valued in space may differ from those most valued on our planet. Passage 2 says this explicitly in lines 74-76: "The resources that are valuable in orbit and beyond may be very different to those we prize on Earth." Meanwhile Passage 1 suggests that water mined from space may be more valuable than metals or other earth elements when creating an "off-plant economy" (lines 25-30).

Choice B is incorrect because neither passage discusses, either implicitly or explicitly, the need for space mining to be inexpensive. Choice C is incorrect because Passage 2 does not specifically identify precious metals or rare earth elements but instead focuses on theoretical problems with space mining. Choice D is incorrect because diminishing resources on Earth is not discussed in Passage 2.

Section 2: Writing and Language Test

QUESTION 1

Choice D is the best answer because "outweigh" is the only choice that appropriately reflects the relationship the sentence sets up between "advantages" and "drawbacks."

Choices A, B, and C are incorrect because each implies a competitive relationship that is inappropriate in this context.

QUESTION 2

Choice B is the best answer because it offers a second action that farmers can undertake to address the problem of acid whey disposal, thus supporting the claim made in the previous sentence ("To address the problem of disposal, farmers have found a *number of uses* for acid whey").

Choices A, C, and D are incorrect because they do not offer examples of how farmers could make use of acid whey.

QUESTION 3

Choice A is the best answer because it results in a sentence that is grammatically correct and coherent. In choice A, "waterways," the correct plural form of "waterway," conveys the idea that acid whey could impact multiple bodies of water. Additionally, the compound verb "can pollute" suggests that acid whey presents an ongoing, potential problem.

Choices B and D are incorrect because both use the possessive form of "waterway." Choice C is incorrect because it creates an unnecessary shift in verb tense. The present tense verb "can pollute" should be used instead, as it is consistent with the other verbs in the paragraph.

QUESTION 4

Choice C is the best answer because it utilizes proper punctuation for items listed in a series. In this case those items are nouns: "Yogurt manufacturers, food scientists, and government officials."

Choices A and B are incorrect because both fail to recognize that the items are a part of a series. Since a comma is used after "manufacturers," a semicolon or colon should not be used after "scientists." Choice D is incorrect because the comma after "and" is unnecessary and deviates from grammatical conventions for presenting items in a series.

QUESTION 5

Choice C is the best answer because sentence 5 logically links sentence 2, which explains why Greek yogurt production yields large amounts of acid whey, and sentence 3, which mentions the need to dispose of acid whey properly.

Choices A, B, and D are incorrect because each would result in an illogical progression of sentences for this paragraph. If sentence 5 were left where it is or placed after sentence 3, it would appear illogically after the discussion of "the problem of disposal." If sentence 5 were placed after sentence 1, it would illogically discuss "acid-whey runoff" before the mention of acid whey being "difficult to dispose of."

QUESTION 6

Choice D is the best answer because the paragraph includes several benefits of consuming Greek yogurt, particularly in regard to nutrition and satisfying hunger, to support the sentence's claim that the conservation efforts are "well worth the effort." This transition echoes the passage's earlier claim that "the advantages of Greek yogurt outweigh the potential drawbacks of its production."

Choices A, B, and C are incorrect because they inaccurately describe the sentence in question.

QUESTION 7

Choice B is the best answer because it provides a grammatically standard preposition that connects the verb "serves" and noun "digestive aid" and accurately depicts their relationship.

Choice A is incorrect because the infinitive form "to be" yields a grammatically incorrect verb construction: "serves to be." Choices C and D are incorrect because both present options that deviate from standard English usage.

QUESTION 8

Choice C is the best answer because it presents a verb tense that is consistent in the context of the sentence. The choice is also free of the redundant "it."

Choice A is incorrect because the subject "it" creates a redundancy. Choices B and D are incorrect because they present verb tenses that are inconsistent in the context of the sentence.

QUESTION 9

Choice A is the best answer because it properly introduces an additional health benefit in a series of sentences that list health benefits. "Also" is the logical and coherent choice to communicate an addition.

Choices B, C, and D are incorrect because none of the transitions they offer logically fits the content that precedes or follows the proposed choice.

QUESTION 10

Choice A is the best answer because "satiated" is the only choice that communicates effectively that Greek yogurt will satisfy hunger for a longer period of time.

Choices B, C, and D are incorrect because each is improper usage in this context. A person can be "fulfilled" spiritually or in other ways, but a person who has eaten until he or she is no longer hungry cannot be described as fulfilled. Neither can he or she be described as being "complacent" or "sufficient."

QUESTION 11

Choice B is the best answer because it provides a syntactically coherent and grammatically correct sentence.

Choices A and C are incorrect because the adverbial conjunctions "therefore" and "so," respectively, are unnecessary following "Because." Choice D is incorrect because it results in a grammatically incomplete sentence (the part of the sentence before the colon must be an independent clause).

QUESTION 12

Choice B is the best answer because the graph clearly indicates that, on March 5, average low temperatures are at their lowest point: 12 degrees Fahrenheit.

Choice A is incorrect because the phrase "as low as" suggests that the temperature falls no lower than 20 degrees Fahrenheit, but the chart shows that in January, February, and March, the temperature frequently falls below that point. Choices C and D are incorrect because the information each provides is inconsistent with the information on the chart.

QUESTION 13

Choice A is the best answer because it concisely combines the two sentences while maintaining the original meaning.

Choices B, C, and D are incorrect because each is unnecessarily wordy, thus undermining one purpose of combining two sentences: to make the phrasing more concise.

QUESTION 14

Choice B is the best answer because it provides a conjunctive adverb that accurately represents the relationship between the two sentences. "However" signals an exception to a case stated in the preceding sentence.

Choices A, C, and D are incorrect because each provides a transition that does not accurately represent the relationship between the two sentences, and as a result each compromises the logical coherence of these sentences.

QUESTION 15

Choice C is the best answer because it provides commas to offset the nonrestrictive modifying clause "an associate professor of geology at Ohio State."

Choices A, B, and D are incorrect because each provides punctuation that does not adequately separate the nonrestrictive modifying clause about Jason Box from the main clause.

QUESTION 16

Choice C is the best answer because the colon signals that the other factor that contributed to the early thaw is about to be provided.

Choice A is incorrect because it results in a sentence that deviates from grammatical standards: a semicolon should be used to separate two independent clauses, but in choice A the second clause only has a subject, not a verb. Choice B is incorrect because it is unnecessarily wordy. Choice D is incorrect because "being" is unnecessary and creates an incoherent clause.

QUESTION 17

Choice C is the best answer because it provides the correct preposition ("of") and relative pronoun ("which") that together create a dependent clause following the comma.

Choices A, B, and D are incorrect because each results in a comma splice. Two independent clauses cannot be joined with only a comma.

QUESTION 18

Choice A is the best answer because the verb tense is consistent with the preceding past tense verbs in the sentence, specifically "produced" and "drifted."

Choices B, C, and D are incorrect because each utilizes a verb tense that is not consistent with the preceding past tense verbs in the sentence.

QUESTION 19

Choice D is the best answer because "their" is the possessive form of a plural noun. In this case, the noun is plural: "snow and ice."

Choices A and B are incorrect because the possessive pronoun must refer to a plural noun, "snow and ice," rather than a singular noun. Choice C is incorrect because "there" would result in an incoherent sentence.

QUESTION 20

Choice D is the best answer. The preceding sentences in the paragraph have established that a darker surface of soot-covered snow leads to more melting because this darker surface absorbs heat, whereas a whiter surface, free of soot, would deflect heat. As the passage points out, exposed land and water are also dark and cannot deflect heat the way ice and snow can. Only choice D reflects the self-reinforcing cycle that the preceding sentences already imply.

Choices A, B, and C are incorrect because the information each provides fails to support the previous claim that the "result" of the soot "is a self-reinforcing cycle."

QUESTION 21

Choice B is the best answer because it is free of redundancies.

Choices A, C, and D are incorrect because each of the three presents a redundancy: Choice A uses "repeat" and "again"; Choice C uses "damage" and "harmful effects"; and Choice D uses "may" and "possibly."

QUESTION 22

Choice D is the best answer because sentence 5 describes the information Box seeks: "to determine just how much the soot is contributing to the melting of the ice sheet." Unless sentence 4 comes after sentence 5, readers will not know what the phrase "this crucial information" in sentence 4 refers to.

Choices A, B, and C are incorrect because each results in an illogical sentence progression. None of the sentences that would precede sentence 4 provides details that could be referred to as "this crucial information."

QUESTION 23

Choice D is the best answer because it is free of redundancies and offers the correct form of the verb "wear" in this context.

Choices A, B, and C are incorrect because all three contain a redundancy. Considering that "quickly" is a fixed part of the sentence, choice A's "soon" and choice B and C's "promptly" all result in redundancies. Choices A and B are also incorrect because each uses an incorrect form of the verb.

QUESTION 24

Choice D is the best answer because it is the only choice that provides a grammatically standard and coherent sentence. The participial phrase "Having become frustrated. . ." functions as an adjective modifying "I," the writer.

Choices A, B, and C are incorrect because each results in a dangling modifier. The participial phrase "Having become frustrated . . ." does not refer to choice A's "no colleagues," choice B's "colleagues," or choice C's "ideas." As such, all three choices yield incoherent and grammatically incorrect sentences.

QUESTION 25

Choice B is the best answer because it provides the correct preposition in this context, "about."

Choices A, C, and D are incorrect because each provides a preposition that deviates from correct usage. One might read an article "about" coworking spaces but not an article "into," "upon," or "for" coworking spaces.

QUESTION 26

Choice A is the best answer because it provides the correct punctuation for the dependent clause that begins with the phrase "such as."

Choices B, C, and D are incorrect because each presents punctuation that deviates from the standard way of punctuating the phrase "such as." When "such as" is a part of a nonrestrictive clause, as it is here, only one comma is needed to separate it from the main independent clause.

QUESTION 27

Choice B is the best answer because it provides a transitional phrase, "In addition to equipment," that accurately represents the relationship between the two sentences connected by the transitional phrase. Together, the sentences describe the key features of coworking spaces, focusing on what the spaces offer (equipment and meeting rooms).

Choices A, C, and D are incorrect because each provides a transition that does not accurately represent the relationship between the two sentences.

QUESTION 28

Choice C is the best answer because the sentence is a distraction from the paragraph's focus. Nothing in the paragraph suggests that the cost of setting up a coworking business is relevant here.

Choices A and D are incorrect because neither accurately represents the information in the paragraph. Choice B is incorrect because it does not accurately represent the information in the next paragraph.

QUESTION 29

Choice B is the best answer because it logically follows the writer's preceding statement about creativity and accurately represents the information in the graph.

Choices A, C, and D are incorrect because they present inaccurate and unsupported interpretations of the information in the graph. In addition, none of these choices provides directly relevant support for the main topic of the paragraph.

QUESTION 30

Choice D is the best answer because it provides a relative pronoun and verb that create a standard and coherent sentence. The relative pronoun "who" refers to the subject "the people," and the plural verb "use" corresponds grammatically with the plural noun "people."

Choices A and B are incorrect because "whom" is the relative pronoun used to represent an object. The noun "people" is a subject performing an action (using the coworking space). Choices B and C are also incorrect because they display a form of the verb "to use" that does not correspond to the plural noun "people."

QUESTION 31

Choice C is the best answer because the proposed sentence offers a necessary and logical transition between sentence 2, which introduces the facility the writer chose, and sentence 3, which tells what happened at the facility "Throughout the morning."

Choices A, B, and D are incorrect because each would result in an illogical progression of sentences.

QUESTION 32

Choice A is the best answer because the punctuation it provides results in a grammatically standard and coherent sentence. When an independent clause is followed by a list, a colon is used to link the two.

Choice B is incorrect because the punctuation creates a fragment (a semicolon should be used to link two independent clauses). Choice C is incorrect because its use of the comma creates a series in which "several of my coworking colleagues" are distinguished from the "website developer" and others, although the logic of the sentence would suggest that they are the same. Choice D is incorrect because it lacks the punctuation necessary to link the independent clause and the list.

QUESTION 33

Choice A is the best answer because it provides a phrase that is consistent with standard English usage and also maintains the tone and style of the passage.

Choice B is incorrect because "give some wisdom" deviates from standard English usage and presents a somewhat colloquial phrase in a text that is generally free of colloquialisms. Choices C and D are incorrect because both are inconsistent with the tone of the passage as well as its purpose. The focus of the paragraph is on sharing, not on proclaiming opinions.

QUESTION 34

Choice A is the best answer because it offers a phrase that introduces a basic definition of philosophy and thereby fits the sentence.

Choices B, C, and D are incorrect because each offers a transition that does not suit the purpose of the sentence.

QUESTION 35

Choice A is the best answer because it offers the most succinct comparison between the basic definition of philosophy and the fact that students can gain specific, practical skills from the study of philosophy. There is no need to include the participle "speaking" in this sentence, as it is clear from context that the writer is offering a different perspective.

Choices B, C, and D are incorrect because they provide options that are unnecessarily wordy.

QUESTION 36

Choice B is the best answer because it provides a verb that creates a grammatically complete, standard, and coherent sentence.

Choices A, C, and D are incorrect because each results in a grammatically incomplete and incoherent sentence.

QUESTION 37

Choice D is the best answer because it most effectively sets up the information in the following sentences, which state that (according to information from the 1990s) "only 18 percent of American colleges required at least one philosophy course," and "more than 400 independent philosophy departments were eliminated" from colleges. These details are most logically linked to the claim that "colleges have not always supported the study of philosophy."

Choices A, B, and C are incorrect because none of these effectively sets up the information that follows, which is about colleges' failure to support the study of philosophy.

QUESTION 38

Choice C is the best answer because it provides a transition that logically connects the information in the previous sentence to the information in this one. Both sentences provide evidence of colleges' lack of support of philosophy programs, so the adverb "Moreover," which means "In addition," accurately captures the relationship between the two sentences.

Choices A, B, and D are incorrect because each presents a transition that does not accurately depict or support the relationship between the two sentences. The second sentence is not a result of the first ("Therefore," "Thus"), and the sentences do not provide a contrast ("However").

QUESTION 39

Choice A is the best answer because it succinctly expresses the idea that "students who major in philosophy often do better . . . as measured by standardized test scores."

Choices B and D are incorrect because they introduce a redundancy and a vague term, "results." The first part of the sentence mentions a research finding or conclusion but does not directly address any "results," so it is confusing to refer to "these results" and indicate that they "can be" or "are measured by standardized test scores." The best way to express the idea is simply to say that some students "often do better" than some other students "in both verbal reasoning and analytical writing as measured by standardized test scores." Choice C is incorrect because there is no indication that multiple criteria are used to evaluate students' "verbal reasoning and analytical writing": test scores and something else. Only test scores are mentioned.

QUESTION 40

Choice B is the best answer because it provides subject-verb agreement and thus creates a grammatically correct and coherent sentence.

Choice A is incorrect because the verb "has scored" does not correspond with the plural subject "students." Similarly, Choice C is incorrect because the verb "scores" would correspond with a singular subject, but not the plural subject present in this sentence. Choice D is incorrect because it results in a grammatically incomplete and incoherent sentence.

QUESTION 41

Choice B is the best answer because it provides a coherent and grammatically standard sentence.

Choices A and D are incorrect because both present "students" in the possessive form, whereas the sentence establishes "students" as the subject ("many students . . . have"). Choice C is incorrect because the verb form it proposes results in an incomplete and incoherent sentence.

QUESTION 42

Choice C is the best answer because it accurately depicts how inserting this sentence would affect the overall paragraph. The fact that Plato used the dialogue form has little relevance to the preceding claim about the usefulness of a philosophy background.

Choices A and B are incorrect because the proposed sentence interrupts the progression of reasoning in the paragraph. Choice D is incorrect because, as with Choice A, Plato's works have nothing to do with "the employability of philosophy majors."

QUESTION 43

Choice D is the best answer because it creates a complete and coherent sentence.

Choices A, B, and C are incorrect because each inserts an unnecessary relative pronoun or conjunction, resulting in a sentence without a main verb.

QUESTION 44

Choice D is the best answer because it provides a possessive pronoun that is consistent with the sentence's plural subject "students," thus creating a grammatically sound sentence.

Choices A, B, and C are incorrect because each proposes a possessive pronoun that is inconsistent with the plural noun "students," the established subject of the sentence.

Section 3: Math Test – No Calculator

QUESTION 1

Choice D is correct. Since $k = 3$, one can substitute 3 for k in the equation $\frac{x-1}{3} = k$, which gives $\frac{x-1}{3} = 3$. Multiplying both sides of $\frac{x-1}{3} = 3$ by 3 gives $x - 1 = 9$ and then adding 1 to both sides of $x - 1 = 9$ gives $x = 10$.

Choices A, B, and C are incorrect because the result of subtracting 1 from the value and dividing by 3 is not the given value of k, which is 3.

QUESTION 2

Choice A is correct. To calculate $(7 + 3i) + (-8 + 9i)$, add the real parts of each complex number, $7 + (-8) = -1$, and then add the imaginary parts, $3i + 9i = 12i$. The result is $-1 + 12i$.

Choices B, C, and D are incorrect and likely result from common errors that arise when adding complex numbers. For example, choice B is the result of adding $3i$ and $-9i$, and choice C is the result of adding 7 and 8.

QUESTION 3

Choice C is correct. The total number of text messages sent by Armand can be found by multiplying his rate of texting, in number of text messages sent per hour, by the total number of hours he spent sending them; that is m texts/hour × 5 hours = $5m$ texts. Similarly, the total number of text messages sent by Tyrone is his hourly rate of texting multiplied by the 4 hours he spent texting: p texts/hour × 4 hours = $4p$ texts. The total number of text messages sent by Armand and Tyrone is the sum of the total number of messages sent by Armand and the total number of messages sent by Tyrone: $5m + 4p$.

Choice A is incorrect and arises from adding the coefficients and multiplying the variables of $5m$ and $4p$. Choice B is incorrect and is the result of multiplying $5m$ and $4p$. The total number of messages sent by Armand and Tyrone should be the sum of $5m$ and $4p$, not the product of these terms. Choice D is incorrect because it multiplies Armand's number of hours spent texting by Tyrone's hourly rate of texting, and vice versa. This mix-up results in an expression that does not equal the total number of messages sent by Armand and Tyrone.

QUESTION 4

Choice B is correct. The value 108 in the equation is the value of P in $P = 108 - 23d$ when $d = 0$. When $d = 0$, Kathy has worked 0 days that week. In other words, 108 is the number of phones left before Kathy has started work for the week. Therefore, the meaning of the value 108 in the equation is that Kathy starts each week with 108 phones to fix.

Choice A is incorrect because Kathy will complete the repairs when $P = 0$. Since $P = 108 - 23d$, this will occur when $0 = 108 - 23d$ or when $d = \frac{108}{23}$, not when $d = 108$. Therefore, the value 108 in the equation does not represent the number of days it will take Kathy to complete the repairs. Choices C and D are incorrect because the number 23 in $P = 108 - 23d$ indicates that the number of phones left will decrease by 23 for each increase in the value of d by 1; in other words, Kathy is repairing phones at a rate of 23 per day, not 108 per hour (choice C) or 108 per day (choice D).

QUESTION 5

Choice C is correct. Only like terms, with the same variables and exponents, can be combined to determine the answer as shown here:

$$\begin{aligned}
&(x^2y - 3y^2 + 5xy^2) - (-x^2y + 3xy^2 - 3y^2)\\
&= (x^2y - (-x^2y)) + (-3y^2 - (-3y^2)) + (5xy^2 - 3xy^2)\\
&= 2x^2y + 0 + 2xy^2\\
&= 2x^2y + 2xy^2
\end{aligned}$$

Choices A, B, and D are incorrect and are the result of common calculation errors or of incorrectly combining like and unlike terms.

QUESTION 6

Choice A is correct. In the equation $h = 3a + 28.6$, if a, the age of the boy, increases by 1, then h becomes $h = 3(a + 1) + 28.6 = 3a + 3 + 28.6 = (3a + 28.6) + 3$. Therefore, the model estimates that the boy's height increases by 3 inches each year.

Alternatively: The height, h, is a linear function of the age, a, of the boy. The coefficient 3 can be interpreted as the rate of change of the function; in this case, the rate of change can be described as a change of 3 inches in height for every additional year in age.

Choices B, C, and D are incorrect and are likely the result of dividing 28.6 by 5, 3, and 2, respectively. The number 28.6 is the estimated height, in inches, of a newborn boy. However, dividing 28.6 by 5, 3, or 2 has no meaning in the context of this question.

QUESTION 7

Choice B is correct. Since the right-hand side of the equation is P times the expression $\frac{\left(\frac{r}{1{,}200}\right)\left(1+\frac{r}{1{,}200}\right)^N}{\left(1+\frac{r}{1{,}200}\right)^N-1}$, multiplying both sides of the equation by the reciprocal of this expression results in $\frac{\left(1+\frac{r}{1{,}200}\right)^N-1}{\left(\frac{r}{1{,}200}\right)\left(1+\frac{r}{1{,}200}\right)^N}m = P$.

Choice A is incorrect and is the result of multiplying both sides of the equation by the rational expression $\frac{\left(\frac{r}{1{,}200}\right)\left(1+\frac{r}{1{,}200}\right)^N}{\left(1+\frac{r}{1{,}200}\right)^N-1}$ rather than by the reciprocal of this expression $\frac{\left(1+\frac{r}{1{,}200}\right)^N-1}{\left(\frac{r}{1{,}200}\right)\left(1+\frac{r}{1{,}200}\right)^N}$. Choices C and D are incorrect and are likely the result of errors while trying to solve for P.

QUESTION 8

Choice C is correct. Since $\frac{a}{b} = 2$, it follows that $\frac{b}{a} = \frac{1}{2}$. Multiplying both sides of the equation by 4 gives $4\left(\frac{b}{a}\right) = 4\left(\frac{1}{2}\right)$, or $\frac{4b}{a} = 2$.

Choice A is incorrect because if $\frac{4b}{a} = 0$, then $\frac{a}{b}$ would be undefined.

Choice B is incorrect because if $\frac{4b}{a} = 1$, then $\frac{a}{b} = 4$. Choice D is incorrect because if $\frac{4b}{a} = 4$, then $\frac{a}{b} = 1$.

QUESTION 9

Choice B is correct. Adding x and 19 to both sides of $2y - x = -19$ gives $x = 2y + 19$. Then, substituting $2y + 19$ for x in $3x + 4y = -23$ gives $3(2y + 19) + 4y = -23$. This last equation is equivalent to $10y + 57 = -23$. Solving $10y + 57 = -23$ gives $y = -8$. Finally, substituting -8 for y in $2y - x = -19$ gives $2(-8) - x = -19$, or $x = 3$. Therefore, the solution (x, y) to the given system of equations is $(3, -8)$.

Choices A, C, and D are incorrect because when the given values of x and y are substituted in $2y - x = -19$, the value of the left side of the equation does not equal -19.

QUESTION 10

Choice A is correct. Since g is an even function, $g(-4) = g(4) = 8$.

Alternatively: First find the value of a, and then find $g(-4)$. Since $g(4) = 8$, substituting 4 for x and 8 for $g(x)$ gives $8 = a(4)^2 + 24 = 16a + 24$. Solving this last equation gives $a = -1$. Thus $g(x) = -x^2 + 24$, from which it follows that $g(-4) = -(-4)^2 + 24$; $g(-4) = -16 + 24$; and $g(-4) = 8$.

Choices B, C, and D are incorrect because g is a function and there can only be one value of $g(-4)$.

QUESTION 11

Choice D is correct. To determine the price per pound of beef when it was equal to the price per pound of chicken, determine the value of x (the number of weeks after July 1) when the two prices were equal. The prices were equal when $b = c$; that is, when $2.35 + 0.25x = 1.75 + 0.40x$. This last equation is equivalent to $0.60 = 0.15x$, and so $x = \frac{0.60}{0.15} = 4$. Then to determine b, the price per pound of beef, substitute 4 for x in $b = 2.35 + 0.25x$, which gives $b = 2.35 + 0.25(4) = 3.35$ dollars per pound.

Choice A is incorrect. It results from substituting the value 1, not 4, for x in $b = 2.35 + 0.25x$. Choice B is incorrect. It results from substituting the value 2, not 4, for x in $b = 2.35 + 0.25x$. Choice C is incorrect. It results from substituting the value 3, not 4, for x in $c = 1.75 + 0.40x$.

QUESTION 12

Choice D is correct. In the xy-plane, all lines that pass through the origin are of the form $y = mx$, where m is the slope of the line. Therefore, the equation of this line is $y = \frac{1}{7}x$, or $x = 7y$. A point with coordinates (a, b) will lie on the line if and only if $a = 7b$. Of the given choices, only choice D, (14, 2), satisfies this condition: $14 = 7(2)$.

Choice A is incorrect because the line determined by the origin (0, 0) and (0, 7) is the vertical line with equation $x = 0$; that is, the y-axis. The slope of the y-axis is undefined, not $\frac{1}{7}$. Therefore, the point (0, 7) does not lie on the line that passes the origin and has slope $\frac{1}{7}$. Choices B and C are incorrect because neither of the ordered pairs has a y-coordinate that is $\frac{1}{7}$ the value of the corresponding x-coordinate.

QUESTION 13

Choice B is correct. To rewrite $\dfrac{1}{\frac{1}{x+2}+\frac{1}{x+3}}$, multiply by $\frac{(x+2)(x+3)}{(x+2)(x+3)}$. This results in the expression $\frac{(x+2)(x+3)}{(x+2)+(x+3)}$, which is equivalent to the expression in choice B.

Choices A, C, and D are incorrect and could be the result of common algebraic errors that arise while manipulating a complex fraction.

QUESTION 14

Choice A is correct. One approach is to express $\frac{8^x}{2^y}$ so that the numerator and denominator are expressed with the same base. Since 2 and 8 are both powers of 2, substituting 2^3 for 8 in the numerator of $\frac{8^x}{2^y}$ gives $\frac{(2^3)^x}{2^y}$, which can be rewritten as $\frac{2^{3x}}{2^y}$. Since the numerator and denominator of $\frac{2^{3x}}{2^y}$ have a common base, this expression can be rewritten as 2^{3x-y}. It is given that $3x - y = 12$, so one can substitute 12 for the exponent, $3x - y$, given that the expression $\frac{8^x}{2^y}$ is equal to 2^{12}.

Choice B is incorrect. The expression $\frac{8^x}{2^y}$ can be rewritten as $\frac{2^{3x}}{2^y}$, or 2^{3x-y}. If the value of 2^{3x-y} is 4^4, which can be rewritten as 28, then $2^{3x-y} = 2^8$, which results in $3x - y = 8$, not 12. Choice C is incorrect. If the value of $\frac{8^x}{2^y}$ is 8^2, then $2^{3x-y} = 8^2$, which results in $3x - y = 6$, not 12. Choice D is incorrect because the value of $\frac{8^x}{2^y}$ can be determined.

QUESTION 15

Choice D is correct. One can find the possible values of a and b in $(ax + 2)(bx + 7)$ by using the given equation $a + b = 8$ and finding another equation that relates the variables a and b. Since $(ax + 2)(bx + 7) = 15x^2 + cx + 14$, one can expand the left side of the equation to obtain $abx^2 + 7ax + 2bx + 14 = 15x^2 + cx + 14$. Since ab is the coefficient of x^2 on the left side of the equation and 15 is the coefficient of x^2 on the right side of the equation, it must be true that $ab = 15$. Since $a + b = 8$, it follows that $b = 8 - a$. Thus, $ab = 15$ can be rewritten as $a(8 - a) = 15$, which in turn can be rewritten as $a^2 - 8a + 15 = 0$. Factoring gives $(a - 3)(a - 5) = 0$. Thus, either $a = 3$ and $b = 5$, or $a = 5$ and $b = 3$. If $a = 3$ and $b = 5$, then $(ax + 2)(bx + 7) = (3x + 2)(5x + 7) = 15x^2 + 31x + 14$. Thus, one of the possible values of c is 31. If $a = 5$ and $b = 3$, then $(ax + 2)(bx + 7) = (5x + 2)(3x + 7) = 15x^2 + 41x + 14$. Thus, another possible value for c is 41. Therefore, the two possible values for c are 31 and 41.

Choice A is incorrect; the numbers 3 and 5 are possible values for a and b, but not possible values for c. Choice B is incorrect; if $a = 5$ and $b = 3$, then 6 and 35 are the coefficients of x when the expression $(5x + 2)(3x + 7)$ is expanded as $15x^2 + 35x + 6x + 14$. However, when the coefficients of x are 6 and 35, the value of c is 41 and not 6 and 35. Choice C is incorrect; if $a = 3$ and $b = 5$, then 10 and 21 are the coefficients of x when the expression $(3x + 2)(5x + 7)$ is expanded as $15x^2 + 21x + 10x + 14$. However, when the coefficients of x are 10 and 21, the value of c is 31 and not 10 and 21.

QUESTION 16

The correct answer is 2. To solve for t, factor the left side of $t^2 - 4 = 0$, giving $(t - 2)(t + 2) = 0$. Therefore, either $t - 2 = 0$ or $t + 2 = 0$. If $t - 2 = 0$, then $t = 2$, and if $t + 2 = 0$, then $t = -2$. Since it is given that $t > 0$, the value of t must be 2.

Another way to solve for t is to add 4 to both sides of $t^2 - 4 = 0$, giving $t^2 = 4$. Then, taking the square root of the left and the right side of the equation gives $t = \pm\sqrt{4} = \pm 2$. Since it is given that $t > 0$, the value of t must be 2.

QUESTION 17

The correct answer is 1600. It is given that $\angle AEB$ and $\angle CDB$ have the same measure. Since $\angle ABE$ and $\angle CBD$ are vertical angles, they have the same measure. Therefore, triangle EAB is similar to triangle DCB because the triangles have two pairs of congruent corresponding angles (angle-angle criterion for similarity of triangles). Since the triangles are similar, the corresponding sides are in the same proportion; thus $\frac{CD}{x} = \frac{BD}{EB}$. Substituting the given values of 800 for CD, 700 for BD, and 1400 for EB in $\frac{CD}{x} = \frac{BD}{EB}$ gives $\frac{800}{x} = \frac{700}{1400}$. Therefore, $x = \frac{(800)(1400)}{700} = 1600$.

QUESTION 18

The correct answer is 7. Subtracting the left and right sides of $x + y = -9$ from the corresponding sides of $x + 2y = -25$ gives $(x + 2y) - (x + y) = -25 - (-9)$, which is equivalent to $y = -16$. Substituting -16 for y in $x + y = -9$ gives $x + (-16) = -9$, which is equivalent to $x = -9 - (-16) = 7$.

QUESTION 19

The correct answer is $\frac{4}{5}$ or 0.8. By the complementary angle relationship for sine and cosine, $\sin(x°) = \cos(90° - x°)$. Therefore, $\cos(90° - x°) = \frac{4}{5}$. Either the fraction 4/5 or its decimal equivalent, 0.8, may be gridded as the correct answer.

Alternatively, one can construct a right triangle that has an angle of measure $x°$ such that $\sin(x°) = \frac{4}{5}$, as shown in the figure below, where $\sin(x°)$ is equal to the ratio of the length of the side opposite the angle measuring $x°$ to the length of the hypotenuse, or $\frac{4}{5}$.

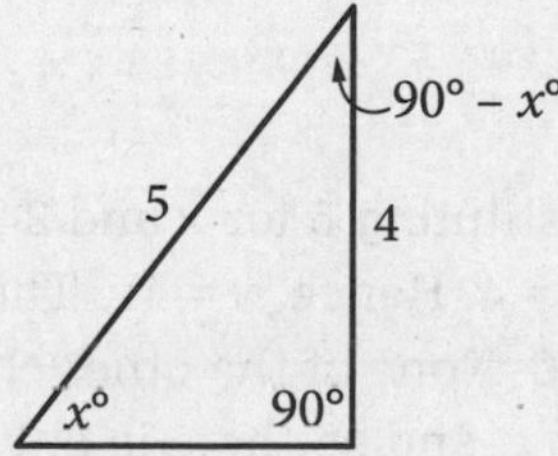

Since two of the angles of the triangle are of measure $x°$ and $90°$, the third angle must have the measure $180° - 90° - x° = 90° - x°$. From the figure, $\cos(90° - x°)$, which is equal to the ratio of the length of the side adjacent to the angle measuring $90° - x°$ to the hypotenuse, is also $\frac{4}{5}$.

QUESTION 20

The correct answer is 100. Since $a = 5\sqrt{2}$, one can substitute $5\sqrt{2}$ for a in $2a = \sqrt{2x}$, giving $10\sqrt{2} = \sqrt{2x}$. Squaring each side of $10\sqrt{2} = \sqrt{2x}$ gives $(10\sqrt{2})^2 = (\sqrt{2x})^2$, which simplifies to $(10)^2(\sqrt{2})^2 = (\sqrt{2x})^2$, or $200 = 2x$. This gives $x = 100$. To verify, substitute 100 for x and $5\sqrt{2}$ for a in the equation $2a = \sqrt{2x}$, which yields $2(5\sqrt{2}) = \sqrt{(2)(100)}$; this is true since $2(5\sqrt{2}) = 10\sqrt{2}$ and $\sqrt{(2)(100)} = \sqrt{2}\sqrt{100} = 10\sqrt{2}$.

Section 4: Math Test – Calculator

QUESTION 1

Choice B is correct. On the graph, a line segment with a positive slope represents an interval over which the target heart rate is strictly increasing as time passes. A horizontal line segment represents an interval over which there is no change in the target heart rate as time passes, and a line segment with a negative slope represents an interval over which the target heart rate is strictly decreasing as time passes. Over the interval between 40 and 60 minutes, the graph consists of a line segment with a positive slope followed by a line segment with a negative slope, with no horizontal line segment in between, indicating that the target heart rate is strictly increasing then strictly decreasing.

Choice A is incorrect because the graph over the interval between 0 and 30 minutes contains a horizontal line segment, indicating a period in which there was no change in the target heart rate. Choice C is incorrect because the graph over the interval between 50 and 65 minutes consists of a line segment with a negative slope followed by a line segment with a positive slope, indicating that the target heart rate is strictly decreasing then strictly increasing. Choice D is incorrect because the graph over the interval between 70 and 90 minutes contains horizontal line segments and no segment with a negative slope.

QUESTION 2

Choice C is correct. Substituting 6 for x and 24 for y in $y = kx$ gives $24 = (k)(6)$, which gives $k = 4$. Hence, $y = 4x$. Therefore, when $x = 5$, the value of y is $(4)(5) = 20$. None of the other choices for y is correct because y is a function of x, and so there is only one y-value for a given x-value.

Choices A, B, and D are incorrect. Choice A is the result of substituting 6 for y and substituting 5 for x in the equation $y = kx$, when solving for k. Choice B results from substituting 3 for k and 5 for x in the equation $y = kx$, when solving for y. Choice D results from using $y = k + x$ instead of $y = kx$.

QUESTION 3

Choice D is correct. Consider the measures of ∠3 and ∠4 in the figure below.

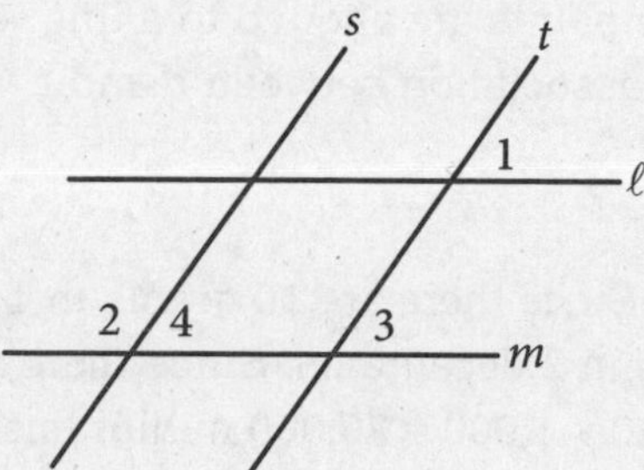

The measure of ∠3 is equal to the measure of ∠1 because they are corresponding angles for the parallel lines ℓ and *m* intersected by the transversal line *t*. Similarly, the measure of ∠3 is equal to the measure of ∠4 because they are corresponding angles for the parallel lines *s* and *t* intersected by the transversal line *m*. Since the measure of ∠1 is 35°, the measures of ∠3 and ∠4 are also 35°. Since ∠4 and ∠2 are supplementary angles, the sum of the measures of these two angles is 180°. Therefore, the measure of ∠2 is 180° − 35° = 145°.

Choice A is incorrect because 35° is the measure of ∠1, and ∠1 is not congruent to ∠2. Choice B is incorrect because it is the measure of the complementary angle of ∠1, and ∠1 and ∠2 are not complementary angles. Choice C is incorrect because it is double the measure of ∠1, which cannot be inferred from the information given.

QUESTION 4

Choice C is correct. The description "$16 + 4x$ is 10 more than 14" can be written as the equation $16 + 4x = 10 + 14$, which is equivalent to $16 + 4x = 24$. Subtracting 16 from each side of $16 + 4x = 24$ gives $4x = 8$. Since $8x$ is 2 times $4x$, multiplying both sides of $4x = 8$ by 2 gives $8x = 16$. Therefore, the value of $8x$ is 16.

Choice A is incorrect because it is the value of x, not $8x$. Choices B and D are incorrect and may be the result of errors made when solving the equation $16 + 4x = 10 + 14$ for x. For example, choice D could be the result of subtracting 16 from the left side of the equation and adding 16 to the right side of the equation $16 + 4x = 10 + 14$, giving $4x = 40$ and $8x = 80$.

QUESTION 5

Choice D is correct. A graph with a strong negative association between *d* and *t* would have the points on the graph closely aligned with a line that has a negative slope. The more closely the points on a graph are aligned with a line, the stronger the association between *d* and *t*, and a negative slope indicates a negative association. Of the four graphs, the points on graph D are most closely aligned with a line with a negative slope. Therefore, the graph in choice D has the strongest negative association between *d* and *t*.

Choice A is incorrect because the points are more scattered than the points in choice D, indicating a weaker negative association between d and t. Choice B is incorrect because the points are aligned to either a curve or possibly a line with a small positive slope. Choice C is incorrect because the points are aligned to a line with a positive slope, indicating a positive association between d and t.

QUESTION 6

Choice D is correct. Since there are 10 grams in 1 decagram, there are $2 \times 10 = 20$ grams in 2 decagrams. Since there are 1,000 milligrams in 1 gram, there are $20 \times 1{,}000 = 20{,}000$ milligrams in 20 grams. Therefore, 20,000 1-milligram doses of the medicine can be stored in a 2-decagram container.

Choice A is incorrect; 0.002 is the number of grams in 2 milligrams. Choice B is incorrect; it could result from multiplying by 1,000 and dividing by 10 instead of multiplying by both 1,000 and 10 when converting from decagrams to milligrams. Choice C is incorrect; 2,000 is the number of milligrams in 2 grams, not the number of milligrams in 2 decagrams.

QUESTION 7

Choice C is correct. Let x represent the number of installations that each unit on the y-axis represents. Then $9x$, $5x$, $6x$, $4x$, and $3.5x$ are the number of rooftops with solar panel installations in cities A, B, C, D, and E, respectively. Since the total number of rooftops is 27,500, it follows that $9x + 5x + 6x + 4x + 3.5x = 27{,}500$, which simplifies to $27.5x = 27{,}500$. Thus, $x = 1{,}000$. Therefore, an appropriate label for the y-axis is "Number of installations (in thousands)."

Choices A, B, and D are incorrect and may result from errors when setting up and calculating the units for the y-axis.

QUESTION 8

Choice D is correct. If the value of $|n - 1| + 1$ is equal to 0, then $|n - 1| + 1 = 0$. Subtracting 1 from both sides of this equation gives $|n - 1| = -1$. The expression $|n - 1|$ on the left side of the equation is the absolute value of $n - 1$, and the absolute value of a quantity can never be negative. Thus $|n - 1| = -1$ has no solution. Therefore, there are no values for n for which the value of $|n - 1| + 1$ is equal to 0.

Choice A is incorrect because $|0 - 1| + 1 = 1 + 1 = 2$, not 0. Choice B is incorrect because $|1 - 1| + 1 = 0 + 1 = 1$, not 0. Choice C is incorrect because $|2 - 1| + 1 = 1 + 1 = 2$, not 0.

QUESTION 9

Choice A is correct. Subtracting 1,052 from both sides of the equation $a = 1{,}052 + 1.08t$ gives $a - 1{,}052 = 1.08t$. Then dividing both sides of $a - 1{,}052 = 1.08t$ by 1.08 gives $t = \frac{a - 1{,}052}{1.08}$.

Choices B, C, and D are incorrect and could arise from errors in rewriting $a = 1{,}052 + 1.08t$. For example, choice B could result if 1,052 is added to the left side of $a = 1{,}052 + 1.08t$ and subtracted from the right side, and then both sides are divided by 1.08.

QUESTION 10

Choice B is correct. The air temperature at which the speed of a sound wave is closest to 1,000 feet per second can be found by substituting 1,000 for a and then solving for t in the given formula. Substituting 1,000 for a in the equation $a = 1{,}052 + 1.08t$ gives $1{,}000 = 1{,}052 + 1.08t$. Subtracting 1,052 from both sides of the equation $1{,}000 = 1{,}052 + 1.08t$ and then dividing both sides of the equation by 1.08 yields $t = \frac{-52}{1.08} \approx -48.15$. Of the choices given, −48°F is closest to −48.15°F.

Choices A, C, and D are incorrect and might arise from errors made when substituting 1,000 for a or solving for t in the equation $a = 1{,}052 + 1.08t$ or in rounding the result to the nearest integer. For example, choice C could be the result of rounding −48.15 to −49 instead of −48.

QUESTION 11

Choice A is correct. Subtracting $3x$ and adding 3 to both sides of $3x - 5 \geq 4x - 3$ gives $-2 \geq x$. Therefore, x is a solution to $3x - 5 \geq 4x - 3$ if and only if x is less than or equal to −2 and x is NOT a solution to $3x - 5 \geq 4x - 3$ if and only if x is greater than −2. Of the choices given, only −1 is greater than −2 and, therefore, cannot be a value of x.

Choices B, C, and D are incorrect because each is a value of x that is less than or equal to −2 and, therefore, could be a solution to the inequality.

QUESTION 12

Choice C is correct. The average number of seeds per apple is the total number of seeds in the 12 apples divided by the number of apples, which is 12. On the graph, the horizontal axis is the number of seeds per apple and the height of each bar is the number of apples with the corresponding number of seeds. The first bar on the left indicates that 2 apples have 3 seeds each, the second bar indicates that 4 apples have 5 seeds each, the third bar indicates that 1 apple has 6 seeds, the fourth bar indicates that 2 apples have 7 seeds each, and the fifth bar indicates that 3 apples have 9 seeds each. Thus, the total number of seeds for the 12 apples is $(2 \times 3) + (4 \times 5) + (1 \times 6) + (2 \times 7) + (3 \times 9) = 73$, and the average number of seeds per apple is $\frac{73}{12} = 6.08$. Of the choices given, 6 is closest to 6.08.

Choice A is incorrect; it is the number of apples represented by the tallest bar but is not the average number of seeds for the 12 apples. Choice B is incorrect; it is the number of seeds per apple corresponding to the tallest bar, but is not the average number of seeds for the 12 apples. Choice D is incorrect; a student might choose this value by correctly calculating the average number of seeds, 6.08, but incorrectly rounding up to 7.

QUESTION 13

Choice C is correct. From the table, there was a total of 310 survey respondents, and 19% of all survey respondents is equivalent to $\frac{19}{100} \times 310 = 58.9$ respondents. Of the choices given, 59, the number of males taking Geometry, is closest to 58.9 respondents.

Choices A, B, and D are incorrect because the number of males taking Geometry is closer to 58.9 (which is 19% of 310) than the number of respondents in each of these categories.

QUESTION 14

Choice C is correct. The range of the lengths of the 21 fish represented in the table is $24 - 8 = 16$ inches, and the range of the remaining 20 lengths after the 24-inch measurement is removed is $16 - 8 = 8$ inches. Therefore, after the 24-inch measurement is removed, the change in range, 8 inches, is much greater than the change in the mean or median.

Choice A is incorrect. Let m be the mean of the lengths, in inches, of the 21 fish. Then the sum of the lengths, in inches, of the 21 fish is $21m$. After the 24-inch measurement is removed, the sum of the lengths, in inches, of the remaining 20 fish is $21m - 24$, and the mean length, in inches, of these 20 fish is $\frac{21m - 24}{20}$, which is a change of $\frac{24 - m}{20}$ inches. Since m must be between the smallest and largest measurements of the 21 fish, it follows that $8 < m < 24$, from which it can be seen that the change in the mean, in inches, is between $\frac{24 - 24}{20} = 0$ and $\frac{24 - 8}{20} = \frac{4}{5}$, and so must be less than the change in the range, 8 inches. Choice B is incorrect because the median length of the 21 fish represented in the table is 12, and after the 24-inch measurement is removed, the median of the remaining 20 lengths is also 12. Therefore, the change in the median (0) is less than the change in the range (8). Choice D is incorrect because the changes in the mean, median, and range of the measurements are different.

QUESTION 15

Choice A is correct. The total cost C of renting a boat is the sum of the initial cost to rent the boat plus the product of the cost per hour and the number of hours, h, that the boat is rented. The C-intercept is the point on the C-axis where h, the number of hours the boat is rented, is 0. Therefore, the C-intercept is the initial cost of renting the boat.

Choice B is incorrect because the graph represents the cost of renting only one boat. Choice C is incorrect because the total number of hours of rental is represented by h-values, each of which corresponds to the first coordinate of a point on the graph not the C-intercept of the graph. Choice D is incorrect because the increase in cost for each additional hour is given by the slope of the line, not by the C-intercept.

QUESTION 16

Choice C is correct. If m is the slope and b is the C-intercept of the line, the relationship between h and C can be represented by $C = mh + b$. The C-intercept of the line is 5. Since the points (0, 5) and (1, 8) lie on the line, the slope of the line is $\frac{8-5}{1-0} = \frac{3}{1} = 3$. Therefore, the relationship between h and C can be represented by $C = 3h + 5$, the slope-intercept equation of the line.

Choices A and D are incorrect because each of these equations represents a line that passes through the origin (0, 0). However, C is not equal to zero when $h = 0$. Choice B is incorrect and may result from errors made when reading the scale on each axis as related to calculating the slope.

QUESTION 17

Choice B is correct. The minimum value of the function corresponds to the y-coordinate of the point on the graph that has the smallest y-coordinate on the graph. Since the smallest y-coordinate belongs to the point with coordinates (−3, −2), the minimum value of the graph is $f(-3) = -2$. Therefore, the minimum value of $f(x)$ is at $x = -3$.

Choice A is incorrect; −5 is the least value for an x-coordinate, not the y-coordinate, of a point on the graph of $y = f(x)$. Choice C is incorrect; it is the minimum value of f, not the value of x that corresponds to the minimum of f. Choice D is incorrect; it is the value of x for which the value of $f(x)$ has its maximum, not minimum.

QUESTION 18

Choice A is correct. Since (0, 0) is a solution to the system of inequalities, substituting 0 for x and 0 for y in the given system must result in two true inequalities. After this substitution, $y < -x + a$ becomes $0 < a$, and $y > x + b$ becomes $0 > b$. Hence, a is positive and b is negative. Therefore, $a > b$.

Choice B is incorrect because $b > a$ cannot be true if b is negative and a is positive. Choice C is incorrect because it is possible to find an example where (0, 0) is a solution to the system, but $|a| < |b|$; for example, if $a = 6$ and $b = -7$. Choice D is incorrect because the equation $a = -b$ doesn't have to be true; for example, (0, 0) is a solution to the system of inequalities if $a = 1$ and $b = -2$.

QUESTION 19

Choice B is correct. To determine the number of salads sold, write and solve a system of two equations. Let x equal the number of salads sold and let y equal the number of drinks sold. Since a total of 209 salads and drinks were sold, the equation $x + y = 209$ must hold. Since salads cost \$6.50 each, drinks cost \$2.00 each, and the total revenue from selling x salads and y drinks was \$836.50, the equation $6.50x + 2.00y = 836.50$ must also hold. The equation $x + y = 209$ is equivalent to $2x + 2y = 418$, and subtracting $(2x + 2y)$ from the left-hand side and subtracting 418 from the right-hand side of $6.50x + 2.00y = 836.50$ gives $4.5x = 418.50$. Therefore, the number of salads sold, x, was $x = \frac{418.50}{4.50} = 93$.

Choices A, C, and D are incorrect and could result from errors in writing the equations and solving the system of equations. For example, choice C could have been obtained by dividing the total revenue, \$836.50, by the total price of a salad and a drink, \$8.50, and then rounding up.

QUESTION 20

Choice D is correct. Let x be the original price of the computer, in dollars. The discounted price is 20 percent off the original price, so $x - 0.2x = 0.8x$ is the discounted price, in dollars. The sales tax is 8 percent of the discounted price, so $0.08(0.8x)$ represents the sales tax Alma paid. The price p, in dollars, that Alma paid the cashiers is the sum of the discounted price and the tax: $p = 0.8x + (0.08)(0.8x)$ which can be rewritten as $p = 1.08(0.8x)$. Therefore, the original price, x, of the computer, in dollars, can be written as $\frac{p}{(0.8)(1.08)}$ in terms of p.

Choices A, B, and C are incorrect. The expression in choice A represents 88% of the amount Alma paid to the cashier, and can be obtained by subtracting the discount of 20% from the original price and adding the sales tax of 8%. However, this is incorrect because 8% of the tax is over the discounted price, not the original one. The expression in choice B is the result of adding the factors associated with the discount and sales tax, 0.8 and .08, rather than multiplying them. The expression in choice C results from assigning p to represent the original price of the laptop, rather than to the amount Alma paid to the cashier.

QUESTION 21

Choice C is correct. The probability that a person from Group Y who recalled at least 1 dream was chosen at random from the group of all people who recalled at least 1 dream is equal to the number of people in Group Y who recalled at least 1 dream divided by the total number of people in the two groups who recalled at least 1 dream. The number of people in Group Y who recalled at least 1 dream is the sum of the 11 people in Group Y who recalled 1 to 4 dreams and the 68 people in Group Y who recalled 5 or more dreams: $11 + 68 = 79$. The total number of people who recalled at least 1 dream is the sum of the 79 people in Group Y who recalled at least 1 dream, the 28 people in Group X who recalled 1 to 4 dreams, and the 57 people in Group X who recalled 5 or more dreams: $79 + 28 + 57 = 164$. Therefore, the probability is $\frac{79}{164}$.

Choice A is incorrect; it is the probability of choosing at random a person from Group Y who recalled 5 or more dreams. Choice B is incorrect; it is the probability of choosing at random a person from Group Y who recalled at least 1 dream. Choice D is incorrect; it is the probability of choosing at random a person from the two groups combined who recalled at least 1 dream.

QUESTION 22

Choice B is correct. The amounts given in the table are in thousands of dollars. Therefore, the amount in the annual budget for agriculture/natural resources is actually \$488,106,000 in 2010 and \$358,708,000 in 2008. Therefore, the change in the budgeted amount is \$488,106,000 – \$358,708,000 = \$129,398,000. Hence, the average change in the annual budget for agriculture/natural resources from 2008 to 2010 is $\frac{\$129,398,000}{2} = \$64,699,000$ per year. Of the options given, this average rate of change is closest to \$65,000,000 per year.

Choices A and C are incorrect and may result from errors in setting up or calculating the average rate of change. Choice D is incorrect; \$130,000,000 is the approximate total change in the annual budget for agriculture/natural resources from 2008 to 2010, not the average rate of change from 2008 to 2010.

QUESTION 23

Choice B is correct. The human resources budget in 2007 was 4,051,050 thousand dollars, and the human resources budget in 2010 was 5,921,379 thousand dollars. Therefore, the ratio of the 2007 budget to the 2010 budget is slightly greater than $\frac{4}{6} = \frac{2}{3}$. Similar estimates for agriculture/natural resources give a ratio of the 2007 budget to the 2010 budget of slightly greater than $\frac{3}{4}$; for education, a ratio of slightly greater than $\frac{2}{3}$; for highways and transportation, a ratio of slightly less than $\frac{5}{6}$; and for public safety, a ratio of slightly greater than $\frac{5}{9}$. Therefore, of the given choices, education's ratio of the 2007 budget to the 2010 budget is closest to that of human resources.

Choices A, C, and D are incorrect because the ratio of the 2007 budget to 2010 budget for each of the programs given in these choices is further from the corresponding ratio for human resources than the corresponding ratio for education.

QUESTION 24

Choice A is correct. The equation of a circle can be written as $(x - h)^2 + (y - k)^2 = r^2$ where (h, k) are the coordinates of the center of the circle and r is the radius of the circle. Since the coordinates of the center of the circle are (0, 4), the equation of the circle is $x^2 + (y - 4)^2 = r^2$. The radius of the circle is the distance from the center, (0, 4), to the given endpoint of a radius, $\left(\frac{4}{3}, 5\right)$. By the distance formula, $r^2 = \left(\frac{4}{3} - 0\right)^2 + (5 - 4)^2 = \frac{25}{9}$. Therefore, an equation of the given circle is $x^2 + (y - 4)^2 = \frac{25}{9}$.

Choices B and D are incorrect. The equations given in these choices represent a circle with center (0, −4), not (0, 4). Choice C is incorrect; it results from using r instead of r^2 in the equation for the circle.

QUESTION 25

Choice D is correct. When the ball hits the ground, its height is 0 meters. Substituting 0 for h in $h = -4.9t^2 + 25t$ gives $0 = -4.9t^2 + 25t$, which can be rewritten as $0 = t(-4.9t + 25)$. Thus, the possible values of t are $t = 0$ and $t = \frac{25}{4.9} \approx 5.1$. The time $t = 0$ seconds corresponds to the time the ball is launched from the ground, and the time $t \approx 5.1$ seconds corresponds to the time after launch that the ball hits the ground. Of the given choices, 5.0 seconds is closest to 5.1 seconds, so the ball returns to the ground approximately 5.0 seconds after it is launched.

Choice A, B, and C are incorrect and could arise from conceptual or computation errors while solving $0 = -4.9t^2 + 25t$ for t.

QUESTION 26

Choice B is correct. Let x represent the number of pears produced by the Type B trees. Type A trees produce 20 percent more pears than Type B trees, or x, which can be represented as $x + 0.20x = 1.20x$ pears. Since Type A trees produce 144 pears, it follows that $1.20x = 144$. Thus $x = \frac{144}{1.20} = 120$. Therefore, the Type B trees produced 120 pears.

Choice A is incorrect because while 144 is reduced by approximately 20 percent, increasing 115 by 20 percent gives 138, not 144. Choice C is incorrect; it results from subtracting 20 from the number of pears produced by the Type A trees. Choice D is incorrect; it results from adding 20 percent of the number of pears produced by Type A trees to the number of pears produced by Type A trees.

QUESTION 27

Choice C is correct. The area of the field is 100 square meters. Each 1-meter-by-1-meter square has an area of 1 square meter. Thus, on average, the earthworm counts to a depth of 5 centimeters for each of the regions investigated by the students should be about $\frac{1}{100}$ of the total number of earthworms to a depth of 5 centimeters in the entire field. Since the counts for the smaller regions are from 107 to 176, the estimate for the entire field should be between 10,700 and 17,600. Therefore, of the given choices, 15,000 is a reasonable estimate for the number of earthworms to a depth of 5 centimeters in the entire field.

Choice A is incorrect; 150 is the approximate number of earthworms in 1 square meter. Choice B is incorrect; it results from using 10 square meters as the area of the field. Choice D is incorrect; it results from using 1,000 square meters as the area of the field.

QUESTION 28

Choice C is correct. To determine which quadrant does not contain any solutions to the system of inequalities, graph the inequalities. Graph the inequality $y \geq 2x + 1$ by drawing a line through the y-intercept (0, 1) and the point (1, 3), as shown. The solutions to this inequality are all points contained on and above this line. Graph the inequality $y > \frac{1}{2}x - 1$ by drawing a dashed line through the y-intercept (0, −1) and the point (2, 0), as shown. The solutions to this inequality are all points above this dashed line.

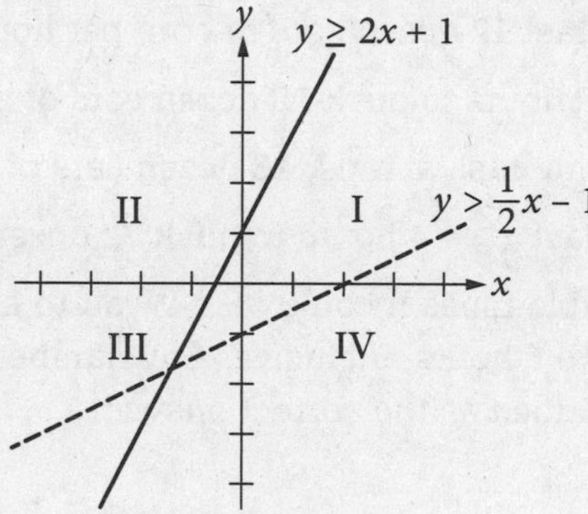

The solution to the system of inequalities is the intersection of the regions above the graphs of both lines. It can be seen that the solutions only include points in quadrants I, II, and III and do not include any points in quadrant IV.

Choices A and B are incorrect because quadrants II and III contain solutions to the system of inequalities, as shown in the figure above. Choice D is incorrect because there are no solutions in quadrant IV.

QUESTION 29

Choice D is correct. If the polynomial $p(x)$ is divided by $x - 3$, the result can be written as $\frac{p(x)}{x-3} = q(x) + \frac{r}{x-3}$, where $q(x)$ is a polynomial and r is the remainder. Since $x - 3$ is a degree 1 polynomial, the remainder is a real number. Hence, $p(x)$ can be written as $p(x) = (x - 3)q(x) + r$, where r is a real number. It is given that $p(3) = -2$ so it must be true that $-2 = p(3) = (3 - 3)q(3) + r = (0)q(3) + r = r$. Therefore, the remainder when $p(x)$ is divided by $x - 3$ is −2.

Choice A is incorrect because $p(3) = -2$ does not imply that $p(5) = 0$. Choices B and C are incorrect because the remainder −2 or its opposite, 2, need not be a root of $p(x)$.

QUESTION 30

Choice D is correct. Any quadratic function q can be written in the form $q(x) = a(x - h)^2 + k$, where a, h, and k are constants and (h, k) is the vertex of the parabola when q is graphed in the coordinate plane. This form can be reached by completing the square in the expression that defines q. The equation of the graph is $y = x^2 - 2x - 15$.

Since the coefficient of x is -2, this equation can be written in terms of $(x-1)^2 = x^2 - 2x + 1$ as follows: $y = x^2 - 2x - 15 = (x^2 - 2x + 1) - 16 = (x-1)^2 - 16$. From this form of the equation, the coefficients of the vertex can be read as $(1, -16)$.

Choices A and C are incorrect because the coordinates of the vertex A do not appear as constants in these equations. Choice B is incorrect because it is not equivalent to the given equation.

QUESTION 31

The correct answer is any number between 4 and 6, inclusive. Since Wyatt can husk at least 12 dozen ears of corn per hour, it will take him no more than $\frac{72}{12} = 6$ hours to husk 72 dozen ears of corn. On the other hand, since Wyatt can husk at most 18 dozen ears of corn per hour, it will take him at least $\frac{72}{18} = 4$ hours to husk 72 dozen ears of corn. Therefore, the possible times it could take Wyatt to husk 72 dozen ears of corn are 4 hours to 6 hours, inclusive. Any number between 4 and 6, inclusive, can be gridded as the correct answer.

QUESTION 32

The correct answer is 107. Since the weight of the empty truck and its driver is 4500 pounds and each box weighs 14 pounds, the weight, in pounds, of the delivery truck, its driver, and x boxes is $4500 + 14x$. This weight is below the bridge's posted weight limit of 6000 pounds if $4500 + 14x < 6000$. Subtracting 4500 from both sides of this inequality and then dividing both sides by 14 yields $x < \frac{1500}{14}$ or $x < 107\frac{1}{7}$. Since the number of packages must be an integer, the maximum possible value for x that will keep the combined weight of the truck, its driver, and the x identical boxes below the bridge's posted weight limit is 107.

QUESTION 33

The correct answer is $\frac{5}{8}$ or .625. Based on the line graph, the number of portable media players sold in 2008 was 100 million, and the number of portable media players sold in 2011 was 160 million. Therefore, the number of portable media players sold in 2008 is $\frac{100 \text{ million}}{160 \text{ million}}$ of the portable media players sold in 2011. This fraction reduces to $\frac{5}{8}$. Either 5/8 or its decimal equivalent, .625, may be gridded as the correct answer.

QUESTION 34

The correct answer is 96. Since each day has a total of 24 hours of time slots available for the station to sell, there is a total of 48 hours of time slots available to sell on Tuesday and Wednesday. Each time slot is a 30-minute interval, which is equal to a $\frac{1}{2}$-hour interval. Therefore, there are $\frac{48 \text{ hours}}{\frac{1}{2} \text{ hours/time slot}} = 96$ time slots of 30 minutes for the station to sell on Tuesday and Wednesday.

QUESTION 35

The correct answer is 6. The volume of a cylinder is $\pi r^2 h$, where r is the radius of the base of the cylinder and h is the height of the cylinder. Since the storage silo is a cylinder with volume 72π cubic yards and height 8 yards, it follows that $72\pi = \pi r^2(8)$, where r is the radius of the base of the cylinder, in yards. Dividing both sides of the equation $72\pi = \pi r^2(8)$ by 8π gives $r^2 = 9$, and so the radius of the base of the cylinder is 3 yards. Therefore, the diameter of the base of the cylinder is 6 yards.

QUESTION 36

The correct answer is 3. The function $h(x)$ is undefined when the denominator of $\frac{1}{(x-5)^2 + 4(x-5) + 4}$ is equal to zero. The expression $(x-5)^2 + 4(x-5) + 4$ is a perfect square: $(x-5)^2 + 4(x-5) + 4 = ((x-5)+2)^2$, which can be rewritten as $(x-3)^2$. The expression $(x-3)^2$ is equal to zero if and only if $x = 3$. Therefore, the value of x for which $h(x)$ is undefined is 3.

QUESTION 37

The correct answer is 1.02. The initial deposit earns 2 percent interest compounded annually. Thus at the end of 1 year, the new value of the account is the initial deposit of \$100 plus 2 percent of the initial deposit: $\$100 + \frac{2}{100}(\$100) = \$100(1.02)$. Since the interest is compounded annually, the value at the end of each succeeding year is the sum of the previous year's value plus 2 percent of the previous year's value. This is again equivalent to multiplying the previous year's value by 1.02. Thus, after 2 years, the value will be $\$100(1.02)(1.02) = \$100(1.02)^2$; after 3 years, the value will be $\$100(1.02)^3$; and after t years, the value will be $\$100(1.02)^t$. Therefore, in the formula for the value for Jessica's account after t years, $\$100(x)^t$, the value of x must be 1.02.

QUESTION 38

The correct answer is 6.11. Jessica made an initial deposit of $100 into her account. The interest on her account is 2 percent compounded annually, so after 10 years, the value of her initial deposit has been multiplied 10 times by the factor $1 + 0.02 = 1.02$. Hence, after 10 years, Jessica's deposit is worth $\$100(1.02)^{10} = \$121.899$ to the nearest tenth of a cent. Tyshaun made an initial deposit of $100 into his account. The interest on his account is 2.5 percent compounded annually, so after 10 years, the value of his initial deposit has been multiplied 10 times by the factor $1 + 0.025 = 1.025$. Hence, after 10 years, Tyshaun's deposit is worth $\$100(1.025)^{10} = \$128.008$ to the nearest tenth of a cent. Hence, Jessica's initial deposit earned $21.899 and Tyshaun's initial deposit earned $28.008. Therefore, to the nearest cent, Tyshaun's initial deposit earned $6.11 more than Jessica's initial deposit.

The SAT®

Practice Test #2

Make time to take the practice test.
It's one of the best ways to get ready for the SAT.

After you've taken the practice test, score it right away at **sat.org/scoring**.

Test begins on the next page.

Reading Test

65 MINUTES, 52 QUESTIONS

Turn to Section 1 of your answer sheet to answer the questions in this section.

DIRECTIONS

Each passage or pair of passages below is followed by a number of questions. After reading each passage or pair, choose the best answer to each question based on what is stated or implied in the passage or passages and in any accompanying graphics (such as a table or graph).

Questions 1-10 are based on the following passage.

This passage is from Charlotte Brontë, *The Professor*, originally published in 1857.

No man likes to acknowledge that he has made a mistake in the choice of his profession, and every man, worthy of the name, will row long against wind and tide before he allows himself to cry out, "I am baffled!" and submits to be floated passively back to land. From the first week of my residence in X— I felt my occupation irksome. The thing itself—the work of copying and translating business-letters—was a dry and tedious task enough, but had that been all, I should long have borne with the nuisance; I am not of an impatient nature, and influenced by the double desire of getting my living and justifying to myself and others the resolution I had taken to become a tradesman, I should have endured in silence the rust and cramp of my best faculties; I should not have whispered, even inwardly, that I longed for liberty; I should have pent in every sigh by which my heart might have ventured to intimate its distress under the closeness, smoke, monotony, and joyless tumult of Bigben Close, and its panting desire for freer and fresher scenes; I should have set up the image of Duty, the fetish of Perseverance, in my small bedroom at Mrs. King's lodgings, and they two should have been my household gods, from which my darling, my cherished-in-secret, Imagination, the tender and the mighty, should never, either by softness or strength, have severed me. But this was not all; the antipathy which had sprung up between myself and my employer striking deeper root and spreading denser shade daily, excluded me from every glimpse of the sunshine of life; and I began to feel like a plant growing in humid darkness out of the slimy walls of a well.

Antipathy is the only word which can express the feeling Edward Crimsworth had for me—a feeling, in a great measure, involuntary, and which was liable to be excited by every, the most trifling movement, look, or word of mine. My southern accent annoyed him; the degree of education evinced in my language irritated him; my punctuality, industry, and accuracy, fixed his dislike, and gave it the high flavour and poignant relish of envy; he feared that I too should one day make a successful tradesman. Had I been in anything inferior to him, he would not have hated me so thoroughly, but I knew all that he knew, and, what was worse, he suspected that I kept the padlock of silence on mental wealth in which he was no sharer. If he could have once placed me in a ridiculous or mortifying position, he would have forgiven me much, but I was guarded by three faculties—Caution, Tact, Observation; and prowling and prying as was Edward's malignity, it could never baffle the lynx-eyes of these, my natural sentinels. Day by day did his malice watch my tact, hoping it would sleep, and prepared to steal snake-like on its slumber; but tact, if it be genuine, never sleeps.

CONTINUE

I had received my first quarter's wages, and was returning to my lodgings, possessed heart and soul with the pleasant feeling that the master who had paid me grudged every penny of that hard-earned pittance—(I had long ceased to regard Mr. Crimsworth as my brother—he was a hard, grinding master; he wished to be an inexorable tyrant: that was all). Thoughts, not varied but strong, occupied my mind; two voices spoke within me; again and again they uttered the same monotonous phrases. One said: "William, your life is intolerable." The other: "What can you do to alter it?" I walked fast, for it was a cold, frosty night in January; as I approached my lodgings, I turned from a general view of my affairs to the particular speculation as to whether my fire would be out; looking towards the window of my sitting-room, I saw no cheering red gleam.

1

Which choice best summarizes the passage?

A) A character describes his dislike for his new job and considers the reasons why.

B) Two characters employed in the same office become increasingly competitive.

C) A young man regrets privately a choice that he defends publicly.

D) A new employee experiences optimism, then frustration, and finally despair.

2

The main purpose of the opening sentence of the passage is to

A) establish the narrator's perspective on a controversy.

B) provide context useful in understanding the narrator's emotional state.

C) offer a symbolic representation of Edward Crimsworth's plight.

D) contrast the narrator's good intentions with his malicious conduct.

3

During the course of the first paragraph, the narrator's focus shifts from

A) recollection of past confidence to acknowledgment of present self-doubt.

B) reflection on his expectations of life as a tradesman to his desire for another job.

C) generalization about job dissatisfaction to the specifics of his own situation.

D) evaluation of factors making him unhappy to identification of alternatives.

4

The references to "shade" and "darkness" at the end of the first paragraph mainly have which effect?

A) They evoke the narrator's sense of dismay.

B) They reflect the narrator's sinister thoughts.

C) They capture the narrator's fear of confinement.

D) They reveal the narrator's longing for rest.

5

The passage indicates that Edward Crimsworth's behavior was mainly caused by his

A) impatience with the narrator's high spirits.

B) scorn of the narrator's humble background.

C) indignation at the narrator's rash actions.

D) jealousy of the narrator's apparent superiority.

6

The passage indicates that when the narrator began working for Edward Crimsworth, he viewed Crimsworth as a

A) harmless rival.

B) sympathetic ally.

C) perceptive judge.

D) demanding mentor.

CONTINUE

7

Which choice provides the best evidence for the answer to the previous question?

A) Lines 28-31 ("the antipathy . . . life")

B) Lines 38-40 ("My southern . . . irritated him")

C) Lines 54-56 ("Day . . . slumber")

D) Lines 61-62 ("I had . . . brother")

8

At the end of the second paragraph, the comparisons of abstract qualities to a lynx and a snake mainly have the effect of

A) contrasting two hypothetical courses of action.

B) conveying the ferocity of a resolution.

C) suggesting the likelihood of an altercation.

D) illustrating the nature of an adversarial relationship.

9

The passage indicates that, after a long day of work, the narrator sometimes found his living quarters to be

A) treacherous.

B) dreary.

C) predictable.

D) intolerable.

10

Which choice provides the best evidence for the answer to the previous question?

A) Lines 17-21 ("I should . . . scenes")

B) Lines 21-23 ("I should . . . lodgings")

C) Lines 64-67 ("Thoughts . . . phrases")

D) Lines 68-74 ("I walked . . . gleam")

CONTINUE

Questions 11-21 are based on the following passage and supplementary material.

This passage is adapted from Iain King, "Can Economics Be Ethical?" ©2013 by Prospect Publishing.

Recent debates about the economy have rediscovered the question, "is that right?", where "right" means more than just profits or efficiency.

Some argue that because the free markets allow for personal choice, they are already ethical. Others have accepted the ethical critique and embraced corporate social responsibility. But before we can label any market outcome as "immoral," or sneer at economists who try to put a price on being ethical, we need to be clear on what we are talking about.

There are different views on where ethics should apply when someone makes an economic decision. Consider Adam Smith, widely regarded as the founder of modern economics. He was a moral philosopher who believed sympathy for others was the basis for ethics (we would call it empathy nowadays). But one of his key insights in *The Wealth of Nations* was that acting on this empathy could be counter-productive—he observed people becoming better off when they put their own empathy aside, and interacted in a self-interested way. Smith justifies selfish behavior by the outcome. Whenever planners use cost-benefit analysis to justify a new railway line, or someone retrains to boost his or her earning power, or a shopper buys one to get one free, they are using the same approach: empathizing with someone, and seeking an outcome that makes that person as well off as possible—although the person they are empathizing with may be themselves in the future.

Instead of judging consequences, Aristotle said ethics was about having the right character—displaying virtues like courage and honesty. It is a view put into practice whenever business leaders are chosen for their good character. But it is a hard philosophy to teach—just how much loyalty should you show to a manufacturer that keeps losing money? Show too little and you're a "greed is good" corporate raider; too much and you're wasting money on unproductive capital. Aristotle thought there was a golden mean between the two extremes, and finding it was a matter of fine judgment. But if ethics is about character, it's not clear what those characteristics should be.

There is yet another approach: instead of rooting ethics in character or the consequences of actions, we can focus on our actions themselves. From this perspective some things are right, some wrong—we should buy fair trade goods, we shouldn't tell lies in advertisements. Ethics becomes a list of commandments, a catalog of "dos" and "don'ts." When a finance official refuses to devalue a currency because they have promised not to, they are defining ethics this way. According to this approach devaluation can still be bad, even if it would make everybody better off.

Many moral dilemmas arise when these three versions pull in different directions but clashes are not inevitable. Take fair trade coffee (coffee that is sold with a certification that indicates the farmers and workers who produced it were paid a fair wage), for example: buying it might have good consequences, be virtuous, and also be the right way to act in a flawed market. Common ground like this suggests that, even without agreement on where ethics applies, ethical economics is still possible.

Whenever we feel queasy about "perfect" competitive markets, the problem is often rooted in a phony conception of people. The model of man on which classical economics is based—an entirely rational and selfish being—is a parody, as John Stuart Mill, the philosopher who pioneered the model, accepted. Most people—even economists—now accept that this "economic man" is a fiction. We behave like a herd; we fear losses more than we hope for gains; rarely can our brains process all the relevant facts.

These human quirks mean we can never make purely "rational" decisions. A new wave of behavioral economists, aided by neuroscientists, is trying to understand our psychology, both alone and in groups, so they can anticipate our decisions in the marketplace more accurately. But psychology can also help us understand why we react in disgust at economic injustice, or accept a moral law as universal. Which means that the relatively new science of human behavior might also define ethics for us. Ethical economics would then emerge from one of the least likely places: economists themselves.

CONTINUE

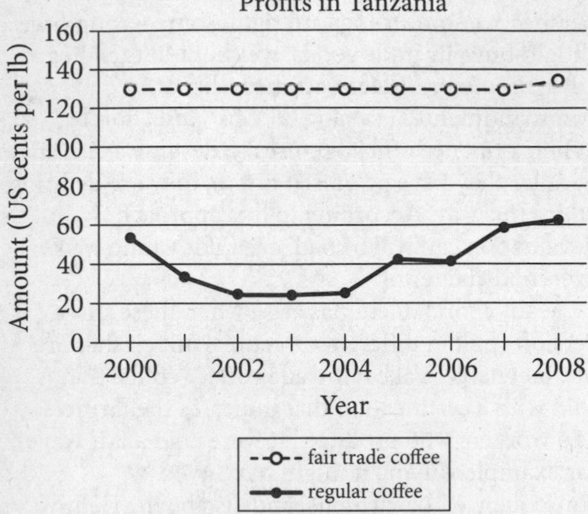

Adapted from the Fair Trade Vancouver website.

11

The main purpose of the passage is to

A) consider an ethical dilemma posed by cost-benefit analysis.

B) describe a psychology study of ethical economic behavior.

C) argue that the free market prohibits ethical economics.

D) examine ways of evaluating the ethics of economics.

12

In the passage, the author anticipates which of the following objections to criticizing the ethics of free markets?

A) Smith's association of free markets with ethical behavior still applies today.

B) Free markets are the best way to generate high profits, so ethics are a secondary consideration.

C) Free markets are ethical because they are made possible by devalued currency.

D) Free markets are ethical because they enable individuals to make choices.

13

Which choice provides the best evidence for the answer to the previous question?

A) Lines 4-5 ("Some . . . ethical")

B) Lines 7-10 ("But . . . about")

C) Lines 21-22 ("Smith . . . outcome")

D) Lines 52-54 ("When . . . way")

CONTINUE

14

As used in line 6, "embraced" most nearly means

A) lovingly held.
B) readily adopted.
C) eagerly hugged.
D) reluctantly used.

15

The main purpose of the fifth paragraph (lines 45-56) is to

A) develop a counterargument to the claim that greed is good.
B) provide support for the idea that ethics is about character.
C) describe a third approach to defining ethical economics.
D) illustrate that one's actions are a result of one's character.

16

As used in line 58, "clashes" most nearly means

A) conflicts.
B) mismatches.
C) collisions.
D) brawls.

17

Which choice best supports the author's claim that there is common ground shared by the different approaches to ethics described in the passage?

A) Lines 11-12 ("There . . . decision")
B) Lines 47-50 ("From . . . advertisements")
C) Lines 59-64 ("Take . . . market")
D) Lines 75-77 ("We . . . facts")

18

The main idea of the final paragraph is that

A) human quirks make it difficult to predict people's ethical decisions accurately.
B) people universally react with disgust when faced with economic injustice.
C) understanding human psychology may help to define ethics in economics.
D) economists themselves will be responsible for reforming the free market.

19

Data in the graph about per-pound coffee profits in Tanzania most strongly support which of the following statements?

A) Fair trade coffee consistently earned greater profits than regular coffee earned.
B) The profits earned from regular coffee did not fluctuate.
C) Fair trade coffee profits increased between 2004 and 2006.
D) Fair trade and regular coffee were earning equal profits by 2008.

20

Data in the graph indicate that the greatest difference between per-pound profits from fair trade coffee and those from regular coffee occurred during which period?

A) 2000 to 2002
B) 2002 to 2004
C) 2004 to 2005
D) 2006 to 2008

CONTINUE

21

Data in the graph provide most direct support for which idea in the passage?

A) Acting on empathy can be counterproductive.

B) Ethical economics is defined by character.

C) Ethical economics is still possible.

D) People fear losses more than they hope for gains.

Questions 22-32 are based on the following passages.

Passage 1 is adapted from Nicholas Carr, "Author Nicholas Carr: The Web Shatters Focus, Rewires Brains." ©2010 by Condé Nast. Passage 2 is from Steven Pinker, "Mind over Mass Media." ©2010 by The New York Times Company.

Passage 1

The mental consequences of our online info-crunching are not universally bad. Certain cognitive skills are strengthened by our use of computers and the Net. These tend to involve more primitive mental functions, such as hand-eye coordination, reflex response, and the processing of visual cues. One much-cited study of video gaming revealed that after just 10 days of playing action games on computers, a group of young people had significantly boosted the speed with which they could shift their visual focus between various images and tasks.

It's likely that Web browsing also strengthens brain functions related to fast-paced problem solving, particularly when it requires spotting patterns in a welter of data. A British study of the way women search for medical information online indicated that an experienced Internet user can, at least in some cases, assess the trustworthiness and probable value of a Web page in a matter of seconds. The more we practice surfing and scanning, the more adept our brain becomes at those tasks.

But it would be a serious mistake to look narrowly at such benefits and conclude that the Web is making us smarter. In a *Science* article published in early 2009, prominent developmental psychologist Patricia Greenfield reviewed more than 40 studies of the effects of various types of media on intelligence and learning ability. She concluded that "every medium develops some cognitive skills at the expense of others." Our growing use of the Net and other screen-based technologies, she wrote, has led to the "widespread and sophisticated development of visual-spatial skills." But those gains go hand in hand with a weakening of our capacity for the kind of "deep processing" that underpins "mindful knowledge acquisition, inductive analysis, critical thinking, imagination, and reflection."

We know that the human brain is highly plastic; neurons and synapses change as circumstances change. When we adapt to a new cultural phenomenon, including the use of a new

CONTINUE

medium, we end up with a different brain, says Michael Merzenich, a pioneer of the field of neuroplasticity. That means our online habits continue to reverberate in the workings of our brain cells even when we're not at a computer. We're exercising the neural circuits devoted to skimming and multitasking while ignoring those used for reading and thinking deeply.

Passage 2

Critics of new media sometimes use science itself to press their case, citing research that shows how "experience can change the brain." But cognitive neuroscientists roll their eyes at such talk. Yes, every time we learn a fact or skill the wiring of the brain changes; it's not as if the information is stored in the pancreas. But the existence of neural plasticity does not mean the brain is a blob of clay pounded into shape by experience.

Experience does not revamp the basic information-processing capacities of the brain. Speed-reading programs have long claimed to do just that, but the verdict was rendered by Woody Allen after he read Leo Tolstoy's famously long novel *War and Peace* in one sitting: "It was about Russia." Genuine multitasking, too, has been exposed as a myth, not just by laboratory studies but by the familiar sight of an SUV undulating between lanes as the driver cuts deals on his cell phone.

Moreover, the effects of experience are highly specific to the experiences themselves. If you train people to do one thing (recognize shapes, solve math puzzles, find hidden words), they get better at doing that thing, but almost nothing else. Music doesn't make you better at math, conjugating Latin doesn't make you more logical, brain-training games don't make you smarter. Accomplished people don't bulk up their brains with intellectual calisthenics; they immerse themselves in their fields. Novelists read lots of novels, scientists read lots of science.

The effects of consuming electronic media are likely to be far more limited than the panic implies. Media critics write as if the brain takes on the qualities of whatever it consumes, the informational equivalent of "you are what you eat." As with ancient peoples who believed that eating fierce animals made them fierce, they assume that watching quick cuts in rock videos turns your mental life into quick cuts or that reading bullet points and online postings turns your thoughts into bullet points and online postings.

22

The author of Passage 1 indicates which of the following about the use of screen-based technologies?

A) It should be thoroughly studied.

B) It makes the brain increasingly rigid.

C) It has some positive effects.

D) It should be widely encouraged.

23

Which choice provides the best evidence for the answer to the previous question?

A) Lines 3-4 ("Certain . . . Net")

B) Lines 23-25 ("But . . . smarter")

C) Lines 25-29 ("In a . . . ability")

D) Lines 29-31 ("She . . . others")

24

The author of Passage 1 indicates that becoming adept at using the Internet can

A) make people complacent about their health.

B) undermine the ability to think deeply.

C) increase people's social contacts.

D) improve people's self-confidence.

25

As used in line 40, "plastic" most nearly means

A) creative.

B) artificial.

C) malleable.

D) sculptural.

CONTINUE

26

The author of Passage 2 refers to the novel *War and Peace* primarily to suggest that Woody Allen

A) did not like Tolstoy's writing style.

B) could not comprehend the novel by speed-reading it.

C) had become quite skilled at multitasking.

D) regretted having read such a long novel.

27

According to the author of Passage 2, what do novelists and scientists have in common?

A) They take risks when they pursue knowledge.

B) They are eager to improve their minds.

C) They are curious about other subjects.

D) They become absorbed in their own fields.

28

The analogy in the final sentence of Passage 2 has primarily which effect?

A) It uses ornate language to illustrate a difficult concept.

B) It employs humor to soften a severe opinion of human behavior.

C) It alludes to the past to evoke a nostalgic response.

D) It criticizes the view of a particular group.

29

The main purpose of each passage is to

A) compare brain function in those who play games on the Internet and those who browse on it.

B) report on the problem-solving skills of individuals with varying levels of Internet experience.

C) take a position on increasing financial support for studies related to technology and intelligence.

D) make an argument about the effects of electronic media use on the brain.

30

Which choice best describes the relationship between the two passages?

A) Passage 2 relates first-hand experiences that contrast with the clinical approach in Passage 1.

B) Passage 2 critiques the conclusions drawn from the research discussed in Passage 1.

C) Passage 2 takes a high-level view of a result that Passage 1 examines in depth.

D) Passage 2 predicts the negative reactions that the findings discussed in Passage 1 might produce.

31

On which of the following points would the authors of both passages most likely agree?

A) Computer-savvy children tend to demonstrate better hand-eye coordination than do their parents.

B) Those who criticize consumers of electronic media tend to overreact in their criticism.

C) Improved visual-spatial skills do not generalize to improved skills in other areas.

D) Internet users are unlikely to prefer reading onscreen text to reading actual books.

32

Which choice provides the best evidence that the author of Passage 2 would agree to some extent with the claim attributed to Michael Merzenich in lines 41-43, Passage 1?

A) Lines 51-53 ("Critics . . . brain")

B) Lines 54-56 ("Yes . . . changes")

C) Lines 57-59 ("But . . . experience")

D) Lines 83-84 ("Media . . . consumes")

Questions 33-42 are based on the following passage.

This passage is adapted from Elizabeth Cady Stanton's address to the 1869 Woman Suffrage Convention in Washington, DC.

I urge a sixteenth amendment, because "manhood suffrage," or a man's government, is civil, religious, and social disorganization. The male element is a destructive force, stern, selfish, aggrandizing, loving war, violence, conquest, acquisition, breeding in the material and moral world alike discord, disorder, disease, and death. See what a record of blood and cruelty the pages of history reveal! Through what slavery, slaughter, and sacrifice, through what inquisitions and imprisonments, pains and persecutions, black codes and gloomy creeds, the soul of humanity has struggled for the centuries, while mercy has veiled her face and all hearts have been dead alike to love and hope!

The male element has held high carnival thus far; it has fairly run riot from the beginning, overpowering the feminine element everywhere, crushing out all the diviner qualities in human nature, until we know but little of true manhood and womanhood, of the latter comparatively nothing, for it has scarce been recognized as a power until within the last century. Society is but the reflection of man himself, untempered by woman's thought; the hard iron rule we feel alike in the church, the state, and the home. No one need wonder at the disorganization, at the fragmentary condition of everything, when we remember that man, who represents but half a complete being, with but half an idea on every subject, has undertaken the absolute control of all sublunary matters.

People object to the demands of those whom they choose to call the strong-minded, because they say "the right of suffrage will make the women masculine." That is just the difficulty in which we are involved today. Though disfranchised, we have few women in the best sense; we have simply so many reflections, varieties, and dilutions of the masculine gender. The strong, natural characteristics of womanhood are repressed and ignored in dependence, for so long as man feeds woman she will try to please the giver and adapt herself to his condition. To keep a foothold in society, woman must be as near like man as possible, reflect his ideas, opinions, virtues, motives, prejudices, and vices. She must respect his statutes, though they strip her of every inalienable right, and conflict with that higher law written by the finger of God on her own soul. . . .

. . . [M]an has been molding woman to his ideas by direct and positive influences, while she, if not a negation, has used indirect means to control him, and in most cases developed the very characteristics both in him and herself that needed repression. And now man himself stands appalled at the results of his own excesses, and mourns in bitterness that falsehood, selfishness, and violence are the law of life. The need of this hour is not territory, gold mines, railroads, or specie payments but a new evangel of womanhood, to exalt purity, virtue, morality, true religion, to lift man up into the higher realms of thought and action.

We ask woman's enfranchisement, as the first step toward the recognition of that essential element in government that can only secure the health, strength, and prosperity of the nation. Whatever is done to lift woman to her true position will help to usher in a new day of peace and perfection for the race.

In speaking of the masculine element, I do not wish to be understood to say that all men are hard, selfish, and brutal, for many of the most beautiful spirits the world has known have been clothed with manhood; but I refer to those characteristics, though often marked in woman, that distinguish what is called the stronger sex. For example, the love of acquisition and conquest, the very pioneers of civilization, when expended on the earth, the sea, the elements, the riches and forces of nature, are powers of destruction when used to subjugate one man to another or to sacrifice nations to ambition.

Here that great conservator of woman's love, if permitted to assert itself, as it naturally would in freedom against oppression, violence, and war, would hold all these destructive forces in check, for woman knows the cost of life better than man does, and not with her consent would one drop of blood ever be shed, one life sacrificed in vain.

CONTINUE

33

The central problem that Stanton describes in the passage is that women have been

A) denied equal educational opportunities, which has kept them from reaching their potential.

B) prevented from exerting their positive influence on men, which has led to societal breakdown.

C) prevented from voting, which has resulted in poor candidates winning important elections.

D) blocked by men from serving as legislators, which has allowed the creation of unjust laws.

34

Stanton uses the phrase "high carnival" (line 15) mainly to emphasize what she sees as the

A) utter domination of women by men.

B) freewheeling spirit of the age.

C) scandalous decline in moral values.

D) growing power of women in society.

35

Stanton claims that which of the following was a relatively recent historical development?

A) The control of society by men

B) The spread of war and injustice

C) The domination of domestic life by men

D) The acknowledgment of women's true character

36

Which choice provides the best evidence for the answer to the previous question?

A) Lines 3-7 ("The male . . . death")

B) Lines 15-22 ("The male . . . century")

C) Lines 22-25 ("Society . . . home")

D) Lines 48-52 ("[M]an . . . repression")

37

As used in line 24, "rule" most nearly refers to

A) a general guideline.

B) a controlling force.

C) an established habit.

D) a procedural method.

38

It can reasonably be inferred that "the strong-minded" (line 32) was a term generally intended to

A) praise women who fight for their long-denied rights.

B) identify women who demonstrate intellectual skill.

C) criticize women who enter male-dominated professions.

D) condemn women who agitate for the vote for their sex.

39

As used in line 36, "best" most nearly means

A) superior.

B) excellent.

C) genuine.

D) rarest.

40

Stanton contends that the situation she describes in the passage has become so dire that even men have begun to

A) lament the problems they have created.

B) join the call for woman suffrage.

C) consider women their social equals.

D) ask women how to improve civic life.

CONTINUE

41

Which choice provides the best evidence for the answer to the previous question?

A) Lines 25-30 ("No one . . . matters")

B) Lines 53-55 ("And now . . . life")

C) Lines 56-60 ("The need . . . action")

D) Lines 61-64 ("We ask . . . nation")

42

The sixth paragraph (lines 67-78) is primarily concerned with establishing a contrast between

A) men and women.

B) the spiritual world and the material world.

C) bad men and good men.

D) men and masculine traits.

CONTINUE

Questions 43-52 are based on the following passage and supplementary material.

This passage is adapted from Geoffrey Giller, "Long a Mystery, How 500-Meter-High Undersea Waves Form Is Revealed." ©2014 by Scientific American.

Some of the largest ocean waves in the world are nearly impossible to see. Unlike other large waves, these rollers, called internal waves, do not ride the ocean surface. Instead, they move underwater, undetectable without the use of satellite imagery or sophisticated monitoring equipment. Despite their hidden nature, internal waves are fundamental parts of ocean water dynamics, transferring heat to the ocean depths and bringing up cold water from below. And they can reach staggering heights—some as tall as skyscrapers.

Because these waves are involved in ocean mixing and thus the transfer of heat, understanding them is crucial to global climate modeling, says Tom Peacock, a researcher at the Massachusetts Institute of Technology. Most models fail to take internal waves into account. "If we want to have more and more accurate climate models, we have to be able to capture processes such as this," Peacock says.

Peacock and his colleagues tried to do just that. Their study, published in November in *Geophysical Research Letters*, focused on internal waves generated in the Luzon Strait, which separates Taiwan and the Philippines. Internal waves in this region, thought to be some of the largest in the world, can reach about 500 meters high. "That's the same height as the Freedom Tower that's just been built in New York," Peacock says.

Although scientists knew of this phenomenon in the South China Sea and beyond, they didn't know exactly how internal waves formed. To find out, Peacock and a team of researchers from M.I.T. and Woods Hole Oceanographic Institution worked with France's National Center for Scientific Research using a giant facility there called the Coriolis Platform. The rotating platform, about 15 meters (49.2 feet) in diameter, turns at variable speeds and can simulate Earth's rotation. It also has walls, which means scientists can fill it with water and create accurate, large-scale simulations of various oceanographic scenarios.

Peacock and his team built a carbon-fiber resin scale model of the Luzon Strait, including the islands and surrounding ocean floor topography. Then they filled the platform with water of varying salinity to replicate the different densities found at the strait, with denser, saltier water below and lighter, less briny water above. Small particles were added to the solution and illuminated with lights from below in order to track how the liquid moved. Finally, they re-created tides using two large plungers to see how the internal waves themselves formed.

The Luzon Strait's underwater topography, with a distinct double-ridge shape, turns out to be responsible for generating the underwater waves. As the tide rises and falls and water moves through the strait, colder, denser water is pushed up over the ridges into warmer, less dense layers above it. This action results in bumps of colder water trailed by warmer water that generate an internal wave. As these waves move toward land, they become steeper—much the same way waves at the beach become taller before they hit the shore—until they break on a continental shelf.

The researchers were also able to devise a mathematical model that describes the movement and formation of these waves. Whereas the model is specific to the Luzon Strait, it can still help researchers understand how internal waves are generated in other places around the world. Eventually, this information will be incorporated into global climate models, making them more accurate. "It's very clear, within the context of these [global climate] models, that internal waves play a role in driving ocean circulations," Peacock says.

CONTINUE

CHANGES IN DEPTH OF ISOTHERMS*
IN AN INTERNAL WAVE OVER A 24-HOUR PERIOD

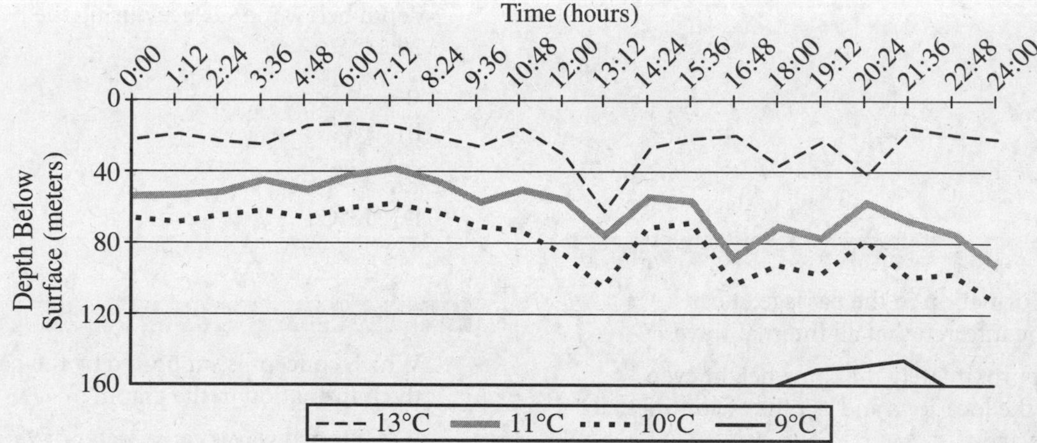

* Bands of water of constant temperatures

Adapted from Justin Small et al., "Internal Solitons in the Ocean: Prediction from SAR." ©1998 by Oceanography, Defence Evaluation and Research Agency.

43

The first paragraph serves mainly to

A) explain how a scientific device is used.

B) note a common misconception about an event.

C) describe a natural phenomenon and address its importance.

D) present a recent study and summarize its findings.

44

As used in line 19, "capture" is closest in meaning to

A) control.

B) record.

C) secure.

D) absorb.

45

According to Peacock, the ability to monitor internal waves is significant primarily because

A) it will allow scientists to verify the maximum height of such waves.

B) it will allow researchers to shift their focus to improving the quality of satellite images.

C) the study of wave patterns will enable regions to predict and prevent coastal damage.

D) the study of such waves will inform the development of key scientific models.

46

Which choice provides the best evidence for the answer to the previous question?

A) Lines 1-2 ("Some . . . see")

B) Lines 4-6 ("they . . . equipment")

C) Lines 17-19 ("If . . . this")

D) Lines 24-26 ("Internal . . . high")

CONTINUE

47

As used in line 65, "devise" most nearly means

A) create.

B) solve.

C) imagine.

D) begin.

48

Based on information in the passage, it can reasonably be inferred that all internal waves

A) reach approximately the same height even though the locations and depths of continental shelves vary.

B) may be caused by similar factors but are influenced by the distinct topographies of different regions.

C) can be traced to inconsistencies in the tidal patterns of deep ocean water located near islands.

D) are generated by the movement of dense water over a relatively flat section of the ocean floor.

49

Which choice provides the best evidence for the answer to the previous question?

A) Lines 29-31 ("Although . . . formed")

B) Lines 56-58 ("As the . . . it")

C) Lines 61-64 ("As these . . . shelf")

D) Lines 67-70 ("Whereas . . . world")

50

In the graph, which isotherm displays an increase in depth below the surface during the period 19:12 to 20:24?

A) 9°C

B) 10°C

C) 11°C

D) 13°C

51

Which concept is supported by the passage and by the information in the graph?

A) Internal waves cause water of varying salinity to mix.

B) Internal waves push denser water above layers of less dense water.

C) Internal waves push bands of cold water above bands of warmer water.

D) Internal waves do not rise to break the ocean's surface.

52

How does the graph support the author's point that internal waves affect ocean water dynamics?

A) It demonstrates that wave movement forces warmer water down to depths that typically are colder.

B) It reveals the degree to which an internal wave affects the density of deep layers of cold water.

C) It illustrates the change in surface temperature that takes place during an isolated series of deep waves.

D) It shows that multiple waves rising near the surface of the ocean disrupt the flow of normal tides.

STOP

If you finish before time is called, you may check your work on this section only.

Do not turn to any other section.

No Test Material On This Page

Writing and Language Test

35 MINUTES, 44 QUESTIONS

Turn to Section 2 of your answer sheet to answer the questions in this section.

DIRECTIONS

Each passage below is accompanied by a number of questions. For some questions, you will consider how the passage might be revised to improve the expression of ideas. For other questions, you will consider how the passage might be edited to correct errors in sentence structure, usage, or punctuation. A passage or a question may be accompanied by one or more graphics (such as a table or graph) that you will consider as you make revising and editing decisions.

Some questions will direct you to an underlined portion of a passage. Other questions will direct you to a location in a passage or ask you to think about the passage as a whole.

After reading each passage, choose the answer to each question that most effectively improves the quality of writing in the passage or that makes the passage conform to the conventions of standard written English. Many questions include a "NO CHANGE" option. Choose that option if you think the best choice is to leave the relevant portion of the passage as it is.

Questions 1-11 are based on the following passage.

Librarians Help Navigate in the Digital Age

In recent years, public libraries in the United States have experienced [1] reducing in their operating funds due to cuts imposed at the federal, state, and local government levels. [2] However, library staffing has been cut by almost four percent since 2008, and the demand for librarians continues to decrease, even though half of public libraries report that they have an insufficient number of staff to meet their patrons' needs. Employment in all job sectors in the United States is projected to grow by fourteen percent over the next

1

A) NO CHANGE
B) reductions
C) deducting
D) deducts

2

A) NO CHANGE
B) Consequently,
C) Nevertheless,
D) Previously,

CONTINUE

decade, yet the expected growth rate for librarians is predicted to be only seven percent, or half of the overall rate. This trend, combined with the increasing accessibility of information via the Internet, [3] has led some to claim that librarianship is in decline as a profession. As public libraries adapt to rapid technological advances in information distribution, librarians' roles are actually expanding.

The share of library materials that is in nonprint formats [4] is increasing steadily; in 2010, at least 18.5 million e-books were available [5] for them to circulate. As a result, librarians must now be proficient curators of electronic information, compiling, [6] catalog, and updating these collections. But perhaps even more importantly, librarians function as first responders for their communities' computer needs. Since

3

A) NO CHANGE
B) have
C) which have
D) which has

4

At this point, the writer is considering adding the following information.

—e-books, audio and video materials, and online journals—

Should the writer make this addition here?

A) Yes, because it provides specific examples of the materials discussed in the sentence.
B) Yes, because it illustrates the reason for the increase mentioned later in the sentence.
C) No, because it interrupts the flow of the sentence by supplying irrelevant information.
D) No, because it weakens the focus of the passage by discussing a subject other than librarians

5

A) NO CHANGE
B) to be circulated by them.
C) for their circulating.
D) for circulation.

6

A) NO CHANGE
B) librarians cataloging,
C) to catalog,
D) cataloging,

CONTINUE

one of the fastest growing library services is public access computer use, there is great demand for computer instruction. 7 In fact, librarians' training now includes courses on research and Internet search methods. Many of whom teach classes in Internet navigation, database and software use, and digital information literacy. While these classes are particularly helpful to young students developing basic research skills, 8 but adult patrons can also benefit from librarian assistance in that they can acquire job-relevant computer skills. 9 Free to all who utilize their services, public libraries and librarians are especially valuable, because they offer free resources that may be difficult to find elsewhere, such as help with online job

7

Which choice most effectively combines the underlined sentences?

A) In fact, librarians' training now includes courses on research and Internet search methods; many librarians teach classes in Internet navigation, database and software use, and digital information literacy is taught by them.

B) In fact, many librarians, whose training now includes courses on research and Internet search methods, teach classes in Internet navigation, database and software use, and digital information literacy.

C) Training now includes courses on research and Internet search methods; many librarians, in fact, are teaching classes in Internet navigation, database and software use, and digital information literacy.

D) Including courses on research and Internet search methods in their training is, in fact, why many librarians teach classes in Internet navigation, database and software use, and digital information literacy.

8

A) NO CHANGE

B) and

C) for

D) DELETE the underlined portion.

9

Which choice most effectively sets up the examples given at the end of the sentence?

A) NO CHANGE

B) During periods of economic recession,

C) Although their value cannot be measured,

D) When it comes to the free services libraries provide,

searches as well as résumé and job material development. An overwhelming number of public libraries also report that they provide help with electronic government resources related to income taxes, **10** law troubles, and retirement programs.

In sum, the Internet does not replace the need for librarians, and librarians are hardly obsolete. **11** Like books, librarians have been around for a long time, but the Internet is extremely useful for many types of research.

10

A) NO CHANGE
B) legal issues,
C) concerns related to law courts,
D) matters for the law courts,

11

Which choice most clearly ends the passage with a restatement of the writer's primary claim?

A) NO CHANGE
B) Although their roles have diminished significantly, librarians will continue to be employed by public libraries for the foreseeable future.
C) The growth of electronic information has led to a diversification of librarians' skills and services, positioning them as savvy resource specialists for patrons.
D) However, given their extensive training and skills, librarians who have been displaced by budget cuts have many other possible avenues of employment.

CONTINUE

Questions 12-22 are based on the following passage.

Tiny Exhibit, Big Impact

— 1 —

The first time I visited the Art Institute of Chicago, I expected to be impressed by its famous large paintings. 12 On one hand, I couldn't wait to view 13 painter, Georges Seurat's, 10-foot-wide *A Sunday Afternoon on the Island of La Grande Jatte* in its full size. It took me by surprise, then, when my favorite exhibit at the museum was one of 14 it's tiniest; the Thorne Miniature Rooms.

12

A) NO CHANGE
B) For instance,
C) However,
D) Similarly,

13

A) NO CHANGE
B) painter, Georges Seurat's
C) painter Georges Seurat's,
D) painter Georges Seurat's

14

A) NO CHANGE
B) its tiniest;
C) its tiniest:
D) it's tiniest,

CONTINUE

— 2 —

Viewing the exhibit, I was amazed by the intricate details of some of the more ornately decorated rooms. I marveled at a replica of a salon (a formal living room) dating back to the reign of French king Louis XV. **15** Built into the dark paneled walls are bookshelves stocked with leather-bound volumes. The couch and chairs, in keeping with the style of the time, are characterized by elegantly curved arms and **16** legs, they are covered in luxurious velvet. A dime-sized portrait of a French aristocratic woman hangs in a golden frame.

— 3 —

This exhibit showcases sixty-eight miniature rooms inserted into a wall at eye level. Each furnished room consists of three walls; the fourth wall is a glass pane through which museumgoers observe. The rooms and their furnishings were painstakingly created to scale at 1/12th their actual size, so that one inch in the exhibit correlates with one foot in real life. A couch, for example, is seven inches long, and **17** that is based on a seven-foot-long couch. Each room represents a distinctive style of European, American, or Asian interior design from the thirteenth to twentieth centuries.

15

At this point, the writer is considering adding the following sentence.

> Some scholars argue that the excesses of King Louis XV's reign contributed significantly to the conditions that resulted in the French Revolution.

Should the writer make this addition here?

A) Yes, because it provides historical context for the Thorne Miniature Rooms exhibit.
B) Yes, because it explains why salons are often ornately decorated.
C) No, because it interrupts the paragraph's description of the miniature salon.
D) No, because it implies that the interior designer of the salon had political motivations.

16

A) NO CHANGE
B) legs, the couch and chairs
C) legs and
D) legs,

17

Which choice gives a second supporting example that is most similar to the example already in the sentence?

A) NO CHANGE
B) a tea cup is about a quarter of an inch.
C) there are even tiny cushions on some.
D) household items are also on this scale.

—4—

The plainer rooms are more sparsely [18] furnished. Their architectural features, furnishings, and decorations are just as true to the periods they represent. One of my favorite rooms in the whole exhibit, in fact, is an 1885 summer kitchen. The room is simple but spacious, with a small sink and counter along one wall, a cast-iron wood stove and some hanging pots and pans against another wall, and [19] a small table under a window of the third wall. Aside from a few simple wooden chairs placed near the edges of the room, the floor is open and obviously well worn.

18

Which choice most effectively combines the sentences at the underlined portion?

A) furnished by their

B) furnished, but their

C) furnished: their

D) furnished, whereas

19

Which choice most closely matches the stylistic pattern established earlier in the sentence?

A) NO CHANGE

B) a small table is under the third wall's window.

C) the third wall has a window and small table.

D) the third wall has a small table against it and a window.

CONTINUE

—5—

As I walked through the exhibit, I overheard a **20** visitors' remark, "You know, that grandfather clock actually runs. Its glass door swings open, and the clock can be wound up." **21** Dotted with pin-sized knobs, another visitor noticed my fascination with a tiny writing desk and its drawers. "All of those little drawers pull out. And you see that hutch? Can you believe it has a secret compartment?" Given the exquisite craftsmanship and level of detail I'd already seen, I certainly could.

Question 22 asks about the previous passage as a whole.

20

A) NO CHANGE
B) visitors remarking,
C) visitor remarked,
D) visitor remark,

21

A) NO CHANGE
B) Another visitor, dotted with pin-sized knobs, noticed my fascination with a tiny writing desk and its drawers.
C) Another visitor dotted with pin-sized knobs noticed my fascination with a tiny writing desk and its drawers.
D) Another visitor noticed my fascination with a tiny writing desk and its drawers, dotted with pin-sized knobs.

Think about the previous passage as a whole as you answer question 22.

22

To make the passage most logical, paragraph 2 should be placed

A) where it is now.
B) after paragraph 3.
C) after paragraph 4.
D) after paragraph 5.

Questions 23-33 are based on the following passage and supplementary material.

Environmentalist Otters

It has long been known that the sea otters **[23]** <u>living along the West Coast of North America help</u> keep kelp forests in their habitat healthy and vital. They do this by feeding on sea urchins and other herbivorous invertebrates that graze voraciously on kelp. With sea otters to keep the population of sea urchins in check, kelp forests can flourish. In fact, **[24]** <u>two years or less of sea otters can completely eliminate sea urchins</u> in a coastal area (see chart).

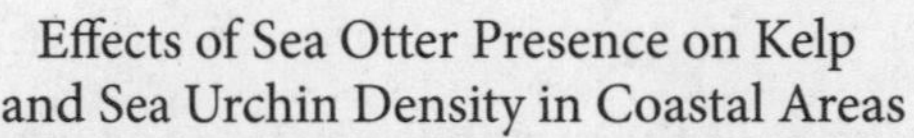

Effects of Sea Otter Presence on Kelp
and Sea Urchin Density in Coastal Areas

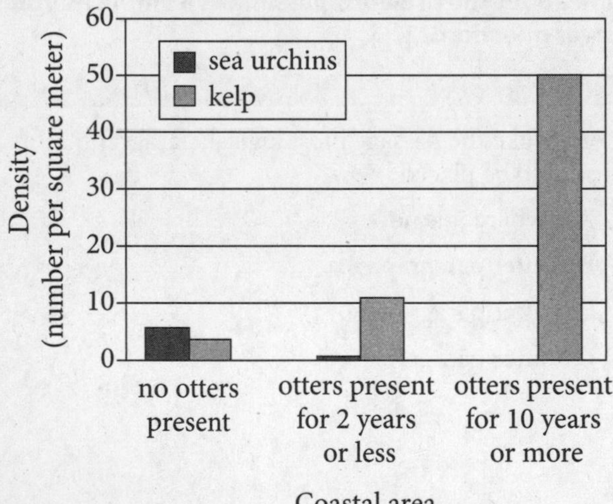

Adapted from David O. Duggins, "Kelp Beds and Sea Otters: An Experimental Approach." ©1980 by the Ecological Society of America.

Without sea otters present, **[25]** <u>nevertheless,</u> kelp forests run the danger of becoming barren stretches of coastal wasteland known as urchin barrens.

23

A) NO CHANGE
B) living along the West Coast of North America, they help
C) that live along the West Coast of North America and help to
D) that live along the West Coast of North America, where they help

24

Which choice offers an accurate interpretation of the data in the chart?

A) NO CHANGE
B) even two years or less of sea otter presence can reduce the sea urchin threat
C) kelp density increases proportionally as sea urchin density increases
D) even after sea otters were present for ten years or more, kelp density was still lower than sea urchin density

25

A) NO CHANGE
B) however,
C) hence,
D) likewise,

CONTINUE

[1] What was less well-known, until recently at least, was how this relationship among sea otters, sea urchins, and kelp forests might help fight global warming. [2] The amount of carbon dioxide in the atmosphere has increased 40 percent **26** . [3] A recent study by two professors at the University of California, Santa Cruz, Chris Wilmers and James Estes, **27** suggests, that kelp forests protected by sea otters can absorb as much as twelve times the amount of carbon dioxide from the atmosphere as those where sea urchins are allowed to **28** devour the kelp. [4] Like **29** their terrestrial plant cousins, kelp removes carbon dioxide from the atmosphere, turning it into sugar fuel through photosynthesis, and releases oxygen back into the air.

26

At this point, the writer is considering adding the following information.

> since the start of the Industrial Revolution, resulting in a rise in global temperatures

Should the writer make this addition here?

A) Yes, because it establishes the relationship between the level of carbon dioxide in the atmosphere and global warming.
B) Yes, because it explains the key role sea otters, sea urchins, and kelp forests play in combating global warming.
C) No, because it contradicts the claim made in the previous paragraph that sea otters help keep kelp forests healthy.
D) No, because it mentions the Industrial Revolution, blurring the focus of the paragraph.

27

A) NO CHANGE
B) suggests—that
C) suggests, "that
D) suggests that

28

A) NO CHANGE
B) dispatch
C) overindulge on
D) dispose of

29

A) NO CHANGE
B) they're
C) its
D) it's

[5] Scientists knew this but did not recognize **30** <u>how large a role they played</u> in helping kelp forests to significantly decrease the amount of carbon dioxide in the atmosphere. [6] Far from making no difference to the ecosystem, the presence of otters was found to increase the carbon storage of kelp forests by 4.4 to 8.7 megatons annually, offsetting the amount of carbon dioxide emitted by three million to six million passenger cars each year. **31**

Wilmers and Estes caution, however, that **32** <u>having more otters</u> will not automatically solve the problem of higher levels of carbon dioxide in the air. But they suggest that the presence of otters provides a good model of how carbon can be sequestered, **33** <u>or removed; from</u> the atmosphere through the management of animal populations. If ecologists can better understand what kinds of impacts animals might have on the environment, Wilmers contends, "there might be opportunities for win-win conservation scenarios, whereby animal species are protected or enhanced, and carbon gets sequestered."

30

A) NO CHANGE
B) how large a role that it played
C) how large a role sea otters played
D) that they played such a large role

31

Where is the most logical place in this paragraph to add the following sentence?

> What Wilmers and Estes discovered in their study, therefore, surprised them.

A) After sentence 1
B) After sentence 3
C) After sentence 4
D) After sentence 5

32

A) NO CHANGE
B) increasing the otter population
C) the otters multiplying
D) having more otters than other locations

33

A) NO CHANGE
B) or removed from,
C) or, removed from,
D) or removed, from

CONTINUE

Questions 34-44 are based on the following passage.

A Quick Fix in a Throwaway Culture

Planned obsolescence, a practice **34** <u>at which</u> products are designed to have a limited period of **35** <u>usefulness,</u> has been a cornerstone of manufacturing strategy for the past 80 years. This approach increases sales, but it also stands in **36** <u>austere</u> contrast to a time when goods were produced to be durable. Planned obsolescence wastes materials as well as energy in making and shipping new products. It also reinforces the belief that it is easier to replace goods than to mend them, as repair shops are rare and **37** <u>repair methods are often specialized.</u> In 2009, an enterprising movement, the Repair Café, challenged this widely accepted belief.

34

A) NO CHANGE
B) from which
C) so that
D) whereby

35

A) NO CHANGE
B) usefulness—
C) usefulness;
D) usefulness

36

A) NO CHANGE
B) egregious
C) unmitigated
D) stark

37

Which choice provides information that best supports the claim made by this sentence?

A) NO CHANGE
B) obsolete goods can become collectible items.
C) no one knows whether something will fall into disrepair again.
D) new designs often have "bugs" that must be worked out.

CONTINUE

[1] More like a **38** fair then an actual café, the first Repair Café took place in Amsterdam, the Netherlands. [2] It was the brainchild of former journalist Martine Postma, **39** wanting to take a practical stand in a throwaway culture. [3] Her goals were **40** straightforward, however: reduce waste, maintain and perpetuate knowledge and skills, and strengthen community. [4] Participants bring all manner of damaged articles—clothing, appliances, furniture, and more—to be repaired by a staff of volunteer specialists including tailors, electricians, and carpenters. [5] Since the inaugural Repair Café, others have been hosted in theater foyers, community centers, hotels, and auditoriums. [6] While **41** they await for service, patrons can enjoy coffee and snacks and mingle with their neighbors in need. **42**

38

A) NO CHANGE
B) fair than
C) fare than
D) fair, then

39

A) NO CHANGE
B) whom wants
C) who wanted
D) she wanted

40

A) NO CHANGE
B) straightforward, therefore:
C) straightforward, nonetheless:
D) straightforward:

41

A) NO CHANGE
B) awaiting
C) they waited
D) waiting

42

To make this paragraph most logical, sentence 5 should be placed

A) where it is now.
B) before sentence 1.
C) after sentence 3.
D) after sentence 6.

CONTINUE

Though only about 3 percent of the Netherlands' municipal waste ends up in landfills, Repair Cafés still raise awareness about what may otherwise be mindless acts of waste by providing a venue for people to share and learn valuable skills that are in danger of being lost. **43** It is easy to classify old but fixable items as "junk" in an era that places great emphasis on the next big thing. In helping people consider how the goods they use on a daily basis work and are made, Repair Cafés restore a sense of relationship between human beings and material goods.

Though the concept remained a local trend at first, international Repair Cafés, all affiliated with the Dutch Repair Café via its website, have since arisen in France, Germany, South Africa, the United States, and other countries **44** on top of that. The original provides a central source for start-up tips and tools, as well as marketing advice to new Repair Cafés. As a result, the Repair Café has become a global network united by common ideals. Ironically, innovators are now looking back to old ways of doing things and applying them in today's cities in an effort to transform the way people relate to and think about the goods they consume.

43

At this point, the writer is considering adding the following sentence.

> As the number of corporate and service-based jobs has increased, the need for people who work with their hands has diminished.

Should the writer make this addition here?

A) Yes, because it provides an example of specific repair skills being lost.
B) Yes, because it elaborates on the statistic about the Netherlands' municipal waste.
C) No, because it blurs the paragraph's focus by introducing a topic that is not further explained.
D) No, because it contradicts the claims made in the rest of the paragraph.

44

A) NO CHANGE
B) in addition.
C) likewise.
D) DELETE the underlined portion, and end the sentence with a period.

STOP

If you finish before time is called, you may check your work on this section only.
Do not turn to any other section.

Math Test – No Calculator

25 MINUTES, 20 QUESTIONS

Turn to Section 3 of your answer sheet to answer the questions in this section.

DIRECTIONS

For questions 1-15, solve each problem, choose the best answer from the choices provided, and fill in the corresponding circle on your answer sheet. **For questions 16-20**, solve the problem and enter your answer in the grid on the answer sheet. Please refer to the directions before question 16 on how to enter your answers in the grid. You may use any available space in your test booklet for scratch work.

NOTES

1. The use of a calculator **is not permitted.**
2. All variables and expressions used represent real numbers unless otherwise indicated.
3. Figures provided in this test are drawn to scale unless otherwise indicated.
4. All figures lie in a plane unless otherwise indicated.
5. Unless otherwise indicated, the domain of a given function f is the set of all real numbers x for which $f(x)$ is a real number.

REFERENCE

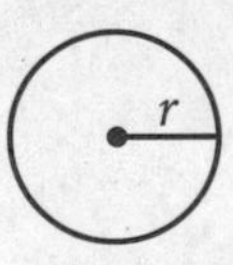

$A = \pi r^2$
$C = 2\pi r$

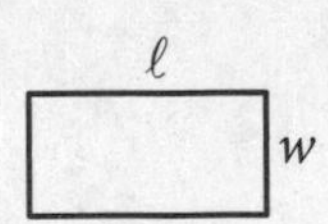

$A = \ell w$

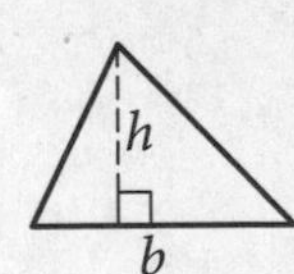

$A = \frac{1}{2}bh$

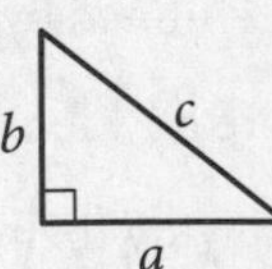

$c^2 = a^2 + b^2$

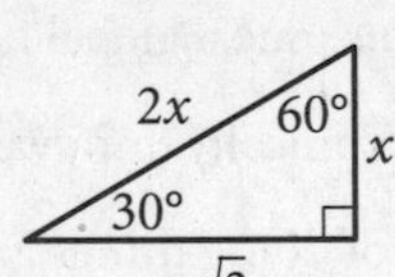

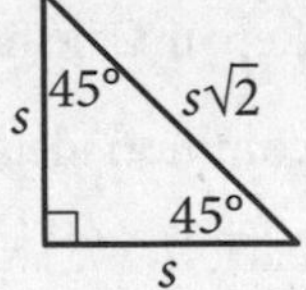

Special Right Triangles

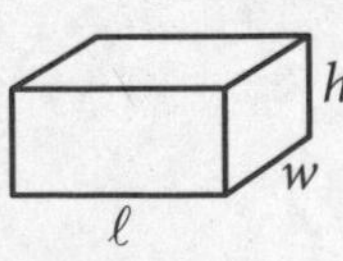

$V = \ell wh$

$V = \pi r^2 h$

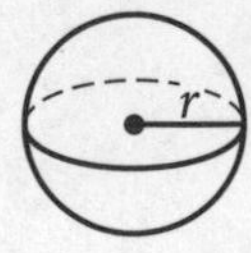

$V = \frac{4}{3}\pi r^3$

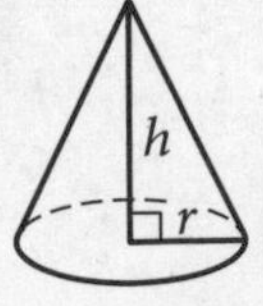

$V = \frac{1}{3}\pi r^2 h$

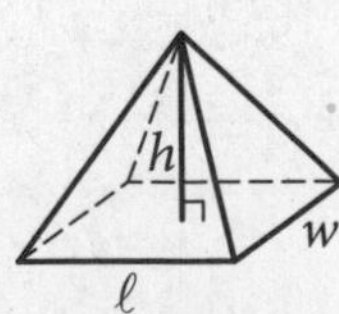

$V = \frac{1}{3}\ell wh$

The number of degrees of arc in a circle is 360.
The number of radians of arc in a circle is 2π.
The sum of the measures in degrees of the angles of a triangle is 180.

CONTINUE

1

If $5x + 6 = 10$, what is the value of $10x + 3$?

A) 4

B) 9

C) 11

D) 20

2

$$x + y = 0$$
$$3x - 2y = 10$$

Which of the following ordered pairs (x, y) satisfies the system of equations above?

A) $(3, -2)$

B) $(2, -2)$

C) $(-2, 2)$

D) $(-2, -2)$

3

A landscaping company estimates the price of a job, in dollars, using the expression $60 + 12nh$, where n is the number of landscapers who will be working and h is the total number of hours the job will take using n landscapers. Which of the following is the best interpretation of the number 12 in the expression?

A) The company charges \$12 per hour for each landscaper.

B) A minimum of 12 landscapers will work on each job.

C) The price of every job increases by \$12 every hour.

D) Each landscaper works 12 hours a day.

4

$$9a^4 + 12a^2b^2 + 4b^4$$

Which of the following is equivalent to the expression shown above?

A) $(3a^2 + 2b^2)^2$

B) $(3a + 2b)^4$

C) $(9a^2 + 4b^2)^2$

D) $(9a + 4b)^4$

5

$$\sqrt{2k^2 + 17} - x = 0$$

If $k > 0$ and $x = 7$ in the equation above, what is the value of k ?

A) 2

B) 3

C) 4

D) 5

6

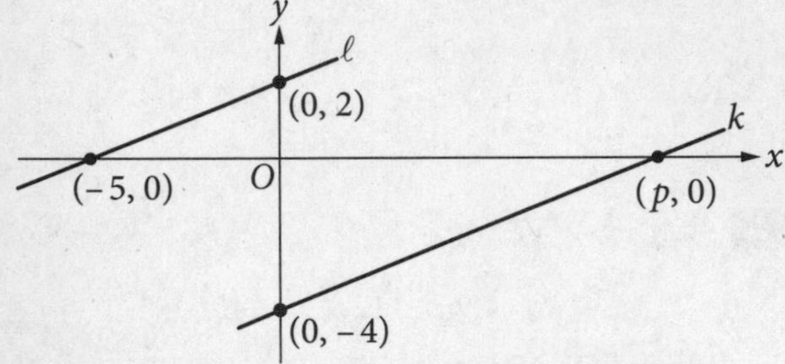

In the xy-plane above, line ℓ is parallel to line k. What is the value of p ?

A) 4

B) 5

C) 8

D) 10

7

If $\frac{x^{a^2}}{x^{b^2}} = x^{16}$, $x > 1$, and $a + b = 2$, what is the value of $a - b$?

A) 8

B) 14

C) 16

D) 18

8

$$nA = 360$$

The measure A, in degrees, of an exterior angle of a regular polygon is related to the number of sides, n, of the polygon by the formula above. If the measure of an exterior angle of a regular polygon is greater than 50°, what is the greatest number of sides it can have?

A) 5

B) 6

C) 7

D) 8

9

The graph of a line in the xy-plane has slope 2 and contains the point $(1, 8)$. The graph of a second line passes through the points $(1, 2)$ and $(2, 1)$. If the two lines intersect at the point (a, b), what is the value of $a + b$?

A) 4

B) 3

C) -1

D) -4

10

Which of the following equations has a graph in the xy-plane for which y is always greater than or equal to -1 ?

A) $y = |x| - 2$

B) $y = x^2 - 2$

C) $y = (x - 2)^2$

D) $y = x^3 - 2$

11

Which of the following complex numbers is equivalent to $\frac{3 - 5i}{8 + 2i}$? (Note: $i = \sqrt{-1}$)

A) $\frac{3}{8} - \frac{5i}{2}$

B) $\frac{3}{8} + \frac{5i}{2}$

C) $\frac{7}{34} - \frac{23i}{34}$

D) $\frac{7}{34} + \frac{23i}{34}$

12

$$R = \frac{F}{N + F}$$

A website uses the formula above to calculate a seller's rating, R, based on the number of favorable reviews, F, and unfavorable reviews, N. Which of the following expresses the number of favorable reviews in terms of the other variables?

A) $F = \frac{RN}{R - 1}$

B) $F = \frac{RN}{1 - R}$

C) $F = \frac{N}{1 - R}$

D) $F = \frac{N}{R - 1}$

CONTINUE

13

What is the sum of all values of m that satisfy $2m^2 - 16m + 8 = 0$?

A) -8

B) $-4\sqrt{3}$

C) $4\sqrt{3}$

D) 8

14

A radioactive substance decays at an annual rate of 13 percent. If the initial amount of the substance is 325 grams, which of the following functions f models the remaining amount of the substance, in grams, t years later?

A) $f(t) = 325(0.87)^t$

B) $f(t) = 325(0.13)^t$

C) $f(t) = 0.87(325)^t$

D) $f(t) = 0.13(325)^t$

15

The expression $\frac{5x-2}{x+3}$ is equivalent to which of the following?

A) $\frac{5-2}{3}$

B) $5 - \frac{2}{3}$

C) $5 - \frac{2}{x+3}$

D) $5 - \frac{17}{x+3}$

CONTINUE

DIRECTIONS

For questions 16–20, solve the problem and enter your answer in the grid, as described below, on the answer sheet.

1. Although not required, it is suggested that you write your answer in the boxes at the top of the columns to help you fill in the circles accurately. You will receive credit only if the circles are filled in correctly.
2. Mark no more than one circle in any column.
3. No question has a negative answer.
4. Some problems may have more than one correct answer. In such cases, grid only one answer.
5. **Mixed numbers** such as $3\frac{1}{2}$ must be gridded as 3.5 or 7/2. (If 3 1 / 2 is entered into the grid, it will be interpreted as $\frac{31}{2}$, not $3\frac{1}{2}$.)
6. **Decimal answers:** If you obtain a decimal answer with more digits than the grid can accommodate, it may be either rounded or truncated, but it must fill the entire grid.

Answer: $\frac{7}{12}$ — Write answer in boxes: 7 / 1 2 — Fraction line — Grid in result.

Answer: 2.5 — 2 . 5 — Decimal point

Acceptable ways to grid $\frac{2}{3}$ are:

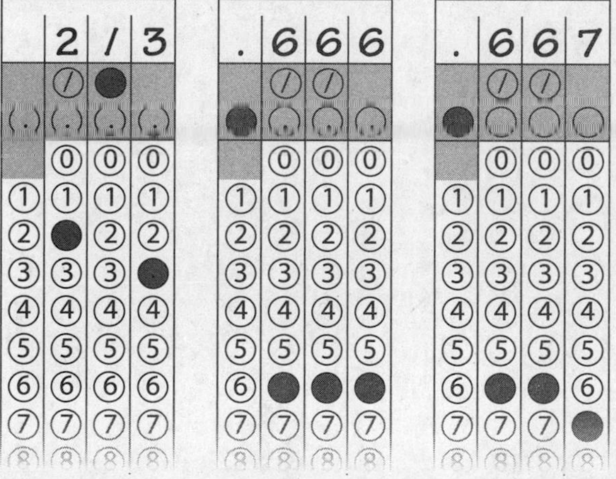

Answer: 201 – either position is correct

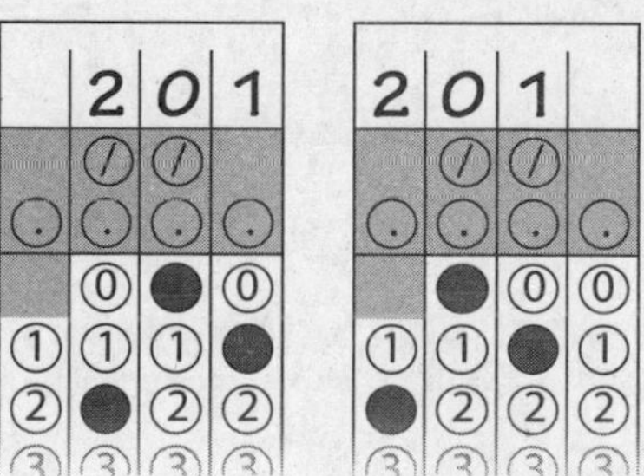

NOTE: You may start your answers in any column, space permitting. Columns you don't need to use should be left blank.

CONTINUE

16

The sales manager of a company awarded a total of \$3000 in bonuses to the most productive salespeople. The bonuses were awarded in amounts of \$250 or \$750. If at least one \$250 bonus and at least one \$750 bonus were awarded, what is one possible number of \$250 bonuses awarded?

17

$$2x(3x + 5) + 3(3x + 5) = ax^2 + bx + c$$

In the equation above, a, b, and c are constants. If the equation is true for all values of x, what is the value of b ?

18

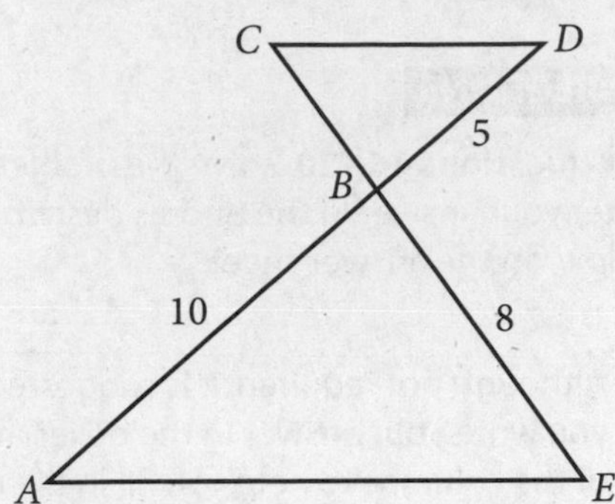

In the figure above, $\overline{AE} \parallel \overline{CD}$ and segment AD intersects segment CE at B. What is the length of segment CE ?

CONTINUE

19

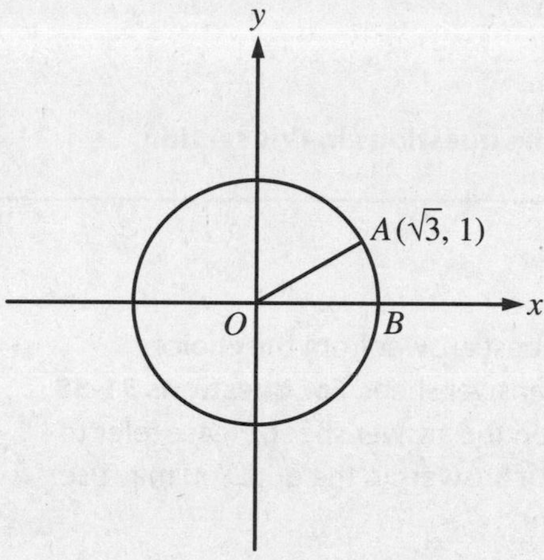

In the xy-plane above, O is the center of the circle, and the measure of $\angle AOB$ is $\frac{\pi}{a}$ radians. What is the value of a ?

20

$$ax + by = 12$$
$$2x + 8y = 60$$

In the system of equations above, a and b are constants. If the system has infinitely many solutions, what is the value of $\frac{a}{b}$?

STOP

If you finish before time is called, you may check your work on this section only.

Do not turn to any other section.

Math Test – Calculator

55 MINUTES, 38 QUESTIONS

Turn to Section 4 of your answer sheet to answer the questions in this section.

DIRECTIONS

For questions 1-30, solve each problem, choose the best answer from the choices provided, and fill in the corresponding circle on your answer sheet. **For questions 31-38**, solve the problem and enter your answer in the grid on the answer sheet. Please refer to the directions before question 31 on how to enter your answers in the grid. You may use any available space in your test booklet for scratch work.

NOTES

1. The use of a calculator **is permitted**.
2. All variables and expressions used represent real numbers unless otherwise indicated.
3. Figures provided in this test are drawn to scale unless otherwise indicated.
4. All figures lie in a plane unless otherwise indicated.
5. Unless otherwise indicated, the domain of a given function f is the set of all real numbers x for which $f(x)$ is a real number.

REFERENCE

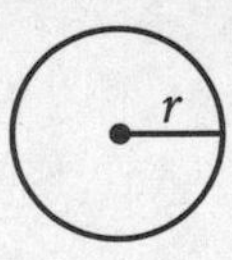

$A = \pi r^2$
$C = 2\pi r$

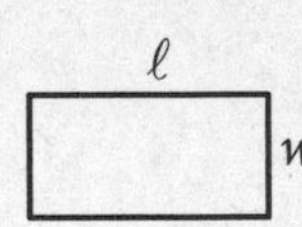

$A = \ell w$

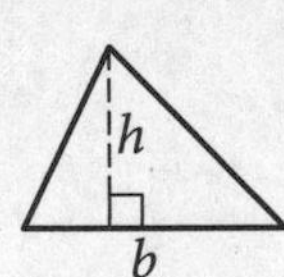

$A = \frac{1}{2}bh$

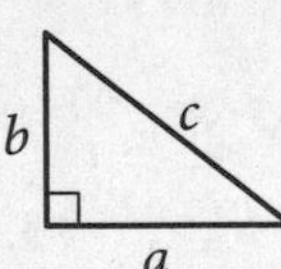

$c^2 = a^2 + b^2$

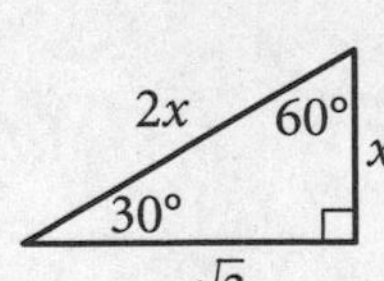

Special Right Triangles

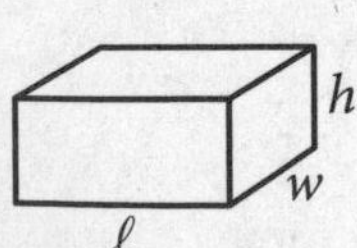

$V = \ell wh$

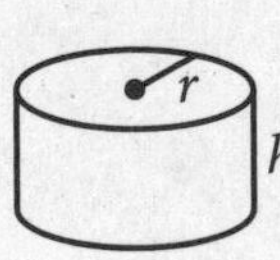

$V = \pi r^2 h$

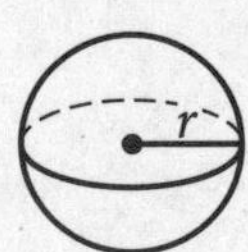

$V = \frac{4}{3}\pi r^3$

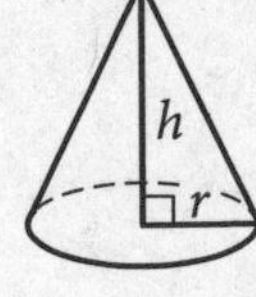

$V = \frac{1}{3}\pi r^2 h$

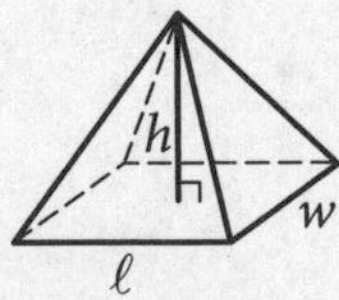

$V = \frac{1}{3}\ell wh$

The number of degrees of arc in a circle is 360.

The number of radians of arc in a circle is 2π.

The sum of the measures in degrees of the angles of a triangle is 180.

CONTINUE

1

A musician has a new song available for downloading or streaming. The musician earns \$0.09 each time the song is downloaded and \$0.002 each time the song is streamed. Which of the following expressions represents the amount, in dollars, that the musician earns if the song is downloaded d times and streamed s times?

A) $0.002d + 0.09s$

B) $0.002d - 0.09s$

C) $0.09d + 0.002s$

D) $0.09d - 0.002s$

2

A quality control manager at a factory selects 7 lightbulbs at random for inspection out of every 400 lightbulbs produced. At this rate, how many lightbulbs will be inspected if the factory produces 20,000 lightbulbs?

A) 300

B) 350

C) 400

D) 450

3

$$\ell = 24 + 3.5m$$

One end of a spring is attached to a ceiling. When an object of mass m kilograms is attached to the other end of the spring, the spring stretches to a length of ℓ centimeters as shown in the equation above. What is m when ℓ is 73 ?

A) 14

B) 27.7

C) 73

D) 279.5

Questions 4 and 5 refer to the following information.

The amount of money a performer earns is directly proportional to the number of people attending the performance. The performer earns \$120 at a performance where 8 people attend.

4

How much money will the performer earn when 20 people attend a performance?

A) \$960

B) \$480

C) \$300

D) \$240

5

The performer uses 43% of the money earned to pay the costs involved in putting on each performance. The rest of the money earned is the performer's profit. What is the profit the performer makes at a performance where 8 people attend?

A) \$51.60

B) \$57.00

C) \$68.40

D) \$77.00

6

When 4 times the number x is added to 12, the result is 8. What number results when 2 times x is added to 7 ?

A) -1

B) 5

C) 8

D) 9

7

$$y = x^2 - 6x + 8$$

The equation above represents a parabola in the xy-plane. Which of the following equivalent forms of the equation displays the x-intercepts of the parabola as constants or coefficients?

A) $y - 8 = x^2 - 6x$

B) $y + 1 = (x - 3)^2$

C) $y = x(x - 6) + 8$

D) $y = (x - 2)(x - 4)$

CONTINUE

8

In a video game, each player starts the game with k points and loses 2 points each time a task is not completed. If a player who gains no additional points and fails to complete 100 tasks has a score of 200 points, what is the value of k ?

A) 0

B) 150

C) 250

D) 400

9

A worker uses a forklift to move boxes that weigh either 40 pounds or 65 pounds each. Let x be the number of 40-pound boxes and y be the number of 65-pound boxes. The forklift can carry up to either 45 boxes or a weight of 2,400 pounds. Which of the following systems of inequalities represents this relationship?

A) $\begin{cases} 40x + 65y \le 2{,}400 \\ x + y \le 45 \end{cases}$

B) $\begin{cases} \dfrac{x}{40} + \dfrac{y}{65} \le 2{,}400 \\ x + y \le 45 \end{cases}$

C) $\begin{cases} 40x + 65y \le 45 \\ x + y \le 2{,}400 \end{cases}$

D) $\begin{cases} x + y \le 2{,}400 \\ 40x + 65y \le 2{,}400 \end{cases}$

10

A function f satisfies $f(2) = 3$ and $f(3) = 5$. A function g satisfies $g(3) = 2$ and $g(5) = 6$. What is the value of $f(g(3))$?

A) 2

B) 3

C) 5

D) 6

11

Number of hours Tony plans to read the novel per day	3
Number of parts in the novel	8
Number of chapters in the novel	239
Number of words Tony reads per minute	250
Number of pages in the novel	1,078
Number of words in the novel	349,168

Tony is planning to read a novel. The table above shows information about the novel, Tony's reading speed, and the amount of time he plans to spend reading the novel each day. If Tony reads at the rates given in the table, which of the following is closest to the number of days it would take Tony to read the entire novel?

A) 6

B) 8

C) 23

D) 324

CONTINUE

12

On January 1, 2000, there were 175,000 tons of trash in a landfill that had a capacity of 325,000 tons. Each year since then, the amount of trash in the landfill increased by 7,500 tons. If y represents the time, in years, after January 1, 2000, which of the following inequalities describes the set of years where the landfill is at or above capacity?

A) $325{,}000 - 7{,}500 \leq y$

B) $325{,}000 \leq 7{,}500y$

C) $150{,}000 \geq 7{,}500y$

D) $175{,}000 + 7{,}500y \geq 325{,}000$

13

A researcher conducted a survey to determine whether people in a certain large town prefer watching sports on television to attending the sporting event. The researcher asked 117 people who visited a local restaurant on a Saturday, and 7 people refused to respond. Which of the following factors makes it least likely that a reliable conclusion can be drawn about the sports-watching preferences of all people in the town?

A) Sample size

B) Population size

C) The number of people who refused to respond

D) Where the survey was given

14

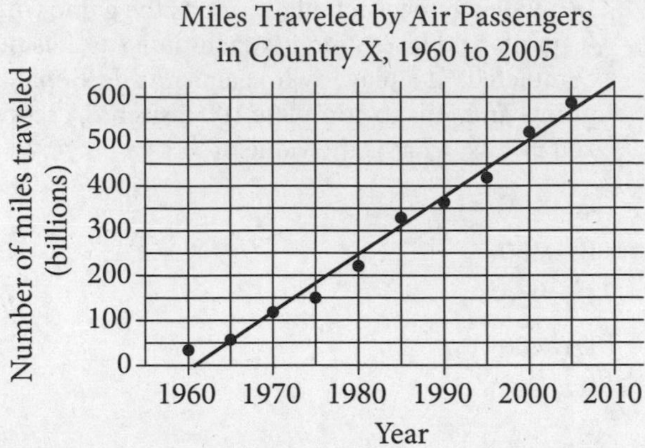

According to the line of best fit in the scatterplot above, which of the following best approximates the year in which the number of miles traveled by air passengers in Country X was estimated to be 550 billion?

A) 1997

B) 2000

C) 2003

D) 2008

CONTINUE

15

The distance traveled by Earth in one orbit around the Sun is about 580,000,000 miles. Earth makes one complete orbit around the Sun in one year. Of the following, which is closest to the average speed of Earth, in miles per hour, as it orbits the Sun?

A) 66,000

B) 93,000

C) 210,000

D) 420,000

16

Results on the Bar Exam of Law School Graduates

	Passed bar exam	Did not pass bar exam
Took review course	18	82
Did not take review course	7	93

The table above summarizes the results of 200 law school graduates who took the bar exam. If one of the surveyed graduates who passed the bar exam is chosen at random for an interview, what is the probability that the person chosen did not take the review course?

A) $\frac{18}{25}$

B) $\frac{7}{25}$

C) $\frac{25}{200}$

D) $\frac{7}{200}$

17

The atomic weight of an unknown element, in atomic mass units (amu), is approximately 20% less than that of calcium. The atomic weight of calcium is 40 amu. Which of the following best approximates the atomic weight, in amu, of the unknown element?

A) 8

B) 20

C) 32

D) 48

18

A survey was taken of the value of homes in a county, and it was found that the mean home value was $165,000 and the median home value was $125,000. Which of the following situations could explain the difference between the mean and median home values in the county?

A) The homes have values that are close to each other.

B) There are a few homes that are valued much less than the rest.

C) There are a few homes that are valued much more than the rest.

D) Many of the homes have values between $125,000 and $165,000.

CONTINUE

Questions 19 and 20 refer to the following information.

A sociologist chose 300 students at random from each of two schools and asked each student how many siblings he or she has. The results are shown in the table below.

Students' Sibling Survey

Number of siblings	Lincoln School	Washington School
0	120	140
1	80	110
2	60	30
3	30	10
4	10	10

There are a total of 2,400 students at Lincoln School and 3,300 students at Washington School.

19

What is the median number of siblings for all the students surveyed?

A) 0
B) 1
C) 2
D) 3

20

Based on the survey data, which of the following most accurately compares the expected total number of students with 4 siblings at the two schools?

A) The total number of students with 4 siblings is expected to be equal at the two schools.
B) The total number of students with 4 siblings at Lincoln School is expected to be 30 more than at Washington School.
C) The total number of students with 4 siblings at Washington School is expected to be 30 more than at Lincoln School.
D) The total number of students with 4 siblings at Washington School is expected to be 900 more than at Lincoln School.

21

A project manager estimates that a project will take x hours to complete, where $x > 100$. The goal is for the estimate to be within 10 hours of the time it will actually take to complete the project. If the manager meets the goal and it takes y hours to complete the project, which of the following inequalities represents the relationship between the estimated time and the actual completion time?

A) $x + y < 10$
B) $y > x + 10$
C) $y < x - 10$
D) $-10 < y - x < 10$

CONTINUE

Questions 22 and 23 refer to the following information.

$$I = \frac{P}{4\pi r^2}$$

At a large distance r from a radio antenna, the intensity of the radio signal I is related to the power of the signal P by the formula above.

22

Which of the following expresses the square of the distance from the radio antenna in terms of the intensity of the radio signal and the power of the signal?

A) $r^2 = \frac{IP}{4\pi}$

B) $r^2 = \frac{P}{4\pi I}$

C) $r^2 = \frac{4\pi I}{P}$

D) $r^2 = \frac{I}{4\pi P}$

23

For the same signal emitted by a radio antenna, Observer A measures its intensity to be 16 times the intensity measured by Observer B. The distance of Observer A from the radio antenna is what fraction of the distance of Observer B from the radio antenna?

A) $\frac{1}{4}$

B) $\frac{1}{16}$

C) $\frac{1}{64}$

D) $\frac{1}{256}$

24

$$x^2 + y^2 + 4x - 2y = -1$$

The equation of a circle in the xy-plane is shown above. What is the radius of the circle?

A) 2

B) 3

C) 4

D) 9

CONTINUE

25

The graph of the linear function f has intercepts at $(a, 0)$ and $(0, b)$ in the xy-plane. If $a + b = 0$ and $a \neq b$, which of the following is true about the slope of the graph of f ?

A) It is positive.

B) It is negative.

C) It equals zero.

D) It is undefined.

26

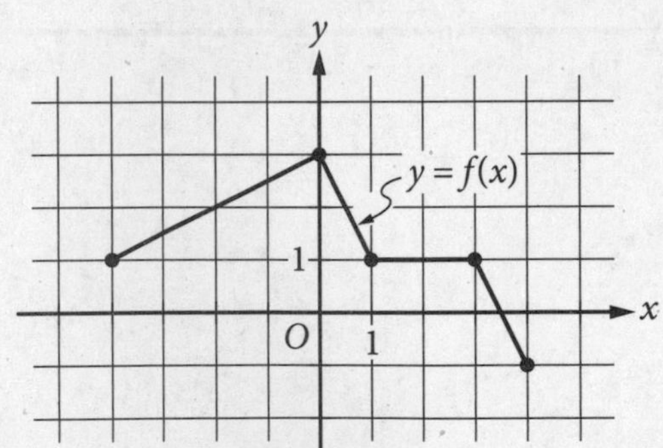

The complete graph of the function f is shown in the xy-plane above. Which of the following are equal to 1 ?

I. $f(-4)$

II. $f\left(\frac{3}{2}\right)$

III. $f(3)$

A) III only

B) I and III only

C) II and III only

D) I, II, and III

27

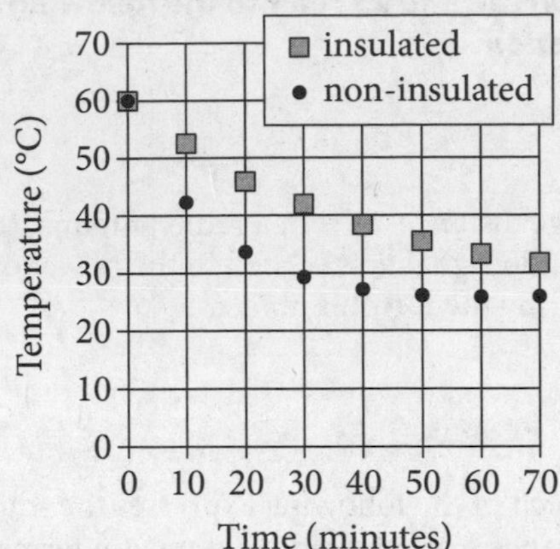

Two samples of water of equal mass are heated to 60 degrees Celsius (°C). One sample is poured into an insulated container, and the other sample is poured into a non-insulated container. The samples are then left for 70 minutes to cool in a room having a temperature of 25°C. The graph above shows the temperature of each sample at 10-minute intervals. Which of the following statements correctly compares the average rates at which the temperatures of the two samples change?

A) In every 10-minute interval, the magnitude of the rate of change of temperature of the insulated sample is greater than that of the non-insulated sample.

B) In every 10-minute interval, the magnitude of the rate of change of temperature of the non-insulated sample is greater than that of the insulated sample.

C) In the intervals from 0 to 10 minutes and from 10 to 20 minutes, the rates of change of temperature of the insulated sample are of greater magnitude, whereas in the intervals from 40 to 50 minutes and from 50 to 60 minutes, the rates of change of temperature of the non-insulated sample are of greater magnitude.

D) In the intervals from 0 to 10 minutes and from 10 to 20 minutes, the rates of change of temperature of the non-insulated sample are of greater magnitude, whereas in the intervals from 40 to 50 minutes and from 50 to 60 minutes, the rates of change of temperature of the insulated sample are of greater magnitude.

CONTINUE

28

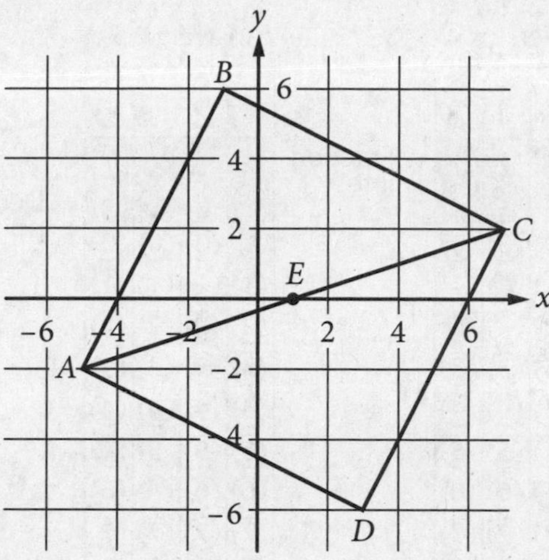

In the xy-plane above, $ABCD$ is a square and point E is the center of the square. The coordinates of points C and E are $(7,2)$ and $(1,0)$, respectively. Which of the following is an equation of the line that passes through points B and D ?

A) $y = -3x - 1$

B) $y = -3(x - 1)$

C) $y = -\frac{1}{3}x + 4$

D) $y = -\frac{1}{3}x - 1$

29

$$y = 3$$
$$y = ax^2 + b$$

In the system of equations above, a and b are constants. For which of the following values of a and b does the system of equations have exactly two real solutions?

A) $a = -2,\ b = 2$

B) $a = -2,\ b = 4$

C) $a = 2,\ b = 4$

D) $a = 4,\ b = 3$

30

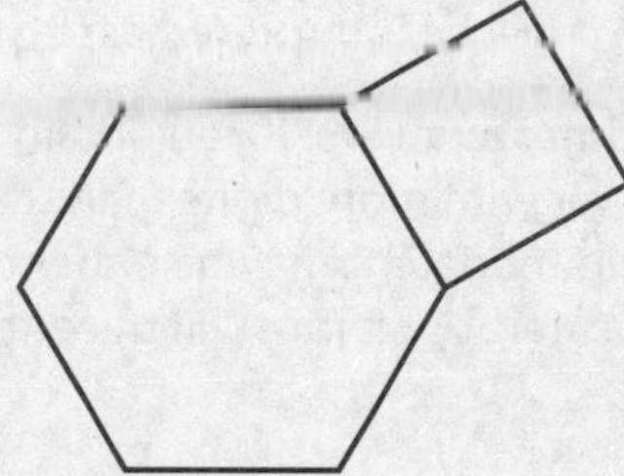

The figure above shows a regular hexagon with sides of length a and a square with sides of length a. If the area of the hexagon is $384\sqrt{3}$ square inches, what is the area, in square inches, of the square?

A) 256

B) 192

C) $64\sqrt{3}$

D) $16\sqrt{3}$

CONTINUE

DIRECTIONS

For questions 31-38, solve the problem and enter your answer in the grid, as described below, on the answer sheet.

1. Although not required, it is suggested that you write your answer in the boxes at the top of the columns to help you fill in the circles accurately. You will receive credit only if the circles are filled in correctly.
2. Mark no more than one circle in any column.
3. No question has a negative answer.
4. Some problems may have more than one correct answer. In such cases, grid only one answer.
5. **Mixed numbers** such as $3\frac{1}{2}$ must be gridded as 3.5 or 7/2. (If 3 1 / 2 is entered into the grid, it will be interpreted as $\frac{31}{2}$, not $3\frac{1}{2}$.)
6. **Decimal answers:** If you obtain a decimal answer with more digits than the grid can accommodate, it may be either rounded or truncated, but it must fill the entire grid.

Answer: $\frac{7}{12}$ — Write answer in boxes: 7 / 1 2 (Fraction line; Grid in result.)

Answer: 2.5 — 2 . 5 (Decimal point)

Acceptable ways to grid $\frac{2}{3}$ are:

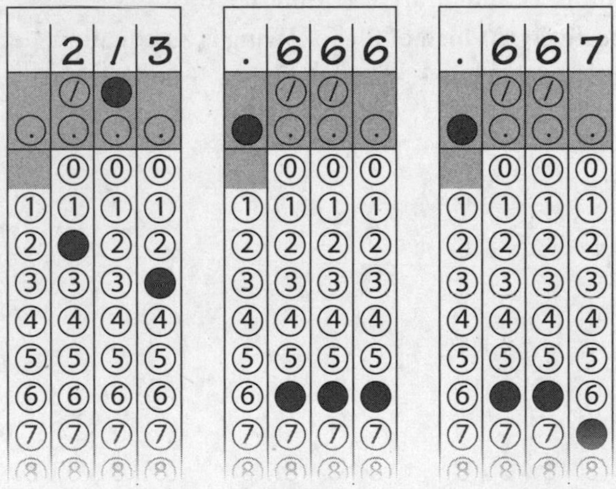

Answer: 201 – either position is correct

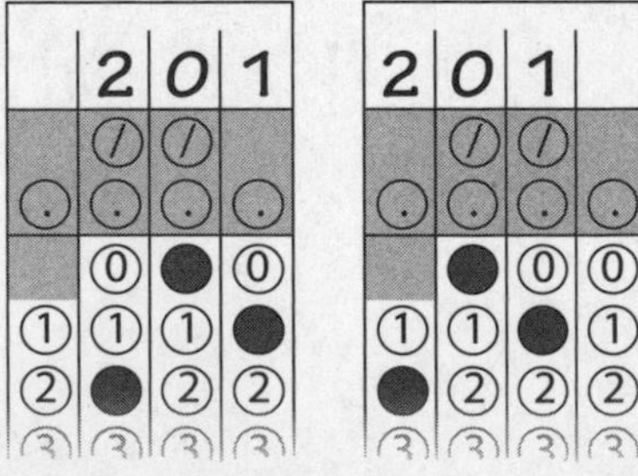

NOTE: You may start your answers in any column, space permitting. Columns you don't need to use should be left blank.

CONTINUE

31

A coastal geologist estimates that a certain country's beaches are eroding at a rate of 1.5 feet per year. According to the geologist's estimate, how long will it take, in years, for the country's beaches to erode by 21 feet?

32

If h hours and 30 minutes is equal to 450 minutes, what is the value of h ?

33

In the xy-plane, the point $(3, 6)$ lies on the graph of the function $f(x) = 3x^2 - bx + 12$. What is the value of b ?

34

In one semester, Doug and Laura spent a combined 250 hours in the tutoring lab. If Doug spent 40 more hours in the lab than Laura did, how many hours did Laura spend in the lab?

CONTINUE

35

$$a = 18t + 15$$

Jane made an initial deposit to a savings account. Each week thereafter she deposited a fixed amount to the account. The equation above models the amount a, in dollars, that Jane has deposited after t weekly deposits. According to the model, how many dollars was Jane's initial deposit? (Disregard the $ sign when gridding your answer.)

36

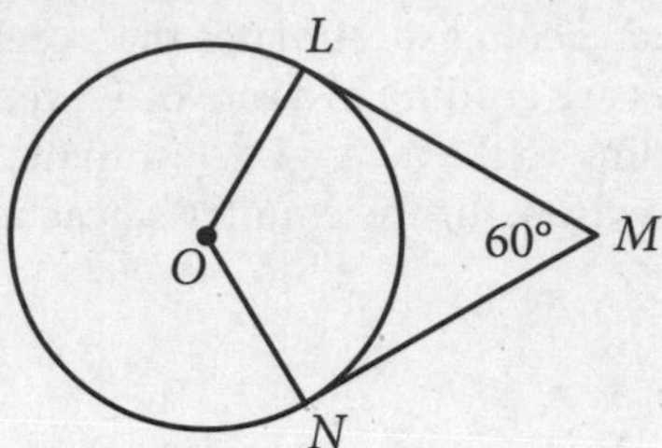

In the figure above, point O is the center of the circle, line segments LM and MN are tangent to the circle at points L and N, respectively, and the segments intersect at point M as shown. If the circumference of the circle is 96, what is the length of minor arc $\overset{\frown}{LN}$?

CONTINUE

Questions 37 and 38 refer to the following information.

A botanist is cultivating a rare species of plant in a controlled environment and currently has 3000 of these plants. The population of this species that the botanist expects to grow next year, $N_{\text{next year}}$, can be estimated from the number of plants this year, $N_{\text{this year}}$, by the equation below.

$$N_{\text{next year}} = N_{\text{this year}} + 0.2\left(N_{\text{this year}}\right)\left(1 - \frac{N_{\text{this year}}}{K}\right)$$

The constant K in this formula is the number of plants the environment is able to support.

37

According to the formula, what will be the number of plants two years from now if $K = 4000$? (Round your answer to the nearest whole number.)

38

The botanist would like to increase the number of plants that the environment can support so that the population of the species will increase more rapidly. If the botanist's goal is that the number of plants will increase from 3000 this year to 3360 next year, how many plants must the modified environment support?

STOP

If you finish before time is called, you may check your work on this section only.

Do not turn to any other section.

This page represents the back cover of the Practice Test.

The SAT®

Practice Essay #2

The essay gives you an opportunity to show how effectively you can read and comprehend a passage and write an essay analyzing the passage. In your essay, you should demonstrate that you have read the passage carefully, present a clear and logical analysis, and use language precisely.

You have 50 minutes to read the passage and write an essay in response to the prompt provided inside this booklet.

For information on scoring your essay, view the SAT Essay scoring rubric at **sat.org/essay**.

As you read the passage below, consider how Martin Luther King Jr. uses

- evidence, such as facts or examples, to support claims.
- reasoning to develop ideas and to connect claims and evidence.
- stylistic or persuasive elements, such as word choice or appeals to emotion, to add power to the ideas expressed.

Adapted from Martin Luther King Jr., "Beyond Vietnam—A Time to Break Silence." The speech was delivered at Riverside Church in New York City on April 4, 1967.

1 Since I am a preacher by calling, I suppose it is not surprising that I have . . . major reasons for bringing Vietnam into the field of my moral vision. There is at the outset a very obvious and almost facile connection between the war in Vietnam and the struggle I, and others, have been waging in America. A few years ago there was a shining moment in that struggle. It seemed as if there was a real promise of hope for the poor—both black and white—through the poverty program. There were experiments, hopes, new beginnings. Then came the buildup in Vietnam, and I watched this program broken and eviscerated, as if it were some idle political plaything of a society gone mad on war, and I knew that America would never invest the necessary funds or energies in rehabilitation of its poor so long as adventures like Vietnam continued to draw men and skills and money like some demonic destructive suction tube. So, I was increasingly compelled to see the war as an enemy of the poor and to attack it as such.

2 Perhaps a more tragic recognition of reality took place when it became clear to me that the war was doing far more than devastating the hopes of the poor at home. It was sending their sons and their brothers and their husbands to fight and to die in extraordinarily high proportions relative to the rest of the population. We were taking the black young men who had been crippled by our society and sending them eight thousand miles away to guarantee liberties in Southeast Asia which they had not found in southwest Georgia and East Harlem. And so we have been repeatedly faced with the cruel irony of watching Negro and white boys on TV screens as they kill and die together for a nation that has been unable to seat them together in the same schools. And so we watch them in brutal solidarity burning the huts of a poor village, but we realize that they would hardly live on the same block in Chicago. I could not be silent in the face of such cruel manipulation of the poor.

3 My [next] reason moves to an even deeper level of awareness, for it grows out of my experience in the ghettoes of the North over the last three years—especially the last three summers. As I have walked among the desperate, rejected, and angry young men, I have told them that Molotov cocktails[1] and rifles would not solve their problems. I have tried to offer them my deepest compassion while maintaining my conviction that social change comes most meaningfully through nonviolent action. But they ask—and rightly so—what about Vietnam? They ask if our own nation wasn't using massive doses of violence to solve its problems, to bring about the changes it wanted. Their questions hit home, and I knew that I could never again raise my voice against the violence of the oppressed in the ghettos without having first spoken clearly to the greatest purveyor of violence in the world today—my own government. For the sake of those boys, for the sake of this government, for the sake of the hundreds of thousands trembling under our violence, I cannot be silent.

4 For those who ask the question, "Aren't you a civil rights leader?" and thereby mean to exclude me from the movement for peace, I have this further answer. In 1957 when a group of us formed the Southern Christian Leadership Conference, we chose as our motto: "To save the soul of America." We were convinced that we could not limit our vision to certain rights for black people, but instead affirmed the conviction that America would never be free or saved from itself until the descendants of its slaves were loosed completely from the shackles they still wear. . . . Now, it should be incandescently clear that no one who has any concern for the integrity and life of America today can ignore the present war. If America's soul becomes totally poisoned, part of the autopsy must read: Vietnam. It can never be saved so long as it destroys the deepest hopes of men the world over. So it is that those of us who are yet determined that America *will* be are led down the path of protest and dissent, working for the health of our land.

Write an essay in which you explain how Martin Luther King Jr. builds an argument to persuade his audience that American involvement in the Vietnam War is unjust. In your essay, analyze how King uses one or more of the features listed in the box above (or features of your own choice) to strengthen the logic and persuasiveness of his argument. Be sure that your analysis focuses on the most relevant features of the passage.

Your essay should not explain whether you agree with King's claims, but rather explain how King builds an argument to persuade his audience.

[1] A crude bomb made from glass bottles filled with flammable liquids and topped with wicks

This page represents the back cover of the Practice Essay.

CollegeBoard

SAT PRACTICE ANSWER SHEET

COMPLETE MARK ● EXAMPLES OF INCOMPLETE MARKS

It is recommended that you use a No. 2 pencil. It is very important that you fill in the entire circle darkly and completely. If you change your response, erase as completely as possible. Incomplete marks or erasures may affect your score.

TEST NUMBER

ENTER TEST NUMBER

For instance, for Practice Test #1, fill in the circle for 0 in the first column and for 1 in the second column.

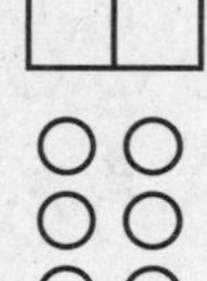

0	○	○
1	○	○
2	○	○
3	○	○
4	○	○
5	○	○
6	○	○
7	○	○
8	○	○
9	○	○

SECTION 1

	A B C D		A B C D		A B C D		A B C D
1	○ ○ ○ ○	14	○ ○ ○ ○	27	○ ○ ○ ○	40	○ ○ ○ ○
2	○ ○ ○ ○	15	○ ○ ○ ○	28	○ ○ ○ ○	41	○ ○ ○ ○
3	○ ○ ○ ○	16	○ ○ ○ ○	29	○ ○ ○ ○	42	○ ○ ○ ○
4	○ ○ ○ ○	17	○ ○ ○ ○	30	○ ○ ○ ○	43	○ ○ ○ ○
5	○ ○ ○ ○	18	○ ○ ○ ○	31	○ ○ ○ ○	44	○ ○ ○ ○
6	○ ○ ○ ○	19	○ ○ ○ ○	32	○ ○ ○ ○	45	○ ○ ○ ○
7	○ ○ ○ ○	20	○ ○ ○ ○	33	○ ○ ○ ○	46	○ ○ ○ ○
8	○ ○ ○ ○	21	○ ○ ○ ○	34	○ ○ ○ ○	47	○ ○ ○ ○
9	○ ○ ○ ○	22	○ ○ ○ ○	35	○ ○ ○ ○	48	○ ○ ○ ○
10	○ ○ ○ ○	23	○ ○ ○ ○	36	○ ○ ○ ○	49	○ ○ ○ ○
11	○ ○ ○ ○	24	○ ○ ○ ○	37	○ ○ ○ ○	50	○ ○ ○ ○
12	○ ○ ○ ○	25	○ ○ ○ ○	38	○ ○ ○ ○	51	○ ○ ○ ○
13	○ ○ ○ ○	26	○ ○ ○ ○	39	○ ○ ○ ○	52	○ ○ ○ ○

Download the College Board SAT Practice app to instantly score this test.
Learn more at sat.org/scoring.

SAT PRACTICE ANSWER SHEET

COMPLETE MARK ● EXAMPLES OF INCOMPLETE MARKS 

It is recommended that you use a No. 2 pencil. It is very important that you fill in the entire circle darkly and completely. If you change your response, erase as completely as possible. Incomplete marks or erasures may affect your score.

SECTION 2

	A B C D		A B C D		A B C D		A B C D		A B C D
1	○ ○ ○ ○	10	○ ○ ○ ○	19	○ ○ ○ ○	28	○ ○ ○ ○	37	○ ○ ○ ○
2	○ ○ ○ ○	11	○ ○ ○ ○	20	○ ○ ○ ○	29	○ ○ ○ ○	38	○ ○ ○ ○
3	○ ○ ○ ○	12	○ ○ ○ ○	21	○ ○ ○ ○	30	○ ○ ○ ○	39	○ ○ ○ ○
4	○ ○ ○ ○	13	○ ○ ○ ○	22	○ ○ ○ ○	31	○ ○ ○ ○	40	○ ○ ○ ○
5	○ ○ ○ ○	14	○ ○ ○ ○	23	○ ○ ○ ○	32	○ ○ ○ ○	41	○ ○ ○ ○
6	○ ○ ○ ○	15	○ ○ ○ ○	24	○ ○ ○ ○	33	○ ○ ○ ○	42	○ ○ ○ ○
7	○ ○ ○ ○	16	○ ○ ○ ○	25	○ ○ ○ ○	34	○ ○ ○ ○	43	○ ○ ○ ○
8	○ ○ ○ ○	17	○ ○ ○ ○	26	○ ○ ○ ○	35	○ ○ ○ ○	44	○ ○ ○ ○
9	○ ○ ○ ○	18	○ ○ ○ ○	27	○ ○ ○ ○	36	○ ○ ○ ○		

If you're scoring with our mobile app we recommend that you cut these pages out of the back of this book. The scoring does best with a flat page.

CollegeBoard

SAT PRACTICE ANSWER SHEET

COMPLETE MARK ● EXAMPLES OF INCOMPLETE MARKS 

It is recommended that you use a No. 2 pencil. It is very important that you fill in the entire circle darkly and completely. If you change your response, erase as completely as possible. Incomplete marks or erasures may affect your score.

SECTION 3

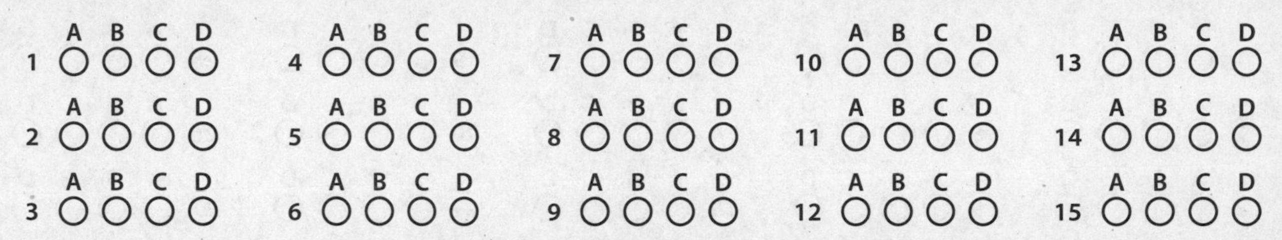

Only answers that are gridded will be scored. You will not receive credit for anything written in the boxes.

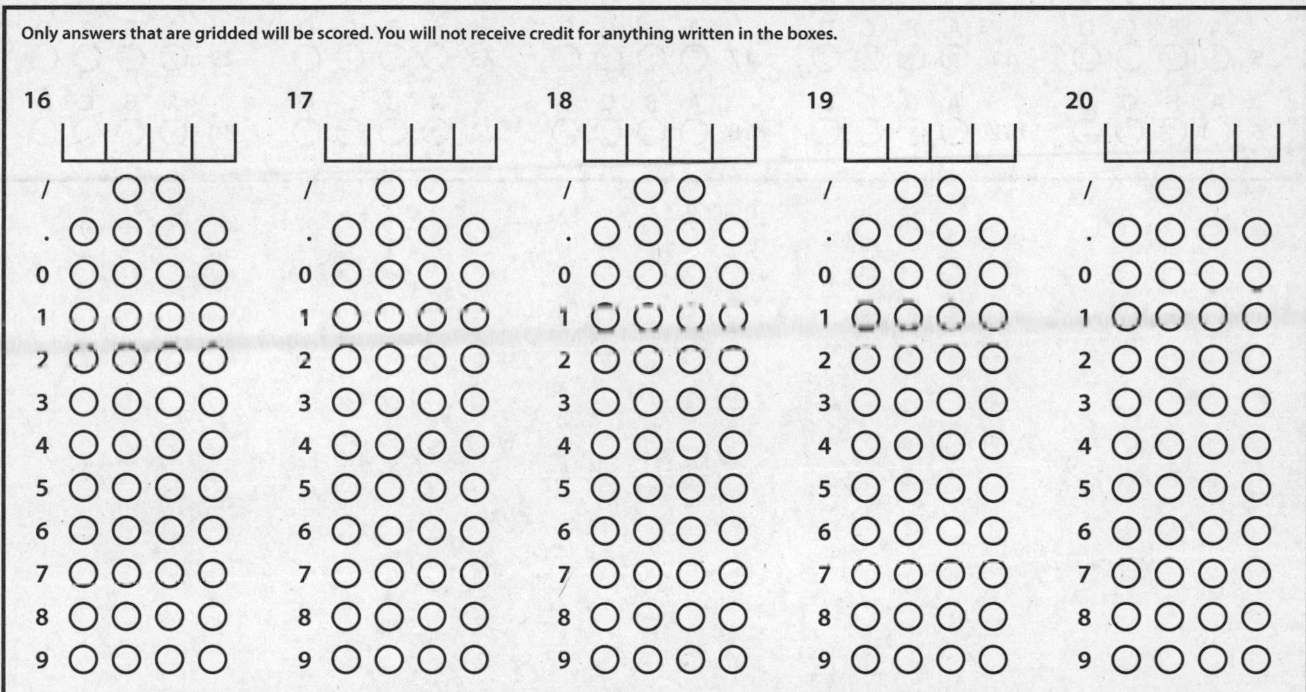

NO CALCULATOR ALLOWED

Did you know that you can print out these test sheets from the web? Learn more at sat.org/scoring.

SAT PRACTICE ANSWER SHEET

COMPLETE MARK ● EXAMPLES OF INCOMPLETE MARKS 

It is recommended that you use a No. 2 pencil. It is very important that you fill in the entire circle darkly and completely. If you change your response, erase as completely as possible. Incomplete marks or erasures may affect your score.

SECTION 4

1 A B C D	7 A B C D	13 A B C D	19 A B C D	25 A B C D
2 A B C D	8 A B C D	14 A B C D	20 A B C D	26 A B C D
3 A B C D	9 A B C D	15 A B C D	21 A B C D	27 A B C D
4 A B C D	10 A B C D	16 A B C D	22 A B C D	28 A B C D
5 A B C D	11 A B C D	17 A B C D	23 A B C D	29 A B C D
6 A B C D	12 A B C D	18 A B C D	24 A B C D	30 A B C D

CALCULATOR ALLOWED

If you're using our mobile app keep in mind that bad lighting and even shadows cast over the answer sheet can affect your score. Be sure to scan this in a well-lit area for best results.

CollegeBoard

SAT PRACTICE ANSWER SHEET

COMPLETE MARK ● EXAMPLES OF INCOMPLETE MARKS 

It is recommended that you use a No. 2 pencil. It is very important that you fill in the entire circle darkly and completely. If you change your response, erase as completely as possible. Incomplete marks or erasures may affect your score.

SECTION 4 (Continued)

Only answers that are gridded will be scored. You will not receive credit for anything written in the boxes.

31 32 33 34 35

/ . 0 1 2 3 4 5 6 7 8 9

Only answers that are gridded will be scored. You will not receive credit for anything written in the boxes.

36 37 38

/ . 0 1 2 3 4 5 6 7 8 9

CALCULATOR ALLOWED

○ I understand that my essay (without my name) may be reproduced in other College Board materials. If I mark this circle, I withhold my permission to reproduce my essay for any purposes beyond score reporting and the assessment of my writing skills. Marking this circle will have no effect on my score, nor will it prevent my essay from being made available to any college to which I send my SAT scores.

IMPORTANT: **USE A NO. 2 PENCIL. DO NOT WRITE OUTSIDE THE BORDER!** Words written outside the essay box or written in ink **WILL NOT APPEAR** in the copy sent to be scored, and your score will be affected.

PLANNING PAGE You may plan your essay in the unlined planning space below, but use only the lined pages following this one to write your essay. Any work on this planning page will not be scored.

Use pages 7 through 10 for your ESSAY →

FOR PLANNING ONLY

Use pages 7 through 10 for your ESSAY →

Page 6

PLEASE DO NOT WRITE IN THIS AREA

○○○○○○○○○○○○○○○○○○○○○○○○○○○○○○

SERIAL #

BEGIN YOUR ESSAY HERE.

You may continue on the next page.

PLEASE DO NOT WRITE IN THIS AREA

SERIAL #

You may continue on the next page.

DO NOT WRITE OUTSIDE OF THE BOX.

You may continue on the next page.

PLEASE DO NOT WRITE IN THIS AREA

SERIAL #

DO NOT WRITE OUTSIDE OF THE BOX.

STOP.

Answer Explanations

SAT Practice Test #2

Section 1: Reading Test

QUESTION 1

Choice A is the best answer. The narrator admits that his job is "irksome" (line 7) and reflects on the reasons for his dislike. The narrator admits that his work is a "dry and tedious task" (line 9) and that he has a poor relationship with his superior: "the antipathy which had sprung up between myself and my employer striking deeper root and spreading denser shade daily, excluded me from every glimpse of the sunshine of life" (lines 28-31).

Choices B, C, and D are incorrect because the narrator does not become increasingly competitive with his employer, publicly defend his choice of occupation, or exhibit optimism about his job.

QUESTION 2

Choice B is the best answer. The first sentence of the passage explains that people do not like to admit when they've chosen the wrong profession and that they will continue in their profession for a while before admitting their unhappiness. This statement mirrors the narrator's own situation, as the narrator admits he finds his own occupation "irksome" (line 7) but that he might "long have borne with the nuisance" (line 10) if not for his poor relationship with his employer.

Choices A, C, and D are incorrect because the first sentence does not discuss a controversy, focus on the narrator's employer, Edward Crimsworth, or provide any evidence of malicious conduct.

QUESTION 3

Choice C is the best answer. The first paragraph shifts from a general discussion of how people deal with choosing an occupation they later regret (lines 1-6) to the narrator's description of his own dissatisfaction with his occupation (lines 6-33).

Choices A, B, and D are incorrect because the first paragraph does not focus on the narrator's self-doubt, his expectations of life as a tradesman, or his identification of alternatives to his current occupation.

QUESTION 4

Choice A is the best answer. In lines 27-33, the narrator is describing the hostile relationship between him and his superior, Edward Crimsworth. This relationship causes the narrator to feel like he lives in the "shade" and in "humid darkness." These words evoke the narrator's feelings of dismay toward his current occupation and his poor relationship with his superior — factors that cause him to live without "the sunshine of life."

Choices B, C, and D are incorrect because the words "shade" and "darkness" do not reflect the narrator's sinister thoughts, his fear of confinement, or his longing for rest.

QUESTION 5

Choice D is the best answer. The narrator states that Crimsworth dislikes him because the narrator may "one day make a successful tradesman" (line 43). Crimsworth recognizes that the narrator is not "inferior to him" but rather more intelligent, someone who keeps "the padlock of silence on mental wealth in which [Crimsworth] was no sharer" (lines 44-48). Crimsworth feels inferior to the narrator and is jealous of the narrator's intellectual and professional abilities.

Choices A and C are incorrect because the narrator is not described as exhibiting "high spirits" or "rash actions," but "Caution, Tact, [and] Observation" (line 51). Choice B is incorrect because the narrator's "humble background" is not discussed.

QUESTION 6

Choice B is the best answer. Lines 61-62 state that the narrator "had long ceased to regard Mr. Crimsworth as my brother." In these lines, the term "brother" means friend or ally, which suggests that the narrator and Crimsworth were once friendly toward one another.

Choices A, C, and D are incorrect because the narrator originally viewed Crimsworth as a friend, or ally, and later as a hostile superior; he never viewed Crimsworth as a harmless rival, perceptive judge, or demanding mentor.

QUESTION 7

Choice D is the best answer. In lines 61-62, the narrator states that he once regarded Mr. Crimsworth as his "brother." This statement provides evidence that the narrator originally viewed Crimsworth as a sympathetic ally.

Choices A, B, and C do not provide the best evidence for the claim that Crimsworth was a sympathetic ally. Rather, choices A, B, and C provide evidence of the hostile relationship that currently exists between the narrator and Crimsworth.

QUESTION 8

Choice D is the best answer. In lines 48-53, the narrator states that he exhibited "Caution, Tact, [and] Observation" at work and watched Mr. Crimsworth with "lynx-eyes." The narrator acknowledges that Crimsworth was "prepared to steal snake-like" if he caught the narrator acting without tact or being disrespectful toward his superiors (lines 53-56). Thus, Crimsworth was trying to find a reason to place the narrator "in a ridiculous or mortifying position" (lines 49-50) by accusing the narrator of acting unprofessionally. The use of the lynx and snake serve to emphasize the narrator and Crimsworth's adversarial, or hostile, relationship.

Choices A and B are incorrect because the description of the lynx and snake does not contrast two hypothetical courses of action or convey a resolution. Choice C is incorrect because while lines 48-56 suggest that Crimsworth is trying to find a reason to fault the narrator's work, they do not imply that an altercation, or heated dispute, between the narrator and Crimsworth is likely to occur.

QUESTION 9

Choice B is the best answer. Lines 73-74 state that the narrator noticed there was no "cheering red gleam" of fire in his sitting-room fireplace. The lack of a "cheering," or comforting, fire suggests that the narrator sometimes found his lodgings to be dreary or bleak.

Choices A and D are incorrect because the narrator does not find his living quarters to be treacherous or intolerable. Choice C is incorrect because while the narrator is walking home he speculates about the presence of a fire in his sitting-room's fireplace (lines 69-74), which suggests that he could not predict the state of his living quarters.

QUESTION 10

Choice D is the best answer. In lines 68-74, the narrator states that he did not see the "cheering" glow of a fire in his sitting-room fireplace. This statement provides evidence that the narrator views his lodgings as dreary or bleak.

Choices A, B, and C do not provide the best evidence that the narrator views his lodgings as dreary. Choices A and C are incorrect because they do not provide the narrator's opinion of his lodgings, and choice B is incorrect because lines 21-23 describe the narrator's lodgings only as "small."

QUESTION 11

Choice D is the best answer. In lines 11-12, the author introduces the main purpose of the passage, which is to examine the "different views on where ethics should apply when someone makes an economic decision." The passage examines what historical figures Adam Smith, Aristotle, and John Stuart Mill believed about the relationship between ethics and economics.

Choices A, B, and C are incorrect because they identify certain points addressed in the passage (cost-benefit analysis, ethical economic behavior, and the role of the free market), but do not describe the passage's main purpose.

QUESTION 12

Choice D is the best answer. In lines 4-5, the author suggests that people object to criticizing ethics in free markets because they believe free markets are inherently ethical, and therefore, the role of ethics in free markets is unnecessary to study. In the opinion of the critics, free markets are ethical because they allow individuals to make their own choices about which goods to purchase and which goods to sell.

Choices A and B are incorrect because they are not objections that criticize the ethics of free markets. Choice C is incorrect because the author does not present the opinion that free markets depend on devalued currency.

QUESTION 13

Choice A is the best answer. In lines 4-5, the author states that some people believe that free markets are "already ethical" because they "allow for personal choice." This statement provides evidence that some people believe criticizing the ethics of free markets is unnecessary because free markets permit individuals to make their own choices.

Choices B, C, and D are incorrect because they do not provide the best evidence of an objection to a critique of the ethics of free markets.

QUESTION 14

Choice B is the best answer. In lines 6-7, the author states that people "have accepted the ethical critique and embraced corporate social responsibility." In this context, people "embrace," or readily adopt, corporate social responsibility by acting in a certain way.

Choices A, C, and D are incorrect because in this context "embraced" does not mean lovingly held, eagerly hugged, or reluctantly used.

QUESTION 15

Choice C is the best answer. The third and fourth paragraphs of the passage present Adam Smith's and Aristotle's different approaches to defining ethics in economics. The fifth paragraph offers a third approach to defining ethical economics, how "instead of rooting ethics in character or the consequences of actions, we can focus on our actions themselves. From this perspective some things are right, some wrong" (lines 45-48).

Choice A is incorrect because the fifth paragraph does not develop a counterargument. Choices B and D are incorrect because although "character" is briefly mentioned in the fifth paragraph, its relationship to ethics is examined in the fourth paragraph.

QUESTION 16

Choice A is the best answer. In lines 57-59, the author states that "Many moral dilemmas arise when these three versions pull in different directions but clashes are not inevitable." In this context, the three different perspectives on ethical economics may "clash," or conflict, with one another.

Choices B, C, and D are incorrect because in this context "clashes" does not mean mismatches, collisions, or brawls.

QUESTION 17

Choice C is the best answer. In lines 59-64, the author states, "Take fair trade coffee . . . for example: buying it might have good consequences, be virtuous, and also be the right way to act in a flawed market." The author is suggesting that in the example of fair trade coffee, all three perspectives about ethical economics — Adam Smith's belief in consequences dictating action, Aristotle's emphasis on character, and the third approach emphasizing the virtue of good actions — can be applied. These three approaches share "common ground" (line 64), as they all can be applied to the example of fair trade coffee without contradicting one another.

Choices A, B, and D are incorrect because they do not show how the three different approaches to ethical economics share common ground. Choice A simply states that there are "different views on ethics" in economics, choice B explains the third ethical economics approach, and choice D suggests that people "behave like a herd" when considering economics.

QUESTION 18

Choice C is the best answer. In lines 83-88, the author states that psychology can help "define ethics for us," which can help explain why people "react in disgust at economic injustice, or accept a moral law as universal."

Choices A and B are incorrect because they identify topics discussed in the final paragraph (human quirks and people's reaction to economic injustice) but not its main idea. Choice D is incorrect because the final paragraph does not suggest that economists may be responsible for reforming the free market.

QUESTION 19

Choice A is the best answer. The data in the graph show that in Tanzania between the years 2000 and 2008, fair trade coffee profits were around \$1.30 per pound, while profits of regular coffee were in the approximate range of 20–60 cents per pound.

Choices B, C, and D are incorrect because they are not supported by information in the graph.

QUESTION 20

Choice B is the best answer. The data in the graph indicate that between 2002 and 2004 the difference in per-pound profits between fair trade and regular coffee was about $1. In this time period, fair trade coffee was valued at around $1.30 per pound and regular coffee was valued at around 20 cents per pound. The graph also shows that regular coffee recorded the lowest profits between the years 2002 and 2004, while fair trade coffee remained relatively stable throughout the entire eight-year span (2000 to 2008).

Choices A, C, and D are incorrect because they do not indicate the greatest difference between per-pound profits for fair trade and regular coffee.

QUESTION 21

Choice C is the best answer. In lines 59-61, the author defines fair trade coffee as "coffee that is sold with a certification that indicates the farmers and workers who produced it were paid a fair wage." This definition suggests that purchasing fair trade coffee is an ethically responsible choice, and the fact that fair trade coffee is being produced and is profitable suggests that ethical economics is still a consideration. The graph's data support this claim by showing how fair trade coffee was more than twice as profitable as regular coffee.

Choice A is incorrect because the graph suggests that people acting on empathy (by buying fair trade coffee) is productive for fair trade coffee farmers and workers. Choices B and D are incorrect because the graph does not provide support for the idea that character or people's fears factor into economic choices.

QUESTION 22

Choice C is the best answer. The author of Passage 1 indicates that people can benefit from using screen-based technologies as these technologies strengthen "certain cognitive skills" (line 3) and the "brain functions related to fast-paced problem solving" (lines 14-15).

Choice A is incorrect because the author of Passage 1 cites numerous studies of screen-based technologies. Choice B is incorrect because it is not supported by Passage 1, and choice D is incorrect because while the author mentions some benefits to screen-based technologies, he does not encourage their use.

QUESTION 23

Choice A is the best answer. In lines 3-4, the author of Passage 1 provides evidence that the use of screen-based technologies has some positive effects: "Certain cognitive skills are strengthened by our use of computers and the Net."

Choices B, C, and D are incorrect because they do not provide the best evidence that the use of screen-based technologies has some positive effects. Choices B, C, and D introduce and describe the author's reservations about screen-based technologies.

QUESTION 24

Choice B is the best answer. The author of Passage 1 cites Patricia Greenfield's study, which found that people's use of screen-based technologies weakened their ability to acquire knowledge, perform "inductive analysis" and "critical thinking," and be imaginative and reflective (lines 34-38). The author of Passage 1 concludes that the use of screen-based technologies interferes with people's ability to think "deeply" (lines 47-50).

Choices A, C, and D are incorrect because the author of Passage 1 does not address how using the Internet affects people's health, social contacts, or self-confidence.

QUESTION 25

Choice C is the best answer. In lines 39-41, the author states, "We know that the human brain is highly plastic; neurons and synapses change as circumstances change." In this context, the brain is "plastic" because it is malleable, or able to change.

Choices A, B, and D are incorrect because in this context "plastic" does not mean creative, artificial, or sculptural.

QUESTION 26

Choice B is the best answer. In lines 60-65, the author of Passage 2 explains how speed-reading does not "revamp," or alter, how the brain processes information. He supports this statement by explaining how Woody Allen's reading of *War and Peace* in one sitting caused him to describe the novel as "about Russia." Woody Allen was not able to comprehend the "famously long" novel by speed-reading it.

Choices A and D are incorrect because Woody Allen's description of *War and Peace* does not suggest he disliked Tolstoy's writing style or that he regretted reading the book. Choice C is incorrect because the anecdote about Woody Allen is unrelated to multitasking.

QUESTION 27

Choice D is the best answer. The author of Passage 2 states that people like novelists and scientists improve in their profession by "immers[ing] themselves in their fields" (line 79). Both novelists and scientists, in other words, become absorbed in their areas of expertise.

Choices A and C are incorrect because the author of Passage 2 does not suggest that novelists and scientists both take risks when they pursue knowledge or are curious about other subjects. Choice B is incorrect because the author of Passage 2 states that "accomplished people" don't perform "intellectual calisthenics," or exercises that improve their minds (lines 77-78).

QUESTION 28

Choice D is the best answer. In lines 83-90, the author of Passage 2 criticizes media critics for their alarmist writing: "Media critics write as if the brain takes on the qualities of whatever it consumes, the informational equivalent of 'you are what you eat.'" The author then compares media critics' "you are what you eat" mentality to ancient people's belief that "eating fierce animals made them fierce." The author uses this analogy to discredit media critics' belief that consumption of electronic media alters the brain.

Choices A, B, and C are incorrect because the final sentence of Passage 2 does not use ornate language, employ humor, or evoke nostalgia for the past.

QUESTION 29

Choice D is the best answer. The author of Passage 1 argues that online and other screen-based technologies affect people's abilities to think deeply (lines 47-50). The author of Passage 2 argues that the effects of consuming electronic media are less drastic than media critics suggest (lines 81-82).

Choices A and B are incorrect because they discuss points made in the passages but not the main purpose of the passages. Choice C is incorrect because neither passage argues in favor of increasing financial support for certain studies.

QUESTION 30

Choice B is the best answer. The author of Passage 1 cites scientific research that suggests online and screen-based technologies have a negative effect on the brain (lines 25-38). The author of Passage 2 is critical of the research highlighted in Passage 1: "Critics of new media sometimes use science itself to press their case, citing research that shows how 'experience can change the brain.' But cognitive neuroscientists roll their eyes at such talk" (lines 51-54).

Choices A, C, and D are incorrect because they do not accurately describe the relationship between the two passages. Passage 1 does not take a clinical approach to the topic. Passage 2 does not take a high-level view of a finding examined in depth in Passage 1, nor does it predict negative reactions to the findings discussed in paragraph 1.

QUESTION 31

Choice C is the best answer. In Passage 1, the author cites psychologist Patricia Greenfield's finding that "'every medium develops some cognitive skills at the expense of others'" (lines 29-31). In Passage 2, the author states "If you train people to do one thing (recognize shapes, solve math puzzles, find hidden words), they get better at doing that thing, but almost nothing else" (lines 71-74). Both authors would agree than an improvement in one cognitive area, such as visual-spatial skills, would not result in improved skills in other areas.

Choice A is incorrect because hand-eye coordination is not discussed in Passage 2. Choice B is incorrect because Passage 1 does not suggest that critics of electronic media tend to overreact. Choice D is incorrect because neither passage discusses whether Internet users prefer reading printed texts or digital texts.

QUESTION 32

Choice B is the best answer. In Passage 1, the author cites Michael Merzenich's claim that when people adapt to a new cultural phenomenon, including the use of a new medium, we end up with a "different brain" (lines 41-43). The author of Passage 2 somewhat agrees with Merzenich's claim by stating, "Yes, every time we learn a fact or skill the wiring of the brain changes" (lines 54-56).

Choices A, C, and D do not provide the best evidence that the author of Passage 2 would agree to some extent with Merzenich's claim. Choices A and D are incorrect because the claims are attributed to critics of new media. Choice C is incorrect because it shows that the author of Passage 2 does not completely agree with Merzenich's claim about brain plasticity.

QUESTION 33

Choice B is the best answer. In lines 15-30, Stanton argues that men make all the decisions in "the church, the state, and the home." This absolute power has led to a disorganized society, a "fragmentary condition of everything." Stanton confirms this claim when she states that society needs women to "lift man up into the higher realms of thought and action" (lines 59-60).

Choices A and D are incorrect because Stanton does not focus on women's lack of equal educational opportunities or inability to hold political positions. Choice C is incorrect because although Stanton implies women are not allowed to vote, she never mentions that "poor candidates" are winning elections.

QUESTION 34

Choice A is the best answer. Stanton argues that women are repressed in society because men hold "high carnival," or have all the power, and make the rules in "the church, the state, and the home" (lines 15-30). Stanton claims that men have total control over women, "overpowering the feminine element everywhere" (line 17).

Choices B, C, and D are incorrect because Stanton does not use the term "high carnival" to emphasize that the time period is freewheeling, or unrestricted; that there has been a scandalous decline in moral values; or that the power of women is growing.

QUESTION 35

Choice D is the best answer. In lines 15-22, Stanton states that men's absolute rule in society is "crushing out all the diviner qualities in human nature," such that society knows very "little of true manhood and womanhood." Stanton argues that society knows less about womanhood than manhood, because womanhood has "scarce been recognized as a power until within the last century." This statement indicates that society's acknowledgment of "womanhood," or women's true character, is a fairly recent historical development.

Choices A, B, and C are incorrect because Stanton describes men's control of society, their domination of the domestic sphere, and the prevalence of war and injustice as long-established realities.

QUESTION 36

Choice B is the best answer. In lines 15-22, Stanton provides evidence for the claim that society's acknowledgment of "womanhood," or women's true character, is a fairly recent historical development: "[womanhood] has scarce been recognized as a power until within the last century."

Choices A, C, and D are incorrect because they do not provide the best evidence that society's acknowledgment of "womanhood," or women's true character, is a fairly recent historical development. Rather, choices A, C, and D discuss men's character, power, and influence.

QUESTION 37

Choice B is the best answer. In lines 22-25, Stanton states, "Society is but the reflection of man himself, untempered by woman's thought; the hard iron rule we feel alike in the church, the state, and the home." In this context, man's "rule" in "the church, the state, and the home" means that men have a controlling force in all areas of society.

Choices A, C, and D are incorrect because in this context "rule" does not mean a general guideline, an established habit, or a procedural method.

QUESTION 38

Choice D is the best answer. In lines 31-34, Stanton argues that people use the term "the strong-minded" to refer to women who advocate for "the right of suffrage," or the right to vote in elections. In this context, people use the term "the strong-minded" to criticize female suffragists, as they believe voting will make women too "masculine."

Choices A and B are incorrect because Stanton does not suggest that people use the term "the strong-minded" as a compliment. Choice C is incorrect because Stanton suggests that "the strong-minded" is a term used to criticize women who want to vote, not those who enter male-dominated professions.

QUESTION 39

Choice C is the best answer. In lines 35-38, Stanton states that society contains hardly any women in the "best sense," and clarifies that too many women are "reflections, varieties, and dilutions of the masculine gender." Stanton is suggesting that there are few "best," or genuine, women who are not completely influenced or controlled by men.

Choices A, B, and D are incorrect because in this context "best" does not mean superior, excellent, or rarest.

QUESTION 40

Choice A is the best answer. In lines 53-55, Stanton argues that man "mourns," or regrets, how his power has caused "falsehood, selfishness, and violence" to become the "law" of society. Stanton is arguing that men are lamenting, or expressing regret about, how their governance has created problems.

Choices B, C, and D are incorrect because Stanton does not suggest that men are advocating for women's right to vote or for female equality, nor are they requesting women's opinions about improving civic life.

QUESTION 41

Choice B is the best answer. In lines 53-55, Stanton provides evidence that men are lamenting the problems they have created, as they recognize that their actions have caused "falsehood, selfishness, and violence [to become] the law of life."

Choices A, C, and D are incorrect because they do not provide the best evidence that men are lamenting the problems they have created. Choice A explains society's current fragmentation. Choices C and D present Stanton's main argument for women's enfranchisement.

QUESTION 42

Choice D is the best answer. In the sixth paragraph, Stanton differentiates between men and masculine traits. Stanton argues that masculine traits or "characteristics," such as a "love of acquisition and conquest," serve to "subjugate one man to another" (lines 67-78). Stanton is suggesting that some masculine traits position men within certain power structures.

Choices A and B are incorrect because the sixth paragraph does not primarily establish a contrast between men and women or between the spiritual and material worlds. Choice C is incorrect because although Stanton argues that not "all men are hard, selfish, and brutal," she does not discuss what constitutes a "good" man.

QUESTION 43

Choice C is the best answer. In the first paragraph, the author identifies the natural phenomenon "internal waves" (line 3), and explains why they are important: "internal waves are fundamental parts of ocean water dynamics, transferring heat to the ocean depths and bringing up cold water from below" (lines 7-9).

Choices A, B, and D are incorrect because they do not identify the main purpose of the first paragraph, as that paragraph does not focus on a scientific device, a common misconception, or a recent study.

QUESTION 44

Choice B is the best answer. In lines 17-19, researcher Tom Peacock argues that in order to create precise global climate models, scientists must be able to "capture processes" such as how internal waves are formed. In this context, to "capture" a process means to record it for scientific study.

Choices A, C, and D are incorrect because in this context "capture" does not mean to control, secure, or absorb.

QUESTION 45

Choice D is the best answer. In lines 17-19, researcher Tom Peacock argues that scientists need to "capture processes" of internal waves to develop "more and more accurate climate models." Peacock is suggesting that studying internal waves will inform the development of scientific models.

Choices A, B, and C are incorrect because Peacock does not state that monitoring internal waves will allow people to verify wave heights, improve satellite image quality, or prevent coastal damage.

QUESTION 46

Choice C is the best answer. In lines 17-19, researcher Tom Peacock provides evidence that studying internal waves will inform the development of key scientific models, such as "more accurate climate models."

Choices A, B, and D are incorrect because they do not provide the best evidence that studying internal waves will inform the development of key scientific models; rather, they provide general information about internal waves.

QUESTION 47

Choice A is the best answer. In lines 65-67, the author notes that Tom Peacock and his team "were able to devise a mathematical model that describes the movement and formation of these waves." In this context, the researchers devised, or created, a mathematical model.

Choices B, C, and D are incorrect because in this context "devise" does not mean to solve, imagine, or begin.

QUESTION 48

Choice B is the best answer. Tom Peacock and his team created a model of the "Luzon's Strait's underwater topography" and determined that its "distinct double-ridge shape . . . [is] responsible for generating the underwater [internal] waves" (lines 53-55). The author notes that this model describes only internal waves in the Luzon Strait but that the team's findings may "help researchers understand how internal waves are generated in other places around the world" (lines 67-70). The author's claim suggests that while internal waves in the Luzon Strait are "some of the largest in the world" (line 25) due to the region's topography, internal waves occurring in other regions may be caused by some similar factors.

Choice A is incorrect because the author notes that the internal waves in the Luzon Strait are "some of the largest in the world" (line 25), which suggests that internal waves reach varying heights. Choices C and D are incorrect because they are not supported by the researchers' findings.

QUESTION 49

Choice D is the best answer. In lines 67-70, the author provides evidence that, while the researchers' findings suggest the internal waves in the Luzon Strait are influenced by the region's topography, the findings may "help researchers understand how internal waves are generated in other places around the world." This statement suggests that all internal waves may be caused by some similar factors.

Choices A, B, and C are incorrect because they do not provide the best evidence that internal waves are caused by similar factors but influenced by the distinct topographies of different regions. Rather, choices A, B, and C reference general information about internal waves or focus solely on those that occur in the Luzon Strait.

QUESTION 50

Choice D is the best answer. During the period 19:12 to 20:24, the graph shows the 13°C isotherm increasing in depth from about 20 to 40 meters.

Choices A, B, and C are incorrect because during the time period 19:12 to 20:24 the 9°C, 10°C, and 11°C isotherms all decreased in depth.

QUESTION 51

Choice D is the best answer. In lines 3-6, the author notes that internal waves "do not ride the ocean surface" but "move underwater, undetectable without the use of satellite imagery or sophisticated monitoring equipment." The graph shows that the isotherms in an internal wave never reach the ocean's surface, as the isotherms do not record a depth of 0.

Choice A is incorrect because the graph provides no information about salinity. Choice B is incorrect because the graph shows layers of less dense water (which, based on the passage, are warmer) riding above layers of denser water (which, based on the passage, are cooler). Choice C is incorrect because the graph shows that internal waves push isotherms of warmer water above bands of colder water.

QUESTION 52

Choice A is the best answer. In lines 7-9, the author notes that internal waves are "fundamental parts of ocean water dynamics" because they transfer "heat to the ocean depths and brin[g] up cold water from below." The graph shows an internal wave forcing the warm isotherms to depths that typically are colder. For example, at 13:12, the internal wave transfers "heat to the ocean depths" by forcing the 10°C, 11°C, and 13°C isotherms to depths that typically are colder.

Choices B, C, and D are incorrect because the graph does not show how internal waves affect the ocean's density, surface temperature, or tide flow.

Section 2: Writing and Language Test

QUESTION 1

Choice B is the best answer because it provides a noun, "reductions," yielding a grammatically complete and coherent sentence.

Choices A, C, and D are incorrect because each provides a verb or gerund, while the underlined portion calls for a noun.

QUESTION 2

Choice B is the best answer because it offers a transitional adverb, "Consequently," that communicates a cause-effect relationship between the funding reduction identified in the previous sentence and the staffing decrease described in this sentence.

Choices A, C, and D are incorrect because each misidentifies the relationship between the preceding sentence and the sentence of which it is a part.

QUESTION 3

Choice A is the best answer because the singular verb "has" agrees with the singular noun "trend" that appears earlier in the sentence.

Choices B, C, and D are incorrect because the plural verb "have" does not agree with the singular subject "trend," and the relative pronoun "which" unnecessarily interrupts the direct relationship between "trend" and the verb.

QUESTION 4

Choice A is the best answer because it states accurately why the proposed clause should be added to the sentence. Without these specific examples, readers have only a vague sense of what "nonprint" formats might be.

Choices B, C, and D are incorrect because each represents a misinterpretation of the relationship between the proposed clause to be added and the surrounding text in the passage.

QUESTION 5

Choice D is the best answer because it includes only the preposition and noun that the sentence requires.

Choices A, B, and C are incorrect because each includes an unnecessary pronoun, either "them" or "their." The sentence contains no referents that would circulate e-books.

QUESTION 6

Choice D is the best answer because the verb form "cataloging" parallels the other verbs in the series.

Choices A, B, and C are incorrect because each interrupts the parallel structure in the verb series, either through an incorrect verb form or with an unnecessary subject.

QUESTION 7

Choice B is the best answer because it consolidates references to the subject, "librarians," by placing the relative pronoun "whose" immediately following "librarians." This results in a logical flow of information within the sentence.

Choices A, C, and D are incorrect because each fails to place "librarians" as the main subject of the sentence without redundancy, resulting in a convoluted sentence whose relevance to the preceding and subsequent sentences is unclear.

QUESTION 8

Choice D is the best answer because no conjunction is necessary to communicate the relationship between the clauses in the sentence. The conjunction "While" at the beginning of the sentence already creates a comparison.

Choices A, B, and C are incorrect because each provides an unnecessary coordinating conjunction.

QUESTION 9

Choice B is the best answer because it mentions time periods when the free services described later in the sentence are particularly useful to library patrons.

Choices A, C, and D are incorrect because each creates redundancy or awkwardness in the remainder of the sentence.

QUESTION 10

Choice B is the best answer because it is concise; it is also consistent with the formal language in the rest of the sentence and the passage overall.

Choices A, C, and D are incorrect because each is either unnecessarily wordy or uses colloquial language that does not correspond with the tone of the passage.

QUESTION 11

Choice C is the best answer because it restates the writer's primary argument, which may be found at the end of the first paragraph: "As public libraries adapt to rapid technological advances in information distribution, librarians' roles are actually expanding."

Choices A, B, and D are incorrect because they do not paraphrase the writer's primary claim.

QUESTION 12

Choice B is the best answer because it clarifies that the sentence, which mentions a specific large-scale painting at the Art Institute of Chicago, is an example supporting the preceding claim about large-scale paintings.

Choices A, C, and D are incorrect because they propose transitional words or phrases that do not accurately represent the relationship between the preceding sentence and the sentence containing the underlined portion.

QUESTION 13

Choice D is the best answer because no punctuation is necessary in the underlined phrase.

Choices A, B, and C are incorrect because each separates parts of the noun phrase "painter Georges Seurat's 10-foot-wide *A Sunday Afternoon on the Island of La Grande Jatte*" from one another with one or more unnecessary commas.

QUESTION 14

Choice C is the best answer because it provides the appropriate possessive form, "its," and a colon to introduce the identifying phrase that follows.

Choices A, B, and D are incorrect because none contains both the appropriate possessive form of "it" and the punctuation that creates a grammatically standard sentence.

QUESTION 15

Choice C is the best answer because an analysis of the consequences of King Louis XV's reign is irrelevant to the paragraph.

Choices A, B, and D are incorrect because each represents a misinterpretation of the relationship between the proposed sentence to be added and the main point of the paragraph.

QUESTION 16

Choice C is the best answer because it provides a coordinating conjunction, "and," to connect the two verb phrases "are characterized" and "are covered."

Choices A, B, and D are incorrect because each lacks the conjunction needed to connect the two verb phrases "are characterized" and "are covered."

QUESTION 17

Choice B is the best answer because it offers an example of an additional household item, a "tea cup," with a specific measurement that is one-twelfth of its actual size.

Choices A, C, D are incorrect because, compared to the example preceding the underlined portion, each is vague and fails to offer a specific measurement of an additional household item.

QUESTION 18

Choice B is the best answer because it provides correct punctuation and the coordinating conjunction "but," which acknowledges the possible contrast between being "sparsely furnished" and displaying "just as true" period details.

Choices A, C, and D are incorrect because each communicates an illogical relationship between the phrases that precede and follow the underlined portion.

QUESTION 19

Choice A is the best answer because it provides a clause that is the most similar to the two preceding clauses, which both end with a reference to a specific wall.

Choices B, C, and D are incorrect because each deviates from the stylistic pattern of the preceding two clauses.

QUESTION 20

Choice D is the best answer because the article "a" requires the singular noun "visitor," and the simple present verb "remark" is the appropriate verb tense in this context.

Choices A, B, and C are incorrect because each contains either a noun or verb that does not fit the context.

QUESTION 21

Choice D is the best answer because it identifies the drawers, rather than the visitor, as being "dotted with pin-sized knobs."

Choices A, B, and C are incorrect because all three contain dangling modifiers that obscure the relationship between the visitor, the drawers, and the pin-sized knobs.

QUESTION 22

Choice B is the best answer because paragraph 3 offers an overview of the exhibit and so serves to introduce the specific aspects of particular miniature rooms described in paragraphs 2 and 4.

Choices A, C, and D are incorrect because each proposes a placement of paragraph 2 that prevents the passage from developing in a logical sequence.

QUESTION 23

Choice A is the best answer because it correctly completes the noun phrase that begins with "sea otters," and directly follows the noun phrase with the verb "help."

Choices B, C, and D are incorrect because each separates the noun "otters" from the verb "help" in a way that results in a grammatically incomplete sentence.

QUESTION 24

Choice B is the best answer because the data in the chart show lower sea urchin density in areas where sea otters have lived for two years or less than in areas where no otters are present.

Choices A, C, and D are incorrect because none accurately describes the data in the chart.

QUESTION 25

Choice B is the best answer because the conjunctive adverb "however" accurately communicates the contrast between an environment shaped by the presence of sea otters, described in the preceding sentence, and an environment shaped by the absence of sea otters, described in this sentence.

Choices A, C, and D are incorrect because each presents a conjunctive adverb that does not accurately depict the relationship between the preceding sentence and the sentence with the underlined word.

QUESTION 26

Choice A is the best answer because the additional information usefully connects the carbon dioxide levels mentioned in this sentence with the global warming mentioned in the previous sentence.

Choices B, C, and D are incorrect because each misinterprets the relationship between the proposed information and the main points of the paragraph and the passage.

QUESTION 27

Choice D is the best answer because it offers the verb "suggests" followed directly by its object, a that-clause, without interruption.

Choices A, B, and C are incorrect because each contains punctuation that unnecessarily separates the study from its findings — that is, separates the verb from its object.

QUESTION 28

Choice A is the best answer because it accurately reflects the fact that sea urchins "graze voraciously on kelp," as stated in the first paragraph, and it also maintains the tone of the passage.

Choices B, C, and D are incorrect because each offers a term that does not accurately describe the behavior of sea otters.

QUESTION 29

Choice C is the best answer because the possessive singular pronoun "its" corresponds with the referent "kelp," which appears later in the sentence, and with the possessive relationship between the pronoun and the "terrestrial plant cousins."

Choices A, B, and D are incorrect because none provides a pronoun that is both singular and possessive.

QUESTION 30

Choice C is the best answer because it provides the noun "sea otters" to identify who or what "played a role."

Choices A, B, and D are incorrect because each provides a pronoun that makes no sense in the context of the paragraph and the passage, which is about the role sea otters play — not the role scientists play or the role kelp plays.

QUESTION 31

Choice D is the best answer because sentence 5 indicates that sea otters' importance in decreasing atmospheric carbon dioxide was not known, and the sentence to be added indicates that a surprise will follow. Sentence 6 provides that surprise: sea otters have a large impact on the amount of carbon dioxide kelp can remove from the atmosphere.

Choices A, B, and C are incorrect because each interrupts the logical flow of ideas in the paragraph.

QUESTION 32

Choice B is the best answer because its clear wording and formal tone correspond with the passage's established style.

Choices A, C, and D are incorrect because each contains vague language that is inconsistent with the passage's clear wording and formal tone.

QUESTION 33

Choice D is the best answer because it provides punctuation that appropriately identifies "removed" as the definition of "sequestered."

Choices A, B, and C are incorrect because each contains punctuation that obscures the relationship between "sequestered," "removed," and the text that follows.

QUESTION 34

Choice D is the best answer because it provides a conjunction that correctly identifies the relationship between "a practice" and the actions involved in the practice.

Choices A, B, and C are incorrect because each contains a conjunction that miscommunicates the relationship between the text that precedes and follows the underlined portion.

QUESTION 35

Choice A is the best answer because it provides a comma to close the appositive clause "a practice whereby products are designed to have a limited period of usefulness," which also begins with a comma.

Choices B, C, and D are incorrect because each provides closing punctuation inconsistent with the punctuation at the beginning of the clause.

QUESTION 36

Choice D is the best answer because it provides an adjective that accurately describes the clear "contrast" between products "designed to have a limited period of usefulness" and those "produced to be durable."

Choices A, B, and C are incorrect because none provides an adjective that appropriately modifies "contrast" in the context of the paragraph.

QUESTION 37

Choice A is the best answer because by mentioning the "specialized" methods used in repair shops, it suggests that repairing goods is seen as a specialty rather than as a common activity. This connects logically with the "rare" repair shops introduced just before the underlined portion.

Choices B, C, and D are incorrect because none provides information that supports the claim made in the sentence.

QUESTION 38

Choice B is the best answer because it provides the correct spelling of the noun "fair," meaning exhibition, and uses the correct word "than" to create the comparison between a "fair" and a "café."

Choices A, C, and D are incorrect because each contains a misspelling of either "fair" or "than."

QUESTION 39

Choice C is the best answer because it offers a relative pronoun that properly links the noun "Martine Postma" with the appropriate verb "wanted."

Choices A, B, and D are incorrect because none contains a pronoun that is appropriate for the referent and placement of the clause.

QUESTION 40

Choice D is the best answer because it provides the most concise phrasing and links the sentence appropriately to the previous sentence.

Choices A, B, and C are incorrect because each provides an unnecessary adverb that obscures the relationship between this sentence and the previous one.

QUESTION 41

Choice D is the best answer because the gerund "waiting" corresponds with the preposition "for" and the present tense used in the rest of the sentence.

Choices A, B, and C are incorrect because each contains a verb form not used with the preposition "for."

QUESTION 42

Choice C is the best answer because it appropriately places sentence 5, which describes the places Repair Cafés can be found today, between a sentence that gives the first Repair Café's location and purpose and a statement about current customers and how they use Repair Cafés.

Choices A, B, and D are incorrect because each creates a paragraph with an inappropriate shift in verb tense and, therefore, an illogical sequence of information.

QUESTION 43

Choice C is the best answer because it accurately states that the issue of "corporate and service-based jobs" is not particularly relevant at this point in the paragraph. The focus here is on repairing objects in a "throwaway culture," not jobs.

Choices A, B, and D are incorrect because each misinterprets the relationship between the proposed text and the information in the paragraph.

QUESTION 44

Choice D is the best answer because the phrase "and other countries" communicates the fact that there are additional items not being named that could be added to the list; no other wording is required to clarify that point.

Choices A, B, and C are incorrect because each presents a word or phrase that results in a redundancy with "and other countries."

Section 3: Math Test – No Calculator

QUESTION 1

Choice C is correct. Subtracting 6 from each side of $5x + 6 = 10$ yields $5x = 4$. Dividing both sides of $5x = 4$ by 5 yields $x = \frac{4}{5}$. The value of x can now be substituted into the expression $10x + 3$, giving $10\left(\frac{4}{5}\right) + 3 = 11$. Alternatively, the expression $10x + 3$ can be rewritten as $2(5x + 6) - 9$, and 10 can be substituted for $5x + 6$, giving $2(10) - 9 = 11$.

Choices A, B, and D are incorrect. Each of these choices leads to $5x + 6 \neq 10$, contradicting the given equation, $5x + 6 = 10$. For example, choice A is incorrect because if the value of $10x + 3$ were 4, then it would follow that $x = 0.1$, and the value of $5x + 6$ would be 6.5, not 10.

QUESTION 2

Choice B is correct. Multiplying each side of $x + y = 0$ by 2 gives $2x + 2y = 0$. Then, adding the corresponding sides of $2x + 2y = 0$ and $3x - 2y = 10$ gives $5x = 10$. Dividing each side of $5x = 10$ by 5 gives $x = 2$. Finally, substituting 2 for x in $x + y = 0$ gives $2 + y = 0$, or $y = -2$. Therefore, the solution to the given system of equations is $(2, -2)$.

Alternatively, the equation $x + y = 0$ can be rewritten as $x = -y$, and substituting x for $-y$ in $3x - 2y = 10$ gives $5x = 10$, or $x = 2$. The value of y can then be found in the same way as before.

Choices A, C, and D are incorrect because when the given values of x and y are substituted into $x + y = 0$ and $3x - 2y = 10$, either one or both of the equations are not true. These answers may result from sign errors or other computational errors.

QUESTION 3

Choice A is correct. The price of the job, in dollars, is calculated using the expression $60 + 12nh$, where 60 is a fixed price and $12nh$ depends on the number of landscapers, n, working the job and the number of hours, h, the job takes those n landscapers. Since nh is the total number of hours of work done when n landscapers work h hours, the cost of the job increases by $12 for each hour each landscaper works. Therefore, of the choices given, the best interpretation of the number 12 is that the company charges $12 per hour for each landscaper.

Choice B is incorrect because the number of landscapers that will work each job is represented by n in the equation, not by the number 12. Choice C is incorrect because the price of the job increases by $12n$ dollars each hour, which will not equal 12 dollars unless $n = 1$. Choice D is incorrect because the total number of hours each landscaper works is equal to h. The number of hours each landscaper works in a day is not provided.

QUESTION 4

Choice A is correct. If a polynomial expression is in the form $(x)^2 + 2(x)(y) + (y)^2$, then it is equivalent to $(x + y)^2$. Because $9a^4 + 12a^2b^2 + 4b^4 = (3a^2)^2 + 2(3a^2)(2b^2) + (2b^2)^2$, it can be rewritten as $(3a^2 + 2b^2)^2$.

Choice B is incorrect. The expression $(3a + 2b)^4$ is equivalent to the product $(3a + 2b)(3a + 2b)(3a + 2b)(3a + 2b)$. This product will contain the term $4(3a)^3(2b) = 216a^3b$. However, the given polynomial, $9a^4 + 12a^2b^2 + 4b^4$, does not contain the term $216a^3b$. Therefore, $9a^4 + 12a^2b^2 + 4b^4 \neq (3a + 2b)^4$. Choice C is incorrect. The expression $(9a^2 + 4b^2)^2$ is equivalent to the product $(9a^2 + 4b^2)(9a^2 + 4b^2)$. This product will contain the term $(9a^2)(9a^2) = 81a^4$. However, the given polynomial, $9a^4 + 12a^2b^2 + 4b^4$, does not contain the term $81a^4$. Therefore, $9a^4 + 12a^2b^2 + 4b^4 \neq (9a^2 + 4b^2)^2$. Choice D is incorrect. The expression $(9a + 4b)^4$ is equivalent to the product $(9a + 4b)(9a + 4b)(9a + 4b)(9a + 4b)$. This product will contain the term $(9a)(9a)(9a)(9a) = 6{,}561a^4$. However, the given polynomial, $9a^4 + 12a^2b^2 + 4b^4$, does not contain the term $6{,}561a^4$. Therefore, $9a^4 + 12a^2b^2 + 4b^4 \neq (9a + 4b)^4$.

QUESTION 5

Choice C is correct. Since $\sqrt{2k^2 + 17} - x = 0$, and $x = 7$, one can substitute 7 for x, which gives $\sqrt{2k^2 + 17} - 7 = 0$. Adding 7 to each side of $\sqrt{2k^2 + 17} - 7 = 0$ gives $\sqrt{2k^2 + 17} = 7$. Squaring each side of $\sqrt{2k^2 + 17} = 7$ will remove the square root symbol: $\left(\sqrt{2k^2 + 17}\right)^2 = (7)^2$, or $2k^2 + 17 = 49$. Then subtracting 17 from each side of $2k^2 + 17 = 49$ gives $2k^2 = 49 - 17 = 32$, and dividing each side of $2k^2 = 32$ by 2 gives $k^2 = 16$. Finally, taking the square root of each side of $k^2 = 16$ gives $k = \pm 4$, and since the problem states that $k > 0$, it follows that $k = 4$.

Since the sides of an equation were squared while solving $\sqrt{2k^2 + 17} - 7 = 0$, it is possible that an extraneous root was produced. However, substituting 4 for k in $\sqrt{2k^2 + 17} - 7 = 0$ confirms that 4 is a solution for k: $\sqrt{2(4)^2 + 17} - 7 = \sqrt{32 + 17} - 7 = \sqrt{49} - 7 = 7 - 7 = 0$.

Choices A, B, and D are incorrect because substituting any of these values for k in $\sqrt{2k^2 + 17} - 7 = 0$ does not yield a true statement.

QUESTION 6

Choice D is correct. Since lines ℓ and k are parallel, the lines have the same slope. The slope m of a line that passes through two points (x_1, y_1) and (x_2, y_2) can be found as $m = \frac{y_2 - y_1}{x_2 - x_1}$. Line ℓ passes through the points (0, 2) and (−5, 0), so its slope is $\frac{0 - 2}{-5 - 0}$, which is $\frac{2}{5}$. The slope of line k must also be $\frac{2}{5}$. Since line k has slope $\frac{2}{5}$ and passes through the points (p, 0) and (0, −4), it follows that $\frac{-4 - 0}{0 - p} = \frac{2}{5}$, or $\frac{4}{p} = \frac{2}{5}$. Multiplying each side of $\frac{4}{p} = \frac{2}{5}$ by $5p$ gives $20 = 2p$, and therefore, $p = 10$.

Choices A, B, and C are incorrect and may result from conceptual or calculation errors.

QUESTION 7

Choice A is correct. Since the numerator and denominator of $\frac{x^{a^2}}{x^{b^2}}$ have a common base, it follows by the laws of exponents that this expression can be rewritten as $x^{a^2 - b^2}$. Thus, the equation $\frac{x^{a^2}}{x^{b^2}} = x^{16}$ can be rewritten as $x^{a^2 - b^2} = x^{16}$. Because the equivalent expressions have the common base x, and $x > 1$, it follows that the exponents of the two expressions must also be equivalent. Hence, the equation $a^2 - b^2 = 16$ must be true. The left-hand side of this new equation is a difference of squares, and so it can be factored: $(a + b)(a - b) = 16$. It is given that $(a + b) = 2$; substituting 2 for the factor $(a + b)$ gives $2(a - b) = 16$. Finally, dividing both sides of $2(a - b) = 16$ by 2 gives $a - b = 8$.

Choices B, C, and D are incorrect and may result from errors in applying the laws of exponents or errors in solving the equation $a^2 - b^2 = 16$.

QUESTION 8

Choice C is correct. The relationship between n and A is given by the equation $nA = 360$. Since n is the number of sides of a polygon, n must be a positive integer, and so $nA = 360$ can be rewritten as $A = \frac{360}{n}$. If the value of A is greater than 50, it follows that $\frac{360}{n} > 50$ is a true statement. Thus, $50n < 360$, or $n < \frac{360}{50} = 7.2$. Since n must be an integer, the greatest possible value of n is 7.

Choices A and B are incorrect. These are possible values for n, the number of sides of a regular polygon, if $A > 50$, but neither is the greatest possible value of n. Choice D is incorrect. If $A < 50$, then $n = 8$ is the least possible value of n, the number of sides of a regular polygon. However, the question asks for the greatest possible value of n if $A > 50$, which is $n = 7$.

QUESTION 9

Choice B is correct. Since the slope of the first line is 2, an equation of this line can be written in the form $y = 2x + c$, where c is the y-intercept of the line. Since the line contains the point (1, 8), one can substitute 1 for x and 8 for y in $y = 2x + c$, which gives $8 = 2(1) + c$, or $c = 6$. Thus, an equation of the first line is $y = 2x + 6$. The slope of the second line is equal to $\frac{1-2}{2-1}$ or -1. Thus, an equation of the second line can be written in the form $y = -x + d$, where d is the y-intercept of the line. Substituting 2 for x and 1 for y gives $1 = -2 + d$, or $d = 3$. Thus, an equation of the second line is $y = -x + 3$.

Since a is the x-coordinate and b is the y-coordinate of the intersection point of the two lines, one can substitute a for x and b for y in the two equations, giving the system $b = 2a + 6$ and $b = -a + 3$. Thus, a can be found by solving the equation $2a + 6 = -a + 3$, which gives $a = -1$. Finally, substituting -1 for a into the equation $b = -a + 3$ gives $b = -(-1) + 3$, or $b = 4$. Therefore, the value of $a + b$ is 3.

Alternatively, since the second line passes through the points (1, 2) and (2, 1), an equation for the second line is $x + y = 3$. Thus, the intersection point of the first line and the second line, (a, b) lies on the line with equation $x + y = 3$. It follows that $a + b = 3$.

Choices A and C are incorrect and may result from finding the value of only a or b, but not calculating the value of $a + b$. Choice D is incorrect and may result from a computation error in finding equations of the two lines or in solving the resulting system of equations.

QUESTION 10

Choice C is correct. Since the square of any real number is nonnegative, every point on the graph of the quadratic equation $y = (x - 2)^2$ in the xy-plane has a nonnegative y-coordinate. Thus, $y \geq 0$ for every point on the graph. Therefore, the equation $y = (x - 2)^2$ has a graph for which y is always greater than or equal to -1.

Choices A, B, and D are incorrect because the graph of each of these equations in the xy-plane has a y-intercept at $(0, -2)$. Therefore, each of these equations contains at least one point where y is less than -1.

QUESTION 11

Choice C is correct. To perform the division $\frac{3-5i}{8+2i}$, multiply the numerator and denominator of $\frac{3-5i}{8+2i}$ by the conjugate of the denominator, $8-2i$. This gives $\frac{(3-5i)(8-2i)}{(8+2i)(8-2i)} = \frac{24-6i-40i+(-5i)(-2i)}{8^2-(2i)^2}$. Since $i^2=-1$, this can be simplified to $\frac{24-6i-40i-10}{64+4} = \frac{14-46i}{68}$, which then simplifies to $\frac{7}{34} - \frac{23i}{34}$.

Choices A and B are incorrect and may result from misconceptions about fractions. For example, $\frac{a+b}{c+d}$ is equal to $\frac{a}{c+d} + \frac{b}{c+d}$, not $\frac{a}{c} + \frac{b}{d}$.

Choice D is incorrect and may result from a calculation error.

QUESTION 12

Choice B is correct. Multiplying each side of $R = \frac{F}{N+F}$ by $N+F$ gives $R(N+F) = F$, which can be rewritten as $RN + RF = F$. Subtracting RF from each side of $RN + RF = F$ gives $RN = F - RF$, which can be factored as $RN = F(1-R)$. Finally, dividing each side of $RN = F(1-R)$ by $1-R$, expresses F in terms of the other variables: $F = \frac{RN}{1-R}$.

Choices A, C, and D are incorrect and may result from calculation errors when rewriting the given equation.

QUESTION 13

Choice D is correct. The problem asks for the sum of the solutions of the quadratic equation $2m^2 - 16m + 8 = 0$. Dividing each side of the equation by 2 gives $m^2 - 8m + 4 = 0$. Applying the quadratic formula to $m^2 - 8m + 4 = 0$ gives $m = \frac{8 \pm \sqrt{(-8)^2 - 4(1)(4)}}{2(1)}$, which simplifies to $m = 4 \pm 2\sqrt{3}$. Thus the two solutions are $4 + \sqrt{3}$ and $4 - \sqrt{3}$, and the sum of the solutions is 8.

Alternatively, the structure of the equation can be used to solve the problem. Dividing both sides of the equation $2m^2 - 16m + 8 = 0$ by 2 gives $m^2 - 8m + 4 = 0$. If the solutions of $m^2 - 8m + 4 = 0$ are s_1 and s_2, then the expression $m^2 - 8m + 4$ can be rewritten as $(m - s_1)(m - s_2)$. Multiplying the two binomials gives $m^2 - (s_1 + s_2)m + s_1 \cdot s_2$. Since the expressions $m^2 - 8m + 4$ and $m^2 - (s_1 + s_2)m + s_1 \cdot s_2$ are equivalent, it follows that $s_1 + s_2 = 8$.

Choices A, B, and C are incorrect and may result from calculation errors when applying the quadratic formula or a sign error when determining the sum of the roots of a quadratic equation from its coefficients.

QUESTION 14

Choice A is correct. Each year, the amount of the radioactive substance is reduced by 13 percent from the prior year's amount; that is, each year, 87 percent of the previous year's amount remains. Since the initial amount of the radioactive substance was 325 grams, after 1 year, 325(0.87) grams remains; after 2 years $325(0.87)(0.87) = 325(0.87)^2$ grams remains; and after t years, $325(0.87)^t$ grams remains. Therefore, the function $f(t) = 325(0.87)^t$ models the remaining amount of the substance, in grams, after t years.

Choice B is incorrect and may result from confusing the amount of the substance remaining with the decay rate. Choices C and D are incorrect and may result from confusing the original amount of the substance and the decay rate.

QUESTION 15

Choice D is correct. The given expression can be rewritten as

$$\frac{5x-2}{x+3} = \frac{(5x+15)-15-2}{x+3}$$

$$= \frac{5(x+3)-17}{x+3}$$

$$= \frac{5(x+3)}{x+3} - \frac{17}{x+3}$$

$$= 5 - \frac{17}{x+3}$$

Therefore, the expression $\frac{5x-2}{x+3}$ can be rewritten as $5 - \frac{17}{x+3}$.

Choices A, B, and C are incorrect and may result from a computation or simplification error such as incorrectly canceling out the x in the expression $\frac{5x-2}{x+3}$.

QUESTION 16

The correct answer is 3, 6, or 9. Let x be the number of \$250 bonuses awarded, and let y be the number of \$750 bonuses awarded. Since \$3000 in bonuses were awarded, and this included at least one \$250 bonus and one \$750 bonus, it follows that $250x + 750y = 3000$, where x and y are positive integers. Dividing each side of $250x + 750y = 3000$ by 250 gives $x + 3y = 12$, where x and y are positive integers. Since $3y$ and 12 are each divisible by 3, it follows that $x = 12 - 3y$ must also be divisible by 3. If $x = 3$, then $y = 3$; if $x = 6$, then $y = 2$; and if $x = 9$, then $y = 1$. If $x = 12$, then $y = 0$, but this is not possible since there was at least one \$750 bonus awarded. Therefore, the possible numbers of \$250 bonuses awarded are 3, 6, and 9. Any of the numbers 3, 6, or 9 may be gridded as the correct answer.

QUESTION 17

The correct answer is 19. Since $2x(3x + 5) + 3(3x + 5) = ax^2 + bx + c$ for all values of x, the two sides of the equation are equal, and the value of b can be determined by simplifying the left-hand side of the equation and writing it in the same form as the right-hand side. Using the distributive property, the equation becomes $(6x^2 + 10x) + (9x + 15) = ax^2 + bx + c$. Combining like terms gives $6x^2 + 19x + 15 = ax^2 + bx + c$. The value of b is the coefficient of x, which is 19.

QUESTION 18

The correct answer is 12. Angles ABE and DBC are vertical angles and thus have the same measure. Since segment AE is parallel to segment CD, angles A and D are of the same measure by the alternate interior angle theorem. Thus, by the angle-angle theorem, triangle ABE is similar to triangle DBC, with vertices A, B, and E corresponding to vertices D, B, and C, respectively. Thus, $\frac{AB}{DB} = \frac{EB}{CB}$, or $\frac{10}{5} = \frac{8}{CB}$. It follows that $CB = 4$, and so $CE = CB + BE = 4 + 8 = 12$.

QUESTION 19

The correct answer is 6. By the distance formula, the length of radius OA is $\sqrt{(\sqrt{3})^2 + 1^2} = \sqrt{3 + 1} = 2$. Thus, $\sin(\angle AOB) = \frac{1}{2}$. Therefore, the measure of $\angle AOB$ is 30°, which is equal to $30\left(\frac{\pi}{180}\right) = \frac{\pi}{6}$ radians. Hence, the value of a is 6.

QUESTION 20

The correct answer is $\frac{2}{8}$ or $\frac{1}{4}$ or .25. In order for a system of two linear equations to have infinitely many solutions, the two equations must be equivalent. Thus, the equation $ax + by = 12$ must be equivalent to the equation $2x + 8y = 60$. Multiplying each side of $ax + by = 12$ by 5 gives $5ax + 5by = 60$, which must be equivalent to $2x + 8y = 60$. Since the right-hand sides of $5ax + 5by = 60$ and $2x + 8y = 60$ are the same, equating coefficients gives $5a = 2$, or $a = \frac{2}{5}$, and $5b = 8$, or $b = \frac{8}{5}$. Therefore, the value of $\frac{a}{b} = \left(\frac{2}{5}\right) \div \left(\frac{8}{5}\right)$, which is equal to $\frac{1}{4}$. Either the fraction 1/4 or its equivalent decimal, .25, may be gridded as the correct answer.

Alternatively, since $ax + by = 12$ is equivalent to $2x + 8y = 60$, the equation $ax + by = 12$ is equal to $2x + 8y = 60$ multiplied on each side by the same constant. Since multiplying $2x + 8y = 60$ by a constant does not change the ratio of the coefficient of x to the coefficient of y, it follows that $\frac{a}{b} = \frac{2}{8} = \frac{1}{4}$.

Section 4: Math Test – Calculator

QUESTION 1

Choice C is correct. Since the musician earns $0.09 for each download, the musician earns $0.09d$ dollars when the song is downloaded d times. Similarly, since the musician earns $0.002 each time the song is streamed, the musician earns $0.002s$ dollars when the song is streamed s times. Therefore, the musician earns a total of $0.09d + 0.002s$ dollars when the song is downloaded d times and streamed s times.

Choice A is incorrect because the earnings for each download and the earnings for time streamed are interchanged in the expression. Choices B and D are incorrect because in both answer choices, the musician will lose money when a song is either downloaded or streamed. However, the musician only earns money, not loses money, when the song is downloaded or streamed.

QUESTION 2

Choice B is correct. The quality control manager selects 7 lightbulbs at random for inspection out of every 400 lightbulbs produced. A quantity of 20,000 lightbulbs is equal to $\frac{20{,}000}{400} = 50$ batches of 400 lightbulbs. Therefore, at the rate of 7 lightbulbs per 400 lightbulbs produced, the quality control manager will inspect a total of $50 \times 7 = 350$ lightbulbs.

Choices A, C, and D are incorrect and may result from calculation errors or misunderstanding of the proportional relationship.

QUESTION 3

Choice A is correct. The value of m when ℓ is 73 can be found by substituting the 73 for ℓ in $\ell = 24 + 3.5m$ and then solving for m. The resulting equation is $73 = 24 + 3.5m$; subtracting 24 from each side gives $49 = 3.5m$. Then, dividing each side of $49 = 3.5m$ by 3.5 gives $14 = m$. Therefore, when ℓ is 73, m is 14.

Choice B is incorrect and may result from adding 24 to 73, instead of subtracting 24 from 73, when solving $73 = 24 + 3.5m$. Choice C is incorrect because 73 is the given value for ℓ, not for m. Choice D is incorrect and may result from substituting 73 for m, instead of for ℓ, in the equation $\ell = 24 + 3.5m$.

QUESTION 4

Choice C is correct. The amount of money the performer earns is directly proportional to the number of people who attend the performance. Thus, by the definition of direct proportionality, $M = kP$, where M is the amount of money the performer earns, in dollars, P is the number of people who attend the performance, and k is a constant.

Since the performer earns \$120 when 8 people attend the performance, one can substitute 120 for M and 8 for P, giving $120 = 8k$. Hence, $k = 15$, and the relationship between the number of people who attend the performance and the amount of money, in dollars, the performer earns is $M = 15P$. Therefore, when 20 people attend the performance, the performer earns $15(20) = 300$ dollars.

Choices A, B, and D are incorrect and may result from either misconceptions about proportional relationships or computational errors.

QUESTION 5

Choice C is correct. If 43% of the money earned is used to pay for costs, then the rest, 57%, is profit. A performance where 8 people attend earns the performer \$120, and 57% of \$120 is $\$120 \times 0.57 = \$68.40$.

Choice A is incorrect. The amount \$51.60 is 43% of the money earned from a performance where 8 people attend, which is the cost of putting on the performance, not the profit from the performance. Choice B is incorrect. It is given that 57% of the money earned is profit, but 57% of \$120 is not equal to \$57.00. Choice D is incorrect. The profit can be found by subtracting 43% of \$120 from \$120, but 43% of \$120 is \$51.60, not \$43.00. Thus, the profit is $\$120 - \$51.60 = \$68.40$, not $\$120 - \$43.00 = \$77.00$.

QUESTION 6

Choice B is correct. When 4 times the number x is added to 12, the result is $12 + 4x$. Since this result is equal to 8, the equation $12 + 4x = 8$ must be true. Subtracting 12 from each side of $12 + 4x = 8$ gives $4x = -4$, and then dividing both sides of $4x = -4$ by 4 gives $x = -1$. Therefore, 2 times x added to 7, or $7 + 2x$, is equal to $7 + 2(-1) = 5$.

Choice A is incorrect because -1 is the value of x, not the value of $7 + 2x$. Choices C and D are incorrect and may result from calculation errors.

QUESTION 7

Choice D is correct. The x-intercepts of the parabola represented by $y = x^2 - 6x + 8$ in the xy-plane are the values of x for which y is equal to 0. The factored form of the equation, $y = (x - 2)(x - 4)$, shows that y equals 0 if and only if $x = 2$ or $x = 4$. Thus, the factored form, $y = (x - 2)(x - 4)$, displays the x-intercepts of the parabola as the constants 2 and 4.

Choices A, B, and C are incorrect because none of these forms shows the x-intercepts 2 and 4 as constants or coefficients.

QUESTION 8

Choice D is correct. Since a player starts with k points and loses 2 points each time a task is not completed, the player's score will be $k - 2n$ after n tasks are not completed (and no additional points are gained). Since a player who fails to complete 100 tasks has a score of 200 points, the equation $200 = k - 100(2)$ must be true. This equation can be solved by adding 200 to each side, giving $k = 400$.

Choices A, B, and C are incorrect and may result from errors in setting up or solving the equation relating the player's score to the number of tasks the player fails to complete. For example, choice A may result from subtracting 200 from the left-hand side of $200 = k - 100(2)$ and adding 200 to the right-hand side.

QUESTION 9

Choice A is correct. Since x is the number of 40-pound boxes, $40x$ is the total weight, in pounds, of the 40-pound boxes; and since y is the number of 65-pound boxes, $65y$ is the total weight, in pounds, of the 65-pound boxes. The combined weight of the boxes is therefore $40x + 65y$, and the total number of boxes is $x + y$. Since the forklift can carry up to 45 boxes or up to 2,400 pounds, the inequalities that represent these relationships are $40x + 65y \leq 2{,}400$ and $x + y \leq 45$.

Choice B is incorrect. The second inequality correctly represents the maximum number of boxes on the forklift, but the first inequality divides, rather than multiplies, the number of boxes by their respective weights. Choice C is incorrect. The combined weight of the boxes, $40x + 65y$, must be less than or equal to 2,400 pounds, not 45; the total number of boxes, $x + y$, must be less than or equal to 45, not 2,400. Choice D is incorrect. The second inequality correctly represents the maximum weight, in pounds, of the boxes on the forklift, but the total number of boxes, $x + y$, must be less than or equal to 45, not 2,400.

QUESTION 10

Choice B is correct. It is given that $g(3) = 2$. Therefore, to find the value of $f(g(3))$, substitute 2 for $g(3)$: $f(g(3)) = f(2) = 3$.

Choices A, C, and D are incorrect and may result from misunderstandings about function notation.

QUESTION 11

Choice B is correct. Tony reads 250 words per minute, and he plans to read for 3 hours, which is 180 minutes, each day. Thus, Tony is planning to read $250 \times 180 = 45{,}000$ words of the novel per day. Since the novel has 349,168 words, it will take Tony $\frac{349{,}168}{45{,}000} \approx 7.76$ days of reading to finish the novel. That is, it will take Tony 7 full days of reading and most of an 8th day of reading to finish the novel. Therefore, it will take Tony 8 days to finish the novel.

Choice A is incorrect and may result from an incorrect calculation or incorrectly using the numbers provided in the table. Choice C is incorrect and may result from taking the total number of words in the novel divided by the rate Tony reads per hour. Choice D is incorrect and may result from taking the total number of words in the novel divided by the number of pages in the novel.

QUESTION 12

Choice D is correct. Since there were 175,000 tons of trash in the landfill on January 1, 2000, and the amount of trash in the landfill increased by 7,500 tons each year after that date, the amount of trash, in tons, in the landfill y years after January 1, 2000, can be expressed as $175{,}000 + 7{,}500y$. The landfill has a capacity of 325,000 tons. Therefore, the set of years where the amount of trash in the landfill is at (equal to) or above (greater than) capacity is described by the inequality $175{,}000 + 7{,}500y \geq 325{,}000$.

Choice A is incorrect. This inequality does not account for the 175,000 tons of trash in the landfill on January 1, 2000, nor does it accurately account for the 7,500 tons of trash that are added to the landfill each year after January 1, 2000. Choice B is incorrect. This inequality does not account for the 175,000 tons of trash in the landfill on January 1, 2000. Choice C is incorrect. This inequality represents the set of years where the amount of trash in the landfill is at or below capacity.

QUESTION 13

Choice D is correct. Survey research is an efficient way to estimate the preferences of a large population. In order to reliably generalize the results of survey research to a larger population, the participants should be randomly selected from all people in that population. Since this survey was conducted with a population that was not randomly selected, the results are not reliably representative of all people in the town. Therefore, of the given factors, where the survey was given makes it least likely that a reliable conclusion can be drawn about the sports-watching preferences of all people in the town.

Choice A is incorrect. In general, larger sample sizes are preferred over smaller sample sizes. However, a sample size of 117 people would have allowed a reliable conclusion about the population if the participants had been selected at random. Choice B is incorrect. Whether the population is large or small, a large enough sample taken from the population is reliably generalizable if the participants are selected at random from that population. Thus, a reliable conclusion could have been drawn about the population if the 117 survey participants had been selected at random. Choice C is incorrect. When giving a survey, participants are not forced to respond. Even though some people refused to respond, a reliable conclusion could have been drawn about the population if the participants had been selected at random.

QUESTION 14

Choice C is correct. According to the graph, the horizontal line that represents 550 billion miles traveled intersects the line of best fit at a point whose horizontal coordinate is between 2000 and 2005, and slightly closer to 2005 than to 2000. Therefore, of the choices given, 2003 best approximates the year in which the number of miles traveled by air passengers in Country X was estimated to be 550 billion.

Choice A is incorrect. According to the line of best fit, in 1997 the estimated number of miles traveled by air passengers in Country X was about 450 billion, not 550 billion. Choice B is incorrect. According to the line of best fit, in 2000 the estimated number of miles traveled by air passengers in Country X was about 500 billion, not 550 billion. Choice D is incorrect. According to the line of best fit, in 2008 the estimated number of miles traveled by air passengers in Country X was about 600 billion, not 550 billion.

QUESTION 15

Choice A is correct. The number of miles Earth travels in its one-year orbit of the Sun is 580,000,000. Because there are about 365 days per year, the number of miles Earth travels per day is $\frac{580,000,000}{365} \approx 1,589,041$. There are 24 hours in one day, so Earth travels at $\frac{1,589,041}{24} \approx 66,210$ miles per hour. Therefore, of the choices given, 66,000 miles per hour is closest to the average speed of Earth as it orbits the Sun.

Choices B, C, and D are incorrect and may result from calculation errors.

QUESTION 16

Choice B is correct. According to the table, there are 18 + 7 = 25 graduates who passed the bar exam, and 7 of them did not take the review course. Therefore, if one of the surveyed graduates who passed the bar exam is chosen at random, the probability that the person chosen did not take the review course is $\frac{7}{25}$.

Choices A, C, and D are incorrect. Each of these choices represents a different probability from the conditional probability that the question asks for. Choice A represents the following probability. If one of the surveyed graduates who passed the bar exam is chosen at random, the probability that the person chosen did take the review course is $\frac{18}{25}$. Choice C represents the following probability. If one of the surveyed graduates is chosen at random, the probability that the person chosen passed the bar exam is $\frac{25}{200}$. Choice D represents the following probability. If one of the surveyed graduates is chosen at random, the probability that the person chosen passed the exam and took the review course is $\frac{7}{200}$.

QUESTION 17

Choice C is correct. To find the atomic weight of an unknown element that is 20% less than the atomic weight of calcium, multiply the atomic weight, in amu, of calcium by (1 − 0.20). This gives (40)(1 − 0.20) = (40)(0.8) = 32.

Choice A is incorrect. This value is 20% of the atomic weight of calcium, not an atomic weight 20% less than that atomic weight of calcium. Choice B is incorrect. This value is 20 amu less, not 20% less, than the atomic weight of calcium. Choice D is incorrect. This value is 20% more, not 20% less, than the atomic weight of calcium.

QUESTION 18

Choice C is correct. The mean and median values of a data set are equal when there is a symmetrical distribution. For example, a normal distribution is symmetrical. If the mean and the median values are not equal, then the distribution is not symmetrical. Outliers are a small group of values that are significantly smaller or larger than the other values in the data. When there are outliers in the data, the mean will be pulled in their direction (either smaller or larger) while the median remains the same. The example in the question has a mean that is larger than the median, and so an appropriate conjecture is that large outliers are present in the data; that is, that there are a few homes that are valued much more than the rest.

Choice A is incorrect because a set of home values that are close to each other will have median and mean values that are also close to each other. Choice B is incorrect because outliers with small values will tend to make the mean lower than the median. Choice D is incorrect because a set of data where many homes are valued between $125,000 and $165,000 will likely have both a mean and a median between $125,000 and $165,000.

QUESTION 19

Choice B is correct. The median of a data set is the middle value when the data points are sorted in either ascending or descending order. There are a total of 600 data points provided, so the median will be the average of the 300th and 301st data points. When the data points are sorted in order:

- Values 1 through 260 will be 0.
- Values 261 through 450 will be 1.
- Values 451 through 540 will be 2.
- Values 541 through 580 will be 3.
- Values 581 through 600 will be 4.

Therefore, both the 300th and 301st values are 1, and hence the median is 1.

Choices A, C, and D are incorrect and may result from either a calculation error or a conceptual error.

QUESTION 20

Choice C is correct. When survey participants are selected at random from a larger population, the sample statistics calculated from the survey can be generalized to the larger population. Since 10 of 300 students surveyed at Lincoln School have 4 siblings, one can estimate that this same ratio holds for all 2,400 students at Lincoln School. Also, since 10 of 300 students surveyed at Washington School have 4 siblings, one can estimate that this same ratio holds for all 3,300 students at Washington School. Therefore, approximately $\frac{10}{300} \times 2{,}400 = 80$ students at Lincoln School and $\frac{10}{300} \times 3{,}300 = 110$ students at Washington School are expected to have 4 siblings. Thus, the total number of students with 4 siblings at Washington School is expected to be $110 - 80 = 30$ more than the total number of students with 4 siblings at Lincoln School.

Choices A, B, and D are incorrect and may result from either conceptual or calculation errors. For example, choice A is incorrect; even though there is the same ratio of survey participants from Lincoln School and Washington School with 4 siblings, the two schools have a different total number of students, and thus, a different expected total number of students with 4 siblings.

QUESTION 21

Choice D is correct. The difference between the number of hours the project takes, y, and the number of hours the project was estimated to take, x, is $|y - x|$. If the goal is met, the difference is less than 10, which can be represented as $|y - x| < 10$, or $-10 < y - x < 10$.

Choice A is incorrect. This inequality states that the estimated number of hours plus the actual number of hours is less than 10, which cannot be true because the estimate is greater than 100. Choice B is incorrect. This inequality states that the actual number of hours is greater than the estimated number of hours plus 10, which could be true only if the goal of being within 10 hours of the estimate were not met. Choice C is incorrect. This inequality states that the actual number of hours is less than the estimated number of hours minus 10, which could be true only if the goal of being within 10 hours of the estimate were not met.

QUESTION 22

Choice B is correct. To rearrange the formula $I = \frac{P}{4\pi r^2}$ in terms of r^2, first multiply each side of the equation by r^2. This yields $r^2 I = \frac{P}{4\pi}$. Then dividing each side of $r^2 I = \frac{P}{4\pi}$ by I gives $r^2 = \frac{P}{4\pi I}$.

Choices A, C, and D are incorrect and may result from algebraic errors during the rearrangement of the formula.

QUESTION 23

Choice A is correct. If I_A is the intensity measured by Observer A from a distance of r_A and I_B is the intensity measured by Observer B from a distance of r_B, then $I_A = 16I_B$. Using the formula $I = \frac{P}{4\pi r^2}$, the intensity measured by Observer A is $I_A = \frac{P}{4\pi r_A^2}$, which can also be written in terms of I_B as $I_A = 16I_B = 16\left(\frac{P}{4\pi r_B^2}\right)$. Setting the right-hand sides of these two equations equal to each other gives $\frac{P}{4\pi r_A^2} = 16\left(\frac{P}{4\pi r_B^2}\right)$, which relates the distance of Observer A from the radio antenna to the distance of Observer B from the radio antenna. Canceling the common factor $\frac{P}{4\pi}$ and rearranging the equation gives $r_B^2 = 16r_A^2$. Taking the square root of each side of $r_B^2 = 16r_A^2$ gives $r_B = 4r_A$, and then dividing each side by 4 yields $r_A = \frac{1}{4}r_B$. Therefore, the distance of Observer A from the radio antenna is $\frac{1}{4}$ the distance of Observer B from the radio antenna.

Choices B, C, and D are incorrect and may result from errors in deriving or using the formula $\frac{P}{4\pi r_A^2} = (16)\left(\frac{P}{4\pi r_B^2}\right)$.

QUESTION 24

Choice A is correct. The equation of a circle with center (h, k) and radius r is $(x - h)^2 + (y - k)^2 = r^2$. To put the equation $x^2 + y^2 + 4x - 2y = -1$ in this form, complete the square as follows:

$$x^2 + y^2 + 4x - 2y = -1$$
$$(x^2 + 4x) + (y^2 - 2y) = -1$$
$$(x^2 + 4x + 4) - 4 + (y^2 - 2y + 1) - 1 = -1$$
$$(x + 2)^2 + (y - 1)^2 - 4 - 1 = -1$$
$$(x + 2)^2 + (y - 1)^2 = 4 = 2^2$$

Therefore, the radius of the circle is 2.

Choice C is incorrect because it is the square of the radius, not the radius. Choices B and D are incorrect and may result from errors in rewriting the given equation in standard form.

QUESTION 25

Choice A is correct. In the xy-plane, the slope m of the line that passes through the points (x_1, y_1) and (x_2, y_2) is given by the formula $m = \frac{y_2 - y_1}{x_2 - x_1}$. Thus, if the graph of the linear function f has intercepts at $(a, 0)$ and $(0, b)$, then the slope of the line that is the graph of $y = f(x)$ is $m = \frac{0 - b}{a - 0} = -\frac{b}{a}$. It is given that $a + b = 0$, and so $a = -b$. Finally, substituting $-b$ for a in $m = -\frac{b}{a}$ gives $m = -\frac{b}{-b} = 1$, which is positive.

Choices B, C, and D are incorrect and may result from a conceptual misunderstanding or a calculation error.

QUESTION 26

Choice D is correct. The definition of the graph of a function f in the xy-plane is the set of all points $(x, f(x))$. Thus, for $-4 \leq a \leq 4$, the value of $f(a)$ is 1 if and only if the unique point on the graph of f with x-coordinate a has y-coordinate equal to 1. The points on the graph of f with x-coordinates -4, $\frac{3}{2}$, and 3 are, respectively, $(-4, 1)$, $\left(\frac{3}{2}, 1\right)$, and $(3, 1)$. Therefore, all of the values of f given in I, II, and III are equal to 1.

Choices A, B, and C are incorrect because they each omit at least one value of x for which $f(x) = 1$.

QUESTION 27

Choice D is correct. According to the graph, in the interval from 0 to 10 minutes, the non-insulated sample decreased in temperature by about 18°C, while the insulated sample decreased by about 8°C; in the interval from 10 to 20 minutes, the non-insulated sample decreased in temperature by about 9°C, while the insulated sample decreased by about 5°C; in the interval from 40 to 50 minutes, the non-insulated sample decreased in temperature by about 1°C, while the insulated sample decreased by about 3°C; and in the interval from 50 to 60 minutes, the non-insulated sample decreased in temperature by about 1°C, while the insulated sample decreased by about 2°C. The description in choice D accurately summarizes these rates of temperature change over the given intervals. (Note that since the two samples of water have equal mass and so must lose the same amount of heat to cool from 60°C to 25°C, the faster cooling of the non-insulated sample at the start of the cooling process must be balanced out by faster cooling of the insulated sample at the end of the cooling process.)

Choices A, B, and C are incorrect. None of these descriptions accurately compares the rates of temperature change shown in the graph for the 10-minute intervals.

QUESTION 28

Choice B is correct. In the xy-plane, the slope m of the line that passes through the points (x_1, y_1) and (x_2, y_2) is $m = \frac{y_2 - y_1}{x_2 - x_1}$. Thus, the slope of the line through the points $E(1, 0)$ and $C(7, 2)$ is $\frac{2 - 0}{7 - 1}$, which simplifies to $\frac{2}{6} = \frac{1}{3}$. Therefore, diagonal AC has a slope of $\frac{1}{3}$. The other diagonal of the square is a segment of the line that passes through points B and D. The diagonals of a square are perpendicular, and so the product of the slopes of the diagonals is equal to -1. Thus, the slope of the line that passes through B and D is -3 because $\frac{1}{3}(-3) = -1$.

Hence, an equation of the line that passes through B and D can be written as $y = -3x + b$, where b is the y-intercept of the line. Since diagonal BD will pass through the center of the square, $E(1, 0)$, the equation $0 = -3(1) + b$ holds. Solving this equation for b gives $b = 3$. Therefore, an equation of the line that passes through points B and D is $y = -3x + 3$, which can be rewritten as $y = -3(x - 1)$.

Choices A, C, and D are incorrect and may result from a conceptual error or a calculation error.

QUESTION 29

Choice B is correct. Substituting 3 for y in $y = ax^2 + b$ gives $3 = ax^2 + b$, which can be rewritten as $3 - b = ax^2$. Since $y = 3$ is one of the equations in the given system, any solution x of $3 - b = ax^2$ corresponds to the solution $(x, 3)$ of the given system. Since the square of a real number is always nonnegative, and a positive number has two square roots, the equation $3 - b = ax^2$ will have two solutions for x if and only if (1) $a > 0$ and $b < 3$ or (2) $a < 0$ and $b > 3$. Of the values for a and b given in the choices, only $a = -2$, $b = 4$ satisfy one of these pairs of conditions.

Alternatively, if $a = -2$ and $b = 4$, then the second equation would be $y = -2x^2 + 4$. The graph of this quadratic equation in the xy-plane is a parabola with y-intercept $(0, 4)$ that opens downward. The graph of the first equation, $y = 3$, is the horizontal line that contains the point $(0, 3)$. As shown below, these two graphs have two points of intersection, and therefore, this system of equations has exactly two real solutions. (Graphing shows that none of the other three choices produces a system with exactly two real solutions.)

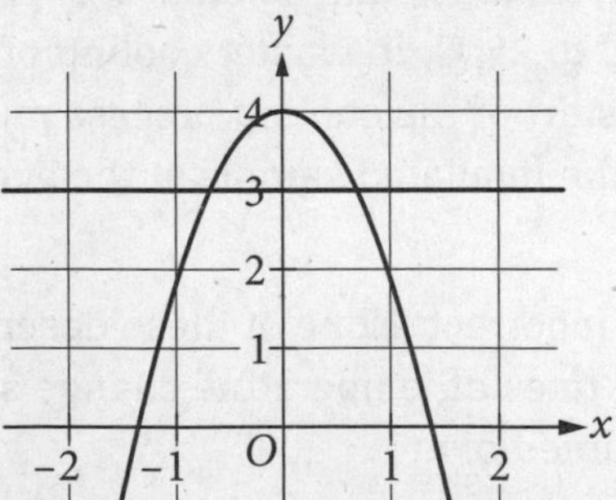

Choices A, C, and D are incorrect and may result from calculation or conceptual errors.

QUESTION 30

Choice A is correct. The regular hexagon can be divided into 6 equilateral triangles of side length a by drawing the six segments from the center of the regular hexagon to each of its 6 vertices. Since the area of the hexagon is $384\sqrt{3}$ square inches, the area of each equilateral triangle will be $\frac{384\sqrt{3}}{6} = 64\sqrt{3}$ square inches. Drawing any altitude of an equilateral triangle divides it into two 30°-60°-90° triangles. If the side length of the equilateral triangle is a, then the hypotenuse of each 30°-60°-90° triangle is a, and the altitude of the equilateral triangle will be the side opposite the 60° angle in each of the 30°-60°-90° triangles. Thus, the altitude of the equilateral triangle is $\frac{\sqrt{3}}{2}a$, and the area of the equilateral triangle is $\frac{1}{2}(a)\left(\frac{\sqrt{3}}{2}a\right) = \frac{\sqrt{3}}{4}a^2$. Since the area of each equilateral triangle is $64\sqrt{3}$ square inches, it follows that $a^2 = \frac{4}{\sqrt{3}}(64\sqrt{3}) = 256$ square inches. And since the area of the square with side length a is a^2, it follows that the square has area 256 square inches.

Choices B, C, and D are incorrect and may result from calculation or conceptual errors.

QUESTION 31

The correct answer is 14. Since the coastal geologist estimates that the country's beaches are eroding at a rate of 1.5 feet every year, they will erode by $1.5x$ feet in x years. Thus, if the beaches erode by 21 feet in x years, the equation $1.5x = 21$ must hold. The value of x is then $\frac{21}{1.5} = 14$. Therefore, according to the geologist's estimate, it will take 14 years for the country's beaches to erode by 21 feet.

QUESTION 32

The correct answer is 7. There are 60 minutes in each hour, and so there are $60h$ minutes in h hours. Since h hours and 30 minutes is equal to 450 minutes, it follows that $60h + 30 = 450$. This equation can be simplified to $60h = 420$, and so the value of h is $\frac{420}{60} = 7$.

QUESTION 33

The correct answer is 11. It is given that the function $f(x)$ passes through the point (3, 6). Thus, if $x = 3$, the value of $f(x)$ is 6 (since the graph of f in the xy-plane is the set of all points $(x, f(x))$). Substituting 3 for x and 6 for $f(x)$ in $f(x) = 3x^2 - bx + 12$ gives $6 = 3(3)^2 - b(3) + 12$. Performing the operations on the right-hand side of this equation gives $6 = 3(9) - 3b + 12 = 27 - 3b + 12 = 39 - 3b$. Subtracting 39 from each side of $6 = 39 - 3b$ gives $-33 = -3b$, and then dividing each side of $-3b = -33$ by -3 gives the value of b as 11.

QUESTION 34

The correct answer is 105. Let D be the number of hours Doug spent in the tutoring lab, and let L be the number of hours Laura spent in the tutoring lab. Since Doug and Laura spent a combined total of 250 hours in the tutoring lab, the equation $D + L = 250$ holds. The number of hours Doug spent in the lab is 40 more than the number of hours Laura spent in the lab, and so the equation $D = L + 40$ holds. Substituting $L + 40$ for D in $D + L = 250$ gives $(L + 40) + L = 250$, or $40 + 2L = 250$. Solving this equation gives $L = 105$. Therefore, Laura spent 105 hours in the tutoring lab.

QUESTION 35

The correct answer is 15. The amount, a, that Jane has deposited after t fixed weekly deposits is equal to the initial deposit plus the total amount of money Jane has deposited in the t fixed weekly deposits. This amount a is given to be $a = 18t + 15$. The amount she deposited in the t fixed weekly deposits is the amount of the weekly deposit times t; hence, this amount must be given by the term $18t$ in $a = 18t + 15$ (and so Jane must have deposited 18 dollars each week after the initial deposit). Therefore, the amount of Jane's original deposit, in dollars, is $a - 18t = 15$.

QUESTION 36

The correct answer is 32. Since segments LM and MN are tangent to the circle at points L and N, respectively, angles OLM and ONM are right angles. Thus, in quadrilateral $OLMN$, the measure of angle O is $360° - (90° + 60° + 90°) = 120°$. Thus, in the circle, central angle O cuts off $\frac{120}{360} = \frac{1}{3}$ of the circumference; that is, minor arc $\overset{\frown}{LN}$ is $\frac{1}{3}$ of the circumference. Since the circumference is 96, the length of minor arc $\overset{\frown}{LN}$ is $\frac{1}{3} \times 96 = 32$.

QUESTION 37

The correct answer is 3284. According to the formula, the number of plants one year from now will be $3000 + 0.2(3000)\left(1 - \frac{3000}{4000}\right)$, which is equal to 3150. Then, using the formula again, the number of plants two years from now will be $3150 + 0.2(3150)\left(1 - \frac{3150}{4000}\right)$, which is 3283.875. Rounding this value to the nearest whole number gives 3284.

QUESTION 38

The correct answer is 7500. If the number of plants is to be increased from 3000 this year to 3360 next year, then the number of plants that the environment can support, K, must satisfy the equation $3360 = 3000 + 0.2(3000)\left(1 - \frac{3000}{K}\right)$. Dividing both sides of this equation by 3000 gives $1.12 = 1 + 0.2\left(1 - \frac{3000}{K}\right)$, and therefore, it must be true that $0.2\left(1 - \frac{3000}{K}\right) = 0.12$, or equivalently, $1 - \frac{3000}{K} = 0.6$. It follows that $\frac{3000}{K} = 0.4$, and so $K = \frac{3000}{0.4} = 7500$.

The SAT®

Practice Test #3

Make time to take the practice test. It's one of the best ways to get ready for the SAT.

After you've taken the practice test, score it right away at **sat.org/scoring**.

CollegeBoard

Test begins on the next page.

Reading Test

65 MINUTES, 52 QUESTIONS

Turn to Section 1 of your answer sheet to answer the questions in this section.

DIRECTIONS

Each passage or pair of passages below is followed by a number of questions. After reading each passage or pair, choose the best answer to each question based on what is stated or implied in the passage or passages and in any accompanying graphics (such as a table or graph).

Questions 1-10 are based on the following passage.

This passage is adapted from Saki, "The Schartz-Metterklume Method." Originally published in 1911.

Lady Carlotta stepped out on to the platform of the small wayside station and took a turn or two up and down its uninteresting length, to kill time till the train should be pleased to proceed on its way. Then, in the roadway beyond, she saw a horse struggling with a more than ample load, and a carter of the sort that seems to bear a sullen hatred against the animal that helps him to earn a living. Lady Carlotta promptly betook her to the roadway, and put rather a different complexion on the struggle. Certain of her acquaintances were wont to give her plentiful admonition as to the undesirability of interfering on behalf of a distressed animal, such interference being "none of her business." Only once had she put the doctrine of non-interference into practice, when one of its most eloquent exponents had been besieged for nearly three hours in a small and extremely uncomfortable may-tree by an angry boar-pig, while Lady Carlotta, on the other side of the fence, had proceeded with the water-colour sketch she was engaged on, and refused to interfere between the boar and his prisoner. It is to be feared that she lost the friendship of the ultimately rescued lady. On this occasion she merely lost the train, which gave way to the first sign of impatience it had shown throughout the journey, and steamed off without her. She bore the desertion with philosophical indifference; her friends and relations were thoroughly well used to the fact of her luggage arriving without her. She wired a vague non-committal message to her destination to say that she was coming on "by another train." Before she had time to think what her next move might be she was confronted by an imposingly attired lady, who seemed to be taking a prolonged mental inventory of her clothes and looks.

"You must be Miss Hope, the governess I've come to meet," said the apparition, in a tone that admitted of very little argument.

"Very well, if I must I must," said Lady Carlotta to herself with dangerous meekness.

"I am Mrs. Quabarl," continued the lady; "and where, pray, is your luggage?"

"It's gone astray," said the alleged governess, falling in with the excellent rule of life that the absent are always to blame; the luggage had, in point of fact, behaved with perfect correctitude. "I've just telegraphed about it," she added, with a nearer approach to truth.

"How provoking," said Mrs. Quabarl; "these railway companies are so careless. However, my maid can lend you things for the night," and she led the way to her car.

During the drive to the Quabarl mansion Lady Carlotta was impressively introduced to the nature of the charge that had been thrust upon her; she learned that Claude and Wilfrid were delicate, sensitive young people, that Irene had the artistic temperament highly developed, and that Viola was

CONTINUE

something or other else of a mould equally commonplace among children of that class and type in the twentieth century.

"I wish them not only to be TAUGHT," said Mrs. Quabarl, "but INTERESTED in what they learn. In their history lessons, for instance, you must try to make them feel that they are being introduced to the life-stories of men and women who really lived, not merely committing a mass of names and dates to memory. French, of course, I shall expect you to talk at meal-times several days in the week."

"I shall talk French four days of the week and Russian in the remaining three."

"Russian? My dear Miss Hope, no one in the house speaks or understands Russian."

"That will not embarrass me in the least," said Lady Carlotta coldly.

Mrs. Quabarl, to use a colloquial expression, was knocked off her perch. She was one of those imperfectly self-assured individuals who are magnificent and autocratic as long as they are not seriously opposed. The least show of unexpected resistance goes a long way towards rendering them cowed and apologetic. When the new governess failed to express wondering admiration of the large newly-purchased and expensive car, and lightly alluded to the superior advantages of one or two makes which had just been put on the market, the discomfiture of her patroness became almost abject. Her feelings were those which might have animated a general of ancient warfaring days, on beholding his heaviest battle-elephant ignominiously driven off the field by slingers and javelin throwers.

1

Which choice best summarizes the passage?

A) A woman weighs the positive and negative aspects of accepting a new job.

B) A woman does not correct a stranger who mistakes her for someone else.

C) A woman impersonates someone else to seek revenge on an acquaintance.

D) A woman takes an immediate dislike to her new employer.

2

In line 2, "turn" most nearly means

A) slight movement.

B) change in rotation.

C) short walk.

D) course correction.

3

The passage most clearly implies that other people regarded Lady Carlotta as

A) outspoken.

B) tactful.

C) ambitious.

D) unfriendly.

4

Which choice provides the best evidence for the answer to the previous question?

A) Lines 10-14 ("Certain . . . business")

B) Lines 22-23 ("It is . . . lady")

C) Lines 23-26 ("On this . . . her")

D) Lines 30-32 ("She . . . train")

CONTINUE

5

The description of how Lady Carlotta "put the doctrine of non-interference into practice" (lines 14-15) mainly serves to

A) foreshadow her capacity for deception.

B) illustrate the subtle cruelty in her nature.

C) provide a humorous insight into her character.

D) explain a surprising change in her behavior.

6

In line 55, "charge" most nearly means

A) responsibility.

B) attack.

C) fee.

D) expense.

7

The narrator indicates that Claude, Wilfrid, Irene, and Viola are

A) similar to many of their peers.

B) unusually creative and intelligent.

C) hostile to the idea of a governess.

D) more educated than others of their age.

8

The narrator implies that Mrs. Quabarl favors a form of education that emphasizes

A) traditional values.

B) active engagement.

C) artistic experimentation.

D) factual retention.

9

As presented in the passage, Mrs. Quabarl is best described as

A) superficially kind but actually selfish.

B) outwardly imposing but easily defied.

C) socially successful but irrationally bitter.

D) naturally generous but frequently imprudent.

10

Which choice provides the best evidence for the answer to the previous question?

A) Lines 49-50 ("How . . . careless")

B) Lines 62-68 ("I wish . . . memory")

C) Lines 70-73 ("I shall . . . Russian")

D) Lines 77-82 ("She was . . . apologetic")

CONTINUE

Questions 11-20 are based on the following passage and supplementary material.

This passage is adapted from Taras Grescoe, *Straphanger: Saving Our Cities and Ourselves from the Automobile*. ©2012 by Taras Grescoe.

Though there are 600 million cars on the planet, and counting, there are also seven billion people, which means that for the vast majority of us getting around involves taking buses, ferryboats, commuter trains, streetcars, and subways. In other words, traveling to work, school, or the market means being a straphanger: somebody who, by choice or necessity, relies on public transport, rather than a privately owned automobile.

Half the population of New York, Toronto, and London do not own cars. Public transport is how most of the people of Asia and Africa, the world's most populous continents, travel. Every day, subway systems carry 155 million passengers, thirty-four times the number carried by all the world's airplanes, and the global public transport market is now valued at $428 billion annually. A century and a half after the invention of the internal combustion engine, private car ownership is still an anomaly.

And yet public transportation, in many minds, is the opposite of glamour—a squalid last resort for those with one too many impaired driving charges, too poor to afford insurance, or too decrepit to get behind the wheel of a car. In much of North America, they are right: taking transit is a depressing experience. Anybody who has waited far too long on a street corner for the privilege of boarding a lurching, overcrowded bus, or wrestled luggage onto subways and shuttles to get to a big city airport, knows that transit on this continent tends to be underfunded, ill-maintained, and ill-planned. Given the opportunity, who wouldn't drive? Hopping in a car almost always gets you to your destination more quickly.

It doesn't have to be like this. Done right, public transport can be faster, more comfortable, and cheaper than the private automobile. In Shanghai, German-made magnetic levitation trains skim over elevated tracks at 266 miles an hour, whisking people to the airport at a third of the speed of sound. In provincial French towns, electric-powered streetcars run silently on rubber tires, sliding through narrow streets along a single guide rail set into cobblestones. From Spain to Sweden, Wi-Fi equipped high-speed trains seamlessly connect with highly ramified metro networks, allowing commuters to work on laptops as they prepare for same-day meetings in once distant capital cities. In Latin America, China, and India, working people board fast-loading buses that move like subway trains along dedicated busways, leaving the sedans and SUVs of the rich mired in dawn-to-dusk traffic jams. And some cities have transformed their streets into cycle-path freeways, making giant strides in public health and safety and the sheer livability of their neighborhoods—in the process turning the workaday bicycle into a viable form of mass transit.

If you credit the demographers, this transit trend has legs. The "Millenials," who reached adulthood around the turn of the century and now outnumber baby boomers, tend to favor cities over suburbs, and are far more willing than their parents to ride buses and subways. Part of the reason is their ease with iPads, MP3 players, Kindles, and smartphones: you can get some serious texting done when you're not driving, and earbuds offer effective insulation from all but the most extreme commuting annoyances. Even though there are more teenagers in the country than ever, only ten million have a driver's license (versus twelve million a generation ago). Baby boomers may have been raised in Leave It to Beaver suburbs, but as they retire, a significant contingent is favoring older cities and compact towns where they have the option of walking and riding bikes. Seniors, too, are more likely to use transit, and by 2025, there will be 64 million Americans over the age of sixty-five. Already, dwellings in older neighborhoods in Washington, D.C., Atlanta, and Denver, especially those near light-rail or subway stations, are commanding enormous price premiums over suburban homes. The experience of European and Asian cities shows that if you make buses, subways, and trains convenient, comfortable, fast, and safe, a surprisingly large percentage of citizens will opt to ride rather than drive.

CONTINUE

Figure 1

Primary Occupation of Public Transportation Passengers in US Cities

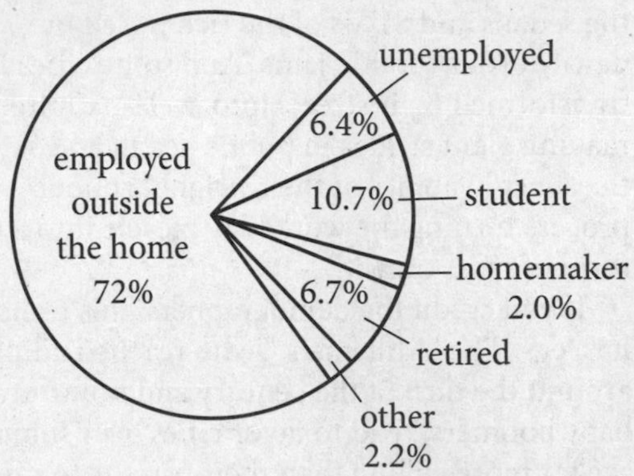

Figure 2

Purpose of Public Transportation Trips in US Cities

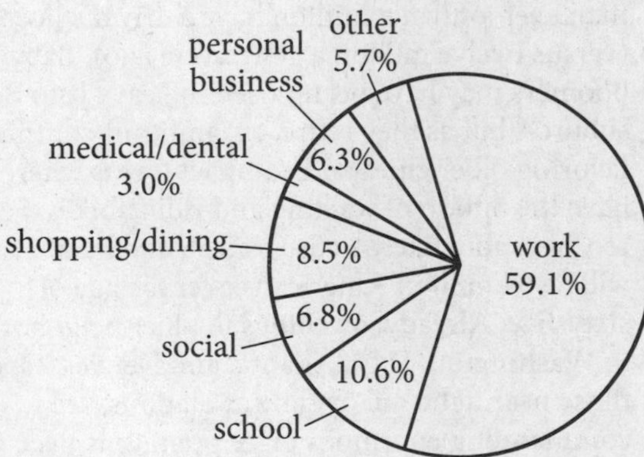

Figure 1 and figure 2 are adapted from the American Public Transportation Association, "A Profile of Public Transportation Passenger Demographics and Travel Characteristics Reported in On-Board Surveys." ©2007 by American Public Transportation Association.

11

What function does the third paragraph (lines 20-34) serve in the passage as a whole?

A) It acknowledges that a practice favored by the author of the passage has some limitations.

B) It illustrates with detail the arguments made in the first two paragraphs of the passage.

C) It gives an overview of a problem that has not been sufficiently addressed by the experts mentioned in the passage.

D) It advocates for abandoning a practice for which the passage as a whole provides mostly favorable data.

12

Which choice does the author explicitly cite as an advantage of automobile travel in North America?

A) Environmental impact

B) Convenience

C) Speed

D) Cost

13

Which choice provides the best evidence for the answer to the previous question?

A) Lines 5-9 ("In . . . automobile")

B) Lines 20-24 ("And . . . car")

C) Lines 24-26 ("In . . . experience")

D) Lines 32-34 ("Hopping . . . quickly")

CONTINUE

14

The central idea of the fourth paragraph (lines 35-57) is that

A) European countries excel at public transportation.

B) some public transportation systems are superior to travel by private automobile.

C) Americans should mimic foreign public transportation systems when possible.

D) much international public transportation is engineered for passengers to work while on board.

15

Which choice provides the best evidence for the answer to the previous question?

A) Line 35 ("It . . . this")

B) Lines 35-37 ("Done . . . automobile")

C) Lines 37-40 ("In . . . sound")

D) Lines 44-48 ("From . . . cities")

16

As used in line 58, "credit" most nearly means

A) endow.

B) attribute.

C) believe.

D) honor.

17

As used in line 61, "favor" most nearly means

A) indulge.

B) prefer.

C) resemble.

D) serve.

18

Which choice best supports the conclusion that public transportation is compatible with the use of personal electronic devices?

A) Lines 59-63 ("The . . . subways")

B) Lines 63-67 ("Part . . . annoyances")

C) Lines 68-70 ("Even . . . ago")

D) Lines 77-81 ("Already . . . homes")

19

Which choice is supported by the data in the first figure?

A) The number of students using public transportation is greater than the number of retirees using public transportation.

B) The number of employed people using public transportation and the number of unemployed people using public transportation is roughly the same.

C) People employed outside the home are less likely to use public transportation than are homemakers.

D) Unemployed people use public transportation less often than do people employed outside the home.

20

Taken together, the two figures suggest that most people who use public transportation

A) are employed outside the home and take public transportation to work.

B) are employed outside the home but take public transportation primarily in order to run errands.

C) use public transportation during the week but use their private cars on weekends.

D) use public transportation only until they are able to afford to buy a car.

CONTINUE

Questions 21-30 are based on the following passage.

This passage is adapted from Thor Hanson, *Feathers*. ©2011 by Thor Hanson. Scientists have long debated how the ancestors of birds evolved the ability to fly. The ground-up theory assumes they were fleet-footed ground dwellers that captured prey by leaping and flapping their upper limbs. The tree-down theory assumes they were tree climbers that leapt and glided among branches.

At field sites around the world, Ken Dial saw a pattern in how young pheasants, quail, tinamous, and other ground birds ran along behind their parents. "They jumped up like popcorn," he said, describing how they would flap their half-formed wings and take short hops into the air. So when a group of graduate students challenged him to come up with new data on the age-old ground-up-tree-down debate, he designed a project to see what clues might lie in how baby game birds learned to fly.

Ken settled on the Chukar Partridge as a model species, but he might not have made his discovery without a key piece of advice from the local rancher in Montana who was supplying him with birds. When the cowboy stopped by to see how things were going, Ken showed him his nice, tidy laboratory setup and explained how the birds' first hops and flights would be measured. The rancher was incredulous. "He took one look and said, in pretty colorful language, 'What are those birds doing on the ground? They hate to be on the ground! Give them something to climb on!' " At first it seemed unnatural—ground birds don't like the ground? But as he thought about it Ken realized that all the species he'd watched in the wild preferred to rest on ledges, low branches, or other elevated perches where they were safe from predators. They really only used the ground for feeding and traveling. So he brought in some hay bales for the Chukars to perch on and then left his son in charge of feeding and data collection while he went away on a short work trip.

Barely a teenager at the time, young Terry Dial was visibly upset when his father got back. "I asked him how it went," Ken recalled, "and he said, 'Terrible! The birds are cheating!' " Instead of flying up to their perches, the baby Chukars were using their legs. Time and again Terry had watched them run right up the side of a hay bale, flapping all the while. Ken dashed out to see for himself, and that was the "aha" moment. "The birds were using their wings and legs cooperatively," he told me, and that single observation opened up a world of possibilities.

Working together with Terry (who has since gone on to study animal locomotion), Ken came up with a series of ingenious experiments, filming the birds as they raced up textured ramps tilted at increasing angles. As the incline increased, the partridges began to flap, but they angled their wings differently from birds in flight. They aimed their flapping down and backward, using the force not for lift but to keep their feet firmly pressed against the ramp. "It's like the spoiler on the back of a race car," he explained, which is a very apt analogy. In Formula One racing, spoilers are the big aerodynamic fins that push the cars downward as they speed along, increasing traction and handling. The birds were doing the very same thing with their wings to help them scramble up otherwise impossible slopes.

Ken called the technique WAIR, for wing-assisted incline running, and went on to document it in a wide range of species. It not only allowed young birds to climb vertical surfaces within the first few weeks of life but also gave adults an energy-efficient alternative to flying. In the Chukar experiments, adults regularly used WAIR to ascend ramps steeper than 90 degrees, essentially running up the wall and onto the ceiling.

In an evolutionary context, WAIR takes on surprising explanatory powers. With one fell swoop, the Dials came up with a viable origin for the flapping flight stroke of birds (something gliding animals don't do and thus a shortcoming of the tree-down theory) and an aerodynamic function for half-formed wings (one of the main drawbacks to the ground-up hypothesis).

CONTINUE

21

Which choice best reflects the overall sequence of events in the passage?

A) An experiment is proposed but proves unworkable; a less ambitious experiment is attempted, and it yields data that give rise to a new set of questions.

B) A new discovery leads to reconsideration of a theory; a classic study is adapted, and the results are summarized.

C) An anomaly is observed and simulated experimentally; the results are compared with previous findings, and a novel hypothesis is proposed.

D) An unexpected finding arises during the early phase of a study; the study is modified in response to this finding, and the results are interpreted and evaluated.

22

As used in line 7, "challenged" most nearly means

A) dared.

B) required.

C) disputed with.

D) competed with.

23

Which statement best captures Ken Dial's central assumption in setting up his research?

A) The acquisition of flight in young birds sheds light on the acquisition of flight in their evolutionary ancestors.

B) The tendency of certain young birds to jump erratically is a somewhat recent evolved behavior.

C) Young birds in a controlled research setting are less likely than birds in the wild to require perches when at rest.

D) Ground-dwelling and tree-climbing predecessors to birds evolved in parallel.

24

Which choice provides the best evidence for the answer to the previous question?

A) Lines 1-4 ("At field . . . parents")

B) Lines 6-11 ("So when . . . fly")

C) Lines 16-19 ("When . . . measured")

D) Lines 23-24 ("At first . . . the ground")

25

In the second paragraph (lines 12-32), the incident involving the local rancher mainly serves to

A) reveal Ken Dial's motivation for undertaking his project.

B) underscore certain differences between laboratory and field research.

C) show how an unanticipated piece of information influenced Ken Dial's research.

D) introduce a key contributor to the tree-down theory.

26

After Ken Dial had his "'aha' moment" (line 41), he

A) tried to train the birds to fly to their perches.

B) studied videos to determine why the birds no longer hopped.

C) observed how the birds dealt with gradually steeper inclines.

D) consulted with other researchers who had studied Chukar Partridges.

27

The passage identifies which of the following as a factor that facilitated the baby Chukars' traction on steep ramps?

A) The speed with which they climbed

B) The position of their flapping wings

C) The alternation of wing and foot movement

D) Their continual hopping motions

CONTINUE

28

As used in line 61, "document" most nearly means

A) portray.
B) record.
C) publish.
D) process.

29

What can reasonably be inferred about gliding animals from the passage?

A) Their young tend to hop along beside their parents instead of flying beside them.
B) Their method of locomotion is similar to that of ground birds.
C) They use the ground for feeding more often than for perching.
D) They do not use a flapping stroke to aid in climbing slopes.

30

Which choice provides the best evidence for the answer to the previous question?

A) Lines 4-6 ("They jumped . . . air")
B) Lines 28-29 ("They really . . . traveling")
C) Lines 57-59 ("The birds . . . slopes")
D) Lines 72-74 ("something . . . theory")

Questions 31-41 are based on the following passages.

Passage 1 is adapted from Talleyrand et al., *Report on Public Instruction*. Originally published in 1791. Passage 2 is adapted from Mary Wollstonecraft, *A Vindication of the Rights of Woman*. Originally published in 1792. Talleyrand was a French diplomat; the *Report* was a plan for national education. Wollstonecraft, a British novelist and political writer, wrote *Vindication* in response to Talleyrand.

Passage 1

That half the human race is excluded by the other half from any participation in government; that they are native by birth but foreign by law in the very land where they were born; and that they are property-owners yet have no direct influence or representation: are all political phenomena apparently impossible to explain on abstract principle. But on another level of ideas, the question changes and may be easily resolved. The purpose of all these institutions must be the happiness of the greatest number. Everything that leads us farther from this purpose is in error; everything that brings us closer is truth. If the exclusion from public employments decreed against women leads to a greater sum of mutual happiness for the two sexes, then this becomes a law that all Societies have been compelled to acknowledge and sanction.

Any other ambition would be a reversal of our primary destinies; and it will never be in women's interest to change the assignment they have received.

It seems to us incontestable that our common happiness, above all that of women, requires that they never aspire to the exercise of political rights and functions. Here we must seek their interests in the wishes of nature. Is it not apparent, that their delicate constitutions, their peaceful inclinations, and the many duties of motherhood, set them apart from strenuous habits and onerous duties, and summon them to gentle occupations and the cares of the home? And is it not evident that the great conserving principle of Societies, which makes the division of powers a source of harmony, has been expressed and revealed by nature itself, when it divided the functions of the two sexes in so obviously distinct a manner? This is sufficient; we need not invoke principles that are inapplicable to the question. Let us not make rivals of life's companions. You must, you truly must allow the persistence of a union that no interest, no rivalry, can possibly undo. Understand that the good of all demands this of you.

CONTINUE

Passage 2

Contending for the rights of woman, my main argument is built on this simple principle, that if she be not prepared by education to become the companion of man, she will stop the progress of knowledge and virtue; for truth must be common to all, or it will be inefficacious with respect to its influence on general practice. And how can woman be expected to co-operate unless she know why she ought to be virtuous? unless freedom strengthen her reason till she comprehend her duty, and see in what manner it is connected with her real good? If children are to be educated to understand the true principle of patriotism, their mother must be a patriot; and the love of mankind, from which an orderly train of virtues spring, can only be produced by considering the moral and civil interest of mankind; but the education and situation of woman, at present, shuts her out from such investigations. . . .

Consider, sir, dispassionately, these observations—for a glimpse of this truth seemed to open before you when you observed, "that to see one half of the human race excluded by the other from all participation of government, was a political phenomenon that, according to abstract principles, it was impossible to explain." If so, on what does your constitution rest? If the abstract rights of man will bear discussion and explanation, those of woman, by a parity of reasoning, will not shrink from the same test: though a different opinion prevails in this country, built on the very arguments which you use to justify the oppression of woman—prescription.

Consider—I address you as a legislator—whether, when men contend for their freedom, and to be allowed to judge for themselves respecting their own happiness, it be not inconsistent and unjust to subjugate women, even though you firmly believe that you are acting in the manner best calculated to promote their happiness? Who made man the exclusive judge, if woman partake with him the gift of reason?

In this style, argue tyrants of every denomination, from the weak king to the weak father of a family; they are all eager to crush reason; yet always assert that they usurp its throne only to be useful. Do you not act a similar part, when you force all women, by denying them civil and political rights, to remain immured in their families groping in the dark?

31

As used in line 21, "common" most nearly means

A) average.
B) shared.
C) coarse.
D) similar.

32

It can be inferred that the authors of Passage 1 believe that running a household and raising children

A) are rewarding for men as well as for women.
B) yield less value for society than do the roles performed by men.
C) entail very few activities that are difficult or unpleasant.
D) require skills similar to those needed to run a country or a business.

33

Which choice provides the best evidence for the answer to the previous question?

A) Lines 4-6 ("they are . . . representation")
B) Lines 13-17 ("If the . . . sanction")
C) Lines 25-30 ("Is it . . . home")
D) Lines 30-35 ("And . . . manner")

34

According to the author of Passage 2, in order for society to progress, women must

A) enjoy personal happiness and financial security.
B) follow all currently prescribed social rules.
C) replace men as figures of power and authority.
D) receive an education comparable to that of men.

CONTINUE

35

As used in line 50, "reason" most nearly means

A) motive.

B) sanity.

C) intellect.

D) explanation.

36

In Passage 2, the author claims that freedoms granted by society's leaders have

A) privileged one gender over the other.

B) resulted in a general reduction in individual virtue.

C) caused arguments about the nature of happiness.

D) ensured equality for all people.

37

Which choice provides the best evidence for the answer to the previous question?

A) Lines 41-45 ("Contending . . . virtue")

B) Lines 45-47 ("truth . . . practice")

C) Lines 65-66 ("If so . . . rest")

D) Lines 72-75 ("Consider . . . happiness")

38

In lines 61-65, the author of Passage 2 refers to a statement made in Passage 1 in order to

A) call into question the qualifications of the authors of Passage 1 regarding gender issues.

B) dispute the assertion made about women in the first sentence of Passage 1.

C) develop her argument by highlighting what she sees as flawed reasoning in Passage 1.

D) validate the concluding declarations made by the authors of Passage 1 about gender roles.

39

Which best describes the overall relationship between Passage 1 and Passage 2?

A) Passage 2 strongly challenges the point of view in Passage 1.

B) Passage 2 draws alternative conclusions from the evidence presented in Passage 1.

C) Passage 2 elaborates on the proposal presented in Passage 1.

D) Passage 2 restates in different terms the argument presented in Passage 1.

40

The authors of both passages would most likely agree with which of the following statements about women in the eighteenth century?

A) Their natural preferences were the same as those of men.

B) They needed a good education to be successful in society.

C) They were just as happy in life as men were.

D) They generally enjoyed fewer rights than men did.

41

How would the authors of Passage 1 most likely respond to the points made in the final paragraph of Passage 2?

A) Women are not naturally suited for the exercise of civil and political rights.

B) Men and women possess similar degrees of reasoning ability.

C) Women do not need to remain confined to their traditional family duties.

D) The principles of natural law should not be invoked when considering gender roles.

Questions 42-52 are based on the following passage and supplementary material.

This passage is adapted from Richard J. Sharpe and Lisa Heyden, "Honey Bee Colony Collapse Disorder is Possibly Caused by a Dietary Pyrethrum Deficiency." ©2009 by Elsevier Ltd. Colony collapse disorder is characterized by the disappearance of adult worker bees from hives.

Honey bees are hosts to the pathogenic large ectoparasitic mite *Varroa destructor* (Varroa mites). These mites feed on bee hemolymph (blood) and can kill bees directly or by increasing their susceptibility to secondary infection with fungi, bacteria or viruses. Little is known about the natural defenses that keep the mite infections under control.

Pyrethrums are a group of flowering plants which include *Chrysanthemum coccineum*, *Chrysanthemum cinerariifolium*, *Chrysanthemum marschalli*, and related species. These plants produce potent insecticides with anti-mite activity. The naturally occurring insecticides are known as pyrethrums. A synonym for the naturally occurring pyrethrums is pyrethrin and synthetic analogues of pyrethrums are known as pyrethroids. In fact, the human mite infestation known as scabies (*Sarcoptes scabiei*) is treated with a topical pyrethrum cream.

We suspect that the bees of commercial bee colonies which are fed mono-crops are nutritionally deficient. In particular, we postulate that the problem is a diet deficient in anti-mite toxins: pyrethrums, and possibly other nutrients which are inherent in such plants. Without, at least, intermittent feeding on the pyrethrum producing plants, bee colonies are susceptible to mite infestations which can become fatal either directly or due to a secondary infection of immunocompromised or nutritionally deficient bees. This secondary infection can be viral, bacterial or fungal and may be due to one or more pathogens. In addition, immunocompromised or nutritionally deficient bees may be further weakened when commercially produced insecticides are introduced into their hives by bee keepers in an effort to fight mite infestation. We further postulate that the proper dosage necessary to prevent mite infestation may be better left to the bees, who may seek out or avoid pyrethrum containing plants depending on the amount necessary to defend against mites and the amount already consumed by the bees, which in higher doses could be potentially toxic to them.

This hypothesis can best be tested by a trial wherein a small number of commercial honey bee colonies are offered a number of pyrethrum producing plants, as well as a typical bee food source such as clover, while controls are offered only the clover. Mites could then be introduced to each hive with note made as to the choice of the bees, and the effects of the mite parasites on the experimental colonies versus control colonies.

It might be beneficial to test wild-type honey bee colonies in this manner as well, in case there could be some genetic difference between them that affects the bees' preferences for pyrethrum producing flowers.

Pathogen Occurence in Honey Bee Colonies With and Without Colony Collapse Disorder

Pathogen	Percent of colonies affected by pathogen: Colonies with colony collapse disorder (%)	Percent of colonies affected by pathogen: Colonies without colony collapse disorder (%)
Viruses		
IAPV	83	5
KBV	100	76
Fungi		
Nosema apis	90	48
Nosema ceranae	100	81
All four pathogens	83	0

Adapted from Diana L. Cox-Foster et al., "A Metagenomic Survey of Microbes in Honey Bee Colony Collapse Disorder." ©2007 by American Association for the Advancement of Science.

The table above shows, for colonies with colony collapse disorder and for colonies without colony collapse disorder, the percent of colonies having honey bees infected by each of four pathogens and by all four pathogens together.

CONTINUE

42

How do the words "can," "may," and "could" in the third paragraph (lines 19-41) help establish the tone of the paragraph?

A) They create an optimistic tone that makes clear the authors are hopeful about the effects of their research on colony collapse disorder.

B) They create a dubious tone that makes clear the authors do not have confidence in the usefulness of the research described.

C) They create a tentative tone that makes clear the authors suspect but do not know that their hypothesis is correct.

D) They create a critical tone that makes clear the authors are skeptical of claims that pyrethrums are inherent in mono-crops.

43

In line 42, the authors state that a certain hypothesis "can best be tested by a trial." Based on the passage, which of the following is a hypothesis the authors suggest be tested in a trial?

A) Honeybees that are exposed to both pyrethrums and mites are likely to develop a secondary infection by a virus, a bacterium, or a fungus.

B) Beekeepers who feed their honeybee colonies a diet of a single crop need to increase the use of insecticides to prevent mite infestations.

C) A honeybee diet that includes pyrethrums results in honeybee colonies that are more resistant to mite infestations.

D) Humans are more susceptible to varroa mites as a result of consuming nutritionally deficient food crops.

44

Which choice provides the best evidence for the answer to the previous question?

A) Lines 3-5 ("These mites . . . viruses")

B) Lines 16-18 ("In fact . . . cream")

C) Lines 19-21 ("We suspect . . . deficient")

D) Lines 24-28 ("Without . . . bees")

45

The passage most strongly suggests that beekeepers' attempts to fight mite infestations with commercially produced insecticides have what unintentional effect?

A) They increase certain mite populations.

B) They kill some beneficial forms of bacteria.

C) They destroy bees' primary food source.

D) They further harm the health of some bees.

46

Which choice provides the best evidence for the answer to the previous question?

A) Lines 1-2 ("Honey bees . . . mites")

B) Lines 6-7 ("Little . . . control")

C) Lines 31-35 ("In addition . . . infestation")

D) Lines 47-50 ("Mites . . . control colonies")

47

As used in line 35, "postulate" most nearly means to

A) make an unfounded assumption.

B) put forth an idea or claim.

C) question a belief or theory.

D) conclude based on firm evidence.

48

The main purpose of the fourth paragraph (lines 42-50) is to

A) summarize the results of an experiment that confirmed the authors' hypothesis about the role of clover in the diets of wild-type honeybees.

B) propose an experiment to investigate how different diets affect commercial honeybee colonies' susceptibility to mite infestations.

C) provide a comparative nutritional analysis of the honey produced by the experimental colonies and by the control colonies.

D) predict the most likely outcome of an unfinished experiment summarized in the third paragraph (lines 19-41).

CONTINUE

49

An unstated assumption made by the authors about clover is that the plants

A) do not produce pyrethrums.

B) are members of the *Chrysanthemum* genus.

C) are usually located near wild-type honeybee colonies.

D) will not be a good food source for honeybees in the control colonies.

50

Based on data in the table, in what percent of colonies with colony collapse disorder were the honeybees infected by all four pathogens?

A) 0 percent

B) 77 percent

C) 83 percent

D) 100 percent

51

Based on data in the table, which of the four pathogens infected the highest percentage of honeybee colonies without colony collapse disorder?

A) IAPV

B) KBV

C) *Nosema apis*

D) *Nosema ceranae*

52

Do the data in the table provide support for the authors' claim that infection with varroa mites increases a honeybee's susceptibility to secondary infections?

A) Yes, because the data provide evidence that infection with a pathogen caused the colonies to undergo colony collapse disorder.

B) Yes, because for each pathogen, the percent of colonies infected is greater for colonies with colony collapse disorder than for colonies without colony collapse disorder.

C) No, because the data do not provide evidence about bacteria as a cause of colony collapse disorder.

D) No, because the data do not indicate whether the honeybees had been infected with mites.

STOP

If you finish before time is called, you may check your work on this section only.

Do not turn to any other section.

Writing and Language Test

35 MINUTES, 44 QUESTIONS

Turn to Section 2 of your answer sheet to answer the questions in this section.

DIRECTIONS

Each passage below is accompanied by a number of questions. For some questions, you will consider how the passage might be revised to improve the expression of ideas. For other questions, you will consider how the passage might be edited to correct errors in sentence structure, usage, or punctuation. A passage or a question may be accompanied by one or more graphics (such as a table or graph) that you will consider as you make revising and editing decisions.

Some questions will direct you to an underlined portion of a passage. Other questions will direct you to a location in a passage or ask you to think about the passage as a whole.

After reading each passage, choose the answer to each question that most effectively improves the quality of writing in the passage or that makes the passage conform to the conventions of standard written English. Many questions include a "NO CHANGE" option. Choose that option if you think the best choice is to leave the relevant portion of the passage as it is.

Questions 1-11 are based on the following passage.

Shed Some Light on the Workplace

Studies have shown that employees are happier, [1] healthier, and more productive when they work in an environment [2] in which temperatures are carefully controlled. New buildings may be designed with these studies in mind, but many older buildings were not, resulting in spaces that often depend primarily on artificial lighting. While employers may balk at the expense of reconfiguring such buildings to increase the amount of natural light, the investment has been shown to be well worth it in the long run—for both employees and employers.

1

A) NO CHANGE
B) healthy, and more
C) healthier, and they are
D) healthier, being more

2

Which choice provides the most appropriate introduction to the passage?

A) NO CHANGE
B) that affords them adequate amounts of natural light.
C) that is thoroughly sealed to prevent energy loss.
D) in which they feel comfortable asking managers for special accommodations.

CONTINUE

For one thing, lack of exposure to natural light has a significant impact on employees' health. A study conducted in 2013 by Northwestern University in Chicago showed that inadequate natural light could result in eye strain, headaches, and fatigue, as well as interference with the body's circadian rhythms. **3** Circadian rhythms, which are controlled by the **4** bodies biological clocks, influence body temperature, hormone release, cycles of sleep and wakefulness, and other bodily functions. Disruptions of circadian rhythms have been linked to sleep disorders, diabetes, depression, and bipolar disorder. Like any other health problems, these ailments can increase employee absenteeism, which, in turn, **5** is costly for employers. Employees who feel less than 100 percent and are sleep deprived are also less prone to work at their maximal productivity. One company in California **6** gained a huge boost in its employees' morale when it moved from an artificially lit distribution facility to one with natural illumination.

3

At this point, the writer is considering adding the following sentence.

> Workers in offices with windows sleep an average of 46 minutes more per night than workers in offices without windows.

Should the writer make this addition here?

A) Yes, because it supplies quantitative data that will be examined in the rest of the paragraph.

B) Yes, because it explains the nature of the bodily functions referred to in the next sentence.

C) No, because it interrupts the discussion of circadian rhythms.

D) No, because it does not take into account whether workers were exposed to sunlight outside the office.

4

A) NO CHANGE

B) bodies' biological clocks',

C) body's biological clocks,

D) body's biological clock's,

5

A) NO CHANGE

B) are

C) is being

D) have been

6

Which choice best supports the statement made in the previous sentence?

A) NO CHANGE

B) saw a 5 percent increase in productivity

C) saved a great deal on its operational costs

D) invested large amounts of time and capital

CONTINUE

[7] Artificial light sources are also costly aside from lowering worker productivity. They typically constitute anywhere from 25 to 50 percent of a building's energy use. When a plant in Seattle, Washington, was redesigned for more natural light, the company was able to enjoy annual electricity cost reductions of $500,000 [8] each year.

7

In context, which choice best combines the underlined sentences?

A) Aside from lowering worker productivity, artificial light sources are also costly, typically constituting anywhere from 25 to 50 percent of a building's energy use.

B) The cost of artificial light sources, aside from lowering worker productivity, typically constitutes anywhere from 25 to 50 percent of a building's energy use.

C) Typically constituting 25 to 50 percent of a building's energy use, artificial light sources lower worker productivity and are costly.

D) Artificial lights, which lower worker productivity and are costly, typically constitute anywhere from 25 to 50 percent of a building's energy use.

8

A) NO CHANGE

B) every year.

C) per year.

D) DELETE the underlined portion and end the sentence with a period.

CONTINUE

Among the possibilities to reconfigure a building's lighting is the installation of full-pane windows to allow the greatest degree of sunlight to reach office interiors. **9** Thus, businesses can install light tubes, **10** these are pipes placed in workplace roofs to capture and funnel sunlight down into a building's interior. Glass walls and dividers can also be used to replace solid walls as a means **11** through distributing natural light more freely. Considering the enormous costs of artificial lighting, both in terms of money and productivity, investment in such improvements should be a natural choice for businesses.

9

A) NO CHANGE
B) Nevertheless,
C) Alternatively,
D) Finally,

10

A) NO CHANGE
B) they are
C) which are
D) those being

11

A) NO CHANGE
B) of
C) from
D) DELETE the underlined portion.

CONTINUE

Questions 12-22 are based on the following passage.

Transforming the American West Through Food and Hospitality

Just as travelers taking road trips today may need to take a break for food at a rest area along the highway, settlers traversing the American West by train in the mid-1800s often found **12** themselves in need of refreshment. However, food available on rail lines was generally of terrible quality. **13** Despite having worked for railroad companies, Fred Harvey, an English-born **14** entrepreneur. He decided to open his own restaurant business to serve rail customers. Beginning in the 1870s, he opened dozens of restaurants in rail stations and dining cars. These Harvey Houses, which constituted the first restaurant chain in the United States, **15** was unique for its high standards of service and quality. The menu was modeled after those of fine restaurants, so the food was leagues beyond the **16** sinister fare travelers were accustomed to receiving in transit.

12

A) NO CHANGE
B) himself or herself
C) their selves
D) oneself

13

Which choice provides the most logical introduction to the sentence?

A) NO CHANGE
B) He had lived in New York and New Orleans, so
C) To capitalize on the demand for good food,
D) DELETE the underlined portion.

14

A) NO CHANGE
B) entrepreneur:
C) entrepreneur; he
D) entrepreneur,

15

A) NO CHANGE
B) were unique for their
C) was unique for their
D) were unique for its

16

Which choice best maintains the tone established in the passage?

A) NO CHANGE
B) surly
C) abysmal
D) icky

CONTINUE

His restaurants were immediately successful, but Harvey was not content to follow conventional business practices. **17** Although women did not traditionally work in restaurants in the nineteenth century, Harvey decided to try employing women as waitstaff. In 1883, he placed an advertisement seeking educated, well-mannered, articulate young women between the ages of 18 and 30. **18** Response to the advertisement was overwhelming, even tremendous, and Harvey soon replaced the male servers at his restaurants with women. Those who were hired as "Harvey Girls" joined an elite group of workers, who were expected to complete a 30-day training program and follow a strict code of rules for conduct and curfews. In the workplace, the women donned identical black-and-white uniforms and carried out their duties with precision. Not only were such regulations meant to ensure the efficiency of the business and the safety of the workers, **19** but also helped to raise people's generally low opinion of the restaurant industry.

17

The writer is considering deleting the previous sentence. Should the writer make this change?

A) Yes, because it introduces information that is irrelevant at this point in the passage.

B) Yes, because it does not logically follow from the previous paragraph.

C) No, because it provides a logical introduction to the paragraph.

D) No, because it provides a specific example in support of arguments made elsewhere in the passage.

18

A) NO CHANGE

B) Response to the advertisement was overwhelming,

C) Overwhelming, even tremendous, was the response to the advertisement,

D) There was an overwhelming, even tremendous, response to the advertisement,

19

A) NO CHANGE

B) but also helping

C) also helping

D) but they also helped

CONTINUE

In return for the servers' work, the position paid quite well for the time: $17.50 a month, plus tips, meals, room and board, laundry service, and travel expenses. **20**

For as long as Harvey Houses served rail travelers through the mid-twentieth century, working there was a steady and lucrative position for women. Living independently and demonstrating an intense work **21** ethic; the Harvey Girls became known as a transformative force in the American **22** West. Advancing the roles of women in the restaurant industry and the American workforce as a whole, the Harvey Girls raised the standards for restaurants and blazed a trail in the fast-changing landscape of the western territories.

20

Which choice most logically follows the previous sentence?

A) The growth of Harvey's business coincided with the expansion of the Santa Fe Railway, which served large sections of the American West.

B) Harvey would end up opening dozens of restaurants and dining cars, plus 15 hotels, over his lucrative career.

C) These benefits enabled the Harvey Girls to save money and build new and exciting lives for themselves in the so-called Wild West.

D) The compensation was considered excellent at the time, though it may not seem like much money by today's standards.

21

A) NO CHANGE

B) ethic:

C) ethic, and

D) ethic,

22

The writer is considering revising the underlined portion of the sentence to read:

> West, inspiring books, documentaries, and even a musical.

Should the writer add this information here?

A) Yes, because it provides examples of the Harvey Girls' influence.

B) Yes, because it serves as a transitional point in the paragraph.

C) No, because it should be placed earlier in the passage.

D) No, because it contradicts the main claim of the passage.

CONTINUE

Questions 23-33 are based on the following passage and supplementary material.

How Do You Like Those Apples?

Marketed as SmartFresh, the chemical 1-MCP (1-methylcyclopropene) has been used by fruit growers since 2002 in the United States and elsewhere to preserve the crispness and lengthen the storage life of apples and other fruit, which often must travel long distances before being eaten by consumers. [23] 1-MCP lengthens storage life by three to four times when applied to apples. This extended life allows producers to sell their apples in the off-season, months after the apples have been harvested. And at a cost of about one cent per pound of apples, 1-MCP is a highly cost-effective treatment. However, 1-MCP is not a panacea for fruit producers or sellers: there are problems and limitations associated with its use.

23

Which choice most effectively combines the underlined sentences?

A) When applied to apples, 1-MCP lengthens storage life by three to four times, allowing producers to sell their apples in the off-season, months after the apples have been harvested.

B) Producers are allowed to sell their apples months after they have been harvested—in the off-season—because 1-MCP, when applied to apples, lengthens their storage life by three to four times.

C) 1-MCP lengthens storage life, when applied to apples, by three to four times, allowing producers to sell their apples months after the apples have been harvested in the off-season.

D) Months after apples have been harvested, producers are allowed to sell their apples, in the off-season, because 1-MCP lengthens storage life when applied to apples by three to four times.

CONTINUE

[1] 1-MCP works by limiting a fruit's production of ethylene, **24** it is a chemical that causes fruit to ripen and eventually rot. [2] While 1-MCP keeps apples **25** tight and crisp for months, it also limits **26** their scent production. [3] This may not be much of a problem with certain kinds of apples that are not naturally very fragrant, such as Granny Smith, but for apples that are prized for their fruity fragrance, such as McIntosh, this can be a problem with consumers, **27** that will reject apples lacking the expected aroma. [4] But some fruits do not respond as well to 1-MCP as others **28** did, and some even respond adversely. [5] Furthermore, some fruits, particularly those that naturally produce a large

24

A) NO CHANGE
B) being
C) that is
D) DELETE the underlined portion.

25

A) NO CHANGE
B) firm
C) stiff
D) taut

26

A) NO CHANGE
B) there
C) its
D) it's

27

A) NO CHANGE
B) they
C) which
D) who

28

A) NO CHANGE
B) do,
C) have,
D) will,

CONTINUE

amount of ethylene, do not respond as well to 1-MCP treatment. [6] Take Bartlett **29** pears, for instance, unless they are treated with exactly the right amount of 1-MCP at exactly the right time, they will remain hard and green until they rot, and consumers who experience this will be unlikely to purchase them again. **30**

29

A) NO CHANGE
B) pears, for instance:
C) pears for instance,
D) pears. For instance,

30

To make this paragraph most logical, sentence 4 should be placed

A) where it is now.
B) after sentence 1.
C) after sentence 2.
D) after sentence 5.

CONTINUE

Finally, researchers have found that 1-MCP actually increases susceptibility to some pathologies in certain apple varieties. For example, Empire apples are prone to a condition that causes the flesh of the apple to turn brown. Traditionally, apple producers have dealt with this problem by leaving the apples in the open air for three weeks before storing them in a controlled atmosphere with tightly regulated temperature, humidity, and carbon dioxide levels. As the graph shows, the flesh of untreated Empire apples that are first stored in the open air undergoes **31** roughly five percent less browning than the flesh of untreated Empire apples that are immediately put into storage in a controlled environment. However, when Empire apples are treated with 1-MCP, **32** their flesh turns brown when the apples are first stored in the open air, though not under other conditions. Although

31

Which choice offers an accurate interpretation of the data in the graph?

A) NO CHANGE

B) slightly more browning than

C) twice as much browning as

D) substantially less browning than

32

Which choice offers an accurate interpretation of the data in the graph?

A) NO CHANGE

B) roughly half of their flesh turns brown, regardless of whether the apples are first stored in the open air.

C) their flesh browns when they are put directly into a controlled atmosphere but not when they are first stored in the open air.

D) their flesh turns brown when they are first stored in the open air, though not as quickly as the apple flesh in an untreated group does.

CONTINUE

researchers continue to search for the right combination of factors that will keep fruits fresh and attractive, 33 the problem may be that consumers are overly concerned with superficial qualities rather than the actual freshness of the fruit.

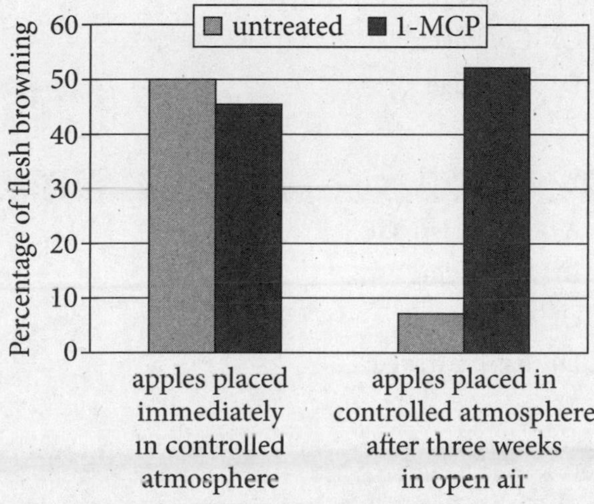

Adapted from Hannah J. James, Jacqueline F. Nock, and Chris B. Watkins, "The Failure of Postharvest Treatments to Control Firm Flesh Browning in Empire Apples." ©2010 by The New York State Horticultural Society.

33

The writer wants a conclusion that conveys how the shortcomings of 1-MCP presented in the passage affect the actions of people in the fruit industry. Which choice best accomplishes this goal?

A) NO CHANGE

B) many of the improvements to fruit quality they have discovered so far have required trade-offs in other properties of the fruit.

C) for now many fruit sellers must weigh the relative values of aroma, color, and freshness when deciding whether to use 1-MCP.

D) it must be acknowledged that 1-MCP, despite some inadequacies, has enabled the fruit industry to ship and store fruit in ways that were impossible before.

CONTINUE

Questions 34-44 are based on the following passage.

More than One Way to Dress a Cat

From Michelangelo's *David* to Vincent van Gogh's series of self-portraits to Grant Wood's iconic image of a farming couple in *American* **34** <u>*Gothic*. These works</u> by human artists have favored representations of members of their own species to those of other species. Indeed, when we think about animals depicted in well-known works of art, the image of dogs playing poker—popularized in a series of paintings by American artist C. M. **35** <u>Coolidge,</u> may be the first and only one that comes to mind. Yet some of the earliest known works of art, including paintings and drawings tens of thousands of years old found on cave walls in Spain and France, **36** <u>portrays</u> animals. Nor has artistic homage to our fellow creatures entirely died out in the millennia since, **37** <u>despite the many years that have passed between then and now.</u>

34

A) NO CHANGE
B) *Gothic*. Works
C) *Gothic*; these works
D) *Gothic*, works

35

A) NO CHANGE
B) Coolidge—
C) Coolidge;
D) Coolidge

36

A) NO CHANGE
B) portraying
C) portray
D) has portrayed

37

The writer wants to link the first paragraph with the ideas that follow. Which choice best accomplishes this goal?

A) NO CHANGE
B) with special attention being paid to domestic animals such as cats.
C) even though most paintings in museums are of people, not animals.
D) as the example of one museum in Russia shows.

CONTINUE

[1] The State Hermitage Museum in St. Petersburg, one of Russia's greatest art museums, has long had a productive partnership with a much loved animal: the cat. [2] For centuries, cats have guarded this famous museum, ridding it of mice, rats, and other rodents that could damage the art, not to mention **38** scared off visitors. [3] Peter the Great introduced the first cat to the Hermitage in the early eighteenth century. [4] Later Catherine the Great declared the cats to be official guardians of the galleries. [5] Continuing the tradition, Peter's daughter Elizaveta introduced the best and strongest cats in Russia to the Hermitage. [6] Today, the museum holds a yearly festival honoring these faithful workers. **39**

38

A) NO CHANGE
B) scaring
C) scare
D) have scared

39

To make this paragraph most logical, sentence 5 should be placed

A) where it is now.
B) after sentence 1.
C) after sentence 3.
D) after sentence 6.

CONTINUE

These cats are so cherished by the museum that officials recently [40] decreed original paintings to be made of six of them. In each, a cat is depicted upright in a humanlike pose and clothed in imperial-era Russian attire. The person chosen for this [41] task, digital artist, Eldar Zakirov painted the cats in the style traditionally used by portrait artists, in so doing [42] presenting the cats as noble individuals worthy of respect. One portrait, *The Hermitage Court Chamber Herald Cat*, includes an

40

A) NO CHANGE
B) commissioned
C) forced
D) licensed

41

A) NO CHANGE
B) task, digital artist, Eldar Zakirov,
C) task digital artist Eldar Zakirov,
D) task, digital artist Eldar Zakirov,

42

Which choice most effectively sets up the examples that follow?

A) NO CHANGE
B) managing to capture unique characteristics of each cat.
C) commenting on the absurdity of dressing up cats in royal robes.
D) indicating that the cats were very talented mouse catchers.

CONTINUE

aristocratic tilt of feline ears as well as a stately sweep of tail emerging from the stiff scarlet and gold of royal court dress. The wise, thoughtful green eyes of the subject of *The Hermitage Court Outrunner Cat* mimic those of a trusted royal advisor. **43** Some may find it peculiar to observe cats portrayed in formal court poses, but these felines, by **44** mastering the art of killing mice and rats, are benefactors of the museum as important as any human.

43

At this point, the writer is considering adding the following sentence.

> The museum occupies six historic buildings, including the Winter Palace, a former residence of Russian emperors.

Should the writer make this addition here?

A) Yes, because it shows the link between Peter the Great and the cat paintings.
B) Yes, because it helps explain why Russian art celebrates animals.
C) No, because it fails to indicate why the Winter Palace became an art museum.
D) No, because it provides background information that is irrelevant to the paragraph.

44

A) NO CHANGE
B) acting as the lead predator in the museum's ecosystem,
C) hunting down and killing all the mice and rats one by one,
D) protecting the museum's priceless artworks from destructive rodents,

STOP

If you finish before time is called, you may check your work on this section only.
Do not turn to any other section.

Math Test – No Calculator

25 MINUTES, 20 QUESTIONS

Turn to Section 3 of your answer sheet to answer the questions in this section.

DIRECTIONS

For questions 1-15, solve each problem, choose the best answer from the choices provided, and fill in the corresponding circle on your answer sheet. **For questions 16-20**, solve the problem and enter your answer in the grid on the answer sheet. Please refer to the directions before question 16 on how to enter your answers in the grid. You may use any available space in your test booklet for scratch work.

NOTES

1. The use of a calculator **is not permitted**.
2. All variables and expressions used represent real numbers unless otherwise indicated.
3. Figures provided in this test are drawn to scale unless otherwise indicated.
4. All figures lie in a plane unless otherwise indicated.
5. Unless otherwise indicated, the domain of a given function *f* is the set of all real numbers *x* for which *f*(*x*) is a real number.

REFERENCE

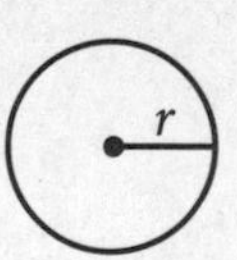

$A = \pi r^2$
$C = 2\pi r$

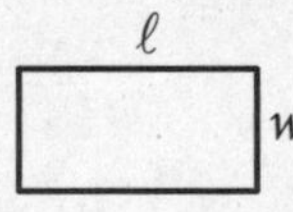

$A = \ell w$

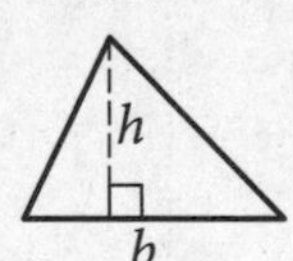

$A = \frac{1}{2}bh$

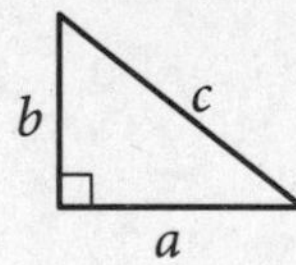

$c^2 = a^2 + b^2$

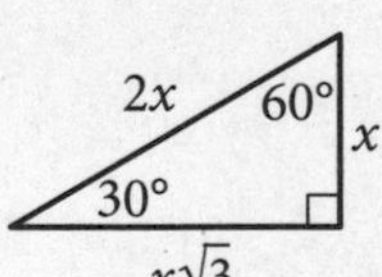

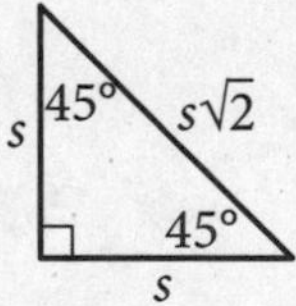

Special Right Triangles

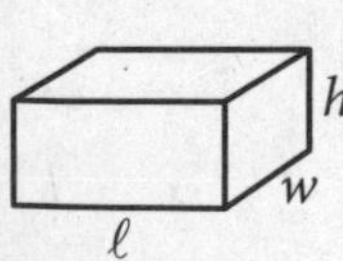

$V = \ell wh$

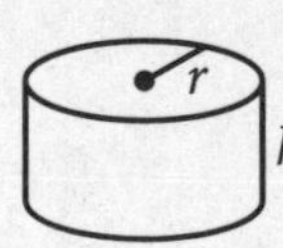

$V = \pi r^2 h$

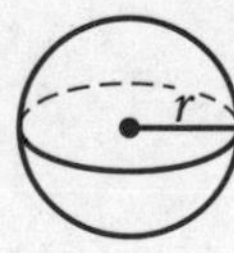

$V = \frac{4}{3}\pi r^3$

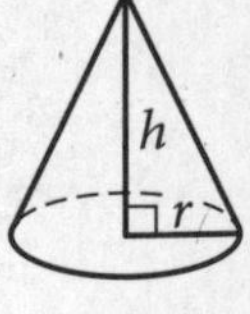

$V = \frac{1}{3}\pi r^2 h$

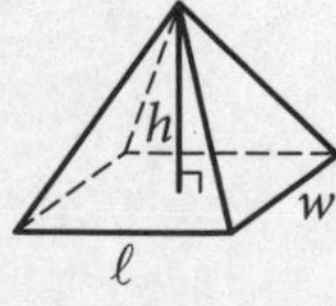

$V = \frac{1}{3}\ell wh$

The number of degrees of arc in a circle is 360.
The number of radians of arc in a circle is 2π.
The sum of the measures in degrees of the angles of a triangle is 180.

CONTINUE

1

A painter will paint n walls with the same size and shape in a building using a specific brand of paint. The painter's fee can be calculated by the expression $nK\ell h$, where n is the number of walls, K is a constant with units of dollars per square foot, ℓ is the length of each wall in feet, and h is the height of each wall in feet. If the customer asks the painter to use a more expensive brand of paint, which of the factors in the expression would change?

A) h

B) ℓ

C) K

D) n

2

If $3r = 18$, what is the value of $6r + 3$?

A) 6

B) 27

C) 36

D) 39

3

Which of the following is equal to $a^{\frac{2}{3}}$, for all values of a ?

A) $\sqrt{a^{\frac{1}{3}}}$

B) $\sqrt{a^3}$

C) $\sqrt[3]{a^{\frac{1}{2}}}$

D) $\sqrt[3]{a^2}$

4

The number of states that joined the United States between 1776 and 1849 is twice the number of states that joined between 1850 and 1900. If 30 states joined the United States between 1776 and 1849 and x states joined between 1850 and 1900, which of the following equations is true?

A) $30x = 2$

B) $2x = 30$

C) $\frac{x}{2} = 30$

D) $x + 30 = 2$

CONTINUE

5

If $\frac{5}{x} = \frac{15}{x+20}$, what is the value of $\frac{x}{5}$?

A) 10

B) 5

C) 2

D) $\frac{1}{2}$

6

$$2x - 3y = -14$$
$$3x - 2y = -6$$

If (x, y) is a solution to the system of equations above, what is the value of $x - y$?

A) -20

B) -8

C) -4

D) 8

7

x	$f(x)$
0	3
2	1
4	0
5	−2

The function f is defined by a polynomial. Some values of x and $f(x)$ are shown in the table above. Which of the following must be a factor of $f(x)$?

A) $x - 2$

B) $x - 3$

C) $x - 4$

D) $x - 5$

8

The line $y = kx + 4$, where k is a constant, is graphed in the xy-plane. If the line contains the point (c, d), where $c \neq 0$ and $d \neq 0$, what is the slope of the line in terms of c and d ?

A) $\frac{d-4}{c}$

B) $\frac{c-4}{d}$

C) $\frac{4-d}{c}$

D) $\frac{4-c}{d}$

CONTINUE

9

$$kx - 3y = 4$$
$$4x - 5y = 7$$

In the system of equations above, k is a constant and x and y are variables. For what value of k will the system of equations have no solution?

A) $\frac{12}{5}$

B) $\frac{16}{7}$

C) $-\frac{16}{7}$

D) $-\frac{12}{5}$

10

In the xy-plane, the parabola with equation $y = (x - 11)^2$ intersects the line with equation $y = 25$ at two points, A and B. What is the length of $\overline{AB}$?

A) 10

B) 12

C) 14

D) 16

11

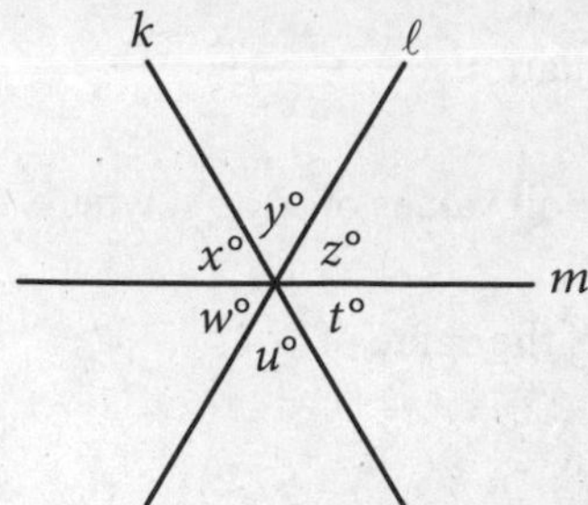

Note: Figure not drawn to scale.

In the figure above, lines k, ℓ, and m intersect at a point. If $x + y = u + w$, which of the following must be true?

I. $x = z$

II. $y = w$

III. $z = t$

A) I and II only

B) I and III only

C) II and III only

D) I, II, and III

12

$$y = a(x - 2)(x + 4)$$

In the quadratic equation above, a is a nonzero constant. The graph of the equation in the xy-plane is a parabola with vertex (c, d). Which of the following is equal to d ?

A) $-9a$

B) $-8a$

C) $-5a$

D) $-2a$

CONTINUE

13

The equation $\dfrac{24x^2 + 25x - 47}{ax - 2} = -8x - 3 - \dfrac{53}{ax - 2}$ is true for all values of $x \neq \dfrac{2}{a}$, where a is a constant.

What is the value of a ?

A) -16

B) -3

C) 3

D) 16

14

What are the solutions to $3x^2 + 12x + 6 = 0$?

A) $x = -2 \pm \sqrt{2}$

B) $x = -2 \pm \dfrac{\sqrt{30}}{3}$

C) $x = -6 \pm \sqrt{2}$

D) $x = -6 \pm 6\sqrt{2}$

15

$$C = \frac{5}{9}(F - 32)$$

The equation above shows how a temperature F, measured in degrees Fahrenheit, relates to a temperature C, measured in degrees Celsius. Based on the equation, which of the following must be true?

I. A temperature increase of 1 degree Fahrenheit is equivalent to a temperature increase of $\dfrac{5}{9}$ degree Celsius.

II. A temperature increase of 1 degree Celsius is equivalent to a temperature increase of 1.8 degrees Fahrenheit.

III. A temperature increase of $\dfrac{5}{9}$ degree Fahrenheit is equivalent to a temperature increase of 1 degree Celsius.

A) I only

B) II only

C) III only

D) I and II only

CONTINUE

DIRECTIONS

For questions 16–20, solve the problem and enter your answer in the grid, as described below, on the answer sheet.

1. Although not required, it is suggested that you write your answer in the boxes at the top of the columns to help you fill in the circles accurately. You will receive credit only if the circles are filled in correctly.
2. Mark no more than one circle in any column.
3. No question has a negative answer.
4. Some problems may have more than one correct answer. In such cases, grid only one answer.
5. **Mixed numbers** such as $3\frac{1}{2}$ must be gridded as 3.5 or 7/2. (If 3 1 / 2 is entered into the grid, it will be interpreted as $\frac{31}{2}$, not $3\frac{1}{2}$.)
6. **Decimal answers:** If you obtain a decimal answer with more digits than the grid can accommodate, it may be either rounded or truncated, but it must fill the entire grid.

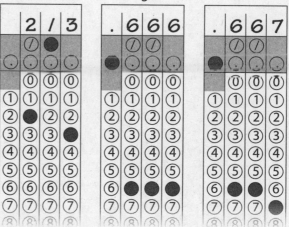

Answer: $\frac{7}{12}$

Write answer in boxes. → 7 / 1 2 ← Fraction line

Grid in result.

Answer: 2.5

2 . 5 ← Decimal point

Acceptable ways to grid $\frac{2}{3}$ are:

2 / 3 .666 .667

Answer: 201 – either position is correct

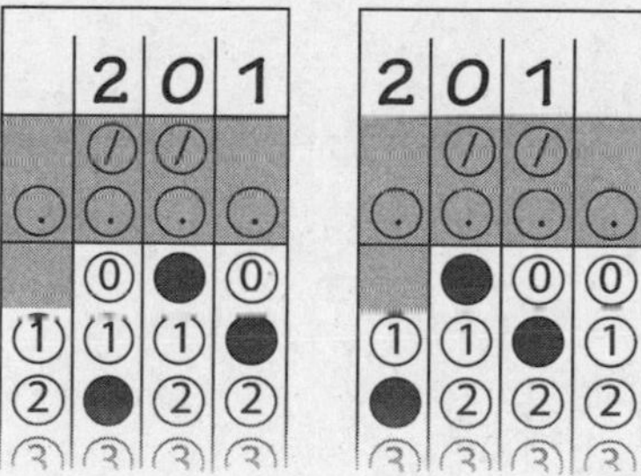

NOTE: You may start your answers in any column, space permitting. Columns you don't need to use should be left blank.

CONTINUE

16

$$x^3(x^2 - 5) = -4x$$

If $x > 0$, what is one possible solution to the equation above?

17

If $\frac{7}{9}x - \frac{4}{9}x = \frac{1}{4} + \frac{5}{12}$, what is the value of x ?

18

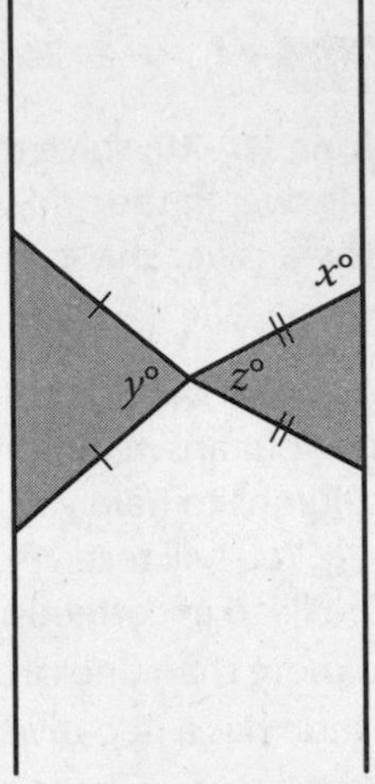

Note: Figure not drawn to scale.

Two isosceles triangles are shown above. If $180 - z = 2y$ and $y = 75$, what is the value of x ?

CONTINUE

19

At a lunch stand, each hamburger has 50 more calories than each order of fries. If 2 hamburgers and 3 orders of fries have a total of 1700 calories, how many calories does a hamburger have?

20

In triangle ABC, the measure of $\angle B$ is $90°$, $BC = 16$, and $AC = 20$. Triangle DEF is similar to triangle ABC, where vertices D, E, and F correspond to vertices A, B, and C, respectively, and each side of triangle DEF is $\frac{1}{3}$ the length of the corresponding side of triangle ABC. What is the value of $\sin F$?

STOP

If you finish before time is called, you may check your work on this section only.

Do not turn to any other section.

Math Test – Calculator

55 MINUTES, 38 QUESTIONS

Turn to Section 4 of your answer sheet to answer the questions in this section.

DIRECTIONS

For questions 1-30, solve each problem, choose the best answer from the choices provided, and fill in the corresponding circle on your answer sheet. **For questions 31-38**, solve the problem and enter your answer in the grid on the answer sheet. Please refer to the directions before question 31 on how to enter your answers in the grid. You may use any available space in your test booklet for scratch work.

NOTES

1. The use of a calculator **is permitted**.
2. All variables and expressions used represent real numbers unless otherwise indicated.
3. Figures provided in this test are drawn to scale unless otherwise indicated.
4. All figures lie in a plane unless otherwise indicated.
5. Unless otherwise indicated, the domain of a given function f is the set of all real numbers x for which $f(x)$ is a real number.

REFERENCE

$A = \pi r^2$
$C = 2\pi r$

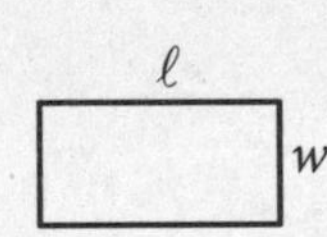

$A = \ell w$

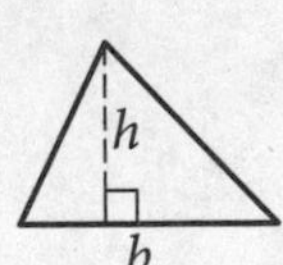

$A = \frac{1}{2}bh$

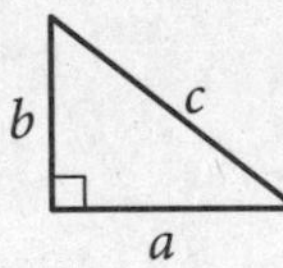

$c^2 = a^2 + b^2$

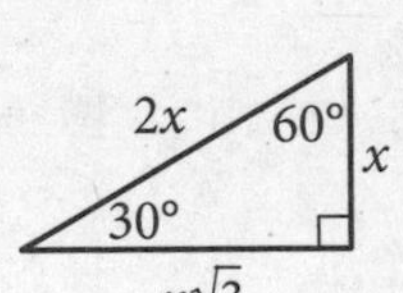

Special Right Triangles

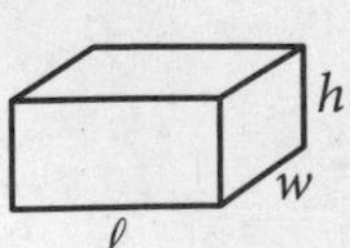

$V = \ell wh$

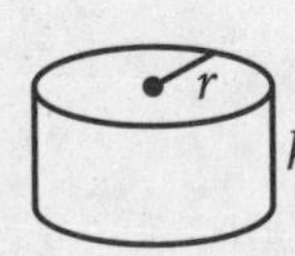

$V = \pi r^2 h$

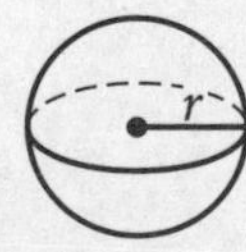

$V = \frac{4}{3}\pi r^3$

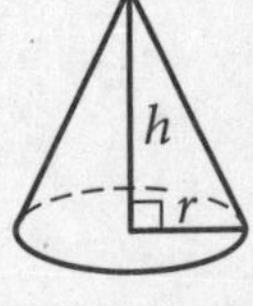

$V = \frac{1}{3}\pi r^2 h$

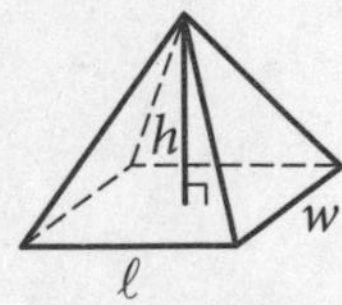

$V = \frac{1}{3}\ell wh$

The number of degrees of arc in a circle is 360.
The number of radians of arc in a circle is 2π.
The sum of the measures in degrees of the angles of a triangle is 180.

CONTINUE

1

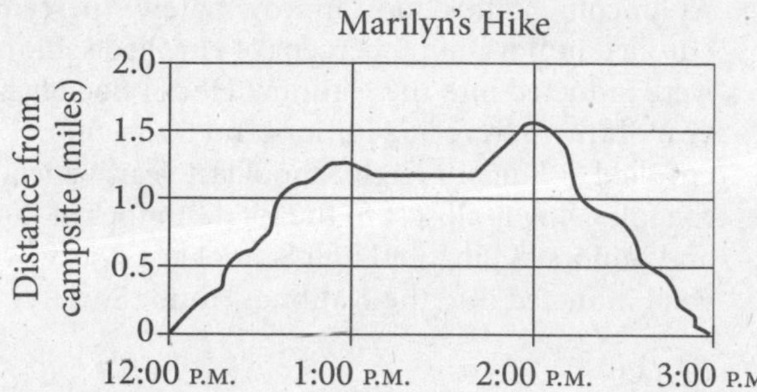

The graph above shows Marilyn's distance from her campsite during a 3-hour hike. She stopped for 30 minutes during her hike to have lunch. Based on the graph, which of the following is closest to the time she finished lunch and continued her hike?

A) 12:40 P.M.

B) 1:10 P.M.

C) 1:40 P.M.

D) 2:00 P.M.

2

Gender	Age: Under 40	Age: 40 or older	Total
Male	12	2	14
Female	8	3	11
Total	20	5	25

The table above shows the distribution of age and gender for 25 people who entered a contest. If the contest winner will be selected at random, what is the probability that the winner will be either a female under age 40 or a male age 40 or older?

A) $\frac{4}{25}$

B) $\frac{10}{25}$

C) $\frac{11}{25}$

D) $\frac{16}{25}$

CONTINUE

3

The graph below shows the total number of music album sales, in millions, each year from 1997 through 2009.

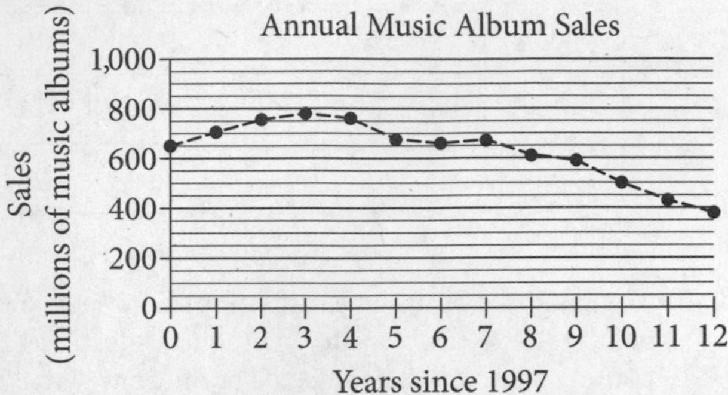

Based on the graph, which of the following best describes the general trend in music album sales from 1997 through 2009 ?

A) Sales generally increased each year since 1997.

B) Sales generally decreased each year since 1997.

C) Sales increased until 2000 and then generally decreased.

D) Sales generally remained steady from 1997 through 2009.

4

n	1	2	3	4
$f(n)$	−2	1	4	7

The table above shows some values of the linear function f. Which of the following defines f ?

A) $f(n) = n - 3$

B) $f(n) = 2n - 4$

C) $f(n) = 3n - 5$

D) $f(n) = 4n - 6$

5

At Lincoln High School, approximately 7 percent of enrolled juniors and 5 percent of enrolled seniors were inducted into the National Honor Society last year. If there were 562 juniors and 602 seniors enrolled at Lincoln High School last year, which of the following is closest to the total number of juniors and seniors at Lincoln High School last year who were inducted into the National Honor Society?

A) 140

B) 69

C) 39

D) 30

6

$$3x^2 - 5x + 2$$
$$5x^2 - 2x - 6$$

Which of the following is the sum of the two polynomials shown above?

A) $8x^2 - 7x - 4$

B) $8x^2 + 7x - 4$

C) $8x^4 - 7x^2 - 4$

D) $8x^4 + 7x^2 - 4$

CONTINUE

7

If $\frac{3}{5}w = \frac{4}{3}$, what is the value of w ?

A) $\frac{9}{20}$

B) $\frac{4}{5}$

C) $\frac{5}{4}$

D) $\frac{20}{9}$

8

The average number of students per classroom at Central High School from 2000 to 2010 can be modeled by the equation $y = 0.56x + 27.2$, where x represents the number of years since 2000, and y represents the average number of students per classroom. Which of the following best describes the meaning of the number 0.56 in the equation?

A) The total number of students at the school in 2000

B) The average number of students per classroom in 2000

C) The estimated increase in the average number of students per classroom each year

D) The estimated difference between the average number of students per classroom in 2010 and in 2000

9

Nate walks 25 meters in 13.7 seconds. If he walks at this same rate, which of the following is closest to the distance he will walk in 4 minutes?

A) 150 meters

B) 450 meters

C) 700 meters

D) 1,400 meters

CONTINUE

Questions 10 and 11 refer to the following information.

Planet	Acceleration due to gravity $\left(\frac{\text{m}}{\text{sec}^2}\right)$
Mercury	3.6
Venus	8.9
Earth	9.8
Mars	3.8
Jupiter	26.0
Saturn	11.1
Uranus	10.7
Neptune	14.1

The chart above shows approximations of the acceleration due to gravity in meters per second squared $\left(\frac{\text{m}}{\text{sec}^2}\right)$ for the eight planets in our solar system. The weight of an object on a given planet can be found by using the formula $W = mg$, where W is the weight of the object measured in newtons, m is the mass of the object measured in kilograms, and g is the acceleration due to gravity on the planet measured in $\frac{\text{m}}{\text{sec}^2}$.

10

What is the weight, in newtons, of an object on Mercury with a mass of 90 kilograms?

A) 25
B) 86
C) 101
D) 324

11

An object on Earth has a weight of 150 newtons. On which planet would the same object have an approximate weight of 170 newtons?

A) Venus
B) Saturn
C) Uranus
D) Neptune

CONTINUE

12

If the function f has five distinct zeros, which of the following could represent the complete graph of f in the xy-plane?

A)
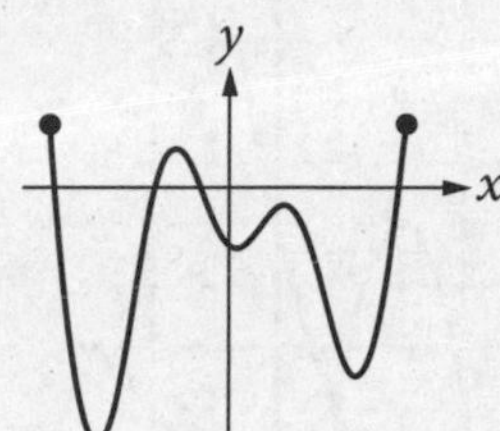

B)
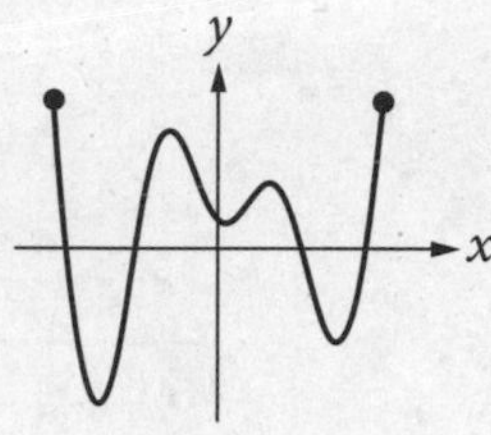

C)
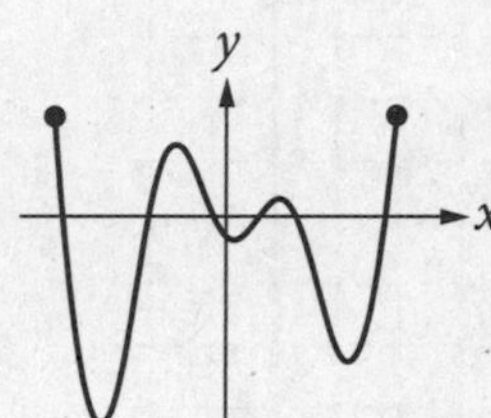

D)
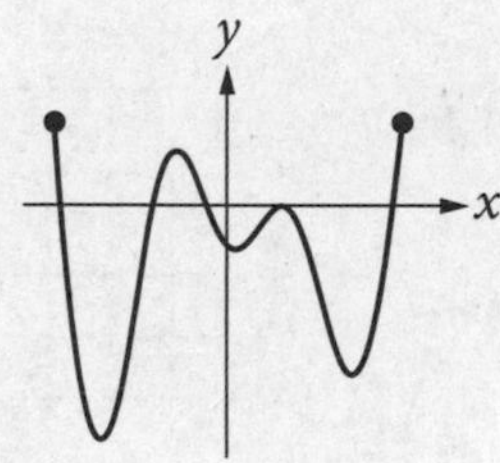

13

$$h = -16t^2 + vt + k$$

The equation above gives the height h, in feet, of a ball t seconds after it is thrown straight up with an initial speed of v feet per second from a height of k feet. Which of the following gives v in terms of h, t, and k ?

A) $v = h + k - 16t$

B) $v = \dfrac{h - k + 16}{t}$

C) $v = \dfrac{h + k}{t} - 16t$

D) $v = \dfrac{h - k}{t} + 16t$

14

The cost of using a telephone in a hotel meeting room is \$0.20 per minute. Which of the following equations represents the total cost c, in dollars, for h hours of phone use?

A) $c = 0.20(60h)$

B) $c = 0.20h + 60$

C) $c = \dfrac{60h}{0.20}$

D) $c = \dfrac{0.20h}{60}$

CONTINUE

15

In order to determine if treatment X is successful in improving eyesight, a research study was conducted. From a large population of people with poor eyesight, 300 participants were selected at random. Half of the participants were randomly assigned to receive treatment X, and the other half did not receive treatment X. The resulting data showed that participants who received treatment X had significantly improved eyesight as compared to those who did not receive treatment X. Based on the design and results of the study, which of the following is an appropriate conclusion?

A) Treatment X is likely to improve the eyesight of people who have poor eyesight.

B) Treatment X improves eyesight better than all other available treatments.

C) Treatment X will improve the eyesight of anyone who takes it.

D) Treatment X will cause a substantial improvement in eyesight.

16

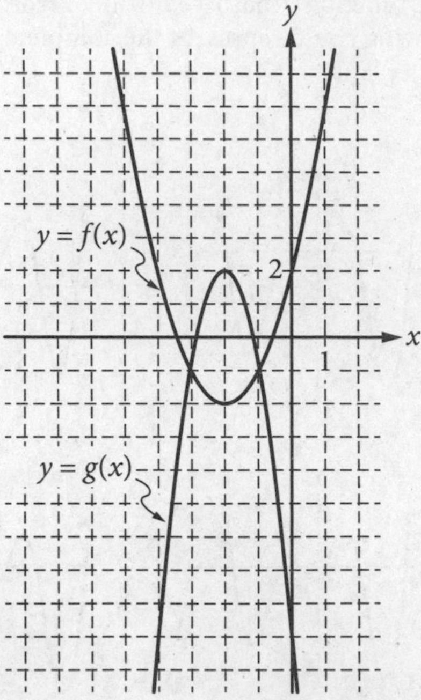

Graphs of the functions f and g are shown in the xy-plane above. For which of the following values of x does $f(x) + g(x) = 0$?

A) -3

B) -2

C) -1

D) 0

CONTINUE

Questions 17 and 18 refer to the following information.

$$S(P) = \frac{1}{2}P + 40$$
$$D(P) = 220 - P$$

The quantity of a product supplied and the quantity of the product demanded in an economic market are functions of the price of the product. The functions above are the estimated supply and demand functions for a certain product. The function $S(P)$ gives the quantity of the product supplied to the market when the price is P dollars, and the function $D(P)$ gives the quantity of the product demanded by the market when the price is P dollars.

17

How will the quantity of the product supplied to the market change if the price of the product is increased by \$10 ?

A) The quantity supplied will decrease by 5 units.
B) The quantity supplied will increase by 5 units.
C) The quantity supplied will increase by 10 units.
D) The quantity supplied will increase by 50 units.

18

At what price will the quantity of the product supplied to the market equal the quantity of the product demanded by the market?

A) \$90
B) \$120
C) \$133
D) \$155

19

Graphene, which is used in the manufacture of integrated circuits, is so thin that a sheet weighing one ounce can cover up to 7 football fields. If a football field has an area of approximately $1\frac{1}{3}$ acres, about how many acres could 48 ounces of graphene cover?

A) 250
B) 350
C) 450
D) 1,350

CONTINUE

20

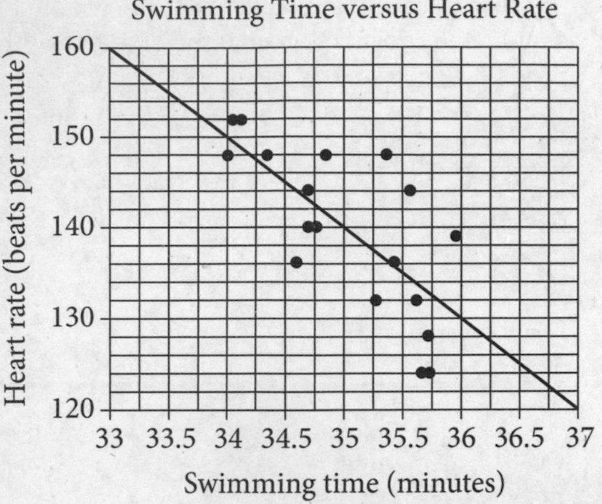

Michael swam 2,000 yards on each of eighteen days. The scatterplot above shows his swim time for and corresponding heart rate after each swim. The line of best fit for the data is also shown. For the swim that took 34 minutes, Michael's actual heart rate was about how many beats per minutes less than the rate predicted by the line of best fit?

A) 1

B) 2

C) 3

D) 4

21

Of the following four types of savings account plans, which option would yield exponential growth of the money in the account?

A) Each successive year, 2% of the initial savings is added to the value of the account.

B) Each successive year, 1.5% of the initial savings and $100 is added to the value of the account.

C) Each successive year, 1% of the current value is added to the value of the account.

D) Each successive year, $100 is added to the value of the account.

22

The sum of three numbers is 855. One of the numbers, x, is 50% more than the sum of the other two numbers. What is the value of x ?

A) 570

B) 513

C) 214

D) 155

CONTINUE

23

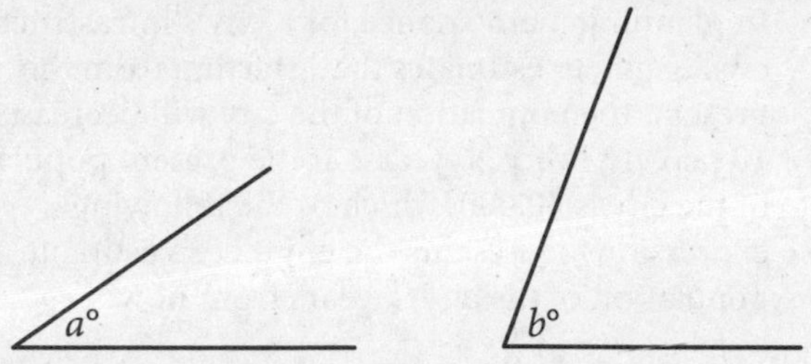

Note: Figures not drawn to scale.

The angles shown above are acute and $\sin(a°) = \cos(b°)$. If $a = 4k - 22$ and $b = 6k - 13$, what is the value of k ?

A) 4.5

B) 5.5

C) 12.5

D) 21.5

24

Mr. Kohl has a beaker containing n milliliters of solution to distribute to the students in his chemistry class. If he gives each student 3 milliliters of solution, he will have 5 milliliters left over. In order to give each student 4 milliliters of solution, he will need an additional 21 milliliters. How many students are in the class?

A) 16

B) 21

C) 23

D) 26

25

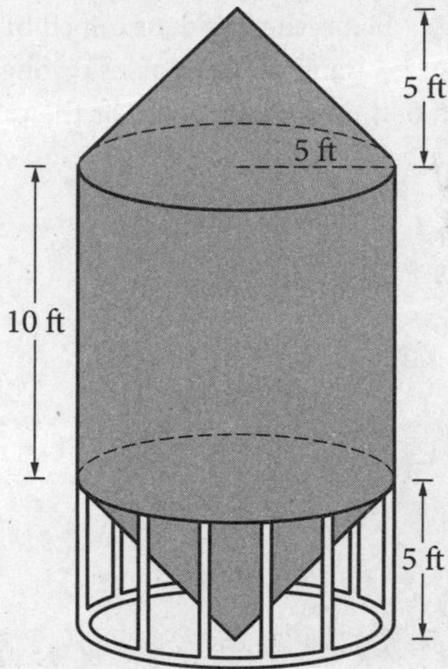

A grain silo is built from two right circular cones and a right circular cylinder with internal measurements represented by the figure above. Of the following, which is closest to the volume of the grain silo, in cubic feet?

A) 261.8

B) 785.4

C) 916.3

D) 1,047.2

26

In the xy-plane, the line determined by the points $(2, k)$ and $(k, 32)$ passes through the origin. Which of the following could be the value of k ?

A) 0

B) 4

C) 8

D) 16

27

A rectangle was altered by increasing its length by 10 percent and decreasing its width by p percent. If these alterations decreased the area of the rectangle by 12 percent, what is the value of p ?

A) 12

B) 15

C) 20

D) 22

28

In planning maintenance for a city's infrastructure, a civil engineer estimates that, starting from the present, the population of the city will decrease by 10 percent every 20 years. If the present population of the city is 50,000, which of the following expressions represents the engineer's estimate of the population of the city t years from now?

A) $50{,}000(0.1)^{20t}$

B) $50{,}000(0.1)^{\frac{t}{20}}$

C) $50{,}000(0.9)^{20t}$

D) $50{,}000(0.9)^{\frac{t}{20}}$

CONTINUE

29

	Handedness	
Gender	Left	Right
Female		
Male		
Total	18	122

The incomplete table above summarizes the number of left-handed students and right-handed students by gender for the eighth-grade students at Keisel Middle School. There are 5 times as many right-handed female students as there are left-handed female students, and there are 9 times as many right-handed male students as there are left-handed male students. If there is a total of 18 left-handed students and 122 right-handed students in the school, which of the following is closest to the probability that a right-handed student selected at random is female? (Note: Assume that none of the eighth-grade students are both right-handed and left-handed.)

A) 0.410

B) 0.357

C) 0.333

D) 0.250

30

$$3x + b = 5x - 7$$
$$3y + c = 5y - 7$$

In the equations above, b and c are constants.

If b is c minus $\frac{1}{2}$, which of the following is true?

A) x is y minus $\frac{1}{4}$.

B) x is y minus $\frac{1}{2}$.

C) x is y minus 1.

D) x is y plus $\frac{1}{2}$.

DIRECTIONS

For questions 31-38, solve the problem and enter your answer in the grid, as described below, on the answer sheet.

1. Although not required, it is suggested that you write your answer in the boxes at the top of the columns to help you fill in the circles accurately. You will receive credit only if the circles are filled in correctly.
2. Mark no more than one circle in any column.
3. No question has a negative answer.
4. Some problems may have more than one correct answer. In such cases, grid only one answer.
5. **Mixed numbers** such as $3\frac{1}{2}$ must be gridded as 3.5 or 7/2. (If 3 1 / 2 is entered into the grid, it will be interpreted as $\frac{31}{2}$, not $3\frac{1}{2}$.)
6. **Decimal answers:** If you obtain a decimal answer with more digits than the grid can accommodate, it may be either rounded or truncated, but it must fill the entire grid.

Answer: $\frac{7}{12}$

Write answer in boxes. → 7 / 1 2 ← Fraction line

Grid in result.

Answer: 2.5

2 . 5 ← Decimal point

Acceptable ways to grid $\frac{2}{3}$ are:

2 / 3   . 6 6 6   . 6 6 7

Answer: 201 – either position is correct

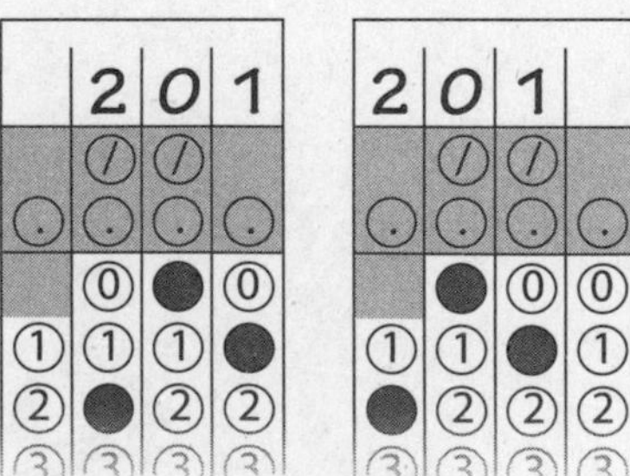

NOTE: You may start your answers in any column, space permitting. Columns you don't need to use should be left blank.

CONTINUE

31

Tickets for a school talent show cost \$2 for students and \$3 for adults. If Chris spends at least \$11 but no more than \$14 on x student tickets and 1 adult ticket, what is one possible value of x ?

32

Ages of the First 12 United States Presidents at the Beginning of Their Terms in Office

President	Age (years)	President	Age (years)
Washington	57	Jackson	62
Adams	62	Van Buren	55
Jefferson	58	Harrison	68
Madison	58	Tyler	51
Monroe	59	Polk	50
Adams	58	Taylor	65

The table above lists the ages of the first 12 United States presidents when they began their terms in office. According to the table, what was the mean age, in years, of these presidents at the beginning of their terms? (Round your answer to the nearest tenth.)

33

$$(-3x^2 + 5x - 2) - 2(x^2 - 2x - 1)$$

If the expression above is rewritten in the form $ax^2 + bx + c$, where a, b, and c are constants, what is the value of b ?

34

In a circle with center O, central angle AOB has a measure of $\frac{5\pi}{4}$ radians. The area of the sector formed by central angle AOB is what fraction of the area of the circle?

CONTINUE

35

An online store receives customer satisfaction ratings between 0 and 100, inclusive. In the first 10 ratings the store received, the average (arithmetic mean) of the ratings was 75. What is the least value the store can receive for the 11th rating and still be able to have an average of at least 85 for the first 20 ratings?

36

$$y \leq -15x + 3000$$
$$y \leq 5x$$

In the xy-plane, if a point with coordinates (a, b) lies in the solution set of the system of inequalities above, what is the maximum possible value of b ?

Questions 37 and 38 refer to the following information.

If shoppers enter a store at an average rate of r shoppers per minute and each stays in the store for an average time of T minutes, the average number of shoppers in the store, N, at any one time is given by the formula $N = rT$. This relationship is known as Little's law.

The owner of the Good Deals Store estimates that during business hours, an average of 3 shoppers per minute enter the store and that each of them stays an average of 15 minutes. The store owner uses Little's law to estimate that there are 45 shoppers in the store at any time.

37

Little's law can be applied to any part of the store, such as a particular department or the checkout lines. The store owner determines that, during business hours, approximately 84 shoppers per hour make a purchase and each of these shoppers spend an average of 5 minutes in the checkout line. At any time during business hours, about how many shoppers, on average, are waiting in the checkout line to make a purchase at the Good Deals Store?

38

The owner of the Good Deals Store opens a new store across town. For the new store, the owner estimates that, during business hours, an average of 90 shoppers per <u>hour</u> enter the store and each of them stays an average of 12 minutes. The average number of shoppers in the new store at any time is what percent less than the average number of shoppers in the original store at any time? (Note: Ignore the percent symbol when entering your answer. For example, if the answer is 42.1%, enter 42.1)

STOP

If you finish before time is called, you may check your work on this section only.

Do not turn to any other section.

This page represents the back cover of the Practice Test.

The SAT®

Practice Essay #3

The essay gives you an opportunity to show how effectively you can read and comprehend a passage and write an essay analyzing the passage. In your essay, you should demonstrate that you have read the passage carefully, present a clear and logical analysis, and use language precisely.

You have <u>50 minutes</u> to read the passage and write an essay in response to the prompt provided inside this booklet.

For information on scoring your essay, view the SAT Essay scoring rubric at **sat.org/essay**.

As you read the passage below, consider how Eliana Dockterman uses

- evidence, such as facts or examples, to support claims.
- reasoning to develop ideas and to connect claims and evidence.
- stylistic or persuasive elements, such as word choice or appeals to emotion, to add power to the ideas expressed.

Adapted from Eliana Dockterman, "The Digital Parent Trap." ©2013 by Time Inc. Originally published August 19, 2013.

1 By all measures, this generation of American kids (ages 3 to 18) is the tech-savviest in history: 27% of them use tablets, 43% use smartphones, and 52% use laptops. And in just a few weeks they will start the most tech-saturated school year ever: Los Angeles County alone will spend $30 million on classroom iPads this year, outfitting 640,000 kids by late 2014.

2 Yet, according to the latest findings from the research firm Grunwald Associates, barely half of U.S. parents agree that mobile technology should play a more prominent role in schools. Some are even paying as much as $24,000 to send their kids to monthlong "digital detox" programs like the one at Capio Nightingale Hospital in the U.K. . . .

3 So who's right—the mom trying to protect her kids from the perils of new technology or the dad who's coaching his kids to embrace it? It's an urgent question at a time when more than 80% of U.S. school districts say they are on the cusp of incorporating Web-enabled tablets into everyday curriculums.

4 For years, the Parental Adage was simple: The less time spent with screens, the better. That thinking stems from, among other things, reports about the rise of cyberbullying . . . as well as the fact that social media—specifically the sight of others looking happy in photos—can make kids feel depressed and insecure.

5 There's also a fundamental aversion to sitting kids in front of screens, thanks to decades of studies proving that watching too much TV can lead to obesity, violence and attention-deficit/hyperactivity disorder.

6 In that vein, the Waldorf Schools—a consortium of private K-12 schools in North America designed to "connect children to nature" and "ignite passion for lifelong learning"—limit tech in the classroom and bar the use of smartphones, laptops, televisions and even radios at home. "You could say some computer games develop creativity," says Lucy Wurtz, an administrator at the Waldorf School in Los Altos, Calif., minutes from Silicon Valley. "But I don't see any benefit. Waldorf kids knit and build things and paint—a lot of really practical and creative endeavors."

7 But it's not that simple. While there are dangers inherent in access to Facebook, new research suggests that social-networking sites also offer unprecedented learning opportunities. "Online, kids can engage with specialized communities of interest,"

says Mimi Ito, an anthropologist at the University of California at Irvine who's studying how technology affects young adults. "They're no longer limited by what's offered in school."

8 Early tech use has cognitive benefits as well. Although parenting experts have questioned the value of educational games—as Jim Taylor, author of *Raising Generation Tech*, puts it, "they're a load of crap . . . meant to make money"—new studies have shown they can add real value. In a recent study by SRI, a nonprofit research firm, kids who played games like Samorost (solving puzzles) did 12% better on logic tests than those who did not. And at MIT's Education Arcade, playing the empire-building game Civilization piqued students' interest in history and was directly linked to an improvement in the quality of their history-class reports.

9 The reason: engagement. On average, according to research cited by MIT, students can remember only 10% of what they read, 20% of what they hear and 50% of what they see demonstrated. But when they're actually doing something themselves—in the virtual worlds on iPads or laptops—that retention rate skyrockets to 90%.

10 This is a main reason researchers like Ito say the American Academy of Pediatrics' recommendation of a two-hour screen-time limit is an outdated concept: actively browsing pages on a computer or tablet is way more brain-stimulating than vegging out in front of the TV.

11 The most convincing argument for early-age tech fluency, however, is more basic: staying competitive. "If you look at applying for college or a job, that's on the computer," says Shawn Jackson, principal of Spencer Tech, a public school in one of Chicago's lower-income neighborhoods. Ditto the essential skills for jobs in fast-growing sectors such as programming, engineering and biotechnology. "If we're not exposing our students to this stuff early," Jackson continues, "they're going to be left behind." . . .

12 None of this means kids deserve unfettered access to the gadget of their choice—especially if, as McGrath notes, they've already been caught abusing it. As with any childhood privilege, monitoring is key. But parents should keep an open mind about the benefits of tech fluency.

Write an essay in which you explain how Eliana Dockterman builds an argument to persuade her audience that there are benefits to early exposure to technology. In your essay, analyze how Dockterman uses one or more of the features listed in the box above (or features of your own choice) to strengthen the logic and persuasiveness of her argument. Be sure that your analysis focuses on the most relevant features of the passage.

Your essay should not explain whether you agree with Dockterman's claims, but rather explain how Dockterman builds an argument to persuade her audience.

This page represents the back cover of the Practice Essay.

CollegeBoard

SAT PRACTICE ANSWER SHEET

COMPLETE MARK ● EXAMPLES OF INCOMPLETE MARKS 

It is recommended that you use a No. 2 pencil. It is very important that you fill in the entire circle darkly and completely. If you change your response, erase as completely as possible. Incomplete marks or erasures may affect your score.

TEST NUMBER

ENTER TEST NUMBER

For instance, for Practice Test #1, fill in the circle for 0 in the first column and for 1 in the second column.

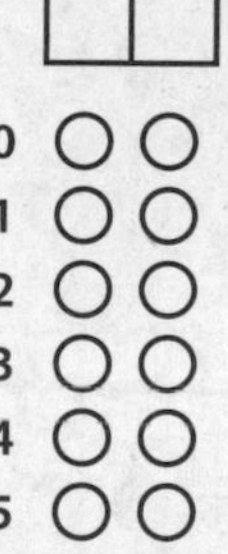

SECTION 1

1	A B C D	14	A B C D	27	A B C D	40	A B C D
2	A B C D	15	A B C D	28	A B C D	41	A B C D
3	A B C D	16	A B C D	29	A B C D	42	A B C D
4	A B C D	17	A B C D	30	A B C D	43	A B C D
5	A B C D	18	A B C D	31	A B C D	44	A B C D
6	A B C D	19	A B C D	32	A B C D	45	A B C D
7	A B C D	20	A B C D	33	A B C D	46	A B C D
8	A B C D	21	A B C D	34	A B C D	47	A B C D
9	A B C D	22	A B C D	35	A B C D	48	A B C D
10	A B C D	23	A B C D	36	A B C D	49	A B C D
11	A B C D	24	A B C D	37	A B C D	50	A B C D
12	A B C D	25	A B C D	38	A B C D	51	A B C D
13	A B C D	26	A B C D	39	A B C D	52	A B C D

Download the College Board SAT Practice app to instantly score this test.
Learn more at sat.org/scoring.

CollegeBoard

SAT PRACTICE ANSWER SHEET

COMPLETE MARK ● EXAMPLES OF INCOMPLETE MARKS 

It is recommended that you use a No. 2 pencil. It is very important that you fill in the entire circle darkly and completely. If you change your response, erase as completely as possible. Incomplete marks or erasures may affect your score.

SECTION 2

1	A B C D	10	A B C D	19	A B C D	28	A B C D	37	A B C D
2	A B C D	11	A B C D	20	A B C D	29	A B C D	38	A B C D
3	A B C D	12	A B C D	21	A B C D	30	A B C D	39	A B C D
4	A B C D	13	A B C D	22	A B C D	31	A B C D	40	A B C D
5	A B C D	14	A B C D	23	A B C D	32	A B C D	41	A B C D
6	A B C D	15	A B C D	24	A B C D	33	A B C D	42	A B C D
7	A B C D	16	A B C D	25	A B C D	34	A B C D	43	A B C D
8	A B C D	17	A B C D	26	A B C D	35	A B C D	44	A B C D
9	A B C D	18	A B C D	27	A B C D	36	A B C D		

If you're scoring with our mobile app we recommend that you cut these pages out of the back of this book. The scoring does best with a flat page.

CollegeBoard

SAT PRACTICE ANSWER SHEET

COMPLETE MARK ● EXAMPLES OF INCOMPLETE MARKS 

It is recommended that you use a No. 2 pencil. It is very important that you fill in the entire circle darkly and completely. If you change your response, erase as completely as possible. Incomplete marks or erasures may affect your score.

SECTION 3

1 A B C D	4 A B C D	7 A B C D	10 A B C D	13 A B C D
2 A B C D	5 A B C D	8 A B C D	11 A B C D	14 A B C D
3 A B C D	6 A B C D	9 A B C D	12 A B C D	15 A B C D

Only answers that are gridded will be scored. You will not receive credit for anything written in the boxes.

16 17 18 19 20

/ . 0 1 2 3 4 5 6 7 8 9

NO CALCULATOR ALLOWED

Did you know that you can print out these test sheets from the web? Learn more at sat.org/scoring.

SAT PRACTICE ANSWER SHEET

COMPLETE MARK ● EXAMPLES OF INCOMPLETE MARKS 

It is recommended that you use a No. 2 pencil. It is very important that you fill in the entire circle darkly and completely. If you change your response, erase as completely as possible. Incomplete marks or erasures may affect your score.

SECTION 4

1 A B C D	7 A B C D	13 A B C D	19 A B C D	25 A B C D
2 A B C D	8 A B C D	14 A B C D	20 A B C D	26 A B C D
3 A B C D	9 A B C D	15 A B C D	21 A B C D	27 A B C D
4 A B C D	10 A B C D	16 A B C D	22 A B C D	28 A B C D
5 A B C D	11 A B C D	17 A B C D	23 A B C D	29 A B C D
6 A B C D	12 A B C D	18 A B C D	24 A B C D	30 A B C D

CALCULATOR ALLOWED

If you're using our mobile app keep in mind that bad lighting and even shadows cast over the answer sheet can affect your score. Be sure to scan this in a well-lit area for best results.

CollegeBoard

SAT PRACTICE ANSWER SHEET

COMPLETE MARK ● EXAMPLES OF INCOMPLETE MARKS 

It is recommended that you use a No. 2 pencil. It is very important that you fill in the entire circle darkly and completely. If you change your response, erase as completely as possible. Incomplete marks or erasures may affect your score.

SECTION 4 (Continued)

Only answers that are gridded will be scored. You will not receive credit for anything written in the boxes.

31 32 33 34 35

/ . 0 1 2 3 4 5 6 7 8 9

Only answers that are gridded will be scored. You will not receive credit for anything written in the boxes.

36 37 38

/ . 0 1 2 3 4 5 6 7 8 9

CALCULATOR ALLOWED

○ I understand that my essay (without my name) may be reproduced in other College Board materials. If I mark this circle, I withhold my permission to reproduce my essay for any purposes beyond score reporting and the assessment of my writing skills. Marking this circle will have no effect on my score, nor will it prevent my essay from being made available to any college to which I send my SAT scores.

IMPORTANT: **USE A NO. 2 PENCIL. DO NOT WRITE OUTSIDE THE BORDER!**
Words written outside the essay box or written in ink **WILL NOT APPEAR** in the copy sent to be scored, and your score will be affected.

PLANNING PAGE You may plan your essay in the unlined planning space below, but use only the lined pages following this one to write your essay. Any work on this planning page will not be scored.

Use pages 7 through 10 for your ESSAY →

FOR PLANNING ONLY

Use pages 7 through 10 for your ESSAY →

PLEASE DO NOT WRITE IN THIS AREA

SERIAL #

BEGIN YOUR ESSAY HERE.

You may continue on the next page.

PLEASE DO NOT WRITE IN THIS AREA

SERIAL #

You may continue on the next page.

DO NOT WRITE OUTSIDE OF THE BOX.

You may continue on the next page.

PLEASE DO NOT WRITE IN THIS AREA

SERIAL #

STOP.

Answer Explanations

SAT Practice Test #3

Section 1: Reading Test

QUESTION 1

Choice B is the best answer. In the passage, Lady Carlotta is approached by the "imposingly attired lady" Mrs. Quabarl while standing at a train station (lines 32-35). Mrs. Quabarl assumes Lady Carlotta is her new nanny, Miss Hope: "You must be Miss Hope, the governess I've come to meet" (lines 36-37). Lady Carlotta does not correct Mrs. Quabarl's mistake and replies, "Very well, if I must I must" (line 39).

Choices A, C, and D are incorrect because the passage is not about a woman weighing a job choice, seeking revenge on an acquaintance, or disliking her new employer.

QUESTION 2

Choice C is the best answer. In lines 1-3, the narrator states that Lady Carlotta "stepped out on to the platform of the small wayside station and took a turn or two up and down its uninteresting length" in order to "kill time." In this context, Lady Carlotta was taking a "turn," or a short walk, along the platform while waiting for the train to leave the station.

Choices A, B, and D are incorrect because in this context "turn" does not mean slight movement, change in rotation, or course correction. While Lady Carlotta may have had to rotate her body while moving across the station, "took a turn" implies that Lady Carlotta took a short walk along the platform's length.

QUESTION 3

Choice A is the best answer. In lines 10-14, the narrator states that some of Lady Carlotta's acquaintances would often admonish, or criticize, Lady Carlotta for meddling in or openly expressing her opinion on other people's affairs.

Choices B, C, and D are incorrect because the narrator does not suggest that other people viewed Lady Carlotta as tactful, ambitious, or unfriendly.

QUESTION 4

Choice A is the best answer. In lines 10-14, the narrator states that people often criticized Lady Carlotta and suggested that she not interfere in other people's affairs, which were "none of her business." The fact that people often were critical of Lady Carlotta's behavior provides evidence that Lady Carlotta was outspoken.

Choices B, C, and D do not provide the best evidence that Lady Carlotta was outspoken. Choices B, C, and D mention Lady Carlotta, but do not specify how others view her.

QUESTION 5

Choice C is the best answer. Lines 4-10 establish that Lady Carlotta intervened on the part of a struggling horse, the kind of behavior for which, lines 10-14 indicate, she received "plentiful admonition" from "certain of her acquaintances," who believed that she should mind her own business. Lines 14-22 indicate that Lady Carlotta had "only once . . . put the doctrine of non-interference into practice," and that was when "one of its most eloquent exponents" had been "besieged for nearly three hours in a small and extremely uncomfortable may-tree by an angry boar-pig" while Lady Carlotta blithely ignored the other woman's hypocritical pleas for interference. This incident provides insight into Lady Carlotta's character and also evokes humor through language choice (e.g., the droll understatement of "it is to be feared that [Lady Carlotta] lost the friendship of the ultimately rescued lady"; lines 22-23) and the sense that, narratively speaking, justice has been served.

Choice A is incorrect because nothing about the incident suggests deception on Lady Carlotta's part. Choice B is incorrect because there is nothing subtle about Lady Carlotta leaving another woman stuck in a tree for nearly three hours. Moreover, the passage does not suggest that this was an act of cruelty on Lady Carlotta's part; rather, the passage suggests that Lady Carlotta was justified in giving the woman stuck in a tree exactly what the woman had so often asked for: noninterference. Choice D is incorrect because the passage indicates that Lady Carlotta was acting consistently with her beliefs and only invoked the doctrine to teach a hypocritical person a lesson.

QUESTION 6

Choice A is the best answer. The narrator explains that Mrs. Quabarl told Lady Carlotta about the "nature of the charge" when she gave Lady Carlotta details about the Quabarl children (line 53-61). Since Lady Carlotta is pretending to be a governess, the term "charge" refers to her responsibilities, or job duties, when caring for the Quabarl children.

Choices B, C, and D are incorrect because in this context "charge" does not mean attack, fee, or expense.

QUESTION 7

Choice A is the best answer. Lady Carlotta learns about Mrs. Quabarl's children Claude, Wilfrid, and Irene (lines 53-58). The narrator then describes Mrs. Quabarl's child Viola as "something or other else of a mould equally commonplace among children of that class and type in the twentieth century" (lines 58-61). This statement about Viola implies that all of the Quabarl children have skills typical, or "of a mould equally commonplace," to other peers in their social class.

Choices B, C, and D are incorrect because the narrator does not indicate that all of the Quabarl children are unusually creative and intelligent, hostile to the idea of having a governess, or more educated than their peers.

QUESTION 8

Choice B is the best answer. In lines 62-69, Mrs. Quabarl explains to Lady Carlotta that she wants her children to actively participate in their education, and that Lady Carlotta should not create lessons that require her children to simply memorize historical figures and dates. Mrs. Quabarl emphasizes an education centered on active engagement when she states that her children should "not only be TAUGHT . . . but INTERESTED in what they learn."

Choices A, C, and D are incorrect because the narrator does not suggest that Mrs. Quabarl favors an education that emphasizes traditional values, artistic experimentation, or factual retention.

QUESTION 9

Choice B is the best answer. In lines 77-82, the narrator describes Mrs. Quabarl as appearing "magnificent and autocratic," or outwardly domineering, but easily "cowed and apologetic" when someone challenges, or defies, her authority.

Choices A, C, and D are incorrect because the narrator does not describe Mrs. Quabarl as selfish, bitter, or frequently imprudent.

QUESTION 10

Choice D is the best answer. In lines 77-82, the narrator provides evidence that Mrs. Quabarl appears imposing, or autocratic, but is easily defied, or opposed: "She was one of those imperfectly self-assured individuals who are magnificent and autocratic as long as they are not seriously opposed. The least show of unexpected resistance goes a long way towards rendering them cowed and apologetic."

Choices A, B, and C do not provide the best evidence that Mrs. Quabarl appears imposing but is easily defied. Choices A and B are incorrect because they present Mrs. Quabarl's opinions on railway companies and education, and choice C is incorrect because it focuses on Lady Carlotta, not Mrs. Quabarl.

QUESTION 11

Choice A is the best answer. While the author predominantly supports the use of public transportation, in the third paragraph he recognizes some limitations to the public transportation system: it is a "depressing experience" (lines 25-26) and "underfunded, ill-maintained, and ill-planned" (line 31).

Choices B, C, and D are incorrect because the third paragraph does not expand upon an argument made in the first two paragraphs, provide an overview of a problem, or advocate ending the use of public transportation.

QUESTION 12

Choice C is the best answer. The author notes that in North America "hopping in a car almost always gets you to your destination more quickly" (lines 32-34). This statement suggests that speed is one advantage to driving in North America.

Choices A, B, and D are incorrect because the author does not cite environmental impact, convenience, or cost as advantages of driving in North America.

QUESTION 13

Choice D is the best answer. In lines 32-34, the author provides evidence that speed is one advantage to driving in North America, because driving "almost always gets you to your destination more quickly."

Choices A, B, and C do not provide the best evidence that speed is one advantage to driving in North America. Choices A and B are incorrect because they offer general information about using public transportation. Choice C is incorrect because although these lines mention North America, they focus on the disadvantages of public transportation.

QUESTION 14

Choice B is the best answer. The author argues in the fourth paragraph that public transportation "can be faster, more comfortable, and cheaper than the private automobile" (lines 36-37) and provides examples of fast and convenient public transportation systems.

Choices A, C, and D are incorrect because they focus on points made in the fourth paragraph rather than the paragraph's central idea.

QUESTION 15

Choice B is the best answer. In lines 35-37, the author provides evidence that some public transportation systems are superior to driving, because public transportation "can be faster, more comfortable, and cheaper than the private automobile."

Choices A, C, and D do not provide the best evidence that some public transportation systems are superior to driving, as they highlight points made in the fourth paragraph rather than the paragraph's central idea.

QUESTION 16

Choice C is the best answer. In the last paragraph, the author explains the trend that people who became adults around the end of the twentieth century are more willing to use public transportation than people from older generations. The author notes, "If you credit the demographers, this transit trend has legs" (lines 58-59). In this context, "credit" means to believe the demographers' claims about the trend.

Choices A, B, and D are incorrect because in this context, "credit" does not mean endow, attribute, or honor.

QUESTION 17

Choice B is the best answer. In lines 59-63, the author explains the trend of people who became adults around the end of the twentieth century "tend[ing] to favor cities over suburbs." In this context, these adults "favor," or prefer, cities over suburbs.

Choices A, C, and D are incorrect because in this context "favor" does not mean indulge, resemble, or serve.

QUESTION 18

Choice B is the best answer. In lines 63-67, the author explains that while riding on public transportation, people can use personal electronic devices, such as "iPads, MP3 players, Kindles, and smartphones."

Choices A, C, and D are incorrect because they do not show that public transportation is compatible with the use of personal electronic devices.

QUESTION 19

Choice A is the best answer. Figure 1 shows that 10.7% of public transportation passengers are students and 6.7% of public transportation passengers are retirees. Thus, more students than retirees use public transportation.

Choices B and C are incorrect because figure 1 shows that more employed than unemployed people use public transportation and that more employed people than homemakers use public transportation.

Choice D is incorrect because figure 1 does not explain how frequently passengers use public transportation; it only identifies public transportation passengers by their primary occupation.

QUESTION 20

Choice A is the best answer. Figure 1 shows that 72% of public transportation passengers are "employed outside the home," and figure 2 indicates that 59.1% of public transportation trips are for "work." It can be inferred from these figures that many public transportation passengers take public transportation to their place of employment.

Choices B, C, and D are incorrect because figure 1 and figure 2 do not indicate that public transportation passengers primarily use the system to run errands, use their own car on weekends, or are planning to purchase a car.

QUESTION 21

Choice D is the best answer. The author explains that Ken Dial created an experiment to study the evolution of flight by observing how baby Chukars learn to fly. During the experiment, Dial noticed the unusual way Chukars use their "'wings and legs cooperatively'" to scale hay bales (lines 38-43), and he created "a series of ingenious experiments" (line 46) to study this observation. After his additional experiments, Dial determined that these baby birds angle "their wings differently from birds in flight" (lines 49-50).

Choices A, B, and C are incorrect because they do not accurately reflect the sequence of events in the passage.

QUESTION 22

Choice A is the best answer. In lines 6-9, the author explains that Dial was "challenged," or dared, by graduate students to develop "new data" on a long-standing scientific debate (the "ground-up-tree-down" theory).

Choices B, C, and D are incorrect because in this context "challenged" does not mean required, disputed with, or competed with.

QUESTION 23

Choice A is the best answer. The author explains that Dial created his initial experiment to try and create "new data on the age-old ground-up-tree-down debate," and that he looked for "clues" in "how baby game birds learned to fly" (lines 8-11). The note at the beginning of the passage explains the "age-old ground-up-tree down debate" and offers two different theories on how birds evolved to fly. Finally, the last paragraph of the passage discusses WAIR in an evolutionary context.

Choices B, C, and D are incorrect because they do not identify Dial's central assumption in setting up his research.

QUESTION 24

Choice B is the best answer. In lines 6-11, the author provides evidence that Dial's central assumption in setting up his research is that the acquisition of flight in young birds is linked to the acquisition of flight in their ancestors. The author notes that Dial created a project to "come up with new data on the age-old ground-up-tree-down debate."

Choices A, C, and D do not provide the best evidence that Dial's central assumption in setting up his research is that the acquisition of flight in young birds is linked to the acquisition of flight in their ancestors. Choices A, C, and D are incorrect because they focus on Dial's experiment and his observations on ground birds.

QUESTION 25

Choice C is the best answer. When a rancher observed Dial's laboratory setup, he was "incredulous" that the Chukars were living on the ground, and he advised Dial to give the birds "something to climb on" (lines 16-23). This "key piece of advice" (line 14) led Dial to add hay bales to his laboratory. Dial later noticed that the Chukars were using their legs and wings to scale the hay bales, and this observation became the focal point of his research.

Choices A, B, and D are incorrect because the incident with the local rancher did not serve to reveal Dial's motivation for creating the project, emphasize differences in laboratory and field research, or introduce a contributor to a scientific theory.

QUESTION 26

Choice C is the best answer. The author explains that Dial's "aha moment" came when he determined the Chukars used "their legs and wings cooperatively" to scale the hay bales (lines 40-42). Dial then created additional experiments to study how the birds dealt with gradually steeper inclines: "[he filmed] the birds as they raced up textured ramps tilted at increasing angles" (lines 46-48).

Choices A, B, and D are incorrect because Dial's "aha moment" was not followed by Dial teaching the birds to fly, studying videos to find out why the birds no longer hopped, or consulting with other researchers.

QUESTION 27

Choice B is the best answer. Dial observed that as the Chukars raced up steep ramps, they "began to flap" and "aimed their flapping down and backward, using the force . . . to keep their feet firmly pressed against the ramp" (lines 49-53). Dial determined that the position of their flapping wings facilitated the baby Chukars' traction on the steep ramps.

Choices A, C, and D are incorrect because the passage does not indicate that the Chukars' speed, alternation of wing and foot movement, or continual hopping motions facilitated their traction on steep ramps.

QUESTION 28

Choice B is the best answer. In lines 61-63, the author explains that Dial named his scientific finding "WAIR, for wing-assisted incline running, and went on to document it in a wide range of species." In this context, Dial "documented," or recorded, the existence of WAIR in numerous bird species.

Choices A, C, and D are incorrect because in this context, "document" does not mean to portray, publish, or process.

QUESTION 29

Choice D is the best answer. In lines 70-74, the author explains that gliding animals do not use a "flapping flight stroke," or WAIR, wing-assisted incline running. Since Chukars, a ground bird, use WAIR to help scale steep inclines, it can be reasonably inferred that gliding animals do not use WAIR to aid in climbing slopes.

Choices A, B, and C are incorrect because the passage does not include information on gliding animals' offspring, their method of locomotion, or their feeding habits.

QUESTION 30

Choice D is the best answer. In lines 73-75, the author provides evidence that "the flapping flight stroke" is "something gliding animals don't do."

Choices A, B, and C do not provide the best evidence that gliding animals do not use a flapping stroke to aid in climbing slopes. These choices do not contain information about gliding animals.

QUESTION 31

Choice B is the best answer. In lines 21-24, the authors of Passage 1 state society's "common happiness" is dependent on women never becoming involved in politics. In this context, the authors of Passage 1 are suggesting that all members of society can have a "common," or shared, happiness.

Choices A, C, and D are incorrect because in this context, "common" does not mean average, coarse, or similar.

QUESTION 32

Choice C is the best answer. In lines 25-30, the authors of Passage 1 state that women should seek "gentle occupations and the cares of the home" so they can avoid performing difficult, or "strenuous," and unpleasant, or "onerous," tasks.

Choices A, B, and D are incorrect because the authors of Passage 1 do not suggest that running a household and raising children are rewarding for both sexes, yield less value for society, or require professional or political skills.

QUESTION 33

Choice C is the best answer. In lines 25-30, the authors of Passage 1 provide evidence that women should run households and raise children because these roles do not require "strenuous habits and onerous duties."

Choices A, B, and D do not provide the best evidence that running a household and raising children entail very few activities that are difficult or unpleasant; rather, these lines offer general information about the differences between the sexes.

QUESTION 34

Choice D is the best answer. In lines 41-46, Wollstonecraft argues that if women do not receive an education "to become the companion of man," or one that is comparable to men's education, then society will not progress in "knowledge and virtue."

Choices A, B, and C are incorrect because Wollstonecraft does not suggest that society can progress only if women have happiness and financial security, follow societal rules, or replace men as figures of power.

QUESTION 35

Choice C is the best answer. Wollstonecraft argues that women should be granted an education comparable to men's so that truth is "common to all" (lines 41-46). Wollstonecraft states that education will "strengthen [women's] reason till she comprehend her duty" (lines 49-50). In this context, Wollstonecraft is arguing that education will improve women's "reason," or intellect, and allow women to consider their role in society.

Choices A, B, and D are incorrect because in this context "reason" does not mean motive, sanity, or explanation.

QUESTION 36

Choice A is the best answer. In lines 72-78, Wollstonecraft argues that the laws passed by society's leaders allow men to "contend for their freedom" but serve to "subjugate women." In this context, "subjugate" means to control. Wollstonecraft is arguing that society's leaders grant men freedoms that are denied to women.

Choices B, C, and D are incorrect because Wollstonecraft does not claim that society's leaders have granted freedoms that created a general reduction in individual virtue, caused arguments about happiness, or ensured equality for all people.

QUESTION 37

Choice D is the best answer. In lines 72-75, Wollstonecraft provides evidence that society's leaders grant freedoms that privilege men. She argues that while society's leaders believe they "are acting in the manner best calculated to promote [women's] happiness," their decisions don't allow women to "contend for their freedom."

Choices A, B, and C do not provide the best evidence that society's leaders grant freedoms that privilege men over women.

QUESTION 38

Choice C is the best answer. Wollstonecraft cites the statement made by the authors of Passage 1 that excluding women from political participation is "according to abstract principles . . . impossible to explain" (lines 61-65). Wollstonecraft then states that if the authors of Passage 1 can discuss "the abstract rights of man" they should be able to discuss the abstract rights of women (lines 66-69). In these lines, Wollstonecraft is developing her argument by highlighting a flaw in the reasoning presented by the authors of Passage 1.

Choices A, B, and D are incorrect because Wollstonecraft does not refer to the statement made in Passage 1 to call into question the authors' qualifications, dispute the assertion that women are excluded by their own government (sentence one of Passage 1), or validate the authors' conclusions on gender roles.

QUESTION 39

Choice A is the best answer. The authors of Passage 1 argue that while restricting women's freedoms may be "impossible to explain" (line 7), this restriction is necessary for society's overall happiness (lines 13-17). Wollstonecraft, however, strongly challenges this argument, asking the authors of Passage 1, "Who made man the exclusive judge" of which freedoms are granted to women, and likening society's male leaders to tyrants as they deny women their "civil and political rights" and leave them "groping in the dark" (lines 78-88).

Choices B, C, and D are incorrect because they do not characterize the overall relationship between Passage 1 and Passage 2.

QUESTION 40

Choice D is the best answer. The authors of Passage 1 admit that women are "excluded by the other half [men] from any participation in government" (lines 1-2), and Wollstonecraft states that society's male leaders create laws that deny women "civil and political rights" (line 86).

Choices A, B, and C are incorrect because the authors of both passages would not agree that women had the same preferences as men, required a good education, or were as happy as men.

QUESTION 41

Choice A is the best answer. Wollstonecraft argues in the final paragraph of Passage 2 that society's male leaders are like "tyrants" that deny women "civil and political rights" (lines 81-88). The authors of Passage 1 would most likely argue that allowing women these rights would be "a reversal of [society's] primary destinies" as society's leaders should only seek women's interests as they pertain to the "wishes of nature," such as women's role as mothers (lines 18-30). The authors of Passage 1 clarify that "nature" created two sexes for a particular reason, so while men can exercise civil and political rights, women are not naturally suited to these activities (lines 30-36).

Choices B and C are incorrect because they are not supported by information in Passage 1. Choice D is incorrect because the authors of Passage 1 do not mention "natural law," only the "wishes of nature."

QUESTION 42

Choice C is the best answer. When discussing problems with bee colonies, the authors use phrases like "we suspect" (line 19) and "we postulate" (line 21) to show they are hypothesizing reasons for bee colonies' susceptibility to mite infestations. The use of "can," "may," and "could" creates a tentative tone and provides further evidence that the authors believe, but are not certain, that their hypothesis is correct.

Choices A, B, and D are incorrect because the authors' use of "can," "may," and "could" does not create an optimistic, dubious, or critical tone.

QUESTION 43

Choice C is the best answer. In lines 24-28, the authors hypothesize that bee colonies will be susceptible to mite infestations if they do not occasionally feed on pyrethrum producing plants. In lines 42-46, they suggest creating a trial where a "small number of commercial honey bee colonies are offered a number of pyrethrum producing plants" to test their hypothesis.

Choices A, B, and D are incorrect because the authors do not hypothesize that honeybees' exposure to both pyrethrums and mites will cause the honeybees to develop secondary infections, that beekeepers should increase their use of insecticides, or that humans are more susceptible to varroa mites.

QUESTION 44

Choice D is the best answer. In lines 24-28, the authors provide evidence that a bee colony may be more resistant to mite infections if the bees eat pyrethrums because this diet may help prevent bees from becoming "immunocompromised or nutritionally deficient." In lines 42-50, the authors suggest testing this hypothesis in a trial on honeybees.

Choices A, B, and C do not describe any of the authors' hypotheses.

QUESTION 45

Choice D is the best answer. The authors explain that when beekeepers use commercially produced insecticides to fight mite infections, they may "further weaken" bees that are "immunocompromised or nutritionally deficient" (lines 31-35).

Choices A, B, and C are incorrect because the authors do not suggest that beekeepers' use of commercially produced insecticides increases mite populations, kills bacteria, or destroys bees' primary food source.

QUESTION 46

Choice C is the best answer. In lines 31-35, the authors provide evidence that beekeepers' use of commercially produced insecticides may cause further harm to "immunocompromised or nutritionally deficient bees."

Choices A, B, and D are incorrect because they do not provide the best evidence that beekeepers' use of commercially produced insecticides may be harmful to bees; choices A, B, and D focus on mite infestations' impact on honeybees.

QUESTION 47

Choice B is the best answer. In lines 31-35, the authors argue that beekeepers' use of insecticides to control mite infestations may be harmful to some bees. The authors then state, "We further postulate that the proper dosage necessary to prevent mite infestation may be better left to the bees" (lines 35-37). In this context, the authors "postulate," or put forth the idea that the bees may naturally control mite infestations better than insecticides.

Choices A, C, and D are incorrect because in this context, "postulate" does not mean to make an unfounded assumption, question a belief or theory, or conclude based on firm evidence.

QUESTION 48

Choice B is the best answer. In the fourth paragraph the authors propose a trial to study if honeybees' consumption of pyrethrum producing plants helps the honeybees defend against mite infestations. In the experiment, the authors plan to offer honey bee colonies both pyrethrum producing plants and "a typical bee food source such as clover" to determine if these different diets affect the bees' susceptibility to mite infestations.

Choices A, C, and D are incorrect because the main purpose of the fourth paragraph is not to summarize the results of an experiment, provide a comparative nutritional analysis, or predict an outcome of an unfinished experiment.

QUESTION 49

Choice A is the best answer. In lines 43-45, the authors propose a scientific trial in which honeybees are "offered a number of pyrethrum producing plants, as well as a typical bee food source such as clover." Since the authors contrast the "pyrethrum producing plants" with clover, a "typical bee food source," it can be assumed that clover does not produce pyrethrums.

Choice B is incorrect because it is stated in the passage. Choices C and D are incorrect because they are not assumptions made by the authors.

QUESTION 50

Choice B is the best answer. The table shows that 77 percent of the honeybee colonies with colony collapse disorder were infected by all four pathogens.

Choices A, C, and D are incorrect because they do not identify the percent of honeybee colonies with colony collapse disorder that were infected by all four pathogens as based on data in the table.

QUESTION 51

Choice D is the best answer. The table shows that 81 percent of colonies without colony collapse disorder were affected by the pathogen *Nosema ceranae.*

Choices A, B, and C are incorrect because they do not identify the pathogen that infected the highest percentage of honeybee colonies without colony collapse disorder as based on data in the table.

QUESTION 52

Choice D is the best answer. The table discusses pathogen occurrence in honeybee colonies, but it includes no information as to whether these honeybees were infected with mites. Because the table does not suggest mites infested the honeybee colonies, no conclusions can be made as to whether mites increased the honeybees' "susceptibility to secondary infection with fungi, bacteria or viruses" (lines 4-5).

Choices A, B, and C are incorrect because the table provides no information about whether these honeybees were infected with mites.

Section 2: Writing and Language Test

QUESTION 1

Choice A is the best answer because by providing the comparative adjective "healthier" and the word "more" to make "productive" comparative, it creates a parallel structure within the list that begins with "happier."

Choices B, C, and D are incorrect because none creates a parallel structure within the list of qualities.

QUESTION 2

Choice B is the best answer. The ways in which exposure to natural light affects employees is the main subject of the passage.

Choices A, C, and D are incorrect because none introduces the topic discussed in the remainder of the passage.

QUESTION 3

Choice C is the best answer. It accurately notes that the proposed sentence would be placed directly between the first mention of circadian rhythms and the explanation of the term.

Choices A, B, and D are incorrect because each misinterprets the relationship between the proposed additional text and the ideas in the paragraph.

QUESTION 4

Choice C is the best answer. It provides the correct possessive construction for "body," which must be a singular noun when discussed in general terms as in this sentence. Choice C also provides the correct plural construction for "clocks."

Choices A, B, and D are incorrect because each applies either a possessive or a plural construction in a place where it doesn't belong.

QUESTION 5

Choice A is the best answer. The singular verb "is" agrees with the singular noun "absenteeism."

Choices B, C, and D are incorrect because each provides a verb that either fails to agree with the singular subject "absenteeism" or introduces redundancy.

QUESTION 6

Choice B is the best answer. It contains a direct reference to productivity, the topic introduced in the previous sentence.

Choices A, C, and D are incorrect because none directly addresses employee productivity, the primary subject of the previous sentence.

QUESTION 7

Choice A is the best answer. It opens with a reference to lowered worker productivity, creating a transition from the previous paragraph, and clearly positions the high energy costs of artificial light sources as an additional disadvantage.

Choices B, C, and D are incorrect because none of the choices offers an adequate transition from the previous paragraph: Each awkwardly inserts the issue of lower worker productivity into a statement about the high energy costs of artificial light sources.

QUESTION 8

Choice D is the best answer. The word "annual" is adequate to communicate that the savings occurred every year.

Choices A, B, and C are incorrect because each proposes an option that would result in a redundancy with "annual."

QUESTION 9

Choice C is the best answer. It provides a transitional adverb that accurately communicates that this sentence describes an option that companies could choose ("light tubes") instead of the option described in the previous sentence ("full-pane windows").

Choices A, B, and D are incorrect because each proposes a transitional adverb that does not accurately reflect the relationship between this sentence and the one preceding it.

QUESTION 10

Choice C is the best answer. It provides the correct relative pronoun to correspond with the plural referent "light tubes" and the correct verb to introduce the definition that follows.

Choices A, B, and D are incorrect because each offers a pronoun inappropriate for opening a dependent clause defining "light tubes."

QUESTION 11

Choice B is the best answer. The preposition "of" idiomatically follows the noun "means," particularly as a way to connect it to another noun or verb.

Choices A, C, and D are incorrect because each results in nonstandard phrasing with "means."

QUESTION 12

Choice A is the best answer. The plural reflexive pronoun "themselves" corresponds with the plural noun "settlers."

Choices B, C, and D are incorrect because each provides either a nonstandard phrase or a singular pronoun that does not correspond with "settlers."

QUESTION 13

Choice C is the best answer. It creates a transition from the poor food quality mentioned in the previous sentence to the information about Harvey in the remainder of the sentence.

Choices A, B, and D are incorrect because none offers a transition from the previous sentence or a detail that corresponds precisely with the information in the remainder of the sentence.

QUESTION 14

Choice D is the best answer. It correctly provides a comma to close the modifying clause "an English-born entrepreneur," which opens with a comma.

Choices A, B, and C are incorrect because each proposes punctuation that creates an inappropriately strong separation between the subject "Fred Harvey" and the verb "decided."

QUESTION 15

Choice B is the best answer. It provides the plural verb and plural possessive pronoun that grammatically correspond to the plural referent "Harvey Houses."

Choices A, C, and D are incorrect because each either fails to provide a verb that corresponds with the plural referent "Harvey Houses" or fails to provide the appropriate possessive pronoun.

QUESTION 16

Choice C is the best answer. It accurately echoes an earlier characterization of the food as being of "terrible quality," while maintaining the established tone of the passage.

Choices A, B, and D are incorrect either because the word is less formal than the established tone of the passage ("icky") or because it illogically attributes agency to food ("sinister," "surly").

QUESTION 17

Choice C is the best answer. It accurately interprets "not content to follow conventional business practices" as logically introducing the new practice of "employing women" described in the following sentences.

Choices A, B, and D are incorrect because none recognizes why the sentence is relevant to this particular location in the passage.

QUESTION 18

Choice B is the best answer. It is concise and free of redundancies.

Choices A, C, and D are incorrect because each pairs "overwhelming" and "tremendous," adjectives so close in meaning that together they present a redundancy.

QUESTION 19

Choice D is the best answer. It contains the pronoun "they," a necessary reference to "such regulations" in the previous clause.

Choices A, B, and C are incorrect because each lacks a necessary subject, such as a pronoun or noun.

QUESTION 20

Choice C is the best answer. It refers directly to benefits for the restaurants' female employees, the subject of the previous sentence.

Choices A, B, and D are incorrect because none logically builds upon the sentence that precedes it.

QUESTION 21

Choice D is the best answer. It provides punctuation that indicates that the opening dependent clause modifies the subject "Harvey Girls."

Choices A, B, and C are incorrect because each uses the punctuation for a dependent clause ("Living independently and demonstrating an intense work ethic") as if it were an independent clause.

QUESTION 22

Choice A is the best answer. It recognizes that the new information supports the previous sentence's claim that "the Harvey Girls became known as a transformative force."

Choices B, C, and D are incorrect because each misinterprets the relationship between the proposed text and the passage.

QUESTION 23

Choice A is the best answer. It opens with a clause that identifies how 1-MCP affects apples, which focuses the sentence on 1-MCP as the subject and allows the ideas in the sentence to progress logically.

Choices B, C, and D are incorrect because each displays awkward or flawed modification and progression of ideas or creates redundancy.

QUESTION 24

Choice D is the best answer. Only the comma is necessary to separate "ethylene" from the appositive noun phrase that defines it.

Choices A, B, and C are incorrect because each creates a comma splice and/or adds unnecessary words.

QUESTION 25

Choice B is the best answer. It offers an adjective that accurately describes fresh apples.

Choices A, C, and D are incorrect because each proposes an adjective that does not describe a plausible fruit texture.

QUESTION 26

Choice A is the best answer. The plural possessive pronoun "their" corresponds with the plural referent "apples."

Choices B, C, and D are incorrect because none provides a pronoun that is both possessive and plural.

QUESTION 27

Choice D is the best answer. It provides the pronoun "who," which accurately identifies the referent "consumers" as people and appropriately begins the relative clause.

Choices A, B, and C are incorrect because each contains a pronoun that either does not correspond with the human referent "consumers" or does not correctly begin the relative clause.

QUESTION 28

Choice B is the best answer. It provides the present tense verb "do," which corresponds to the present tense established earlier in the sentence.

Choices A, C, and D are incorrect because each contains a verb that deviates from the simple present tense established in the sentence.

QUESTION 29

Choice B is the best answer. It provides a colon to appropriately introduce the clause that follows, an elaboration on the preceding claim that Bartlett pears are an example of fruit that "do not respond as well to 1-MCP treatment."

Choices A, C, and D are incorrect because each either creates a comma splice or uses a transitional phrase ("For instance") illogically.

QUESTION 30

Choice B is the best answer. Sentence 4 begins with "But," indicating a contrast with a previous idea, and goes on to mention that 1-MCP can have negative effects. Sentence 1 continues the discussion of benefits of 1-MCP, and sentence 2 names the adverse effect of limiting scent production, so the most logical spot for sentence 4 is between these sentences.

Choices A, C, and D are incorrect because each proposes placing the sentence at a point where it would compromise the logical development of ideas in the paragraph.

QUESTION 31

Choice D is the best answer. It most accurately reflects the data in the graph, which shows a steep decrease in percentage of flesh browning when untreated apples are left in the open air for three weeks rather than placed immediately into a controlled atmosphere.

Choices A, B, and C are incorrect because each presents an inaccurate interpretation of the data in the graph.

QUESTION 32

Choice B is the best answer. It accurately interprets the data as indicating that "roughly half of their flesh turns brown" when apples are treated with 1-MCP: both bars representing 1-MCP treatment are near the 50% line.

Choices A, C, and D are incorrect because each proposes an inaccurate interpretation of the data.

QUESTION 33

Choice C is the best answer. It describes an action, weighing the relative values, that fruit sellers must take as a result of 1-MCP's limitations.

Choices A, B, and D are incorrect because none specifically connects the shortcomings of 1-MCP with any action on the part of fruit sellers.

QUESTION 34

Choice D is the best answer. It clearly communicates that the preceding dependent clause modifies "works by human artists."

Choices A, B, and C are incorrect because each fails to link the preceding dependent clause to an independent clause, resulting in an incomplete sentence.

QUESTION 35

Choice B is the best answer. It provides the necessary em dash to close the aside about artist C.M. Coolidge, which opens with an em dash.

Choices A, C, and D are incorrect because each provides closing punctuation for the aside that does not correspond with the opening punctuation.

QUESTION 36

Choice C is the best answer. The plural verb "portray" corresponds with the plural noun "works of art."

Choices A, B, and D are incorrect because none provides the plural verb in the present tense that the sentence requires.

QUESTION 37

Choice D is the best answer. It names a "museum in Russia," which is the subject of the next paragraph.

Choices A, B, and C are incorrect because each provides an overly general phrase that does not specifically link to the paragraph that follows.

QUESTION 38

Choice C is the best answer. It creates parallelism with the verb "could damage" that appears earlier in the clause ("rodents that could damage . . . [and could] scare off visitors").

Choices A, B, and D are incorrect because each presents a verb tense that is inconsistent with the sentence's other present tense verb ("could damage") that shares "mice, rats, and other rodents" as its subject.

QUESTION 39

Choice C is the best answer. Sentence 5, which discusses Peter the Great's daughter continuing his tradition, most logically follows the sentence about Peter the Great.

Choices A, B, and D are incorrect because each presents a placement that would compromise the logical development of the paragraph.

QUESTION 40

Choice B is the best answer. "Commissioned" describes the act of hiring an artist to create a specific work.

Choices A, C, and D are incorrect because each provides a word that does not correspond logically with the context.

QUESTION 41

Choice D is the best answer. It provides punctuation that clearly places the noun phrase "digital artist Eldar Zakirov" as an appositive identifying the person mentioned in the previous phrase, "The person chosen for this task."

Choices A, B, and C are incorrect because each fails to open and close the uninterrupted appositive noun phrase "digital artist Eldar Zakirov" with commas.

QUESTION 42

Choice A is the best answer. The phrase "noble individuals" corresponds with the subsequent examples of portraits where the cats are depicted as "aristocratic," "stately," and like a "trusted royal advisor."

Choices B, C, and D are incorrect because each provides a statement that does not logically connect to the examples that follow.

QUESTION 43

Choice D is the best answer. It accurately states that the information in the proposed additional sentence is not related to formal portraits of cats, the main topic of the paragraph.

Choices A, B, and C are incorrect because each fails to recognize that the proposed sentence interrupts the logical development of the paragraph.

QUESTION 44

Choice D is the best answer. The tone corresponds with that established in the passage, and the phrasing appropriately focuses on the cats' contribution to protecting artwork rather than on simply killing rodents.

Choices A, B, and C are incorrect because none makes explicit the link between the cats' hunting activities and the service to the museum.

Section 3: Math Test – No Calculator

QUESTION 1

Choice C is correct. The painter's fee is given by $nK\ell h$, where n is the number of walls, K is a constant with units of dollars per square foot, ℓ is the length of each wall in feet, and h is the height of each wall in feet. Examining this equation shows that ℓ and h will be used to determine the area of each wall. The variable n is the number of walls, so n times the area of each wall will give the amount of area that will need to be painted. The only remaining variable is K, which represents the cost per square foot and is determined by the painter's time and the price of paint. Therefore, K is the only factor that will change if the customer asks for a more expensive brand of paint.

Choice A is incorrect because a more expensive brand of paint would not cause the height of each wall to change. Choice B is incorrect because a more expensive brand of paint would not cause the length of each wall to change. Choice D is incorrect because a more expensive brand of paint would not cause the number of walls to change.

QUESTION 2

Choice D is correct. Dividing each side of the equation $3r = 18$ by 3 gives $r = 6$. Substituting 6 for r in the expression $6r + 3$ gives $6(6) + 3 = 39$.

Alternatively, the expression $6r + 3$ can be rewritten as $2(3r) + 3$. Substituting 18 for $3r$ in the expression $2(3r) + 3$ yields $2(18) + 3$, or $36 + 3 = 39$.

Choice A is incorrect because 6 is the value of r; however, the question asks for the value of the expression $6r + 3$. Choices B and C are incorrect because if $6r + 3$ were equal to either of these values, then it would not be possible for $3r$ to be equal to 18, as stated in the question.

QUESTION 3

Choice D is correct. By definition, $a^{\frac{m}{n}} = \sqrt[n]{a^m}$ for any positive integers m and n. It follows, therefore, that $a^{\frac{2}{3}} = \sqrt[3]{a^2}$.

Choice A is incorrect. By definition, $a^{\frac{1}{n}} = \sqrt[n]{a}$ for any positive integer n. Applying this definition as well as the power property of exponents to the expression $\sqrt{a^{\frac{1}{3}}}$ yields $\sqrt{a^{\frac{1}{3}}} = \left(a^{\frac{1}{3}}\right)^{\frac{1}{2}} = a^{\frac{1}{6}}$. Because $a^{\frac{1}{6}} \neq a^{\frac{2}{3}}$, $\sqrt{a^{\frac{1}{3}}}$ is not the correct answer. Choice B is incorrect. By definition, $a^{\frac{1}{n}} = \sqrt[n]{a}$ for any positive integer n. Applying this definition as well as the power property of exponents to the expression $\sqrt{a^3}$ yields $\sqrt{a^3} = (a^3)^{\frac{1}{2}} = a^{\frac{3}{2}}$. Because $a^{\frac{3}{2}} \neq a^{\frac{2}{3}}$, $\sqrt{a^3}$ is not the correct answer. Choice C is incorrect. By definition, $a^{\frac{1}{n}} = \sqrt[n]{a}$ for any positive integer n. Applying this definition as well as the power property of exponents to the expression $\sqrt[3]{a^{\frac{1}{2}}}$ yields $\sqrt[3]{a^{\frac{1}{2}}} = \left(a^{\frac{1}{2}}\right)^{\frac{1}{3}} = a^{\frac{1}{6}}$. Because $a^{\frac{1}{6}} \neq a^{\frac{2}{3}}$, $\sqrt[3]{a^{\frac{1}{2}}}$ is not the correct answer.

QUESTION 4

Choice B is correct. To fit the scenario described, 30 must be twice as large as x. This can be written as $2x = 30$.

Choices A, C, and D are incorrect. These equations do not correctly relate the numbers and variables described in the stem. For example, the expression in choice C states that 30 is half as large as x, not twice as large as x.

QUESTION 5

Choice C is correct. Multiplying each side of $\frac{5}{x} = \frac{15}{x+20}$ by $x(x + 20)$ gives $5(x + 20) = 15x$. Using the distributive property to eliminate the parentheses yields $5x + 100 = 15x$, and then subtracting $5x$ from each side of the equation $5x + 100 = 15x$ gives $100 = 10x$. Finally, dividing both sides of the equation $100 = 10x$ by 10 gives $10 = x$. Therefore, the value of $\frac{x}{5}$ is $\frac{10}{5} = 2$.

Choice A is incorrect because it is the value of x, not $\frac{x}{5}$. Choices B and D are incorrect and may be the result of errors in arithmetic operations on the given equation.

QUESTION 6

Choice C is correct. Multiplying each side of the equation $2x - 3y = -14$ by 3 gives $6x - 9y = -42$. Multiplying each side of the equation $3x - 2y = -6$ by 2 gives $6x - 4y = -12$. Then, subtracting the sides of $6x - 4y = -12$ from the corresponding sides of $6x - 9y = -42$ gives $-5y = -30$. Dividing each side of the equation $-5y = -30$ by -5 gives $y = 6$. Finally, substituting 6 for y in $2x - 3y = -14$ gives $2x - 3(6) = -14$, or $x = 2$. Therefore, the value of $x - y$ is $2 - 6 = -4$.

Alternatively, adding the corresponding sides of $2x - 3y = -14$ and $3x - 2y = -6$ gives $5x - 5y = -20$, from which it follows that $x - y = -4$.

Choices A and B are incorrect and may be the result of an arithmetic error when solving the system of equations. Choice D is incorrect and may be the result of finding $x + y$ instead of $x - y$.

QUESTION 7

Choice C is correct. If $x - b$ is a factor of $f(x)$, then $f(b)$ must equal 0. Based on the table, $f(4) = 0$. Therefore, $x - 4$ must be a factor of $f(x)$.

Choice A is incorrect because $f(2) \neq 0$. Choice B is incorrect because no information is given about the value of $f(3)$, so $x - 3$ may or may not be a factor of $f(x)$. Choice D is incorrect because $f(5) \neq 0$.

QUESTION 8

Choice A is correct. The linear equation $y = kx + 4$ is in slope-intercept form, and so the slope of the line is k. Since the line contains the point (c, d), the coordinates of this point satisfy the equation $y = kx + 4$; therefore, $d = kc + 4$. Solving this equation for the slope, k, gives $k = \frac{d-4}{c}$.

Choices B, C, and D are incorrect and may be the result of errors in substituting the coordinates of (c, d) in $y = kx + 4$ or of errors in solving for k in the resulting equation.

QUESTION 9

Choice A is correct. If a system of two linear equations has no solution, then the lines represented by the equations in the coordinate plane are parallel. The equation $kx - 3y = 4$ can be rewritten as $y = \frac{k}{3}x - \frac{4}{3}$, where $\frac{k}{3}$ is the slope of the line, and the equation $4x - 5y = 7$ can be rewritten as $y = \frac{4}{5}x - \frac{7}{5}$, where $\frac{4}{5}$ is the slope of the line. If two lines are parallel, then the slopes of the line are equal. Therefore, $\frac{4}{5} = \frac{k}{3}$, or $k = \frac{12}{5}$. (Since the y-intercepts of the lines represented by the equations are $-\frac{4}{3}$ and $-\frac{7}{5}$, the lines are parallel, not identical.)

Choices B, C, and D are incorrect and may be the result of a computational error when rewriting the equations or solving the equation representing the equality of the slopes for k.

QUESTION 10

Choice A is correct. Substituting 25 for y in the equation $y = (x - 11)^2$ gives $25 = (x - 11)^2$. It follows that $x - 11 = 5$ or $x - 11 = -5$, so the x-coordinates of the two points of intersection are $x = 16$ and $x = 6$, respectively. Since both points of intersection have a y-coordinate of 25, it follows that the two points are (16, 25) and (6, 25). Since these points lie on the horizontal line $y = 25$, the distance between these points is the positive difference of the x-coordinates: $16 - 6 = 10$.

Alternatively, since a translation is a rigid motion, the distance between points A and B would be the same as the distance between the points of intersection of the line $y = 25$ and the parabola $y = x^2$. Since those graphs intersect at (0, 5) and (0, −5), the distance between the two points, and thus the distance between A and B, is 10.

Choices B, C, and D are incorrect and may be the result of an error in solving the quadratic equation that results when substituting 25 for y in the given quadratic equation.

QUESTION 11

Choice B is correct. Since the angles marked $y°$ and $u°$ are vertical angles, $y = u$. Substituting y for u in the equation $x + y = u + w$ gives $x = w$. Since the angles marked $w°$ and $z°$ are vertical angles, $w = z$. Therefore, by the transitive property, $x = z$, and so I must be true.

The equation in II need not be true. For example, if $x = w = z = t = 70$ and $y = u = 40$, then all three pairs of vertical angles in the figure have equal measure and the given condition $x + y = u + w$ holds. But it is not true in this case that y is equal to w. Therefore, II need not be true.

Since the top three angles in the figure form a straight angle, it follows that $x + y + z = 180$. Similarly, $w + u + t = 180$, and so $x + y + z = w + u + t$. Subtracting the sides of the given equation $x + y = u + w$ from the corresponding sides of $x + y + z = w + u + t$ gives $z = t$. Therefore, III must be true. Since only I and III must be true, the correct answer is choice B.

Choices A, C, and D are incorrect because each of these choices includes II, which need not be true.

QUESTION 12

Choice A is correct. The parabola with equation $y = a(x - 2)(x + 4)$ crosses the x-axis at the points $(-4, 0)$ and $(2, 0)$. By symmetry, the x-coordinate of the vertex of the parabola is halfway between the x-coordinates of $(-4, 0)$ and $(2, 0)$. Thus, the x-coordinate of the vertex is $\frac{-4 + 2}{2} = -1$. This is the value of c. To find the y-coordinate of the vertex, substitute -1 for x in $y = a(x - 2)(x + 4)$:

$$y = a(x - 2)(x + 4) = a(-1 - 2)(-1 + 4) = a(-3)(3) = -9a$$

Therefore, the value of d is $-9a$.

Choice B is incorrect because the value of the constant term in the equation is not the y-coordinate of the vertex, unless there were no linear terms in the quadratic. Choice C is incorrect and may be the result of a sign error in finding the x-coordinate of the vertex. Choice D is incorrect because the negative of the coefficient of the linear term in the quadratic equation is not the y-coordinate of the vertex.

QUESTION 13

Choice B is correct. Since $24x^2 + 25x - 47$ divided by $ax - 2$ is equal to $-8x - 3$ with remainder -53, it is true that $(-8x - 3)(ax - 2) - 53 = 24x^2 + 25x - 47$. (This can be seen by multiplying each side of the given equation by $ax - 2$). This can be rewritten as $-8ax^2 + 16x - 3ax + 6 - 53 = 24x^2 + 25x - 47$. Since the coefficients of the x^2-term have to be equal on both sides of the equation, $-8a = 24$, or $a = -3$.

Choices A, C, and D are incorrect and may be the result of either a conceptual misunderstanding or a computational error when trying to solve for the value of a.

QUESTION 14

Choice A is correct. Dividing each side of the given equation by 3 gives the equivalent equation $x^2 + 4x + 2 = 0$. Then using the quadratic formula, $\frac{-b \pm \sqrt{b^2 - 4ac}}{2a}$ with $a = 1$, $b = 4$, and $c = 2$, gives the solutions $x = -2 \pm \sqrt{2}$.

Choices B, C, and D are incorrect and may be the result of errors when applying the quadratic formula.

QUESTION 15

Choice D is correct. If C is graphed against F, the slope of the line is equal to $\frac{5}{9}$ degrees Celsius/degrees Fahrenheit, which means that for an increase of 1 degree Fahrenheit, the increase is $\frac{5}{9}$ of 1 degree Celsius. Thus, statement I is true. This is the equivalent to saying that an increase of 1 degree Celsius is equal to an increase of $\frac{9}{5}$ degrees Fahrenheit.

Since $\frac{9}{5} = 1.8$, statement II is true. On the other hand, statement III is not true, since a temperature increase of $\frac{9}{5}$ degrees Fahrenheit, not $\frac{5}{9}$ degree Fahrenheit, is equal to a temperature increase of 1 degree Celsius.

Choices A, B, and C are incorrect because each of these choices omits a true statement or includes a false statement.

QUESTION 16

The correct answer is either 1 or 2. The given equation can be rewritten as $x^5 - 5x^3 + 4x = 0$. Since the polynomial expression on the left has no constant term, it has x as a factor: $x(x^4 - 5x^2 + 4) = 0$. The expression in parentheses is a quadratic equation in x^2 that can be factored, giving $x(x^2 - 1)(x^2 - 4) = 0$. This further factors as $x(x - 1)(x + 1)(x - 2)(x + 2) = 0$. The solutions for x are $x = 0$, $x = 1$, $x = -1$, $x = 2$, and $x = -2$. Since it is given that $x > 0$, the possible values of x are $x = 1$ and $x = 2$. Either 1 or 2 may be gridded as the correct answer.

QUESTION 17

The correct answer is 2. First, clear the fractions from the given equation by multiplying each side of the equation by 36 (the least common multiple of 4, 9, and 12). The equation becomes $28x - 16x = 9 + 15$. Combining like terms on each side of the equation yields $12x = 24$. Finally, dividing both sides of the equation by 12 yields $x = 2$.

Alternatively, since $\frac{7}{9}x - \frac{4}{9}x = \frac{3}{9}x = \frac{1}{3}x$ and $\frac{1}{4} + \frac{5}{12} = \frac{3}{12} + \frac{5}{12} = \frac{8}{12} = \frac{2}{3}$, the given equation simplifies to $\frac{1}{3}x = \frac{2}{3}$. Multiplying each side of $\frac{1}{3}x = \frac{2}{3}$ by 3 yields $x = 2$.

QUESTION 18

The correct answer is 105. Since $180 - z = 2y$ and $y = 75$, it follows that $180 - z = 150$, and so $z = 30$. Thus, each of the base angles of the isosceles triangle on the right has measure $\frac{180° - 30°}{2} = 75°$. Therefore, the measure of the angle marked $x°$ is $180° - 75° = 105°$, and so the value of x is 105.

QUESTION 19

The correct answer is 370. A system of equations can be used where h represents the number of calories in a hamburger and f represents the number of calories in an order of fries. The equation $2h + 3f = 1700$ represents the fact that 2 hamburgers and 3 orders of fries contain a total of 1700 calories, and the equation $h = f + 50$ represents the fact that one hamburger contains 50 more calories than an order of fries. Substituting $f + 50$ for h in $2h + 3f = 1700$ gives $2(f + 50) + 3f = 1700$. This equation can be solved as follows:

$$2f + 100 + 3f = 1700$$

$$5f + 100 = 1700$$

$$5f = 1600$$

$$f = 320$$

The number of calories in an order of fries is 320, so the number of calories in a hamburger is 50 more than 320, or 370.

QUESTION 20

The correct answer is $\frac{3}{5}$ or .6. Triangle ABC is a right triangle with its right angle at B. Thus, $\overline{AC}$ is the hypotenuse of right triangle ABC, and $\overline{AB}$ and $\overline{BC}$ are the legs of right triangle ABC. By the Pythagorean theorem, $AB = \sqrt{20^2 - 16^2} = \sqrt{400 - 256} = \sqrt{144} = 12$. Since triangle DEF is similar to triangle ABC, with vertex F corresponding to vertex C, the measure of angle F equals the measure of angle C. Thus, $\sin F = \sin C$. From the side lengths of triangle ABC, $\sin C = \frac{\text{opposite side}}{\text{hypotenuse}} = \frac{AB}{AC} = \frac{12}{20} = \frac{3}{5}$. Therefore, $\sin F = \frac{3}{5}$. Either 3/5 or its decimal equivalent, .6, may be gridded as the correct answer.

Section 4: Math Test – Calculator

QUESTION 1

Choice C is correct. Marilyn's distance from her campsite remained the same during the time she ate lunch. This is represented by a horizontal segment in the graph. The only horizontal segment in the graph starts at a time of about 1:10 P.M. and ends at about 1:40 P.M. Therefore, Marilyn finished her lunch and continued her hike at about 1:40 P.M.

Choices A, B, and D are incorrect and may be the result of a misinterpretation of the graph. For example, choice B is the time Marilyn started her lunch, and choice D is the time Marilyn was at the maximum distance from her campsite.

QUESTION 2

Choice B is correct. Of the 25 people who entered the contest, there are 8 females under age 40 and 2 males age 40 or older. Because there is no overlap in the categories, the probability that the contest winner will be either a female under age 40 or a male age 40 or older is $\frac{8}{25} + \frac{2}{25} = \frac{10}{25}$.

Choice A is incorrect and may be the result of dividing 8 by 2, instead of adding 8 to 2, to find the probability. Choice C is incorrect; it is the probability that the contest winner will be either a female under age 40 or a female age 40 or older. Choice D is incorrect and may be the result of multiplying 8 and 2, instead of adding 8 and 2, to find the probability.

QUESTION 3

Choice C is correct. Based on the graph, sales increased in the first 3 years since 1997, which is until year 2000, and then generally decreased thereafter.

Choices A, B, and D are incorrect; each of these choices contains inaccuracies in describing the general trend of music album sales from 1997 through 2009.

QUESTION 4

Choice C is correct. The graph of $y = f(n)$ in the coordinate plane is a line that passes through each of the points given in the table. From the table, one can see that an increase of 1 unit in n results in an increase of 3 units in $f(n)$; for example, $f(2) - f(1) = 1 - (-2) = 3$. Therefore, the graph of $y = f(n)$ in the coordinate plane is a line with slope 3. Only choice C is a line with slope 3. The y-intercept of the line is the value of $f(0)$. Since an increase of 1 unit in n results in an increase of 3 units in $f(n)$, it follows that $f(1) - f(0) = 3$. Since $f(1) = -2$, it follows that $f(0) = f(1) - 3 = -5$. Therefore, the y-intercept of the graph of $f(n)$ is -5, and the equation in slope-intercept form that defined f is $f(n) = 3n - 5$.

Choices A, B, and D are incorrect because each equation has the incorrect slope of the line (the y-intercept in each equation is also incorrect).

QUESTION 5

Choice B is correct. Since 7 percent of the 562 juniors is 0.07(562) and 5 percent of the 602 seniors is 0.05(602), the expression 0.07(562) + 0.05(602) can be evaluated to determine the total number of juniors and seniors inducted into the National Honor Society. Of the given choices, 69 is closest to the value of the expression.

Choice A is incorrect and may be the result of adding the number of juniors and seniors and the percentages given and then using the expression (0.07 + 0.05)(562 + 602). Choices C and D are incorrect and may be the result of finding either only the number of juniors inducted or only the number of seniors inducted.

QUESTION 6

Choice A is correct. The sum of the two polynomials is $(3x^2 - 5x + 2) + (5x^2 - 2x - 6)$. This can be rewritten by combining like terms:

$$(3x^2 - 5x + 2) + (5x^2 - 2x - 6) = (3x^2 + 5x^2) + (-5x - 2x) + (2 - 6) = 8x^2 - 7x - 4$$

Choice B is incorrect and may be the result of a sign error when combining the coefficients of the x-term. Choice C is incorrect and may be the result of adding the exponents, as well as the coefficients, of like terms. Choice D is incorrect and may be the result of a combination of the errors described in choice B and choice C.

QUESTION 7

Choice D is correct. To solve the equation for w, multiply both sides of the equation by the reciprocal of $\frac{3}{5}$, which is $\frac{5}{3}$. This gives $\left(\frac{5}{3}\right) \cdot \frac{3}{5}w = \frac{4}{3} \cdot \left(\frac{5}{3}\right)$, which simplifies to $w = \frac{20}{9}$.

Choices A, B, and C are incorrect and may be the result of errors in arithmetic when simplifying the given equation.

QUESTION 8

Choice C is correct. In the equation $y = 0.56x + 27.2$, the value of x increases by 1 for each year that passes. Each time x increases by 1, y increases by 0.56 since 0.56 is the slope of the graph of this equation. Since y represents the average number of students per classroom in the year represented by x, it follows that, according to the model, the estimated increase each year in the average number of students per classroom at Central High School is 0.56.

Choice A is incorrect because the total number of students in the school in 2000 is the product of the average number of students per classroom and the total number of classrooms, which would appropriately be approximated by the y-intercept (27.2) times the total number of classrooms, which is not given. Choice B is incorrect because the average number of students per classroom in 2000 is given by the y-intercept of the graph of the equation, but the question is asking for the meaning of the number 0.56, which is the slope. Choice D is incorrect because 0.56 represents the estimated yearly change in the average number of students per classroom. The estimated difference between the average number of students per classroom in 2010 and 2000 is 0.56 times the number of years that have passed between 2000 and 2010, that is, $0.56 \times 10 = 5.6$.

QUESTION 9

Choice B is correct. Because Nate walks 25 meters in 13.7 seconds, and 4 minutes is equal to 240 seconds, the proportion $\frac{25 \text{ meters}}{13.7 \text{ sec}} = \frac{x \text{ meters}}{240 \text{ sec}}$ can be used to find out how many meters, x, Nate walks in 4 minutes. The proportion can be simplified to $\frac{25}{13.7} = \frac{x}{240}$, because the units of meters per second cancel, and then each side of the equation can be multiplied by 240, giving $\frac{(240)(25)}{13.7} = x \approx 438$. Therefore, of the given options, 450 meters is closest to the distance Nate will walk in 4 minutes.

Choice A is incorrect and may be the result of setting up the proportion as $\frac{13.7 \text{ sec}}{25 \text{ meters}} = \frac{x \text{ meters}}{240 \text{ sec}}$ and finding that $x \approx 132$, which is close to 150. Choices C and D are incorrect and may be the result of errors in calculation.

QUESTION 10

Choice D is correct. On Mercury, the acceleration due to gravity is 3.6 m/sec^2. Substituting 3.6 for g and 90 for m in the formula $W = mg$ gives $W = 90(3.6) = 324$ newtons.

Choice A is incorrect and may be the result of dividing 90 by 3.6. Choice B is incorrect and may be the result of subtracting 3.6 from 90 and rounding to the nearest whole number. Choice C is incorrect because an object with a weight of 101 newtons on Mercury would have a mass of about 28 kilograms, not 90 kilograms.

QUESTION 11

Choice B is correct. On Earth, the acceleration due to gravity is 9.8 m/sec^2. Thus, for an object with a weight of 150 newtons, the formula $W = mg$ becomes $150 = m(9.8)$, which shows that the mass of an object with a weight of 150 newtons on Earth is about 15.3 kilograms. Substituting this mass into the formula $W = mg$ and now using the weight of 170 newtons gives $170 = 15.3g$, which shows that the second planet's acceleration due to gravity is about 11.1 m/sec^2. According to the table, this value for the acceleration due to gravity holds on Saturn.

Choices A, C, and D are incorrect. Using the formula $W = mg$ and the values for g in the table shows that an object with a weight of 170 newtons on these planets would not have the same mass as an object with a weight of 150 newtons on Earth.

QUESTION 12

Choice D is correct. A zero of a function corresponds to an x-intercept of the graph of the function in the xy-plane. Therefore, the complete graph of the function f, which has five distinct zeros, must have five x-intercepts. Only the graph in choice D has five x-intercepts, and therefore, this is the only one of the given graphs that could be the complete graph of f in the xy-plane.

Choices A, B, and C are incorrect. The number of x-intercepts of each of these graphs is not equal to five; therefore, none of these graphs could be the complete graph of f, which has five distinct zeros.

QUESTION 13

Choice D is correct. Starting with the original equation, $h = -16t^2 + vt + k$, in order to get v in terms of the other variables, $-16t^2$ and k need to be subtracted from each side. This yields $vt = h + 16t^2 - k$, which when divided by t will give v in terms of the other variables. However, the equation $v = \frac{h + 16t^2 - k}{t}$ is not one of the options, so the right side needs to be further simplified. Another way to write the previous equation is $v = \frac{h - k}{t} + \frac{16t^2}{t}$, which can be simplified to $v = \frac{h - k}{t} + 16t$.

Choices A, B, and C are incorrect and may be the result of arithmetic errors when rewriting the original equation to express v in terms of h, t, and k.

QUESTION 14

Choice A is correct. The hotel charges $0.20 per minute to use the meeting-room phone. This per-minute rate can be converted to the hourly rate using the conversion 1 hour = 60 minutes, as shown below.

$$\frac{\$0.20}{\text{minute}} \times \frac{60 \text{ minutes}}{1 \text{ hour}} = \frac{\$(0.20 \times 60)}{\text{hour}}$$

Thus, the hotel charges $\$(0.20 \times 60)$ per hour to use the meeting-room phone. Therefore, the cost c, in dollars, for h hours of use is $c = (0.20 \times 60)h$, which is equivalent to $c = 0.20(60h)$.

Choice B is incorrect because in this expression the per-minute rate is multiplied by h, the number of hours of phone use. Furthermore, the equation indicates that there is a flat fee of $60 in addition to the per-minute or per-hour rate. This is not the case. Choice C is incorrect because the expression indicates that the hotel charges $\$\left(\frac{60}{0.20}\right)$ per hour for use of the meeting-room phone, not $0.20(60) per hour. Choice D is incorrect because the expression indicates that the hourly rate is $\frac{1}{60}$ times the per-minute rate, not 60 times the per-minute rate.

QUESTION 15

Choice A is the correct answer. Experimental research is a method used to study a small group of people and generalize the results to a larger population. However, in order to make a generalization involving cause and effect:

- The population must be well defined.
- The participants must be selected at random.
- The participants must be randomly assigned to treatment groups.

When these conditions are met, the results of the study can be generalized to the population with a conclusion about cause and effect. In this study, all conditions are met and the population from which the participants were selected are people with poor eyesight. Therefore, a general conclusion can be drawn about the effect of Treatment X on the population of people with poor eyesight.

Choice B is incorrect. The study did not include all available treatments, so no conclusion can be made about the relative effectiveness of all available treatments. Choice C is incorrect. The participants were selected at random from a large population of people with poor eyesight. Therefore, the results can be generalized only to that population and not to anyone in general. Also, the conclusion is too strong: an experimental study might show that people are likely to be helped by a treatment, but it cannot show that anyone who takes the treatment will be helped. Choice D is incorrect. This conclusion is too strong. The study shows that Treatment X is likely to improve the eyesight of people with poor eyesight, but it cannot show that the treatment definitely will cause improvement in eyesight for every person. Furthermore, since the people undergoing the treatment in the study were selected from people with poor eyesight, the results can be generalized only to this population, not to all people.

QUESTION 16

Choice B is correct. The graphs of $y = f(x)$ and $y = g(x)$ are given. In order for $f(x) + g(x)$ to be 0, there must be one or more values of x for which the y-coordinates of the graphs are opposites. Looking at the graphs, one can see that this occurs at $x = -2$: the point $(-2, -2)$ lies on the graph of f, and the point $(-2, 2)$ lies on the graph of g. Thus, at $x = -2$, the value of $f(x) + g(x)$ is $-2 + 2 = 0$.

Choices A, C, and D are incorrect because none of these x-values satisfies the given equation, $f(x) + g(x) = 0$.

QUESTION 17

Choice B is correct. The quantity of the product supplied to the market is given by the function $S(P) = \frac{1}{2}P + 40$. If the price P of the product increases by \$10, the effect on the quantity of the product supplied can be determined by substituting $P + 10$ for P in the function $S(P) = \frac{1}{2}P + 40$. This gives $S(P + 10) = \frac{1}{2}(P + 10) + 40 = \frac{1}{2}P + 45$, which shows that $S(P + 10) = S(P) + 5$. Therefore, the quantity supplied to the market will increase by 5 units when the price of the product is increased by \$10.

Alternatively, look at the coefficient of P in the linear function S. This is the slope of the graph of the function, where P is on the horizontal axis and $S(P)$ is on the vertical axis. Since the slope is $\frac{1}{2}$, for every increase of 1 in P, there will be an increase of $\frac{1}{2}$ in $S(P)$, and therefore, an increase of 10 in P will yield an increase of 5 in $S(P)$.

Choice A is incorrect. If the quantity supplied decreases as the price of the product increases, the function $S(P)$ would be decreasing, but $S(P) = \frac{1}{2}P + 40$ is an increasing function. Choice C is incorrect and may be the result of assuming the slope of the graph of $S(P)$ is equal to 1. Choice D is incorrect and may be the result of confusing the y-intercept of the graph of $S(P)$ with the slope, and then adding 10 to the y-intercept.

QUESTION 18

Choice B is correct. The quantity of the product supplied to the market will equal the quantity of the product demanded by the market if $S(P)$ is equal to $D(P)$, that is, if $\frac{1}{2}P + 40 = 220 - P$. Solving this equation gives $P = 120$, and so \$120 is the price at which the quantity of the product supplied will equal the quantity of the product demanded.

Choices A, C, and D are incorrect. At these dollar amounts, the quantities given by $S(P)$ and $D(P)$ are not equal.

QUESTION 19

Choice C is correct. It is given that 1 ounce of graphene covers 7 football fields. Therefore, 48 ounces can cover $7 \times 48 = 336$ football fields. If each football field has an area of $1\frac{1}{3}$ acres, then 336 football fields have a total area of $336 \times 1\frac{1}{3} = 448$ acres. Therefore, of the choices given, 450 acres is closest to the number of acres 48 ounces of graphene could cover.

Choice A is incorrect and may be the result of dividing, instead of multiplying, the number of football fields by $1\frac{1}{3}$. Choice B is incorrect and may be the result of finding the number of football fields, not the number of acres, that can be covered by 48 ounces of graphene. Choice D is incorrect and may be the result of setting up the expression $\frac{7 \times 48 \times 4}{3}$ and then finding only the numerator of the fraction.

QUESTION 20

Choice B is correct. To answer this question, find the point in the graph that represents Michael's 34-minute swim and then compare the actual heart rate for that swim with the expected heart rate as defined by the line of best fit. To find the point that represents Michael's swim that took 34 minutes, look along the vertical line of the graph that is marked "34" on the horizontal axis. That vertical line intersects only one point in the scatterplot, at 148 beats per minute. On the other hand, the line of best fit intersects the vertical line representing 34 minutes at 150 beats per minute. Therefore, for the swim that took 34 minutes, Michael's actual heart rate was $150 - 148 = 2$ beats per minute less than predicted by the line of best fit.

Choices A, C, and D are incorrect and may be the result of misreading the graph.

QUESTION 21

Choice C is correct. Linear growth is characterized by an increase of a quantity at a constant rate. Exponential growth is characterized by an increase of a quantity at a relative rate; that is, an increase by the same factor over equal increments of time. In choice C, the value of the account increases by 1% each year; that is, the value is multiplied by the same factor, 1.01, each year. Therefore, the value described in choice C grows exponentially.

Choices A and B are incorrect because the rate depends only on the initial value, and thus the value increases by the same amount each year. Both options A and B describe linear growth. Choice D is incorrect; it is is also a description of linear growth, as the increase is constant each year.

QUESTION 22

Choice B is correct. One of the three numbers is x; let the other two numbers be y and z. Since the sum of three numbers is 855, the equation $x + y + z = 855$ is true. The statement that x is 50% more than the sum of the other two numbers can be represented as $x = 1.5(y + z)$, or $x = \frac{3}{2}(y + z)$. Multiplying both sides of the equation $x = \frac{3}{2}(y + z)$ by $\frac{2}{3}$ gives $\frac{2}{3}x = y + z$. Substituting $\frac{2}{3}x$ in $x + y + z = 855$ gives $x + \frac{2}{3}x = 855$, or $\frac{5x}{3} = 855$. Therefore, x equals $\frac{3}{5} \times 855 = 513$.

Choices A, C, and D are incorrect and may be the result of computational errors.

QUESTION 23

Choice C is correct. Since the angles are acute and $\sin(a°) = \cos(b°)$, it follows from the complementary angle property of sines and cosines that $a + b = 90$. Substituting $4k - 22$ for a and $6k - 13$ for b gives $(4k - 22) + (6k - 13) = 90$, which simplifies to $10k - 35 = 90$. Therefore, $10k = 125$, and $k = 12.5$.

Choice A is incorrect and may be the result of mistakenly assuming that $a = b$ and making a sign error. Choices B and D are incorrect because they result in values for a and b such that $\sin(a°) \neq \cos(b°)$.

QUESTION 24

Choice D is correct. Let c be the number of students in Mr. Kohl's class. The conditions described in the question can be represented by the equations $n = 3c + 5$ and $n + 21 = 4c$. Substituting $3c + 5$ for n in the second equation gives $3c + 5 + 21 = 4c$, which can be solved to find $c = 26$.

Choices A, B, and C are incorrect because the values given for the number of students in the class cannot fulfill both conditions given in the question. For example, if there were 16 students in the class, then the first condition would imply that there are $3(16) + 5 = 53$ milliliters of solution in the beaker, but the second condition would imply that there are $4(16) - 21 = 43$ milliliters of solution in the beaker. This contradiction shows that there cannot be 16 students in the class.

QUESTION 25

Choice D is correct. The volume of the grain silo can be found by adding the volumes of all the solids of which it is composed. The silo is made up of a cylinder with height 10 feet (ft) and base radius 5 ft and two cones, each having height 5 ft and base radius 5 ft. The formulas $V_{cylinder} = \pi r^2 h$ and $V_{cone} = \frac{1}{3}\pi r^2 h$ can be used to determine the total volume of the silo. Since the two cones have identical dimensions, the total volume, in cubic feet, of the silo is given by $V_{silo} = \pi(5)^2(10) + (2)\left(\frac{1}{3}\right)\pi(5)^2(5) = \left(\frac{4}{3}\right)(250)\pi$, which is approximately equal to 1,047.2 cubic feet.

Choice A is incorrect because this is the volume of only the two cones. Choice B is incorrect because this is the volume of only the cylinder. Choice C is incorrect because this is the volume of only one of the cones plus the cylinder.

QUESTION 26

Choice C is correct. The line passes through the origin, $(2, k)$, and $(k, 32)$. Any two of these points can be used to find the slope of the line. Since the line passes through $(0, 0)$ and $(2, k)$, the slope of the line is equal to $\frac{k-0}{2-0} = \frac{k}{2}$. Similarly, since the line passes through $(0, 0)$ and $(k, 32)$, the slope of the line is equal to $\frac{32-0}{k-0} = \frac{32}{k}$. Since each expression gives the slope of the same line, it must be true that $\frac{k}{2} = \frac{32}{k}$. Multiplying each side of $\frac{k}{2} = \frac{32}{k}$ by $2k$ gives $k^2 = 64$, from which it follows that $k = 8$ or $k = -8$. Therefore, of the given choices, only 8 could be the value of k.

Choices A, B, and D are incorrect and may be the result of computational errors.

QUESTION 27

Choice C is correct. Let ℓ and w be the length and width, respectively, of the original rectangle. The area of the original rectangle is $A = \ell w$. The rectangle is altered by increasing its length by 10 percent and decreasing its width by p percent; thus, the length of the altered rectangle is 1.1ℓ, and the width of the altered rectangle is $\left(1 - \frac{p}{100}\right)w$. The alterations decrease the area by 12 percent, so the area of the altered rectangle is $(1 - 0.12)A = 0.88A$. The area of the altered rectangle is the product of its length and width, so $0.88A = (1.1\ell)\left(1 - \frac{p}{100}\right)w$. Since $A = \ell w$, this last equation can be rewritten as $0.88A = (1.1)\left(1 - \frac{p}{100}\right)\ell w = (1.1)\left(1 - \frac{p}{100}\right)A$, from which it follows that $0.88 = (1.1)\left(1 - \frac{p}{100}\right)$, or $0.8 = \left(1 - \frac{p}{100}\right)$. Therefore, $\frac{p}{100} = 0.2$, and so the value of p is 20.

Choice A is incorrect and may be the result of confusing the 12 percent decrease in area with the percent decrease in width. Choice B is incorrect because decreasing the width by 15 percent results in a 6.5 percent decrease in area, not a 12 percent decrease. Choice D is incorrect and may be the result of adding the percents given in the question (10 + 12).

QUESTION 28

Choice D is correct. For the present population to decrease by 10 percent, it must be multiplied by the factor 0.9. Since the engineer estimates that the population will decrease by 10 percent every 20 years, the present population, 50,000, must be multiplied by $(0.9)^n$, where n is the number of 20-year periods that will have elapsed t years from now. After t years, the number of 20-year periods that have elapsed is $\frac{t}{20}$. Therefore, $50{,}000(0.9)^{\frac{t}{20}}$ represents the engineer's estimate of the population of the city t years from now.

Choices A, B, and C are incorrect because each of these choices either confuses the percent decrease with the multiplicative factor that represents the percent decrease or mistakenly multiplies t by 20 to find the number of 20-year periods that will have elapsed in t years.

QUESTION 29

Choice A is correct. Let x be the number of left-handed female students and let y be the number of left-handed male students. Then the number of right-handed female students will be $5x$ and the number of right-handed male students will be $9y$. Since the total number of left-handed students is 18 and the total number of right-handed students is 122, the system of equations below must be satisfied.

$$\begin{cases} x + y = 18 \\ 5x + 9y = 122 \end{cases}$$

Solving this system gives $x = 10$ and $y = 8$. Thus, 50 of the 122 right-handed students are female. Therefore, the probability that a right-handed student selected at random is female is $\frac{50}{122}$, which to the nearest thousandth is 0.410.

Choices B, C, and D are incorrect and may be the result of incorrectly calculating the missing values in the table.

QUESTION 30

Choice A is correct. Subtracting the sides of $3y + c = 5y - 7$ from the corresponding sides of $3x + b = 5x - 7$ gives $(3x - 3y) + (b - c) = (5x - 5y) + (-7 - (-7))$. Since $b = c - \frac{1}{2}$, or $b - c = -\frac{1}{2}$, it follows that $(3x - 3y) + \left(-\frac{1}{2}\right) = (5x - 5y)$. Solving this equation for x in terms of y gives $x = y - \frac{1}{4}$. Therefore, x is y minus $\frac{1}{4}$.

Choices B, C, and D are incorrect and may be the result of making a computational error when solving the equations for x in terms of y.

QUESTION 31

The correct answer is either 4 or 5. Because each student ticket costs \$2 and each adult ticket costs \$3, the total amount, in dollars, that Chris spends on x student tickets and 1 adult ticket is $2(x) + 3(1)$. Because Chris spends at least \$11 but no more than \$14 on the tickets, one can write the compound inequality $2x + 3 \geq 11$ and $2x + 3 \leq 14$. Subtracting 3 from each side of both inequalities and then dividing each side of both inequalities by 2 yields $x \geq 4$ and $x \leq 5.5$. Thus, the value of x must be an integer that is both greater than or equal to 4 and less than or equal to 5.5. Therefore, $x = 4$ or $x = 5$. Either 4 or 5 may be gridded as the correct answer.

QUESTION 32

The correct answer is 58.6. The mean of a data set is determined by calculating the sum of the values and dividing by the number of values in the data set. The sum of the ages, in years, in the data set is 703, and the number of values in the data set is 12. Thus, the mean of the ages, in years, of the first 12 United States presidents at the beginning of their terms is $\frac{703}{12}$. The question asks for an answer rounded to the nearest tenth, so the decimal equivalent, rounded to the nearest tenth, is the correct answer. This rounded decimal equivalent is 58.6.

QUESTION 33

The correct answer is 9. To rewrite the difference $(-3x^2 + 5x - 2) - 2(x^2 - 2x - 1)$ in the form $ax^2 + bx + c$, the expression can be simplified by using the distributive property and combining like terms as follows:

$$(-3x^2 + 5x - 2) - (2x^2 - 4x - 2)$$

$$(-3x^2 - 2x^2) + (5x - (-4x)) + (-2 - (-2))$$

$$-5x^2 + 9x + 0$$

The coefficient of x is the value of b, which is 9.

Alternatively, since b is the coefficient of x in the difference $(-3x^2 + 5x - 2) - 2(x^2 - 2x - 1)$, one need only compute the x-term in the difference. The x-term is $5x - 2(-2x) = 5x + 4x = 9x$, so the value of b is 9.

QUESTION 34

The correct answer is $\frac{5}{8}$ or .625. A complete rotation around a point is 360° or 2π radians. Since the central angle AOB has measure $\frac{5\pi}{4}$ radians, it represents $\frac{\frac{5\pi}{4}}{2\pi} = \frac{5}{8}$ of a complete rotation around point O. Therefore, the sector formed by central angle AOB has area equal to $\frac{5}{8}$ the area of the entire circle. Either the fraction 5/8 or its decimal equivalent, .625, may be gridded as the correct answer.

QUESTION 35

The correct answer is 50. The mean of a data set is the sum of the values in the data set divided by the number of values in the data set. The mean of 75 is obtained by finding the sum of the first 10 ratings and dividing by 10. Thus, the sum of the first 10 ratings was 750. In order for the mean of the first 20 ratings to be at least 85, the sum of the first 20 ratings must be at least $(85)(20) = 1700$. Therefore, the sum of the next 10 ratings must be at least $1700 - 750 = 950$. The maximum rating is 100, so the maximum possible value of the sum of the 12th through 20th ratings is $9 \times 100 = 900$. Therefore, for the store to be able to have an average of at least 85 for the first 20 ratings, the least possible value for the 11th rating is $950 - 900 = 50$.

QUESTION 36

The correct answer is 750. The inequalities $y \leq -15x + 3000$ and $y \leq 5x$ can be graphed in the xy-plane. They are represented by the lower half-planes with the boundary lines $y = -15x + 3000$ and $y = 5x$, respectively. The solution set of the system of inequalities will be the intersection of these half-planes, including the boundary lines, and the solution (a, b) with the greatest possible value of b will be the point of intersection of the boundary lines. The intersection of boundary lines of these inequalities can be found by substituting $5x$ for y in the equation for the first line: $5x = -15x + 3000$, which has solution $x = 150$. Thus, the x-coordinate of the point of intersection is 150. Therefore, the y-coordinate of the point of intersection of the boundary lines is $5(150) = -15(150) + 3000 = 750$. This is the maximum possible value of b for a point (a, b) that is in the solution set of the system of inequalities.

QUESTION 37

The correct answer is 7. The average number of shoppers, N, in the checkout line at any time is $N = rt$, where r is the number of shoppers entering the checkout line per minute and T is the average number of minutes each shopper spends in the checkout line. Since 84 shoppers per hour make a purchase, 84 shoppers per hour enter the checkout line. This needs to be converted to the number of shoppers per minute. Since there are 60 minutes in one hour, the rate is $\frac{84 \text{ shoppers}}{60 \text{ minutes}} = 1.4$ shoppers per minute. Using the given formula with $r = 1.4$ and $t = 5$ yields $N = rt = (1.4)(5) = 7$. Therefore, the average number of shoppers, N, in the checkout line at any time during business hours is 7.

QUESTION 38

The correct answer is 60. The estimated average number of shoppers in the original store at any time is 45. In the new store, the manager estimates that an average of 90 shoppers per hour enter the store, which is equivalent to 1.5 shoppers per minute. The manager also estimates that each shopper stays in the store for an average of 12 minutes. Thus, by Little's law, there are, on average, $N = rt = (1.5)(12) = 18$ shoppers in the new store at any time. This is $\frac{45 - 18}{45} \times 100 = 60$ percent less than the average number of shoppers in the original store at any time.

The SAT®

Practice Test #4

Make time to take the practice test. It's one of the best ways to get ready for the SAT.

After you've taken the practice test, score it right away at **sat.org/scoring**.

Test begins on the next page.

Reading Test

65 MINUTES, 52 QUESTIONS

Turn to Section 1 of your answer sheet to answer the questions in this section.

DIRECTIONS

Each passage or pair of passages below is followed by a number of questions. After reading each passage or pair, choose the best answer to each question based on what is stated or implied in the passage or passages and in any accompanying graphics (such as a table or graph).

Questions 1-10 are based on the following passage.

This passage is adapted from MacDonald Harris, *The Balloonist*. ©2011 by The Estate of Donald Heiney. During the summer of 1897, the narrator of this story, a fictional Swedish scientist, has set out for the North Pole in a hydrogen-powered balloon.

My emotions are complicated and not readily verifiable. I feel a vast yearning that is simultaneously a pleasure and a pain. I am certain of the consummation of this yearning, but I don't know yet what form it will take, since I do not understand quite what it is that the yearning desires. For the first time there is borne in upon me the full truth of what I myself said to the doctor only an hour ago: that my motives in this undertaking are not entirely clear. For years, for a lifetime, the machinery of my destiny has worked in secret to prepare for this moment; its clockwork has moved exactly toward this time and place and no other. Rising slowly from the earth that bore me and gave me sustenance, I am carried helplessly toward an uninhabited and hostile, or at best indifferent, part of the earth, littered with the bones of explorers and the wrecks of ships, frozen supply caches, messages scrawled with chilled fingers and hidden in cairns that no eye will ever see. Nobody has succeeded in this thing, and many have died. Yet in freely willing this enterprise, in choosing this moment and no other when the south wind will carry me exactly northward at a velocity of eight knots, I have converted the machinery of my fate into the servant of my will. All this I understand, as I understand each detail of the technique by which this is carried out. What I don't understand is why I am so intent on going to this particular place. Who wants the North Pole! What good is it! Can you eat it? Will it carry you from Gothenburg to Malmö like a railway? The Danish ministers have declared from their pulpits that participation in polar expeditions is beneficial to the soul's eternal well-being, or so I read in a newspaper. It isn't clear how this doctrine is to be interpreted, except that the Pole is something difficult or impossible to attain which must nevertheless be sought for, because man is condemned to seek out and know everything whether or not the knowledge gives him pleasure. In short, it is the same unthinking lust for knowledge that drove our First Parents out of the garden.

And suppose you were to find it in spite of all, this wonderful place that everybody is so anxious to stand on! *What* would you find? Exactly nothing. A point precisely identical to all the others in a completely featureless wasteland stretching around it for hundreds of miles. It is an abstraction, a mathematical fiction. No one but a Swedish madman could take the slightest interest in it. Here I am. The wind is still from the south, bearing us steadily northward at the speed of a trotting dog. Behind us, perhaps forever, lie the Cities of Men with their

CONTINUE

teacups and their brass bedsteads. I am going forth of my own volition to join the ghosts of Bering and poor Franklin, of frozen De Long and his men. What I am on the brink of knowing, I now see, is not an ephemeral mathematical spot but myself. The doctor was right, even though I dislike him. Fundamentally I am a dangerous madman, and what I do is both a challenge to my egotism and a surrender to it.

1

Over the course of the passage, the narrator's attitude shifts from

A) fear about the expedition to excitement about it.
B) doubt about his abilities to confidence in them.
C) uncertainty of his motives to recognition of them.
D) disdain for the North Pole to appreciation of it.

2

Which choice provides the best evidence for the answer to the previous question?

A) Lines 10-12 ("For . . . moment")
B) Lines 21-25 ("Yet . . . will")
C) Lines 42-44 ("And . . . stand on")
D) Lines 56-57 ("What . . . myself")

3

As used in lines 1-2, "not readily verifiable" most nearly means

A) unable to be authenticated.
B) likely to be contradicted.
C) without empirical support.
D) not completely understood.

4

The sentence in lines 10-13 ("For years . . . other") mainly serves to

A) expose a side of the narrator that he prefers to keep hidden.
B) demonstrate that the narrator thinks in a methodical and scientific manner.
C) show that the narrator feels himself to be influenced by powerful and independent forces.
D) emphasize the length of time during which the narrator has prepared for his expedition.

5

The narrator indicates that many previous explorers seeking the North Pole have

A) perished in the attempt.
B) made surprising discoveries.
C) failed to determine its exact location.
D) had different motivations than his own.

6

Which choice provides the best evidence for the answer to the previous question?

A) Lines 20-21 ("Nobody . . . died")
B) Lines 25-27 ("All . . . out")
C) Lines 31-34 ("The . . . newspaper")
D) Lines 51-53 ("Behind . . . bedsteads")

7

Which choice best describes the narrator's view of his expedition to the North Pole?

A) Immoral but inevitable
B) Absurd but necessary
C) Socially beneficial but misunderstood
D) Scientifically important but hazardous

CONTINUE

8

The question the narrator asks in lines 30-31 ("Will it . . . railway") most nearly implies that

A) balloons will never replace other modes of transportation.

B) the North Pole is farther away than the cities usually reached by train.

C) people often travel from one city to another without considering the implications.

D) reaching the North Pole has no foreseeable benefit to humanity.

9

As used in line 49, "take the slightest interest in" most nearly means

A) accept responsibility for.

B) possess little regard for.

C) pay no attention to.

D) have curiosity about.

10

As used in line 50, "bearing" most nearly means

A) carrying.

B) affecting.

C) yielding.

D) enduring.

Questions 11-21 are based on the following passage and supplementary material.

This passage is adapted from Alan Ehrenhalt, *The Great Inversion and the Future of the American City*. ©2013 by Vintage. Ehrenhalt is an urbanologist—a scholar of cities and their development. Demographic inversion is a phenomenon that describes the rearrangement of living patterns throughout a metropolitan area.

We are not witnessing the abandonment of the suburbs, or a movement of millions of people back to the city all at once. The 2010 census certainly did not turn up evidence of a middle-class stampede to the nation's cities. The news was mixed: Some of the larger cities on the East Coast tended to gain population, albeit in small increments. Those in the Midwest, including Chicago, tended to lose substantial numbers. The cities that showed gains in overall population during the entire decade tended to be in the South and Southwest. But when it comes to measuring demographic inversion, raw census numbers are an ineffective blunt instrument. A closer look at the results shows that the most powerful demographic events of the past decade were the movement of African Americans out of central cities (180,000 of them in Chicago alone) and the settlement of immigrant groups in suburbs, often ones many miles distant from downtown. Central-city areas that gained affluent residents in the first part of the decade maintained that population in the recession years from 2007 to 2009. They also, according to a 2011 study by Brookings, suffered considerably less from increased unemployment than the suburbs did. Not many young professionals moved to new downtown condos in the recession years because few such residences were being built. But there is no reason to believe that the demographic trends prevailing prior to the construction bust will not resume once that bust is over. It is important to remember that demographic inversion is not a proxy for population growth; it can occur in cities that are growing, those whose numbers are flat, and even in those undergoing a modest decline in size.

America's major cities face enormous fiscal problems, many of them the result of public pension obligations they incurred in the more prosperous years of the past two decades. Some, Chicago

CONTINUE

prominent among them, simply are not producing enough revenue to support the level of public services to which most of the citizens have grown to feel entitled. How the cities are going to solve this problem, I do not know. What I do know is that if fiscal crisis were going to drive affluent professionals out of central cities, it would have done so by now. There is no evidence that it has.

The truth is that we are living at a moment in which the massive outward migration of the affluent that characterized the second half of the twentieth century is coming to an end. And we need to adjust our perceptions of cities, suburbs, and urban mobility as a result.

Much of our perspective on the process of metropolitan settlement dates, whether we realize it or not, from a paper written in 1925 by the University of Chicago sociologist Ernest W. Burgess. It was Burgess who defined four urban/suburban zones of settlement: a central business district; an area of manufacturing just beyond it; then a residential area inhabited by the industrial and immigrant working class; and finally an outer enclave of single-family dwellings.

Burgess was right about the urban America of 1925; he was right about the urban America of 1974. Virtually every city in the country had a downtown, where the commercial life of the metropolis was conducted; it had a factory district just beyond; it had districts of working-class residences just beyond that; and it had residential suburbs for the wealthy and the upper middle class at the far end of the continuum. As a family moved up the economic ladder, it also moved outward from crowded working-class districts to more spacious apartments and, eventually, to a suburban home. The suburbs of Burgess's time bore little resemblance to those at the end of the twentieth century, but the theory still essentially worked. People moved ahead in life by moving farther out.

But in the past decade, in quite a few places, this model has ceased to describe reality. There are still downtown commercial districts, but there are no factory districts lying next to them. There are scarcely any factories at all. These close-in parts of the city, whose few residents Burgess described as dwelling in "submerged regions of poverty, degradation and disease," are increasingly the preserve of the affluent who work in the commercial core. And just as crucially newcomers to America are not settling on the inside and accumulating the resources to move out; they are living in the suburbs from day one.

United States Population by Metropolitan Size/Status, 1980 – 2010

Chart 1

2010 Population Shares by Metro Size (%)

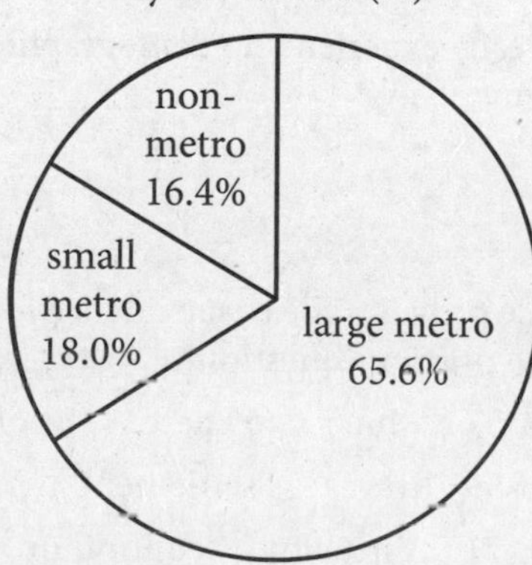

Chart 2

Growth Rates by Metro Size

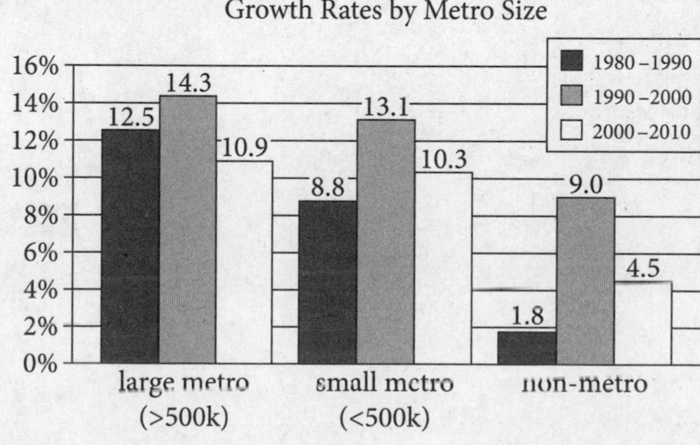

Adapted from William H. Frey, "Population Growth in Metro America since 1980: Putting the Volatile 2000s in Perspective." Published 2012 by Metropolitan Policy Program, Brookings Institution.

CONTINUE

11

Which choice best summarizes the first paragraph of the passage (lines 1-35)?

A) The 2010 census demonstrated a sizeable growth in the number of middle-class families moving into inner cities.

B) The 2010 census is not a reliable instrument for measuring population trends in American cities.

C) Population growth and demographic inversion are distinct phenomena, and demographic inversion is evident in many American cities.

D) Population growth in American cities has been increasing since roughly 2000, while suburban populations have decreased.

12

According to the passage, members of which group moved away from central-city areas in large numbers in the early 2000s?

A) The unemployed

B) Immigrants

C) Young professionals

D) African Americans

13

In line 34, "flat" is closest in meaning to

A) static.

B) deflated.

C) featureless.

D) obscure.

14

According to the passage, which choice best describes the current financial situation in many major American cities?

A) Expected tax increases due to demand for public works

B) Economic hardship due to promises made in past years

C) Greater overall prosperity due to an increased inner-city tax base

D) Insufficient revenues due to a decrease in manufacturing

15

Which choice provides the best evidence for the answer to the previous question?

A) Lines 36-39 ("America's . . . decades")

B) Lines 43-44 ("How . . . not know")

C) Lines 44-46 ("What . . . now")

D) Lines 48-51 ("The truth . . . end")

16

The passage implies that American cities in 1974

A) were witnessing the flight of minority populations to the suburbs.

B) had begun to lose their manufacturing sectors.

C) had a traditional four-zone structure.

D) were already experiencing demographic inversion.

17

Which choice provides the best evidence for the answer to the previous question?

A) Lines 54-57 ("Much . . . Ernest W. Burgess")

B) Lines 58-59 ("It was . . . settlement")

C) Lines 66-71 ("Virtually . . . continuum")

D) Lines 72-75 ("As . . . home")

CONTINUE

18

As used in line 68, "conducted" is closest in meaning to

A) carried out.

B) supervised.

C) regulated.

D) inhibited.

19

The author of the passage would most likely consider the information in chart 1 to be

A) excellent evidence for the arguments made in the passage.

B) possibly accurate but too crude to be truly informative.

C) compelling but lacking in historical information.

D) representative of a perspective with which the author disagrees.

20

According to chart 2, the years 2000–2010 were characterized by

A) less growth in metropolitan areas of all sizes than had taken place in the 1990s.

B) more growth in small metropolitan areas than in large metropolitan areas.

C) a significant decline in the population of small metropolitan areas compared to the 1980s.

D) roughly equal growth in large metropolitan areas and nonmetropolitan areas.

21

Chart 2 suggests which of the following about population change in the 1990s?

A) Large numbers of people moved from suburban areas to urban areas in the 1990s.

B) Growth rates fell in smaller metropolitan areas in the 1990s.

C) Large numbers of people moved from metropolitan areas to nonmetropolitan areas in the 1990s.

D) The US population as a whole grew more in the 1990s than in the 1980s.

Questions 22-31 are based on the following passage.

This passage is adapted from Emily Anthes, *Frankenstein's Cat.* ©2013 by Emily Anthes.

When scientists first learned how to edit the genomes of animals, they began to imagine all the ways they could use this new power. Creating brightly colored novelty pets was not a high priority. Instead, most researchers envisioned far more consequential applications, hoping to create genetically engineered animals that saved human lives. One enterprise is now delivering on this dream. Welcome to the world of "pharming," in which simple genetic tweaks turn animals into living pharmaceutical factories.

Many of the proteins that our cells crank out naturally make for good medicine. Our bodies' own enzymes, hormones, clotting factors, and antibodies are commonly used to treat cancer, diabetes, autoimmune diseases, and more. The trouble is that it's difficult and expensive to make these compounds on an industrial scale, and as a result, patients can face shortages of the medicines they need. Dairy animals, on the other hand, are expert protein producers, their udders swollen with milk. So the creation of the first transgenic animals—first mice, then other species—in the 1980s gave scientists an idea: What if they put the gene for a human antibody or enzyme into a cow, goat, or sheep? If they put the gene in just the right place, under the control of the right molecular switch, maybe they could engineer animals that produced healing human proteins in their milk. Then doctors could collect medicine by the bucketful.

Throughout the 1980s and '90s, studies provided proof of principle, as scientists created transgenic mice, sheep, goats, pigs, cattle, and rabbits that did in fact make therapeutic compounds in their milk. At first, this work was merely gee-whiz, scientific geekery, lab-bound thought experiments come true. That all changed with ATryn, a drug produced by the Massachusetts firm GTC Biotherapeutics. ATryn is antithrombin, an anticoagulant that can be used to prevent life-threatening blood clots. The compound, made by our liver cells, plays a key role in keeping our bodies clot-free. It acts as a molecular bouncer, sidling up to clot-forming compounds and escorting them out of the bloodstream. But as many as 1 in 2,000 Americans are born with a genetic mutation that prevents them from making antithrombin. These patients are prone to clots, especially in their legs and lungs, and they are at elevated risk of suffering from fatal complications during surgery and childbirth. Supplemental antithrombin can reduce this risk, and GTC decided to try to manufacture the compound using genetically engineered goats.

To create its special herd of goats, GTC used microinjection, the same technique that produced GloFish and AquAdvantage salmon. The company's scientists took the gene for human antithrombin and injected it directly into fertilized goat eggs. Then they implanted the eggs in the wombs of female goats. When the kids were born, some of them proved to be transgenic, the human gene nestled safely in their cells. The researchers paired the antithrombin gene with a promoter (which is a sequence of DNA that controls gene activity) that is normally active in the goat's mammary glands during milk production. When the transgenic females lactated, the promoter turned the transgene on and the goats' udders filled with milk containing antithrombin. All that was left to do was to collect the milk, and extract and purify the protein. *Et voilà*—human medicine! And, for GTC, liquid gold. ATryn hit the market in 2006, becoming the world's first transgenic animal drug. Over the course of a year, the "milking parlors" on GTC's 300-acre farm in Massachusetts can collect more than a kilogram of medicine from a single animal.

22

The primary purpose of the passage is to

A) present the background of a medical breakthrough.

B) evaluate the research that led to a scientific discovery.

C) summarize the findings of a long-term research project.

D) explain the development of a branch of scientific study.

CONTINUE

23

The author's attitude toward pharming is best described as one of

A) apprehension.
B) ambivalence.
C) appreciation.
D) astonishment.

24

As used in line 20, "expert" most nearly means

A) knowledgeable.
B) professional.
C) capable.
D) trained.

25

What does the author suggest about the transgenic studies done in the 1980s and 1990s?

A) They were limited by the expensive nature of animal research.
B) They were not expected to yield products ready for human use.
C) They were completed when an anticoagulant compound was identified.
D) They focused only on the molecular properties of cows, goats, and sheep.

26

Which choice provides the best evidence for the answer to the previous question?

A) Lines 16-19 ("The trouble . . . need")
B) Lines 25-29 ("If they . . . milk")
C) Lines 35-36 ("At first . . . true")
D) Lines 37-40 ("That all . . . clots")

27

According to the passage, which of the following is true of antithrombin?

A) It reduces compounds that lead to blood clots.
B) It stems from a genetic mutation that is rare in humans.
C) It is a sequence of DNA known as a promoter.
D) It occurs naturally in goats' mammary glands.

28

Which choice provides the best evidence for the answer to the previous question?

A) Lines 12-16 ("Many . . . more")
B) Lines 42-44 ("It acts . . . bloodstream")
C) Lines 44-46 ("But as . . . antithrombin")
D) Lines 62-65 ("The researchers . . . production")

29

Which of the following does the author suggest about the "female goats" mentioned in line 59?

A) They secreted antithrombin in their milk after giving birth.
B) Some of their kids were not born with the antithrombin gene.
C) They were the first animals to receive microinjections.
D) Their cells already contained genes usually found in humans.

30

The most likely purpose of the parenthetical information in lines 63-64 is to

A) illustrate an abstract concept.
B) describe a new hypothesis.
C) clarity a claim.
D) define a term.

31

The phrase "liquid gold" (line 71) most directly suggests that

A) GTC has invested a great deal of money in the microinjection technique.

B) GTC's milking parlors have significantly increased milk production.

C) transgenic goats will soon be a valuable asset for dairy farmers.

D) ATryn has proved to be a financially beneficial product for GTC.

Questions 32-41 are based on the following passages.

Passage 1 is adapted from Edmund Burke, *Reflections on the Revolution in France*. Originally published in 1790. Passage 2 is adapted from Thomas Paine, *Rights of Man*. Originally published in 1791.

Passage 1

To avoid . . . the evils of inconstancy and versatility, ten thousand times worse than those of obstinacy and the blindest prejudice, we have consecrated the state, that no man should approach to look into its defects or corruptions but with due caution; that he should never dream of beginning its reformation by its subversion; that he should approach to the faults of the state as to the wounds of a father, with pious awe and trembling solicitude. By this wise prejudice we are taught to look with horror on those children of their country who are prompt rashly to hack that aged parent in pieces, and put him into the kettle of magicians, in hopes that by their poisonous weeds, and wild incantations, they may regenerate the paternal constitution, and renovate their father's life.

Society is indeed a contract. Subordinate contracts for objects of mere occasional interest may be dissolved at pleasure—but the state ought not to be considered as nothing better than a partnership agreement in a trade of pepper and coffee, calico or tobacco, or some other such low concern, to be taken up for a little temporary interest, and to be dissolved by the fancy of the parties. It is to be looked on with other reverence; because it is not a partnership in things subservient only to the gross animal existence of a temporary and perishable nature. It is a partnership in all science; a partnership in all art; a partnership in every virtue, and in all perfection. As the ends of such a partnership cannot be obtained in many generations, it becomes a partnership not only between those who are living, but between those who are living, those who are dead, and those who are to be born. . . . The municipal corporations of that universal kingdom are not morally at liberty at their pleasure, and on their speculations of a contingent improvement, wholly to separate and tear asunder the bands of their subordinate community, and to dissolve it into an unsocial, uncivil, unconnected chaos of elementary principles.

CONTINUE

Passage 2

Every age and generation must be as free to act for itself, *in all cases*, as the ages and generations which preceded it. The vanity and presumption of governing beyond the grave, is the most ridiculous and insolent of all tyrannies.

Man has no property in man; neither has any generation a property in the generations which are to follow. The Parliament or the people of 1688, or of any other period, had no more right to dispose of the people of the present day, or to bind or to control them in any shape whatever, than the parliament or the people of the present day have to dispose of, bind, or control those who are to live a hundred or a thousand years hence.

Every generation is, and must be, competent to all the purposes which its occasions require. It is the living, and not the dead, that are to be accommodated. When man ceases to be, his power and his wants cease with him; and having no longer any participation in the concerns of this world, he has no longer any authority in directing who shall be its governors, or how its government shall be organized, or how administered. . . .

Those who have quitted the world, and those who are not yet arrived at it, are as remote from each other, as the utmost stretch of mortal imagination can conceive. What possible obligation, then, can exist between them; what rule or principle can be laid down, that two nonentities, the one out of existence, and the other not in, and who never can meet in this world, that the one should control the other to the end of time? . . .

The circumstances of the world are continually changing, and the opinions of men change also; and as government is for the living, and not for the dead, it is the living only that has any right in it. That which may be thought right and found convenient in one age, may be thought wrong and found inconvenient in another. In such cases, who is to decide, the living, or the dead?

32

In Passage 1, Burke indicates that a contract between a person and society differs from other contracts mainly in its

A) brevity and prominence.

B) complexity and rigidity.

C) precision and usefulness.

D) seriousness and permanence.

33

As used in line 4, "state" most nearly refers to a

A) style of living.

B) position in life.

C) temporary condition.

D) political entity.

34

As used in line 22, "low" most nearly means

A) petty.

B) weak.

C) inadequate.

D) depleted.

35

It can most reasonably be inferred from Passage 2 that Paine views historical precedents as

A) generally helpful to those who want to change society.

B) surprisingly difficult for many people to comprehend.

C) frequently responsible for human progress.

D) largely irrelevant to current political decisions.

CONTINUE

36

How would Paine most likely respond to Burke's statement in lines 30-34, Passage 1 ("As the . . . born")?

A) He would assert that the notion of a partnership across generations is less plausible to people of his era than it was to people in the past.

B) He would argue that there are no politically meaningful links between the dead, the living, and the unborn.

C) He would question the possibility that significant changes to a political system could be accomplished within a single generation.

D) He would point out that we cannot know what judgments the dead would make about contemporary issues.

37

Which choice provides the best evidence for the answer to the previous question?

A) Lines 41-43 ("Every . . . it")

B) Lines 43-45 ("The vanity . . . tyrannies")

C) Lines 56-58 ("It is . . . accommodated")

D) Lines 67-72 ("What . . . time")

38

Which choice best describes how Burke would most likely have reacted to Paine's remarks in the final paragraph of Passage 2?

A) With approval, because adapting to new events may enhance existing partnerships.

B) With resignation, because changing circumstances are an inevitable aspect of life.

C) With skepticism, because Paine does not substantiate his claim with examples of governments changed for the better.

D) With disapproval, because changing conditions are insufficient justification for changing the form of government.

39

Which choice provides the best evidence for the answer to the previous question?

A) Lines 1-4 ("To avoid . . . state")

B) Lines 7-9 ("he should . . . solicitude")

C) Lines 27-29 ("It is . . . perfection")

D) Lines 34-38 ("The municipal . . . community")

40

Which choice best states the relationship between the two passages?

A) Passage 2 challenges the primary argument of Passage 1.

B) Passage 2 advocates an alternative approach to a problem discussed in Passage 1.

C) Passage 2 provides further evidence to support an idea introduced in Passage 1.

D) Passage 2 exemplifies an attitude promoted in Passage 1.

41

The main purpose of both passages is to

A) suggest a way to resolve a particular political struggle.

B) discuss the relationship between people and their government.

C) evaluate the consequences of rapid political change.

D) describe the duties that governments have to their citizens.

CONTINUE

Questions 42-52 are based on the following passage and supplementary material.

This passage is adapted from Carolyn Gramling, "Source of Mysterious Medieval Eruption Identified." ©2013 by American Association for the Advancement of Science.

About 750 years ago, a powerful volcano erupted somewhere on Earth, kicking off a centuries-long cold snap known as the Little Ice Age. Identifying the volcano responsible has been tricky.

That a powerful volcano erupted somewhere in the world, sometime in the Middle Ages, is written in polar ice cores in the form of layers of sulfate deposits and tiny shards of volcanic glass. These cores suggest that the amount of sulfur the mystery volcano sent into the stratosphere put it firmly among the ranks of the strongest climate-perturbing eruptions of the current geological epoch, the Holocene, a period that stretches from 10,000 years ago to the present. A haze of stratospheric sulfur cools the climate by reflecting solar energy back into space.

In 2012, a team of scientists led by geochemist Gifford Miller strengthened the link between the mystery eruption and the onset of the Little Ice Age by using radiocarbon dating of dead plant material from beneath the ice caps on Baffin Island and Iceland, as well as ice and sediment core data, to determine that the cold summers and ice growth began abruptly between 1275 and 1300 C.E. (and became intensified between 1430 and 1455 C.E.). Such a sudden onset pointed to a huge volcanic eruption injecting sulfur into the stratosphere and starting the cooling. Subsequent, unusually large and frequent eruptions of other volcanoes, as well as sea-ice/ocean feedbacks persisting long after the aerosols have been removed from the atmosphere, may have prolonged the cooling through the 1700s.

Volcanologist Franck Lavigne and colleagues now think they've identified the volcano in question: Indonesia's Samalas. One line of evidence, they note, is historical records. According to Babad Lombok, records of the island written on palm leaves in Old Javanese, Samalas erupted catastrophically before the end of the 13th century, devastating surrounding villages—including Lombok's capital at the time, Pamatan—with ash and fast-moving sweeps of hot rock and gas called pyroclastic flows.

The researchers then began to reconstruct the formation of the large, 800-meter-deep caldera [a basin-shaped volcanic crater] that now sits atop the volcano. They examined 130 outcrops on the flanks of the volcano, exposing sequences of pumice—ash hardened into rock—and other pyroclastic material. The volume of ash deposited, and the estimated height of the eruption plume (43 kilometers above sea level) put the eruption's magnitude at a minimum of 7 on the volcanic explosivity index (which has a scale of 1 to 8)—making it one of the largest known in the Holocene.

The team also performed radiocarbon analyses on carbonized tree trunks and branches buried within the pyroclastic deposits to confirm the date of the eruption; it could not, they concluded, have happened before 1257 C.E., and certainly happened in the 13th century.

It's not a total surprise that an Indonesian volcano might be the source of the eruption, Miller says. "An equatorial eruption is more consistent with the apparent climate impacts." And, he adds, with sulfate appearing in both polar ice caps—Arctic and Antarctic—there is "a strong consensus" that this also supports an equatorial source.

Another possible candidate—both in terms of timing and geographical location—is Ecuador's Quilotoa, estimated to have last erupted between 1147 and 1320 C.E. But when Lavigne's team examined shards of volcanic glass from this volcano, they found that they didn't match the chemical composition of the glass found in polar ice cores, whereas the Samalas glass is a much closer match. That, they suggest, further strengthens the case that Samalas was responsible for the medieval "year without summer" in 1258 C.E.

Estimated Temperature in Central England
1000 CE to 2000 CE

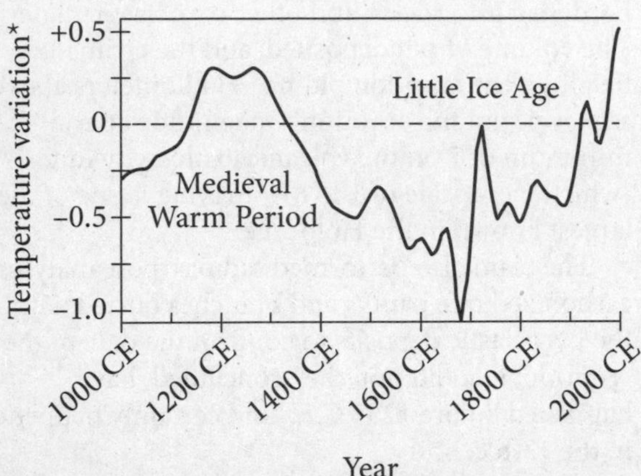

*Variation from the 1961-1990 average temperature, in °C, represented at 0.

Adapted from John P. Rafferty, "Little Ice Age." Originally published in 2011. ©2014 by Encyclopedia Britannica, Inc.

42

The main purpose of the passage is to

A) describe periods in Earth's recent geologic history.

B) explain the methods scientists use in radiocarbon analysis.

C) describe evidence linking the volcano Samalas to the Little Ice Age.

D) explain how volcanic glass forms during volcanic eruptions.

43

Over the course of the passage, the focus shifts from

A) a criticism of a scientific model to a new theory.

B) a description of a recorded event to its likely cause.

C) the use of ice core samples to a new method of measuring sulfates.

D) the use of radiocarbon dating to an examination of volcanic glass.

44

Which choice provides the best evidence for the answer to the previous question?

A) Lines 17-25 ("In 2012 . . . 1455 C.E.")

B) Lines 43-46 ("The researchers . . . atop the volcano")

C) Lines 46-48 ("They examined . . . material")

D) Lines 55-60 ("The team . . . 13th century")

45

The author uses the phrase "is written in" (line 6) most likely to

A) demonstrate the concept of the hands-on nature of the work done by scientists.

B) highlight the fact that scientists often write about their discoveries.

C) underscore the sense of importance that scientists have regarding their work.

D) reinforce the idea that the evidence is there and can be interpreted by scientists.

46

Where does the author indicate the medieval volcanic eruption most probably was located?

A) Near the equator, in Indonesia

B) In the Arctic region

C) In the Antarctic region

D) Near the equator, in Ecuador

47

Which choice provides the best evidence for the answer to the previous question?

A) Lines 1-3 ("About 750 . . . Ice Age")

B) Lines 26-28 ("Such a . . . the cooling")

C) Lines 49-54 ("The volume . . . the Holocene")

D) Lines 61-64 ("It's not . . . climate impacts")

CONTINUE

48

As used in line 68, the phrase “Another possible candidate” implies that

A) powerful volcanic eruptions occur frequently.

B) the effects of volcanic eruptions can last for centuries.

C) scientists know of other volcanoes that erupted during the Middle Ages.

D) other volcanoes have calderas that are very large.

49

Which choice best supports the claim that Quilotoa was not responsible for the Little Ice Age?

A) Lines 3-4 (“Identifying . . . tricky”)

B) Lines 26-28 (“Such a . . . cooling”)

C) Lines 43-46 (“The researchers . . . atop the volcano”)

D) Lines 71-75 (“But . . . closer match”)

50

According to the data in the figure, the greatest below-average temperature variation occurred around what year?

A) 1200 CE

B) 1375 CE

C) 1675 CE

D) 1750 CE

51

The passage and the figure are in agreement that the onset of the Little Ice Age began

A) around 1150 CE.

B) just before 1300 CE.

C) just before 1500 CE.

D) around 1650 CE.

52

What statement is best supported by the data presented in the figure?

A) The greatest cooling during the Little Ice Age occurred hundreds of years after the temperature peaks of the Medieval Warm Period.

B) The sharp decline in temperature supports the hypothesis of an equatorial volcanic eruption in the Middle Ages.

C) Pyroclastic flows from volcanic eruptions continued for hundreds of years after the eruptions had ended.

D) Radiocarbon analysis is the best tool scientists have to determine the temperature variations after volcanic eruptions.

STOP

If you finish before time is called, you may check your work on this section only. Do not turn to any other section.

Writing and Language Test

35 MINUTES, 44 QUESTIONS

Turn to Section 2 of your answer sheet to answer the questions in this section.

DIRECTIONS

Each passage below is accompanied by a number of questions. For some questions, you will consider how the passage might be revised to improve the expression of ideas. For other questions, you will consider how the passage might be edited to correct errors in sentence structure, usage, or punctuation. A passage or a question may be accompanied by one or more graphics (such as a table or graph) that you will consider as you make revising and editing decisions.

Some questions will direct you to an underlined portion of a passage. Other questions will direct you to a location in a passage or ask you to think about the passage as a whole.

After reading each passage, choose the answer to each question that most effectively improves the quality of writing in the passage or that makes the passage conform to the conventions of standard written English. Many questions include a "NO CHANGE" option. Choose that option if you think the best choice is to leave the relevant portion of the passage as it is.

Questions 1-11 are based on the following passage.

Ghost Mural

In 1932 the well-known Mexican muralist David Alfaro Siqueiros was commissioned to paint a mural on the second-story exterior wall of a historic building in downtown Los Angeles. Siqueiros was asked to celebrate tropical America in his work, [1] he accordingly titled it "América Tropical." He painted the mural's first two sections, featuring images of a tropical rainforest and a Maya pyramid, during the day. [2] Also, to avoid

1

A) NO CHANGE
B) which he accordingly titled
C) accordingly he titled it
D) it was titled accordingly

2

A) NO CHANGE
B) However,
C) Although,
D) Moreover,

CONTINUE

scrutiny, Siqueiros painted the final section of the mural, the **3** centerpiece at night.

4 The reason for Siqueiros's secrecy became clear when the mural was **5** confided. The centerpiece of the work was dominated by images of native people being oppressed and **6** including an eagle symbolizing the United States. Siqueiros's political message did not please the wealthy citizens who had commissioned his work. They eventually ordered the mural to be literally whitewashed, or painted over with white paint.

However, by the 1970s, the white paint had begun to fade, and the bright colors of the mural were beginning to show through. At the same time, a social and civil rights movement for Mexican Americans was working to raise awareness of Mexican American cultural identity. Artists associated with **7** this began to rediscover and promote the work of the Mexican muralists, particularly Siqueiros. To them, "América Tropical" was an example of how art in public spaces could be used to celebrate Mexican American heritage while at the same time making a political statement. Inspired by Siqueiros and the other muralists, this new generation of artists strove to emulate the old mural masters.

3

A) NO CHANGE
B) centerpiece,
C) centerpiece;
D) centerpiece—

4

Which choice best connects the sentence with the previous paragraph?

A) NO CHANGE
B) All three sections of the mural were on display
C) The community turned out in large numbers
D) Siqueiros was informed of people's reactions

5

A) NO CHANGE
B) promulgated.
C) imparted.
D) unveiled.

6

A) NO CHANGE
B) included
C) includes
D) had included

7

A) NO CHANGE
B) it
C) them
D) this movement

8 The result was an explosion of mural painting that spread throughout California and the southwestern United States in the 1970s. It was the Chicano mural movement. Hundreds of large, colorful new murals depicting elements of Mexican American life and history appeared during this period, some in designated cultural locations but many more in abandoned lots, on unused buildings, or 9 painted on infrastructure such as highways and bridges. Many of these murals can still be seen today, although some have not been well maintained.

8

Which choice most effectively combines the underlined sentences?

A) The result was an explosion, the Chicano mural movement, of mural painting that spread throughout California and the southwestern United States in the 1970s.

B) The result was the Chicano mural movement, an explosion of mural painting that spread throughout California and the southwestern United States in the 1970s.

C) The explosion of mural painting that spread throughout California and the southwestern United States in the 1970s was the resulting Chicano mural movement.

D) An explosion of mural painting resulted and it spread throughout California and the southwestern United States in the 1970s; it was the Chicano mural movement.

9

A) NO CHANGE

B) they were painted on

C) on

D) DELETE the underlined portion.

CONTINUE

Fortunately, a new group of artists has discovered the murals, and efforts are underway to clean, restore, and repaint them. Once again, Siqueiros's "América Tropical" is **10** leading the way. After a lengthy and complex restoration process, this powerful work is now a tourist attraction, complete with a visitor center and a rooftop viewing platform. **11** Advocates hope that Siqueiros's mural will once more serve as an inspiration, this time inspiring viewers to save and restore an important cultural and artistic legacy.

10

Which choice most effectively sets up the information that follows?

A) NO CHANGE
B) being cleaned and restored.
C) at risk of destruction.
D) awaiting its moment of appreciation.

11

At this point, the writer is considering adding the following sentence.

> When it was painted in 1932, Siqueiros's mural was considered offensive, but now it is acclaimed.

Should the writer make this addition here?

A) Yes, because it provides historical context for the changes discussed in the passage.
B) Yes, because it provides a useful reminder of how people once viewed Siqueiros's work.
C) No, because it unnecessarily repeats information from earlier in the passage.
D) No, because it makes a claim about Siqueiros's work that is not supported by the passage.

CONTINUE

Questions 12-22 are based on the following passage.

The Hype of Healthier Organic Food

Some people buy organic food because they believe organically grown crops are more nutritious and safer for consumption than [12] the people who purchase their conventionally grown counterparts, which are usually produced with pesticides and synthetic fertilizers. In the name of health, [13] spending $1.60 for every dollar they would have spent on food that is [14] grown in a manner that is considered conventional. Scientific evidence, [15] therefore, suggests that consumers do not reap significant benefits, in terms of either nutritional value or safety, from organic food.

12

A) NO CHANGE
B) the purchase of
C) purchasing
D) DELETE the underlined portion.

13

A) NO CHANGE
B) these consumers spend
C) having spent
D) to spend

14

A) NO CHANGE
B) grown with conventional methods, using pesticides and synthetic fertilizers.
C) conventionally and therefore not organically grown.
D) conventionally grown.

15

A) NO CHANGE
B) furthermore,
C) however,
D) subsequently,

CONTINUE

Although advocates of organic food **16** preserve that organic produce is healthier than conventionally grown produce because it has more vitamins and minerals, this assertion is not supported by scientific research. **17** For instance, one review published in *The American Journal of Clinical Nutrition* provided analysis of the results of comparative studies conducted over a span of 50 years; researchers consistently found no evidence that organic crops are more nutritious than conventionally grown ones in terms of their vitamin and mineral content. **18** Similarly, Stanford University researchers who examined almost 250 studies comparing the nutritional content of different kinds of organic foods with that of their nonorganic counterparts found very little difference between the two.

16

A) NO CHANGE
B) carry on
C) maintain
D) sustain

17

A) NO CHANGE
B) However,
C) In addition,
D) Likewise,

18

At this point, the writer is considering adding the following sentence.

> The United States Department of Agriculture (USDA) reports that organic agricultural products are now available in approximately 20,000 markets specializing in natural foods.

Should the writer make this addition here?

A) Yes, because it adds a relevant research finding from a government agency
B) Yes, because it supports the passage's argument that organic food is less nutritious than conventionally grown food.
C) No, because it is not relevant to the paragraph's discussion of scientific evidence.
D) No, because it introduces a term that has not been defined in the passage.

CONTINUE

Evidence also undermines the claim that organic food is safer to eat. While researchers have found lower levels of pesticide residue in organic produce than in nonorganic produce, the pesticide residue detected in conventional produce falls within acceptable safety limits. According to such organizations as the US Environmental Protection Agency, the minute amounts of residue falling within such limits **19** have no negative impact on human health. **20**

19

A) NO CHANGE
B) is having
C) has had
D) has

20

At this point, the writer wants to further reinforce the paragraph's claim about the safety of nonorganic food. Which choice most effectively accomplishes this goal?

A) To be labeled organic, a product must meet certain standards determined and monitored by the US Department of Agriculture.
B) Organic food, however, is regulated to eliminate artificial ingredients that include certain types of preservatives, sweeteners, colorings, and flavors.
C) Moreover, consumers who are concerned about ingesting pesticide residue can eliminate much of it by simply washing or peeling produce before eating it.
D) In fact, the Environmental Protection Agency estimates that about one-fifth of the pesticides used worldwide are applied to crops in the United States.

CONTINUE

Based on scientific evidence, organic food offers neither significant nutritional nor safety benefits for consumers. Proponents of organic food, of course, are quick to add that **21** their are numerous other reasons to buy organic **22** food, such as, a desire to protect the environment from potentially damaging pesticides or a preference for the taste of organically grown foods. Research regarding these issues is less conclusive than the findings regarding nutritional content and pesticide residue safety limits. What is clear, though, is this: if a consumer's goal is to buy the healthiest and safest food to eat, the increased cost of organic food is a waste of money.

21

A) NO CHANGE
B) there are
C) there is
D) their is

22

A) NO CHANGE
B) food such as:
C) food such as,
D) food, such as

Questions 23-33 are based on the following passage and supplementary material.

You Are Where You Say

Research on regional variations in English-language use has not only yielded answers to such **23** life-altering questions as how people in different parts of the United States refer to carbonated beverages ("soda"? "pop"? "coke"?) **24** it also illustrates how technology can change the very nature of research. While traditional, human-intensive data collection **25** has all but disappeared in language studies, the explosion of social media has opened new avenues for investigation.

[1] Perhaps the epitome of traditional methodology is the *Dictionary of American Regional English*, colloquially known as *DARE*. [2] Its fifth and final alphabetical volume—ending with "zydeco"—released in 2012, the dictionary represents decades of arduous work. [3] Over a six-year period from 1965 to 1970, university graduate students conducted interviews in more than a thousand communities across the nation. [4] Their goal was to determine what names people used for such everyday objects and concepts as a submarine sandwich

23

The writer wants to convey an attitude of genuine interest and to avoid the appearance of mockery. Which choice best accomplishes this goal?

A) NO CHANGE
B) galvanizing
C) intriguing
D) weird

24

A) NO CHANGE
B) and also illustrates
C) but also illustrates
D) illustrating

25

Which choice most effectively sets up the contrast in the sentence and is consistent with the information in the rest of the passage?

A) NO CHANGE
B) still has an important place
C) remains the only option
D) yields questionable results

CONTINUE

(a "hero" in New York City but a "dagwood" in many parts of Minnesota, Iowa, and Colorado) and a heavy rainstorm (variously a "gully washer," "pour-down," or "stump mover"). [5] The work that dictionary founder Frederic G. Cassidy had expected to be finished by 1976 was not, in fact, completed in his lifetime. [6] The wait did not dampen enthusiasm among **26** scholars. Scholars consider the work a signal achievement in linguistics. **27**

Not all research into regional English varieties **28** requires such time, effort, and resources, however. Today's researchers have found that the veritable army of trained volunteers traveling the country conducting face-to-face interviews can sometimes be **29** replaced by another army the vast array of individuals volunteering details about their lives—and, inadvertently, their language—through social media. Brice Russ of Ohio State University, for example, has employed software to sort through postings on one social media **30** cite in search of particular words and phrases of interest as well as the location from which users are posting. From these data,

26

A) NO CHANGE
B) scholars, and these scholars
C) scholars, but scholars
D) scholars, who

27

To improve the cohesion and flow of this paragraph, the writer wants to add the following sentence.

> Data gathering proved to be the quick part of the project.

The sentence would most logically be placed after

A) sentence 2.
B) sentence 3.
C) sentence 4.
D) sentence 5.

28

A) NO CHANGE
B) are requiring
C) have required
D) require

29

A) NO CHANGE
B) replaced—by another army,
C) replaced by another army;
D) replaced by another army:

30

A) NO CHANGE
B) site in search of
C) sight in search for
D) cite in search for

he was able, among other things, to confirm regional variations in people's terms for soft drinks. As the map shows, "soda" is commonly heard in the middle and western portions of the United States; "pop" is frequently used in many southern states; and "coke" is predominant in the northeastern and southwest regions but used elsewhere as well. **31** As interesting as Russ's findings are, though, **32** <u>they're true value lies in their</u> reminder that the Internet is not merely a sophisticated tool for collecting data but is also **33** <u>itself a rich source of data.</u>

Soft Drink Descriptions by State
Highest Percentage Reported

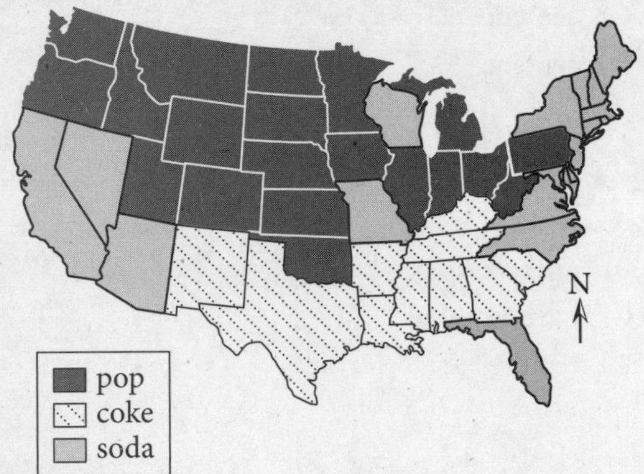

Adapted from Jennifer M. Smith, Department of Geography, The Pennsylvania State University, with data from www.popvssoda.com

31

The writer wants the information in the passage to correspond as closely as possible with the information in the map. Given that goal and assuming that the rest of the previous sentence would remain unchanged, in which sequence should the three terms for soft drinks be discussed?

A) NO CHANGE
B) "pop," "soda," "coke"
C) "pop," "coke," "soda"
D) "soda," "coke," "pop"

32

A) NO CHANGE
B) their true value lies in their
C) there true value lies in they're
D) their true value lies in there

33

Which choice most effectively concludes the sentence and paragraph?

A) NO CHANGE
B) where we can learn what terms people use to refer to soft drinks.
C) a useful way to stay connected to friends, family, and colleagues.
D) helpful to researchers.

CONTINUE

Questions 34-44 are based on the following passage.

Creating Worlds: A Career in Game Design

If you love video games and have thought about how the games you play might be changed or improved, or if you've imagined creating a video game of your own, you might want to consider a career as a video game designer. There [34] were a number of steps you can take to determine whether game design is the right field for you and, if it is, to prepare yourself for such a career.

Before making the choice, you should have some sense of what a video game designer does. Every video game, whether for a console, computer, or mobile device, starts with a concept that originates in the mind of a designer. The designer envisions the game's fundamental [35] elements: the settings, characters, and plots that make each game unique, and is thus a primary creative force behind a video game.

Conceptualizing a game is only the beginning of a video game designer's [36] job, however, no matter how good a concept is, it will never be translated into a video game unless it is communicated effectively to all the other members of the video game development team. [37] A designer must generate extensive documentation and

34

A) NO CHANGE
B) has been
C) are
D) was

35

A) NO CHANGE
B) elements: the settings, characters, and plots that make each game unique—
C) elements—the settings, characters, and plots that make each game unique—
D) elements; the settings, characters, and plots that make each game unique;

36

A) NO CHANGE
B) job, however. No
C) job—however, no
D) job however no

37

At this point, the writer is considering adding the following sentence.

> Successful communication is essential if a designer's idea is to become a reality.

Should the writer make this addition here?

A) Yes, because it supports the conclusion drawn in the following sentence.
B) Yes, because it illustrates a general principle discussed in the paragraph.
C) No, because it distracts from the focus of the paragraph by introducing irrelevant material.
D) No, because it merely reformulates the thought expressed in the preceding sentence.

CONTINUE

38 explain his or her ideas clearly in order to ensure that the programmers, artists, and others on the team all share the same vision. 39 Likewise, anyone considering a career as a video game designer must be 40 skilled writers and speakers. In addition, because video game development is a collaborative effort and because the development of any one game may take months or even years, a designer must be an effective team player as well as detail oriented.

[1] A basic understanding of computer programming is essential. [2] In fact, many designers 41 initially begin their pursuits as programmers. [3] Consider taking some general computer science courses as well as courses in artificial intelligence and graphics in order to increase your understanding of the technical challenges involved in developing a video game. [4] Courses in psychology and human behavior may help you develop 42 emphatic collaboration skills, while courses in the humanities, such as in literature and film, should give you the background necessary to develop effective narrative structures. [5] A

38

Which choice results in a sentence that best supports the point developed in this paragraph?

A) NO CHANGE
B) possess a vivid imagination
C) assess his or her motivations carefully
D) learn to accept constructive criticism

39

A) NO CHANGE
B) Nevertheless,
C) Consequently,
D) However,

40

A) NO CHANGE
B) a skilled writer and speaker.
C) skilled both as writers and speakers.
D) both skilled writers and speakers.

41

A) NO CHANGE
B) start to begin their work
C) initiate their progression
D) begin their careers

42

A) NO CHANGE
B) paramount
C) eminent
D) important

CONTINUE

designer also needs careful educational preparation. [6] Finally, because a designer should understand the business aspects of the video game industry, such as budgeting and marketing, you may want to consider taking some business courses. [7] Although demanding and deadline driven, **43** video game design can be a lucrative and rewarding field for people who love gaming and have prepared themselves with the necessary skills and knowledge. **44**

43

A) NO CHANGE
B) the choice of video game design
C) you should choose video game design because it
D) choosing to design video games

44

To make this paragraph most logical, sentence 5 should be

A) placed where it is now.
B) placed before sentence 1.
C) placed after sentence 3.
D) DELETED from the paragraph.

STOP

If you finish before time is called, you may check your work on this section only. Do not turn to any other section.

Math Test – No Calculator

25 MINUTES, 20 QUESTIONS

Turn to Section 3 of your answer sheet to answer the questions in this section.

DIRECTIONS

For questions 1-15, solve each problem, choose the best answer from the choices provided, and fill in the corresponding circle on your answer sheet. **For questions 16-20**, solve the problem and enter your answer in the grid on the answer sheet. Please refer to the directions before question 16 on how to enter your answers in the grid. You may use any available space in your test booklet for scratch work.

NOTES

1. The use of a calculator **is not permitted**.
2. All variables and expressions used represent real numbers unless otherwise indicated.
3. Figures provided in this test are drawn to scale unless otherwise indicated.
4. All figures lie in a plane unless otherwise indicated.
5. Unless otherwise indicated, the domain of a given function *f* is the set of all real numbers *x* for which *f*(*x*) is a real number.

REFERENCE

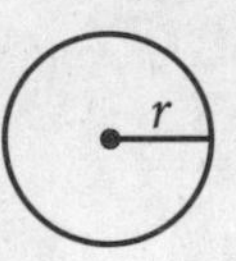

$A = \pi r^2$
$C = 2\pi r$

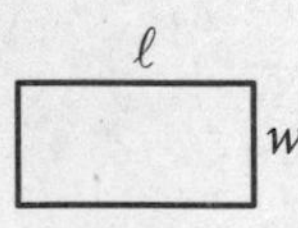

$A = \ell w$

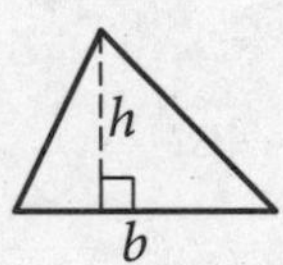

$A = \frac{1}{2}bh$

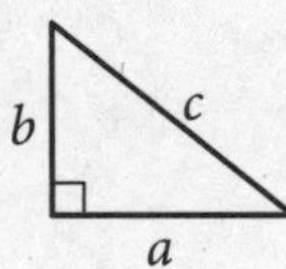

$c^2 = a^2 + b^2$

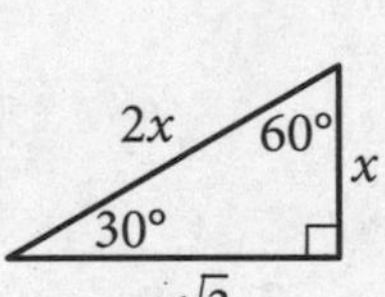

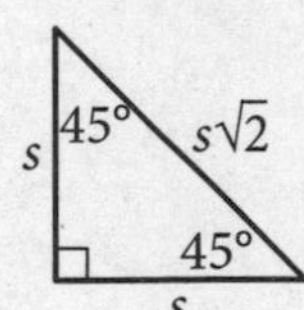

Special Right Triangles

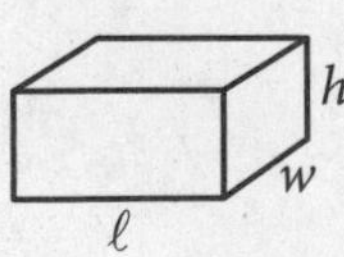

$V = \ell wh$

$V = \pi r^2 h$

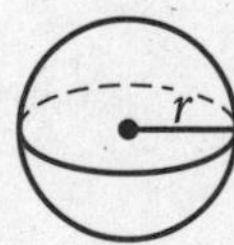

$V = \frac{4}{3}\pi r^3$

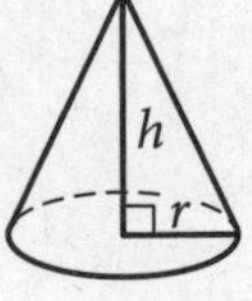

$V = \frac{1}{3}\pi r^2 h$

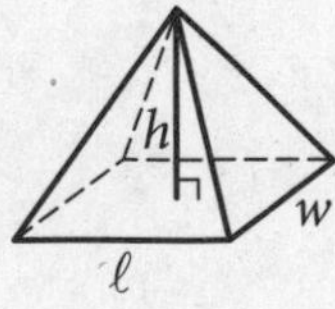

$V = \frac{1}{3}\ell wh$

The number of degrees of arc in a circle is 360.
The number of radians of arc in a circle is 2π.
The sum of the measures in degrees of the angles of a triangle is 180.

CONTINUE

1

Which of the following expressions is equal to 0 for some value of x ?

A) $|x-1|-1$

B) $|x+1|+1$

C) $|1-x|+1$

D) $|x-1|+1$

2

$$f(x)=\frac{3}{2}x+b$$

In the function above, b is a constant. If $f(6)=7$, what is the value of $f(-2)$?

A) -5

B) -2

C) 1

D) 7

3

$$\frac{x}{y}=6$$

$$4(y+1)=x$$

If (x, y) is the solution to the system of equations above, what is the value of y ?

A) 2

B) 4

C) 12

D) 24

4

If $f(x)=-2x+5$, what is $f(-3x)$ equal to?

A) $-6x-5$

B) $6x+5$

C) $6x-5$

D) $6x^2-15x$

5

$$3(2x + 1)(4x + 1)$$

Which of the following is equivalent to the expression above?

A) $45x$

B) $24x^2 + 3$

C) $24x^2 + 18x + 3$

D) $18x^2 + 6$

6

If $\frac{a-b}{b} = \frac{3}{7}$, which of the following must also be true?

A) $\frac{a}{b} = -\frac{4}{7}$

B) $\frac{a}{b} = \frac{10}{7}$

C) $\frac{a+b}{b} = \frac{10}{7}$

D) $\frac{a-2b}{b} = -\frac{11}{7}$

7

While preparing to run a marathon, Amelia created a training schedule in which the distance of her longest run every week increased by a constant amount. If Amelia's training schedule requires that her longest run in week 4 is a distance of 8 miles and her longest run in week 16 is a distance of 26 miles, which of the following best describes how the distance Amelia runs changes between week 4 and week 16 of her training schedule?

A) Amelia increases the distance of her longest run by 0.5 miles each week.

B) Amelia increases the distance of her longest run by 2 miles each week.

C) Amelia increases the distance of her longest run by 2 miles every 3 weeks.

D) Amelia increases the distance of her longest run by 1.5 miles each week.

CONTINUE

8

Which of the following equations represents a line that is parallel to the line with equation $y = -3x + 4$?

A) $6x + 2y = 15$

B) $3x - y = 7$

C) $2x - 3y = 6$

D) $x + 3y = 1$

9

$$\sqrt{x - a} = x - 4$$

If $a = 2$, what is the solution set of the equation above?

A) $\{3, 6\}$

B) $\{2\}$

C) $\{3\}$

D) $\{6\}$

10

If $\frac{t + 5}{t - 5} = 10$, what is the value of t ?

A) $\frac{45}{11}$

B) 5

C) $\frac{11}{2}$

D) $\frac{55}{9}$

11

$$x = 2y + 5$$
$$y = (2x - 3)(x + 9)$$

How many ordered pairs (x, y) satisfy the system of equations shown above?

A) 0

B) 1

C) 2

D) Infinitely many

12

Ken and Paul each ordered a sandwich at a restaurant. The price of Ken's sandwich was x dollars, and the price of Paul's sandwich was \$1 more than the price of Ken's sandwich. If Ken and Paul split the cost of the sandwiches evenly and each paid a 20% tip, which of the following expressions represents the amount, in dollars, each of them paid? (Assume there is no sales tax.)

A) $0.2x + 0.2$

B) $0.5x + 0.1$

C) $1.2x + 0.6$

D) $2.4x + 1.2$

13

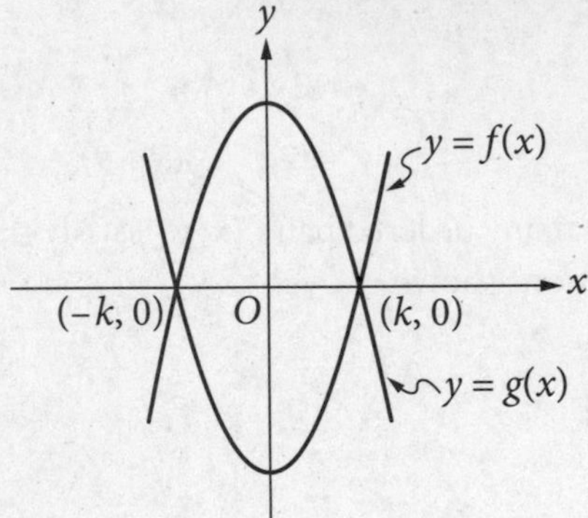

The functions f and g, defined by $f(x) = 8x^2 - 2$ and $g(x) = -8x^2 + 2$, are graphed in the xy-plane above. The graphs of f and g intersect at the points $(k, 0)$ and $(-k, 0)$. What is the value of k ?

A) $\frac{1}{4}$

B) $\frac{1}{2}$

C) 1

D) 2

14

$$\frac{8 - i}{3 - 2i}$$

If the expression above is rewritten in the form $a + bi$, where a and b are real numbers, what is the value of a ? (Note: $i = \sqrt{-1}$)

A) 2

B) $\frac{8}{3}$

C) 3

D) $\frac{11}{3}$

15

$$x^2 - \frac{k}{2}x = 2p$$

In the quadratic equation above, k and p are constants. What are the solutions for x ?

A) $x = \frac{k}{4} \pm \frac{\sqrt{k^2 + 2p}}{4}$

B) $x = \frac{k}{4} \pm \frac{\sqrt{k^2 + 32p}}{4}$

C) $x = \frac{k}{2} \pm \frac{\sqrt{k^2 + 2p}}{2}$

D) $x = \frac{k}{2} \pm \frac{\sqrt{k^2 + 32p}}{4}$

CONTINUE

DIRECTIONS

For questions 16–20, solve the problem and enter your answer in the grid, as described below, on the answer sheet.

1. Although not required, it is suggested that you write your answer in the boxes at the top of the columns to help you fill in the circles accurately. You will receive credit only if the circles are filled in correctly.
2. Mark no more than one circle in any column.
3. No question has a negative answer.
4. Some problems may have more than one correct answer. In such cases, grid only one answer.
5. **Mixed numbers** such as $3\frac{1}{2}$ must be gridded as 3.5 or 7/2. (If 3 1 / 2 is entered into the grid, it will be interpreted as $\frac{31}{2}$, not $3\frac{1}{2}$.)
6. **Decimal answers:** If you obtain a decimal answer with more digits than the grid can accommodate, it may be either rounded or truncated, but it must fill the entire grid.

Answer: $\frac{7}{12}$

Write answer in boxes. → 7 / 1 2

← Fraction line

Grid in result.

Answer: 2.5

2 . 5

← Decimal point

Acceptable ways to grid $\frac{2}{3}$ are:

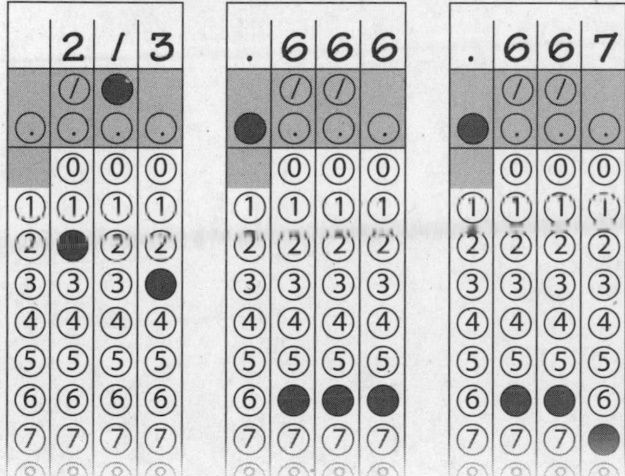

Answer: 201 – either position is correct

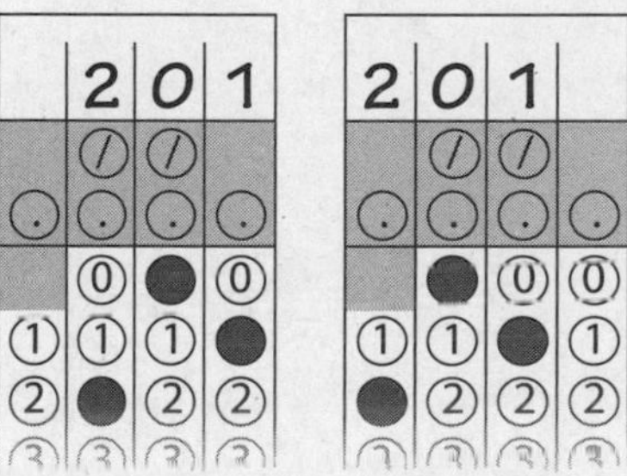

NOTE: You may start your answers in any column, space permitting. Columns you don't need to use should be left blank.

16

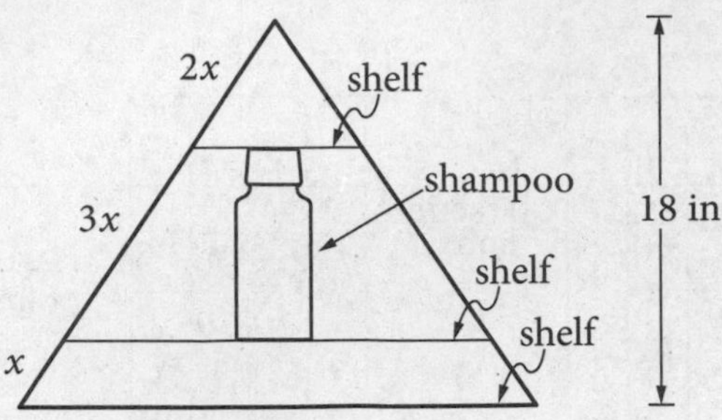

Jim has a triangular shelf system that attaches to his showerhead. The total height of the system is 18 inches, and there are three parallel shelves as shown above. What is the maximum height, in inches, of a shampoo bottle that can stand upright on the middle shelf?

17

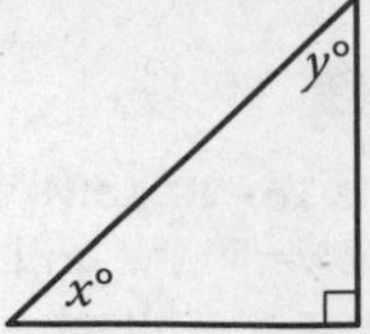

In the triangle above, the sine of $x°$ is 0.6. What is the cosine of $y°$?

18

$$x^3 - 5x^2 + 2x - 10 = 0$$

For what real value of x is the equation above true?

19

$$-3x + 4y = 20$$
$$6x + 3y = 15$$

If (x, y) is the solution to the system of equations above, what is the value of x ?

20

The mesosphere is the layer of Earth's atmosphere between 50 kilometers and 85 kilometers above Earth's surface. At a distance of 50 kilometers from Earth's surface, the temperature in the mesosphere is $-5°$ Celsius, and at a distance of 80 kilometers from Earth's surface, the temperature in the mesosphere is $-80°$ Celsius. For every additional 10 kilometers from Earth's surface, the temperature in the mesosphere decreases by $k°$ Celsius, where k is a constant. What is the value of k ?

STOP

If you finish before time is called, you may check your work on this section only.
Do not turn to any other section.

Math Test – Calculator

55 MINUTES, 38 QUESTIONS

Turn to Section 4 of your answer sheet to answer the questions in this section.

DIRECTIONS

For questions 1-30, solve each problem, choose the best answer from the choices provided, and fill in the corresponding circle on your answer sheet. **For questions 31-38**, solve the problem and enter your answer in the grid on the answer sheet. Please refer to the directions before question 31 on how to enter your answers in the grid. You may use any available space in your test booklet for scratch work.

NOTES

1. The use of a calculator **is permitted**.
2. All variables and expressions used represent real numbers unless otherwise indicated.
3. Figures provided in this test are drawn to scale unless otherwise indicated.
4. All figures lie in a plane unless otherwise indicated.
5. Unless otherwise indicated, the domain of a given function f is the set of all real numbers x for which $f(x)$ is a real number.

REFERENCE

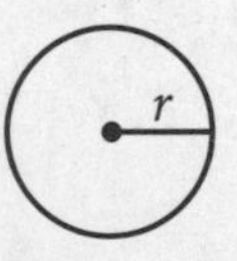

$A = \pi r^2$
$C = 2\pi r$

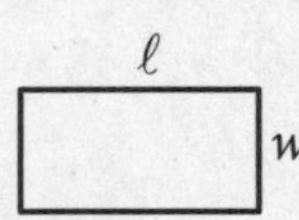

$A = \ell w$

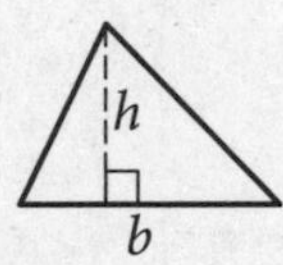

$A = \frac{1}{2}bh$

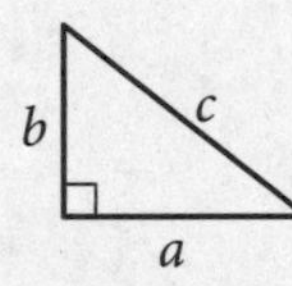

$c^2 = a^2 + b^2$

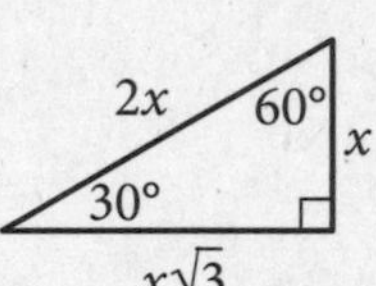

Special Right Triangles

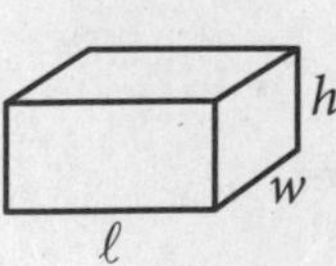

$V = \ell wh$

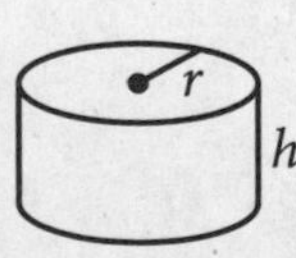

$V = \pi r^2 h$

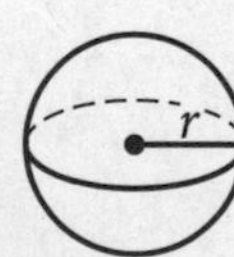

$V = \frac{4}{3}\pi r^3$

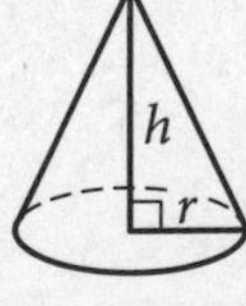

$V = \frac{1}{3}\pi r^2 h$

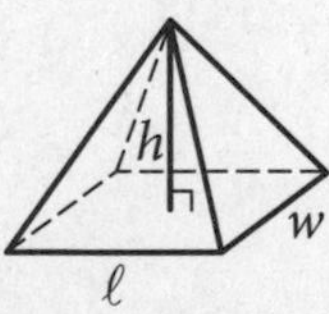

$V = \frac{1}{3}\ell wh$

The number of degrees of arc in a circle is 360.
The number of radians of arc in a circle is 2π.
The sum of the measures in degrees of the angles of a triangle is 180.

CONTINUE

1

The monthly membership fee for an online television and movie service is \$9.80. The cost of viewing television shows online is included in the membership fee, but there is an additional fee of \$1.50 to rent each movie online. For one month, Jill's membership and movie rental fees were \$12.80. How many movies did Jill rent online that month?

A) 1

B) 2

C) 3

D) 4

2

One of the requirements for becoming a court reporter is the ability to type 225 words per minute. Donald can currently type 180 words per minute, and believes that with practice he can increase his typing speed by 5 words per minute each month. Which of the following represents the number of words per minute that Donald believes he will be able to type m months from now?

A) $5 + 180m$

B) $225 + 5m$

C) $180 + 5m$

D) $180 - 5m$

3

If a 3-pound pizza is sliced in half and each half is sliced into thirds, what is the weight, in ounces, of each of the slices? (1 pound = 16 ounces)

A) 4

B) 6

C) 8

D) 16

4

Nick surveyed a random sample of the freshman class of his high school to determine whether the Fall Festival should be held in October or November. Of the 90 students surveyed, 25.6% preferred October. Based on this information, about how many students in the entire 225-person class would be expected to prefer having the Fall Festival in October?

A) 50

B) 60

C) 75

D) 80

5

The density of an object is equal to the mass of the object divided by the volume of the object. What is the volume, in milliliters, of an object with a mass of 24 grams and a density of 3 grams per milliliter?

A) 0.125

B) 8

C) 21

D) 72

6

Last week Raul worked 11 more hours than Angelica. If they worked a combined total of 59 hours, how many hours did Angelica work last week?

A) 24

B) 35

C) 40

D) 48

7

Movies with Greatest Ticket Sales in 2012

MPAA rating	Type of movie				
	Action	Animated	Comedy	Drama	Total
PG	2	7	0	2	11
PG-13	10	0	4	8	22
R	6	0	5	6	17
Total	18	7	9	16	50

The table above represents the 50 movies that had the greatest ticket sales in 2012, categorized by movie type and Motion Picture Association of America (MPAA) rating. What proportion of the movies are comedies with a PG-13 rating?

A) $\frac{2}{25}$

B) $\frac{9}{50}$

C) $\frac{2}{11}$

D) $\frac{11}{25}$

8

Line ℓ in the xy-plane contains points from each of Quadrants II, III, and IV, but no points from Quadrant I. Which of the following must be true?

A) The slope of line ℓ is undefined.

B) The slope of line ℓ is zero.

C) The slope of line ℓ is positive.

D) The slope of line ℓ is negative.

CONTINUE

9

Number of Registered Voters
in the United States in 2012, in Thousands

Region	Age, in years					Total
	18 to 24	25 to 44	45 to 64	65 to 74	75 and older	
Northeast	2,713	8,159	10,986	3,342	2,775	27,975
Midwest	3,453	11,237	13,865	4,221	3,350	36,126
South	5,210	18,072	21,346	7,272	4,969	56,869
West	3,390	10,428	11,598	3,785	2,986	32,187
Total	14,766	47,896	57,795	18,620	14,080	153,157

The table above shows the number of registered voters in 2012, in thousands, in four geographic regions and five age groups. Based on the table, if a registered voter who was 18 to 44 years old in 2012 is chosen at random, which of the following is closest to the probability that the registered voter was from the Midwest region?

A) 0.10
B) 0.25
C) 0.40
D) 0.75

CONTINUE

Questions 10 and 11 refer to the following information.

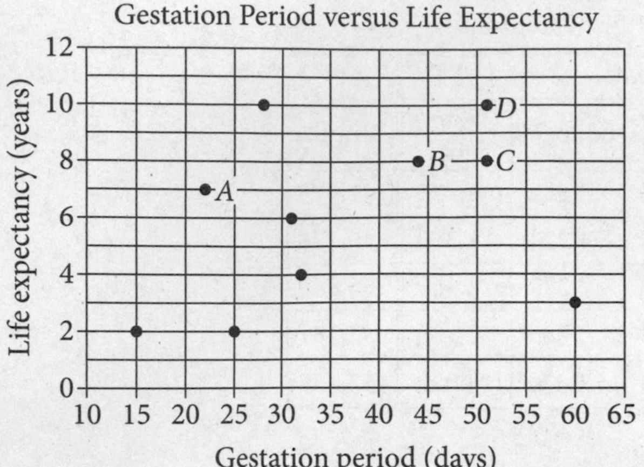

A curator at a wildlife society created the scatterplot above to examine the relationship between the gestation period and life expectancy of 10 species of animals.

10

What is the life expectancy, in years, of the animal that has the longest gestation period?

A) 3

B) 4

C) 8

D) 10

11

Of the labeled points, which represents the animal for which the ratio of life expectancy to gestation period is greatest?

A) A

B) B

C) C

D) D

12

In the xy-plane, the graph of function f has x-intercepts at -3, -1, and 1. Which of the following could define f?

A) $f(x) = (x - 3)(x - 1)(x + 1)$

B) $f(x) = (x - 3)(x - 1)^2$

C) $f(x) = (x - 1)(x + 1)(x + 3)$

D) $f(x) = (x + 1)^2(x + 3)$

CONTINUE

13

The population of mosquitoes in a swamp is estimated over the course of twenty weeks, as shown in the table.

Time (weeks)	Population
0	100
5	1,000
10	10,000
15	100,000
20	1,000,000

Which of the following best describes the relationship between time and the estimated population of mosquitoes during the twenty weeks?

A) Increasing linear

B) Decreasing linear

C) Exponential growth

D) Exponential decay

14

$$1{,}000\left(1+\frac{r}{1{,}200}\right)^{12}$$

The expression above gives the amount of money, in dollars, generated in a year by a \$1,000 deposit in a bank account that pays an annual interest rate of r%, compounded monthly. Which of the following expressions shows how much additional money is generated at an interest rate of 5% than at an interest rate of 3% ?

A) $1{,}000\left(1+\frac{5-3}{1{,}200}\right)^{12}$

B) $1{,}000\left(1+\frac{\frac{5}{3}}{1{,}200}\right)^{12}$

C) $\dfrac{1{,}000\left(1+\frac{5}{1{,}200}\right)^{12}}{1{,}000\left(1+\frac{3}{1{,}200}\right)^{12}}$

D) $1{,}000\left(1+\frac{5}{1{,}200}\right)^{12} - 1{,}000\left(1+\frac{3}{1{,}200}\right)^{12}$

CONTINUE

15

Which of the following scatterplots shows a relationship that is appropriately modeled with the equation $y = ax^b$, where a is positive and b is negative?

A) 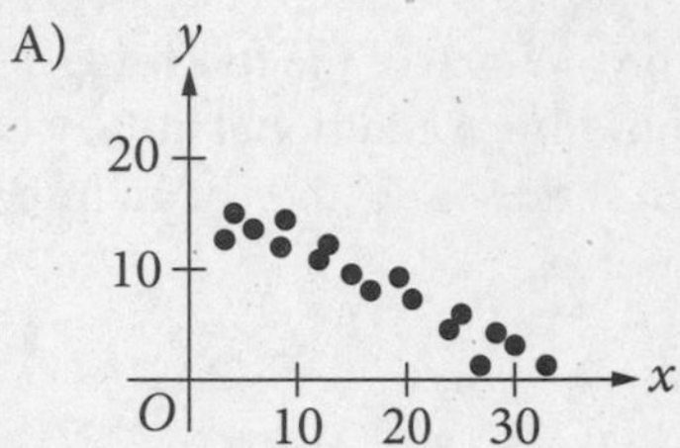

B) 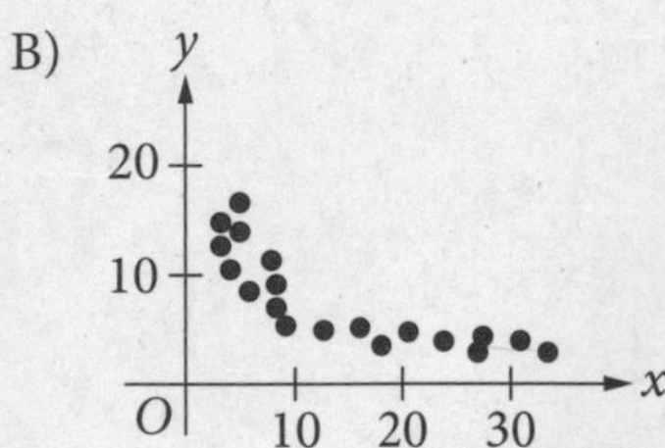

C) 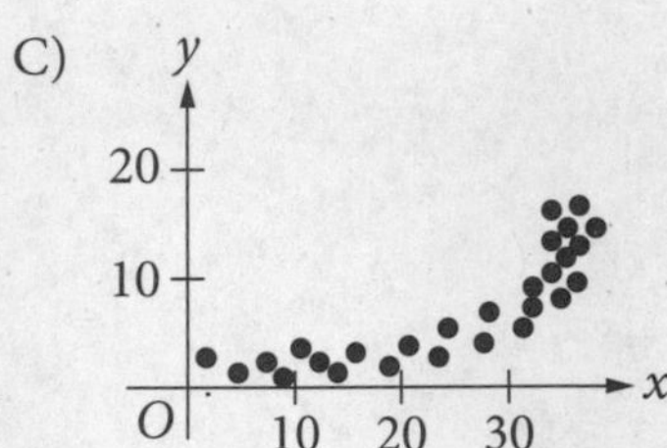

D) 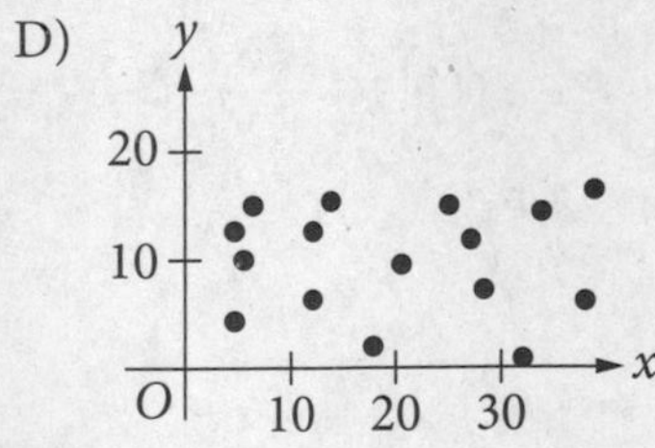

Questions 16 and 17 refer to the following information.

Mr. Martinson is building a concrete patio in his backyard and deciding where to buy the materials and rent the tools needed for the project. The table below shows the materials' cost and daily rental costs for three different stores.

Store	Materials' Cost, M (dollars)	Rental cost of wheelbarrow, W (dollars per day)	Rental cost of concrete mixer, K (dollars per day)
A	750	15	65
B	600	25	80
C	700	20	70

The total cost, y, for buying the materials and renting the tools in terms of the number of days, x, is given by $y = M + (W + K)x$.

16

For what number of days, x, will the total cost of buying the materials and renting the tools from Store B be less than or equal to the total cost of buying the materials and renting the tools from Store A ?

A) $x \leq 6$

B) $x \geq 6$

C) $x \leq 7.3$

D) $x \geq 7.3$

CONTINUE

17

If the relationship between the total cost, y, of buying the materials and renting the tools at Store C and the number of days, x, for which the tools are rented is graphed in the xy-plane, what does the slope of the line represent?

A) The total cost of the project

B) The total cost of the materials

C) The total daily cost of the project

D) The total daily rental costs of the tools

18

Jim has identical drinking glasses each in the shape of a right circular cylinder with internal diameter of 3 inches. He pours milk from a gallon jug into each glass until it is full. If the height of milk in each glass is about 6 inches, what is the largest number of full milk glasses that he can pour from one gallon of milk? (Note: There are 231 cubic inches in 1 gallon.)

A) 2

B) 4

C) 5

D) 6

19

If $3p - 2 \geq 1$, what is the least possible value of $3p + 2$?

A) 5

B) 3

C) 2

D) 1

CONTINUE

20

The mass of living organisms in a lake is defined to be the biomass of the lake. If the biomass in a lake doubles each year, which of the following graphs could model the biomass in the lake as a function of time? (Note: In each graph below, O represents $(0, 0)$.)

A)

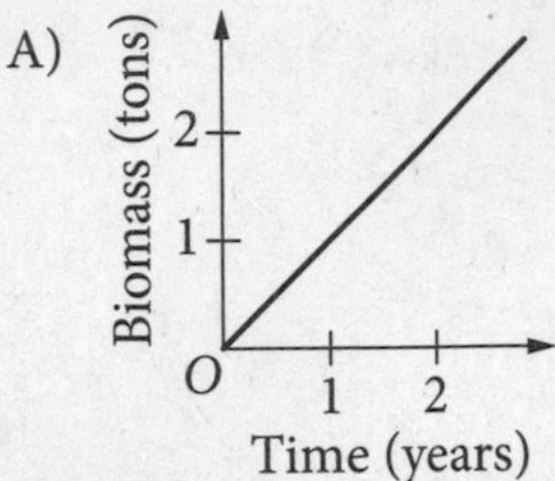

B)

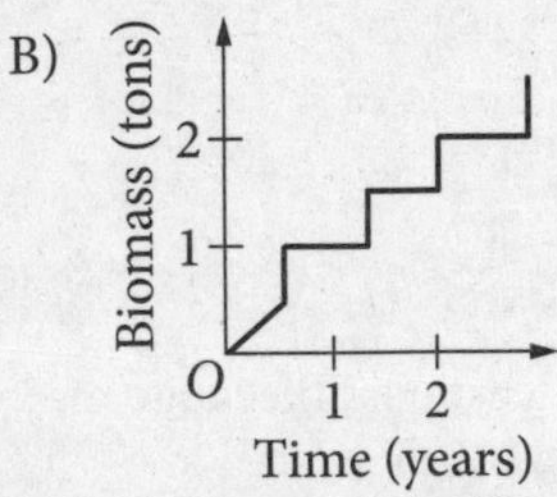

C)

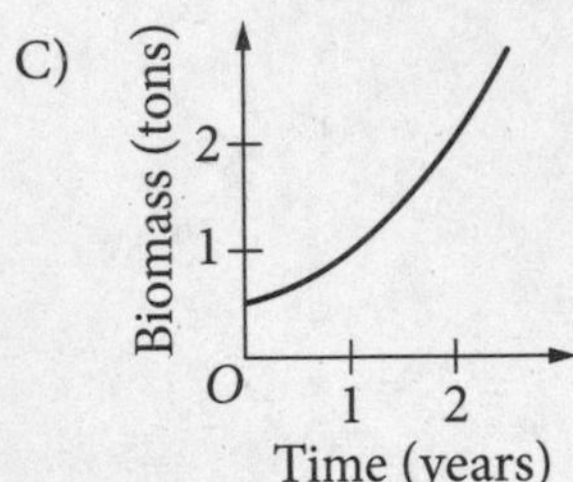

D)

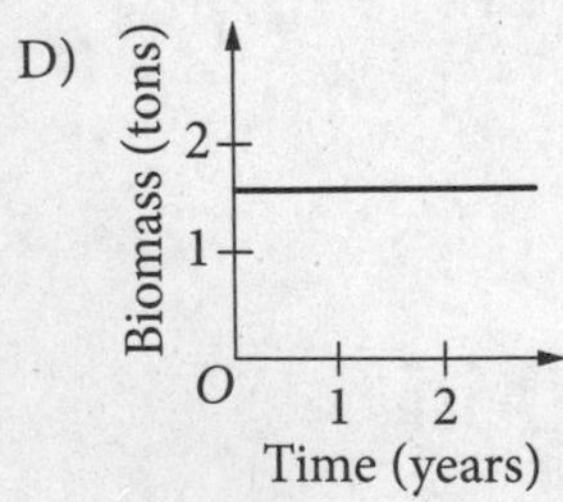

Questions 21 and 22 refer to the following information.

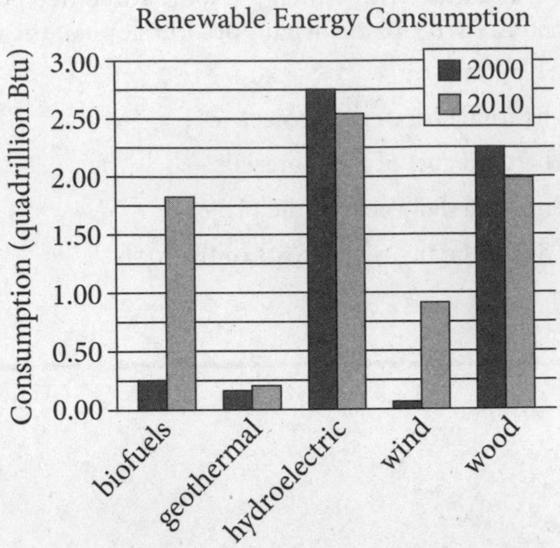

The bar graph above shows renewable energy consumption in quadrillions of British thermal units (Btu) in the United States, by energy source, for several energy sources in the years 2000 and 2010.

21

In a scatterplot of this data, where renewable energy consumption in the year 2000 is plotted along the x-axis and renewable energy consumption in the year 2010 is plotted along the y-axis for each of the given energy sources, how many data points would be above the line $y = x$?

A) 1

B) 2

C) 3

D) 4

CONTINUE

22

Of the following, which best approximates the percent decrease in consumption of wood power in the United States from 2000 to 2010 ?

A) 6%

B) 11%

C) 21%

D) 26%

23

The tables below give the distribution of high temperatures in degrees Fahrenheit (°F) for City A and City B over the same 21 days in March.

City A

Temperature (°F)	Frequency
80	3
79	14
78	2
77	1
76	1

City B

Temperature (°F)	Frequency
80	6
79	3
78	2
77	4
76	6

Which of the following is true about the data shown for these 21 days?

A) The standard deviation of temperatures in City A is larger.

B) The standard deviation of temperatures in City B is larger.

C) The standard deviation of temperatures in City A is the same as that of City B.

D) The standard deviation of temperatures in these cities cannot be calculated with the data provided.

CONTINUE

24

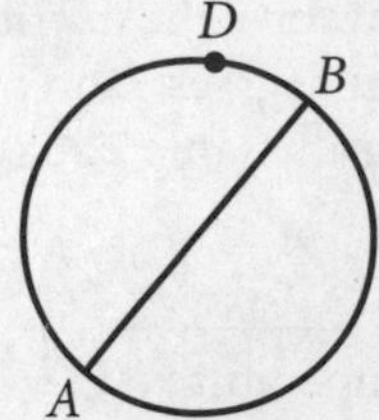

In the circle above, segment AB is a diameter. If the length of arc $\overset{\frown}{ADB}$ is 8π, what is the length of the radius of the circle?

A) 2
B) 4
C) 8
D) 16

25

$$f(x) = 2x^3 + 6x^2 + 4x$$
$$g(x) = x^2 + 3x + 2$$

The polynomials $f(x)$ and $g(x)$ are defined above. Which of the following polynomials is divisible by $2x + 3$?

A) $h(x) = f(x) + g(x)$
B) $p(x) = f(x) + 3g(x)$
C) $r(x) = 2f(x) + 3g(x)$
D) $s(x) = 3f(x) + 2g(x)$

26

Let x and y be numbers such that $-y < x < y$. Which of the following must be true?

I. $|x| < y$
II. $x > 0$
III. $y > 0$

A) I only
B) I and II only
C) I and III only
D) I, II, and III

CONTINUE

27

The relative housing cost for a US city is defined to be the ratio $\frac{\text{average housing cost for the city}}{\text{national average housing cost}}$, expressed as a percent.

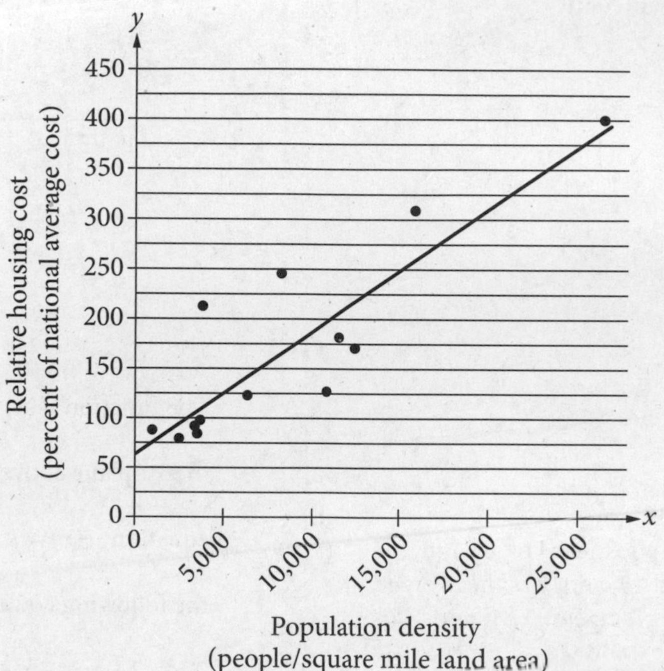

The scatterplot above shows the relative housing cost and the population density for several large US cities in the year 2005. The line of best fit is also shown and has equation $y = 0.0125x + 61$. Which of the following best explains how the number 61 in the equation relates to the scatterplot?

A) In 2005, the lowest housing cost in the United States was about \$61 per month.

B) In 2005, the lowest housing cost in the United States was about 61% of the highest housing cost.

C) In 2005, even in cities with low population densities, housing costs were never below 61% of the national average.

D) In 2005, even in cities with low population densities, housing costs were likely at least 61% of the national average.

CONTINUE

28

$$f(x) = (x + 6)(x - 4)$$

Which of the following is an equivalent form of the function f above in which the minimum value of f appears as a constant or coefficient?

A) $f(x) = x^2 - 24$

B) $f(x) = x^2 + 2x - 24$

C) $f(x) = (x - 1)^2 - 21$

D) $f(x) = (x + 1)^2 - 25$

29

If x is the average (arithmetic mean) of m and 9, y is the average of $2m$ and 15, and z is the average of $3m$ and 18, what is the average of x, y, and z in terms of m ?

A) $m + 6$

B) $m + 7$

C) $2m + 14$

D) $3m + 21$

30

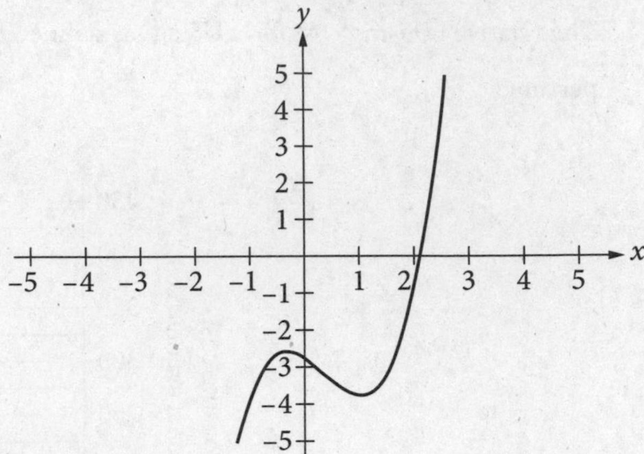

The function $f(x) = x^3 - x^2 - x - \frac{11}{4}$ is graphed in the xy-plane above. If k is a constant such that the equation $f(x) = k$ has three real solutions, which of the following could be the value of k ?

A) 2

B) 0

C) −2

D) −3

CONTINUE

DIRECTIONS

For questions 31–38, solve the problem and enter your answer in the grid, as described below, on the answer sheet.

1. Although not required, it is suggested that you write your answer in the boxes at the top of the columns to help you fill in the circles accurately. You will receive credit only if the circles are filled in correctly.
2. Mark no more than one circle in any column.
3. No question has a negative answer.
4. Some problems may have more than one correct answer. In such cases, grid only one answer.
5. **Mixed numbers** such as $3\frac{1}{2}$ must be gridded as 3.5 or 7/2. (If 3 1 / 2 is entered into the grid, it will be interpreted as $\frac{31}{2}$, not $3\frac{1}{2}$.)
6. **Decimal answers:** If you obtain a decimal answer with more digits than the grid can accommodate, it may be either rounded or truncated, but it must fill the entire grid.

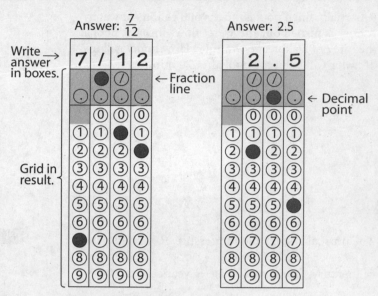

Answer: $\frac{7}{12}$

Write answer in boxes. → 7 / 1 2

← Fraction line

Grid in result.

Answer: 2.5

2 . 5

← Decimal point

Acceptable ways to grid $\frac{2}{3}$ are:

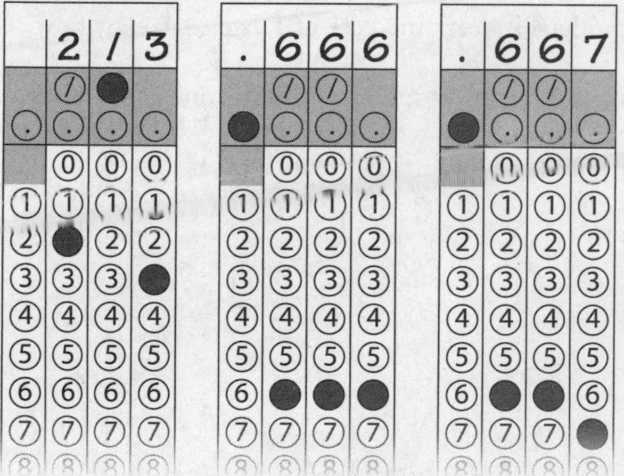

Answer: 201 – either position is correct

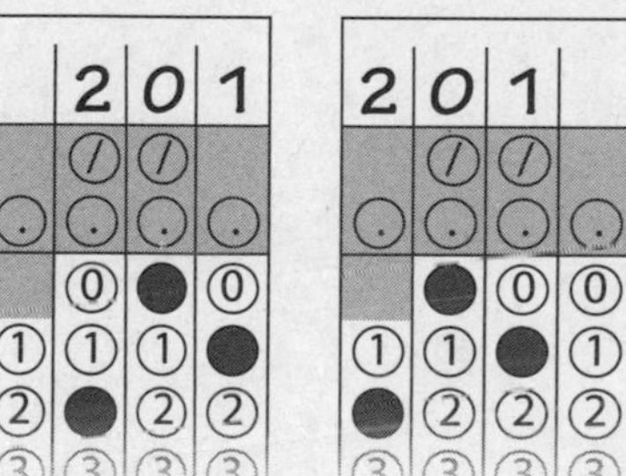

NOTE: You may start your answers in any column, space permitting. Columns you don't need to use should be left blank.

CONTINUE

31

A partially filled pool contains 600 gallons of water. A hose is turned on, and water flows into the pool at the rate of 8 gallons per minute. How many gallons of water will be in the pool after 70 minutes?

32

The normal systolic blood pressure P, in millimeters of mercury, for an adult male x years old can be modeled by the equation $P = \frac{x + 220}{2}$. According to the model, for every increase of 1 year in age, by how many millimeters of mercury will the normal systolic blood pressure for an adult male increase?

33

The *pes*, a Roman measure of length, is approximately equal to 11.65 inches. It is also equivalent to 16 smaller Roman units called digits. Based on these relationships, 75 Roman digits is equivalent to how many <u>feet</u>, to the nearest hundredth? (12 inches = 1 foot)

34

In a study of bat migration habits, 240 male bats and 160 female bats have been tagged. If 100 more female bats are tagged, how many more male bats must be tagged so that $\frac{3}{5}$ of the total number of bats in the study are male?

CONTINUE

35

$$q = \frac{1}{2}nv^2$$

The dynamic pressure q generated by a fluid moving with velocity v can be found using the formula above, where n is the constant density of the fluid. An aeronautical engineer uses the formula to find the dynamic pressure of a fluid moving with velocity v and the same fluid moving with velocity $1.5v$. What is the ratio of the dynamic pressure of the faster fluid to the dynamic pressure of the slower fluid?

36

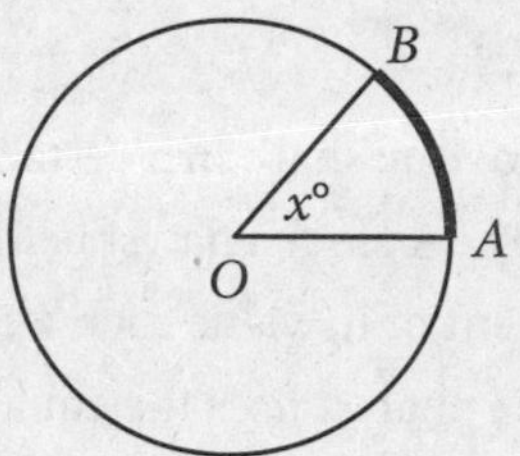

Note: Figure not drawn to scale.

In the figure above, the circle has center O and has radius 10. If the length of arc $\widehat{AB}$ (shown in bold) is between 5 and 6, what is one possible integer value of x ?

CONTINUE

Questions 37 and 38 refer to the following information.

The stock price of one share in a certain company is worth $360 today. A stock analyst believes that the stock will lose 28 percent of its value each week for the next three weeks. The analyst uses the equation $V = 360(r)^t$ to model the value, V, of the stock after t weeks.

37

What value should the analyst use for r ?

38

To the nearest dollar, what does the analyst believe the value of the stock will be at the end of three weeks? (Note: Disregard the $ sign when gridding your answer.)

STOP

If you finish before time is called, you may check your work on this section only. Do not turn to any other section.

No Test Material On This Page

This page represents the back cover of the Practice Test.

The SAT®

Practice Essay #4

The essay gives you an opportunity to show how effectively you can read and comprehend a passage and write an essay analyzing the passage. In your essay, you should demonstrate that you have read the passage carefully, present a clear and logical analysis, and use language precisely.

You have 50 minutes to read the passage and write an essay in response to the prompt provided inside this booklet.

For information on scoring your essay, view the SAT Essay scoring rubric at **sat.org/essay**.

As you read the passage below, consider how Paul Bogard uses

- evidence, such as facts or examples, to support claims.
- reasoning to develop ideas and to connect claims and evidence.
- stylistic or persuasive elements, such as word choice or appeals to emotion, to add power to the ideas expressed.

Adapted from Paul Bogard, "Let There Be Dark." ©2012 by Los Angeles Times. Originally published December 21, 2012.

1 At my family's cabin on a Minnesota lake, I knew woods so dark that my hands disappeared before my eyes. I knew night skies in which meteors left smoky trails across sugary spreads of stars. But now, when 8 of 10 children born in the United States will never know a sky dark enough for the Milky Way, I worry we are rapidly losing night's natural darkness before realizing its worth. This winter solstice, as we cheer the days' gradual movement back toward light, let us also remember the irreplaceable value of darkness.

2 All life evolved to the steady rhythm of bright days and dark nights. Today, though, when we feel the closeness of nightfall, we reach quickly for a light switch. And too little darkness, meaning too much artificial light at night, spells trouble for all.

3 Already the World Health Organization classifies working the night shift as a probable human carcinogen, and the American Medical Association has voiced its unanimous support for "light pollution reduction efforts and glare reduction efforts at both the national and state levels." Our bodies need darkness to produce the hormone melatonin, which keeps certain cancers from developing, and our bodies need darkness for sleep. Sleep disorders have been linked to diabetes, obesity, cardiovascular disease and depression, and recent research suggests one main cause of "short sleep" is "long light." Whether we work at night or simply take our tablets, notebooks and smartphones to bed, there isn't a place for this much artificial light in our lives.

4 The rest of the world depends on darkness as well, including nocturnal and crepuscular species of birds, insects, mammals, fish and reptiles. Some examples are well known—the 400 species of birds that migrate at night in North America, the sea turtles that come ashore to lay their eggs—and some are not, such as the bats that save American farmers billions in pest control and the moths that pollinate 80% of the world's flora. Ecological light pollution is like the bulldozer of the night, wrecking habitat and disrupting ecosystems several billion years in the making. Simply put, without darkness, Earth's ecology would collapse. . . .

5 In today's crowded, louder, more fast-paced world, night's darkness can provide solitude, quiet and stillness, qualities increasingly in short supply. Every religious tradition has considered darkness invaluable for a soulful life, and the chance to witness the universe has inspired artists, philosophers and everyday stargazers since time began. In a world awash with electric light . . . how would Van Gogh have given the world his "Starry Night"? Who knows what this vision of the night sky might inspire in each of us, in our children or grandchildren?

6 Yet all over the world, our nights are growing brighter. In the United States and Western Europe, the amount of light in the sky increases an average of about 6% every year. Computer images of the United States at night, based on NASA photographs, show that what was a very dark country as recently as the 1950s is now nearly covered with a blanket of light. Much of this light is wasted energy, which means wasted dollars. Those of us over 35 are perhaps among the last generation to have known truly dark nights. Even the northern lake where I was lucky to spend my summers has seen its darkness diminish.

7 It doesn't have to be this way. Light pollution is readily within our ability to solve, using new lighting technologies and shielding existing lights. Already, many cities and towns across North America and Europe are changing to LED streetlights, which offer dramatic possibilities for controlling wasted light. Other communities are finding success with simply turning off portions of their public lighting after midnight. Even Paris, the famed "city of light," which already turns off its monument lighting after 1 a.m., will this summer start to require its shops, offices and public buildings to turn off lights after 2 a.m. Though primarily designed to save energy, such reductions in light will also go far in addressing light pollution. But we will never truly address the problem of light pollution until we become aware of the irreplaceable value and beauty of the darkness we are losing.

Write an essay in which you explain how Paul Bogard builds an argument to persuade his audience that natural darkness should be preserved. In your essay, analyze how Bogard uses one or more of the features listed in the box above (or features of your own choice) to strengthen the logic and persuasiveness of his argument. Be sure that your analysis focuses on the most relevant features of the passage.

Your essay should not explain whether you agree with Bogard's claims, but rather explain how Bogard builds an argument to persuade his audience.

This page represents the back cover of the Practice Essay.

CollegeBoard

SAT PRACTICE ANSWER SHEET

COMPLETE MARK ● EXAMPLES OF INCOMPLETE MARKS 

It is recommended that you use a No. 2 pencil. It is very important that you fill in the entire circle darkly and completely. If you change your response, erase as completely as possible. Incomplete marks or erasures may affect your score.

TEST NUMBER

ENTER TEST NUMBER

For instance, for Practice Test #1, fill in the circle for 0 in the **first** column and for 1 in the **second** column.

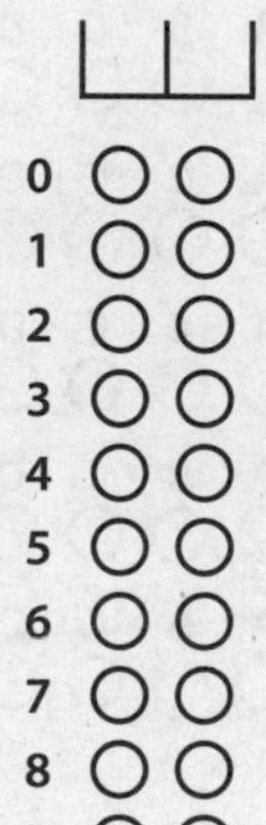

0 ○ ○
1 ○ ○
2 ○ ○
3 ○ ○
4 ○ ○
5 ○ ○
6 ○ ○
7 ○ ○
8 ○ ○
9 ○ ○

SECTION 1

	A B C D		A B C D		A B C D		A B C D
1	○ ○ ○ ○	14	○ ○ ○ ○	27	○ ○ ○ ○	40	○ ○ ○ ○
2	○ ○ ○ ○	15	○ ○ ○ ○	28	○ ○ ○ ○	41	○ ○ ○ ○
3	○ ○ ○ ○	16	○ ○ ○ ○	29	○ ○ ○ ○	42	○ ○ ○ ○
4	○ ○ ○ ○	17	○ ○ ○ ○	30	○ ○ ○ ○	43	○ ○ ○ ○
5	○ ○ ○ ○	18	○ ○ ○ ○	31	○ ○ ○ ○	44	○ ○ ○ ○
6	○ ○ ○ ○	19	○ ○ ○ ○	32	○ ○ ○ ○	45	○ ○ ○ ○
7	○ ○ ○ ○	20	○ ○ ○ ○	33	○ ○ ○ ○	46	○ ○ ○ ○
8	○ ○ ○ ○	21	○ ○ ○ ○	34	○ ○ ○ ○	47	○ ○ ○ ○
9	○ ○ ○ ○	22	○ ○ ○ ○	35	○ ○ ○ ○	48	○ ○ ○ ○
10	○ ○ ○ ○	23	○ ○ ○ ○	36	○ ○ ○ ○	49	○ ○ ○ ○
11	○ ○ ○ ○	24	○ ○ ○ ○	37	○ ○ ○ ○	50	○ ○ ○ ○
12	○ ○ ○ ○	25	○ ○ ○ ○	38	○ ○ ○ ○	51	○ ○ ○ ○
13	○ ○ ○ ○	26	○ ○ ○ ○	39	○ ○ ○ ○	52	○ ○ ○ ○

Download the College Board SAT Practice app to instantly score this test.
Learn more at sat.org/scoring.

CollegeBoard

SAT PRACTICE ANSWER SHEET

COMPLETE MARK ● EXAMPLES OF INCOMPLETE MARKS 

It is recommended that you use a No. 2 pencil. It is very important that you fill in the entire circle darkly and completely. If you change your response, erase as completely as possible. Incomplete marks or erasures may affect your score.

SECTION 2

	A	B	C	D		A	B	C	D		A	B	C	D		A	B	C	D		A	B	C	D
1	○	○	○	○	10	○	○	○	○	19	○	○	○	○	28	○	○	○	○	37	○	○	○	○
2	○	○	○	○	11	○	○	○	○	20	○	○	○	○	29	○	○	○	○	38	○	○	○	○
3	○	○	○	○	12	○	○	○	○	21	○	○	○	○	30	○	○	○	○	39	○	○	○	○
4	○	○	○	○	13	○	○	○	○	22	○	○	○	○	31	○	○	○	○	40	○	○	○	○
5	○	○	○	○	14	○	○	○	○	23	○	○	○	○	32	○	○	○	○	41	○	○	○	○
6	○	○	○	○	15	○	○	○	○	24	○	○	○	○	33	○	○	○	○	42	○	○	○	○
7	○	○	○	○	16	○	○	○	○	25	○	○	○	○	34	○	○	○	○	43	○	○	○	○
8	○	○	○	○	17	○	○	○	○	26	○	○	○	○	35	○	○	○	○	44	○	○	○	○
9	○	○	○	○	18	○	○	○	○	27	○	○	○	○	36	○	○	○	○					

If you're scoring with our mobile app we recommend that you cut these pages out of the back of this book. The scoring does best with a flat page.

CollegeBoard

SAT PRACTICE ANSWER SHEET

COMPLETE MARK

EXAMPLES OF INCOMPLETE MARKS

It is recommended that you use a No. 2 pencil. It is very important that you fill in the entire circle darkly and completely. If you change your response, erase as completely as possible. Incomplete marks or erasures may affect your score.

SECTION 3

1 A B C D	4 A B C D	7 A B C D	10 A B C D	13 A B C D
2 A B C D	5 A B C D	8 A B C D	11 A B C D	14 A B C D
3 A B C D	6 A B C D	9 A B C D	12 A B C D	15 A B C D

Only answers that are gridded will be scored. You will not receive credit for anything written in the boxes.

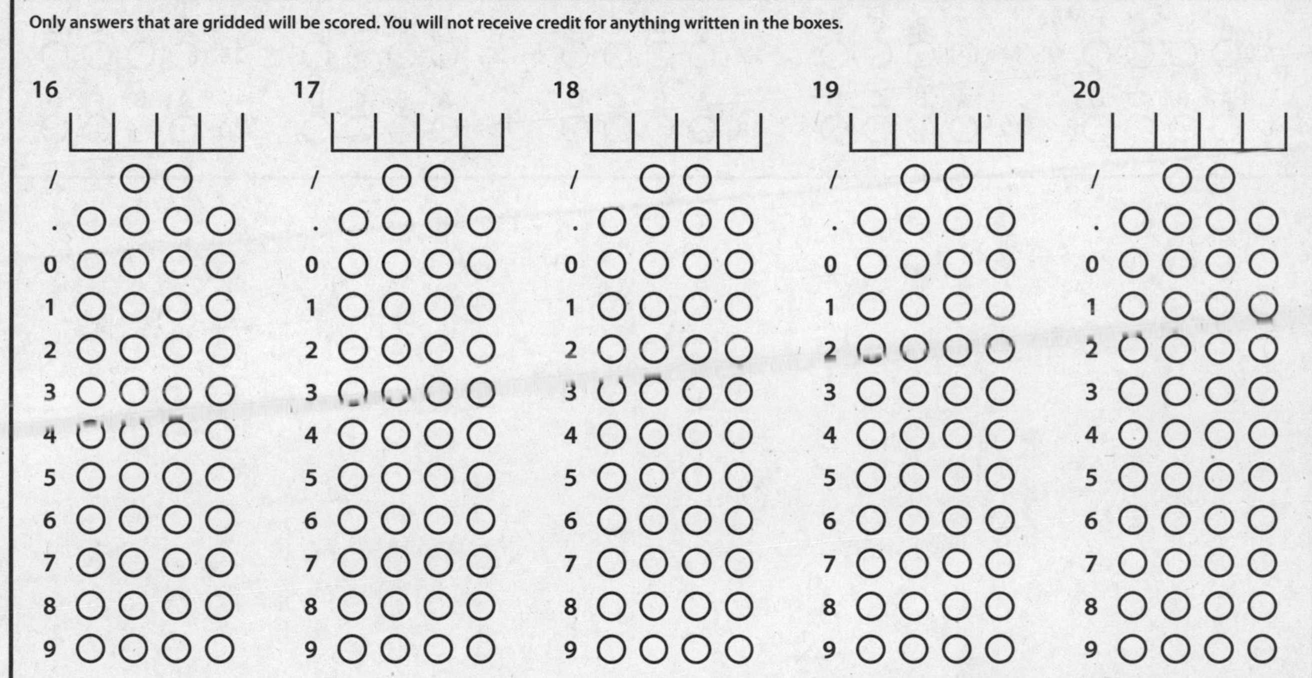

Did you know that you can print out these test sheets from the web? Learn more at sat.org/scoring.

NO CALCULATOR ALLOWED

SAT PRACTICE ANSWER SHEET

COMPLETE MARK ● EXAMPLES OF INCOMPLETE MARKS 

It is recommended that you use a No. 2 pencil. It is very important that you fill in the entire circle darkly and completely. If you change your response, erase as completely as possible. Incomplete marks or erasures may affect your score.

SECTION 4

	A B C D		A B C D		A B C D		A B C D		A B C D
1	○ ○ ○ ○	7	○ ○ ○ ○	13	○ ○ ○ ○	19	○ ○ ○ ○	25	○ ○ ○ ○
2	○ ○ ○ ○	8	○ ○ ○ ○	14	○ ○ ○ ○	20	○ ○ ○ ○	26	○ ○ ○ ○
3	○ ○ ○ ○	9	○ ○ ○ ○	15	○ ○ ○ ○	21	○ ○ ○ ○	27	○ ○ ○ ○
4	○ ○ ○ ○	10	○ ○ ○ ○	16	○ ○ ○ ○	22	○ ○ ○ ○	28	○ ○ ○ ○
5	○ ○ ○ ○	11	○ ○ ○ ○	17	○ ○ ○ ○	23	○ ○ ○ ○	29	○ ○ ○ ○
6	○ ○ ○ ○	12	○ ○ ○ ○	18	○ ○ ○ ○	24	○ ○ ○ ○	30	○ ○ ○ ○

CALCULATOR ALLOWED

If you're using our mobile app keep in mind that bad lighting and even shadows cast over the answer sheet can affect your score. Be sure to scan this in a well-lit area for best results.

SAT PRACTICE ANSWER SHEET

COMPLETE MARK ● EXAMPLES OF INCOMPLETE MARKS

It is recommended that you use a No. 2 pencil. It is very important that you fill in the entire circle darkly and completely. If you change your response, erase as completely as possible. Incomplete marks or erasures may affect your score.

SECTION 4 (Continued)

Only answers that are gridded will be scored. You will not receive credit for anything written in the boxes.

31 32 33 34 35

/ . 0 1 2 3 4 5 6 7 8 9

Only answers that are gridded will be scored. You will not receive credit for anything written in the boxes.

36 37 38

/ . 0 1 2 3 4 5 6 7 8 9

CALCULATOR ALLOWED

○ I understand that my essay (without my name) may be reproduced in other College Board materials. If I mark this circle, I withhold my permission to reproduce my essay for any purposes beyond score reporting and the assessment of my writing skills. Marking this circle will have no effect on my score, nor will it prevent my essay from being made available to any college to which I send my SAT scores.

IMPORTANT: **USE A NO. 2 PENCIL. DO NOT WRITE OUTSIDE THE BORDER!** Words written outside the essay box or written in ink **WILL NOT APPEAR** in the copy sent to be scored, and your score will be affected.

PLANNING PAGE You may plan your essay in the unlined planning space below, but use only the lined pages following this one to write your essay. Any work on this planning page will not be scored.

Use pages 7 through 10 for your ESSAY →

FOR PLANNING ONLY

Use pages 7 through 10 for your ESSAY →

PLEASE DO NOT WRITE IN THIS AREA

○○○○○○○○○○○○○○○○○○○○○○○○○○○○○○

SERIAL #

BEGIN YOUR ESSAY HERE.

You may continue on the next page.

PLEASE DO NOT WRITE IN THIS AREA

SERIAL #

DO NOT WRITE OUTSIDE OF THE BOX.

You may continue on the next page.

DO NOT WRITE OUTSIDE OF THE BOX.

You may continue on the next page.

PLEASE DO NOT WRITE IN THIS AREA

SERIAL #

DO NOT WRITE OUTSIDE OF THE BOX.

STOP.

Answer Explanations

SAT Practice Test #4

Section 1: Reading Test

QUESTION 1

Choice C is the best answer. The narrator initially expresses uncertainty, or uneasiness, over his decision to set out for the North Pole: "my motives in this undertaking are not entirely clear" (lines 9-10). At the end of the passage, the narrator recognizes that because of this journey he is "on the brink of knowing . . . not an ethereal mathematical spot," the North Pole, but himself (lines 56-57).

Choices A, B, and D are incorrect because the narrator does not suggest that he fears going on the expedition, doubts his own abilities, or feels disdain for the North Pole.

QUESTION 2

Choice D is the best answer. Lines 56-57 provide evidence that the narrator eventually recognizes his motives for traveling to the North Pole: "What I am on the brink of knowing, I now see, is not an ephemeral mathematical spot but myself." The narrator initially was unsure of why he was traveling to the North Pole, but realizes that he has embarked on a journey to find himself.

Choices A, B, and C are incorrect because they do not provide the best evidence that the narrator eventually recognizes his motives for traveling to the North Pole. Rather, choices A, B, and C all focus on the narrator's preparations and expectations for the journey.

QUESTION 3

Choice D is the best answer. In lines 1-6, the narrator says that he feels a "vast yearning" and that his emotions are "complicated." He explains that he does "not understand quite what it is that the yearning desires." In this context, his emotions are "not readily verifiable," or not completely understood.

Choices A, B, and C are incorrect because in this context, "not readily verifiable" does not mean unable to be authenticated, likely to be contradicted, or without empirical support.

QUESTION 4

Choice C is the best answer. In lines 10-13, the narrator explains that "the machinery of [his] destiny has worked in secret" to prepare him for this journey, as "its clockwork" has propelled him to "this time and place." By using the phrases "the machinery" and "its clockwork," the narrator is showing that powerful and independent forces are causing him to journey to the North Pole.

Choices A, B, and D are incorrect because they do not indicate the main purpose of lines 10-13. While lines 10-13 mention that these powerful and independent forces have been working "for years, for a lifetime" to convince the narrator to journey to the North Pole, they do not expose a hidden side of the narrator, demonstrate the narrator's manner, or explain the amount of time the narrator has spent preparing for his expedition.

QUESTION 5

Choice A is the best answer. In lines 20-21, the narrator states that many people have perished while journeying to the North Pole: "Nobody has succeeded in this thing, and many have died."

Choices B, C, and D are incorrect because the narrator does not indicate that previous explorers have made surprising discoveries, have failed to determine the exact location of the North Pole, or had different motivations than his own.

QUESTION 6

Choice A is the best answer. In lines 20-21, the narrator provides evidence that many previous explorers seeking the North Pole have perished in the attempt: "Nobody has succeeded in this thing, and many have died."

Choices B, C, and D do not mention previous explorers; therefore, these lines do not provide the best evidence that explorers died while seeking the North Pole.

QUESTION 7

Choice B is the best answer. In lines 27-39, the narrator states that he is "intent" on traveling to the North Pole but acknowledges that the journey is absurd: "Who wants the North Pole! What good is it! Can you eat it? Will it carry you from Gothenburg to Malmö like a railway?" By asking these questions, the narrator recognizes that the North Pole has no practical value. Still, the narrator admits that finding the North Pole is necessary, as it "must nevertheless be sought for."

Choices A, C, and D are incorrect because the narrator does not view his expedition to the North Pole as immoral, socially beneficial, or scientifically important.

QUESTION 8

Choice D is the best answer. In lines 27-31, the narrator asks a series of rhetorical questions about the North Pole: "Who wants the North Pole! What good is it! Can you eat it? Will it carry you from Gothenburg to Malmö like a railway?" In this context, the narrator is suggesting that reaching the North Pole has no foreseeable benefit or value to humanity; unlike trains that bring travelers to specific destinations, the North Pole does not provide humans with a specific benefit or form of convenience.

Choices A, B, and C are incorrect because the question posed in lines 30-31 does not debate modes of travel, examine the proximity of cities that can be reached by trains, or question how often people travel.

QUESTION 9

Choice D is the best answer. In lines 48-49, the narrator states that the North Pole "is an abstraction, a mathematical fiction" and that "no one but a Swedish madman could take the slightest interest in it." In this context, the narrator is stating that people would not "take the slightest interest in," or be curious about, the North Pole.

Choices A, B, and C are incorrect because in this context, "take the slightest interest in" does not mean to accept responsibility for, to possess little regard for, or to pay no attention to something.

QUESTION 10

Choice A is the best answer. In lines 49-51, the narrator describes his balloon journey toward the North Pole: "The wind is still from the south, bearing us steadily northward at the speed of a trotting dog." In this context, the wind is "bearing," or carrying, the narrator in a direction to the North.

Choices B, C, and D are incorrect because in this context, "bearing" does not mean affecting, yielding, or enduring.

QUESTION 11

Choice C is the best answer. The author states that "demographic inversion is not a proxy for population growth" (lines 32-33). In other words, demographic inversion is distinct from population growth. The author also notes that demographic inversion is evident in many American cities, as it "can occur in cities that are growing, those whose numbers are flat, and even in those undergoing a modest decline in size" (lines 33-35).

Choices A, B, and D are incorrect because they do not summarize the first paragraph.

QUESTION 12

Choice D is the best answer. The author notes that one of "the most powerful demographic events of the past decade [was] the movement of African Americans out of central cities" (lines 14-17).

Choices A, B, and C are incorrect because the author does not state that the unemployed, immigrants, or young professionals moved away from central-city areas in large numbers in the early 2000s.

QUESTION 13

Choice A is the best answer. The author states that democratic inversion "can occur in cities that are growing, those whose numbers are flat, and even in those undergoing a modest decline in size" (lines 33-35). In this context, cities whose "numbers," or population size, are "flat" have static, or unchanging, populations.

Choices B, C, and D are incorrect because in this context, "flat" does not mean deflated, featureless, or obscure.

QUESTION 14

Choice B is the best answer. The author states that many major American cities are currently experiencing economic hardship, or "enormous fiscal problems," because of "public pension obligations they incurred in the more prosperous years of the past two decades" (lines 36-39). The author then provides the example of Chicago, a city that can no longer afford to pay the "public services to which most of [its] citizens have grown to feel entitled" (lines 41-43). The author is arguing that many major American cities face economic hardship due to past promises (such as public services) they made to their constituents.

Choices A, C, and D are incorrect because the passage does not discuss expected tax increases, an inner-city tax base, or manufacturing production as they relate to the financial status of many major American cities.

QUESTION 15

Choice A is the best answer. In lines 36-39, the author provides evidence that many major American cities are currently experiencing economic hardship due to promises made in past years: "America's major cities face enormous fiscal problems, many of them the result of public pension obligations they incurred in the more prosperous years of the past two decades." America's major cities made past promises, such as "public pension obligations," to their citizens, which caused their current financial situation.

Choices B, C, and D are incorrect because they do not provide evidence that many major American cities are currently experiencing economic hardship due to promises made in past years.

QUESTION 16

Choice C is the best answer. The author explains how sociologist Ernest W. Burgess determined that urban areas have a traditional four-zone structure (lines 54-63). He then states that Burgess was "right about the urban America of 1974" (line 65) as it also followed the traditional four-zone structure: "Virtually every city in the country had a downtown, where the commercial life of the metropolis was conducted; it had a factory district just beyond; it had districts of working-class residences just beyond that; and it had residential suburbs for the wealthy and the upper middle class at the far end of the continuum" (lines 66-71).

Choices A, B, and D are incorrect because the passage does not imply that American cities in 1974 were witnessing the flight of minority populations to the suburbs, had begun to lose their manufacturing sectors, or were already experiencing demographic inversion.

QUESTION 17

Choice C is the best answer. In lines 66-71, the author provides evidence that American cities in 1974 had a traditional four-zone structure: "Virtually every city in the country had a downtown, where the commercial life of the metropolis was conducted; it had a factory district just beyond; it had districts of working-class residences just beyond that; and it had residential suburbs for the wealthy and the upper middle class at the far end of the continuum."

Choices A, B, and D are incorrect because they do not provide evidence that American urban cities in 1974 had a traditional four-zone structure. Choice A references a seminal paper on the layout of American cities, choice B identifies Burgess's original theory, and choice D focuses on movement to the suburbs.

QUESTION 18

Choice A is the best answer. In lines 66-68, the author notes that American cities in 1974 each had a "downtown, where the commercial life of the metropolis was conducted." In this context, the author is stating that these cities "conducted," or carried out, business, the "commercial life," in downtown areas.

Choices B, C, and D are incorrect because in this context, "conducted" does not mean supervised, regulated, or inhibited.

QUESTION 19

Choice B is the best answer. Chart 1 shows the percentage of the US population in 2010 that lived in non-metro, small metro, and large metro areas. While the author cites census numbers, he notes that "when it comes to measuring demographic inversion, raw census numbers are an ineffective blunt instrument" (lines 11-13). Census data refer to the number of people living in a specific area and the demographic information that's been collected on them. The author would most likely consider the information in chart 1 to be possibly accurate but an "ineffective blunt instrument" that's not truly informative.

Choices A and C are incorrect because the author would not consider census data to be excellent or compelling. Choice D is incorrect because while the author does not believe the census completely explains demographic inversion, he would be unlikely to disagree with the census data.

QUESTION 20

Choice A is the best answer. Chart 2 shows that the growth of all metropolitan areas in the 1990s was higher than the growth in all metropolitan areas in the 2000s: large metro areas experienced a growth of 14.3% in the 1990s versus a growth of 10.9% in the 2000s, small metro areas experienced a growth of 13.1% in the 1990s versus a growth of 10.3% in the 2000s, and non-metro areas experienced a growth of 9.0% in the 1990s versus a growth of 4.5% in the 2000s.

Choices B, C, and D are incorrect because they do not accurately characterize the US growth rate by metro size from 2000-2010 as illustrated in chart 2.

QUESTION 21

Choice D is the best answer. Chart 2 shows that in the 1990s the US population increased in large metro, small metro, and non-metro areas when compared to the population growth experienced in the 1980s. Large metro areas experienced a growth of 12.5% in the 1980s versus a growth of 14.3% in the 1990s, small metro areas experienced a growth of 8.8% in the 1980s versus a growth of 13.1% in the 1990s, and non-metro areas experienced a growth of 1.8% in the 1980s versus a growth of 9.0% in the 1990s. Given this information, the population grew more in all metro areas in the 1990s when compared to the growth of those areas in the 1980s.

Choices A, B, and C are incorrect because they do not draw an accurate conclusion about the US growth rate in the 1990s.

QUESTION 22

Choice A is the best answer. Lines 9-11 introduce the focus of the passage: "Welcome to the world of 'pharming,' in which simple genetic tweaks turn animals into living pharmaceutical factories." The passage then discusses the chronological development of "pharming," and describes ATryn, a useful drug produced after decades of laboratory experiments.

Choices B and C are incorrect because the passage does not primarily evaluate research or summarize long-term research findings. Choice D is incorrect because "pharming" is not a branch of scientific study.

QUESTION 23

Choice C is the best answer. The author is appreciative of pharming and describes it as turning "animals into living pharmaceutical factories" (lines 10-11). She expresses a positive view of pharming in line 70, when she describes its end result: "*Et voilà* — human medicine!"

Choices A, B, and D are incorrect because the author's attitude about pharming is not accurately characterized as one of fear, disinterest, or surprise.

QUESTION 24

Choice C is the best answer. In lines 19-21, the author explains that dairy animals are "expert," or capable, "protein producers."

Choices A, B, and D are incorrect because in this context "expert" does not mean knowledgeable, professional, or trained.

QUESTION 25

Choice B is the best answer. In line 36, the author explains that the initial transgenic studies were "lab-bound thought experiments come true." Those first studies, in other words, were considered to be of theoretical value only. They were not expected to yield products ready for human use.

Choices A and D are incorrect because the cost of animal research and the molecular properties of certain animals are not discussed in the passage. Choice C is incorrect because the passage does not suggest that all of the transgenic studies were focused on anticoagulants.

QUESTION 26

Choice C is the best answer. In lines 35-36, the author provides evidence that the transgenic studies done in the 1980s and 1990s were not expected to yield products ready for human use. The author explains that the initial transgenic studies were "merely gee-whiz, scientific geekery, lab-bound thought experiments come true."

Choices A, B, and D are incorrect because they do not provide evidence that the transgenic studies done in the 1980s and 1990s were not expected to yield products ready for human use. Choices A and B do not address the transgenic studies, and choice D focuses on ATryn, a drug that was intended for human use.

QUESTION 27

Choice A is the best answer. Lines 42-44 explain that ATryn "acts as a molecular bouncer, sidling up to clot-forming compounds and escorting them out of the bloodstream." Antithrombin can thus be seen as an agent that reduces the amount of dangerous clots in the bloodstream.

Choices B, C, and D are incorrect because the passage does not suggest that antithrombin stems from a rare genetic mutation, is a sequence of DNA, or occurs naturally in goats' mammary glands.

QUESTION 28

Choice B is the best answer. Lines 42-44 provide evidence that antithrombin reduces compounds that lead to blood clots, as it acts as a "molecular bouncer, sidling up to clot-forming compounds and escorting them out of the bloodstream."

Choices A, C, and D do not provide evidence that antithrombin reduces compounds that lead to blood clots; these lines describe proteins, people unable to produce antithrombin, and the production of ATryn.

QUESTION 29

Choice B is the best answer. In lines 60-62, the description of female goats' kids mentions that "some of them proved to be transgenic, the human gene nestled safely in their cells." The statement "some of them" indicates that while a number of the newborn goats were transgenic, others were not.

Choices A, C, and D are incorrect because the passage does not suggest that the female goats used in the initial experiment secreted antithrombin in their milk after giving birth, were the first animals to receive the microinjections, or had cells that contained genes usually found in humans.

QUESTION 30

Choice D is the best answer. In lines 63-64, the parenthetical is added after the phrase "a promoter," which is "(. . . a sequence of DNA that controls gene activity)." The parenthetical's purpose is to define the term "promoter."

Choices A, B, and C are incorrect because they do not correctly identify the purpose of the parenthetical information in lines 63-64.

QUESTION 31

Choice D is the best answer. Gold is a valuable element that commands high prices, so calling something "liquid gold" implies that it has great value. Because the pharmaceutical company GTC was producing the drug in order to sell it, it can be inferred that describing ATryn as "liquid gold" means it proved to be a lucrative product for GTC.

Choices A, B, and C are incorrect because the phrase "liquid gold" does not refer to the microinjection technique, efficiency in dairy production, or transgenic goats being beneficial to dairy farmers.

QUESTION 32

Choice D is the best answer. In lines 25-29, Burke describes the contract between a person and society as one that is "not a partnership in things subservient only to the gross animal existence of a temporary and perishable nature. It is a partnership in all science; a partnership in all art; a partnership in every virtue, and in all perfection." Describing that contract as a partnership in all things indicates its seriousness, while describing it as not being a "temporary and perishable nature" implies its permanence.

Choice A is incorrect because line 27 states that the contract between a person and society is not "temporary or perishable," meaning it is not brief. Choices B and C are incorrect because the passage does not compare the contracts in terms of complexity or precision.

QUESTION 33

Choice D is the best answer. In lines 1-9, Burke explains that people have "consecrated the state" to "avoid . . . the evils of inconstancy and versatility," and that people should examine "the faults of the state . . . with pious awe and trembling solitude." Burke then explains that society is taught to "look with horror on those children of their country who want to hack that aged parent in pieces" (lines 10-12). Burke is arguing that children want to revise the state, or "this aged parent," by amending its faults. In this context, "state" refers to a political entity, or government, that attempts to protect its citizens from "the evils of inconstancy and versatility."

Choices A, B, and C are incorrect because in this context, "state" does not mean style of living, position in life, or temporary condition.

QUESTION 34

Choice A is the best answer. In lines 17-29, Burke argues that "subordinate contracts," are simply business agreements over traded goods, while the state is not merely "a partnership agreement in a trade . . . or some other such low concern . . . but a partnership in all science; a partnership in all art; a partnership in every virtue, and in all perfection." In this context, Burke is stating that the state is not a contract consisting of "low" or petty concerns.

Choices B, C, and D are incorrect because in this context, "low" does not mean weak, inadequate, or depleted.

QUESTION 35

Choice D is the best answer. In lines 41-43, Paine asserts that "Every age and generation must be as free to act for itself, *in all cases*, as the ages and generations which preceded it." He later states that deceased citizens of a state should no longer have "any authority in directing who shall be its governors, or how its government shall be organized, or how administered" (lines 61-63). Paine doesn't believe, in other words, that the decisions of previous generations should dictate the conditions of modern life and government.

Choices A, B, and C are incorrect because they do not accurately characterize the way Paine views historical precedents.

QUESTION 36

Choice B is the best answer. In lines 30-34, Burke describes societal contracts as long-term agreements that preserve the interests of past generations and link the living and the dead into a "partnership." Paine, however, states that past generations have no "control" over the decisions made by living (line 71) because the dead have "no longer any participation in the concerns of this world" (lines 59-60).

Choices A, C, and D are incorrect because they do not accurately characterize how Paine would respond to Burke's claim that societal contracts link past and current generations.

QUESTION 37

Choice D is the best answer. Lines 67-72 provide the best evidence that Paine would respond to Burke's statement that society is a "partnership" between past and current generations (lines 30-34) with the explanation that the current generation cannot know what judgments the dead would make about contemporary issues. In these lines Paine explains: "What possible obligation, then, can exist between them; what rule or principle can be laid down, that two nonentities, the one out of existence, and the other not in, and who never can meet in this world, that the one should control the other to the end of time?"

Choices A, B, and C are incorrect because the lines cited do not provide the best evidence that Paine would respond to Burke's statement that society is a "partnership" between past and current generations (lines 30-34) by arguing that the current generation cannot know what judgments the dead would make about contemporary issues.

QUESTION 38

Choice D is the best answer. Paine concludes Passage 2 with the argument that because social issues change over time, the living should not try to adhere to decisions made by former generations (lines 73-80). Burke, however, states that living citizens exist within a "universal kingdom" (line 35) comprised of the living, the dead, and those who are not yet born. Burke argues that the living do not have the right to change their government based on "their speculations of a contingent improvement" (lines 36-37). Therefore, Burke would disapprove of Paine's concluding argument, as he believes the living do not have sufficient justification for changing the existing governmental structure.

Choices A, B, and C are incorrect because they do not accurately describe how Burke would likely have responded to Paine's remarks in the final paragraph of Passage 2.

QUESTION 39

Choice D is the best answer. Lines 34-38 provide the best evidence that Burke would disapprove of Paine's remarks in the final paragraph of Passage 2: "The municipal corporations of that universal kingdom are not morally at liberty at [the living's] pleasure, and on their speculations of a contingent improvement, wholly to separate and tear asunder the bands of their subordinate community." In these lines, Burke is arguing that the living do not have sufficient justification to change the existing governmental structure.

Choices A, B, and C do not provide the best evidence that Burke would disapprove of Paine's remarks in the final paragraph of Passage 2, as Burke believes the living do not have sufficient justification for changing the existing governmental structure.

QUESTION 40

Choice A is the best answer. The primary argument of Passage 1 is that an inviolable contract exists between a people and its government, one that is to be "looked on with other reverence" (lines 24-25). Passage 1 suggests that this contract exists between past and future generations as well; in effect, current and future generations should be governed by decisions made in the past. Passage 2 challenges these points, as it argues that current and future generations are not obligated to preserve past generations' beliefs: "The Parliament or the people of 1688, or of any other period, had no more right to dispose of the people of the present day, or to bind or to control them in any shape whatever, than the parliament or the people of the present day have to dispose of, bind, or control those who are to live a hundred or a thousand years hence" (lines 48-54).

Choices B, C, and D are incorrect because Passage 2 does not offer an alternative approach to Passage 1, support an idea introduced in Passage 1, or exemplify an attitude promoted in Passage 1.

QUESTION 41

Choice B is the best answer. Passage 1 argues that the government is sacred (lines 3-6) and that no person should interfere with it (lines 6-9). Passage 2 argues that people have the right to make changes to their government: "The circumstances of the world are continually changing, and the opinions of men change also; and as government is for the living, and not for the dead, it is the living only that has any right in it" (lines 73-76).

Choices A, C, and D are incorrect because they do not identify the main purpose of both passages.

QUESTION 42

Choice C is the best answer. The author explains that a "powerful volcano" erupted around 750 years ago and caused "a centuries-long cold snap known as the Little Ice Age" (lines 1-3). The author then states that a group of scientists believe the volcano Samalas was this "powerful volcano," and she explains how the scientists' research supports this claim (lines 17-78).

Choices A, B, and D are incorrect because they do not identify the main purpose of the passage.

QUESTION 43

Choice B is the best answer. The author begins the passage by explaining how the Little Ice Age was a "centuries-long cold snap" that was likely caused by a volcanic eruption (lines 1-3). The author then explains how scientists used radiocarbon analysis to determine when the Little Ice Age began and how a volcanic eruption triggered the cooling temperatures (lines 17-25).

Choices A, C, and D are incorrect because the passage does not criticize a scientific model, offer a new method of measuring sulfates, or shift from the use of radiocarbon dating to an examination of volcanic glass.

QUESTION 44

Choice A is the best answer. In lines 17-25, the passage shifts focus from describing a recorded event to providing evidence that the Little Ice Age was likely caused by a volcanic eruption. The passage states that scientists used "radiocarbon dating of dead plant material from beneath the ice caps on Baffin Island and Iceland, as well as ice and sediment core data" to determine when the Little Ice Age began and how it was connected to the "mystery" volcanic eruption.

Choices B, C, and D are incorrect because they do not provide the best evidence that the passage shifts focus from a description of a recorded event to its likely cause. Choices B, C, and D all focus on the scientists' research but do not explain what caused the Little Ice Age.

QUESTION 45

Choice D is the best answer. According to lines 5-8, "That a powerful volcano erupted somewhere in the world, sometime in the Middle Ages, is written in polar ice cores in the form of layers of sulfate deposits and tiny shards of volcanic glass." The phrase "is written in" reinforces the idea that the polar ice caps contain evidence of the volcanic eruption, and that scientists can interpret this evidence by examining the "sulfate deposits and tiny shards of volcanic glass."

Choices A, B, and C are incorrect because the author does not use the phrase "is written in" to demonstrate the concept of the hands-on nature of the scientists' work, highlight the fact that scientists often write about their work, or underscore the sense of importance scientists have about their work.

QUESTION 46

Choice A is the best answer. The scientists believe the volcano Samalas, located in Indonesia, was most likely the medieval volcanic eruption (lines 33-35). The eruption likely occurred near the equator because an equatorial location is "consistent with the apparent climate impacts" the scientists observed (lines 61-67).

Choices B, C, and D are incorrect because the scientists do not suggest that the medieval volcanic eruption was located in the Arctic region, the Antarctic region, or Ecuador.

QUESTION 47

Choice D is the best answer. In lines 61-64, the author cites geochemist Gifford Miller's findings that provide evidence that the medieval volcanic eruption most likely occurred in Indonesia near the equator: "It's not a total surprise that an Indonesian volcano might be the source of the eruption, Miller says. 'An equatorial eruption is more consistent with the apparent climate impacts.'"

Choices A, B, and C are incorrect because they do not provide evidence that the medieval volcanic eruption most likely occurred in Indonesia near the equator. Rather, choices A, B, and C focus on the medieval volcano's power, impact, and magnitude.

QUESTION 48

Choice C is the best answer. In lines 68-71, the author states, "Another possible candidate — both in terms of timing and geographical location — is Ecuador's Quilotoa, estimated to have last erupted between 1147 and 1320 C.E." The phrase "another possible candidate" implies that the scientists believe that in the Middle Ages a different volcanic eruption, such as an eruption from the volcano Quilotoa, could have been responsible for the onset of the Little Ice Age.

Choices A, B, and D are incorrect because the phrase "another possible candidate" does not imply the frequency or effects of volcanic eruptions, or that some volcanoes have large calderas.

QUESTION 49

Choice D is the best answer. In lines 71-75, the author explains how Lavigne's team proved that Quilotoa's eruption did not cause the Little Ice Age:

"But when Lavigne's team examined shards of volcanic glass from this volcano, they found that they didn't match the chemical composition of the glass found in polar ice cores, whereas the Samalas glass is a much closer match." These findings show that Samalas, not Quilotoa, was responsible for the onset of the Little Ice Age.

Choices A, B, and C are incorrect because they focus on the difficulty of identifying the volcano responsible for the Little Ice Age, the magnitude of the volcanic eruption, and the researchers' experiment.

QUESTION 50

Choice C is the best answer. The data in the figure show the greatest below-average temperature variation occurred in 1675 CE, as the temperature reached a variation of −1.0° Celsius.

Choice A is incorrect because the figure shows that the temperature in 1200 CE was above average (+0.25° Celsius). Choices B and D are incorrect because the below-average temperature variation reported in 1675 CE (at −1.0° Celsius) was greater than the below-average temperature variation reported for 1375 CE (around −0.25° Celsius) and 1750 CE (around (−0.5° Celsius).

QUESTION 51

Choice B is the best answer. The passage says that the Little Ice Age began "about 750 years ago" (line 1) and that "the cold summers and ice growth began abruptly between 1275 and 1300 C.E." (lines 23-24). The figure indicates that average temperatures in central England began to drop around 1275 CE, and this drop in temperatures continued "through the 1700s" (line 32).

Choices A, C, and D are incorrect because the passage and figure do not indicate that the Little Ice Again began around 1150 CE, just before 1500 CE, or around 1650 CE.

QUESTION 52

Choice A is the best answer. The figure shows that the greatest cooling period of the Little Ice Age occurred between 1500 and 1700 CE; it also shows that the greatest warming period of the Medieval Warm Period occurred between 1150 and 1250 CE. Therefore, the Little Ice Age's greatest cooling occurred a couple of centuries, or "hundreds of years," after the temperature peaks of the Medieval Warm Period.

Choices B, C, and D are incorrect because the figure does not focus on equatorial volcanic eruptions, pyroclastic flows, or radiocarbon analysis.

Section 2: Writing and Language Test

QUESTION 1

Choice B is the best answer because the relative clause appropriately modifies the noun "work" in the preceding independent clause.

Choices A, C, and D are incorrect because each creates a comma splice.

QUESTION 2

Choice B is the best answer because it creates the appropriate contrasting transition from the fact that the first two panels were painted during the day to the fact that the third panel was painted at night.

Choices A, C, and D are incorrect because each creates an inappropriate transition from the previous sentence. Choice A and choice D imply addition rather than contrast. Choice C results in an incomplete sentence.

QUESTION 3

Choice B is the best answer because it creates an appropriate appositive to the subject "mural," and is correctly set off by commas on both sides.

Choices A, C, and D are incorrect because each is incorrectly punctuated. Choice A lacks a comma after "centerpiece," choice C unnecessarily introduces an independent clause, and choice D contains an em dash that has no parallel earlier in the sentence.

QUESTION 4

Choice A is the best answer because it explicitly introduces the explanation for the behavior (painting at night) described in the previous paragraph.

Choices B, C, and D are incorrect because none alludes to the artist's painting at night, which is described at the end of the previous paragraph and explained in this paragraph.

QUESTION 5

Choice D is the best answer because it refers to an action that can be performed on a physical object such as a mural.

Choices A, B, and C are incorrect because each refers to an action that is performed on information rather than on a physical object.

QUESTION 6

Choice B is the best answer because it creates a past tense construction consistent with the verb "was dominated."

Choices A, C, and D are incorrect because none is consistent with the verb tense established earlier in the sentence.

QUESTION 7

Choice D is the best answer because it is the most precise choice, specifying the noun that the demonstrative pronoun "this" refers to.

Choices A, B, and C are incorrect because each provides a vague, nonspecific pronoun that does not concretely define a referent.

QUESTION 8

Choice B is the best answer because it correctly places and punctuates the appositive phrase that describes the "Chicano mural movement."

Choices A, C, and D are incorrect because each contains awkward syntax that obscures the relationship between the key noun phrases "an explosion of mural painting" and "the Chicano mural movement."

QUESTION 9

Choice C is the best answer because it creates parallel construction within the list of locations ("*in* abandoned lots, *on* unused buildings, or *on* infrastructure").

Choices A, B, and D are incorrect because none follows the construction established within the list of locations.

QUESTION 10

Choice A is the best answer because it alludes to the uniquely high level of investment, described in the next sentence, that the new group of artists is making in restoring and publicizing "América Tropical."

Choices B, C, and D are incorrect because each fails to express the connection between the general restoration efforts mentioned in the previous sentence and the specific role of "América Tropical" in these efforts, which is described in the next sentence.

QUESTION 11

Choice C is the best answer because details of the initial reaction to Siqueiros's mural and its subsequent rediscovery are given previously in the passage and are not needed to set up the forward-looking sentence that follows.

Choices A, B, and D are incorrect because each provides an inaccurate interpretation of the sentence that the writer is considering adding.

QUESTION 12

Choice D is the best answer because without the underlined portion, the sentence contains an appropriate parallel contrast between the phrases "organically grown crops" and "conventionally grown counterparts," each of which describes crops.

Choices A, B, and C are incorrect because each creates an illogical comparison: crops to "people," crops to "purchase," and crops to "purchasing."

QUESTION 13

Choice B is the best answer because it provides the subject "consumers," creating a complete sentence and providing a referent for the pronoun "they" that appears later in the sentence.

Choices A, C, and D are incorrect because each lacks the subject that the sentence requires and none provide a referent for "they."

QUESTION 14

Choice D is the best answer because it efficiently creates a contrast with "organically grown."

Choices A, B, and C are incorrect because they are unnecessarily wordy and repeat information given in previous sentences.

QUESTION 15

Choice C is the best answer because it sets up the contrast between the added expense of organic food and the evidence that suggests a lack of benefits from eating organic food.

Choices A, B, and D are incorrect because each fails to acknowledge the contrast between the last sentence in the paragraph and the previous sentences.

QUESTION 16

Choice C is the best answer because "maintain" is commonly used to describe advocating a position in an argument.

Choices A, B, and D are incorrect because none is appropriate in the context of describing an opinion advocated by a group of people.

QUESTION 17

Choice A is the best answer because the transitional phrase "For instance" sets up an example supporting the point, made in the previous sentence, that organic food may not contain more vitamins and minerals than conventionally grown food.

Choices B, C, and D are incorrect because none indicates that the sentence is providing an example supporting the point made in the previous sentence.

QUESTION 18

Choice C is the best answer because it accurately identifies the reason that the writer should not add the proposed sentence: the paragraph is about evidence of nutritional content, not the availability of organic food.

Choices A, B, and D are incorrect because each provides an inaccurate interpretation of the proposed sentence's relationship to the passage.

QUESTION 19

Choice A is the best answer because the plural verb "have" is consistent with the plural subject "amounts."

Choices B, C, and D are incorrect because each is a singular verb, which is inconsistent with the plural subject "amounts."

QUESTION 20

Choice C is the best answer because the example it supplies, that pesticides can be minimized by washing or peeling produce, supports the claim that nonorganic food is safe.

Choices A, B, and D are incorrect because none supports the paragraph's claim about the safety of nonorganic food.

QUESTION 21

Choice B is the best answer because the plural noun phrase "numerous other reasons" must be preceded by a plural verb and a pronoun that does not indicate possession: "there are."

Choices A, C, and D are incorrect because each contains the singular verb "is," the possessive pronoun "their," or both.

QUESTION 22

Choice D is the best answer because a nonrestrictive clause must be preceded by a comma; in addition, "such as" is never followed by a comma. In this case, the list of reasons supporting the claim that there are benefits to buying organic food is nonrestrictive; the list tells the reader something about organic food but does not restrict or place limits on organic food.

Choices A, B, and C are incorrect because each places erroneous punctuation after the phrase "such as." Choices B and C also lack the necessary comma preceding "such as."

QUESTION 23

Choice C is the best answer because "intriguing" conveys a realistic level of interest for the entertaining but ultimately inconsequential question of regional differences in words for carbonated beverages.

Choices A, B, and D are incorrect because each mocks the topic of regional words for carbonated beverages.

QUESTION 24

Choice C is the best answer because "but also" is the appropriate transition to complete the correlative pair "not only . . . but also," which begins earlier in the sentence.

Choices A, B, and D are incorrect because each fails to complete the phrase "not only . . . but also."

QUESTION 25

Choice B is the best answer because it is consistent with the fact that there remains a "veritable army of trained volunteers traveling the country" and because it uses "still" to contrast this method with the "new avenues."

Choices A, C, and D are incorrect because none is consistent with the information contained later in the passage.

QUESTION 26

Choice D is the best answer because it uses the relative pronoun "who" to avoid needless repetition of the word "scholars."

Choices A, B, and C are incorrect because each unnecessarily repeats the word "scholars."

QUESTION 27

Choice C is the best answer because the new sentence provides a logical transition from sentences 3 and 4, which describe the data collection, to sentence 5, which explains that completing the dictionary took far longer than expected.

Choices A, B, and D are incorrect because each fails to create a logical transition between the preceding and subsequent sentences.

QUESTION 28

Choice A is the best answer because the singular verb "requires" agrees with the singular subject "research."

Choices B, C, and D are incorrect because they do not create subject-verb agreement.

QUESTION 29

Choice D is the best answer because a colon is the correct punctuation to introduce the elaborating phrase that follows the word "army."

Choices A, B, and C are incorrect because none provides the appropriate punctuation.

QUESTION 30

Choice B is the best answer because it contains both the correct word to refer to an Internet location — "site" — and the correct preposition to complete the collocation "in search of."

Choices A, C, and D are incorrect because each contains a word that does not refer to an Internet location, and choices C and D contain the wrong preposition.

QUESTION 31

Choice C is the best answer because it correctly associates each beverage term with the region described in the sentence according to the information contained in the map.

Choices A, B, and D are incorrect because each contradicts the information contained in the map.

QUESTION 32

Choice B is the best answer because it contains the two plural possessive pronouns needed to refer to the subject "findings" — "their" and "their."

Choices A, C, and D are incorrect because each contains a word frequently confused with "their."

QUESTION 33

Choice A is the best answer because it provides a summary and evaluation of gathering data from the Internet, which is the focus of the paragraph.

Choices B, C, and D are incorrect because each is either irrelevant to the main point of the paragraph or unnecessarily repeats information.

QUESTION 34

Choice C is the best answer because it uses the present tense, which is consistent with the verbs that appear later in the sentence.

Choices A, B, and D are incorrect because they create awkward shifts in tense.

QUESTION 35

Choice C is the best answer because the em dashes correctly bracket the examples of the types of elements.

Choices A, B, and D are incorrect because each uses either inconsistent or incorrect punctuation to set off the types of elements.

QUESTION 36

Choice B is the best answer because a period is an appropriate way to separate the two independent clauses that meet at the underlined text.

Choices A, C, and D are incorrect because each either creates a comma splice or lacks necessary punctuation.

QUESTION 37

Choice D is the best answer because the proposed sentence to be added is a paraphrase of the sentence before it, containing the same ideas.

Choices A, B, and C are incorrect because none fully acknowledges the relationship between the proposed sentence to be added and the other sentences in the paragraph.

QUESTION 38

Choice A is the best answer because it highlights the importance of the game designer's communication with others, which is the paragraph's main point.

Choices B, C, and D are incorrect because none describes communication originating with the game designer, which is the main focus of the paragraph.

QUESTION 39

Choice C is the best answer because the importance of communication is established in the previous sentences. The transition "consequently" best captures the fact that the designer must be skilled in this area.

Choices A, B, and D are incorrect because each contains a transition that either repeats information or creates an illogical relationship between this sentence and the previous sentences.

QUESTION 40

Choice B is the best answer because it provides the singular nouns "writer" and "speaker" to agree with the singular pronoun "anyone."

Choices A, C, and D are incorrect because none creates pronoun-referent agreement.

QUESTION 41

Choice D is the best answer because it expresses in the clearest, simplest way the idea that many game designers start out as programmers.

Choices A, B, and C are incorrect because each is unnecessarily wordy and obscures meaning.

QUESTION 42

Choice D is the best answer because it logically and appropriately modifies the phrase "collaboration skills."

Choices A, B, and C are incorrect because none appropriately describes the value of collaboration skills.

QUESTION 43

Choice A is the best answer because it provides a logical subject for the modifying phrase "demanding and deadline driven."

Choices B, C, and D are incorrect because each creates a dangling modifier.

QUESTION 44

Choice B is the best answer because sentence 5 expresses the main point upon which the paragraph elaborates.

Choices A, C, and D are incorrect because none places sentence 5 in the appropriate position to set up the details contained in the paragraph.

Section 3: Math Test – No Calculator

QUESTION 1

Choice A is correct. The expression $|x - 1| - 1$ will equal 0 if $|x - 1| = 1$. This is true for $x = 2$ and for $x = 0$. For example, substituting $x = 2$ into the expression $|x - 1| - 1$ and simplifying the result yields $|2 - 1| - 1 = |1| - 1 = 1 - 1 = 0$. Therefore, there is a value of x for which $|x - 1| - 1$ is equal to 0.

Choices B, C, and D are incorrect. By definition, the absolute value of any expression is a nonnegative number. For example, in answer choice B, substituting any value for x into the expression $|x + 1|$ will yield a nonnegative number. Because the sum of a nonnegative number and a positive number is positive, $|x + 1| + 1$ will be a positive number for any value of x. Therefore, $|x + 1| + 1 \neq 0$ for any value of x. Similarly, the expressions given in answer choices C and D are not equivalent to zero for any value of x.

QUESTION 2

Choice A is correct. Since $f(x) = \frac{3}{2}x + b$ and $f(6) = 7$, substituting 6 for x in $f(x) = \frac{3}{2}x + b$ gives $f(6) = \frac{3}{2}(6) + b = 7$. Then, solving the equation $\frac{3}{2}(6) + b = 7$ for b gives $\frac{18}{2} + b = 7$, or $9 + b = 7$. Thus, $b = 7 - 9 = -2$. Substituting -2 for the constant b gives $f(x) = \frac{3}{2}x - 2$; therefore, one can evaluate $f(-2)$ by substituting -2 for x: $\frac{3}{2}(-2) - 2 = -\frac{6}{2} - 2 = -3 - 2 = -5$.

Choice B is incorrect as it is the value of b, not of $f(-2)$. Choice C is incorrect as it is the value of $f(2)$, not of $f(-2)$. Choice D is incorrect as it is the value of $f(6)$, not of $f(-2)$.

QUESTION 3

Choice A is correct. The first equation can be rewritten as $x = 6y$. Substituting $6y$ for x in the second equation gives $4(y + 1) = 6y$. The left-hand side can be rewritten as $4y + 4$, giving $4y + 4 = 6y$. Subtracting $4y$ from both sides of the equation gives $4 = 2y$, or $y = 2$.

Choices B, C, and D are incorrect and may be the result of a computational or conceptual error when solving the system of equations.

QUESTION 4

Choice B is correct. If $f(x) = -2x + 5$, then one can evaluate $f(-3x)$ by substituting $-3x$ for every instance of x. This yields $f(-3x) = -2(-3x) + 5$, which simplifies to $6x + 5$.

Choices A, C, and D are incorrect and may be the result of miscalculations in the substitution or of misunderstandings of how to evaluate $f(-3x)$.

QUESTION 5

Choice C is correct. The expression $3(2x + 1)(4x + 1)$ can be simplified by first distributing the 3 to yield $(6x + 3)(4x + 1)$, and then multiplying the binomials together to obtain $24x^2 + 12x + 6x + 3$. Combining like terms gives $24x^2 + 18x + 3$.

Choice A is incorrect and may be the result of performing the multiplication of $3(2x + 1)(4x + 1)$ to result in $24x^2 + 18x + 3$, then incorrectly combining terms to result in $45x$. Choice B is incorrect and may be the result of correctly finding $(6x + 3)(4x + 1)$, but then multiplying only the first terms, $(6x)(4x)$, and the last terms, $(3)(1)$, but not the outer or inner terms, $(6x)(1)$ and $(3)(4x)$. Choice D is incorrect and may be the result of incorrectly distributing the 3 to both $(2x + 1)$ and $(4x + 1)$ to obtain $(6x + 3)(12x + 3)$, and then adding $3 + 3$ and $6x + 12x$ and incorrectly adding the exponents of x.

QUESTION 6

Choice B is correct. The equation $\frac{a-b}{b} = \frac{3}{7}$ can be rewritten as $\frac{a}{b} - \frac{b}{b} = \frac{3}{7}$, from which it follows that $\frac{a}{b} - 1 = \frac{3}{7}$, or $\frac{a}{b} = \frac{3}{7} + 1 = \frac{10}{7}$.

Choices A, C, and D are incorrect and may be the result of calculation errors in rewriting $\frac{a-b}{b} = \frac{3}{7}$. For example, choice A may be the result of a sign error in rewriting $\frac{a-b}{b}$ as $\frac{a}{b} + \frac{b}{b} = \frac{a}{b} + 1$.

QUESTION 7

Choice D is correct. In Amelia's training schedule, her longest run in week 16 will be 26 miles and her longest run in week 4 will be 8 miles. Thus, Amelia increases the distance of her longest run by 18 miles over the course of 12 weeks. Since Amelia increases the distance of her longest run each week by a constant amount, her rate of increase is $\frac{26-8}{16-4} = \frac{18}{12}$ miles per week, which is equal to 1.5 miles per week. So each week she increases the distance of her longest run by 1.5 miles.

Choices A, B, and C are incorrect because none of these training schedules would result in increasing Amelia's longest run from 8 miles in week 4 to 26 miles in week 16. For example, choice A is incorrect because if Amelia increases the distance of her longest run by 0.5 miles each week and has her longest run of 8 miles in week 4, her longest run in week 16 would be $8 + 0.5 \cdot 12 = 14$ miles, not 26 miles.

QUESTION 8

Choice A is correct. For an equation of a line in the form $y = mx + b$, the constant m is the slope of the line. Thus, the line represented by $y = -3x + 4$ has slope -3. Lines that are parallel have the same slope. To determine which of the given equations represents a line with the same slope as the line represented by $y = -3x + 4$, one can rewrite each equation in the form $y = mx + b$, that is, solve each equation for y. Choice A, $6x + 2y = 15$, can be rewritten as $2y = -6x + 15$ by subtracting $6x$ from each side of the equation. Then, dividing each side of $2y = -6x + 15$ by 2 gives $y = -\frac{6}{2}x + \frac{15}{2}$, which simplifies to $y = -3x + \frac{15}{2}$. Therefore, this line has slope -3 and is parallel to the line represented by $y = -3x + 4$. (The lines are parallel, not coincident, because they have different y-intercepts.)

Choices B, C, and D are incorrect and may be the result of common misunderstandings about which value in the equation of a line represents the slope of the line.

QUESTION 9

Choice D is correct. The question states that $\sqrt{x - a} = x - 4$ and that $a = 2$, so substituting 2 for a in the equation yields $\sqrt{x - 2} = x - 4$. To solve for x, square each side of the equation, which gives $\left(\sqrt{x - 2}\right)^2 = (x - 4)^2$, or $x - 2 = (x - 4)^2$. Then, expanding $(x - 4)^2$ yields $x - 2 = x^2 - 8x + 16$, or $0 = x^2 - 9x + 18$. Factoring the right-hand side gives $0 = (x - 3)(x - 6)$, and so $x = 3$ or $x = 6$. However, for $x = 3$, the original equation becomes $\sqrt{3 - 2} = 3 - 4$, which yields $1 = -1$, which is not true. Hence, $x = 3$ is an extraneous solution that arose from squaring each side of the equation. For $x = 6$, the original equation becomes $\sqrt{6 - 2} = 6 - 4$, which yields $\sqrt{4} = 2$, or $2 = 2$. Since this is true, the solution set of $\sqrt{x - 2} = x - 4$ is $\{6\}$.

Choice A is incorrect because it includes the extraneous solution in the solution set. Choice B is incorrect and may be the result of a calculation or factoring error. Choice C is incorrect because it includes only the extraneous solution, and not the correct solution, in the solution set.

QUESTION 10

Choice D is correct. Multiplying each side of $\frac{t+5}{t-5} = 10$ by $t - 5$ gives $t + 5 = 10(t - 5)$. Distributing the 10 to the binomial $(t - 5)$ yields $t + 5 = 10t - 50$. Subtracting t from each side of this equation gives $5 = 9t - 50$, and then adding 50 to each side gives $55 = 9t$. Finally, dividing each side of the equation $55 = 9t$ by 9 yields $t = \frac{55}{9}$.

Choices A, B, and C are incorrect and may be the result of calculation errors or incorrectly applying the distribution property.

QUESTION 11

Choice C is correct. It is given that $x = 2y + 5$ and $y = (2x - 3)(x + 9)$. To solve the system of equations, the quantity $(2x - 3)(x + 9)$ can be substituted for y in the first equation to yield $x = 2((2x - 3)(x + 9)) + 5$, which simplifies to $x = 4x^2 + 30x - 49$ and can be rewritten as $4x^2 + 29x - 49 = 0$. The discriminant of a quadratic equation in the form $ax^2 + bx + c = 0$, where a, b, and c are constants, is $b^2 - 4ac$. The discriminant for this quadratic equation is $29^2 - 4(4)(-49)$. This is a positive number which indicates that this quadratic equation has 2 distinct roots. The roots to the quadratic equation are the two x-coordinates of the ordered pairs which satisfy the system of equations. Since no other value of x satisfies $4x^2 + 29x - 49 = 0$, there are no other ordered pairs that satisfy the given system. Therefore, there are 2 ordered pairs (x, y) that satisfy the given system of equations.

Choices A and B are incorrect and may be the result of either a miscalculation or a conceptual error. Choice D is incorrect because a system of one quadratic equation and one linear equation cannot have infinitely many solutions.

QUESTION 12

Choice C is correct. Since the price of Ken's sandwich was x dollars, and Paul's sandwich was \$1 more, the price of Paul's sandwich was $x + 1$ dollars. Thus, the total cost of the sandwiches was $2x + 1$ dollars. Since this cost was split evenly between two people, Ken and Paul each paid $\frac{2x+1}{2} = x + 0.5$ dollars plus a 20% tip. After adding the 20% tip, each of them paid $(x + 0.5) + 0.2(x + 0.5) = 1.2(x + 0.5) = 1.2x + 0.6$ dollars.

Choices A, B, and D are incorrect. These expressions do not model the given context. They may be the result of errors in setting up the expression or of calculation errors.

QUESTION 13

Choice B is correct. The points where the two graphs intersect can be found by setting the functions $f(x)$ and $g(x)$ equal to one another and then solving for x. This yields $8x^2 - 2 = -8x^2 + 2$. Adding $8x^2$ and 2 to each side of the equation gives $16x^2 = 4$. Then dividing each side by 16 gives $x^2 = \frac{1}{4}$; therefore, x must be either $\frac{1}{2}$ or $-\frac{1}{2}$. From the graph, the value of k is the x-coordinate of the point of intersection on the positive x-axis. Therefore, $k = \frac{1}{2}$.

Alternatively, since $(k, 0)$ lies on the graph of both f and g, it follows that $f(k) = g(k) = 0$. Thus, evaluating $f(x) = 8x^2 - 2$ at $x = k$ gives $0 = 8k^2 - 2$. Adding 2 to each side yields $2 = 8k^2$ and then dividing each side by 8 gives $\frac{1}{4} = k^2$. Therefore, the value of k must be $\frac{1}{2}$ or $-\frac{1}{2}$. From the graph, k is positive, so $k = \frac{1}{2}$.

Choices A, C, and D are incorrect and may be the result of calculation errors in solving for x or k.

QUESTION 14

Choice A is correct. To rewrite $\frac{8-i}{3-2i}$ in the standard form $a+bi$, multiply the numerator and denominator of $\frac{8-i}{3-2i}$ by the conjugate of the denominator, $3+2i$. This gives $\left(\frac{8-i}{3-2i}\right)\left(\frac{3+2i}{3+2i}\right)=\frac{24+16i-3i+(-i)(2i)}{3^2-6i+6i-(2i)^2}$. Since $i^2=-1$, this can be rewritten as $\frac{24+16i-3i+2}{9-(-4)}=\frac{26+13i}{13}$, which simplifies to $2+i$. Therefore, when $\frac{8-i}{3-2i}$ is rewritten in the standard form $a+bi$, the value of a is 2.

Choices B, C, and D are incorrect and may be the result of errors in symbolic manipulation. For example, choice B could be the result of mistakenly rewriting $\frac{8-i}{3-2i}$ as $\frac{8}{3}+\frac{1}{2}i$.

QUESTION 15

Choice B is correct. The given quadratic equation can be rewritten as $2x^2-kx-4p=0$. Applying the quadratic formula, $\frac{-b\pm\sqrt{b^2-4ac}}{2a}$, to this equation with $a=2$, $b=-k$, and $c=-4p$ gives the solutions $\frac{k}{4}\pm\frac{\sqrt{k^2+32p}}{4}$.

Choices A, C, and D are incorrect and may be the result of errors in applying the quadratic formula.

QUESTION 16

The correct answer is 9. Since the three shelves of the triangular shelf system are parallel, the three triangles in the figure are similar. Since the shelves divide the left side of the largest triangle in the ratio 2 to 3 to 1, the similarity ratios of the triangles are as follows.

- Smallest to middle: 2 to 5
- Smallest to largest: 2 to 6, or 1 to 3
- Middle to largest: 5 to 6

The height of the largest shampoo bottle that can stand upright on the middle shelf is equal to the height of the middle shelf. The height of the entire triangular shelf system is 18 inches. This is the height of the largest triangle. The height of the middle shelf is the height of the middle triangle minus the height of the smallest triangle. Since the similarity ratio of the middle triangle to the largest triangle is 5 to 6, the height of the middle triangle is $\frac{5}{6}(18)=15$ inches. Since the similarity ratio of the smallest triangle to the largest triangle is 1 to 3, the height of the smallest triangle is $\frac{1}{3}(18) = 6$ inches. Therefore the height of the largest shampoo bottle that can fit on the middle shelf is $15 - 6 = 9$ inches.

Alternatively, in the diagram below, the altitude of the largest triangle has been drawn and is a line segment that intersects and is perpendicular to each of the parallel lines.

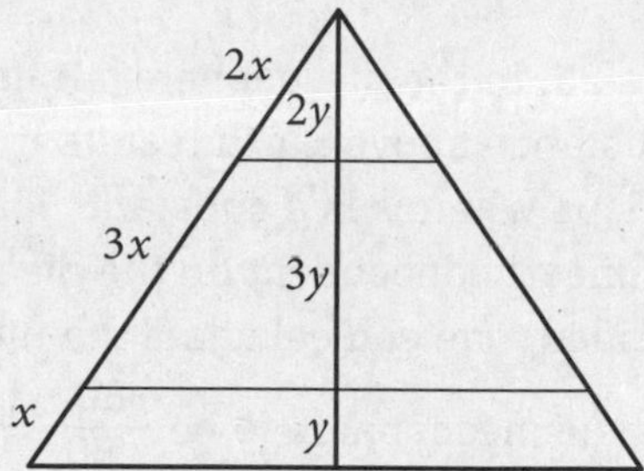

Using the proportional segment theorem, it follows that the lengths of the three segments formed by the altitude are in the ratio 2:3:1 (from top to bottom). If y is the length of the shortest segment, then the lengths of the three segments are $2y$, $3y$, and y, with $3y$ being the height of the middle shelf. Since $2y + 3y + y = 18$, it follows that $3y = 9$.

QUESTION 17

The correct answer is .6 or $\frac{3}{5}$. The angles marked $x°$ and $y°$ are acute angles in a right triangle. Thus, they are complementary angles. By the complementary angle relationship between sine and cosine, it follows that $\sin(x°) = \cos(y°)$. Therefore, the cosine of $y°$ is .6. Either .6 or the equivalent fraction 3/5 may be gridded as the correct answer.

Alternatively, since the sine of $x°$ is .6, the ratio of the side opposite the $x°$ angle to the hypotenuse is .6. The side opposite the $x°$ angle is the side adjacent to the $y°$ angle. Thus, the ratio of the side adjacent to the $y°$ angle to the hypotenuse, which is equal to the cosine of $y°$, is equal to .6.

QUESTION 18

The correct answer is 5. The four-term polynomial expression can be factored completely, by grouping, as follows:

$$(x^3 - 5x^2) + (2x - 10) = 0$$

$$x^2(x - 5) + 2(x - 5) = 0$$

$$(x - 5)(x^2 + 2) = 0$$

By the zero product property, set each factor of the polynomial equal to 0 and solve each resulting equation for x. This gives $x = 5$ or $x = \pm i\sqrt{2}$, respectively. Because the question asks for the real value of x that satisfies the equation, the correct answer is 5.

QUESTION 19

The correct answer is 0. Multiplying each side of $-3x + 4y = 20$ by 2 gives $-6x + 8y = 40$. Adding each side of $-6x + 8y = 40$ to the corresponding side of $6x + 3y = 15$ gives $11y = 55$, or $y = 5$. Finally, substituting 5 for y in $6x + 3y = 15$ gives $6x + 3(5) = 15$, or $x = 0$.

QUESTION 20

The correct answer is 25. In the mesosphere, an increase of 10 kilometers in the distance above Earth results in a decrease in the temperature by $k°$ Celsius where k is a constant. Thus, the temperature in the mesosphere is linearly dependent on the distance above Earth. Using the values provided, one can calculate the unit rate of change for the temperature in the mesosphere to be $\frac{-80 - (-5)}{80 - 50} = \frac{-75}{30} = \frac{-25}{10}$.

Therefore, within the mesosphere, if the distance above Earth increases by 1 kilometer, the temperature decreases by 2.5° Celsius. Therefore, if the distance above Earth increases by $(1 \times 10) = 10$ kilometers, the temperature will decrease by $(2.5 \times 10) = 25°$ Celsius. Thus, the value of k is 25.

Section 4: Math Test – Calculator

QUESTION 1

Choice B is correct. Let m be the number of movies Jill rented online during the month. Since the monthly membership fee is \$9.80 and there is an additional fee of \$1.50 to rent each movie online, the total of the membership fee and the movie rental fees, in dollars, can be written as $9.80 + 1.50m$. Since the total of these fees for the month was \$12.80, the equation $9.80 + 1.50m = 12.80$ must be true. Subtracting 9.80 from each side and then dividing each side by 1.50 yields $m = 2$.

Choices A, C, and D are incorrect and may be the result of errors in setting up or solving the equation that represents the context.

QUESTION 2

Choice C is correct. Donald believes he can increase his typing speed by 5 words per minute each month. Therefore, in m months, he believes he can increase his typing speed by $5m$ words per minute. Because he is currently able to type at a speed of 180 words per minute, he believes that in m months, he will be able to increase his typing speed to $180 + 5m$ words per minute.

Choice A is incorrect because the expression indicates that Donald currently types 5 words per minute and will increase his typing speed by 180 words per minute each month. Choice B is incorrect because the expression indicates that Donald currently types 225 words per minute, not 180 words per minute. Choice D is incorrect because the expression indicates that Donald will decrease, not increase, his typing speed by 5 words per minute each month.

QUESTION 3

Choice C is correct. Because there are 16 ounces in 1 pound, a 3-pound pizza weighs $3 \times 16 = 48$ ounces. One half of the pizza weighs $\frac{1}{2} \times 48 = 24$ ounces, and one-third of the half weighs $\frac{1}{3} \times 24 = 8$ ounces.

Alternatively, since $\frac{1}{2} \times \frac{1}{3} = \frac{1}{6}$, cutting the pizza into halves and then into thirds results in a pizza that is cut into sixths. Therefore, each slice of the 48-ounce pizza weighs $\frac{1}{6} \times 48 = 8$ ounces.

Choice A is incorrect and is the result of cutting each half into sixths rather than thirds. Choice B is incorrect and is the result of cutting each half into fourths rather than thirds. Choice D is incorrect and is the result of cutting the whole pizza into thirds.

QUESTION 4

Choice B is correct. Because Nick surveyed a random sample of the freshman class, his sample was representative of the entire freshman class. Thus, the percent of students in the entire freshman class expected to prefer the Fall Festival in October is appropriately estimated by the percent of students who preferred it in the sample, 25.6%. Thus, of the 225 students in the freshman class, approximately $225 \times 0.256 = 57.6$ or about 60 students would be expected to prefer having the Fall Festival in October.

Choices A, C, and D are incorrect. These choices may be the result of misapplying the concept of percent or of calculation errors.

QUESTION 5

Choice B is correct. The density of an object is equal to the mass of the object divided by the volume of the object, which can be expressed as density $= \frac{\text{mass}}{\text{volume}}$. Thus, if an object has a density of 3 grams per milliliter and a mass of 24 grams, the equation becomes 3 grams/milliliter $= \frac{24 \text{ grams}}{\text{volume}}$. This can be rewritten as volume $= \frac{24 \text{ grams}}{3 \text{ grams/milliliter}} = 8$ milliliters.

Choice A is incorrect and be may be the result of confusing the density and the volume and setting up the density equation as $24 = \frac{3}{\text{volume}}$. Choice C is incorrect and may be the result of a conceptual error that leads to subtracting 3 from 24. Choice D is incorrect and may be the result of confusing the mass and the volume and setting up the density equation as $24 = \frac{\text{volume}}{3}$.

QUESTION 6

Choice A is correct. Let a be the number of hours Angelica worked last week. Since Raul worked 11 more hours than Angelica, Raul worked $a + 11$ hours last week. Since they worked a combined total of 59 hours, the equation $a + (a + 11) = 59$ can represent this situation This equation can be simplified to $2a + 11 = 59$, or $2a = 48$. Therefore, $a = 24$, and Angelica worked 24 hours last week.

Choice B is incorrect because it is the number of hours Raul worked last week. Choice C is incorrect. If Angelica worked 40 hours and Raul worked 11 hours more, Raul would have worked 51 hours, and the combined total number of hours they worked would be 91, not 59. Choice D is incorrect and may be the result of solving the equation $a + 11 = 59$ rather than $a + (a + 11) = 59$.

QUESTION 7

Choice A is correct. According to the table, of the 50 movies with the greatest ticket sales in 2012, 4 are comedy movies with a PG-13 rating. Therefore, the proportion of the 50 movies with the greatest ticket sales in 2012 that are comedy movies with a PG-13 rating is $\frac{4}{50}$, or equivalently, $\frac{2}{25}$.

Choice B is incorrect; $\frac{9}{50}$ is the proportion of the 50 movies with the greatest ticket sales in 2012 that are comedy movies, regardless of rating. Choice C is incorrect; $\frac{2}{11} = \frac{4}{22}$ is the proportion of movies with a PG-13 rating that are comedy movies. Choice D is incorrect; $\frac{11}{25} = \frac{22}{50}$ is the proportion of the 50 movies with the greatest ticket sales in 2012 that have a rating of PG-13.

QUESTION 8

Choice D is correct. The quadrants of the xy-plane are defined as follows: Quadrant I is above the x-axis and to the right of the y-axis; Quadrant II is above the x-axis and to the left of the y-axis; Quadrant III is below the x-axis and to the left of the y-axis; and Quadrant IV is below the x-axis and to the right of the y-axis. It is possible for line ℓ to pass through Quadrants II, III, and IV, but not Quadrant I, only if line ℓ has negative x- and y-intercepts. This implies that line ℓ has a negative slope, since between the negative x-intercept and the negative y-intercept the value of x increases (from negative to zero) and the value of y decreases (from zero to negative); so the quotient of the change in y over the change in x, that is, the slope of line ℓ, must be negative.

Choice A is incorrect because a line with an undefined slope is a vertical line, and if a vertical line passes through Quadrant IV, it must pass through Quadrant I as well. Choice B is incorrect because a line with a slope of zero is a horizontal line and, if a horizontal line passes through Quadrant II, it must pass through Quadrant I as well. Choice C is incorrect because if a line with a positive slope passes through Quadrant IV, it must pass through Quadrant I as well.

QUESTION 9

Choice B is correct. According to the table, in 2012 there was a total of 14,766 + 47,896 = 62,662 registered voters between 18 and 44 years old, and 3,453 + 11,237 = 14,690 of them were from the Midwest region. Therefore, the probability that a randomly chosen registered voter who was between 18 and 44 years old in 2012 was from the Midwest region is $\frac{14{,}690}{62{,}662} \approx 0.234$. Of the given choices, 0.25 is closest to this value.

Choice A is incorrect; this is the probability of selecting at random a registered voter from the Midwest who is 18 to 24 years old. Choice C is incorrect; this is the probability of selecting at random a registered voter from the Midwest who is 18 to 44 years old. Choice D is incorrect and may be the result of errors made when choosing the correct proportion or in calculating the probability.

QUESTION 10

Choice A is correct. According to the graph, the animal with the longest gestation period (60 days) has a life expectancy of 3 years.

Choices B, C, and D are incorrect. All the animals that have a life expectancy of 4, 8, or 10 years have a gestation period that is shorter than 60 days, which is the longest gestation period.

QUESTION 11

Choice A is correct. The ratio of life expectancy to gestation period for the animal represented by point A is approximately $\frac{7 \text{ years}}{23 \text{ days}}$, or about 0.3 years/day, which is greater than the ratio for the animals represented by the other labeled points (the ratios for points B, C, and D, in units of years of life expectancy per day of gestation, are approximately $\frac{8}{44}$, $\frac{8}{51}$, and $\frac{10}{51}$ respectively, each of which is less than 0.2 years/day).

Choices B, C, and D are incorrect and may be the result of errors in calculating the ratio or in reading the graph.

QUESTION 12

Choice C is correct. All of the given choices are polynomials. If the graph of a polynomial function f in the xy-plane has an x-intercept at b, then $(x - b)$ must be a factor of $f(x)$. Since -3, -1, and 1 are each x-intercepts of the graph of f, it follows that $(x + 3)$, $(x + 1)$, and $(x - 1)$ must each be a factor of $f(x)$. Of the given equations, only the equation in choice C has these 3 factors. Therefore, only the equation in choice C could define the function f.

Choices A, B, and D are incorrect because these equations do not contain all three factors necessary in order for the graph of the polynomial function f to have x-intercepts at -3, -1, and 1.

QUESTION 13

Choice C is correct. The mosquito population starts at 100 in week 0 and then is multiplied by a factor of 10 every 5 weeks. Thus, if $P(t)$ is the mosquito population after t weeks, then based on the table, $P(t) = 100\,(10)^{\frac{t}{5}}$, which indicates an exponential growth relationship.

Choice A is incorrect. Increasing linearly means that the estimated population grows by the same amount every 5 weeks. According to the table, from week 0 to week 5, the estimated population grows by 900 mosquitoes, and from week 5 to week 10, it grows by 9,900 mosquitoes. Therefore, the estimated population is not increasing linearly. Choices B and C are incorrect because according to the table, the estimated population is increasing, not decreasing.

QUESTION 14

Choice D is correct. According to the given formula, the amount of money generated for a year at 5% interest, compounded monthly, is $1{,}000\left(1 + \frac{5}{1{,}200}\right)^{12}$, whereas the amount of money generated at 3% interest, compounded monthly, is $1{,}000\left(1 + \frac{3}{1{,}200}\right)^{12}$. Therefore, the difference between these two amounts, $1{,}000\left(1 + \frac{5}{1{,}200}\right)^{12} - 1{,}000\left(1 + \frac{3}{1{,}200}\right)^{12}$, shows how much additional money is generated at an interest rate of 5% than at an interest rate of 3%.

Choices A, B, and C are incorrect and may be the result of misinterpreting the given formula. For example, the expression in choice C gives how many times as much money, not how much additional money, is generated at an interest rate of 5% than at an interest rate of 3%.

QUESTION 15

Choice B is correct. The graph of $y = ax^b$, where a is positive and b is negative, would show a trend that is decreasing, but with a rate of decrease that slows as x increases. Of the scatterplots shown, only the one in choice B would be appropriately modeled by such a function.

Choice A is incorrect, as this scatterplot is appropriately modeled by a linear function. Choice C is incorrect, as this scatterplot is appropriately modeled by an increasing function. Choice D is incorrect, as this scatterplot shows no clear relationship between x and y.

QUESTION 16

Choice A is correct. The total cost y, in dollars, of buying the materials and renting the tools for x days from Store A and Store B is found by substituting the respective values for these stores from the table into the given equation, $y = M + (W + K)x$, as shown below.

$$\text{Store A: } y = 750 + (15 + 65)x = 750 + 80x$$

$$\text{Store B: } y = 600 + (25 + 80)x = 600 + 105x$$

Thus, the number of days, x, for which the total cost of buying the materials and renting the tools from Store B is less than or equal to the total cost of buying the materials and renting the tools from Store A can be found by solving the inequality $600 + 105x \leq 750 + 80x$. Subtracting $80x$ and 600 from each side of $600 + 105x \leq 750 + 80x$ and combining like terms yields $25x \leq 150$. Dividing each side of $25x \leq 150$ by 25 yields $x \leq 6$.

Choice B is incorrect. The inequality $x \geq 6$ is the number of days for which the total cost of buying the materials and renting the tools from Store B is greater than or equal to the total cost of buying the materials and renting the tools from Store A. Choices C and D are incorrect and may be the result of an error in setting up or simplifying the inequality.

QUESTION 17

Choice D is correct. The total cost, y, of buying the materials and renting the tools in terms of the number of days, x, is given as $y = M + (W + K)x$. If this relationship is graphed in the xy-plane, the slope of the graph is equal to $W + K$, which is the daily rental cost of the wheelbarrow plus the daily rental cost of the concrete mixer, that is, the total daily rental costs of the tools.

Choice A is incorrect because the total cost of the project is y. Choice B is incorrect because the total cost of the materials is M, which is the y-intercept of the graph of $y = M + (W + K)x$. Choice C is incorrect because the total daily cost of the project is the total cost of the project divided by the total number of days the project took and, since materials cost more than 0 dollars, this is not the same as the total daily rental costs.

QUESTION 18

Choice C is correct. The volume V of a right circular cylinder is given by the formula $V = \pi r^2 h$, where r is the base radius of the cylinder and h is the height of the cylinder. Since each glass has an internal diameter of 3 inches, each glass has a base radius of $\frac{3}{2}$ inches. Since the height of the milk in each glass is 6 inches, the volume of milk in each glass is $V = \pi\left(\frac{3}{2}\right)^2(6) \approx 42.41$ cubic inches. The total number of glasses Jim can pour from 1 gallon is equal to $\frac{\text{number of cubic inches in 1 gallon}}{\text{number of cubic inches in 1 glass}} = \frac{231}{42.41}$, which is approximately 5.45 glasses. Since the question asks for the largest number of full glasses Jim can pour, the number of glasses needs to be rounded down to 5.

Choices A, B, and D are incorrect and may be the result of conceptual errors or calculation errors. For example, choice D is incorrect because even though Jim can pour more than 5 full glasses, he will not have enough milk to pour a full 6th glass.

QUESTION 19

Choice A is correct. Adding 4 to each side of the inequality $3p - 2 \geq 1$ yields the inequality $3p + 2 \geq 5$. Therefore, the least possible value of $3p + 2$ is 5.

Choice B is incorrect because it gives the least possible value of $3p$, not of $3p + 2$. Choice C is incorrect. If the least possible value of $3p + 2$ were 2, then it would follow that $3p + 2 \geq 2$. Subtracting 4 from each side of this inequality would yield $3p - 2 \geq -2$. This contradicts the given inequality, $3p - 2 \geq 1$. Therefore, the least possible value of $3p + 2$ cannot be 2. Choice D is incorrect because it gives the least possible value of p, not of $3p + 2$.

QUESTION 20

Choice C is correct. Since the biomass of the lake doubles each year, the biomass starts at a positive value and then increases exponentially over time. Of the graphs shown, only the graph in choice C is of an increasing exponential function.

Choice A is incorrect because the biomass of the lake must start at a positive value, not zero. Furthermore, this graph shows linear growth, not exponential growth. Choice B is incorrect because the biomass of the lake must start at a positive value, not zero. Furthermore, this graph has vertical segments and is not a function. Choice D is incorrect because the biomass of the lake does not remain the same over time.

QUESTION 21

Choice C is correct. For a data point to be above the line $y = x$, the value of y must be greater than the value of x. That is, the consumption in 2010 must be greater than the consumption in 2000. This occurs for 3 types of energy sources shown in the bar graph: biofuels, geothermal, and wind.

Choices A, B, and D are incorrect and may be the result of a conceptual error in presenting the data shown in a scatterplot. For example, choice B is incorrect because there are 2 data points in the scatterplot that lie <u>below</u> the line $y = x$.

QUESTION 22

Choice B is correct. Reading the graph, the amount of wood power used in 2000 was 2.25 quadrillion BTUs and the amount used in 2010 was 2.00 quadrillion BTUs. To find the percent decrease, find the positive difference between the two amounts, divide by the earlier amount (from 2000), and then multiply by 100: $\frac{2.25 - 2.00}{2.25} \times 100 = \frac{0.25}{2.25} \times 100 \approx 11.1$ percent. Of the choices given, 11% is closest to the percent decrease in the consumption of wood power from 2000 to 2010.

Choices A, C, and D are incorrect and may be the result of errors in reading the bar graph or in calculating the percent decrease.

QUESTION 23

Choice B is correct. The standard deviation is a measure of how far the data set values are from the mean. In the data set for City A, the large majority of the data are in three of the five possible values, which are the three values closest to the mean. In the data set for City B, the data are more spread out, with many values at the minimum and maximum values. Therefore, by observation, the data for City B have a larger standard deviation.

Alternatively, one can calculate the mean and visually inspect the difference between the data values and the mean. For City A the mean is $\frac{1,655}{21} \approx 78.8$, and for City B the mean is $\frac{1,637}{21} \approx 78.0$. The data for City A are closely clustered near 79, which indicates a small standard deviation. The data for City B are spread out away from 78, which indicates a larger standard deviation.

Choices A, C, and D are incorrect and may be the result of misconceptions about the standard deviation.

QUESTION 24

Choice C is correct. Since segment AD is a diameter of the circle, it follows that arc $\overset{\frown}{ADB}$ is a semicircle. Thus, the circumference of the circle is twice the length of arc $\overset{\frown}{ADB}$ which is $2(8\pi) = 16\pi$. Since the circumference of a circle is 2π times the radius of the circle, the radius of this circle is 16π divided by 2π, which is equal to 8.

Choice A is incorrect. If the radius of the circle is 2, the circumference of the circle would be $2(2\pi)$ and the length of arc $\overset{\frown}{ADB}$ would be 2π, not 8π. Choice B is incorrect. If the radius of the circle is 4, the circumference of the circle would be $2(4\pi)$ and the length of arc $\overset{\frown}{ADB}$ would be 4π, not 8π. Choice D is incorrect; 16 is the length of the diameter of the circle, not of the radius.

QUESTION 25

Choice B is correct. In $f(x)$, factoring out the greatest common factor, $2x$, yields $f(x) = 2x(x^2 + 3x + 2)$. It is given that $g(x) = x^2 + 3x + 2$, so using substitution, $f(x)$ can be rewritten as $f(x) = 2x \cdot g(x)$. In the equation $p(x) = f(x) + 3g(x)$, substituting $2x \cdot g(x)$ for $f(x)$ yields $p(x) = 2x \cdot g(x) + 3 \cdot g(x)$. In $p(x)$, factoring out the greatest common factor, $g(x)$, yields $p(x) = (g(x))(2x + 3)$. Because $2x + 3$ is a factor of $p(x)$, it follows that $p(x)$ is divisible by $2x + 3$.

Choices A, C, and D are incorrect because $2x + 3$ is not a factor of the polynomials $h(x)$, $r(x)$, or $s(x)$. Using the substitution $f(x) = 2x \cdot g(x)$, and factoring further, $h(x)$, $r(x)$, and $s(x)$ can be rewritten as follows:

$$h(x) = (x + 1)(x + 2)(2x + 1)$$

$$r(x) = (x + 1)(x + 2)(4x + 3)$$

$$s(x) = 2(x + 1)(x + 2)(3x + 1)$$

Because $2x + 3$ is not a factor of $h(x)$, $r(x)$, or $s(x)$, it follows that $h(x)$, $r(x)$, and $s(x)$ are each not divisible by $2x + 3$.

QUESTION 26

Choice C is correct. If $-y < x < y$, the value of x is either 0 or between $-y$ and 0 or between 0 and y, so statement I, $|x| < y$ is true. It is possible that the value of x is greater than zero, but x could be negative. For example, a counterexample to statement II, $x > 0$, is $x = -2$ and $y = 3$, yielding $-3 < -2 < 3$, so the given condition is satisfied. Statement III must be true since $-y < x < y$ implies that $-y < y$, so y must be greater than 0. Therefore, statements I and III are the only statements that must be true.

Choices A, B, and D are incorrect because each of these choices either omits a statement that must be true or includes a statement that could be false.

QUESTION 27

Choice D is correct. To interpret what the number 61 in the equation of the line of best fit represents, one must first understand what the data in the scatterplot represent. Each of the points in the scatterplot represents a large US city, graphed according to its population density (along the horizontal axis) and its relative housing cost (along the vertical axis). The line of best fit for this data represents the expected relative housing cost for a certain population density, based on the data points in the graph. Thus, one might say, on average, a city of population density x is expected to have a relative housing cost of y%, where $y = 0.0125x + 61$. The number 61 in the equation represents the y-intercept of the line of best fit, in that when the population density, x, is 0, there is an expected relative housing cost of 61%. This might not have meaning within the context of the problem, in that when the population density is 0, the population is 0, so there probably wouldn't be any housing costs. However, it could be interpreted that for cities with low population densities, housing costs were likely around or above 61% (since below 61% would be for cities with negative population densities, which is impossible).

Choice A is incorrect because it interprets the values of the vertical axis as dollars and not percentages. Choice B is incorrect because the lowest housing cost is about 61% of the national average, not 61% of the highest housing cost. Choice C is incorrect because one cannot absolutely assert that no city with a low population density had housing costs below 61% of the national average, as the model shows that it is unlikely, but not impossible.

QUESTION 28

Choice D is correct. The minimum value of a quadratic function appears as a constant in the vertex form of its equation, which can be found from the standard form by completing the square. Rewriting $f(x) = (x + 6)(x - 4)$ in standard form gives $f(x) = x^2 + 2x - 24$. Since the coefficient of the linear term is 2, the equation for $f(x)$ can be rewritten in terms of $(x + 1)^2$ as follows:

$$f(x) = x^2 + 2x - 24 = (x^2 + 2x + 1) - 1 - 24 = (x + 1)^2 - 25$$

The vertex form $f(x) = (x + 1)^2 - 25$ shows that the minimum value of f is -25 (and occurs at $x = -1$).

Alternatively, since $f(-6) = f(4) = 0$, by symmetry the vertex must have an x-coordinate at the midpoint between -6 and 4, which is -1. Since $f(-1) = (5)(-5) = -25$, the vertex must be at $(-1, -25)$. Finally since the coefficient of x^2 is 1, the vertex form must be $f(x) = (x + 1)^2 - 25$.

Choices A and C are incorrect because they are not equivalent to the given equation for f. Choice B is incorrect because the minimum value of f, which is -25, does not appear as a constant or a coefficient.

QUESTION 29

Choice B is correct. Since the average of 2 numbers is the sum of the 2 numbers divided by 2, the equations $x = \frac{m + 9}{2}$, $y = \frac{2m + 15}{2}$ and $z = \frac{3m + 18}{2}$ are true. The average of x, y, and z is given by $\frac{x + y + z}{3}$. Because x, y, and z are defined in terms of m, the expressions in terms of m can be substituted for each variable to give $\frac{\frac{m + 9}{2} + \frac{2m + 15}{2} + \frac{3m + 18}{2}}{3}$. This fraction can be simplified to $\frac{6m + 42}{6}$, or $m + 7$.

Choices A, C, and D are incorrect and may be the result of conceptual errors or calculation errors. For example, choice D is the sum of x, y, and z, not the average.

QUESTION 30

Choice D is correct. The equation $f(x) = k$ gives the solutions to the system of equations $y = f(x) = x^3 - x^2 - x - \frac{11}{4}$ and $y = k$. A real solution of a system of two equations corresponds to a point of intersection of the graphs of the two equations in the xy-plane. The graph of $y = k$ is a horizontal line that contains the point $(0, k)$. Thus, the line with equation $y = -3$ is a horizontal line that intersects the graph of the cubic equation three times, and it follows that the equation $f(x) = x^3 - x^2 - x - \frac{11}{4} = -3$ has three real solutions.

Choices A, B, and C are incorrect because the graphs of $y = 2$, $y = 0$, and $y = -2$ are horizontal lines that do not intersect the graph of the cubic equation three times.

QUESTION 31

The correct answer is 1160. The pool contains 600 gallons of water before the hose is turned on, and water flows from the hose into the pool at a rate of 8 gallons per minute. Thus, the number of gallons of water in the pool m minutes after the hose is turned on is given by the expression $600 + 8m$. Therefore, after 70 minutes, there will be $600 + 8(70) = 1160$ gallons of water in the pool.

QUESTION 32

The correct answer is $\frac{1}{2}$ or .5. The equation that models the normal systolic blood pressure P, in millimeters of mercury, for a male x years old, $P = \frac{x + 220}{2}$, can be rewritten as $P = \frac{1}{2}x + 110$. For each increase of 1 year in age, the value of x increases by 1; hence, P becomes $\frac{1}{2}(x + 1) + 110 = \left(\frac{1}{2}x + 110\right) + \frac{1}{2}$. That is, P increases by $\frac{1}{2}$ millimeter of mercury. Either the fraction 1/2 or its decimal equivalent, .5, may be gridded as the correct answer.

QUESTION 33

The correct answer is 4.55. Since there are 16 Roman digits in a Roman pes, 75 digits is equal to $\frac{75}{16}$ pes. Since 1 pes is equal to 11.65 inches, $\frac{75}{16}$ pes is equal to $\frac{75}{16}(11.65)$ inches. Since 12 inches is equal to 1 foot, $\frac{75}{16}(11.65)$ inches is equal to $\frac{75}{16}(11.65)\left(\frac{1}{12}\right) = 4.55078125$ feet. Therefore, 75 digits is equal to $\frac{75}{16}(11.65)\left(\frac{1}{12}\right) = 4.55078125$ feet. Rounded to the nearest hundredth of a foot, 75 Roman digits is equal to 4.55 feet.

QUESTION 34

The correct answer is 150. In the study, 240 male and 160 plus another 100 female bats have been tagged, so that 500 bats have been tagged altogether. If x more male bats must be tagged for $\frac{3}{5}$ of the total number of bats to be male, the proportion $\frac{\text{male bats}}{\text{total bats}} = \frac{240 + x}{500 + x} = \frac{3}{5}$ must be true. Multiplying each side of $\frac{240 + x}{500 + x} = \frac{3}{5}$ by $5(500 + x)$ gives $5(240 + x) = 3(500 + x)$, which simplifies to $1200 + 5x = 1500 + 3x$. Subtracting 1200 from both sides and subtracting $3x$ from both sides yields $2x = 300$, and dividing both sides by 2 gives $x = 150$. Therefore, 150 more male bats must be tagged; this will bring the total to 390 male bats out of 650 bats, which is equal to $\frac{3}{5}$.

QUESTION 35

The correct answer is 2.25 or $\frac{9}{4}$. Let q_s be the dynamic pressure of the slower fluid moving with velocity v_s, and let q_f be the dynamic pressure of the faster fluid moving with velocity v_f. Then $v_f = 1.5v_s$.

Given the equation $q = \frac{1}{2}nv^2$, substituting the dynamic pressure and velocity of the faster fluid gives $q_f = \frac{1}{2}nv_f^2$. Since $v_f = 1.5v_s$, the expression $1.5v_s$ can be substituted for v_f in this equation, giving $q_t = \frac{1}{2}n(1.5v_s)^2$. This can be rewritten as $q_f = (2.25)\frac{1}{2}nv_s^2 = (2.25)q_s$.

Therefore, the ratio of the dynamic pressure of the faster fluid is $\frac{q_f}{q_s} = \frac{2.25q_s}{q_s} = 2.25$. Either 2.25 or the equivalent improper fraction 9/4 may be gridded as the correct answer.

Alternatively, since q is directly proportional to the square of v, scaling v by 1.5 should scale q by $(1.5)^2 = 2.25$.

QUESTION 36

The correct answer is 29, 30, 31, 32, 33, or 34. Since the radius of the circle is 10, its circumference is 20π. The full circumference of a circle is 360°. Thus, an arc of length s on the circle corresponds to a central angle of $x°$, where $\frac{x}{360} = \frac{s}{20\pi}$, or $x = \frac{360}{20\pi}(s)$. Since $5 < s < 6$, it follows that $\frac{360}{20\pi}(5) < x < \frac{360}{20\pi}(6)$, which becomes, to the nearest tenth, $28.6 < x < 34.4$. Therefore, the possible integer values of x are 29, 30, 31, 32, 33, and 34. Any one of these numbers may be gridded as the correct answer.

QUESTION 37

The correct answer is .72. According to the analyst's estimate, the value V, in dollars, of the stock will decrease by 28% each week for t weeks, where $t = 1$, 2, or 3, with its value being given by the formula $V = 360(r)^t$. This equation is an example of exponential decay. A stock losing 28% of its value each week is the same as the stock's value decreasing to 72% of its value from the previous week, since $V - (.28)V = (.72)V$. Using this information, after 1 week the value, in dollars, of the stock will be $V = 360(.72)$; after 2 weeks the value of the stock will be $V = 360(.72)(.72) = 360(.72)^2$; and after 3 weeks the value of the stock will be $V = 360(.72)(.72)(.72) = 360(.72)^3$. For all of the values of t in question, namely $t = 1$, 2, and 3, the equation $V = 360(.72)^t$ is true. Therefore, the analyst should use .72 as the value of r.

QUESTION 38

The correct answer is 134. The analyst's prediction is that the stock will lose 28 percent of its value for each of the next three weeks. Thus, the predicted value of the stock after 1 week is \$360 – (.28)\$360 = \$259.20; after 2 weeks, \$259.20 – (.28)\$259.20 ≈ \$186.62; and after 3 weeks, \$186.62 – (.28)\$186.62 ≈ \$134.37. Therefore, to the nearest dollar, the stock analyst believes the stock will be worth 134 dollars after three weeks.

The SAT®

Practice Test #5

Make time to take the practice test.
It's one of the best ways to get ready for the SAT.

After you've taken the practice test, score it right away at **sat.org/scoring**.

Test begins on the next page.

Reading Test

65 MINUTES, 52 QUESTIONS

Turn to Section 1 of your answer sheet to answer the questions in this section.

DIRECTIONS

Each passage or pair of passages below is followed by a number of questions. After reading each passage or pair, choose the best answer to each question based on what is stated or implied in the passage or passages and in any accompanying graphics (such as a table or graph).

Questions 1-10 are based on the following passage.

This passage is adapted from William Maxwell, *The Folded Leaf.* ©1959 by William Maxwell. Originally published in 1945.

The Alcazar Restaurant was on Sheridan Road near Devon Avenue. It was long and narrow, with tables for two along the walls and tables for four down the middle. The decoration was *art moderne*, except for the series of murals depicting the four seasons, and the sick ferns in the front window. Lymie sat down at the second table from the cash register, and ordered his dinner. The history book, which he propped against the catsup and the glass sugar bowl, had been used by others before him. Blank pages front and back were filled in with maps, drawings, dates, comic cartoons, and organs of the body; also with names and messages no longer clear and never absolutely legible. On nearly every other page there was some marginal notation, either in ink or in very hard pencil. And unless someone had upset a glass of water, the marks on page 177 were from tears.

While Lymie read about the Peace of Paris, signed on the thirtieth of May, 1814, between France and the Allied powers, his right hand managed again and again to bring food up to his mouth. Sometimes he chewed, sometimes he swallowed whole the food that he had no idea he was eating. The Congress of Vienna met, with some allowance for delays, early in November of the same year, and all the powers engaged in the war on either side sent plenipotentiaries. It was by far the most splendid and important assembly ever convoked to discuss and determine the affairs of Europe. The Emperor of Russia, the King of Prussia, the Kings of Bavaria, Denmark, and Wurttemberg, all were present in person at the court of the Emperor Francis I in the Austrian capital. When Lymie put down his fork and began to count them off, one by one, on the fingers of his left hand, the waitress, whose name was Irma, thought he was through eating and tried to take his plate away. He stopped her. Prince Metternich (his right thumb) presided over the Congress, and Prince Talleyrand (the index finger) represented France.

A party of four, two men and two women, came into the restaurant, all talking at once, and took possession of the center table nearest Lymie. The women had shingled hair and short tight skirts which exposed the underside of their knees when they sat down. One of the women had the face of a young boy but disguised by one trick or another (rouge, lipstick, powder, wet bangs plastered against the high forehead, and a pair of long pendent earrings) to look like a woman of thirty-five, which as a matter of fact she was. The men were older. They laughed more than there seemed any occasion for, while they were deciding between soup and shrimp cocktail, and their laughter was too loud. But it was the women's voices, the terrible not quite sober pitch of the women's voices which caused Lymie to skim over two whole pages without knowing what was on them. Fortunately he realized this and went back. Otherwise he might never have known about the

CONTINUE

secret treaty concluded between England, France, and Austria, when the pretensions of Prussia and Russia, acting in concert, seemed to threaten a renewal of the attack. The results of the Congress were stated clearly at the bottom of page 67 and at the top of page 68, but before Lymie got halfway through them, a coat that he recognized as his father's was hung on the hook next to his chair. Lymie closed the book and said, "I didn't think you were coming."

Time is probably no more unkind to sporting characters than it is to other people, but physical decay unsustained by respectability is somehow more noticeable. Mr. Peters' hair was turning gray and his scalp showed through on top. He had lost weight also; he no longer filled out his clothes the way he used to. His color was poor, and the flower had disappeared from his buttonhole. In its place was an American Legion button.

Apparently he himself was not aware that there had been any change. He straightened his tie self-consciously and when Irma handed him a menu, he gestured with it so that the two women at the next table would notice the diamond ring on the fourth finger of his right hand. Both of these things, and also the fact that his hands showed signs of the manicurist, one can blame on the young man who had his picture taken with a derby hat on the back of his head, and also sitting with a girl in the curve of the moon. The young man had never for one second deserted Mr. Peters. He was always there, tugging at Mr. Peters' elbow, making him do things that were not becoming in a man of forty-five.

1

Over the course of the passage, the primary focus shifts from

A) Lymie's inner thoughts to observations made by the other characters.

B) an exchange between strangers to a satisfying personal relationship.

C) the physical setting of the scene to the different characters' personality traits.

D) Lymie's experience reading a book to descriptions of people in the restaurant.

2

The main purpose of the first paragraph is to

A) introduce the passage's main character by showing his nightly habits.

B) indicate the date the passage takes place by presenting period details.

C) convey the passage's setting by describing a place and an object.

D) foreshadow an event that is described in detail later in the passage.

3

It can reasonably be inferred that Irma, the waitress, thinks Lymie is "through eating" (line 37) because

A) he has begun reading his book.

B) his plate is empty.

C) he is no longer holding his fork.

D) he has asked her to clear the table.

4

Lymie's primary impression of the "party of four" (line 42) is that they

A) are noisy and distracting.

B) are a refreshing change from the other customers.

C) resemble characters from his history book.

D) represent glamour and youth.

5

Which choice provides the best evidence for the answer to the previous question?

A) Lines 45-47 ("The women . . . down")

B) Lines 47-52 ("One . . . was")

C) Lines 55-59 ("But . . . them")

D) Line 69 ("Lymie . . . book")

CONTINUE

6

The narrator indicates that Lymie finally closes the history book because

A) his father has joined him at the table.

B) the people at the other table are too disruptive.

C) he has finished the chapter about the Congress.

D) he is preparing to leave the restaurant.

7

The primary impression created by the narrator's description of Mr. Peters in lines 74-79 is that he is

A) healthy and fit.

B) angry and menacing.

C) nervous and hesitant.

D) aging and shriveled.

8

The main idea of the last paragraph is that Mr. Peters

A) neglects to spend any time with his family members.

B) behaves as if he is a younger version of himself.

C) is very conscious of symbols of wealth and power.

D) is preoccupied with the knowledge that he is growing old.

CONTINUE

9

Which choice best supports the conclusion that Mr. Peters wants to attract attention?

A) Lines 80-81 ("Apparently . . . change")

B) Lines 81-85 ("He straightened . . . hand")

C) Lines 90-91 ("The young . . . Mr. Peters")

D) Lines 91-93 ("He was . . . forty-five")

10

As used in line 93, "becoming" most nearly means

A) emerging.

B) fitting.

C) developing.

D) happening.

CONTINUE

Questions 11-21 are based on the following passages.

Passage 1 is adapted from Catharine Beecher, *Essay on Slavery and Abolitionism*. Originally published in 1837. Passage 2 is adapted from Angelina E. Grimké, *Letters to Catharine Beecher*. Originally published in 1838. Grimké encouraged Southern women to oppose slavery publicly. Passage 1 is Beecher's response to Grimké's views. Passage 2 is Grimké's response to Beecher.

Passage 1

Heaven has appointed to one sex the superior, and to the other the subordinate station, and this without any reference to the character or conduct of either. It is therefore as much for the dignity as it is for the interest of females, in all respects to conform to the duties of this relation. . . . But while woman holds a subordinate relation in society to the other sex, it is not because it was designed that her duties or her influence should be any the less important, or all-pervading. But it was designed that the mode of gaining influence and of exercising power should be altogether different and peculiar. . . .

A man may act on society by the collision of intellect, in public debate; he may urge his measures by a sense of shame, by fear and by personal interest; he may coerce by the combination of public sentiment; he may drive by physical force, and he does not outstep the boundaries of his sphere. But all the power, and all the conquests that are lawful to woman, are those only which appeal to the kindly, generous, peaceful and benevolent principles.

Woman is to win every thing by peace and love; by making herself so much respected, esteemed and loved, that to yield to her opinions and to gratify her wishes, will be the free-will offering of the heart. But this is to be all accomplished in the domestic and social circle. There let every woman become so cultivated and refined in intellect, that her taste and judgment will be respected; so benevolent in feeling and action; that her motives will be reverenced;—so unassuming and unambitious, that collision and competition will be banished;—so "gentle and easy to be entreated," as that every heart will repose in her presence; then, the fathers, the husbands, and the sons, will find an influence thrown around them, to which they will yield not only willingly but proudly. . . .

A woman may seek the aid of co-operation and combination among her own sex, to assist her in her appropriate offices of piety, charity, maternal and domestic duty; but whatever, in any measure, throws a woman into the attitude of a combatant, either for herself or others—whatever binds her in a party conflict—whatever obliges her in any way to exert coercive influences, throws her out of her appropriate sphere. If these general principles are correct, they are entirely opposed to the plan of arraying females in any Abolition movement.

Passage 2

The investigation of the rights of the slave has led me to a better understanding of my own. I have found the Anti-Slavery cause to be the high school of morals in our land—the school in which *human rights* are more fully investigated, and better understood and taught, than in any other. Here a great fundamental principle is uplifted and illuminated, and from this central light, rays innumerable stream all around.

Human beings have *rights*, because they are *moral* beings: the rights of *all* men grow out of their moral nature; and as all men have the same moral nature, they have essentially the same rights. These rights may be wrested from the slave, but they cannot be alienated: his title to himself is as perfect now, as is that of Lyman Beecher:[1] it is stamped on his moral being, and is, like it, imperishable. Now if rights are founded in the nature of our moral being, then the *mere circumstance of sex* does not give to man higher rights and responsibilities, than to woman. To suppose that it does, would be to deny the self-evident truth, that the "physical constitution is the mere instrument of the moral nature." To suppose that it does, would be to break up utterly the relations, of the two natures, and to reverse their functions, exalting the animal nature into a monarch, and humbling the moral into a slave; making the former a proprietor, and the latter its property.

When human beings are regarded as *moral* beings, *sex*, instead of being enthroned upon the summit, administering upon rights and responsibilities, sinks into insignificance and nothingness. My doctrine then is, that whatever it is morally right for man to do, it is morally right for woman to do. Our duties originate, not from difference of sex, but from the diversity of our relations in life, the various gifts and talents committed to our care, and the different eras in which we live.

[1] Lyman Beecher was a famous minister and the father of Catharine Beecher.

CONTINUE

11

In Passage 1, Beecher makes which point about the status of women relative to that of men?

A) Women depend on men for their safety and security, but men are largely independent of women.

B) Women are inferior to men, but women play a role as significant as that played by men.

C) Women have fewer rights than men do, but women also have fewer responsibilities.

D) Women are superior to men, but tradition requires women to obey men.

12

Which choice provides the best evidence for the answer to the previous question?

A) Lines 6-10 ("But . . . all-pervading")

B) Lines 13-14 ("A man . . . debate")

C) Lines 16-18 ("he may coerce . . . sphere")

D) Lines 41-46 ("but whatever . . . sphere")

13

In Passage 1, Beecher implies that women's effect on public life is largely

A) overlooked, because few men are interested in women's thoughts about politics.

B) indirect, because women exert their influence within the home and family life.

C) unnecessary, because men are able to govern society themselves.

D) symbolic, because women tend to be more idealistic about politics than men are.

14

As used in line 2, "station" most nearly means

A) region.

B) studio.

C) district.

D) rank.

15

As used in line 12, "peculiar" most nearly means

A) eccentric.

B) surprising.

C) distinctive.

D) infrequent.

16

What is Grimké's central claim in Passage 2?

A) The rights of individuals are not determined by race or gender.

B) Men and women must learn to work together to improve society.

C) Moral rights are the most important distinction between human beings and animals.

D) Men and women should have equal opportunities to flourish.

17

In Passage 2, Grimké makes which point about human rights?

A) They are viewed differently in various cultures around the world.

B) They retain their moral authority regardless of whether they are recognized by law.

C) They are sometimes at odds with moral responsibilities.

D) They have become more advanced and refined throughout history.

18

Which choice provides the best evidence for the answer to the previous question?

A) Lines 58-61 ("Human . . . same rights")

B) Lines 61-65 ("These . . . imperishable")

C) Lines 71-76 ("To suppose . . . property")

D) Lines 77-81 ("When . . . nothingness")

CONTINUE

19

Which choice best states the relationship between the two passages?

A) Passage 2 illustrates the practical difficulties of a proposal made in Passage 1.

B) Passage 2 takes issue with the primary argument of Passage 1.

C) Passage 2 provides a historical context for the perspective offered in Passage 1.

D) Passage 2 elaborates upon several ideas implied in Passage 1.

20

Based on the passages, both authors would agree with which of the following claims?

A) Women have moral duties and responsibilities.

B) Men often work selflessly for political change.

C) The ethical obligations of women are often undervalued.

D) Political activism is as important for women as it is for men.

21

Beecher would most likely have reacted to lines 65-68 ("Now . . . woman") of Passage 2 with

A) sympathy, because she feels that human beings owe each other a debt to work together in the world.

B) agreement, because she feels that human responsibilities are a natural product of human rights.

C) dismay, because she feels that women actually have a more difficult role to play in society than men do.

D) disagreement, because she feels that the natures of men and women are fundamentally different.

Questions 22-31 are based on the following passage and supplementary material.

This passage is adapted from Bryan Walsh, "Whole Food Blues: Why Organic Agriculture May Not Be So Sustainable." ©2012 by Time Inc.

When it comes to energy, everyone loves efficiency. Cutting energy waste is one of those goals that both sides of the political divide can agree on, even if they sometimes diverge on how best to get there. Energy efficiency allows us to get more out of our given resources, which is good for the economy and (mostly) good for the environment as well. In an increasingly hot and crowded world, the only sustainable way to live is to get more out of less. Every environmentalist would agree.

But change the conversation to food, and suddenly efficiency doesn't look so good. Conventional industrial agriculture has become incredibly efficient on a simple land to food basis. Thanks to fertilizers, mechanization and irrigation, each American farmer feeds over 155 people worldwide. Conventional farming gets more and more crop per square foot of cultivated land—over 170 bushels of corn per acre in Iowa, for example—which can mean less territory needs to be converted from wilderness to farmland. And since a third of the planet is already used for agriculture—destroying forests and other wild habitats along the way—anything that could help us produce more food on less land would seem to be good for the environment.

Of course, that's not how most environmentalists regard their arugula [a leafy green]. They have embraced organic food as better for the planet—and healthier and tastier, too—than the stuff produced by agricultural corporations. Environmentalists disdain the enormous amounts of energy needed and waste created by conventional farming, while organic practices—forgoing artificial fertilizers and chemical pesticides—are considered far more sustainable. Sales of organic food rose 7.7% in 2010, up to $26.7 billion—and people are making those purchases for their consciences as much as their taste buds.

Yet a new meta-analysis in *Nature* does the math and comes to a hard conclusion: organic farming yields 25% fewer crops on average than conventional agriculture. More land is therefore needed to produce fewer crops—and that means organic farming may not be as good for the planet as we think.

CONTINUE

In the *Nature* analysis, scientists from McGill University in Montreal and the University of Minnesota performed an analysis of 66 studies comparing conventional and organic methods across 34 different crop species, from fruits to grains to legumes. They found that organic farming delivered a lower yield for every crop type, though the disparity varied widely. For rain-watered legume crops like beans or perennial crops like fruit trees, organic trailed conventional agriculture by just 5%. Yet for major cereal crops like corn or wheat, as well as most vegetables—all of which provide the bulk of the world's calories—conventional agriculture outperformed organics by more than 25%.

The main difference is nitrogen, the chemical key to plant growth. Conventional agriculture makes use of 171 million metric tons of synthetic fertilizer each year, and all that nitrogen enables much faster plant growth than the slower release of nitrogen from the compost or cover crops used in organic farming. When we talk about a Green Revolution, we really mean a nitrogen revolution—along with a lot of water.

But not all the nitrogen used in conventional fertilizer ends up in crops—much of it ends up running off the soil and into the oceans, creating vast polluted dead zones. We're already putting more nitrogen into the soil than the planet can stand over the long term. And conventional agriculture also depends heavily on chemical pesticides, which can have unintended side effects.

What that means is that while conventional agriculture is more efficient—sometimes much more efficient—than organic farming, there are trade-offs with each. So an ideal global agriculture system, in the views of the study's authors, may borrow the best from both systems, as Jonathan Foley of the University of Minnesota explained:

> The bottom line? Today's organic farming practices are probably best deployed in fruit and vegetable farms, where growing nutrition (not just bulk calories) is the primary goal. But for delivering sheer calories, especially in our staple crops of wheat, rice, maize, soybeans and so on, conventional farms have the advantage right now.
>
> Looking forward, I think we will need to deploy different kinds of practices (especially new, mixed approaches that take the best of organic and conventional farming systems) where they are best suited—geographically, economically, socially, etc.

CONTINUE

Figure 1

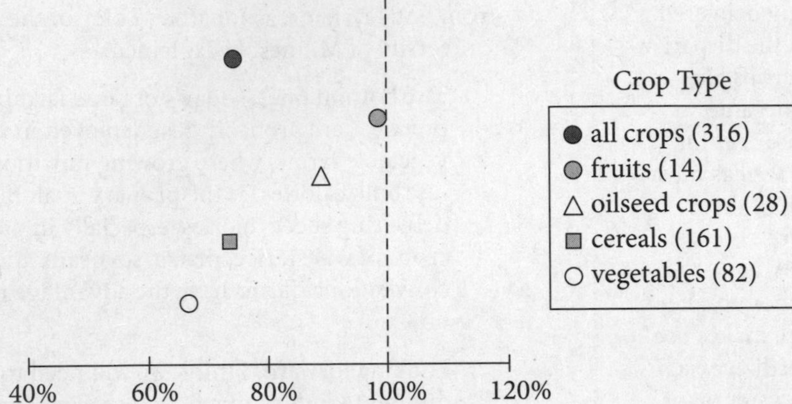

At 100%, the organic yield is the same as the conventional yield. The number of observations for each crop type is shown in parentheses.

Figure 2

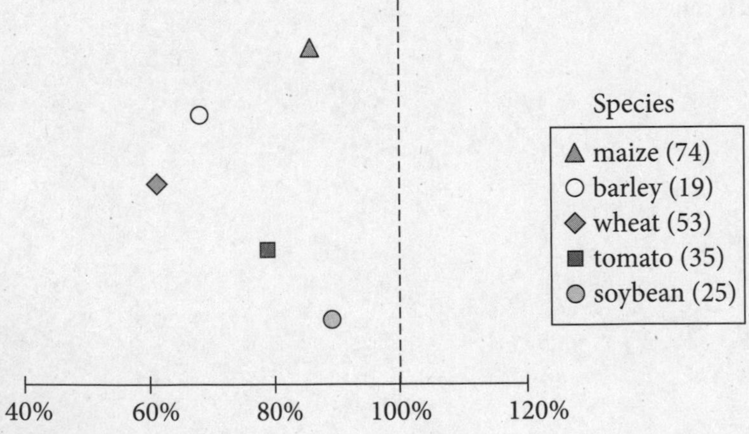

At 100%, the organic yield is the same as the conventional yield. The number of observations for each species is shown in parentheses.

Figures adapted from Verena Seufert, Navin Ramankutty, and Jonathan A. Foley, "Comparing the Yields of Organic and Conventional Agriculture." ©2012 by Nature Publishing Group.

CONTINUE

22

As used in line 14, "simple" most nearly means

A) straightforward.

B) modest.

C) unadorned.

D) easy.

23

According to the passage, a significant attribute of conventional agriculture is its ability to

A) produce a wide variety of fruits and vegetables.

B) maximize the output of cultivated land.

C) satisfy the dietary needs of the world's population.

D) lessen the necessity of nitrogen in plant growth.

24

Which choice best reflects the perspective of the "environmentalists" (line 27) on conventional agriculture?

A) It produces inferior fruits and vegetables and is detrimental to the environment.

B) It is energy efficient and reduces the need to convert wilderness to farmland.

C) It is good for the environment only in the short run.

D) It depletes critical resources but protects wildlife habitats.

25

Which choice provides the best evidence for the answer to the previous question?

A) Lines 27-28 ("Of course . . . green")

B) Lines 28-31 ("They . . . corporations")

C) Lines 31-35 ("Environmentalists . . . sustainable")

D) Lines 42-45 ("More . . . think")

CONTINUE

26

Which statement best expresses a relationship between organic farming and conventional farming that is presented in the passage?

A) Both are equally sustainable, but they differ dramatically in the amount of land they require to produce equivalent yields.

B) Both rely on artificial chemicals for pest control, but organic farmers use the chemicals sparingly in conjunction with natural remedies.

C) Both use nitrogen to encourage plant growth, but the nitrogen used in conventional farming comes from synthetic sources.

D) Both create a substantial amount of nitrogen runoff, but only the type of nitrogen found in fertilizers used in conventional farming can be dangerous.

27

Which choice provides the best evidence for the answer to the previous question?

A) Lines 13-14 ("Conventional . . . basis")

B) Lines 22-26 ("And since . . . environment")

C) Lines 51-53 ("They . . . widely")

D) Lines 61-65 ("Conventional . . . farming")

28

According to Foley, an "ideal global agriculture system" (line 80)

A) focuses primarily on yield percentages and global markets.

B) considers multiple factors in the selection of farming techniques.

C) weighs the economic interests of farmers against the needs of consumers.

D) puts the nutritional value of produce first and foremost.

29

In line 88, "sheer" most nearly means

A) transparent.

B) abrupt.

C) steep.

D) pure.

CONTINUE

30

Which statement is best supported by the information provided in figure 1?

A) The organic yield as a percentage of conventional yield is greater for vegetables than for fruits.

B) The organic yield as a percentage of conventional yield is similar for cereals and all crops.

C) The reported number of observations for each crop type exceeds 82.

D) The organic yield as a percentage of conventional yield is greater for vegetable crops than it is for oilseed crops.

31

Which of the following claims is supported by figure 2?

A) Of the organically grown species represented, soybeans have the lowest yield.

B) The organically grown maize and barley represented are comparable in their yields to conventionally grown maize and barley.

C) Of the organically grown species represented, tomatoes have the highest yield.

D) The organically grown species represented have lower yields than their conventionally grown counterparts do.

Questions 32-41 are based on the following passage and supplementary material.

This passage is adapted from John Bohannon, "Why You Shouldn't Trust Internet Comments." ©2013 by American Association for the Advancement of Science.

The "wisdom of crowds" has become a mantra of the Internet age. Need to choose a new vacuum cleaner? Check out the reviews on online merchant Amazon. But a new study suggests that such online scores don't always reveal the best choice. A massive controlled experiment of Web users finds that such ratings are highly susceptible to irrational "herd behavior"—and that the herd can be manipulated.

Sometimes the crowd really is wiser than you. The classic examples are guessing the weight of a bull or the number of gumballs in a jar. Your guess is probably going to be far from the mark, whereas the average of many people's choices is remarkably close to the true number.

But what happens when the goal is to judge something less tangible, such as the quality or worth of a product? According to one theory, the wisdom of the crowd still holds—measuring the aggregate of people's opinions produces a stable, reliable value. Skeptics, however, argue that people's opinions are easily swayed by those of others. So nudging a crowd early on by presenting contrary opinions—for example, exposing them to some very good or very bad attitudes—will steer the crowd in a different direction. To test which hypothesis is true, you would need to manipulate huge numbers of people, exposing them to false information and determining how it affects their opinions.

A team led by Sinan Aral, a network scientist at the Massachusetts Institute of Technology in Cambridge, did exactly that. Aral has been secretly working with a popular website that aggregates news stories. The website allows users to make comments about news stories and vote each other's comments up or down. The vote tallies are visible as a number next to each comment, and the position of the comments is chronological. (Stories on the site get an average of about ten comments and about three votes per comment.) It's a follow-up to his experiment using people's ratings of movies to measure how much individual people influence each other online (answer: a lot). This time, he wanted to know how much the crowd influences the individual, and whether it can be controlled from outside.

For five months, every comment submitted by a user randomly received an "up" vote (positive); a "down" vote (negative); or as a control, no vote at all. The team then observed how users rated those comments. The users generated more than 100,000 comments that were viewed more than 10 million times and rated more than 300,000 times by other users.

At least when it comes to comments on news sites, the crowd is more herdlike than wise. Comments that received fake positive votes from the researchers were 32% more likely to receive more positive votes compared with a control, the team reports. And those comments were no more likely than the control to be down-voted by the next viewer to see them. By the end of the study, positively manipulated comments got an overall boost of about 25%. However, the same did not hold true for negative manipulation. The ratings of comments that got a fake down vote were usually negated by an up vote by the next user to see them.

"Our experiment does not reveal the psychology behind people's decisions," Aral says, "but an intuitive explanation is that people are more skeptical of negative social influence. They're more willing to go along with positive opinions from other people."

Duncan Watts, a network scientist at Microsoft Research in New York City, agrees with that conclusion. "[But] one question is whether the positive [herding] bias is specific to this site" or true in general, Watts says. He points out that the category of the news items in the experiment had a strong effect on how much people could be manipulated. "I would have thought that 'business' is pretty similar to 'economics,' yet they find a much stronger effect (almost 50% stronger) for the former than the latter. What explains this difference? If we're going to apply these findings in the real world, we'll need to know the answers."

Will companies be able to boost their products by manipulating online ratings on a massive scale? "That is easier said than done," Watts says. If people detect—or learn—that comments on a website are being manipulated, the herd may spook and leave entirely.

CONTINUE

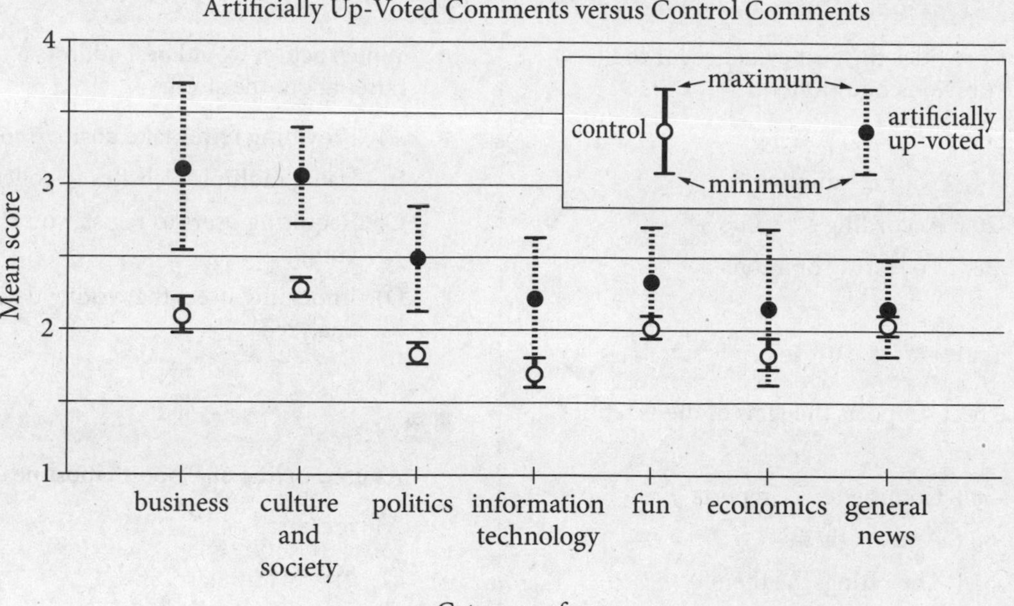

Mean score: mean of scores for the comments in each category, with the score for each comment being determined by the number of positive votes from website users minus the number of negative votes

Adapted from Lev Muchnik, Sinan Aral, and Sean J. Taylor, "Social Influence Bias: A Randomized Experiment." ©2013 by American Association for the Advancement of Science.

32

Over the course of the passage, the main focus shifts from a discussion of an experiment and its results to

A) an explanation of the practical applications of the results.

B) a consideration of the questions prompted by the results.

C) an analysis of the defects undermining the results.

D) a conversation with a scientist who disputes the results.

33

The author of the passage suggests that crowds may be more effective at

A) creating controversy than examining an issue in depth.

B) reinforcing members' ideas than challenging those ideas.

C) arriving at accurate quantitative answers than producing valid qualitative judgments.

D) ranking others' opinions than developing genuinely original positions.

34

Which choice provides the best evidence for the answer to the previous question?

A) Line 9 ("Sometimes . . . you")

B) Lines 11-14 ("Your . . . number")

C) Lines 17-20 ("According . . . value")

D) Lines 25-28 ("To test . . . opinions")

35

Which choice best supports the view of the "skeptics" (line 20)?

A) Lines 55-58 ("Comments . . . reports")

B) Lines 58-60 ("And . . . them")

C) Lines 63-65 ("The ratings . . . them")

D) Lines 76-79 ("He . . . manipulated")

36

Which action would best address a question Watts raises about the study?

A) Providing fewer fake positive comments

B) Using multiple websites to collect ratings

C) Requiring users to register on the website before voting

D) Informing users that voting data are being analyzed

37

As used in line 85, "boost" most nearly means

A) increase.

B) accelerate.

C) promote.

D) protect.

CONTINUE

38

As used in line 86, "scale" most nearly means

A) level.
B) wage.
C) interval.
D) scheme.

39

In the figure, which category of news has an artificially up-voted mean score of 2.5?

A) Business
B) Politics
C) Fun
D) General news

40

According to the figure, which category of news showed the smallest difference in mean score between artificially up-voted comments and control comments?

A) Culture and society
B) Information technology
C) Fun
D) General news

41

Data presented in the figure most directly support which idea from the passage?

A) The mean score of artificially down-voted comments is similar to that of the control.
B) The patterns observed in the experiment suggest that people are suspicious of negative social influence.
C) The positive bias observed in users of the news site may not apply to human behavior in other contexts.
D) The type of story being commented on has an impact on the degree to which people can be influenced.

CONTINUE

Questions 42-52 are based on the following passage.

This passage is adapted from Joshua Foer, *Moonwalking with Einstein: The Art and Science of Remembering Everything*. ©2011 by Joshua Foer.

In 2000, a neuroscientist at University College London named Eleanor Maguire wanted to find out what effect, if any, all that driving around the labyrinthine streets of London might have on cabbies' brains. When she brought sixteen taxi drivers into her lab and examined their brains in an MRI scanner, she found one surprising and important difference. The right posterior hippocampus, a part of the brain known to be involved in spatial navigation, was 7 percent larger than normal in the cabbies—a small but very significant difference. Maguire concluded that all of that way-finding around London had physically altered the gross structure of their brains. The more years a cabbie had been on the road, the more pronounced the effect.

The brain is a mutable organ, capable—within limits—of reorganizing itself and readapting to new kinds of sensory input, a phenomenon known as neuroplasticity. It had long been thought that the adult brain was incapable of spawning new neurons—that while learning caused synapses to rearrange themselves and new links between brain cells to form, the brain's basic anatomical structure was more or less static. Maguire's study suggested the old inherited wisdom was simply not true.

After her groundbreaking study of London cabbies, Maguire decided to turn her attention to mental athletes. She teamed up with Elizabeth Valentine and John Wilding, authors of the academic monograph *Superior Memory*, to study ten individuals who had finished near the top of the World Memory Championship. They wanted to find out if the memorizers' brains were—like the London cabbies'—structurally different from the rest of ours, or if they were somehow just making better use of memory abilities that we all possess.

The researchers put both the mental athletes and a group of matched control subjects into MRI scanners and asked them to memorize three-digit numbers, black-and-white photographs of people's faces, and magnified images of snowflakes, while their brains were being scanned. Maguire and her team thought it was possible that they might discover anatomical differences in the brains of the memory champs, evidence that their brains had somehow reorganized themselves in the process of doing all that intensive remembering. But when the researchers reviewed the imaging data, not a single significant structural difference turned up. The brains of the mental athletes appeared to be indistinguishable from those of the control subjects. What's more, on every single test of general cognitive ability, the mental athletes' scores came back well within the normal range. The memory champs weren't smarter, and they didn't have special brains.

But there was one telling difference between the brains of the mental athletes and the control subjects: When the researchers looked at which parts of the brain were lighting up when the mental athletes were memorizing, they found that they were activating entirely different circuitry. According to the functional MRIs [fMRIs], regions of the brain that were less active in the control subjects seemed to be working in overdrive for the mental athletes.

Surprisingly, when the mental athletes were learning new information, they were engaging several regions of the brain known to be involved in two specific tasks: visual memory and spatial navigation, including the same right posterior hippocampal region that the London cabbies had enlarged with all their daily way-finding. At first glance, this wouldn't seem to make any sense. Why would mental athletes be conjuring images in their mind's eye when they were trying to learn three-digit numbers? Why should they be navigating like London cabbies when they're supposed to be remembering the shapes of snowflakes?

Maguire and her team asked the mental athletes to describe exactly what was going through their minds as they memorized. The mental athletes said they were consciously converting the information they were being asked to memorize into images, and distributing those images along familiar spatial journeys. They weren't doing this automatically, or because it was an inborn talent they'd nurtured since childhood. Rather, the unexpected patterns of neural activity that Maguire's fMRIs turned up were the result of training and practice.

CONTINUE

42

According to the passage, Maguire's findings regarding taxi drivers are significant because they

A) demonstrate the validity of a new method.
B) provide evidence for a popular viewpoint.
C) call into question an earlier consensus.
D) challenge the authenticity of previous data.

43

Which choice provides the best evidence for the answer to the previous question?

A) Lines 8-12 ("The right . . . difference")
B) Lines 12-16 ("Maguire . . . effect")
C) Lines 17-20 ("The brain . . . neuroplasticity")
D) Lines 20-26 ("It had . . . true")

44

As used in line 24, "basic" most nearly means

A) initial.
B) simple.
C) necessary.
D) fundamental.

45

Which question was Maguire's study of mental athletes primarily intended to answer?

A) Does the act of memorization make use of different brain structures than does the act of navigation?
B) Do mental athletes inherit their unusual brain structures, or do the structures develop as a result of specific activities?
C) Does heightened memorization ability reflect abnormal brain structure or an unusual use of normal brain structure?
D) What is the relationship between general cognitive ability and the unusual brain structures of mental athletes?

46

Which choice provides the best evidence for the answer to the previous question?

A) Lines 27-29 ("After . . . athletes")
B) Lines 33-37 ("They . . . possess")
C) Lines 38-43 ("The researchers . . . scanned")
D) Lines 52-54 ("What's . . . range")

CONTINUE

47

As used in line 39, “matched” most nearly means

A) comparable.

B) identical.

C) distinguishable.

D) competing.

48

The main purpose of the fifth paragraph (lines 57-65) is to

A) relate Maguire’s study of mental athletes to her study of taxi drivers.

B) speculate on the reason for Maguire’s unexpected results.

C) identify an important finding of Maguire’s study of mental athletes.

D) transition from a summary of Maguire’s findings to a description of her methods.

49

According to the passage, when compared to mental athletes, the individuals in the control group in Maguire’s second study

A) showed less brain activity overall.

B) demonstrated a wider range of cognitive ability.

C) exhibited different patterns of brain activity.

D) displayed noticeably smaller hippocampal regions.

50

The passage most strongly suggests that mental athletes are successful at memorization because they

A) exploit parts of the brain not normally used in routine memorization.

B) convert information they are trying to memorize into abstract symbols.

C) organize information into numerical lists prior to memorization.

D) exercise their brains regularly through puzzles and other mental challenges.

CONTINUE

51

Which choice provides the best evidence for the answer to the previous question?

A) Lines 66-72 ("Surprisingly . . . way-finding")

B) Lines 72-73 ("At first . . . sense")

C) Lines 79-81 ("Maguire . . . memorized")

D) Lines 85-87 ("They . . . childhood")

52

The questions in lines 74-78 primarily serve to

A) raise doubts about the reliability of the conclusions reached by Maguire.

B) emphasize and elaborate on an initially puzzling result of Maguire's study of mental athletes.

C) imply that Maguire's findings undermine earlier studies of the same phenomenon.

D) introduce and explain a connection between Maguire's two studies and her earlier work.

STOP

If you finish before time is called, you may check your work on this section only.

Do not turn to any other section.

Writing and Language Test

35 MINUTES, 44 QUESTIONS

Turn to Section 2 of your answer sheet to answer the questions in this section.

DIRECTIONS

Each passage below is accompanied by a number of questions. For some questions, you will consider how the passage might be revised to improve the expression of ideas. For other questions, you will consider how the passage might be edited to correct errors in sentence structure, usage, or punctuation. A passage or a question may be accompanied by one or more graphics (such as a table or graph) that you will consider as you make revising and editing decisions.

Some questions will direct you to an underlined portion of a passage. Other questions will direct you to a location in a passage or ask you to think about the passage as a whole.

After reading each passage, choose the answer to each question that most effectively improves the quality of writing in the passage or that makes the passage conform to the conventions of standard written English. Many questions include a "NO CHANGE" option. Choose that option if you think the best choice is to leave the relevant portion of the passage as it is.

Questions 1-11 are based on the following passage.

Prehistoric Printing

Paleontologists are using modern technology to gain a greater understanding of the distant past. With the aid of computed tomography (CT) scanning and 3-D printing, researchers are able to create accurate models of prehistoric fossils. [1] These models have expanded

1

At this point, the writer is considering adding the following sentence.

> Fossils provide paleontologists with a convenient way of estimating the age of the rock in which the fossils are found.

Should the writer make this addition here?

A) Yes, because it supports the paragraph's argument with an important detail.

B) Yes, because it provides a logical transition from the preceding sentence.

C) No, because it is not directly related to the main point of the paragraph.

D) No, because it undermines the main claim of the paragraph.

CONTINUE

researchers' knowledge of ancient species and [2] swear to advance the field of paleontology in the years to come.

CT scanners use X-rays to map the surface of a fossil in minute detail, recording as many as one million data points to create a digital blueprint. A 3-D printer then builds a polymer model based on this blueprint, much as a regular computer printer reproduces digital documents on paper. [3] Whereas the head of an ordinary computer printer moves back and forth while printing ink onto paper, the corresponding part of a 3-D printer moves in multiple dimensions while squirting out thin layers of melted polymer plastic. The plastic hardens quickly, [4] it allows the printer to build the layers of the final model. Compared with older ways of modeling fossils, scanning and printing in this way is extremely versatile.

2

A) NO CHANGE
B) subscribe
C) vow
D) promise

3

The writer is considering deleting the underlined sentence. Should the sentence be kept or deleted?

A) Kept, because it helps explain why X-rays are used in CT scanners.
B) Kept, because it provides details to illustrate how a 3-D printer works.
C) Deleted, because it contradicts the passage's information about digital blueprints.
D) Deleted, because it creates confusion about how researchers gather data.

4

A) NO CHANGE
B) this
C) which
D) that

CONTINUE

[1] One significant benefit of 3-D printing technology is its ability to create scale reproductions of fossils. [2] But now 3-D scale models can be rearranged with ease, which is a huge boon to scientists. [3] A team led by Drexel University professor Kenneth Lacovara is making models of dinosaur bones one-tenth the bones' original sizes **5** in order to learn how they fit together when the animals were alive. [4] In the past, such research was limited by the weight and bulk of the fossils as well as **6** its preciousness and fragility. [5] In many cases, scientists had to rearrange bones virtually, using artists' renderings. **7**

Because CT scanners can map objects that are impossible to excavate, CT scanning and 3-D printing can also be used to reproduce fossils that scientists cannot observe firsthand. **8** By contrast, researchers

5

A) NO CHANGE
B) in order for learning
C) so that one is learning
D) so to learn

6

A) NO CHANGE
B) it's
C) their
D) there

7

To make this paragraph most logical, sentence 2 should be placed

A) where it is now.
B) before sentence 1.
C) after sentence 4.
D) after sentence 5.

8

A) NO CHANGE
B) Nonetheless,
C) Besides,
D) For example,

CONTINUE

from the National Museum of Brazil **9** has relied on this technique to study a fossilized skeleton that was discovered protruding from a rock at an old São Paulo railroad site. **10** The fossil was too delicate to be removed from the rock. Because of the fossil's delicate nature, the team dug up a block of stone around the fossil and brought it to their lab. With the aid of a CT scanner and a 3-D printer, they were able to produce a resin model of the fossil. Examining the model, the researchers determined that **11** one had found a new species, a 75-million-year-old crocodile. While not every discovery will be as dramatic as this one, paleontologists anticipate further expanding their knowledge of ancient life-forms as CT scanning and 3-D printing continue to make fossils more accessible.

9

A) NO CHANGE
B) relied
C) will rely
D) is relying

10

Which choice most effectively combines the underlined sentences?

A) The fossil could not be removed from the rock on account of it being too delicate; moreover, the team dug up a block of stone around it and brought it to their lab.
B) The team thought the fossil was too delicate to remove from the rock, and their next decision was to dig up a block of stone around the fossil and bring it to their lab.
C) The fossil was too delicate to be removed from the rock, so the team dug up a block of stone around the fossil and brought it to their lab.
D) In removing the fossil from the rock, the team found it was too delicate; then they dug up a block of stone around the fossil and brought it to their lab.

11

A) NO CHANGE
B) he or she
C) they
D) it

CONTINUE

Questions 12-22 are based on the following passage.

Thomas Nast, the Crusading Cartoonist

"Stop them pictures!" Legend has it that the corrupt politician William "Boss" Tweed once used those words when ordering someone to offer a bribe to Thomas Nast, an artist who had become famous for cartoons that called for reforms to end corruption. **12** As a result, Tweed's attempt to silence the artist failed, and Nast's cartoons, published in magazines like *Harper's Weekly*, actually played a key role in bringing Boss Tweed and his cronies to justice.

13 There were powerful political organizations in the 1860s and the 1870s. The organizations were known as "political machines" and started taking control of city governments. These political machines were able to pack legislatures and courts with hand-picked supporters by purchasing **14** votes, a form of election fraud involving the exchange of money or favors for votes. Once a political machine had control of enough important positions, its members were able to use public funds to enrich themselves and their friends. Boss Tweed's Tammany Hall group, which controlled New York **15** City in the 1860s—stole more than $30 million,

12

A) NO CHANGE
B) Therefore,
C) Furthermore,
D) DELETE the underlined portion.

13

Which choice most effectively combines the underlined sentences?

A) Powerful political organizations in the 1860s and the 1870s started taking control of city governments, and they were known as "political machines."
B) Known as "political machines," in the 1860s and the 1870s, political organizations that were powerful started taking control of city governments.
C) City governments were taken control of in the 1860s and the 1870s, and powerful political organizations known as "political machines" did so.
D) In the 1860s and the 1870s, powerful political organizations known as "political machines" started taking control of city governments.

14

A) NO CHANGE
B) votes, being
C) votes, that is
D) votes, which it is

15

A) NO CHANGE
B) City in the 1860s,
C) City, in the 1860s,
D) City in the 1860s

CONTINUE

the equivalent of more than $365 million today. [16] Tweed had been elected to a single two-year term in Congress in 1852. Tammany Hall was so powerful and [17] corrupt that, the *New York Times*, commented "There is absolutely nothing . . . in the city which is beyond the reach of the insatiable gang."

Given the extent of Tweed's power, it is remarkable that a single cartoonist could have played such a significant role in bringing about his downfall. Nast's cartoons depicted Tweed as a great big bloated thief. One of the artist's most [18] famous images showed Tweed with a bag of money in place of his [19] head. Another featured Tweed leaning against a ballot box with the caption "As long as I count the votes, what are you going to do about it?" These cartoons were so effective in part because many of the citizens who supported Tweed were illiterate and thus could not read the newspaper accounts of his criminal activities. Nast's cartoons, though, widely exposed the public to the injustice of Tweed's political machine.

16

The writer is considering deleting the underlined sentence. Should the sentence be kept or deleted?

A) Kept, because it introduces the quote from the *New York Times* in the next sentence.
B) Kept, because it adds a vital detail about Tweed that is necessary to understand his power.
C) Deleted, because it blurs the focus of the paragraph by introducing loosely related information.
D) Deleted, because it contains information that undermines the main claim of the passage.

17

A) NO CHANGE
B) corrupt, that the *New York Times* commented,
C) corrupt that the *New York Times* commented,
D) corrupt that the *New York Times*, commented

18

A) NO CHANGE
B) famous and well-known
C) famous and commonly known
D) famous, commonly known

19

Which choice adds the most relevant supporting information to the paragraph?

A) head; like many other Nast cartoons, that one was published in *Harper's Weekly*.
B) head; Nast would later illustrate Tweed's escape from prison.
C) head, one depiction that omits Tweed's signature hat.
D) head, an image that perfectly captured Tweed's greedy nature.

Nast's campaign to bring down Tweed and the Tammany Hall gang was ultimately successful. In the elections of 1871, the public voted against most of the Tammany Hall candidates, greatly weakening Tweed's power. Eventually, Tweed and his gang were **20** persecuted for a number of charges, including fraud and larceny, and many of them were sent to jail. In 1875 Tweed escaped from jail and fled to Spain and unwittingly **21** brought about one final **22** pinnacle for the power of political cartoons: A Spanish police officer recognized Tweed from one of Nast's cartoons. Consequently, Tweed was sent back to jail, and Nast was hailed as the man who toppled the great Tammany Hall machine.

20

A) NO CHANGE
B) persecuted on
C) persecuted with
D) prosecuted on

21

A) NO CHANGE
B) bringing
C) brings
D) has brought

22

A) NO CHANGE
B) triumph
C) culmination
D) apex

CONTINUE

Questions 23-33 are based on the following passage and supplementary material.

Rethinking Crowdfunding in the Arts

Crowdfunding is a popular way to raise money using the Internet. The process sounds simple: an artist, entrepreneur, or other innovator takes his or her ideas straight to the public via a crowdfunding website. The innovator creates a video about the project and offers, in exchange for donations, a series of "perks," from acknowledgment on a social media site to a small piece of art. Many crowdfunding programs are all-or-nothing; in other words, the innovator must garner 100 percent funding for the project or the money is refunded to the donors. At **23** it's best, the system can give creators direct access to millions of potential backers.

The home page of one leading crowdfunding site features a project to manufacture pinhole cameras on a 3-D printer. **24** The idea is obviously very attractive. An obscure method of photography may be made available to many with little expense. Within weeks, the project was 621 percent funded. In contrast, on the same page, a small Brooklyn performance venue is attempting to raise money for its current season. The venue features works of performance art showcased in a storefront window. Those who have seen the space consider it vital. **25** However, that group may not be large enough; with just fourteen days to go in the fund-raising period, the campaign is only 46 percent funded.

23

A) NO CHANGE
B) its
C) its'
D) their

24

Which choice most effectively combines the underlined sentences?

A) With the idea being obviously very attractive, an obscure method of photography may be made available to many at little expense.
B) The idea is obviously very attractive: an obscure method of photography may be made available to many at little expense.
C) An obscure method of photography may be made available to many at little expense, and the idea is obviously very attractive.
D) An obscure method of photography, an idea that is obviously very attractive, may be made available to many at little expense.

25

A) NO CHANGE
B) Therefore,
C) In effect,
D) As a rule,

CONTINUE

Artists such as these Brooklyn performers find that crowdfunding exacerbates problems that already exist. **26** Work, that is easily understood and appreciated, is supported, while more complex work goes unnoticed. **27** Time that could be used creating art is spent devising clever perks to draw the attention of potential contributors. **28** In addition, audiences may contain many "free **29** riders," they did not make contributions.

26

A) NO CHANGE

B) Work that is easily understood and appreciated is supported,

C) Work that is easily understood, and appreciated is supported

D) Work—that is easily understood and appreciated—is supported,

27

At this point, the writer is considering adding the following sentence.

> Crowdfunding tends to attract contributors from a wide variety of professional fields.

Should the writer make this addition here?

A) Yes, because it gives more information about the people who donate to crowdfunding campaigns.

B) Yes, because it reinforces the writer's point about the funding of artistic projects.

C) No, because it fails to take into account project funding received from public institutions.

D) No, because it blurs the focus of the paragraph by introducing a poorly integrated piece of information.

28

A) NO CHANGE

B) Conversely,

C) However,

D) Thus,

29

A) NO CHANGE

B) riders," not making

C) riders," who did not make

D) riders" to not make

Ironically, the success of crowdfunding may weaken overall funding for the arts if people begin to feel that paying for the art **30** loved by them is someone else's responsibility.

[1] One innovative playwright has woven the deficiencies of the system into her crowdfunding model. [2] Though the price for her tickets was higher than that of tickets for comparable shows, it was still affordable to most theatergoers—and reflected the real cost of the performance. [3] She presented the total cost for producing her play on a crowdfunding site. [4] Then she divided the total cost by the number of people she expected to attend the performance. [5] The result of the calculation was the minimum donor price, and only donors who paid at least the minimum ticket price were allowed to attend the performance. [6] By subverting the presumption that money used for her project is an altruistic donation, the playwright showed that **31** our work has monetary value to those who enjoy it. **32**

30

A) NO CHANGE
B) they love
C) loved by him or her
D) he or she loves

31

A) NO CHANGE
B) their
C) her
D) its

32

To make this paragraph most logical, sentence 2 should be placed

A) where it is now.
B) after sentence 3.
C) after sentence 4.
D) after sentence 5.

CONTINUE

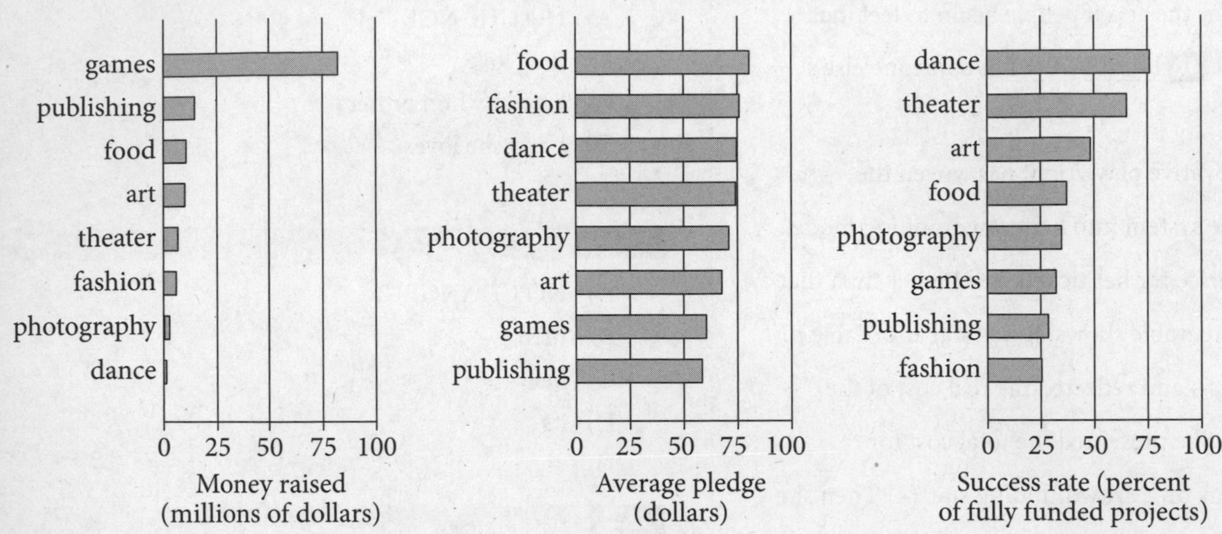

Adapted from "These Were the Most Successful Projects on Kickstarter Last Year." ©2013 by The Economist Newspaper Limited.

Question 33 asks about the graphic.

33

Which choice offers an accurate interpretation of the data in the graphs?

A) The project category with the lowest amount of money raised was also the most successfully funded project category.

B) The project category with the highest average pledge amount was also the most successfully funded project category.

C) The project category with the lowest average pledge amount was also the project category that raised the most money.

D) The project category with the highest average pledge amount was also the project category with the most money raised.

CONTINUE

Questions 34-44 are based on the following passage.

Investigative Journalism: An Evolving American Tradition

[1] The recent precipitous decline of print journalism as a viable profession has exacerbated long-held concerns about the state of investigative reporting in the United States. [2] Facing lower print circulation and diminished advertising revenue, many major newspapers have reduced or eliminated investigative resources. [3] Newspapers, the traditional nurturing ground for investigative journalism, have been hit especially hard by the widespread availability of free news online. [4] To survive, investigative journalism must continue to adapt to the digital age. 34

It is not difficult to understand why a cash-strapped, understaffed publication might feel pressure to cut teams of investigative 35 reporter's—their work is expensive and time-consuming. 36 Taking on the public interest, investigative journalism involves original, often long-form reporting on such topics as 37 illegal activities, street crime, corporate wrongdoing, and political corruption. An investigative story involves one or more experienced journalists dedicating their full energy and the resources of the publisher to a piece for a prolonged period of time. Expensive legal battles may ensue. The results of this work, though costly, have

34

For the sake of the logic and cohesion of the paragraph, sentence 3 should be

A) placed where it is now.
B) placed before sentence 1.
C) placed after sentence 1.
D) DELETED from the paragraph.

35

A) NO CHANGE
B) reporters:
C) reporters,
D) reporter's;

36

A) NO CHANGE
B) Undertaken in
C) Overtaking
D) Taking off from

37

A) NO CHANGE
B) business scandals,
C) abuse of government power,
D) DELETE the underlined portion.

CONTINUE

helped keep those in power accountable. The exposure by *Washington Post* reporters Bob Woodward and Carl Bernstein of government misconduct in the Watergate scandal resulted in the resignation of President Richard Nixon in 1974. More recently, Seymour Hersh, reporting for the *New Yorker* in 2004, helped publicize the mistreatment of Iraqi prisoners by US personnel at Abu Ghraib during the Iraq War. **38** In these and other cases, exposure from reporters has served as an important **39** <u>blockade to or scolding of</u> malfeasance.

38

At this point, the writer is considering adding the following sentence.

> In 1954, Edward R. Murrow and Fred Friendly produced episodes of the CBS television show *See It Now* that contributed to the end of US senator Joseph McCarthy's anticommunist "witch hunts."

Should the writer make this addition here?

A) Yes, because it helps clarify that the passage's main focus is on investigations of political corruption.

B) Yes, because it offers an important counterpoint to the other cases previously described in the paragraph.

C) No, because it gives an example that is both chronologically and substantively out of place in the paragraph.

D) No, because it provides an example that is inconsistent with the passage's definition of investigative journalism.

39

A) NO CHANGE

B) interference to or condemnation of

C) drag on or reproof of

D) deterrent or rebuke to

While worrisome, the decline of traditional print media **40** could not entail the end of investigative journalism. **41** Although many newsrooms have reduced their staff, some still employ investigative reporters. Nonprofit **42** enterprises such as the Organized Crime and Corruption Reporting Project have begun to fill the void created by staff losses at newspapers and magazines. Enterprising freelance reporters, newly funded by nonprofits, make extensive use of social media,

40

Which choice most effectively suggests that the "end of investigative journalism" is a real possibility but one that can be prevented?

A) NO CHANGE
B) need
C) will
D) must

41

Which choice most effectively sets up the examples in the following sentences?

A) NO CHANGE
B) Investigative journalism also declined between the 1930s and 1950s, only to be revived in the 1960s.
C) According to the Pew Research Center, more people get their national and international news from the Internet than from newspapers.
D) Indeed, recent years have witnessed innovative adjustments to changing times.

42

A) NO CHANGE
B) enterprises: such as
C) enterprises such as:
D) enterprises, such as

CONTINUE

including blogs and Twitter, to foster a public conversation about key issues. The Help Me Investigate project, **43** for example, solicited readers to submit tips and information related to ongoing stories to its website. Far from marking the end of investigative journalism, **44** cooperation among journalists and ordinary citizens has been facilitated by the advent of the digital age through an increase in the number of potential investigators.

43

A) NO CHANGE
B) therefore,
C) however,
D) in any case,

44

A) NO CHANGE
B) the number of potential investigators has increased since the advent of the digital age owing to the facilitation of cooperation among journalists and ordinary citizens.
C) the advent of the digital age has increased the number of potential investigators by facilitating cooperation among journalists and ordinary citizens.
D) by facilitating cooperation among journalists and ordinary citizens the advent of the digital age has increased the number of potential investigators.

STOP

If you finish before time is called, you may check your work on this section only.

Do not turn to any other section.

No Test Material On This Page

Math Test – No Calculator

25 MINUTES, 20 QUESTIONS

Turn to Section 3 of your answer sheet to answer the questions in this section.

DIRECTIONS

For questions 1-15, solve each problem, choose the best answer from the choices provided, and fill in the corresponding circle on your answer sheet. **For questions 16-20**, solve the problem and enter your answer in the grid on the answer sheet. Please refer to the directions before question 16 on how to enter your answers in the grid. You may use any available space in your test booklet for scratch work.

NOTES

1. The use of a calculator **is not permitted**.
2. All variables and expressions used represent real numbers unless otherwise indicated.
3. Figures provided in this test are drawn to scale unless otherwise indicated.
4. All figures lie in a plane unless otherwise indicated.
5. Unless otherwise indicated, the domain of a given function f is the set of all real numbers x for which $f(x)$ is a real number.

REFERENCE

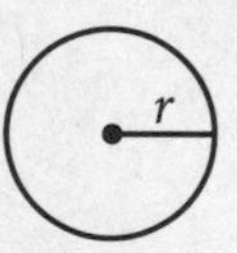

$A = \pi r^2$
$C = 2\pi r$

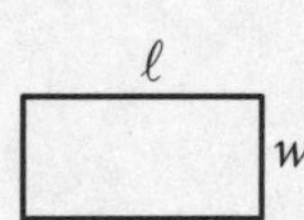

$A = \ell w$

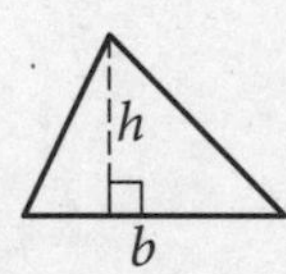

$A = \frac{1}{2}bh$

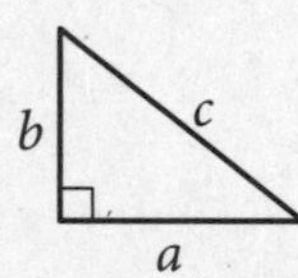

$c^2 = a^2 + b^2$

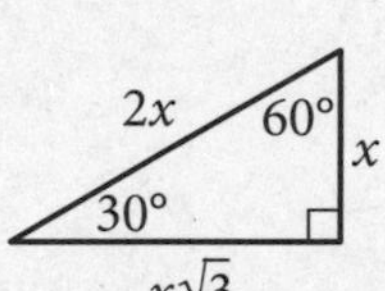

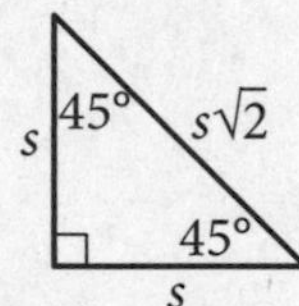

Special Right Triangles

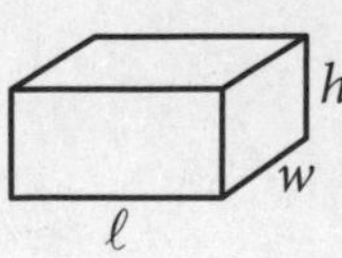

$V = \ell wh$

$V = \pi r^2 h$

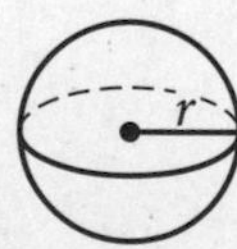

$V = \frac{4}{3}\pi r^3$

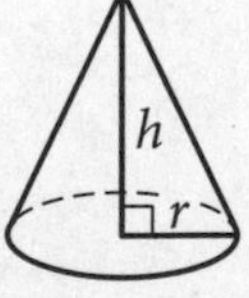

$V = \frac{1}{3}\pi r^2 h$

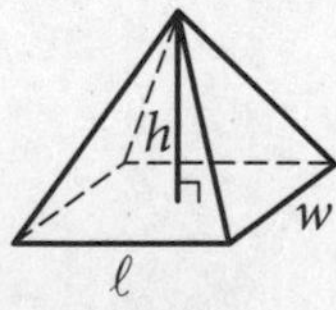

$V = \frac{1}{3}\ell wh$

The number of degrees of arc in a circle is 360.
The number of radians of arc in a circle is 2π.
The sum of the measures in degrees of the angles of a triangle is 180.

CONTINUE

1

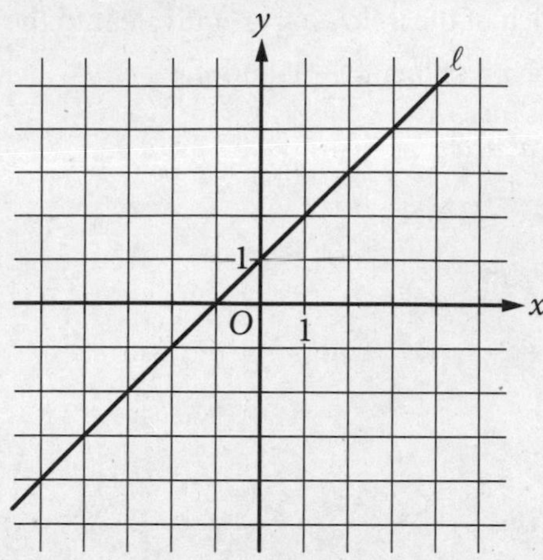

Which of the following is an equation of line ℓ in the xy-plane above?

A) $x = 1$

B) $y = 1$

C) $y = x$

D) $y = x + 1$

2

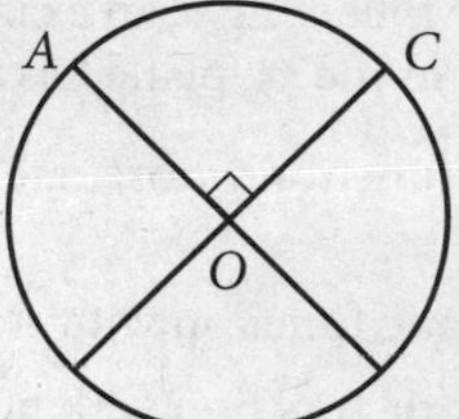

The circle above with center O has a circumference of 36. What is the length of minor arc $\overset{\frown}{AC}$?

A) 9

B) 12

C) 18

D) 36

3

What are the solutions of the quadratic equation $4x^2 - 8x - 12 = 0$?

A) $x = -1$ and $x = -3$

B) $x = -1$ and $x = 3$

C) $x = 1$ and $x = -3$

D) $x = 1$ and $x = 3$

CONTINUE

4

Which of the following is an example of a function whose graph in the xy-plane has no x-intercepts?

A) A linear function whose rate of change is not zero
B) A quadratic function with real zeros
C) A quadratic function with no real zeros
D) A cubic polynomial with at least one real zero

5

$$\sqrt{k+2} - x = 0$$

In the equation above, k is a constant. If $x = 9$, what is the value of k ?

A) 1
B) 7
C) 16
D) 79

6

Which of the following is equivalent to the sum of the expressions $a^2 - 1$ and $a + 1$?

A) $a^2 + a$
B) $a^3 - 1$
C) $2a^2$
D) a^3

7

Jackie has two summer jobs. She works as a tutor, which pays \$12 per hour, and she works as a lifeguard, which pays \$9.50 per hour. She can work no more than 20 hours per week, but she wants to earn at least \$220 per week. Which of the following systems of inequalities represents this situation in terms of x and y, where x is the number of hours she tutors and y is the number of hours she works as a lifeguard?

A) $12x + 9.5y \le 220$
$x + y \ge 20$

B) $12x + 9.5y \le 220$
$x + y \le 20$

C) $12x + 9.5y \ge 220$
$x + y \le 20$

D) $12x + 9.5y \ge 220$
$x + y \ge 20$

8

In air, the speed of sound S, in meters per second, is a linear function of the air temperature T, in degrees Celsius, and is given by $S(T) = 0.6T + 331.4$. Which of the following statements is the best interpretation of the number 331.4 in this context?

A) The speed of sound, in meters per second, at 0°C

B) The speed of sound, in meters per second, at 0.6°C

C) The increase in the speed of sound, in meters per second, that corresponds to an increase of 1°C

D) The increase in the speed of sound, in meters per second, that corresponds to an increase of 0.6°C

9

$$y = x^2$$
$$2y + 6 = 2(x + 3)$$

If (x, y) is a solution of the system of equations above and $x > 0$, what is the value of xy ?

A) 1

B) 2

C) 3

D) 9

10

If $a^2 + b^2 = z$ and $ab = y$, which of the following is equivalent to $4z + 8y$?

A) $(a + 2b)^2$

B) $(2a + 2b)^2$

C) $(4a + 4b)^2$

D) $(4a + 8b)^2$

CONTINUE

11

The volume of right circular cylinder A is 22 cubic centimeters. What is the volume, in cubic centimeters, of a right circular cylinder with twice the radius and half the height of cylinder A?

A) 11

B) 22

C) 44

D) 66

12

Which of the following is equivalent to $9^{\frac{3}{4}}$?

A) $\sqrt[3]{9}$

B) $\sqrt[4]{9}$

C) $\sqrt{3}$

D) $3\sqrt{3}$

13

At a restaurant, n cups of tea are made by adding t tea bags to hot water. If $t = n + 2$, how many additional tea bags are needed to make each additional cup of tea?

A) None

B) One

C) Two

D) Three

CONTINUE

14

$$f(x) = 2^x + 1$$

The function f is defined by the equation above. Which of the following is the graph of $y = -f(x)$ in the xy-plane?

A)

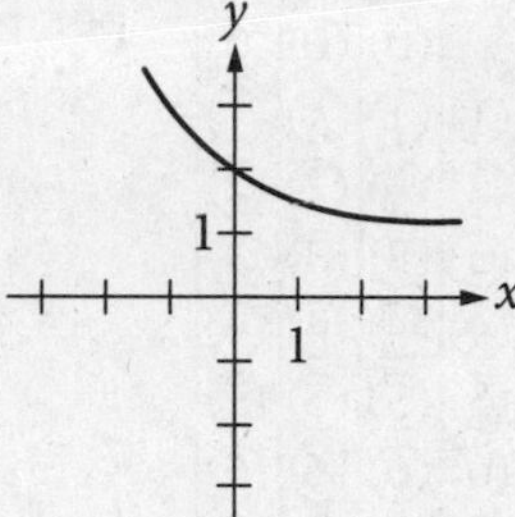

B)

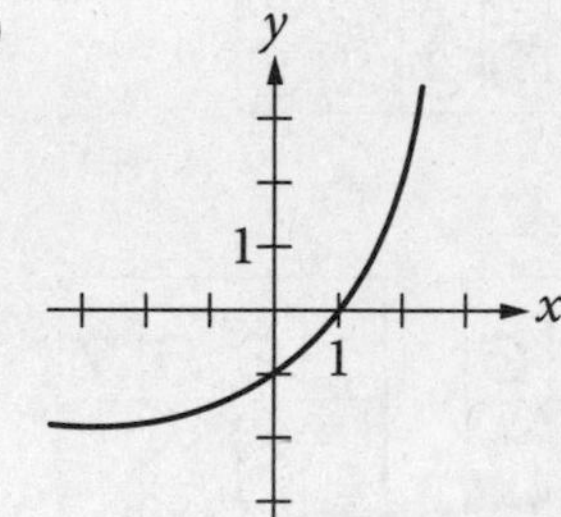

C)

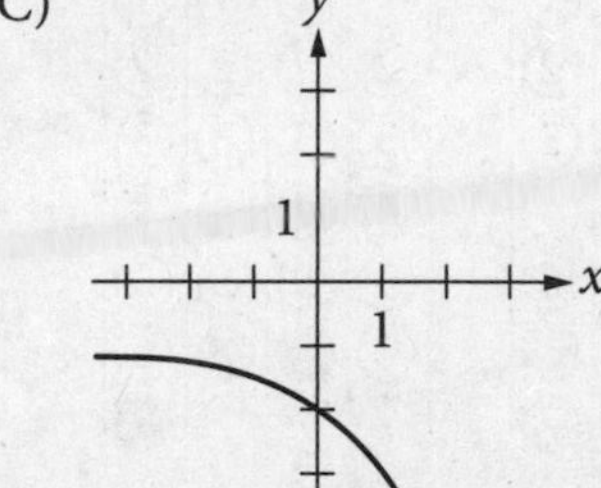

D)

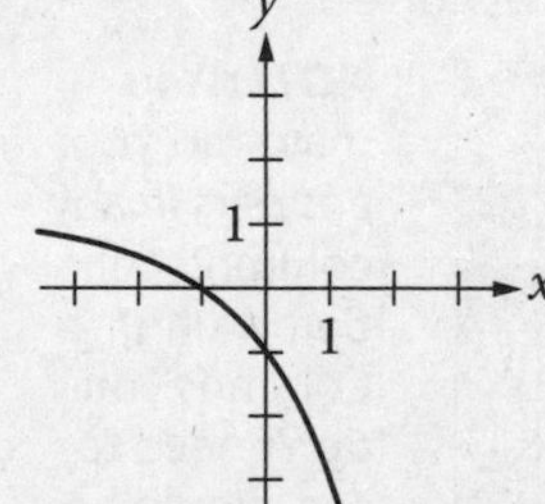

15

Alan drives an average of 100 miles each week. His car can travel an average of 25 miles per gallon of gasoline. Alan would like to reduce his weekly expenditure on gasoline by \$5. Assuming gasoline costs \$4 per gallon, which equation can Alan use to determine how many fewer average miles, m, he should drive each week?

A) $\frac{25}{4}m = 95$

B) $\frac{25}{4}m = 5$

C) $\frac{4}{25}m = 95$

D) $\frac{4}{25}m = 5$

CONTINUE

DIRECTIONS

For questions 16-20, solve the problem and enter your answer in the grid, as described below, on the answer sheet.

1. Although not required, it is suggested that you write your answer in the boxes at the top of the columns to help you fill in the circles accurately. You will receive credit only if the circles are filled in correctly.
2. Mark no more than one circle in any column.
3. No question has a negative answer.
4. Some problems may have more than one correct answer. In such cases, grid only one answer.
5. **Mixed numbers** such as $3\frac{1}{2}$ must be gridded as 3.5 or 7/2. (If 3 1 / 2 is entered into the grid, it will be interpreted as $\frac{31}{2}$, not $3\frac{1}{2}$.)
6. **Decimal answers:** If you obtain a decimal answer with more digits than the grid can accommodate, it may be either rounded or truncated, but it must fill the entire grid.

Answer: $\frac{7}{12}$

Write answer in boxes. → 7 / 1 2 ← Fraction line

Grid in result.

Answer: 2.5

2 . 5 ← Decimal point

Acceptable ways to grid $\frac{2}{3}$ are:

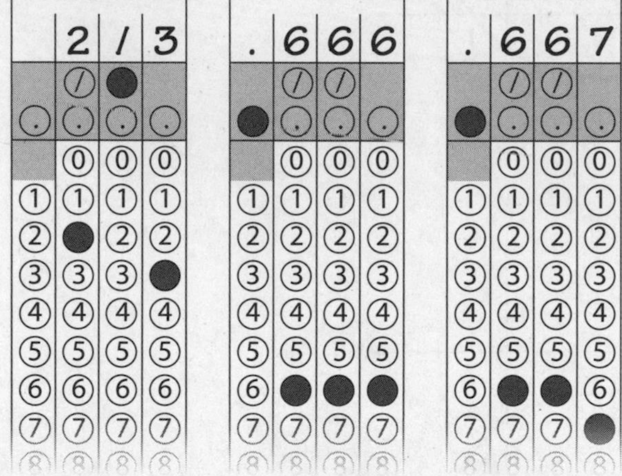

Answer: 201 – either position is correct

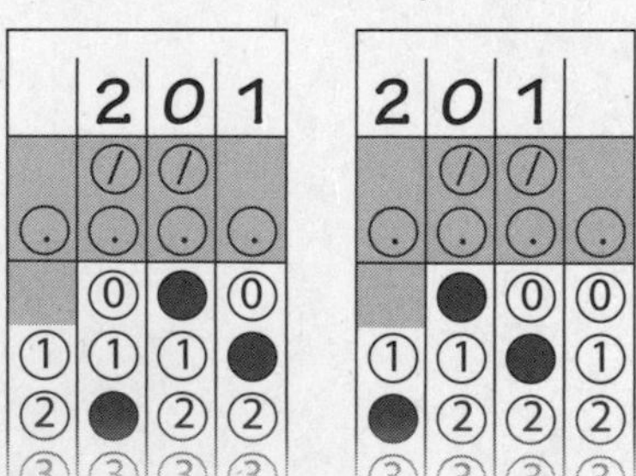

NOTE: You may start your answers in any column, space permitting. Columns you don't need to use should be left blank.

CONTINUE

16

Maria plans to rent a boat. The boat rental costs \$60 per hour, and she will also have to pay for a water safety course that costs \$10. Maria wants to spend no more than \$280 for the rental and the course. If the boat rental is available only for a whole number of hours, what is the maximum number of hours for which Maria can rent the boat?

17

$$2(p+1)+8(p-1)=5p$$

What value of p is the solution of the equation above?

18

$$\frac{1}{2}(2x+y)=\frac{21}{2}$$
$$y=2x$$

The system of equations above has solution (x, y). What is the value of x ?

CONTINUE

19

$$\frac{2x+6}{(x+2)^2} - \frac{2}{x+2}$$

The expression above is equivalent to $\frac{a}{(x+2)^2}$, where a is a positive constant and $x \neq -2$.

What is the value of a ?

20

Intersecting lines r, s, and t are shown below.

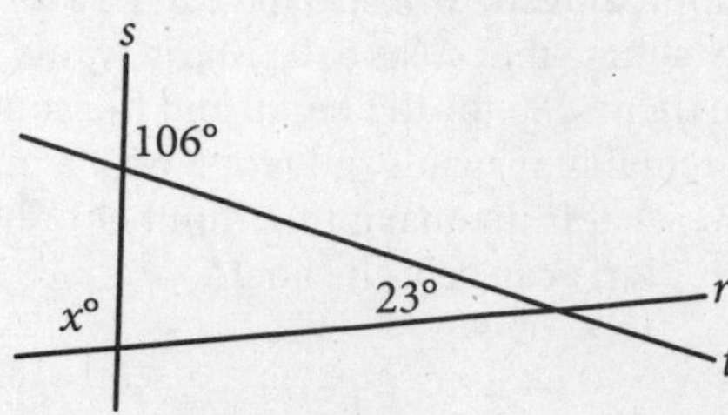

What is the value of x ?

STOP

If you finish before time is called, you may check your work on this section only.
Do not turn to any other section.

No Test Material On This Page

Math Test – Calculator

55 MINUTES, 38 QUESTIONS

Turn to Section 4 of your answer sheet to answer the questions in this section.

DIRECTIONS

For questions 1-30, solve each problem, choose the best answer from the choices provided, and fill in the corresponding circle on your answer sheet. **For questions 31-38**, solve the problem and enter your answer in the grid on the answer sheet. Please refer to the directions before question 31 on how to enter your answers in the grid. You may use any available space in your test booklet for scratch work.

NOTES

1. The use of a calculator **is permitted**.
2. All variables and expressions used represent real numbers unless otherwise indicated.
3. Figures provided in this test are drawn to scale unless otherwise indicated.
4. All figures lie in a plane unless otherwise indicated.
5. Unless otherwise indicated, the domain of a given function f is the set of all real numbers x for which $f(x)$ is a real number.

REFERENCE

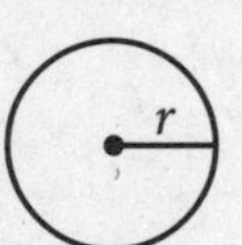

$A = \pi r^2$
$C = 2\pi r$

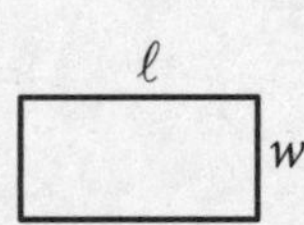

$A = \ell w$

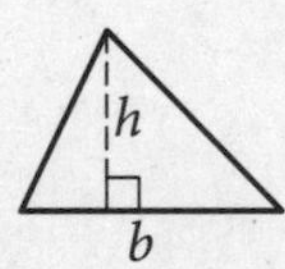

$A = \frac{1}{2}bh$

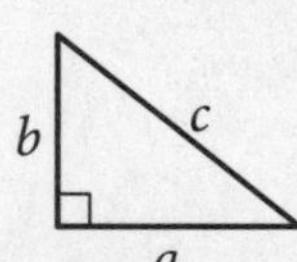

$c^2 = a^2 + b^2$

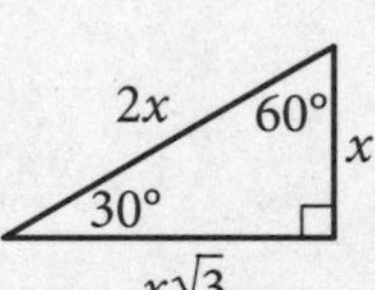

Special Right Triangles

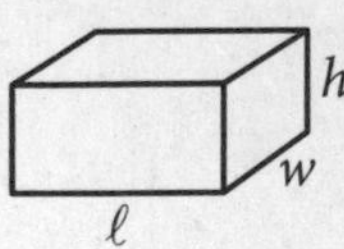

$V = \ell wh$

$V = \pi r^2 h$

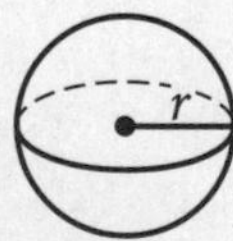

$V = \frac{4}{3}\pi r^3$

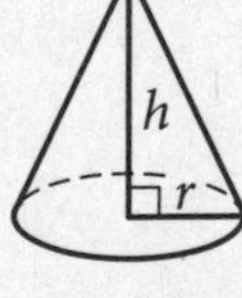

$V = \frac{1}{3}\pi r^2 h$

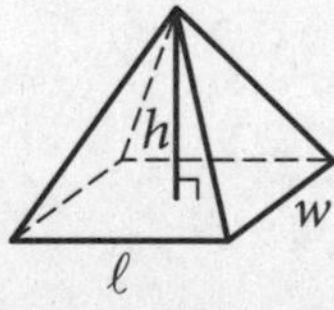

$V = \frac{1}{3}\ell wh$

The number of degrees of arc in a circle is 360.
The number of radians of arc in a circle is 2π.
The sum of the measures in degrees of the angles of a triangle is 180.

CONTINUE

1

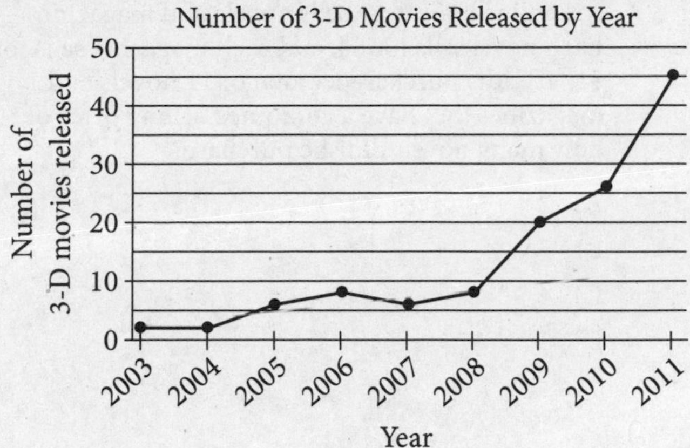

According to the line graph above, between which two consecutive years was there the greatest change in the number of 3-D movies released?

A) 2003–2004

B) 2008–2009

C) 2009–2010

D) 2010–2011

2

x	$f(x)$
1	5
3	13
5	21

Some values of the linear function f are shown in the table above. Which of the following defines f ?

A) $f(x) = 2x + 3$

B) $f(x) = 3x + 2$

C) $f(x) = 4x + 1$

D) $f(x) = 5x$

3

To make a bakery's signature chocolate muffins, a baker needs 2.5 ounces of chocolate for each muffin. How many pounds of chocolate are needed to make 48 signature chocolate muffins?
(1 pound = 16 ounces)

A) 7.5

B) 10

C) 50.5

D) 120

4

If $3(c+d)=5$, what is the value of $c+d$?

A) $\frac{3}{5}$

B) $\frac{5}{3}$

C) 3

D) 5

5

The weight of an object on Venus is approximately $\frac{9}{10}$ of its weight on Earth. The weight of an object on Jupiter is approximately $\frac{23}{10}$ of its weight on Earth. If an object weighs 100 pounds on Earth, approximately how many more pounds does it weigh on Jupiter than it weighs on Venus?

A) 90

B) 111

C) 140

D) 230

6

An online bookstore sells novels and magazines. Each novel sells for \$4, and each magazine sells for \$1. If Sadie purchased a total of 11 novels and magazines that have a combined selling price of \$20, how many novels did she purchase?

A) 2

B) 3

C) 4

D) 5

CONTINUE

7

The Downtown Business Association (DBA) in a certain city plans to increase its membership by a total of n businesses per year. There were b businesses in the DBA at the beginning of this year. Which function best models the total number of businesses, y, the DBA plans to have as members x years from now?

A) $y = nx + b$

B) $y = nx - b$

C) $y = b(n)^x$

D) $y = n(b)^x$

8

Which of the following is an equivalent form of $(1.5x - 2.4)^2 - (5.2x^2 - 6.4)$?

A) $-2.2x^2 + 1.6$

B) $-2.2x^2 + 11.2$

C) $-2.95x^2 - 7.2x + 12.16$

D) $-2.95x^2 - 7.2x + 0.64$

9

In the 1908 Olympic Games, the Olympic marathon was lengthened from 40 kilometers to approximately 42 kilometers. Of the following, which is closest to the increase in the distance of the Olympic marathon, in miles? (1 mile is approximately 1.6 kilometers.)

A) 1.00

B) 1.25

C) 1.50

D) 1.75

CONTINUE

10

The density d of an object is found by dividing the mass m of the object by its volume V. Which of the following equations gives the mass m in terms of d and V ?

A) $m = dV$

B) $m = \frac{d}{V}$

C) $m = \frac{V}{d}$

D) $m = V + d$

11

$$-2x + 3y = 6$$

In the xy-plane, the graph of which of the following equations is perpendicular to the graph of the equation above?

A) $3x + 2y = 6$

B) $3x + 4y = 6$

C) $2x + 4y = 6$

D) $2x + 6y = 3$

12

$$\frac{1}{2}y = 4$$
$$x - \frac{1}{2}y = 2$$

The system of equations above has solution (x, y). What is the value of x ?

A) 3

B) $\frac{7}{2}$

C) 4

D) 6

13

$$y \leq 3x + 1$$
$$x - y > 1$$

Which of the following ordered pairs (x, y) satisfies the system of inequalities above?

A) $(-2, -1)$

B) $(-1, 3)$

C) $(1, 5)$

D) $(2, -1)$

CONTINUE

14

Type of surgeon	Major professional activity		Total
	Teaching	Research	
General	258	156	414
Orthopedic	119	74	193
Total	377	230	607

In a survey, 607 general surgeons and orthopedic surgeons indicated their major professional activity. The results are summarized in the table above. If one of the surgeons is selected at random, which of the following is closest to the probability that the selected surgeon is an orthopedic surgeon whose indicated professional activity is research?

A) 0.122
B) 0.196
C) 0.318
D) 0.379

CONTINUE

15

A polling agency recently surveyed 1,000 adults who were selected at random from a large city and asked each of the adults, “Are you satisfied with the quality of air in the city?” Of those surveyed, 78 percent responded that they were satisfied with the quality of air in the city. Based on the results of the survey, which of the following statements must be true?

I. Of all adults in the city, 78 percent are satisfied with the quality of air in the city.

II. If another 1,000 adults selected at random from the city were surveyed, 78 percent of them would report they are satisfied with the quality of air in the city.

III. If 1,000 adults selected at random from a different city were surveyed, 78 percent of them would report they are satisfied with the quality of air in the city.

A) None

B) II only

C) I and II only

D) I and III only

Questions 16-18 refer to the following information.

Species of tree	Growth factor
Red maple	4.5
River birch	3.5
Cottonwood	2.0
Black walnut	4.5
White birch	5.0
American elm	4.0
Pin oak	3.0
Shagbark hickory	7.5

One method of calculating the approximate age, in years, of a tree of a particular species is to multiply the diameter of the tree, in inches, by a constant called the growth factor for that species. The table above gives the growth factors for eight species of trees.

16

According to the information in the table, what is the approximate age of an American elm tree with a diameter of 12 inches?

A) 24 years

B) 36 years

C) 40 years

D) 48 years

CONTINUE

17

Tree Diameter versus Age

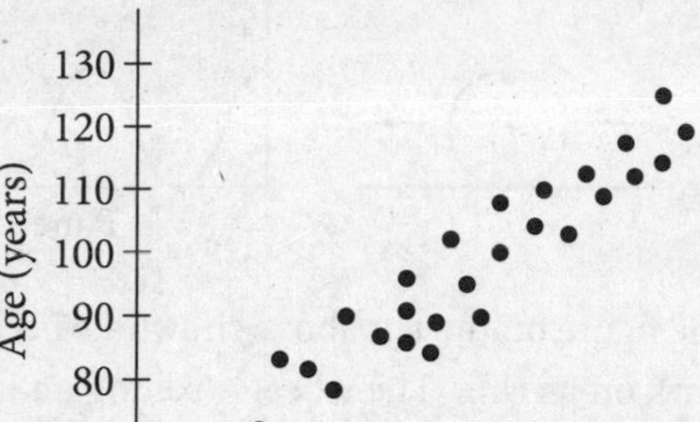

The scatterplot above gives the tree diameter plotted against age for 26 trees of a single species. The growth factor of this species is closest to that of which of the following species of tree?

A) Red maple

B) Cottonwood

C) White birch

D) Shagbark hickory

18

If a white birch tree and a pin oak tree each now have a diameter of 1 foot, which of the following will be closest to the difference, in inches, of their diameters 10 years from now? (1 foot = 12 inches)

A) 1.0

B) 1.2

C) 1.3

D) 1.4

CONTINUE

19

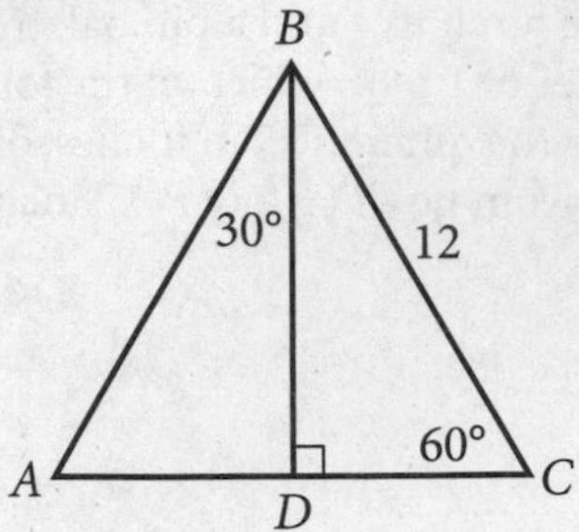

In $\triangle ABC$ above, what is the length of $\overline{AD}$?

A) 4

B) 6

C) $6\sqrt{2}$

D) $6\sqrt{3}$

20

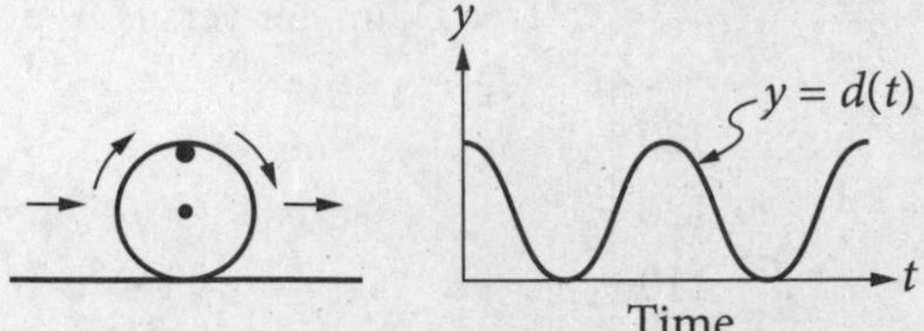

The figure on the left above shows a wheel with a mark on its rim. The wheel is rolling on the ground at a constant rate along a level straight path from a starting point to an ending point. The graph of $y = d(t)$ on the right could represent which of the following as a function of time from when the wheel began to roll?

A) The speed at which the wheel is rolling

B) The distance of the wheel from its starting point

C) The distance of the mark on the rim from the center of the wheel

D) The distance of the mark on the rim from the ground

CONTINUE

21

$$\frac{a-b}{a}=c$$

In the equation above, if a is negative and b is positive, which of the following must be true?

A) $c>1$

B) $c=1$

C) $c=-1$

D) $c<-1$

22

In State X, Mr. Camp's eighth-grade class consisting of 26 students was surveyed and 34.6 percent of the students reported that they had at least two siblings. The average eighth-grade class size in the state is 26. If the students in Mr. Camp's class are representative of students in the state's eighth-grade classes and there are 1,800 eighth-grade classes in the state, which of the following best estimates the number of eighth-grade students in the state who have fewer than two siblings?

A) 16,200

B) 23,400

C) 30,600

D) 46,800

CONTINUE

Questions 23 and 24 refer to the following information.

Townsend Realty Group Investments		
Property address	Purchase price (dollars)	Monthly rental price (dollars)
Clearwater Lane	128,000	950
Driftwood Drive	176,000	1,310
Edgemont Street	70,000	515
Glenview Street	140,000	1,040
Hamilton Circle	450,000	3,365

The Townsend Realty Group invested in the five different properties listed in the table above. The table shows the amount, in dollars, the company paid for each property and the corresponding monthly rental price, in dollars, the company charges for the property at each of the five locations.

23

The relationship between the monthly rental price r, in dollars, and the property's purchase price p, in thousands of dollars, can be represented by a linear function. Which of the following functions represents the relationship?

A) $r(p) = 2.5p - 870$

B) $r(p) = 5p + 165$

C) $r(p) = 6.5p + 440$

D) $r(p) = 7.5p - 10$

24

Townsend Realty purchased the Glenview Street property and received a 40% discount off the original price along with an additional 20% off the discounted price for purchasing the property in cash. Which of the following best approximates the original price, in dollars, of the Glenview Street property?

A) \$350,000

B) \$291,700

C) \$233,300

D) \$175,000

CONTINUE

25

A psychologist set up an experiment to study the tendency of a person to select the first item when presented with a series of items. In the experiment, 300 people were presented with a set of five pictures arranged in random order. Each person was asked to choose the most appealing picture. Of the first 150 participants, 36 chose the first picture in the set. Among the remaining 150 participants, p people chose the first picture in the set. If more than 20% of all participants chose the first picture in the set, which of the following inequalities best describes the possible values of p ?

A) $p > 0.20(300 - 36)$, where $p \leq 150$

B) $p > 0.20(300 + 36)$, where $p \leq 150$

C) $p - 36 > 0.20(300)$, where $p \leq 150$

D) $p + 36 > 0.20(300)$, where $p \leq 150$

26

The surface area of a cube is $6\left(\frac{a}{4}\right)^2$, where a is a positive constant. Which of the following gives the perimeter of one face of the cube?

A) $\frac{a}{4}$

B) a

C) $4a$

D) $6a$

27

The mean score of 8 players in a basketball game was 14.5 points. If the highest individual score is removed, the mean score of the remaining 7 players becomes 12 points. What was the highest score?

A) 20

B) 24

C) 32

D) 36

CONTINUE

28

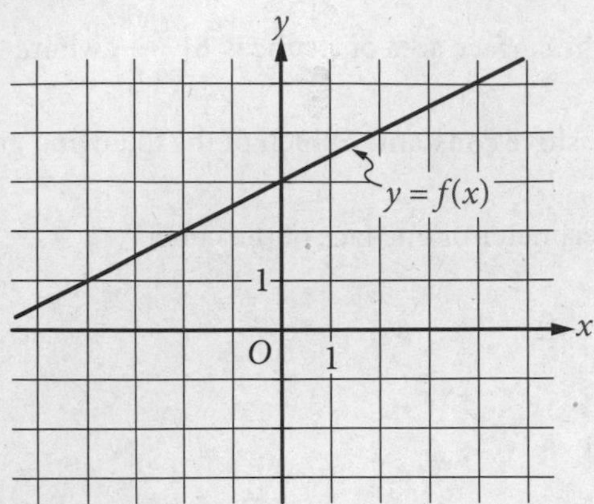

The graph of the linear function f is shown in the xy-plane above. The slope of the graph of the linear function g is 4 times the slope of the graph of f. If the graph of g passes through the point $(0, -4)$, what is the value of $g(9)$?

A) 5

B) 9

C) 14

D) 18

29

$$x^2 + 20x + y^2 + 16y = -20$$

The equation above defines a circle in the xy-plane. What are the coordinates of the center of the circle?

A) $(-20, -16)$

B) $(-10, -8)$

C) $(10, 8)$

D) $(20, 16)$

30

$$y = x^2 - a$$

In the equation above, a is a positive constant and the graph of the equation in the xy-plane is a parabola. Which of the following is an equivalent form of the equation?

A) $y = (x + a)(x - a)$

B) $y = (x + \sqrt{a})(x - \sqrt{a})$

C) $y = \left(x + \frac{a}{2}\right)\left(x - \frac{a}{2}\right)$

D) $y = (x + a)^2$

CONTINUE

DIRECTIONS

For questions 31-38, solve the problem and enter your answer in the grid, as described below, on the answer sheet.

1. Although not required, it is suggested that you write your answer in the boxes at the top of the columns to help you fill in the circles accurately. You will receive credit only if the circles are filled in correctly.
2. Mark no more than one circle in any column.
3. No question has a negative answer.
4. Some problems may have more than one correct answer. In such cases, grid only one answer.
5. **Mixed numbers** such as $3\frac{1}{2}$ must be gridded as 3.5 or 7/2. (If 3 1 / 2 is entered into the grid, it will be interpreted as $\frac{31}{2}$, not $3\frac{1}{2}$.)
6. **Decimal answers:** If you obtain a decimal answer with more digits than the grid can accommodate, it may be either rounded or truncated, but it must fill the entire grid.

Answer: $\frac{7}{12}$

Write answer in boxes. → 7 / 1 2 ← Fraction line

Grid in result.

Answer: 2.5

2 . 5 ← Decimal point

Acceptable ways to grid $\frac{2}{3}$ are:

2 / 3   . 6 6 6   . 6 6 7

Answer: 201 – either position is correct

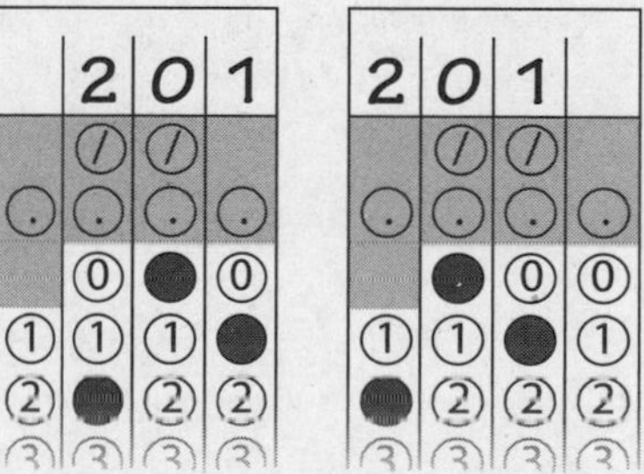

NOTE: You may start your answers in any column, space permitting. Columns you don't need to use should be left blank.

31

Horsepower and watts are units of measure of power. They are directly proportional such that 5 horsepower is equal to 3730 watts. How much power, in watts, is equal to 2 horsepower?

32

The painting *The Starry Night* by Vincent van Gogh is rectangular in shape with height 29 inches and width 36.25 inches. If a reproduction was made where each dimension is $\frac{1}{3}$ the corresponding original dimension, what is the height of the reproduction, in inches?

33

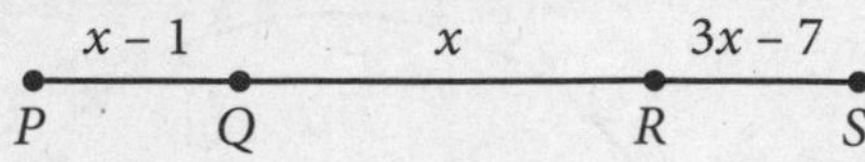

Note: Figure not drawn to scale.

On $\overline{PS}$ above, $PQ = RS$. What is the length of $\overline{PS}$?

34

In the xy-plane, the point $(2, 5)$ lies on the graph of the function f. If $f(x) = k - x^2$, where k is a constant, what is the value of k ?

35

A landscaper is designing a rectangular garden. The length of the garden is to be 5 feet longer than the width. If the area of the garden will be 104 square feet, what will be the length, in feet, of the garden?

36

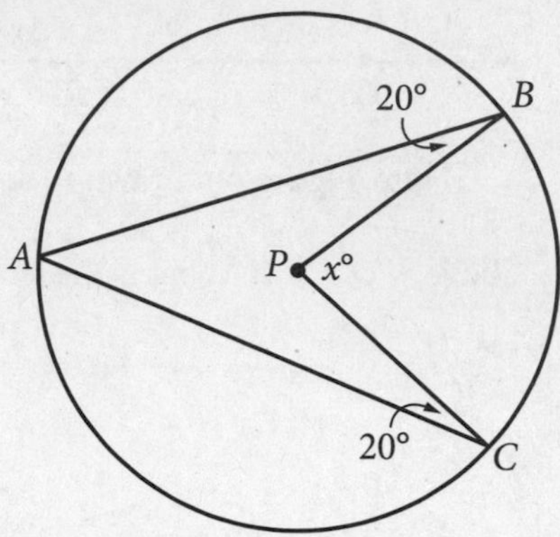

Point P is the center of the circle in the figure above. What is the value of x ?

CONTINUE

Questions 37 and 38 refer to the following information.

Ms. Simon's Workday Morning Drive

Segment of drive	Distance (miles)	Average driving speed with no traffic delay (mph)
From home to freeway entrance	0.6	25
From freeway entrance to freeway exit	15.4	50
From freeway exit to workplace	1.4	35

Ms. Simon drives her car from her home to her workplace every workday morning. The table above shows the distance, in miles, and her average driving speed, in miles per hour (mph), when there is no traffic delay, for each segment of her drive.

37

One morning, Ms. Simon drove directly from her home to her workplace in 24 minutes. What was her average speed, in miles per hour, during her drive that morning?

38

If Ms. Simon starts her drive at 6:30 a.m., she can drive at her average driving speed with no traffic delay for each segment of the drive. If she starts her drive at 7:00 a.m., the travel time from the freeway entrance to the freeway exit increases by 33% due to slower traffic, but the travel time for each of the other two segments of her drive does not change. Based on the table, how many more minutes does Ms. Simon take to arrive at her workplace if she starts her drive at 7:00 a.m. than if she starts her drive at 6:30 a.m.? (Round your answer to the nearest minute.)

STOP

If you finish before time is called, you may check your work on this section only.

Do not turn to any other section.

No Test Material On This Page

No Test Material On This Page

No Test Material On This Page

No Test Material On This Page

This page represents the back cover of the Practice Test.

The SAT®

Practice Essay #5

The essay gives you an opportunity to show how effectively you can read and comprehend a passage and write an essay analyzing the passage. In your essay, you should demonstrate that you have read the passage carefully, present a clear and logical analysis, and use language precisely.

You have <u>50 minutes</u> to read the passage and write an essay in response to the prompt provided inside this booklet.

For information on scoring your essay, view the SAT Essay scoring rubric at **sat.org/essay**.

As you read the passage below, consider how Eric Klinenberg uses

- evidence, such as facts or examples, to support claims.
- reasoning to develop ideas and to connect claims and evidence.
- stylistic or persuasive elements, such as word choice or appeals to emotion, to add power to the ideas expressed.

Adapted from Eric Klinenberg, "Viewpoint: Air-Conditioning Will Be the End of Us." ©2013 by Time Inc. Originally published July 17, 2013.

1 Earlier this week, as the temperature in New York City hit the upper 90s and the heat index topped 100, my utility provider issued a heat alert and advised customers to use air-conditioning "wisely." It was a nice, polite gesture but also an utterly ineffectual one. After all, despite our other green tendencies, most Americans still believe that the wise way to use air conditioners is to crank them up, cooling down every room in the house—or even better, relax in the cold blasts of a movie theater or shopping mall, where someone else pays the bills. Today Americans use twice as much energy for air-conditioning as we did 20 years ago, and more than the rest of the world's nations combined. As a climate-change adaptation strategy, this is as dumb as it gets.

2 I'm hardly against air-conditioning. During heat waves, artificial cooling can save the lives of old, sick and frail people, and epidemiologists have shown that owning an AC unit is one of the strongest predictors of who survives during dangerously hot summer weeks. I've long advocated public-health programs that help truly vulnerable people, whether isolated elders in broiling urban apartments or farm workers who toil in sunbaked fields, by giving them easy access to air-conditioning.

3 I also recognize that air conditioners can enhance productivity in offices and make factories safer for workers who might otherwise wilt in searing temperatures. Used conservatively—say, to reduce indoor temperatures to the mid-70s in rooms that, because of shortsighted design, cannot be cooled by cross-ventilation from fans and windows—air conditioners may well generate enough benefits to balance the indisputable, irreversible damage they generate. But in most situations, the case for air-conditioning is made of hot air.

4 What's indefensible is our habit of converting homes, offices and massive commercial outlets into igloos on summer days, regardless of how hot it is outdoors. Recently, New York City prohibited stores from pumping arctic air out onto the searing sidewalks in an attempt to lure customers while burning through fossil fuels in suicidal fashion. I can't help but wonder whether cities like New York will ever prohibit stores from cooling their facilities below, say, 70°F. No doubt a law like that would raise even more objections than Mayor Michael Bloomberg's attempt to ban big sodas, but it might well be necessary if we can't turn down the dial on our own.

5 I'm skeptical that American businesses and consumers will reduce their use of air-conditioning without new rules and regulations, especially now that natural gas has helped bring down energy bills and the short-term costs of cranking the AC are relatively low. Part of the problem is that in recent decades, the fastest-growing U.S. cities—places like Las Vegas, Phoenix and Austin—have effectively been built on air-conditioning. (This is also true in the Middle East and Asia, and as a result, global energy consumption is soaring precisely when it needs to be lowered.) Throughout the country, most designs for new office, commercial and residential property rely entirely on AC, rather than on time-honored cooling technologies such as shading from trees and cross-ventilation from windows and fans. As a result, there is now an expectation that indoor air will be frigid on even the steamiest days everywhere from the Deep South to the Great West. What's worse, this expectation is spreading to the nations where American culture carries influence; sales of air conditioners rose 20% in India and China last year.

6 Trying to engineer hot weather out of existence rather than adjust our culture of consumption for the age of climate change is one of our biggest environmental blind spots. If you can't stand the heat, you should know that blasting the AC will ultimately make us all even hotter. Let's put our air conditioners on ice before it's too late.

Write an essay in which you explain how Eric Klinenberg builds an argument to persuade his audience that Americans need to greatly reduce their reliance on air-conditioning. In your essay, analyze how Klinenberg uses one or more of the features listed in the box above (or features of your own choice) to strengthen the logic and persuasiveness of his argument. Be sure that your analysis focuses on the most relevant features of the passage.

Your essay should not explain whether you agree with Klinenberg's claims, but rather explain how Klinenberg builds an argument to persuade his audience.

This page represents the back cover of the Practice Essay.

CollegeBoard

SAT PRACTICE ANSWER SHEET

COMPLETE MARK | EXAMPLES OF INCOMPLETE MARKS

It is recommended that you use a No. 2 pencil. It is very important that you fill in the entire circle darkly and completely. If you change your response, erase as completely as possible. Incomplete marks or erasures may affect your score.

TEST NUMBER

ENTER TEST NUMBER

For instance, for Practice Test #1, fill in the circle for 0 in the **first column** and for 1 in the **second column.**

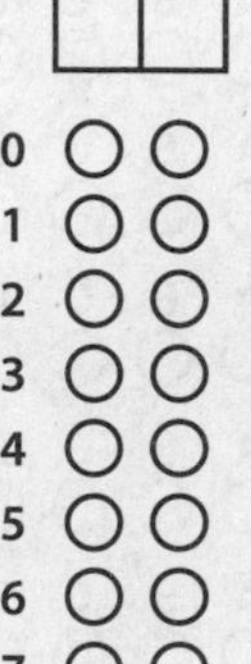

SECTION 1

1 A B C D	14 A B C D	27 A B C D	40 A B C D
2 A B C D	15 A B C D	28 A B C D	41 A B C D
3 A B C D	16 A B C D	29 A B C D	42 A B C D
4 A B C D	17 A B C D	30 A B C D	43 A B C D
5 A B C D	18 A B C D	31 A B C D	44 A B C D
6 A B C D	19 A B C D	32 A B C D	45 A B C D
7 A B C D	20 A B C D	33 A B C D	46 A B C D
8 A B C D	21 A B C D	34 A B C D	47 A B C D
9 A B C D	22 A B C D	35 A B C D	48 A B C D
10 A B C D	23 A B C D	36 A B C D	49 A B C D
11 A B C D	24 A B C D	37 A B C D	50 A B C D
12 A B C D	25 A B C D	38 A B C D	51 A B C D
13 A B C D	26 A B C D	39 A B C D	52 A B C D

Download the College Board SAT Practice app to instantly score this test.
Learn more at sat.org/scoring.

CollegeBoard

SAT PRACTICE ANSWER SHEET

COMPLETE MARK ● EXAMPLES OF INCOMPLETE MARKS 

It is recommended that you use a No. 2 pencil. It is very important that you fill in the entire circle darkly and completely. If you change your response, erase as completely as possible. Incomplete marks or erasures may affect your score.

SECTION 2

1 A B C D	10 A B C D	19 A B C D	28 A B C D	37 A B C D
2 A B C D	11 A B C D	20 A B C D	29 A B C D	38 A B C D
3 A B C D	12 A B C D	21 A B C D	30 A B C D	39 A B C D
4 A B C D	13 A B C D	22 A B C D	31 A B C D	40 A B C D
5 A B C D	14 A B C D	23 A B C D	32 A B C D	41 A B C D
6 A B C D	15 A B C D	24 A B C D	33 A B C D	42 A B C D
7 A B C D	16 A B C D	25 A B C D	34 A B C D	43 A B C D
8 A B C D	17 A B C D	26 A B C D	35 A B C D	44 A B C D
9 A B C D	18 A B C D	27 A B C D	36 A B C D	

If you're scoring with our mobile app we recommend that you cut these pages out of the back of this book. The scoring does best with a flat page.

CollegeBoard

SAT PRACTICE ANSWER SHEET

COMPLETE MARK ● EXAMPLES OF INCOMPLETE MARKS 

It is recommended that you use a No. 2 pencil. It is very important that you fill in the entire circle darkly and completely. If you change your response, erase as completely as possible. Incomplete marks or erasures may affect your score.

SECTION 3

1 A B C D	4 A B C D	7 A B C D	10 A B C D	13 A B C D
2 A B C D	5 A B C D	8 A B C D	11 A B C D	14 A B C D
3 A B C D	6 A B C D	9 A B C D	12 A B C D	15 A B C D

Only answers that are gridded will be scored. You will not receive credit for anything written in the boxes.

16 17 18 19 20

	16	17	18	19	20
/	○○	○○	○○	○○	○○
.	○○○○	○○○○	○○○○	○○○○	○○○○
0	○○○○	○○○○	○○○○	○○○○	○○○○
1	○○○○	○○○○	○○○○	○○○○	○○○○
2	○○○○	○○○○	○○○○	○○○○	○○○○
3	○○○○	○○○○	○○○○	○○○○	○○○○
4	○○○○	○○○○	○○○○	○○○○	○○○○
5	○○○○	○○○○	○○○○	○○○○	○○○○
6	○○○○	○○○○	○○○○	○○○○	○○○○
7	○○○○	○○○○	○○○○	○○○○	○○○○
8	○○○○	○○○○	○○○○	○○○○	○○○○
9	○○○○	○○○○	○○○○	○○○○	○○○○

NO CALCULATOR ALLOWED

Did you know that you can print out these test sheets from the web? Learn more at sat.org/scoring.

SAT PRACTICE ANSWER SHEET

COMPLETE MARK ● EXAMPLES OF INCOMPLETE MARKS 

It is recommended that you use a No. 2 pencil. It is very important that you fill in the entire circle darkly and completely. If you change your response, erase as completely as possible. Incomplete marks or erasures may affect your score.

SECTION 4

1 A B C D	7 A B C D	13 A B C D	19 A B C D	25 A B C D
2 A B C D	8 A B C D	14 A B C D	20 A B C D	26 A B C D
3 A B C D	9 A B C D	15 A B C D	21 A B C D	27 A B C D
4 A B C D	10 A B C D	16 A B C D	22 A B C D	28 A B C D
5 A B C D	11 A B C D	17 A B C D	23 A B C D	29 A B C D
6 A B C D	12 A B C D	18 A B C D	24 A B C D	30 A B C D

CALCULATOR ALLOWED

If you're using our mobile app keep in mind that bad lighting and even shadows cast over the answer sheet can affect your score. Be sure to scan this in a well-lit area for best results.

CollegeBoard

SAT PRACTICE ANSWER SHEET

COMPLETE MARK ● EXAMPLES OF INCOMPLETE MARKS 

It is recommended that you use a No. 2 pencil. It is very important that you fill in the entire circle darkly and completely. If you change your response, erase as completely as possible. Incomplete marks or erasures may affect your score.

SECTION 4 (Continued)

Only answers that are gridded will be scored. You will not receive credit for anything written in the boxes.

31

/ ○○
. ○○○○
0 ○○○○
1 ○○○○
2 ○○○○
3 ○○○○
4 ○○○○
5 ○○○○
6 ○○○○
7 ○○○○
8 ○○○○
9 ○○○○

32

/ ○○
. ○○○○
0 ○○○○
1 ○○○○
2 ○○○○
3 ○○○○
4 ○○○○
5 ○○○○
6 ○○○○
7 ○○○○
8 ○○○○
9 ○○○○

33

/ ○○
. ○○○○
0 ○○○○
1 ○○○○
2 ○○○○
3 ○○○○
4 ○○○○
5 ○○○○
6 ○○○○
7 ○○○○
8 ○○○○
9 ○○○○

34

/ ○○
. ○○○○
0 ○○○○
1 ○○○○
2 ○○○○
3 ○○○○
4 ○○○○
5 ○○○○
6 ○○○○
7 ○○○○
8 ○○○○
9 ○○○○

35

/ ○○
. ○○○○
0 ○○○○
1 ○○○○
2 ○○○○
3 ○○○○
4 ○○○○
5 ○○○○
6 ○○○○
7 ○○○○
8 ○○○○
9 ○○○○

Only answers that are gridded will be scored. You will not receive credit for anything written in the boxes.

36

/ ○○
. ○○○○
0 ○○○○
1 ○○○○
2 ○○○○
3 ○○○○
4 ○○○○
5 ○○○○
6 ○○○○
7 ○○○○
8 ○○○○
9 ○○○○

37

/ ○○
. ○○○○
0 ○○○○
1 ○○○○
2 ○○○○
3 ○○○○
4 ○○○○
5 ○○○○
6 ○○○○
7 ○○○○
8 ○○○○
9 ○○○○

38

/ ○○
. ○○○○
0 ○○○○
1 ○○○○
2 ○○○○
3 ○○○○
4 ○○○○
5 ○○○○
6 ○○○○
7 ○○○○
8 ○○○○
9 ○○○○

CALCULATOR ALLOWED

○ I understand that my essay (without my name) may be reproduced in other College Board materials. If I mark this circle, I withhold my permission to reproduce my essay for any purposes beyond score reporting and the assessment of my writing skills. Marking this circle will have no effect on my score, nor will it prevent my essay from being made available to any college to which I send my SAT scores.

IMPORTANT: **USE A NO. 2 PENCIL. DO NOT WRITE OUTSIDE THE BORDER!**
Words written outside the essay box or written in ink **WILL NOT APPEAR** in the copy sent to be scored, and your score will be affected.

PLANNING PAGE You may plan your essay in the unlined planning space below, but use only the lined pages following this one to write your essay. Any work on this planning page will not be scored.

Use pages 7 through 10 for your ESSAY →

FOR PLANNING ONLY

Use pages 7 through 10 for your ESSAY →

Page 6

PLEASE DO NOT WRITE IN THIS AREA

SERIAL #

BEGIN YOUR ESSAY HERE.

You may continue on the next page.

PLEASE DO NOT WRITE IN THIS AREA

SERIAL #

DO NOT WRITE OUTSIDE OF THE BOX.

You may continue on the next page.

DO NOT WRITE OUTSIDE OF THE BOX.

You may continue on the next page.

PLEASE DO NOT WRITE IN THIS AREA

SERIAL #

DO NOT WRITE OUTSIDE OF THE BOX.

STOP.

Answer Explanations

SAT Practice Test #5

Section 1: Reading Test

QUESTION 1

Choice D is the best answer. The passage begins with the main character, Lymie, sitting in a restaurant and reading a history book. The first paragraph describes the book in front of him ("Blank pages front and back were filled in with maps, drawings, dates, comic cartoons, and organs of the body," lines 11-13). The second paragraph reveals what Lymie is reading about (the Peace of Paris and the Congress of Vienna) and suggests his intense concentration on the book ("sometimes he swallowed whole the food that he had no idea he was eating," lines 23-24). In the third paragraph, the focus of the passage shifts to a description and discussion of others in the restaurant, namely "A party of four, two men and two women . . . " (lines 42-43).

Choice A is incorrect because the passage does not provide observations made by other characters, only offering Lymie's and the narrator's observations. Choice B is incorrect because the beginning of the passage focuses on Lymie as he reads by himself and the end of the passage focuses on the arrival of Lymie's father, with whom Lymie's relationship seems somewhat strained. Choice C is incorrect because the setting is described in the beginning of the first paragraph but is never the main focus of the passage.

QUESTION 2

Choice C is the best answer. The main purpose of the first paragraph is to establish the passage's setting by describing a place and an object. The place is the Alcazar Restaurant, which is described as being "long and narrow" and decorated with "*art moderne*," murals, and plants (lines 2-6), and the object is the history book Lymie is reading.

Choice A is incorrect because rather than establishing what Lymie does every night, the first paragraph describes what Lymie is doing on *one* night. Choice B is incorrect because nothing in the first paragraph indicates when the passage takes place, as the details provided (such as the restaurant and the book) are not specific to one era. Choice D is incorrect because nothing in the first paragraph clearly foreshadows a later event.

QUESTION 3

Choice C is the best answer. The passage states that "when Lymie put down his fork and began to count. . . the waitress, whose name was Irma, thought he was through eating and tried to take his plate away" (lines 34-38). It is reasonable to assume that Irma thinks Lymie is finished eating because he is no longer holding his fork.

Choice A is incorrect because Lymie has already been reading his book while eating for some time before Irma thinks he is finished eating. Choice B is incorrect because the passage doesn't state that Lymie's plate is empty, and the fact that Lymie stops Irma from taking his plate suggests that it is not empty. Choice D is incorrect because the passage gives no indication that Lymie asks Irma to clear the table.

QUESTION 4

Choice A is the best answer. The passage makes it clear that Lymie finds the party of four who enter the restaurant to be loud and bothersome, as their entrance means he is no longer able to concentrate on his book: "They laughed more than there seemed any occasion for . . . and their laughter was too loud. But it was the women's voices . . . which caused Lymie to skim over two whole pages without knowing what was on them" (lines 52-59).

Choices B, C, and D are incorrect because lines 55-59 make clear that Lymie is annoyed by the party of four, not that he finds their presence refreshing (choice B), thinks they resemble the people he is reading about (choice C), or thinks they represent glamour and youth (choice D).

QUESTION 5

Choice C is the best answer. The previous question asks about Lymie's impression of the party of four who enter the restaurant, with the correct answer being that he finds them noisy and distracting. This is supported in lines 55-59: "But it was the women's voices, the terrible not quite sober pitch of the women's voices, which caused Lymie to skim over two whole pages without knowing what was on them."

Choices A, B, and D are incorrect because the lines cited do not support the answer to the previous question about Lymie's impression of the party of four who enter the restaurant. Rather than showing that Lymie finds the group of strangers noisy and distracting, the lines simply describe how two of the four people look (choices A and B) and indicate what Lymie does when his father joins him in the restaurant (choice D).

QUESTION 6

Choice A is the best answer. In the passage, Lymie closes his book only after "a coat that he recognized as his father's was hung on the hook next to his chair" (lines 67-68). It is Lymie's father's arrival that causes him to close the book.

Choices B, C, and D are incorrect because lines 67-70 of the passage clearly establish that Lymie closes his book because his father has arrived, not that he does so because the party of four is too loud (choice B), because he has finished reading a section of the book (choice C), or because he is getting ready to leave (choice D).

QUESTION 7

Choice D is the best answer. In lines 74-79, the narrator describes Mr. Peters as "gray" and balding, noting that he has "lost weight" and his color is "poor." This description suggests Mr. Peters is aging and losing strength and vigor.

Choices A, B, and C are incorrect because the description of Mr. Peters in lines 74-79 suggests he is a person who is wan and losing vitality, not someone who is healthy and in good shape (choice A), angry and intimidating (choice B), or emotionally anxious (choice C).

QUESTION 8

Choice B is the best answer. In the last paragraph of the passage, Mr. Peters is described as being unaware "that there had been any change" in his appearance since he was younger (lines 80-81). Later in the paragraph, the passage states that "the young man" Mr. Peters once was "had never for one second deserted" him (lines 90-91). The main idea of the last paragraph is that Mr. Peters still thinks of himself as young, or at least acts as if he is a younger version of himself.

Choice A is incorrect because Mr. Peters is spending time with Lymie, his son, and there is no indication that he generally does not spend time with his family. Choice C is incorrect because although there are brief mentions of a diamond ring and manicured fingers, the paragraph focuses on Mr. Peters's overall appearance, not on his awareness of status symbols. Choice D is incorrect because the last paragraph clearly states that Mr. Peters is "not aware that there had been any change" and thinks of himself as young.

QUESTION 9

Choice B is the best answer. In lines 81-85, Mr. Peters is described as having "straightened his tie self-consciously" and gestured with a menu "so that the two women at the next table would notice the diamond ring on the fourth finger of his right hand." Mr. Peters's actions are those of someone who wants to attract attention and be noticed.

Choices A, C, and D are incorrect because the lines cited do not support the idea Mr. Peters wants to attract attention to himself. Choices A and C address Mr. Peters's view of himself. Choice D indicates that Mr. Peters's view of himself affects his behavior but does not reveal that he acts in a way meant to draw attention.

QUESTION 10

Choice B is the best answer. The last sentence of the passage states that Mr. Peters's mischaracterization of himself makes him act in ways that are not "becoming" for a man of his age. In this context, "becoming" suggests behavior that is appropriate or fitting.

Choices A, C, and D are incorrect because in the context of describing one's behavior, "becoming" means appropriate or fitting, not becoming known (choice A), becoming more advanced (choice C), or simply occurring (choice D).

QUESTION 11

Choice B is the best answer. In Passage 1, Beecher makes the point that even if women in her society are perceived as being inferior to men, they are still able to effect considerable influence on that society: "But while woman holds a subordinate relation in society to the other sex, it is not because it was designed that her duties or her influence should be any the less important, or all-pervading" (lines 6-10).

Choice A is incorrect because Beecher describes the dynamic between men and women in terms of the way they can change society, not in terms of security and physical safety. Choice C is incorrect because even though Beecher implies that women have fewer rights in society than men do, she doesn't say that women have fewer responsibilities. Choice D is incorrect because Beecher does not assert that women are superior to men.

QUESTION 12

Choice A is the best answer. The previous question asks what point Beecher makes regarding the relationship between men and women in her society, with the answer being that women are considered inferior but can still have influence. This is supported in lines 6-10: "But while woman holds a subordinate relation in society to the other sex, it is not because it was designed that her duties or her influence should be any the less important, or all-pervading."

Choices B, C, and D are incorrect because the lines cited do not support the answer to the previous question about the point Beecher makes regarding the relationship between men and women in her society. Instead, they describe ways men can affect society (choices B and C) and explain how certain actions undertaken by a woman can be viewed negatively (choice D).

QUESTION 13

Choice B is the best answer. In the third paragraph (lines 22-37), Beecher suggests that women can be "so much respected, esteemed and loved" by those around them that men will accede to their wishes: "then, the fathers, the husbands, and the sons, will find an influence thrown around them, to which they will yield not only willingly but proudly. . . ." These lines show that Beecher believes women can influence society by influencing the men around them; in other words, women have an indirect influence on public life.

Choices A, C, and D are incorrect because lines 34-37 make it clear that Beecher believes women do have an effect on society, even if it is an indirect effect. Beecher does not indicate that women's effect on public life is ignored because most men are not interested (choice A), unnecessary because men do not need help governing society (choice C), or merely symbolic because women tend to be idealistic (choice D).

QUESTION 14

Choice D is the best answer. Regarding the dynamic of men and women in society, Beecher says that one sex is given "the subordinate station" while the other is given the "superior" station (lines 1-2). In the context of how one gender exists in comparison to the other, the word "station" suggests a standing or rank.

Choices A, B, and C are incorrect because in the context of the relative standing of men and women in Beecher's society, the word "station" suggests a standing or rank, not a physical location or area (choices A, B, and C).

QUESTION 15

Choice C is the best answer. When describing how men and women can influence society, Beecher says the ways they can do so "should be altogether different and peculiar" (lines 11-12). In the context of the "altogether different" ways men and women can influence society, the word "peculiar" implies being unique or distinctive.

Choices A, B, and D are incorrect because in the context of the "altogether different" ways men and women can influence society, the word "peculiar" suggests something unique or distinctive, not something unusual and odd (choice A), unexpected (choice B), or rare (choice D).

QUESTION 16

Choice A is the best answer. In Passage 2, Grimké makes the main point that people have rights because they are human, not because of their gender or race. This is clear in lines 58-60, when Grimké states that "human beings have *rights*, because they are *moral* beings: the rights of *all* men grow out of their moral nature" and lines 65-68, when Grimké writes, "Now if rights are founded in the nature of our moral being, then the *mere circumstance of sex* does not give to man higher rights and responsibilities, than to woman."

Choices B, C, and D are incorrect because Grimké primarily emphasizes that all men and women inherently have the same rights ("rights are founded in the nature of our moral being," lines 65-66). Her central claim is not that men and women need to work together to change society (choice B), that moral rights are the distinguishing characteristic separating humans from animals (choice C), or that there should be equal opportunities for men and women to advance and succeed.

QUESTION 17

Choice B is the best answer. In Passage 2, Grimké makes the point that human rights are not fleeting or changeable but things that remain, regardless of the circumstances, because they are tied to humans' moral nature. She emphasizes that human rights exist even if societal laws attempt to contradict or override them, citing slavery as an example: "These rights may be wrested from the slave, but they cannot be alienated: his title to himself is as perfect now, as is that of Lyman Beecher: it is stamped on his moral being, and is, like it, imperishable" (lines 61-65).

Choices A and D are incorrect because in Passage 2, Grimké makes the point that human rights are inherent and unchanging, not that they are viewed differently in different societies (choice A) or that they have changed and developed over time (choice D). Choice C is incorrect because Grimké doesn't describe a clash between human rights and moral responsibilities; instead, she says that humans have rights "because they are *moral* beings" (lines 58-59).

QUESTION 18

Choice B is the best answer. The previous question asks what point Grimké makes about human rights in Passage 2, with the answer being that they exist and have moral authority whether or not they are established by societal law. This is supported in lines 61-65: "These rights may be wrested from the slave, but they cannot be alienated: his title to himself is as perfect now, as is that of Lyman Beecher: it is stamped on his moral being, and is, like it, imperishable."

Choices A, C, and D are incorrect because the lines cited do not support the answer to the previous question about the point Grimké makes about human rights in Passage 2. Instead, they explain the source of all people's human rights (choice A), indicate what would happen if rights were determined by gender (choice C), and discuss why gender is irrelevant to rights (choice D).

QUESTION 19

Choice B is the best answer. In Passage 1, Beecher asserts that men and women naturally have different positions in society: "Heaven has appointed to one sex the superior, and to the other the subordinate station" (lines 1-2). She goes on to argue that a woman should act within her subordinate role to influence men but should not "exert coercive influences" that would put her "out of her appropriate sphere" (lines 44-46). In Passage 2, Grimké takes issue with the idea that men and women have different rights and roles. She asserts that as moral beings all people have the same inherent rights and states that "the *mere circumstance of sex* does not give to man higher rights and responsibilities, than to woman" (lines 66-68).

Choice A is incorrect because Passage 2 does not discuss the practical difficulties of something that is proposed in Passage 1 but rather argues against the main point of Passage 1. Choice C is incorrect because Passage 2 does not provide historical context for the view expressed in Passage 1; the passages were published at around the same time and both discuss contemporary society. Choice D is incorrect because Passage 2 does not elaborate on implications found in Passage 1 as much as it disputes the ideas explicitly expressed in Passage 1.

QUESTION 20

Choice A is the best answer. While Beecher and Grimké clearly disagree regarding a woman's role in society, the passages suggest that both authors share the belief that women do have moral duties and responsibilities in society. In Passage 1, Beecher writes that "while woman holds a subordinate relation in society to the other sex, it is not because it was designed that her duties or her influence should be any the less important, or all-pervading" (lines 6-10). She suggests that women do have an obligation to use their influence to bring about beneficial changes in society. In Passage 2, Grimké asserts that all people "are *moral* beings" (lines 58-59) and that both men and women have "rights and responsibilities" (line 68). She concludes that "whatever it is morally right for man to do, it is morally right for woman to do" (lines 81-83).

Choice B is incorrect because neither author suggests that when men work to bring about political changes, they often do so out of consideration for others rather than considerations for themselves. Choice C is incorrect because neither passage discusses the value given to women's ethical obligations, although both authors suggest that women do have ethical and moral obligations. Choice D is incorrect because in Passage 1 Beecher argues that women should avoid direct political activism, cautioning against actions that would put them outside their "appropriate sphere" (line 46).

QUESTION 21

Choice D is the best answer. In lines 65-68 of Passage 2, Grimké writes, "Now if rights are founded in the nature of our moral being, then the *mere circumstance of sex* does not give to man higher rights and responsibilities, than to woman." In other words, gender does not make men's rights and duties superior to women's. Beecher, on the other hand, begins Passage 1 by stating that "heaven has appointed to one sex the superior, and to the other the subordinate station," suggesting that men and women have fundamentally different natures. Therefore, Beecher most likely would have disagreed with Grimké's assertion.

Choices A and B are incorrect because Beecher fundamentally disagrees with Grimké regarding the basic nature and societal roles of men and women, making it very unlikely that she would have viewed Grimké's statement in lines 65-68 with either sympathy or agreement. Choice C is incorrect because Beecher wouldn't necessarily have been dismayed by Grimké's belief as much as she would have simply disagreed with it, and she does not indicate that the role of women in society is more difficult to play than is that of men.

QUESTION 22

Choice A is the best answer. In line 14, the passage states that industrial agriculture has become "incredibly efficient on a simple land to food basis." In this context, "simple" suggests something basic or straightforward.

Choices B, C, and D are incorrect because in the context of a land to food dynamic, the word "simple" suggests something basic or straightforward, not something humble (choice B), something without any decoration or ornamentation (choice C), or something that requires little effort (choice D).

QUESTION 23

Choice B is the best answer. The passage clearly states that conventional agriculture is very efficient, especially when compared to organic farming: "organic farming yields 25% fewer crops on average than conventional agriculture" (lines 40-42) and in a study "organic farming delivered a lower yield for every crop type" (lines 51-52). It can therefore be understood from the passage that conventional agriculture does a good job maximizing the output of the land that is farmed.

Choice A is incorrect because the passage states how efficient conventional agriculture is in regard to the amount of food it can produce but does not indicate that it produces a significantly wide variety of fruits and vegetables. Choice C is incorrect because even if the passage does say that each American farmer can produce crops to feed "over 155 people worldwide" (lines 16-17), it never claims that conventional agriculture can satisfactorily feed everyone in the world. Choice D is incorrect because the passage states that conventional agriculture uses a great deal of nitrogen, not that it changes the need for nitrogen in plant growth one way or the other.

QUESTION 24

Choice A is the best answer. The passage makes it clear that "most environmentalists" (line 27) believe conventional agriculture produces food that is not as healthy as food produced through organic farming and that it is more harmful to the environment than organic farming is: many environmentalists "have embraced organic food as better for the planet — and healthier and tastier, too — than the stuff produced by agricultural corporations" (lines 28-31).

Choices B, C, and D are incorrect because they are not supported by the passage. The passage never states that many environmentalists believe that conventional farming reduces the need to convert wilderness to farmland (choice B), is in any way good for the environment (choice C), or protects wildlife habitats (choice D).

QUESTION 25

Choice B is the best answer. The previous question asks how environmentalists perceive conventional agriculture, with the answer being that they believe it produces a product that is less healthy and more environmentally destructive than that produced by organic farming. This is supported in lines 28-31: "They have embraced organic food as better for the planet — and healthier and tastier, too — than the stuff produced by agricultural corporations."

Choices A, C, and D are incorrect because the lines cited do not support the answer to the previous question about how environmentalists perceive the efforts of conventional agriculture. Although the lines in choice A do touch on environmentalists' views, they indicate only that most environmentalists don't view conventional agriculture's ability to "produce more food on less land" (line 25) as beneficial to the environment. Choice C is incorrect because these lines address environmentalists' view of the environmental effects of conventional and organic farming but not the taste or nutritional value of the food produced. Choice D is incorrect because these lines focus on a drawback to organic farming.

QUESTION 26

Choice C is the best answer. The passage makes it clear that while both conventional and organic farming need nitrogen for plant growth, conventional farming uses synthetic fertilizers and organic does not: "Conventional agriculture makes use of 171 million metric tons of synthetic fertilizer each year, and all that nitrogen enables much faster plant growth than the slower release of nitrogen from the compost or cover crops used in organic farming" (lines 61-65).

Choice A is incorrect because the passage does not state that conventional and organic farming are equally sustainable and does state that organic farming needs "more land" to produce "fewer crops" (lines 42-43) but does not indicate that it always requires dramatically more land. Choice B is incorrect because the passage does not state that organic farming uses artificial chemicals. Choice D is incorrect because the passage mentions nitrogen runoff only as a product of conventional farming, not organic farming, and does not indicate that only the nitrogen in conventional fertilizers is dangerous.

QUESTION 27

Choice D is the best answer. The previous question asks about the relationship between conventional agriculture and organic farming, with the answer being that unlike organic farms, conventional farms use synthetic fertilizers. This is supported in lines 61-65: "Conventional agriculture makes use of 171 million metric tons of synthetic fertilizer each year, and all that nitrogen enables much faster plant growth than the slower release of nitrogen from the compost or cover crops used in organic farming."

Choices A, B, and C are incorrect because the lines cited do not support the answer to the previous question about the relationship between conventional and organic farming, instead describing the efficiency only of conventional agriculture (choice A), discussing one perceived positive aspect of conventional agriculture (choice B), and highlighting a drawback of organic farming (choice C).

QUESTION 28

Choice B is the best answer. The passage states that the authors of the study comparing conventional and organic farming have come to the conclusion that an "ideal global agriculture system" would "borrow the best from both systems" (lines 80-82). The quote from Jonathan Foley in lines 84-97 indicates that this ideal system would take into consideration many different factors, including the nutrition and calories offered by specific types of foods as well as different geographic, economic, and social needs.

Choices A and D are incorrect because the passage makes it clear that the "ideal global agriculture system" would give consideration to multiple factors, not that it would focus mainly on productivity (choice A) or nutritional value (choice D). Choice C is incorrect because Foley states that the ideal system would take economics into consideration but does not indicate that farmers' economic interests would be weighed against consumers' needs.

QUESTION 29

Choice D is the best answer. The passage states that conventional agriculture can be superior to organic farming in terms of producing "sheer calories" (line 88). In this context, "sheer" most nearly means pure; the passage is referring to the pure number of calories delivered by foods.

Choices A, B, and C are incorrect because in the context of discussing the calories foods can provide, "sheer" suggests the pure number of calories. Also, it does not make sense to say that calories can be seen through (choice A), are somehow sudden or happen unexpectedly (choice B), or are at a very sharp angle (choice C).

QUESTION 30

Choice B is the best answer. Figure 1 shows that the organic yield as a percentage of conventional yield is similar for cereals and all crops, with both yielding roughly 75%.

Choice A is incorrect because figure 1 shows that the organic yield as a percentage of conventional yield is higher for fruits (just under 100%) than for vegetables (just under 70%). Choice C is incorrect because figure 1 shows there were only 28 observations for oilseed crops. Choice D is incorrect because figure 1 shows that the organic yield as a percentage of conventional yield is higher for oilseed crops (approximately 90%) than for vegetables (just under 70%).

QUESTION 31

Choice D is the best answer. Every organically grown species represented in figure 2 produces a smaller yield than do their conventional counterparts. All of the organically grown species are within a range of approximately 60–90% of the conventional yield.

Choice A is incorrect because figure 2 shows that soybeans have the highest yield (approximately 90%), not the lowest. Choice B is incorrect because figure 2 shows that organically grown barley and maize are produced at a lower yield than the conventionally grown species (just below 70% and just below 90%, respectively), not a comparable one. Choice C is incorrect because figure 2 shows that soybeans, not tomatoes, have the highest yield of the organically grown species.

QUESTION 32

Choice B is the best answer. The majority of the passage focuses on the experiment concerning "how much the crowd influences the individual, and whether it can be controlled from outside" (lines 42-44). After explaining the experiment and the results it produced, the passage moves on to consider questions raised by the results, such as whether the findings are site specific or "true in general" (lines 75-76), why different findings are observed, and whether companies can "boost their products by manipulating online ratings on a massive scale" (lines 85-86).

Choice A is incorrect because the passage does not conclude by explaining the practical ways the experiment's findings have been applied but rather by considering questions the findings raise. Choices C and D are incorrect because the passage does not indicate that there were any flaws in the experiment's findings and does not include statements from anyone who disputes the findings.

QUESTION 33

Choice C is the best answer. The author of the passage suggests that a group of people can be "wiser" and more effective than a single person at assessing a quantitative answer, or a measurement, versus producing a valid qualitative judgment, or a judgment of the quality of something. This is most clear in lines 11-14, which state that when guessing a bull's weight or how many gumballs are in a jar, "your guess is probably going to be far from the mark, whereas the average of many people's choices is remarkably close to the true number."

Choices A, B, and D are incorrect because lines 11-14 indicate that the author believes that crowds may be more effective than individuals when arriving at quantitative answers rather than qualitative results. Nothing in the passage suggests that the author believes that crowds are better at starting disagreements than studying an issue in depth (choice A), supporting ideas rather than challenging them (choice B), or ranking opinions rather than coming up with new ideas (choice D).

QUESTION 34

Choice B is the best answer. The previous question asks what the author of the passage suggests about the wisdom of crowds, with the answer being that crowds can be more effective at producing quantitative answers than qualitative results. This is supported in lines 11-14: when it comes to guessing a bull's weight or how many gumballs are in a jar, "your guess is probably going to be far from the mark, whereas the average of many people's choices is remarkably close to the true number."

Choices A, C, and D are incorrect because the lines cited do not support the answer to the previous question about the author's belief about when the wisdom of a crowd is effective. Instead, they simply state that crowds are sometimes wiser than individuals, without explaining when (choice A), put forth a theory held by someone other than the author (choice C), and explain how hypotheses about the wisdom of crowds could be tested (choice D).

QUESTION 35

Choice A is the best answer. In the passage, the author explains that those who are skeptical of the theory that "measuring the aggregate of people's opinions produces a stable, reliable value" (lines 18-20) believe that "people's opinions are easily swayed by those of others" (lines 20-21). This idea is best supported in lines 55-58, which describe a finding from a study of opinions in crowds: "Comments that received fake positive votes from the researchers were 32% more likely to receive more positive votes compared with a control, the team reports." In other words, people were more likely to give a positive vote when they thought other people had given positive votes.

Choices B, C, and D are incorrect because the lines cited do not provide support for the skeptics' idea that people's opinions are easily influenced by the thoughts of others. Instead, they cite findings concerning people giving ratings *different* from those already given (choices B and C) and share an observation that the degree to which others can be influenced depends in part on the context of the situation (choice D).

QUESTION 36

Choice B is the best answer. One question Watts asks in regard to the experiment is whether the results would hold true on a larger scale. The passage quotes him in lines 74-76: "'[But] one question is whether the positive [herding] bias is specific to this site' or true in general." Doing the experiment again but collecting ratings on multiple websites would address Watts's question, as it would show whether or not the same results occur on other sites.

Choices A, C, and D are incorrect. Providing fewer fake positive comments during the experiment (choice A), requiring users to be registered on the website (choice C), or telling users that their answers will be studied (choice D) are actions that likely would affect the results of the experiment involving users voting on comments about stories on one news website, but they would not address Watts's questions about whether the study would produce the same results on *other* websites or why different categories of news items had different effects on the news website.

QUESTION 37

Choice C is the best answer. In lines 85-86 the author asks, "Will companies be able to boost their products by manipulating online ratings on a massive scale?" In the context of selling products by manipulating user reviews, "boost" most nearly means promote.

Choices A, B, and D are incorrect because in the context of selling products by manipulating user reviews, the word "boost" refers to promoting the products, not making them larger or bigger (choice A), faster (choice B), or safe (choice D).

QUESTION 38

Choice A is the best answer. In lines 85-86 the author asks, "Will companies be able to boost their products by manipulating online ratings on a massive scale?" In the context of selling products by manipulating user reviews on a massive scale, the word "scale" most nearly means level or size.

Choices B, C, and D are incorrect because in the context of selling products by manipulating user reviews, a massive "scale" refers to a great level or size, not to a payment (choice B), an interval or space between things (choice C), or a plan (choice D).

QUESTION 39

Choice B is the best answer. The figure shows that while the mean score of the control comments in the politics category is below 2.0, the artificially up-voted mean score for that category is exactly 2.5.

Choice A is incorrect because the artificially up-voted mean score of comments in the business category is higher than 3.0. Choice C is incorrect because the artificially up-voted mean score of comments in the fun category is less than 2.5. Choice D is incorrect because the artificially up-voted mean score of the comments in the general news category is just over 2.0.

QUESTION 40

Choice D is the best answer. The figure shows that the mean score for both control comments and artificially up-voted comments in the general news category is just above 2.0.

Choice A is incorrect because the mean score for the control comments in the culture and society category is a little below 2.5 while the mean score for the artificially up-voted comments is over 3.0. Choice B is incorrect because the mean score for the control comments in the information technology category is a little above 1.5 while the mean score for the artificially up-voted comments is above 2.0. Choice C is incorrect because the mean score for the control comments in the fun category is exactly 2.0 while the mean score for the artificially up-voted comments is nearly 2.5.

QUESTION 41

Choice D is the best answer. In the passage Watts notes that "the category of the news items . . . had a strong effect on how much people could be manipulated" (lines 76-79). That idea is directly supported by the data in the figure, which show that the difference in mean score between the control comments and the artificially up-voted comments varies by subject (for example, in the general news category there is virtually no difference between the mean scores of the two types of comments, while for the business category there is almost a 1.0-point difference between the mean scores).

Choices A and B are incorrect because the passage provides no data for artificially down-voted comments or negative social influence. Choice C is incorrect because the figure applies only to one context (mean score of control comments versus mean score of artificially up-voted comments on the news site); there is no way to tell what patterns would be observed in other contexts.

QUESTION 42

Choice C is the best answer. According to the passage, Maguire found that taxi drivers' hippocampi are "7 percent larger than normal," which is evidence that "way-finding around London had physically altered the gross structure of their brains" (lines 10-14). In lines 20-26, the passage indicates that this finding challenges an earlier consensus: "It had long been thought that the adult brain was incapable of spawning new neurons — that . . . the brain's basic anatomical structure was more or less static. Maguire's study suggested the old inherited wisdom was simply not true."

Choice A is incorrect because the passage does not indicate that Maguire used a new method in her study or that her findings demonstrate the validity of a method. Choice B is incorrect because lines 20-26 show that Maguire's findings disprove a popular viewpoint, not that they support one. Choice D is incorrect because although Maguire's findings call into question a previous idea, there is no indication that they challenge the authenticity of any previous data.

QUESTION 43

Choice D is the best answer. The previous question asks about the significance of Maguire's findings, with the answer being that her findings call into question a previous belief. This is supported in lines 20-26: "It had long been thought that the adult brain was incapable of spawning new neurons — that . . . the brain's basic anatomical structure was more or less static. Maguire's study suggested the old inherited wisdom was simply not true."

Choices A, B, and C are incorrect because the lines cited do not support the answer to the previous question about the significance of Maguire's findings. Choices A and B are incorrect because these lines present Maguire's observation and her conclusion but do not indicate that her findings call into question a previous belief. Choice C is incorrect because these lines simply explain one capability of the human brain.

QUESTION 44

Choice D is the best answer. In line 24, the passage discusses the "brain's basic anatomical structure." In this context, the word "basic" most nearly means fundamental.

Choices A, B, and C are incorrect because in the context of discussing the brain's structure, the word "basic" most nearly means fundamental, not first (choice A), uncomplicated (choice B), or required (choice C).

QUESTION 45

Choice C is the best answer. The purpose of Maguire's study of the mental athletes was to try to determine what it is that makes them so good at memorization, and in particular if they have structurally different brains than people without such extraordinary memorization skills or if they have normal brain structures but use them in unusual ways. This is supported in lines 33-37, which state that Maguire and her team "wanted to find out if the memorizers' brains were — like the London cabbies' — structurally different from the rest of ours, or if they were somehow just making better use of memory abilities that we all possess."

Choice A is incorrect because the study was an attempt to compare the brains of mental athletes to the brains of the general population, not to compare the use of different brain structures in memorization and navigation. Choices B and D are incorrect because the passage makes it clear that it was not known if mental athletes have unusual brain structures; finding out if they do was actually one of the goals of the study.

QUESTION 46

Choice B is the best answer. The previous question asks what Maguire's study of mental athletes attempted to answer, with the answer being the question of whether it is brain structure or an unusual use of the brain that gives certain people extraordinary memorization skills. This is supported in lines 33-37: "They wanted to find out if the memorizers' brains were — like the London cabbies' — structurally different from the rest of ours, or if they were somehow just making better use of memory abilities that we all possess."

Choices A, C, and D are incorrect because the lines cited do not support the answer to the previous question about what Maguire's study of mental athletes was investigating. Instead they simply identify the subject of the study (choice A), explain what the study involved (choice C), and state a finding concerning the cognitive ability of the mental athletes (choice D).

QUESTION 47

Choice A is the best answer. In lines 38-39, the passage describes part of Maguire's study by stating that "the researchers put both the mental athletes and a group of matched control subjects into MRI scanners." In the context of a study that has two groups of subjects, the word "matched" suggests subjects that are similar or comparable.

Choices B, C, and D are incorrect because in the context of a study with two groups of subjects, the word "matched" suggests subjects that are similar or comparable, not ones that are exactly the same (choice B), ones that are recognizably different (choice C), or ones that are rivals (choice D).

QUESTION 48

Choice C is the best answer. The main purpose of the fifth paragraph (lines 57-65) is to relate what Maguire discovered about the mental athletes, namely that their brain structures are not different from those of the control group but that the mental athletes use their brains differently: "there was one telling difference . . . regions of the brain that were less active in the control subjects seemed to be working in overdrive for the mental athletes."

Choice A is incorrect because the fifth paragraph does not mention the taxi drivers or the study involving them. Choice B is incorrect because the fifth paragraph describes some of the unexpected results of Maguire's study but does not address the possible reasons for those results. Choice D is incorrect because the fifth paragraph describes only Maguire's findings, not her methods.

QUESTION 49

Choice C is the best answer. The passage indicates that Maguire's second study revealed that people in the control group don't have different brain structures than the mental athletes but that they use their brains differently. In particular, the two groups use different pathways in the brain: "regions of the brain that were less active in the control subjects seemed to be working in overdrive for the mental athletes" (lines 63-65).

Choices A and D are incorrect because the passage states that there was only "one telling difference between the brains of the mental athletes and the control subjects" (lines 57-58); there is no indication that the control group showed less total brain activity or had smaller hippocampal regions. Choice B is incorrect because the passage mentions only the general cognitive ability of the mental athletes, noting that their scores were "within the normal range" (line 54).

QUESTION 50

Choice A is the best answer. After establishing in lines 50-52 that the brains of the control group and the mental athletes seemed to be "indistinguishable," the passage suggests that the reason mental athletes are so good at memorization is that they use parts of their brains that most other people don't use when memorizing: "Surprisingly, when the mental athletes were learning new information, they were engaging several regions of the brain known to be involved in two specific tasks: visual memory and spatial navigation, including the same right posterior hippocampal region that the London cabbies had enlarged with all their daily way-finding" (lines 66-72).

Choices B and C are incorrect because the passage explains that the mental athletes were converting information into images, not abstract symbols or numerical lists. Choice D is incorrect because it is not supported by the passage, as the author discusses the mental athletes' actions while memorizing but not any brain exercises the mental athletes regularly do.

QUESTION 51

Choice A is the best answer. The previous question asks what the passage suggests about the mental athletes' success with memorization, with the answer being that they use parts of the brain that most other people don't use when memorizing. This is supported in lines 66-72: "Surprisingly, when the mental athletes were learning new information, they were engaging several regions of the brain known to be involved in two specific tasks: visual memory and spatial navigation, including the same right posterior hippocampal region that the London cabbies had enlarged with all their daily way-finding."

Choices B, C, and D are incorrect because the lines cited do not support the answer to the previous question about what the passage suggests about the mental athletes' success with memorization. Instead, they acknowledge that Maguire's findings seem odd (choice B), describe how Maguire first responded to the results (choice C), and explain things that *don't* account for the mental athletes' ability (choice D).

QUESTION 52

Choice B is the best answer. According to the passage, Maguire's study revealed that the mental athletes were using the same parts of the brain for memorization as were the London cabbies from the first study, a result that was initially puzzling. The questions in lines 74-78 highlight and expand on that result, making it clear that it is surprising to find that the mental athletes use images to remember numbers or use a part of the brain associated with navigation when trying to remember shapes. Although it became clear *how* the mental athletes were memorizing things, it was not clear why they were doing it that way.

Choice A is incorrect because the questions in lines 74-78 seem to reflect additional questions Maguire and others had based on their result and do not suggest that Maguire's conclusions may not be reliable. Choice C is incorrect because the passage makes no mention of any earlier studies of the phenomenon of using images to remember numbers or to use a part of the brain associated with navigation when trying to remember shapes. Choice D is incorrect because the questions in lines 74-78 specifically address Maguire's two studies but not her earlier work.

Section 2: Writing and Language Test

QUESTION 1

Choice C is the best answer because the sentence is not directly related to the main point of the paragraph and should not be added. The main idea of the paragraph is that new high-tech fossil models help expand scientists' knowledge of ancient species. There is no indication in the paragraph that these scientists are concerned about the age of the rocks in which fossils are found.

Choices A and B are incorrect because the sentence should not be added. It neither adds support to an argument nor provides a transition from one sentence to another. Choice D is incorrect because the sentence does not undermine any claim made in the paragraph.

QUESTION 2

Choice D is the best answer because "promise" suggests the hope of good things to come. The models offer the possibility of advancing the field of paleontology in the future.

Choices A, B, and C are incorrect because they do not make sense in the context of the passage.

QUESTION 3

Choice B is the best answer because the sentence should be kept: it provides a brief but useful explanation of how a 3-D printer works.

Choice A is incorrect. The sentence should be kept because it provides important information about 3-D printers, not because it explains why X-rays are used in CT scanners. Choices C and D are incorrect because the sentence is neither contradictory nor confusing and should not be deleted.

QUESTION 4

Choice C is the best answer because the relative pronoun "which" appropriately follows the independent clause "The plastic hardens quickly." It introduces the relative clause explaining what the fact that the plastic hardens quickly allows the printer to do.

Choices A, B, and D are incorrect because each results in a comma splice (the joining of two independent clauses with only a comma).

QUESTION 5

Choice A is the best answer because no change is needed. The prepositional phrase "in order" and the infinitive "to learn" are appropriately used in conjunction to create an idiomatic phrase.

Choices B and D are incorrect because the phrases "in order for learning" and "so to learn" are not idiomatic. Choice C is incorrect because the pronoun "one" is inconsistent with the noun "team," which identifies a specific team.

QUESTION 6

Choice C is the best answer because the personal plural pronoun "their" agrees in number with its antecedent, the plural noun "fossils."

Choice A is incorrect because the pronoun "its" is singular and doesn't agree with the plural antecedent "fossils." Choices B and D are incorrect because a personal pronoun is needed in the sentence. Neither "it's" (the contraction of "it is") nor "there" is a personal pronoun.

QUESTION 7

Choice D is the best answer because sentence 2 should be placed after sentence 5 to make the paragraph most logical. Sentence 2 begins "But now," signaling a contrast with the past. Sentences 4 and 5 tell what scientists did in the past, so it makes sense for sentence 2 to follow sentence 5.

Choices A, B, and C are incorrect because they result in a paragraph that does not proceed logically. Keeping sentence 2, which begins "But now," where it is now (choice A) or placing it at the beginning of the paragraph (choice B) signals a contrast with the past that doesn't make sense in context. Placing sentence 2 after sentence 4 (choice C) appropriately signals a contrast with the past but creates problems for sentence 5, which needs to be placed directly after sentence 4 to continue the discussion of past research limitations.

QUESTION 8

Choice D is the best answer because the phrase "for example" indicates that an example will follow. In this paragraph, the sentence that follows the phrase provides a relevant example of the use of technology to "reproduce fossils that scientists cannot observe firsthand."

Choices A, B, and C are incorrect because they set up expectations that are not carried out in the paragraph. "By contrast" in choice A and "nonetheless" in choice B suggest that contrary information will follow. "Besides" in choice C suggests that additional information will follow. None of these choices indicates what should be indicated: that an example will follow.

QUESTION 9

Choice B is the best answer because the simple past tense verb "relied" is consistent with the other past tense verbs in the National Museum of Brazil example, such as "dug" and "determined."

Choices A and D are incorrect because they provide singular verbs that don't agree in number with the plural subject "researchers." Choice C is incorrect because the future tense helping verb "will" is inconsistent with the other past tense verbs in the National Museum of Brazil example.

QUESTION 10

Choice C is the best answer because it clearly and concisely combines the sentences in a way that shows the cause-effect relationship between the condition of the fossil and the decision by the research team.

Choices A, B, and D are incorrect because they do not effectively combine the sentences. In each of these choices, the sentence mischaracterizes the relationship between the condition of the fossil and the decision by the research team.

QUESTION 11

Choice C is the best answer because the plural pronoun "they" correctly refers to its plural antecedent "researchers."

Choices A, B, and D are incorrect because "one," "he or she," and "it" are singular pronouns. A plural pronoun is needed to agree in number with the plural antecedent "researchers."

QUESTION 12

Choice D is the best answer because no transitional phrase is needed between the two sentences. The first sentence indicates that Tweed wanted to silence Nast, and the second sentence simply states what happened next: that his attempt to do so failed.

Choices A, B, and C are incorrect because no transitional phrase or conjunctive adverb such as "therefore" or "furthermore" is needed between the sentences. The information in the second sentence neither results from information in the first nor adds to it. Rather, it tells what happened next: the first sentence indicates that Tweed wanted to silence Nast, and the second states that his attempt to do so failed.

QUESTION 13

Choice D is the best answer because it is the only choice that clearly and concisely conveys the key information that "in the 1860s and the 1870s, . . . organizations known as 'political machines' started taking control of city governments."

Choices A, B, and C are incorrect because they all contain unnecessary words or invert the logical order of words in ways that lead to vagueness and redundancy. In choice A, it is unclear if the pronoun "they" refers to "organizations" or "governments." In choices B and C, word order is inverted, creating a lack of concision ("political organizations that were powerful" is used instead of "powerful political organizations"; "city governments were taken control of" and "organizations . . . did so" are used instead of "organizations . . . started taking control of city governments").

QUESTION 14

Choice A is the best answer because no words are needed between the noun phrase "purchasing votes" and the explanatory appositive phrase that follows it ("a form of . . .").

Choices B, C, and D are incorrect because the participle "being" and the relative pronouns "that" and "which" are not needed to introduce the appositive phrase "a form of . . .," which explains the concept of "purchasing votes."

QUESTION 15

Choice B is the best answer because the comma after "1860s" is used correctly with the comma after "group" to set off the nonessential (nonrestrictive) clause "which controlled New York City in the 1860s."

Choice A is incorrect because a dash cannot be used in conjunction with a comma to set off a nonessential clause. Either two commas or two dashes may be used, but not one of each. Choice C is incorrect because a comma is not needed after "City." Choice D is incorrect because a comma is necessary to separate the nonessential clause from the rest of the sentence.

QUESTION 16

Choice C is the best answer because the sentence should be deleted. Although the information is true, it is not essential to the paragraph, which is focused on political machines in general and the Tammany Hall group in particular, not on Tweed himself.

Choices A and B are incorrect because the sentence should not be kept. Choice D is incorrect because, while the sentence should be deleted, it does not undermine or challenge the main claim of the passage.

QUESTION 17

Choice C is the best answer because no comma is needed after "that" or before "commented," and the comma after "commented" correctly separates the first part of the sentence from the quotation it introduces.

Choices A, B, and D are incorrect because each includes one or more unnecessary commas.

QUESTION 18

Choice A is the best answer because the adjective "famous," which means widely known, clearly and concisely describes "images."

Choices B, C, and D are incorrect because "well-known" and "commonly known" are repetitive when used with the adjective "famous," which means widely known.

QUESTION 19

Choice D is the best answer because it adds the most relevant supporting information. The paragraph is focused on the cartoons' depictions of Tweed as a thief, so making an explicit connection between one cartoon and "Tweed's greedy nature" is extremely relevant to the paragraph.

Choices A, B, and C are incorrect because they all contain irrelevant information. Information about Nast's other cartoons, Tweed's prison escape, and Tweed's hat is not important to add to the paragraph, which is focused on the cartoons' depictions of Tweed as a thief.

QUESTION 20

Choice D is the best answer because the word "prosecuted" correctly indicates that Tweed was charged and tried for his crimes. The preposition "on" is idiomatic when used with the verb "prosecuted."

Choices A, B, and C are incorrect because the word "persecuted" means that someone is harassed or oppressed, not that he or she is charged with a crime. "Persecuted" doesn't fit into the context of this sentence, which is about the legal troubles of Tweed and his gang.

QUESTION 21

Choice A is the best answer because the past tense verb "brought" is consistent with the other past tense verbs in the sentence, such as "escaped" and "fled."

Choices B, C, and D are incorrect because the participle "bringing," the present tense verb "brings," and the present perfect tense verb "has brought" are not consistent with the other verbs in the sentence.

QUESTION 22

Choice B is the best answer because "triumph" indicates victory. It could be considered a victory for political cartoons that Tweed was recaptured because he was recognized from a Nast cartoon.

Choices A, C, and D are incorrect because "pinnacle," "culmination," and "apex" all suggest the highest point or end of something. None of these words indicates the appropriate relationship between the recapture of Tweed and the impact of Nast's cartoons.

QUESTION 23

Choice B is the best answer because the singular possessive pronoun "its" is used correctly to refer to the singular noun "system."

Choice A is incorrect because the contraction "it's" cannot be used to show possession. Choice C is incorrect because "its" is already possessive; an apostrophe is unnecessary. Choice D is incorrect because "their" is a plural possessive pronoun that does not agree in number with the singular noun "system."

QUESTION 24

Choice B is the best answer because it clearly and concisely combines the sentences to show the relationship between the claim ("the idea is obviously very attractive") and the supporting information about the cameras' cost.

Choices A, C, and D are incorrect because they mischaracterize the relationship between the claim ("the idea is obviously very attractive") and the supporting information about the cameras' cost. The claim about the idea's attractiveness is not *in addition to* the information about the cost; rather, the information about the cameras' cost supports the claim that the idea is very attractive.

QUESTION 25

Choice A is the best answer because "however" is used correctly to indicate contrast. Some people consider the art space vital, but that group of people may be too small to generate necessary funding for the project.

Choices B, C, and D are incorrect because neither "therefore," "in effect," nor "as a rule" indicates the appropriate relationship between the two sentences being connected. The two sentences form a contrast: some people consider the art space vital, but that group of people may be too small to generate necessary funding for the project.

QUESTION 26

Choice B is the best answer because no commas are needed to set off the restrictive clause ("that is easily understood and appreciated") that follows the subject.

Choices A and D are incorrect because the clause that describes "work" is essential and should not be set off with punctuation. Setting off a clause with two commas or dashes indicates that it is nonessential to the sentence (nonrestrictive). Choice C is incorrect because no comma is needed between the two verbs.

QUESTION 27

Choice D is the best answer because the sentence should not be added. The general information it contains is not relevant to this paragraph's discussion of crowdfunding for the arts.

Choices A and B are incorrect because the sentence should not be added. Information about the types of people who donate to crowdfunding campaigns is not relevant to the discussion of the arts in this paragraph. Additionally, the sentence doesn't support the writer's point about funding of artistic projects. Choice C is incorrect because, while the sentence should not be added, "funding received from public institutions" is not an idea that is developed in the passage.

QUESTION 28

Choice A is the best answer because "in addition" appropriately introduces an additional problem with crowdfunding in the arts.

Choices B, C, and D are incorrect because "conversely," "however," and "thus" do not indicate the appropriate relationship between what is said earlier in the paragraph about problems with crowdfunding in the arts and the additional problem that follows.

QUESTION 29

Choice C is the best answer because the pronoun "who" appropriately introduces a dependent clause defining "free riders."

Choice A is incorrect because it results in a comma splice (two independent clauses cannot be joined by only a comma). Choice B is incorrect because it is not clear which people don't contribute: "audiences" or "free riders." Choice D is incorrect because the infinitive phrase "to not make" doesn't make sense in the sentence.

QUESTION 30

Choice B is the best answer because the plural pronoun "they" agrees in number with the plural noun "people" and results in a clear, straightforward clause: "if people begin to feel that paying for the art they love is someone else's responsibility."

Choice A is incorrect because the passive voice is unnecessary and adds some confusion about which antecedent the pronoun "them" is referring to: "arts" or "people." Choices C and D are incorrect because the pronouns "him" and "her" and "he" and "she" are singular and do not agree in number with the plural antecedent "people."

QUESTION 31

Choice C is the best answer because the singular pronoun "her" is consistent with the pronoun "her" that is used earlier in the sentence to refer to the playwright.

Choices A and B are incorrect because they are plural pronouns that are not consistent with the singular pronoun "her" used earlier in the sentence to refer to the singular noun "playwright." Choice D is incorrect because the singular pronoun "its" is not consistent with "her" and is not used to refer to a person.

QUESTION 32

Choice D is the best answer because sentence 2, which mentions the high price of the playwright's tickets, logically follows sentence 5, which addresses how the price of tickets was determined.

Choices A, B, and C are incorrect because sentence 2 does not logically follow sentences 1, 3, or 4. Sentences 3, 4, and 5 present a logical sequence of activities that establish the ticket price: first the playwright presents the total cost of her production, then she projects the attendance, and then she sets a per-person cost and prices tickets accordingly. Sentence 2, which addresses the ticket price, must come after the completion of this sequence; it can't come before the sequence (choice A) or interrupt the sequence (choices B and C).

QUESTION 33

Choice A is the best answer because it accurately interprets data in the graph. The category "dance" had the lowest amount of money raised but also had the highest percentage of projects fully funded.

Choices B, C, and D are incorrect because they do not accurately interpret the information provided in the graph.

QUESTION 34

Choice C is the best answer because sentence 3 needs to be placed before sentence 2 for the paragraph to be cohesive. Sentence 3 presents a cause ("Newspapers . . . have been hit especially hard by the widespread availability of free news online") and sentence 2 presents an effect of that cause ("newspapers have reduced or eliminated investigative resources").

Choice A is incorrect because sentence 3 needs to precede sentence 2, not follow it: sentence 3 presents a cause ("newspapers . . . have been hit especially hard"), and sentence 2 presents an effect ("newspapers have reduced or eliminated investigative resources"). Choice B is incorrect because sentence 1 needs to precede sentence 3, not follow it: sentence 1 offers a general assessment of "print journalism as a viable profession," and sentence 3 offers information about one form of print journalism (newspapers). Choice D is incorrect because sentence 3 is needed to provide an explanation for the "lower print circulation and diminished advertising revenue" noted in sentence 2.

QUESTION 35

Choice B is the best answer because the plural noun "reporters" is used correctly as the object of the preposition "of" and because the colon appropriately joins two independent clauses, indicating that the second clause ("their work is expensive and time-consuming") follows logically from the first ("It is not difficult . . . reporters").

Choices A and D are incorrect because the singular possessive "reporter's" does not provide an object for the preposition "of." Choice C is incorrect because the comma after "reporters" creates a comma splice (the comma is used without a conjunction to join two independent clauses).

QUESTION 36

Choice B is the best answer because the phrase "undertaken in" appropriately identifies why and for whom investigative journalism is conducted ("in the public interest" — that is, to serve the interests of all of the people instead of only a few).

Choice A is incorrect because "taking on the public interest" implies that investigative journalism is the adversary of the public interest (that is, it "takes on," or confronts, the interests of ordinary people). Choice C is incorrect because it implies that investigative journalism overpowers or takes control of the public interest. Choice D is incorrect because it is unclear what "taking off from the public interest" might mean in this context.

QUESTION 37

Choice D is the best answer because the general term "illegal activities" creates redundancy with the specific examples provided in the sentence and should be deleted. "Street crime," "corporate wrongdoing," and "political corruption" are all specific examples of "illegal activities," so it is unnecessary to mention "illegal activities" as a separate item in the list.

Choice A is incorrect because the general term "illegal activities" creates redundancy with the specific examples of illegal activities provided in the sentence. Choices B and C are incorrect because they repeat ideas that are already in the sentence: "corporate wrongdoing" is a type of business scandal, and "political corruption" is a type of abuse of government power.

QUESTION 38

Choice C is the best answer because the sentence is out of place in the paragraph: the year 1954 breaks the chronology of the other examples (1974, 2004), and the example is about television news instead of print journalism.

Choices A and B are incorrect because the sentence is out of place in the paragraph and should not be added. Choice D is incorrect because, while the sentence should not be added, the reason is not the one specified. The example of journalists reporting a story that exposes a person in power is consistent with the passage's definition of investigative journalism.

QUESTION 39

Choice D is the best answer because "deterrent" and "rebuke to" appropriately indicate the effect that exposure by reporters has had on "malfeasance" (misconduct).

Choices A, B, and C are incorrect because they do not appropriately indicate the effect that exposure by reporters has had on "malfeasance" (misconduct). It is unclear how journalism would act as a "blockade" to misconduct, and it is not idiomatic to say that these reports have acted as an important "interference to" or "drag on" misconduct.

QUESTION 40

Choice B is the best answer because the verb phrase "need not entail" — an inverted form of "does not need to entail" — appropriately conveys the writer's point that the decline in traditional print media does not *necessarily* mean "the end of investigative journalism." In other words, this possibility is real but can be prevented.

Choices A and C are incorrect because "could not" and "will not" indicate certainty — in other words, that there is no possibility of an end to investigative journalism. Choice D is incorrect because "must not" suggests a call to action by the writer ("this *must* be prevented"), which is inconsistent with the approach taken in the paragraph.

QUESTION 41

Choice D is the best answer because the noun phrase "innovative adjustments" sets up the examples that follow. The examples of the Organized Crime and Corruption Reporting Project, blogs and Twitter, and Help Me Investigate all refer to innovative projects and media that enable investigative journalism to thrive outside of traditional newspapers and magazines.

Choices A, B, and C are incorrect because they do not set up the specific examples of innovative projects and media that are helping fill the void left by the decline of investigative journalism in traditional newspapers and magazines.

QUESTION 42

Choice A is the best answer because no punctuation is needed to separate the subject of the sentence, "enterprises," from the adjective phrase beginning "such as."

Choices B and C are incorrect because placing a colon before or after "such as" would create an error in sentence structure: a colon must be preceded by an independent clause. Choice D is incorrect because no comma is necessary here.

QUESTION 43

Choice A is the best answer because the transitional phrase "for example" appropriately indicates that the Help Me Investigate project discussed in the sentence is an example of the use of social media mentioned in the previous sentence.

Choices B, C, and D are incorrect because neither "therefore," "however," nor "in any case" indicates the true relationship between this and the previous sentence. The Help Me Investigate project discussed in the current sentence is an example of the use of social media mentioned in the previous sentence.

QUESTION 44

Choice C is the best answer because the full subject of the independent clause, "the advent of the digital age," directly follows the dependent clause that introduces it.

Choices A, B, and D are incorrect because the subjects of their independent clauses do not directly follow the introductory dependent clause. "Far from marking the end of investigative journalism" refers to the "advent of the digital age," not to "cooperation among journalists and ordinary citizens" (choice A) or "the number of potential investigators" (choice B). In choice D, an interrupting phrase ("by facilitating cooperation among journalists and ordinary citizens") separates the subject from the dependent clause that modifies it.

Section 3: Math Test – No Calculator

QUESTION 1

Choice D is correct. From the graph, the y-intercept of line ℓ is (0, 1). The line also passes through the point (1, 2). Therefore, the slope of the line is $\frac{2-1}{1-0} = \frac{1}{1}$. In slope-intercept form, the equation for line ℓ is $y = mx + b$, where m is the slope and b is the y-intercept. The resulting equation for line ℓ is $y = 1x + 1$, or $y = x + 1$.

Choice A is incorrect. This is the equation of the vertical line that passes through the point (1, 0). Choice B is incorrect. This is the equation of the horizontal line that passes through the point (0, 1). Choice C is incorrect. The line defined by this equation has y-intercept (0, 0), whereas line ℓ has y-intercept (0, 1).

QUESTION 2

Choice A is correct. A circle has 360 degrees of arc. In the circle shown, O is the center of the circle and $\angle AOC$ is a central angle of the circle. From the figure, the two diameters that meet to form $\angle AOC$ are perpendicular, so the measure of $\angle AOC$ is 90°. Therefore, the length of minor arc $\overset{\frown}{AC}$ is $\frac{90}{360}$ of the circumference of the circle. Since the circumference of the circle is 36, the length of minor arc $\overset{\frown}{AC}$ is $\frac{90}{360} \times 36 = 9$.

Choices B, C, and D are incorrect. The perpendicular diameters divide the circumference of the circle into four equal arcs; therefore, minor arc $\overset{\frown}{AC}$ is $\frac{1}{4}$ of the circumference. However, the lengths in choices B and C are, respectively, $\frac{1}{3}$ and $\frac{1}{2}$ the circumference of the circle, and the length in choice D is the length of the entire circumference. None of these lengths is $\frac{1}{4}$ the circumference.

QUESTION 3

Choice B is correct. Dividing both sides of the quadratic equation $4x^2 - 8x - 12 = 0$ by 4 yields $x^2 - 2x - 3 = 0$. The equation $x^2 - 2x - 3 = 0$ can be factored as $(x + 1)(x - 3) = 0$. This equation is true when $x + 1 = 0$ or $x - 3 = 0$. Solving for x gives the solutions to the original quadratic equation: $x = -1$ and $x = 3$.

Alternate approach: After dividing both sides of the given equation by 4, the equation obtained can be rewritten as $x^2 - 2x + 1 = 4$, or equivalently $(x - 1)^2 = 4$. Therefore, $x - 1$ must either equal -2 or 2, so x must either equal -1 or 3.

Choices A and C are incorrect because -3 is not a solution of $4x^2 - 8x - 12 = 0$: $4(-3)^2 - 8(-3) - 12 = 36 + 24 - 12 \neq 0$. Choice D is incorrect because 1 is not a solution of $4x^2 - 8x - 12 = 0$: $4(1)^2 - 8(1) - 12 = 4 - 8 - 12 \neq 0$.

QUESTION 4

Choice C is correct. If f is a function of x, then the graph of f in the xy-plane consists of all points $(x, f(x))$. An x-intercept is where the graph intersects the x-axis; since all points on the x-axis have y-coordinate 0, the graph of f will cross the x-axis at values of x such that $f(x) = 0$. Therefore, the graph of a function f will have no x-intercepts if and only if f has no real zeros. Thus the graph of a quadratic function with no real zeros will have no x-intercepts.

Choice A is incorrect. The graph of a linear function in the xy-plane whose rate of change is not zero is a line with a nonzero slope. The x-axis is a horizontal line and thus has slope 0, so the graph of the linear function whose rate of change is not zero is a line that is not parallel to the x-axis. Thus, the graph must intersect the x-axis at some point, and this point is an x-intercept of the graph. Choices B and D are incorrect because the graph of any function with a real zero must have an x-intercept.

QUESTION 5

Choice D is correct. Substituting 9 for x in the equation $\sqrt{k+2} - x = 0$ gives $\sqrt{k+2} - 9 = 0$, which can be rewritten as $\sqrt{k+2} = 9$. It follows that $k + 2$ must equal 81; thus, $k = 79$.

Choices A, B, and C are incorrect because substituting any of these values for k in the equation $\sqrt{k+2} - 9 = 0$ gives a false statement. For example, if $k = 7$, the equation becomes $\sqrt{(7+2)} - 9 = \sqrt{9} - 9 = 3 - 9 = 0$, which is false.

QUESTION 6

Choice A is correct. The sum of $(a^2 - 1)$ and $(a + 1)$ can be rewritten as $(a^2 - 1) + (a + 1)$, or $a^2 - 1 + a + 1$, which is equivalent to $a^2 + a$. Therefore, the sum of the two expressions is equivalent to $a^2 + a$.

Choices B and D are incorrect. Since neither of the two expressions being added has a term with a^3, the sum of the two expressions cannot have the term a^3 when simplified. Choice C is incorrect. This choice may result from incorrectly adding the terms a^2 and a, which cannot be added because they are not like terms.

QUESTION 7

Choice C is correct. If Jackie works x hours as a tutor, which pays \$12 per hour, she earns $12x$ dollars. If Jackie works y hours as a lifeguard, which pays \$9.50 per hour, she earns $9.5y$ dollars. Thus the total, in dollars, Jackie earns in a week that she works x hours as a tutor and y hours as a lifeguard is $12x + 9.5y$. Therefore, the condition that Jackie wants to earn at least \$220 is represented by the inequality $12x + 9.5y \geq 220$. The condition that Jackie can work no more than 20 hours per week is represented by the inequality $x + y \leq 20$. These two inequalities form the system shown in choice C.

Choice A is incorrect. This system represents the conditions that Jackie earns no more than \$220 and works at least 20 hours. Choice B is incorrect.

The first inequality in this system represents the condition that Jackie earns no more than $220. Choice D is incorrect. The second inequality in this system represents the condition that Jackie works at least 20 hours.

QUESTION 8

Choice A is correct. The constant term 331.4 in $S(T) = 0.6T + 331.4$ is the value of S when $T = 0$. The value $T = 0$ corresponds to a temperature of 0°C. Since $S(T)$ represents the speed of sound, 331.4 is the speed of sound, in meters per second, when the temperature is 0°C.

Choice B is incorrect. When $T = 0.6$°C, $S(T) = 0.6(0.6) + 331.4 = 331.76$, not 331.4, meters per second. Choice C is incorrect. Based on the given function, the speed of sound increases by 0.6 meters per second for every increase of temperature by 1°C, as shown by the equation $0.6(T + 1) + 331.4 = (0.6T + 331.4) + 0.6$. Choice D is incorrect. An increase in the speed of sound, in meters per second, that corresponds to an increase of 0.6°C is $0.6(0.6) = 0.36$.

QUESTION 9

Choice A is correct. Substituting x^2 for y in the second equation gives $2(x^2) + 6 = 2(x + 3)$. This equation can be solved as follows:

$2x^2 + 6 = 2x + 6$	Apply the distributive property.
$2x^2 + 6 - 2x - 6 = 0$	Subtract $2x$ and 6 from both sides of the equation.
$2x^2 - 2x = 0$	Combine like terms.
$2x(x - 1) = 0$	Factor both terms on the left side of the equation by $2x$.

Thus, $x = 0$ and $x = 1$ are the solutions to the system. Since $x > 0$, only $x = 1$ needs to be considered. The value of y when $x = 1$ is $y = x^2 = 1^2 = 1$. Therefore, the value of xy is $(1)(1) = 1$.

Choices B, C, and D are incorrect and likely result from a computational or conceptual error when solving this system of equations.

QUESTION 10

Choice B is correct. Substituting $a^2 + b^2$ for z and ab for y into the expression $4z + 8y$ gives $4(a^2 + b^2) + 8ab$. Multiplying $a^2 + b^2$ by 4 gives $4a^2 + 4b^2 + 8ab$, or equivalently $4(a^2 + 2ab + b^2)$. Since $(a^2 + 2ab + b^2) = (a + b)^2$, it follows that $4z + 8y$ is equivalent to $4(a + b)^2$, which may be rewritten as $2^2(a + b)^2$, or $(2a + 2b)^2$.

Choices A, C, and D are incorrect and likely result from errors made when substituting or factoring.

QUESTION 11

Choice C is correct. The volume of right circular cylinder A is given by the expression $\pi r^2 h$, where r is the radius of its circular base and h is its height. The volume of a cylinder with twice the radius and half the height of cylinder A is given by $\pi(2r)^2\left(\frac{1}{2}\right)h$, which is equivalent to $4\pi r^2\left(\frac{1}{2}\right)h = 2\pi r^2 h$. Therefore, the volume is twice the volume of cylinder A, or $2 \times 22 = 44$.

Choice A is incorrect and likely results from not multiplying the radius of cylinder A by 2. Choice B is incorrect and likely results from not squaring the 2 in $2r$ when applying the volume formula. Choice D is incorrect and likely results from a conceptual error.

QUESTION 12

Choice D is correct. Since 9 can be rewritten as 3^2, $9^{\frac{3}{4}}$ is equivalent to $\sqrt[4]{9^3}$. Applying the properties of exponents, this can be written as $\sqrt[4]{3^6}$, which can further be rewritten as $\sqrt{3^3}$, an expression that is equivalent to $3\sqrt{3}$.

Choice A is incorrect; it is equivalent to $9^{\frac{1}{3}}$. Choice B is incorrect; it is equivalent to $9^{\frac{1}{4}}$. Choice C is incorrect; it is equivalent to $3^{\frac{1}{2}}$.

QUESTION 13

Choice B is correct. When n is increased by 1, t increases by the coefficient of n, which is 1.

Choices A, C, and D are incorrect and likely result from a conceptual error when interpreting the equation.

QUESTION 14

Choice C is correct. The graph of $y = -f(x)$ is the graph of the equation $y = -(2^x + 1)$, or $y = -2^x - 1$. This should be the graph of a decreasing exponential function. The y-intercept of the graph can be found by substituting the value $x = 0$ into the equation, as follows: $y = -2^0 - 1 = -1 - 1 = -2$. Therefore, the graph passes through the point $(0, -2)$. Choice C is the only graph that passes through this point.

Choices A, B, and D are incorrect because the graphs of these functions do not pass through the point $(0, -2)$.

QUESTION 15

Choice D is correct. Since gasoline costs \$4 per gallon, and since Alan's car travels an average of 25 miles per gallon, the expression $\frac{4}{25}$ gives the cost, in dollars per mile, to drive the car. Multiplying $\frac{4}{25}$ by m gives the cost for Alan to drive m miles in his car. Alan wants to reduce his weekly spending by \$5, so setting $\frac{4}{25}m$ equal to 5 gives the number of miles, m, by which he must reduce his driving.

Choices A, B, and C are incorrect. Choices A and B transpose the numerator and the denominator in the fraction. The fraction $\frac{25}{4}$ would result in the unit miles per dollar, but the question requires a unit of dollars per mile. Choices A and C set the expression equal to 95 instead of 5, a mistake that may result from a misconception that Alan wants to reduce his driving by 5 miles each week; instead, the question says he wants to reduce his weekly expenditure by $5.

QUESTION 16

The correct answer is 4. The equation $60h + 10 \leq 280$, where h is the number of hours the boat has been rented, can be written to represent the situation. Subtracting 10 from both sides and then dividing by 60 yields $h \leq 4.5$. Since the boat can be rented only for whole numbers of hours, the maximum number of hours for which Maria can rent the boat is 4.

QUESTION 17

The correct answer is $\frac{6}{5}$, or 1.2. One way to solve the equation $2(p + 1) + 8(p - 1) = 5p$ is to first distribute the terms outside the parentheses to the terms inside the parentheses: $2p + 2 + 8p - 8 = 5p$. Next, combine like terms on the left side of the equal sign: $10p - 6 = 5p$. Subtracting $10p$ from both sides yields $-6 = -5p$. Finally, dividing both sides by -5 gives $p = \frac{6}{5} = 1.2$. Either 6/5 or 1.2 can be gridded as the correct answer.

QUESTION 18

The correct answer is $\frac{21}{4}$, or 5.25. Use substitution to create a one-variable equation that can be solved for x. The second equation gives that $y = 2x$. Substituting $2x$ for y in the first equation gives $\frac{1}{2}(2x + 2x) = \frac{21}{2}$. Dividing both sides of this equation by $\frac{1}{2}$ yields $2x + 2x = 21$. Combining like terms results in $4x = 21$. Finally, dividing both sides by 4 gives $x = \frac{21}{4} = 5.25$. Either 21/4 or 5.25 can be gridded as the correct answer.

QUESTION 19

The correct answer is 2. To subtract the two fractions, first obtain common denominators. Multiplying the numerator and the denominator of the second fraction by $(x + 2)$ will result in common denominators: $\frac{2x+6}{(x+2)^2} - \frac{2(x+2)}{(x+2)^2}$, which is equivalent to $\frac{2x+6-2x-4}{(x+2)^2}$, or $\frac{2}{(x+2)^2}$. This is in the form $\frac{a}{(x+2)^2}$; therefore, $a = 2$.

QUESTION 20

The correct answer is 97. The intersecting lines form a triangle, and the angle with measure of $x°$ is an exterior angle of this triangle. The measure of an exterior angle of a triangle is equal to the sum of the measures of the two nonadjacent interior angles of the triangle. One of these angles has measure of 23° and the other, which is supplementary to the angle with measure 106°, has measure of $180° - 106° = 74°$. Therefore, the value of x is $23 + 74 = 97$.

Section 4: Math Test – Calculator

QUESTION 1

Choice D is correct. The change in the number of 3-D movies released between any two consecutive years can be found by first estimating the number of 3-D movies released for each of the two years and then finding the positive difference between these two estimates. Between 2003 and 2004, this change is approximately $2 - 2 = 0$ movies; between 2008 and 2009, this change is approximately $20 - 8 = 12$ movies; between 2009 and 2010, this change is approximately $26 - 20 = 6$ movies; and between 2010 and 2011, this change is approximately $46 - 26 = 20$ movies. Therefore, of the pairs of consecutive years in the choices, the greatest increase in the number of 3-D movies released occurred during the time period between 2010 and 2011.

Choices A, B, and C are incorrect. Between 2010 and 2011, approximately 20 more 3-D movies were released. The change in the number of 3-D movies released between any of the other pairs of consecutive years is significantly smaller than 20.

QUESTION 2

Choice C is correct. Because f is a linear function of x, the equation $f(x) = mx + b$, where m and b are constants, can be used to define the relationship between x and $f(x)$. In this equation, m represents the increase in the value of $f(x)$ for every increase in the value of x by 1. From the table, it can be determined that the value of $f(x)$ increases by 8 for every increase in the value of x by 2. In other words, for the function f the value of m is $\frac{8}{2}$, or 4. The value of b can be found by substituting the values of x and $f(x)$ from any row of the table and the value of m into the equation $f(x) = mx + b$ and solving for b. For example, using $x = 1$, $f(x) = 5$, and $m = 4$ yields $5 = 4(1) + b$. Solving for b yields $b = 1$. Therefore, the equation defining the function f can be written in the form $f(x) = 4x + 1$.

Choices A, B, and D are incorrect. Any equation defining the linear function f must give values of $f(x)$ for corresponding values of x, as shown in each row of the table. According to the table, if $x = 3$, $f(x) = 13$. However, substituting $x = 3$ into the equation given in choice A gives $f(3) = 2(3) + 3$, or $f(3) = 9$, not 13. Similarly, substituting $x = 3$ into the equation given in choice B gives $f(3) = 3(3) + 2$, or $f(3) = 11$, not 13. Lastly, substituting $x = 3$ into the equation given in choice D gives $f(3) = 5(3)$, or $f(3) = 15$, not 13. Therefore, the equations in choices A, B, and D cannot define f.

QUESTION 3

Choice A is correct. If 2.5 ounces of chocolate are needed for each muffin, then the number of ounces of chocolate needed to make 48 muffins is $48 \times 2.5 = 120$ ounces. Since 1 pound = 16 ounces, the number of pounds that is equivalent to 120 ounces is $\frac{120}{16} = 7.5$ pounds. Therefore, 7.5 pounds of chocolate are needed to make the 48 muffins.

Choice B is incorrect. If 10 pounds of chocolate were needed to make 48 muffins, then the total number of ounces of chocolate needed would be $10 \times 16 = 160$ ounces. The number of ounces of chocolate per muffin would then be $\frac{160}{48} = 3.33$ ounces per muffin, not 2.5 ounces per muffin. Choices C and D are also incorrect. Following the same procedures as used to test choice B gives 16.8 ounces per muffin for choice C and 40 ounces per muffin for choice D, not 2.5 ounces per muffin. Therefore, 50.5 and 120 pounds cannot be the number of pounds needed to make 48 signature chocolate muffins.

QUESTION 4

Choice B is correct. The value of $c + d$ can be found by dividing both sides of the given equation by 3. This yields $c + d = \frac{5}{3}$.

Choice A is incorrect. If the value of $c + d$ is $\frac{3}{5}$, then substituting $\frac{3}{5}$ for $(c + d)$ into the given equation yields $3 \times \frac{3}{5} = 5$, which is false. Choice C is incorrect. If the value of $c + d$ is 3, then substituting 3 for $(c + d)$ into the given equation yields $3 \times 3 = 5$, which is false. Choice D is incorrect. If the value of $c + d$ is 5, then substituting 5 for $(c + d)$ into the given equation yields $3 \times 5 = 5$, which is false.

QUESTION 5

Choice C is correct. The weight of an object on Venus is approximately $\frac{9}{10}$ of its weight on Earth. If an object weighs 100 pounds on Earth, then the object's weight on Venus is approximately $\frac{9}{10}(100) = 90$ pounds. The same object's weight on Jupiter is approximately $\frac{23}{10}$ of its weight on Earth; therefore, the object weighs approximately $\frac{23}{10}(100) = 230$ pounds on Jupiter. The difference between the object's weight on Jupiter and the object's weight on Venus is approximately $230 - 90 = 140$ pounds. Therefore, an object that weighs 100 pounds on Earth weighs 140 more pounds on Jupiter than it weighs on Venus.

Choice A is incorrect because it is the weight, in pounds, of the object on Venus. Choice B is incorrect because it is the weight, in pounds, of an object on Earth if it weighs 100 pounds on Venus. Choice D is incorrect because it is the weight, in pounds, of the object on Jupiter.

QUESTION 6

Choice B is correct. Let n be the number of novels and m be the number of magazines that Sadie purchased. If Sadie purchased a total of 11 novels and magazines, then $n + m = 11$. It is given that the combined price of 11 novels and magazines is \$20. Since each novel sells for \$4 and each magazine sells for \$1, it follows that $4n + m = 20$. So the system of equations below must hold.

$$4n + m = 20$$
$$n + m = 11$$

Subtracting corresponding sides of the second equation from the first equation yields $3n = 9$, so $n = 3$. Therefore, Sadie purchased 3 novels.

Choice A is incorrect. If 2 novels were purchased, then a total of \$8 was spent on novels. That leaves \$12 to be spent on magazines, which means that 12 magazines would have been purchased. However, Sadie purchased a total of 11 novels and magazines. Choices C and D are incorrect. If 4 novels were purchased, then a total of \$16 was spent on novels. That leaves \$4 to be spent on magazines, which means that 4 magazines would have been purchased. By the same logic, if Sadie purchased 5 novels, she would have no money at all (\$0) to buy magazines. However, Sadie purchased a total of 11 novels and magazines.

QUESTION 7

Choice A is correct. The DBA plans to increase its membership by n businesses each year, so x years from now, the association plans to have increased its membership by nx businesses. Since there are already b businesses at the beginning of this year, the total number of businesses, y, the DBA plans to have as members x years from now is modeled by $y = nx + b$.

Choice B is incorrect. The equation given in choice B correctly represents the increase in membership x years from now as nx. However, the number of businesses at the beginning of the year, b, has been subtracted from this amount of increase, not added to it. Choices C and D are incorrect because they use exponential models to represent the increase in membership. Since the membership increases by n businesses each year, this situation is correctly modeled by a linear relationship.

QUESTION 8

Choice C is correct. The first expression $(1.5x - 2.4)^2$ can be rewritten as $(1.5x - 2.4)(1.5x - 2.4)$. Applying the distributive property to this product yields $(2.25x^2 - 3.6x - 3.6x + 5.76) - (5.2x^2 - 6.4)$. This difference can be rewritten as $(2.25x^2 - 3.6x - 3.6x + 5.76) + (-1)(5.2x^2 - 6.4)$. Distributing the factor of -1 through the second expression yields

$2.25x^2 - 3.6x - 3.6x + 5.76 - 5.2x^2 + 6.4$. Regrouping like terms, the expression becomes $(2.25x^2 - 5.2x^2) + (-3.6x - 3.6x) + (5.76 + 6.4)$. Combining like terms yields $-2.95x^2 - 7.2x + 12.16$.

Choices A, B, and D are incorrect and likely result from errors made when applying the distributive property or combining the resulting like terms.

QUESTION 9

Choice B is correct. In 1908, the marathon was lengthened by $42 - 40 = 2$ kilometers. Since 1 mile is approximately 1.6 kilometers, the increase of 2 kilometers can be converted to miles by multiplying as shown: $2 \text{ kilometers} \times \frac{1 \text{ mile}}{1.6 \text{ kilometers}} = 1.25 \text{ miles}$.

Choices A, C, and D are incorrect and may result from errors made when applying the conversion rate or other computational errors.

QUESTION 10

Choice A is correct. The density d of an object can be found by dividing the mass m of the object by its volume V. Symbolically this is expressed by the equation $d = \frac{m}{V}$. Solving this equation for m yields $m = dV$.

Choices B, C, and D are incorrect and are likely the result of errors made when translating the definition of density into an algebraic equation and errors made when solving this equation for m. If the equations given in choices B, C, and D are each solved for density d, none of the resulting equations are equivalent to $d = \frac{m}{V}$.

QUESTION 11

Choice A is correct. The equation $-2x + 3y = 6$ can be rewritten in the slope-intercept form as follows: $y = \frac{2}{3}x + 2$. So the slope of the graph of the given equation is $\frac{2}{3}$. In the xy-plane, when two nonvertical lines are perpendicular, the product of their slopes is -1. So, if m is the slope of a line perpendicular to the line with equation $y = \frac{2}{3}x + 2$, then $m \times \frac{2}{3} = -1$, which yields $m = -\frac{3}{2}$. Of the given choices, only the equation in choice A can be rewritten in the form $y = -\frac{3}{2}x + b$, for some constant b. Therefore, the graph of the equation in choice A is perpendicular to the graph of the given equation.

Alternate approach: A line with an equation in the form $ax + by = c$ is perpendicular to a line with an equation that can be written in the form $bx - ay = d$. So the line with equation $-2x + 3y = 6$ is perpendicular to the line with an equation of the form $3x + 2y = d$. Only the equation in choice A has this form.

Choices B, C, and D are incorrect because the graphs of the equations in these choices have slopes, respectively, of $-\frac{3}{4}$, $-\frac{1}{2}$, and $-\frac{1}{3}$, not $-\frac{3}{2}$.

QUESTION 12

Choice D is correct. Adding the corresponding sides of the two equations eliminates y and yields $x = 6$, as shown.

$$\begin{array}{r} \frac{1}{2}y = 4 \\ x - \frac{1}{2}y = 2 \\ \hline x + 0 = 6 \end{array}$$

If (x, y) is a solution to the system, then (x, y) satisfies both equations in the system and any equation derived from them. Therefore, $x = 6$.

Choices A, B, and C are incorrect and may be the result of errors when solving the system.

QUESTION 13

Choice D is correct. Any point (x, y) that is a solution to the given system of inequalities must satisfy both inequalities in the system. The second inequality in the system can be rewritten as $x > y + 1$. Of the given answer choices, only choice D satisfies this inequality, because inequality $2 > -1 + 1$ is a true statement. The point $(2, -1)$ also satisfies the first inequality.

Alternate approach: Substituting $(2, -1)$ into the first inequality gives $-1 \leq 3(2) + 1$, or $-1 \leq 7$, which is a true statement. Substituting $(2, -1)$ into the second inequality gives $2 - (-1) > 1$, or $3 > 1$, which is a true statement. Therefore, since $(2, -1)$ satisfies both inequalities, it is a solution to the system.

Choice A is incorrect because substituting -2 for x and -1 for y in the first inequality gives $-1 \leq 3(-2) + 1$, or $-1 \leq -5$, which is false. Choice B is incorrect because substituting -1 for x and 3 for y in the first inequality gives $3 \leq 3(-1) + 1$, or $3 \leq -2$, which is false. Choice C is incorrect because substituting 1 for x and 5 for y in the first inequality gives $5 \leq 3(1) + 1$, or $5 \leq 4$, which is false.

QUESTION 14

Choice A is correct. According to the table, 74 orthopedic surgeons indicated that research is their major professional activity. Since a total of 607 surgeons completed the survey, it follows that the probability that the randomly selected surgeon is an orthopedic surgeon whose indicated major professional activity is research is 74 out of 607, or $\frac{74}{607}$, which is approximately 0.122.

Choices B, C, and D are incorrect and may be the result of finding the probability that the randomly selected surgeon is an orthopedic surgeon whose major professional activity is teaching (choice B), an orthopedic surgeon whose major professional activity is either teaching or research (choice C), or a general surgeon or orthopedic surgeon whose major professional activity is research (choice D).

QUESTION 15

Choice A is correct. Statement I need not be true. The fact that 78% of the 1,000 adults who were surveyed responded that they were satisfied with the air quality in the city does not mean that the exact same percentage of all adults in the city will be satisfied with the air quality in the city. Statement II need not be true because random samples, even when they are of the same size, are not necessarily identical with regard to percentages of people in them who have a certain opinion. Statement III need not be true for the same reason that statement II need not be true: results from different samples can vary. The variation may be even bigger for this sample since it would be selected from a different city. Therefore, none of the statements must be true.

Choices B, C, and D are incorrect because none of the statements must be true.

QUESTION 16

Choice D is correct. According to the given information, multiplying a tree species' growth factor by the tree's diameter is a method to approximate the age of the tree. Multiplying the growth factor, 4.0, of the American elm given in the table by the given diameter of 12 inches yields an approximate age of 48 years.

Choices A, B, and C are incorrect because they do not result from multiplying the given diameter of an American elm tree with that tree species' growth factor.

QUESTION 17

Choice D is correct. The growth factor of a tree species is approximated by the slope of a line of best fit that models the relationship between diameter and age. A line of best fit can be visually estimated by identifying a line that goes in the same direction of the data and where roughly half the given data points fall above and half the given data points fall below the line. Two points that fall on the line can be used to estimate the slope and y-intercept of the equation of a line of best fit. Estimating a line of best fit for the given scatterplot could give the points (11, 80) and (15, 110). Using these two points, the slope of the equation of the line of best fit can be calculated as $\frac{110 - 80}{15 - 11}$, or 7.5. The slope of the equation is interpreted as the growth factor for a species of tree. According to the table, the species of tree with a growth factor of 7.5 is shagbark hickory.

Choices A, B, and C are incorrect and likely result from errors made when estimating a line of best fit for the given scatterplot and its slope.

QUESTION 18

Choice C is correct. According to the given information, multiplying a tree species' growth factor by the tree's diameter is a method to approximate the age of the tree. A white birch with a diameter of 12 inches (or 1 foot) has a given growth factor of 5 and is approximately 60 years old. A pin oak with a diameter of 12 inches (or 1 foot) has a given growth factor of 3 and is approximately 36 years old. The diameters of the two trees 10 years from now can be found by dividing each tree's age in 10 years, 70 years, and 46 years, by its respective growth factor. This yields 14 inches and $15\frac{1}{3}$ inches. The difference between $15\frac{1}{3}$ and 14 is $1\frac{1}{3}$, or approximately 1.3 inches. Alternate approach: Since a white birch has a growth factor of 5, the age increases at a rate of 5 years per inch or, equivalently, the diameter increases at a rate of $\frac{1}{5}$ of an inch per year. Likewise, the pin oak has a growth factor of 3, so its diameter increases at a rate of $\frac{1}{3}$ of an inch per year. Thus, the pin oak grows $\frac{2}{15}$ of an inch per year more than the white birch. In 10 years it will grow $\left(\frac{2}{15}\right)10 = \frac{4}{3}$ of an inch more, which is approximately 1.3 inches.

Choices A, B, and D are incorrect and a result of incorrectly calculating the diameters of the two trees in 10 years.

QUESTION 19

Choice B is correct. Triangles *ADB* and *CDB* are both 30°-60°-90° triangles and share $\overline{BD}$. Therefore, triangles *ADB* and *CDB* are congruent by the angle-side-angle postulate. Using the properties of 30°-60°-90° triangles, the length of $\overline{AD}$ is half the length of hypotenuse $\overline{AB}$. Since the triangles are congruent, $AB = BC = 12$. So the length of $\overline{AD}$ is $\frac{12}{2} = 6$.

Alternate approach: Since angle *CBD* has a measure of 30°, angle *ABC* must have a measure of 60°. It follows that triangle *ABC* is equilateral, so side *AC* also has length 12. It also follows that the altitude *BD* is also a median, and therefore the length of *AD* is half of the length of *AC*, which is 6.

Choice A is incorrect. If the length of $\overline{AD}$ were 4, then the length of $\overline{AB}$ would be 8. However, this is incorrect because $\overline{AB}$ is congruent to $\overline{BC}$, which has a length of 12. Choices C and D are also incorrect. Following the same procedures as used to test choice A gives $\overline{AB}$ a length of $12\sqrt{2}$ for choice C and $12\sqrt{3}$ for choice D. However, these results cannot be true because $\overline{AB}$ is congruent to $\overline{BC}$, which has a length of 12.

QUESTION 20

Choice D is correct. The graph on the right shows the change in distance from the ground of the mark on the rim over time. The *y*-intercept of the graph corresponds to the mark's position at the start of the motion ($t = 0$); at this moment, the mark is at its highest point from the ground. As the wheel rolls, the mark approaches the ground, its distance from the ground decreasing until it reaches 0 — the point where it touches the ground. After that, the mark moves up and away from the ground, its distance from the ground increasing until it reaches its maximum height from the ground. This is the moment when the wheel has completed a full rotation. The remaining part of the graph shows the distance of the mark from the ground during the second rotation of the wheel. Therefore, of the given choices, only choice D is in agreement with the given information.

Choice A is incorrect because the speed at which the wheel is rolling does not change over time, meaning the graph representing the speed would be a horizontal line. Choice B is incorrect because the distance of the wheel from its starting point to its ending point increases continuously; the graph shows a quantity that changes periodically over time, alternately decreasing and increasing. Choice C is incorrect because the distance of the mark from the center of the wheel is constant and equals the radius of the wheel. The graph representing this distance would be a horizontal line, not the curved line of the graph shown.

QUESTION 21

Choice A is correct. The equation can be rewritten as $1 - \frac{b}{a} = c$, or equivalently $1 - c = \frac{b}{a}$. Since $a < 0$ and $b > 0$, it follows that $\frac{b}{a} < 0$, and so $1 - c < 0$, or equivalently $c > 1$.

Choice B is incorrect. If $c = 1$, then $a - b = a$, or $b = 0$. But it is given that $b > 0$, so $c = 1$ cannot be true. Choice C is incorrect. If $c = -1$, then $a - b = -a$, or $2a = b$. But this equation contradicts the premise that $a < 0$ and $b > 0$, so $c = -1$ cannot be true. Choice D is incorrect. For example, if $c = -2$, then $a - b = -2a$, or $3a = b$. But this contradicts the fact that a and b have opposite signs, so $c < -1$ cannot be true.

QUESTION 22

Choice C is correct. It is given that 34.6% of 26 students in Mr. Camp's class reported that they had at least two siblings. Since 34.6% of 26 is 8.996, there must have been 9 students in the class who reported having at least two siblings and 17 students who reported that they had fewer than two siblings. It is also given that the average eighth-grade class size in the state is 26 and that Mr. Camp's class is representative of all eighth-grade classes in the state. This means that in each eighth-grade class in the state there are about 17 students who have fewer than two siblings. Therefore, the best estimate of the number of eighth-grade students in the state who have fewer than two siblings is $17 \times$ (number of eighth-grade classes in the state), or $17 \times 1{,}800 = 30{,}600$.

Choice A is incorrect because 16,200 is the best estimate for the number of eighth-grade students in the state who have at least, not fewer than, two siblings. Choice B is incorrect because 23,400 is half of the estimated total number of eighth-grade students in the state; however, since the students in Mr. Camp's class are representative of students in the eighth-grade classes in the state and more than half of the students in Mr. Camp's class have fewer than two siblings, more than half of the students in each eighth-grade class in the state have fewer than two siblings, too. Choice D is incorrect because 46,800 is the estimated total number of eighth-grade students in the state.

QUESTION 23

Choice D is correct. The linear function that represents the relationship will be in the form $r(p) = ap + b$, where a and b are constants and $r(p)$ is the monthly rental price, in dollars, of a property that was purchased with p thousands of dollars. According to the table, (70, 515) and (450, 3,365) are ordered pairs that should satisfy the function, which leads to the system of equations below.

$$\begin{cases} 70a + b = 515 \\ 450a + b = 3{,}365 \end{cases}$$

Subtracting corresponding sides of the first equation from the second eliminates b and gives $380a = 2{,}850$; solving for a gives $a = \frac{2{,}850}{380} = 7.5$. Substituting 7.5 for a in the first equation of the system gives $525 + b = 515$; solving for b gives $b = -10$. Therefore, the linear function that represents the relationship is $r(p) = 7.5p - 10$.

Choices A, B, and C are incorrect because the coefficient of p, or the rate at which the rental price, in dollars, increases for every thousand-dollar increase of the purchase price is different from what is suggested by these choices. For example, the Glenview Street property was purchased for $140,000, but the rental price that each of the functions in these choices provides is significantly off from the rental price given in the table, $1,040.

QUESTION 24

Choice B is correct. Let x be the original price, in dollars, of the Glenview Street property. After the 40% discount, the price of the property became $0.6x$ dollars, and after the additional 20% off the discounted price, the price of the property became $0.8(0.6x)$. Thus, in terms of the original price of the property, x, the purchase price of the property is $0.48x$. It follows that $0.48x = 140{,}000$. Solving this equation for x gives $x = 291{,}666.\overline{6}$. Therefore, of the given choices, $291,700 best approximates the original price of the Glenview Street property.

Choice A is incorrect because it is the result of dividing the purchase price of the property by 0.4, as though the purchase price were 40% of the original price. Choice C is incorrect because it is the closest to dividing the purchase price of the property by 0.6, as though the purchase price were 60% of the original price. Choice D is incorrect because it is the result of dividing the purchase price of the property by 0.8, as though the purchase price were 80% of the original price.

QUESTION 25

Choice D is correct. Of the first 150 participants, 36 chose the first picture in the set, and of the 150 remaining participants, p chose the first picture in the set. Hence, the proportion of the participants who chose the first picture in the set is $\frac{36 + p}{300}$. Since more than 20% of all the participants chose the first picture, it follows that $\frac{36 + p}{300} > 0.20$. This inequality can be rewritten as $p + 36 > 0.20(300)$. Since p is a number of people among the remaining 150 participants, $p \leq 150$.

Choices A, B, and C are incorrect and may be the result of some incorrect interpretations of the given information or of computational errors.

QUESTION 26

Choice B is correct. A cube has 6 faces of equal area, so if the total surface area of a cube is $6\left(\frac{a}{4}\right)^2$, then the area of one face is $\left(\frac{a}{4}\right)^2$. Likewise, the area of one face of a cube is the square of one of its edges; therefore, if the area of one face is $\left(\frac{a}{4}\right)^2$, then the length of one edge of the cube is $\frac{a}{4}$. Since the perimeter of one face of a cube is four times the length of one edge, the perimeter is $4\left(\frac{a}{4}\right) = a$.

Choice A is incorrect because if the perimeter of one face of the cube is $\frac{a}{4}$, then the total surface area of the cube is $6\left(\frac{\frac{a}{4}}{4}\right)^2 = 6\left(\frac{a}{16}\right)^2$, which is not $6\left(\frac{a}{4}\right)^2$. Choice C is incorrect because if the perimeter of one face of the cube is $4a$, then the total surface area of the cube is $6\left(\frac{4a}{4}\right)^2 = 6a^2$, which is not $6\left(\frac{a}{4}\right)^2$. Choice D is incorrect because if the perimeter of one face of the cube is $6a$, then the total surface area of the cube is $6\left(\frac{6a}{4}\right)^2 = 6\left(\frac{3a}{2}\right)^2$, which is not $6\left(\frac{a}{4}\right)^2$.

QUESTION 27

Choice C is correct. If the mean score of 8 players is 14.5, then the total of all 8 scores is $14.5 \times 8 = 116$. If the mean of 7 scores is 12, then the total of all 7 scores is $12 \times 7 = 84$. Since the set of 7 scores was made by removing the highest score of the set of 8 scores, then the difference between the total of all 8 scores and the total of all 7 scores is equal to the removed score: $116 - 84 = 32$.

Choice A is incorrect because if 20 is removed from the group of 8 scores, then the mean score of the remaining 7 players is $\frac{(14.5 \times 8) - 20}{7}$ is approximately 13.71, not 12. Choice B is incorrect because if 24 is removed from the group of 8 scores, then the mean score of the remaining 7 players is $\frac{(14.5 \times 8) - 24}{7}$ is approximately 13.14, not 12. Choice D is incorrect because if 36 is removed from the group of 8 scores, then the mean score of the remaining 7 players is $\frac{(14.5 \times 8) - 36}{7}$ or approximately 11.43, not 12.

QUESTION 28

Choice C is correct. The slope of a line is $\frac{(y_2 - y_1)}{(x_2 - x_1)}$, or $\frac{\text{rise}}{\text{run}}$, and can be calculated using the coordinates of any two points on the line. For example, the graph of f passes through the points (0, 3) and (2, 4), so the slope of the graph of f is $\frac{4-3}{2-0} = \frac{1}{2}$. The slope of the graph of function g is 4 times the slope of the graph of f, so the slope of the graph of g is $4\left(\frac{1}{2}\right) = 2$. Since the point (0, −4) is the y-intercept of g, g is defined as $g(x) = 2x - 4$. It follows that $g(9) = 2(9) - 4 = 14$.

Choice A is incorrect because if $g(9) = 5$, then the slope of the graph of function g is $\frac{-4-5}{0-9} = 1$ which is not 4 times the slope of the graph of f. Choices B and D are also incorrect. The same procedures used to test choice A yields $\frac{-4-9}{0-9} = \frac{13}{9}$ and $\frac{-4-18}{0-9} = \frac{22}{9}$ for the slope of the graph of g for choices B and D, respectively. Neither of these slopes is 4 times the slope of the graph of f.

QUESTION 29

Choice B is correct. The standard equation of a circle in the xy-plane is of the form $(x - h)^2 + (y - k)^2 = r^2$, where (h, k) are the coordinates of the center of the circle and r is the radius. The given equation can be rewritten in standard form by completing the squares. So the sum of the first two terms, $x^2 + 20x$, needs a 100 to complete the square, and the sum of the second two terms, $y^2 + 16y$, needs a 64 to complete the square. Adding 100 and 64 to both sides of the given equation yields $(x^2 + 20x + 100) + (y^2 + 16y + 64) = -20 + 100 + 64$, which is equivalent to $(x + 10)^2 + (y + 8)^2 = 144$. Therefore, the coordinates of the center of the circle are (−10, −8).

Choices A, C, and D are incorrect and may result from computational errors made when attempting to complete the squares or when identifying the coordinates of the center.

QUESTION 30

Choice B is correct. The given equation can be thought of as the difference of two squares, where one square is x^2 and the other square is $(\sqrt{a})^2$. Using the difference of squares formula, the equation can be rewritten as $y = (x + \sqrt{a})(x - \sqrt{a})$.

Choices A, C, and D are incorrect because they are not equivalent to the given equation. Choice A is incorrect because it is equivalent to $y = x^2 - a^2$. Choice C is incorrect because it is equivalent to $y = x^2 - \frac{a^2}{4}$. Choice D is incorrect because it is equivalent to $y = x^2 + 2ax + a^2$.

QUESTION 31

The correct answer is 1492. Let x be the number of watts that is equal to 2 horsepower. Since 5 horsepower is equal to 3730 watts, it follows that $\frac{2}{5} = \frac{x}{3730}$. This is equivalent to $5x = 7460$, so $x = \frac{7460}{5} = 1492$.

QUESTION 32

The correct answer is $\frac{29}{3}$, 9.66, or 9.67. It is given that the height of the original painting is 29 inches and the reproduction's height is $\frac{1}{3}$ the original height. It follows that $\frac{1}{3} \times 29 = \frac{29}{3}$, or $9.\overline{6}$. Either the fraction 29/3 or the decimals 9.66 or 9.67 can be gridded as the correct answer.

QUESTION 33

The correct answer is 7. It is given that $PQ = RS$, and the diagram shows that $PQ = x - 1$ and $RS = 3x - 7$. Therefore, the equation $x - 1 = 3x - 7$ must be true. Solving this equation for x gives $2x = 6$, so $x = 3$. The length of segment PS is the sum of the lengths of PQ, QR, and RS, which is $(x - 1) + x + (3x - 7)$, or equivalently $5x - 8$. Substituting 3 for x in this expression gives $5(3) - 8 = 7$.

QUESTION 34

The correct answer is 9. Since the point (2, 5) lies on the graph of $y = f(x)$ in the xy-plane, the ordered pair (2, 5) must satisfy the equation $y = f(x)$. That is, $5 = f(2)$, or $5 = k - 2^2$. This equation simplifies to $5 = k - 4$. Therefore, the value of the constant k is 9.

QUESTION 35

The correct answer is 13. Let w represent the width of the rectangular garden, in feet. Since the length of the garden will be 5 feet longer than the width of the garden, the length of the garden will be $w + 5$ feet. Thus the area of the garden will be $w(w + 5)$. It is also given that the area of the garden will be 104 square feet. Therefore, $w(w + 5) = 104$, which is equivalent to $w^2 + 5w - 104 = 0$. Factoring this equation results in $(w + 13)(w - 8) = 0$. Therefore, $w = 8$ and $w = -13$. Because width cannot be negative, the width of the garden must be 8 feet. This means the length of the garden must be $8 + 5 = 13$ feet.

QUESTION 36

The correct answer is 80. If points *A* and *P* are joined, then the triangles that will be formed, *APB* and *APC*, are isosceles because $PA = PB = PC$. It follows that the base angles on both triangles each measure 20°. Angle *BAC* consists of two base angles; therefore, the measure of angle $BAC = 40°$. Since the measure of an angle inscribed in a circle is half the measure of the central angle that intercepts the same arc, it follows that the value of *x* is 80°.

QUESTION 37

The correct answer is $\frac{87}{2}$, 43.5, 43, or 44. The distance from Ms. Simon's home to her workplace is $0.6 + 15.4 + 1.4 = 17.4$ miles. Ms. Simon took 24 minutes to drive this distance. Since there are 60 minutes in one hour, her average speed, in miles per hour, for this trip is $\frac{17.4}{24} \times 60 = 43.5$ miles per hour. Based on the directions, 87/2 or 43.5 can be gridded as the correct answer. Numbers 43 and 44 are additional correct answers because the precision of the measurements provided does not support an answer with three significant digits.

QUESTION 38

The correct answer is 6. Ms. Simon travels 15.4 miles on the freeway, and her average speed for this portion of the trip is 50 miles per hour when there is no traffic delay. Therefore, when there is no traffic delay, Ms. Simon spends $\frac{15.4 \text{ miles}}{50 \text{ mph}} = 0.308$ hours on the freeway. Since there are 60 minutes in one hour, she spends $(0.308)(60) = 18.48$ minutes on the freeway when there is no delay. Leaving at 7:00 a.m. results in a trip that is 33% longer, and 33% of 18.48 minutes is 6.0984; the travel time for each of the other two segments does not change. Therefore, rounded to the nearest minute, it takes Ms. Simon 6 more minutes to drive to her workplace when she leaves at 7:00 a.m.

The SAT®

Practice Test #6

Make time to take the practice test. It's one of the best ways to get ready for the SAT.

After you've taken the practice test, score it right away at **sat.org/scoring**.

CollegeBoard

Test begins on the next page.

Reading Test

65 MINUTES, 52 QUESTIONS

Turn to Section 1 of your answer sheet to answer the questions in this section.

DIRECTIONS

Each passage or pair of passages below is followed by a number of questions. After reading each passage or pair, choose the best answer to each question based on what is stated or implied in the passage or passages and in any accompanying graphics (such as a table or graph).

Questions 1-10 are based on the following passage.

This passage is adapted from Daniyal Mueenuddin, "Nawabdin Electrician." ©2009 by Daniyal Mueenuddin.

Another man might have thrown up his hands—but not Nawabdin. His twelve daughters acted as a spur to his genius, and he looked with satisfaction in the mirror each morning at the face of a warrior going out to do battle. Nawab of course knew that he must proliferate his sources of revenue—the salary he received from K. K. Harouni for tending the tube wells would not even begin to suffice. He set up a little one-room flour mill, run off a condemned electric motor—condemned by him. He tried his hand at fish-farming in a little pond at the edge of his master's fields. He bought broken radios, fixed them, and resold them. He did not demur even when asked to fix watches, though that enterprise did spectacularly badly, and in fact earned him more kicks than kudos, for no watch he took apart ever kept time again.

K. K. Harouni rarely went to his farms, but lived mostly in Lahore. Whenever the old man visited, Nawab would place himself night and day at the door leading from the servants' sitting area into the walled grove of ancient banyan trees where the old farmhouse stood. Grizzled, his peculiar aviator glasses bent and smudged, Nawab tended the household machinery, the air conditioners, water heaters, refrigerators, and water pumps, like an engineer tending the boilers on a foundering steamer in an Atlantic gale. By his superhuman efforts he almost managed to maintain K. K. Harouni in the same mechanical cocoon, cooled and bathed and lighted and fed, that the landowner enjoyed in Lahore.

Harouni of course became familiar with this ubiquitous man, who not only accompanied him on his tours of inspection, but morning and night could be found standing on the master bed rewiring the light fixture or in the bathroom poking at the water heater. Finally, one evening at teatime, gauging the psychological moment, Nawab asked if he might say a word. The landowner, who was cheerfully filing his nails in front of a crackling rosewood fire, told him to go ahead.

"Sir, as you know, your lands stretch from here to the Indus, and on these lands are fully seventeen tube wells, and to tend these seventeen tube wells there is but one man, me, your servant. In your service I have earned these gray hairs"—here he bowed his head to show the gray—"and now I cannot fulfill my duties as I should. Enough, sir, enough. I beg you, forgive me my weakness. Better a darkened house and proud hunger within than disgrace in the light of day. Release me, I ask you, I beg you."

The old man, well accustomed to these sorts of speeches, though not usually this florid, filed away at his nails and waited for the breeze to stop.

"What's the matter, Nawabdin?"

CONTINUE

"Matter, sir? O what could be the matter in your service. I've eaten your salt for all my years. But sir, on the bicycle now, with my old legs, and with the many injuries I've received when heavy machinery fell on me—I cannot any longer bicycle about like a bridegroom from farm to farm, as I could when I first had the good fortune to enter your employment. I beg you, sir, let me go."

"And what's the solution?" asked Harouni, seeing that they had come to the crux. He didn't particularly care one way or the other, except that it touched on his comfort—a matter of great interest to him.

"Well, sir, if I had a motorcycle, then I could somehow limp along, at least until I train up some younger man."

The crops that year had been good, Harouni felt expansive in front of the fire, and so, much to the disgust of the farm managers, Nawab received a brand-new motorcycle, a Honda 70. He even managed to extract an allowance for gasoline.

The motorcycle increased his status, gave him weight, so that people began calling him "Uncle," and asking his opinion on world affairs, about which he knew absolutely nothing. He could now range further, doing a much wider business. Best of all, now he could spend every night with his wife, who had begged to live not on the farm but near her family in Firoza, where also they could educate at least the two eldest daughters. A long straight road ran from the canal headworks near Firoza all the way to the Indus, through the heart of the K. K. Harouni lands. Nawab would fly down this road on his new machine, with bags and cloths hanging from every knob and brace, so that the bike, when he hit a bump, seemed to be flapping numerous small vestigial wings; and with his grinning face, as he rolled up to whichever tube well needed servicing, with his ears almost blown off, he shone with the speed of his arrival.

1

The main purpose of the first paragraph is to

A) characterize Nawab as a loving father.

B) outline the schedule of a typical day in Nawab's life.

C) describe Nawab's various moneymaking ventures.

D) contrast Nawab's and Harouni's lifestyles.

2

As used in line 16, "kicks" most nearly means

A) thrills.

B) complaints.

C) jolts.

D) interests.

3

The author uses the image of an engineer at sea (lines 23-28) most likely to

A) suggest that Nawab often dreams of having a more exciting profession.

B) highlight the fact that Nawab's primary job is to tend to Harouni's tube wells.

C) reinforce the idea that Nawab has had many different occupations in his life.

D) emphasize how demanding Nawab's work for Harouni is.

4

Which choice best supports the claim that Nawab performs his duties for Harouni well?

A) Lines 28-32 ("By his . . . Lahore")
B) Lines 40-42 ("The landowner . . . ahead")
C) Lines 46-49 ("In your . . . should")
D) Line 58 ("I've . . . years")

5

In the context of the conversation between Nawab and Harouni, Nawab's comments in lines 43-52 ("Sir . . . beg you") mainly serve to

A) flatter Harouni by mentioning how vast his lands are.
B) boast to Harouni about how competent and reliable Nawab is.
C) emphasize Nawab's diligence and loyalty to Harouni.
D) notify Harouni that Nawab intends to quit his job tending the tube wells.

6

Nawab uses the word "bridegroom" (line 62) mainly to emphasize that he's no longer

A) in love.
B) naive.
C) busy.
D) young.

7

It can reasonably be inferred from the passage that Harouni provides Nawab with a motorcycle mainly because

A) Harouni appreciates that Nawab has to work hard to support his family.
B) Harouni sees benefit to himself from giving Nawab a motorcycle.
C) Nawab's speech is the most eloquent that Harouni has ever heard.
D) Nawab threatens to quit if Harouni doesn't agree to give him a motorcycle.

CONTINUE

8

Which choice provides the best evidence for the answer to the previous question?

A) Lines 65-66 ("And . . . crux")

B) Lines 66-68 ("He didn't . . . him")

C) Lines 75-76 ("He even . . . gasoline")

D) Lines 80-81 ("He could . . . business")

9

The passage states that the farm managers react to Nawab receiving a motorcycle with

A) disgust.

B) happiness.

C) envy.

D) indifference.

10

According to the passage, what does Nawab consider to be the best result of getting the motorcycle?

A) People start calling him "Uncle."

B) He's able to expand his business.

C) He's able to educate his daughters.

D) He can spend more time with his wife.

CONTINUE

Questions 11-21 are based on the following passage and supplementary material.

This passage is adapted from Stephen Coleman, Scott Anthony, and David E. Morrison, "Public Trust in the News." ©2009 by Stephen Coleman.

The news is a form of public knowledge. Unlike personal or private knowledge (such as the health of one's friends and family; the conduct of a private hobby; a secret liaison), public knowledge increases in value as it is shared by more people. The date of an election and the claims of rival candidates; the causes and consequences of an environmental disaster; a debate about how to frame a particular law; the latest reports from a war zone—these are all examples of public knowledge that people are generally expected to know in order to be considered informed citizens. Thus, in contrast to personal or private knowledge, which is generally left to individuals to pursue or ignore, public knowledge is promoted even to those who might not think it matters to them. In short, the circulation of public knowledge, including the news, is generally regarded as a public good which cannot be solely demand-driven.

The production, circulation, and reception of public knowledge is a complex process. It is generally accepted that public knowledge should be authoritative, but there is not always common agreement about what the public needs to know, who is best placed to relate and explain it, and how authoritative reputations should be determined and evaluated. Historically, newspapers such as *The Times* and broadcasters such as the BBC were widely regarded as the trusted shapers of authoritative agendas and conventional wisdom. They embodied the *Oxford English Dictionary's* definition of authority as the "power over, or title to influence, the opinions of others." As part of the general process of the transformation of authority whereby there has been a reluctance to uncritically accept traditional sources of public knowledge, the demand has been for all authority to make explicit the frames of value which determine their decisions. Centres of news production, as our focus groups show, have not been exempt from this process. Not surprisingly perhaps some news journalists feel uneasy about this renegotiation of their authority:

Editors are increasingly casting a glance at the "most read" lists on their own and other websites to work out which stories matter to readers and viewers. And now the audience—which used to know its place—is being asked to act as a kind of journalistic ombudsman, ruling on our credibility (broadcast journalist, 2008).

The result of democratising access to TV news could be political disengagement by the majority and a dumbing down through a popularity contest of stories (online news editor, 2007).

Despite the rhetorical bluster of these statements, they amount to more than straightforward professional defensiveness. In their reference to an audience "which used to know its place" and conflation between democratisation and "dumbing down," they are seeking to argue for a particular mode of public knowledge: one which is shaped by experts, immune from populist pressures; and disseminated to attentive, but mainly passive recipients. It is a view of citizenship that closes down opportunities for popular involvement in the making of public knowledge by reinforcing the professional claims of experts. The journalists quoted above are right to feel uneasy, for there is, at almost every institutional level in contemporary society, scepticism towards the epistemological authority of expert elites. There is a growing feeling, as expressed by several of our focus group participants, that the news media should be "informative rather than authoritative"; the job of journalists should be to "give the news as raw as it is, without putting their slant on it"; and people should be given "sufficient information" from which "we would be able to form opinions of our own."

At stake here are two distinct conceptions of authority. The journalists we have quoted are resistant to the democratisation of news: the supremacy of the clickstream (according to which editors raise or lower the profile of stories according to the number of readers clicking on them online); the parity of popular culture with "serious" news; the demands of some audience members for raw news rather than constructed narratives.

CONTINUE

Percentage of Respondents Seeing News Stories as Inaccurate or Favoring One Side

	1985	1992	2003	2007	2011
News organizations...					
• Get the facts straight	55	49	36	39	25
• Often have inaccurate stories	34	44	56	53	66
• Don't know	11	7	8	8	9
• Are pretty independent	37	35	23	23	15
• Are often influenced by powerful people and organizations	53	58	70	69	80
• Don't know	10	7	7	8	5
On political and social issues, news organizations...					
• Deal fairly with all sides	34	31	26	26	16
• Tend to favor one side	53	63	66	66	77
• Don't know	13	6	8	8	7

Adapted from "Pew Research Center for the People & the Press Report on Views of the News Media, 1985–2011." ©2011 by Pew Research Center.

CONTINUE

11

The main purpose of the passage is to

A) analyze the technological developments that have affected the production, circulation, and reception of news stories.

B) discuss changes in the perception of the news media as a source of public knowledge.

C) show how journalists' frames of value influence the production of news stories.

D) challenge the conventional view that news is a form of public knowledge.

12

According to the passage, which expectation do traditional authorities now face?

A) They should be uninfluenced by commercial considerations.

B) They should be committed to bringing about positive social change.

C) They should be respectful of the difference between public and private knowledge.

D) They should be transparent about their beliefs and assumptions.

13

Which choice provides the best evidence for the answer to the previous question?

A) Lines 2-5 ("Unlike . . . people")

B) Lines 20-21 ("The production . . . process")

C) Lines 33-38 ("As part . . . decisions")

D) Lines 43-46 ("Editors . . . viewers")

14

As used in line 24, "common" most nearly means

A) numerous.

B) familiar.

C) widespread.

D) ordinary.

15

The authors most likely include the extended quotations in lines 43-53 to

A) present contradictory examples.

B) cite representative opinions.

C) criticize typical viewpoints.

D) suggest viable alternatives.

16

The authors indicate that the public is coming to believe that journalists' reports should avoid

A) personal judgments about the events reported.

B) more information than is absolutely necessary.

C) quotations from authorities on the subject matter.

D) details that the subjects of news reports wish to keep private.

CONTINUE

17

Which choice provides the best evidence for the answer to the previous question?

A) Lines 12-16 ("Thus . . . them")

B) Lines 30-33 ("They . . . others")

C) Lines 40-42 ("Not surprisingly . . . authority")

D) Lines 70-77 ("There . . . own")

18

As used in line 74, "raw" most nearly means

A) unfiltered.

B) exposed.

C) harsh.

D) inexperienced.

19

Based on the table, in which year were people the most trusting of the news media?

A) 1985

B) 1992

C) 2003

D) 2011

20

Which statement is best supported by information presented in the table?

A) Between 1985 and 2011, the proportion of inaccurate news stories rose dramatically.

B) Between 1992 and 2003, the proportion of people who believed that news organizations were biased almost doubled.

C) Between 2003 and 2007, people's views of the accuracy, independence, and fairness of news organizations changed very little.

D) Between 2007 and 2011, people's perception that news organizations are accurate increased, but people's perception that news organizations are fair diminished.

21

The 2011 data in the table best serve as evidence of

A) "political disengagement by the majority" (line 51).

B) "the professional claims of experts" (lines 65-66).

C) "scepticism towards the epistemological authority of expert elites" (lines 69-70).

D) "the supremacy of the clickstream" (line 81).

Questions 22-32 are based on the following passage.

This passage is adapted from Elsa Youngsteadt, "Decoding a Flower's Message." ©2012 by Sigma Xi, The Scientific Research Society.

Texas gourd vines unfurl their large, flared blossoms in the dim hours before sunrise. Until they close at noon, their yellow petals and mild, squashy aroma attract bees that gather nectar and shuttle pollen from flower to flower. But "when you advertise [to pollinators], you advertise in an open communication network," says chemical ecologist Ian Baldwin of the Max Planck Institute for Chemical Ecology in Germany. "You attract not just the good guys, but you also attract the bad guys." For a Texas gourd plant, striped cucumber beetles are among the very bad guys. They chew up pollen and petals, defecate in the flowers and transmit the dreaded bacterial wilt disease, an infection that can reduce an entire plant to a heap of collapsed tissue in mere days.

In one recent study, Nina Theis and Lynn Adler took on the specific problem of the Texas gourd—how to attract enough pollinators but not too many beetles. The Texas gourd vine's main pollinators are honey bees and specialized squash bees, which respond to its floral scent. The aroma includes 10 compounds, but the most abundant—and the only one that lures squash bees into traps—is 1,4-dimethoxybenzene.

Intuition suggests that more of that aroma should be even more appealing to bees. "We have this assumption that a really fragrant flower is going to attract a lot of pollinators," says Theis, a chemical ecologist at Elms College in Chicopee, Massachusetts. But, she adds, that idea hasn't really been tested—and extra scent could well call in more beetles, too. To find out, she and Adler planted 168 Texas gourd vines in an Iowa field and, throughout the August flowering season, made half the plants more fragrant by tucking dimethoxybenzene-treated swabs deep inside their flowers. Each treated flower emitted about 45 times more fragrance than a normal one; the other half of the plants got swabs without fragrance.

The researchers also wanted to know whether extra beetles would impose a double cost by both damaging flowers and deterring bees, which might not bother to visit (and pollinate) a flower laden with other insects and their feces. So every half hour throughout the experiments, the team plucked all the beetles off of half the fragrance-enhanced flowers and half the control flowers, allowing bees to respond to the blossoms with and without interference by beetles.

Finally, they pollinated by hand half of the female flowers in each of the four combinations of fragrance and beetles. Hand-pollinated flowers should develop into fruits with the maximum number of seeds, providing a benchmark to see whether the fragrance-related activities of bees and beetles resulted in reduced pollination.

"It was very labor intensive," says Theis. "We would be out there at four in the morning, three in the morning, to try and set up before these flowers open." As soon as they did, the team spent the next several hours walking from flower to flower, observing each for two-minute intervals "and writing down everything we saw."

What they saw was double the normal number of beetles on fragrance-enhanced blossoms. Pollinators, to their surprise, did not prefer the highly scented flowers. Squash bees were indifferent, and honey bees visited enhanced flowers less often than normal ones. Theis thinks the bees were repelled not by the fragrance itself, but by the abundance of beetles: The data showed that the more beetles on a flower, the less likely a honey bee was to visit it.

That added up to less reproduction for fragrance-enhanced flowers. Gourds that developed from those blossoms weighed 9 percent less and had, on average, 20 fewer seeds than those from normal flowers. Hand pollination didn't rescue the seed set, indicating that beetles damaged flowers directly —regardless of whether they also repelled pollinators. (Hand pollination did rescue fruit weight, a hard-to-interpret result that suggests that lost bee visits did somehow harm fruit development.)

CONTINUE

The new results provide a reason that Texas gourd plants never evolved to produce a stronger scent: "If you really ramp up the odor, you don't get more pollinators, but you can really get ripped apart by your enemies," says Rob Raguso, a chemical ecologist at Cornell University who was not involved in the Texas gourd study.

22

The primary purpose of the passage is to

A) discuss the assumptions and reasoning behind a theory.
B) describe the aim, method, and results of an experiment.
C) present and analyze conflicting data about a phenomenon.
D) show the innovative nature of a procedure used in a study.

23

As presented in the passage, Theis and Adler's research primarily relied on which type of evidence?

A) Direct observation
B) Historical data
C) Expert testimony
D) Random sampling

24

Which statement about striped cucumber beetles can most reasonably be inferred from the passage?

A) They feed primarily on Texas gourd plants.
B) They are less attracted to dimethoxybenzene than honey bees are.
C) They experience only minor negative effects as a result of carrying bacterial wilt disease.
D) They are attracted to the same compound in Texas gourd scent that squash bees are.

25

The author indicates that it seems initially plausible that Texas gourd plants could attract more pollinators if they

A) did not have aromatic flowers.
B) targeted insects other than bees.
C) increased their floral scent.
D) emitted more varied fragrant compounds.

CONTINUE

26

As used in line 38, "treated" most nearly means

A) altered.
B) restored.
C) provided.
D) preserved.

27

What did Theis and Adler do as part of their study that most directly allowed Theis to reason that "bees were repelled not by the fragrance itself" (lines 70-71)?

A) They observed the behavior of bees and beetles both before and after the flowers opened in the morning.
B) They increased the presence of 1,4-dimethoxybenzene only during the August flowering season.
C) They compared the gourds that developed from naturally pollinated flowers to the gourds that developed from hand-pollinated flowers.
D) They gave bees a chance to choose between beetle-free enhanced flowers and beetle-free normal flowers.

28

Which choice provides the best evidence for the answer to the previous question?

A) Lines 45-50 ("So every . . . beetles")
B) Lines 51-53 ("Finally . . . beetles")
C) Lines 59-61 ("We would . . . open")
D) Lines 76-79 ("Gourds . . . flowers")

29

The primary function of the seventh and eighth paragraphs (lines 65-84) is to

A) summarize Theis and Adler's findings.
B) describe Theis and Adler's hypotheses.
C) illustrate Theis and Adler's methods.
D) explain Theis and Adler's reasoning.

CONTINUE

30

In describing squash bees as "indifferent" (line 68), the author most likely means that they

A) could not distinguish enhanced flowers from normal flowers.

B) visited enhanced flowers and normal flowers at an equal rate.

C) largely preferred normal flowers to enhanced flowers.

D) were as likely to visit beetle-infested enhanced flowers as to visit beetle-free enhanced flowers.

31

According to the passage, Theis and Adler's research offers an answer to which of the following questions?

A) How can Texas gourd plants increase the number of visits they receive from pollinators?

B) Why is there an upper limit on the intensity of the aroma emitted by Texas gourd plants?

C) Why does hand pollination rescue the fruit weight of beetle-infested Texas gourd plants?

D) Why do Texas gourd plants stop producing fragrance attractive to pollinators when beetles are present?

32

Which choice provides the best evidence for the answer to the previous question?

A) Lines 17-20 ("In one . . . beetles")

B) Lines 22-25 ("The aroma . . . 1,4-dimethoxybenzene")

C) Lines 79-84 ("Hand . . . development")

D) Lines 85-86 ("The new . . . scent")

Questions 33-42 are based on the following passages.

Passage 1 is adapted from Abraham Lincoln, "Address to the Young Men's Lyceum of Springfield, Illinois." Originally delivered in 1838. Passage 2 is from Henry David Thoreau, "Resistance to Civil Government." Originally published in 1849.

Passage 1

Let every American, every lover of liberty, every well wisher to his posterity, swear by the blood of the Revolution, never to violate in the least particular, the laws of the country; and never to tolerate their violation by others. As the patriots of seventy-six did to the support of the Declaration of Independence, so to the support of the Constitution and Laws, let every American pledge his life, his property, and his sacred honor;—let every man remember that to violate the law, is to trample on the blood of his father, and to tear the character of his own, and his children's liberty. Let reverence for the laws, be breathed by every American mother, to the lisping babe, that prattles on her lap—let it be taught in schools, in seminaries, and in colleges;—let it be written in Primers, spelling books, and in Almanacs;—let it be preached from the pulpit, proclaimed in legislative halls, and enforced in courts of justice. And, in short, let it become the *political religion* of the nation; and let the old and the young, the rich and the poor, the grave and the gay, of all sexes and tongues, and colors and conditions, sacrifice unceasingly upon its altars. . . .

When I so pressingly urge a strict observance of all the laws, let me not be understood as saying there are no bad laws, nor that grievances may not arise, for the redress of which, no legal provisions have been made. I mean to say no such thing. But I do mean to say, that, although bad laws, if they exist, should be repealed as soon as possible, still while they continue in force, for the sake of example, they should be religiously observed. So also in unprovided cases. If such arise, let proper legal provisions be made for them with the least possible delay; but, till then, let them if not too intolerable, be borne with.

There is no grievance that is a fit object of redress by mob law. In any case that arises, as for instance, the promulgation of abolitionism, one of two positions is necessarily true; that is, the thing is right within itself, and therefore deserves the protection of all law and all good citizens; or, it is wrong, and therefore proper to be prohibited by legal enactments; and in neither case, is the interposition of mob law, either necessary, justifiable, or excusable.

Passage 2

Unjust laws exist; shall we be content to obey them, or shall we endeavor to amend them, and obey them until we have succeeded, or shall we transgress them at once? Men generally, under such a government as this, think that they ought to wait until they have persuaded the majority to alter them. They think that, if they should resist, the remedy would be worse than the evil. But it is the fault of the government itself that the remedy is worse than the evil. It makes it worse. Why is it not more apt to anticipate and provide for reform? Why does it not cherish its wise minority? Why does it cry and resist before it is hurt? . . .

If the injustice is part of the necessary friction of the machine of government, let it go, let it go; perchance it will wear smooth—certainly the machine will wear out. If the injustice has a spring, or a pulley, or a rope, or a crank, exclusively for itself, then perhaps you may consider whether the remedy will not be worse than the evil; but if it is of such a nature that it requires you to be the agent of injustice to another, then, I say, break the law. Let your life be a counter friction to stop the machine. What I have to do is to see, at any rate, that I do not lend myself to the wrong which I condemn.

As for adopting the ways which the State has provided for remedying the evil, I know not of such ways. They take too much time, and a man's life will be gone. I have other affairs to attend to. I came into this world, not chiefly to make this a good place to live in, but to live in it, be it good or bad. A man has not everything to do, but something; and because he cannot do everything, it is not necessary that he should do something wrong. . . .

CONTINUE

I do not hesitate to say, that those who call themselves Abolitionists should at once effectually withdraw their support, both in person and property, from the government . . . and not wait till they constitute a majority of one, before they suffer the right to prevail through them. I think that it is enough if they have God on their side, without waiting for that other one. Moreover, any man more right than his neighbors constitutes a majority of one already.

33

In Passage 1, Lincoln contends that breaking the law has which consequence?

A) It slows the repeal of bad laws.

B) It undermines and repudiates the nation's values.

C) It leads slowly but inexorably to rule by the mob.

D) It creates divisions between social groups.

34

Which choice provides the best evidence for the answer to the previous question?

A) Lines 9-12 ("let every man . . . liberty")

B) Lines 20-23 ("and let . . . altars")

C) Lines 33-35 ("If such . . . borne with")

D) Lines 36-37 ("There . . . law")

35

As used in line 24, "urge" most nearly means

A) hasten.

B) stimulate.

C) require.

D) advocate.

36

The sentence in lines 24-28 ("When . . . made") primarily serves which function in Passage 1?

A) It raises and refutes a potential counterargument to Lincoln's argument.

B) It identifies and concedes a crucial shortcoming of Lincoln's argument.

C) It acknowledges and substantiates a central assumption of Lincoln's argument.

D) It anticipates and corrects a possible misinterpretation of Lincoln's argument.

CONTINUE

37

As used in line 32, “observed” most nearly means

A) followed.

B) scrutinized.

C) contemplated.

D) noticed.

38

In Passage 2, Thoreau indicates that some unjust aspects of government are

A) superficial and can be fixed easily.

B) subtle and must be studied carefully.

C) self-correcting and may be beneficial.

D) inevitable and should be endured.

39

Which choice provides the best evidence for the answer to the previous question?

A) Lines 45-48 (“Unjust . . . once”)

B) Lines 51-52 (“They . . . evil”)

C) Lines 58-59 (“If the injustice . . . go”)

D) Lines 75-78 (“A man . . . wrong”)

CONTINUE

40

The primary purpose of each passage is to

A) make an argument about the difference between legal duties and moral imperatives.
B) discuss how laws ought to be enacted and changed in a democracy.
C) advance a view regarding whether individuals should follow all of the country's laws.
D) articulate standards by which laws can be evaluated as just or unjust.

41

Based on the passages, Lincoln would most likely describe the behavior that Thoreau recommends in lines 64-66 ("if it . . . law") as

A) an excusable reaction to an intolerable situation.
B) a rejection of the country's proper forms of remedy.
C) an honorable response to an unjust law.
D) a misapplication of a core principle of the Constitution.

42

Based on the passages, one commonality in the stances Lincoln and Thoreau take toward abolitionism is that

A) both authors see the cause as warranting drastic action.
B) both authors view the cause as central to their argument.
C) neither author expects the cause to win widespread acceptance.
D) neither author embraces the cause as his own.

CONTINUE

Questions 43-52 are based on the following passage and supplementary material.

This passage is adapted from Kevin Bullis, "What Tech Is Next for the Solar Industry?" ©2013 by MIT Technology Review.

Solar panel installations continue to grow quickly, but the solar panel manufacturing industry is in the doldrums because supply far exceeds demand. The poor market may be slowing innovation, but advances continue; judging by the mood this week at the IEEE Photovoltaics Specialists Conference in Tampa, Florida, people in the industry remain optimistic about its long-term prospects.

The technology that's surprised almost everyone is conventional crystalline silicon. A few years ago, silicon solar panels cost $4 per watt, and Martin Green, professor at the University of New South Wales and one of the leading silicon solar panel researchers, declared that they'd never go below $1 a watt. "Now it's down to something like 50 cents a watt, and there's talk of hitting 36 cents per watt," he says.

The U.S. Department of Energy has set a goal of reaching less than $1 a watt—not just for the solar panels, but for complete, installed systems—by 2020. Green thinks the solar industry will hit that target even sooner than that. If so, that would bring the direct cost of solar power to six cents per kilowatt-hour, which is cheaper than the average cost expected for power from new natural gas power plants.

All parts of the silicon solar panel industry have been looking for ways to cut costs and improve the power output of solar panels, and that's led to steady cost reductions. Green points to something as mundane as the pastes used to screen-print some of the features on solar panels. Green's lab built a solar cell in the 1990s that set a record efficiency for silicon solar cells—a record that stands to this day. To achieve that record, he had to use expensive lithography techniques to make fine wires for collecting current from the solar cell. But gradual improvements have made it possible to use screen printing to produce ever-finer lines. Recent research suggests that screen-printing techniques can produce lines as thin as 30 micrometers—about the width of the lines Green used for his record solar cells, but at costs far lower than his lithography techniques.

Meanwhile, researchers at the National Renewable Energy Laboratory have made flexible solar cells on a new type of glass from Corning called Willow Glass, which is thin and can be rolled up. The type of solar cell they made is the only current challenger to silicon in terms of large-scale production—thin-film cadmium telluride. Flexible solar cells could lower the cost of installing solar cells, making solar power cheaper.

One of Green's former students and colleagues, Jianhua Zhao, cofounder of solar panel manufacturer China Sunergy, announced this week that he is building a pilot manufacturing line for a two-sided solar cell that can absorb light from both the front and back. The basic idea, which isn't new, is that during some parts of the day, sunlight falls on the land between rows of solar panels in a solar power plant. That light reflects onto the back of the panels and could be harvested to increase the power output. This works particularly well when the solar panels are built on sand, which is highly reflective. Where a one-sided solar panel might generate 340 watts, a two-sided one might generate up to 400 watts. He expects the panels to generate 10 to 20 percent more electricity over the course of a year.

Even longer-term, Green is betting on silicon, aiming to take advantage of the huge reductions in cost already seen with the technology. He hopes to greatly increase the efficiency of silicon solar panels by combining silicon with one or two other semiconductors, each selected to efficiently convert a part of the solar spectrum that silicon doesn't convert efficiently. Adding one semiconductor could boost efficiencies from the 20 to 25 percent range to around 40 percent. Adding another could make efficiencies as high as 50 percent feasible, which would cut in half the number of solar panels needed for a given installation. The challenge is to produce good connections between these semiconductors, something made challenging by the arrangement of silicon atoms in crystalline silicon.

CONTINUE

Figure 1

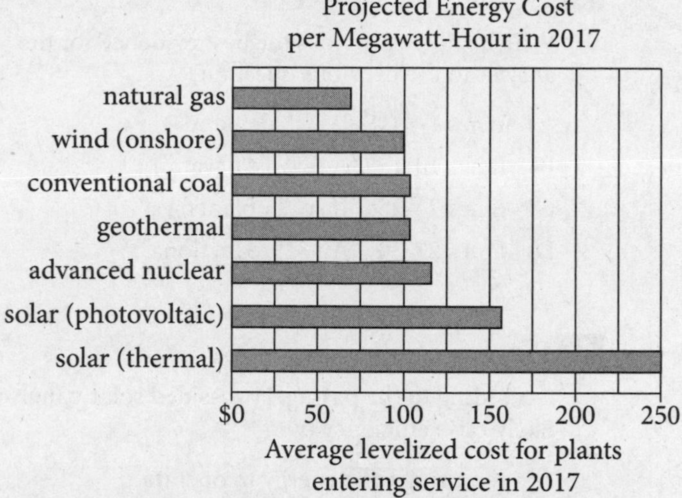

Adapted from Peter Schwartz, "Abundant Natural Gas and Oil Are Putting the Kibosh on Clean Energy." ©2012 by Condé Nast.

Figure 2

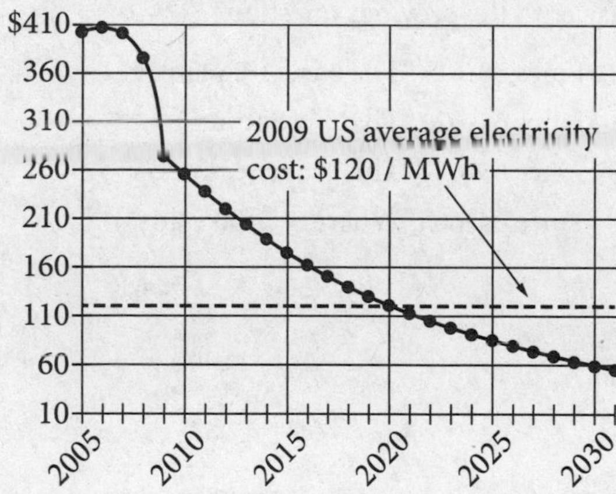

Adapted from Ramez Naam, "Smaller, Cheaper, Faster: Does Moore's Law Apply to Solar Cells?" ©2011 by Scientific American.

43

The passage is written from the point of view of a

A) consumer evaluating a variety of options.

B) scientist comparing competing research methods.

C) journalist enumerating changes in a field.

D) hobbyist explaining the capabilities of new technology.

44

As used in line 4, "poor" most nearly means

A) weak.

B) humble.

C) pitiable.

D) obsolete.

45

It can most reasonably be inferred from the passage that many people in the solar panel industry believe that

A) consumers don't understand how solar panels work.

B) two-sided cells have weaknesses that have not yet been discovered.

C) the cost of solar panels is too high and their power output too low.

D) Willow Glass is too inefficient to be marketable.

46

Which choice provides the best evidence for the answer to the previous question?

A) Lines 1-3 ("Solar . . . demand")

B) Lines 10-15 ("A few . . . a watt")

C) Lines 22-26 ("If so . . . plants")

D) Lines 27-30 ("All . . . reductions")

47

According to the passage, two-sided solar panels will likely raise efficiency by

A) requiring little energy to operate.

B) absorbing reflected light.

C) being reasonably inexpensive to manufacture.

D) preventing light from reaching the ground.

48

Which choice provides the best evidence for the answer to the previous question?

A) Lines 58-61 ("The basic . . . plant")

B) Lines 61-62 ("That . . . output")

C) Lines 63-64 ("This . . . reflective")

D) Lines 64-66 ("Where . . . 400 watts")

CONTINUE

49

As used in line 69, "betting on" most nearly means

A) dabbling in.

B) gambling with.

C) switching from.

D) optimistic about.

50

The last sentence of the passage mainly serves to

A) express concern about the limitations of a material.

B) identify a hurdle that must be overcome.

C) make a prediction about the effective use of certain devices.

D) introduce a potential new area of study.

51

According to figure 1, in 2017, the cost of which of the following fuels is projected to be closest to the 2009 US average electricity cost shown in figure 2?

A) Natural gas

B) Wind (onshore)

C) Conventional coal

D) Advanced nuclear

52

According to figure 2, in what year is the average cost of solar photovoltaic power projected to be equal to the 2009 US average electricity cost?

A) 2018

B) 2020

C) 2025

D) 2027

STOP

If you finish before time is called, you may check your work on this section only.

Do not turn to any other section.

Writing and Language Test

35 MINUTES, 44 QUESTIONS

Turn to Section 2 of your answer sheet to answer the questions in this section.

DIRECTIONS

Each passage below is accompanied by a number of questions. For some questions, you will consider how the passage might be revised to improve the expression of ideas. For other questions, you will consider how the passage might be edited to correct errors in sentence structure, usage, or punctuation. A passage or a question may be accompanied by one or more graphics (such as a table or graph) that you will consider as you make revising and editing decisions.

Some questions will direct you to an underlined portion of a passage. Other questions will direct you to a location in a passage or ask you to think about the passage as a whole.

After reading each passage, choose the answer to each question that most effectively improves the quality of writing in the passage or that makes the passage conform to the conventions of standard written English. Many questions include a "NO CHANGE" option. Choose that option if you think the best choice is to leave the relevant portion of the passage as it is.

Questions 1-11 are based on the following passage.

A Necessary Resource for Science

In the winter of 1968, scientists David Schindler and Gregg Brunskill poured nitrates and phosphates into Lake [1] 227, this is one of the 58 freshwater bodies that compose Canada's remotely located Experimental Lakes Area. Schindler and Brunskill were contaminating the water not out of malice but in the name of research. While deliberately adding chemical compounds to a lake may seem [2] destructive and irresponsible, this method of experimenting is sometimes the most effective way to influence policy and save the environment from even more damaging pollution.

1

A) NO CHANGE
B) 227. Which is one
C) 227. One
D) 227, one

2

A) NO CHANGE
B) destructive, and irresponsible this method
C) destructive and, irresponsible, this method
D) destructive and irresponsible this method,

CONTINUE

Schindler and Brunskill were investigating possible causes for the large blooms of blue-green algae, or cyanobacteria, that had been affecting bodies of water such as Lake Erie. **3** In addition to being unsightly and odorous, these algal blooms cause oxygen depletion. Oxygen depletion kills fish and other wildlife in the lakes. Just weeks after the scientists added the nitrates and phosphates, the water in Lake 227 turned bright **4** green. It was thick with: the same type of algal blooms that had plagued Lake Erie.

3

Which choice most effectively combines the underlined sentences?

A) In addition to being unsightly and odorous, these algal blooms cause oxygen depletion: the result being that it kills fish and other wildlife in the lakes.

B) In addition to being unsightly and odorous, these algal blooms cause oxygen depletion; the algal blooms cause oxygen depletion that kills fish and other wildlife in the lakes.

C) In addition to being unsightly and odorous, these algal blooms cause oxygen depletion, and oxygen depletion caused by the algal blooms kills fish and other wildlife in the lakes.

D) In addition to being unsightly and odorous, these algal blooms cause oxygen depletion, which kills fish and other wildlife in the lakes.

4

A) NO CHANGE

B) green: it was thick with

C) green. It was thick with—

D) green, it was thick with

CONTINUE

5 One mission of the Experimental Lakes Area is to conduct research that helps people better understand threats to the environment. The scientists divided the lake in half by placing a nylon barrier through the narrowest part of its figure-eight shape. In one half of Lake 226, they added phosphates, nitrates, and a source of carbon; in the other, they added just nitrates **6** and a source of carbon was added. Schindler and Brunskill hypothesized that phosphates were responsible for the growth of cyanobacteria. The experiment confirmed their suspicions when the half of the lake containing the phosphates **7** was teeming with blue-green algae.

5

Which choice provides the best transition from the previous paragraph to this one?

A) NO CHANGE
B) The Experimental Lakes Area is located in a sparsely inhabited region that experiences few effects of human and industrial activity.
C) To isolate the cause of the algae, Schindler and Brunskill performed another experiment, this time using Lake 226.
D) The process by which water becomes enriched by dissolved nutrients, such as phosphates, is called eutrophication.

6

A) NO CHANGE
B) and a source of carbon.
C) plus also a source of carbon.
D) but also adding a source of carbon.

7

A) NO CHANGE
B) were teeming
C) are teeming
D) teems

CONTINUE

Schindler and Brunskill's findings were **8** <u>shown off by</u> the journal *Science*. The research demonstrated a clear correlation between introducing phosphates and the growth of blue-green algae. **9** <u>For example,</u> legislators in Canada passed laws banning phosphates in laundry detergents, which had been entering the water supply. **10**

8

A) NO CHANGE
B) put in the spotlight of
C) published in
D) put into

9

A) NO CHANGE
B) Similarly,
C) However,
D) Subsequently,

10

At this point, the writer wants to add a second policy outcome of the research described. Which choice best accomplishes this goal?

A) Lake 226 continued to develop blooms of blue-green algae for eight consecutive years after the experiment took place.
B) In the United States, many individual states have also adopted legislation to eliminate, or at least reduce, phosphorous content in laundry detergents.
C) In 1974, Schindler initiated a study of the effects of acid rain, using Lake 223 to examine how sulfuric acid altered aquatic ecosystems.
D) Aerial photos of the lakes taken before and during algal blooms helped convey the effects of phosphates in water to the public.

CONTINUE

Experiments like these can help people understand the unintended consequences of using certain household products. **11** Of course, regulating the use of certain chemical compounds can be a controversial issue. Selectively establishing remote study locations, such as the Experimental Lakes Area, can provide scientists with opportunities to safely conduct controlled research. This research can generate evidence solid enough to persuade policy makers to take action in favor of protecting the larger environment.

11

Which choice most effectively anticipates and addresses a relevant counterargument to the argument in favor of the types of experiments described in the passage?

A) NO CHANGE

B) Many companies now offer phosphate-free alternatives for household cleaning products.

C) Obviously, scientists should not be allowed to randomly perform experiments on just any body of water.

D) Phosphates are sometimes used in agricultural fertilizers, in addition to being used in cleaning products.

CONTINUE

Questions 12-22 are based on the following passage.

A Little to the Left, but Not Too Much!

Italy's Tower of Pisa has been leaning southward since the initial **12** stages of it's construction over 800 years ago. **13** Indeed, if the tower's construction had not taken two centuries and involved significant breaks due to war and civil unrest, which allowed the ground beneath the tower to settle, the tower would likely have collapsed before it was completed.

12

A) NO CHANGE
B) stage's of its'
C) stage's of it's
D) stages of its

13

A) NO CHANGE
B) Therefore,
C) Nevertheless,
D) However,

CONTINUE

Luckily, the tower survived, and its tilt has made it an Italian **14** icon, it attracts visitors from all over who flock to Pisa to see one of the greatest architectural **15** weirdnesses in the world. **16** By the late twentieth century, the angle of the tower's tilt had reached an astonishing 5.5 degrees; in **17** 1990, Italy's government closed the tower to visitors and appointed a committee to find a way to save it.

14

A) NO CHANGE
B) icon, attracting
C) icon, its attracting
D) icon; attracting

15

A) NO CHANGE
B) deviations
C) oddities
D) abnormalities

16

At this point, the writer is considering adding the following sentence.

> Unfortunately, the tower's tilt has steadily increased over the centuries, placing the structure in danger of collapse.

Should the writer make this addition here?

A) Yes, because it provides an important restatement of the main claim in the previous sentence.
B) Yes, because it establishes an important shift in emphasis in the paragraph's discussion about the tower's tilt.
C) No, because it interrupts the paragraph's discussion with irrelevant information.
D) No, because it repeats information that is already presented in the first paragraph.

17

A) NO CHANGE
B) 1990, Italy's government, closed
C) 1990 Italy's government, closed,
D) 1990: Italy's government closed

CONTINUE

The committee was charged with saving the tower without ruining its aesthetic, **18** which no one had yet managed to achieve. The committee's first attempt to reduce the angle of the tower's tilt—placing 600 tons of iron ingots (molded pieces of metal) on the tower's north side to create a counterweight—was derided because the bulky weights ruined the tower's appearance. The attempt at a less visible solution—sinking anchors into the ground below the tower—almost caused the tower to fall.

18

Which choice best supports the main point of the paragraph?

A) NO CHANGE
B) although not everyone on the committee agreed completely about what that aesthetic was.
C) which meant somehow preserving the tower's tilt while preventing that tilt from increasing and toppling the tower.
D) which included the pristine white marble finish that has come to be widely associated with the tower's beauty.

[1] Enter committee member John Burland, **19** he is a geotechnical engineer from England who saved London's clock tower Big Ben from collapse. [2] Burland began a years-long process of drilling out small amounts of soil from under the tower **20** that took several years to complete and then monitoring the tower's resulting movement. [3] Twice daily, Burland evaluated these movements and made recommendations as to how much soil should be removed in the next drilling. [4] By 2001, almost 77 tons of soil had been removed, and the tower's tilt had decreased by over 1.5 degrees; the ugly iron weights were removed, and the tower was reopened to visitors. [5] Burland **21** advocated using soil extraction: removing small amounts of soil from under the tower's north side, opposite its tilt, to enable gravity to straighten the tower. **22**

The tower's tilt has not increased since, and the committee is confident that the tower will be safe for another 200 years. Burland is now working on a more permanent solution for keeping the tower upright, but he is adamant that the tower never be completely straightened. In an interview with PBS's *Nova*, Burland explained that it is very important "that we don't really change the character of the monument. That would be quite wrong and quite inappropriate."

19

A) NO CHANGE
B) Burland is
C) his being
D) DELETE the underlined portion.

20

A) NO CHANGE
B) —taking several years to complete—
C) that took him several years to complete
D) DELETE the underlined portion.

21

A) NO CHANGE
B) advocated to use
C) advocated the using of
D) advocating to use

22

To make this paragraph most logical, sentence 5 should be

A) placed after sentence 1.
B) placed after sentence 2.
C) placed after sentence 3.
D) DELETED from the paragraph.

CONTINUE

Questions 23-33 are based on the following passage and supplementary material.

The Physician Assistant Will See You Now

[23] The term "paramedics" refers to health care workers who provide routine and clinical services. While the pressures of an aging population, insurance reforms, and health epidemics have increased demand for care, the supply of physicians is not expected to [24] keep pace. The Association of American Medical Colleges predicts a shortage of over 90,000 physicians by 2020; by 2025, that number could climb to more than 130,000. In some parts of the country, shortages are already a sad fact of life. A 2009 report by the Bureau of Health Professions notes that although a fifth of the US population lives in rural areas, less than a tenth of US physicians serves that population. Because a traditionalist response to the crisis—[25] amping up medical-college enrollments and expanding physician training programs—is too slow and costly to address the near-term problem, alternatives are being explored. One promising avenue has been greater reliance on physician assistants (PAs).

23

Which choice is the best introduction to the paragraph?

A) NO CHANGE
B) For many Americans, finding a physician is likely to become a growing challenge.
C) Getting treatment for an illness usually requires seeing either a general practitioner or a specialist.
D) Worldwide the costs of health care are increasing at an alarming rate.

24

A) NO CHANGE
B) maintain the tempo.
C) get in line.
D) move along.

25

A) NO CHANGE
B) bolstering
C) arousing
D) revving up

CONTINUE

26 By virtue of 27 there medical training, PAs can perform many of the jobs traditionally done by doctors, including treating chronic and acute conditions, performing minor 28 surgeries: and prescribing some medications. However, although well 29 compensated earning in 2012 a median annual salary of $90,930, PAs cost health care providers less than do the physicians who

26

At this point, the writer is considering adding the following sentence.

> Several factors argue in favor of such an expanded role.

Should the writer make this addition here?

A) Yes, because it introduces a counterargument for balance.
B) Yes, because it frames the points that the paragraph will examine.
C) No, because it does not specify the education required to be a PA.
D) No, because it presents information that is only tangential to the main argument.

27

A) NO CHANGE
B) they're
C) their
D) his or her

28

A) NO CHANGE
B) surgeries; and
C) surgeries, and,
D) surgeries, and

29

A) NO CHANGE
B) compensated (earning in 2012 a median annual salary of $90,930),
C) compensated, earning in 2012 a median annual salary of $90,930
D) compensated: earning in 2012 a median annual salary of $90,930,

CONTINUE

might otherwise undertake these tasks. Moreover, the training period for PAs is markedly shorter than **30** those for physicians—two to three years versus the seven to eleven required for physicians.

Physician assistants already offer vital primary care in many locations. Some 90,000 PAs were employed nationwide in 2012. Over and above their value in partially compensating for the general physician shortage has been their extraordinary contribution to rural health care. A recent review of the scholarly literature by Texas researchers found that PAs lend cost-efficient, widely appreciated services in underserved areas. **31** In addition, rural-based PAs often provide a broader spectrum of such services than do their urban and suburban counterparts, possibly as a consequence of the limited pool of rural-based physicians.

30

A) NO CHANGE
B) that compared with
C) that for
D) DELETE the underlined portion.

31

A) NO CHANGE
B) Thus,
C) Despite this,
D) On the other hand,

CONTINUE

Increasingly, PAs and other such medical practitioners have become a critical complement to physicians. A 2013 RAND Corporation report estimates that while the number of primary care physicians will increase slowly from 2010 to 2025, the number of physician assistants and nurse-practitioners in primary care will grow at much faster rates. **32** Both by merit and from necessity, PAs are likely to greet more **33** patience than ever before.

Supply of Physicians, Physician Assistants, and Nurse-Practitioners in Primary Care Clinical Practice in 2010 and 2025

	2010		2025 (predicted)	
Provider type	Number	Percent of total	Number	Percent of total
Physicians	210,000	71	216,000	60
Physician assistants	30,000	10	42,000	12
Nurse-practitioners	56,000	19	103,000	28
Total	296,000	100	361,000	100

Adapted from David I. Auerbach et al., "Nurse-Managed Health Centers and Patient-Centered Medical Homes Could Mitigate Expected Primary Care Physician Shortage." ©2013 by Project HOPE: The People-to-People Health Foundation, Inc.

32

At this point, the writer is considering adding the following sentence.

In fact, according to the data presented in the table, physician assistants will likely outnumber physicians by 2025.

Should the writer make this addition here?

A) Yes, because it provides additional support for the main point of the paragraph.
B) Yes, because it addresses a possible counterargument to the writer's main claim.
C) No, because it is not an accurate interpretation of the data.
D) No, because it introduces irrelevant information that interrupts the flow of the passage.

33

A) NO CHANGE
B) patience, than
C) patients then
D) patients than

CONTINUE

Questions 34-44 are based on the following passage.

Gold into Silver: The "Reverse Alchemy" of Superhero Comics History

[34] Popular film franchises are often "rebooted" in an effort to make their characters and stories fresh and relevant for new audiences. Superhero comic books are periodically reworked to try to increase their appeal to contemporary readers. This practice is almost as [35] elderly as the medium itself and has in large part established the "ages" that compose comic book history. The shift from the Golden to the Silver Age is probably the most successful [36] example: of publishers responding to changing times and tastes.

34

Which choice most effectively combines the underlined sentences?

A) In an effort to make their characters and stories fresh and relevant for new audiences, popular film franchises, which are often "rebooted," are similar to superhero comic books, which are periodically reworked to try to increase their appeal to contemporary readers.

B) Just as popular film franchises are often "rebooted" in an effort to make their characters and stories fresh and relevant for new audiences, superhero comic books are periodically reworked to try to increase their appeal to contemporary readers.

C) Superhero comic books are periodically reworked to try to increase their appeal to contemporary readers, while popular film franchises are often "rebooted" in an effort to make their characters and stories fresh and relevant for new audiences.

D) Superhero comic books are much like popular film franchises in being often "rebooted" in an effort to make their characters and stories fresh and relevant for new audiences and periodically reworked to try to increase their appeal to contemporary readers.

35

A) NO CHANGE

B) old

C) mature

D) geriatric

36

A) NO CHANGE

B) example, of publishers

C) example of publishers,

D) example of publishers

CONTINUE

The start of the first ("Golden") age of comic books is often dated to 1938 with the debut of Superman in *Action Comics* #1. Besides beginning the age, Superman in many respects defined it, becoming the model on which many later superheroes were based. His characterization, as established in *Superman* #1 (1939), was relatively simple. He could "hurdle skyscrapers" and "leap an eighth of a mile"; "run faster than a streamline train"; withstand anything less than a "bursting shell"; and **37** lift a car over his head. Sent to Earth from the "doomed planet" Krypton, he was raised by human foster parents, whose love helped infuse him with an unapologetic desire to "benefit mankind." Admirable but aloof, the Golden Age Superman was arguably more paragon than character, a problem only partially solved by giving him a human alter ego. Other Golden Age superheroes were similarly archetypal: Batman was a crime-fighting millionaire, Wonder Woman a warrior princess from a mythical island.

37

Which choice is most consistent with the previous examples in the sentence?

A) NO CHANGE

B) hold down a regular job as a newspaper reporter.

C) wear a bright blue costume with a flowing red cape.

D) live in the big city of Metropolis instead of the small town where he grew up.

CONTINUE

By contrast, the second ("Silver") age of comics was marked by characters that, though somewhat simplistic by today's standards, **38** were provided with origin stories often involving scientific experiments gone wrong. In addition to super villains, the new, soon-to-be-iconic characters of the **39** age: Spider-Man, the Fantastic Four, and the Hulk among them—had to cope with mundane, real-life problems, including paying the rent, dealing with family squabbles, and facing anger, loneliness, and ostracism. Their interior lives were richer and their motivations more complex. Although sales remained strong for Golden Age stalwarts Superman and, to a lesser extent, Batman, **40** subsequent decades would show the enduring appeal of these characters.

38

Which choice most effectively sets up the main idea of the following two sentences?

A) NO CHANGE
B) reflected the increasing conservatism of the United States in the 1950s.
C) engaged in bizarre adventures frequently inspired by science fiction.
D) were more "realistic" than their Golden Age counterparts.

39

A) NO CHANGE
B) age;
C) age,
D) age—

40

The writer wants a conclusion to the sentence and paragraph that logically completes the discussion of the Silver Age and provides an effective transition into the next paragraph. Which choice best accomplishes these goals?

A) NO CHANGE
B) the distinctions between later stages of comic book history are less well defined than the one between the Golden and Silver Ages.
C) readers increasingly gravitated to the upstarts as the 1960s and the Silver Age drew to a close.
D) these characters themselves underwent significant changes over the course of the Silver Age.

CONTINUE

More transformations would take place in the medium as the Silver Age gave way to the Bronze and Modern (and possibly Postmodern) Ages. Such efforts **41** have yielded diminishing returns, as even the complete relaunch of DC **42** Comics' superhero's, line in 2011 has failed to arrest the steep two-decade decline of comic book sales. For both commercial and, arguably, creative reasons, **43** then, no transition was more successful than **44** those from the Golden to Silver Age.

41

A) NO CHANGE
B) would have yielded
C) were yielding
D) will yield

42

A) NO CHANGE
B) Comic's superhero's
C) Comics superhero's
D) Comics' superhero

43

A) NO CHANGE
B) however,
C) nevertheless,
D) yet,

44

A) NO CHANGE
B) these
C) that
D) DELETE the underlined portion.

STOP

If you finish before time is called, you may check your work on this section only.
Do not turn to any other section.

No Test Material On This Page

Math Test – No Calculator

25 MINUTES, 20 QUESTIONS

Turn to Section 3 of your answer sheet to answer the questions in this section.

DIRECTIONS

For questions 1-15, solve each problem, choose the best answer from the choices provided, and fill in the corresponding circle on your answer sheet. **For questions 16-20**, solve the problem and enter your answer in the grid on the answer sheet. Please refer to the directions before question 16 on how to enter your answers in the grid. You may use any available space in your test booklet for scratch work.

NOTES

1. The use of a calculator **is not permitted**.
2. All variables and expressions used represent real numbers unless otherwise indicated.
3. Figures provided in this test are drawn to scale unless otherwise indicated.
4. All figures lie in a plane unless otherwise indicated.
5. Unless otherwise indicated, the domain of a given function f is the set of all real numbers x for which $f(x)$ is a real number.

REFERENCE

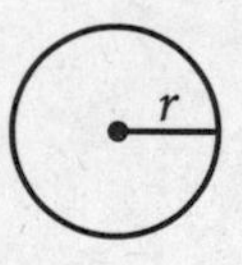

$A = \pi r^2$
$C = 2\pi r$

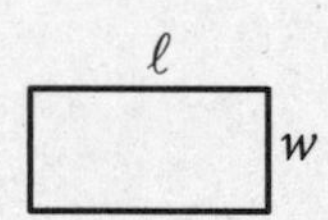

$A = \ell w$

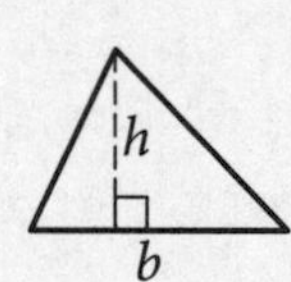

$A = \frac{1}{2}bh$

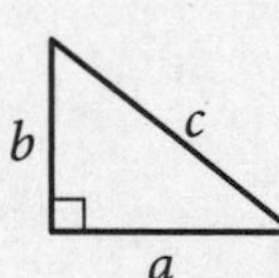

$c^2 = a^2 + b^2$

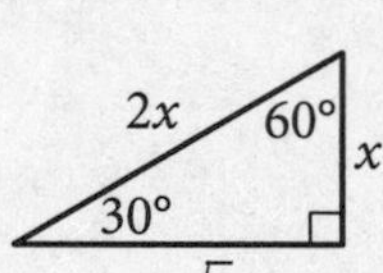

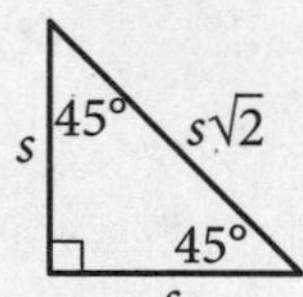

Special Right Triangles

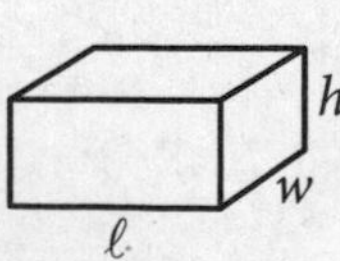

$V = \ell wh$

$V = \pi r^2 h$

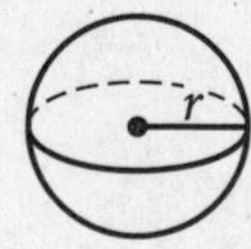

$V = \frac{4}{3}\pi r^3$

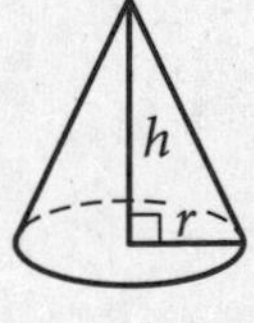

$V = \frac{1}{3}\pi r^2 h$

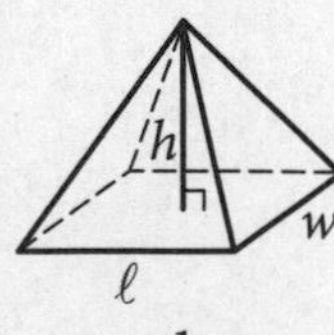

$V = \frac{1}{3}\ell wh$

The number of degrees of arc in a circle is 360.
The number of radians of arc in a circle is 2π.
The sum of the measures in degrees of the angles of a triangle is 180.

CONTINUE

1

Salim wants to purchase tickets from a vendor to watch a tennis match. The vendor charges a one-time service fee for processing the purchase of the tickets. The equation $T = 15n + 12$ represents the total amount T, in dollars, Salim will pay for n tickets. What does 12 represent in the equation?

A) The price of one ticket, in dollars

B) The amount of the service fee, in dollars

C) The total amount, in dollars, Salim will pay for one ticket

D) The total amount, in dollars, Salim will pay for any number of tickets

2

A gardener buys two kinds of fertilizer. Fertilizer A contains 60% filler materials by weight and Fertilizer B contains 40% filler materials by weight. Together, the fertilizers bought by the gardener contain a total of 240 pounds of filler materials. Which equation models this relationship, where x is the number of pounds of Fertilizer A and y is the number of pounds of Fertilizer B?

A) $0.4x + 0.6y = 240$

B) $0.6x + 0.4y = 240$

C) $40x + 60y = 240$

D) $60x + 40y = 240$

3

What is the sum of the complex numbers $2 + 3i$ and $4 + 8i$, where $i = \sqrt{-1}$?

A) 17

B) $17i$

C) $6 + 11i$

D) $8 + 24i$

4

$$4x^2 - 9 = (px + t)(px - t)$$

In the equation above, p and t are constants. Which of the following could be the value of p ?

A) 2

B) 3

C) 4

D) 9

CONTINUE

5

Which of the following is the graph of the equation $y = 2x - 5$ in the xy-plane?

A)

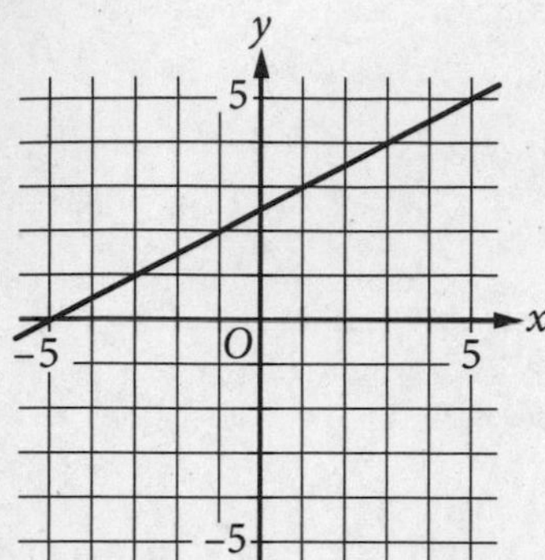

B)

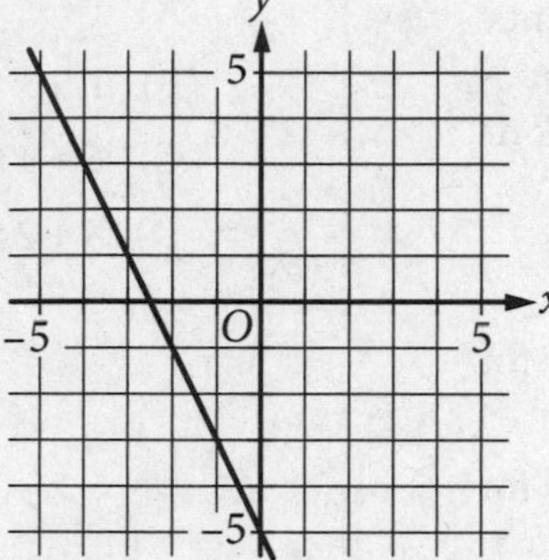

C)

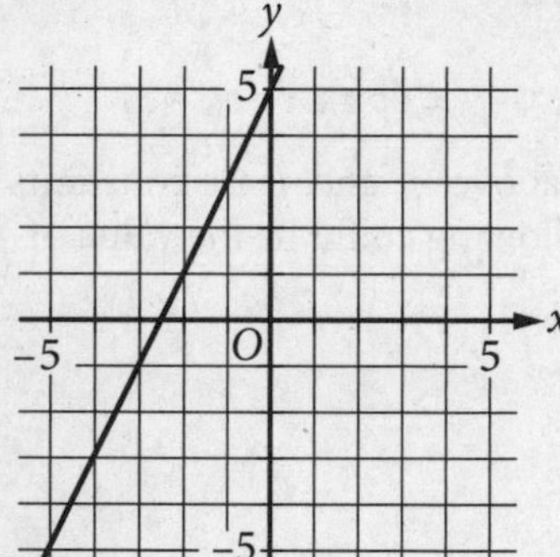

D)

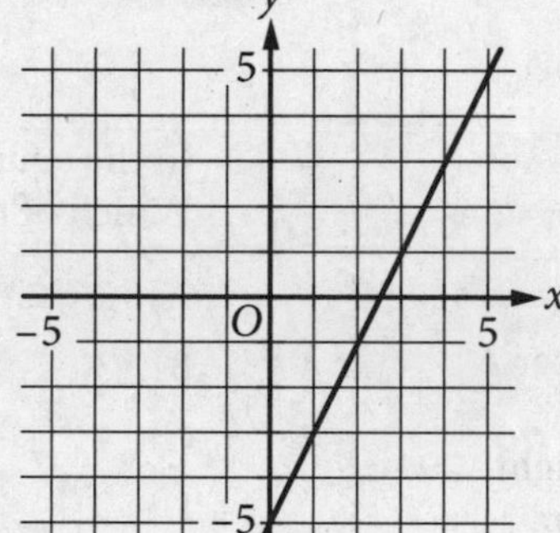

CONTINUE

14

A laundry service is buying detergent and fabric softener from its supplier. The supplier will deliver no more than 300 pounds in a shipment. Each container of detergent weighs 7.35 pounds, and each container of fabric softener weighs 6.2 pounds. The service wants to buy at least twice as many containers of detergent as containers of fabric softener. Let d represent the number of containers of detergent, and let s represent the number of containers of fabric softener, where d and s are nonnegative integers. Which of the following systems of inequalities best represents this situation?

A) $7.35d + 6.2s \leq 300$
$d \geq 2s$

B) $7.35d + 6.2s \leq 300$
$2d \geq s$

C) $14.7d + 6.2s \leq 300$
$d \geq 2s$

D) $14.7d + 6.2s \leq 300$
$2d \geq s$

15

Which of the following is equivalent to $\left(a + \frac{b}{2}\right)^2$?

A) $a^2 + \frac{b^2}{2}$

B) $a^2 + \frac{b^2}{4}$

C) $a^2 + \frac{ab}{2} + \frac{b^2}{2}$

D) $a^2 + ab + \frac{b^2}{4}$

CONTINUE

DIRECTIONS

For questions 16-20, solve the problem and enter your answer in the grid, as described below, on the answer sheet.

1. Although not required, it is suggested that you write your answer in the boxes at the top of the columns to help you fill in the circles accurately. You will receive credit only if the circles are filled in correctly.
2. Mark no more than one circle in any column.
3. No question has a negative answer.
4. Some problems may have more than one correct answer. In such cases, grid only one answer.
5. **Mixed numbers** such as $3\frac{1}{2}$ must be gridded as 3.5 or 7/2. (If 3 1 / 2 is entered into the grid, it will be interpreted as $\frac{31}{2}$, not $3\frac{1}{2}$.)
6. **Decimal answers:** If you obtain a decimal answer with more digits than the grid can accommodate, it may be either rounded or truncated, but it must fill the entire grid.

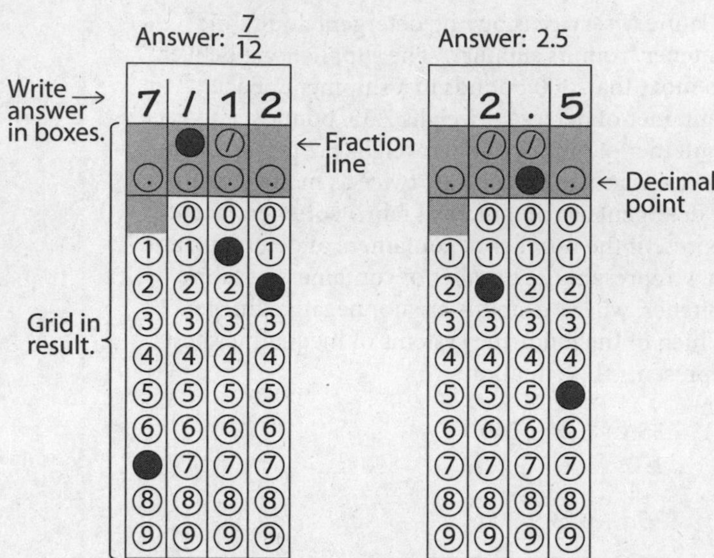

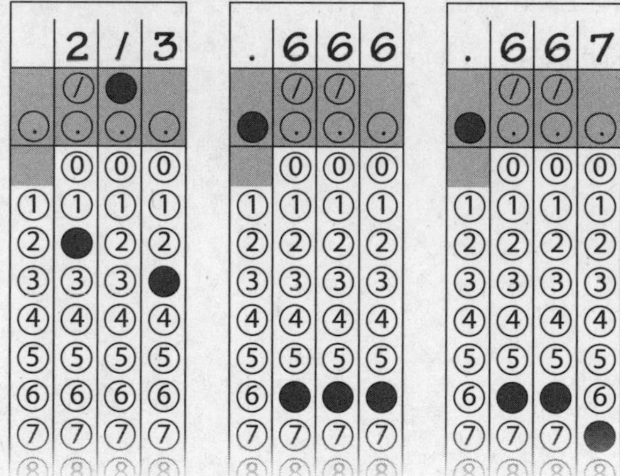

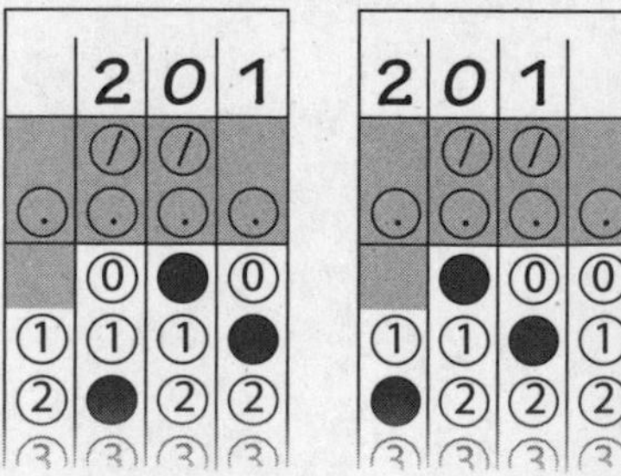

NOTE: You may start your answers in any column, space permitting. Columns you don't need to use should be left blank.

CONTINUE

16

If $a^{\frac{b}{4}} = 16$ for positive integers a and b, what is one possible value of b ?

17

$$\frac{2}{3}t = \frac{5}{2}$$

What value of t is the solution of the equation above?

18

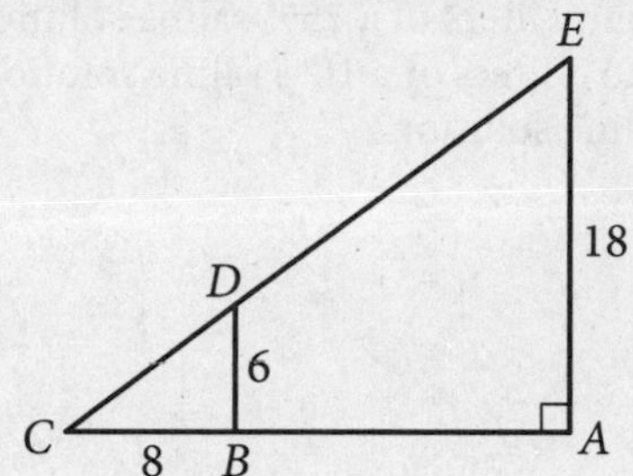

In the figure above, $\overline{BD}$ is parallel to $\overline{AE}$. What is the length of $\overline{CE}$?

CONTINUE

19

How many liters of a 25% saline solution must be added to 3 liters of a 10% saline solution to obtain a 15% saline solution?

20

Points A and B lie on a circle with radius 1, and arc $\widehat{AB}$ has length $\frac{\pi}{3}$. What fraction of the circumference of the circle is the length of arc $\widehat{AB}$?

STOP

If you finish before time is called, you may check your work on this section only. Do not turn to any other section.

No Test Material On This Page

Math Test – Calculator

55 MINUTES, 38 QUESTIONS

Turn to Section 4 of your answer sheet to answer the questions in this section.

DIRECTIONS

For questions 1-30, solve each problem, choose the best answer from the choices provided, and fill in the corresponding circle on your answer sheet. **For questions 31-38**, solve the problem and enter your answer in the grid on the answer sheet. Please refer to the directions before question 31 on how to enter your answers in the grid. You may use any available space in your test booklet for scratch work.

NOTES

1. The use of a calculator **is permitted**.
2. All variables and expressions used represent real numbers unless otherwise indicated.
3. Figures provided in this test are drawn to scale unless otherwise indicated.
4. All figures lie in a plane unless otherwise indicated.
5. Unless otherwise indicated, the domain of a given function f is the set of all real numbers x for which $f(x)$ is a real number.

REFERENCE

$A = \pi r^2$
$C = 2\pi r$

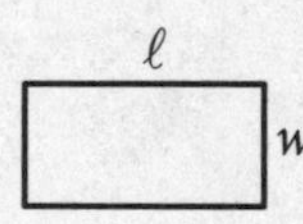

$A = \ell w$

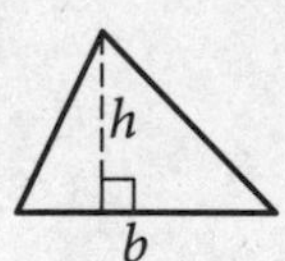

$A = \frac{1}{2}bh$

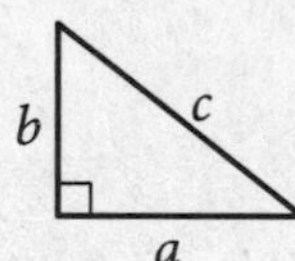

$c^2 = a^2 + b^2$

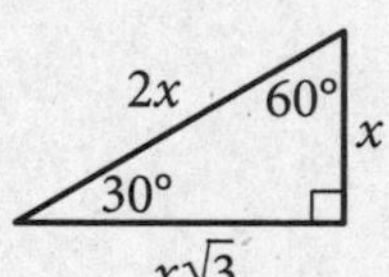

Special Right Triangles

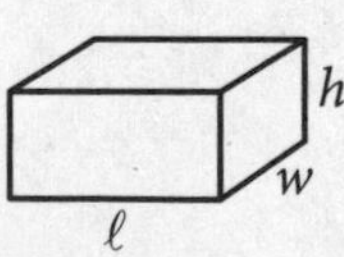

$V = \ell wh$

$V = \pi r^2 h$

$V = \frac{4}{3}\pi r^3$

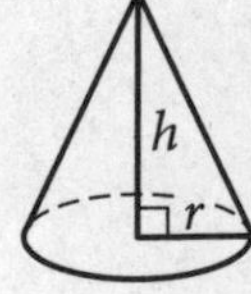

$V = \frac{1}{3}\pi r^2 h$

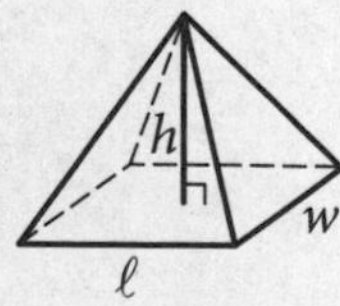

$V = \frac{1}{3}\ell wh$

The number of degrees of arc in a circle is 360.
The number of radians of arc in a circle is 2π.
The sum of the measures in degrees of the angles of a triangle is 180.

CONTINUE

1

Which expression is equivalent to
$(2x^2 - 4) - (-3x^2 + 2x - 7)$?

A) $5x^2 - 2x + 3$

B) $5x^2 + 2x - 3$

C) $-x^2 - 2x - 11$

D) $-x^2 + 2x - 11$

2

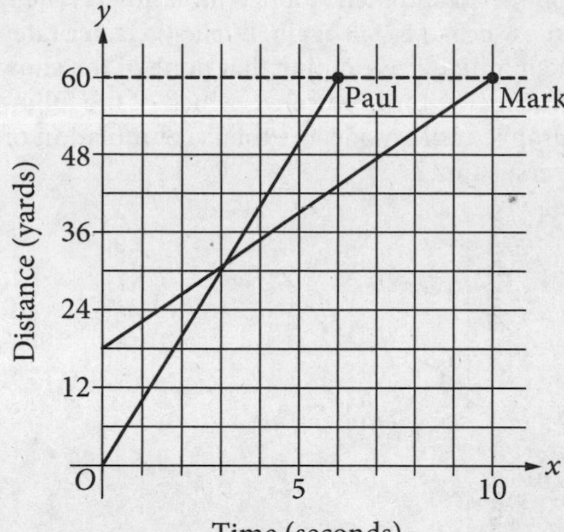

The graph above shows the positions of Paul and Mark during a race. Paul and Mark each ran at a constant rate, and Mark was given a head start to shorten the distance he needed to run. Paul finished the race in 6 seconds, and Mark finished the race in 10 seconds. According to the graph, Mark was given a head start of how many yards?

A) 3

B) 12

C) 18

D) 24

CONTINUE

3

Snow fell and then stopped for a time. When the snow began to fall again, it fell at a faster rate than it had initially. Assuming that none of the snow melted during the time indicated, which of the following graphs could model the total accumulation of snow versus time?

A) 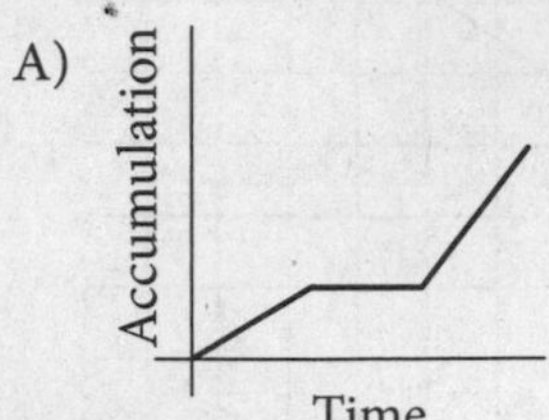

B) 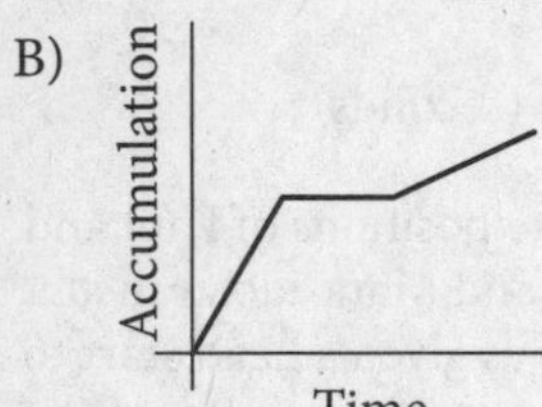

C) 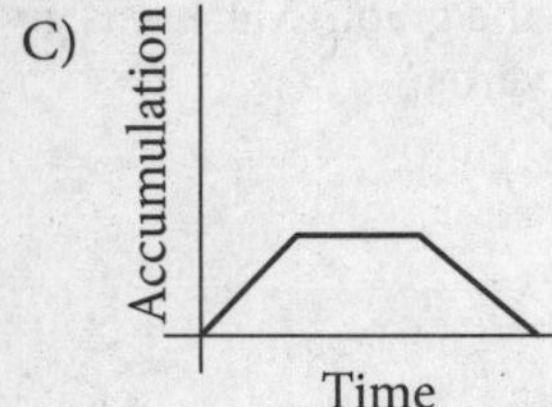

D) 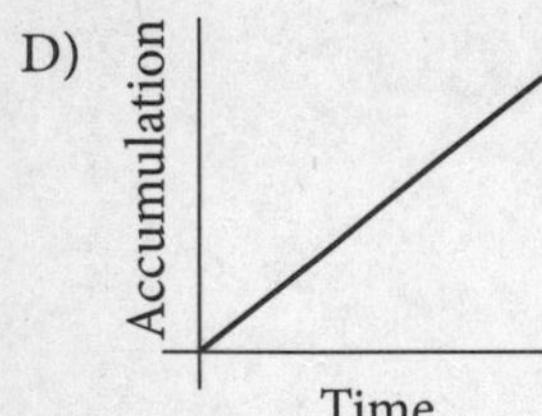

4

A website-hosting service charges businesses a onetime setup fee of \$350 plus d dollars for each month. If a business owner paid \$1,010 for the first 12 months, including the setup fee, what is the value of d ?

A) 25

B) 35

C) 45

D) 55

5

$$6x - 9y > 12$$

Which of the following inequalities is equivalent to the inequality above?

A) $x - y > 2$

B) $2x - 3y > 4$

C) $3x - 2y > 4$

D) $3y - 2x > 2$

CONTINUE

6

Where Do People Get Most of
Their Medical Information?

Source	Percent of those surveyed
Doctor	63%
Internet	13%
Magazines/brochures	9%
Pharmacy	6%
Television	2%
Other/none of the above	7%

The table above shows a summary of 1,200 responses to a survey question. Based on the table, how many of those surveyed get most of their medical information from either a doctor or the Internet?

A) 865
B) 887
C) 912
D) 926

7

The members of a city council wanted to assess the opinions of all city residents about converting an open field into a dog park. The council surveyed a sample of 500 city residents who own dogs. The survey showed that the majority of those sampled were in favor of the dog park. Which of the following is true about the city council's survey?

A) It shows that the majority of city residents are in favor of the dog park.
B) The survey sample should have included more residents who are dog owners.
C) The survey sample should have consisted entirely of residents who do not own dogs.
D) The survey sample is biased because it is not representative of all city residents.

CONTINUE

8

Ice Cream and Topping Selections

		Flavor	
		Vanilla	Chocolate
Topping	Hot fudge	8	6
	Caramel	5	6

The table above shows the flavors of ice cream and the toppings chosen by the people at a party. Each person chose one flavor of ice cream and one topping. Of the people who chose vanilla ice cream, what fraction chose hot fudge as a topping?

A) $\frac{8}{25}$

B) $\frac{5}{13}$

C) $\frac{13}{25}$

D) $\frac{8}{13}$

9

The total area of a coastal city is 92.1 square miles, of which 11.3 square miles is water. If the city had a population of 621,000 people in the year 2010, which of the following is closest to the population density, in people per square mile of land area, of the city at that time?

A) 6,740

B) 7,690

C) 55,000

D) 76,000

CONTINUE

10

Between 1497 and 1500, Amerigo Vespucci embarked on two voyages to the New World. According to Vespucci's letters, the first voyage lasted 43 days longer than the second voyage, and the two voyages combined lasted a total of 1,003 days. How many days did the second voyage last?

A) 460

B) 480

C) 520

D) 540

11

$$7x + 3y = 8$$
$$6x - 3y = 5$$

For the solution (x, y) to the system of equations above, what is the value of $x - y$?

A) $-\frac{4}{3}$

B) $\frac{2}{3}$

C) $\frac{4}{3}$

D) $\frac{22}{3}$

CONTINUE

Questions 12-14 refer to the following information.

Sunflower Growth

Day	Height (cm)
0	0.00
7	17.93
14	36.36
21	67.76
28	98.10
35	131.00
42	169.50
49	205.50
56	228.30
63	247.10
70	250.50
77	253.80
84	254.50

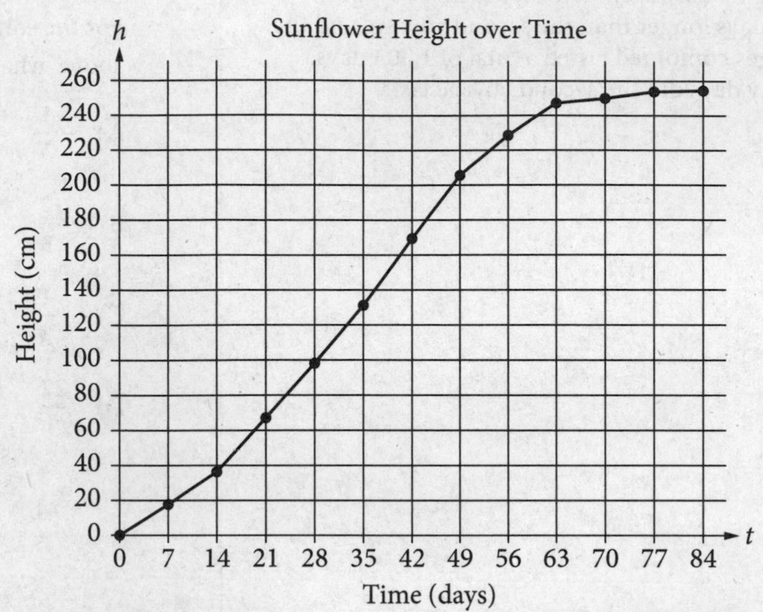

In 1919, H. S. Reed and R. H. Holland published a paper on the growth of sunflowers. Included in the paper were the table and graph above, which show the height h, in centimeters, of a sunflower t days after the sunflower begins to grow.

12

Over which of the following time periods is the average growth rate of the sunflower least?

A) Day 0 to Day 21

B) Day 21 to Day 42

C) Day 42 to Day 63

D) Day 63 to Day 84

13

The function h, defined by $h(t) = at + b$, where a and b are constants, models the height, in centimeters, of the sunflower after t days of growth during a time period in which the growth is approximately linear. What does a represent?

A) The predicted number of centimeters the sunflower grows each day during the period

B) The predicted height, in centimeters, of the sunflower at the beginning of the period

C) The predicted height, in centimeters, of the sunflower at the end of the period

D) The predicted total increase in the height of the sunflower, in centimeters, during the period

CONTINUE

14

The growth rate of the sunflower from day 14 to day 35 is nearly constant. On this interval, which of the following equations best models the height h, in centimeters, of the sunflower t days after it begins to grow?

A) $h = 2.1t - 15$

B) $h = 4.5t - 27$

C) $h = 6.8t - 12$

D) $h = 13.2t - 18$

15

x	1	2	3	4	5
y	$\frac{11}{4}$	$\frac{25}{4}$	$\frac{39}{4}$	$\frac{53}{4}$	$\frac{67}{4}$

Which of the following equations relates y to x for the values in the table above?

A) $y = \frac{1}{2} \cdot \left(\frac{5}{2}\right)^x$

B) $y = 2 \cdot \left(\frac{3}{4}\right)^x$

C) $y = \frac{3}{4}x + 2$

D) $y = \frac{7}{2}x - \frac{3}{4}$

16

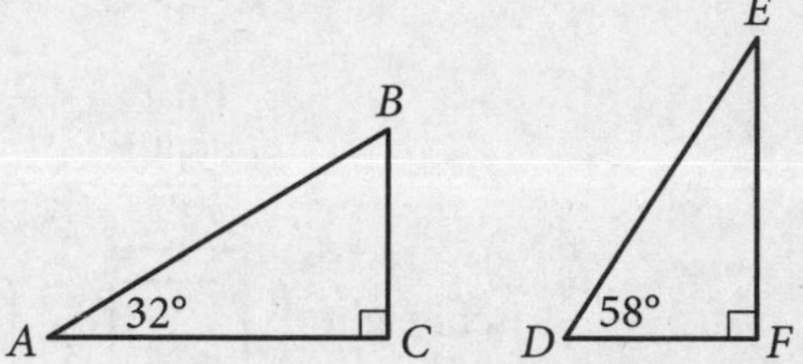

Triangles ABC and DEF are shown above. Which of the following is equal to the ratio $\frac{BC}{AB}$?

A) $\frac{DE}{DF}$

B) $\frac{DF}{DE}$

C) $\frac{DF}{EF}$

D) $\frac{EF}{DE}$

Questions 17-19 refer to the following information.

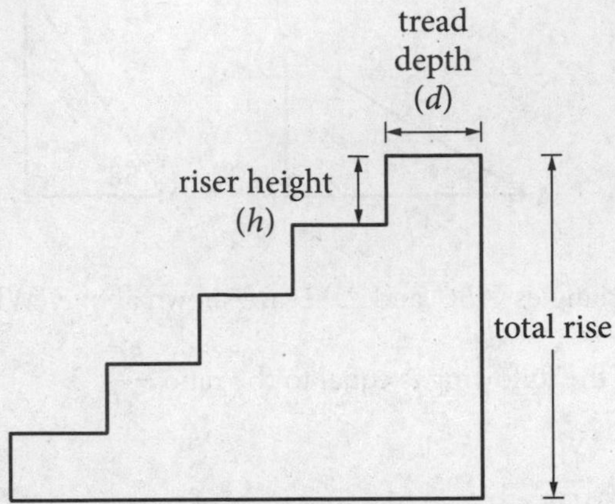

Note: Figure not drawn to scale.

When designing a stairway, an architect can use the riser-tread formula $2h + d = 25$, where h is the riser height, in inches, and d is the tread depth, in inches. For any given stairway, the riser heights are the same and the tread depths are the same for all steps in that stairway.

The number of steps in a stairway is the number of its risers. For example, there are 5 steps in the stairway in the figure above. The total rise of a stairway is the sum of the riser heights as shown in the figure.

17

Which of the following expresses the riser height in terms of the tread depth?

A) $h = \frac{1}{2}(25 + d)$

B) $h = \frac{1}{2}(25 - d)$

C) $h = -\frac{1}{2}(25 + d)$

D) $h = -\frac{1}{2}(25 - d)$

18

Some building codes require that, for indoor stairways, the tread depth must be at least 9 inches and the riser height must be at least 5 inches. According to the riser-tread formula, which of the following inequalities represents the set of all possible values for the riser height that meets this code requirement?

A) $0 \le h \le 5$

B) $h \ge 5$

C) $5 \le h \le 8$

D) $8 \le h \le 16$

19

An architect wants to use the riser-tread formula to design a stairway with a total rise of 9 feet, a riser height between 7 and 8 inches, and an odd number of steps. With the architect's constraints, which of the following must be the tread depth, in inches, of the stairway? (1 foot = 12 inches)

A) 7.2

B) 9.5

C) 10.6

D) 15

CONTINUE

20

What is the sum of the solutions to $(x-6)(x+0.7)=0$?

A) -6.7

B) -5.3

C) 5.3

D) 6.7

21

A study was done on the weights of different types of fish in a pond. A random sample of fish were caught and marked in order to ensure that none were weighed more than once. The sample contained 150 largemouth bass, of which 30% weighed more than 2 pounds. Which of the following conclusions is best supported by the sample data?

A) The majority of all fish in the pond weigh less than 2 pounds.

B) The average weight of all fish in the pond is approximately 2 pounds.

C) Approximately 30% of all fish in the pond weigh more than 2 pounds.

D) Approximately 30% of all largemouth bass in the pond weigh more than 2 pounds.

22

Number of States with 10 or More Electoral Votes in 2008

Electoral votes	Frequency
10	4
11	4
12	1
13	1
15	3
17	1
20	1
21	2
27	1
31	1
34	1
55	1

In 2008, there were 21 states with 10 or more electoral votes, as shown in the table above. Based on the table, what was the median number of electoral votes for the 21 states?

A) 13

B) 15

C) 17

D) 20

CONTINUE

23

Height versus Time for a Bouncing Ball

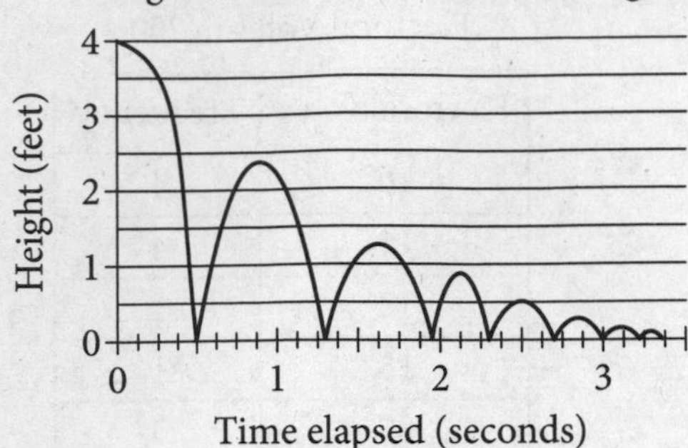

As part of an experiment, a ball was dropped and allowed to bounce repeatedly off the ground until it came to rest. The graph above represents the relationship between the time elapsed after the ball was dropped and the height of the ball above the ground. After it was dropped, how many times was the ball at a height of 2 feet?

A) One

B) Two

C) Three

D) Four

24

A customer's monthly water bill was \$75.74. Due to a rate increase, her monthly bill is now \$79.86. To the nearest tenth of a percent, by what percent did the amount of the customer's water bill increase?

A) 4.1%

B) 5.1%

C) 5.2%

D) 5.4%

25

x	$f(x)$
0	−2
2	4
6	16

Some values of the linear function f are shown in the table above. What is the value of $f(3)$?

A) 6

B) 7

C) 8

D) 9

CONTINUE

26

A gear ratio $r{:}s$ is the ratio of the number of teeth of two connected gears. The ratio of the number of revolutions per minute (rpm) of two gear wheels is $s{:}r$. In the diagram below, Gear A is turned by a motor. The turning of Gear A causes Gears B and C to turn as well.

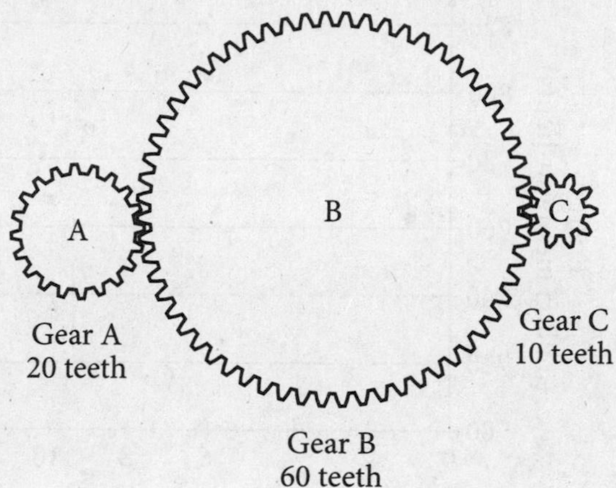

If Gear A is rotated by the motor at a rate of 100 rpm, what is the number of revolutions per minute for Gear C?

A) 50

B) 110

C) 200

D) 1,000

27

In the xy-plane, the graph of $2x^2 - 6x + 2y^2 + 2y = 45$ is a circle. What is the radius of the circle?

A) 5

B) 6.5

C) $\sqrt{40}$

D) $\sqrt{50}$

28

Two different points on a number line are both 3 units from the point with coordinate -4. The solution to which of the following equations gives the coordinates of both points?

A) $|x + 4| = 3$

B) $|x - 4| = 3$

C) $|x + 3| = 4$

D) $|x - 3| = 4$

29

A motor powers a model car so that after starting from rest, the car travels s inches in t seconds, where $s = 16t\sqrt{t}$. Which of the following gives the average speed of the car, in inches per second, over the first t seconds after it starts?

A) $4\sqrt{t}$

B) $16\sqrt{t}$

C) $\dfrac{16}{\sqrt{t}}$

D) $16t$

30

The scatterplot below shows the amount of electric energy generated, in millions of megawatt-hours, by nuclear sources over a 10-year period.

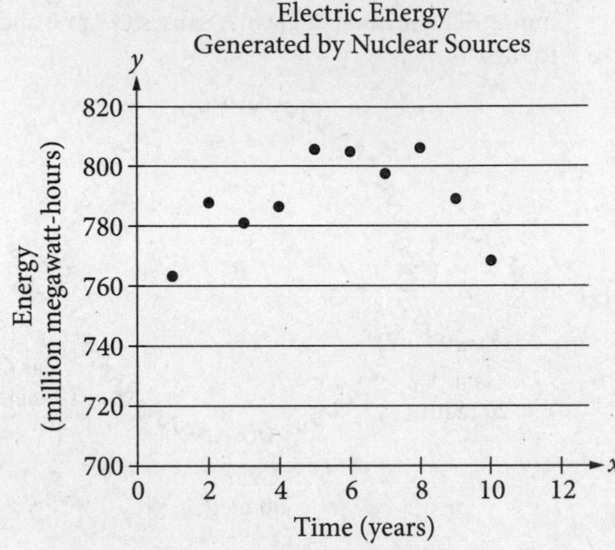

Of the following equations, which best models the data in the scatterplot?

A) $y = 1.674x^2 + 19.76x - 745.73$

B) $y = -1.674x^2 - 19.76x - 745.73$

C) $y = 1.674x^2 + 19.76x + 745.73$

D) $y = -1.674x^2 + 19.76x + 745.73$

CONTINUE

DIRECTIONS

For questions 31-38, solve the problem and enter your answer in the grid, as described below, on the answer sheet.

1. Although not required, it is suggested that you write your answer in the boxes at the top of the columns to help you fill in the circles accurately. You will receive credit only if the circles are filled in correctly.
2. Mark no more than one circle in any column.
3. No question has a negative answer.
4. Some problems may have more than one correct answer. In such cases, grid only one answer.
5. **Mixed numbers** such as $3\frac{1}{2}$ must be gridded as 3.5 or 7/2. (If 3 1 / 2 is entered into the grid, it will be interpreted as $\frac{31}{2}$, not $3\frac{1}{2}$.)
6. **Decimal answers:** If you obtain a decimal answer with more digits than the grid can accommodate, it may be either rounded or truncated, but it must fill the entire grid.

Answer: $\frac{7}{12}$ — Write answer in boxes: 7 / 1 2 — Fraction line — Grid in result.

Answer: 2.5 — 2 . 5 — Decimal point

Acceptable ways to grid $\frac{2}{3}$ are: 2 / 3 — .666 — .667

Answer: 201 – either position is correct

NOTE: You may start your answers in any column, space permitting. Columns you don't need to use should be left blank.

31

A group of friends decided to divide the $800 cost of a trip equally among themselves. When two of the friends decided not to go on the trip, those remaining still divided the $800 cost equally, but each friend's share of the cost increased by $20. How many friends were in the group originally?

32

$$2(5x - 20) - (15 + 8x) = 7$$

What value of x satisfies the equation above?

33

A laboratory supply company produces graduated cylinders, each with an internal radius of 2 inches and an internal height between 7.75 inches and 8 inches. What is one possible volume, rounded to the nearest cubic inch, of a graduated cylinder produced by this company?

34

In the xy-plane, the graph of $y = 3x^2 - 14x$ intersects the graph of $y = x$ at the points $(0, 0)$ and (a, a). What is the value of a ?

35

The line with the equation $\frac{4}{5}x + \frac{1}{3}y = 1$ is graphed in the xy-plane. What is the x-coordinate of the x-intercept of the line?

36

	Masses (kilograms)					
Andrew	2.4	2.5	3.6	3.1	2.5	2.7
Maria	x	3.1	2.7	2.9	3.3	2.8

Andrew and Maria each collected six rocks, and the masses of the rocks are shown in the table above. The mean of the masses of the rocks Maria collected is 0.1 kilogram greater than the mean of the masses of the rocks Andrew collected. What is the value of x ?

CONTINUE

37

Jeremy deposited x dollars in his investment account on January 1, 2001. The amount of money in the account doubled each year until Jeremy had 480 dollars in his investment account on January 1, 2005. What is the value of x ?

38

A school district is forming a committee to discuss plans for the construction of a new high school. Of those invited to join the committee, 15% are parents of students, 45% are teachers from the current high school, 25% are school and district administrators, and the remaining 6 individuals are students. How many more teachers were invited to join the committee than school and district administrators?

STOP

If you finish before time is called, you may check your work on this section only.

Do not turn to any other section.

No Test Material On This Page

No Test Material On This Page

This page represents the back cover of the Practice Test.

The SAT®

Practice Essay #6

The essay gives you an opportunity to show how effectively you can read and comprehend a passage and write an essay analyzing the passage. In your essay, you should demonstrate that you have read the passage carefully, present a clear and logical analysis, and use language precisely.

You have 50 minutes to read the passage and write an essay in response to the prompt provided inside this booklet.

For information on scoring your essay, view the SAT Essay scoring rubric at **sat.org/essay**.

As you read the passage below, consider how Christopher Hitchens uses

- evidence, such as facts or examples, to support claims.
- reasoning to develop ideas and to connect claims and evidence.
- stylistic or persuasive elements, such as word choice or appeals to emotion, to add power to the ideas expressed.

Adapted from Christopher Hitchens, "The Lovely Stones." ©2009 by Condé Nast Digital. Originally published July 2009.

1 The great classicist A. W. Lawrence . . . once remarked of the Parthenon[1] that it is "the one building in the world which may be assessed as absolutely *right*." . . .

2 Not that the beauty and symmetry of the Parthenon have not been abused and perverted and mutilated. Five centuries after the birth of Christianity the Parthenon was closed and desolated. . . . Turkish forces also used it for centuries as a garrison[2] and an arsenal, with the tragic result that in 1687 . . . a powder magazine was detonated and huge damage inflicted on the structure. Most horrible of all, perhaps, the Acropolis was made to fly a Nazi flag during the German occupation of Athens. . . .

3 The damage done by the ages to the building, and by past empires and occupations, cannot all be put right. But there is one desecration and dilapidation that can at least be partially undone. Early in the 19th century, Britain's ambassador to the Ottoman Empire, Lord Elgin, sent a wrecking crew to the Turkish-occupied territory of Greece, where it sawed off approximately half of the adornment of the Parthenon and carried it away. As with all things Greek, there were three elements to this, the most lavish and beautiful sculptural treasury in human history. Under the direction of the artistic genius Phidias, the temple had two massive pediments decorated with the figures of Pallas Athena, Poseidon, and the gods of the sun and the moon. It then had a series of 92 high-relief panels, or metopes, depicting a succession of mythical and historical battles. The most intricate element was the frieze, carved in bas-relief,[3] which showed the gods, humans, and animals that made up the annual Pan-Athens procession: there were 192 equestrian warriors and auxiliaries featured, which happens to be the exact number of the city's heroes who fell at the Battle of Marathon. Experts differ on precisely what story is being told here, but the frieze was quite clearly carved as a continuous narrative. Except that half the cast of the tale is still in Bloomsbury, in London, having been sold well below cost by Elgin to the British government in 1816 for $2.2 million in today's currency to pay off his many debts. . . .

---

1 An ancient Greek temple located on the grounds of the ancient citadel, the Acropolis of Athens

2 A military fort or base

3 Raised carvings made of stone

4 . . . [T]here has been a bitter argument about the legitimacy of the British Museum's deal. I've written a whole book about this controversy and won't oppress you with all the details, but would just make this one point. If the *Mona Lisa* had been sawed in two during the Napoleonic Wars and the separated halves had been acquired by different museums in, say, St. Petersburg and Lisbon, would there not be a general wish to see what they might look like if re-united? If you think my analogy is overdrawn, consider this: the body of the goddess Iris is at present in London, while her head is in Athens. The front part of the torso of Poseidon is in London, and the rear part is in Athens. And so on. This is grotesque. . . .

5 It is unfortunately true that [Athens] allowed itself to become very dirty and polluted in the 20th century, and as a result the remaining sculptures and statues on the Parthenon were nastily eroded by "acid rain." . . . But gradually and now impressively, the Greeks have been living up to their responsibilities. Beginning in 1992, the endangered marbles were removed from the temple, given careful cleaning with ultraviolet and infra-red lasers, and placed in a climate-controlled interior. . . .

6 About a thousand feet southeast of the temple [is] the astonishing new Acropolis Museum. . . . With 10 times the space of the old repository, it display[s] all the marvels that go with the temples on top of the hill. Most important, it show[s], for the first time in centuries, how the Parthenon sculptures looked to the citizens of old. . . .

7 The British may continue in their constipated fashion to cling to what they have so crudely amputated, but . . . the Acropolis Museum has hit on the happy idea of exhibiting . . . its own original sculptures with the London-held pieces represented by beautifully copied casts. This creates a natural thirst to see the actual re-assembly completed. So, far from emptying or weakening a museum, this controversy has created another [museum], which is destined to be among Europe's finest galleries. And one day, surely, there will be an agreement to do the right thing by the world's most "right" structure.

Write an essay in which you explain how Christopher Hitchens builds an argument to persuade his audience that the original Parthenon sculptures should be returned to Greece. In your essay, analyze how Hitchens uses one or more of the features listed in the box above (or features of your own choice) to strengthen the logic and persuasiveness of his argument. Be sure that your analysis focuses on the most relevant features of the passage.

Your essay should not explain whether you agree with Hitchens's claims, but rather explain how Hitchens builds an argument to persuade his audience.

This page represents the back cover of the Practice Essay.

CollegeBoard

SAT PRACTICE ANSWER SHEET

COMPLETE MARK ● EXAMPLES OF INCOMPLETE MARKS 

It is recommended that you use a No. 2 pencil. It is very important that you fill in the entire circle darkly and completely. If you change your response, erase as completely as possible. Incomplete marks or erasures may affect your score.

TEST NUMBER

ENTER TEST NUMBER

For instance, for Practice Test #1, fill in the circle for 0 in the first column and for 1 in the second column.

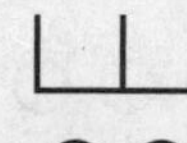

	Column 1	Column 2
0	○	○
1	○	○
2	○	○
3	○	○
4	○	○
5	○	○
6	○	○
7	○	○
8	○	○
9	○	○

SECTION 1

	A B C D		A B C D		A B C D		A B C D
1	○ ○ ○ ○	14	○ ○ ○ ○	27	○ ○ ○ ○	40	○ ○ ○ ○
2	○ ○ ○ ○	15	○ ○ ○ ○	28	○ ○ ○ ○	41	○ ○ ○ ○
3	○ ○ ○ ○	16	○ ○ ○ ○	29	○ ○ ○ ○	42	○ ○ ○ ○
4	○ ○ ○ ○	17	○ ○ ○ ○	30	○ ○ ○ ○	43	○ ○ ○ ○
5	○ ○ ○ ○	18	○ ○ ○ ○	31	○ ○ ○ ○	44	○ ○ ○ ○
6	○ ○ ○ ○	19	○ ○ ○ ○	32	○ ○ ○ ○	45	○ ○ ○ ○
7	○ ○ ○ ○	20	○ ○ ○ ○	33	○ ○ ○ ○	46	○ ○ ○ ○
8	○ ○ ○ ○	21	○ ○ ○ ○	34	○ ○ ○ ○	47	○ ○ ○ ○
9	○ ○ ○ ○	22	○ ○ ○ ○	35	○ ○ ○ ○	48	○ ○ ○ ○
10	○ ○ ○ ○	23	○ ○ ○ ○	36	○ ○ ○ ○	49	○ ○ ○ ○
11	○ ○ ○ ○	24	○ ○ ○ ○	37	○ ○ ○ ○	50	○ ○ ○ ○
12	○ ○ ○ ○	25	○ ○ ○ ○	38	○ ○ ○ ○	51	○ ○ ○ ○
13	○ ○ ○ ○	26	○ ○ ○ ○	39	○ ○ ○ ○	52	○ ○ ○ ○

Download the College Board SAT Practice app to instantly score this test. Learn more at sat.org/scoring.

SAT PRACTICE ANSWER SHEET

COMPLETE MARK ● EXAMPLES OF INCOMPLETE MARKS 

It is recommended that you use a No. 2 pencil. It is very important that you fill in the entire circle darkly and completely. If you change your response, erase as completely as possible. Incomplete marks or erasures may affect your score.

SECTION 2

1 A B C D	10 A B C D	19 A B C D	28 A B C D	37 A B C D
2 A B C D	11 A B C D	20 A B C D	29 A B C D	38 A B C D
3 A B C D	12 A B C D	21 A B C D	30 A B C D	39 A B C D
4 A B C D	13 A B C D	22 A B C D	31 A B C D	40 A B C D
5 A B C D	14 A B C D	23 A B C D	32 A B C D	41 A B C D
6 A B C D	15 A B C D	24 A B C D	33 A B C D	42 A B C D
7 A B C D	16 A B C D	25 A B C D	34 A B C D	43 A B C D
8 A B C D	17 A B C D	26 A B C D	35 A B C D	44 A B C D
9 A B C D	18 A B C D	27 A B C D	36 A B C D	

If you're scoring with our mobile app we recommend that you cut these pages out of the back of this book. The scoring does best with a flat page.

SAT PRACTICE ANSWER SHEET

COMPLETE MARK

EXAMPLES OF INCOMPLETE MARKS 

It is recommended that you use a No. 2 pencil. It is very important that you fill in the entire circle darkly and completely. If you change your response, erase as completely as possible. Incomplete marks or erasures may affect your score.

SECTION 3

1 A B C D
2 A B C D
3 A B C D
4 A B C D
5 A B C D
6 A B C D
7 A B C D
8 A B C D
9 A B C D
10 A B C D
11 A B C D
12 A B C D
13 A B C D
14 A B C D
15 A B C D

Only answers that are gridded will be scored. You will not receive credit for anything written in the boxes.

16 17 18 19 20

/ . 0 1 2 3 4 5 6 7 8 9

NO CALCULATOR ALLOWED

Did you know that you can print out these test sheets from the web? Learn more at sat.org/scoring.

SAT PRACTICE ANSWER SHEET

COMPLETE MARK ● EXAMPLES OF INCOMPLETE MARKS 

It is recommended that you use a No. 2 pencil. It is very important that you fill in the entire circle darkly and completely. If you change your response, erase as completely as possible. Incomplete marks or erasures may affect your score.

SECTION 4

1 A B C D	7 A B C D	13 A B C D	19 A B C D	25 A B C D
2 A B C D	8 A B C D	14 A B C D	20 A B C D	26 A B C D
3 A B C D	9 A B C D	15 A B C D	21 A B C D	27 A B C D
4 A B C D	10 A B C D	16 A B C D	22 A B C D	28 A B C D
5 A B C D	11 A B C D	17 A B C D	23 A B C D	29 A B C D
6 A B C D	12 A B C D	18 A B C D	24 A B C D	30 A B C D

CALCULATOR ALLOWED

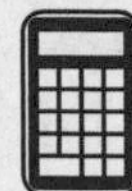

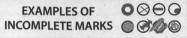

If you're using our mobile app keep in mind that bad lighting and even shadows cast over the answer sheet can affect your score. Be sure to scan this in a well-lit area for best results.

CollegeBoard

SAT PRACTICE ANSWER SHEET

COMPLETE MARK ● EXAMPLES OF INCOMPLETE MARKS 

It is recommended that you use a No. 2 pencil. It is very important that you fill in the entire circle darkly and completely. If you change your response, erase as completely as possible. Incomplete marks or erasures may affect your score.

SECTION 4 (Continued)

Only answers that are gridded will be scored. You will not receive credit for anything written in the boxes.

31

/
.
0
1
2
3
4
5
6
7
8
9

32

/
.
0
1
2
3
4
5
6
7
8
9

33

/
.
0
1
2
3
4
5
6
7
8
9

34

/
.
0
1
2
3
4
5
6
7
8
9

35

/
.
0
1
2
3
4
5
6
7
8
9

Only answers that are gridded will be scored. You will not receive credit for anything written in the boxes.

36

/
.
0
1
2
3
4
5
6
7
8
9

37

/
.
0
1
2
3
4
5
6
7
8
9

38

/
.
0
1
2
3
4
5
6
7
8
9

CALCULATOR ALLOWED

○ I understand that my essay (without my name) may be reproduced in other College Board materials. If I mark this circle, I withhold my permission to reproduce my essay for any purposes beyond score reporting and the assessment of my writing skills. Marking this circle will have no effect on my score, nor will it prevent my essay from being made available to any college to which I send my SAT scores.

IMPORTANT: **USE A NO. 2 PENCIL. DO NOT WRITE OUTSIDE THE BORDER!**
Words written outside the essay box or written in ink **WILL NOT APPEAR** in the copy sent to be scored, and your score will be affected.

PLANNING PAGE You may plan your essay in the unlined planning space below, but use only the lined pages following this one to write your essay. Any work on this planning page will not be scored.

Use pages 7 through 10 for your ESSAY →

FOR PLANNING ONLY

Use pages 7 through 10 for your ESSAY →

PLEASE DO NOT WRITE IN THIS AREA

SERIAL #

BEGIN YOUR ESSAY HERE.

You may continue on the next page.

PLEASE DO NOT WRITE IN THIS AREA

SERIAL #

DO NOT WRITE OUTSIDE OF THE BOX.

You may continue on the next page.

DO NOT WRITE OUTSIDE OF THE BOX.

You may continue on the next page.

PLEASE DO NOT WRITE IN THIS AREA

SERIAL #

DO NOT WRITE OUTSIDE OF THE BOX.

STOP.

Answer Explanations

SAT Practice Test #6

Section 1: Reading Test

QUESTION 1

Choice C is the best answer. In the first paragraph the reader is introduced to Nawab, a father of twelve daughters who feels compelled to make more money to care for his family: "he must proliferate his sources of revenue" (lines 6-7). The remainder of the paragraph focuses on the way Nawab attempts to "proliferate" those income sources by identifying some of the moneymaking schemes Nawab undertakes, including setting up a flour mill and a fish farm and attempting to fix both radios and watches.

Choice A is incorrect because even if the first paragraph does indicate that Nawab is willing to work hard to take care of his family, it does not specifically address how he interacts with his daughters emotionally. Choice B is incorrect because the first paragraph describes some of Nawab's activities but not the specifics of his schedule. Choice D is incorrect because the first paragraph introduces Harouni as Nawab's employer but does not describe his lifestyle.

QUESTION 2

Choice B is the best answer. The passage states that Nawab earned "more kicks than kudos" (line 16) for his failed attempts at fixing watches. In the context of not doing a job well, this means Nawab was not given compliments ("kudos") for his efforts but complaints ("kicks") about them.

Choices A and D are incorrect because the passage clearly states that Nawab was not successful fixing watches, which earned him a negative response ("kicks," or complaints). In this context it would be illogical to suggest that Nawab's unsuccessful efforts at fixing watches would result in the sort of positive response implied by choice A ("thrills") or choice D ("interests"). Choice C is incorrect because even though "jolts" might be unpleasant, they're not the kind of negative response one would get instead of compliments.

QUESTION 3

Choice D is the best answer. The passage states that Nawab works "like an engineer tending the boilers on a foundering steamer in an Atlantic gale" (lines 26-28) in his attempts to keep his employer comfortable. The author likely uses this image because it highlights the challenging nature of Nawab's work—work that is described in the next sentence as requiring "superhuman efforts" (line 28).

Choices A, B, and C are incorrect because the author's use of the image of an engineer working hard on a "foundering steamer" describes the effort Nawab is making in keeping his employer comfortable, not what Nawab might be dreaming about, anything to do with tube wells (which are not mentioned in the second paragraph), or that Nawab has had many different jobs in his life.

QUESTION 4

Choice A is the best answer because lines 28-32 show that Nawab is an efficient employee, stating that due to his "superhuman efforts," Nawab is able to keep his employer comfortable, or in almost "the same mechanical cocoon . . . that the landowner enjoyed in Lahore."

Choice B is incorrect because lines 40-42 describe the actions of Nawab's employer only and do not address the employer's feelings about Nawab's work. Choice C is incorrect because lines 46-49 show Nawab characterizing himself as an old and ineffective employee, not one who performs his job well. Choice D is incorrect because line 58 addresses the fact Nawab had always lived in his employer's household but not his effectiveness as an employee.

QUESTION 5

Choice C is the best answer. The main purpose of Nawab's comments in lines 43-52 is to highlight the labor and service he has provided for Harouni over the years. Nawab says "there is but one man, me, your servant" to take care of the tube wells on all Harouni's vast lands and that the extensive work has resulted in Nawab earning gray hairs on his employer's behalf.

Choice A is incorrect because even though lines 43-52 initially highlight the vastness of Harouni's lands, those lines primarily focus on Nawab's dedication and service to Harouni. Choice B is incorrect because lines 43-52 emphasize not that Nawab is competent and reliable but that he feels he is no longer able to adequately fulfill his duties. Choice D is incorrect because in lines 43-52, Nawab doesn't say he intends to quit his job, asking instead only for help doing it.

QUESTION 6

Choice D is the best answer. In lines 61-62, Nawab says to his employer that he "cannot any longer bicycle about like a bridegroom from farm to farm." In this context, Nawab uses the word "bridegroom" to imply he is no longer a young man who can easily travel such great distances on his bike.

Choices A, B, and C are incorrect because in the context of Nawab not being able to bike so far, he uses the word "bridegroom" to imply that he is no longer young, not that he is no longer in love (choice A), naive (choice B), or busy (choice C).

QUESTION 7

Choice B is the best answer. Harouni's reaction to Nawab's request for a new motorcycle can be found in lines 66-68, where the employer is said not to "particularly care one way or the other, except that it touched on his comfort—a matter of great interest to him." For Harouni, in other words, the issue of Nawab getting a new motorcycle came down to what was best for Harouni, not what was best for Nawab.

Choice A is incorrect because in the passage Harouni is said not to be particularly impressed with how hard Nawab works; he cares about the issue of the motorcycle only in regard to its effect on his own comfort. Choice C is incorrect because Harouni is said to find Nawab's speech not eloquent but "florid" (line 54), meaning flamboyant or ostentatious. Choice D is incorrect because Nawab does not threaten to quit his job but politely asks his employer to "let me go" (line 64).

QUESTION 8

Choice B is the best answer. The previous question asks why Harouni purchases his employee Nawab a new motorcycle, with the correct answer (that Harouni did so because it was in his own best interest) being supported in lines 66-68: "He didn't particularly care one way or the other, except that it touched on his comfort — a matter of great interest to him."

Choices A, C, and D are incorrect because the lines cited do not support the answer to the previous question about why Harouni buys Nawab a new motorcycle. Instead, they simply identify the issue (choice A), note that Harouni also gave Nawab money for gas (choice C), and show how the motorcycle affects Nawab's side businesses (choice D).

QUESTION 9

Choice A is the best answer. The passage states that Nawab's new motorcycle leads to the "disgust of the farm managers" (line 74).

Choices B, C, and D are incorrect because the passage specifically says Nawab's new motorcycle leads to the "disgust of the farm managers," not their happiness (choice B), envy (choice C), or indifference (choice D).

QUESTION 10

Choice D is the best answer. The passage specifically states what Nawab considers the greatest part of his getting a new motorcycle: "Best of all, now he could spend every night with his wife" (lines 81-82).

Choices A, B, and C are incorrect because the passage explicitly states that Nawab believes the best thing about his new motorcycle is that he can "spend every night with his wife," not that people start calling him "Uncle" (choice A), that he is able to expand his business (choice B), or that he is able to educate his daughters (choice C).

QUESTION 11

Choice B is the best answer. The passage states that "historically, newspapers such as *The Times* and broadcasters such as the BBC were widely regarded as the trusted shapers of authoritative agendas and conventional wisdom" (lines 27-30). But the passage goes on to say that "there is a growing feeling . . . that the news media should be 'informative rather than authoritative'" (lines 70-73). Together these lines indicate the main purpose of the passage, which is to discuss how people's perception of the news media is changing from its being an authoritative voice to simply an informative one.

Choice A is incorrect because the passage deals with changes in the way news is perceived but does not primarily focus on the technological changes that may have resulted in those or other changes. Choice C is incorrect because even if the passage implies that viewers might increasingly believe a journalist's values can affect the news stories being produced, it does not provide specific examples of that happening. Choice D is incorrect because the passage begins with the simple sentence "The news is a form of public knowledge" (line 1) and makes no attempt to refute that claim.

QUESTION 12

Choice D is the best answer. Although the passage initially states that traditional news authorities were once implicitly "trusted" (line 29) regarding the content they produced, it goes on to note that "as part of the general process of the transformation of authority . . . the demand has been for all authority to make explicit the frames of value which determine their decisions" (lines 33-38). The modern audience, in other words, wants to hear not only the stories a news organization produces but also the values that form the foundation of that organization's beliefs.

Choices A, B, and C are incorrect because lines 33-38 make clear that the expectation traditional authorities now face is the need to "make explicit the frames of value which determine their decisions," not that they shouldn't be affected by commercial interests (choice A), that they should work for the common good (choice B), or that they should consider the context of public versus private knowledge (choice C).

QUESTION 13

Choice C is the best answer. The previous question asks what expectation traditional authorities now face, with the answer being that they must make their perspectives or beliefs clear to the audience.

This is supported in lines 33-38: "As part of the general process of the transformation of authority . . . the demand has been for all authority to make explicit the frames of value which determine their decisions."

Choices A, B, and D are incorrect because the lines cited do not support the answer to the previous question about what expectation traditional authorities now face, instead contrasting private and public knowledge (choice A), explaining the complexity of news dissemination (choice B), and providing one way news has changed in modern times (choice D).

QUESTION 14

Choice C is the best answer. In lines 23-25, the passage states that "there is not always common agreement about what the public needs to know." In this context, a "common" agreement is a widespread one shared by many people.

Choices A, B, and D are incorrect because in the context of something shared by many people, the word "common" implies that it is widespread, not that it is plentiful or abundant (choice A), recognizable to others (choice B), or normal (choice D).

QUESTION 15

Choice B is the best answer. Two quotations are provided in lines 43-53, one highlighting the way editors work differently in modern times due to the demands of the audience and one offering an opinion about the perceived negative effects of that new reality of news. Those extended quotations were added by the authors most likely because they provide concrete examples of how some journalists feel about modern news dissemination.

Choice A is incorrect because the two quotations provided in lines 43-53 are not contradictory: the first offers a description of how news editors work differently in modern times, and the second describes how certain changes might affect news stories or the audience. Choices C and D are incorrect because the two quotations illustrate how some feel about the way the dissemination of news might be changing and are not used to either criticize or make suggestions.

QUESTION 16

Choice A is the best answer. The passage explains that although the major news organizations were once considered "trusted shapers" (line 29) of public knowledge, that perception is changing due to the "growing feeling . . . that the news media should be 'informative rather than authoritative'; the job of journalists should be to 'give the news as raw as it is, without putting their slant on it'; and people should be given 'sufficient information' from which 'we would be able to form opinions of our own'" (lines 70-77). In other words, the audience now wants raw facts about the world, not facts constructed in support of a certain opinion.

Choice B is incorrect because the passage presents the public as wanting information without any slant on it, not as wanting only a limited amount of information. Choices C and D are incorrect because the passage does not specifically identify the public's feelings about including quotations from authorities in news stories or how they would want journalists to handle private details that the subjects of news stories do not want revealed.

QUESTION 17

Choice D is the best answer. The previous question asks what the public is beginning to believe should be avoided in news stories, with the answer being the personal opinions or feelings of journalists. This is supported in lines 70-77: "There is a growing feeling . . . that the news media should be 'informative rather than authoritative'; the job of journalists should be to 'give the news as raw as it is, without putting their slant on it'; and people should be given 'sufficient information' from which 'we would be able to form opinions of our own.'"

Choices A, B, and C are incorrect because the lines cited do not support the answer that the modern public wants journalists to avoid personal judgments when telling news stories, instead contrasting personal or private knowledge with public knowledge (choice A), characterizing how trusted broadcasters were once viewed (choice B), and explaining how some professional journalists feel about the new reality of the news (choice C).

QUESTION 18

Choice A is the best answer. In lines 73-75, the passage states the modern belief that "the job of journalists should be to 'give the news as raw as it is, without putting their slant on it.'" In this context, the word "raw" means unfiltered or in its most basic state.

Choices B, C, and D are incorrect because in the context of news without any "slant on it," the word "raw" implies something unfiltered, not something unprotected or uncovered (choice B), severe (choice C), or untried or unproven (choice D).

QUESTION 19

Choice A is the best answer. The table shows that in 1985, 55% of respondents believed news organizations "get the facts straight," which was the highest percentage for that choice for any of the years provided.

Choices B, C, and D are incorrect because the table shows that the percentage of respondents who believed news organizations "get the facts straight" was smaller in 1992 (49%), 2003 (36%), and 2011 (25%) than in 1985 (55%).

QUESTION 20

Choice C is the best answer. The table shows that from 2003 to 2007, the percentage of people who believed news organizations "get the facts straight" rose only minimally, from 36 to 39%, while their perception of the independence and fairness of those organizations changed not at all, remaining at 23% and 26%, respectively.

Choice A is incorrect because the table indicates viewers' perceptions of the accuracy of news organizations but does not identify how many inaccurate news stories there were in any of the years listed. Choice B is incorrect because the number of people who believe news organizations "tend to favor one side" did not double between 1992 and 2003, rising only from 63% to 66%. Choice D is incorrect because the table shows that between 2007 and 2011, people's perception of the accuracy of news organizations decreased rather than increased, dropping from 39% to 25%.

QUESTION 21

Choice C is the best answer. The 2011 data in the table indicate that only 25% of respondents believed news organizations were accurate, 15% believed they were independent, and 16% believed they were fair. Combined, these data support the idea put forth in lines 69-70 that modern audiences are becoming skeptical of the authority of experts.

Choices A, B, and D are incorrect because the 2011 data in the table show the public's lack of faith in the accuracy, independence, and fairness of news organizations but do not indicate how politically involved that public was (choice A), demonstrate the claims of experts (choice B), or reveal the importance of viewer mouse clicks in modern news (choice D).

QUESTION 22

Choice B is the best answer. The first paragraph of the passage identifies and describes Texas gourd vines (line 1), but the primary focus of the passage is introduced in the first sentence of the second paragraph: "In one recent study, Nina Theis and Lynn Adler took on the specific problem of the Texas gourd — how to attract enough pollinators but not too many beetles" (lines 17-20). The remainder of the passage focuses on describing the purpose, process, and results of the recent research done on those Texas gourd vines.

Choice A is incorrect because the passage doesn't focus on the assumptions behind a theory but rather on the way in which that theory was tested. Choice C is incorrect because the passage does not present much conflicting data; most of it supports the idea there can be too much fragrance for the Texas gourd vine. Choice D is incorrect because the passage explains that the procedures used in the study conducted by Theis and Adler were "very labor intensive" (line 58) but does not necessarily present them as innovative.

QUESTION 23

Choice A is the best answer. The passage says that to test their hypothesis, the scientists "planted 168 Texas gourd vines in an Iowa field" (lines 33-34) and then ultimately walked "from flower to flower, observing each for two-minute intervals" (lines 62-63). Because the scientists gathered data by looking at and studying the plants in question, their research is best characterized as relying on direct observation.

Choices B, C, and D are incorrect because lines 62-63 make clear that the research emphasized direct observation, not historical data (choice B), expert testimony (choice C), or random sampling (choice D).

QUESTION 24

Choice D is the best answer. The passage states that by using the smell of their nectar to lure pollinators like bees, Texas gourd vines are employing an "open communication network" that attracts "not just the good guys, but . . . also . . . the bad guys" (lines 7-10). Because cucumber beetles are then identified as some of "the very bad guys" (line 12) as far as the Texas gourd plant is concerned, it can be inferred that both the beetles and the bees are attracted to the same scent.

Choices A and C are incorrect because they are not supported by the text; the passage states that cucumber beetles "chew up pollen and petals" (lines 12-13) from the Texas gourd vines but not that those vines are their "primary" food source, and the passage does not address any effects, positive or negative, that cucumber beetles experience as a result of carrying bacterial wilt disease. Choice B is incorrect because the passage states that treating the Texas gourd vines with dimethoxybenzene led to "double the normal number of beetles" (lines 65-66) but that pollinators like bees "did not prefer" (line 67) the treated flowers, which implies that cucumber beetles are not less attracted but more attracted to dimethoxybenzene than honey bees are.

QUESTION 25

Choice C is the best answer. The author indicates that it is reasonable to think that the Texas gourd plants might lure more pollinators if their smell was stronger. This is clear from lines 26-27, which state that "intuition suggests that more of that aroma should be even more appealing to bees."

Choices A and D are incorrect because lines 26-27 support the idea that it was initially thought that Texas gourd vines could lure more pollinators through "more of that aroma," not by lacking an aroma (choice A) or giving off a more varied aroma (choice D). Choice B is incorrect because bees are the only pollinators specifically discussed in the passage, and there is no suggestion that targeting other insects would attract more bees.

QUESTION 26

Choice A is the best answer. The passage explains that as part of their research, the scientists "made half the plants more fragrant by tucking dimethoxybenzene-treated swabs deep inside their flowers. Each treated flower emitted about 45 times more fragrance than a normal one" (lines 35-39). In this context, a flower that was "treated" would be one that was changed or altered.

Choices B, C, and D are incorrect because in the context of a flower having a compound like dimethoxybenzene added to it, the word "treated" means changed or altered, not returned to normal (choice B), given (choice C), or kept for future use (choice D).

QUESTION 27

Choice D is the best answer. According to the passage, Theis reasons that honey bees were likely repelled not by the enhanced fragrance of the dimethoxybenzene-treated flowers but "by the abundance of beetles" (lines 71-72) present on such flowers. She was able to make that assumption because the honey bees were able to choose between both normal flowers and fragrance-enhanced flowers without any beetles on them. That the bees were able to do so is evident from the passage's description of one of the conditions of the study: "every half hour throughout the experiments, the team plucked all the beetles off of half the fragrance-enhanced flowers and half the control flowers, allowing bees to respond to the blossoms with and without interference by beetles" (lines 45-50).

Choice A is incorrect because the passage states only that the scientists observed the bees and beetles on the flowers as soon as they opened (lines 59-61), not both before and after they opened. Choice B is incorrect because although the passage does state that the experiment only took place during the "August flowering season" (line 35), there is no suggestion that this was a variable in the experiment or had any effect on it. Choice C is incorrect because comparing gourds based on the type of pollination is not related to the issue of what repelled bees from the fragrance-enhanced plants.

QUESTION 28

Choice A is the best answer. The previous question asks what Theis and Adler did to allow Theis to theorize that the bees were repelled not by the enhanced fragrance of certain flowers but by the excessive number of beetles on them, with the answer (they give the bees the chance to visit both normal and fragrance-enhanced flowers that did not have beetles on them) being supported in lines 45-50: "So every half hour throughout the experiments, the team plucked all the beetles off of half the fragrance-enhanced flowers and half the control flowers, allowing bees to respond to the blossoms with and without interference by beetles."

Choices B, C, and D are incorrect because the lines cited do not support the answer to the previous question about what allowed Theis and Adler to theorize that the bees were repelled not by fragrance but by insects, instead highlighting a variable that didn't directly address the effect of fragrance on bees (choice B), describing the timing of one of the steps undertaken in the experiment (choice C), and discussing an aspect of gourd growth that was not related to the question of why bees may or may not have wanted to visit fragrance-enhanced flowers (choice D).

QUESTION 29

Choice A is the best answer. The first six paragraphs (lines 1-64) of the passage introduce a plant (the Texas gourd vine) and its problem (luring enough insects to pollinate it but not too many of those that will harm it) and then describe a study undertaken to deal with that problem. After the specifics of that experiment are described in detail, the results are explained and summarized in the seventh and eighth paragraphs (lines 65-84): "What they saw was double the normal number of beetles. . . . Squash bees were indifferent, and honey bees visited enhanced flowers less often. . . . That added up to less reproduction for fragrance-enhanced flowers" (lines 65-76).

Choice B is incorrect because Theis and Adler's hypothesis (that more fragrance would make the flowers "even more appealing to bees," line 27) is found in the third paragraph (lines 26-40). Choice C is incorrect because Theis and Adler's methods are described in the third through sixth paragraphs (lines 26-64), not the seventh and eighth (lines 65-84). Choice D is incorrect because the seventh and eighth paragraphs detail the results in an experiment but do not focus on the researchers' reasoning.

QUESTION 30

Choice B is the best answer. To be "indifferent" is to be apathetic, or without care or concern. In the context of an experiment that tested whether or not insects preferred normally scented flowers or ones with enhanced fragrance, the description of the squash bees as "indifferent" (line 68) implies they did not care about the scents and were equally drawn to both types of flowers.

Choice A is incorrect because "indifference" suggests the amount of concern one has about something but not anything to do with physical capabilities (such as being able to distinguish between the flowers). Choice C is incorrect because "indifference" suggests that one has no preference. Choice D is incorrect because the squash bees are said to be "indifferent" to certain flowers based on their fragrance, not on the number of beetles that may or may not be on them.

QUESTION 31

Choice B is the best answer. Theis and Adler's research clearly provided an answer to the question of why there is an upper limit on the intensity of the aroma emitted by Texas gourd plants. This can be inferred from the last paragraph, which describes their experiment as having been able to "provide a reason that Texas gourd plants never evolved to produce a stronger scent" (lines 85-86).

Choice A is incorrect because Theis and Adler's research was not able to show how to increase pollinator visits to the Texas gourd vine; instead, as the passage explains, the results of their experiment showed that "pollinators, to their surprise, did not prefer the highly scented flowers" (lines 67-68). Choice C is incorrect because Theis and Adler's research was not able to explain how hand pollination rescued fruit weight, a finding the passage describes as "a hard-to-interpret result" (line 83). Choice D is incorrect because the passage never indicates that the flowers stop producing fragrance when beetles are present.

QUESTION 32

Choice D is the best answer. The previous question asks what question from among the answer choices Theis and Adler's research was able to answer regarding Texas gourd vines. The answer (they determined why there was an upper limit to the amount of fragrance produced) is supported in lines 85-86: "The new results provide a reason that Texas gourd plants never evolved to produce a stronger scent."

Choices A, B, and C are incorrect because the lines cited do not support the answer to the previous question about what Theis and Adler's research revealed about Texas gourd vines, instead explaining the goal of the experiment undertaken (choice A), identifying some of the fragrance compounds found in the plant's aroma (choice B), and describing results related to hand pollination rather than fragrance (choice C).

QUESTION 33

Choice B is the best answer. In Passage 1, Lincoln asserts that citizens of the United States should never break the laws of their land, for any reason, because to do so undermines the nation's values. This is clearly demonstrated when he says, "let every man remember that to violate the law, is to trample on the blood of his father, and to tear the character of his own, and his children's liberty" (lines 9-12).

Choice A is incorrect because Lincoln's argument regarding bad laws, as presented in Passage 1, is not that breaking the law would slow the repeal of bad laws but that such laws "should be repealed as soon as possible" (line 30). Choice C is incorrect because Lincoln's argument regarding "mob law" in Passage 1 is not that breaking the law will lead to mob rule but instead that "there is no grievance that is a fit object of redress by mob law" (lines 36-37). Choice D is incorrect because in his speech Lincoln doesn't discuss divisions between social groups.

QUESTION 34

Choice A is the best answer. The previous question asks what Lincoln believes is the result of breaking the laws, with the answer being that such actions undermine a nation's values. This is supported in lines 9-12: "let every man remember that to violate the law, is to trample on the blood of his father, and to tear the character of his own, and his children's liberty."

Choices B, C, and D are incorrect because the lines cited do not support the answer to the previous question regarding what Lincoln contends happens when citizens break the law, instead explaining exactly which groups Lincoln believes should vow to follow the laws (choice B), illustrating how Lincoln believes unjust laws should be dealt with (choice C), and stating Lincoln's belief that no law is ever improved through mob rule (choice D).

QUESTION 35

Choice D is the best answer. In lines 24-25, Lincoln says, "I so pressingly urge a strict observance of all the laws." In this context, the word "urge" most nearly means advocate, because when Lincoln urges people to obey the laws, he is pleading in favor of them doing so.

Choices A and C are incorrect because in the context of lines 24-25 ("I so pressingly urge a strict observance of all the laws"), to urge that laws be followed is to advocate for them to be obeyed, not to speed up such adherence (choice A) or make such adherence necessary (choice C). Choice B is incorrect because Lincoln is asking people to follow the laws but not directly causing people to obey them.

QUESTION 36

Choice D is the best answer. After counseling citizens "never to violate in the least particular, the laws of the country" (lines 3-4), Lincoln begins the second paragraph by making another point: "When I so pressingly urge a strict observance of all the laws, let me not be understood as saying there are no bad laws, nor that grievances may not arise, for the redress of which, no legal provisions have been made" (lines 24-28). This sentence is an attempt on Lincoln's part to anticipate a potential misinterpretation of his position ("let me not be understood") and to correct that misinterpretation. Lincoln doesn't want people to believe he is saying all laws are always good, but rather that those laws need to be followed as long as they are on the books.

Choices A and B are incorrect because the sentence in lines 24-28 does not raise and refute a possible counterargument to Lincoln's argument or identify a shortcoming of his argument, but instead represents an attempt on Lincoln's part to make sure he is not misunderstood. Choice C is incorrect because that sentence does not acknowledge and provide support for a central assumption of Lincoln's argument but instead looks at a different aspect of the issue.

QUESTION 37

Choice A is the best answer. In the passage Lincoln states his belief that any laws that "continue in force, for the sake of example, they should be religiously observed" (lines 31-32). In this context, "observed" most nearly means followed, as Lincoln is urging citizens to heed or follow the country's laws.

Choices B, C, and D are incorrect because in the context of Lincoln advocating that laws be religiously "observed," he means those laws should be followed, not that they should be studied closely (choice B), considered at length (choice C), or merely recognized (choice D).

QUESTION 38

Choice D is the best answer. Passage 2 begins with Thoreau's assertion that "unjust laws exist" (line 45). His philosophy regarding how to deal with those unjust laws is evident in lines 58-59: "If the injustice is part of the necessary friction of the machine of government, let it go, let it go." Thoreau believes, in other words, that some injustices are an unfortunate part of normal governance and just need to be endured ("let it go, let it go").

Choice A is incorrect because Thoreau does not say some unjust aspects of government can be fixed easily or that they are merely superficial. Choice B is incorrect because Thoreau does not argue that such injustices are subtle and should be studied, but rather that in certain cases it is best to "let it go, let it go" (line 59), while in other cases one should act or "break the law" (line 66). Choice C is incorrect because Thoreau does not say that any such unjust aspects of government are beneficial or helpful.

QUESTION 39

Choice C is the best answer. The previous question asks what Thoreau feels about some unjust aspects of government, with the answer being that he finds them inevitable and something that needs to be endured. This is supported in lines 58-59: "If the injustice is part of the necessary friction of the machine of government, let it go, let it go."

Choices A, B, and D are incorrect because the lines cited do not support the answer to the previous question about Thoreau's thoughts regarding certain injustices in government, instead asking a theoretical question about how one should respond to unjust laws (choice A), providing an observation about how some view acting out against unjust laws (choice B), and acknowledging that in some questions of conscience, one may or may not choose to act (choice D).

QUESTION 40

Choice C is the best answer. In Passage 1, Lincoln makes clear his belief that individuals should always heed the laws: "Let every American . . . swear . . . never to violate in the least particular, the laws of the country" (lines 1-4). Even bad laws, he states, "while they continue in force, for the sake of example, they should be religiously observed" (lines 30-32). In Passage 2, Thoreau is less rigid in his beliefs regarding the need for individuals to heed the laws of the country, arguing at times that some laws should be broken: "but if it is of such a nature that it requires you to be the agent of injustice to another, then, I say, break the law" (lines 64-66). While Lincoln and Thoreau can therefore be said to disagree about the moral imperative to follow existing laws, both passages advance an opinion regarding the need to follow or not follow all of the country's laws.

Choice A is incorrect because the passages do not make arguments about differences between legal duties and moral imperatives but rather address the need to follow (or not) the laws of a land. Choice B is incorrect because although both passages address the question of changing existing laws in the United States, that question is only a secondary consideration within the larger debate about following unjust laws. Choice D is incorrect because neither passage addresses the standards for determining whether or not laws are just, only whether laws should be heeded or not.

QUESTION 41

Choice B is the best answer. In Passage 2, Thoreau says that if a law "is of such a nature that it requires you to be the agent of injustice to another, then, I say, break the law" (lines 64-66). It is clear from Passage 1 that Lincoln would reject this stance since he argues that individuals should never break the law ("Let every American . . . swear . . . never to violate in the least particular, the laws of the country," lines 1-4) and should wait for bad laws to be repealed rather than violate them ("bad laws, if they exist, should be repealed . . . still while they continue . . . they should be religiously observed," lines 29-32).

Choices A and C are incorrect because in Passage 1, Lincoln is absolutely clear that all laws "should be religiously observed" (line 32); he does not describe anyone's suggestion to break the law as either excusable (choice A) or honorable (choice C). Choice D is incorrect because it is not supported by the passage, as Lincoln does not discuss the core principles of the Constitution in Passage 1.

QUESTION 42

Choice D is the best answer. In Passage 1, Lincoln uses abolitionism solely as an example to illustrate the argument he is making about heeding the law: "In any case that arises, as for instance, the promulgation of abolitionism, one of two positions is necessarily true" (lines 37-39). In Passage 2, Thoreau does the same thing by noting that "those who call themselves Abolitionists should at once effectually withdraw their support . . . from the government" (lines 79-82). Although Lincoln and Thoreau use the cause of abolitionism to argue different points, a commonality they share is that neither embraces the cause personally in the passage; Lincoln simply uses it as an example ("as for instance") while Thoreau specifically talks of *other people* "who call themselves Abolitionists."

Choice A is incorrect because in Passage 1, Lincoln argues against drastic action, saying that even in the case of abolitionism, such a response is not "necessary, justifiable, or excusable" (line 44). Choice B is incorrect because it's not accurate to say abolitionism was central to the arguments, only that each used that subject as an example. Choice C is incorrect because neither Lincoln nor Thoreau offers an opinion about whether or not abolitionism will gain widespread acceptance, instead they incorporate it only as an example in their discussions of just and unjust laws.

QUESTION 43

Choice C is the best answer. The first three paragraphs of the passage discuss the steps by which the cost of solar energy has dropped in recent years. The last four paragraphs are largely concerned with describing some of the new technology in the solar energy field, with each paragraph focusing on a specific advancement and its cost-saving potential. Therefore, the passage as a whole can be regarded as an objective overview of the solar panel industry delivered by a journalist covering the field.

Choices A and D are incorrect because the author does not present himself as either a consumer who plans to buy solar panels or a hobbyist with a personal interest in solar panel technology. Rather, the author focuses on developments in solar technology. Choice B is incorrect because the passage does not discuss research methods used in the solar panel field but rather the technologies that exist in the field.

QUESTION 44

Choice A is the best answer. In the context of a description of the solar panel manufacturing industry as being "in the doldrums because supply far exceeds demand" (lines 2-3), to refer to the market as "poor" (line 4) implies that it is a weak, or slow, market.

Choices B, C, and D are incorrect because in the context of a solar panel manufacturing industry that is "in the doldrums," to refer to a market as "poor" implies that it is a weak market, not a humble one (choice B), a pitiable one (choice C), or an obsolete or outdated one (choice D).

QUESTION 45

Choice C is the best answer. The passage explains that the solar panel industry has sought to reduce the expense and boost the efficiency of solar technology: "All parts of the silicon solar panel industry have been looking for ways to cut costs and improve the power output of solar panels, and that's led to steady cost reductions" (lines 27-30). It can reasonably be inferred from these lines that many in the industry feel that current solar technology is both too costly and too inefficient.

Choice A is incorrect because the passage explains how solar panels work but never states or implies that consumers do not understand the technology. Choice B is incorrect because while the passage explains how two-sided solar cells can increase solar electric output, it does not suggest that they have any existing or possible weaknesses. Choice D is incorrect because the passage characterizes Willow Glass as entirely promising and doesn't imply that it is not efficient enough to be marketed.

QUESTION 46

Choice D is the best answer. The previous question asks what can be inferred from the passage about beliefs in the solar panel industry, with the answer being that many in the industry believe current solar technology is too expensive and too inefficient. This is supported in lines 27-30: "All parts of the silicon solar panel industry have been looking for ways to cut costs and improve the power output of solar panels, and that's led to steady cost reductions."

Choices A, B, and C are incorrect because the lines cited do not support the answer to the previous question, which is that much of the solar panel industry believes current solar technology is too expensive and inefficient. Choice A highlights the industry's current limited sales. Choice B addresses the high cost of solar panels but not their inefficiency. Choice C addresses a potential decrease in the cost of solar panels and does not mention efficiency.

QUESTION 47

Choice B is the best answer. The passage explains that light that would otherwise be lost in a one-sided solar panel system could be harvested by two-sided solar panels: "That light reflects onto the back of the panels and could be harvested to increase the power output" (lines 61-62). It can thus be inferred that two-sided panels' absorption of this reflected light will likely increase the efficiency of solar electricity units.

Choices A, C, and D are incorrect because the passage explains only that two-sided solar panels can raise efficiency by harvesting reflected light, not that they can raise efficiency because they take little energy to operate (choice A), are cost-effective (choice C), or keep sunlight from reaching the ground (choice D).

QUESTION 48

Choice B is the best answer. The previous question asks how two-sided solar panels can raise the efficiency of solar electricity units, with the answer being they can increase solar power input by catching excess reflected light. This is supported in lines 61-62: "That light reflects onto the back of the panels and could be harvested to increase the power output."

Choices A, C, and D are incorrect because the lines cited do not support the answer to the previous question about how two-sided solar panels can raise the efficiency of solar electricity units, instead highlighting that some sunlight is missed by current units (choice A), explaining why two-sided solar panels work well in sand (choice C), and projecting how much more effective those two-sided solar panels could be (choice D).

QUESTION 49

Choice D is the best answer. In lines 69-71, the passage states that "even longer-term, Green is betting on silicon, aiming to take advantage of the huge reductions in cost already seen with the technology." In this context, the phrase "betting on" most nearly means "optimistic about," as the sentence implies that Green has positive expectations for silicon use now and in the future.

Choice A is incorrect because "dabbling in" a subject implies being only minimally involved with it, but in lines 69-71, Green is shown to be committed to silicon use. Choice B is incorrect because in this context the phrase "betting on" is figurative and implies believing in something, not actually being involved with games of chance. Choice C is incorrect because Green is said to want to "take advantage" of silicon use, meaning he does not intend to switch from it.

QUESTION 50

Choice B is the best answer. The passage concludes by stating that "the challenge is to produce good connections between these semiconductors, something made challenging by the arrangement of silicon atoms in crystalline silicon" (lines 81-84). As this last sentence identifies an ongoing issue faced by the solar panel industry and describes that issue as a "challenging" one, the sentence mainly serves to identify a problem or hurdle that must be dealt with by the industry.

Choices A, C, and D are incorrect because the main point of the passage's last sentence is that there is a "challenge" or hurdle that the solar panel industry has to deal with; the sentence doesn't express concerns about what a material won't be able to do (choice A), make predictions (choice C), or introduce a new idea for study (choice D).

QUESTION 51

Choice D is the best answer. Figure 2 shows that in 2009, the US average electricity cost per megawatt-hour (MWh) was $120. Of the projected 2017 energy costs for fuels listed in figure 1, the one closest to the 2009 US average electricity cost 120 dollars per megawatt-hour is the projected cost of advanced nuclear energy, estimated at just below 125 dollars per megawatt-hour.

Choices A, B, and C are incorrect because figure 1 shows the projected energy costs of natural gas, wind (onshore), and conventional coal as just below 75 dollars per megawatt-hour, 100 dollars per megawatt-hour, and approximately 105 dollars per megawatt-hour, respectively. None of these costs is as close to the 2009 US average electricity cost of 120 dollars per megawatt-hour as the projected 2017 cost of advanced nuclear energy, which is just below 125 dollars per megawatt-hour.

QUESTION 52

Choice B is the best answer. Figure 2 shows that the dropping cost of solar photovoltaic power per megawatt-hour is projected to intersect with the 2009 US average electricity cost of 120 dollars per megawatt-hour in the year 2020.

Choice A is incorrect because figure 2 projects that the solar photovoltaic cost per megawatt-hour in 2018 will be approximately $140, which is more than the 2009 US average electricity cost of 120 dollars per megawatt-hour. Choices C and D are incorrect because figure 2 projects that the solar photovoltaic cost per megawatt-hour will be around $90 in 2025 and $70 in 2027, both of which are less than the 2009 US average electricity cost of 120 dollars per megawatt-hour.

Section 2: Writing and Language Test

QUESTION 1

Choice D is the best answer because a comma is needed to separate the main independent clause ("In the winter . . . Lake 227") from the dependent clause that describes the lake. The pronoun "one" is used correctly to refer to its antecedent "Lake 227."

Choice A is incorrect because it creates a comma splice (two independent clauses joined by only a comma). Choices B and C are incorrect because both choices create sentence fragments.

QUESTION 2

Choice A is the best answer because the comma is used correctly to separate the introductory dependent clause ("While . . . irresponsible") from the independent clause that follows it.

Choices B, C, and D are incorrect because the comma in each is misplaced. Choices B and D lack a comma where one is needed after the dependent clause ("While . . . irresponsible"). In choice C, while a comma is provided after "irresponsible," there is an unnecessary comma after "and."

QUESTION 3

Choice D is the best answer because it most clearly and concisely combines the sentences using the correct punctuation. This choice eliminates unnecessary words, and the commas are placed correctly between the clauses.

Choice A is incorrect because the phrase "the result being that it" is wordy and could be replaced with the single word "which." Choice B is incorrect because the words "algal blooms cause oxygen depletion" need not be repeated. Choice C is incorrect because there is unnecessary repetition of the words "oxygen depletion" and "algal blooms."

QUESTION 4

Choice B is the best answer because the colon is used properly to introduce an independent clause ("it was . . . Erie") that explains or elaborates on the information that came before in the sentence.

Choice A is incorrect because the colon is misplaced. It should be placed after the word "green," not after "with." Choice C is incorrect because the dash is not placed correctly. If it were placed after the word "green," it could be used. Choice D is incorrect because the comma creates a comma splice. A comma cannot be used without a conjunction to join two independent clauses.

QUESTION 5

Choice C is the best answer because it contains the best transition between the two paragraphs. The previous paragraphs describe an experiment that Schindler and Brunskill conducted in Lake 227. This paragraph is about an experiment they performed in Lake 226. Only choice C provides a transition that introduces the new experiment performed in Lake 226.

Choice A is incorrect because it contains no specific reference to the previous paragraph and is too general to be tied to this paragraph. Choices B and D are incorrect because they contain unnecessary details that do not connect the ideas in the paragraphs.

QUESTION 6

Choice B is the best answer because it is concise. It does not repeat the idea of addition.

Choices A, C, and D are incorrect because they are repetitive. The conjunction "and" is sufficient after "they added just nitrates" to indicate that "a source of carbon" was also added. Choice A needlessly contains "was added." In choice C "plus also" and in choice D "also adding" are similarly repetitive.

QUESTION 7

Choice A is the best answer because the singular past tense verb "was teeming" agrees in number with the singular subject "half" and is consistent with the other past tense verbs in the paragraph.

Choices B and C are incorrect because they contain plural verbs instead of the singular one that is needed to agree with the singular subject "half." Choice D is incorrect because it contains a present tense verb that is inconsistent with the past tense verbs in the paragraph.

QUESTION 8

Choice C is the best answer because the verb "published" most effectively indicates the relationship between research findings and a journal, *Science*. Scientific research is published in scientific journals.

Choices A, B, and D are incorrect because they don't feature the specific vocabulary required, and the tone of the answer choices is too informal for the content of the passage.

QUESTION 9

Choice D is the best answer because "subsequently" logically indicates that after the research demonstrated a clear correlation between the growth of blue-green algae and the introduction of phosphates into the water, Canadian legislators passed laws banning phosphates in laundry detergent.

Choices A, B, and C are incorrect because the transitional phrase "for example" and the conjunctive adverbs "similarly" and "however" do not indicate a logical relationship between what the research demonstrated and what the Canadian legislators did with that knowledge.

QUESTION 10

Choice B is the best answer because it deals with a "policy outcome" related to the research. The adoption of legislation to reduce or eliminate phosphates in detergents is a policy outcome (a change in official policy concerning detergents) that was clearly informed by Schindler and Brunskill's research.

Choices A, C, and D are incorrect because they do not mention legislation or policies that were adopted as a result of Schindler and Brunskill's research on the effects of phosphates in laundry detergents.

QUESTION 11

Choice C is the best answer because it offers a counterargument to the previous sentence's claim in favor of "experiments like these." Acknowledging that "scientists should not be allowed to randomly perform experiments on just any body of water" shows that the writer is aware of the potential problems with these experiments.

Choices A, B, and D are incorrect because none of them offers a counterargument. They all make factual statements.

QUESTION 12

Choice D is the best answer because it correctly provides the plural noun "stages" and the singular possessive pronoun "its" (no apostrophe).

Choices A and C are incorrect because a possessive pronoun is needed to replace the proper noun "Tower of Pisa," not the contraction "it's." Choices B and C are incorrect because there is no reason to make "stage" possessive; nothing belongs to it.

QUESTION 13

Choice A is the best answer because the conjunctive adverb "indeed" appropriately points back to and elaborates on the fact provided in the previous sentence (that the Tower has been leaning from the very beginning).

Choices B, C, and D are incorrect because they do not accurately present the relationship between the first and second sentences. Choice B, "therefore," indicates that what follows is a consequence of what came before. Choice C, "nevertheless," and choice D, "however," suggest that what follows contrasts with what was stated previously.

QUESTION 14

Choice B is the best answer because the participle "attracting" introduces a dependent clause ("attracting . . . world") that appropriately modifies the noun "icon."

Choice A is incorrect because it creates a comma splice. A comma cannot be used without a conjunction to separate two independent clauses. Choice C is incorrect because the possessive pronoun "its" makes no sense in the context of the sentence. Choice D is incorrect because a semicolon is used to join two independent clauses, not an independent and a dependent clause.

QUESTION 15

Choice C is the best answer because it would be appropriate to characterize a famous and unusual building like the Tower of Pisa as "one of the greatest architectural oddities in the world."

Choices A, B, and D are incorrect. The words "weirdnesses," "deviations," and "abnormalities" would all result in inappropriate characterizations. The Tower is a beloved icon and tourist magnet; as such, it is more fitting to describe it as an architectural oddity than as an architectural weirdness, architectural deviation, or architectural abnormality.

QUESTION 16

Choice B is the best answer because it confirms that the sentence should be added and provides the appropriate reason: it establishes a key shift in the passage between the introduction of the tower and the discussion of recent attempts to save it.

Choice A is incorrect because the suggested sentence does not repeat a previous idea. Choices C and D are incorrect because the sentence should be added. The suggested sentence does not contain irrelevant information that interrupts the flow of the paragraph, nor does it repeat information.

QUESTION 17

Choice A is the best answer because the comma is used correctly after the prepositional phrase "in 1990" to introduce the independent clause "Italy's government closed the tower. . . ."

Choices B and C are incorrect because each places a comma between the subject "government" and the verb "closed." Choice D is incorrect because a comma can be used, but not a colon, after an introductory prepositional phrase.

QUESTION 18

Choice C is the best answer because it supports the main point of the paragraph. The paragraph suggests that the committee's goal was to maintain the tower's "aesthetic" by reducing (but not eliminating) the tilt without ruining the tower's appearance or causing it to fall.

Choices A, B, and D are incorrect because none of the choices supports the main point of the paragraph — the need to both keep the tower from falling and maintain its charming appearance. Choice A repeats an idea from earlier in the passage. Choices B and D provide information that is only loosely related to the paragraph's discussion of efforts to save the tower.

QUESTION 19

Choice D is the best answer because deleting "he is" eliminates the comma splice that exists in the original sentence. Two independent clauses cannot be joined by only a comma.

Choice A is incorrect because two independent clauses cannot be joined by only a comma. Choice B is incorrect because it creates a comma splice and also needlessly repeats Burland's name. Choice C is incorrect because "his being" is unnecessary and unidiomatic in this context.

QUESTION 20

Choice D is the best answer because the earlier phrase "a years-long process" is sufficient to indicate that Burland's work spanned several years.

Choices A, B, and C are incorrect because they all repeat information provided in the earlier phrase "a years-long process."

QUESTION 21

Choice A is the best answer because the verb "advocated" and the participle "using" are appropriate in this context: "advocated" functions as the main verb and "using" introduces the clause that tells what Burland advocated.

Choices B and C are incorrect because they are unidiomatic. Choice D doesn't provide a main verb necessary to create an independent clause before the semicolon.

QUESTION 22

Choice A is the best answer because sentence 5 introduces Burland's plan for using gravity to straighten the tower—a plan that is presented in detail in the subsequent sentences 2, 3, and 4.

Choices B and C are incorrect because if sentence 5 were to be placed after either sentence 2 or sentence 3, the sequencing and logic of the paragraph would be impaired. Choice D is incorrect because if sentence 5 were to be deleted, a key aspect of the plan — its use of gravity to straighten the tower — would never be mentioned. The reader would then have to infer what Burland was doing by "drilling out small amounts of soil from under the tower."

QUESTION 23

Choice B is the best answer because the main point of the paragraph is that the supply of physicians in the United States is not expected to keep up with the demand or need for them in the future. Choice B introduces the idea that it may become increasingly difficult for Americans to find a physician.

Choice A is not correct because it discusses "paramedics," health care workers who are not mentioned elsewhere in the paragraph. Choice C is incorrect because it does not introduce the doctor shortage problem, which is the main topic of the paragraph. Choice D is incorrect because the paragraph is not focused on the costs of health care.

QUESTION 24

Choice A is the best answer because "keep pace" is an appropriate idiomatic expression that clearly indicates the writer's concern that the supply of doctors won't be able to match the growing demand for them.

Choices B, C, and D are incorrect because they are unidiomatic in the context of the sentence. The sentence discusses the mismatch between the "increased demand for care" and the limited "supply of physicians." The writer is concerned with the extent to which supply can grow to meet the growth in demand — or, in other words, "keep pace" with increased demand. The phrases "maintain the tempo," "get in line," and "move along" are inappropriate to convey this idea.

QUESTION 25

Choice B is the best answer because "bolstering" means supporting, which is appropriate in the context of "medical-college enrollments." It makes sense in a discussion of a doctor shortage to mention the idea of providing support for enrollments — that is, maintaining and perhaps increasing the numbers of students enrolled in medical colleges.

Choices A and D are incorrect because they are excessively casual and unclear in context: it is not clear what it would mean for "medical-college enrollments" (the numbers of students enrolled in medical colleges) to be amped or revved up. Choice C is incorrect because it would be inappropriate to describe enrollments as being aroused.

QUESTION 26

Choice B is the best answer because it provides an appropriate reason for adding the sentence. In context, the sentence sets up the "several factors" that follow in the paragraph: the services that a PA can provide, the monetary advantages associated with employing a PA, and the short training period required for becoming a PA.

Choice A is incorrect because the sentence does not introduce a counterargument; rather, it supports the claim made in the previous sentence. Choices C and D are incorrect because the sentence should be added.

QUESTION 27

Choice C is the best answer because the plural possessive pronoun "their" correctly refers to its plural antecedent "PAs."

Choice A is incorrect because the word "there" does not show possession and does not make sense in the context of the sentence. Choice B is incorrect because the contraction "they're" does not show possession and does not make sense in the context of the sentence. Choice D is incorrect because the singular pronoun phrase "his or her" does not agree in number with the plural antecedent "PAs."

QUESTION 28

Choice D is the best answer because the comma is used correctly to separate the items in the list of jobs that PAs can perform.

Choice A is incorrect because a colon should not be used to separate items in a list. Choice B is incorrect because, while semicolons may be used to separate items in a list, they must be used consistently (that is, after "conditions" as well as after "surgeries"). Choice C is incorrect because a comma should not be used after the conjunction "and" in a list of items.

QUESTION 29

Choice B is the best answer because the parentheses are used correctly to enclose information that is interesting but not essential to the sentence. If the parenthetical information were to be deleted, the sentence would still make sense.

Choice A is incorrect because a comma or other punctuation is necessary to separate "well compensated" from the nonessential clause "earning in 2012 a median annual salary of $90,930." Choice C is incorrect because a comma is necessary after "$90,930" to set off the clause from the rest of the sentence. Choice D is incorrect because a colon is typically preceded by an independent clause and because a nonessential clause should be set off from the sentence by matching punctuation, such as two commas or parentheses.

QUESTION 30

Choice C is the best answer because "that for" agrees with the singular antecedent "period" and compares two similar things: the training period for PAs and that (the training period) for physicians.

Choice A is incorrect because the plural pronoun "those" doesn't agree with the singular antecedent "period." Choice B is incorrect because "compared with" repeats the idea of comparison already provided in the word "shorter." Choice D is incorrect because the underlined portion cannot be deleted without eliminating a necessary element in the comparison. A "training period" can't be compared to "physicians."

QUESTION 31

Choice A is the best answer because the transitional phrase "in addition" correctly introduces another example of PAs' "extraordinary contribution to rural health care."

Choices B, C, and D are incorrect because they do not convey the appropriate relationship between ideas. In choice B, "Thus" does not make sense because the claim that PAs "provide a broader spectrum of such services" is not a result or consequence of the claim that they provide "cost-efficient, widely appreciated services." Choices C and D, "despite this" and "on the other hand," incorrectly indicate that the claim about the "broader spectrum of such services" is in contrast to the previous claim rather than in addition to it.

QUESTION 32

Choice C is the best answer because it gives an appropriate explanation for why the sentence should not be added. While relevant, the sentence does not accurately interpret the data in the table, which indicates that the number of physicians in 2025 will be 216,000 and the number of physician assistants will be 42,000.

Choices A and B are incorrect because the sentence incorrectly interprets the data in the table and should not be added. Choice D is incorrect because the sentence contains false information, not irrelevant information.

QUESTION 33

Choice D is the best answer because the word "patients" correctly identifies the people served by PAs. Additionally, the comparative conjunction "than" is used correctly in the comparison introduced by the adverb "more."

Choices A and B are incorrect because the noun "patience" refers to a human quality of tolerance or perseverance. It cannot be used to refer to people served by PAs. Choice C is incorrect because the word "then" refers to a time sequence or tells when something happened.

QUESTION 34

Choice B is the best answer because it most effectively combines the underlined sentences. The introductory dependent clause clearly and concisely sets up the comparison between the "rebooting" of films and the reworking of comic books. It also provides a clear and logical referent for the phrase "This practice" in the second sentence.

Choices A, C, and D are incorrect because the combinations do not connect the two sentences logically and concisely to demonstrate the comparison between the "rebooting" of films and the reworking of comic books. In addition, none provides a clear and logical referent for the phrase "This practice" in the second sentence.

QUESTION 35

Choice B is the best answer because the adjective "old" is used appropriately to describe a long-standing practice.

Choices A and D, "elderly" and "geriatric," are incorrect in this context because they are generally used to refer to people, not to a practice. Choice C, "mature," is incorrect because it does not fit the context of the sentence, which is about a long-standing practice, not a fully developed one.

QUESTION 36

Choice D is the best answer because no punctuation is needed to set off the prepositional phrase "of publishers."

Choices A and B are incorrect because neither a colon nor a comma is needed to separate the noun "example" from the prepositional phrase that describes it. Choice C is incorrect because no comma is needed to separate the noun "publishers" from the participle "responding" that describes it.

QUESTION 37

Choice A is the best answer because the phrase "lift a car over his head" is consistent with the other examples of Superman's superhuman physical abilities: "hurdle skyscrapers," "leap an eighth of a mile," etc.

Choices B, C, and D are incorrect because they are inconsistent with the other examples in the sentence of Superman's superhuman physical abilities. Holding a job, wearing a costume, and living in a city describe the original Superman but do not characterize his physical abilities.

QUESTION 38

Choice D is the best answer because it most effectively sets up the following sentences, which describe the "realistic" nature of superheroes in the Silver Age. According to these sentences, Silver Age superheroes dealt with everyday problems and had richer interior lives and more complex motivations than their Golden Age counterparts.

Choices A, B, and C are incorrect because neither "scientific experiments gone wrong," conservatism in the United States in the 1950s, nor the influence of science fiction on comics is addressed in the following two sentences.

QUESTION 39

Choice D is the best answer because it uses punctuation correctly. Because there is a dash between "them" and the verb "had," another dash is required before "Spider-Man" to set off the nonessential clause "Spider-Man, the Fantastic Four, and the Hulk among them." A nonessential clause should be set off from the sentence by matching punctuation, such as two dashes or commas.

Choice A is incorrect because a colon needs to be preceded by an independent clause. Choice B is incorrect because, when used in this way, a semicolon needs to be preceded and followed by independent clauses. Choice C is incorrect because a comma and a dash cannot be used to enclose a nonessential clause. Two dashes or two commas should be used instead.

QUESTION 40

Choice C is the best answer because, as the only choice that focuses on Silver Age characters ("the upstarts"), it most logically completes the discussion of the Silver Age. It also provides an effective transition to the next paragraph: by indicating that "the Silver Age drew to a close," it sets up the next paragraph's discussion of the Bronze and other ages.

Choices A and D are incorrect because each focuses on Golden Age characters and thus fails to logically complete the discussion of the Silver Age. Choice B is incorrect because it prematurely discusses a topic that would be better addressed in the next paragraph.

QUESTION 41

Choice A is the best answer because the present perfect verb "have yielded" is used correctly to indicate that the action of the sentence began in the past and is ongoing in the present. In this case, the transformation of comics from the Silver Age to subsequent ages began in the past and continues today.

Choice B is incorrect because the verb "would have yielded" indicates that an action was possible but never happened. Choice C is incorrect because the past tense verb "were yielding" indicates that the action happened and ended in the past. Choice D is incorrect because the verb "will yield" means that the action will happen in the future, which is not necessarily true.

QUESTION 42

Choice D is the best answer because the possessive plural noun "Comics'" and adjective "superhero" appropriately indicate that the "superhero line" is a feature of the comics.

Choices A, B, and C are incorrect because the possessive singular noun "superhero's" is not correctly used in the sentence. Nothing belongs to a singular "superhero" in the sentence. Furthermore, in choice B, the singular possessive noun "Comic's" is used incorrectly since more than one comic is being referred to. In choice C, "Comics" is plural, but it needs to be possessive, too.

QUESTION 43

Choice A is the best answer because the conjunctive adverb "then" correctly shows that given previously stated information, the conclusion that can be drawn is that the transition between the Golden and Silver Ages of comic books was more successful than others.

Choices B, C, and D are incorrect because they do not indicate the correct relationship between the information presented earlier and conclusions that can be drawn from the information. "However," "nevertheless," and "yet" are ordinarily used to indicate that in spite of some action, a different or unexpected result occurs.

QUESTION 44

Choice C is the best answer because the singular pronoun "that" agrees in number with its singular antecedent "transition."

Choices A and B are incorrect because the plural pronouns "those" and "these" do not agree with the singular antecedent "transition." Additionally, choice B is incorrect because "these" implies that whatever is being referred to is at hand, not in the past. Choice D is incorrect because a pronoun is needed to complete the comparison of transitions between comic book ages.

Section 3: Math Test – No Calculator

QUESTION 1

Choice B is correct. The total amount T, in dollars, Salim will pay for n tickets is given by $T = 15n + 12$, which consists of both a per-ticket charge and a one-time service fee. Since n represents the number of tickets that Salim purchases, it follows that $15n$ represents the price, in dollars, of n tickets. Therefore, 15 must represent the per-ticket charge. At the same time, no matter how many tickets Salim purchases, he will be charged the $12 fee only once. Therefore, 12 must represent the amount of the service fee, in dollars.

Choice A is incorrect. Since n represents the total number of tickets that Salim purchases, it follows that $15n$ represents the price, in dollars, of n tickets, excluding the service fee. Therefore, 15, not 12, must represent the price of 1 ticket. Choice C is incorrect. If Salim purchases only 1 ticket, the total amount, in dollars, Salim will pay can be found by substituting $n = 1$ into the equation for T. If $n = 1$, $T = 15(1) + 12 = 27$. Therefore, the total amount Salim will pay for one ticket is $27, not $12. Choice D is incorrect. The total amount, in dollars, Salim will pay for n tickets is given by $15n + 12$. The value 12 represents only a portion of this total amount. Therefore, the value 12 does not represent the total amount, in dollars, for any number of tickets.

QUESTION 2

Choice B is correct. Since Fertilizer A contains 60% filler materials by weight, it follows that x pounds of Fertilizer A consists of $0.6x$ pounds of filler materials. Similarly, y pounds of Fertilizer B consists of $0.4y$ pounds of filler materials. When x pounds of Fertilizer A and y pounds of Fertilizer B are combined, the result is 240 pounds of filler materials. Therefore, the total amount, in pounds, of filler materials in a mixture of x pounds of Fertilizer A and y pounds of Fertilizer B can be expressed as $0.6x + 0.4y = 240$.

Choice A is incorrect. This choice transposes the percentages of filler materials for Fertilizer A and Fertilizer B. Fertilizer A consists of $0.6x$ pounds of filler materials and Fertilizer B consists of $0.4y$ pounds of filler materials. Therefore, $0.6x + 0.4y$ is equal to 240, not $0.4x + 0.6y$. Choice C is incorrect. This choice transposes the percentages of filler materials for Fertilizer A and Fertilizer B and incorrectly represents how to take the percentage of a value mathematically. Choice D is incorrect. This choice incorrectly represents how to take the percentage of a value mathematically. Fertilizer A consists of $0.6x$ pounds of filler materials, not $60x$ pounds of filler materials, and Fertilizer B consists of $0.4y$ pounds of filler materials, not $40y$ pounds of filler materials.

QUESTION 3

Choice C is correct. For a complex number written in the form $a + bi$, a is called the real part of the complex number and b is called the imaginary part. The sum of two complex numbers, $a + bi$ and $c + di$, is found by adding real parts and imaginary parts, respectively; that is, $(a + bi) + (c + di) = (a + c) + (b + d)i$. Therefore, the sum of $2 + 3i$ and $4 + 8i$ is $(2 + 4) + (3 + 8)i = 6 + 11i$.

Choice A is incorrect and is the result of disregarding i and adding all parts of the two complex numbers together, $2 + 3 + 4 + 8 = 17$. Choice B is incorrect and is the result of adding all parts of the two complex numbers together and multiplying the sum by i. Choice D is incorrect and is the result of multiplying the real parts and imaginary parts of the two complex numbers, $(2)(4) = 8$ and $(3)(8) = 24$, instead of adding those parts together.

QUESTION 4

Choice A is correct. The right side of the equation can be multiplied using the distributive property: $(px + t)(px - t) = p^2x^2 - ptx + ptx - t^2$. Combining like terms gives $p^2x^2 - t^2$. Substituting this expression for the right side of the equation gives $4x^2 - 9 = p^2x^2 - t^2$, where p and t are constants. This equation is true for all values of x only when $4 = p^2$ and $9 = t^2$. If $4 = p^2$, then $p = 2$ or $p = -2$. Therefore, of the given answer choices, only 2 could be the value of p.

Choices B, C, and D are incorrect. For the equation to be true for all values of x, the coefficients of x^2 on both sides of the equation must be equal; that is, $4 = p^2$. Therefore, the value of p cannot be 3, 4, or 9.

QUESTION 5

Choice D is correct. In the xy-plane, the graph of the equation $y = mx + b$, where m and b are constants, is a line with slope m and y-intercept $(0, b)$. Therefore, the graph of $y = 2x - 5$ in the xy-plane is a line with slope 2 and a y-intercept $(0, -5)$. Having a slope of 2 means that for each increase in x by 1, the value of y increases by 2. Only the graph in choice D has a slope of 2 and crosses the y-axis at $(0, -5)$. Therefore, the graph shown in choice D must be the correct answer.

Choices A, B, and C are incorrect. The graph of $y = 2x - 5$ in the xy-plane is a line with slope 2 and a y-intercept at $(0, -5)$. The graph in choice A crosses the y-axis at the point $(0, 2.5)$, not $(0, -5)$, and it has a slope of $\frac{1}{2}$, not 2. The graph in choice B crosses the y-axis at $(0, -5)$; however, the slope of this line is -2, not 2. The graph in choice C has a slope of 2; however, the graph crosses the y-axis at $(0, 5)$, not $(0, -5)$.

QUESTION 6

Choice A is correct. Substituting the given value of $y = 18$ into the equation $x = \frac{2}{3}y$ gives $x = \left(\frac{2}{3}\right)(18)$, or $x = 12$. The value of the expression $2x - 3$ when $x = 12$ is $2(12) - 3 = 21$.

Choice B is incorrect and may be the result of a computation error. If $2x - 3 = 15$, then adding 3 to both sides of the equation and then dividing both sides of the equation by 2 gives $x = 9$. Substituting 9 for x and 18 for y into the equation $x = \frac{2}{3}y$ gives $9 = \left(\frac{2}{3}\right)18 = 12$, which is false. Therefore, the value of $2x - 3$ cannot be 15. Choice C is incorrect and may be the result of solving to find $x = 12$ and not substituting the value of x into the expression. Choice D is incorrect. As with choice B, assuming the value of $2x - 3$ is 10 will lead to a false statement.

QUESTION 7

Choice C is correct. By properties of multiplication, the formula $n = 7\ell h$ can be rewritten as $n = (7h)\ell$. To solve for ℓ in terms of n and h, divide both sides of the equation by the factor $7h$. Solving this equation for ℓ gives $\ell = \frac{n}{7h}$.

Choices A, B, and D are incorrect and may result from algebraic errors when rewriting the given equation.

QUESTION 8

Choice B is correct. This question can be answered by making a connection between the table and the algebraic equation. Each row of the table gives a value of x and its corresponding values in both $w(x)$ and $t(x)$. For instance, the first row gives $x = 1$ and the corresponding values $w(1) = -1$ and $t(1) = -3$. The row in the table where $x = 2$ is the only row that has the property $x = w(x) + t(x)$: $2 = 3 + (-1)$. Therefore, choice B is the correct answer.

Choice A is incorrect because when $x = 1$, the equation $w(x) + t(x) = x$ is not true. According to the table, $w(1) = -1$ and $t(1) = -3$. Substituting the values of each term when $x = 1$ gives $-1 + (-3) = 1$, an equation that is not true. Choice C is incorrect because when $x = 3$, the equation $w(x) + t(x) = x$ is not true. According to the table, $w(3) = 4$ and $t(3) = 1$. Substituting the values of each term when $x = 3$ gives $4 + 1 = 3$, an equation that is not true. Choice D is incorrect because when $x = 4$, the equation $w(x) + t(x) = x$ is not true. According to the table, $w(4) = 3$ and $t(4) = 3$. Substituting the values of each term when $x = 4$ gives $3 + 3 = 4$, an equation that is not true.

QUESTION 9

Choice C is correct. The two numerical expressions in the given equation can be simplified as $\sqrt{9} = 3$ and $\sqrt{64} = 8$, so the equation can be rewritten as $\sqrt{x} + 3 = 8$, or $\sqrt{x} = 5$. Squaring both sides of the equation gives $x = 25$.

Choice A is incorrect and may result from a misconception about how to square both sides of $\sqrt{x} = 5$ to determine the value of x. Choice B is incorrect. The value of $\sqrt{x}$, not x, is 5. Choice D is incorrect and represents a misconception about the properties of radicals. While it is true that $55 + 9 = 64$, it is not true that $\sqrt{55} + \sqrt{9} = \sqrt{64}$.

QUESTION 10

Choice D is correct. Jaime's goal is to bicycle an average of at least 280 miles per week for 4 weeks. If T is the total number of miles Jaime will bicycle in 4 weeks, then his goal can be represented symbolically by the inequality $\frac{T}{4} \geq 280$, or equivalently $T \geq 4(280)$. The total number of miles Jaime will bicycle during this time is the sum of the distances he has completed and has yet to complete. Thus $T = 240 + 310 + 320 + x$. Substituting this expression into the inequality $T \geq 4(280)$ gives $240 + 310 + 320 + x \geq 4(280)$. Therefore, choice D is the correct answer.

Choices A, B, and C are incorrect because they do not correctly capture the relationship between the total number of miles Jaime will ride his bicycle $(240 + 310 + 320 + x)$ and the minimum number of miles he is attempting to bicycle for the four weeks $4(280)$.

QUESTION 11

Choice B is correct. Since the shown parabola opens upward, the coefficient of x^2 in the equation $y = ax^2 + c$ must be positive. Given that a is positive, $-a$ is negative, and therefore the graph of the equation $y = -a(x - b)^2 + c$ will be a parabola that opens downward. The vertex of this parabola is (b, c), because the maximum value for y of c is reached when $x = b$. Therefore, the answer must be choice B.

Choices A and C are incorrect. The coefficient of x^2 in the equation $y = -a(x - b)^2 + c$ is negative. Therefore, the parabola with this equation opens downward, not upward. Choice D is incorrect because the vertex of this parabola is (b, c), not $(-b, c)$, because the maximum value for y of c is reached when $x = b$.

QUESTION 12

Choice D is correct. Dividing $4x^2 + 6x$ by $4x + 2$ gives:

$$\begin{array}{r} x + 1 \\ 4x + 2 \overline{)\, 4x^2 + 6x} \\ \underline{-(4x^2 + 2x)} \\ 4x \\ \underline{-(4x + 2)} \\ -2 \end{array}$$

Therefore, the expression $\frac{4x^2 + 6x}{4x + 2}$ is equivalent to $x + 1 - \frac{2}{4x + 2}$.

Alternate approach: The numerator of the given expression, $4x^2 + 6x$, can be rewritten in terms of the denominator, $4x + 2$, as follows: $4x^2 + 2x + 4x + 2 - 2$, or $x(4x + 2) + (4x + 2) - 2$. So the given expression can be rewritten as

$$\frac{x(4x + 2) + (4x + 2) - 2}{4x + 2} = x + 1 - \frac{2}{4x + 2}.$$

Choices A and B are incorrect and may result from incorrectly factoring the numerator and denominator of the expression $\frac{4x^2 + 6x}{4x + 2}$ and then incorrectly identifying common factors in the two factored expressions. Choice C is incorrect and may result from a variety of mistakes made when performing long division.

QUESTION 13

Choice A is correct. The number of solutions to any quadratic equation in the form $ax^2 + bx + c = 0$, where a, b, and c are constants, can be found by evaluating the expression $b^2 - 4ac$, which is called the discriminant. If the value of $b^2 - 4ac$ is a positive number, then there will be exactly two real solutions to the equation. If the value of $b^2 - 4ac$ is zero, then there will be exactly one real solution to the equation. Finally, if the value of $b^2 - 4ac$ is negative, then there will be no real solutions to the equation.

The given equation $2x^2 - 4x = t$ is a quadratic equation in one variable, where t is a constant. Subtracting t from both sides of the equation gives $2x^2 - 4x - t = 0$. In this form, $a = 2$, $b = -4$, and $c = -t$. The values of t for which the equation has no real solutions are the same values of t for which the discriminant of this equation is a negative value. The discriminant is equal to $(-4)^2 - 4(2)(-t)$; therefore, $(-4)^2 - 4(2)(-t) < 0$. Simplifying the left side of the inequality gives $16 + 8t < 0$. Subtracting 16 from both sides of the inequality and then dividing both sides by 8 gives $t < -2$. Of the values given in the options, -3 is the only value that is less than -2. Therefore, choice A must be the correct answer.

Choices B, C, and D are incorrect and may result from a misconception about how to use the discriminant to determine the number of solutions of a quadratic equation in one variable.

QUESTION 14

Choice A is correct. The number of containers in a shipment must have a weight less than or equal to 300 pounds. The total weight, in pounds, of detergent and fabric softener that the supplier delivers can be expressed as the weight of each container multiplied by the number of each type of container, which is $7.35d$ for detergent and $6.2s$ for fabric softener. Since this total cannot exceed 300 pounds, it follows that $7.35d + 6.2s \leq 300$. Also, since the laundry service wants to buy at least twice as many containers of detergent as containers of fabric softener, the number of containers of detergent should be greater than or equal to two times the number of containers of fabric softener. This can be expressed by the inequality $d \geq 2s$.

Choice B is incorrect because it misrepresents the relationship between the numbers of each container that the laundry service wants to buy. Choice C is incorrect because the first inequality of the system incorrectly doubles the weight per container of detergent. The weight of each container of detergent is 7.35, not 14.7 pounds. Choice D is incorrect because it doubles the weight per container of detergent and transposes the relationship between the numbers of containers.

QUESTION 15

Choice D is correct. The expression $\left(a+\frac{b}{2}\right)^2$ can be rewritten as $\left(a+\frac{b}{2}\right)\left(a+\frac{b}{2}\right)$. Using the distributive property, the expression yields $\left(a+\frac{b}{2}\right)\left(a+\frac{b}{2}\right)=a^2+\frac{ab}{2}+\frac{ab}{2}+\frac{b^2}{4}$. Combining like terms gives $a^2+ab+\frac{b^2}{4}$.

Choices A, B, and C are incorrect and may result from errors using the distributive property on the given expression or combining like terms.

QUESTION 16

The correct answers are 1, 2, 4, 8, or 16. The number 16 can be written in exponential form $a^{\frac{b}{4}}$, where a and b are positive integers as follows: 2^4, 4^2, 16^1, $(16^2)^{\frac{1}{2}}$, $(16^4)^{\frac{1}{4}}$. Hence, if $a^{\frac{b}{4}}=16$, where a and b are positive integers, then $\frac{b}{4}$ can be 4, 2, 1, $\frac{1}{2}$, or $\frac{1}{4}$. So the value of b can be 16, 8, 4, 2, or 1. Any of these values may be gridded as the correct answer.

QUESTION 17

The correct answer is $\frac{15}{4}$ or 3.75. Multiplying both sides of the equation $\frac{2}{3}t=\frac{5}{2}$ by $\frac{3}{2}$ results in $t=\frac{15}{4}$, or $t=3.75$.

QUESTION 18

The correct answer is 30. In the figure given, since $\overline{BD}$ is parallel to $\overline{AE}$ and both segments are intersected by $\overline{CE}$, then angle BDC and angle AEC are corresponding angles and therefore congruent. Angle BCD and angle ACE are also congruent because they are the same angle. Triangle BCD and triangle ACE are similar because if two angles of one triangle are congruent to two angles of another triangle, the triangles are similar. Since triangle BCD and triangle ACE are similar, their corresponding sides are proportional. So in triangle BCD and triangle ACE, $\overline{BD}$ corresponds to $\overline{AE}$ and $\overline{CD}$ corresponds to $\overline{CE}$. Therefore, $\frac{BD}{CD}=\frac{AE}{CE}$. Since triangle BCD is a right triangle, the Pythagorean theorem can be used to give the value of CD: $6^2 + 8^2 = CD^2$. Taking the square root of each side gives $CD = 10$. Substituting the values in the proportion $\frac{BD}{CD} = \frac{AE}{CE}$ yields $\frac{6}{10} = \frac{18}{CE}$. Multiplying each side by CE, and then multiplying by $\frac{10}{6}$ yields $CE = 30$. Therefore, the length of $\overline{CE}$ is 30.

QUESTION 19

The correct answer is 1.5 or $\frac{3}{2}$. The total amount, in liters, of a saline solution can be expressed as the liters of each type of saline solution multiplied by the percent concentration of the saline solution. This gives $3(0.10)$, $x(0.25)$, and $(x + 3)(0.15)$, where x is the amount, in liters, of 25% saline solution and 10%, 15%, and 25% are represented as 0.10, 0.15, and 0.25, respectively. Thus, the equation $3(0.10) + 0.25x = 0.15(x + 3)$ must be true. Multiplying 3 by 0.10 and distributing 0.15 to $(x + 3)$ yields $0.30 + 0.25x = 0.15x + 0.45$. Subtracting $0.15x$ and 0.30 from each side of the equation gives $0.10x = 0.15$. Dividing each side of the equation by 0.10 yields $x = 1.5$, or $x = \frac{3}{2}$.

QUESTION 20

The correct answer is $\frac{1}{6}$, .166, or .167. The circumference, C, of a circle is $C = 2\pi r$, where r is the length of the radius of the circle. For the given circle with a radius of 1, the circumference is $C = 2(\pi)(1)$, or $C = 2\pi$. To find what fraction of the circumference the length of arc $\overset{\frown}{AB}$ is, divide the length of the arc by the circumference, which gives $\frac{\pi}{3} \div 2\pi$. This division can be represented by $\frac{\pi}{3} \cdot \frac{1}{2\pi} = \frac{1}{6}$. The fraction $\frac{1}{6}$ can also be rewritten as .166 or .167.

Section 4: Math Test – Calculator

QUESTION 1

Choice A is correct. The given expression $(2x^2 - 4) - (-3x^2 + 2x - 7)$ can be rewritten as $2x^2 - 4 + 3x^2 - 2x + 7$. Combining like terms yields $5x^2 - 2x + 3$.

Choices B, C, and D are incorrect and may be the result of errors when applying the distributive property.

QUESTION 2

Choice C is correct. The lines shown on the graph give the positions of Paul and Mark during the race. At the start of the race, 0 seconds have elapsed. The y-intercepts of these lines represent the positions at the start of the race, or when 0 seconds have elapsed. The y-intercept of the line that represents Paul's position during the race is at 0. The y-intercept of the line that represents Mark's position during the race represents the number of yards Mark was from Paul's position (at 0 yards) at the start of the race. Because the y-intercept of the line that represents Mark's position is at the grid line that is halfway between 12 and 24, the value of the y-intercept is 18, and therefore Mark had a head start of 18 yards.

Choices A, B, and D are incorrect. The y-intercept of the line that represents Mark's position shows that he was 18 yards from Paul's position at the start of the race, so he did not have a head start of 3, 12, or 24 yards.

QUESTION 3

Choice A is correct. The leftmost segment in choice A, which represents the first time period, shows that the snow accumulated at a certain rate; the middle segment, which represents the second time period, is horizontal, showing that the snow stopped accumulating; and the rightmost segment, which represents the third time period, is steeper than the first segment, indicating that the snow accumulated at a faster rate than it did during the first time period.

Choice B is incorrect. This graph shows snow accumulating faster during the first time period than during the third time period; however, the question says that the rate of snow accumulation in the third time period is higher than in the first time period. Choice C is incorrect. This graph shows snow accumulation increasing during the first time period, not accumulating during the second time period, and then decreasing during the third time period; however, the question says that no snow melted (accumulation did not decrease) during this time. Choice D is incorrect. This graph shows snow accumulating at a constant rate, not stopping for a period of time or accumulating at a faster rate during a third time period.

QUESTION 4

Choice D is correct. The equation $12d + 350 = 1{,}010$ can be used to determine d, the number of dollars charged per month for the first 12 months. Subtracting 350 from both sides of this equation yields $12d = 660$, and then dividing both sides of the equation by 12 yields $d = 55$.

Choice A is incorrect. If d were equal to 25, the first 12 months would cost $350 + (12)(25) = 650$ dollars, not \$1,010. Choice B is incorrect. If d were equal to 35, the first 12 months would cost $350 + (12)(35) = 770$ dollars, not \$1,010. Choice C is incorrect. If d were equal to 45, the first 12 months would cost $350 + (12)(45) = 890$ dollars, not \$1,010.

QUESTION 5

Choice B is correct. Both sides of the given inequality can be divided by 3 to yield $2x - 3y > 4$.

Choices A, C, and D are incorrect because they are not equivalent to (do not have the same solution set as) the given inequality. For example, the ordered pair $(0, -1.5)$ is a solution to the given inequality, but it is not a solution to any of the inequalities in choices A, C, or D.

QUESTION 6

Choice C is correct. According to the table, 63% of survey respondents get most of their medical information from a doctor and 13% get most of their medical information from the Internet. Therefore, 76% of the 1,200 survey respondents get their information from either a doctor or the Internet, and 76% of 1,200 is 912.

Choices A, B, and D are incorrect. According to the table, 76% of survey respondents get their information from either a doctor or the Internet. Choice A is incorrect because 865 is about 72% (the percent of survey respondents who get most of their medical information from a doctor or from magazines/brochures), not 76%, of 1,200. Choice B is incorrect because 887 is about 74%, not 76%, of 1,200. Choice D is incorrect because 926 is about 77%, not 76%, of 1,200.

QUESTION 7

Choice D is correct. The members of the city council wanted to assess opinions of all city residents. To gather an unbiased sample, the council should have used a random sampling design to select subjects from all city residents. The given survey introduced a sampling bias because the 500 city residents surveyed were all dog owners. This sample is not representative of all city residents because not all city residents are dog owners.

Choice A is incorrect because when the sampling method isn't random, there is no guarantee that the survey results will be reliable; hence, they cannot be generalized to the entire population. Choice B is incorrect because a larger sample of residents who are dog owners would not correct the sampling bias. Choice C is incorrect because a survey sample of entirely non–dog owners would likely have a biased opinion, just as a sample of dog owners would likely have a biased opinion.

QUESTION 8

Choice D is correct. According to the table, 13 people chose vanilla ice cream. Of those people, 8 chose hot fudge as a topping. Therefore, of the people who chose vanilla ice cream, the fraction who chose hot fudge as a topping is $\frac{8}{13}$.

Choice A is incorrect because it represents the fraction of people at the party who chose hot fudge as a topping and vanilla ice cream. Choice B is incorrect because it represents the fraction of people at the party who chose caramel as a topping and vanilla ice cream. Choice C is incorrect because it represents the fraction of people at the party who chose vanilla ice cream.

QUESTION 9

Choice B is correct. The land area of the coastal city can be found by subtracting the area of the water from the total area of the coastal city; that is, $92.1 - 11.3 = 80.8$ square miles. The population density is the population divided by the land area, or $\frac{621,000}{80.8} = 7,686$, which is closest to 7,690 people per square mile.

Choice A is incorrect and may be the result of dividing the population by the total area, instead of the land area. Choice C is incorrect and may be the result of dividing the population by the area of water. Choice D is incorrect and may be the result of making a computational error with the decimal place.

QUESTION 10

Choice B is correct. Let x represent the number of days the second voyage lasted. The number of days the first voyage lasted is then $x + 43$. Since the two voyages combined lasted a total of 1,003 days, the equation $x + (x + 43) = 1{,}003$ must hold. Combining like terms yields $2x + 43 = 1{,}003$, and solving for x gives $x = 480$.

Choice A is incorrect because $460 + (460 + 43) = 963$, not 1,003, days. Choice C is incorrect because $520 + (520 + 43) = 1{,}083$, not 1,003, days. Choice D is incorrect because $540 + (540 + 43) = 1{,}123$, not 1,003, days.

QUESTION 11

Choice B is correct. One way to solve the system of equations is using the method of elimination. Adding the equations as follows eliminates y:

$$\begin{array}{r} 7x + 3y = 8 \\ 6x - 3y = 5 \\ \hline 13x + 0 = 13 \end{array}$$

Solving the obtained equation for x gives $x = 1$. Substituting 1 for x in the first equation gives $7(1) + 3y = 8$. Subtracting 7 from both sides of the equation yields $3y = 1$, so $y = \frac{1}{3}$. Therefore, the value of $x - y$ is $1 - \frac{1}{3}$, or $\frac{2}{3}$.

Choice C is incorrect because $1 + \frac{1}{3} = \frac{4}{3}$ is the value of $x + y$, not $x - y$. Choices A and D are incorrect and may be the result of some computational errors.

QUESTION 12

Choice D is correct. The average growth rate of the sunflower over a certain time period is the increase in height of the sunflower over the time period divided by the change in time. Symbolically, this rate is $\frac{h(b) - h(a)}{b - a}$, where a and b are the first and the last day of the time period, respectively, and $h(a)$ and $h(b)$ are the heights at the beginning and end of the time period, respectively. Since the time period for each option is the same (21 days), the total growth over the period can be used to evaluate in which time period the sunflower grew the least. According to the graph, the 21-day time period during which the sunflower grew the least over the period was from day 63 to day 84. Therefore, the sunflower's average growth rate was the least from day 63 to day 84.

Alternate approach: The average growth rate of the sunflower over a certain time period is the slope of the line segment that joins the point on the graph at the beginning of the time period with the point on the graph at the end of the time period. Based on the graph, of the four time periods, the slope of the line segment is least between the sunflower's height on day 63 and its height on day 84.

Choices A, B, and C are incorrect. On the graph, the line segment from day 63 to 84 is less steep than each of the three other line segments representing other periods. Therefore, the average growth rate of the sunflower is the least from day 63 to 84.

QUESTION 13

Choice A is correct. Based on the definition and contextual interpretation of the function h, when the value of t increases by 1, the height of the sunflower increases by a centimeters. Therefore, a represents the predicted number of centimeters the sunflower grows each day during the period the function models.

Choice B is incorrect. In the given model, the beginning of the period corresponds to $t = 0$, and since $h(0) = b$, the predicted height, in centimeters, of the sunflower at the beginning of the period is represented by b, not by a. Choice C is incorrect. If the period of time modeled by the function is c days long, then the predicted height, in centimeters, of the sunflower at the end of the period is represented by $ac + b$, not by a. Choice D is incorrect. If the period of time modeled by the function is c days long, the predicted total increase in the height of the sunflower, in centimeters, during that period is represented by the difference $h(c) - h(0) = (ac + b) - (a \cdot 0 + b)$, which is equivalent to ac, not a.

QUESTION 14

Choice B is correct. According to the table, the height of the sunflower is 36.36 cm on day 14 and 131.00 cm on day 35. Since the height of the sunflower between day 14 and day 35 changes at a nearly constant rate, the height of the sunflower increases by approximately $\frac{131.00 - 36.36}{35 - 14} \approx 4.5$ cm per day. Therefore, the equation that models the height of the sunflower t days after it begins to grow is of the form $h = 4.5t + b$. Any ordered pair (t, h) from the table between day 14 and day 35 can be used to estimate the value of b. For example, substituting the ordered pair (14, 36.36) for (t, h) into the equation $h = 4.5t + b$ gives $36.36 = 4.5(14) + b$. Solving this for b yields $b = -26.64$. Therefore, of the given choices, the equation $h = 4.5t - 27$ best models the height h, in centimeters, of the sunflower t days after it begins to grow.

Choices A, C, and D are incorrect because the growth rates of the sunflower from day 14 to day 35 in these choices are significantly higher or lower than the true growth rate of the sunflower as shown in the graph or the table. These choices may result from considering time periods different from the period indicated in the question or from calculation errors.

QUESTION 15

Choice D is correct. According to the table, the value of y increases by $\frac{14}{4} = \frac{7}{2}$ every time the value of x increases by 1. It follows that the simplest equation relating y to x is linear and of the form $y = \frac{7}{2}x + b$ for some constant b. Furthermore, the ordered pair $\left(1, \frac{11}{4}\right)$ from the table must satisfy this equation. Substituting 1 for x and $\frac{11}{4}$ for y in the equation $y = \frac{7}{2}x + b$ gives $\frac{11}{4} = \frac{7}{2}(1) + b$. Solving this equation for b gives $b = -\frac{3}{4}$. Therefore, the equation in choice D correctly relates y to x.

Choices A and B are incorrect. The relationship between x and y cannot be exponential because the differences, not the ratios, of y-values are the same every time the x-values change by the same amount. Choice C is incorrect because the ordered pair $\left(2, \frac{25}{4}\right)$ is not a solution to the equation $y = \frac{3}{4}x + 2$. Substituting 2 for x and $\frac{25}{4}$ for y in this equation gives $\frac{25}{4} = \frac{3}{2} + 2$, which is false.

QUESTION 16

Choice B is correct. In right triangle ABC, the measure of angle B must be 58° because the sum of the measure of angle A, which is 32°, and the measure of angle B is 90°. Angle D in the right triangle DEF has measure 58°. Hence, triangles ABC and DEF are similar (by angle-angle similarity). Since $\overline{BC}$ is the side opposite to the angle with measure 32° and AB is the hypotenuse in right triangle ABC, the ratio $\frac{BC}{AB}$ is equal to $\frac{DF}{DE}$.

Alternate approach: The trigonometric ratios can be used to answer this question. In right triangle ABC, the ratio $\frac{BC}{AB} = \sin(32°)$. The angle E in triangle DEF has measure 32° because $m(\angle D) + m(\angle E) = 90°$. In triangle DEF, the ratio $\frac{DF}{DE} = \sin(32°)$. Therefore, $\frac{DF}{DE} = \frac{BC}{AB}$.

Choice A is incorrect because $\frac{DE}{DF}$ is the reciprocal of the ratio $\frac{BC}{AB}$. Choice C is incorrect because $\frac{DF}{EF} = \frac{BC}{AC}$, not $\frac{BC}{AB}$. Choice D is incorrect because $\frac{EF}{DE} = \frac{AC}{AB}$, not $\frac{BC}{AB}$.

QUESTION 17

Choice B is correct. Isolating the term that contains the riser height, h, in the formula $2h + d = 25$ gives $2h = 25 - d$. Dividing both sides of this equation by 2 yields $h = \frac{25 - d}{2}$, or $h = \frac{1}{2}(25 - d)$.

Choices A, C, and D are incorrect and may result from incorrect transformations of the riser-tread formula $2h + d = 25$ when expressing h in terms of d.

QUESTION 18

Choice C is correct. Since the tread depth, d, must be at least 9 inches, and the riser height, h, must be at least 5 inches, it follows that $d \geq 9$ and $h \geq 5$, respectively. Solving for d in the riser-tread formula $2h + d = 25$ gives $d = 25 - 2h$. Thus the first inequality, $d \geq 9$, is equivalent to $25 - 2h \geq 9$. This inequality can be solved for h as follows:

$$-2h \geq 9 - 25$$

$$2h \leq 25 - 9$$

$$2h \leq 16$$

$$h \leq 8$$

Therefore, the inequality $5 \leq h \leq 8$, derived from combining the inequalities $h \geq 5$ and $h \leq 8$, represents the set of all possible values for the riser height that meets the code requirement.

Choice A is incorrect because the riser height, h, cannot be less than 5 inches because the question states that the riser height must be at least, not at most, 5 inches. Choices B and D are incorrect because the riser height, h, cannot be greater than 8. For example, if $h = 10$, then according to the riser-tread formula $2h + d = 25$, it follows that $d = 5$ inches. However, d must be at least 9 inches according to the building codes, so h cannot be 10.

QUESTION 19

Choice C is correct. Let h be the riser height, in inches, and n be the number of the steps in the stairway. According to the architect's design, the total rise of the stairway is 9 feet, or $9 \times 12 = 108$ inches. Hence, $nh = 108$, and solving for n gives $n = \frac{108}{h}$. It is given that $7 < h < 8$. It follows that $\frac{108}{8} < \frac{108}{h} < \frac{108}{7}$, or equivalently, $\frac{108}{8} < n < \frac{108}{7}$. Since $\frac{108}{8} < 14$ and $\frac{108}{7} > 15$ and n is an integer, it follows that

$14 \leq n \leq 15$. Since n can be an odd number, n can only be 15; therefore, $h = \frac{108}{15} = 7.2$ inches. Substituting 7.2 for h in the riser-tread formula $2h + d = 25$ gives $14.4 + d = 25$. Solving for d gives $d = 10.6$ inches.

Choice A is incorrect because 7.2 inches is the riser height, not the tread depth of the stairs. Choice B is incorrect and may be the result of calculation errors. Choice D is incorrect because 15 is the number of steps, not the tread depth of the stairs.

QUESTION 20

Choice C is correct. Since the product of $x - 6$ and $x + 0.7$ equals 0, by the zero product property either $x - 6 = 0$ or $x + 0.7 = 0$. Therefore, the solutions to the equation are 6 and -0.7. The sum of 6 and -0.7 is 5.3.

Choice A is incorrect and is the result of subtracting 6 from −0.7 instead of adding. Choice B is incorrect and may be the result of erroneously calculating the sum of −6 and 0.7 instead of 6 and −0.7. Choice D is incorrect and is the sum of 6 and 0.7, not 6 and −0.7.

QUESTION 21

Choice D is correct. The sample of 150 largemouth bass was selected at random from all the largemouth bass in the pond, and since 30% of the fish in the sample weighed more than 2 pounds, it can be concluded that approximately 30% of all largemouth bass in the pond weigh more than 2 pounds.

Choices A, B, and C are incorrect. Since the sample contained 150 largemouth bass, of which 30% weighed more than 2 pounds, this result can be generalized only to largemouth bass in the pond, not to all fish in the pond.

QUESTION 22

Choice B is correct. The median of a list of numbers is the middle value when the numbers are listed in order from least to greatest. For the electoral votes shown in the table, their frequency should also be taken into account. Since there are 21 states represented in the table, the middle number will be the eleventh number in the ordered list. Counting the frequencies from the top of the table (4 + 4 + 1 + 1 + 3 = 13) shows that the median number of electoral votes for the 21 states is 15.

Choice A is incorrect. If the electoral votes are ordered from least to greatest taking into account the frequency, 13 will be in the tenth position, not the middle. Choice C is incorrect because 17 is in the fourteenth position, not in the middle, of the ordered list. Choice D is incorrect because 20 is in the fifteenth position, not in the middle, of the ordered list.

QUESTION 23

Choice C is correct. Since the graph shows the height of the ball above the ground after it was dropped, the number of times the ball was at a height of 2 feet is equal to the number of times the graph crosses the horizontal grid line that corresponds to a height of 2 feet. The graph crosses this grid line three times.

Choices A, B, and D are incorrect. According to the graph, the ball was at a height of 2 feet three times, not one, two, or four times.

QUESTION 24

Choice D is correct. To find the percent increase of the customer's water bill, the absolute increase of the bill, in dollars, is divided by the original amount of the bill, and the result is multiplied by 100%, as follows: $\frac{79.86 - 75.74}{75.74} \approx 0.054$; $0.054 \times 100\% = 5.4\%$.

Choice A is incorrect. This choice is the difference $79.86 - 75.74$ rounded to the nearest tenth, which is the (absolute) increase of the bill's amount, not its percent increase. Choice B is incorrect and may be the result of some calculation errors. Choice C is incorrect and is the result of dividing the difference between the two bill amounts by the new bill amount instead of the original bill amount.

QUESTION 25

Choice B is correct. A linear function has a constant rate of change, and any two rows of the table shown can be used to calculate this rate. From the first row to the second, the value of x is increased by 2 and the value of $f(x)$ is increased by $6 = 4 - (-2)$. So the values of $f(x)$ increase by 3 for every increase by 1 in the value of x. Since $f(2) = 4$, it follows that $f(2 + 1) = 4 + 3 = 7$. Therefore, $f(3) = 7$.

Choice A is incorrect. This is the third x-value in the table, not $f(3)$. Choices C and D are incorrect and may result from errors when calculating the function's rate of change.

QUESTION 26

Choice C is correct. Since Gear A has 20 teeth and Gear B has 60 teeth, the gear ratio for Gears A and B is 20:60. Thus the ratio of the number of revolutions per minute (rpm) for the two gears is 60:20, or 3:1. That is, when Gear A turns at 3 rpm, Gear B turns at 1 rpm. Similarly, since Gear B has 60 teeth and Gear C has 10 teeth, the gear ratio for Gears B and C is 60:10, and the ratio of the rpms for the two gears is 10:60, or 1:6. That is, when Gear B turns at 1 rpm, Gear C turns at 6 rpm. Therefore, if Gear A turns at 100 rpm, then Gear B turns at $\frac{100}{3}$ rpm, and Gear C turns at $\frac{100}{3} \times 6 = 200$ rpm.

Alternate approach: Gear A and Gear C can be considered as directly connected since their "contact" speeds are the same. Gear A has twice as many teeth as Gear C, and since the ratios of the number of teeth are equal to the reverse of the ratios of rotation speeds, in rpm, Gear C would be rotated at a rate that is twice the rate of Gear A. Therefore, Gear C will be rotated at a rate of 200 rpm since Gear A is rotated at 100 rpm.

Choice A is incorrect and may result from using the gear ratio instead of the ratio of the rpm when calculating the rotational speed of Gear C. Choice B is incorrect and may result from comparing the rpm of the gears using addition instead of multiplication. Choice D is incorrect and may be the result of multiplying the 100 rpm for Gear A by the number of teeth in Gear C.

QUESTION 27

Choice A is correct. One way to find the radius of the circle is to rewrite the given equation in standard form, $(x - h)^2 + (y - k)^2 = r^2$, where (h, k) is the center of the circle and the radius of the circle is r. To do this, divide the original equation, $2x^2 - 6x + 2y^2 + 2y = 45$, by 2 to make the leading coefficients of x^2 and y^2 each equal to 1: $x^2 - 3x + y^2 + y = 22.5$. Then complete the square to put the equation in standard form. To do so, first rewrite $x^2 - 3x + y^2 + y = 22.5$ as $(x^2 - 3x + 2.25) - 2.25 + (y^2 + y + 0.25) - 0.25 = 22.5$. Second, add 2.25 and 0.25 to both sides of the equation: $(x^2 - 3x + 2.25) + (y^2 + y + 0.25) = 25$. Since $x^2 - 3x + 2.25 = (x - 1.5)^2$, $y^2 + y + 0.25 = (y + 0.5)^2$, and $25 = 5^2$, it follows that $(x - 1.5)^2 + (y + 0.5)^2 = 5^2$. Therefore, the radius of the circle is 5.

Choices B, C, and D are incorrect and may be the result of errors in manipulating the equation or of a misconception about the standard form of the equation of a circle in the *xy*-plane.

QUESTION 28

Choice A is correct. The coordinates of the points at a distance d units from the point with coordinate a on the number line are the solutions to the equation $|x - a| = d$. Therefore, the coordinates of the points at a distance of 3 units from the point with coordinate −4 on the number line are the solutions to the equation $|x - (-4)| = 3$, which is equivalent to $|x + 4| = 3$.

Choice B is incorrect. The solutions of $|x - 4| = 3$ are the coordinates of the points on the number line at a distance of 3 units from the point with coordinate 4. Choice C is incorrect. The solutions of $|x + 3| = 4$ are the coordinates of the points on the number line at a distance of 4 units from the point with coordinate −3. Choice D is incorrect. The solutions of $|x - 3| = 4$ are the coordinates of the points on the number line at a distance of 4 units from the point with coordinate 3.

QUESTION 29

Choice B is correct. The average speed of the model car is found by dividing the total distance traveled by the car by the total time the car traveled. In the first t seconds after the car starts, the time changes from 0 to t seconds. So the total distance the car traveled is the distance it traveled at t seconds minus the distance it traveled at 0 seconds. At 0 seconds, the car has traveled $16(0)\sqrt{0}$ inches, which is equal to 0 inches. According to the equation given, after t seconds, the car has traveled $16t\sqrt{t}$ inches. In other words, after the car starts, it travels a total of $16t\sqrt{t}$ inches in t seconds. Dividing this total distance traveled by the total time shows the car's average speed: $\frac{16t\sqrt{t}}{t} = 16\sqrt{t}$ inches per second.

Choices A, C, and D are incorrect and may result from misconceptions about how average speed is calculated.

QUESTION 30

Choice D is correct. The data in the scatterplot roughly fall in the shape of a downward-opening parabola; therefore, the coefficient for the x^2 term must be negative. Based on the location of the data points, the y-intercept of the parabola should be somewhere between 740 and 760. Therefore, of the equations given, the best model is $y = -1.674x^2 + 19.76x + 745.73$.

Choices A and C are incorrect. The positive coefficient of the x^2 term means that these equations each define upward-opening parabolas, whereas a parabola that fits the data in the scatterplot must open downward. Choice B is incorrect because it defines a parabola with a y-intercept that has a negative y-coordinate, whereas a parabola that fits the data in the scatterplot must have a y-intercept with a positive y-coordinate.

QUESTION 31

The correct answer is 10. Let n be the number of friends originally in the group. Since the cost of the trip was \$800, the share, in dollars, for each friend was originally $\frac{800}{n}$. When two friends decided not to go on the trip, the number of friends who split the \$800 cost became $n - 2$, and each friend's cost became $\frac{800}{n-2}$. Since this share represented a \$20 increase over the original share, the equation $\frac{800}{n} + 20 = \frac{800}{n-2}$ must be true. Multiplying each side of $\frac{800}{n} + 20 = \frac{800}{n-2}$ by $n(n - 2)$ to clear all the denominators gives

$$800(n - 2) + 20n(n - 2) = 800n$$

This is a quadratic equation and can be rewritten in the standard form by expanding, simplifying, and then collecting like terms on one side, as shown below:

$$800n - 1600 + 20n^2 - 40n = 800n$$

$$40n - 80 + n^2 - 2n = 40n$$

$$n^2 - 2n - 80 = 0$$

After factoring, this becomes $(n + 8)(n - 10) = 0$.

The solutions of this equation are -8 and 10. Since a negative solution makes no sense for the number of people in a group, the number of friends originally in the group was 10.

QUESTION 32

The correct answer is 31. The equation can be solved using the steps shown below.

$2(5x - 20) - (15 + 8x) = 7$	
$2(5x) - 2(20) - 15 - 8x = 7$	Apply the distributive property.
$10x - 40 - 15 - 8x = 7$	Multiply.
$2x - 55 = 7$	Combine like terms.
$2x = 62$	Add 55 to both sides of the equation.
$x = 31$	Divide both sides of the equation by 2.

QUESTION 33

The possible correct answers are 97, 98, 99, 100, and 101. The volume of a cylinder can be found by using the formula $V = \pi r^2 h$, where r is the radius of the circular base and h is the height of the cylinder. The smallest possible volume, in cubic inches, of a graduated cylinder produced by the laboratory supply company can be found by substituting 2 for r and 7.75 for h, giving $V = \pi(2^2)(7.75)$. This gives a volume of approximately 97.39 cubic inches, which rounds to 97 cubic inches. The largest possible volume, in cubic inches, can be found by substituting 2 for r and 8 for h, giving $V = \pi(2^2)(8)$. This gives a volume of approximately 100.53 cubic inches, which rounds to 101 cubic inches. Therefore, the possible volumes are all the integers greater than or equal to 97 and less than or equal to 101, which are 97, 98, 99, 100, and 101. Any of these numbers may be gridded as the correct answer.

QUESTION 34

The correct answer is 5. The intersection points of the graphs of $y = 3x^2 - 14x$ and $y = x$ can be found by solving the system consisting of these two equations. To solve the system, substitute x for y in the first equation. This gives $x = 3x^2 - 14x$. Subtracting x from both sides of the equation gives $0 = 3x^2 - 15x$. Factoring $3x$ out of each term on the left-hand side of the equation gives $0 = 3x(x - 5)$. Therefore, the possible values for x are 0 and 5. Since $y = x$, the two intersection points are (0, 0) and (5, 5). Therefore, $a = 5$.

QUESTION 35

The correct answer is 1.25 or $\frac{5}{4}$. The y-coordinate of the x-intercept is 0, so 0 can be substituted for y, giving $\frac{4}{5}x + \frac{1}{3}(0) = 1$. This simplifies to $\frac{4}{5}x = 1$. Multiplying both sides of $\frac{4}{5}x = 1$ by 5 gives $4x = 5$. Dividing both sides of $4x = 5$ by 4 gives $x = \frac{5}{4}$, which is equivalent to 1.25. Either 5/4 or 1.25 may be gridded as the correct answer.

QUESTION 36

The correct answer is 2.6 or $\frac{13}{5}$. Since the mean of a set of numbers can be found by adding the numbers together and dividing by how many numbers there are in the set, the mean mass, in kilograms, of the rocks Andrew collected is $\frac{2.4 + 2.5 + 3.6 + 3.1 + 2.5 + 2.7}{6} = \frac{16.8}{6} = 2.8$. Since the mean mass of the rocks Maria collected is 0.1 kilogram greater than the mean mass of rocks Andrew collected, the mean mass of the rocks Maria collected is $2.8 + 0.1 = 2.9$ kilograms. The value of x can be found by writing an equation for finding the mean: $\frac{x + 3.1 + 2.7 + 2.9 + 3.3 + 2.8}{6} = 2.9$. Solving this equation gives $x = 2.6$, which is equivalent to $\frac{13}{5}$. Either 2.6 or 13/5 may be gridded as the correct answer.

QUESTION 37

The correct answer is 30. The situation can be represented by the equation $x(2^4) = 480$, where the 2 represents the fact that the amount of money in the account doubled each year and the 4 represents the fact that there are 4 years between January 1, 2001, and January 1, 2005. Simplifying $x(2^4) = 480$ gives $16x = 480$. Therefore, $x = 30$.

QUESTION 38

The correct answer is 8. The 6 students represent $(100 - 15 - 45 - 25)\% = 15\%$ of those invited to join the committee. If x people were invited to join the committee, then $0.15x = 6$. Thus, there were $\frac{6}{0.15} = 40$ people invited to join the committee. It follows that there were $0.45(40) = 18$ teachers and $0.25(40) = 10$ school and district administrators invited to join the committee. Therefore, there were 8 more teachers than school and district administrators invited to join the committee.

The SAT®

Practice Test #7

Make time to take the practice test.
It's one of the best ways to get ready for the SAT.

After you've taken the practice test, score it right away at **sat.org/scoring**.

CollegeBoard

Test begins on the next page.

Reading Test

65 MINUTES, 52 QUESTIONS

Turn to Section 1 of your answer sheet to answer the questions in this section.

DIRECTIONS

Each passage or pair of passages below is followed by a number of questions. After reading each passage or pair, choose the best answer to each question based on what is stated or implied in the passage or passages and in any accompanying graphics (such as a table or graph).

Questions 1-10 are based on the following passage.

This passage is adapted from George Eliot, *Silas Marner*. Originally published in 1861. Silas was a weaver and a notorious miser, but then the gold he had hoarded was stolen. Shortly after, Silas adopted a young child, Eppie, the daughter of an impoverished woman who had died suddenly.

Unlike the gold which needed nothing, and must be worshipped in close-locked solitude—which was hidden away from the daylight, was deaf to the song of birds, and started to no human tones—Eppie was a creature of endless claims and ever-growing desires, seeking and loving sunshine, and living sounds, and living movements; making trial of everything, with trust in new joy, and stirring the human kindness in all eyes that looked on her. The gold had kept his thoughts in an ever-repeated circle, leading to nothing beyond itself; but Eppie was an object compacted of changes and hopes that forced his thoughts onward, and carried them far away from their old eager pacing towards the same blank limit—carried them away to the new things that would come with the coming years, when Eppie would have learned to understand how her father Silas cared for her; and made him look for images of that time in the ties and charities that bound together the families of his neighbors. The gold had asked that he should sit weaving longer and longer, deafened and blinded more and more to all things except the monotony of his loom and the repetition of his web; but Eppie called him away from his weaving, and made him think all its pauses a holiday, reawakening his senses with her fresh life, even to the old winter-flies that came crawling forth in the early spring sunshine, and warming him into joy because *she* had joy.

And when the sunshine grew strong and lasting, so that the buttercups were thick in the meadows, Silas might be seen in the sunny mid-day, or in the late afternoon when the shadows were lengthening under the hedgerows, strolling out with uncovered head to carry Eppie beyond the Stone-pits to where the flowers grew, till they reached some favorite bank where he could sit down, while Eppie toddled to pluck the flowers, and make remarks to the winged things that murmured happily above the bright petals, calling "Dad-dad's" attention continually by bringing him the flowers. Then she would turn her ear to some sudden bird-note, and Silas learned to please her by making signs of hushed stillness, that they might listen for the note to come again: so that when it came, she set up her small back and laughed with gurgling triumph. Sitting on the banks in this way, Silas began to look for the once familiar herbs again; and as the leaves, with their unchanged outline and markings, lay on his palm, there was a sense of crowding remembrances from which he turned away timidly, taking refuge in Eppie's little world, that lay lightly on his enfeebled spirit.

CONTINUE

As the child's mind was growing into knowledge, his mind was growing into memory: as her life unfolded, his soul, long stupefied in a cold narrow prison, was unfolding too, and trembling gradually into full consciousness.

It was an influence which must gather force with every new year: the tones that stirred Silas' heart grew articulate, and called for more distinct answers; shapes and sounds grew clearer for Eppie's eyes and ears, and there was more that "Dad-dad" was imperatively required to notice and account for. Also, by the time Eppie was three years old, she developed a fine capacity for mischief, and for devising ingenious ways of being troublesome, which found much exercise, not only for Silas' patience, but for his watchfulness and penetration. Sorely was poor Silas puzzled on such occasions by the incompatible demands of love.

1

Which choice best describes a major theme of the passage?

A) The corrupting influence of a materialistic society

B) The moral purity of young children

C) The bittersweet brevity of childhood naïveté

D) The restorative power of parental love

2

As compared with Silas's gold, Eppie is portrayed as having more

A) vitality.

B) durability.

C) protection.

D) self-sufficiency.

3

Which statement best describes a technique the narrator uses to represent Silas's character before he adopted Eppie?

A) The narrator emphasizes Silas's former obsession with wealth by depicting his gold as requiring certain behaviors on his part.

B) The narrator underscores Silas's former greed by describing his gold as seeming to reproduce on its own.

C) The narrator hints at Silas's former antisocial attitude by contrasting his present behavior toward his neighbors with his past behavior toward them.

D) The narrator demonstrates Silas's former lack of self-awareness by implying that he is unable to recall life before Eppie.

4

The narrator uses the phrase "making trial of everything" (line 7) to present Eppie as

A) friendly.

B) curious.

C) disobedient.

D) judgmental.

5

According to the narrator, one consequence of Silas adopting Eppie is that he

A) has renounced all desire for money.

B) better understands his place in nature.

C) seems more accepting of help from others.

D) looks forward to a different kind of future.

CONTINUE

6

Which choice provides the best evidence for the answer to the previous question?

A) Lines 9-11 ("The gold . . . itself")
B) Lines 11-16 ("but Eppie . . . years")
C) Lines 41-43 ("Then . . . stillness")
D) Lines 61-63 ("shapes . . . for")

7

What function does the second paragraph (lines 30-52) serve in the passage as a whole?

A) It presents the particular moment at which Silas realized that Eppie was changing him.
B) It highlights Silas's love for Eppie by depicting the sacrifices that he makes for her.
C) It illustrates the effect that Eppie has on Silas by describing the interaction between them.
D) It reveals a significant alteration in the relationship between Silas and Eppie.

8

In describing the relationship between Eppie and Silas, the narrator draws a connection between Eppie's

A) physical vulnerability and Silas's emotional fragility.
B) expanding awareness and Silas's increasing engagement with life.
C) boundless energy and Silas's insatiable desire for wealth.
D) physical growth and Silas's painful perception of his own mortality.

9

Which choice provides the best evidence for the answer to the previous question?

A) Lines 1-9 ("Unlike . . . her")
B) Lines 30-41 ("And when . . . flowers")
C) Lines 46-48 ("Sitting . . . again")
D) Lines 53-57 ("As the . . . consciousness")

10

As used in line 65, "fine" most nearly means

A) acceptable.
B) delicate.
C) ornate.
D) keen.

CONTINUE

Questions 11-21 are based on the following passage and supplementary material.

This passage is adapted from David Rotman, "How Technology Is Destroying Jobs." ©2013 by MIT Technology Review.

MIT business scholars Erik Brynjolfsson and Andrew McAfee have argued that impressive advances in computer technology—from improved industrial robotics to automated translation services—are largely behind the sluggish employment growth of the last 10 to 15 years. Even more ominous for workers, they foresee dismal prospects for many types of jobs as these powerful new technologies are increasingly adopted not only in manufacturing, clerical, and retail work but in professions such as law, financial services, education, and medicine.

That robots, automation, and software can replace people might seem obvious to anyone who's worked in automotive manufacturing or as a travel agent. But Brynjolfsson and McAfee's claim is more troubling and controversial. They believe that rapid technological change has been destroying jobs faster than it is creating them, contributing to the stagnation of median income and the growth of inequality in the United States. And, they suspect, something similar is happening in other technologically advanced countries.

As evidence, Brynjolfsson and McAfee point to a chart that only an economist could love. In economics, productivity—the amount of economic value created for a given unit of input, such as an hour of labor—is a crucial indicator of growth and wealth creation. It is a measure of progress. On the chart Brynjolfsson likes to show, separate lines represent productivity and total employment in the United States. For years after World War II, the two lines closely tracked each other, with increases in jobs corresponding to increases in productivity. The pattern is clear: as businesses generated more value from their workers, the country as a whole became richer, which fueled more economic activity and created even more jobs. Then, beginning in 2000, the lines diverge; productivity continues to rise robustly, but employment suddenly wilts. By 2011, a significant gap appears between the two lines, showing economic growth with no parallel increase in job creation. Brynjolfsson and McAfee call it the "great decoupling." And Brynjolfsson says he is confident that technology is behind both the healthy growth in productivity and the weak growth in jobs.

It's a startling assertion because it threatens the faith that many economists place in technological progress. Brynjolfsson and McAfee still believe that technology boosts productivity and makes societies wealthier, but they think that it can also have a dark side: technological progress is eliminating the need for many types of jobs and leaving the typical worker worse off than before. Brynjolfsson can point to a second chart indicating that median income is failing to rise even as the gross domestic product soars. "It's the great paradox of our era," he says. "Productivity is at record levels, innovation has never been faster, and yet at the same time, we have a falling median income and we have fewer jobs. People are falling behind because technology is advancing so fast and our skills and organizations aren't keeping up."

While technological changes can be painful for workers whose skills no longer match the needs of employers, Lawrence Katz, a Harvard economist, says that no historical pattern shows these shifts leading to a net decrease in jobs over an extended period. Katz has done extensive research on how technological advances have affected jobs over the last few centuries—describing, for example, how highly skilled artisans in the mid-19th century were displaced by lower-skilled workers in factories. While it can take decades for workers to acquire the expertise needed for new types of employment, he says, "we never have run out of jobs. There is no long-term trend of eliminating work for people. Over the long term, employment rates are fairly stable. People have always been able to create new jobs. People come up with new things to do."

Still, Katz doesn't dismiss the notion that there is something different about today's digital technologies—something that could affect an even broader range of work. The question, he says, is whether economic history will serve as a useful

CONTINUE

guide. Will the job disruptions caused by technology be temporary as the workforce adapts, or will we see a science-fiction scenario in which automated processes and robots with superhuman skills take over a broad swath of human tasks? Though Katz expects the historical pattern to hold, it is "genuinely a question," he says. "If technology disrupts enough, who knows what will happen?"

Figure 1

United States Productivity and Employment

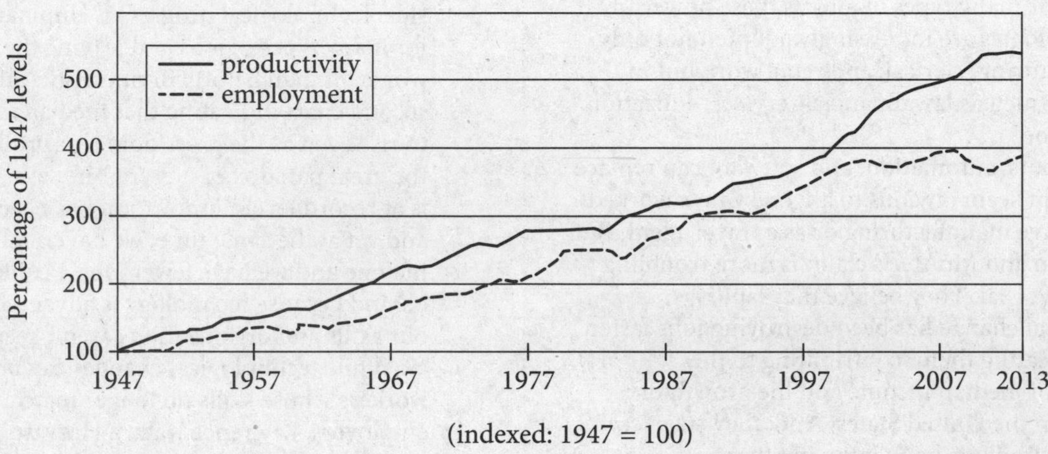

(indexed: 1947 = 100)

Figure 2

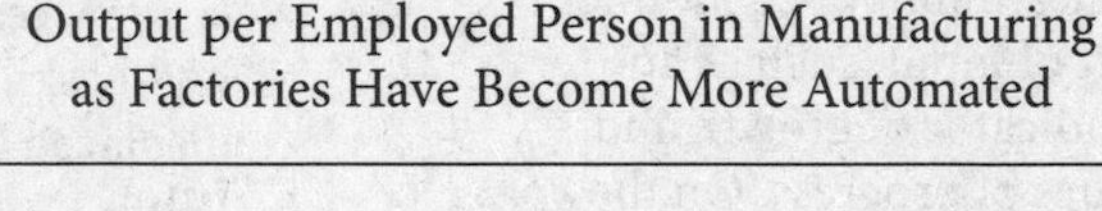

Output per Employed Person in Manufacturing as Factories Have Become More Automated

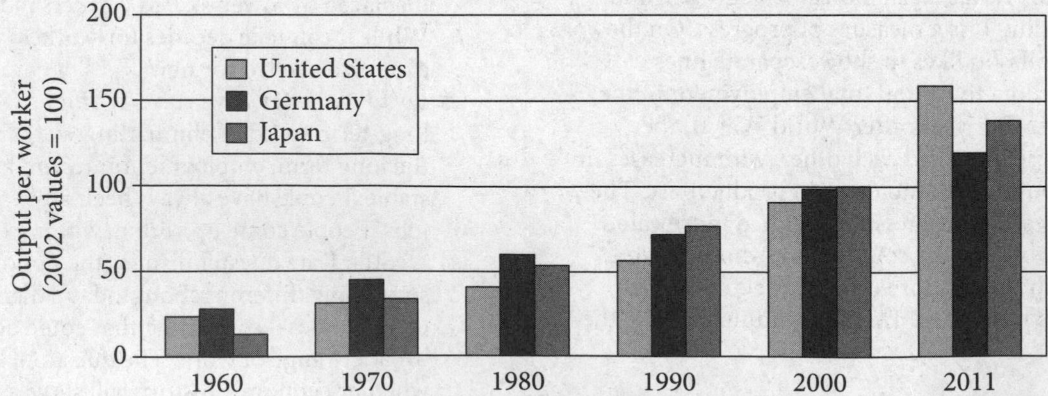

CONTINUE

11

The main purpose of the passage is to

A) examine the role of technology in workers' lives during the last century.
B) advocate for better technology to enhance workplace conditions.
C) argue for changes in how technology is deployed in the workplace.
D) assess the impact of advancements in technology on overall job growth.

12

According to Brynjolfsson and McAfee, advancements in technology since approximately the year 2000 have resulted in

A) low job growth in the United States.
B) global workplace changes.
C) more skilled laborers in the United States.
D) no global creation of new jobs.

13

Which choice provides the best evidence for the answer to the previous question?

A) Lines 1-6 ("MIT . . . years")
B) Lines 13-15 ("That . . . agent")
C) Lines 21-23 ("And . . . countries")
D) Lines 35-38 ("as businesses . . . jobs")

14

The primary purpose of lines 26-28 ("the amount . . . labor") is to

A) describe a process.
B) highlight a dilemma.
C) clarify a claim.
D) explain a term.

15

As used in line 35, "clear" most nearly means

A) pure.
B) keen.
C) untroubled.
D) unmistakable.

16

Which of the following best characterizes Katz's attitude toward "today's digital technologies" (lines 81-82)?

A) He is alarmed about countries' increasing reliance on them.
B) He is unconcerned about their effect on the economy.
C) He is uncertain how they might affect job growth.
D) He is optimistic that they will spur job creation to a degree not seen since the mid-nineteenth century.

CONTINUE

17

Which choice provides the best evidence for the answer to the previous question?

A) Lines 68-72 ("Katz . . . factories")

B) Lines 73-75 ("While . . . jobs")

C) Line 79 ("People come . . . do")

D) Lines 91-92 ("If . . . happen")

18

As used in line 83, "range" most nearly means

A) region.

B) scope.

C) distance.

D) position.

19

According to figure 1, which of the following years showed the widest gap between percentages of productivity and employment?

A) 1987

B) 1997

C) 2007

D) 2013

20

Which statement is supported by figure 2?

A) The country with the greatest growth in output per manufacturing worker from 1960 to 1990 was Germany.

B) Japan experienced its smallest increase in output per manufacturing worker from 2000 to 2011.

C) Each of the three countries experienced an increase in its output per manufacturing worker from 1960 to 2011.

D) Of the three countries, the United States had the greatest output per manufacturing worker for each of the years shown.

21

Which additional information, if presented in figure 2, would be most useful in evaluating the statement in lines 57-60 ("Productivity . . . jobs")?

A) The median income of employees as it compares across all three countries in a single year

B) The number of people employed in factories from 1960 to 2011

C) The types of organizations at which output of employed persons was measured

D) The kinds of manufacturing tasks most frequently taken over by machines

CONTINUE

Questions 22-31 are based on the following passage.

This passage is adapted from Patricia Waldron, "Why Birds Fly in a V Formation." ©2014 by American Association for the Advancement of Science.

Anyone watching the autumn sky knows that migrating birds fly in a V formation, but scientists have long debated why. A new study of ibises finds that these big-winged birds carefully position their wingtips and sync their flapping, presumably to catch the preceding bird's updraft—and save energy during flight.

There are two reasons birds might fly in a V formation: It may make flight easier, or they're simply following the leader. Squadrons of planes can save fuel by flying in a V formation, and many scientists suspect that migrating birds do the same. Models that treated flapping birds like fixed-wing airplanes estimate that they save energy by drafting off each other, but currents created by airplanes are far more stable than the oscillating eddies coming off of a bird. "Air gets pretty unpredictable behind a flapping wing," says James Usherwood, a locomotor biomechanist at the Royal Veterinary College at the University of London in Hatfield, where the research took place.

The study, published in *Nature*, took advantage of an existing project to reintroduce endangered northern bald ibises (*Geronticus eremita*) to Europe. Scientists used a microlight plane to show hand-raised birds their ancestral migration route from Austria to Italy. A flock of 14 juveniles carried data loggers specially built by Usherwood and his lab. The device's GPS determined each bird's flight position to within 30 cm, and an accelerometer showed the timing of the wing flaps.

Just as aerodynamic estimates would predict, the birds positioned themselves to fly just behind and to the side of the bird in front, timing their wing beats to catch the uplifting eddies. When a bird flew directly behind another, the timing of the flapping reversed so that it could minimize the effects of the downdraft coming off the back of the bird's body. "We didn't think this was possible," Usherwood says, considering that the feat requires careful flight and incredible awareness of one's neighbors. "Perhaps these big V formation birds can be thought of quite like an airplane with wings that go up and down."

The findings likely apply to other long-winged birds, such as pelicans, storks, and geese, Usherwood says. Smaller birds create more complex wakes that would make drafting too difficult. The researchers did not attempt to calculate the bird's energy savings because the necessary physiological measurements would be too invasive for an endangered species. Previous studies estimate that birds can use 20 percent to 30 percent less energy while flying in a V.

"From a behavioral perspective it's really a breakthrough," says David Lentink, a mechanical engineer at Stanford University in Palo Alto, California, who was not involved in the work. "Showing that birds care about syncing their wing beats is definitely an important insight that we didn't have before."

Scientists do not know how the birds find that aerodynamic sweet spot, but they suspect that the animals align themselves either by sight or by sensing air currents through their feathers. Alternatively, they may move around until they find the location with the least resistance. In future studies, the researchers will switch to more common birds, such as pigeons or geese. They plan to investigate how the animals decide who sets the course and the pace, and whether a mistake made by the leader can ripple through the rest of the flock to cause traffic jams.

"It's a pretty impressive piece of work as it is, but it does suggest that there's a lot more to learn," says Ty Hedrick, a biologist at the University of North Carolina, Chapel Hill, who studies flight aerodynamics in birds and insects. However they do it, he says, "birds are awfully good hang-glider pilots."

22

The main purpose of the passage is to

A) describe how squadrons of planes can save fuel by flying in a V formation.

B) discuss the effects of downdrafts on birds and airplanes.

C) explain research conducted to study why some birds fly in a V formation.

D) illustrate how birds sense air currents through their feathers.

23

The author includes the quotation "Air gets pretty unpredictable behind a flapping wing" (lines 17-18) to

A) explain that the current created by a bird differs from that of an airplane.

B) stress the amount of control exerted by birds flying in a V formation.

C) indicate that wind movement is continuously changing.

D) emphasize that the flapping of a bird's wings is powerful.

24

What can reasonably be inferred about the reason Usherwood used northern bald ibises as the subjects of his study?

A) The ibises were well acquainted with their migration route.

B) Usherwood knew the ibises were familiar with carrying data loggers during migration.

C) The ibises have a body design that is similar to that of a modern airplane.

D) The ibises were easily accessible for Usherwood and his team to track and observe.

25

Which choice provides the best evidence for the answer to the previous question?

A) Lines 3-7 ("A new . . . flight")

B) Lines 10-12 ("Squadrons . . . same")

C) Lines 22-24 ("The study . . . Europe")

D) Lines 29-31 ("The device's . . . flaps")

26

What is the most likely reason the author includes the 30 cm measurement in line 30?

A) To demonstrate the accuracy with which the data loggers collected the data

B) To present recorded data about how far an ibis flies between successive wing flaps

C) To provide the wingspan length of a juvenile ibis

D) To show how far behind the microlight plane each ibis flew

27

What does the author imply about pelicans, storks, and geese flying in a V formation?

A) They communicate with each other in the same way as do ibises.

B) They have the same migration routes as those of ibises.

C) They create a similar wake to that of ibises.

D) They expend more energy than do ibises.

28

Which choice provides the best evidence for the answer to the previous question?

A) Lines 35-38 ("When . . . body")

B) Lines 47-48 ("Smaller . . . difficult")

C) Lines 52-54 ("Previous . . . a V")

D) Lines 66-67 ("Alternatively . . . resistance")

29

What is a main idea of the seventh paragraph (lines 62-73)?

A) Different types of hierarchies exist in each flock of birds.

B) Mistakes can happen when long-winged birds create a V formation.

C) Future research will help scientists to better understand V formations.

D) Long-winged birds watch the lead bird closely to keep a V formation intact.

30

The author uses the phrase "aerodynamic sweet spot" in line 63 most likely to

A) describe how the proper structural design of an airplane helps to save fuel.

B) show that flying can be an exhilarating experience.

C) describe the birds' synchronized wing movement.

D) suggest that a certain position in a V formation has the least amount of wind resistance.

31

As used in line 72, "ripple" most nearly means

A) fluctuate.

B) spread.

C) wave.

D) undulate.

CONTINUE

Questions 32-41 are based on the following passages.

Passage 1 is adapted from Alexis de Tocqueville, *Democracy in America, Volume 2*. Originally published in 1840. Passage 2 is adapted from Harriet Taylor Mill, "Enfranchisement of Women." Originally published in 1851. As United States and European societies grew increasingly democratic during the nineteenth century, debates arose about whether freedoms enjoyed by men should be extended to women as well.

Passage 1

I have shown how democracy destroys or modifies the different inequalities which originate in society; but is this all? or does it not ultimately affect that great inequality of man and woman which has seemed, up to the present day, to be eternally based in human nature? I believe that the social changes which bring nearer to the same level the father and son, the master and servant, and superiors and inferiors generally speaking, will raise woman and make her more and more the equal of man. But here, more than ever, I feel the necessity of making myself clearly understood; for there is no subject on which the coarse and lawless fancies of our age have taken a freer range.

There are people in Europe who, confounding together the different characteristics of the sexes, would make of man and woman beings not only equal but alike. They would give to both the same functions, impose on both the same duties, and grant to both the same rights; they would mix them in all things—their occupations, their pleasures, their business. It may readily be conceived, that by thus attempting to make one sex equal to the other, both are degraded; and from so preposterous a medley of the works of nature nothing could ever result but weak men and disorderly women.

It is not thus that the Americans understand that species of democratic equality which may be established between the sexes. They admit, that as nature has appointed such wide differences between the physical and moral constitution of man and woman, her manifest design was to give a distinct employment to their various faculties; and they hold that improvement does not consist in making beings so dissimilar do pretty nearly the same things, but in getting each of them to fulfill their respective tasks in the best possible manner. The Americans have applied to the sexes the great principle of political economy which governs the manufactures of our age, by carefully dividing the duties of man from those of woman, in order that the great work of society may be the better carried on.

Passage 2

As society was constituted until the last few generations, inequality was its very basis; association grounded on equal rights scarcely existed; to be equals was to be enemies; two persons could hardly coöperate in anything, or meet in any amicable relation, without the law's appointing that one of them should be the superior of the other. Mankind have outgrown this state, and all things now tend to substitute, as the general principle of human relations, a just equality, instead of the dominion of the strongest. But of all relations, that between men and women, being the nearest and most intimate, and connected with the greatest number of strong emotions, was sure to be the last to throw off the old rule, and receive the new; for, in proportion to the strength of a feeling is the tenacity with which it clings to the forms and circumstances with which it has even accidentally become associated. . . .

. . . The proper sphere for all human beings is the largest and highest which they are able to attain to. What this is, cannot be ascertained without complete liberty of choice. . . . Let every occupation be open to all, without favor or discouragement to any, and employments will fall into the hands of those men or women who are found by experience to be most capable of worthily exercising them. There need be no fear that women will take out of the hands of men any occupation which men perform better than they. Each individual will prove his or her capacities, in the only way in which capacities can be proved,—by trial; and the world will have the benefit of the best faculties of all its inhabitants. But to interfere beforehand by an arbitrary limit, and declare that whatever be the genius, talent, energy, or force of

CONTINUE

mind, of an individual of a certain sex or class, those faculties shall not be exerted, or shall be exerted only in some few of the many modes in which others are permitted to use theirs, is not only an injustice to the individual, and a detriment to society, which loses what it can ill spare, but is also the most effectual way of providing that, in the sex or class so fettered, the qualities which are not permitted to be exercised shall not exist.

32

As used in line 9, "raise" most nearly means

A) increase.

B) cultivate.

C) nurture.

D) elevate.

33

In Passage 1, Tocqueville implies that treatment of men and women as identical in nature would have which consequence?

A) Neither sex would feel oppressed.

B) Both sexes would be greatly harmed.

C) Men would try to reclaim their lost authority.

D) Men and women would have privileges they do not need.

34

Which choice provides the best evidence for the answer to the previous question?

A) Lines 15-18 ("There . . . alike")

B) Lines 18-20 ("They . . . rights")

C) Lines 22-24 ("It may . . . degraded")

D) Lines 27-29 ("It is . . . sexes")

35

As used in line 53, "dominion" most nearly means

A) omnipotence.

B) supremacy.

C) ownership.

D) territory.

36

In Passage 2, Mill most strongly suggests that gender roles are resistant to change because they

A) have long served as the basis for the formal organization of society.

B) are matters of deeply entrenched tradition.

C) can be influenced by legislative reforms only indirectly.

D) benefit the groups and institutions currently in power.

37

Which choice provides the best evidence for the answer to the previous question?

A) Lines 43-44 ("As society . . . basis")

B) Lines 46-49 ("two . . . other")

C) Lines 58-61 ("in proportion . . . associated")

D) Lines 67-69 ("employments . . . them")

38

Both authors would most likely agree that the changes in gender roles that they describe would be

A) part of a broad social shift toward greater equality.

B) unlikely to provide benefits that outweigh their costs.

C) inevitable given the economic advantages of gender equality.

D) at odds with the principles of American democracy.

CONTINUE

39

Tocqueville in Passage 1 would most likely characterize the position taken by Mill in lines 65-69 in Passage 2 ("Let . . . them") as

A) less radical about gender roles than it might initially seem.

B) persuasive in the abstract but difficult to implement in practice.

C) ill-advised but consistent with a view held by some other advocates of gender equality.

D) compatible with economic progress in the United States but not in Europe.

40

Which choice best describes the ways that the two authors conceive of the individual's proper position in society?

A) Tocqueville believes that an individual's position should be defined in important ways by that individual's sex, while Mill believes that an individual's abilities should be the determining factor.

B) Tocqueville believes that an individual's economic class should determine that individual's position, while Mill believes that class is not a legitimate consideration.

C) Tocqueville believes that an individual's temperament should determine that individual's position, while Mill believes that temperament should not be a factor in an individual's position.

D) Tocqueville believes that an individual's position should be determined by what is most beneficial to society, while Mill believes it should be determined by what an individual finds most rewarding.

41

Based on Passage 2, Mill would most likely say that the application of the "great principle of political economy" (lines 38-39, Passage 1) to gender roles has which effect?

A) It prevents many men and women from developing to their full potential.

B) It makes it difficult for men and women to sympathize with each other.

C) It unintentionally furthers the cause of gender equality.

D) It guarantees that women take occupations that men are better suited to perform.

CONTINUE

Questions 42-52 are based on the following passage and supplementary material.

This passage is adapted from Brian Greene, "How the Higgs Boson Was Found." ©2013 by Smithsonian Institution. The Higgs boson is an elementary particle associated with the Higgs field. Experiments conducted in 2012–2013 tentatively confirmed the existence of the Higgs boson and thus of the Higgs field.

Nearly a half-century ago, Peter Higgs and a handful of other physicists were trying to understand the origin of a basic physical feature: mass. You can think of mass as an object's heft or, a little more precisely, as the resistance it offers to having its motion changed. Push on a freight train (or a feather) to increase its speed, and the resistance you feel reflects its mass. At a microscopic level, the freight train's mass comes from its constituent molecules and atoms, which are themselves built from fundamental particles, electrons and quarks. But where do the masses of these and other fundamental particles come from?

When physicists in the 1960s modeled the behavior of these particles using equations rooted in quantum physics, they encountered a puzzle. If they imagined that the particles were all massless, then each term in the equations clicked into a perfectly symmetric pattern, like the tips of a perfect snowflake. And this symmetry was not just mathematically elegant. It explained patterns evident in the experimental data. But—and here's the puzzle—physicists knew that the particles did have mass, and when they modified the equations to account for this fact, the mathematical harmony was spoiled. The equations became complex and unwieldy and, worse still, inconsistent.

What to do? Here's the idea put forward by Higgs. Don't shove the particles' masses down the throat of the beautiful equations. Instead, keep the equations pristine and symmetric, but consider them operating within a peculiar environment. Imagine that all of space is uniformly filled with an invisible substance—now called the Higgs field—that exerts a drag force on particles when they accelerate through it. Push on a fundamental particle in an effort to increase its speed and, according to Higgs, you would feel this drag force as a resistance. Justifiably, you would interpret the resistance as the particle's mass. For a mental toehold, think of a ping-pong ball submerged in water. When you push on the ping-pong ball, it will feel much more massive than it does outside of water. Its interaction with the watery environment has the effect of endowing it with mass. So with particles submerged in the Higgs field.

In 1964, Higgs submitted a paper to a prominent physics journal in which he formulated this idea mathematically. The paper was rejected. Not because it contained a technical error, but because the premise of an invisible something permeating space, interacting with particles to provide their mass, well, it all just seemed like heaps of overwrought speculation. The editors of the journal deemed it "of no obvious relevance to physics."

But Higgs persevered (and his revised paper appeared later that year in another journal), and physicists who took the time to study the proposal gradually realized that his idea was a stroke of genius, one that allowed them to have their cake and eat it too. In Higgs's scheme, the fundamental equations can retain their pristine form because the dirty work of providing the particles' masses is relegated to the environment.

While I wasn't around to witness the initial rejection of Higgs's proposal in 1964 (well, I was around, but only barely), I can attest that by the mid-1980s, the assessment had changed. The physics community had, for the most part, fully bought into the idea that there was a Higgs field permeating space. In fact, in a graduate course I took that covered what's known as the Standard Model of Particle Physics (the quantum equations physicists have assembled to describe the particles of matter and the dominant forces by which they influence each other), the professor presented the Higgs field with such certainty that for a long while I had no idea it had yet to be established experimentally.
On occasion, that happens in physics. Mathematical equations can sometimes tell such a convincing tale, they can seemingly radiate reality so strongly, that they become entrenched in the vernacular of working physicists, even before there's data to confirm them.

CONTINUE

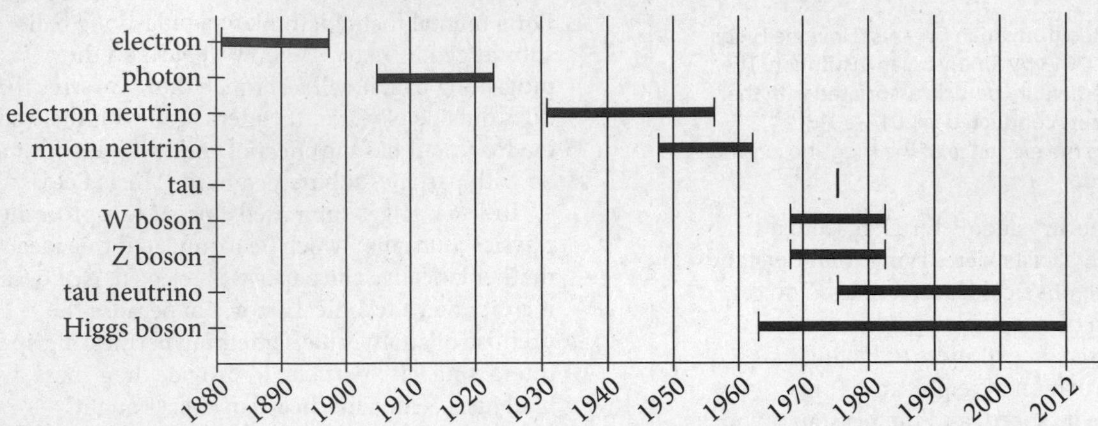

Adapted from the editors of *The Economist*, "Worth the Wait." ©2012 by The Economist Newspaper Limited.

42

Over the course of the passage, the main focus shifts from

A) a technical account of the Higgs field to a description of it aimed at a broad audience.

B) a review of Higgs's work to a contextualization of that work within Higgs's era.

C) an explanation of the Higgs field to a discussion of the response to Higgs's theory.

D) an analysis of the Higgs field to a suggestion of future discoveries that might build upon it.

43

The main purpose of the analogy of the ping-pong ball (line 40) is to

A) popularize a little-known fact.

B) contrast competing scientific theories.

C) criticize a widely accepted explanation.

D) clarify an abstract concept.

44

The author most strongly suggests that the reason the scientific community initially rejected Higgs's idea was that the idea

A) addressed a problem unnoticed by other physicists.

B) only worked if the equations were flawless.

C) rendered accepted theories in physics obsolete.

D) appeared to have little empirical basis.

45

Which choice provides the best evidence for the answer to the previous question?

A) Lines 30-32 ("Instead . . . environment")

B) Lines 46-48 ("In 1964 . . . mathematically")

C) Lines 48-53 ("Not . . . speculation")

D) Lines 67-70 ("The physics . . . space")

CONTINUE

46

The author notes that one reason Higgs's theory gained acceptance was that it

A) let scientists accept two conditions that had previously seemed irreconcilable.

B) introduced an innovative approach that could be applied to additional problems.

C) answered a question that earlier scientists had not even raised.

D) explained why two distinct phenomena were being misinterpreted as one phenomenon.

47

Which choice provides the best evidence for the answer to the previous question?

A) Lines 36-39 ("Push . . . mass")

B) Lines 43-45 ("Its interaction . . . field")

C) Lines 55-63 ("But . . . environment")

D) Lines 78-83 ("On occasion . . . them")

48

Which statement best describes the technique the author uses to advance the main point of the last paragraph?

A) He recounts a personal experience to illustrate a characteristic of the discipline of physics.

B) He describes his own education to show how physics has changed during his career.

C) He provides autobiographical details to demonstrate how Higgs's theory was confirmed.

D) He contrasts the status of Higgs's theory at two time periods to reveal how the details of the theory evolved.

49

As used in line 77, "established" most nearly means

A) validated.

B) founded.

C) introduced.

D) enacted.

50

What purpose does the graph serve in relation to the passage as a whole?

A) It indicates that the scientific community's quick acceptance of the Higgs boson was typical.

B) It places the discussion of the reception of the Higgs boson into a broader scientific context.

C) It demonstrates that the Higgs boson was regarded differently than were other hypothetical particles.

D) It clarifies the ways in which the Higgs boson represented a major discovery.

CONTINUE

51

Which statement is best supported by the data presented in the graph?

A) The W boson and the Z boson were proposed and experimentally confirmed at about the same time.

B) The Higgs boson was experimentally confirmed more quickly than were most other particles.

C) The tau neutrino was experimentally confirmed at about the same time as the tau.

D) The muon neutrino took longer to experimentally confirm than did the electron neutrino.

52

Based on the graph, the author's depiction of Higgs's theory in the mid-1980s is most analogous to which hypothetical situation?

A) The muon neutrino was widely disputed until being confirmed in the early 1960s.

B) Few physicists in 2012 doubted the reality of the tau neutrino.

C) No physicists prior to 1960 considered the possibility of the W or Z boson.

D) Most physicists in 1940 believed in the existence of the electron neutrino.

STOP

If you finish before time is called, you may check your work on this section only.

Do not turn to any other section.

No Test Material On This Page

Writing and Language Test

35 MINUTES, 44 QUESTIONS

Turn to Section 2 of your answer sheet to answer the questions in this section.

DIRECTIONS

Each passage below is accompanied by a number of questions. For some questions, you will consider how the passage might be revised to improve the expression of ideas. For other questions, you will consider how the passage might be edited to correct errors in sentence structure, usage, or punctuation. A passage or a question may be accompanied by one or more graphics (such as a table or graph) that you will consider as you make revising and editing decisions.

Some questions will direct you to an underlined portion of a passage. Other questions will direct you to a location in a passage or ask you to think about the passage as a whole.

After reading each passage, choose the answer to each question that most effectively improves the quality of writing in the passage or that makes the passage conform to the conventions of standard written English. Many questions include a "NO CHANGE" option. Choose that option if you think the best choice is to leave the relevant portion of the passage as it is.

Questions 1-11 are based on the following passage.

NASA: A Space Program with Down-to-Earth Benefits

The National Aeronautics and Space Administration (NASA) is a US government agency whose budget is frequently [1] many times contested. Many people think of NASA's programs as trivial. In truth, the agency has a widespread positive [2] effect on society by serving as a catalyst for innovation and scientific understanding,

1

A) NO CHANGE

B) oftentimes

C) repeatedly

D) DELETE the underlined portion.

2

A) NO CHANGE

B) affect on

C) effect to

D) affects on

CONTINUE

3 to create jobs, and showing humanity its place within the universe.

In 1958, the program's first year, very few people believed that it was even possible for a manned spacecraft to leave the atmosphere and orbit Earth. But by initiating and collaborating on projects such as the Apollo Moon missions, the space shuttle program, the Hubble Space 4 Telescope, and unmanned planetary exploration, NASA has continually challenged its scientists and engineers to do things that were previously thought impossible. All along, these NASA projects have 5 greatly increased international cooperation. A short list of inventions 6 elaborated by NASA includes communications satellites, invisible braces, and cordless tools. All these inventions 7 spawns new industries, and with those industries, jobs. NASA also sponsors the Small Business Innovation Research and Small Business Technology Transfer programs, which are specifically designed to support technological development in the private sector.

3

A) NO CHANGE
B) creating jobs,
C) for job creation,
D) the creation of jobs,

4

A) NO CHANGE
B) Telescope; and
C) Telescope and;
D) Telescope and,

5

Which choice most effectively sets up the list of examples that follows in the next sentence?

A) NO CHANGE
B) garnered national publicity for the agency.
C) generated a steady stream of new technology.
D) made a lot of money for the agency.

6

A) NO CHANGE
B) evolved
C) developed
D) progressed

7

A) NO CHANGE
B) spawned
C) has spawned
D) spawning

[1] A report by the Space Foundation estimated that NASA contributed $180 billion to the economy in 2005. [2] More than 60 percent of the contribution **8** coming from commercial goods and services created by companies using space-related technology. [3] This translates as excellent returns from an agency that received approximately 17.7 billion in tax dollars in 2014. [4] This investment by taxpayers enhances not only the national economy but also the United States' competitiveness in the international market.

[5] Moreover, the benefits of NASA funding extend beyond the purely economic, as astrophysicist Neil deGrasse Tyson indicated in his testimony before the US Senate: "For . . . a penny on a dollar—we can transform the country from a sullen, dispirited nation, weary of economic struggle, to one where it has reclaimed its twentieth-century birthright to dream of tomorrow." **9**

8

A) NO CHANGE
B) which came
C) to come
D) came

9

To make this paragraph most logical, sentence 1 should be placed

A) where it is now.
B) after sentence 2.
C) after sentence 3.
D) after sentence 4.

CONTINUE

Tyson's expansive vision for the agency hints at another mission of NASA's, illuminated in this observation by Apollo 14 astronaut Edgar Mitchell: "You develop an instant global consciousness, a people orientation, an intense dissatisfaction with the state of the world, and a compulsion to do something about it." **10** With world population topping seven billion, humanity is in need of some perspective. **11** Therefore, we should continue to support NASA not only for practical reasons but also because it is a necessary vehicle for increasing our awareness of how we can fulfill our responsibilities to the planet and each other.

10

At this point, the writer is considering adding the following sentence.

> In addition, NASA has facilities in Washington, DC, Florida, Texas, California, and other states.

Should the writer make this addition here?

A) Yes, because it serves as a counterargument to the quotation from astrophysicist Neil deGrasse Tyson.

B) Yes, because it reinforces the passage's point about the importance of NASA's work.

C) No, because it undermines the passage's claim about the economic benefits of NASA's work.

D) No, because it blurs the paragraph's focus by introducing information that does not support the paragraph's claim about the importance of NASA's work.

11

A) NO CHANGE

B) Instead,

C) For example,

D) However,

CONTINUE

Questions 12-22 are based on the following passage and supplementary material.

Professional Development: A Shared Responsibility

New theories, **12** new practices too, and technologies are transforming the twenty-first-century workplace at lightning speed. To perform their jobs successfully in this dynamic environment, workers in many **13** fields—from social services to manufacturing, must continually acquire relevant knowledge and update key skills. This practice of continued education, also known as professional development, benefits not only employees but also their employers. **14** Accordingly, meaningful professional development is a shared responsibility: it is the responsibility of employers to provide useful programs, and it is also the responsibility of employees to take advantage of the opportunities offered to them.

Critics of employer-provided professional development argue that employees **15** might consider a popular career path. If employees find themselves falling behind in the workplace, these critics **16** contend. Then it is the duty of those employees to identify, and even pay

12

A) NO CHANGE
B) also new practices,
C) in addition to practices,
D) practices,

13

A) NO CHANGE
B) fields
C) fields,
D) fields;

14

A) NO CHANGE
B) Nevertheless,
C) Regardless,
D) Similarly,

15

Which choice best establishes the argument that follows?

A) NO CHANGE
B) should lean heavily on their employers.
C) must be in charge of their own careers.
D) will be ready for changes in the job market.

16

A) NO CHANGE
B) contend; then
C) contend then
D) contend, then

CONTINUE

for, appropriate resources to **17** show them how and why they are falling behind and what they should do about it. This argument ignores research pointing to high employee turnover and training of new staff as significant costs plaguing employers in many fields. Forward-thinking employers recognize the importance of investing in the employees they have rather than hiring new staff when the skills of current workers **18** get old and worn out.

17

A) NO CHANGE
B) address their deficiencies.
C) deal with their flaws and shortcomings.
D) allow them to meet their employers' needs in terms of the knowledge they are supposed to have.

18

A) NO CHANGE
B) are no good anymore.
C) become obsolete.
D) have lost their charm.

The most common forms of professional development provided to employees **19** includes coaching, mentoring, technical assistance, and workshops. Some employers utilize several approaches simultaneously, developing a framework that suits the particular needs of their employees. **20** Around the same time, the figure illustrates a simple yet comprehensive professional-development model created for special education personnel. As the figure suggests, **21** receiving coaching and consultation is the overarching framework, while the opportunity to belong to professional networks and participate in activities such as foundation and skill-building workshops is relatively unimportant.

Professional-Development Framework

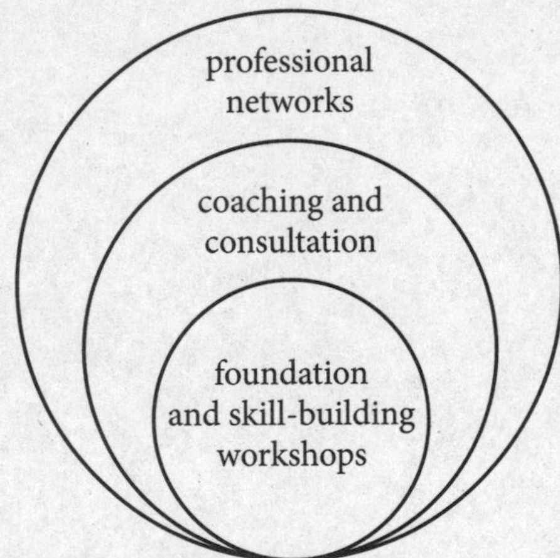

Adapted from Northern Suburban Special Education District, "Professional Development Framework." ©2014 by Northern Suburban Special Education Program.

19

A) NO CHANGE
B) include
C) including
D) has included

20

A) NO CHANGE
B) Besides that,
C) Nevertheless,
D) DELETE the underlined portion and begin the sentence with a capital letter.

21

Which choice makes the writer's description of the figure most accurate?

A) NO CHANGE
B) participation in foundation and skill-building workshops is the overarching framework within which staff receive coaching and consultation as well as the opportunity to belong to a professional network.
C) membership in a professional network is the overarching framework within which staff receive coaching and consultation as well as the opportunity to attend foundation and skill-building workshops.
D) receiving coaching and consultation is the overarching framework within which staff have the opportunity to belong to a professional network as well as attend foundation and skill-building workshops.

CONTINUE

A recent trend in professional development that has provided advantages to both employers and employees is online instruction. From an employer perspective, the first and perhaps most obvious advantage is the lower cost of online professional development compared with that of in-person workshops and training. Employers can also 22 identify, which employees have successfully completed instructional modules and which need to be offered additional training. For employees, online professional development provides the opportunity to receive instruction at their own pace and interact with other professionals online. This exciting trend has the potential to make the shared responsibility of professional development less burdensome for both employers and employees.

22

A) NO CHANGE
B) identify:
C) identify
D) identify—

CONTINUE

Questions 23-33 are based on the following passage.

The Evolution of Slow Food

In 1986, McDonald's caused a stir in Italy when it opened a restaurant next to Rome's historic Spanish Steps. Young, on-the-go eaters were thrilled; [23] specifically, those who prized regional foods and Italy's convivial culture built on cooking and long meals feared that the restaurant signaled the death of a way of life. To counter the rise of fast food and fast [24] life, a cohort of chefs, journalists, and sociologists spearheaded a Slow Food movement, declaring loyalty to unhurried enjoyment. [25]

From its beginning, the movement [26] had opposed the standardization of taste that fast food chains promote. For example, a McDonald's hamburger made in Boston tastes more or less the same as one made in Beijing. This consistency is made possible by industrial mass production. Slow Food supporters, by contrast, back methods of growing and preparing food based on regional culinary traditions. When produced using traditional methods, goat cheese made in France tastes different from goat cheese made in Vermont. A goat

23

A) NO CHANGE
B) for example,
C) however,
D) in fact,

24

A) NO CHANGE
B) life; a
C) life: a
D) life. A

25

At this point, the writer is considering adding the following sentence.

> The group's philosophy was connected to the tale of the hare and the tortoise, in which the tortoise wins the race.

Should the writer make this addition here?

A) Yes, because it explains the primary belief that led to the development of the Slow Food movement.
B) Yes, because it reinforces a claim that the writer makes earlier in the paragraph.
C) No, because it blurs the paragraph's focus by introducing a new idea that is not clearly explained.
D) No, because it distracts from the paragraph's emphasis on the Slow Food movement's origins and beliefs.

26

A) NO CHANGE
B) opposes
C) will oppose
D) has opposed

CONTINUE

ingests the vegetation particular to the meadow in which it grazes, which, along with other environmental **27** factors such as altitude and weather shapes the cheese's taste and texture. If all foods were produced under the industrial model, **28** we would have meals that are not very flavorful.

During **29** their early years, the movement also focused on the value of **30** spending lots of time with friends and family during long meals. It emphasized the importance of preserving these "easygoing, slow

27

A) NO CHANGE
B) factors, such as altitude and weather,
C) factors such as, altitude and weather,
D) factors, such as altitude and weather

28

Which choice most effectively supports the central point of the paragraph?

A) NO CHANGE
B) the public would not be interested in learning about traditional foods.
C) people would not be able to determine how a particular food was made.
D) consumers would lose this diversity of flavors.

29

A) NO CHANGE
B) there
C) its
D) it's

30

A) NO CHANGE
B) leisurely meals with friends and family.
C) eating slowly and in the company of loved ones such as friends and family.
D) joining friends as well as family for time-consuming meals.

CONTINUE

pleasures." As the movement grew beyond Italy's borders—today Slow Food International boasts more than 100,000 members in 150 countries—this emphasis on pleasure **31** pictured criticism for being elitist. Critics have also asked if growing food using traditional methods, as opposed to mass production, **32** can adequately and affordably feed the world? Given the hectic pace of modern life, who among us has the time and resources for elaborate meals? Such questions, in addition to environmental concerns, are at the heart of perennial debates about food production.

Over time, Slow Food has broadened its mission to focus on food that is good, clean, and fair for all. Members assert that food should be flavorful, carrying the properties of a particular region; it should be raised using environmentally sustainable practices that preserve biodiversity; and it should be accessible to all without exploiting the labors of those who produced it. **33** In short, Slow Food runs programs that support small-scale producers in marketing regional foods in a world where food corporations threaten to drive them out of the marketplace and homogenize food choices.

31

A) NO CHANGE
B) portrayed
C) drew
D) sketched

32

A) NO CHANGE
B) adequately and affordably can feed the world?
C) can adequately and affordably feed the world.
D) adequately and affordably can feed the world.

33

A) NO CHANGE
B) Nonetheless,
C) To these ends,
D) By the same token,

CONTINUE

Questions 34-44 are based on the following passage.

Was the Hoax a Hoax?

For an hour on the evening of October 30, 1938, Orson Welles and other performers from the Mercury Theatre flooded the airwaves with alarming "news bulletins" about a Martian invasion supposedly occurring in Grover's Mill, New Jersey. They were performing a radio play adapted from *The War of the Worlds*, a science fiction novel by H. G. Wells. The next day, a front-page **34** headline in the *New York Times* declared, "Radio Listeners in Panic, Taking War Drama as Fact." **35** The *Times* article claimed that people had fled their homes and that police stations had been swamped with calls. This version of events persisted, and the legend became that Welles's broadcast had as many as twelve million people **36** who feared that Martians had invaded Earth.

Recently, however, scholars have questioned the accuracy of this legend, suggesting the degree of public hysteria has been grossly exaggerated. The authors of an article published in October 2013 go **37** so far to assign blame for the distortion to the newspaper industry.

34

A) NO CHANGE
B) headline in the *New York Times*, declared
C) headline, in the *New York Times* declared,
D) headline, in the *New York Times*, declared

35

The writer wants to add a supporting detail to indicate that the story was widely reported. Which choice best accomplishes this goal?

A) NO CHANGE
B) Other newspapers also ran stories claiming that the broadcast had incited mass hysteria.
C) In 2013, many newspapers and magazines featured articles about the seventy-fifth anniversary of the broadcast.
D) The *Times* was then and is now one of the United States' most popular news sources.

36

A) NO CHANGE
B) that feared
C) fearing
D) to fear

37

A) NO CHANGE
B) as far
C) as far and
D) so far as

CONTINUE

38 At this time, Jefferson Pooley and Michael Socolow, both professors of communication studies, argue that the newspaper industry sought to discredit the newly emerging technology of radio, which was cutting into newspapers' **39** profits. The newspaper industry tried to do this by portraying the new medium as irresponsible.

[1] Proof of ulterior motives is scarce, **40** consequently weakening Pooley and Socolow's argument. [2] For instance, the C. E. Hooper ratings indicate that a mere 2 percent of households had tuned in to the broadcast. [3] Pooley and Socolow also call into question the validity of an oft-cited report that was based on a survey conducted six weeks after the broadcast. [4] Just because some people found the broadcast unsettling, the authors contend, doesn't mean they believed it and reacted with real terror. [5] According to this report, one million people indicated that they had been "frightened" by the broadcast. [6] Ratings, however, reveal that **41** far fewer than a million people had been

38

A) NO CHANGE
B) On one hand,
C) In the article,
D) Next,

39

Which choice most effectively combines the sentences at the underlined portion?

A) profits, which is what the newspaper industry tried to do when it portrayed
B) profits, by which the newspaper industry portrayed
C) profits and tried to do this by portraying
D) profits, by portraying

40

Which choice best establishes the main idea of the paragraph?

A) NO CHANGE
B) but evidence does suggest that reports of panic have been overblown.
C) yet Pooley and Socolow maintain that the newspaper industry intentionally distorted the story.
D) making it difficult to determine what really happened in 1938.

41

A) NO CHANGE
B) many less than
C) much less then
D) much fewer then

CONTINUE

listening to the broadcast. [7] Furthermore, Pooley and Socolow note that this survey "conflated being 'frightened,' 'disturbed,' or 'excited' by the program with being 'panicked.'" 42

Pooley and Socolow describe a more likely scenario: most people who heard the broadcast understood they were listening to a piece of fiction, but 43 some being influenced by the sensationalized news coverage afterward, later "remembered" being more afraid than they had been. The researchers also suggest that, 44 not unlike people who got caught up in the excitement of the story when reading about it in the newspaper, the American public may have been willing to embrace the legend because of its appeal to the imagination.

42

To make this paragraph most logical, sentence 4 should be placed

A) where it is now.
B) after sentence 2.
C) after sentence 5.
D) after sentence 7.

43

A) NO CHANGE
B) some, they were
C) some,
D) some

44

Which choice most effectively signals the comparison the writer is making between the two groups mentioned?

A) NO CHANGE
B) unlike
C) not like
D) different from

STOP

If you finish before time is called, you may check your work on this section only. Do not turn to any other section.

Math Test – No Calculator

25 MINUTES, 20 QUESTIONS

Turn to Section 3 of your answer sheet to answer the questions in this section.

DIRECTIONS

For questions 1-15, solve each problem, choose the best answer from the choices provided, and fill in the corresponding circle on your answer sheet. **For questions 16-20**, solve the problem and enter your answer in the grid on the answer sheet. Please refer to the directions before question 16 on how to enter your answers in the grid. You may use any available space in your test booklet for scratch work.

NOTES

1. The use of a calculator **is not permitted.**
2. All variables and expressions used represent real numbers unless otherwise indicated.
3. Figures provided in this test are drawn to scale unless otherwise indicated.
4. All figures lie in a plane unless otherwise indicated.
5. Unless otherwise indicated, the domain of a given function f is the set of all real numbers x for which $f(x)$ is a real number.

REFERENCE

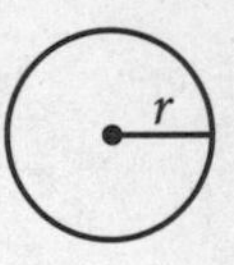

$A = \pi r^2$
$C = 2\pi r$

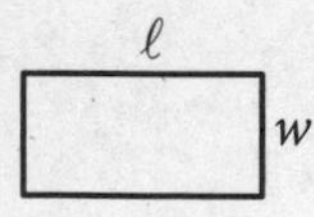

$A = \ell w$

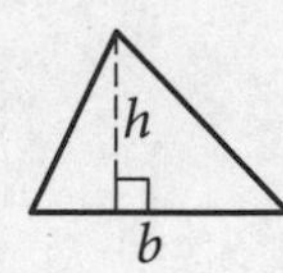

$A = \frac{1}{2}bh$

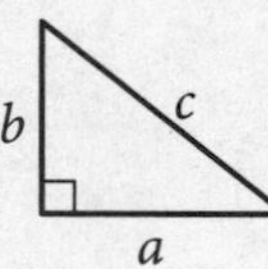

$c^2 = a^2 + b^2$

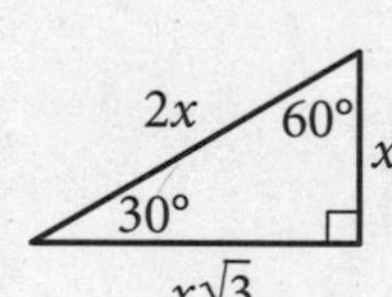

Special Right Triangles

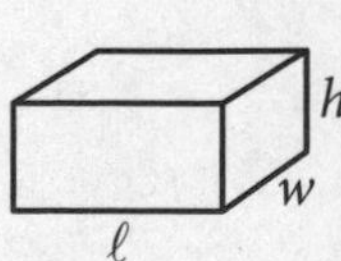

$V = \ell wh$

$V = \pi r^2 h$

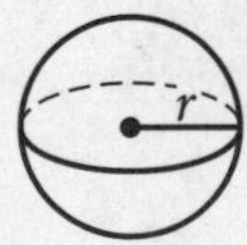

$V = \frac{4}{3}\pi r^3$

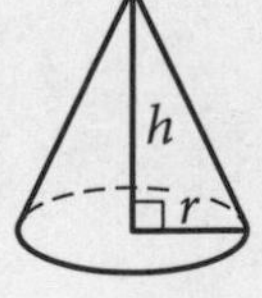

$V = \frac{1}{3}\pi r^2 h$

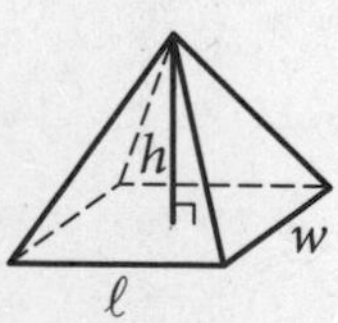

$V = \frac{1}{3}\ell wh$

The number of degrees of arc in a circle is 360.
The number of radians of arc in a circle is 2π.
The sum of the measures in degrees of the angles of a triangle is 180.

CONTINUE

1

$$x + y = 75$$

The equation above relates the number of minutes, x, Maria spends running each day and the number of minutes, y, she spends biking each day. In the equation, what does the number 75 represent?

A) The number of minutes spent running each day
B) The number of minutes spent biking each day
C) The total number of minutes spent running and biking each day
D) The number of minutes spent biking for each minute spent running

2

Which of the following is equivalent to $3(x + 5) - 6$?

A) $3x - 3$
B) $3x$ [illegible] 1
C) $3x + 9$
D) $15x - 6$

3

$$x = y - 3$$
$$\frac{x}{2} + 2y = 6$$

Which ordered pair (x, y) satisfies the system of equations shown above?

A) $(-3, 0)$
B) $(0, 3)$
C) $(6, -3)$
D) $(36, -6)$

4

Which of the following complex numbers is equal to $(5 + 12i) - (9i^2 - 6i)$, for $i = \sqrt{-1}$?

A) $-14 - 18i$
B) $-4 - 6i$
C) $4 + 6i$
D) $14 + 18i$

CONTINUE

5

If $f(x) = \dfrac{x^2 - 6x + 3}{x - 1}$, what is $f(-1)$?

A) -5

B) -2

C) 2

D) 5

6

A company that makes wildlife videos purchases camera equipment for $32,400. The equipment depreciates in value at a constant rate for 12 years, after which it is considered to have no monetary value. How much is the camera equipment worth 4 years after it is purchased?

A) $10,800

B) $16,200

C) $21,600

D) $29,700

7

$$x^2 + 6x + 4$$

Which of the following is equivalent to the expression above?

A) $(x+3)^2 + 5$

B) $(x+3)^2 - 5$

C) $(x-3)^2 + 5$

D) $(x-3)^2 - 5$

8

Ken is working this summer as part of a crew on a farm. He earned $8 per hour for the first 10 hours he worked this week. Because of his performance, his crew leader raised his salary to $10 per hour for the rest of the week. Ken saves 90% of his earnings from each week. What is the least number of hours he must work the rest of the week to save at least $270 for the week?

A) 38

B) 33

C) 22

D) 16

CONTINUE

9

Marisa needs to hire at least 10 staff members for an upcoming project. The staff members will be made up of junior directors, who will be paid \$640 per week, and senior directors, who will be paid \$880 per week. Her budget for paying the staff members is no more than \$9,700 per week. She must hire at least 3 junior directors and at least 1 senior director. Which of the following systems of inequalities represents the conditions described if x is the number of junior directors and y is the number of senior directors?

A) $640x + 880y \geq 9{,}700$
$x + y \leq 10$
$x \geq 3$
$y \geq 1$

B) $640x + 880y \leq 9{,}700$
$x + y \geq 10$
$x \geq 3$
$y \geq 1$

C) $640x + 880y \geq 9{,}700$
$x + y \geq 10$
$x \leq 3$
$y \leq 1$

D) $640x + 880y \leq 9{,}700$
$x + y \leq 10$
$x \leq 3$
$y \leq 1$

10

$$ax^3 + bx^2 + cx + d = 0$$

In the equation above, a, b, c, and d are constants. If the equation has roots -1, -3, and 5, which of the following is a factor of $ax^3 + bx^2 + cx + d$?

A) $x - 1$

B) $x + 1$

C) $x - 3$

D) $x + 5$

CONTINUE

11

The expression $\dfrac{x^{-2}y^{\frac{1}{2}}}{x^{\frac{1}{3}}y^{-1}}$, where $x > 1$ and $y > 1$, is equivalent to which of the following?

A) $\dfrac{\sqrt{y}}{\sqrt[3]{x^2}}$

B) $\dfrac{y\sqrt{y}}{\sqrt[3]{x^2}}$

C) $\dfrac{y\sqrt{y}}{x\sqrt{x}}$

D) $\dfrac{y\sqrt{y}}{x^2\sqrt[3]{x}}$

12

The function f is defined by $f(x) = (x+3)(x+1)$. The graph of f in the xy-plane is a parabola. Which of the following intervals contains the x-coordinate of the vertex of the graph of f?

A) $-4 < x < -3$

B) $-3 < x < 1$

C) $1 < x < 3$

D) $3 < x < 4$

CONTINUE

13

Which of the following expressions is equivalent to

$\dfrac{x^2 - 2x - 5}{x - 3}$?

A) $x - 5 - \dfrac{20}{x - 3}$

B) $x - 5 - \dfrac{10}{x - 3}$

C) $x + 1 - \dfrac{8}{x - 3}$

D) $x + 1 - \dfrac{2}{x - 3}$

14

A shipping service restricts the dimensions of the boxes it will ship for a certain type of service. The restriction states that for boxes shaped like rectangular prisms, the sum of the perimeter of the base of the box and the height of the box cannot exceed 130 inches. The perimeter of the base is determined using the width and length of the box. If a box has a height of 60 inches and its length is 2.5 times the width, which inequality shows the allowable width x, in inches, of the box?

A) $0 < x \leq 10$

B) $0 < x \leq 11\frac{2}{3}$

C) $0 < x \leq 17\frac{1}{2}$

D) $0 < x \leq 20$

15

The expression $\frac{1}{3}x^2 - 2$ can be rewritten as $\frac{1}{3}(x - k)(x + k)$, where k is a positive constant. What is the value of k ?

A) 2

B) 6

C) $\sqrt{2}$

D) $\sqrt{6}$

DIRECTIONS

For questions 16-20, solve the problem and enter your answer in the grid, as described below, on the answer sheet.

1. Although not required, it is suggested that you write your answer in the boxes at the top of the columns to help you fill in the circles accurately. You will receive credit only if the circles are filled in correctly.
2. Mark no more than one circle in any column.
3. No question has a negative answer.
4. Some problems may have more than one correct answer. In such cases, grid only one answer.
5. **Mixed numbers** such as $3\frac{1}{2}$ must be gridded as 3.5 or 7/2. (If 3 1 / 2 is entered into the grid, it will be interpreted as $\frac{31}{2}$, not $3\frac{1}{2}$.)
6. **Decimal answers:** If you obtain a decimal answer with more digits than the grid can accommodate, it may be either rounded or truncated, but it must fill the entire grid.

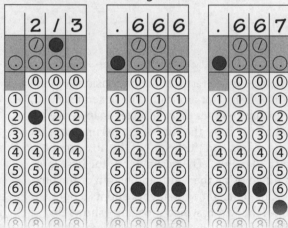

Answer: $\frac{7}{12}$

Write answer in boxes. → 7 / 1 2

← Fraction line

Grid in result.

Answer: 2.5

2 . 5

← Decimal point

Acceptable ways to grid $\frac{2}{3}$ are:

2 / 3   . 6 6 6   . 6 6 7

Answer: 201 – either position is correct

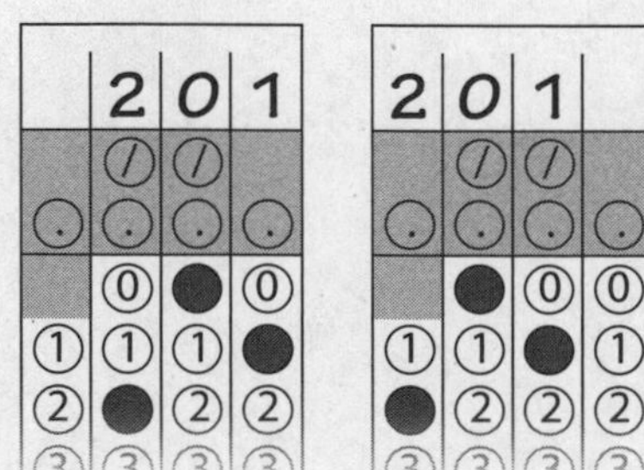

NOTE: You may start your answers in any column, space permitting. Columns you don't need to use should be left blank.

16

If $2x + 8 = 16$, what is the value of $x + 4$?

17

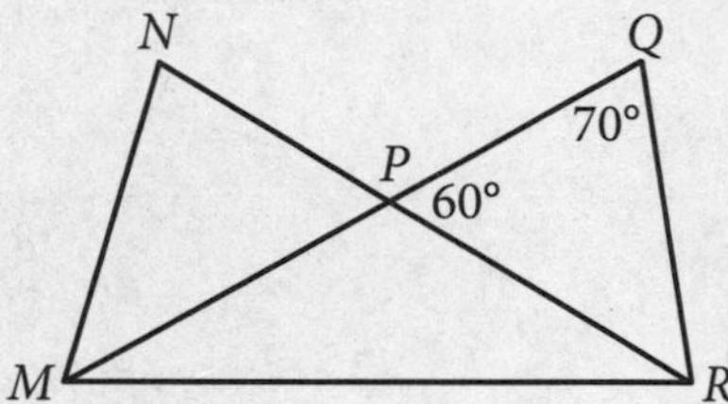

In the figure above, $\overline{MQ}$ and $\overline{NR}$ intersect at point P, $NP = QP$, and $MP = PR$. What is the measure, in degrees, of $\angle QMR$? (Disregard the degree symbol when gridding your answer.)

18

The number of radians in a 720-degree angle can be written as $a\pi$, where a is a constant. What is the value of a ?

CONTINUE

19

The graph of a line in the xy-plane passes through the point $(1, 4)$ and crosses the x-axis at the point $(2, 0)$. The line crosses the y-axis at the point $(0, b)$. What is the value of b ?

20

$$(7532 + 100y^2) + 10(10y^2 - 110)$$

The expression above can be written in the form $ay^2 + b$, where a and b are constants. What is the value of $a + b$?

STOP

If you finish before time is called, you may check your work on this section only.

Do not turn to any other section.

No Test Material On This Page

Math Test – Calculator

55 MINUTES, 38 QUESTIONS

Turn to Section 4 of your answer sheet to answer the questions in this section.

DIRECTIONS

For questions 1-30, solve each problem, choose the best answer from the choices provided, and fill in the corresponding circle on your answer sheet. **For questions 31-38**, solve the problem and enter your answer in the grid on the answer sheet. Please refer to the directions before question 31 on how to enter your answers in the grid. You may use any available space in your test booklet for scratch work.

NOTES

1. The use of a calculator **is permitted**.
2. All variables and expressions used represent real numbers unless otherwise indicated.
3. Figures provided in this test are drawn to scale unless otherwise indicated.
4. All figures lie in a plane unless otherwise indicated.
5. Unless otherwise indicated, the domain of a given function f is the set of all real numbers x for which $f(x)$ is a real number.

REFERENCE

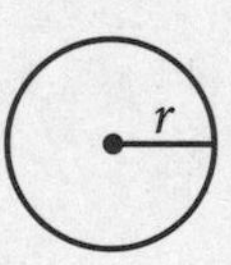

$A = \pi r^2$
$C = 2\pi r$

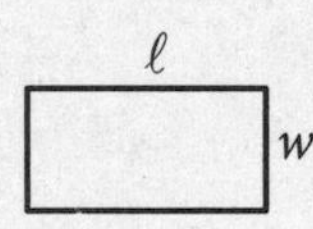

$A = \ell w$

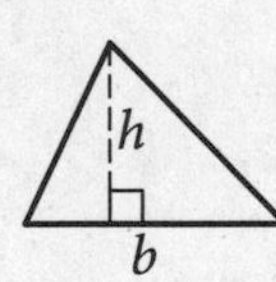

$A = \frac{1}{2}bh$

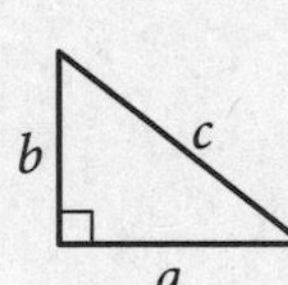

$c^2 = a^2 + b^2$

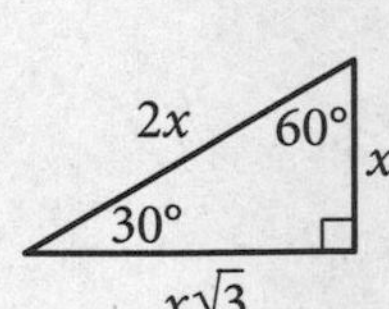

Special Right Triangles

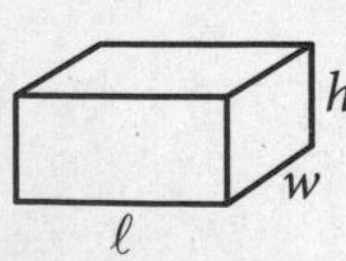

$V = \ell wh$

$V = \pi r^2 h$

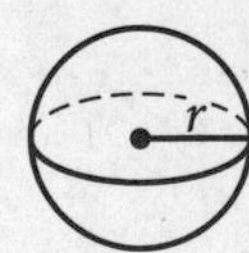

$V = \frac{4}{3}\pi r^3$

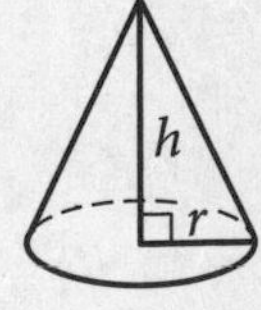

$V = \frac{1}{3}\pi r^2 h$

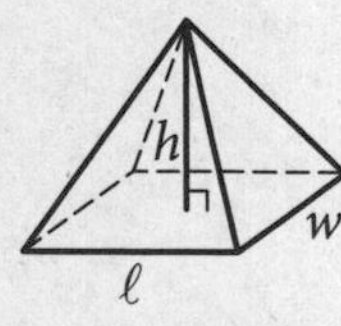

$V = \frac{1}{3}\ell wh$

The number of degrees of arc in a circle is 360.
The number of radians of arc in a circle is 2π.
The sum of the measures in degrees of the angles of a triangle is 180.

CONTINUE

1

Feeding Information for Boarded Pets

	Fed only dry food	Fed both wet and dry food	Total
Cats	5	11	16
Dogs	2	23	25
Total	7	34	41

The table above shows the kinds of foods that are fed to the cats and dogs currently boarded at a pet care facility. What fraction of the dogs are fed only dry food?

A) $\frac{2}{41}$

B) $\frac{2}{25}$

C) $\frac{7}{41}$

D) $\frac{2}{7}$

2

$$(x^2 - 3) - (-3x^2 + 5)$$

Which of the following expressions is equivalent to the one above?

A) $4x^2 - 8$

B) $4x^2 - 2$

C) $-2x^2 - 8$

D) $-2x^2 - 2$

3

A certain package requires 3 centimeters of tape to be closed securely. What is the maximum number of packages of this type that can be secured with 6 meters of tape? (1 meter = 100 cm)

A) 100

B) 150

C) 200

D) 300

4

A market researcher selected 200 people at random from a group of people who indicated that they liked a certain book. The 200 people were shown a movie based on the book and then asked whether they liked or disliked the movie. Of those surveyed, 95% said they disliked the movie. Which of the following inferences can appropriately be drawn from this survey result?

A) At least 95% of people who go see movies will dislike this movie.

B) At least 95% of people who read books will dislike this movie.

C) Most people who dislike this book will like this movie.

D) Most people who like this book will dislike this movie.

CONTINUE

5

Which of the following ordered pairs (x, y) satisfies the inequality $5x - 3y < 4$?

I. $(1, 1)$

II. $(2, 5)$

III. $(3, 2)$

A) I only
B) II only
C) I and II only
D) I and III only

6

In the equation $(ax + 3)^2 = 36$, a is a constant. If $x = -3$ is one solution to the equation, what is a possible value of a ?

A) -11
B) -5
C) -1
D) 0

Questions 7 and 8 refer to the following information.

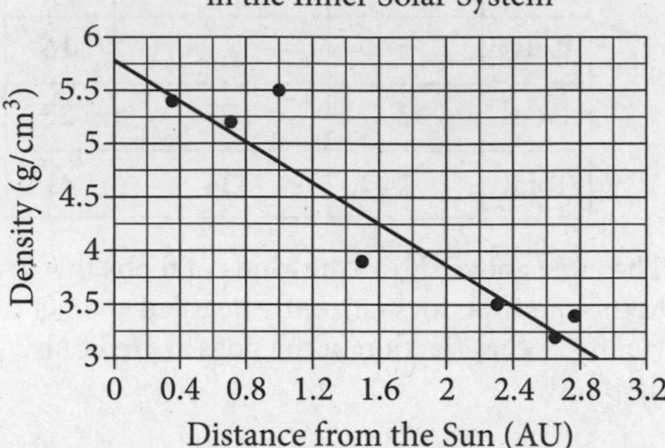

The scatterplot above shows the densities of 7 planetoids, in grams per cubic centimeter, with respect to their average distances from the Sun in astronomical units (AU). The line of best fit is also shown.

7

According to the scatterplot, which of the following statements is true about the relationship between a planetoid's average distance from the Sun and its density?

A) Planetoids that are more distant from the Sun tend to have lesser densities.
B) Planetoids that are more distant from the Sun tend to have greater densities.
C) The density of a planetoid that is twice as far from the Sun as another planetoid is half the density of that other planetoid.
D) The distance from a planetoid to the Sun is unrelated to its density.

CONTINUE

8

An astronomer has discovered a new planetoid about 1.2 AU from the Sun. According to the line of best fit, which of the following best approximates the density of the planetoid, in grams per cubic centimeter?

A) 3.6

B) 4.1

C) 4.6

D) 5.5

9

$$9ax + 9b - 6 = 21$$

Based on the equation above, what is the value of $ax + b$?

A) 3

B) 6

C) 8

D) 12

10

Lani spent 15% of her 8-hour workday in meetings. How many minutes of her workday did she spend in meetings?

A) 1.2

B) 15

C) 48

D) 72

11

A software company is selling a new game in a standard edition and a collector's edition. The box for the standard edition has a volume of 20 cubic inches, and the box for the collector's edition has a volume of 30 cubic inches. The company receives an order for 75 copies of the game, and the total volume of the order to be shipped is 1,870 cubic inches. Which of the following systems of equations can be used to determine the number of standard edition games, s, and collector's edition games, c, that were ordered?

A) $75 - s = c$
$20s + 30c = 1{,}870$

B) $75 - s = c$
$30s + 20c = 1{,}870$

C) $s - c = 75$
$25(s + c) = 1{,}870$

D) $s - c = 75$
$30s + 20c = 1{,}870$

CONTINUE

12

A customer paid $53.00 for a jacket after a 6 percent sales tax was added. What was the price of the jacket before the sales tax was added?

A) $47.60

B) $50.00

C) $52.60

D) $52.84

13

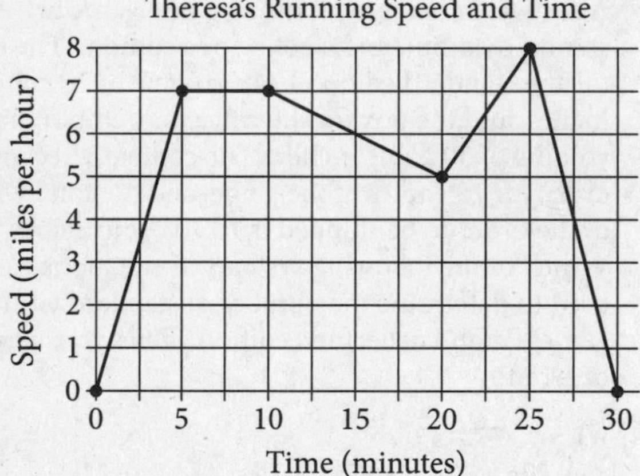

Theresa ran on a treadmill for thirty minutes, and her time and speed are shown on the graph above. According to the graph, which of the following statements is NOT true concerning Theresa's run?

A) Theresa ran at a constant speed for five minutes.

B) Theresa's speed was increasing for a longer period of time than it was decreasing.

C) Theresa's speed decreased at a constant rate during the last five minutes.

D) Theresa's speed reached its maximum during the last ten minutes.

14

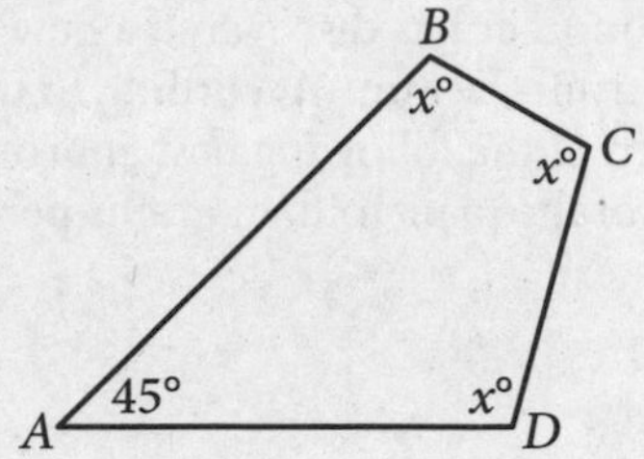

In the figure above, what is the value of x ?

A) 45

B) 90

C) 100

D) 105

15

If 50 one-cent coins were stacked on top of each other in a column, the column would be approximately $3\frac{7}{8}$ inches tall. At this rate, which of the following is closest to the number of one-cent coins it would take to make an 8-inch-tall column?

A) 75

B) 100

C) 200

D) 390

CONTINUE

16

If $a - b = 12$ and $\frac{b}{2} = 10$, what is the value of $a + b$?

A) 2
B) 12
C) 32
D) 52

17

$$y = 19.99 + 1.50x$$

The equation above models the total cost y, in dollars, that a company charges a customer to rent a truck for one day and drive the truck x miles. The total cost consists of a flat fee plus a charge per mile driven. When the equation is graphed in the xy-plane, what does the y-intercept of the graph represent in terms of the model?

A) A flat fee of \$19.99
B) A charge per mile of \$1.50
C) A charge per mile of \$19.99
D) Total daily charges of \$21.49

18

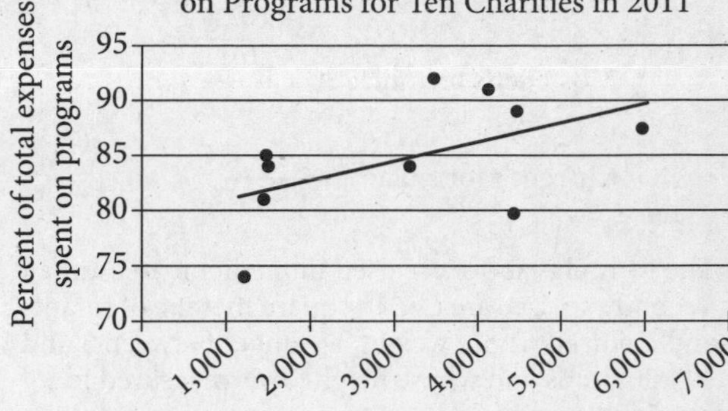

The scatterplot above shows data for ten charities along with the line of best fit. For the charity with the greatest percent of total expenses spent on programs, which of the following is closest to the difference of the actual percent and the percent predicted by the line of best fit?

A) 10%
B) 7%
C) 4%
D) 1%

Questions 19 and 20 refer to the following information.

Mosteller's formula: $A = \frac{\sqrt{hw}}{60}$

Current's formula: $A = \frac{4 + w}{30}$

The formulas above are used in medicine to estimate the body surface area A, in square meters, of infants and children whose weight w ranges between 3 and 30 kilograms and whose height h is measured in centimeters.

19

Based on Current's formula, what is w in terms of A ?

A) $w = 30A - 4$

B) $w = 30A + 4$

C) $w = 30(A - 4)$

D) $w = 30(A + 4)$

20

If Mosteller's and Current's formulas give the same estimate for A, which of the following expressions is equivalent to $\sqrt{hw}$?

A) $\frac{4 + w}{2}$

B) $\frac{4 + w}{1,800}$

C) $2(4 + w)$

D) $\frac{(4 + w)^2}{2}$

CONTINUE

21

Total Protein and Total Fat for Eight Sandwiches

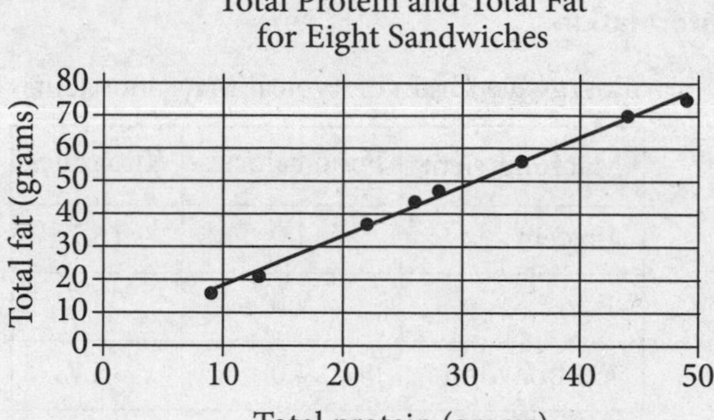

The scatterplot above shows the numbers of grams of both total protein and total fat for eight sandwiches on a restaurant menu. The line of best fit for the data is also shown. According to the line of best fit, which of the following is closest to the predicted increase in total fat, in grams, for every increase of 1 gram in total protein?

A) 2.5
B) 2.0
C) 1.5
D) 1.0

22

Percent of Residents Who Earned a Bachelor's Degree or Higher

State	Percent of residents
State A	21.9%
State B	27.9%
State C	25.9%
State D	19.5%
State E	30.1%
State F	36.4%
State G	35.5%

A survey was given to residents of all 50 states asking if they had earned a bachelor's degree or higher. The results from 7 of the states are given in the table above. The median percent of residents who earned a bachelor's degree or higher for all 50 states was 26.95%. What is the difference between the median percent of residents who earned a bachelor's degree or higher for these 7 states and the median for all 50 states?

A) 0.05%
B) 0.95%
C) 1.22%
D) 7.45%

23

A cylindrical can containing pieces of fruit is filled to the top with syrup before being sealed. The base of the can has an area of 75 cm^2, and the height of the can is 10 cm. If 110 cm^3 of syrup is needed to fill the can to the top, which of the following is closest to the total volume of the pieces of fruit in the can?

A) 7.5 cm^3

B) 185 cm^3

C) 640 cm^3

D) 750 cm^3

24

$$h(t) = -16t^2 + 110t + 72$$

The function above models the height h, in feet, of an object above ground t seconds after being launched straight up in the air. What does the number 72 represent in the function?

A) The initial height, in feet, of the object

B) The maximum height, in feet, of the object

C) The initial speed, in feet per second, of the object

D) The maximum speed, in feet per second, of the object

Questions 25 and 26 refer to the following information.

Energy per Gram of Typical Macronutrients

Macronutrient	Food calories	Kilojoules
Protein	4.0	16.7
Fat	9.0	37.7
Carbohydrate	4.0	16.7

The table above gives the typical amounts of energy per gram, expressed in both food calories and kilojoules, of the three macronutrients in food.

25

If x food calories is equivalent to k kilojoules, of the following, which best represents the relationship between x and k ?

A) $k = 0.24x$

B) $k = 4.2x$

C) $x = 4.2k$

D) $xk = 4.2$

CONTINUE

26

If the 180 food calories in a granola bar come entirely from p grams of protein, f grams of fat, and c grams of carbohydrate, which of the following expresses f in terms of p and c ?

A) $f = 20 + \frac{4}{9}(p + c)$

B) $f = 20 - \frac{4}{9}(p + c)$

C) $f = 20 - \frac{4}{9}(p - c)$

D) $f = 20 + \frac{9}{4}(p + c)$

27

The world's population has grown at an average rate of 1.9 percent per year since 1945. There were approximately 4 billion people in the world in 1975. Which of the following functions represents the world's population P, in billions of people, t years since 1975 ? (1 billion = 1,000,000,000)

A) $P(t) = 4(1.019)^t$

B) $P(t) = 4(1.9)^t$

C) $P(t) = 1.19t + 4$

D) $P(t) = 1.019t + 4$

28

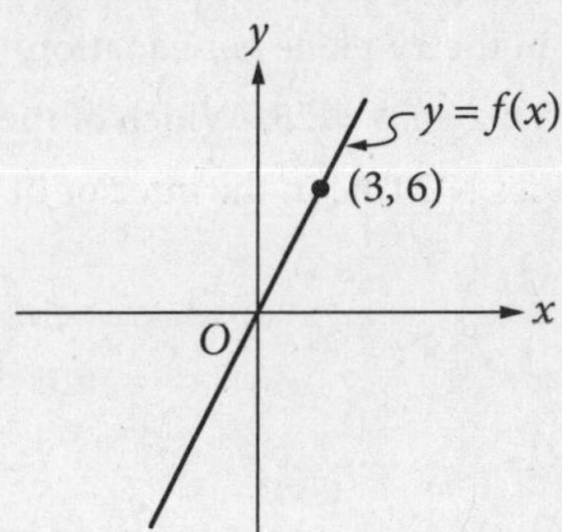

In the xy-plane above, a point (not shown) with coordinates (s, t) lies on the graph of the linear function f. If s and t are positive integers, what is the ratio of t to s ?

A) 1 to 3

B) 1 to 2

C) 2 to 1

D) 3 to 1

CONTINUE

29

A circle in the xy-plane has equation $(x+3)^2+(y-1)^2=25$. Which of the following points does NOT lie in the interior of the circle?

A) $(-7, 3)$

B) $(-3, 1)$

C) $(0, 0)$

D) $(3, 2)$

30

Year	Subscriptions sold
2012	5,600
2013	5,880

The manager of an online news service received the report above on the number of subscriptions sold by the service. The manager estimated that the percent increase from 2012 to 2013 would be double the percent increase from 2013 to 2014. How many subscriptions did the manager expect would be sold in 2014?

A) 6,020

B) 6,027

C) 6,440

D) 6,468

CONTINUE

DIRECTIONS

For questions 31-38, solve the problem and enter your answer in the grid, as described below, on the answer sheet.

1. Although not required, it is suggested that you write your answer in the boxes at the top of the columns to help you fill in the circles accurately. You will receive credit only if the circles are filled in correctly.
2. Mark no more than one circle in any column.
3. No question has a negative answer.
4. Some problems may have more than one correct answer. In such cases, grid only one answer.
5. **Mixed numbers** such as $3\frac{1}{2}$ must be gridded as 3.5 or 7/2. (If 3 1 / 2 is entered into the grid, it will be interpreted as $\frac{31}{2}$, not $3\frac{1}{2}$.)
6. **Decimal answers:** If you obtain a decimal answer with more digits than the grid can accommodate, it may be either rounded or truncated, but it must fill the entire grid.

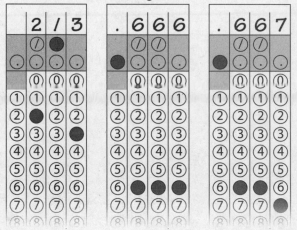

Answer: $\frac{7}{12}$

Write answer in boxes. → 7 / 1 2 ← Fraction line

Grid in result.

Answer: 2.5

2 . 5 ← Decimal point

Acceptable ways to grid $\frac{2}{3}$ are:

2 / 3 | . 6 6 6 | . 6 6 7

Answer: 201 – either position is correct

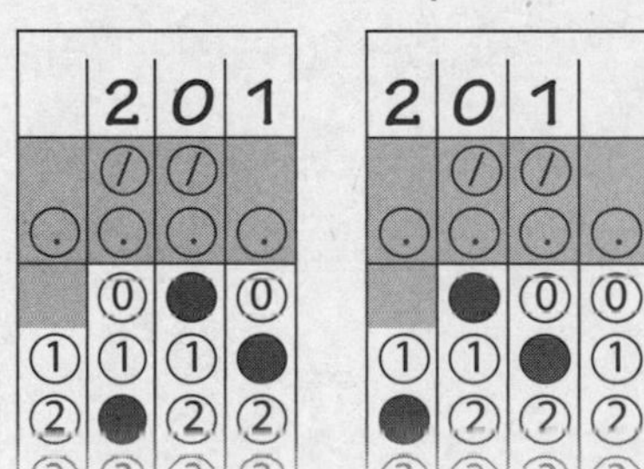

NOTE: You may start your answers in any column, space permitting. Columns you don't need to use should be left blank.

31

In 1854, during the California gold rush, each ounce of gold was worth \$20, and the largest known mass of gold found in California was worth \$62,400 in that year. What was the weight, in pounds, of this mass of gold? (16 ounces = 1 pound)

32

Line t is shown in the xy-plane below.

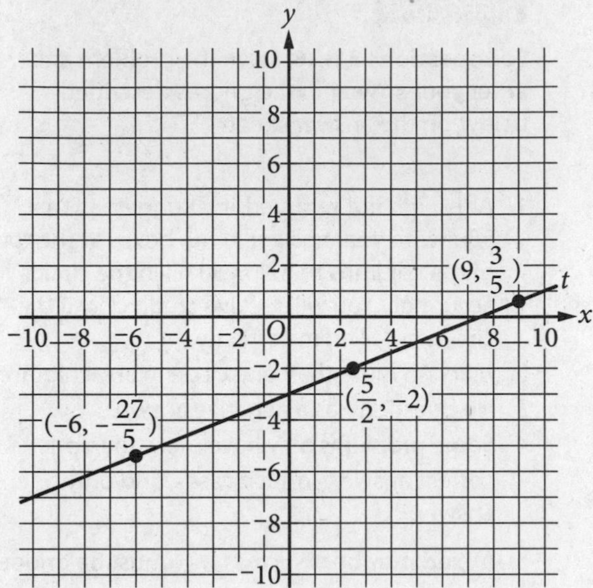

What is the slope of line t ?

CONTINUE

33

The score on a trivia game is obtained by subtracting the number of incorrect answers from twice the number of correct answers. If a player answered 40 questions and obtained a score of 50, how many questions did the player answer correctly?

34

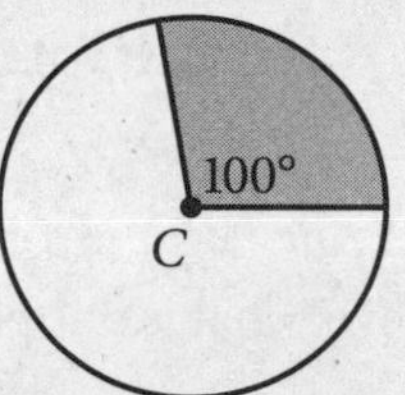

Point C is the center of the circle above. What fraction of the area of the circle is the area of the shaded region?

CONTINUE

35

$$y = x^2 - 4x + 4$$
$$y = 4 - x$$

If the ordered pair (x, y) satisfies the system of equations above, what is one possible value of x ?

36

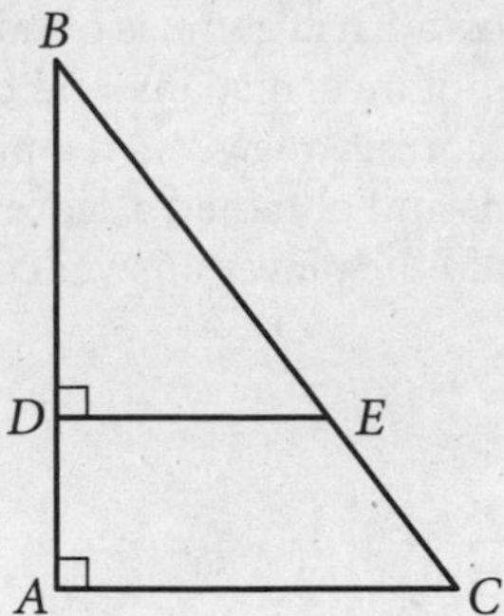

In the figure above, $\tan B = \frac{3}{4}$. If $BC = 15$ and $DA = 4$, what is the length of $\overline{DE}$?

CONTINUE

Questions 37 and 38 refer to the following information.

Number of Contestants by Score and Day

	5 out of 5	4 out of 5	3 out of 5	2 out of 5	1 out of 5	0 out of 5	Total
Day 1	2	3	4	6	2	3	20
Day 2	2	3	5	5	4	1	20
Day 3	3	3	4	5	3	2	20
Total	7	9	13	16	9	6	60

The same 20 contestants, on each of 3 days, answered 5 questions in order to win a prize. Each contestant received 1 point for each correct answer. The number of contestants receiving a given score on each day is shown in the table above.

37

What was the mean score of the contestants on Day 1 ?

38

No contestant received the same score on two different days. If a contestant is selected at random, what is the probability that the selected contestant received a score of 5 on Day 2 or Day 3, given that the contestant received a score of 5 on one of the three days?

STOP

If you finish before time is called, you may check your work on this section only. Do not turn to any other section.

No Test Material On This Page

No Test Material On This Page

This page represents the back cover of the Practice Test.

The SAT®

Practice Essay #7

The essay gives you an opportunity to show how effectively you can read and comprehend a passage and write an essay analyzing the passage. In your essay, you should demonstrate that you have read the passage carefully, present a clear and logical analysis, and use language precisely.

You have 50 minutes to read the passage and write an essay in response to the prompt provided inside this booklet.

For information on scoring your essay, view the SAT Essay scoring rubric at **sat.org/essay**.

As you read the passage below, consider how Zadie Smith uses

- evidence, such as facts or examples, to support claims.
- reasoning to develop ideas and to connect claims and evidence.
- stylistic or persuasive elements, such as word choice or appeals to emotion, to add power to the ideas expressed.

Adapted from Zadie Smith, "The North West London Blues." ©2012 by NYREV, Inc. Originally published June 2, 2012. Writer Zadie Smith wrote the following piece in response to news that several local libraries in the greater London area, including Kensal Rise and Willesden Green Libraries, would be closed down.

1 What kind of a problem is a library? It's clear that for many people it is not a problem at all, only a kind of obsolescence.[1] At the extreme pole of this view is the technocrat's total faith: with every book in the world online, what need could there be for the physical reality? This kind of argument thinks of the library as a function rather than a plurality of individual spaces. But each library is a different kind of problem and "the Internet" is no more a solution for all of them than it is their universal death knell. Each morning I struggle to find a seat in the packed university library in which I write this, despite the fact every single student in here could be at home in front of their macbook browsing Google Books. . . . Kensal Rise is being closed not because it is unpopular but because it is unprofitable, this despite the fact that the friends of Kensal Rise library are willing to run their library themselves. . . . Meanwhile it is hard not to conclude that Willesden Green is being mutilated not least because the members of the council see the opportunity for a sweet real estate deal.

2 All libraries have a different character and setting. Some are primarily for children or primarily for students, or the general public, primarily full of books or microfilms or digitized material or with a café in the basement or a market out front. Libraries are not failing "because they are libraries." Neglected libraries get neglected, and this cycle, in time, provides the excuse to close them. Well-run libraries are filled with people because what a good library offers cannot be easily found elsewhere: an indoor public space in which you do not have to buy anything in order to stay.

3 In the modern state there are very few sites where this is possible. . . . It would seem the most obvious thing in the world to say that the reason why the market is not an efficient solution to libraries is because the market has no use for a library. Nor can the experience of library life be recreated online. It's not just a matter of free books. A library is a different kind of social reality (of the three dimensional kind), which by its very existence teaches a system of values beyond the fiscal.

---

[1] The condition of being old-fashioned or no longer useful

4 I don't think the argument in favor of libraries is especially ideological or ethical. I would even agree with those who say it's not especially logical. I think for most people it's emotional. Not logos or ethos but pathos. This is not a denigration: emotion also has a place in public policy. We're humans, not robots. The people protesting the closing of Kensal Rise Library love that library. They were open to any solution on the left or on the right if it meant keeping their library open. . . . A library is one of those social goods that matter to people of many different political attitudes. All that the friends of Kensal Rise and Willesden Library and similar services throughout the country are saying is: these places are important to us. We get that money is tight, we understand that there is a hierarchy of needs, and that [libraries] are not hospital beds and classroom size. But they are still a significant part of our social reality, the only thing left on the . . . street that doesn't want either your soul or your wallet.

5 If the losses of private companies are to be socialized within already struggling communities the very least we can do is listen to people when they try to tell us where in the hierarchy of their needs things like public space, access to culture, and preservation of environment lie. "But I never use the damn things!" says Mr. Notmytaxes, under the line. Sir, I believe you. However. British libraries received over 300 million visits last year, and this despite the common neglect of the various councils that oversee them. In North West London people are even willing to form human chains in front of them. People have taken to writing long pieces in newspapers to "defend" them. Just saying the same thing over and over again. Defend our libraries. We like libraries. Can we keep our libraries? We need to talk about libraries. Pleading, like children. Is that really where we are?

Write an essay in which you explain how Zadie Smith builds an argument to persuade her audience that public libraries are important and should remain open. In your essay, analyze how Smith uses one or more of the features listed in the box above (or features of your own choice) to strengthen the logic and persuasiveness of her argument. Be sure that your analysis focuses on the most relevant features of the passage.

Your essay should not explain whether you agree with Smith's claims, but rather explain how Smith builds an argument to persuade her audience.

This page represents the back cover of the Practice Essay.

CollegeBoard

SAT PRACTICE ANSWER SHEET

COMPLETE MARK ● EXAMPLES OF INCOMPLETE MARKS 

It is recommended that you use a No. 2 pencil. It is very important that you fill in the entire circle darkly and completely. If you change your response, erase as completely as possible. Incomplete marks or erasures may affect your score.

TEST NUMBER

ENTER TEST NUMBER

For instance, for Practice Test #1, fill in the circle for 0 in the first column and for 1 in the second column.

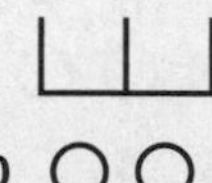

0	○	○
1	○	○
2	○	○
3	○	○
4	○	○
5	○	○
6	○	○
7	○	○
8	○	○
9	○	○

SECTION 1

	A B C D		A B C D		A B C D		A B C D
1	○ ○ ○ ○	14	○ ○ ○ ○	27	○ ○ ○ ○	40	○ ○ ○ ○
2	○ ○ ○ ○	15	○ ○ ○ ○	28	○ ○ ○ ○	41	○ ○ ○ ○
3	○ ○ ○ ○	16	○ ○ ○ ○	29	○ ○ ○ ○	42	○ ○ ○ ○
4	○ ○ ○ ○	17	○ ○ ○ ○	30	○ ○ ○ ○	43	○ ○ ○ ○
5	○ ○ ○ ○	18	○ ○ ○ ○	31	○ ○ ○ ○	44	○ ○ ○ ○
6	○ ○ ○ ○	19	○ ○ ○ ○	32	○ ○ ○ ○	45	○ ○ ○ ○
7	○ ○ ○ ○	20	○ ○ ○ ○	33	○ ○ ○ ○	46	○ ○ ○ ○
8	○ ○ ○ ○	21	○ ○ ○ ○	34	○ ○ ○ ○	47	○ ○ ○ ○
9	○ ○ ○ ○	22	○ ○ ○ ○	35	○ ○ ○ ○	48	○ ○ ○ ○
10	○ ○ ○ ○	23	○ ○ ○ ○	36	○ ○ ○ ○	49	○ ○ ○ ○
11	○ ○ ○ ○	24	○ ○ ○ ○	37	○ ○ ○ ○	50	○ ○ ○ ○
12	○ ○ ○ ○	25	○ ○ ○ ○	38	○ ○ ○ ○	51	○ ○ ○ ○
13	○ ○ ○ ○	26	○ ○ ○ ○	39	○ ○ ○ ○	52	○ ○ ○ ○

Download the College Board SAT Practice app to instantly score this test.
Learn more at sat.org/scoring.

CollegeBoard

SAT PRACTICE ANSWER SHEET

COMPLETE MARK ● EXAMPLES OF INCOMPLETE MARKS 

It is recommended that you use a No. 2 pencil. It is very important that you fill in the entire circle darkly and completely. If you change your response, erase as completely as possible. Incomplete marks or erasures may affect your score.

SECTION 2

1 ○A ○B ○C ○D	10 ○A ○B ○C ○D	19 ○A ○B ○C ○D	28 ○A ○B ○C ○D	37 ○A ○B ○C ○D
2 ○A ○B ○C ○D	11 ○A ○B ○C ○D	20 ○A ○B ○C ○D	29 ○A ○B ○C ○D	38 ○A ○B ○C ○D
3 ○A ○B ○C ○D	12 ○A ○B ○C ○D	21 ○A ○B ○C ○D	30 ○A ○B ○C ○D	39 ○A ○B ○C ○D
4 ○A ○B ○C ○D	13 ○A ○B ○C ○D	22 ○A ○B ○C ○D	31 ○A ○B ○C ○D	40 ○A ○B ○C ○D
5 ○A ○B ○C ○D	14 ○A ○B ○C ○D	23 ○A ○B ○C ○D	32 ○A ○B ○C ○D	41 ○A ○B ○C ○D
6 ○A ○B ○C ○D	15 ○A ○B ○C ○D	24 ○A ○B ○C ○D	33 ○A ○B ○C ○D	42 ○A ○B ○C ○D
7 ○A ○B ○C ○D	16 ○A ○B ○C ○D	25 ○A ○B ○C ○D	34 ○A ○B ○C ○D	43 ○A ○B ○C ○D
8 ○A ○B ○C ○D	17 ○A ○B ○C ○D	26 ○A ○B ○C ○D	35 ○A ○B ○C ○D	44 ○A ○B ○C ○D
9 ○A ○B ○C ○D	18 ○A ○B ○C ○D	27 ○A ○B ○C ○D	36 ○A ○B ○C ○D	

If you're scoring with our mobile app we recommend that you cut these pages out of the back of this book. The scoring does best with a flat page.

SAT PRACTICE ANSWER SHEET

COMPLETE MARK | EXAMPLES OF INCOMPLETE MARKS

It is recommended that you use a No. 2 pencil. It is very important that you fill in the entire circle darkly and completely. If you change your response, erase as completely as possible. Incomplete marks or erasures may affect your score.

SECTION 3

1 A B C D	4 A B C D	7 A B C D	10 A B C D	13 A B C D
2 A B C D	5 A B C D	8 A B C D	11 A B C D	14 A B C D
3 A B C D	6 A B C D	9 A B C D	12 A B C D	15 A B C D

Only answers that are gridded will be scored. You will not receive credit for anything written in the boxes.

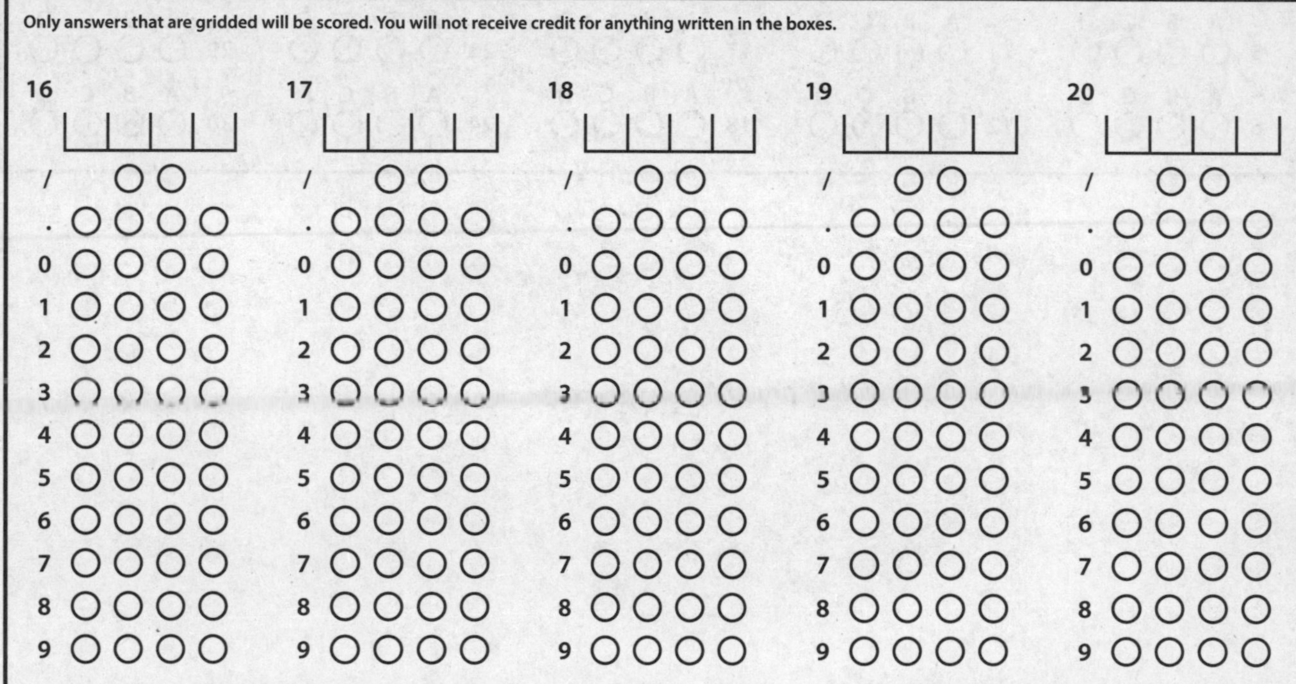

NO CALCULATOR ALLOWED

Did you know that you can print out these test sheets from the web? Learn more at sat.org/scoring.

SAT PRACTICE ANSWER SHEET

COMPLETE MARK ● EXAMPLES OF INCOMPLETE MARKS 

It is recommended that you use a No. 2 pencil. It is very important that you fill in the entire circle darkly and completely. If you change your response, erase as completely as possible. Incomplete marks or erasures may affect your score.

SECTION 4

1 A B C D	7 A B C D	13 A B C D	19 A B C D	25 A B C D
2 A B C D	8 A B C D	14 A B C D	20 A B C D	26 A B C D
3 A B C D	9 A B C D	15 A B C D	21 A B C D	27 A B C D
4 A B C D	10 A B C D	16 A B C D	22 A B C D	28 A B C D
5 A B C D	11 A B C D	17 A B C D	23 A B C D	29 A B C D
6 A B C D	12 A B C D	18 A B C D	24 A B C D	30 A B C D

CALCULATOR ALLOWED

If you're using our mobile app keep in mind that bad lighting and even shadows cast over the answer sheet can affect your score. Be sure to scan this in a well-lit area for best results.

CollegeBoard

SAT PRACTICE ANSWER SHEET

COMPLETE MARK ● EXAMPLES OF INCOMPLETE MARKS 

It is recommended that you use a No. 2 pencil. It is very important that you fill in the entire circle darkly and completely. If you change your response, erase as completely as possible. Incomplete marks or erasures may affect your score.

SECTION 4 (Continued)

Only answers that are gridded will be scored. You will not receive credit for anything written in the boxes.

31 32 33 34 35

/ . 0 1 2 3 4 5 6 7 8 9

Only answers that are gridded will be scored. You will not receive credit for anything written in the boxes.

36 37 38

/ . 0 1 2 3 4 5 6 7 8 9

CALCULATOR ALLOWED

○ I understand that my essay (without my name) may be reproduced in other College Board materials. If I mark this circle, I withhold my permission to reproduce my essay for any purposes beyond score reporting and the assessment of my writing skills. Marking this circle will have no effect on my score, nor will it prevent my essay from being made available to any college to which I send my SAT scores.

IMPORTANT: **USE A NO. 2 PENCIL. DO NOT WRITE OUTSIDE THE BORDER!** Words written outside the essay box or written in ink **WILL NOT APPEAR** in the copy sent to be scored, and your score will be affected.

PLANNING PAGE You may plan your essay in the unlined planning space below, but use only the lined pages following this one to write your essay. Any work on this planning page will not be scored.

Use pages 7 through 10 for your ESSAY →

FOR PLANNING ONLY

Use pages 7 through 10 for your ESSAY →

PLEASE DO NOT WRITE IN THIS AREA

SERIAL #

BEGIN YOUR ESSAY HERE.

You may continue on the next page.

DO NOT WRITE OUTSIDE OF THE BOX.

You may continue on the next page.

DO NOT WRITE OUTSIDE OF THE BOX.

You may continue on the next page.

PLEASE DO NOT WRITE IN THIS AREA

SERIAL #

DO NOT WRITE OUTSIDE OF THE BOX.

STOP.

Answer Explanations

SAT Practice Test #7

Section 1: Reading Test

QUESTION 1

Choice D is the best answer. The final sentence of the first paragraph makes clear that before adopting his daughter, the weaver Silas was greedy for gold and chained to his work, "deafened and blinded more and more to all things except the monotony of his loom." But after adopting Eppie, Silas became more interested in life outside his job: "Eppie called him away from his weaving, and made him think all its pauses a holiday, reawakening his senses with her fresh life." A major theme of the passage can be seen in this transformation, as it represents how loving a child can improve or change a parent's life.

Choice A is incorrect because even if the passage implies that Silas was too materialistic before his daughter's arrival in his life, his greediness was a personal characteristic only, not a societal one; whether the society Silas lives in is overly materialistic is never addressed. Choice B is incorrect because even if the passage represents the "moral purity" of children, it does so only indirectly and not as a major theme. Choice C is incorrect because the passage addresses childhood enthusiasm and curiosity more than "naïveté" and never discusses the length or "brevity" of that naïveté.

QUESTION 2

Choice A is the best answer. The first sentence of the first paragraph notes that "Unlike the gold . . . Eppie was a creature of endless claims and ever-growing desires, seeking and loving sunshine, and living sounds, and living movements; making trial of everything, with trust in new joy, and stirring the human kindness in all eyes that looked on her." These lines make clear that in contrast to Silas's gold, his new daughter is vibrant and alive.

Choices B, C, and D are incorrect because the lines from the first paragraph cited above reveal Eppie's interest in "living sounds" and "living movements" and thus characterize her vitality in comparison to the gold, rather than her durability, protection, or self-sufficiency.

QUESTION 3

Choice A is the best answer. In the first paragraph, the narrator describes Silas as having been so obsessed as to have felt required to worship the gold "in close-locked solitude," with "his thoughts in an ever-repeated circle" centered on his hoard. Moreover, this obsession compelled him to "sit weaving longer and longer, deafened and blinded more and more to all things except the monotony of his loom and the repetition of his web." These lines convey the extent to which Silas's behaviors were determined by his obsession.

Choice B is incorrect because the narrator does not make it seem as if Silas's gold could reproduce on its own, with the first paragraph suggesting that his hoard was a consequence of hard work, his being "deafened and blinded more and more to all things except the monotony of his loom and the repetition of his web." Choice C is incorrect because even if the first paragraph mentions that, after Eppie's arrival, Silas thinks about "the ties and charities that bound together the families of his neighbors," the passage never addresses how Silas interacted with those neighbors previously. Choice D is incorrect because the third paragraph makes clear that Silas is not only able to recall life before Eppie, but that with her in his life, "his mind was growing into memory."

QUESTION 4

Choice B is the best answer. The first paragraph of the passage describes Eppie as "a creature of endless claims and ever-growing desires," one who is "making trial of everything." In this context, her "making trial of everything" can be read as her acting on her curiosity by striving to experience the world around her.

Choices A, C, and D are incorrect because in the context of her "making trial of everything," Eppie can be seen as curious, not friendly (choice A), disobedient (choice C), or judgmental (choice D).

QUESTION 5

Choice D is the best answer. In the first paragraph, the narrator indicates that with the arrival of Eppie, Silas's thoughts turn from his work and his gold toward Eppie's future and his life with her: "Eppie was an object compacted of changes and hopes that forced his thoughts onward, and carried them far away from their old eager pacing towards the same blank limit — carried them away to the new things that would come with the coming years." By influencing Silas to think "onward" and of "the coming years," Eppie prompts Silas to envision a far different future than he would experience otherwise.

Choice A is incorrect because although the passage implies that Silas is less obsessed with money than before, there is no indication that he has actually renounced his desire for it. Choice B is incorrect because although the passage explains that Silas spends time outdoors after the arrival of Eppie, there is no indication that her presence has necessarily changed his understanding of his place in nature. Choice C is incorrect because at no point in the passage is Silas shown accepting help from anyone.

QUESTION 6

Choice B is the best answer. The previous question asks what consequence Silas has experienced as a result of adopting Eppie. The answer, that he begins to imagine a new future for himself and her, is supported in the first paragraph: "but Eppie was an object compacted of changes and hopes that forced his thoughts onward, and carried them far away from their old eager pacing towards the same blank limit — carried them away to the new things that would come with the coming years."

Choices A, C, and D are incorrect because the lines cited do not support the answer to the previous question about the consequence of Silas's adoption of Eppie, instead describing Silas's life before Eppie entered it (choice A), how he occasionally acts in her presence (choice C), and the changes in Eppie's perception of the world as she ages (choice D).

QUESTION 7

Choice C is the best answer. In the second paragraph, the description of Silas and Eppie's interaction outdoors conveys the extent to which he has changed since her arrival: where he once worked all day at his loom to earn more and more money, he now "might be seen in the sunny mid-day" strolling with her, accepting the flowers she brings him, or listening to birdcalls with her. With these experiences also come "crowding remembrances" of his early life — the life he led before amassing his hoard of gold. In its entirety, the paragraph can therefore be seen as illustrating the profound change into a more sociable being that Silas has undergone as a result of parenting Eppie.

Choice A is incorrect because the second paragraph does not present a particular moment when Silas realizes that Eppie has changed him but instead describes a pattern of behavior indicative of that change. Choice B is incorrect because the second paragraph shows the benefits Silas derives from Eppie's presence, rather than any sacrifices he has made for her. Choice D is incorrect because the second paragraph dramatizes a change in Silas's life overall, rather than showing a change in the dynamic that has arisen between Silas and Eppie.

QUESTION 8

Choice B is the best answer. The third paragraph of the passage shows that as Eppie learns more and more, Silas reengages with life: "As the child's mind was growing into knowledge, his mind was growing into memory: as her life unfolded, his soul, long stupefied in a cold narrow prison, was unfolding too, and trembling gradually into full consciousness." As Eppie grows into a world that is new to her, Silas recovers a world he'd largely forgotten.

Choice A is incorrect because the narrator portrays Eppie as being curious and eager, not physically vulnerable, and also implies that Silas is becoming ever more emotionally robust, not psychologically fragile. Choice C is incorrect because the only connection the narrator makes regarding Silas's former greed and Eppie's presence in his life is that she has brought an end to his obsessive pursuit of wealth. Choice D is incorrect because the narrator does not address Silas's mortality in any way but rather shows him becoming more and more alive through Eppie's love.

QUESTION 9

Choice D is the best answer. The previous question asks what connection the narrator draws between Eppie and Silas. The answer, that as she learns more about the world, he becomes more involved in it, is supported in the third paragraph: "As the child's mind was growing into knowledge, his mind was growing into memory: as her life unfolded, his soul, long stupefied in a cold narrow prison, was unfolding too, and trembling gradually into full consciousness."

Choices A, B, and C are incorrect because the lines cited do not support the answer to the previous question about the connection between Eppie and Silas, instead contrasting Silas's fixation on his gold with Eppie's curiosity (choice A) and describing Silas's habitual behavior when accompanying Eppie outdoors (choices B and C).

QUESTION 10

Choice D is the best answer. In the last paragraph, the narrator states, "Also, by the time Eppie was three years old, she developed a fine capacity for mischief, and for devising ingenious ways of being troublesome." In this context, the word "fine" most nearly means keen, or acute.

Choices A, B, and C are incorrect because in the context of a description in which Eppie was said to have a "fine capacity for mischief," the word "fine" most nearly means keen, or acute, not acceptable (choice A), delicate (choice B), or ornate (choice C).

QUESTION 11

Choice D is the best answer. The first paragraph of the passage explains the theory of two MIT business scholars who believe that technological advances in the workplace could lead to fewer jobs for human workers, explaining that they "foresee dismal prospects for many types of jobs as these powerful new technologies are increasingly adopted not only in manufacturing, clerical, and retail work but in professions such as law, financial services, education, and medicine." The fifth paragraph of the passage, however, offers a contrasting view, citing a Harvard economist who "says that no historical pattern shows these shifts leading to a net decrease in jobs over an extended period." Combined, these different opinions indicate the main purpose of the passage, which is to assess how new technologies in the workplace might affect job growth as a whole.

Choice A is incorrect because the passage does not examine how workers' lives have been affected by technology during the last century. Choices B and C are incorrect because the passage does not advocate or argue for a course of action; instead, the passage considers both sides of an issue, taking no position of its own.

QUESTION 12

Choice A is the best answer. In the first paragraph of the passage, Brynjolfsson and McAfee clearly state that technological advances since the year 2000 have led to low job growth in the United States: "MIT business scholars Erik Brynjolfsson and Andrew McAfee have argued that impressive advances in computer technology — from improved industrial robotics to automated translation services — are largely behind the sluggish employment growth of the last 10 to 15 years."

Choice B is incorrect because although Brynjolfsson and McAfee assert that certain "changes" have occurred in the workplace as a result of technological advancement, they offer only tentative speculation that those changes may be reflected globally. Choice C is incorrect because the passage notes a decrease, rather than an increase, in skilled laborers. Choice D is incorrect because the passage makes no mention of the global creation of new jobs, even speculating that jobs may have been negatively impacted in technologically advanced nations.

QUESTION 13

Choice A is the best answer. The previous question asks what Brynjolfsson and McAfee say has resulted in the workplace from advances in technology since the year 2000. The answer, that low job growth has resulted from these advances, is supported in the first sentence of the first paragraph: "MIT business scholars Erik Brynjolfsson and Andrew McAfee have argued that impressive advances in computer technology — from improved industrial robotics to automated translation services — are largely behind the sluggish employment growth of the last 10 to 15 years."

Choices B, C, and D are incorrect because the lines cited do not support the answer to the previous question about what Brynjolfsson and McAfee say has resulted in the workplace from advances in technology since the year 2000; instead they point to industries not under specific consideration by Brynjolfsson and McAfee (choice B), speculate as to whether changes might also be happening in other countries (choice C), and explain the importance of productivity in the marketplace in the decades following World War II. (choice D).

QUESTION 14

Choice D is the best answer. The second sentence of the third paragraph reads, "In economics, productivity — the amount of economic value created for a given unit of input, such as an hour of labor — is a crucial indicator of growth and wealth creation." In this context, the primary purpose of the appositive ("the amount of economic value . . . such as an hour of labor") is to define "productivity."

Choices A, B, and C are incorrect because in the context of the third paragraph, the appositive ("the amount of economic value . . . such as an hour of labor") is clearly provided to help explain the term "productivity," not to describe a process (choice A), highlight a dilemma (choice B), or clarify a claim (choice C).

QUESTION 15

Choice D is the best answer. The third paragraph states that "the pattern is clear: as businesses generated more value from their workers, the country as a whole became richer." In this context, the word "clear" most nearly means obvious, or unmistakable.

Choices A, B, and C are incorrect because in the context of the third paragraph, the word "clear" can be seen to mean obvious, or unmistakable, not pure (choice A), keen (choice B), or untroubled (choice C).

QUESTION 16

Choice C is the best answer. Katz doesn't necessarily agree with Brynjolfsson and McAfee that new technologies will lead to sluggish job growth, saying in the fifth paragraph that "no historical pattern shows these shifts leading to a net decrease in jobs over an extended period." However, he's not sure that will remain true, explaining in the sixth paragraph that no one can be certain what is going to happen to the workplace as a result of these new technologies: "If technology disrupts enough, who knows what will happen?"

Choices A, B, and D are incorrect because it would not be accurate to characterize Katz as being alarmed (choice A), unconcerned (choice B), or optimistic (choice D) about today's digital technologies. Rather, it's clear from the conclusion of the sixth paragraph that Katz isn't sure how technological advancement will affect the workplace: "If technology disrupts enough, who knows what will happen?"

QUESTION 17

Choice D is the best answer. The previous question asks how Katz's attitude toward "today's digital technologies" can best be characterized. The answer, that he is uncertain about their possible effects, is supported in the final sentence of the sixth paragraph: "If technology disrupts enough, who knows what will happen?"

Choices A, B, and C are incorrect because the lines cited do not support the answer to the previous question Katz's attitude toward "today's digital technologies"; instead, they describe some of his earlier research (choice A) and provide insight only into his initial thoughts but not his final conclusion on the matter (choices B and C).

QUESTION 18

Choice B is the best answer. The sixth paragraph of the passage states that "Katz doesn't dismiss the notion that there is something different about today's digital technologies — something that could affect an even broader range of work." In the context of this sentence, the "range" of work being discussed means the scope of work or all the various kinds of work.

Choices A, C, and D are incorrect because in the context of the sentence, the "range" of work being discussed means the array or scope of work, not a physical delineation like a region (choice A) or distance (choice C), or the professional position of those who perform particular jobs (choice D).

QUESTION 19

Choice D is the best answer. Figure 1 shows the highest gap between the percentages of productivity and employment in relation to 1947 levels occurring in 2013, when there was a difference of approximately 150 percentage points between 2013 employment (under 400%) and 2013 productivity (well over 500%).

Choices A, B, and C are incorrect because Figure 1 shows a gap of well over 100 percentage points between 2013 employment and 2013 productivity in relation to 1947 levels, while 1987 (choice A) and 1997 (choice B) show a difference of about 30 percentage points or less between employment and productivity, and 2007 (choice C) indicates a difference of approximately 100 percentage points.

QUESTION 20

Choice C is the best answer. Figure 2 clearly shows an increase of worker output in all three countries between 1960 and 2011, with workers in each country producing on average less than 50 units of output in 1960 but more than 100 units by 2011.

Choice A is incorrect because figure 2 shows that Japan saw greater growth in output between 1960 and 1990 than Germany saw. Choice B is incorrect because figure 2 shows that Japan experienced its greatest increase in output from 2000 to 2011, not its smallest. Choice D is incorrect because figure 2 shows that the United States had the greatest output of all three countries only in 2011, not in each of the years shown.

QUESTION 21

Choice B is the best answer. In the fourth paragraph, Brynjolfsson asserts, "Productivity is at record levels, innovation has never been faster, and yet at the same time, we have a falling median income and we have fewer jobs." In order to evaluate his statement that today "we have fewer jobs," figure 2 would need to include accurate information about the number of jobs held by people employed in factories from 1960 to 2011. Without knowing those numbers, it's not possible to determine whether Brynjolfsson's statement is correct.

Choice A is incorrect because a comparison of the median income of all three nations' factory workers within a single year would not aid in the evaluation of Brynjolfsson's statement regarding changes in worker productivity over a span of 10 to 15 years. Choices C and D are incorrect because knowing either the types of organizations where those outputs were measured or which specific manufacturing jobs might have been lost to new technologies would not be helpful in evaluating Brynjolfsson's statement about how median incomes have fallen and job growth has reduced over time.

QUESTION 22

Choice C is the best answer. The main purpose of the passage is conveyed by the first sentence: "Anyone watching the autumn sky knows that migrating birds fly in a V formation, but scientists have long debated why." The first paragraph continues by focusing on new research that might answer the question of why birds fly in that formation ("presumably to catch the preceding bird's updraft — and save energy during flight"). As a whole, the passage can therefore be seen as a discussion of the biological motivation behind migrating birds' reliance on the V formation.

Choice A is incorrect because the squadrons of planes mentioned in the second paragraph are used as an example to discuss migrating birds but are not themselves the main subject of this passage. Choice B is incorrect because although the fourth paragraph does discuss the role of downdrafts in V-formation flight, this discussion is brief and does not constitute a main purpose. Choice D is incorrect because the passage does not illustrate how birds sense air currents through their feathers; instead, the seventh paragraph suggests in passing that such sensation may play a role in maintaining the V formation: "Scientists do not know how the birds find that aerodynamic sweet spot, but they suspect that the animals align themselves either by sight or by sensing air currents through their feathers."

QUESTION 23

Choice A is the best answer. In the second paragraph of the passage, the quotation "Air gets pretty unpredictable behind a flapping wing" immediately follows the statement that "currents created by airplanes are far more stable than the oscillating eddies coming off of a bird."

The inclusion of the above quotation can therefore be seen as a way to explain that the current created by a bird's flapping wings is different from the current coming off the fixed wing of an airplane.

Choice B is incorrect because the quotation's explanation that air is "unpredictable" behind a bird's wing stresses the bird's lack of control over the air current. Choice C is incorrect because the quotation attributes the unpredictability of the current "behind a flapping wind" to the action of the wing rather than to wind, and in fact the passage makes no mention of wind. Choice D is incorrect because the quotation characterizes the flapping of the bird's wings in terms of the unpredictability of its effects, not of its comparative strength.

QUESTION 24

Choice D is the best answer. The reason Usherwood used northern bald ibises as the subjects of his study is clearly stated at the beginning of the third paragraph: "The study, published in *Nature*, took advantage of an existing project to reintroduce endangered northern bald ibises (*Geronticus eremita*) to Europe." Because the project reintroducing those birds was already underway, it was therefore easy for Usherwood and his team to join it.

Choice A is incorrect because it would not be accurate to say that ibises were well acquainted with their migration route, as the third paragraph explains that scientists needed to "show hand-raised birds their ancestral migration route." Choice B is incorrect because the third paragraph states that the ibises wore "data loggers specially built by Usherwood and his lab" but never indicates that they had worn any such device before or undertaken migration previously. Choice C is incorrect because the passage never claims that ibises' body shape is similar to the design of a modern airplane, instead comparing only a V formation of birds to an airplane in the fourth paragraph.

QUESTION 25

Choice C is the best answer. The previous question asks why Usherwood used northern bald ibises as the subject of his study. The answer, that he had easy access to them because they were being used in another scientific study, is supported at the beginning of the passage's third paragraph: "The study, published in *Nature*, took advantage of an existing project to reintroduce endangered northern bald ibises (*Geronticus eremita*) to Europe."

Choices A, B, and D are incorrect because the lines cited do not support the answer to the previous question as to why Usherwood chose northern bald ibises as the subject of his study; instead, they describe the results of the study (choice A), compare birds and planes in flight (choice B), and describe one element of the actual study (choice D) but not the reason ibises were chosen.

QUESTION 26

Choice A is the best answer. At the end of the third paragraph the author notes that the GPS tracking devices attached to the birds "determined each bird's flight position to within 30 cm." This detail, along with the author's mention in the same sentence of another device that measured the timing of the wing flaps, provides evidence for the inference that the author likely specified 30 cm to underscore Usherwood's use of precise data-collection methods.

Choice B is incorrect because the passage does not state that the distance an ibis flies between wing flaps was something that could be ascertained by Usherwood's study. Choice C is incorrect because the passage does not discuss the wingspan length of juvenile ibises or suggest that this length could be determined from Usherwood's tracking data. Choice D is incorrect because the passage does not discuss the distance maintained between the plane and the ibises in flight.

QUESTION 27

Choice C is the best answer. At the beginning of the fifth paragraph the passage states that "the findings likely apply to other long-winged birds, such as pelicans, storks, and geese, Usherwood says. Smaller birds create more complex wakes that would make drafting too difficult." In these lines the author therefore implies that unlike smaller birds, pelicans, storks, and geese flying in a V formation likely create a similar wake to that of ibises.

Choice A is incorrect because the passage focuses entirely on bird flight, not bird communication. Choices B and D are incorrect because the passage discusses pelicans, storks, and geese only with respect to their drafting behavior, not in terms of their migration routes or how much energy they might expend when flying.

QUESTION 28

Choice B is the best answer. The previous question asks what the author implies about pelicans, storks, and geese flying in a V formation. The answer, that they produce a similar wake to ibises, is supported at the beginning of the fifth paragraph: "Smaller birds create more complex wakes that would make drafting too difficult." This sentence, in conjunction with the preceding sentence's assertion of the probable applicability of Usherwood's findings to pelicans, storks, and geese, underscores that the point of probable similarity between ibises and those other species is in their wake and the drafting it makes possible.

Choices A, C, and D are incorrect because the lines cited do not support the answer to the previous question regarding what the author implies about pelicans, storks, and geese flying in a V formation. Instead, they explain one finding in the ibis study, with no reference to other long-winged species (choice A); highlight the findings of a previous study of energy use in bird flight, with no reference to the relationship between ibises and other species (choice C); and offer a theory about ibises in flight, again with no reference to other species (choice D).

QUESTION 29

Choice C is the best answer. The seventh paragraph speculates that further research may provide insight into how and why birds fly in formation: "In future studies, the researchers will switch to more common birds, such as pigeons or geese. They plan to investigate how the animals decide who sets the course and the pace." In sum, the seventh paragraph can therefore be seen as recognizing that more research is needed to explain the phenomenon of flight formation more completely.

Choice A is incorrect because neither the seventh paragraph nor the passage as a whole is concerned with bird hierarchies; the decision as to which bird sets the "course" or "pace" is mentioned only as another aspect of bird flight that scientists have yet to explain fully. Choice B is incorrect because the seventh paragraph only briefly mentions mistakes in V-formation flight, and this subject is not a central focus of the paragraph. Choice D is incorrect because although the seventh paragraph mentions the sighting of a lead bird or "leader" as a possible factor in the V formation, this factor is mentioned briefly and in conjunction with other factors, so that to describe it as a main idea would misrepresent the paragraph as a whole.

QUESTION 30

Choice D is the best answer. In describing the way that long-winged birds like ibises fly in a V formation by drafting off each other, the seventh paragraph begins by stating, "scientists do not know how the birds find that aerodynamic sweet spot." In context, the phrase "aerodynamic sweet spot" characterizes the particular spatial relationship among birds in the formation that affords the least amount of wind resistance and is thus beneficial for flock members to maintain.

Choice A is incorrect because the author uses the phrase "aerodynamic sweet spot" in relation to bird flight, not plane flight. Choice B is incorrect because the phrase is not meant to imply the joy of flight so much as the optimum efficiency that can be found by flying in a certain position. Choice C is incorrect because the phrase is not used to discuss synchronized wing movement among birds, nor is synchronization addressed anywhere in the seventh paragraph.

QUESTION 31

Choice B is the best answer. In the seventh paragraph, the passage explains that one aspect of bird flight that awaits further study by scientists is the question of whether "a mistake made by the leader can ripple through the rest of the flock to cause traffic jams." In this context, to say that a mistake might "ripple" through the flock most nearly means that it might progressively spread through the flock.

Choices A, C, and D are incorrect because in the context of the seventh paragraph, to "ripple" through the flock means to spread through it progressively, not to fluctuate (choice A), to wave, or move in the pattern of the ebb and flow of waves (choice C), or to undulate, or move in a manner that creates a textured, undulating appearance (choice D).

QUESTION 32

Choice D is the best answer. In the first paragraph of Passage 1, Tocqueville predicts that "the social changes which bring nearer to the same level the father and son, the master and servant, and superiors and inferiors generally speaking, will raise woman and make her more and more the equal of man." In this context, to "raise" women to a higher social position most nearly means to elevate, or lift, them.

Choices A, B, and C are incorrect because in the context of Tocqueville's prediction that women will attain a higher social position, the word "raise" most nearly means elevate, not increase (choice A), cultivate, or support (choice B), or nurture (choice C).

QUESTION 33

Choice B is the best answer. In Passage 1, Tocqueville expresses concern that treating men and women as identical would likely harm both genders, rather than benefit them. This sentiment can be seen most clearly in the second paragraph, when he writes that "it may readily be conceived, that by thus attempting to make one sex equal to the other, both are degraded."

Choice A is incorrect because Tocqueville says treating men and women as identical in nature would result in the degradation of both genders, a condition closer to oppression than to freedom from oppression. Choice C is incorrect because Tocqueville does not address the issue of whether men might ultimately try to reclaim any authority they lost as a result of the treatment of both genders as identical. Choice D is incorrect because in the passage, Tocqueville never claims that treating men and women the same would result in superfluous privileges for either.

QUESTION 34

Choice C is the best answer. The previous question asks what Tocqueville implies would result from treating men and women as identical in nature. The answer, that he believes such treatment would harm both men and women, is supported in the second paragraph of Passage 1: "It may readily be conceived, that by thus attempting to make one sex equal to the other, both are degraded."

Choices A, B, and D are incorrect because the lines cited do not support the answer to the previous question about what Tocqueville implies would result from treating men and women as identical; instead, they discuss European approaches to such treatment, with no reference to the actual effects of it on men and women (choices A and B), and what Tocqueville considers Americans' proper conception of equality as it relates to gender roles (choice D).

QUESTION 35

Choice B is the best answer. In the first paragraph of Passage 2, when discussing changing social relations, Mill writes that in her time there had come to exist "a just equality, instead of the dominion of the strongest." In this context of a society where some had once wielded much greater power than others, the word "dominion" most nearly means supremacy, or greater power.

Choices A, C, and D are incorrect because in the context of a paragraph discussing differences in the amount of power possessed by members of a society, "dominion" means supremacy, or greater power, not omnipotence, or the state of being all-powerful (choice A), ownership (choice C), or territory (choice D).

QUESTION 36

Choice B is the best answer. In the first paragraph of Passage 2, Mill suggests that social roles are resistant to change in part because of their being entrenched in the cultural tradition: "for, in proportion to the strength of a feeling is the tenacity with which it clings to the forms and circumstances with which it has even accidentally become associated." In the context of a discussion of equality between men and women, Mill's statement serves to imply that gender roles change so slowly precisely because they are so deeply ingrained in society and culture.

Choice A is incorrect because although Mill suggests in Passage 2 that gender roles are deeply entrenched, she does not imply that they serve as the foundation of society. Choice C is incorrect because Passage 2 does not address the issue of legislative reforms, only societal ones. Choice D is incorrect because although Mill addresses the difficulty of reforming traditional gender roles, she does not attribute it to the benefits that certain groups or institutions derive from those roles.

QUESTION 37

Choice C is the best answer. The previous question asks about what Mill implies is the reason it is hard to change gender roles. The answer, that they are deeply entrenched in tradition, is supported in the first paragraph of Passage 2: "In proportion to the strength of a feeling is the tenacity with which it clings to the forms and circumstances with which it has even accidentally become associated."

Choices A, B, and D are incorrect because the lines cited do not support the answer to the previous question about what Mill implies is the reason it is hard to change gender roles, instead describing the condition of general inequality in prior eras (choices A and B) and optimistically considering a future society that she imagines will be less unequal (choice D).

QUESTION 38

Choice A is the best answer. Although the authors generally disagree about the roles men and women should occupy, both Tocqueville and Mill share the idea that gender equality is one small part of a societal shift toward equality in general. This can be seen in the first paragraph of Passage 1, where Tocqueville explains that raising woman to be "more and more the equal of man" is part of the overall "social changes which bring nearer to the same level the father and son, the master and servant," and in the first paragraph of Passage 2, where Mill writes that "mankind have outgrown" the state of inequality and "now tend to substitute, as the general principle of human relations, a just equality," with gender roles being the last of these relations to undergo such a shift.

Choice B is incorrect because although in Passage 1 Tocqueville argues that there are costs to treating men and women the same, in Passage 2 Mill characterizes gender equality as a source of benefits only. Choice C is incorrect because neither author considers changing gender roles in terms of economic ramifications, focusing instead on questions of fairness and justice and the fulfillment of people's potential. Choice D is incorrect because Mill does not discuss the issue in terms of American democracy, though Tocqueville does.

QUESTION 39

Choice C is the best answer. In the second paragraph of Passage 2, Mill writes that she believes job opportunities in her society should be open to all: "Let every occupation be open to all, without favor or discouragement to any, and employments will fall into the hands of those men or women who are found by experience to be most capable of worthily exercising them." In the second paragraph of Passage 1, Tocqueville argues that equality between men and women would leave both degraded; nonetheless, he recognizes that the belief in such equality is widespread: "There are people in Europe who . . . would give to both the same functions, impose on both the same duties, and grant to both the same rights; they would mix them in all things — their occupations." It can be inferred, then, that although Tocqueville would consider Mill's position ill-advised, he does recognize this position as one that is held by a number of reformers.

Choice A is incorrect because Tocqueville in Passage 1 never characterizes advocacy on behalf of gender equality (such as Mill engages in, in Passage 2) as less radical than it initially seems. Choice B is incorrect because Mill's stated belief that all jobs should be open to both men and women would clearly be refuted by Tocqueville as harmful to men and women alike. Choice D is incorrect because what Tocqueville praises the United States for is not gender equality as a component of economic progress, but rather the United States' division of activity into masculine and feminine spheres, which he likens to the division of labor in industrial production.

QUESTION 40

Choice A is the best answer. In Passage 1, Tocqueville argues that equality is generally beneficial for society, but he moderates that claim in the third paragraph by further stating that even if men and women should be considered equal, they should not work in the same jobs: "As nature has appointed such wide differences between the physical and moral constitution of man and woman, her manifest design was to give a distinct employment to their various faculties." In contrast, Mill argues in the second paragraph of Passage 2 that men and women should be awarded work based on individual ability: "Let every occupation be open to all, without favor or discouragement to any, and employments will fall into the hands of those men or women who are found by experience to be most capable of worthily exercising them." It can therefore be said that Tocqueville believes one's gender should play a determining factor in one's position in society, whereas Mill believes it should not.

Choice B is incorrect because both Tocqueville in Passage 1 and Mill in Passage 2 would likely argue against limiting an individual to the social class he or she was born to. Choice C is incorrect because it is Mill, not Tocqueville, who argues that individual temperament is the proper determining factor for social position. Choice D is incorrect because although it accurately represents Tocqueville's implicit stance that an individual's social position should contribute to society as a whole, it misrepresents Mill's argument, which conceives of social position in relation to individual aptitude, not individual satisfaction.

QUESTION 41

Choice A is the best answer. In the third paragraph of Passage 1, Tocqueville credits the Americans of his time for applying "to the sexes the great principle of political economy . . . by carefully dividing the duties of man from those of woman." In contrast, in the second paragraph of Passage 2, Mill argues that rigid social roles function to "declare that whatever be the genius, talent, energy, or force of mind, of an individual of a certain sex or class, those faculties shall not be exerted." It can be inferred, then, that Mill would argue that the principle praised by Tocqueville tends to limit both men and women from developing their full potential.

Choice B is incorrect because in Passage 2, Mill focuses her argument on gender roles and equality between sexes but never addresses the idea of sympathy between them. Choice C is incorrect because Mill considers the division of professions by gender as a perpetuation of a long tradition of gender inequality. Choice D is incorrect because although Mill suggests that gender equality would involve rethinking the professional options available to men and women, she dismisses the notion that one gender is better suited to certain professions or would displace the other gender in certain professions.

QUESTION 42

Choice C is the best answer. The passage's first two paragraphs describe how "Peter Higgs and a handful of other physicists were trying to understand the origin of a basic physical feature: mass," and the third paragraph discusses the idea put forth ("now called the Higgs field") to explain the environment where mathematical equations are most helpful in understanding mass. The passage shifts its focus, however: the fourth and fifth paragraphs describe how the idea of the Higgs field was not initially well-received in the scientific community, and the last paragraph illustrates that in modern times, the idea ultimately became an accepted fact to most scientists. Over the course of the passage, then, it can be seen that the main focus of the passage changes from an explanation of what the Higgs field is to an explanation of how the theory of it was received.

Choice A is incorrect because the passage makes no shift from a more to a less technical mode of description, and indeed the entire passage is aimed at readers with no specialized knowledge of physics. Choice B is incorrect because the passage never provides any contextualization of Higgs's work within other lines of inquiry in physics contemporary to Higgs. Choice D is incorrect because the passage offers no speculation regarding future discoveries that may result from the confirmation of the Higgs field's existence.

QUESTION 43

Choice D is the best answer. The third paragraph of the passage provides the following analogy: "For a mental toehold, think of a ping-pong ball submerged in water." Since this analogy occurs in a discussion of how mass operates within the Higgs field, it functions to explain an abstract concept in terms more readily grasped by readers with no background in physics.

Choices A, B, and C are incorrect because the analogy of the ping-pong ball is used in the passage to help laypeople understand the difficult concept of the Higgs field, rather than to make a little-known fact more widely known (choice A), draw a contrast between oppositional scientific theories (choice B), or refute any established explanation (choice C).

QUESTION 44

Choice D is the best answer. The fourth paragraph of the passage explains why Higgs's idea of the Higgs field was initially rebuffed by the scientific community: "The paper was rejected. Not because it contained a technical error, but because the premise of an invisible something permeating space, interacting with particles to provide their mass, well, it all just seemed like heaps of overwrought speculation." In other words, the scientific community was skeptical of Higgs's idea because it appeared to be mere theoretical speculation, with no empirical evidence to support it.

Choice A is incorrect because the passage makes clear that Higgs's idea addressed a theoretical problem already recognized by scientists, rather than a problem yet to be noticed by them. Choice B is incorrect because the fourth paragraph implies that Higgs's paper was rigorous (free from "technical error"), rather than problematic at the level of its equations. Choice C is incorrect because the passage never indicates that the acceptance of the Higgs field had the effect of rendering other, earlier theories in physics obsolete.

QUESTION 45

Choice C is the best answer. The previous question asks why the scientific community initially rejected the idea of the Higgs field. The answer, that Higgs offered only theoretical speculation for the existence of the field, not actual evidence, is supported in the fourth paragraph: "The paper was rejected. Not because it contained a technical error, but because the premise of an invisible something permeating space, interacting with particles to provide their mass, well, it all just seemed like heaps of overwrought speculation."

Choices A, B, and D are incorrect because the lines cited do not support the answer to the previous question about why the scientific community initially rejected the idea of the Higgs field, instead discussing how Higgs dealt with established equations in physics when he theorized the field (choice A), describing the circumstances in which Higgs revealed his theory to the scientific community (choice B), and illustrating the fact that the Higgs field eventually came to be an accepted fact to most scientists (choice D).

QUESTION 46

Choice A is the best answer. The fifth paragraph of the passage explains how the idea of the Higgs field eventually came to be accepted in the scientific community: "But Higgs persevered (and his revised paper appeared later that year in another journal), and physicists who took the time to study the proposal gradually realized that his idea was a stroke of genius, one that allowed them to have their cake and eat it too. In Higgs's scheme, the fundamental equations can retain their pristine form because the dirty work of providing the particles' masses is relegated to the environment." In saying that the Higgs field came to be accepted because it allowed scientists to "have their cake and eat it too," the author suggests that Higgs's theory was ultimately accepted as fact in part because it allowed physicists to reconcile what had seemed to be contradictory conditions: the harmony of the mathematical equations and the particles' apparent mass.

Choice B is incorrect because the passage does not suggest that the Higgs field was necessarily a concept that could be applied to other problems in physics than those immediately under Higgs's consideration. Choice C is incorrect because the passage does not suggest that Higgs's theory was accepted because it provided an answer to a question that earlier scientists had failed to anticipate. Choice D is incorrect because the passage never addresses any two phenomena being misinterpreted as a single phenomenon.

QUESTION 47

Choice C is the best answer. The previous question asks for one reason Higgs's theory eventually gained acceptance in the scientific community. The answer, that it reconciled two seemingly irreconcilable conditions, is supported in the passage's fifth paragraph: "But Higgs persevered (and his revised paper appeared later that year in another journal), and physicists who took the time to study the proposal gradually realized that his idea was a stroke of genius, one that allowed them to have their cake and eat it too. In Higgs's scheme, the fundamental equations can retain their pristine form because the dirty work of providing the particles' masses is relegated to the environment." These lines make clear that Higgs's theory allowed for the particles' mass, while at the same time accepting the fundamental equations as valid.

Choices A, B, and D are incorrect because the lines cited do not support the answer to the previous question about why the Higgs field eventually gained acceptance in the scientific community, instead explaining certain aspects of the Higgs field (choices A and B) and discussing how certain scientific theories become accepted as fact even before they are proven (choice D).

QUESTION 48

Choice A is the best answer. The main point of the last paragraph can be seen in its final sentence, which states that "mathematical equations can sometimes tell such a convincing tale, they can seemingly radiate reality so strongly, that they become entrenched in the vernacular of working physicists, even before there's data to confirm them." This point is borne out by the preceding lines of the paragraph, which recount the author's own experience of studying the still unproven Higgs field as it if were already a settled fact.

Choice B is incorrect because the anecdote the author shares about his own education does not demonstrate that physics, as a discipline, has come to operate differently over the course of his career. Choice C is incorrect because the details of the author's experience do not point to the process by which the existence of the Higgs field was confirmed, and indeed the passage does not describe that process at all. Choice D is incorrect because the passage broadly discusses the status of Higgs's theory at two different times (its initial rejection and later acceptance by physicists) and never considers how the details of the theory may have evolved.

QUESTION 49

Choice A is the best answer. In the last paragraph, the author states that "the professor presented the Higgs field with such certainty that for a long while I had no idea it had yet to be established experimentally." In this context, for a scientific theory to be established most nearly means that it is validated, or proven.

Choices B, C, and D are incorrect because in the context of the last paragraph describing a scientific theory as being "established experimentally," the word "established" means validated, or proven, not founded (choice B), introduced (choice C), or enacted (choice D).

QUESTION 50

Choice B is the best answer. The graph shows the periods of time that transpired between the moment when certain scientific concepts were introduced and the moment when those concepts were scientifically proven. Given the passage's discussion of the Higgs field, which was initially rejected by the scientific community before ultimately being accepted by it, the graph can therefore be seen as a means to put Higgs's work on mass into a greater context with other radical concepts that were ultimately accepted by the scientific community.

Choice A is incorrect because the graph illustrates that the Higgs boson required significantly more time to be confirmed than did any of the other theorized particles. Choice C is incorrect because the graph displays information only on the length of time necessary for any of the particles to be confirmed experimentally and does not indicate how any of them were regarded by scientists. Choice D is incorrect because the graph does not clarify anything about the Higgs boson other than the time that transpired between its being introduced and being confirmed.

QUESTION 51

Choice A is the best answer. Both the W boson and Z boson were introduced in the late 1960s and experimentally confirmed in the early 1980s. It is therefore accurate to say that they were both proposed and proven at about the same time.

Choice B is incorrect because the graph shows that it took more than forty years for the Higgs boson to be experimentally confirmed, while all the other particles were confirmed in a significantly shorter period of time than that. Choice C is incorrect because the graph shows that the tau neutrino was experimentally confirmed in 2000, while tau itself was experimentally confirmed in approximately 1975. Choice D is incorrect because the muon neutrino took approximately fifteen years to be confirmed, while the electron neutrino took well over twenty years.

QUESTION 52

Choice D is the best answer. In the last paragraph of the passage, the author explains that by the mid-1980s, "the physics community had, for the most part, fully bought into the idea that there was a Higgs field permeating space." That was fifteen years after the concept was introduced but decades before it would be confirmed, which would be analogous to most physicists believing in the existence of the electron neutrino in 1940, well after it had been introduced but many years before it was confirmed via experiment.

Choices A, B, and C are incorrect because the author depicts the Higgs field in the mid-1980s as being virtually an accepted fact, even though it had not yet been proven experimentally. This situation is not analogous to a proposed particle that is widely disputed until it is confirmed experimentally (choice A), a particle that has already been confirmed and consequently elicits widespread acceptance (choice B), or particles that are not considered as possibilities before the date on which they are formally proposed (choice C).

Section 2: Writing and Language Test

QUESTION 1

Choice D is the best answer. Since "frequently" and "many times" repeat the same idea, "many times" can be deleted without changing the meaning of the sentence.

Choices A, B, and C are incorrect. They all provide options that repeat the idea of "frequently" and are unnecessary in the sentence.

QUESTION 2

Choice A is the best answer. The noun "effect" is needed in the sentence to provide a direct object for the verb "has." Furthermore, the article "a" indicates that a noun will follow. In this sentence the noun "effect" is used to suggest a positive influence. The preposition "on" is idiomatic when used with "effect."

Choice B is incorrect because "affect" is a verb and the noun "effect" is needed in the sentence. (There is also the noun "affect," but it means a "display of emotion" and is not appropriate in this context.) Choice C is incorrect because the preposition "to" is not idiomatic in this context. Choice D is incorrect because a noun is needed, not the verb "affects."

QUESTION 3

Choice B is the best answer. The participle "creating" is consistent with "serving" and "showing," the other participles in the sentence, and provides parallel structure in the sentence.

Choices A, C, and D are incorrect and do not provide options that create parallel structure in the sentence.

QUESTION 4

Choice A is the best answer. The comma between "Telescope" and the conjunction "and" correctly separates the series of projects listed in the sentence.

Choices B and C are incorrect because there is no reason to use a semicolon in the sentence. Choices C and D are incorrect because when listing a series of items in a sentence, punctuation should be placed before the conjunction.

QUESTION 5

Choice C is the best answer. It most effectively sets up the list of examples of new technology that are listed in the sentence that follows: "communications satellites, invisible braces, and cordless tools."

Choices A, B, and D are incorrect because they mention "international cooperation," "national publicity," and "money for the agency," respectively; however, the sentence that follows lists examples of technology.

QUESTION 6

Choice C is the best answer because this option makes the most sense within the context of the paragraph. The inventions listed in the sentence were created or "developed" by NASA.

Choices A, B, and D are incorrect because they don't clearly convey the idea that NASA created the inventions.

QUESTION 7

Choice B is the best answer. The past tense verb "spawned" is consistent with the other past tense verbs in the paragraph.

Choice A is incorrect because the present tense verb "spawns" is inconsistent with the past tense verbs in the paragraph. Choice C is incorrect because the helping verb "has" is not needed since the action took place in the past. Choice D is incorrect because the sentence needs a simple verb to create a complete sentence, and the participle "spawning" doesn't provide that.

QUESTION 8

Choice D is the best answer. The contribution of money occurred in 2005, so the simple past tense verb "came" makes the most sense in the sentence. It also acts as a main verb, which creates a complete sentence.

Choices A, B, and C are incorrect because the participle "coming," the relative clause that begins "which came," and the infinitive phrase "to come" would each result in a sentence fragment and not a complete sentence in this context.

QUESTION 9

Choice A is the best answer. Leaving the sentence where it is now makes the paragraph logical. Sentence 1 serves as a topic sentence for the paragraph by introducing the idea that NASA contributed a significant amount of money to the economy in 2005. The supporting sentences that follow develop the topic sentence by explaining why the benefits of the NASA funding are significant.

Choices B, C, and D are incorrect because if sentence 1 were to be placed after any other sentence, the paragraph would not be logical and would therefore be confusing.

QUESTION 10

Choice D is the best answer. The sentence should not be added because the information it contains — the locations of various NASA facilities — is not relevant to the claim about the importance of NASA's work.

Choices A and B are incorrect because the sentence should not be added. Choice C is incorrect because the information it contains is not true. A statement about the locations of various NASA facilities does not undermine the claim about the economic benefits of NASA's work.

QUESTION 11

Choice A is the best answer. "Therefore" conveys the true relationship between the previous sentence and the statement that follows by indicating that, in addition to the practical benefits it contributes to the economy and society, NASA needs to be supported for global reasons as well.

Choices B, C, and D are incorrect because the transitional words "instead," "for example," and "however" would change the meaning of the sentence and do not convey the idea that a result or reason will follow.

QUESTION 12

Choice D is the best answer because it is clear and concise and provides parallel structure in the sentence. This choice eliminates unnecessary words and creates a list in which the topics "theories," "practices," and "technologies" are equally important.

Choices A, B, and C are incorrect because they contain words that are unnecessary and interrupt the flow of the sentence.

QUESTION 13

Choice C is the best answer. A pair of commas is needed to set off the phrase "from social services to manufacturing" to indicate that this information is explanatory but not crucial for understanding the sentence.

Choices A and D are incorrect because they both provide an incorrect punctuation mark. Choice B is incorrect because it doesn't provide a comma.

QUESTION 14

Choice A is the best answer. The adverb "accordingly" indicates correctly that because professional development provides a joint benefit to employers and employees, both parties share a joint responsibility to take advantage of the opportunities offered.

Choices B, C, and D are incorrect because they provide transitions that don't indicate the true relationship of shared responsibility between employees and employers.

QUESTION 15

Choice C is the best answer. Employees "must be in charge of their own careers." This claim provides an argument for what follows — "it is the duty of . . . employees to identify . . . resources" should they find themselves "falling behind in the workplace" — and supports the previous statement about shared responsibility, as well.

Choices A, B, and D are incorrect because they do not provide an argument for what must happen if employees find themselves "falling behind in the workplace."

QUESTION 16

Choice D is the best answer. A comma is needed between the dependent and independent clauses in order to create one sentence. The introductory conditional dependent clause beginning with "if" cannot stand alone and needs to be separated from the independent clause by a comma.

Choice A is incorrect because the dependent clause needs to be attached to an independent clause. Choice B is incorrect because a semicolon would be correct in this context only if it were connecting two independent clauses. Choice C is incorrect because there is no comma between the dependent and independent clauses.

QUESTION 17

Choice B is the best answer. It provides a clear and concise sentence that doesn't repeat ideas and specifically focuses on workers' "deficiencies."

Choices A and D are incorrect because they are wordy and repeat previously stated ideas. Choice C uses the casual expression "deal with," which is not the appropriate tone for the passage, and "flaws and shortcomings" mean the same thing.

QUESTION 18

Choice C is the best answer. "Obsolete" clearly and concisely conveys the idea that skills can become outdated.

Choices A, B, and D are incorrect either because they are not clear or they convey a tone that is inappropriate for the passage.

QUESTION 19

Choice B is the best answer. "Include" is a plural, present tense verb that agrees in number with the plural noun "forms" and the other present tense verbs in the paragraph.

Choice A is incorrect because the singular verb "includes" does not agree in number with the plural noun "forms." Choice C is incorrect because a simple present tense verb is needed to provide a predicate for the sentence. The participle "including" doesn't provide a predicate. Choice D is incorrect because the present perfect verb form is inconsistent with the present tense verbs in the paragraph.

QUESTION 20

Choice D is the best answer. No transitional link is needed between the two sentences.

In addition to the fact that no transition is needed, choice A is incorrect because "around the same time" indicates that time has been discussed earlier in the passage, but it hasn't. Choice B incorrectly indicates that additional information will be added to the previous statement. Choice C wrongly indicates that regardless of what has been said already, what follows is true.

QUESTION 21

Choice C is the best answer. Since "professional networks" is the largest circle in the illustration, it is therefore the overarching framework "within which staff receive coaching and consultation as well as the opportunity to attend foundation and skill-building workshops."

Choices A, B, and D are incorrect because as shown in the illustration, "coaching and consultation" and "foundation and skill-building workshops" occupy smaller circles within the professional-development framework, and thus cannot be the overarching framework.

QUESTION 22

Choice C is the best answer. No punctuation is needed between the main verb "can identify" and the clause that begins with "which" and functions as the object of the verb.

Choices A, B, and D are incorrect because they all contain punctuation marks.

QUESTION 23

Choice C is the best answer. The transition "however" indicates that a contrast or difference will follow. In this sentence two types of diners are being contrasted: "on-the-go eaters" and those who value "regional foods" and "culture built on cooking and long meals."

Choices A, B, and D are incorrect because these transitions do not indicate the contrast that sets up the resistance to the Slow Food movement discussed in the passage.

QUESTION 24

Choice A is the best answer. A comma is needed to separate the introductory infinitive phrase beginning with "to counter" from the independent main clause of the sentence beginning with "a cohort."

Choice B is incorrect because a semicolon is used in this context between two independent clauses. Choice C is incorrect because a colon is used before a list or to set off an important idea. Choice D is incorrect because the infinitive phrase beginning with "to counter" is not a complete sentence.

QUESTION 25

Choice C is the best answer. The sentence should not be added because the fact that the Slow Food movement's philosophy "was connected to the tale of the hare and the tortoise" blurs the focus of the paragraph, which is the contrast between two attitudes toward eating. The idea is also not clearly explained.

Choices A and B are incorrect because the sentence is irrelevant without further explanation. Choice D is incorrect because the paragraph doesn't emphasize the "Slow Food movement's origins and beliefs."

QUESTION 26

Choice D is the best answer. The auxiliary verb "has" correctly indicates that the Slow Food movement's opposition to fast food's standardization of taste is ongoing.

Choices A, B, and C provide verb tenses that do not indicate an opposition that began in the past and is ongoing: choice A provides a past perfect tense verb; choice B, a present tense verb; and choice C, a future tense verb.

QUESTION 27

Choice B is the best answer. The comma, which is necessary to set off information that may be informative but is not necessary for understanding the sentence, is placed correctly after the noun "factors" and after the noun "weather."

Choice A is incorrect because commas are needed to set off the nonrestrictive phrase. Choice C is incorrect because the first comma is misplaced. Choice D is incorrect because there should be a comma after "weather."

QUESTION 28

Choice D is the best answer. This choice most effectively supports the central point of the paragraph — the factors that influence the diversity of food flavors.

Choices A, B, and C are incorrect because they contain ideas that are not consistent with those in the paragraph. Choice A is subjective and mentions flavor quality instead of diversity, choice B addresses learning about traditional food, and choice C addresses how food is made.

QUESTION 29

Choice C is the best answer. The singular possessive pronoun “its” refers correctly to the singular noun “movement.”

Choice A is incorrect because “their” is a plural possessive pronoun, which cannot be used with a singular noun. Choice B is incorrect because the pronoun “there” refers to a place or is used to introduce a clause, and it is not possessive. Choice D is incorrect because “it’s” is a contraction for “it is,” not a possessive pronoun, and does not make sense in the sentence.

QUESTION 30

Choice B is the best answer. “Leisurely meals with friends and family” is clear and concise and eliminates unnecessary repetition.

Choices A and C are wordy and contain unnecessary repetition: In choice A, “lots of time” and “long meals” are the same. In choice C, “loved ones such as friends and family” is redundant. In choice D, “time-consuming meals” has a negative connotation, which is not consistent with the Slow Food movement’s belief that long, leisurely meals are beneficial.

QUESTION 31

Choice C is the best answer. “Drew criticism” is an idiomatic phrase meaning “caused criticism to flow forth,” which fits in the context of the sentence.

Choices A, B, and D are incorrect. All contain synonyms for “drew,” but they refer to drawing as an artistic exercise. None of these choices works, within the context of the sentence, since drawing here means enticing or attracting.

QUESTION 32

Choice C is the best answer. The sentence contains an indirect question, which does not take a question mark.

Choices A and B are incorrect because they contain question marks. Choice D is incorrect because the word order is confusing.

QUESTION 33

Choice C is the best answer. The prepositional phrase "to these ends" is used correctly as a transition to show that the three beliefs identified in the previous sentence cause the action (supporting small-scale producers) in the sentence that the prepositional phrase introduces.

Choices A, B, and D are incorrect. None of these options shows the true relationship between the sentences. "In short" (choice A) means that a summary will follow; "nonetheless" (choice B) means that in spite of the fact that something has been stated as being a certain way, an exception or contrasting statement will follow; and "by the same token" (choice D) indicates that a similar idea will follow.

QUESTION 34

Choice A is the best answer. The comma is placed correctly after "declared" to set off the headline that follows.

Choices B, C, and D are incorrect because they contain misplaced commas. Additionally, the inclusion of a second comma in choices C and D suggests incorrectly that the information between the commas could be eliminated without changing the meaning of the sentence.

QUESTION 35

Choice B is the best answer. This choice clearly says that "other newspapers also ran stories claiming that the broadcast had incited mass hysteria," which suggests that the story was widely reported.

Choice A is incorrect because it identifies only one news source. Choices C and D are incorrect because they are not relevant to the paragraph.

QUESTION 36

Choice C is the best answer. The participle "fearing" clearly describes the people who thought that Martians had invaded Earth and places the focus on "fear."

Choice A is incorrect because it changes the meaning of the sentence. A broadcast can't "have" people. Choice A would also require a comma before "who feared" to make it grammatically correct. Choice B is incorrect because the relative pronoun "that" isn't used to begin clauses describing people. Choice D is incorrect because the infinitive "to fear" doesn't make sense in the sentence.

QUESTION 37

Choice D is the best answer. "Go so far as to" is an idiomatic expression meaning "proceed to the point of doing something."

Choices A, B, and C are incorrect because they are not idiomatic.

QUESTION 38

Choice C is the best answer. The prepositional phrase "in the article" is used correctly to link the article mentioned in the previous sentence to a statement that was made in the article.

Choices A, B, and D are incorrect because they don't show the true relationship between the sentences. The previous sentence makes a statement that the following sentence expands upon.

QUESTION 39

Choice D is the best answer. The prepositional phrase "by portraying the new medium as irresponsible" clearly and concisely tells how the newspaper industry "sought to discredit the newly emerging technology of radio."

Choices A and B are incorrect because they include unnecessary words that do not add meaning to the sentence. Choice C is incorrect because the conjunction "and" is unnecessary and confusing.

QUESTION 40

Choice B is the best answer. It best establishes the main idea of the paragraph by focusing on the overblown reports of panic. The paragraph lists various pieces of evidence to support the claim that reports were exaggerated; for instance, "a mere 2 percent of households had tuned in to the broadcast" and the validity of "an oft-cited report" is called into question.

Choices A, C, and D are incorrect. Choice A is too specific since the paragraph doesn't evaluate the strength of Pooley and Socolow's argument. Choice C is too specific since the paragraph doesn't focus on Pooley and Socolow's insistence on newspapers' distortions. Choice D is too general and doesn't focus on a topic.

QUESTION 41

Choice A is the best answer. "Fewer" is an adjective that is used with things that can be counted and therefore is used correctly in this sentence to describe "people." "Far" is an adverb that describes the adjective "fewer" and is used to indicate the extent to which the number of people listening to the broadcast differed from a million.

Choices B and C are incorrect because the adjective "less" is used when describing things that cannot be counted. Choices C and D are incorrect because they use "then" and not the appropriate comparison preposition "than."

QUESTION 42

Choice D is the best answer. Sentence 4 is most logically placed after sentence 7 because sentence 7 implies that the words used in the survey were used synonymously, even though the words convey different levels of reaction. Sentence 4 supports this idea with further explanation.

Choices A, B, and C are incorrect because it would be illogical and confusing to place sentence 4 after sentence 2, 3, or 5.

QUESTION 43

Choice C is the best answer. The pronoun "some" is used correctly as the subject of the independent clause. The comma after "some" is needed to set off the nonrestrictive clause ("influenced by the sensationalized news coverage afterward") that follows it.

Choice A is incorrect because without a comma, the resulting restrictive clause changes the meaning of the sentence. Choice B is incorrect because the pronoun "they" introduces an independent clause and provides another, unnecessary subject for the sentence. Choice D is incorrect because a comma is needed to set off the nonrestrictive clause.

QUESTION 44

Choice A is the best answer. "Not unlike," which means the same as "like," most effectively signals the similarity between the two groups mentioned by the researchers.

Choices B, C, and D are incorrect because they all indicate difference instead of similarity.

Section 3: Math Test – No Calculator

QUESTION 1

Choice C is correct. Maria spends x minutes running each day and y minutes biking each day. Therefore, $x + y$ represents the total number of minutes Maria spent running and biking each day. Because $x + y = 75$, it follows that 75 is the total number of minutes that Maria spent running and biking each day.

Choices A and B are incorrect. The number of minutes Maria spent running each day is represented by x and need not be 75. Similarly, the number of minutes that Maria spends biking each day is represented by y and need not be 75. The number of minutes Maria spends running each day and biking each day may vary; however, the total number of minutes she spends each day on these activities is constant and equal to 75. Choice D is incorrect. The number of minutes Maria spent biking for each minute spent running cannot be determined from the information provided.

QUESTION 2

Choice C is correct. Using the distributive property to multiply 3 and $(x + 5)$ gives $3x + 15 - 6$, which can be rewritten as $3x + 9$.

Choice A is incorrect and may result from rewriting the given expression as $3(x + 5 - 6)$. Choice B is incorrect and may result from incorrectly rewriting the expression as $(3x + 5) - 6$. Choice D is incorrect and may result from incorrectly rewriting the expression as $3(5x) - 6$.

QUESTION 3

Choice B is correct. The first equation can be rewritten as $y - x = 3$ and the second as $\frac{x}{4} + y = 3$, which implies that $-x = \frac{x}{4}$, and so $x = 0$. The ordered pair (0, 3) satisfies the first equation and also the second, since $0 + 2(3) = 6$ is a true equality.

Alternatively, the first equation can be rewritten as $y = x + 3$. Substituting $x + 3$ for y in the second equation gives $\frac{x}{2} + 2(x + 3) = 6$. This can be rewritten using the distributive property as $\frac{x}{2} + 2x + 6 = 6$. It follows that $2x + \frac{x}{2}$ must be 0. Thus, $x = 0$. Substituting 0 for x in the equation $y = x + 3$ gives $y = 3$. Therefore, the ordered pair (0, 3) satisfies the system of equations shown.

Choice A is incorrect; it satisfies the first equation but not the second. Choices C and D are incorrect because neither satisfies the first equation, $x = y - 3$.

QUESTION 4

Choice D is correct. Applying the distributive property, the original expression is equivalent to $5 + 12i - 9i^2 + 6i$. Since $i = \sqrt{-1}$, it follows that $i^2 = -1$. Substituting -1 for i^2 in the expression and simplifying yields $5 + 12i + 9 + 6i$, which is equal to $14 + 18i$.

Choices A, B, and C are incorrect and may result from substituting 1 for i^2 or errors made when rewriting the given expression.

QUESTION 5

Choice A is correct. Substituting -1 for x in the equation that defines f gives $f(-1) = \frac{(-1)^2 - 6(-1) + 3}{(-1) - 1}$. Simplifying the expressions in the numerator and denominator yields $\frac{1 + 6 + 3}{-2}$, which is equal to $\frac{10}{-2}$ or -5.

Choices B, C, and D are incorrect and may result from misapplying the order of operations when substituting -1 for x.

QUESTION 6

Choice C is correct. The value of the camera equipment depreciates from its original purchase value at a constant rate for 12 years. So if x is the amount, in dollars, by which the value of the equipment depreciates each year, the value of the camera equipment, in dollars, t years after it is purchased would be $32{,}400 - tx$. Since the value of the camera equipment after 12 years is \$0, it follows that $32{,}400 - 12x = 0$. To solve for x, rewrite the equation as $32{,}400 = 12x$. Dividing both sides of the equation by 12 gives $x = 2{,}700$. It follows that the value of the camera equipment depreciates by \$2,700 each year. Therefore, the value of the equipment after 4 years, represented by the expression $32{,}400 - 2{,}700(4)$, is \$21,600.

Choice A is incorrect. The value given in choice A is equivalent to \$2,700 × 4. This is the amount, in dollars, by which the value of the camera equipment depreciates 4 years after it is purchased, not the dollar value of the camera equipment 4 years after it is purchased. Choice B is incorrect. The value given in choice B is equal to \$2,700 × 6, which is the amount, in dollars, by which the value of the camera equipment depreciates 6 years after it is purchased, not the dollar value of the camera equipment 4 years after it is purchased. Choice D is incorrect. The value given in choice D is equal to \$32,400 – \$2,700. This is the dollar value of the camera equipment 1 year after it is purchased.

Alternative approach: Since the camera equipment loses all of its value at a constant rate for 12 years, it will lose one-third of its value after 4 years; therefore, its value would be two-thirds of its original purchase price of \$32,400. Since two-thirds of \$32,400 is \$21,600, that is the value of the camera equipment after 4 years.

QUESTION 7

Choice B is correct. The given quadratic expression is in standard form, and each answer choice is in vertex form. Completing the square converts the expression from standard form to vertex form. The first step is to rewrite the expression as follows: $x^2 + 6x + 4 = x^2 + 6x + 9 + 4 - 9$. The first three terms of the revised expression can be rewritten as a perfect square as follows: $x^2 + 6x + 9 + 4 - 9 = (x + 3)^2 + 4 - 9$. Combining the constant terms gives $(x + 3)^2 - 5$.

Choice A is incorrect. Squaring the binomial and simplifying the expression in choice A gives $x^2 + 6x + 9 + 5$. Combining like terms gives $x^2 + 6x + 14$, not $x^2 + 6x + 4$. Choice C is incorrect. Squaring the binomial and simplifying the expression in choice C gives $x^2 - 6x + 9 + 5$. Combining like terms gives $x^2 - 6x + 14$, not $x^2 + 6x + 4$. Choice D is incorrect. Squaring the binomial and simplifying the expression in choice D gives $x^2 - 6x + 9 - 5$. Combining like terms gives $x^2 - 6x + 4$, not $x^2 + 6x + 4$.

QUESTION 8

Choice C is correct. Ken earned \$8 per hour for the first 10 hours he worked, so he earned a total of \$80 for the first 10 hours he worked. For the rest of the week, Ken was paid at the rate of \$10 per hour. Let x be the number of hours he will work for the rest of the week. The total of Ken's earnings, in dollars, for the week will be $10x + 80$. He saves 90% of his earnings each week, so this week he will save $0.9(10x + 80)$ dollars. The inequality $0.9(10x + 80) \geq 270$ represents the condition that he will save at least \$270 for the week. Factoring 10 out of the expression $10x + 80$ gives $10(x + 8)$. The product of 10 and 0.9 is 9, so the inequality can be rewritten as $9(x + 8) \geq 270$. Dividing both sides of this inequality by 9 yields $x + 8 \geq 30$, so $x \geq 22$. Therefore, the least number of hours Ken must work the rest of the week to save at least \$270 for the week is 22.

Choices A and B are incorrect because Ken can save \$270 by working fewer hours than 38 or 33 for the rest of the week. Choice D is incorrect. If Ken worked 16 hours for the rest of the week, his total earnings for the week will be \$80 + \$160 = \$240, which is less than \$270. Since he saves only 90% of his earnings each week, he would save even less than \$240 for the week.

QUESTION 9

Choice B is correct. Marisa will hire x junior directors and y senior directors. Since she needs to hire at least 10 staff members, $x + y \geq 10$. Each junior director will be paid \$640 per week, and each senior director will be paid \$880 per week. Marisa's budget for paying the new staff is no more than \$9,700 per week; in terms of x and y, this condition is $640x + 880y \leq 9{,}700$. Since Marisa must hire at least 3 junior directors and at least 1 senior director, it follows that $x \geq 3$ and $y \geq 1$. All four of these conditions are represented correctly in choice B.

Choices A and C are incorrect. For example, the first condition, $640x + 880y \geq 9{,}700$, in each of these options implies that Marisa can pay the new staff members more than her budget of \$9,700. Choice D is incorrect because Marisa needs to hire at least 10 staff members, not at most 10 staff members, as the inequality $x + y \leq 10$ implies.

QUESTION 10

Choice B is correct. The factor theorem states that a polynomial equation with roots -1, -3, and 5 must have factors of $(x + 1)$, $(x + 3)$, and $(x - 5)$. Of the answer choices provided, only $x + 1$ appears from this list of possible factors.

Choices A, C, and D are incorrect because a third-degree equation cannot have more than three roots. Based on the factor theorem, choice A implies that 1 is a root of the equation, choice C implies that 3 is a root of the equation, and choice D implies that –5 is a root of the equation. However, none of these roots appears in the given list.

QUESTION 11

Choice D is correct. For $x > 1$ and $y > 1$, $x^{\frac{1}{3}}$ and $y^{\frac{1}{2}}$ are equivalent to $\sqrt[3]{x}$ and $\sqrt{y}$, respectively. Also, x^{-2} and y^{-1} are equivalent to $\frac{1}{x^2}$ and $\frac{1}{y}$, respectively. Therefore, the given expression can be rewritten as $\frac{y\sqrt{y}}{x^2\sqrt[3]{x}}$.

Choices A, B, and C are incorrect because these choices are not equivalent to the given expression for $x > 1$ and $y > 1$.

For example, for $x = 2$ and $y = 2$, the value of the given expression is $2^{-\frac{5}{6}}$; the values of the choices, however, are $2^{-\frac{1}{3}}$, $2^{\frac{5}{6}}$, and 1, respectively.

QUESTION 12

Choice B is correct. The graph of a quadratic function in the *xy*-plane is a parabola. The axis of symmetry of the parabola passes through the vertex of the parabola. Therefore, the vertex of the parabola and the midpoint of the segment between the two *x*-intercepts of the graph have the same *x*-coordinate. Since $f(-3) = f(-1) = 0$, the *x*-coordinate of the vertex is $\frac{(-3) + (-1)}{2} = -2$. Of the shown intervals, only the interval in choice B contains –2.

Choices A, C, and D are incorrect and may result from either calculation errors or misidentification of the graph's *x*-intercepts.

QUESTION 13

Choice D is correct. The numerator of the given expression can be rewritten in terms of the denominator, $x - 3$, as follows: $x^2 - 2x - 5 = x^2 - 3x + x - 3 - 2$, which is equivalent to $x(x - 3) + (x - 3) - 2$. So the given expression is equivalent to $\frac{x(x-3) + (x-3) - 2}{x-3} = \frac{x(x-3)}{x-3} + \frac{x-3}{x-3} - \frac{2}{x-3}$. Since the given expression is defined for $x \neq 3$, the expression can be rewritten as $x + 1 - \frac{2}{x-3}$.

Long division can also be used as an alternate approach.

Choices A, B, and C are incorrect and may result from errors made when dividing the two polynomials or making use of structure.

QUESTION 14

Choice A is correct. If x is the width, in inches, of the box, then the length of the box is $2.5x$ inches. It follows that the perimeter of the base is $2(2.5x + x)$, or $7x$ inches. The height of the box is given to be 60 inches. According to the restriction, the sum of the perimeter of the base and the height of the box should not exceed 130 inches. Algebraically, this can be represented by $7x + 60 \leq 130$, or $7x \leq 70$. Dividing both sides of the inequality by 7 gives $x \leq 10$. Since x represents the width of the box, x must also be a positive number. Therefore, the inequality $0 < x \leq 10$ represents all the allowable values of x that satisfy the given conditions.

Choices B, C, and D are incorrect and may result from calculation errors or misreading the given information.

QUESTION 15

Choice D is correct. Factoring out the coefficient $\frac{1}{3}$, the given expression can be rewritten as $\frac{1}{3}(x^2 - 6)$. The expression $x^2 - 6$ can be approached as a difference of squares and rewritten as $(x - \sqrt{6})(x + \sqrt{6})$. Therefore, k must be $\sqrt{6}$.

Choice A is incorrect. If k were 2, then the expression given would be rewritten as $\frac{1}{3}(x - 2)(x + 2)$, which is equivalent to $\frac{1}{3}x^2 - \frac{4}{3}$, not $\frac{1}{3}x^2 - 2$. Choice B is incorrect. This may result from incorrectly factoring the expression and finding $(x - 6)(x + 6)$ as the factored form of the expression. Choice C is incorrect. This may result from incorrectly distributing the $\frac{1}{3}$ and rewriting the expression as $\frac{1}{3}(x^2 - 2)$.

QUESTION 16

The correct answer is 8. The expression $2x + 8$ contains a factor of $x + 4$. It follows that the original equation can be rewritten as $2(x + 4) = 16$. Dividing both sides of the equation by 2 gives $x + 4 = 8$.

QUESTION 17

The correct answer is 30. It is given that the measure of $\angle QPR$ is 60°. Angle MPR and $\angle QPR$ are collinear and therefore are supplementary angles. This means that the sum of the two angle measures is 180°, and so the measure of $\angle MPR$ is 120°. The sum of the angles in a triangle is 180°. Subtracting the measure of $\angle MPR$ from 180° yields the sum of the other angles in the triangle MPR. Since $180 - 120 = 60$, the sum of the measures of $\angle QMR$ and $\angle NRM$ is 60°. It is given that $MP = PR$, so it follows that triangle MPR is isosceles. Therefore $\angle QMR$ and $\angle NRM$ must be congruent. Since the sum of the measure of these two angles is 60°, it follows that the measure of each angle is 30°.

An alternate approach would be to use the exterior angle theorem, noting that the measure of $\angle QPR$ is equal to the sum of the measures of $\angle QMR$ and $\angle NRM$. Since both angles are equal, each of them has a measure of 30°.

QUESTION 18

The correct answer is 4. There are π radians in a 180° angle. An angle measure of 720° is 4 times greater than an angle measure of 180°. Therefore, the number of radians in a 720° angle is 4π.

QUESTION 19

The correct answer is 8. Since the line passes through the point (2, 0), its equation can be written in the form $y = m(x - 2)$. The coordinates of the point (1, 4) must also satisfy this equation. So $4 = m(1 - 2)$, or $m = -4$. Substituting -4 for m in the equation of the line gives $y = -4(x - 2)$, or equivalently $y = -4x + 8$. Therefore, $b = 8$.

Alternate approach: Given the coordinates of two points through which the line passes, the slope of the line is $\frac{4 - 0}{1 - 2} = -4$. So an equation of the line is of the form $y = -4x + b$. Since (2, 0) satisfies this equation, $0 = -4(2) + b$ must be true. Solving this equation for b gives $b = 8$.

QUESTION 20

The correct answer is 6632. Applying the distributive property to the expression yields $(7532 + 100y^2) + (100y^2 - 1100)$. Then adding together $7532 + 100y^2$ and $100y^2 - 1100$ and collecting like terms results in $200y^2 + 6432$. This is written in the form $ay^2 + b$, where $a = 200$ and $b = 6432$. Therefore $a + b = 200 + 6432 = 6632$.

Section 4: Math Test – Calculator

QUESTION 1

Choice B is correct. There are 2 dogs that are fed only dry food and a total of 25 dogs. Therefore, the fraction of dogs fed only dry food is $\frac{2}{25}$.

Choice A is incorrect. This fraction is the number of dogs fed only dry food divided by the total number of pets instead of the total number of dogs. Choice C is incorrect because it is the fraction of all pets fed only dry food. Choice D is incorrect. This fraction is the number of dogs fed only dry food divided by the total number of pets fed only dry food.

QUESTION 2

Choice A is correct. Applying the distributive property, the given expression can be rewritten as $x^2 - 3 + 3x^2 - 5$. Combining like terms yields $4x^2 - 8$.

Choice B is incorrect and is the result of disregarding the negative sign in front of the first 3 before combining like terms. Choice C is incorrect and is the result of not multiplying $-3x^2$ by -1 before combining like terms. Choice D is incorrect and is the result of disregarding the negative sign in front of the first 3 and not multiplying $-3x^2$ by -1 before combining like terms.

QUESTION 3

Choice C is correct. Multiplying each side of 1 meter = 100 cm by 6 gives 6 meters = 600 cm. Each package requires 3 centimeters of tape. The number of packages that can be secured with 600 cm of tape is $\frac{600}{3}$, or 200 packages.

Choices A, B, and D are incorrect and may be the result of incorrect interpretations of the given information or of computation errors.

QUESTION 4

Choice D is correct. The sample was selected from a group of people who indicated that they liked the book. It is inappropriate to generalize the result of the survey beyond the population from which the participants were selected. Choice D is the most appropriate inference from the survey results because it describes a conclusion about people who liked the book, and the results of the survey indicate that most people who like the book disliked the movie.

Choices A, B, and C are incorrect because none of these inferences can be drawn from the survey results. Choices A and B need not be true. The people surveyed all liked the book on which the movie was based, which is not necessarily true of all people who go see movies or all people who read books. Thus, the people surveyed are not representative of all people who go see movies or all people who read books. Therefore, the results of this survey cannot appropriately be extended to at least 95% of people who go see movies or to at least 95% of people who read books. Choice C need not be true because the sample includes only people who liked the book, and so the results do not extend to people who dislike the book.

QUESTION 5

Choice C is correct. Substituting (1, 1) into the inequality gives $5(1) - 3(1) < 4$, or $2 < 4$, which is a true statement. Substituting (2, 5) into the inequality gives $5(2) - 3(5) < 4$, or $-5 < 4$, which is a true statement. Substituting (3, 2) into the inequality gives $5(3) - 3(2) < 4$, or $9 < 4$, which is not a true statement. Therefore, (1, 1) and (2, 5) are the only ordered pairs shown that satisfy the given inequality.

Choice A is incorrect because the ordered pair (2, 5) also satisfies the inequality. Choice B is incorrect because the ordered pair (1, 1) also satisfies the inequality. Choice D is incorrect because the ordered pair (3, 2) does not satisfy the inequality.

QUESTION 6

Choice C is correct. Since $x = -3$ is a solution to the equation, substituting -3 for x gives $(-3a + 3)^2 = 36$. It follows that $-3a + 3 = 6$ or $-3a + 3 = -6$. Solving each of these for a yields $a = -1$ or $a = 3$. Therefore, -1 is a possible value of a.

Choice A is incorrect and may be the result of ignoring the squared expression and solving $-3a + 3 = 36$ for a. Choice B is incorrect and may be the result of dividing 36 by 2 instead of taking the square root of 36 when solving for a. Choice D is incorrect and may be the result of taking the sum of the value of x, -3, and the constant, 3.

QUESTION 7

Choice A is correct. The slope of the line of best fit is negative, meaning the greater the distance of a planetoid from the Sun, the less the predicted density of the planetoid. Therefore, planetoids that are more distant from the Sun tend to have lesser densities.

Choice B is incorrect because the further the distance of a planetoid from the Sun, the less the predicted density of the planetoid. Choice C is incorrect. For example, according to the line of best fit, a planetoid that is 0.8 AU from the Sun has a predicted density of 5 g/cm^3, but a planetoid that is twice as far from the Sun with a distance of 1.6 AU has a predicted density of 4.25 g/cm^3. However, the predicted density of 4.25 g/cm^3 is not half the predicted density of 5 g/cm^3. Choice D is incorrect because there is a relationship between the distance from a planetoid to the Sun and predicted density, as shown by the line of best fit.

QUESTION 8

Choice C is correct. According to the line of best fit, a planetoid with a distance from the Sun of 1.2 AU has a predicted density between 4.5 g/cm^3 and 4.75 g/cm^3. The only choice in this range is 4.6.

Choices A, B, and D are incorrect and may result from misreading the information in the scatterplot.

QUESTION 9

Choice A is correct. To isolate the terms that contain ax and b, 6 can be added to both sides of the equation, which gives $9ax + 9b = 27$. Then, both sides of this equation can be divided by 9, which gives $ax + b = 3$.

Choices B, C, and D are incorrect and may result from computation errors.

QUESTION 10

Choice D is correct. There are 60 minutes in one hour, so an 8-hour workday has $(60)(8) = 480$ minutes. To calculate 15% of 480, multiply 0.15 by 480: $(0.15)(480) = 72$. Therefore, Lani spent 72 minutes of her workday in meetings.

Choice A is incorrect because 1.2 is 15% of 8, which gives the time Lani spent of her workday in meetings in hours, not minutes. Choices B and C are incorrect and may be the result of computation errors.

QUESTION 11

Choice A is correct. The total number of copies of the game the company will ship is 75, so one equation in the system is $s + c = 75$, which can be written as $75 - s = c$. Because each standard edition of the game has a volume of 20 cubic inches and s represents the number of standard edition games, the expression $20s$ represents the volume of the shipment that comes from standard edition copies of the game. Similarly, the expression $30c$ represents the volume of the shipment that comes from collector's edition copies of the games. Because these volumes combined are 1,870 cubic inches, the equation $20s + 30c = 1{,}870$ represents this situation. Therefore, the correct answer is choice A.

Choice B is incorrect. This equation gives the volume of each standard edition game as 30 cubic inches and the volume of each collector's edition game as 20 cubic inches. Choice C is incorrect. This is the result of finding the average volume of the two types of games, using that average volume (25) for both types of games, and assuming that there are 75 more standard editions of the game than there are collector's editions of the game. Choice D is incorrect. This is the result of assuming that the volume of each standard edition game is 30 cubic inches, that the volume of each collector's edition game is 20 cubic inches, and that there are 75 more standard editions than there are collector's editions.

QUESTION 12

Choice B is correct. Let x be the price, in dollars, of the jacket before sales tax. The price of the jacket after the 6% sales tax is added was \$53. This can be expressed by the equation $x + 0.06x = 53$, or $1.06x = 53$. Dividing each side of this equation by 1.06 gives $x = 50$. Therefore, the price of the jacket before sales tax was \$50.

Choices A, C, and D are incorrect and may be the result of computation errors.

QUESTION 13

Choice B is correct. Theresa's speed was increasing from 0 to 5 minutes and from 20 to 25 minutes, which is a total of 10 minutes. Theresa's speed was decreasing from 10 minutes to 20 minutes and from 25 to 30 minutes, which is a total of 15 minutes. Therefore, Theresa's speed was NOT increasing for a longer period of time than it was decreasing.

Choice A is incorrect. Theresa ran at a constant speed for the 5-minute period from 5 to 10 minutes. Choice C is incorrect. Theresa's speed decreased at a constant rate during the last 5 minutes, which can be seen since the graph is linear during that time. Choice D is incorrect. Theresa's speed reached its maximum at 25 minutes, which is within the last 10 minutes.

QUESTION 14

Choice D is correct. The figure is a quadrilateral, so the sum of the measures of its interior angles is 360°. The value of x can be found by using the equation $45 + 3x = 360$. Subtracting 45 from both sides of the equation results in $3x = 315$, and dividing both sides of the resulting equation by 3 yields $x = 105$. Therefore, the value of x in the figure is 105.

Choice A is incorrect. If the value of x were 45, the sum of the measures of the angles in the figure would be $45 + 3(45)$, or 180°, but the sum of the measures of the angles in a quadrilateral is 360°. Choice B is incorrect. If the value of x were 90, the sum of the measures of the angles in the figure would be $45 + 3(90)$, or 315°, but the sum of the measures of the angles in a quadrilateral is 360°. Choice C is incorrect. If the value of x were 100, the sum of the measures of the angles in the figure would be $45 + 3(100)$, or 345°, but the sum of the measures of the angles in a quadrilateral is 360°.

QUESTION 15

Choice B is correct. A column of 50 stacked one-cent coins is about $3\frac{7}{8}$ inches tall, which is slightly less than 4 inches tall and equivalent to $\frac{31}{8}$. Therefore, a column of stacked one-cent coins that is 4 inches tall would contain slightly more than 50 one-cent coins. It can then be reasoned that because 8 inches is twice 4 inches, a column of stacked one-cent coins that is 8 inches tall would contain slightly more than twice as many coins; that is, slightly more than 100 one-cent coins. An alternate approach is to set up a proportion comparing the column height to the number of one-cent coins, or $\frac{\frac{31}{8}\text{ inches}}{50\text{ coins}} = \frac{8\text{ inches}}{x\text{ coins}}$, where x is the number of coins in an 8-inch-tall column. Multiplying each side of the proportion by $50x$ gives $\frac{31}{8}x = 400$. Solving for x gives $x = 400\left(\frac{8}{31}\right)$, which is approximately 103. Therefore, of the given choices, 100 is closest to the number of one-cent coins it would take to build an 8-inch-tall column.

Choice A is incorrect. A column of 75 stacked one-cent coins would be slightly less than 6 inches tall. Choice C is incorrect. A column of 200 stacked one-cent coins would be more than 15 inches tall. Choice D is incorrect. A column of 390 stacked one-cent coins would be over 30 inches tall.

QUESTION 16

Choice D is correct. If $\frac{b}{2} = 10$, then multiplying each side of this equation by 2 gives $b = 20$. Substituting 20 for b in the equation $a - b = 12$ gives $a - 20 = 12$. Adding 20 to each side of this equation gives $a = 32$. Since $a = 32$ and $b = 20$, it follows that the value of $a + b$ is $32 + 20$, or 52.

Choice A is incorrect. If the value of $a + b$ were less than the value of $a - b$, it would follow that b is negative. But if $\frac{b}{2} = 10$, then b must be positive. This contradiction shows that the value of $a + b$ cannot be 2. Choice B is incorrect. If the value of $a + b$ were equal to the value of $a - b$, then it would follow that $b = 0$. However, b cannot equal zero because it is given that $\frac{b}{2} = 10$. Choice C is incorrect. This is the value of a, but the question asks for the value of $a + b$.

QUESTION 17

Choice A is correct. The y-intercept of the graph of $y = 19.99 + 1.50x$ in the xy-plane is the point on the graph with an x-coordinate equal to 0. In the model represented by the equation, the x-coordinate represents the number of miles a rental truck is driven during a one-day rental, and so the y-intercept represents the charge, in dollars, for the rental when the truck is driven 0 miles; that is, the y-intercept represents the cost, in dollars, of the flat fee. Since the y-intercept of the graph of $y = 19.99 + 1.50x$ is $(0, 19.99)$, the y-intercept represents a flat fee of \$19.99 in terms of the model.

Choice B is incorrect. The slope of the graph of $y = 19.99 + 1.50x$ in the xy-plane, not the y-intercept, represents a driving charge per mile of \$1.50 in terms of the model. Choice C is incorrect. Since the coefficient of x in the equation is 1.50, the charge per mile for driving the rental truck is \$1.50, not \$19.99. Choice D is incorrect. The sum of 19.99 and 1.50, which is 21.49, represents the cost, in dollars, for renting the truck for one day and driving the truck 1 mile; however, the total daily charges for renting the truck does not need to be \$21.49.

QUESTION 18

Choice B is correct. The charity with the greatest percent of total expenses spent on programs is represented by the highest point on the scatterplot; this is the point that has a vertical coordinate slightly less than halfway between 90 and 95 and a horizontal coordinate slightly less than halfway between 3,000 and 4,000. Thus, the charity represented by this point has a total income of about \$3,400 million and spends about 92% of its total expenses on programs. The percent predicted by the line of best fit is the vertical coordinate of the point on the line of best fit with horizontal coordinate \$3,400 million; this vertical coordinate is very slightly more than 85. Thus, the line of best fit predicts that the charity with the greatest percent of total expenses spent on programs will spend slightly more than 85% on programs. Therefore, the difference between the actual percent (92%) and the prediction (slightly more than 85%) is slightly less than 7%.

Choice A is incorrect. There is no charity represented in the scatterplot for which the difference between the actual percent of total expenses spent on programs and the percent predicted by the line of best fit is as much as 10%. Choices C and D are incorrect. These choices may result from misidentifying in the scatterplot the point that represents the charity with the greatest percent of total expenses spent on programs.

QUESTION 19

Choice A is correct. Current's formula is $A = \frac{4 + w}{30}$. Multiplying each side of the equation by 30 gives $30A = 4 + w$. Subtracting 4 from each side of $30A = 4 + w$ gives $w = 30A - 4$.

Choices B, C, and D are incorrect and may result from errors in choosing and applying operations to isolate w as one side of the equation in Current's formula.

QUESTION 20

Choice C is correct. If Mosteller's and Current's formulas give the same estimate for A, then the right-hand sides of these two equations are equal; that is, $\frac{\sqrt{hw}}{60} = \frac{4 + w}{30}$. Multiplying each side of this equation by 60 to isolate the expression $\sqrt{hw}$ gives $\sqrt{hw} = 60\left(\frac{4 + w}{30}\right)$ or $\sqrt{hw} = 2(4 + w)$. Therefore, if Mosteller's and Current's formulas give the same estimate for A, then $\sqrt{hw}$ is equivalent to $2(4 + w)$.

An alternate approach is to multiply the numerator and denominator of Current's formula by 2, which gives $\frac{2(4 + w)}{60}$. Since it is given that Mosteller's and Current's formulas give the same estimate for A, $\frac{2(4 + w)}{60} = \frac{\sqrt{hw}}{60}$. Therefore, $\sqrt{hw} = 2(4 + w)$.

Choices A, B, and D are incorrect and may result from errors in the algebraic manipulation of the equations.

QUESTION 21

Option C is correct. The predicted increase in total fat, in grams, for every increase of 1 gram in total protein is represented by the slope of the line of best fit. Any two points on the line can be used to calculate the slope of the line as the change in total fat over the change in total protein. For instance, it can be estimated that the points (20, 34) and (30, 48) are on the line of best fit, and the slope of the line that passes through them is $\frac{48 - 34}{30 - 20} = \frac{14}{10}$, or 1.4. Of the choices given, 1.5 is the closest to the slope of the line of best fit.

Choices A, B, and D are incorrect and may be the result of incorrectly finding ordered pairs that lie on the line of best fit or of incorrectly calculating the slope.

QUESTION 22

Choice B is correct. The median of a set of numbers is the middle value of the set values when ordered from least to greatest. If the percents in the table are ordered from least to greatest, the middle value is 27.9%. The difference between 27.9% and 26.95% is 0.95%.

Choice A is incorrect and may be the result of calculation errors or not finding the median of the data in the table correctly. Choice C is incorrect and may be the result of finding the mean instead of the median. Choice D is incorrect and may be the result of using the middle value of the unordered list.

QUESTION 23

Choice C is correct. The total volume of the cylindrical can is found by multiplying the area of the base of the can, 75 cm^2, by the height of the can, 10 cm, which yields 750 cm^3. If the syrup needed to fill the can has a volume of 110 cm^3, then the remaining volume for the pieces of fruit is $750 - 110 = 640$ cm^3.

Choice A is incorrect because if the fruit had a volume of 7.5 cm^3, there would be $750 - 7.5 = 742.5$ cm^3 of syrup needed to fill the can to the top. Choice B is incorrect because if the fruit had a volume of 185 cm^3, there would be $750 - 185 = 565$ cm^3 of syrup needed to fill the can to the top. Choice D is incorrect because it is the total volume of the can, not just of the pieces of fruit.

QUESTION 24

Choice A is correct. The variable t represents the seconds after the object is launched. Since $h(0) = 72$, this means that the height, in feet, at 0 seconds, or the initial height, is 72 feet.

Choices B, C, and D are incorrect and may be the result of misinterpreting the function in context.

QUESTION 25

Choice B is correct. The relationship between x food calories and k kilojoules can be modeled as a proportional relationship. Let (x_1, k_1) and (x_2, k_2) represent the values in the first two rows in the table: (4.0, 16.7) and (9.0, 37.7). The rate of change, or $\frac{(k_2 - k_1)}{(x_2 - x_1)}$, is $\frac{21}{5} = 4.2$; therefore, the equation that best represents the relationship between x and k is $k = 4.2x$.

Choice A is incorrect and may be the result of calculating the rate of change using $\frac{(x_2 - x_1)}{(k_2 - k_1)}$. Choice C is incorrect because the number of kilojoules is greater than the number of food calories. Choice D is incorrect and may be the result of an error when setting up the equation.

QUESTION 26

Choice B is correct. It is given that there are 4.0 food calories per gram of protein, 9.0 food calories per gram of fat, and 4.0 food calories per gram of carbohydrate. If 180 food calories in a granola bar came from p grams of protein, f grams of fat, and c grams of carbohydrate, then the situation can be represented by the equation $180 = 4p + 9f + 4c$. The equation can then be rewritten in terms of f by subtracting $4p$ and $4c$ from both sides of the equation and then dividing both sides of the equation by 9. The result is the equation $f = 20 - \frac{4}{9}(p + c)$.

Choices A, C, and D are incorrect and may be the result of not representing the situation with the correct equation or incorrectly rewriting the equation in terms of f.

QUESTION 27

Choice A is correct. Because the world's population has grown at an average rate of 1.9% per year since 1945, it follows that the world's population has been growing by a constant factor of 1.019 since 1945. If the world's population in 1975 was about 4 billion, in 1976 the world's population would have been about $4(1.019)$; in 1977 the world's population would have been about $4(1.019)(1.019)$, or $4(1.019)^2$; and so forth. Therefore, the world's population, $P(t)$, t years since 1975 could be represented by the function $P(t) = 4(1.019)^t$.

Choice B is incorrect because it represents a 90% increase in population each year. Choices C and D are incorrect because they are linear models, which represent situations that have a constant growth.

QUESTION 28

Choice C is correct. The line shown has a slope of $\frac{6-0}{3-0} = 2$ and a y-intercept of $(0, 0)$; therefore, the equation of the line is $y = 2x$. This means that for each point on the line, the value of the y-coordinate is twice the value of the x-coordinate. Therefore, for the point (s, t), the ratio of t to s is 2 to 1.

Choice A is incorrect and would be the ratio of t to s if the slope of the line were $\frac{1}{3}$. Choice B is incorrect and would be the ratio of t to s if the slope of the line were $\frac{1}{2}$. Choice D is incorrect and would be the ratio of t to s if the slope of the line were 3.

QUESTION 29

Choice D is correct. The circle with equation $(x + 3)^2 + (y - 1)^2 = 25$ has center $(-3, 1)$ and radius 5. For a point to be inside of the circle, the distance from that point to the center must be less than the radius, 5. The distance between $(3, 2)$ and $(-3, 1)$ is $\sqrt{(-3 - 3)^2 + (1 - 2)^2} = \sqrt{(-6)^2 + (-1)^2} = \sqrt{37}$, which is greater than 5. Therefore, $(3, 2)$ does NOT lie in the interior of the circle.

Choice A is incorrect. The distance between (–7, 3) and (–3, 1) is $\sqrt{(-7+3)^2+(3-1)^2} = \sqrt{(-4)^2+(2)^2} = \sqrt{20}$, which is less than 5, and therefore (–7, 3) lies in the interior of the circle. Choice B is incorrect because it is the center of the circle. Choice C is incorrect because the distance between (0, 0) and (–3, 1) is $\sqrt{(0+3)^2+(0-1)^2} = \sqrt{(3)^2+(1)^2} = \sqrt{8}$, which is less than 5, and therefore (0, 0) lies in the interior of the circle.

QUESTION 30

Choice B is correct. The percent increase from 2012 to 2013 was $\frac{5{,}880 - 5{,}600}{5{,}600} = 0.05$, or 5%. Since the percent increase from 2012 to 2013 was estimated to be double the percent increase from 2013 to 2014, the percent increase from 2013 to 2014 was expected to be 2.5%. Therefore, the number of subscriptions sold in 2014 is expected to be the number of subscriptions sold in 2013 multiplied by (1 + 0.025), or 5,880(1.025) = 6,027.

Choice A is incorrect and is the result of adding half of the value of the increase from 2012 to 2013 to the 2013 result. Choice C is incorrect and is the result adding twice the value of the increase from 2012 to 2013 to the 2013 result. Choice D is incorrect and is the result of interpreting the percent increase from 2013 to 2014 as double the percent increase from 2012 to 2013.

QUESTION 31

The correct answer is 195. Since the mass of gold was worth \$62,400 and each ounce of gold was worth \$20, the mass of the gold was $\frac{62{,}400}{20} = 3120$ ounces. Since 1 pound = 16 ounces, 3120 ounces is equivalent to $\frac{3120}{16} = 195$ pounds.

Alternative approach: Since each ounce of gold was worth \$20 and there are 16 ounces in a pound, each pound of gold was worth \$320. Thus, the mass of gold was $\frac{62{,}400}{320} = 195$ pounds.

QUESTION 32

The correct answer is $\frac{2}{5}$. The slope of the line can be found by selecting any two points (x_1, y_1) and (x_2, y_2) on the line and then dividing the difference of the y-coordinates $(y_2 - y_1)$ by the difference of the x-coordinates $(x_2 - x_1)$. Using the points $(-6, -\frac{27}{5})$ and $(9, \frac{3}{5})$, the slope is $\frac{\frac{3}{5} - \left(-\frac{27}{5}\right)}{9-(-6)} = \frac{\frac{30}{5}}{15}$. This can be rewritten as $\frac{6}{15}$, which reduces to $\frac{2}{5}$. Any of the following equivalent expressions can be gridded as the correct answer: 2/5, 6/15, .4, .40, .400, 4/10, 8/20.

QUESTION 33

The correct answer is 30. Let x represent the number of correct answers from the player and y represent the number of incorrect answers from the player. Since the player answered 40 questions in total, the equation $x + y = 40$ represents this situation. Also, since the score is found by subtracting the number of incorrect answers from twice the number of correct answers and the player received a score of 50, the equation $2x - y = 50$ represents this situation. Adding the equations in the system of two equations together yields $(x + y) + (2x - y) = 40 + 50$. This can be rewritten as $3x = 90$. Finally, solving for x by dividing both sides of the equation by 3 yields $x = 30$.

QUESTION 34

The correct answer is $\frac{5}{18}$. There are 360° in a circle, and it is shown that the central angle of the shaded region is 100°. Therefore, the area of the shaded region can be represented as a fraction of the area of the entire circle, $\frac{100}{360}$, which can be reduced to $\frac{5}{18}$. Either 5/18, .277, or .278 can be gridded as the correct answer.

QUESTION 35

The correct answer is 0 or 3. For an ordered pair to satisfy a system of equations, both the x- and y-values of the ordered pair must satisfy each equation in the system. Both expressions on the right-hand side of the given equations are equal to y, therefore it follows that both expressions on the right-hand side of the equations are equal to each other: $x^2 - 4x + 4 = 4 - x$. This equation can be rewritten as $x^2 - 3x = 0$, and then through factoring, the equation becomes $x(x - 3) = 0$. Because the product of the two factors is equal to 0, it can be concluded that either $x = 0$ or $x - 3 = 0$, or rather, $x = 0$ or $x = 3$. Either 0 or 3 can be gridded as the correct answer.

QUESTION 36

The correct answer is 6. Since $\tan B = \frac{3}{4}$, ΔABC and ΔDBE are both similar to 3-4-5 triangles. This means that they are both similar to the right triangle with sides of lengths 3, 4, and 5. Since $BC = 15$, which is 3 times as long as the hypotenuse of the 3-4-5 triangle, the similarity ratio of ΔABC to the 3-4-5 triangle is 3:1. Therefore, the length of $\overline{AC}$ (the side opposite to $\angle B$) is $3 \times 3 = 9$, and the length of $\overline{AB}$ (the side adjacent to $\angle B$) is $4 \times 3 = 12$. It is also given that $DA = 4$. Since $AB = DA + DB$ and $AB = 12$, it follows that $DB = 8$, which means that the similarity ratio of ΔDBE to the 3-4-5 triangle is 2:1 ($\overline{DB}$ is the side adjacent to $\angle B$). Therefore, the length of $\overline{DE}$, which is the side opposite to $\angle B$, is $3 \times 2 = 6$.

QUESTION 37

The correct answer is 2.4. The mean score of the 20 contestants on Day 1 is found by dividing the sum of the total scores of the contestants by the number of contestants. It is given that each contestant received 1 point for each correct answer. The table shows that on Day 1, 2 contestants each answered 5 questions correctly, so those 2 contestants scored 10 points in total ($2 \times 5 = 10$). Similarly, the table shows 3 contestants each answered 4 questions correctly, so those 3 contestants scored 12 points in total ($3 \times 4 = 12$). Continuing these calculations reveals that the 4 contestants who answered 3 questions correctly scored 12 points in total ($4 \times 3 = 12$); the 6 contestants who answered 2 questions correctly scored 12 points in total ($6 \times 2 = 12$); the 2 contestants who answered 1 question correctly scored 2 points in total ($2 \times 1 = 2$); and the 3 contestants who answered 0 questions correctly scored 0 points in total ($3 \times 0 = 0$). Adding up the total of points scored by these 20 contestants gives $10 + 12 + 12 + 12 + 2 + 0 = 48$. Therefore, the mean score of the contestants is $\frac{48}{20} = 2.4$. Either 12/5, 2.4, or 2.40 can be gridded as the correct answer.

QUESTION 38

The correct answer is $\frac{5}{7}$. It is given that no contestant received the same score on two different days, so each of the contestants who received a score of 5 is represented in the "5 out of 5" column of the table exactly once. Therefore, the probability of selecting a contestant who received a score of 5 on Day 2 or Day 3, given that the contestant received a score of 5 on one of the three days, is found by dividing the total number of contestants who received a score of 5 on Day 2 or Day 3 ($2 + 3 = 5$) by the total number of contestants who received a score of 5, which is given in the table as 7. So the probability is $\frac{5}{7}$. Either 5/7 or .714 can be gridded as the correct answer.

The SAT®

Practice Test #8

Make time to take the practice test.
It's one of the best ways to get ready for the SAT.

After you've taken the practice test, score it right away at **sat.org/scoring**.

Test begins on the next page.

Reading Test

65 MINUTES, 52 QUESTIONS

Turn to Section 1 of your answer sheet to answer the questions in this section.

DIRECTIONS

Each passage or pair of passages below is followed by a number of questions. After reading each passage or pair, choose the best answer to each question based on what is stated or implied in the passage or passages and in any accompanying graphics (such as a table or graph).

Questions 1-10 are based on the following passage.

This passage is from Carlos Ruiz Zafón, *The Angel's Game*. ©2008 by Dragonworks, S.L. Translation ©2009 by Lucia Graves. The narrator, a writer, recalls his childhood in early twentieth-century Barcelona.

Even then my only friends were made of paper and ink. At school I had learned to read and write long before the other children. Where my school friends saw notches of ink on incomprehensible pages, I saw light, streets, and people. Words and the mystery of their hidden science fascinated me, and I saw in them a key with which I could unlock a boundless world, a safe haven from that home, those streets, and those troubled days in which even I could sense that only a limited fortune awaited me. My father didn't like to see books in the house. There was something about them—apart from the letters he could not decipher—that offended him. He used to tell me that as soon as I was ten he would send me off to work and that I'd better get rid of all my scatterbrained ideas if I didn't want to end up a loser, a nobody. I used to hide my books under the mattress and wait for him to go out or fall asleep so that I could read. Once he caught me reading at night and flew into a rage. He tore the book from my hands and flung it out of the window.

"If I catch you wasting electricity again, reading all this nonsense, you'll be sorry."

My father was not a miser and, despite the hardships we suffered, whenever he could he gave me a few coins so that I could buy myself some treats like the other children. He was convinced that I spent them on licorice sticks, sunflower seeds, or sweets, but I would keep them in a coffee tin under the bed, and when I'd collected four or five reales I'd secretly rush out to buy myself a book.

My favorite place in the whole city was the Sempere & Sons bookshop on Calle Santa Ana. It smelled of old paper and dust and it was my sanctuary, my refuge. The bookseller would let me sit on a chair in a corner and read any book I liked to my heart's content. He hardly ever allowed me to pay for the books he placed in my hands, but when he wasn't looking I'd leave the coins I'd managed to collect on the counter before I left. It was only small change—if I'd had to buy a book with that pittance, I would probably have been able to afford only a booklet of cigarette papers. When it was time for me to leave, I would do so dragging my feet, a weight on my soul. If it had been up to me, I would have stayed there forever.

One Christmas Sempere gave me the best gift I have ever received. It was an old volume, read and experienced to the full.

"*Great Expectations*, by Charles Dickens," I read on the cover.

I was aware that Sempere knew a few authors who frequented his establishment and, judging by the care with which he handled the volume, I thought perhaps this Mr. Dickens was one of them.

"A friend of yours?"

"A lifelong friend. And from now on, he's your friend too."

CONTINUE

That afternoon I took my new friend home, hidden under my clothes so that my father wouldn't see it. It was a rainy winter, with days as gray as lead, and I read *Great Expectations* about nine times, partly because I had no other book at hand, partly because I did not think there could be a better one in the whole world and I was beginning to suspect that Mr. Dickens had written it just for me. Soon I was convinced that I didn't want to do anything else in life but learn to do what Mr. Dickens had done.

1

Over the course of the passage, the main focus shifts from a

A) general discussion of the narrator's love of reading to a portrayal of an influential incident.
B) depiction of the narrator's father to an examination of an author with whom the narrator becomes enchanted.
C) symbolic representation of a skill the narrator possesses to an example of its application.
D) tale about the hardships of the narrator's childhood to an analysis of the effects of those hardships.

2

The main purpose of lines 1-10 ("Even . . . awaited me") is to

A) introduce the characters who play a part in the narrator's story.
B) list the difficult conditions the narrator endured in childhood.
C) describe the passion that drives the actions the narrator recounts.
D) depict the narrator's aspirations before he met Sempere.

3

With which of the following statements about his father would the narrator most likely agree?

A) He lacked affection for the narrator.
B) He disliked any unnecessary use of money.
C) He would not have approved of Sempere's gift.
D) He objected to the writings of Charles Dickens.

4

Which choice provides the best evidence for the answer to the previous question?

A) Lines 24-27 ("My father . . . children")
B) Lines 35-37 ("The bookseller . . . content")
C) Lines 37-38 ("He hardly . . . hands")
D) Lines 59-61 ("That afternoon . . . see it")

5

It can reasonably be inferred from the passage that the main reason that the narrator considers *Great Expectations* to be the best gift he ever received is because

A) reading the book convinced him that he wanted to be a writer.
B) he'd only ever been given sweets and snacks as gifts in the past.
C) the gift meant that Sempere held him in high regard.
D) Sempere was a friend of the book's author.

6

Which choice provides the best evidence for the answer to the previous question?

A) Lines 38-40 ("when . . . left")
B) Lines 48-49 ("It was . . . full")
C) Lines 52-55 ("I was . . . them")
D) Lines 66-68 ("Soon . . . done")

CONTINUE

7

The narrator indicates that he pays Sempere

A) less than Sempere expects him to pay for the books.

B) nothing, because Sempere won't take his money.

C) the money he makes selling sweets to the other children.

D) much less for the books than they are worth.

8

As used in line 44, "weight" most nearly means

A) bulk.

B) burden.

C) force.

D) clout.

9

The word "friend" is used twice in lines 57-58 to

A) underline the importance of the narrator's connection to Sempere.

B) stress how friendships helped the narrator deal with his difficult home situation.

C) emphasize the emotional connection Sempere feels to reading.

D) imply that the narrator's sentiments caused him to make an irrational decision.

10

Which statement best characterizes the relationship between Sempere and Charles Dickens?

A) Sempere models his own writing after Dickens's style.

B) Sempere is an avid admirer of Dickens's work.

C) Sempere feels a personal connection to details of Dickens's biography.

D) Sempere considers himself to be Dickens's most appreciative reader.

Questions 11-21 are based on the following passage and supplementary material.

This passage is adapted from Jeffrey Mervis, "Why Null Results Rarely See the Light of Day." ©2014 by American Association for the Advancement of Science.

The question of what to do with null results—when researchers fail to see an effect that should be detectable—has long been hotly debated among those conducting medical trials, where the results can have a big impact on lives and corporate bottom lines. More recently, the debate has spread to the social and behavioral sciences, which also have the potential to sway public and social policy. There were little hard data, however, on how often or why null results were squelched. "Yes, it's true that null results are not as exciting," political scientist Gary King of Harvard University says. "But I suspect another reason they are rarely published is that there are many, many ways to produce null results by messing up. So they are much harder to interpret."

In a recent study, Stanford political economist Neil Malhotra and two of his graduate students examined every study since 2002 that was funded by a competitive grants program called TESS (Time-sharing Experiments for the Social Sciences). TESS allows scientists to order up Internet-based surveys of a representative sample of US adults to test a particular hypothesis (for example, whether voters tend to favor legislators who boast of bringing federal dollars to their districts over those who tout a focus on policy matters).

Malhotra's team tracked down working papers from most of the experiments that weren't published, and for the rest asked grantees what had happened to their results. In their e-mailed responses, some scientists cited deeper problems with a study or more pressing matters—but many also believed the journals just wouldn't be interested. "The unfortunate reality of the publishing world [is] that null effects do not tell a clear story," said one scientist. Said another, "Never published, definitely disappointed to not see any major effects."

Their answers suggest to Malhotra that rescuing findings from the file drawer will require a shift in expectations. "What needs to change is the culture—the author's belief about what will happen if the research is written up," he says.

Not unexpectedly, the statistical strength of the findings made a huge difference in whether they were ever published. Overall, 42% of the experiments

CONTINUE

produced statistically significant results. Of those, 62% were ultimately published, compared with 21% of the null results. However, the Stanford team was surprised that researchers didn't even write up 65% of the experiments that yielded a null finding.

Scientists not involved in the study praise its "clever" design. "It's a very important paper" that "starts to put numbers on things we want to understand," says economist Edward Miguel of the University of California, Berkeley.

He and others note that the bias against null studies can waste time and money when researchers devise new studies replicating strategies already found to be ineffective. Worse, if researchers publish significant results from similar experiments in the future, they could look stronger than they should because the earlier null studies are ignored. Even more troubling to Malhotra was the fact that two scientists whose initial studies "didn't work out" went on to publish results based on a smaller sample. "The non-TESS version of the same study, in which we used a student sample, did yield fruit," noted one investigator.

A registry for data generated by all experiments would address these problems, the authors argue. They say it should also include a "preanalysis" plan, that is, a detailed description of what the scientist hopes to achieve and how the data will be analyzed. Such plans would help deter researchers from tweaking their analyses after the data are collected in search of more publishable results.

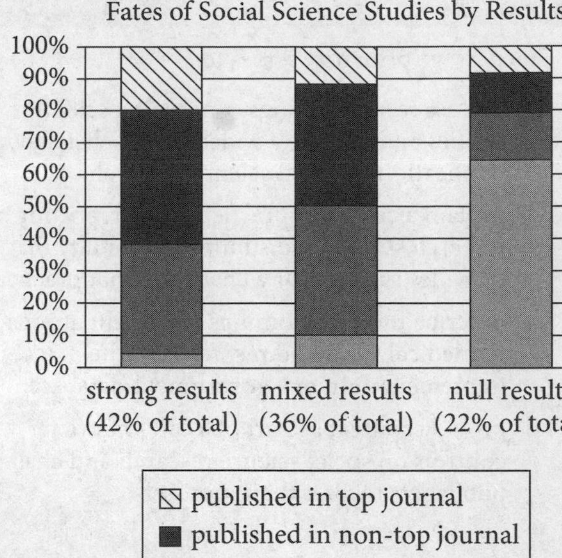

Adapted from Annie Franco, Neil Malhotra, and Gabor Simonovits, "Publication Bias in the Social Sciences: Unlocking the File Drawer." ©2014 by American Association for the Advancement of Science.

CONTINUE

11

The passage primarily serves to

A) discuss recent findings concerning scientific studies and dispute a widely held belief about the publication of social science research.

B) explain a common practice in the reporting of research studies and summarize a study that provides support for a change to that practice.

C) describe the shortcomings in current approaches to medical trials and recommend the implementation of a government database.

D) provide context as part of a call for stricter controls on social science research and challenge publishers to alter their mindsets.

12

As used in line 21, "allows" most nearly means

A) admits.

B) tolerates.

C) grants.

D) enables.

13

As used in line 43, "strength" most nearly means

A) attribution.

B) exertion.

C) toughness.

D) significance.

14

The passage indicates that a problem with failing to document null results is that

A) the results of related studies will be misleading.

B) researchers may overlook promising areas of study.

C) mistakes in the collection of null results may be overlooked.

D) the bias against null results will be disregarded.

15

Which choice provides the best evidence for the answer to the previous question?

A) Lines 38-40 ("Their . . . expectations")

B) Lines 48-50 ("However . . . finding")

C) Lines 56-59 ("He and . . . ineffective")

D) Lines 59-62 ("Worse . . . ignored")

16

Based on the passage, to which of the following hypothetical situations would Malhotra most strongly object?

A) A research team refuses to publish null results in anything less than a top journal.

B) A research team excludes the portion of data that produced null results when reporting its results in a journal.

C) A research team unknowingly repeats a study that produced null results for another research team.

D) A research team performs a follow-up study that expands the scope of an initial study that produced null results.

17

Which choice provides the best evidence for the answer to the previous question?

A) Lines 36-37 ("Said . . . effects")
B) Lines 45-48 ("Overall . . . null results")
C) Lines 62-68 ("Even . . . investigator")
D) Lines 69-73 ("A registry . . . analyzed")

18

The last paragraph serves mainly to

A) propose a future research project to deal with some of the shortcomings of current publishing practices noted in the passage.
B) introduce a possible solution to problems discussed in the passage regarding the reporting of social science studies.
C) summarize the findings of a study about experimental results explained in the passage.
D) reinforce the importance of reexamining the results of all social science trials.

19

According to the graph, social science studies yielding strong results were

A) unwritten over 50 percent of the time.
B) unpublished but written 50 percent of the time.
C) published in a top journal approximately 20 percent of the time.
D) published in a non-top journal almost 80 percent of the time.

20

Which of the following statements is supported by the graph?

A) Studies with mixed results were just as likely to be published as they were to be left either unpublished or unwritten.
B) Studies with mixed results occurred more frequently than did studies with strong and null results combined.
C) Studies with mixed results were more likely to be published in top journals than they were to be published in non-top journals.
D) Studies with mixed results were the most common type of social science studies.

21

Which statement from the passage is most directly reflected by the data presented in the graph?

A) Lines 30-33 ("In their . . . interested")
B) Lines 33-36 ("The unfortunate . . . scientist")
C) Lines 43-45 ("Not unexpectedly . . . published")
D) Lines 52-55 ("It's a . . . Berkeley")

CONTINUE

Questions 22-31 are based on the following passage and supplementary material.

This passage is adapted from Rachel Ehrenberg, "Salt Stretches in Nanoworld." ©2009 by Society for Science & the Public. The "nanoworld" is the world observed on a scale one billionth that of ordinary human experience.

Inflexible old salt becomes a softy in the nanoworld, stretching like taffy to more than twice its length, researchers report. The findings may lead to new approaches for making nanowires that could end up in solar cells or electronic circuits. The work also suggests that these ultra-tiny salt wires may already exist in sea spray and large underground salt deposits.

"We think nanowires are special and go to great lengths to make them," says study coauthor Nathan Moore of Sandia National Laboratories in Albuquerque. "Maybe they are more common than we think."

Metals such as gold or lead, in which bonding angles are loosey-goosey, can stretch out at temperatures well below their melting points. But scientists don't expect this superplasticity in a rigid, crystalline material like salt, Moore says.

This unusual behavior highlights that different forces rule the nanoworld, says theoretical physicist Krzysztof Kempa of Boston College. "Forget about gravity. It plays no role," he says. Surface tension and electrostatic forces are much more important at this scale.

Moore and his colleagues discovered salt's stretchiness accidently. They were investigating how water sticks to a surface such as salt and created a super-dry salt sample for testing. After cleaving a chunk of salt about the size of a sugar cube with a razor, the scientists guided a microscope that detects forces toward the surface. When the tip was far away there was no measured force, but within about seven nanometers a very strong attraction rapidly developed between the diamond tip of the microscope and the salt. The salt actually stretched out to glom on to the microscope tip. Using an electron microscope to see what was happening, the researchers observed the nanowires.

The initial attraction between the tip and salt might be due to electrostatic forces, perhaps good old van der Waals interactions,[1] the researchers speculate. Several mechanisms might lead to the elasticity, including the excessive surface tension found in the nanoworld (the same tension that allows a water strider to skim the surface of a pond).

The surface tension is so strong that as the microscope pulls away from the salt, the salt stretches, Kempa says. "The inside has no choice but to rearrange the atoms, rather than break," he says.

This bizarre behavior is actually mirrored in the macroworld, the researchers say. Huge underground deposits of salt can bend like plastic, but water is believed to play a role at these scales. Perhaps salty nanowires are present in these deposits as well.

"Sodium chloride[2] is everywhere—in the air, in our bodies," Moore says. "This may change our view of things, of what's happening at the nanoscale."

The work also suggests new techniques for making nanowires, which are often created through nano-imprinting techniques, Kempa says. "We invoke the intuition of the macroworld," he says. "Maybe instead of stamping [nanowires] we should be nano-pulling them."

[1] Attractive forces between nearby atoms

[2] Common salt

CONTINUE

Interaction of Microscope Tip with Salt Surface

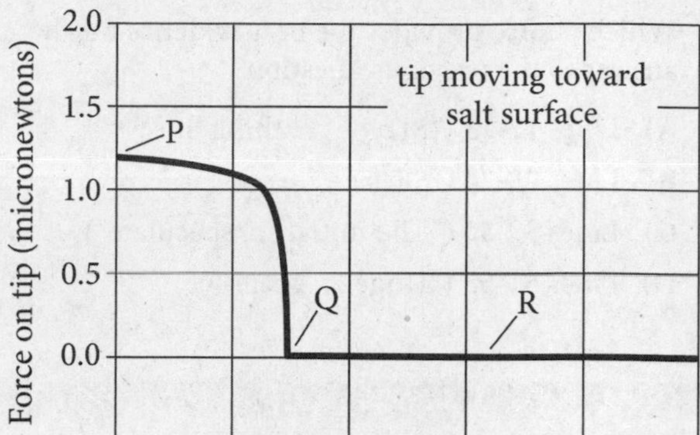

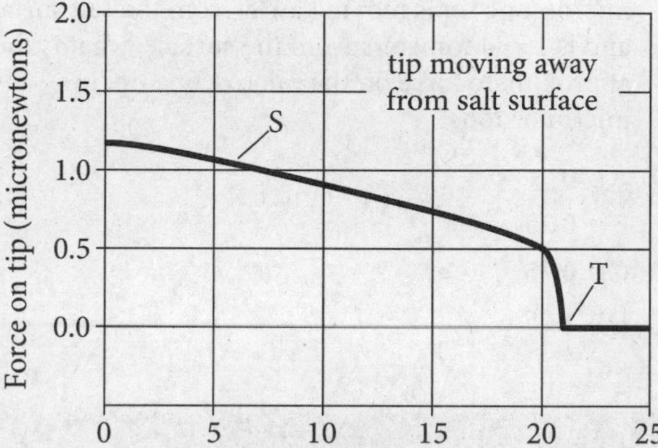

Adapted from Moore et al., "Superplastic Nanowires Pulled from the Surface of Common Salt." ©2009 by American Chemical Society.

22

One central idea of the passage is that

A) sometimes materials behave contrary to expectations.

B) systems can be described in terms of inputs and outputs.

C) models of materials have both strengths and weaknesses.

D) properties of systems differ from the properties of their parts.

23

Which choice best describes the overall structure of the passage?

A) A list of several ways in which salt's properties differ from researchers' expectations

B) A presentation of a hypothesis regarding salt behavior, description of an associated experiment, and explanation of why the results weaken the hypothesis

C) A description of two salt crystal experiments, the apparent disagreement in their results, and the resolution by more sensitive equipment

D) An introduction to an interesting salt property, description of its discovery, and speculation regarding its application

24

Which choice provides the best evidence for the claim that Moore's group was surprised to observe salt stretching?

A) Lines 17-18 ("But . . . says")

B) Lines 26-28 ("They were . . . testing")

C) Lines 36-38 ("Using . . . nanowires")

D) Lines 55-56 ("Sodium . . . says")

25

As used in line 20, "rule" most nearly means

A) mark.

B) control.

C) declare.

D) restrain.

CONTINUE

26

According to the passage, researchers have identified which mechanism as potentially responsible for the initial attraction between the microscope tip and the salt?

A) Gravity

B) Nano-imprinting

C) Surface tension

D) Van der Waals interactions

27

As used in line 42, “lead to” most nearly means

A) guide to.

B) result in.

C) point toward.

D) start with.

28

Based on the passage, which choice best describes the relationship between salt behavior in the nanoworld and in the macroworld?

A) In both the nanoworld and the macroworld, salt can be flexible.

B) Salt flexibility is expected in the nanoworld but is surprising in the macroworld.

C) Salt nanowires were initially observed in the nanoworld and later observed in the macroworld.

D) In the nanoworld, salt’s interactions with water lead to very different properties than they do in the macroworld.

29

Which choice provides the best evidence for the answer to the previous question?

A) Lines 12-13 (“Maybe . . . think”)

B) Lines 22-24 (“Surface . . . scale”)

C) Lines 39-42 (“The initial . . . speculate”)

D) Lines 51-53 (“Huge . . . scales”)

30

According to the information in the graph, when the microscope tip is moving away from the salt surface and is 15 nanometers from the surface, what is the approximate force on the microscope tip, in micronewtons?

A) 0

B) 0.25

C) 0.75

D) 1.25

31

Based on the passage and the graph, which label on the graph indicates the point at which a salt nanowire breaks?

A) P

B) Q

C) R

D) T

CONTINUE

Questions 32-41 are based on the following passages.

These passages are adapted from the Lincoln-Douglas debates. Passage 1 is from a statement by Stephen Douglas. Passage 2 is from a statement by Abraham Lincoln. Douglas and Lincoln engaged in a series of debates while competing for a US Senate seat in 1858.

Passage 1

Mr. Lincoln likens that bond of the Federal Constitution, joining Free and Slave States together, to a house divided against itself, and says that it is contrary to the law of God, and cannot stand. When did he learn, and by what authority does he proclaim, that this Government is contrary to the law of God and cannot stand? It has stood thus divided into Free and Slave States from its organization up to this day. During that period we have increased from four millions to thirty millions of people; we have extended our territory from the Mississippi to the Pacific Ocean; we have acquired the Floridas and Texas, and other territory sufficient to double our geographical extent; we have increased in population, in wealth, and in power beyond any example on earth; we have risen from a weak and feeble power to become the terror and admiration of the civilized world; and all this has been done under a Constitution which Mr. Lincoln, in substance, says is in violation of the law of God; and under a Union divided into Free and Slave States, which Mr. Lincoln thinks, because of such division, cannot stand. Surely, Mr. Lincoln is a wiser man than those who framed the Government. . . .

I now come back to the question, why cannot this Union exist forever, divided into Free and Slave States, as our fathers made it? It can thus exist if each State will carry out the principles upon which our institutions were founded; to wit, the right of each State to do as it pleases, without meddling with its neighbors. Just act upon that great principle, and this Union will not only live forever, but it will extend and expand until it covers the whole continent, and makes this confederacy one grand, ocean-bound Republic. We must bear in mind that we are yet a young nation, growing with a rapidity unequalled in the history of the world, that our national increase is great, and that the emigration from the old world is increasing, requiring us to expand and acquire new territory from time to time, in order to give our people land to live upon. If we live upon the principle of State rights and State sovereignty, each State regulating its own affairs and minding its own business, we can go on and extend indefinitely, just as fast and as far as we need the territory. . . .

Passage 2

In complaining of what I said in my speech at Springfield, in which he says I accepted my nomination for the Senatorship . . . he again quotes that portion in which I said that "a house divided against itself cannot stand." Let me say a word in regard to that matter. He tries to persuade us that there must be a variety in the different institutions of the States of the Union; that that variety necessarily proceeds from the variety of soil, climate, of the face of the country, and the difference in the natural features of the States. I agree to all that. Have these very matters ever produced any difficulty among us? Not at all. Have we ever had any quarrel over the fact that they have laws in Louisiana designed to regulate the commerce that springs from the production of sugar? Or because we have a different class relative to the production of flour in this State? Have they produced any differences? Not at all. They are the very cements of this Union. They don't make the house a "house divided against itself." They are the props that hold up the house and sustain the Union.

But has it been so with this element of slavery? Have we not always had quarrels and difficulties over it? And when will we cease to have quarrels over it? Like causes produce like effects. It is worth while to observe that we have generally had comparative peace upon the slavery question, and that there has been no cause for alarm until it was excited by the effort to spread it into new territory. Whenever it has been limited to its present bounds, and there has been no effort to spread it, there has been peace. All the trouble and convulsion has proceeded from efforts to spread it over more territory. It was thus at the date of the Missouri Compromise. It was so again with the annexation of Texas; so with the territory acquired by the Mexican War; and it is so now. Whenever there has been an effort to spread it there has been agitation and resistance. . . . Do you think that the nature of man will be changed, that the same causes that produced agitation at one time will not have the same effect at another?

CONTINUE

32

In the first paragraph of Passage 1, the main purpose of Douglas's discussion of the growth of the territory and population of the United States is to

A) provide context for Douglas's defense of continued expansion.
B) suggest that the division into free and slave states does not endanger the Union.
C) imply that Lincoln is unaware of basic facts concerning the country.
D) account for the image of the United States as powerful and admirable.

33

What does Passage 1 suggest about the US government's provisions for the institution of slavery, as framed in the Constitution?

A) They included no means for reconciling differences between free states and slave states.
B) They anticipated the Union's expansion into western territories.
C) They provided a good basic structure that does not need to be changed.
D) They were founded on an assumption that slavery was necessary for economic growth.

34

Which choice provides the best evidence for the answer to the previous question?

A) Lines 10-16 ("we have . . . earth")
B) Lines 25-27 ("I now . . . made it")
C) Lines 35-39 ("We must . . . increasing")
D) Lines 41-45 ("If we . . . territory")

35

As used in line 67, "element" most nearly means

A) ingredient.
B) environment.
C) factor.
D) quality.

36

Based on Passage 2, Lincoln would be most likely to agree with which claim about the controversy over slavery?

A) It can be ended only if Northern states act unilaterally to abolish slavery throughout the United States.
B) It would abate if attempts to introduce slavery to regions where it is not practiced were abandoned.
C) It has been exacerbated by the ambiguity of laws regulating the holding of slaves.
D) It is fueled in part by differences in religion and social values from state to state.

37

Which choice provides the best evidence for the answer to the previous question?

A) Lines 56-61 ("I agree . . . sugar")
B) Lines 64-66 ("They don't . . . Union")
C) Lines 74-76 ("Whenever . . . peace")
D) Lines 83-86 ("Do you . . . another")

CONTINUE

38

As used in line 84, "nature" most nearly means

A) force.

B) simplicity.

C) world.

D) character.

39

Which choice identifies a central tension between the two passages?

A) Douglas proposes changes to federal policies on slavery, but Lincoln argues that such changes would enjoy no popular support.

B) Douglas expresses concerns about the economic impact of abolition, but Lincoln dismisses those concerns as irrelevant.

C) Douglas criticizes Lincoln for finding fault with the Constitution, and Lincoln argues that this criticism misrepresents his position.

D) Douglas offers an interpretation of federal law that conflicts with Lincoln's, and Lincoln implies that Douglas's interpretation is poorly reasoned.

40

Both passages discuss the issue of slavery in relationship to

A) the expansion of the Union.

B) questions of morality.

C) religious toleration.

D) laws regulating commerce.

41

In the context of each passage as a whole, the questions in lines 25-27 of Passage 1 and lines 67-69 of Passage 2 primarily function to help each speaker

A) cast doubt on the other's sincerity.

B) criticize the other's methods.

C) reproach the other's actions.

D) undermine the other's argument.

CONTINUE

Questions 42-52 are based on the following passage.

This passage is adapted from Daniel Chamovitz, *What a Plant Knows: A Field Guide to the Senses*. ©2012 by Daniel Chamovitz.

The Venus flytrap [*Dionaea muscipula*] needs to know when an ideal meal is crawling across its leaves. Closing its trap requires a huge expense of energy, and reopening the trap can take several hours, so *Dionaea* only wants to spring closed when it's sure that the dawdling insect visiting its surface is large enough to be worth its time. The large black hairs on their lobes allow the Venus flytraps to literally feel their prey, and they act as triggers that spring the trap closed when the proper prey makes its way across the trap. If the insect touches just one hair, the trap will not spring shut; but a large enough bug will likely touch two hairs within about twenty seconds, and that signal springs the Venus flytrap into action.

We can look at this system as analogous to short-term memory. First, the flytrap encodes the information (forms the memory) that something (it doesn't know what) has touched one of its hairs. Then it stores this information for a number of seconds (retains the memory) and finally retrieves this information (recalls the memory) once a second hair is touched. If a small ant takes a while to get from one hair to the next, the trap will have forgotten the first touch by the time the ant brushes up against the next hair. In other words, it loses the storage of the information, doesn't close, and the ant happily meanders on. How does the plant encode and store the information from the unassuming bug's encounter with the first hair? How does it remember the first touch in order to react upon the second?

Scientists have been puzzled by these questions ever since John Burdon-Sanderson's early report on the physiology of the Venus flytrap in 1882. A century later, Dieter Hodick and Andreas Sievers at the University of Bonn in Germany proposed that the flytrap stored information regarding how many hairs have been touched in the electric charge of its leaf. Their model is quite elegant in its simplicity. In their studies, they discovered that touching a trigger hair on the Venus flytrap causes an electric action potential [a temporary reversal in the electrical polarity of a cell membrane] that induces calcium channels to open in the trap (this coupling of action potentials and the opening of calcium channels is similar to the processes that occur during communication between human neurons), thus causing a rapid increase in the concentration of calcium ions.

They proposed that the trap requires a relatively high concentration of calcium in order to close and that a single action potential from just one trigger hair being touched does not reach this level. Therefore, a second hair needs to be stimulated to push the calcium concentration over this threshold and spring the trap. The encoding of the information requires maintaining a high enough level of calcium so that a second increase (triggered by touching the second hair) pushes the total concentration of calcium over the threshold. As the calcium ion concentrations dissipate over time, if the second touch and potential don't happen quickly, the final concentration after the second trigger won't be high enough to close the trap, and the memory is lost.

Subsequent research supports this model. Alexander Volkov and his colleagues at Oakwood University in Alabama first demonstrated that it is indeed electricity that causes the Venus flytrap to close. To test the model they rigged up very fine electrodes and applied an electrical current to the open lobes of the trap. This made the trap close without any direct touch to its trigger hairs (while they didn't measure calcium levels, the current likely led to increases). When they modified this experiment by altering the amount of electrical current, Volkov could determine the exact electrical charge needed for the trap to close. As long as fourteen microcoulombs—a tiny bit more than the static electricity generated by rubbing two balloons together—flowed between the two electrodes, the trap closed. This could come as one large burst or as a series of smaller charges within twenty seconds. If it took longer than twenty seconds to accumulate the total charge, the trap would remain open.

CONTINUE

42

The primary purpose of the passage is to

A) discuss findings that offer a scientific explanation for the Venus flytrap's closing action.

B) present research that suggests that the Venus flytrap's predatory behavior is both complex and unique among plants.

C) identify the process by which the Venus flytrap's closing action has evolved.

D) provide a brief overview of the Venus flytrap and its predatory behavior.

43

Based on the passage, a significant advantage of the Venus flytrap's requirement for multiple triggers is that it

A) enables the plant to identify the species of its prey.

B) conserves the plant's calcium reserves.

C) safeguards the plant's energy supply.

D) prevents the plant from closing before capturing its prey.

44

Which choice provides the best evidence for the answer to the previous question?

A) Lines 3-7 ("Closing . . . time")

B) Lines 7-11 ("The large . . . across the trap")

C) Lines 11-14 ("If the . . . action")

D) Lines 16-18 ("First . . . hairs")

45

The use of the phrases "dawdling insect" (line 6), "happily meanders" (line 27), and "unassuming bug's encounter" (lines 28-29) in the first two paragraphs establishes a tone that is

A) academic.

B) melodramatic.

C) informal.

D) mocking.

CONTINUE

46

In the second paragraph (lines 15-31), the discussion of short-term memory primarily functions to

A) clarify an explanation of what prompts the Venus flytrap to close.
B) advance a controversial hypothesis about the function of electric charges found in the leaf of the Venus flytrap.
C) stress the distinction between the strategies of the Venus flytrap and the strategies of human beings.
D) emphasize the Venus flytrap's capacity for retaining detailed information about its prey.

47

According to the passage, which statement best explains why the Venus flytrap requires a second trigger hair to be touched within a short amount of time in order for its trap to close?

A) The second trigger produces an electrical charge that reverses the charge produced by the first trigger.
B) The second trigger stabilizes the surge of calcium ions created by the first trigger.
C) The second trigger prompts the calcium channels to open.
D) The second trigger provides a necessary supplement to the calcium concentration released by the first trigger.

48

Which choice describes a scenario in which Hodick and Sievers's model predicts that a Venus flytrap will NOT close around an insect?

A) A large insect's second contact with the plant's trigger hairs results in a total calcium ion concentration above the trap's threshold.
B) A large insect makes contact with a second trigger hair after a period of inactivity during which calcium ion concentrations have diminished appreciably.
C) A large insect's contact with the plant's trigger hairs causes calcium channels to open in the trap.
D) A large insect's contact with a second trigger hair occurs within ten seconds of its contact with the first trigger hair.

49

As used in line 67, "demonstrated" most nearly means

A) protested.
B) established.
C) performed.
D) argued.

CONTINUE

50

Based on the passage, what potential criticism might be made of Volkov's testing of Hodick and Sievers's model?

A) Volkov's understanding of Hodick and Sievers's model was incorrect.

B) Volkov's measurements did not corroborate a central element of Hodick and Sievers's model.

C) Volkov's direct application of an electrical current would have been objectionable to Hodick and Sievers.

D) Volkov's technology was not available to Hodick and Sievers.

51

Which choice provides the best evidence for the answer to the previous question?

A) Lines 66-69 ("Alexander . . . close")

B) Lines 69-71 ("To test . . . trap")

C) Lines 71-74 ("This . . . increases")

D) Lines 74-77 ("When . . . close")

52

Based on the passage, in studying the Venus flytrap, Volkov and his colleagues made the most extensive use of which type of evidence?

A) Mathematical models to predict the electrical charge required to close the Venus flytrap

B) Analysis of data collected from previous researchers' work involving the Venus flytrap's response to electricity

C) Information obtained from monitoring the Venus flytrap's response to varying amounts of electrical current

D) Published theories of scientists who developed earlier models of the Venus flytrap

STOP

If you finish before time is called, you may check your work on this section only.
Do not turn to any other section.

Writing and Language Test

35 MINUTES, 44 QUESTIONS

Turn to Section 2 of your answer sheet to answer the questions in this section.

DIRECTIONS

Each passage below is accompanied by a number of questions. For some questions, you will consider how the passage might be revised to improve the expression of ideas. For other questions, you will consider how the passage might be edited to correct errors in sentence structure, usage, or punctuation. A passage or a question may be accompanied by one or more graphics (such as a table or graph) that you will consider as you make revising and editing decisions.

Some questions will direct you to an underlined portion of a passage. Other questions will direct you to a location in a passage or ask you to think about the passage as a whole.

After reading each passage, choose the answer to each question that most effectively improves the quality of writing in the passage or that makes the passage conform to the conventions of standard written English. Many questions include a "NO CHANGE" option. Choose that option if you think the best choice is to leave the relevant portion of the passage as it is.

Questions 1-11 are based on the following passage and supplementary material.

Compost: Don't Waste This Waste

Over the past generation, people in many parts of the United States have become accustomed to dividing their household waste products into different categories for recycling. [1] Regardless, paper may go in one container, glass and aluminum in another, regular garbage in a third. Recently, some US cities have added a new category: compost, organic matter such as food scraps and yard debris. Like paper or glass recycling, composting demands a certain amount of effort from the

1

A) NO CHANGE
B) However,
C) Furthermore,
D) For example,

CONTINUE

public in order to be successful. But the inconveniences of composting are far outweighed by its benefits.

Most people think of banana peels, eggshells, and dead leaves as "waste," but compost is actually a valuable resource with multiple practical uses. When utilized as a garden fertilizer, compost provides nutrients to soil and improves plant growth while deterring or killing pests and preventing some plant diseases. It also enhances soil texture, encouraging healthy roots and minimizing or **2** <u>annihilating</u> the need for chemical fertilizers. Better than soil at holding moisture, compost minimizes water waste and storm runoff, **3** <u>it increases savings</u> on watering costs, and helps reduce erosion on embankments near bodies of water. In large **4** <u>quantities, which</u> one would expect to see when it is collected for an entire municipality), compost can be converted into a natural gas that can be used as fuel for transportation or heating and cooling systems.

2

Which choice best maintains the style and tone of the passage?

A) NO CHANGE
B) eliminating
C) ousting
D) closing the door on

3

A) NO CHANGE
B) savings increase
C) increases savings
D) also it increases savings

4

A) NO CHANGE
B) quantities (which
C) quantities which
D) quantities; (which

CONTINUE

In spite of all compost's potential uses, however, most of this so-called waste is wasted. According to the Environmental Protection Agency (EPA), over **5** 13 million tons of metal ended up in US landfills in 2009, along with over 13 million tons of yard debris. Remarkably, **6** less glass was discarded in landfills in that year than any other substance, including plastics or paper. Even **7** worse, then the squandering of this useful resource is the fact that compost in landfills cannot break down due to the lack of necessary air and moisture.

5

The writer wants to include information from the graph that is consistent with the description of compost in the passage. Which choice most effectively accomplishes this goal?

A) NO CHANGE
B) 6 million tons of rubber and leather
C) 10 million tons of textiles
D) 33 million tons of food waste

6

The writer wants to support the paragraph's main idea with accurate, relevant information from the graph. Which choice most effectively accomplishes this goal?

A) NO CHANGE
B) more metal
C) more food waste
D) more yard waste

7

A) NO CHANGE
B) worse than
C) worse then
D) worse, than

CONTINUE

As a result, organic material that is sent to landfills **8** <u>contribute</u> to the release of methane, a very **9** <u>potent</u> greenhouse gas.

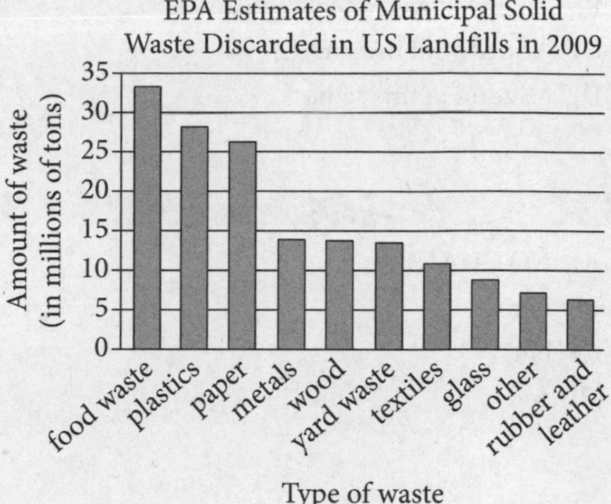

Adapted from Food Waste Disposal. ©n.d. by Food Waste Disposal, LLC.

8

A) NO CHANGE
B) are contributing
C) contributes
D) have contributed

9

A) NO CHANGE
B) sturdy
C) influential
D) commanding

CONTINUE

10 <u>While composting can sometimes lead to accidental pollution through the release of methane gas,</u> cities such as San Francisco and Seattle have instituted mandatory composting laws requiring individuals and businesses to use separate bins for compostable waste. This strict approach may not work everywhere. However, given the clear benefits of composting and the environmental costs of not composting, all municipalities should encourage their residents either to create their own compost piles for use in backyard gardens **11** <u>or</u> to dispose of compostable materials in bins for collection.

10

Which choice provides the most effective transition from the previous paragraph?

A) NO CHANGE
B) Though government regulations vary,
C) Armed with these facts,
D) Mindful of this setback,

11

A) NO CHANGE
B) nor
C) but
D) and

CONTINUE

Questions 12-22 are based on the following passage.

A Lion's Share of Luck

It's the beginning of February, and as they do every year, thousands of people line H Street, the heart of Chinatown in Washington, DC. The crowd has gathered to celebrate Lunar New Year. The street is a sea of **12** red. Red is the traditional Chinese color of luck and happiness. Buildings are **13** draped with festive, red, banners, and garlands. Lampposts are strung with crimson paper lanterns, which bob in the crisp winter breeze. The eager spectators await the highlight of the New Year parade: the lion dance.

Experts agree that the lion dance originated in the Han dynasty (206 BCE–220 CE); however, there is little agreement about the dance's original purpose. Some evidence suggests that the earliest version of the dance was an attempt to ward off an evil spirit; **14** lions are obviously very fierce. Another theory is that an emperor, upon waking from a dream about a lion, hired an artist to

12

Which choice most effectively combines the sentences at the underlined portion?

A) red,

B) red; in addition, red is

C) red; in other words, red is

D) red, the color; that is

13

A) NO CHANGE

B) draped, with festive red banners,

C) draped with festive red banners—

D) draped with festive red banners

14

Which choice most effectively completes the explanation of a possible origin of the lion dance?

A) NO CHANGE

B) the evil spirit was called Nian.

C) villagers dressed in lion costumes to scare the spirit away

D) the precise location of the village remains lost to history.

choreograph the dance. **15** <u>The current function of the dance is celebration.</u>

The lion dance requires the strength, grace, and coordination of two dancers, **16** <u>both of whom</u> are almost completely hidden by the elaborate bamboo and papier-mâché lion costume that they maneuver. One person operates the lion's head as the other guides the torso and tail. Many of the moves in the dance, such as jumps, rolls, and kicks, are similar to **17** <u>martial arts and acrobatics.</u> The dancers must be synchronized with the music accompanying the dance—drums, cymbals, and gongs that supply the lion's roar—as well as with each other.

15

Which choice most effectively concludes the paragraph?

A) NO CHANGE

B) It turns out that the origins of the lion dance are irrelevant.

C) Whatever its origins, today the lion dance is a joyous spectacle, a celebration of the promise of the New Year.

D) Things are different these days, of course.

16

A) NO CHANGE

B) of which both

C) both of them

D) both

17

A) NO CHANGE

B) the disciplines of martial arts and acrobatics.

C) martial artists and acrobats.

D) those in martial arts and acrobatics.

CONTINUE

[1] While there are many regional variations of the lion dance costume, all make extensive use of symbols and colors. [2] The lion's head is often adorned with a phoenix **18** (a mythical bird) or a tortoise (for longevity). [3] Green lions encourage friendliness. [4] Golden and red lions represent liveliness and bravery, respectively. [5] Their older counterparts, yellow and white lions, dance more slowly and deliberately. [6] In some variations, lions of different colors are different ages, and they move accordingly. [7] Black lions are the youngest; therefore, they dance quickly and playfully. [8] The appearance of the lions varies, but their message is consistent: Happy New Year. **19**

18

Which choice provides information that is most consistent in style and content with the information about the symbolism of the tortoise?

A) NO CHANGE
B) (for new beginnings)
C) (from Chinese mythology)
D) (for symbolic reasons)

19

To make this paragraph most logical, sentence 5 should be placed

A) where it is now.
B) after sentence 1.
C) after sentence 3.
D) after sentence 7.

CONTINUE

As the parade winds its way through Chinatown, the music crescendos, and the lion dance reaches **20** it's climax with the "plucking of the greens." Approaching a doorway in which dangles a red envelope filled with green paper money, the **21** lion's teeth snare the envelope. It then chews up the bills and spits out the **22** money-filled envelope instead of chewing it up. The crowd cheers for the lion dancers and for the prosperity and good fortune their dance foretells.

20

A) NO CHANGE
B) its
C) there
D) their

21

A) NO CHANGE
B) lion snares the envelope with its teeth.
C) envelope is snared by the lion with its teeth.
D) teeth of the lion snare the envelope.

22

A) NO CHANGE
B) envelope that had been dangling from the doorway.
C) envelope that had the money in it.
D) envelope.

Questions 23-33 are based on the following passage.

Court Reporting: Humans v. Machines

Court reporters for years have been the record keepers of the court, taking **23** scrupulous notes during **24** hearings; depositions, and other legal proceedings. Despite the increasing use of digital recording technologies, court reporters still play a vital role in

23

Which choice best fits with the tone of the rest of the passage?

A) NO CHANGE
B) super-rigorous
C) spot-on
D) intense

24

A) NO CHANGE
B) hearings; depositions;
C) hearings, depositions,
D) hearings, depositions;

CONTINUE

courtrooms. 25 Although machines can easily make digital audio recordings of court events, they lack the nuance of human court reporters in providing a precise record.

[1] Court reporters record the spoken word in real time, most commonly using the technique of stenography. [2] A stenotype machine allows a person to type about 200 words per minute (the speed of speech is about 180 words per minute). [3] The typed words are instantaneously translated onto a computer screen for the judge to view, and the transcript is used later by people who want to review the case, such as journalists and lawyers. [4] Digital audio recording is becoming increasingly popular in courtrooms across the United States, with six states using solely audio recordings for

25

At this point, the writer is considering adding the following graph.

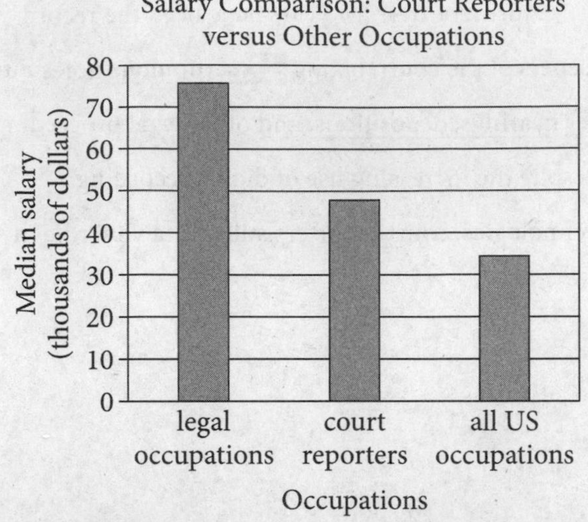

Adapted from Bureau of Labor Statistics, US Department of Labor, *Occupational Outlook Handbook, 2014–15 Edition.*

Should the writer make this addition here?

A) Yes, because it supports the claim that court reporting is an important part of a trial.

B) Yes, because it offers a relevant counterpoint to the argument that the use of digital recorders is on the rise.

C) No, because it presents information that is not directly related to the paragraph's discussion of the role of court reporters.

D) No, because it does not provide information about the pay scale for more experienced court reporters.

CONTINUE

general jurisdiction sessions. [5] Proponents of going digital say that technology is the easiest way to get the most accurate record of the proceedings, as the machine records everything faithfully as it occurs and is not **26** subject to human errors such as mishearing or mistyping. [6] However, with the rise of high-quality recording technology, reliance on court reporters **27** as a record keeper is decreasing. **28**

26

A) NO CHANGE
B) subjected to
C) subjected from
D) subject for

27

A) NO CHANGE
B) each as record keepers
C) as record keepers
D) to be a record keeper

28

To make this paragraph most logical, sentence 6 should be placed

A) where it is now.
B) after sentence 1.
C) after sentence 3.
D) after sentence 4.

Champions of court reporting, though, argue the **29** opposite. They argue that with the increased reliance on technology, errors actually increase. Because digital systems record **30** indiscriminately; they cannot discern important parts of the proceedings from other noises in the courtroom. **31** Despite this, a digital device does indeed record everything, but that includes loud noises, such as a book dropping, that can make the actual words spoken impossible to hear. A court reporter, however,

29

Which choice most effectively combines the sentences at the underlined portion?

A) opposite, such
B) opposite—
C) opposite, which is
D) opposite; their opinion is

30

A) NO CHANGE
B) indiscriminately, they
C) indiscriminately. They
D) indiscriminately, therefore they

31

A) NO CHANGE
B) In other words,
C) Therefore,
D) Consequently,

CONTINUE

can distinguish between the words **32** <u>and distinguish between the</u> extrinsic noises that need not be recorded. Also, if a witness mumbles, a human court reporter can pause court proceedings to ask the witness to repeat what he or she said. In some cases, digital recording **33** <u>makes it necessary for the judge to make additional announcements at the beginning of a trial.</u> Increasing use of technology is "a transition from accurate records to adequate records," says Bob Tate, president of the Certified Court Reporters Association of New Jersey.

Despite the apparent benefits of using digital recording systems in courtrooms, there is still a need for the human touch in legal proceedings. At least for the foreseeable future, machines simply cannot replicate the invaluable clarification skills and adaptability of human court reporters.

32

A) NO CHANGE
B) also between the
C) and when there are
D) and the

33

Which choice provides the best supporting example for the main idea of the paragraph?

A) NO CHANGE
B) requires a courtroom monitor to ensure the equipment is functioning properly.
C) leads to changes in the roles and duties of several members of the courtroom staff.
D) has led to the need for retrial because of indistinct testimony from key witnesses.

Questions 34-44 are based on the following passage.

Fire in Space

On Earth, fire provides light, heat, and comfort. Its creation, by a process called combustion, requires a chemical reaction between a fuel source and oxygen. The shape that fire assumes on Earth is a result of gravitational influence and the movement of molecules. In the microgravity environment of space, **34** moreover, combustion and the resulting fire behave in fundamentally different ways than they do on Earth—differences that have important implications for researchers.

A group of engineering students from the University of California at San Diego (UCSD), for example, **35** tried to find a method to make their biofuel combustion study (fuels derived from once-living material) free of the drawbacks researchers face on Earth. The standard method involves burning droplets of fuel, but Earth's gravitational influence causes the droplets to lose

34

A) NO CHANGE
B) however,
C) accordingly,
D) subsequently,

35

A) NO CHANGE
B) strove for a method to make their study of biofuel combustion
C) looked for a method to study biofuel combustion
D) sought a method to study combustion of biofuels

CONTINUE

spherical symmetry while burning. This **36** deformation results in subtle variations in density that both **37** causes uneven heat flow and limits the size of the droplets that can be tested. Specially designed "drop towers" **38** built for this purpose reduce these problems, but they provide no more than 10 seconds of microgravity, and droplet size is still too small to produce accurate models of combustion rates. **39** The UCSD students understood that these limitations had to be surmounted. As part of the program, researchers fly their experiments aboard aircraft that simulate the microgravity environment of space. The aircraft accomplish this feat by flying in parabolic paths instead of horizontal ones. On the plane's ascent, passengers feel twice Earth's gravitational pull, but for brief periods at the peak of the trajectory,

36

Which choice provides the most precise description of the phenomenon depicted in the previous sentence?

A) NO CHANGE
B) alteration
C) transformation
D) modification

37

A) NO CHANGE
B) cause uneven heat flow and limit
C) cause uneven heat flow and limits
D) has caused uneven heat flow and has limited

38

A) NO CHANGE
B) intended for this use
C) constructed for this function
D) DELETE the underlined portion.

39

Which choice provides the most effective transition between ideas in the paragraph?

A) NO CHANGE
B) The UCSD group sought to overcome these difficulties by participating in NASA's Microgravity University program.
C) The engineering group realized that aircraft might be the tools they were looking for.
D) Thus, for the UCSD group, drop towers were not an adequate solution.

40 "weightlessness" or microgravity similar to what is experienced in space, is achieved.

These flights allowed the UCSD students to experience microgravity **41**. Specifically, they **42** investigated the combustion of biofuel droplets in microgravity for twice as long as could be accomplished

40

A) NO CHANGE
B) "weightlessness" or microgravity, similar to what is experienced, in space
C) "weightlessness" or, microgravity, similar to what is experienced in space
D) "weightlessness," or microgravity similar to what is experienced in space,

41

At this point, the writer is considering adding the following.

> and perform their experiment without traveling into space

Should the writer make this addition here?

A) Yes, because it elaborates on the advantage the students gained from the flights.
B) Yes, because it reveals that the students did not actually go into space, a point that the previous paragraph does not address.
C) No, because it shifts focus away from the students' experiences while on the flights.
D) No, because it restates what has already been said in the sentence.

42

A) NO CHANGE
B) could investigate
C) were investigating
D) were able to investigate

CONTINUE

in drop towers and to perform tests with larger droplets. The larger, **43** spherically symmetric droplets burned longer and gave the students more reliable data on combustion rates of biofuels because the droplets' uniform shape reduced the variations in density that hinder tests performed in normal gravity. The students hope the new data will aid future research by improving theoretical models of biofuel combustion. Better combustion-rate models may even lead to the production of more fuel-efficient engines and improved **44** techniques, for fighting fires in space or at future outposts on the Moon and Mars.

43

Which choice most effectively establishes that the UCSD students' approach had solved a problem, mentioned earlier in the passage, relating to burning fuel on Earth?

A) NO CHANGE
B) combustible
C) microgravity-influenced
D) biofuel-derived

44

A) NO CHANGE
B) techniques for fighting fires, in space or at future outposts
C) techniques for fighting fires in space or at future outposts
D) techniques for fighting fires in space, or at future outposts,

STOP

If you finish before time is called, you may check your work on this section only.
Do not turn to any other section.

Math Test – No Calculator

25 MINUTES, 20 QUESTIONS

Turn to Section 3 of your answer sheet to answer the questions in this section.

DIRECTIONS

For questions 1-15, solve each problem, choose the best answer from the choices provided, and fill in the corresponding circle on your answer sheet. **For questions 16-20**, solve the problem and enter your answer in the grid on the answer sheet. Please refer to the directions before question 16 on how to enter your answers in the grid. You may use any available space in your test booklet for scratch work.

NOTES

1. The use of a calculator **is not permitted**.
2. All variables and expressions used represent real numbers unless otherwise indicated.
3. Figures provided in this test are drawn to scale unless otherwise indicated.
4. All figures lie in a plane unless otherwise indicated.
5. Unless otherwise indicated, the domain of a given function *f* is the set of all real numbers *x* for which *f*(*x*) is a real number.

REFERENCE

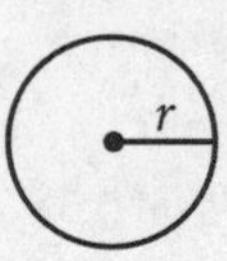

$A = \pi r^2$
$C = 2\pi r$

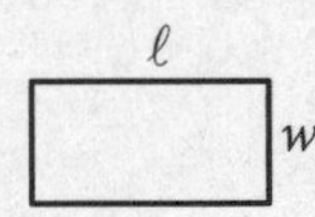

$A = \ell w$

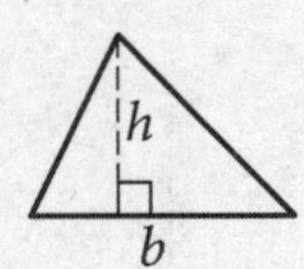

$A = \frac{1}{2}bh$

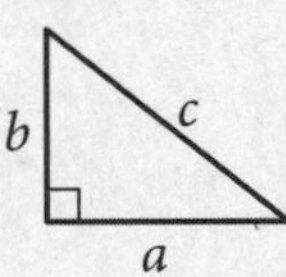

$c^2 = a^2 + b^2$

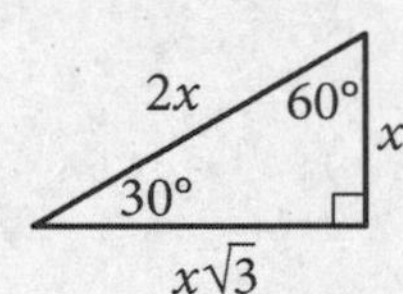

Special Right Triangles

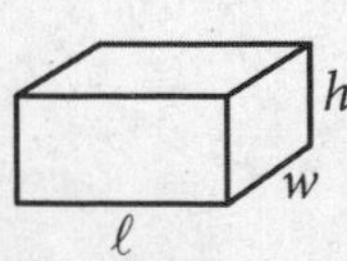

$V = \ell wh$

$V = \pi r^2 h$

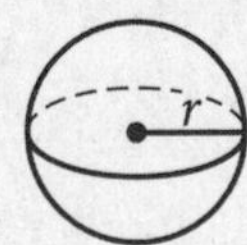

$V = \frac{4}{3}\pi r^3$

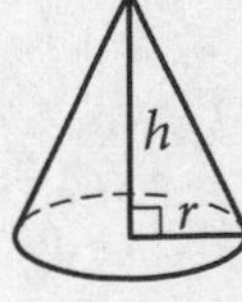

$V = \frac{1}{3}\pi r^2 h$

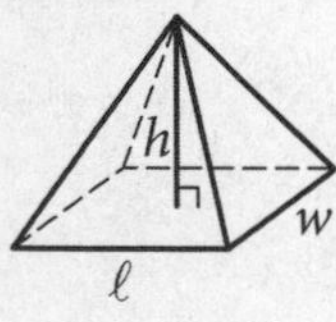

$V = \frac{1}{3}\ell wh$

The number of degrees of arc in a circle is 360.
The number of radians of arc in a circle is 2π.
The sum of the measures in degrees of the angles of a triangle is 180.

CONTINUE

1

$$3x + x + x + x - 3 - 2 = 7 + x + x$$

In the equation above, what is the value of x ?

A) $-\frac{5}{7}$

B) 1

C) $\frac{12}{7}$

D) 3

2

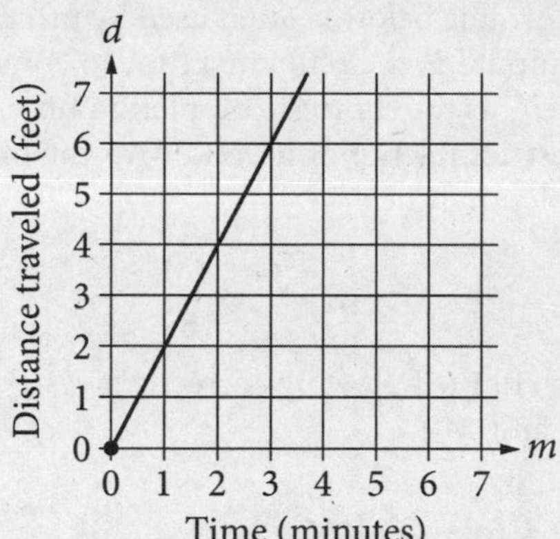

The graph above shows the distance traveled d, in feet, by a product on a conveyor belt m minutes after the product is placed on the belt. Which of the following equations correctly relates d and m ?

A) $d = 2m$

B) $d = \frac{1}{2}m$

C) $d = m + 2$

D) $d = 2m + 2$

CONTINUE

3

The formula below is often used by project managers to compute E, the estimated time to complete a job, where O is the shortest completion time, P is the longest completion time, and M is the most likely completion time.

$$E = \frac{O + 4M + P}{6}$$

Which of the following correctly gives P in terms of E, O, and M ?

A) $P = 6E - O - 4M$

B) $P = -6E + O + 4M$

C) $P = \frac{O + 4M + E}{6}$

D) $P = \frac{O + 4M - E}{6}$

4

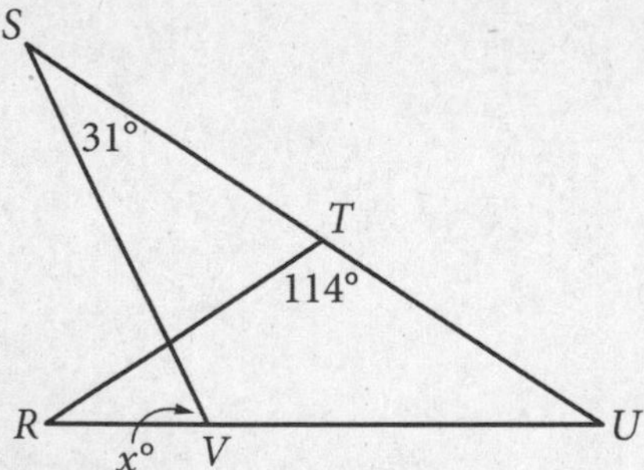

In the figure above, $RT = TU$. What is the value of x ?

A) 72

B) 66

C) 64

D) 58

5

The width of a rectangular dance floor is w feet. The length of the floor is 6 feet longer than its width. Which of the following expresses the perimeter, in feet, of the dance floor in terms of w ?

A) $2w + 6$

B) $4w + 12$

C) $w^2 + 6$

D) $w^2 + 6w$

6

$$y > 2x - 1$$
$$2x > 5$$

Which of the following consists of the y-coordinates of all the points that satisfy the system of inequalities above?

A) $y > 6$

B) $y > 4$

C) $y > \frac{5}{2}$

D) $y > \frac{3}{2}$

CONTINUE

7

$$\sqrt{2x+6}+4=x+3$$

What is the solution set of the equation above?

A) $\{-1\}$

B) $\{5\}$

C) $\{-1, 5\}$

D) $\{0, -1, 5\}$

8

$$f(x) = x^3 - 9x$$
$$g(x) = x^2 - 2x - 3$$

Which of the following expressions is equivalent to

$\dfrac{f(x)}{g(x)}$, for $x > 3$?

A) $\dfrac{1}{x+1}$

B) $\dfrac{x+3}{x+1}$

C) $\dfrac{x(x-3)}{x+1}$

D) $\dfrac{x(x+3)}{x+1}$

9

$$(x-6)^2 + (y+5)^2 = 16$$

In the xy-plane, the graph of the equation above is a circle. Point P is on the circle and has coordinates $(10, -5)$. If $\overline{PQ}$ is a diameter of the circle, what are the coordinates of point Q ?

A) $(2, -5)$

B) $(6, -1)$

C) $(6, -5)$

D) $(6, -9)$

10

A group of 202 people went on an overnight camping trip, taking 60 tents with them. Some of the tents held 2 people each, and the rest held 4 people each. Assuming all the tents were filled to capacity and every person got to sleep in a tent, exactly how many of the tents were 2-person tents?

A) 30

B) 20

C) 19

D) 18

CONTINUE

11

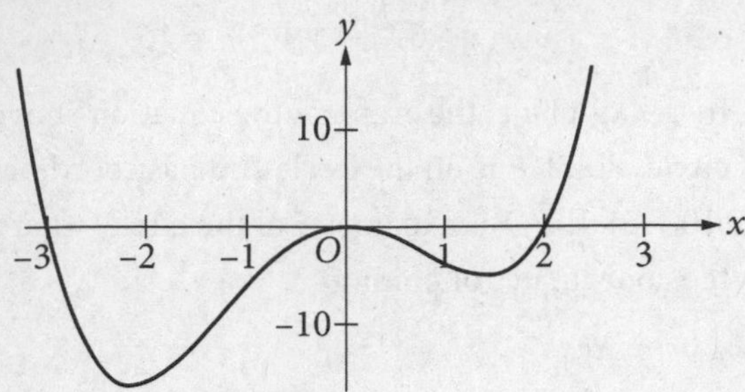

Which of the following could be the equation of the graph above?

A) $y = x(x - 2)(x + 3)$

B) $y = x^2(x - 2)(x + 3)$

C) $y = x(x + 2)(x - 3)$

D) $y = x^2(x + 2)(x - 3)$

12

If $\dfrac{2a}{b} = \dfrac{1}{2}$, what is the value of $\dfrac{b}{a}$?

A) $\dfrac{1}{8}$

B) $\dfrac{1}{4}$

C) 2

D) 4

13

Oil and gas production in a certain area dropped from 4 million barrels in 2000 to 1.9 million barrels in 2013. Assuming that the oil and gas production decreased at a constant rate, which of the following linear functions f best models the production, in millions of barrels, t years after the year 2000?

A) $f(t) = \dfrac{21}{130}t + 4$

B) $f(t) = \dfrac{19}{130}t + 4$

C) $f(t) = -\dfrac{21}{130}t + 4$

D) $f(t) = -\dfrac{19}{130}t + 4$

CONTINUE

14

$$y = x^2 + 3x - 7$$
$$y - 5x + 8 = 0$$

How many solutions are there to the system of equations above?

A) There are exactly 4 solutions.

B) There are exactly 2 solutions.

C) There is exactly 1 solution.

D) There are no solutions.

15

$$g(x) = 2x - 1$$
$$h(x) = 1 - g(x)$$

The functions g and h are defined above. What is the value of $h(0)$?

A) -2

B) 0

C) 1

D) 2

DIRECTIONS

For questions 16-20, solve the problem and enter your answer in the grid, as described below, on the answer sheet.

1. Although not required, it is suggested that you write your answer in the boxes at the top of the columns to help you fill in the circles accurately. You will receive credit only if the circles are filled in correctly.
2. Mark no more than one circle in any column.
3. No question has a negative answer.
4. Some problems may have more than one correct answer. In such cases, grid only one answer.
5. **Mixed numbers** such as $3\frac{1}{2}$ must be gridded as 3.5 or 7/2. (If 3 1 / 2 is entered into the grid, it will be interpreted as $\frac{31}{2}$, not $3\frac{1}{2}$.)
6. **Decimal answers:** If you obtain a decimal answer with more digits than the grid can accommodate, it may be either rounded or truncated, but it must fill the entire grid.

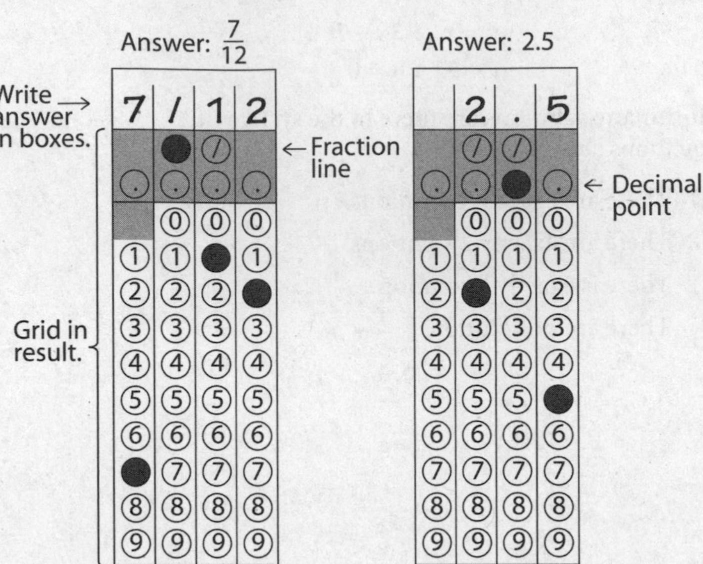

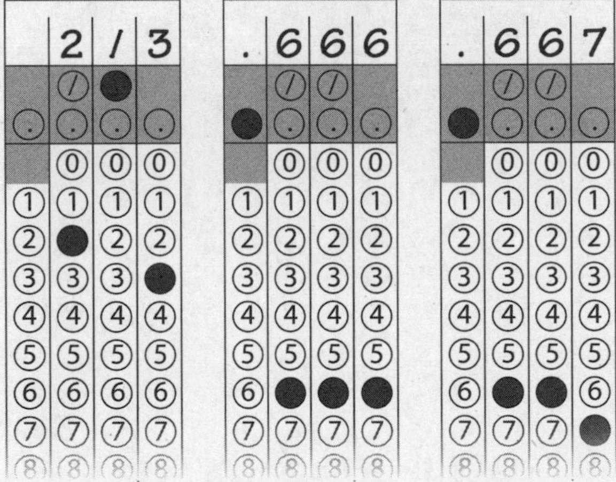

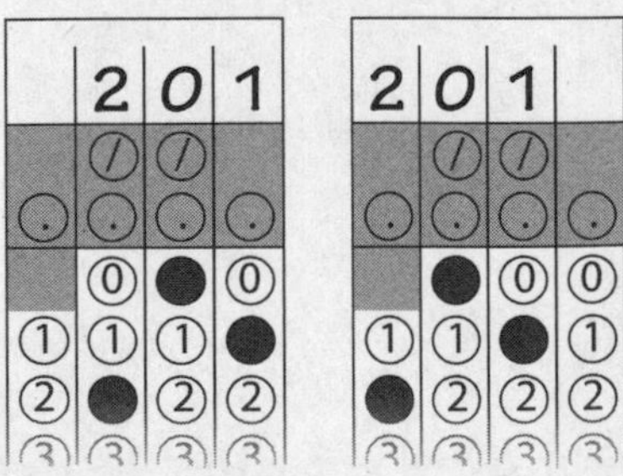

NOTE: You may start your answers in any column, space permitting. Columns you don't need to use should be left blank.

CONTINUE

16

$$x^2 + x - 12 = 0$$

If a is a solution of the equation above and $a > 0$, what is the value of a ?

17

The sum of $-2x^2 + x + 31$ and $3x^2 + 7x - 8$ can be written in the form $ax^2 + bx + c$, where a, b, and c are constants. What is the value of $a + b + c$?

18

$$-x + y = -3.5$$
$$x + 3y = 9.5$$

If (x, y) satisfies the system of equations above, what is the value of y ?

19

A start-up company opened with 8 employees. The company's growth plan assumes that 2 new employees will be hired each quarter (every 3 months) for the first 5 years. If an equation is written in the form $y = ax + b$ to represent the number of employees, y, employed by the company x quarters after the company opened, what is the value of b ?

20

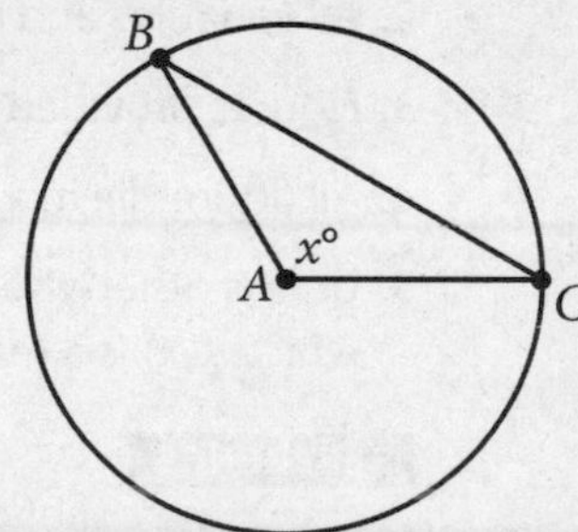

Note: Figure not drawn to scale.

In the circle above, point A is the center and the length of arc $\overset{\frown}{BC}$ is $\frac{2}{5}$ of the circumference of the circle. What is the value of x ?

STOP

If you finish before time is called, you may check your work on this section only. Do not turn to any other section.

Math Test – Calculator

55 MINUTES, 38 QUESTIONS

Turn to Section 4 of your answer sheet to answer the questions in this section.

DIRECTIONS

For questions 1-30, solve each problem, choose the best answer from the choices provided, and fill in the corresponding circle on your answer sheet. **For questions 31-38**, solve the problem and enter your answer in the grid on the answer sheet. Please refer to the directions before question 31 on how to enter your answers in the grid. You may use any available space in your test booklet for scratch work.

NOTES

1. The use of a calculator **is permitted**.
2. All variables and expressions used represent real numbers unless otherwise indicated.
3. Figures provided in this test are drawn to scale unless otherwise indicated.
4. All figures lie in a plane unless otherwise indicated.
5. Unless otherwise indicated, the domain of a given function *f* is the set of all real numbers *x* for which *f*(*x*) is a real number.

REFERENCE

$A = \pi r^2$
$C = 2\pi r$

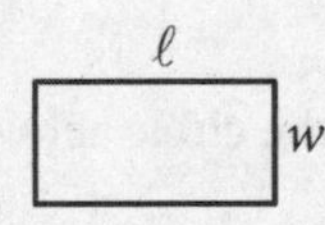

$A = \ell w$

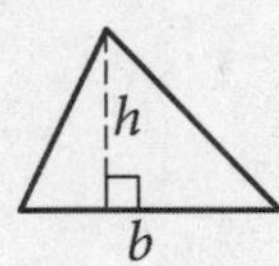

$A = \frac{1}{2}bh$

$c^2 = a^2 + b^2$

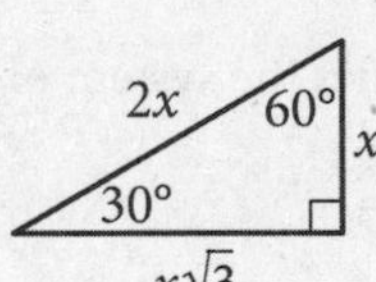

Special Right Triangles

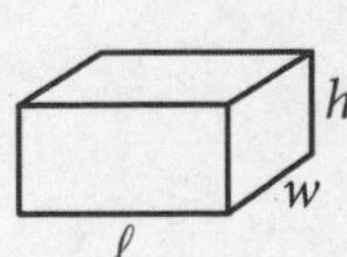

$V = \ell wh$

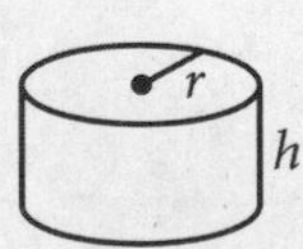

$V = \pi r^2 h$

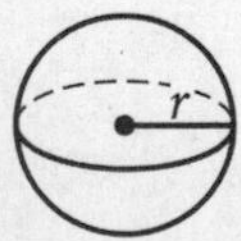

$V = \frac{4}{3}\pi r^3$

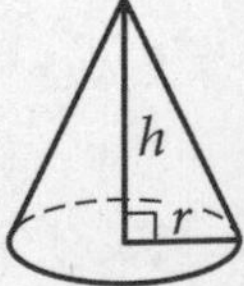

$V = \frac{1}{3}\pi r^2 h$

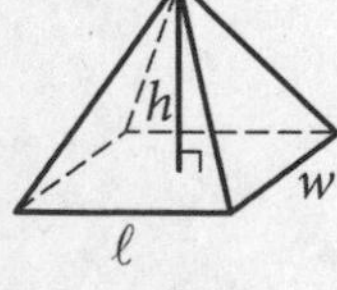

$V = \frac{1}{3}\ell wh$

The number of degrees of arc in a circle is 360.
The number of radians of arc in a circle is 2π.
The sum of the measures in degrees of the angles of a triangle is 180.

CONTINUE

1

One pound of grapes costs \$2. At this rate, how many dollars will c pounds of grapes cost?

A) $2c$

B) $2 + c$

C) $\frac{2}{c}$

D) $\frac{c}{2}$

2

Tracy collects, sells, and trades figurines, and she tracks the number of figurines in her collection on the graph below.

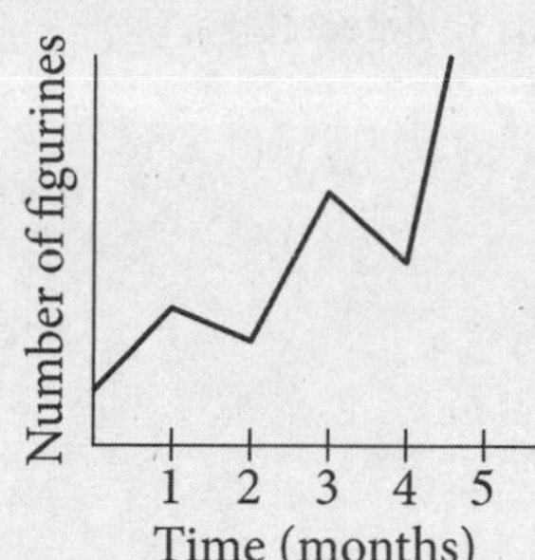

On what interval did the number of figurines decrease the fastest?

A) Between 1 and 2 months

B) Between 2 and 3 months

C) Between 3 and 4 months

D) Between 4 and 5 months

3

In a random sample of 200 cars of a particular model, 3 have a manufacturing defect. At this rate, how many of 10,000 cars of the same model will have a manufacturing defect?

A) 150

B) 200

C) 250

D) 300

4

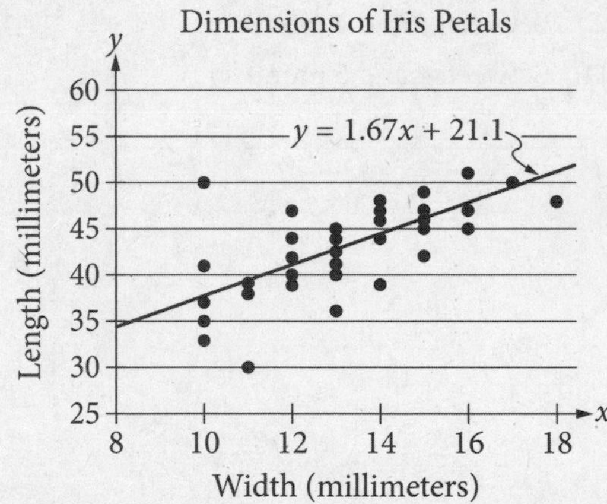

The scatterplot above shows data collected on the lengths and widths of *Iris setosa* petals. A line of best fit for the data is also shown. Based on the line of best fit, if the width of an *Iris setosa* petal is 19 millimeters, what is the predicted length, in millimeters, of the petal?

A) 21.10

B) 31.73

C) 52.83

D) 55.27

5

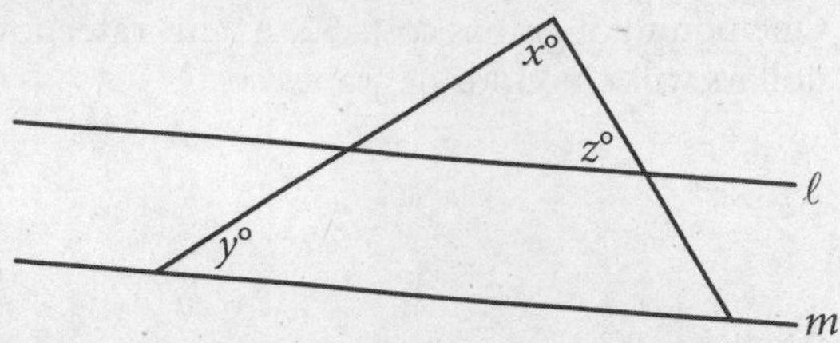

Note: Figure not drawn to scale.

In the figure above, lines ℓ and m are parallel, $y = 20$, and $z = 60$. What is the value of x ?

A) 120

B) 100

C) 90

D) 80

6

Two types of tickets were sold for a concert held at an amphitheater. Tickets to sit on a bench during the concert cost \$75 each, and tickets to sit on the lawn during the concert cost \$40 each. Organizers of the concert announced that 350 tickets had been sold and that \$19,250 had been raised through ticket sales alone. Which of the following systems of equations could be used to find the number of tickets for bench seats, B, and the number of tickets for lawn seats, L, that were sold for the concert?

A) $(75B)(40L) = 1{,}950$
$B + L = 350$

B) $40B + 75L = 19{,}250$
$B + L = 350$

C) $75B + 40L = 350$
$B + L = 19{,}250$

D) $75B + 40L = 19{,}250$
$B + L = 350$

7

In the xy-plane, the graph of which of the following equations is a line with a slope of 3 ?

A) $y = \frac{1}{3}x$

B) $y = x - 3$

C) $y = 3x + 2$

D) $y = 6x + 3$

8

$$x + 1 = \frac{2}{x + 1}$$

In the equation above, which of the following is a possible value of $x + 1$?

A) $1 - \sqrt{2}$

B) $\sqrt{2}$

C) 2

D) 4

Questions 9-11 refer to the following information.

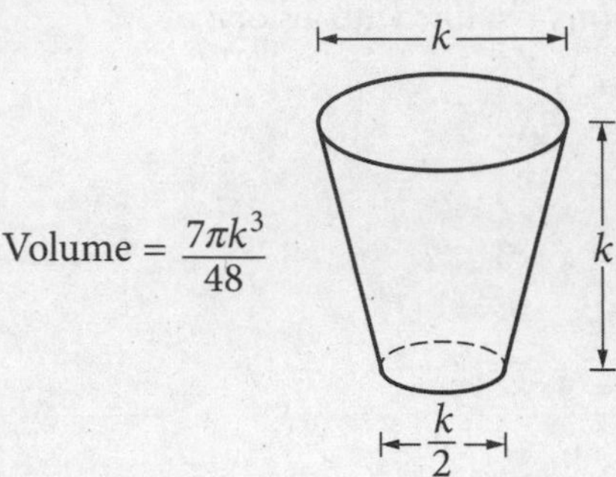

The glass pictured above can hold a maximum volume of 473 cubic centimeters, which is approximately 16 fluid ounces.

9

What is the value of k, in centimeters?

A) 2.52
B) 7.67
C) 7.79
D) 10.11

10

Water pours into the glass slowly and at a constant rate. Which of the following graphs best illustrates the height of the water level in the glass as it fills?

A)

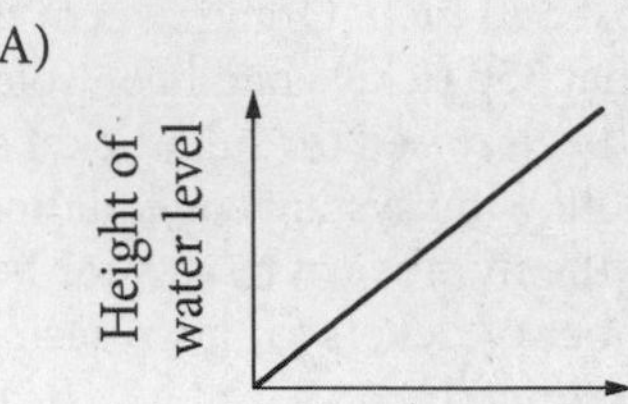

B)

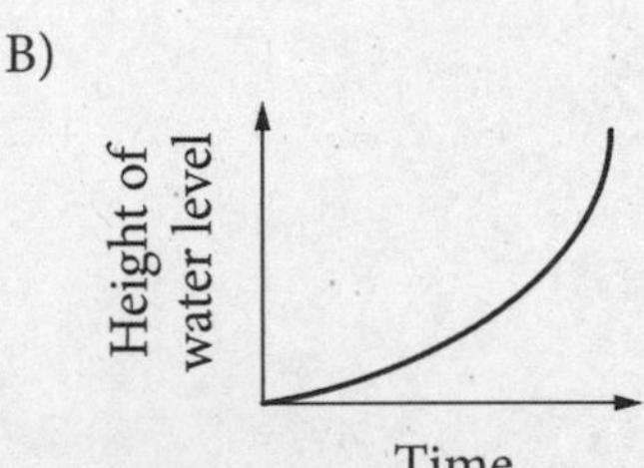

C)

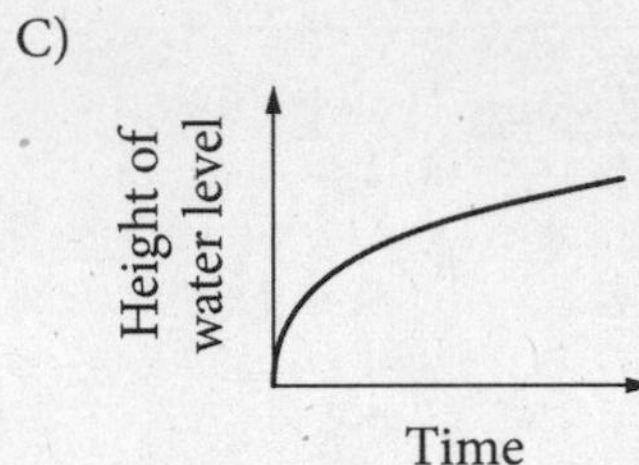

D)

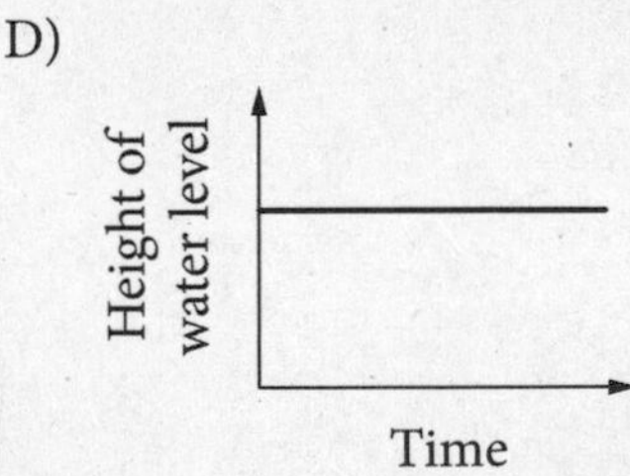

CONTINUE

11

Jenny has a pitcher that contains 1 gallon of water. How many times could Jenny completely fill the glass with 1 gallon of water? (1 gallon = 128 fluid ounces)

A) 16
B) 8
C) 4
D) 3

12

Roberto is an insurance agent who sells two types of policies: a \$50,000 policy and a \$100,000 policy. Last month, his goal was to sell at least 57 insurance policies. While he did not meet his goal, the total value of the policies he sold was over \$3,000,000. Which of the following systems of inequalities describes x, the possible number of \$50,000 policies, and y, the possible number of \$100,000 policies, that Roberto sold last month?

A) $x + y < 57$
$50{,}000x + 100{,}000y < 3{,}000{,}000$

B) $x + y > 57$
$50{,}000x + 100{,}000y > 3{,}000{,}000$

C) $x + y < 57$
$50{,}000x + 100{,}000y > 3{,}000{,}000$

D) $x + y > 57$
$50{,}000x + 100{,}000y < 3{,}000{,}000$

13

If $a^{-\frac{1}{2}} = x$, where $a > 0$, what is a in terms of x ?

A) $\sqrt{x}$

B) $-\sqrt{x}$

C) $\frac{1}{x^2}$

D) $-\frac{1}{x^2}$

14

Which of the following is a value of x for which the expression $\frac{-3}{x^2 + 3x - 10}$ is undefined?

A) -3
B) -2
C) 0
D) 2

CONTINUE

15

A granite block in the shape of a right rectangular prism has dimensions 30 centimeters by 40 centimeters by 50 centimeters. The block has a density of 2.8 grams per cubic centimeter. What is the mass of the block, in grams? (Density is mass per unit volume.)

A) 336

B) 3,360

C) 16,800

D) 168,000

16

Number of Adults Contracting Colds

	Cold	No cold	Total
Vitamin C	21	129	150
Sugar pill	33	117	150
Total	54	246	300

The table shows the results of a research study that investigated the therapeutic value of vitamin C in preventing colds. A random sample of 300 adults received either a vitamin C pill or a sugar pill each day during a 2-week period, and the adults reported whether they contracted a cold during that time period. What proportion of adults who received a sugar pill reported contracting a cold?

A) $\frac{11}{18}$

B) $\frac{11}{50}$

C) $\frac{9}{50}$

D) $\frac{11}{100}$

17

Ages of 20 Students Enrolled in a College Class

Age	Frequency
18	6
19	5
20	4
21	2
22	1
23	1
30	1

The table above shows the distribution of ages of the 20 students enrolled in a college class. Which of the following gives the correct order of the mean, median, and mode of the ages?

A) mode < median < mean

B) mode < mean < median

C) median < mode < mean

D) mean < mode < median

CONTINUE

18

The figure below shows the relationship between the percent of leaf litter mass remaining after decomposing for 3 years and the mean annual temperature, in degrees Celsius (°C), in 18 forests in Canada. A line of best fit is also shown.

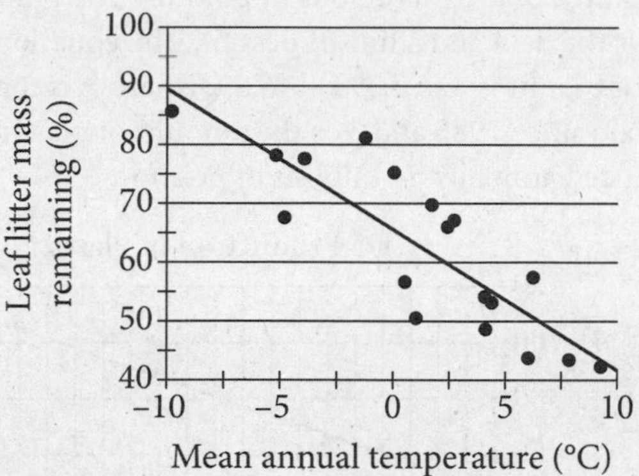

A particular forest in Canada, whose data is not included in the figure, had a mean annual temperature of −2°C. Based on the line of best fit, which of the following is closest to the predicted percent of leaf litter mass remaining in this particular forest after decomposing for 3 years?

A) 50%

B) 63%

C) 70%

D) 82%

19

The range of the polynomial function f is the set of real numbers less than or equal to 4. If the zeros of f are -3 and 1, which of the following could be the graph of $y = f(x)$ in the xy-plane?

A)

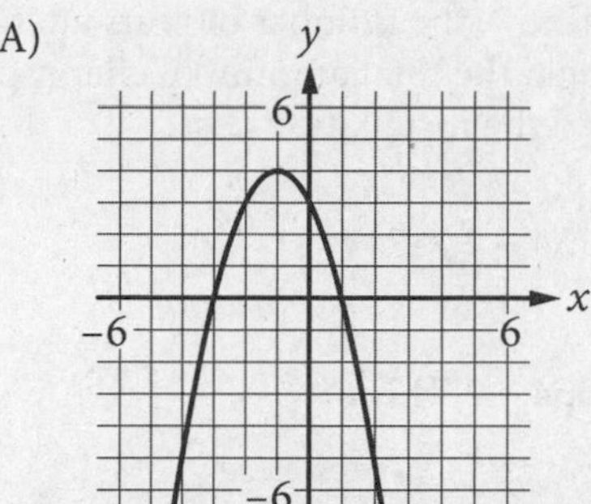

B)

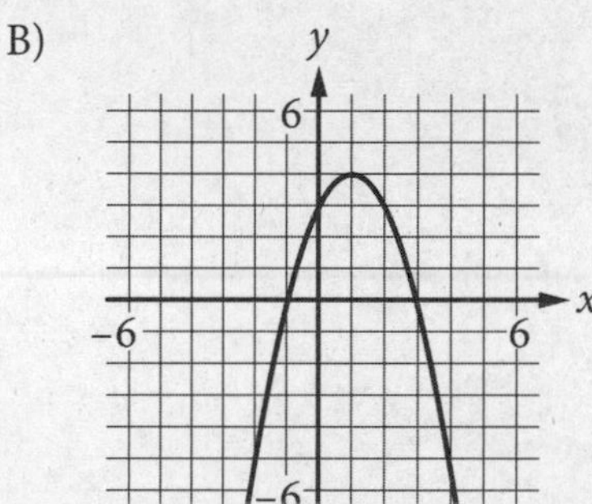

C)

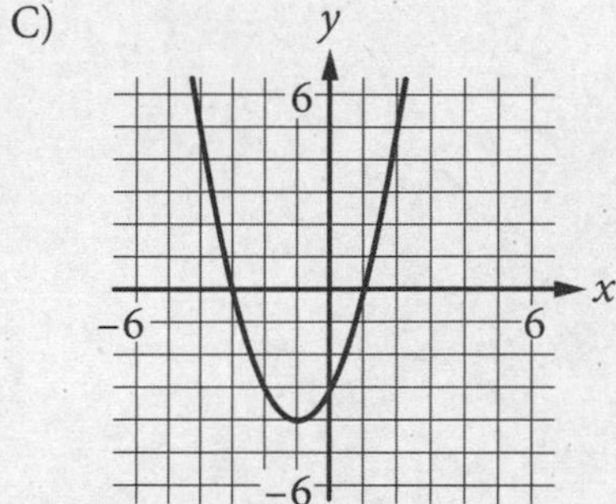

D)

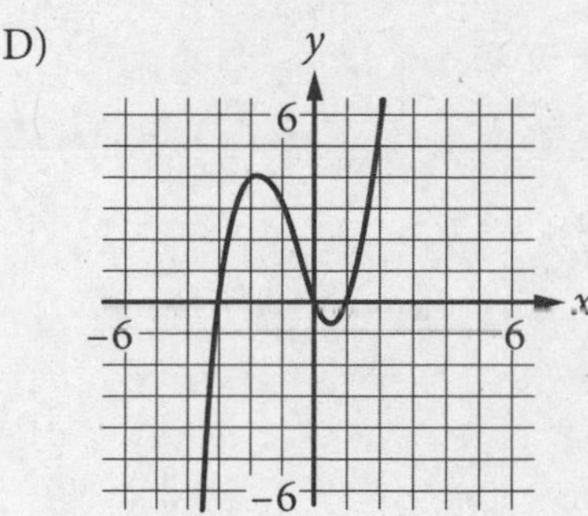

CONTINUE

20

The average annual energy cost for a certain home is \$4,334. The homeowner plans to spend \$25,000 to install a geothermal heating system. The homeowner estimates that the average annual energy cost will then be \$2,712. Which of the following inequalities can be solved to find t, the number of years after installation at which the total amount of energy cost savings will exceed the installation cost?

A) $25{,}000 > (4{,}334 - 2{,}712)\,t$

B) $25{,}000 < (4{,}334 - 2{,}712)\,t$

C) $25{,}000 - 4{,}334 > 2{,}712t$

D) $25{,}000 > \dfrac{4{,}332}{2{,}712}\,t$

Questions 21 and 22 refer to the following information.

Between 1985 and 2003, data were collected every three years on the amount of plastic produced annually in the United States, in billions of pounds. The graph below shows the data and a line of best fit. The equation of the line of best fit is $y = 3.39x + 46.89$, where x is the number of years since 1985 and y is the amount of plastic produced annually, in billions of pounds.

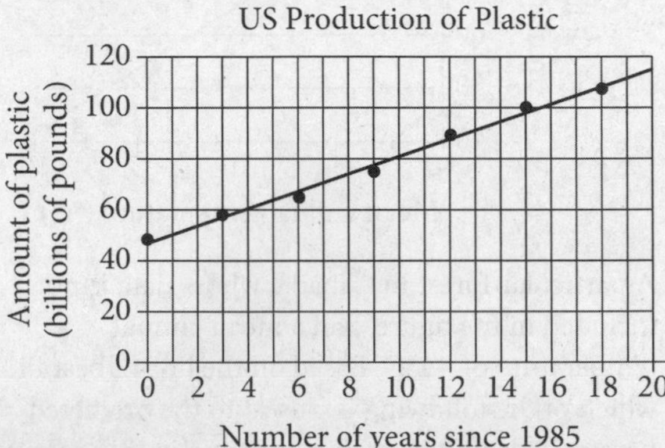

21

Which of the following is the best interpretation of the number 3.39 in the context of the problem?

A) The amount of plastic, in billions of pounds, produced in the United States during the year 1985

B) The number of years it took the United States to produce 1 billion pounds of plastic

C) The average annual plastic production, in billions of pounds, in the United States from 1985 to 2003

D) The average annual increase, in billions of pounds, of plastic produced per year in the United States from 1985 to 2003

CONTINUE

22

Which of the following is closest to the percent increase in the billions of pounds of plastic produced in the United States from 2000 to 2003?

A) 10%

B) 44%

C) 77%

D) 110%

23

$$M = 1{,}800(1.02)^t$$

The equation above models the number of members, M, of a gym t years after the gym opens. Of the following, which equation models the number of members of the gym q quarter years after the gym opens?

A) $M = 1{,}800(1.02)^{\frac{q}{4}}$

B) $M = 1{,}800(1.02)^{4q}$

C) $M = 1{,}800(1.005)^{4q}$

D) $M = 1{,}800(1.082)^{q}$

24

For the finale of a TV show, viewers could use either social media or a text message to vote for their favorite of two contestants. The contestant receiving more than 50% of the vote won. An estimated 10% of the viewers voted, and 30% of the votes were cast on social media. Contestant 2 earned 70% of the votes cast using social media and 40% of the votes cast using a text message. Based on this information, which of the following is an accurate conclusion?

A) If all viewers had voted, Contestant 2 would have won.

B) Viewers voting by social media were likely to be younger than viewers voting by text message.

C) If all viewers who voted had voted by social media instead of by text message, Contestant 2 would have won.

D) Viewers voting by social media were more likely to prefer Contestant 2 than were viewers voting by text message.

25

Population of Greenleaf, Idaho

Year	Population
2000	862
2010	846

The table above shows the population of Greenleaf, Idaho, for the years 2000 and 2010. If the relationship between population and year is linear, which of the following functions P models the population of Greenleaf t years after 2000?

A) $P(t) = 862 - 1.6t$

B) $P(t) = 862 - 16t$

C) $P(t) = 862 + 16(t - 2{,}000)$

D) $P(t) = 862 - 1.6(t - 2{,}000)$

26

To determine the mean number of children per household in a community, Tabitha surveyed 20 families at a playground. For the 20 families surveyed, the mean number of children per household was 2.4. Which of the following statements must be true?

A) The mean number of children per household in the community is 2.4.

B) A determination about the mean number of children per household in the community should not be made because the sample size is too small.

C) The sampling method is flawed and may produce a biased estimate of the mean number of children per household in the community.

D) The sampling method is not flawed and is likely to produce an unbiased estimate of the mean number of children per household in the community.

CONTINUE

27

In the xy-plane, the point (p, r) lies on the line with equation $y = x + b$, where b is a constant. The point with coordinates $(2p, 5r)$ lies on the line with equation $y = 2x + b$. If $p \neq 0$, what is the value of $\frac{r}{p}$?

A) $\frac{2}{5}$

B) $\frac{3}{4}$

C) $\frac{4}{3}$

D) $\frac{5}{2}$

28

The 22 students in a health class conducted an experiment in which they each recorded their pulse rates, in beats per minute, before and after completing a light exercise routine. The dot plots below display the results.

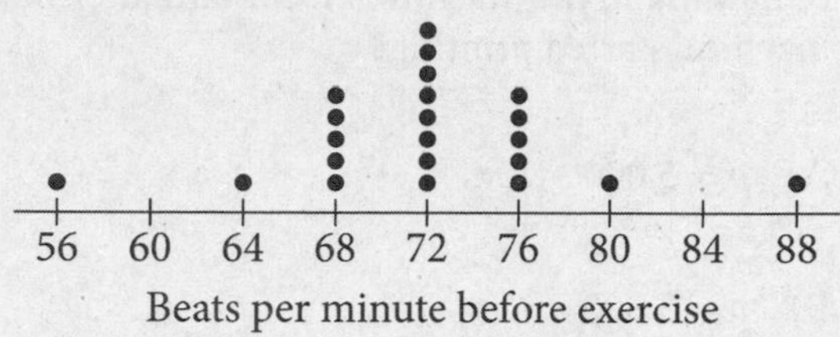

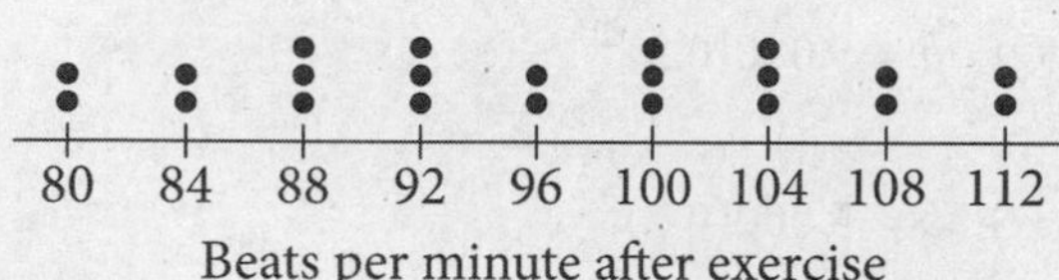

Let s_1 and r_1 be the standard deviation and range, respectively, of the data before exercise, and let s_2 and r_2 be the standard deviation and range, respectively, of the data after exercise. Which of the following is true?

A) $s_1 = s_2$ and $r_1 = r_2$

B) $s_1 < s_2$ and $r_1 < r_2$

C) $s_1 > s_2$ and $r_1 > r_2$

D) $s_1 \neq s_2$ and $r_1 = r_2$

CONTINUE

29

A photocopy machine is initially loaded with 5,000 sheets of paper. The machine starts a large job and copies at a constant rate. After 20 minutes, it has used 30% of the paper. Which of the following equations models the number of sheets of paper, p, remaining in the machine m minutes after the machine started printing?

A) $p = 5{,}000 - 20m$

B) $p = 5{,}000 - 75m$

C) $p = 5{,}000(0.3)^{\frac{m}{20}}$

D) $p = 5{,}000(0.7)^{\frac{m}{20}}$

30

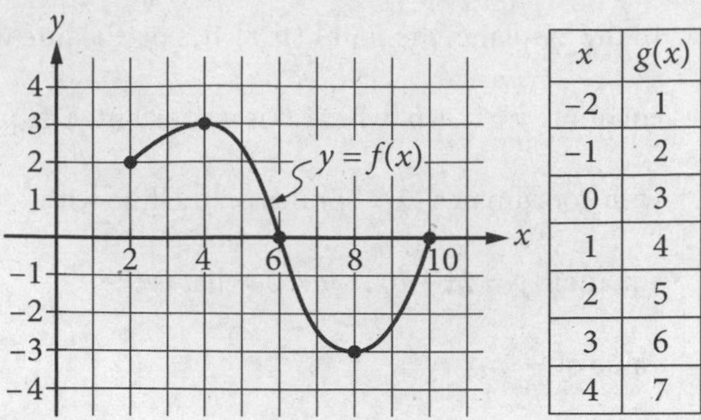

x	$g(x)$
−2	1
−1	2
0	3
1	4
2	5
3	6
4	7

The complete graph of the function f and a table of values for the function g are shown above. The maximum value of f is k. What is the value of $g(k)$?

A) 7

B) 6

C) 3

D) 0

CONTINUE

DIRECTIONS

For questions 31-38, solve the problem and enter your answer in the grid, as described below, on the answer sheet.

1. Although not required, it is suggested that you write your answer in the boxes at the top of the columns to help you fill in the circles accurately. You will receive credit only if the circles are filled in correctly.
2. Mark no more than one circle in any column.
3. No question has a negative answer.
4. Some problems may have more than one correct answer. In such cases, grid only one answer.
5. **Mixed numbers** such as $3\frac{1}{2}$ must be gridded as 3.5 or 7/2. (If 3 1 / 2 is entered into the grid, it will be interpreted as $\frac{31}{2}$, not $3\frac{1}{2}$.)
6. **Decimal answers:** If you obtain a decimal answer with more digits than the grid can accommodate, it may be either rounded or truncated, but it must fill the entire grid.

Answer: $\frac{7}{12}$

Write answer in boxes. → 7 / 1 2

← Fraction line

Grid in result.

Answer: 2.5

2 . 5

← Decimal point

Acceptable ways to grid $\frac{2}{3}$ are:

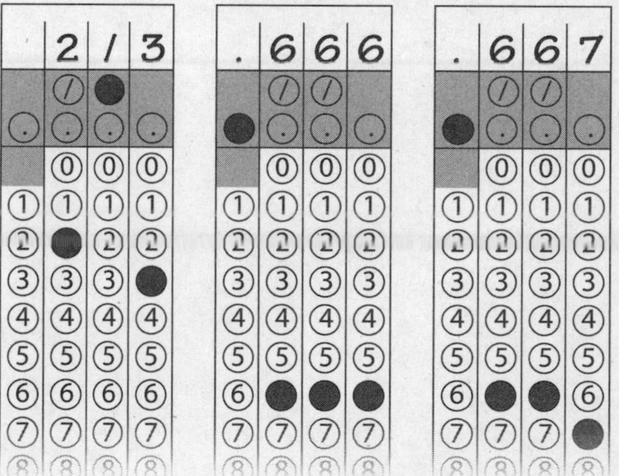

Answer: 201 – either position is correct

NOTE: You may start your answers in any column, space permitting. Columns you don't need to use should be left blank.

CONTINUE

31

There are two atoms of hydrogen and one atom of oxygen in one molecule of water. How many atoms of hydrogen are there in 51 molecules of water?

32

$$x - \frac{1}{2}a = 0$$

If $x = 1$ in the equation above, what is the value of a ?

33

In the xy-plane, the equations $x + 2y = 10$ and $3x + 6y = c$ represent the same line for some constant c. What is the value of c ?

34

On April 18, 1775, Paul Revere set off on his midnight ride from Charlestown to Lexington. If he had ridden straight to Lexington without stopping, he would have traveled 11 miles in 26 minutes. In such a ride, what would the average speed of his horse have been, to the nearest tenth of a mile per <u>hour</u>?

CONTINUE

35

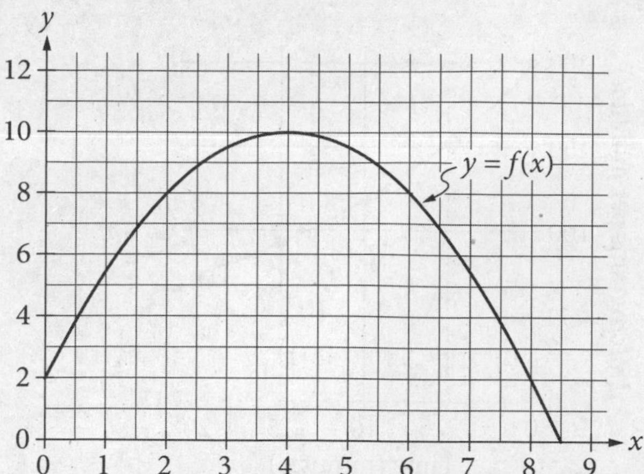

The graph of the function *f*, defined by $f(x) = -\frac{1}{2}(x-4)^2 + 10$, is shown in the *xy*-plane above. If the function g (not shown) is defined by $g(x) = -x + 10$, what is one possible value of a such that $f(a) = g(a)$?

36

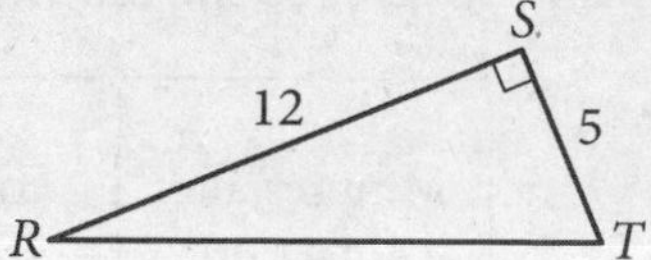

In triangle RST above, point W (not shown) lies on $\overline{RT}$. What is the value of $\cos(\angle RSW) - \sin(\angle WST)$?

CONTINUE

Questions 37 and 38 refer to the following information.

Minutes after injection	Penicillin concentration (micrograms per milliliter)
0	200
5	152
10	118
15	93
20	74

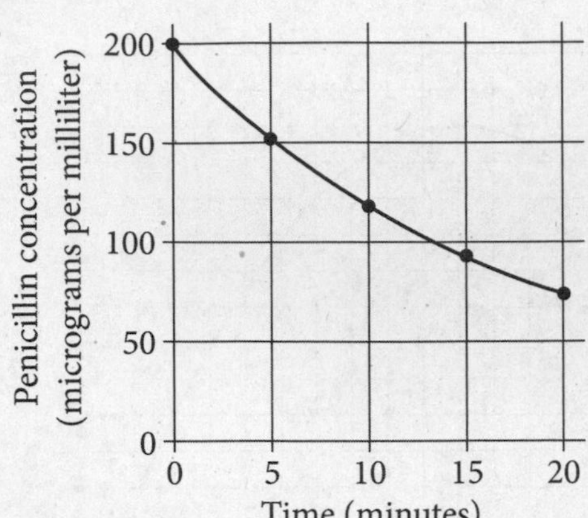

When a patient receives a penicillin injection, the kidneys begin removing the penicillin from the body. The table and graph above show the penicillin concentration in a patient's bloodstream at 5-minute intervals for the 20 minutes immediately following a one-time penicillin injection.

CONTINUE

37

According to the table, how many more micrograms of penicillin are present in 10 milliliters of blood drawn from the patient 5 minutes after the injection than are present in 8 milliliters of blood drawn 10 minutes after the injection?

38

The penicillin concentration, in micrograms per milliliter, in the patient's bloodstream t minutes after the penicillin injection is modeled by the function P defined by $P(t) = 200b^{\frac{t}{5}}$. If P approximates the values in the table to within 10 micrograms per milliliter, what is the value of b, rounded to the nearest tenth?

STOP

If you finish before time is called, you may check your work on this section only.

Do not turn to any other section.

No Test Material On This Page

No Test Material On This Page

No Test Material On This Page

No Test Material On This Page

No Test Material On This Page

No Test Material On This Page

No Test Material On This Page

No Test Material On This Page

This page represents the back cover of the Practice Test.

The SAT®

Practice Essay #8

The essay gives you an opportunity to show how effectively you can read and comprehend a passage and write an essay analyzing the passage. In your essay, you should demonstrate that you have read the passage carefully, present a clear and logical analysis, and use language precisely.

You have 50 minutes to read the passage and write an essay in response to the prompt provided inside this booklet.

For information on scoring your essay, view the SAT Essay scoring rubric at **sat.org/essay**.

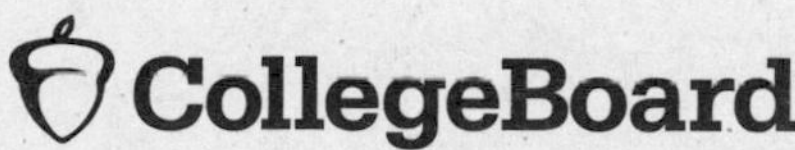

As you read the passage below, consider how Bobby Braun uses

- evidence, such as facts or examples, to support claims.
- reasoning to develop ideas and to connect claims and evidence.
- stylistic or persuasive elements, such as word choice or appeals to emotion, to add power to the ideas expressed.

Adapted from Bobby Braun, "Space Technology: A Critical Investment for Our Nation's Future." ©2014 by Capitol Hill Publishing Corp. Originally published in the *Hill*, October 27, 2011.

1 Aerospace remains a strong component of our national fabric and is the largest positive contributor to our nation's trade balance. However, this technological leadership position is not a given. To remain the leader in aerospace technology, we must continue to perform research and invest in the people who will create the breakthroughs of tomorrow, preserving a critical component of our nation's economic competitiveness for future generations.

2 For NASA,[1] past cutting-edge technology investments led to design and flight of the Apollo missions, the space shuttle, the International Space Station and a myriad of robotic explorers that allowed us to reach destinations across our solar system and peer across the universe. NASA remains one of the nation's premiere research and development agencies, pursuing breakthrough technologies that will expand the frontiers of aeronautics and space.

3 Unfortunately, the pioneering spirit embodied by this storied agency is endangered as a result of chronic underinvestment in basic and applied research. In a recent report on the state of NASA's technology plans, the National Research Council offered a stark assessment: "Success in executing future NASA space missions will depend on advanced technology developments that should already be underway. However, it has been years since NASA has had a vigorous, broad-based program in advanced space technology. NASA's technology base is largely depleted. Currently, available technology is insufficient to accomplish many intended space missions. Future U.S. leadership in space requires a foundation of sustained technology advances."

4 America is beginning an exciting new chapter in human space exploration. This chapter centers on full use of the International Space Station, maturation of multiple American vehicles for delivering astronauts and cargo to low-Earth orbit, development of a crew vehicle and an evolvable heavy-lift rocket—two critical building blocks for our nation's deep-space exploration future—and advancement of a suite of new in-space technologies that will allow us to send explorers safely into deep space for the first time.

---

1 National Aeronautics and Space Administration

5 By investing in the high payoff, transformative technology that the aerospace industry cannot tackle today, NASA will mature the systems required for its future missions while proving the capabilities and lowering the cost of other government agency and commercial space activities. Developing these solutions will create high-tech jobs.

6 NASA's technology investments continue to make a difference in the world around us. Knowledge provided by weather and navigational spacecraft, efficiency improvements in both ground and air transportation, super computers, solar- and wind-generated energy, the cameras found in many of today's cellphones, improved biomedical applications including advanced medical imaging and more nutritious infant formula, and the protective gear that keeps our military, firefighters and police safe, have all benefitted from our nation's investments in aerospace technology.

7 For many of the tens of thousands of engineering and science students in our nation's universities today, the space program provides the opportunity to invent technologies today that will form the foundation for humanity's next great leap across the solar system. For this new generation of engineers and scientists, and for those working across NASA at this moment, the future starts today. Modest, sustained federal investment in space technology, at a funding level approaching 5 percent of NASA's budget (well below the R&D[2] budget of many corporations), is the key ingredient to their success. A NASA that is reaching for grand challenges and operating at the cutting-edge is critical not only for our country's future in space but also for America's technological leadership position in the world.

8 Nearly 50 years ago, a young president gave NASA a grand challenge—one chosen not for its simplicity, but for its audacity, not for its ultimate goal or destination, but to "organize and measure the best of our energies and skills." In accomplishing that goal, NASA not only defined what we now call "rocket science," but also made a lasting imprint on the economic, national security and geopolitical landscape of the time.

9 NASA can do the same today. This is the task for which this agency was built. This is the task this agency can complete. America expects no less.

Write an essay in which you explain how Bobby Braun builds an argument to persuade his audience that the US government must continue to invest in NASA. In your essay, analyze how Braun uses one or more of the features listed in the box above (or features of your own choice) to strengthen the logic and persuasiveness of his argument. Be sure that your analysis focuses on the most relevant features of the passage.

Your essay should not explain whether you agree with Braun's claims, but rather explain how Braun builds an argument to persuade his audience.

---

2 Research and development

This page represents the back cover of the Practice Essay.

CollegeBoard

SAT PRACTICE ANSWER SHEET

COMPLETE MARK ●

EXAMPLES OF INCOMPLETE MARKS 

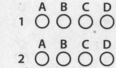

It is recommended that you use a No. 2 pencil. It is very important that you fill in the entire circle darkly and completely. If you change your response, erase as completely as possible. Incomplete marks or erasures may affect your score.

TEST NUMBER

ENTER TEST NUMBER

For instance, for Practice Test #1, fill in the circle for 0 in the **first column** and for 1 in the **second column.**

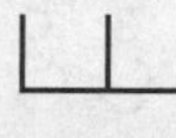

0	○	○
1	○	○
2	○	○
3	○	○
4	○	○
5	○	○
6	○	○
7	○	○
8	○	○
9	○	○

SECTION 1

	A	B	C	D		A	B	C	D		A	B	C	D		A	B	C	D
1	○	○	○	○	14	○	○	○	○	27	○	○	○	○	40	○	○	○	○
2	○	○	○	○	15	○	○	○	○	28	○	○	○	○	41	○	○	○	○
3	○	○	○	○	16	○	○	○	○	29	○	○	○	○	42	○	○	○	○
4	○	○	○	○	17	○	○	○	○	30	○	○	○	○	43	○	○	○	○
5	○	○	○	○	18	○	○	○	○	31	○	○	○	○	44	○	○	○	○
6	○	○	○	○	19	○	○	○	○	32	○	○	○	○	45	○	○	○	○
7	○	○	○	○	20	○	○	○	○	33	○	○	○	○	46	○	○	○	○
8	○	○	○	○	21	○	○	○	○	34	○	○	○	○	47	○	○	○	○
9	○	○	○	○	22	○	○	○	○	35	○	○	○	○	48	○	○	○	○
10	○	○	○	○	23	○	○	○	○	36	○	○	○	○	49	○	○	○	○
11	○	○	○	○	24	○	○	○	○	37	○	○	○	○	50	○	○	○	○
12	○	○	○	○	25	○	○	○	○	38	○	○	○	○	51	○	○	○	○
13	○	○	○	○	26	○	○	○	○	39	○	○	○	○	52	○	○	○	○

Download the College Board SAT Practice app to instantly score this test.
Learn more at sat.org/scoring.

CollegeBoard

SAT PRACTICE ANSWER SHEET

COMPLETE MARK ● | EXAMPLES OF INCOMPLETE MARKS

It is recommended that you use a No. 2 pencil. It is very important that you fill in the entire circle darkly and completely. If you change your response, erase as completely as possible. Incomplete marks or erasures may affect your score.

SECTION 2

1 A B C D	10 A B C D	19 A B C D	28 A B C D	37 A B C D
2 A B C D	11 A B C D	20 A B C D	29 A B C D	38 A B C D
3 A B C D	12 A B C D	21 A B C D	30 A B C D	39 A B C D
4 A B C D	13 A B C D	22 A B C D	31 A B C D	40 A B C D
5 A B C D	14 A B C D	23 A B C D	32 A B C D	41 A B C D
6 A B C D	15 A B C D	24 A B C D	33 A B C D	42 A B C D
7 A B C D	16 A B C D	25 A B C D	34 A B C D	43 A B C D
8 A B C D	17 A B C D	26 A B C D	35 A B C D	44 A B C D
9 A B C D	18 A B C D	27 A B C D	36 A B C D	

If you're scoring with our mobile app we recommend that you cut these pages out of the back of this book. The scoring does best with a flat page.

CollegeBoard

SAT PRACTICE ANSWER SHEET

COMPLETE MARK ● EXAMPLES OF INCOMPLETE MARKS 

It is recommended that you use a No. 2 pencil. It is very important that you fill in the entire circle darkly and completely. If you change your response, erase as completely as possible. Incomplete marks or erasures may affect your score.

SECTION 3

1 A B C D	4 A B C D	7 A B C D	10 A B C D	13 A B C D
2 A B C D	5 A B C D	8 A B C D	11 A B C D	14 A B C D
3 A B C D	6 A B C D	9 A B C D	12 A B C D	15 A B C D

Only answers that are gridded will be scored. You will not receive credit for anything written in the boxes.

16 17 18 19 20

/
.
0
1
2
3
4
5
6
7
8
9

NO CALCULATOR ALLOWED

Did you know that you can print out these test sheets from the web? Learn more at sat.org/scoring.

SAT PRACTICE ANSWER SHEET

COMPLETE MARK ● EXAMPLES OF INCOMPLETE MARKS 

It is recommended that you use a No. 2 pencil. It is very important that you fill in the entire circle darkly and completely. If you change your response, erase as completely as possible. Incomplete marks or erasures may affect your score.

SECTION 4

1 A B C D	7 A B C D	13 A B C D	19 A B C D	25 A B C D
2 A B C D	8 A B C D	14 A B C D	20 A B C D	26 A B C D
3 A B C D	9 A B C D	15 A B C D	21 A B C D	27 A B C D
4 A B C D	10 A B C D	16 A B C D	22 A B C D	28 A B C D
5 A B C D	11 A B C D	17 A B C D	23 A B C D	29 A B C D
6 A B C D	12 A B C D	18 A B C D	24 A B C D	30 A B C D

CALCULATOR ALLOWED

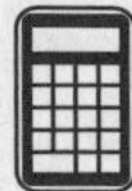

If you're using our mobile app keep in mind that bad lighting and even shadows cast over the answer sheet can affect your score. Be sure to scan this in a well-lit area for best results.

CollegeBoard

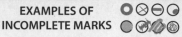

SAT PRACTICE ANSWER SHEET

COMPLETE MARK ● EXAMPLES OF INCOMPLETE MARKS 

It is recommended that you use a No. 2 pencil. It is very important that you fill in the entire circle darkly and completely. If you change your response, erase as completely as possible. Incomplete marks or erasures may affect your score.

SECTION 4 (Continued)

Only answers that are gridded will be scored. You will not receive credit for anything written in the boxes.

31 32 33 34 35

/ . 0 1 2 3 4 5 6 7 8 9

Only answers that are gridded will be scored. You will not receive credit for anything written in the boxes.

36 37 38

/ . 0 1 2 3 4 5 6 7 8 9

CALCULATOR ALLOWED

○ I understand that my essay (without my name) may be reproduced in other College Board materials. If I mark this circle, I withhold my permission to reproduce my essay for any purposes beyond score reporting and the assessment of my writing skills. Marking this circle will have no effect on my score, nor will it prevent my essay from being made available to any college to which I send my SAT scores.

IMPORTANT: **USE A NO. 2 PENCIL. DO NOT WRITE OUTSIDE THE BORDER!** Words written outside the essay box or written in ink **WILL NOT APPEAR** in the copy sent to be scored, and your score will be affected.

PLANNING PAGE You may plan your essay in the unlined planning space below, but use only the lined pages following this one to write your essay. Any work on this planning page will not be scored.

Use pages 7 through 10 for your ESSAY →

FOR PLANNING ONLY

Use pages 7 through 10 for your ESSAY →

PLEASE DO NOT WRITE IN THIS AREA

○○○○○○○○○○○○○○○○○○○○○○○○○○○○○○○

SERIAL #

BEGIN YOUR ESSAY HERE.

You may continue on the next page.

PLEASE DO NOT WRITE IN THIS AREA

SERIAL #

You may continue on the next page.

DO NOT WRITE OUTSIDE OF THE BOX.

You may continue on the next page.

PLEASE DO NOT WRITE IN THIS AREA

SERIAL #

DO NOT WRITE OUTSIDE OF THE BOX.

STOP.

Answer Explanations

SAT Practice Test #8

Section 1: Reading Test

QUESTION 1

Choice A is the best answer. The first paragraph explains the narrator's love of reading: "Even then my only friends were made of paper and ink. . . . Where my school friends saw notches of ink on incomprehensible pages, I saw light, streets, and people." The fourth paragraph reiterates this love in its description of the bookshop as a "sanctuary" and "refuge." The shift in focus occurs in the last six paragraphs, which recount the gift of a book that transforms the narrator's love of reading into a desire to write: "I did not think there could be a better [book] in the whole world and I was beginning to suspect that Mr. Dickens had written it just for me. Soon I was convinced that I didn't want to do anything else in life but learn to do what Mr. Dickens had done." Thus the passage's overall focus shifts from the narrator's love of reading to a specific incident that influences his decision to become a writer.

Choice B is incorrect because the passage never focuses on the narrator's father, who primarily serves to illustrate the narrator's determination to read books despite all obstacles. Choice C is incorrect because the passage focuses on the narrator's desire to write rather than on whatever skill he may have as a writer. Choice D is incorrect because the passage doesn't make the narrator's childhood hardships its central focus or analyze the effects of those hardships.

QUESTION 2

Choice C is the best answer. In the first paragraph, the third sentence describes the narrator's love of reading ("where my school friends saw notches of ink on incomprehensible pages, I saw light, streets, and people"), and the fourth sentence describes the role that reading played in the narrator's life ("a safe haven from that home, those streets, and those troubled days in which even I could sense that only a limited fortune awaited me"). The remainder of the passage recounts incidents in which the narrator's actions arise from his love of, and dependence on, reading. Thus the third and fourth sentences can be seen as describing a passion that accounts for those actions.

Choice A is incorrect because although the narrator's "school friends" are mentioned in passing in the third sentence, they aren't introduced as proper characters and make no further appearance in the passage. Choice B is incorrect because the passage doesn't list the difficult conditions of the narrator's childhood until after these sentences. Choice D is incorrect because the narrator's aspirations aren't discussed until the last paragraph of the passage.

QUESTION 3

Choice C is the best answer. The tenth paragraph shows that upon returning home, the narrator hides the gift (the "new friend") that Sempere had given him: "That afternoon I took my new friend home, hidden under my clothes so that my father wouldn't see it." It can be inferred from this sentence that the narrator's concern arises from an awareness that his father would disapprove of the gift.

Choice A is incorrect because although the passage discusses the father's hostility toward the narrator's love of reading, there is no indication that the father is not affectionate to the narrator more generally; indeed, the third paragraph depicts the father's generosity toward the narrator. Choice B is incorrect because the father's generosity toward the narrator, as depicted in the third paragraph, clearly shows that the father encourages unnecessary purchases of such things as candy. Choice D is incorrect because although the first paragraph shows that the father is hostile toward books in general, there is no indication in the passage that Dickens or any other author is a specific object of the father's disdain.

QUESTION 4

Choice D is the best answer. The previous question asks which statement about the narrator's father would the narrator most likely agree with. The answer, that his father wouldn't have approved of Sempere's gift to the narrator, is best supported in the tenth paragraph: "That afternoon I took my new friend home, hidden under my clothes so that my father wouldn't see it." It can be inferred from this sentence that the narrator is aware of his father's likely disapproval of the gift (the "new friend").

Choices A, B, and C are incorrect because the cited lines don't support the answer to the previous question. Instead, they show the father giving his own gift to the narrator (choice A) and illustrate how the narrator was treated when in Sempere's bookshop (choices B and C).

QUESTION 5

Choice A is the best answer. The last paragraph makes clear the narrator's enthusiasm for Charles Dickens's *Great Expectations*, and it can be inferred from the last sentence of this paragraph that this enthusiasm motivated the narrator to aspire to a career as a writer: "Soon I was convinced that I didn't want to do anything else in life but learn to do what Mr. Dickens had done."

Choice B is incorrect because the passage doesn't discuss gifts the narrator has received in the past; although the father sometimes gave the narrator money to buy sweets and snacks, these weren't gifts since the narrator made the purchases himself. Choice C is incorrect because although it is clear from the passage that Sempere was kind and even indulgent to the narrator, there is no suggestion that this treatment was inspired by respect for the narrator. Choice D is incorrect because there is no suggestion that the narrator took Sempere's figurative designation of Dickens as a "lifelong friend" in the ninth paragraph to be a literal statement.

QUESTION 6

Choice D is the best answer. The previous question asks why the narrator considers *Great Expectations* to be the greatest gift he ever received. The answer, that the book convinced him to become a writer, is best supported by the last sentence of the last paragraph: "Soon I was convinced that I didn't want to do anything else in life but learn to do what Mr. Dickens had done."

Choices A, B, and C are incorrect because the cited lines don't support the answer to the previous question. Instead, they explain the narrator's interactions with the bookseller (choice A), describe the book's physical condition (choice B), and indicate the narrator's initial, erroneous assumption that Sempere knew Charles Dickens personally (choice C).

QUESTION 7

Choice D is the best answer. In the fourth paragraph, the narrator explains that although Sempere normally didn't charge him for books, he still left Sempere a few coins as payment: "It was only small change—if I'd had to buy a book with that pittance, I would probably have been able to afford only a booklet of cigarette papers." These lines signal the narrator's awareness that he was paying less for the books than they were worth.

Choice A is incorrect because the passage states that Sempere didn't expect or want the narrator to pay: "He hardly ever allowed me to pay for the books." Choice B is incorrect because the fourth paragraph makes clear that even if Sempere didn't want the narrator's money, the narrator would still "leave the coins I'd managed to collect." Choice C is incorrect because the third paragraph states that the money with which the narrator paid Sempere was originally given to the narrator by his father.

QUESTION 8

Choice B is the best answer. In the fourth paragraph, the narrator describes his reluctance to leave Sempere's bookshop: "When it was time for me to leave, I would do so dragging my feet, a weight on my soul." In this context, "weight" most nearly means burden.

Choices A, C, and D are incorrect because in the context of the narrator having to do something he doesn't want to, a "weight" he had to carry most nearly means a burden, not a bulk (choice A), force (choice C), or clout (choice D).

QUESTION 9

Choice C is the best answer. When, in the eighth paragraph, the narrator asks Sempere if the author Charles Dickens is a friend of his, Sempere replies, in the ninth paragraph, that Dickens is a "lifelong friend. And from now on, he's your friend too." Sempere designated Dickens a "friend" of both himself and the narrator, who had never heard of the author before. This signals that the use of "friend" in these lines is figurative and emphasizes Sempere's emotional connection to Dickens and, more generally, to reading. It also signals Sempere's hope that the narrator will come to have a similar connection to Dickens.

Choices A, B, and D are incorrect because the word "friend" is used in these lines to emphasize Sempere's connection to reading, rather than his connection to the narrator (choice A), the narrator's relationships or home life (choice B), or the narrator's emotional state or decision making (choice D).

QUESTION 10

Choice B is the best answer. In the ninth paragraph, Sempere describes the author Charles Dickens to the narrator: "A lifelong friend. And from now on, he's your friend too." As the reader can reasonably assume that Sempere doesn't actually know Dickens, this description can be read as signaling Sempere as an avid admirer of Dickens's work.

Choice A is incorrect because the passage describes Sempere as a bookseller, not a writer. Choice C is incorrect because although the passage implies Sempere feels an emotional connection to Dickens, it doesn't suggest that this connection arises from any similarity between Sempere's life and that of Dickens. Choice D is incorrect because even if the passage implies that Sempere admires Dickens's work, Sempere's admiration isn't discussed in relation to that felt by other readers of Dickens, nor is Sempere shown to compare himself to other such readers.

QUESTION 11

Choice B is the best answer. The first paragraph describes the widespread practice of not reporting null results, or results in which researchers fail to see an effect that should be detectable. The second through sixth paragraphs discuss a study that examined how scientists have dealt with null results. The seventh and eighth paragraphs discuss the negative consequences that null results pose for future research and the possible creation of a registry for all data produced by research studies, reported and unreported alike, as a remedy for those consequences. Therefore, the purpose of the passage as a whole is to explain a common practice in the reporting of research studies and summarize a study that provides support for a change to that practice.

Choice A is incorrect because the passage doesn't dispute a widely held belief about the publication of social science research; rather, it suggests a solution to deal with a long-debated problem. Choice C is incorrect because while the passage hints at possible shortcomings in research trials, it doesn't describe them in detail; because it addresses other kinds of research besides medical trials; and because it doesn't call for a government database, specifically. Choice D is incorrect because the passage calls for changes to the reporting of research results, rather than to research methodology itself, and because it doesn't address the publishers of research at all.

QUESTION 12

Choice D is the best answer. The second paragraph states that "TESS allows scientists to order up Internet-based surveys." In the context of the service that the TESS program provides to scientists, "allows" most nearly means enables.

Choices A, B, and C are incorrect because in the context of the passage's discussion of TESS, "allows" most nearly means enables, not admits (choice A), tolerates (choice B), or grants (choice C).

QUESTION 13

Choice D is the best answer. The fifth paragraph of the passage addresses the "statistical strength" of certain scientific findings. In this context, "strength" most nearly means significance, or importance.

Choices A, B, and C are incorrect because in the context of the statistical importance of scientific findings, "strength" most nearly means significance, not attribution (choice A), exertion (choice B), or toughness (choice C).

QUESTION 14

Choice A is the best answer. The seventh paragraph discusses the negative consequences of not publishing null results, emphasizing that "worse, if researchers publish significant results from similar experiments in the future, they could look stronger than they should because the earlier null studies are ignored." In other words, failing to document null results means that the results of later, related studies will not be as accurate as they appear.

Choices B, C, and D are incorrect because the passage does not indicate that failing to document null results can cause promising areas of research to be overlooked (choice B), cause errors in data collection practices that lead to null results being overlooked (choice C), or lessen bias against null results (choice D).

QUESTION 15

Choice D is the best answer. The previous question asks what the passage indicates could result from failing to document null results. The answer, that the results of future studies will be misleading, is best supported in the seventh paragraph: "Worse, if researchers publish significant results from similar experiments in the future, they could look stronger than they should because the earlier null studies are ignored."

Choices A, B, and C are incorrect because the cited lines don't support the answer to the previous question. Instead, choice A suggests how the findings of a study about null results may affect existing beliefs about such results; choice B explains how infrequently null results had been written up, according to Malhotra's study; and choice C illustrates a problem resulting from the failure to document null results, but one that is unrelated to the fact that this documentation failure may make the results of future, related studies appear more valid than they are.

QUESTION 16

Choice B is the best answer. The last two sentences of the seventh paragraph identify a particular research scenario that Malhotra uncovered in his study: "Even more troubling to Malhotra was the fact that two scientists whose initial studies 'didn't work out' went on to publish results based on a smaller sample. 'The non-TESS version of the same study, in which we used a student sample, did yield fruit,' noted one investigator." Since Malhotra especially objected to these researchers' suppression of data that produced null results and their subsequent publication of related data that were statistically significant, it can be inferred that the hypothetical situation to which he would most strongly object is one in which researchers publish their study results in a journal but exclude the portion of data that produced null results.

Choices A and D are incorrect because the seventh paragraph, which identifies a research scenario that Malhotra disapproved of, provides no basis for an inference that he would especially object to a team's insisting on publishing null results in a top journal only (choice A) or a team's expanding the scope of a study that had produced null results (choice D). Choice C is incorrect because although the first sentence of the seventh paragraph indicates Malhotra's concern that failing to publish null results can mean that other researchers unwittingly replicate strategies that produced null results in prior studies, the paragraph goes on to identify other scenarios as being "worse" and "even more troubling" from Malhotra's perspective.

QUESTION 17

Choice C is the best answer. The previous question asks about which hypothetical situation Malhotra would most strongly object to. The answer, that he would most strongly object to researchers' reporting their findings but failing to disclose the null results, is best supported at the end of the seventh paragraph: "Even more troubling to Malhotra was the fact that two scientists whose initial studies 'didn't work out' went on to publish results based on a smaller sample. 'The non-TESS version of the same study, in which we used a student sample, did yield fruit,' noted one investigator."

Choices A, B, and D are incorrect because the cited lines don't support the answer to the previous question about which situation Malhotra would most strongly object to. Instead, they cite another researcher's attitude toward null results from his or her own study (choice A), compare the publication rate for studies that produce null results with that for studies that produce statistically significant results (choice B), and describe the recommendation by Malhotra and his team for the creation of a database to remedy problems resulting from the nonpublication of null results (choice D).

QUESTION 18

Choice B is the best answer. After describing problems that could arise from the failure to report null results, the passage shifts in the last paragraph to a potential solution to such problems: "A registry for data generated by all experiments would address these problems, the authors argue." The paragraph goes on to imply that a registry could solve such problems by deterring the suppression of null results.

Choice A is incorrect because the last paragraph proposes a "registry for data" rather than a future research project. Choice C is incorrect because the summary of the results of Malhotra's study occurs in the fifth paragraph, not in the last. Choice D is incorrect because the last paragraph of the passage does not mention reexamining results already obtained in social science trials.

QUESTION 19

Choice C is the best answer. The far left bar of the graph pertains to social science studies that produced strong results. This bar shows that approximately 20 percent (or two full increments of 10 percent) of such studies were published in a top journal.

Choice A is incorrect because the graph shows that approximately 5 percent of social science studies that produced strong results were unwritten, rather than over 50 percent. Choice B is incorrect because the graph shows that about 30 percent of social science studies that produced strong results were unpublished but written, rather than 50 percent. Choice D is incorrect because the graph shows that slightly over 40 percent of social science studies that produced strong results were published in a non-top journal, rather than almost 80 percent.

QUESTION 20

Choice A is the best answer. The middle bar of the graph pertains to social science studies that produced mixed results. The top 50 percent of this bar represents studies that were published. The bottom 50 percent of this bar represents studies that were either unpublished or went unwritten. Since each of the two categories accounts for 50 percent of the total, it can be said that studies with mixed results were just as likely to be published as they were to be left either unpublished or unwritten.

Choice B is incorrect because the graph indicates that roughly 42 percent of social science studies produced strong results and roughly 22 percent produced null results; together, these two percentages far exceed the 36 percent accounted for by studies that produced mixed results. Choice C is incorrect because the graph shows that roughly 12 percent of studies that produced mixed results were published in top journals, well less than the percentage published in non-top journals (approximately 38 percent). Choice D is incorrect because the graph indicates that studies that produced strong results accounted for approximately 42 percent of all studies, while those that produced mixed results only accounted for around 36 percent of all studies.

QUESTION 21

Choice C is the best answer. The first sentence of the fifth paragraph states, "Not unexpectedly, the statistical strength of the findings made a huge difference in whether they were ever published." This statement is supported by the graph, which shows that more than 60 percent of social science studies that produced strong results were published, while only about 50 percent of studies with mixed results and about 20 percent of studies with null results were published.

Choices A, B, and D are incorrect because none of the cited lines contain information that is represented by the data in the graph. Instead, they recount scientists' explanations for why they didn't publish their null results (choices A and B) and highlight claims about the importance of Malhotra's study (choice D).

QUESTION 22

Choice A is the best answer. The first paragraph explains that in the nanoworld, salt can be seen "stretching like taffy." The third paragraph notes that while this elasticity was expected in metals, it wasn't imagined for salt: "But scientists don't expect this superplasticity in a rigid, crystalline material like salt." The rest of the passage explores this unexpected behavior of salt. Therefore it can be said that one of the central ideas of the passage is that materials don't always behave as scientists might expect them to.

Choices B, C, and D are incorrect because the passage focuses on the unexpected way that salt reacts in the nanoworld, not on the role of inputs and outputs in systems (choice B), the relative strengths and weaknesses of models (choice C), or how the properties of systems differ from the properties of their parts (choice D).

QUESTION 23

Choice D is the best answer. The first five paragraphs introduce salt's ability to stretch "like taffy to more than twice its length." In the fifth paragraph, the passage shifts into an explanation of how "Moore and his colleagues discovered salt's stretchiness." The last paragraph speculates about the possible application of this discovery: "The work also suggests new techniques for making nanowires, which are often created through nano-imprinting techniques." The passage's overall structure can therefore be seen as consisting of an introduction to an interesting salt property, followed by a description of how the property was discovered, followed by a speculation regarding applications of this property.

Choice A is incorrect because the passage discusses only one way in which salt differed from researchers' expectations. Choice B is incorrect because the passage begins not with a hypothesis about salt's behavior but with an explanation of its behaviors. Choice C is incorrect because the passage discusses complementary observations of salt crystals rather than two experiments involving salt that yield seemingly conflicting results.

QUESTION 24

Choice A is the best answer. That Moore's group was surprised to observe salt stretching is most directly suggested by the last sentence of the third paragraph: "But scientists don't expect this superplasticity in a rigid, crystalline material like salt, Moore says."

Choices B, C, and D are incorrect because the cited lines don't support the idea that Moore's group was surprised to observe salt stretching. Instead, they explain how the group happened upon their observation (choice B), the measures the group took to investigate the stretching further (choice C), and how common salt is in nature (choice D).

QUESTION 25

Choice B is the best answer. The first sentence of the fourth paragraph states, "This unusual behavior highlights that different forces rule the nanoworld." In this context, to "rule" most nearly means to control.

Choices A, C, and D are incorrect because in the context of a discussion of forces that operate on the nanoworld, to "rule" most nearly means to control, not to mark (choice A), declare (choice C), or restrain (choice D).

QUESTION 26

Choice D is the best answer. The first sentence of the sixth paragraph identifies "electrostatic forces, perhaps good old van der Waals interactions" as the potential cause of the initial attraction between the microscope tip and the salt.

Choices A, B, and C are incorrect because the first sentence of the sixth paragraph clearly identifies the potential cause of the initial attraction between the microscope tip and the salt as van der Waals interactions, not as gravity (choice A), nano-imprinting (choice B), or surface tension (choice C).

QUESTION 27

Choice B is the best answer. The sixth paragraph says that "several mechanisms might lead to" salt's elasticity. In this context, the phrase "lead to" most nearly means result in.

Choices A, C, and D are incorrect because in the context of something causing salt molecules to exhibit elasticity, the phrase "lead to" most nearly means result in, not guide to (choice A), point toward (choice C), or start with (choice D).

QUESTION 28

Choice A is the best answer. The first paragraph of the passage makes clear that salt exhibits elasticity ("stretching like taffy") in the nanoworld, and the eighth paragraph explains that salt possesses some degree of elasticity in the macroworld as well: "Huge underground deposits of salt can bend like plastic, but water is believed to play a role at these scales." Thus flexibility describes the relationship between salt's behavior in both the nanoworld and the macroworld.

Choice B is incorrect because the third paragraph explains that "scientists don't expect" salt's flexibility in the nanoworld, not that they do expect it; moreover, there is no indication that salt's flexibility in the macroworld is surprising. Choice C is incorrect because the passage doesn't make clear whether nanowires were first observed in the nanoworld or the macroworld. Choice D is incorrect because the passage does not examine the interaction of salt and water in the nanoworld or suggest that such interaction causes salt to have properties that are different from those it possesses in the macroworld.

QUESTION 29

Choice D is the best answer. The previous question asks about which description of the relationship between salt behavior in the nanoworld and in the macroworld can be inferred from the passage. The answer, that salt is flexible or elastic in both worlds, is best supported in the eighth paragraph: "Huge underground deposits of salt can bend like plastic, but water is believed to play a role at these scales." These lines suggest that in the macroworld, as in the nanoworld, salt possesses flexibility.

Choices A, B, and C are incorrect because the cited lines don't support the answer to the previous question. Instead, they highlight the prevalence of nanowires (choice A), identify which forces dominate the nanoworld (choice B), and offer a tentative explanation for an observation discussed in the passage (choice C).

QUESTION 30

Choice C is the best answer. The lower graph, which shows the "tip moving away from salt surface," indicates that when the microscope tip was 15 nanometers from the surface, the force on the tip was approximately 0.75 micronewtons.

Choices A, B, and D are incorrect because the graph shows that when the microscope tip was 15 nanometers from the salt surface, the force on the tip was approximately 0.75 micronewtons, not 0 micronewtons (choice A), 0.25 micronewtons (choice B), or 1.25 micronewtons (choice D).

QUESTION 31

Choice D is the best answer. The bottom graph illustrates the process described in the first sentence of the seventh paragraph of the passage: "as the microscope pulls away from the salt, the salt stretches." On the graph, the stretching of the salt is represented by the amount of force, in micronewtons, exerted on the microscope tip as the tip moves away from the salt surface. The graph shows that force was exerted on the tip until the tip reached point T at approximately 22 nanometers from the salt surface; from point T on, the force was 0 micronewtons. It can be inferred that since no force is being exerted after point T, point T is the point at which a salt nanowire breaks.

Choices A, B, and C are incorrect because the labels P, Q, and R all appear on the top graph, which represents data on the movement of the microscope tip toward the salt surface. As the fifth sentence of the fifth paragraph explains, when the microscope tip moved toward the salt, "the salt actually stretched out to glom on to the microscope tip." Therefore, the first graph shows the salt attaching itself to the microscope tip and forming nanowires, not the breaking of a nanowire.

QUESTION 32

Choice B is the best answer. In the first paragraph of Passage 1, Douglas argues that throughout the period in which the United States had both free and slave states, the nation as a whole "increased from four millions to thirty millions of people . . . extended our territory from the Mississippi to the Pacific Ocean . . . acquired the Floridas and Texas . . . [and had] risen from a weak and feeble power to become the terror and admiration of the civilized world." It can reasonably be inferred that Douglas cites such growth in territory and population to make the point that the division into free and slave states was obviously not a threat to the country's health or survival.

Choice A is incorrect because although it can be inferred that Douglas would argue for continued expansion of the United States, he cites the expansion it has already undergone as support for perpetuating the division into free and slave states. Choice C is incorrect because although Douglas implies that basic facts pertaining to the historical growth of the nation cast doubt on Lincoln's political agenda, he doesn't imply that Lincoln is unaware of those facts. Choice D is incorrect because although Douglas notes that the United States is globally perceived to be powerful, he doesn't imply that this perception can be accounted for by the nation's record of growth.

QUESTION 33

Choice C is the best answer. In the second paragraph of Passage 1, Douglas uses a rhetorical question to stress that the division into slave and free states has existed since the beginning of the United States: "I now come back to the question, why cannot this Union exist forever, divided into Free and Slave States, as our fathers made it?" It can be inferred from this question that Douglas believes that since this division is long-standing, the provisions for it in the US Constitution have provided a good basic structure that doesn't need to be changed.

Choice A is incorrect because in Passage 1, Douglas doesn't observe that the US Constitution's provisions for slavery lack a means for reconciling differences between slave states and free states. Choice B is incorrect because although Douglas stresses that the provisions for slavery are long-standing, he doesn't characterize them as having somehow anticipated the Union's expansion to the west. Choice D is correct because although it can be inferred from Passage 1 that Douglas believes the provisions for slavery have had a positive economic impact, he nowhere implies that the founders based them on an assumption that slavery was economically necessary.

QUESTION 34

Choice B is the best answer. The previous question asks about how Douglas, in Passage 1, characterizes the Constitution's provisions for slavery. The answer, that Douglas believes they provided a good basic structure and don't need to be changed, is best supported in the first sentence of the second paragraph of Passage 1: "I now come back to the question, why cannot this Union exist forever, divided into Free and Slave States, as our fathers made it?"

Choices A, C, and D are incorrect because the cited lines don't support the answer to the previous question. Instead, they describe the various ways in which the nation has expanded since its founding (choice A), stress the likelihood that the nation will only continue to expand (choice C), and assert the importance of the sovereignty of individual states to the future expansion of the nation (choice D).

QUESTION 35

Choice C is the best answer. In the first sentence of the second paragraph of Passage 2, Lincoln raises a question about how the consequences of the division of the United States into slave states and free states compare with the consequences of the other ways in which states differ from each other: "But has it been so with this element of slavery?" In this context, the word "element" most nearly means factor.

Choices A, B, and D are incorrect because in the context of Lincoln's discussion of the "element of slavery," the word "element" most nearly means factor, not ingredient (choice A), environment (choice B), or quality (choice D).

QUESTION 36

Choice B is the best answer. In the second paragraph of Passage 2, Lincoln asserts that the controversy surrounding slavery in the United States has died down whenever the institution of slavery has been restricted geographically: "Whenever it has been limited to its present bounds, and there has been no effort to spread it, there has been peace." Since Lincoln associates peace on this issue with geographical limits on the institution of slavery itself, it can be inferred that he would agree that the controversy would abate if all attempts to establish slavery in new regions ceased.

Choice A is incorrect because Lincoln neither urges Northern states to attempt to abolish slavery unilaterally nor implies that such an attempt would extinguish the controversy over slavery. Choice C is incorrect because Lincoln neither suggests that the laws regulating slavery are ambiguous nor that such ambiguity exacerbates controversy over slavery. Choice D is incorrect because Lincoln never attributes the controversy over slavery to differences in religion or social values from one state to another.

QUESTION 37

Choice C is the best answer. The previous question asks which claim about the controversy over slavery would Lincoln agree with. The answer, that the controversy would abate if attempts to spread slavery to regions where it isn't practiced were abandoned, is best supported in the second paragraph of Passage 2: "Whenever [slavery] has been limited to its present bounds, and there has been no effort to spread it, there has been peace."

Choices A, B, and D are incorrect because the cited lines don't support the answer to the previous question. Instead, they discuss state-to-state differences in laws regulating issues other than slavery (choice A), assert that the differences among the various states generally benefit the nation (choice B), and ask a philosophical question that doesn't directly address the issue of slavery (choice D).

QUESTION 38

Choice D is the best answer. In the last sentence of Passage 2, Lincoln asks about the likelihood that people will fundamentally change: "Do you think that the nature of man will be changed?" In this context, the word "nature" most nearly means character.

Choices A, B, and C are incorrect because in the context of a discussion of the "nature of man," the word "nature" most nearly means character, not force (choice A), simplicity (choice B), or world (choice C).

QUESTION 39

Choice C is the best answer. In the first paragraph of Passage 1, Douglas claims that Lincoln considers the Constitution to be "a house divided against itself," due to its provisions for the division of the nation into slave states and free states, and to be "in violation of the law of God." In Passage 2, Lincoln objects to this characterization of his position and devotes the majority of the passage to clarifying that it isn't the Constitution he finds fault with, or even its provisions for slavery, but rather with attempts to spread slavery to regions where it isn't currently practiced. Therefore it can be said that a central tension between the two passages arises from, on the one hand, Douglas's criticism of Lincoln for finding fault with the Constitution and, on the other, Lincoln's insistence that Douglas has misrepresented his position.

Choice A is incorrect because Douglas (Passage 1) proposes no changes to federal policies on slavery and because Lincoln (Passage 2) doesn't consider whether changes to such policies would enjoy popular support. Choice B is incorrect because Douglas (Passage 1) never expresses concern about the potential impact of abolition on the US economy and because Lincoln (Passage 2) neither discusses such an impact nor dismisses concerns about it. Choice D is incorrect because neither passage offers any interpretation of federal law.

QUESTION 40

Choice A is the best answer. In the first paragraph of Passage 1, Douglas discusses the issue of slavery in the context of the division of free states and slave states throughout the period when the United States "extended our territory from the Mississippi to the Pacific Ocean" and "acquired the Floridas and Texas, and other territory sufficient to double our geographical extent." In the second paragraph of Passage 2, Lincoln asserts that the controversy over slavery has historically been "excited by the effort to spread [slavery] into new territory," as in the case of Missouri, Texas, and "the territory acquired by the Mexican War." Therefore, it can be said that, notwithstanding their differences of opinion, both Douglas and Lincoln discuss the issue of slavery in relationship to the expansion of the Union.

Choices B, C, and D are incorrect because it is in relationship to the nation's expansion that both passages discuss the issue of slavery, not in relationship to questions of morality (choice B), religious toleration (choice C), or laws regulating commerce (choice D).

QUESTION 41

Choice D is the best answer. In the second paragraph of Passage 1, Douglas asks the rhetorical question: "why cannot this Union exist forever, divided into Free and Slave States, as our fathers made it?" The remainder of the paragraph amounts to an answer to this rhetorical question and a refutation of Lincoln's viewpoint on slavery, as represented by Douglas. In the second paragraph of Passage 2, Lincoln asks a series of rhetorical questions: "But has it been so with this element of slavery? Have we not always had quarrels and difficulties over it? And when will we cease to have quarrels over it?" These questions imply that there are flaws in Douglas's equating the division into slave states and free states with other, more unambiguously beneficial differences from state to state. The remainder of the second paragraph expands on these flaws. Therefore, it can be said that in context, the rhetorical questions asked by each speaker serve to undermine the argument of the other speaker.

Choice A is incorrect because in asking rhetorical questions, neither Douglas nor Lincoln casts doubt on the sincerity of his opponent. Choices B and C are incorrect because although Douglas and Lincoln find fault with each other's ideas, they don't criticize each other's methods (choice B) or reproach each other's actions (choice C).

QUESTION 42

Choice A is the best answer. The first two paragraphs of the passage describe the physical process by which the Venus flytrap closes its trap but also note certain long-standing questions about that process: "How does the plant encode and store the information from the unassuming bug's encounter with the first hair? How does it remember the first touch in order to react upon the second?" The passage then answers those questions by discussing, in the third and fourth paragraphs, a study conducted by Dieter Hodick and Andreas Sievers that identified the physiological means behind the closing of the Venus flytrap's trap and, in the last paragraph, a study conducted by Alexander Volkov that confirmed and built on Hodick and Sievers's findings. The primary purpose of the passage can therefore be seen as discussing scientific findings that explain how the Venus flytrap closes its trap.

Choice B is incorrect because the passage doesn't discuss the Venus flytrap's ability to close its trap in the context of the abilities of other plants. Choice C is incorrect because the passage discusses how the closing action operates but not how it has evolved. Choice D is incorrect because the passage doesn't provide an overview of the Venus flytrap and its predatory behavior; it merely notes in passing that the closing action has a predatory function.

QUESTION 43

Choice C is the best answer. The first paragraph discusses the challenge posed to the Venus flytrap by the opening and closing of its trap: "Closing its trap requires a huge expense of energy, and reopening the trap can take several hours, so *Dionaea* only wants to spring closed when it's sure that the dawdling insect visiting its surface is large enough to be worth its time." Since closing and reopening the trap requires the expense of precious energy, it can be inferred that by guarding against unnecessary closing, multiple triggers safeguard the plant's energy supply.

Choice A is incorrect because the passage never indicates that multiple triggers allow the Venus flytrap to identify which species its prey belongs to, only that they allow it to gauge the prey's size. Choice B is incorrect because although the passage implies that the plant needs to conserve energy and indicates that calcium is involved in the trap-closing mechanism, there is no indication that the plant's calcium reserves themselves require conservation. Choice D is incorrect because it can be inferred from the passage that the advantage of multiple triggers is that they prevent the Venus flytrap from closing on the improper prey rather than from prematurely closing on the proper prey; the passage never implies that when touched by its proper prey, the Venus flytrap is at risk of closing too soon to capture it.

QUESTION 44

Choice A is the best answer. The previous question asks what the Venus flytrap gains from requiring multiple triggers before closing. The answer, that multiple triggers allow the plant to conserve energy, is best supported near the beginning of the first paragraph: "Closing its trap requires a huge expense of energy, and reopening the trap can take several hours, so *Dionaea* only wants to spring closed when it's sure that the dawdling insect visiting its surface is large enough to be worth its time."

Choices B, C, and D are incorrect because the cited lines don't support the answer to the previous question. Instead, they describe how the hairs on the Venus flytrap function and how the system of multiple triggers works (choices B and C) and explain how the plant preserves a memory, as it were, that something has touched the trigger hairs (choice D).

QUESTION 45

Choice C is the best answer. The phrases "dawdling insect," "happily meanders," and "unassuming bug's encounter" are less typical of word choices made in formal, scientific writing than of those made in less formal writing modes. Therefore, the tone that these phrases establish is best described as informal.

Choices A, B, and D are incorrect because the phrases establish a tone that is informal, not academic (choice A), melodramatic (choice B), or mocking (choice D).

QUESTION 46

Choice A is the best answer. The first paragraph describes the mechanism that prompts the Venus flytrap to close its trap. The second paragraph makes an analogy of each step of that mechanism to an aspect of short-term memory formation in humans and then poses questions about the precise physiological terms in which those steps are carried out. It can therefore be said that the discussion of short-term memory serves to clarify the first paragraph's explanation of what prompts the trap of the Venus flytrap to close.

Choice B is incorrect because it is the third paragraph, not the second, that discusses the function of electric charges in the Venus flytrap; moreover, the passage presents this function as a fact, not as a controversial hypothesis. Choice C is incorrect because rather than stressing the differences between Venus flytraps and humans, the analogy in the second paragraph stresses their superficial similarities. Choice D is incorrect because the second paragraph implies that the Venus flytrap's capacity for retaining information is far from detailed: "something (it doesn't know what) has touched one of its hairs."

QUESTION 47

Choice D is the best answer. The third paragraph explains that touching a single trigger hair results in "a rapid increase in the concentration of calcium ions" in the plant. The fourth paragraph further explains that the calcium concentration produced by this initial touch isn't enough to cause the trap to close, but that a second hair touch will bring the total concentration to the level necessary to close the trap: "a second hair needs to be stimulated to push the calcium concentration over this threshold and spring the trap."

Choices A and B are incorrect because the fourth paragraph explains that the second trigger supplements the action of the first trigger, not that it reverses it (choice A) or stabilizes its effect (choice B). Choice C is incorrect because the third paragraph clearly states that the calcium channels open after the first trigger hair is touched, not the second.

QUESTION 48

Choice B is the best answer. The fourth paragraph explains that the Venus flytrap will close only if a second hair is stimulated to "push the calcium concentration over this threshold and spring the trap." But the last sentence of the paragraph notes that the calcium concentrations "dissipate over time," and if enough time elapses after the first trigger, "the final concentration after the second trigger won't be high enough to close the trap." It can be inferred, then, that if a large insect didn't touch a second trigger hair until after the calcium ion concentrations had diminished appreciably, the Venus flytrap would fail to close.

Choice A is incorrect because the fourth paragraph makes clear that if the calcium concentration goes above the trap's threshold, the plant will close, not remain open. Choice C is incorrect because as the third paragraph explains, the touching of the trigger hair and opening of the calcium ion channels don't act to keep the trap open but are instead a precondition for the closing of the trap (though closing will occur only if a second trigger hair is touched). Choice D is incorrect because the last sentence of the fifth paragraph explains that the threshold for the time that can elapse between the touching of the first and second trigger hairs is twenty seconds, meaning that a large insect touching two hairs within ten seconds would almost certainly make the plant close.

QUESTION 49

Choice B is the best answer. The second sentence of the last paragraph says that Alexander Volkov and his colleagues "first demonstrated that it is indeed electricity that causes the Venus flytrap to close." In this context, the word "demonstrated" most nearly means established.

Choices A, C, and D are incorrect because in the context of scientists showing what causes the Venus flytrap to close, the word "demonstrated" most nearly means established, not protested (choice A), performed (choice C), or argued (choice D).

QUESTION 50

Choice B is the best answer. As described in the third paragraph, Hodick and Sievers's model emphasizes that the Venus flytrap closes by means of an electrical charge triggered when the plant's hairs are touched. But as explained in the last paragraph, when Alexander Volkov tested this model, the design of his experiment involved the direct application of an electrical charge, which "made the trap close without any direct touch to its trigger hairs." Therefore, Volkov's work could be criticized because his design omitted, rather than corroborated, a central element of Hodick and Sievers's model—namely, the physical stimulation of the hairs.

Choice A is incorrect because although the last paragraph explains that Volkov omitted an element of Hodick and Sievers's model when designing his own experiment, there is no suggestion that he did so out of a faulty understanding of their model. Choice C is incorrect because it is impossible to know from the passage if Hodick and Sievers would have objected to Volkov's methods. Choice D is incorrect because the passage doesn't indicate whether the technology Volkov used had been available to Hodick and Sievers when they formulated their model.

QUESTION 51

Choice C is the best answer. The previous question asks what potential criticism might be made of Volkov's testing of Hodick and Sievers's model. The answer, that a central element of that model wasn't corroborated by Volkov's measurements, is best supported in the last paragraph: "This made the trap close without any direct touch to its trigger hairs (while they didn't measure calcium levels, the current likely led to increases)." Because the physical touch to the hairs figured in Hodick and Sievers's model, it can be said that Volkov's decision to apply an electrical current directly to the plant means that he failed to corroborate a central element of their model.

Choices A, B, and D are incorrect because the cited lines don't support the answer to the previous question. Instead, they summarize the basic agreement of Volkov's work with Hodick and Sievers's model (choice A) and describe steps in Volkov's experimental design that are related to the application of an electrical current but don't directly address the omission of the central element of the physical touch to the hairs (choices B and D).

QUESTION 52

Choice C is the best answer. The second sentence of the last paragraph says that the focus of Volkov's work was the role of electricity in the Venus flytrap's closing mechanism. The paragraph goes on to explain that by applying electricity directly to the plant and "altering the amount of electrical current, Volkov could determine the exact electrical charge needed for the trap to close." It is therefore accurate to say that Volkov and his colleagues made the most extensive use of information obtained from measuring the plant's response to varying amounts of electrical current.

Choice A is incorrect because although the last paragraph explains that Volkov's work was based on Hodick and Sievers's mathematical model in which an electrical charge is required to close the Venus flytrap, that model isn't described as predicting the precise amount of charge required; moreover, although Volkov made use of this earlier model, it served as a starting point, and his work made greater use of the findings generated by his experiment. Choice B is incorrect because the passage doesn't describe Volkov's work as having involved analysis of data from earlier studies on the plant's response to electricity. Choice D is incorrect because although the last paragraph explains that Volkov based his work on Hodick and Sievers's earlier model, this was the sole model that Volkov relied on, and there is no suggestion that he made use of multiple "published theories" or "earlier models"; moreover, he made more extensive use of data generated by his own experiment than of Hodick and Sievers's model.

Section 2: Writing and Language Test

QUESTION 1

Choice D is the best answer. The prepositional phrase "for example" logically connects the two sentences and correctly indicates that what follows in the second sentence will be examples of household waste products: paper, glass, aluminum, and garbage.

Choices A, B, and C are incorrect because they don't indicate the true relationship between the two sentences. "Regardless" (choice A) means in spite of something, "however" (choice B) indicates a contrast, and "furthermore" (choice C) means in addition. None of these transitions indicates that an example will follow.

QUESTION 2

Choice B is the best answer. The verb "eliminate" means to remove, and it makes the most sense in the sentence because the object of the verb is "need." "Eliminating the need" is an idiomatic expression for "removing the need."

Choices A, C, and D are incorrect. Although all the choices mean "to get rid of," their connotations are different. "Annihilating" (choice A) is usually used to refer to the act of completely destroying, which is too intense in this context. "Ousting" (choice C) is generally used when referring to the act of forcibly removing a person from a position. "Closing the door on" (choice D) is a colloquial expression that usually means shutting out the possibility of something happening or not being willing to consider an idea. This expression doesn't fit the tone of the passage and is not idiomatic when used with "need."

QUESTION 3

Choice C is the best answer. The singular present tense verb "increases" agrees in number with the singular noun "compost" and maintains the parallel structure of the other two compound verbs in the sentence, "minimizes" and "helps."

Choices A and D are incorrect because the use of the pronoun "it" (choice A) and "also it" (choice D) to begin new independent clauses creates comma splices. Choice B is incorrect because "savings increase" doesn't maintain the parallel structure of the verbs in the sentence: "minimizes water waste and storm runoff" and "helps reduce erosion."

QUESTION 4

Choice B is the best answer. When setting off nonessential information, a pair of parentheses needs to be used. This choice provides the initial parenthesis that the parenthesis after "municipality" requires.

Choice A is incorrect because the initial parenthesis is missing and no comma is needed between the noun "quantities" and the modifying information. Choice C is incorrect because the initial parenthesis is missing. Choice D is incorrect because no semicolon is needed before the parenthetical information.

QUESTION 5

Choice D is the best answer. According to the information from the graph, 33 million tons of food waste were discarded in US landfills in 2009, which is consistent with the discussion of food waste in the passage.

Choices A, B, and C are incorrect because the passage thus far has focused on compost. Metal, rubber, leather, and textiles are not materials that are composted.

QUESTION 6

Choice C is the best answer. According to the graph, this is the only choice that makes the sentence true. More food waste was discarded in landfills in 2009 "than any other substance, including plastics or paper."

Choices A, B, and D are incorrect because they are not true, according to the graph. The graph indicates that less glass, metal, and yard waste were discarded in the landfills than plastics and paper.

QUESTION 7

Choice B is the best answer. No comma is needed between the comparative adjective "worse" and the comparative conjunction "than."

Choices A, C, and D are incorrect because the word "then" indicates "when" and is not used in comparisons (choices A and C), and no comma is needed after worse (choice D).

QUESTION 8

Choice C is the best answer. The present tense singular verb "contributes" agrees in number with the singular noun "material," and the present tense verb is consistent with the other present tense verbs in the passage.

Choices A and B are incorrect because "contribute" (choice A) and "are contributing" (choice B) are plural present tense verbs. Choice D is incorrect because "have contributed" is a plural past tense verb.

QUESTION 9

Choice A is the best answer. "Potent" means strong or powerful, which makes sense in the context of discussing greenhouse gas.

Choice B is incorrect because "sturdy" is usually used to refer to the physical strength or solidity of something. Choice C is incorrect because "influential" refers to the power of a person to affect or sway others or events without any apparent effort. Choice D is incorrect because "commanding" indicates that the inanimate greenhouse gas is actually commanding something.

QUESTION 10

Choice C is the best answer. "Armed with these facts" is the most effective transition from the previous paragraph, which discusses the amounts of various substances that end up in landfills and the resulting methane gas that is released from the organic matter. The paragraph that this transition introduces goes on to discuss laws that some cities have instituted to control the handling of compost in landfills to reduce the release of methane gas.

Choices A, B, and D are incorrect because they do not offer transitions that indicate a connection between the problem identified in the previous paragraph—the release of dangerous methane gas from the compost in landfills—and the concluding paragraph that identifies what some cities have done to help alleviate the problem.

QUESTION 11

Choice A is the best answer. No change is needed because the correlative conjunctions "either" and "or" are used together to indicate that one choice or another should be considered. In this sentence, residents are encouraged to choose the option to create their own compost piles or to dispose of compostable materials in bins for collection.

Choices B, C, and D are incorrect because they do not provide the correlating conjunction for "either" used earlier in the sentence.

QUESTION 12

Choice A is the best answer. The sentences are effectively combined by placing a comma after "red" and making the second sentence an appositive that explains the significance of the color red.

Choices B, C, and D are incorrect because they all contain excessive words that add no meaning to the resulting sentence.

QUESTION 13

Choice D is the best answer. Punctuation is not necessary in the underlined portion of the sentence.

Choice A is incorrect because no commas are needed after "festive" and "red" because the adjectives don't equally modify "banners." No comma is needed after "banners" because there is no reason to put one between "banners" and "and garlands," the two objects of the preposition "with." Choice B is incorrect because placing commas around the prepositional phrase "with festive red banners" wrongly indicates that the information is nonessential and could be eliminated without changing the meaning of the sentence. Choice C is incorrect because there should not be a dash or any other kind of punctuation between "banners" and "and garlands."

QUESTION 14

Choice C is the best answer. This choice expands on the idea that the lion dance may have originated to ward off an evil spirit and that dressing in a lion costume was part of the effort to scare the spirit away.

Choice A is incorrect because it doesn't make a connection between the fierce quality of a lion and scaring away spirits. Choices B and D are incorrect because the name of the spirit (choice B) and the location of the village where the dance originated (choice D) are not as important as why a lion was incorporated into the dance.

QUESTION 15

Choice C is the best answer. It ties the information about the possible origins and historical purpose of the lion dance to its present purpose as a New Year's celebration of hope.

Choices A, B, and D are incorrect because they don't effectively bring the paragraph to a conclusion. Each of these options is vague and calls for elaboration: choice A lacks specific information, choice B lacks proof for the idea of irrelevance, and choice D lacks a connection to the subject of the paragraph.

QUESTION 16

Choice A is the best answer. The pronoun "both" and prepositional phrase "of whom" refer to "dancers" and are used correctly to introduce a clause that describes how the dancers are hidden by the lion costume. "Whom" is used correctly as the object of the preposition "of."

Choice B is incorrect because the word order doesn't make grammatical sense and the pronoun "which" can't be used to refer to people. Choices C and D are incorrect because they create comma splices.

QUESTION 17

Choice D is the best answer. The pronoun "those" correctly indicates that the moves in dance are being compared to the moves in martial arts. "Those" takes the place of the noun "moves" in the comparison.

Choices A, B, and C are incorrect because they do not compare similar things. "Moves" can't be compared to "martial arts," "acrobatics," "disciplines," "martial artists," or "acrobats."

QUESTION 18

Choice B is the best answer. This choice indicates that the phoenix represents new beginnings, which is consistent in content with the information explaining that the tortoise represents longevity. Additionally, this choice is presented as a parenthetical prepositional phrase beginning with the preposition "for," which is consistent in structure with the parenthetical prepositional phrase "for longevity."

Choice A is incorrect because the parenthetical information indicates what a phoenix is, not what it represents. Furthermore, the information is not presented in a prepositional phrase. Choice C is incorrect because this choice indicates the source of the phoenix, not what it represents. Choice D is incorrect because it is vague and doesn't identify what the phoenix symbolizes.

QUESTION 19

Choice D is the best answer. Sentence 5 most logically should follow sentence 7. The pronoun "their" in sentence 5 refers to the "black lions" (which are the youngest lions and dance quickly) in sentence 7. Sentence 5 indicates that the "older counterparts" to the young lions don't move as quickly.

Choices A, B, and C are incorrect because placing sentence 5 after any other sentence in the paragraph would not be logical and would interrupt the flow of the passage.

QUESTION 20

Choice B is the best answer. The singular possessive pronoun "its" agrees in number with the singular antecedent "dance" and correctly indicates that the "climax" belongs to the dance.

Choice A is incorrect because "it's" is the contraction for "it is" and doesn't make sense in the sentence. Choice C is incorrect because "there" is not a possessive pronoun. Choice D is incorrect because "their" is a plural possessive pronoun that doesn't agree with the singular antecedent "dance."

QUESTION 21

Choice B is the best answer. This choice correctly indicates that the lion is doing the approaching and the snaring, not the teeth.

Choices A and D are incorrect because the teeth don't do the approaching or the snaring; only an animate object can do either. Choice C is incorrect because it is written in the passive voice, which changes the subject of the sentence from "lion" to "envelope." Furthermore, an "envelope" cannot approach a doorway.

QUESTION 22

Choice D is the best answer. The single word "envelope" is concise and clearly refers to the envelope that has been described earlier in the paragraph.

Choices A, B, and C are incorrect because they are wordy and contain information that has been given previously in the paragraph. Additionally, choice A contains inaccurate information because once the money has been chewed up, the envelope is no longer "money-filled."

QUESTION 23

Choice A is the best answer. No change is needed because "scrupulous" fits the formal tone of the passage. "Scrupulous" means exact and conscientious, and it is appropriate when discussing notes taken during a court proceeding.

Choices B and C are incorrect because they are too informal and therefore do not fit the tone of the passage. Choice D is incorrect because "intense" is an adjective that is used to describe something that is done to an extreme degree, such as putting forth effort or performing a physical act.

QUESTION 24

Choice C is the best answer. Commas after "hearings" and "depositions" are correct because they separate the first two items in a series of three.

Choices A, B, and D are incorrect because they all contain semicolons either after "hearings," "depositions," or both of the words. Semicolons can be used to separate items in a series that already contains commas, but not to separate individual items in a simple series of words or phrases.

QUESTION 25

Choice C is the best answer. The graph should not be added because it doesn't support the information in the paragraph. The paragraph describes what a court reporter does. The graph provides information that compares the median salary of court reporters to that of other jobs.

Choices A and B are incorrect because the graph should not be added. It neither supports the claim that court reporting is an important part of a trial nor offers a relevant counterpoint to the argument that the use of digital recorders is on the rise. Choice D is incorrect because it doesn't matter that there is no information provided in the graph about the pay scale for more experienced court reporters. The paragraph doesn't deal with the subject of pay, so therefore the graph doesn't support the paragraph.

QUESTION 26

Choice A is the best answer. No change needs to be made because the word "to" is the idiomatic preposition to connect "subject" with the phrase "human errors" to show that technology such as a digital recorder doesn't make the same mistakes that people make, such as "mishearing or mistyping."

Choices B and C are incorrect because the verb "subjected" is a transitive verb that requires a direct object, which is not present in the sentence. Furthermore, "subjected from" is not idiomatic. Choice D is incorrect because "subject for human errors" doesn't make sense.

QUESTION 27

Choice C is the best answer. The preposition "as" means "functioning in the same way" or "in the capacity of." The plural noun "record keepers" agrees in number with the plural noun "court reporters." The sentence indicates that court reporters are functioning as record keepers.

Choices A and D are incorrect because the singular "record keeper" can't be used to refer to plural "court reporters." Additionally, in choice D the infinitive verb phrase "to be" can't be used in place of a preposition. Choice B is incorrect because the word "each" is unnecessary and makes the sentence confusing.

QUESTION 28

Choice C is the best answer. To make the paragraph most logical, sentence 6 should be placed after sentence 3. Sentence 3 explains that the words the recorder types are "instantaneously" available to a judge to view on a computer screen. Sentence 6 explains, by using the transition "however," that even though words are available instantly, recording technology continues to improve and therefore the need for court reporters is decreasing.

Choices A, B, and D are incorrect because placing sentence 6 after any other sentence would not be logical and would interrupt the flow of the paragraph.

QUESTION 29

Choice B is the best answer. The dash most effectively combines the two sentences. It correctly indicates that what follows is explanatory information. In this case, the information after the dash could be inferred from what has already been stated because the opposite of making fewer mistakes is making more mistakes. The information after the dash in this sentence makes the conclusion overt.

Choice A is incorrect because the word "such" indicates incorrectly that an example of something will follow it. Choices C and D are incorrect because they are wordy and not as succinct as using a dash.

QUESTION 30

Choice B is the best answer. The comma is used correctly to separate the introductory dependent clause from the main independent clause that follows it.

Choice A is incorrect because a semicolon can't be used to separate a dependent and an independent clause. Choice C is incorrect because a period can't be used at the end of a dependent clause. Choice D is incorrect because the adverb "therefore" doesn't make sense in this context; what follows does not result from something said earlier in the sentence.

QUESTION 31

Choice B is the best answer. "In other words" indicates correctly that what follows will be an elaboration of the idea that digital recorders can't distinguish "important parts of the proceedings from other noises in the courtroom," "such as a book dropping."

Choices A, C, and D are incorrect because they don't show the true relationship between the two sentences. "Despite this" means that in spite of something already said, what follows will be the case. "Therefore" and "consequently" indicate that what follows will be the result of something said earlier. None of these offers a further explanation of what was previously said.

QUESTION 32

Choice D is the best answer. The prepositional phrase "between the words and the extrinsic noises" clearly and concisely identifies what a court reporter is able to distinguish. It is also the only parallel option, using two noun phrases after "between," which are joined by "and."

Choice A is incorrect because it needlessly repeats "distinguish between." Choice B is incorrect because it is not parallel or grammatical. Choice C is incorrect because it is wordy and wrongly suggests that court reporters distinguish between words and a time period (when).

QUESTION 33

Choice D is the best answer. The main idea of the paragraph is that court reporters can distinguish between words and extraneous noises in the courtroom, which digital recorders can't always do. This choice offers an example of what can go wrong in a courtroom because digital recorders can't always pick up "indistinct testimony": the need for retrial because of indistinct testimony from witnesses.

Choices A, B, and C are incorrect because they don't support the main idea of the paragraph. Making additional announcements at the beginning of a trial (choice A), monitoring to ensure equipment is functioning properly (choice B), and changing roles and duties of several members of the courtroom staff (choice C) are not examples of what can happen as a result of using digital recorders that can't distinguish words from other courtroom noises.

QUESTION 34

Choice B is the best answer. The adverb "however" indicates that regardless of the conditions that affect "combustion and the resulting fire" on Earth, their behavior in space is different.

Choices A, C, and D are incorrect because they do not show the true relationship between the information that comes before and what follows the linking adverb. "Moreover" means that additional information will follow; "accordingly" means that what follows corresponds to what has already been said or that what follows is a consequence; and "subsequently" means that what follows happens after what was previously stated. None of these choices indicates the difference between the behaviors of combustion and fire on Earth and in space.

QUESTION 35

Choice D is the best answer. The past tense verb "sought" clearly and concisely conveys the idea that the students were trying to find a method to study combustion of biofuels. Additionally, the word "biofuels" is correctly placed immediately in front of the parenthetical information that defines it to prevent confusion.

Choices A and B are incorrect because they are wordy and the word "biofuel" is not placed immediately in front of the parenthetical information that defines it. Choice C is incorrect because it uses the verb "looked," which is not preferable to "sought" in this science context.

QUESTION 36

Choice A is the best answer. No change needs to be made because the word "deformation" provides the most precise description of what results when fuel droplets lose their symmetrical form while burning. A droplet that is deformed loses some good attribute due to the influence of some external condition.

Choices B and D are incorrect because "alteration" and "modification" imply that something is changed on purpose. Choice C is incorrect because "transformation" means that one thing is changed into another. None of these choices is accurate when discussing the effect of "gravitational influence" and the "movement of molecules" on droplets of fuel.

QUESTION 37

Choice B is the best answer. The plural verbs "cause" and "limit" agree in number with the plural pronoun "both," which refers to the plural noun "variations."

Choices A and C are incorrect because "causes" and "limits" are singular verbs that don't agree in number with the plural pronoun "both." Choice D is incorrect because "has caused" and "has limited" are also singular verbs. Additionally, they are present perfect tense verbs that are used to describe a past event that has an influence on the present, which is not the case in this context.

QUESTION 38

Choice D is the best answer. The underlined portion should be deleted because "built for this purpose" repeats the idea of being "specially designed" used previously in the sentence.

Choices A, B, and C are incorrect because they are redundant. There is no reason to repeat the idea of "specially designed."

QUESTION 39

Choice B is the best answer. This choice offers the most effective transition because it links the previously mentioned problems of conducting the biofuel experiment to the UCSD students' solution: participating in NASA's Microgravity University program.

Choices A, C, and D are incorrect because they don't link the previously identified problems with the specific solution: a program that could help the students overcome too little microgravity time and too small droplets.

QUESTION 40

Choice D is the best answer. The commas after "weightlessness" and "space" are used correctly to set off the nonessential information between them. The information between the commas could be removed and the sentence would still make sense.

Choice A is incorrect because it is missing the comma after "weightlessness." In this context, choices B and C are incorrect because the commas are misplaced. In each of these choices, if the information between the commas were removed, the sentence would not make sense.

QUESTION 41

Choice A is the best answer. The addition should be made because the information specifically identifies an advantage the students gained by working with NASA's Microgravity University program: not traveling to space.

Choice B is incorrect because it isn't accurate. The previous paragraph does suggest that the students didn't actually go into space by stating that researchers fly their experiments aboard aircraft that simulate the microgravity environment. Choices C and D are incorrect because the addition should be made. The addition neither shifts focus away from the students' experiences while on the flight nor restates what has already been said in the sentence.

QUESTION 42

Choice D is the best answer. This choice, "were able to investigate," focuses on what the flights enabled the UCSD students to do that they were not able to do previously using the drop towers. It is consistent with the previous sentence, which states what the flights allowed the students to do.

Choices A, B, and C are incorrect because their focus is on "investigating" and not on allowing or enabling the students to investigate combustion in an environment that provided larger droplets and microgravity similar to that experienced in space.

QUESTION 43

Choice A is the best answer. No change is needed because the larger "spherically symmetric" droplets indicate that the flights remedied the problem of smaller deformed droplets mentioned earlier in the passage.

Choices B, C, and D are incorrect because none of these choices refers to the size or shape of the biofuel droplets, which is what made the investigation of combustion and fire on Earth problematic.

QUESTION 44

Choice C is the best answer. No comma is needed in the underlined phrase, which clearly and concisely expresses the improved techniques for fighting fires in space or at future outposts on the Moon and Mars that may result from better combustion-rate models.

Choices A and B are incorrect because the commas are incorrectly separating the prepositional phrases from the noun "techniques." Choice D is incorrect because the pair of commas indicate that the information contained between them is nonessential, which isn't accurate.

Section 3: Math Test – No Calculator

QUESTION 1

Choice D is correct. Combining like terms on each side of the given equation yields $6x - 5 = 7 + 2x$. Adding 5 to both sides of $6x - 5 = 7 + 2x$ and subtracting $2x$ from both sides yields $4x = 12$. Dividing both sides of $4x = 12$ by 4 yields $x = 3$.

Choices A, B, and C are incorrect because substituting those values into the equation $3x + x + x + x - 3 - 2 = 7 + x + x$ will result in a false statement. For example, in choice B, substituting 1 for x in the equation would give $3(1) + 1 + 1 + 1 - 3 - 2 = 7 + 1 + 1$, which yields the false statement $1 = 9$; therefore, x cannot equal 1.

QUESTION 2

Choice A is correct. The line passes through the origin. Therefore, this is a relationship of the form $d = km$, where k is a constant representing the slope of the graph. To find the value of k, choose a point (m, d) on the graph of the line other than the origin and substitute the values of m and d into the equation. For example, if the point (2, 4) is chosen, then $4 = k(2)$, and $k = 2$. Therefore, the equation of the line is $d = 2m$.

Choice B is incorrect and may result from calculating the slope of the line as the change in time over the change in distance traveled instead of the change in distance traveled over the change in time. Choices C and D are incorrect because each of these equations represents a line with a d-intercept of 2. However, the graph shows a line with a d-intercept of 0.

QUESTION 3

Choice A is correct. Multiplying both sides of the equation by 6 results in $6E = O + 4M + P$. Then, subtracting $O + 4M$ from both sides of $6E = O + 4M + P$ gives $P = 6E - O - 4M$.

Choice B is incorrect. This choice may result from solving for $-P$ instead of for P. Choice C is incorrect and may result from transposing P with E in the given equation rather than solving for P. Choice D is incorrect and may result from transposing P with E and changing the sign of E rather than solving for P.

QUESTION 4

Choice C is correct. Since $RT = TU$, it follows that ΔRTU is an isosceles triangle with base RU. Therefore, $\angle TRU$ and $\angle TUR$ are the base angles of an isosceles triangle and are congruent. Let the measures of both $\angle TRU$ and $\angle TUR$ be $t°$. According to the triangle sum theorem, the sum of the measures of the three angles of a triangle is 180°. Therefore, $114° + 2t° = 180°$, so $t = 33$.

Note that $\angle TUR$ is the same angle as $\angle SUV$. Thus, the measure of $\angle SUV$ is 33°. According to the triangle exterior angle theorem, an external angle of a triangle is equal to the sum of the opposite interior angles. Therefore, $x°$ is equal to the sum of the measures of $\angle VSU$ and $\angle SUV$; that is, $31° + 33° = 64°$. Thus, the value of x is 64.

Choice B is incorrect. This is the measure of $\angle STR$, but $\angle STR$ is not congruent to $\angle SVR$. Choices A and D are incorrect and may result from a calculation error.

QUESTION 5

Choice B is correct. It is given that the width of the dance floor is w feet. The length is 6 feet longer than the width; therefore, the length of the dance floor is $w + 6$. So the perimeter is $w + w + (w + 6) + (w + 6) = 4w + 12$.

Choice A is incorrect because it is the sum of one length and one width, which is only half the perimeter. Choice C is incorrect and may result from using the formula for the area instead of the formula for the perimeter and making a calculation error. Choice D is incorrect because this is the area, not the perimeter, of the dance floor.

QUESTION 6

Choice B is correct. Subtracting the same number from each side of an inequality gives an equivalent inequality. Hence, subtracting 1 from each side of the inequality $2x > 5$ gives $2x - 1 > 4$. So the given system of inequalities is equivalent to the system of inequalities $y > 2x - 1$ and $2x - 1 > 4$, which can be rewritten as $y > 2x - 1 > 4$. Using the transitive property of inequalities, it follows that $y > 4$.

Choice A is incorrect because there are points with a y-coordinate less than 6 that satisfy the given system of inequalities. For example, (3, 5.5) satisfies both inequalities. Choice C is incorrect. This may result from solving the inequality $2x > 5$ for x, then replacing x with y. Choice D is incorrect because this inequality allows y-values that are not the y-coordinate of any point that satisfies both inequalities. For example, $y = 2$ is contained in the set $y > \frac{3}{2}$; however, if 2 is substituted into the first inequality for y, the result is $x < \frac{3}{2}$. This cannot be true because the second inequality gives $x > \frac{5}{2}$.

QUESTION 7

Choice B is correct. Subtracting 4 from both sides of $\sqrt{2x + 6} + 4 = x + 3$ isolates the radical expression on the left side of the equation as follows: $\sqrt{2x + 6} = x - 1$. Squaring both sides of $\sqrt{2x + 6} = x - 1$ yields $2x + 6 = x^2 - 2x + 1$. This equation can be rewritten as a quadratic equation in standard form: $x^2 - 4x - 5 = 0$. One way to solve this quadratic equation is to factor the expression $x^2 - 4x - 5$ by identifying two numbers with a sum of -4 and a product of -5. These numbers are -5 and 1. So the quadratic equation can be factored as $(x - 5)(x + 1) = 0$. It follows that 5 and -1 are the solutions to the quadratic equation. However, the solutions must be verified by checking whether 5 and -1 satisfy the original equation, $\sqrt{2x + 6} + 4 = x + 3$. When $x = -1$, the original equation gives $\sqrt{2(-1) + 6} + 4 = (-1) + 3$, or $6 = 2$, which is false. Therefore, -1 does not satisfy the original equation. When $x = 5$, the original equation gives $\sqrt{2(5) + 6} + 4 = 5 + 3$, or $8 = 8$, which is true. Therefore, $x = 5$ is the only solution to the original equation, and so the solution set is $\{5\}$.

Choices A, C, and D are incorrect because each of these sets contains at least one value that results in a false statement when substituted into the given equation. For instance, in choice D, when 0 is substituted for x into the given equation, the result is $\sqrt{2(0) + 6} + 4 = (0) + 3$, or $\sqrt{6} + 4 = 3$. This is not a true statement, so 0 is not a solution to the given equation.

QUESTION 8

Choice D is correct. Since $x^3 - 9x = x(x + 3)(x - 3)$ and $x^2 - 2x - 3 = (x + 1)(x - 3)$, the fraction $\frac{f(x)}{g(x)}$ can be written as $\frac{x(x + 3)(x - 3)}{(x + 1)(x - 3)}$. It is given that $x > 3$, so the common factor $x - 3$ is not equal to 0. Therefore, the fraction can be further simplified to $\frac{x(x + 3)}{x + 1}$.

Choice A is incorrect. The expression $\frac{1}{x+1}$ is not equivalent to $\frac{f(x)}{g(x)}$ because at $x = 0$, $\frac{1}{x+1}$ as a value of 1 and $\frac{f(x)}{g(x)}$ has a value of 0.

Choice B is incorrect and results from omitting the factor x in the factorization of $f(x)$. Choice C is incorrect and may result from incorrectly factoring $g(x)$ as $(x + 1)(x + 3)$ instead of $(x + 1)(x - 3)$.

QUESTION 9

Choice A is correct. The standard form for the equation of a circle is $(x - h)^2 + (y - k)^2 = r^2$, where (h, k) are the coordinates of the center and r is the length of the radius. According to the given equation, the center of the circle is $(6, -5)$. Let (x_1, y_1) represent the coordinates of point Q. Since point P $(10, -5)$ and point Q (x_1, y_1) are the endpoints of a diameter of the circle, the center $(6, -5)$ lies on the diameter, halfway between P and Q. Therefore, the following relationships hold: $\frac{x_1 + 10}{2} = 6$ and $\frac{y_1 + (-5)}{2} = -5$. Solving the equations for x_1 and y_1, respectively, yields $x_1 = 2$ and $y_1 = -5$. Therefore, the coordinates of point Q are $(2, -5)$.

Alternate approach: Since point P $(10, -5)$ on the circle and the center of the circle $(6, -5)$ have the same y-coordinate, it follows that the radius of the circle is $10 - 6 = 4$. In addition, the opposite end of the diameter $\overline{PQ}$ must have the same y-coordinate as P and be 4 units away from the center. Hence, the coordinates of point Q must be $(2, -5)$.

Choices B and D are incorrect because the points given in these choices lie on a diameter that is perpendicular to the diameter $\overline{PQ}$. If either of these points were point Q, then $\overline{PQ}$ would not be the diameter of the circle. Choice C is incorrect because $(6, -5)$ is the center of the circle and does not lie on the circle.

QUESTION 10

Choice C is correct. Let x represent the number of 2-person tents and let y represent the number of 4-person tents. It is given that the total number of tents was 60 and the total number of people in the group was 202. This situation can be expressed as a system of two equations, $x + y = 60$ and $2x + 4y = 202$. The first equation can be rewritten as $y = -x + 60$. Substituting $-x + 60$ for y in the equation $2x + 4y = 202$ yields $2x + 4(-x + 60) = 202$. Distributing and combining like terms gives $-2x + 240 = 202$. Subtracting 240 from both sides of $-2x + 240 = 202$ and then dividing both sides by -2 gives $x = 19$. Therefore, the number of 2-person tents is 19.

Alternate approach: If each of the 60 tents held 4 people, the total number of people that could be accommodated in tents would be 240. However, the actual number of people who slept in tents was 202. The difference of 38 accounts for the 2-person tents. Since each of these tents holds 2 people fewer than a 4-person tent, $\frac{38}{2} = 19$ gives the number of 2-person tents.

Choice A is incorrect. This choice may result from assuming exactly half of the tents hold 2 people. If that were true, then the total number of people who slept in tents would be $2(30) + 4(30) = 180$; however, the total number of people who slept in tents was 202, not 180. Choice B is incorrect. If 20 tents were 2-person tents, then the remaining 40 tents would be 4-person tents. Since all the tents were filled to capacity, the total number of people who slept in tents would be $2(20) + 4(40) = 40 + 160 = 200$; however, the total number of people who slept in tents was 202, not 200. Choice D is incorrect. If 18 tents were 2-person tents, then the remaining 42 tents would be 4-person tents. Since all the tents were filled to capacity, the total number of people who slept in tents would be $2(18) + 4(42) = 36 + 168 = 204$; however, the total number of people who slept in tents was 202, not 204.

QUESTION 11

Choice B is correct. The x-coordinates of the x-intercepts of the graph are -3, 0, and 2. This means that if $y = f(x)$ is the equation of the graph, where f is a polynomial function, then $(x + 3)$, x, and $(x - 2)$ are factors of f. Of the choices given, A and B have the correct factors. However, in choice A, x is raised to the first power, and in choice B, x is raised to the second power. At $x = 0$, the graph touches the x-axis but doesn't cross it. This means that x, as a factor of f, is raised to an even power. If x were raised to an odd power, then the graph would cross the x-axis. Alternatively, in choice A, f is a third-degree polynomial, and in choice B, f is a fourth-degree polynomial. The y-coordinates of points on the graph become large and positive as x becomes large and negative; this is consistent with a fourth-degree polynomial, but not with a third-degree polynomial. Therefore, of the choices given, only choice B could be the equation of the graph.

Choice A is incorrect. The graph of the equation in this answer choice has the correct factors. However, at $x = 0$ the graph of the equation in this choice crosses the x-axis; the graph shown touches the x-axis but doesn't cross it. Choices C and D are incorrect and are likely the result of misinterpreting the relationship between the x-intercepts of a graph of a polynomial function and the factors of the polynomial expression.

QUESTION 12

Choice D is correct. Dividing both sides of equation $\frac{2a}{b} = \frac{1}{2}$ by 2 gives $\frac{a}{b} = \frac{1}{4}$. Taking the reciprocal of both sides yields $\frac{b}{a} = 4$.

Choice A is incorrect. This is the value of $\frac{a}{2b}$, not $\frac{b}{a}$. Choice B is incorrect. This is the value of $\frac{a}{b}$, not $\frac{b}{a}$. Choice C is incorrect. This is the value of $\frac{b}{2a}$, not $\frac{b}{a}$.

QUESTION 13

Choice C is correct. It is assumed that the oil and gas production decreased at a constant rate. Therefore, the function f that best models the production t years after the year 2000 can be written as a linear function, $f(t) = mt + b$, where m is the rate of change of the oil and gas production and b is the oil and gas production, in millions of barrels, in the year 2000. Since there were 4 million barrels of oil and gas produced in 2000, $b = 4$. The rate of change, m, can be calculated as $\frac{4 - 1.9}{0 - 13} = -\frac{2.1}{13}$, which is equivalent to $-\frac{21}{130}$, the rate of change in choice C.

Choices A and B are incorrect because each of these functions has a positive rate of change. Since the oil and gas production decreased over time, the rate of change must be negative. Choice D is incorrect. This model may result from misinterpreting 1.9 million barrels as the amount by which the production decreased.

QUESTION 14

Choice C is correct. The second equation of the system can be rewritten as $y = 5x - 8$. Substituting $5x - 8$ for y in the first equation gives $5x - 8 = x^2 + 3x - 7$. This equation can be solved as shown below:

$$x^2 + 3x - 7 - 5x + 8 = 0$$

$$x^2 - 2x + 1 = 0$$

$$(x - 1)^2 = 0$$

$$x = 1$$

Substituting 1 for x in the equation $y = 5x - 8$ gives $y = -3$. Therefore, $(1, -3)$ is the only solution to the system of equations.

Choice A is incorrect. In the xy-plane, a parabola and a line can intersect at no more than two points. Since the graph of the first equation is a parabola and the graph of the second equation is a line, the system cannot have more than 2 solutions. Choice B is incorrect. There is a single ordered pair (x, y) that satisfies both equations of the system. Choice D is incorrect because the ordered pair $(1, -3)$ satisfies both equations of the system.

QUESTION 15

Choice D is correct. Since $h(x) = 1 - g(x)$, substituting 0 for x yields $h(0) = 1 - g(0)$. Evaluating $g(0)$ gives $g(0) = 2(0) - 1 = -1$. Therefore, $h(0) = 1 - (-1) = 2$.

Choice A is incorrect. This choice may result from an arithmetic error. Choice B is incorrect. This choice may result from incorrectly evaluating $g(0)$ to be 1. Choice C is incorrect. This choice may result from evaluating $1 - 0$ instead of $1 - g(0)$.

QUESTION 16

The correct answer is 3. The solution to the given equation can be found by factoring the quadratic expression. The factors can be determined by finding two numbers with a sum of 1 and a product of −12. The two numbers that meet these constraints are 4 and −3. Therefore, the given equation can be rewritten as $(x + 4)(x - 3) = 0$. It follows that the solutions to the equation are $x = -4$ or $x = 3$. Since it is given that $a > 0$, a must equal 3.

QUESTION 17

The correct answer is 32. The sum of the given expressions is $(-2x^2 + x + 31) + (3x^2 + 7x - 8)$. Combining like terms yields $x^2 + 8x + 23$. Based on the form of the given equation, $a = 1$, $b = 8$, and $c = 23$. Therefore, $a + b + c = 32$.

Alternate approach: Because $a + b + c$ is the value of $ax^2 + bx + c$ when $x = 1$, it is possible to first make that substitution into each polynomial before adding them. When $x = 1$, the first polynomial is equal to $-2 + 1 + 31 = 30$ and the second polynomial is equal to $3 + 7 - 8 = 2$. The sum of 30 and 2 is 32.

QUESTION 18

The correct answer is $\frac{3}{2}$. One method for solving the system of equations for y is to add corresponding sides of the two equations. Adding the left-hand sides gives $(-x + y) + (x + 3y)$, or $4y$. Adding the right-hand sides yields $-3.5 + 9.5 = 6$. It follows that $4y = 6$. Finally, dividing both sides of $4y = 6$ by 4 yields $y = \frac{6}{4}$ or $\frac{3}{2}$. Any of 3/2, 6/4, 9/6, 12/8 or the decimal equivalent 1.5 will be scored as correct.

QUESTION 19

The correct answer is 8. The number of employees, y, expected to be employed by the company x quarters after the company opened can be modeled by the equation $y = ax + b$, where a represents the constant rate of change in the number of employees each quarter and b represents the number of employees with which the company opened. The company's growth plan assumes that 2 employees will be hired each quarter, so $a = 2$. The number of employees the company opened with was 8, so $b = 8$.

QUESTION 20

The correct answer is 144. In a circle, the ratio of the length of a given arc to the circle's circumference is equal to the ratio of the measure of the arc, in degrees, to 360°. The ratio between the arc length and the circle's circumference is given as $\frac{2}{5}$. It follows that $\frac{2}{5} = \frac{x}{360}$. Solving this proportion for x gives $x = 144$.

Section 4: Math Test – Calculator

QUESTION 1

Choice A is correct. If one pound of grapes costs \$2, two pounds of grapes will cost 2 times \$2, three pounds of grapes will cost 3 times \$2, and so on. Therefore, c pounds of grapes will cost c times \$2, which is $2c$ dollars.

Choice B is incorrect and may result from incorrectly adding instead of multiplying. Choice C is incorrect and may result from assuming that c pounds cost \$2, and then finding the cost per pound. Choice D is incorrect and could result from incorrectly assuming that 2 pounds cost \$$c$, and then finding the cost per pound.

QUESTION 2

Choice C is correct. According to the graph, the number of figurines decreased between 1 and 2 months and between 3 and 4 months. Because the line segment between 3 and 4 months is steeper than the line segment between 1 and 2 months, it follows that the number of figurines decreased the fastest between 3 and 4 months.

Choice A is incorrect. Between 1 and 2 months, the number of figurines decreased. However, the number of figurines decreased faster during the interval between 3 and 4 months. Choices B and D are incorrect. The number of figurines during these intervals was increasing, not decreasing.

QUESTION 3

Choice A is correct. The fraction of the cars in the random sample that have a manufacturing defect is $\frac{3}{200} = 0.015$. At this rate, out of 10,000 cars there would be $0.015 \times 10{,}000 = 150$ cars that have a manufacturing defect.

Choices B, C, and D are incorrect because the fractions of cars in the population that have a defect, $\frac{200}{10{,}000} = 0.02$ in choice B, $\frac{250}{10{,}000} = 0.025$ in choice C, and $\frac{300}{10{,}000} = 0.03$ in choice D, are all different from the fraction of cars in the sample with a manufacturing defect, which is 0.015.

QUESTION 4

Choice C is correct. The given line of best fit can be used to predict the length when the width is known. The equation of the line of best fit is given as $y = 1.67x + 21.1$, where x is the width in millimeters and y is the predicted length in millimeters. If the width of the petal is 19 millimeters, then $x = 19$ and $y = 1.67(19) + 21.1 = 52.83$.

Choice A is incorrect and may result from incorrectly using $x = 0$ in the equation. Choice B is incorrect and may result from neglecting to add 21.1 in the computation. Choice D is incorrect and may result from an arithmetic error.

QUESTION 5

Choice B is correct. Let the measure of the third angle in the smaller triangle be $a°$. Since lines ℓ and m are parallel and cut by transversals, it follows that the corresponding angles formed are congruent. So $a° = y° = 20°$. The sum of the measures of the interior angles of a triangle is 180°, which for the interior angles in the smaller triangle yields $a + x + z = 180$. Given that $z = 60$ and $a = 20$, it follows that $20 + x + 60 = 180$. Solving for x gives $x = 180 - 60 - 20$, or $x = 100$.

Choice A is incorrect and may result from incorrectly assuming that angles $x + z = 180$. Choice C is incorrect and may result from incorrectly assuming that the smaller triangle is a right triangle, with x as the right angle. Choice D is incorrect and may result from a misunderstanding of the exterior angle theorem and incorrectly assuming that $x = y + z$.

QUESTION 6

Choice D is correct. Since only two types of tickets were sold and a total of 350 tickets were sold, the sum of the numbers of both types of ticket sold must be 350. Therefore, $B + L = 350$. Since the bench tickets were \$75 each, the income from B bench tickets was $75B$. Similarly, since the lawn tickets were \$40 each, the income from L lawn tickets sold was $40L$. The total income from all tickets was \$19,250. So the sum of the income from bench tickets and lawn tickets sold must equal 19,250. Therefore, $75B + 40L = 19{,}250$. Only choice D has both correct equations.

Choice A is incorrect and may result from incorrectly multiplying the income from each type of ticket instead of adding them. It also incorrectly uses 1,950 instead of 19,250. Choice B is incorrect and may result from confusing the cost of bench tickets with the cost of lawn tickets. Choice C is incorrect and may result from confusing the total number of tickets sold with the total amount raised.

QUESTION 7

Choice C is correct. The graph of an equation given in the form $y = mx + b$ has slope m. The equation in choice C is $y = 3x + 2$, so the slope of its graph is 3.

Choices A, B, and D are incorrect. They are all given in the form $y = mx + b$, where m is the slope. Therefore, choice A has a graph with a slope of $\frac{1}{3}$, choice B has a graph with a slope of 1 (because $x = 1 \cdot x$), and choice D has a graph with a slope of 6.

QUESTION 8

Choice B is correct. Multiplying both sides of the equation by $x + 1$ gives $(x + 1)^2 = 2$. This means $x + 1$ is a number whose square is 2, so $(x + 1)$ is either $\sqrt{2}$ or $-\sqrt{2}$. Therefore, $\sqrt{2}$ is a possible value for $x + 1$.

Choice A is incorrect and may result from trying to find the value of x instead of $x + 1$ and making a sign error. Choice C is incorrect and may result from solving for $(x + 1)^2$ instead of $x + 1$. Choice D is incorrect and may result from squaring instead of taking the square root to find the value of $x + 1$.

QUESTION 9

Choice D is correct. Using the volume formula $V = \frac{7\pi k^3}{48}$ and the given information that the volume of the glass is 473 cubic centimeters, the value of k can be found as follows:

$$473 = \frac{7\pi k^3}{48}$$

$$k^3 = \frac{473(48)}{7\pi}$$

$$k = \sqrt[3]{\frac{473(48)}{7\pi}} \approx 10.10690$$

Therefore, the value of k is approximately 10.11 centimeters.

Choices A, B, and C are incorrect. Substituting the values of k from these choices in the formula results in volumes of approximately 7 cubic centimeters, 207 cubic centimeters, and 217 cubic centimeters, respectively, all of which contradict the given information that the volume of the glass is 473 cubic centimeters.

QUESTION 10

Choice C is correct. Due to the shape of the glass, if the water is poured at a constant rate, the height of the water level will increase faster initially, where the diameter of the glass is smaller, and increase more slowly later, as the diameter of the glass increases. Choice C is the only graph that shows this behavior: it is steeper initially and then gets less steep.

Choice A is incorrect since it shows the height of the water level increasing at a constant rate over time. Choice B is incorrect since it shows the height of the water level increasing slowly at first and faster later. Choice D is incorrect since it shows the height of the water level staying constant even as water is being poured into the glass.

QUESTION 11

Choice B is correct. It is given that the volume of the glass is approximately 16 fluid ounces. If Jenny has 1 gallon of water, which is 128 fluid ounces, she could fill the glass $\frac{128}{16} = 8$ times.

Choice A is incorrect because Jenny would need 16 × 16 fluid ounces = 256 fluid ounces, or 2 gallons, of water to fill the glass 16 times. Choice C is incorrect because Jenny would need only 4 × 16 fluid ounces = 64 fluid ounces of water to fill the glass 4 times. Choice D is incorrect because Jenny would need only 3 × 16 fluid ounces = 48 fluid ounces to fill the glass 3 times.

QUESTION 12

Choice C is correct. Since Roberto sells only two types of policies and he didn't meet his goal of selling at least 57 policies, the sum of x, the number of $50,000 policies, and y, the number of $100,000 policies, must be less than 57. Symbolically, that is $x + y < 57$. The total value, in dollars, from selling x number of $50,000 policies is $50,000x$. The total value, in dollars, from selling y number of $100,000 policies is $100,000y$. Since the total value of the policies he sold was over $3,000,000, it follows that $50,000x + 100,000y > 3,000,000$. Only choice C has both correct inequalities.

Choice A is incorrect because the total value, in dollars, of the policies Roberto sold was greater than, not less than, 3,000,000. Choice B is incorrect because Roberto didn't meet his goal, so $x + y$ should be less than, not greater than, 57. Choice D is incorrect because both inequalities misrepresent the situation.

QUESTION 13

Choice C is correct. Since a has the exponent $-\frac{1}{2}$, a can be isolated by raising both sides of the equation to the −2 power.

$$a^{\left(-\frac{1}{2}\right)(-2)} = x^{-2}$$

$$a = x^{-2}$$

$$a = \frac{1}{x^2}$$

Alternate method:

$$a^{-\frac{1}{2}} = \frac{1}{a^{\frac{1}{2}}} = \frac{1}{\sqrt{a}}$$

So,

$$\frac{1}{\sqrt{a}} = x$$

Square both sides of the equation:

$$\frac{1}{a} = x^2$$

Then take the reciprocal of both sides:

$$a = \frac{1}{x^2}$$

Choice A is incorrect and may result from incorrectly taking the square root of both sides to eliminate the exponent of a. Choice B is incorrect and may result from incorrectly taking the square root of both sides to eliminate the exponent of a, and incorrectly multiplying by −1 to make the exponent positive. Choice D is incorrect and may result from incorrectly multiplying by −1 to make the exponent positive.

QUESTION 14

Choice D is correct. A rational expression is undefined when the denominator is 0. To determine the values of x that result in a denominator of 0, set the denominator equal to 0 and solve for x:

$x^2 + 3x - 10 = 0$

$(x + 5)(x - 2) = 0$

$x + 5 = 0$ or $x - 2 = 0$

$x = -5$ or $x = 2$

Among the answer choices, only the value $x = 2$ is listed, so choice D is correct.

Choice A is incorrect. When $x = -3$, the denominator is $(-3)^2 + 3(-3) - 10 = -10$, so the given expression is not undefined. Choice B is incorrect and may result from incorrectly factoring the denominator or incorrectly assuming that if $(x - 2)$ is a factor, then $x = -2$ is a solution. Choice C is incorrect and may result from giving the value of the denominator that makes the given expression undefined rather than the value of x that makes the denominator equal to 0.

QUESTION 15

Choice D is correct. Since density is mass per unit volume, the mass is the density times volume. The volume of a right rectangular prism is the product of the lengths of the sides. Therefore:

mass = (2.8 grams per cubic centimeter) × (30 centimeters × 40 centimeters × 50 centimeters)

mass = (2.8 grams per cubic centimeter) × (60,000 cubic centimeters)

mass = 168,000 grams

Choice A is incorrect and may result from adding, instead of multiplying, the lengths of the sides to find the volume. Choice B is incorrect and may result from the same error as in choice A, as well as a place value error. Choice C is incorrect and may result from a place value error when finding the volume.

QUESTION 16

Choice B is correct. A total of 150 adults received the sugar pill. Of those, 33 reported contracting a cold. Therefore, $\frac{33}{150}$, or the equivalent $\frac{11}{50}$, is the proportion of adults receiving a sugar pill who reported contracting a cold.

Choice A is incorrect. This is the proportion of adults receiving a sugar pill and contracting a cold to all adults contracting a cold $\left(\frac{33}{54}\right)$. Choice C is incorrect. This is the proportion of adults who reported contracting a cold to all the participants in the study $\left(\frac{54}{300} = \frac{9}{50}\right)$. Choice D is incorrect. This is the proportion of adults who received a sugar pill and reported contracting a cold to all the participants in the study $\left(\frac{33}{300} = \frac{11}{100}\right)$.

QUESTION 17

Choice A is correct. The mode is the data value with the highest frequency. So for the data shown, the mode is 18. The median is the middle data value when the data values are sorted from least to greatest. Since there are 20 ages ordered, the median is the average of the two middle values, the 10th and 11th, which for these data are both 19. Therefore, the median is 19. The mean is the sum of the data values divided by the number of the data values. So for these data, the mean is

$$\frac{(18 \times 6) + (19 \times 5) + (20 \times 4) + (21 \times 2) + (22 \times 1) + (23 \times 1) + (30 \times 1)}{20} = 20.$$

Since the mode is 18, the median is 19, and the mean is 20, mode < median < mean.

Choice B and D are incorrect because the mean is greater than the median. Choice C is incorrect because the median is greater than the mode.

Alternate approach: After determining the mode, 18, and the median, 19, it remains to determine whether the mean is less than 19 or more than 19. Because the mean is a balancing point, there is as much deviation below the mean as above the mean. It is possible to compare the data to 19 to determine the balance of deviation above and below the mean. There is a total deviation of only 6 below 19 (the 6 values of 18); however, the data value 30 alone deviates by 11 above 19. Thus the mean must be greater than 19.

QUESTION 18

Choice C is correct. Based on the line of best fit shown, the predicted percent of leaf litter mass remaining for a forest with a mean annual temperature of −2°C is about 70%.

Choice A is incorrect; it is the predicted percent of leaf litter mass remaining at about 6.5°C. Choice B is incorrect; it is the predicted percent of leaf litter mass remaining at 2°C instead of at −2°C. Choice D is incorrect; it is the predicted percent of leaf litter mass remaining at about −7°C.

QUESTION 19

Choice A is correct. Since zeros of f correspond to the x-intercepts of the graph of f, and the range of f gives all the possible y-values on the graph of the function, the correct graph of the function has only points with y-values less than or equal to 4, and crosses the x-axis at only $(-3, 0)$ and $(1, 0)$. The graph in choice A satisfies both of these conditions.

Choice B is incorrect. The graph of the function matches the range given, but the zeros are at -1 and 3, not -3 and 1. Choice C is incorrect. The graph has y-values greater than 4. Choice D is incorrect. Even though the graph has zeros at -3 and 1, it has an additional zero at 0, and the range of the graph is the set of all real numbers.

QUESTION 20

Choice B is correct. The savings each year from installing the geothermal heating system will be the average annual energy cost for the home before the geothermal heating system installation minus the average annual energy cost after the geothermal heating system installation, which is $(4{,}334 - 2{,}712)$ dollars. In t years, the savings will be $(4{,}334 - 2{,}712)t$ dollars. Therefore, the inequality that can be solved to find the number of years after installation at which the total amount of energy cost savings will exceed (be greater than) the installation cost, \$25,000, is $25{,}000 < (4{,}334 - 2{,}712)t$.

Choice A is incorrect. It gives the number of years after installation at which the total amount of energy cost savings will be less than the installation cost. Choice C is incorrect and may result from subtracting the average annual energy cost for the home from the onetime cost of the geothermal heating system installation. To find the predicted total savings, the predicted average cost should be subtracted from the average annual energy cost before the installation, and the result should be multiplied by the number of years, t. Choice D is incorrect and may result from misunderstanding the context. The ratio $\frac{4{,}332}{2{,}712}$ compares the average energy cost before installation and the average energy cost after installation; it does not represent the savings.

QUESTION 21

Choice D is correct. The number 3.39 in the equation $y = 3.39x + 46.89$ is the slope, which is the change in y per unit change in x. Because y represents the amount of plastic produced annually, in billions of pounds, and x represents the number of years since 1985, the number 3.39 represents the rate of change of the amount of plastic produced with respect to time, in units of billions of pounds per year. The change is an increase since 3.39 is positive, and it is described as an average change because the data show increases that are sometimes more and sometimes less than 3.39.

Choice A is incorrect. It is the interpretation of the number 46.89 in the line of best fit equation, $y = 3.39x + 46.89$. Choices B and C are incorrect because they are expressed in the wrong units. The number 3.39 has units of billions of pounds per year, but choice B has units of years and choice C has units of billions of pounds.

QUESTION 22

Choice A is correct. Since x is the number of years since 1985, the year 2000 corresponds to $x = 15$ and the year 2003 corresponds to $x = 18$. The corresponding points on the line of best fit are approximately (15, 98) and (18, 107). This means that approximately 98 billion pounds of plastic were produced in 2000 and approximately 107 billion pounds of plastic were produced in 2003. To calculate the percent increase, subtract the amount of plastic produced in 2000 from the amount of plastic produced in 2003 and then divide the result by the amount of plastic produced in 2000 and multiply by 100. This yields $\left(\frac{107 - 98}{98}\right) \cdot 100 = 9.2$, or approximately 10%.

Choices B and C are incorrect and may be the result of misreading the graph or making an arithmetic error. Choice D is incorrect and may be the result of approximating the amount of plastic produced, in billions of pounds, in the year 2003 ($x = 18$).

QUESTION 23

Choice A is correct. In 1 year, there are 4 quarter years, so the number of quarter years, q, is 4 times the number of years, t; that is, $q = 4t$. This is equivalent to $t = \frac{q}{4}$, and substituting this into the expression for M in terms of t gives $M = 1{,}800(1.02)^{\frac{q}{4}}$.

Choices B and D are incorrect and may be the result of incorrectly using $t = 4q$. In choice D, $1.02^{4q} = 1.02^{4(q)}$, which is approximately 1.082^{q}. Choice C is incorrect and may be the result of incorrectly using $t = 4q$ and unnecessarily dividing 0.02 by 4.

QUESTION 24

Choice D is correct. It is given that Contestant 2 earned 70% of the votes cast using social media and 40% of the votes cast using a text message. Based on this information, viewers voting by social media were more likely to prefer Contestant 2 than were viewers voting by text message.

Choices A, B, and C are incorrect. There is not enough information about the viewers to reach these conclusions.

QUESTION 25

Choice A is correct. It is given that the relationship between population and year is linear; therefore, the function that models the population t years after 2000 is of the form $P(t) = mt + b$, where m is the slope and b is the population when $t = 0$. In the year 2000, $t = 0$. Therefore, $b = 862$. The slope is given by $m = \frac{P(10) - P(0)}{10 - 0} = \frac{846 - 862}{10 - 0} = \frac{-16}{10} = -1.6$. Therefore, $P(t) = -1.6t + 862$, which is equivalent to the equation in choice A.

Choice B is incorrect and may be the result of incorrectly calculating the slope as just the change in the value of P. Choice C is incorrect and may be the result of the same error as in choice B, in addition to incorrectly using t to represent the year, instead of the number of years after 2000. Choice D is incorrect and may be the result of incorrectly using t to represent the year instead of the number of years after 2000.

QUESTION 26

Choice C is correct. In order to use a sample mean to estimate the mean for a population, the sample must be representative of the population (for example, a simple random sample). In this case, Tabitha surveyed 20 families in a playground. Families in the playground are more likely to have children than other households in the community. Therefore, the sample isn't representative of the population. Hence, the sampling method is flawed and may produce a biased estimate.

Choices A and D are incorrect because they incorrectly assume the sampling method is unbiased. Choice B is incorrect because a sample of size 20 could be large enough to make an estimate if the sample had been representative of all the families in the community.

QUESTION 27

Choice B is correct. Since the point (p, r) lies on the line with equation $y = x + b$, the point must satisfy the equation. Substituting p for x and r for y in the equation $y = x + b$ gives $r = p + b$. Similarly, since the point $(2p, 5r)$ lies on the line with the equation $y = 2x + b$, the point must satisfy the equation. Substituting $2p$ for x and $5r$ for y in the equation $y = 2x + b$ gives $5r = 2(2p) + b$, or $5r = 4p + b$. Solving each equation for b gives $b = r - p$ and $b = 5r - 4p$, respectively. Substituting $r - p$ for b in the equation $b = 5r - 4p$ gives $r - p = 5r - 4p$. Subtracting r from each side of the equation and adding $4p$ to each side of the equation gives $3p = 4r$. Dividing each side of the equation by p and dividing each side of the equation by 4 gives $\frac{3}{4} = \frac{r}{p}$.

Choices A, C, and D are incorrect. Choices A and D may be the result of incorrectly forming the answer out of the coefficients in the point $(2p, 5r)$. Choice C may be the result of confusing r and p.

QUESTION 28

Choice D is correct. The two data sets have the same range. The first data set has a range of $88 - 56 = 32$, and the second data set has a range of $112 - 80 = 32$. Alternatively, it can be seen visually that the ranges are the same because the two dot plots are aligned, the scales of the graphs are the same, and the graphs have the same width. The two data sets have different standard deviations. Both dot plots show distributions that have a mean near the center value of the dot plot. The first dot plot shows most values clustered near the mean, while the second dot plot shows most values farther from the mean. Therefore, the standard deviations of the two data sets are not equal—the data represented by the second dot plot has a greater standard deviation.

Choices A, B, and C are incorrect because they incorrectly assert either that the standard deviations are the same or that the ranges are different.

QUESTION 29

Choice B is correct. Since the machine copies at a constant rate, the relationship between p, the number of sheets of paper remaining, and m, the time in minutes since the machine started printing, is modeled by a linear equation. The initial number of sheets of paper is given as 5,000. It is also given that the machine used 30% of those 5,000 sheets in 20 minutes, so it used $0.30 \times 5{,}000 = 1{,}500$ sheets in 20 minutes. Therefore, the number of sheets used per minute is $\frac{1{,}500}{20} = 75$. To determine the number of sheets of paper used m minutes after the machine started printing, multiply 75 by m, which gives $75m$. Therefore, a linear equation modeling this relationship is the number of sheets remaining equals the initial number of sheets of paper minus the number of sheets of paper used m minutes after the machine started printing, which is $p = 5{,}000 - 75m$.

Choice A is incorrect and may be the result of using the given number of minutes, 20, as the rate at which the copy machine uses paper. However, the rate is 75, not 20, sheets per minute. Choices C and D are incorrect because they aren't linear equations; they assume that the copy machine prints at a nonconstant rate.

QUESTION 30

Choice B is correct. The maximum value of the function f occurs at the highest point on the graph of $y = f(x)$; the highest point on the graph is (4, 3). For any point on the graph of f, the y-coordinate gives the value of the function at the x-coordinate; therefore, the maximum value of the function f is 3. It is stated that k is the maximum value of f, so $k = 3$. Thus, $g(k) = g(3)$. From the table of values for g, it can be seen that when $x = 3$, $g(3) = 6$.

Choice A is incorrect and may result from using the x-coordinate of the maximum point as the value of k. Choice C is incorrect; it is the value of k, not of $g(k)$. Choice D is incorrect and may be the result of giving the value of x that makes $g(x) = 3$ instead of finding the value of $g(x)$ when $x = 3$.

QUESTION 31

The correct answer is 102. Since each molecule of water has 2 atoms of hydrogen, 51 molecules of water have a total of (51)(2) = 102 atoms of hydrogen.

QUESTION 32

The correct answer is 2. Substituting $x = 1$ in the equation $x - \frac{1}{2}a = 0$ gives $1 - \frac{1}{2}a = 0$. Adding $\frac{1}{2}a$ to both sides of this equation gives $1 = \frac{1}{2}a$. Multiplying both sides of this last equation by 2 gives $2 = a$.

QUESTION 33

The correct answer is 30. Since the equations $x + 2y = 10$ and $3x + 6y = c$ represent the same line in the xy-plane, they must be equivalent equations. The expression $3x + 6y$ on the left-hand side of the second equation is equivalent to $3(x + 2y)$, which is 3 times the left-hand side of the first equation. Thus, to be equivalent, the right-hand side of the second equation, c, must be 3 times the right-hand side of the first equation, 10. Therefore, $c = 30$.

QUESTION 34

The correct answer is 25.4. The average speed is the total distance divided by the total time. The total distance is 11 miles and the total time is 26 minutes. Thus, the average speed is $\frac{11}{26}$ miles per minute. The question asks for the average speed in miles per hour, and there are 60 minutes in an hour; converting miles per minute to miles per hour gives the following:

$$\text{Average speed} = \frac{11 \text{ miles}}{26 \text{ minutes}} \times \frac{60 \text{ minutes}}{1 \text{ hour}}$$
$$= \frac{660}{26} \text{ miles per hour}$$
$$\approx 25.38 \text{ miles per hour}$$

Therefore, to the nearest tenth of a mile per hour, the average speed of Paul Revere's ride would have been 25.4 miles per hour.

QUESTION 35

The correct answers are 2 and 8. Substituting $x = a$ in the definitions for f and g gives $f(a) = -\frac{1}{2}(a - 4)^2 + 10$ and $g(a) = -a + 10$, respectively. If $f(a) = g(a)$, then $-\frac{1}{2}(a - 4)^2 + 10 = -a + 10$. Subtracting 10 from both sides of this equation gives $-\frac{1}{2}(a - 4)^2 = -a$. Multiplying both sides by -2 gives $(a - 4)^2 = 2a$. Expanding $(a - 4)^2$ gives $a^2 - 8a + 16 = 2a$. Combining the like terms on one side of the equation gives $a^2 - 10a + 16 = 0$. One way to solve this equation is to factor $a^2 - 10a + 16$ by identifying two numbers with a sum of -10 and a product of 16. These numbers are -2 and -8, so the quadratic equation can be factored as $(a - 2)(a - 8) = 0$. Therefore, the possible values of a are either 2 or 8. Either 2 or 8 will be scored as a correct answer.

Alternate approach: Graphically, the condition $f(a) = g(a)$ implies the graphs of the functions $y = f(x)$ and $y = g(x)$ intersect at $x = a$. The graph $y = f(x)$ is given, and the graph of $y = g(x)$ may be sketched as a line with y-intercept 10 and a slope of -1 (taking care to note the different scales on each axis). These two graphs intersect at $x = 2$ and $x = 8$.

QUESTION 36

The correct answer is 0. Note that no matter where point W is on $\overline{RT}$, the sum of the measures of $\angle RSW$ and $\angle WST$ is equal to the measure of $\angle RST$, which is 90°. Thus, $\angle RSW$ and $\angle WST$ are complementary angles. Since the cosine of an angle is equal to the sine of its complementary angle, $\cos(\angle RSW) = \sin(\angle WST)$. Therefore, $\cos(\angle RSW) - \sin(\angle WST) = 0$.

QUESTION 37

The correct answer is 576. According to the table, 5 minutes after the injection, the penicillin in the patient's bloodstream is 152 micrograms per milliliter. Thus, there are $10 \times 152 = 1520$ micrograms of penicillin in 10 milliliters of blood drawn 5 minutes after the injection. Similarly, 10 minutes after the injection, the penicillin concentration is 118 micrograms per milliliter. Thus, there are $8 \times 118 = 944$ micrograms of penicillin in 8 milliliters of blood drawn 10 minutes after the injection. Therefore, there are $1520 - 944 = 576$ more micrograms of penicillin in 10 milliliters of blood drawn 5 minutes after the injection than in 8 milliliters of blood drawn 10 minutes after the injection.